THE COMPLETE SCHOLARSHIP BOOK

3rd Edition

FastWeb.com

SOURCEBOOKS, INC.
NAPERVILLE, ILLINOIS

Disclaimer

Scholarships in this book were up-to-date at the time of this book's most recent printing. Every effort has been made to provide you with the best, most current information on private sector financial aid. Care has been taken in collecting and presenting the material contained in this book. Unfortunately, awards, addresses, requirements, etc., change often, and neither Fastweb.com nor Sourcebooks, Inc., guarantee its accuracy. Fastweb.com and Sourcebooks, Inc., are private corporations and are not affiliated in any way with the U.S. Department of Education or any other government agency.

Published by Sourcebooks
P.O. Box 4410, Naperville, Illinois 60567-4410
(630) 961-3900
FAX: 630-961-2168

Library of Congress Cataloging-in-Publication Data

The complete scholarship book / Fastweb.com — 3rd ed.
     p. cm.
   Includes index.
   ISBN 1-57071-530-0 (alk. paper)
   1. Scholarships—United States—Directories. 2. Associations, institutions, etc.—Charitable contributions—United States—Directories. 3. Student aid—United States—Handbooks, manuals, etc. I. Fastweb.com (Firm).
LB2338.C653 2000
378.3′4′0973—dc21

                                              00-024787

Printed and bound in the United States of America

DR 10 9 8 7 6 5 4 3 2 1

Table of Contents

The Complete Scholarship Book

A college education is a valuable asset. According the 1998 U.S. Census report, heads of household with bachelor's degrees earned nearly double the yearly income earned by those with high school diplomas.

But for many, a college education can seem out of reach. Currently, the average student graduates with $20,000 worth of debt due to college costs. Tuition takes its own bite, and additional costs (books, supplies, room and board, living expenses) can make college hard to afford.

These costs are increasing all the time. In the year 2000, the average annual total cost of attending a private college was $22,000; the average annual total cost of attending a public school was $9,000. Within five years, those costs are projected to increase to nearly $28,000 for private colleges and $12,000 for public colleges.

Financial aid provides a much needed solution. Through a variety of sources, most students qualify for some kind of college funding, including:

Scholarships and Grants: "free money" awarded based on merit, need, or both.

Loans: funds that must be repaid either by students or their families.

Work-Study: financial aid funds that are paid back through on-campus jobs.

While loans and work-study are often most readily available, scholarships offer a better alternative: funding that doesn't need to be paid back.

The best place to find this "free money" is *The Complete Scholarship Book*. Here you'll find listings for more than 5,000 awards, grants, and scholarships, from sources such as schools, corporations, philanthropic organizations, professional societies, employers, clubs, and service groups.

Scholarship Eligibility

You may think that scholarships are only for the straight-A students, the super-achievers, or the very needy. In reality, scholarships require varying levels of achievement and frequently award students based on specific criteria, such as background, field of study, or hobbies. The result is that virtually any student can find scholarships for which they qualify.

In this book, you'll find scholarships that are awarded based on:

➤ Career objectives

➤ Gender

➤ Disabilities

➤ Financial need

➤ Academic performance

➤ Race and heritage

➤ Military service

➤ Religious affiliation

➤ Region of residence

➤ Club affiliation

➤ Work experience

Paying for College

The Cost of College

Your college price tag is made up of two parts:

Direct costs: tuition and fees; books and supplies; room and board. In some cases (such as with tuition), the amount can be fixed and unchanging. In other cases (books and supplies; room and board), the cost may not be fixed—you won't be billed at the beginning of each semester—but they are costs you will have to pay during college.

Indirect costs: transportation, phone service, personal expenses, and entertainment. Your indirect costs are much more variable, depending on your habits and choices.

When determining how much money you'll need for your college education, be sure to include both direct and indirect costs in your budget.

Types of Aid

With college costs rising, most students need help paying for higher education. That aid can come in a variety of forms:

Scholarships and Grants

Scholarships and grants are the best kind of aid because they're "free money" that you don't have to pay back. This includes federally sponsored grants, such as the Pell Grant and the Federal Supplemental Educational Opportunity Grant (FSEOG), state grants, and scholarships offered by schools or private organizations.

Work-Study

Work-study aid is typically provided through the Federal Work-Study Program as a part of the financial aid package you receive from your college. With work-study, you earn your financial aid by working on campus. Work-study can be a good option, especially if you want to gain on-the-job experience while in college. Be careful about how work-study fits into your financial aid package: If too much of your award is made up of work-study, you won't be able to fulfill your work requirement and keep up with your classes.

Loans

Loans are funds that must be repaid either by students or their families. Loans offered through the Federal Direct Student Loan Program (FDSLP) and the Federal Family Education Loan Program (FFELP), such as the Stafford Loan and the Perkins Loan, generally offer the best terms to students. The federal government also sponsors a loan for parents of students, the federal Parent Loan for Undergraduate Students (PLUS). To learn more about federal loans, read the federal government's Student Guide for federal aid at www.ed.gov/prog_info/SFA/StudentGuide/. Students may also take out loans from private lenders to supplement the aid provided by the federal government.

Other Ways to Pay

In addition to these basic types of aid, you may benefit from other assistance programs and options:

National Service: The Corporation for National Service (Americorps) offers a number of opportunities for funding in exchange for community service.

Tuition Payment Plans: Many schools offer short-term installment plans that split your tuition into equal monthly payments. Many such plans are essentially interest-free, but some have fees or finance charges.

Employer Support: Many companies recognize the value of investing in an employee's educational development. Ask your employer about tuition reimbursement programs.

Benefits for Military Service: The military offers a number of tuition assistance programs in exchange for military service, including ROTC, Army/Navy/Marine Corps College Funds, and U.S. Service Academies.

Tax Credit: The HOPE Scholarship and Lifetime Learning credits establish a tax credit for higher education.

Prepaid Tuition Plans: These plans allow parents to lock in future tuition rates at current prices by paying years before attendance.

Applying for Financial Aid and Scholarships

The Free Application for Federal Student Aid (FAFSA)

Applying for aid starts with the Free Application for Federal Student Aid (the FAFSA). The federal government uses the FAFSA to determine your eligibility for federal assistance (grants, work-study appointments, and loans). Schools also base their financial aid package on the FAFSA. As the name implies, the FAFSA is completely free. The new FAFSA becomes available each year on January 1. Submit your application as soon after January 1 as possible to ensure that funding is still available. The FAFSA is available online at www.fafsa.ed.gov. It can also be found at libraries and schools.

School-based Aid Applications

You should also check with your school to learn about their requirements for applying for financial aid. They may require additional forms and information, and frequently set their own deadlines for their financial aid applications.

Private Scholarship Applications

In addition to government and school-sponsored aid, there is a wealth of aid available in the form of scholarships sponsored by private foundations, associations, and organizations. In most cases, you must apply for these awards individually. Eligibility requirements and criteria vary and are established by the providers who sponsor the awards. To apply for private awards, call or write to the provider and request a scholarship application. If sending your request through the mail, enclose a self-addressed, stamped envelope with your letter.

Top Tips for Scholarships and Financial Aid

Tip 1:

Apply for financial aid every year you're in college. Even small changes in your situation can alter (and possibly increase) your eligibility for assistance.

Tip 2:

Be sure to fill out the Free Application for Federal Student Aid (FAFSA). The FAFSA is the first step for qualifying for federal grants, loans, and work-study, as well as many school-sponsored forms of aid. Submit your FAFSA as soon after January 1 as possible.

Tip 4:

In addition to filling out the FAFSA, check with your school to learn about their financial aid application process. Some schools require additional forms and more detailed financial information.

Tip 5:

Be sure to stay in contact with your financial aid administrators and inform them about atypical expenses. Certain allowances may be made to assist you.

Tip 6:

When applying to college, keep your options open. If you suspect that your top-choice school may be out of your price range, apply to a "safety school" that's closer to what you can afford.

Tip 7:

Take advantage of tuition breaks you may receive for going to a college in your home state. Tuition for in-state students at public colleges is often cheaper than tuition for students from out of state. Some states also offer additional grants for students who stay in-state for college.

Tip 8:

Investigate alternate ways to help pay for college, such as company-sponsored tuition reimbursement programs, tuition tax credits such as the Hope Scholarship and Lifetime Learning credit, tuition payment plans, aid in exchange for military service, and prepaid tuition plans. Visit http://www.finaid.org to learn all you can about financial aid.

Tip 9:

Consider living at home during college. While you may miss out on some "classic" college experiences, you can save a lot in food and housing bills.

Tip 10:

Apply for as many scholarships as you can, even the smaller awards. The small awards can really add up, and they'll make you a better applicant for other awards. Check *The Complete Scholarship Book* and http://www.fastweb.com to learn about scholarship opportunities.

Tip 11:

To maximize your eligibility for scholarships, use your extracurricular time to develop hobbies, join clubs, and build a strong resume. Don't spread yourself too thin, though. Make sure you're putting a worthwhile effort into your activities.

Tip 12:

When preparing your scholarship application, neatness counts. Remember to type your application and use large, legible font. Always proofread your application and essay, and ask someone else to proofread them as well.

Tip 13:

Get ready for scholarship applications early by writing practice essays during the summer or other vacations. It's easier to rewrite the drafts for specific applications than to start from scratch later on.

Tip 14:

For a strong scholarship application essay, be original and creative. Use stories, examples, and anecdotes to make your own mark. Choose a single theme you want to convey and focus your essay on developing that theme.

Tip 15:

When writing your scholarship essay, think about the sponsor you're writing for. Your essay should reflect that organization's goals and mission. Keep in mind that they're looking for a candidate to serve as their representative.

Tip 16:

To get the best letters of recommendation, give your recommenders ample time to produce their letter—at least three weeks advance notice. Supply everything they need to write a great letter, including a list of your achievements and a description of the scholarship.

Tip 17:

Make a great impression at your scholarship interview by preparing in advance. Be ready to talk about your background, academic achievements, future plans, hobbies, financial circumstances, and your personal values. Also, do some research on the sponsoring organization so you can discuss their mission as well.

Tip 18:

Be sure to talk to your financial aid officer about any outside awards you win. Schools vary regarding their policies on external scholarships.

Tip 19:

Ask about the ongoing eligibility requirements for any scholarships or grants you receive. Make sure you understand what you need to do to keep the awards you've won.

Tip 20:

Don't be taken in by scholarship scams. Be cautious if anyone asks you to pay a fee to apply for financial aid or learn about awards.

Searching for Free Money

Scholarships come from a variety of sources. *The Complete Scholarship Book* can help you find those sources. It also helps to know the kinds of sponsors who may offer free money.

Sources of Scholarships

College-Based Scholarships

Colleges and universities attract new students by offering scholarships. They also have award programs to help current students with their academic careers. Some of these are scholarships for which you must apply; others you receive automatically when you apply for admissions or financial aid. These can include:

Merit Scholarships: These scholarships award students based on a variety of achievements, from high academic performance to leadership ability to artistic accomplishment. Financial need may also be considered. Often, you won't apply for these awards; appropriate recipients are chosen based on entrance applications.

Departmental Awards: Some college departments offer awards to students who show promise and achievement in one of their majors. To find out about these opportunities, call the Dean's office in your area of study.

Athletic Scholarships: Schools use scholarships to attract top athletes. You can receive anything from a small award to a full ride. Talk to your high school coach or counselor to learn more.

Fellowships: Fellowships are awards offered to

incoming graduate students. Generally these awards accompany admission to a graduate program and cover all expenses, including tuition and a living stipend. Some graduate fellowship programs require research or teaching duties.

Private Scholarships

Your school isn't the only one who wants to give you money. Some private scholarships are available as early as your junior year in high school. They are a little harder to find, but resources like *The Complete Scholarship Book* can help.

Businesses and Corporations: Corporations use scholarships to advertise the company name and attract future employees, while giving the student financial assistance and professional contacts. Start with local businesses and move on to bigger companies like Coca-Cola and Procter & Gamble.

Professional Associations: Many professional associations, like the American Federation of Teachers International and the Society for Pharmaceutical Engineers, offer scholarships to encourage students in their field.

Clubs and Groups in Your Community: Local civic groups and organizations, like the Rotary Clubs and the Jaycees, offer scholarships. Scan your local newspaper, visit the Chamber of Commerce, and speak with your high school counselor to learn more.

The Religious Community: Churches and other places of worship often sponsor scholarships. Also check with worship-oriented service groups. You may not have to be a member to receive an award. Some use criteria like community service or financial need to determine eligibility.

Minority Organizations: To encourage minority involvement and increase diversity, many organizations, like the Hispanic College Fund or Women In Communication, use race, ethnicity, religion, gender, or sexual orientation as eligibility requirements for their scholarships.

Your Parents' Employers and Affiliations: Employers, labor unions, clubs, and associations frequently offer awards to children of their employees and members.

Maximizing Your Scholarship Eligibility

You may be eligible for more kinds of awards than you think. The secret is to "type" yourself. Think about who you are and what you do to find the maximum number of scholarship opportunities.

College Major/Field of Interest

If you're in college, start with your major or academic area. Departments and schools, as well as academic and professional organizations, offer scholarships for students based on their majors.

Don't limit yourself. If you're a double major, check under both majors to make sure you're not missing anything. Also, don't be too specific. For example, if you're an English major, you can look for scholarships listed under "English," "Literature," and "Literary Studies," as well as broader categories like "Humanities." If you're majoring in Physics, don't look for scholarships only under "Physics"; check "Physical Sciences" and "Science" too.

Also don't forget to include what you'll *become*. Whether you want to be a lawyer, doctor, journalist, or teacher, you may find awards to help you pursue the career of your dreams—regardless of your major.

State of Residence/State of Study

Many state governments offer financial assistance to in-state students. Check with your state of residence to find out about these programs.

Private organizations also offer state-specific scholarships that reward academic merit and extra-curricular achievements. Some scholarships are also available for residents of certain counties or cities.

Student Affiliations

Also think about things you like to do. Start with clubs and organizations. As a member or officer, you'll qualify for awards sponsored by your club.

But don't stop there. What are your hobbies? Have you trained in any special skills or sports? Do you attend religious services? Have you worked a part-time job? All these activities are part of your "type" and can lead to scholarships.

Ethnic Background

Awards are given to students of certain ethnic or minority groups. If your parents are from different ethnic groups, look for awards for each group. Also look for scholarships targeting students from broader ethnic categories like "Asian" or "Hispanic."

Disability

A wide variety of students may qualify for awards because they are physically challenged, learning-disabled, or suffer from long-term illness. Look for scholarships listed under your specific disability or illness, as well as more general awards for disabled students.

International Students

If you are a citizen of a country other than the U.S., that's part of your "type" as well. You'll find that some awards are restricted to students from certain countries, but many more target international students in general. Look for awards in both categories.

The key to finding scholarships is to think broadly. Do your own personal inventory and try to figure out how many "types" you fit into. Be true to your "type" to find the scholarships you need.

Preparing Your Application

The Parts of the Scholarship Application

All scholarship applications vary, but they frequently consist of a few basic parts:

1. A scholarship application form.

2. A transcript of your scholastic performance.

3. An essay. The topics vary. Some providers ask general questions to learn more about you; others ask more specific questions that relate to their particular interests.

4. Letters of recommendation.

5. An interview with the scholarship judging committee. Some providers require interviews

of all applicants; others select finalists or semi-finalists to interview to help determine the final winner.

Top Ten Tips for Winning Scholarship Applications

Before you submit your scholarship application, check out these tips, provided by scholarship sponsors nationwide.

Tip #1: Apply only if you are eligible.

Read all the scholarship requirements and directions carefully and make sure you're eligible before you apply.

Tip #2: Complete the application in full.

If a question doesn't apply, note that on the application. Don't just leave a blank. Be sure to supply all additional supporting material, such as transcripts, letters of recommendation, and essays.

Tip #3: Follow directions.

Provide everything that is required. But don't supply things that aren't requested—you could be disqualified.

Tip #4: Neatness counts.

Always type the application, or if you must print, do so neatly and legibly. Make a couple of photocopies of all the forms you receive before you fill them out. Use the copies as working drafts as you develop your application packet.

Tip #5: Write an essay that makes a strong impression.

The key to writing a strong essay is to be personal and specific. Include concrete details to make your experience come alive: the "who," "what," "where," and "when" of your topic. The simplest experience can be monumental if you honestly present how you were affected.

Tip #6: Watch all deadlines.

Impose your own deadline that is at least two weeks prior to the official deadline. Use the buffer time to make sure everything is ready on time.

Don't rely on extensions—very few scholarship providers allow them.

Tip #7: Make sure your application gets where it needs to go.

Make sure your name appears on all pages of the application. Pieces of your application may get lost unless they are clearly identified.

Tip #8: Keep a back-up file in case anything goes wrong.

Before sending the application, make a copy of the entire packet. If your application goes astray, you'll be able to reproduce it quickly.

Tip #9: Give it a final "once-over."

Proofread the entire application carefully. Be on the lookout for misspelled words and grammatical errors. Ask a friend, teacher, or parent to proofread it as well.

Tip #10: Ask for help if you need it.

If you have problems with the application, do not hesitate to call the funding organization. It's better to ask questions than lose a chance at winning a scholarship.

Writing the Scholarship Essay

Writing scholarship essays is hard work, but it's work that pays off. The essay is the part of the application where the "real you" can shine through. Follow these tips to make a good impression:

Think before you write. Take some time to organize your thoughts before you sit down to write. Brainstorm to generate some good ideas and then create an outline to help you get going.

Be original. Your essay should reflect what is unique about you. Be honest and true to yourself and write about something that sets you apart. Remember, in most cases readers are faced with hundreds of essays to read. It's your job to make your essay stand out from the rest.

Show, don't tell. Use stories, examples, and anecdotes to individualize your essay and demonstrate the point you want to make. By

using specifics, you'll avoid vagueness and generalities.

Develop a theme. Don't simply list all your achievements. Decide on a theme you want to convey that sums up the impression you want to make. Write about experiences which develop that theme.

Know your audience. Personal essays are not "one size fits all." Write a new essay for each application—one that fits the interests and requirements of that scholarship organization. You're asking to be selected as the represent- ative for that group. The essay is your chance to show how you are the ideal representative.

Submit an essay that is neat and readable. Make sure your essay is neatly typed, and that there is a lot of "white space" on the page. Double-space the essay, and provide adequate margins (1″-1 1/2″) on all sides.

Make sure your essay is well written. Proofread carefully, check spelling and grammar, and share your essay with friends or teachers. Another pair of eyes can catch errors you might miss.

Practice Session: Common Essay Questions

A great way to prepare for upcoming scholarship applications is to practice writing responses to essay questions that scholarship providers often use. Later, you can use and rewrite your "practice essays" when it's time to apply. Try your hand at these common essay questions:

Your Field of Specialization and Academic Plans

Some scholarship applications will ask you to write about your major or field of study. These questions are used to determine how serious you are about your area of specialization.

How will your study of _____ contribute to your immediate or long-range career plans?

Why do you want to be a _____?

Explain the importance of (your major) in today's society.

What do you think the industry of _____ will be like in the next 10 years?

What are the most important issues your field is facing today?

Current Events and Social Issues

To test your skills at problem-solving and check how up-to-date you are on current issues, many scholarship applications include questions about problems and issues facing society.

What do you consider to be the single most important societal problem? Why?

If you had the authority to change your school in a positive way, what specific changes would you make?

Pick a controversial problem on college campuses and suggest a solution.

What do you see as the greatest threat to the environment today?

Personal Achievements

You may be asked to write about special achievements, projects, or accomplishments. To create the strongest impression, select specific events or activities and use them to build a theme. Avoid simply listing your activities.

Describe how you have demonstrated leadership ability both in and out of school.

Discuss a special attribute or accomplishment that sets you apart.

Describe your most meaningful achievements and how they relate to your field of study and your future goals.

Why are you a good candidate to receive this award?

Background and Influences

An essay about the people, organizations, and experiences that have influenced you is a great way for scholarship judges to learn more about you.

Pick an experience from your own life and explain how it has influenced your development.

Who in your life has been your biggest influence and why?

How has your family background affected the way you see the world?

How has your education contributed to who you are today?

Future Plans and Goals

Scholarship sponsors look for applicants with vision and motivation, so you may be asked to write about your goals and aspirations. Use your essay to show not just what your goals are, but how you plan to reach those goals.

Briefly describe your long- and short-term goals.

Where do you see yourself 10 years from now?

Why do you want to get a college education?

Financial Need

Detailed information about your financial situation can help scholarship providers decide which applicant most needs their assistance.

From a financial standpoint, what impact would this scholarship have on your education?

State any special personal or family circumstances affecting your need for financial assistance.

How have you been financing your college education?

"Creative" Topics

Some essay questions don't relate directly to your education or the scholarship organization's mission, but committees use them to test your creativity and get a more well-rounded sense of your personality.

Choose a person or persons you admire and explain why.

Choose a book or books and that have affected you deeply and explain why.

The Guide to Great Letters of Recommendation

Many scholarship providers ask for letters of recommendation from teachers, employers, and others who know you well. Even though someone else writes your letter of recommendation, you're responsible for making sure it gets written. And there's a lot you can do to ensure it's the best letter possible.

Who?

The best recommendations come from people who have worked closely with you and who understand the award for which you are applying. Teachers and professors are excellent sources, but also consider previous employers, coaches, clergy members, and community leaders.

Pick someone who can address the award's special criteria or the sponsoring organization's particular interests. For example, the director of the homeless shelter where you volunteer would be a great reference for an award sponsored by a community service group.

Don't ask a family member for a recommendation. Their praise won't have the proper level of credibility to impress the admissions staff.

When?

In most cases, you'll ask for recommendations as you need them; for example, when you apply for college admissions or for scholarships. But you should also plan ahead. Start by making a list of potential letter-writers, including names, addresses, email addresses, and phone numbers.

It's also a good idea to compile a file of letters before you need them, especially once you've started college. Ask for letters right after you've finished a course with a professor who likes your work. If you wait until you need the letter (maybe two or three years down the line), you risk losing it because the professor doesn't remember you.

Some colleges can help by maintaining a dossier, or official letter file. When requested, letters from your dossier are sent directly and (if you waive your right to see them) can carry more weight with the judges because they know the recommender was able to express his or her true opinion.

How?

There's an art to getting the best letters of recommendation. The key is to make it easy for your recommenders. Provide ample time for the letter to be written—at least three weeks advance notice. When you request your recommendation, schedule an appointment to discuss the letter and the application fully.

Once your recommender has agreed to write a letter for you, supply as much information as possible, including:

Your correct contact information (your full name as it appears on the application, address, e-mail address, and phone number).

Materials/information needed for the application, including two copies of any forms to be filled out (for a "rough draft" and a "final draft"); the full title and description of the award; the correct name, title, and mailing address of the recipient; a copy of your completed scholarship application/essay; complete instructions on how the letters should be handled; and correct deadline information.

Information about your achievements, such as your transcripts, resume, and samples of your past work with the recommender (e.g., a description of coursework, a copy of an essay or class project, etc.).

Provide an addressed, stamped envelope if the recommendation is to be sent separate from the rest of your application.

Check back with your recommender a few weeks before the due date to ask if they need anything else, and then verify that your letter has been sent. Afterwards, send a thank-you note to your recommender.

The Scholarship Interview

A good interview is vital to your scholarship application. It's an opportunity to supplement your credentials with the kind of impression that can't be put on paper. But for most, interviews are a major source of stress. Keep the anxiety level under control by following these tips.

It's a Conversation

To keep yourself relaxed, think of your interview as a conversation rather than a test. It's an opportunity to discuss your goals, plans, and concerns with experienced professionals.

Be Prepared

You can also decrease your anxiety level and improve your experience by anticipating the questions you'll be asked. Be prepared to discuss:

Your background: your educational history, your employment experiences, family background, and upbringing.

Your academic achievements: class-ranking, grade point average, awards you have won or projects you have undertaken (science fairs, debate competitions, etc.).

Your future plans: academic plans, career plans.

Your hobbies and interests: extracurricular activities, skills, jobs, etc.

Your financial profile and needs: income, savings, parents' resources, level of financial need, anticipated expenses, etc. Information about your financial resources is especially important if the scholarship is need-based.

Your personal "value structure": the things you think are important in your life. Information about your personal value structure helps the interviewers determine whether you would serve as an appropriate representative for their organization.

Don't Forget the Basics

Be punctual. Check the interview time and location before leaving home.

Dress appropriately. Select conservative, semi-formal wear: slacks and a jacket or a dress shirt for men; dresses, skirts, or pantsuits for women. Never wear jeans or a T-shirt to an interview.

Make a good first impression. When you meet the interviewers, introduce yourself, make eye contact, and use a firm handshake.

Be brief and honest with your answers. Try to sum up your thoughts quickly. Interviewers will ask follow-up questions if they want to know more.

Have some questions ready for the interviewers. Prepare these questions in advance by researching the sponsoring organization, school, or company.

Be prepared to reiterate the basic information

you supplied on your application. Review your application before the interview to jog your memory.

Don't be negative. Interviewers value the individual who perceives difficult situations as challenging and interesting.

Don't be afraid to say "I don't know" or ask questions. It's better to ask for clarification than to miss an opportunity to produce an insightful answer.

Don't chew gum, bite nails, smoke, yawn, stretch, or slouch. Avoid wearing perfume or cologne.

Show your appreciation. Thank the interviewers for their time at the end of the interview. Afterwards, send a thank-you note.

How Are Scholarships Judged?

Understanding the judge's role can help you put together a winning scholarship application.

At First Glance

The judges' first evaluation of your application is a quick one—usually only 15 to 30 seconds. Even though it's quick, it's important; most applications don't get past this first stage. To be sure yours makes it through, give your application one last review.

Is your application complete? Check to see that you've included all the requirements.

Is your application neat and easy to read? Use a legible and large font (12 point) to make the judge's job easier and more pleasant.

Are all of the required documents included? Be sure you're not leaving out references, transcripts, photographs, or anything else the application requires.

Are all of the questions answered? Scan your application to see if you've left anything out.

The Second Cut

After an application makes it past the first round, the judges separate "OK" from "great." The applications that make it through are those that have thorough and well-thought-out responses.

Make sure your essay responses are complete and answer the question. It's very important that your grammar and spelling are correct, so check and re-check all of your essays.

The Final Decision

This is the most difficult part of the process for judges. They've narrowed it down to a few highly qualified students. Now they must examine and compare every detail of the applications.

Judges pay special attention to:

Academics—It's important to have a competitive GPA. However, providers also consider how challenging your course load and school are. They also check to see if you're taking the right courses to reach your goals and how well you did in those courses.

Leadership—If leadership is part of the criteria they're looking for, judges will examine your activities. They'll also look for a range of leadership positions.

Service—Some providers are interested in knowing what community service you've done. If volunteer work is required by your school, they'll look for activities that go above and beyond the required service job.

Creativity—You can show your creative side if you play an instrument, write stories, paint pictures, or act in plays. Demonstrate your ability by letting the judges know if you've won any awards.

Special Circumstances—If you've overcome any obstacles to achieve your goals, the judges want to know about it. Let them know how you achieved all that you've done, in spite of the roadblocks you've encountered.

It's not an easy job being a scholarship judge. Each provider has only so much to give and must make a tough decision: who will receive the award. By knowing what's on the minds of scholarship judges, you'll have a better chance at being one of those winners.

After You've Won

Winning a scholarship is cause for celebration—but it's also cause for planning. Scholarships can affect your school's financial package, and you may find that keeping your scholarship after you've won it takes some care. So plan ahead!

Scholarship Dollars and Your Financial Aid Package

Scholarships are a valuable part of college financing. But if you win a scholarship from an outside source, it could affect your school's financial aid package. To maximize your aid package, make sure you know about how scholarships fit into your financial aid picture.

When you apply for financial aid, your college constructs a financial aid package consisting of the federal, state, and school-based assistance you're eligible to receive, such as loans, grants, school-sponsored scholarships, and work-study. If you win an outside scholarship (one that is not sponsored by the school), the financial assistance office has to reconsider their initial financial aid package in order to comply with the federal government's regulations.

But what happens next varies from school to school. In some cases, the school "replaces" existing institutional grants and scholarships with the outside award. The result is that the student's aid dollars remain the same even though the scholarship dollars have been added.

In other cases, outside scholarships can still help out. For example, if your school compensates for the scholarship by reducing your loans (instead of reducing grants), your financial aid package will end up with a smaller proportion of debt (money you must repay) and more "free money" (in the form of scholarships and grants).

Ask your financial aid officer how your school treats outside scholarships. But keep looking for scholarships—you may not lose anything and you may have a lot to gain!

Keeping Your Scholarship

Winning scholarships is hard work, but the work doesn't end after the check is cut. Find out about the policies surrounding your award so you can keep your scholarship.

Renewable Scholarships

The first question you need to ask is whether your scholarship is renewable. Renewable awards can be extended beyond the initial award year—in some cases, for your entire college career. If your scholarship is renewable, find out about all the policies and procedures for renewal. Be sure to ask:

How often is scholarship eligibility reviewed? When does the review occur?

Do you need to reapply to ensure renewal? How often? What forms do you need to submit?

General Eligibility Requirements

Renewable or not, your scholarship may carry ongoing eligibility requirements. If you fail to fulfill these requirements, you may lose funding. Typical requirements include:

Designated expenditures: What does your scholarship cover? Tuition? On-campus room and board? General living expenses? School-related supplies?

GPA: You may need to maintain a minimum GPA in order to remain eligible (often, the same GPA that won you the scholarship). Find out when your GPA will be reviewed and whether you will need to supply transcripts.

Satisfactory academic progress: You may also be required to meet standards for academic progress, including completion of general education requirements or the degree within a designated time frame. Check with your school or provider to learn the standards that are applied for satisfactory academic progress.

Full-time status: Scholarships frequently require a minimum level of enrollment. If you fall below the minimum or fail to enroll, you may lose the award. Check with your school for its definition of "full-time." You should also find out what happens if you drop a course (and drop below full-time status for a term). Will you lose the award, or will you be granted a "grace period" to make up the units?

Time off from school: What happens if you take time off in order to work, study abroad, or attend to personal responsibilities? Will your scholarship be waiting for you when you return? Can the scholarship be applied to study abroad?

Study within a designated field of study: Can you lose the award if you change majors?

College choice: Some awards apply only to enrollment at a particular college. Can your award can be "moved" if you enroll at a different school or if you transfer schools?

Service requirements: Certain awards require a set number of community service hours. Find out how to document and report your service.

Progress reports: Some providers require periodic reports on your progress. Regardless of the requirements, you should always write a progress report and thank-you note. Donors appreciate knowing about your progress; it's further confirmation that they selected the right candidate for the award.

Military service: ROTC funding and scholarships for military academies require service after graduation as well as military training during college.

Participation in sports: Athletic scholarships often require participation in sports. Anything that impedes your participation (injury, unsatisfactory academic performance, etc.) may put your funding in jeopardy.

Eligibility Reinstatement

If you fail to fulfill the terms of your award, you could lose eligibility—and your scholarship. To avoid disaster, ask about your scholarship's reinstatement policies. Under what circumstances can you get the scholarship back after losing eligibility? Is there a probationary period prior to losing it? What procedures do you need to follow?

Plan ahead, and get your provider/school's renewal and eligibility policies in writing in advance. Keep records on these policies, as well as any conversations you have with staff members regarding eligibility issues. A scholarship worth winning is worth keeping!

Protecting Yourself from Scams

Guess what? You're a "finalist" for a scholarship. And you never even applied! Too good to be true? Probably so.

The sad truth is that there are scammers out there—posing as scholarship providers or scholarship matching services—who take your money and leave you with nothing. The good news is that you can protect yourself.

Know Your Scams

Scams come in many flavors, but there are a few typical moves you should be aware of:

The phony scholarship: you receive a notice about a scholarship that promises you cash. All you need to do is pay the registration fee. So why not apply? Because there is no award. Or there is one small award used to lure you in.

The phony scholarship matching service: pay a fee, and they'll do all the work. They'll find information that you can't get anywhere else! Not only that, they will guarantee that you'll win. The outcome? You never hear from them again or (even more frustrating) you receive a list of inappropriate or defunct awards. And forget your money-back guarantee; the company is long gone.

The phony educational loan: a low-interest loan in exchange for an up-front fee. You pay the fee, but never receive the loan.

The phony free financial-aid seminar: a thinly disguised sales pitch for a bogus scholarship search or insurance offer.

Scam Warning Signs

A fee. Your best rule of thumb: financial aid should never cost you. Never invest anything beyond the cost of a postage stamp in your search for financial aid.

The "money-back guarantee"—especially if the company tries to "guarantee" that you will win an award. Also be suspicious of services that claim to "do all the work for you"—filling out the application, contacting the scholarship provider, securing the award.

Credit card verification. If they ask for a checking account or credit card number—for "verification" or to "confirm eligibility"—stop listening. Scammers use this ploy to get your financial information and then drain your account or run up charges on your credit card.

No application. If you're told you've won an award for which you did not apply, be suspicious. Legitimate scholarship providers send you information about their award only after you request it.

Suspicious contact information. Make sure that a telephone and full address is available. Scammers frequently refuse to release their phone number and provide only a PO box where you can mail their payment.

Don't be fooled by an "official sounding" name. Just because a company uses words like "National," "Federal," "Foundation," or "Administration" in its title doesn't mean it's legit.

What to Do If You Suspect a Scam

1. Document all your dealings with any company that you suspect of fraud. Include details about the offer, your response, and the dates of your communications.

2. Take notes during any telephone conversations with these organizations. Record the date and time of the conversation, the name of the person with whom you spoke, and a detailed account of your conversation.

3. Report them! Any of the following organizations can help:

National Fraud Information Center (NFIC)

Call their toll-free hotline at (800) 876-7060 or write:

National Fraud Information Center
PO Box 65868
Washington, DC 20035

Federal Trade Commission (FTC)

To report suspected fraud, call (202) FTC-HELP (202-382-4357) or write:

Correspondence Branch
Federal Trade Commission, Room 200
6th Street & Pennsylvania Avenue, NW
Washington, DC 20580

State Attorney General's Office

File your complaint with the Bureau of Consumer Protection in your state.

Better Business Bureau (BBB)

Report business fraud, ask for information about a company or request the BBB's publications about scholarship scams: BBB Warning: Scholarship Search Services (July/August 1994) and Tips for Consumers from your Better Business Bureau (Scholarships, March 1996). Call (703) 525-8277 or write:

Council of Better Business Bureaus
845 Third Avenue
New York, NY 10022

Additional Tips

Keeping Down College Costs

Follow these strategies to reduce the sticker cost of your education.

Ask about application fee waivers.

The cost of applying to college, taking standardized test scores, and having those scores sent to schools can really add up. If you're strapped for cash, consider asking about application fee waivers. But keep in mind:

availability is limited, and you must meet some pretty stringent standards to qualify.

Apply for financial aid.

Even if you think you're not eligible, be sure to apply for financial aid by filling out the FAFSA (Free Application for Federal Student Aid). This form is the first step for applying for all kinds of aid, from federal aid (grants, loans, and work-study) to state-based funding (grants and other programs) to college-based aid (special awards, grants, and work-study programs).

Search for free money.

And since every little bit counts, you should also apply for scholarships. Use The Complete Scholarship Book and free, online services like www.fastweb.com to help you find awards and then apply! And to learn more about all your funding options, visit www.finaid.org.

Complete some of your credits at a lower-cost school.

You can save a lot by completing your general education requirements at a community college or less expensive school and then transferring to complete the degree. Talk to an admissions counselor to be sure your credits will transfer, and learn as much as you can about the financial aid policy. Some schools restrict financial aid for transfer students.

Get to know the financial aid officer at your college.

Specific rules apply for financial aid calculations, but your financial aid officers may be able to work with you to find ways to make college more affordable. Let your financial aid officer know about any special circumstances that affect your ability to pay for college.

Look for ways to pay in-state tuition.

Most public colleges and universities charge considerably less tuition to in-state students in comparison to students from out of state. Pick a college in your state to keep costs down.

Accumulate credits before college.

You may be able to save some tuition costs by

earning college credits while you're still in high school through Advanced Placement courses or courses at a local community college. Be sure to check with your prospective college to see whether the credits you earn will be applied toward your college degree.

Combine degrees to save time and money.

If you're planning to earn multiple degrees, you may be able to cut tuition costs by enrolling in a combined degree program. Some schools will allow you to combine a bachelor's degree with a master's degree or a master's degree with a doctoral degree, reducing the number of credit hours you must earn.

Live at home during college.

You can save a lot if you live in your parents' home when you go to college. You might miss out on some "classic" college experiences, but your food and housing bills will be a lot lower. Or if you really want the residential college experience, compromise by spending some years at home and some years living on campus.

Apply for "life experience credit."

If you're entering school from the work force, you may be able to earn college credit for your employment and life experience. Some schools administer their own tests and standards while others allow you to take CLEPÆ(College-Level Examination Program) tests for college credit. Policies vary, so check with your prospective school.

Keep costs down and maximize your financial aid, and you'll look forward to graduation day all the more!

What to Do When Your Financial Aid Is Not Enough

It's a common dilemma. You want to go to college, you apply for financial aid, but the award you receive from your school is still not enough. All is not lost, though. You may still be able to get the aid you need.

Getting enough aid starts long before financial aid season. To maximize your aid, take some

precautions:

Even if you think you don't qualify, be sure to apply for financial aid. You have nothing to lose by applying, and you could find you're eligible.

Keep detailed records of your family's income and assets. These documents will be invaluable if you have to appeal to a college for more aid.

Be timely. Submit your financial aid application as early as you can. As enrollment season progresses, the school will have fewer and fewer financial aid dollars to distribute.

Even with these precautions, you might find that the college you wish to attend is still out of your price range. If this is the case, don't give up. While your school may not be able to allot more aid to you, it's worth your while to ask.

Start by contacting your school about your situation. Let them know that you want to attend, but tuition is still not affordable. Ask if there is anything you can do to help. Be ready to explain why you can't meet the cost and be ready to verify your claims with extra information and documentation.

Throughout your discussion, remain polite and considerate. Don't approach the situation as if you're "bargaining" for a better deal. Financial aid officers do all they can to help students; let them know that you appreciate their efforts. Be patient, communicate honestly, and you may discover a solution that works for all.

Finally, keep your options open. While your top college choice may be out of your price range, other schools may be more affordable and provide a good alternative. Apply to schools from a variety of price ranges to ensure you find a college you can afford.

Web Resources

Scholarships and Financial Aid

FastWeb—free online scholarship search
www.fastweb.com

FinAid—free information about financial aid
www.finaid.org

The Scholarship Coach
www.fastweb.com/sp/coach

Financial Aid Calculators
www.finaid.org/calculators

College Is Possible   www.collegeispossible.org

The Student Guide to Financial Aid
www.ed.gov/prog_info/SFA/StudentGuide/

Government Resources

FAFSA—the Free Application for Federal Student
Aid   www.fafsa.ed.gov

U.S. Department of Education   www.ed.gov

The Student Guide to Financial Aid
www.ed.gov/prog_info/SFA/StudentGuide/

U.S. State Government Aid
www.finaid.org/otheraid/state.phtml

Office of Postsecondary Education
www.ed.gov/offices/ope

U.S. Direct Loans
www.ed.gov/DirectLoan/students.html

Direct Consolidated Loans
www.loanconsolidation.ed.gov

Access America for Students   www.students.gov

Getting Ready for College Early
www.ed.gov/pubs/GettingReadyCollegeEarly/

Alternate Forms of Aid:

Corporation for National Service/Americorps
www.cns.gov

Hope Scholarships and Lifetime Learning Credits
www.ed.gov/inits/hope/

U.S. State Government Aid
www.finaid.org/otheraid/state.phtml

Army ROTC   www-
rotc.monroe.army.mil/Information/information.htm

Navy ROTC   www.nadn.navy.mil/

Air Force ROTC
www.airforce.com/welcome/welcome.ptml

Marine Corps ROTC   www.marines.com/

Bureau of Indian Affairs
www.doi.gov/bureau-indian-affairs.ptml

Tuition Payment Plans
www.finaid.org/otheraid/tuition.phtml

Prepaid Tuition Programs
www.finaid.org/otheraid/prepaid.phtml

1

102nd Infantry Division Scholarship

AMOUNT: $500-$1200 DEADLINE: May 15
MAJOR: All Areas of Study

The 102nd Infantry Division Scholarship is open to applicants whose father or grandfather was an active dues-paying member of the 102nd Infantry Division between August 1942 and March 1946. If the father or grandfather is deceased, they must have been a dues-paying member at the time of death in order for the applicant to qualify for the scholarship. Award requirements change regularly. Please send a self-addressed, stamped envelope to receive your application and any further instructions from the scholarship provider. Scholarship Information at the 102nd Infantry Division Association may also be reached by calling (615) 292-2469. No GPA requirement specified.

102nd Infantry Division
Attn: Scholarships
1821 Shackleford Road
Nashville, TN 37215

2

37th Infantry Division Award

AMOUNT: $1000 DEADLINE: April 1
MAJOR: All Areas of Study

The 37th Infantry Division Award is available to the son or daughter of a 37th Division veteran of World War I, World War II or the Korean conflict. Award is based on financial need, and is renewable every year. Award requirements change regularly. Please send a self-addressed, stamped envelope to receive your application and for any further instructions from the scholarship provider. No GPA requirement specified.

37th Division Veterans Association
Attn: James W. Wallace, Secretary
183 East Mound Street, Suite 103
Columbus, OH 43215

3

3M Company Scholarship

AMOUNT: $1050 DEADLINE: May 15
MAJOR: Chemical Engineering, Electrical Engineering, Industrial Engineering, Mechanical Engineering

This scholarship is open to freshmen women majoring in chemical, electrical, industrial or mechanical engineering. The applicants must have been accepted into an ABET-accredited program or an SWE-approved school. Recipients must be U.S. citizens. Award requirements change regularly. Please send a self-addressed, stamped envelope to receive your application. For further instructions, please browse the SWE website at www.swe.org or email hq@swe.org. No GPA requirement specified.

Society of Women Engineers Headquarters
Scholarship Coordinator
120 Wall Street, FL 11
New York, NY 10005-3902

4

3M Company Scholarship

AMOUNT: $2000 DEADLINE: March 15
MAJOR: All Fields of Study

The 3M Company Scholarship is open to employees of Business Products Industry Association member firms and their families. Persons holding academic records sufficient for acceptance by accredited colleges, junior colleges or technical schools, or persons already enrolled in one of those institutions are eligible for this two-year award. Selection is made by a committee from the Student Financial Aid Department of The George Washington University, Washington, DC, Award requirements change regularly. Please send a self-addressed, stamped envelope to receive your application and any further instructions from the scholarship provider or email: info@bpia.org. No GPA requirement specified.

Business Products Industry Association
Attn: Scholarship Committee
301 North Fairfax Street
Alexandria, VA 22314-2633

5

4-H Scholarship

AMOUNT: $350 DEADLINE: Varies
MAJOR: All Areas of Study

Open to 4-H members planning to continue their education beyond high school. Applicants must be attending four-year universities or colleges, two-year business schools, two-year trade or tech schools, or the Vo-Ag short course. Awards will be granted upon completion of the following conditions: proof of completed semester, minimum cumulative GPA of 2.0 verified by school transcript, and proof of enrollment for 2nd semester. Award requirements change regularly. Applications are available from your club general leader or by calling the UW-Extension Office (414) 857-1945. GPA must be 2.0-4.0.

Kenosha County UW-Extension Office
Scholarship Coordinator
PO Box 550
Bristol, WI 53104-0550

6

A.O. Putnam Memorial Scholarship

AMOUNT: $700 DEADLINE: November 15
MAJOR: Industrial Engineering

This scholarship is open to undergraduate students who are enrolled in an industrial engineering program on a full-time basis, who are members of the institute and have a minimum 3.4 GPA. Priority consideration is given to, but not limited to, students who have demonstrated an interest in management consulting. The program enrolled in may be located in the United States and its territories, Canada or Mexico provided that the school's engineering program or equivalent is accredited by an accrediting agency recognized by IIE. The applicants must have a graduation date of May/June 2001 or later and must be nominated by their IE Department heads. Award requirements change regularly. GPA must be 3.4-4.0.

Institute of Industrial Engineers
Attn: Chapter Operations Board
25 Technology Park
Norcross, GA 30092-2988

7
A.W. Bodine-Sunkist Memorial Scholarship

AMOUNT: Maximum: $3000 DEADLINE: April 30
MAJOR: All Areas of Study

The A.W. Bodine-Sunkist Memorial Scholarship is open to students entering any undergraduate grade level in an accredited college. To be considered for this award you must have a background in Arizona or California agriculture (you or someone in your immediate family must have derived the majority of your/their income from agriculture), have financial need and have a minimum 3.0 GPA. Selection is also based on a combination of test scores, an essay and references. The award is renewable. Award requirements change regularly. For an application and further information, please write to the address listed and enclose a self-addressed, stamped envelope. GPA must be 3.0.

Sunkist Growers, Inc.
Attn: Scholarship Programs
PO Box 7888
Van Nuys, CA 91409-7888

8
AAJUW Scholarship

AMOUNT: $1000 DEADLINE: September 30
MAJOR: Japan Studies

This scholarship is awarded to female juniors, seniors or graduate students enrolled in an accredited California college or university. Applicants should be contributors to U.S.-Japan relations, participate in cultural exchanges and the development of leadership in the areas of their designated study field. Award requirements change regularly. Write to the address listed, enclosing a self-addressed, stamped envelope (4 1/2 x 9 1/2) for an application and further information. No GPA requirement specified.

American Association of Japanese University Women
Scholarship Committee Chair
3812 Inlet Isle Drive
Corona Del Mar, CA 92625-1602

9
AALL Educational Scholarship Type I

AMOUNT: None Specified DEADLINE: April 1
MAJOR: Library Science

The AALL Educational Scholarship Type I is open to law school graduates working toward a degree in an ALA-accredited library school. Preference is given to AALL members with meaningful law library experience. Applicants must have at least one quarter/semester remaining after scholarship is awarded. Evidence of financial need must be submitted. Award requirements change regularly. Please send a self-addressed, stamped envelope to receive your application and any further instructions from the scholarship provider; or download the scholarship application and instructions from

their website at www.aallnet.org/services/scholarships.asp. No GPA requirement specified.

American Association of Law Libraries
Attn: Scholarship Committee
53 West Jackson Blvd, Suite 940
Chicago, IL 60604

10
AALL Educational Scholarship Type II

AMOUNT: None Specified DEADLINE: April 1
MAJOR: Law

The AALL Educational Scholarship Type II is open to library school graduates working toward a degree in an ABA-accredited law school who have meaningful law library experience and have no more than 36 semester (54 quarter) credit hours remaining before qualifying for the law degree. Preference is given to members of AALL. Evidence of financial need must be submitted. Award requirements change regularly. Please send a self-addressed, stamped envelope to receive your application and any further instructions from the scholarship provider; or download the scholarship application and instructions from their website at www.aallnet.org/services/scholarships.asp. No GPA requirement specified.

American Association of Law Libraries
Attn: Scholarship Committee
53 West Jackson Blvd, Suite 940
Chicago, IL 60604

11
AALL Educational Scholarship Type III

AMOUNT: None Specified DEADLINE: April 1
MAJOR: Library Science

The AALL Educational Scholarship Type III is open to college graduates with meaningful law library experience who are degree candidates in an ALA-accredited library school. Preference is given to members of AALL and to applicants working for degrees with emphasis on courses in law librarianship. Applicants must have at least one quarter/semester remaining after scholarship is awarded. Evidence of financial need must be submitted. Award requirements change regularly. Please send a self-addressed, stamped envelope to receive your application and any further instructions from the scholarship provider; or download the scholarship application and instructions from their website at www.aallnet.org/services/scholarships.asp. No GPA requirement specified.

American Association of Law Libraries
Attn: Scholarship Committee
53 West Jackson Blvd, Suite 940
Chicago, IL 60604

12
AALL Educational Scholarship Type IV

AMOUNT: None Specified DEADLINE: April 1
MAJOR: Fields to Complement a Career in Law Librarianship Except Law

The AALL Educational Scholarship Type IV is open to library school graduates who are degree candidates in an area other than law, which will be beneficial to the development of a professional career in law librarianship. The scholarship is restricted to members of AALL. Evidence of financial need must be submitted. Award requirements change regularly. Please send a self-addressed, stamped envelope to receive your application and any further instructions from the scholarship provider; or download the scholarship application and instructions from their website at www.aallnet.org/services/scholarships.asp. No GPA requirement specified.

American Association of Law Libraries
Attn: Scholarship Committee
53 West Jackson Blvd, Suite 940
Chicago, IL 60604

13
AALL Educational Scholarship Type V

AMOUNT: None Specified DEADLINE: Varies
MAJOR: Continuing Education Courses Related to Law Librarianship

The AALL Educational Scholarship Type V is open to law librarians with a degree from an ALA-accredited library school or an ABA-accredited law school who are registrants in continuing education courses related to law librarianship. Applications must be received on or before October 1, February 1, or April 1. Award requirements change regularly. Please send a self-addressed, stamped envelope to receive your application and any further instructions from the scholarship provider; or download the scholarship application and instructions from their website at www.aallnet.org/services/scholarships.asp. No GPA requirement specified.

American Association of Law Libraries
Attn: Scholarship Committee
53 West Jackson Blvd, Suite 940
Chicago, IL 60604

14
AALL/John Johnson LEXIS Publishing Memorial Scholarship

AMOUNT: None Specified DEADLINE: April 1
MAJOR: Library Science, Law

The AALL/John Johnson LEXIS Publishing Memorial Scholarship is open to individuals with meaningful law library experience who plan to pursue graduate-level studies related to their professional interests in law librarianship. Award requirements change regularly. Candidates who apply for AALL Educational Scholarships, Type I - IV, will automatically be reviewed for this scholarship. No separate application is needed. This scholarship is awarded annually at the discretion

of the Scholarship Committee. For additional information, please visit the AALL website at www.aallnet.org/services/scholarships.asp. No GPA requirement specified.

American Association of Law Libraries
Attn: Scholarship Committee
53 West Jackson Blvd, Suite 940
Chicago, IL 60604

15
AASL/School Librarian's Workshop Scholarship

AMOUNT: $2500 DEADLINE: April 1
MAJOR: Library Science

The AASL/School Librarian's Workshop Scholarship is open to students who intend to pursue full-time graduate study in an ALA-accredited program, an ALA-accredited library program or in a school library media program that meets ALA curriculum guidelines for an NCATE-accredited unit. To be considered for this award, you must demonstrate a strong interest in working with children or young adults in a school library media program in either a public or private educational setting. You should have received a bachelor's degree and have a record of academic excellence and leadership potential. This award has no citizenship requirement. Award requirements change regularly. No GPA requirement specified.

American Library Association
HRDR/Staff Liaison - Scholarship Juries
50 East Huron Street
Chicago, IL 60611-2795

16
AAUW Recognition Award for Emerging Scholars

AMOUNT: $5000 DEADLINE: February 10
MAJOR: All Areas of Study

Open to women scholars who have a record of exceptional early accomplishments and who show promise of future distinction. Recipients must be untenured and have earned a Ph.D. or its equivalent in the past five years. Selection is based on demonstrated excellence in teaching, a documented research record, and evidence of potentially significant contribution to her field of study. Award requirements change regularly. For an application and further information, please write to the address listed, including a self-addressed, stamped envelope or email foundation@mail.aauw.org. GPA must be 3.2-4.0.

AAUW Educational Foundation
Recognition Award for Emerging Scholars
111 Sixteenth Street, N.W.
Washington, DC 20036

17
AAUW Scholarships for Local Area Women

AMOUNT: $1000 DEADLINE: March 1
MAJOR: All Areas of Study

Open to women who are residents of Livermore, Pleasanton, Dublin, or Sunol, or who are graduates of one of the high schools serving those communities. Applicants must be planning to attend an accredited college or university, and be planning to complete her full course of study. Selection is based on GPA, financial need, work experience related to major, personal statement, letters of recommendation, letter grades for major classes, and a personal interview. Award requirements change regularly. For further information and an application, please write to the address listed, including a self-addressed, stamped envelope. Requests for application forms must be postmarked between October 1 and January 15. GPA must be 2.8-4.0.

L-P-D AAUW Foundation for Education
Scholarship Coordinator
PO Box 661
Livermore, CA 94551-0661

AAUW, Poway-Penasquitos Branch Scholarship, San Diego, CA

AMOUNT: Maximum: $500 DEADLINE: May 15
MAJOR: All Areas of Study

This scholarship is open to female high school graduates residing in San Diego in one of the following areas: Poway, Rancho Bernardo, Sabre Springs, Carmel Mountain, Mira Mesa, Rancho Penasquitos, Scripps Ranch or Ramona. You must be a re-entry student who is currently enrolled in or accepted at a four-year school. Re-entry is defined as having been out of school for at least three years prior to re-entry. Two scholarships of up to $500 each are offered. Award requirements change regularly. No GPA requirement specified.

American Association of University Women, Poway-Penasquitos Branch
AAUW Scholarship Chair
113816 Lewiston Street
San Diego, CA 92128

19
AAUW/Racine Branch Scholarship

AMOUNT: $1000 DEADLINE: April 1
MAJOR: All Areas of Study

This scholarship is open to Racine County women who are juniors at an accredited college or university. The scholarship is based on academic achievement and financial need. Award requirements change regularly. Please write to the address listed, enclosing a self-addressed, stamped envelope for an application and further information. GPA must be 2.8-4.0.

American Association of University Women-Racine Branch
Attn: Elaine Fish
3620 Osborne Blvd
Racine, WI 53405-2032

20
Abafazi-Africana Women's Studies Essay Award

AMOUNT: $400 DEADLINE: February 1
MAJOR: African-American Women's Studies

The Abafazi-Africana Women's Studies Essay Award is open to African-American women writing an essay on feminist/womanist issues among women of color. Your essay can cover any subject relevant to African-American girlchildren, women's issues and/or experiences in the U.S. or throughout the diaspora. You must be an undergraduate or graduate student and a member of NWSA. Award requirements change regularly. No GPA requirement specified.

National Women's Studies Association
University of Maryland
7100 Baltimore Avenue, Suite 500
College Park, MD 20740-3636

21
Abbie Sargent Memorial Scholarship

AMOUNT: $400 DEADLINE: March 15
MAJOR: Agriculture, Agribusiness, Horticulture, Veterinary Medicine, Animal Science, Home Economics

This scholarship is open to undergraduates or graduate students who are attending school full-time or part-time. You must be concentrating in the areas listed above, be a resident of New Hampshire and demonstrate financial need. Award requirements change regularly. Please write to the address listed, enclosing a self-addressed, stamped envelope for an application and further information. GPA must be 2.0-4.0.

Abbie Sargent Memorial Scholarship
295 Sheep Davis Road
Concord, NH 03301-5747

22
Academic Scholarships

AMOUNT: $1000 DEADLINE: April 1
MAJOR: Real Estate

Open to students who are enrolled in a degree program with an emphasis on real estate at any accredited two- or four-year junior college, college, or university in Illinois. Applicants must have completed at least 30 college credit hours, be U.S. citizens, and be residents of the state of Illinois. Award requirements change regularly. For further information and an application, please write to the address listed, including a self-addressed, stamped envelope. No GPA requirement specified.

Illinois Real Estate Educational Foundation
Academic Scholarships
PO Box 19457
Springfield, IL 62794

23
ACB of Colorado Scholarship

AMOUNT: $1500 DEADLINE: March 1
MAJOR: All Areas of Study

These scholarships are available to legally blind students who are residents of Colorado. Award requirements change regularly. Write to the address listed, enclosing a self-addressed envelope for an application and further information. No GPA requirement specified.

American Council of the Blind
Attn: Billie Jean Keith
1155 15th Street NW, Suite 720
Washington, DC 20005-2706

24

ACB of Maine Scholarships

AMOUNT: $1000 DEADLINE: March 1
MAJOR: All Areas of Study

Scholarships are available to legally blind students who are residents of Maine. Award requirements change regularly. Write to the address listed, enclosing a self-addressed envelope for an application and further information. No GPA requirement specified.

American Council of the Blind
Attn: Billie Jean Keith
1155 15th Street NW, Suite 720
Washington, DC 20005-2706

25

ACCO World Corporation Scholarship

AMOUNT: $2000 DEADLINE: March 15
MAJOR: All Fields of Study

The ACCO World Corporation Scholarship is open to employees of Business Products Industry Association member firms and their families. You may be eligible for this scholarship if you have been accepted by an accredited college, university, junior college or technical school, or are already enrolled in an accredited institution. Selection for this scholarship is made by a committee from the Student Financial Aid Department of George Washington University, Washington, DC. Award requirements change regularly. Please send a self-addressed, stamped envelope to receive your application and any further instructions from the scholarship provider or email: info@bpia.org. No GPA requirement specified.

Business Products Industry Association
Attn: Scholarship Committee
301 North Fairfax Street
Alexandria, VA 22314-2633

26

ACRES Scholarship

AMOUNT: Maximum $1000 DEADLINE: December 10
MAJOR: Special Education

The ACRES Scholarship is for teachers who are currently (or have been) employed by a rural school district as a certified teacher in regular or special education. Applicants must be working with students with disabilities or with regular education students and preparing for work in a special education setting. Applicants must be U.S. citizens. An essay is required. Award requirements change regularly. For additional information regarding the awards process, please contact the sponsor at the address provided, enclosing a self-addressed, stamped envelope or you may send them an email: acres@ksu.edu or browse their website: www.ksu.edu. No GPA requirement specified.

American Council on Rural Special Education (ACRES)
Kansas State University
2323 Anderson Avenue, Suite 226
Manhattan, KS 66502-7732

27

Actions Speak Scholarship

AMOUNT: $1000-$4000 DEADLINE: April 15
MAJOR: All Areas of Study

The Actions Speak Scholarship recognizes young FBLA members for exemplary entrepreneurial spirit and fundraising skills as demonstrated through their volunteer activities in support of their high school and/or community. This award is open to high school seniors who plan on pursuing a full-time two- or four-year course of study and who have demonstrated a commitment to serving their school and/or community through activities including, but not limited to, fundraising activities. You must be a national and state dues-paying member of the FBLA. A brief description of the student, school and/or community fundraising project should be submitted to the FBLA-PBL National Center. An official transcript and two letters of recommendation are required. Award requirements change regularly. No GPA requirement specified.

Future Business Leaders of America
Attn: Scholarship Coordinator
1912 Association Drive
Reston, VA 22091

28

Actuarial Scholarships for Minority Students

AMOUNT: None Specified DEADLINE: May 1
MAJOR: Actuarial Science

Scholarships for undergraduates who are African-American, Hispanic-American or Native North American citizens or permanent residents. Recipients must be enrolled/accepted into a program in actuarial science or courses that will serve to prepare for an actuarial career. Applicants must demonstrate mathematical ability and evidence of some understanding of the actuarial field. Based on financial need and merit. Award requirements change regularly. Write to the address listed, enclosing a self-addressed, stamped envelope for an application and further information. Applicants must submit the Financial Aid Form (FAF) to CSS (College Scholarship Service) no later than March 31, giving CSS permission to send information from their FAF to the Society of Actuaries. Completed applications are due by May 1. GPA must be 2.5-4.0.

Society of Actuaries
Minority Scholarship Coordinator
475 North Martingale Road, Suite 800
Schaumburg, IL 60173-2226

29
Addison H. Gibson Student Loan Program

AMOUNT: $9000-$15000 DEADLINE: Varies
MAJOR: Most Areas of Study

Low-interest student loans are available to residents of Western Pennsylvania who have successfully completed one or more years of their undergraduate or graduate education. In order to apply, you must demonstrate financial need. If you are an undergraduate, you may be eligible to receive up to $9,000. As a graduate student, you are eligible to receive up to $15,000. Award requirements change regularly. GPA must be 2.3-4.0.

Addison H. Gibson Foundation
One PPG Place, Suite 2230
Pittsburgh, PA 15222-5401

30
Adele Filene Travel Award

AMOUNT: Maximum: $500 DEADLINE: March 15
MAJOR: Costume Design

Open to Costume Society of America members currently enrolled as students to assist their travel to CSA national symposia to present their juried paper or poster. Included as travel costs are: airfare, mileage to and from home to the airport, parking at airport, bus or taxi fare to and from hotel, mileage if traveling by private auto and hotel parking during symposium. Award requirements change regularly. For further information and an application, please write to the address listed, including a self-addressed, stamped envelope, call (410) 275-1619, or browse their website: www.costumesocietyamerica.com. No GPA requirement specified.

Costume Society of America
Stella Blum Research Grant, PO Box 73
55 Edgewater
Earleville, MD 21919-0073

31
Adele Kagan Scholarship

AMOUNT: None Specified DEADLINE: March 1
MAJOR: Mathematics, Engineering, Sciences

The Adele Kagan Scholarship is for Jewish men and women living in the Chicago area or Cook County, Illinois. To be considered for this award, you must have career goals in mathematics, engineering or other sciences. Award requirements change regularly. No GPA requirement specified.

Jewish Vocational Service
Attn: Scholarship Secretary
One South Franklin Street
Chicago, IL 60606-4694

32
Adeline Godfrey-Dilley Memorial Scholarship

AMOUNT: $250 DEADLINE: May 1
MAJOR: Teaching, Education

The Adeline Godfrey-Dilley Memorial Scholarship is open to seniors at Camden-Frontier School (Camden, MI). To be considered for this award, you must be officially accepted into a postsecondary school which offers either two-or four-year degrees. You must also have a minimum 2.5 cumulative GPA. If you aspire to become a teacher of English, foreign language or speech, you will be given preference for this award. Award requirements change regularly. Please send a self-addressed, stamped envelope to receive your application and any further instructions from the scholarship provider. GPA must be 2.5-4.0.

Camden-Frontier Schools
Attn: Scholarship Coordinator
4971 Montgomery Road
Camden, MI 49232

33
Admiral Grace Murray Hopper Scholarship

AMOUNT: $1000 DEADLINE: May 15
MAJOR: Computer Engineering, Computer Science

This scholarship is open to a freshmen female student majoring in computer engineering or computer science. In order to apply, you must have been accepted into an ABET-accredited program or an SWE-approved school. The program you enter must also be a four-year program. Award requirements change regularly. Please send a self-addressed, stamped envelope to receive your application. For further instructions, please browse the SWE website at www.swe.org or email hq@swe.org. No GPA requirement specified.

Society of Women Engineers Headquarters
Scholarship Coordinator
120 Wall Street, FL 11
New York, NY 10005-3902

34
Adrian Arca Automobile Dealers Association Scholarship

AMOUNT: $1000 DEADLINE: March 12
MAJOR: Automotive Related

The Adrian Arca Automobile Dealers Association Scholarship is open to Lenawee County (MI) graduating seniors. You qualify for the award if you if you have already been accepted at a college and plan to study in an automotive-related field. You must have successfully completed Vo-Tech's auto body, auto mechanics or marketing education programs. Award requirements change regularly. Please send a self-addressed, stamped envelope to receive your application and any further instructions from the scholarship provider. No GPA requirement specified.

Morenci High School
Attn: Mrs. Melissa Parnell
788 Coomer Street
Morenci, MI 49256

35
Adrian Breakfast Lions Club Scholarship

AMOUNT: $1000 DEADLINE: March 31
MAJOR: Special Education

The Adrian Breakfast Lions Club Scholarship is open to Lenawee County (MI) graduates. To be considered for the award, you must be enrolled in a program leading to a career assisting people with visual or auditory problems. Award requirements change regularly. Please send a self-addressed, stamped envelope to receive your application and any further instructions from the scholarship provider. No GPA requirement specified.

Morenci High School
Attn: Mrs. Melissa Parnell
788 Coomer Street
Morenci, MI 49256

36
Adrian Breakfast Lions Club Scholarship

AMOUNT: $500 DEADLINE: March 31
MAJOR: All Fields of Study

The Adrian Breakfast Lions Club Scholarship is open to Lenawee County (MI) graduating seniors. To be considered for the award, you must have visual or auditory impairment. Award requirements change regularly. Please send a self-addressed, stamped envelope to receive your application and any further instructions from the scholarship provider. No GPA requirement specified.

Morenci High School
Attn: Mrs. Melissa Parnell
788 Coomer Street
Morenci, MI 49256

37
Adrian Morning Rotary Club Scholarship

AMOUNT: $1000 DEADLINE: March 31
MAJOR: All Fields of Study

The Adrian Breakfast Lions Club Scholarship is open to students from Lenawee County (MI) high schools. To qualify, you must be a graduating senior. Award requirements change regularly. Please send a self-addressed, stamped envelope to receive your application and any further instructions from the scholarship provider. No GPA requirement specified.

Morenci High School
Attn: Mrs. Melissa Parnell
788 Coomer Street
Morenci, MI 49256

38
Adrian Rotary Club 4-Way Test Scholarship

AMOUNT: $1000 DEADLINE: March 31
MAJOR: All Fields of Study

The Adrian Rotary Club 4-Way Test Scholarship is open to Lenawee County (MI) graduating seniors. Selection will be based on an essay in which you will discuss the implications of the Rotary 4-Way test in your life. Award requirements change regularly. Please send a self-addressed, stamped envelope to receive your application and any further instructions from the scholarship provider. No GPA requirement specified.

Morenci High School
Attn: Mrs. Melissa Parnell
788 Coomer Street
Morenci, MI 49256

39
Adrian Rotary Club Counseling/Social Work Scholarship

AMOUNT: $1000 DEADLINE: March 31
MAJOR: Counseling, Social Work

The Adrian Rotary Club Counseling/Social Work Scholarship is open to high school seniors from Lenawee County (MI). To qualify for the award, you must be planning to pursue a career in counseling or social work. A preferred candidate will demonstrate an interest in substance abuse prevention. Award requirements change regularly. Please send a self-addressed, stamped envelope to receive your application and any further instructions from the scholarship provider. No GPA requirement specified.

Morenci High School
Attn: Mrs. Melissa Parnell
788 Coomer Street
Morenci, MI 49256

40
Adult Vocational Training Grant Assistance Program

AMOUNT: Maximum: $2800 DEADLINE: March 1
MAJOR: All Areas of Study

Scholarships are available for members of the Blackfeet Tribe who are between the ages of 18 and 35 years. In order to apply, you should accept full-time employment as soon as possible after completion of training. Award requirements change regularly. No GPA requirement specified.

Blackfeet Tribe
PO Box 850
Browning MT, 59417-0850

41
Aero Club Memorial Scholarship

AMOUNT: Maximum: $1000 DEADLINE: May 28
MAJOR: Aviation

This scholarship is open to students between the ages of 17 and 30 who are interested in pursuing a career in flying.

Students must be residents of the Greater Delaware Valley area (PA) and have reached the point of first solo. A personal interview with the scholarship review board in June will be required. Award requirements change regularly. Write to the address listed, enclosing a self-addressed, stamped envelope for an application and further information. No GPA requirement specified.

Aero Club of Pennsylvania
Scholarship Coordinator
PO Box 748
Blue Bell, PA 19422-0108

AESF Graduate Scholarship

AMOUNT: $1500 DEADLINE: April 15
MAJOR: Finishing Technologies, Chemical/Environmental Engineering, Materials Science

This scholarship is open to students who have completed an accredited undergraduate program leading to a master's or Ph.D. Selection is based on, but not limited to: career interest in surface finishing technologies, scholarship, achievement, motivation and potential. Awards are not necessarily based on financial need. Award requirements change regularly. No GPA requirement specified.

American Electroplaters and Surface Finishers Society
Central Florida Research Park
12644 Research Parkway
Orlando, FL 32826

43
AESF Undergraduate Scholarship

AMOUNT: $1500 DEADLINE: April 15
MAJOR: Chemistry, Chemical/Environmental Engineering, Metallurgy, Materials Science

This scholarship is open to junior and senior undergraduates majoring in a chemistry, chemical engineering, environmental engineering, metallurgy, or materials science program where the focus of the curriculum is in surface science subjects. Selection is based on, but not limited to: career interest in surface finishing, scholarship, achievement, motivation and potential. Awards are not necessarily based on financial need. Award requirements change regularly. GPA must be 2.7-4.0.

American Electroplaters and Surface Finishers Society
Central Florida Research Park
12644 Research Parkway
Orlando, FL 32826

44
AFCEA Fellowship

AMOUNT: $25000 DEADLINE: February 1
MAJOR: Electrical Engineering, Electronic Engineering, Communications Engineering, Physics, Mathematics, Computer Science

This fellowship is open to postgraduate students working toward doctoral degrees in electrical, electronic, or communications engineering, physics, mathematics, or computer science. In order to apply, you must be a U.S. citizen and have a personal endorsement by the Dean of the College of Engineering at any accredited university in the U.S. Award requirements change regularly. No GPA requirement specified.

Armed Forces Communications and Electronics Association
AFCEA Educational Foundation
4400 Fair Lakes Court
Fairfax, VA 22033-3801

AFCEA General Emmett Paige Scholarship

AMOUNT: $2000 DEADLINE: March 1
MAJOR: Electrical Engineering, Electronics, Computer Science, Computer Engineering, Physics, Mathematics

The AFCEA General Emmett Paige Scholarship is open to veterans, to persons on active duty in the uniformed military services and to their spouses or dependents who are working toward a degree in an accredited four-year college or university in the U.S. You must major in electrical engineering, electronics, computer science, computer engineering, physics or mathematics, and have a minimum 3.4 GPA. Graduating high school seniors are not eligible, but veterans enrolled as freshmen are eligible to apply. Spouses or dependents must be enrolled as sophomores or juniors at the time of application. Award requirements change regularly. GPA must be 3.4-4.0.

Armed Forces Communications and Electronics Association
AFCEA Educational Foundation
4400 Fair Lakes Court
Fairfax, VA 22033-3801

46
AFCEA General John A. Wickham Scholarship

AMOUNT: $2000 DEADLINE: May 1
MAJOR: Electrical Engineering, Electronics, Computer Engineering, Computer Science, Physics, Mathematics

This scholarship is open to juniors and seniors enrolled full-time in an accredited degree-granting four-year college or university in the U.S. In order to apply, you must be a U.S. citizen working towards a degree in electrical engineering, electronics, computer science, computer engineering, physics, or mathematics, and have a minimum 3.4 GPA. You must also be enrolled as a sophomore or junior at the time of your application. Award requirements change regularly. GPA must be 3.4-4.0.

Armed Forces Communications and Electronics Association
AFCEA Educational Foundation
4400 Fair Lakes Court
Fairfax, VA 22033-3801

47
AFCEA Ralph W. Shrader Scholarship

AMOUNT: $3000 DEADLINE: February 1
MAJOR: Electrical Engineering, Electronic Engineering, Communications Engineering, Physics, Mathematics, Computer Science, Information Management

This scholarship is open to postgraduate students working toward master's degrees in electrical, electronic, or communications engineering, physics, mathematics, computer science, or information management. In order to apply, you must be a U.S. citizen attending an accredited college or university in

...r's program. Award require-
...equirement specified.

...d Electronics Association

...olarship

MAJOR: Electrical Engineering, Electronics, Computer
Science, Computer Engineering, Physics, Mathematics

This scholarship is open to sophomore and junior ROTC students majoring in electrical engineering, electronics, computer
science, computer engineering, physics, or mathematics. You
must be attending an accredited degree-granting four-year college or university in the U.S. In order to apply, you must also
be nominated by professors of military science, naval science
or aerospace studies. U.S. citizenship, enrollment in the
ROTC, good moral character, academic excellence, demonstration of the potential to serve as an officer in the U.S.
Armed Forces and financial need are also required. Award
requirements change regularly. GPA must be 3.4-4.0.

Armed Forces Communications and Electronics Association
AFCEA Educational Foundation
4400 Fair Lakes Court
Fairfax, VA 22033-3801

49
AFSA/AAFSW Academic Merit Awards

AMOUNT: $200-$1000 DEADLINE: February 6
MAJOR: All Areas of Study

This scholarship is open to high school seniors who are
dependents of U.S. Government Foreign Service personnel
(active, retired with pension or deceased) who have served
with a Foreign Service Agency for at least one year. Awards
acknowledge academic excellence and accomplishments at
home and abroad. Selection is based on a personal essay,
extracurricular activities, two letters of recommendation, SAT
scores, and your high school GPA. Award requirements
change regularly. No GPA requirement specified.

American Foreign Service Association (AFSA)
Scholarship Coordinator
2101 E Street NW
Washington, DC 20037-2916

50
AFSA/AAFSW Art Merit Award Program

AMOUNT: $1000 DEADLINE: February 6
MAJOR: Visual, Musical Arts, Dance, Drama, Creative Writing

This scholarship is open to high school seniors who are
dependents of Foreign Service personnel (active, retired with
pension or deceased) who have served with a Foreign Service
Agency for at least one year. You must have an extraordinary
talent in the fields of visual arts, musical arts, dance, drama or
creative writing. Award requirements change regularly. No
GPA requirement specified.

American Foreign Service Association (AFSA)
Scholarship Coordinator
2101 E Street NW
Washington, DC 20037-2916

51
AFSA Financial Aid Awards

AMOUNT: $500-$3000 DEADLINE: February 6
MAJOR: All Areas of Study

This award is open to entering freshmen and undergraduates
attending a U.S. college, university, or community college
full-time (a minimum of 12 hours). In order to apply, you
must maintain a minimum 2.0 GPA and be a dependent child
of a U.S. Government Foreign Service personnel (active,
retired w/pension, or deceased) who has served abroad with a
Foreign Service Agency for at least one year. Award requirements change regularly. GPA must be 2.0-4.0.

American Foreign Service Association (AFSA)
Scholarship Coordinator
2101 E Street NW
Washington, DC 20037-2916

52
AGC of Maine Scholarship Program

AMOUNT: $1000-$3000 DEADLINE: March 17
MAJOR: Construction and related areas

The AGC of Maine Scholarship Program is open to Maine
residents entering their second, third or fourth year at an
accredited postsecondary Maine institution. You must be able
to demonstrate financial need. These awards are based on academic achievement, extracurricular activities and submitted
essays. Award requirements change regularly. No GPA
requirement specified.

Associated General Contractors of Maine, Inc.
Attn: Education Foundation
P.O. Box 5519
Augusta, ME 04332-5519

53
AICPA Scholarship for Minority Accounting Students

AMOUNT: Maximum: $5000 DEADLINE: July 1
MAJOR: Accounting

The AICPA Scholarship for Minority Accounting Students is
open to full-time undergraduate and graduate students who are
African-American, Native American/Alaskan Native, Pacific
Islander or Hispanic. If you are an undergraduate student, you
must be a declared accounting major, have completed at least
30 semester hours (45 quarter hours) with at least six semester
hours in accounting and have a minimum 3.0 GPA. If you are
a graduate student, you are eligible if you meet one of the following criteria: you are in the final year of a five-year
accounting program; you are an undergraduate accounting
major who is presently accepted or enrolled in a master-level
accounting, business administration, finance or taxation program; you have an undergraduate degree in any field and have
been accepted to a master-level accounting program. In addition to the scholarship application, you must submit the
FAFSA. Award requirements change regularly. The scholar-

ship application can be downloaded or submitted online from the AICPA website at www.aicpa.org/members/div/career/mini/smas.htm. GPA must be 3.0-4.0.

American Institute of Certified Public Accountants
AICPA Order Dept, Product 870110
PO Box 2209
Jersey City, NJ 07303-2209

54
AILA Yamagami Hope Fellowship

AMOUNT: $1000 DEADLINE: August 2
MAJOR: Landscape Architecture

The AILA Yamagami Hope Fellowship is open to landscape architects who already have a Bachelor or master's degree in landscape architecture and have been in practice for a minimum of three years. Submissions will be evaluated on: 1) the innovative nature of the proposed endeavor; 2) the benefits that may accrue to other members of the profession and the profession in general; 3) the personal goals to be achieved; and 4) the qualifications of the applicant. The fellowship may be used to support credit or noncredit courses, seminars or workshops; for travel or related expenses in support of an independent research project; or for development of postsecondary educational materials or curriculum plans. Award requirements change regularly. No GPA requirement specified.

Landscape Architecture Foundation
Scholarship Program
636 'I' Street NW
Washington, DC 20001-3736

55
Air Force Sergeants Association Scholarship

AMOUNT: $2000-$2500 DEADLINE: April 15
MAJOR: All Areas of Study

The Air Force Sergeants Association Scholarship is open to single, dependent children of the Air Force Sergeants Association (AFSA) or an AFSA Auxiliary Member. Selection is based upon academic ability, character, leadership, writing ability and potential for success. The applicant must under 23 years of age. Award requirements change regularly. For more information, please send a self-addressed, stamped envelope to the scholarship provider, or they can be reached at (800) 638-0594. No GPA requirement specified.

Air Force Sergeants Association (AFSA)
Scholarship Program
PO Box 50
Temple Hills, MD 20757-0050

56
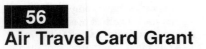
Air Travel Card Grant

AMOUNT: $3000 DEADLINE: July 28
MAJOR: Travel and Tourism

Open to students who are currently enrolled in a travel program in an accredited two- or four-year college/university. Applicants will be required to submit a 500-word paper defining the importance and challenges of managing business travel, and a brief description of his/her career goals, and why he/she wants a career in the field of travel and tourism. Award

requirements change regularly. Write to the address listed, enclosing a self-addressed, stamped envelope for an application and further information. You can browse their website: www.astanet.com or email: myriaml@astahq.com. No GPA requirement specified.

American Society of Travel Agents
Attn: ASTA Foundation
1101 King Street, Suite 200
Alexandria, VA 22314-2944

57
Airgas-Terry Jarvis Memorial Scholarship

AMOUNT: $2500 DEADLINE: January 15
MAJOR: Welding Engineering, Welding Engineering Technology

The Airgas-Terry Jarvis Memorial Scholarship is awarded to full-time undergraduates pursuing a minimum four-year bachelor's degree in welding engineering or welding engineering technology. Priority will be given to welding engineering students interested in pursuing a career with an industrial gas or welding equipment distributor by prior work experience, clubs or extracurricular activities. Applicants must reside in or attend school in the states of Alabama, Georgia or Florida. A minimum overall GPA of 2.8 is required. Demonstrated financial need is also considered. Students must have U.S. or Canadian citizenship. This award is renewable. Award requirements change regularly. Please send a self-addressed, stamped envelope to receive your application and any further instructions from the scholarship provider. GPA must be 2.8-4.0.

American Welding Society Foundation, Inc.
National Education Scholarship Committee
550 Northwest LeJeune Road
Miami, FL 33126-4165

58
Airline Pilots Association Scholarship

AMOUNT: $3000 DEADLINE: April 1
MAJOR: All Areas of Study

This scholarship is open to undergraduates who are children of medically retired, long-term disabled or deceased pilot members of the Airline Pilots Association. You must be enrolled in a program of studies principally creditable toward a baccalaureate degree, have a minimum 3.0 GPA and demonstrate financial need. This scholarship is renewable up to four years. Award requirements change regularly. For further information and an application, please write to the address provided, including a self-addressed, stamped envelope or call (703) 689-2270. GPA must be 3.0-4.0.

Air Line Pilots Association
Scholarship Committee
1625 Massachusetts Ave NW
Washington, DC 20036

Airmen Memorial Foundation CMSAF Richard D. Kisling Scholarship

AMOUNT: $1000-$3000 DEADLINE: April 15
MAJOR: All Areas of Study

The Airmen Memorial Foundation CMSAF Richard D. Kisling Scholarship is open to single dependent children of an enlisted member serving in the U.S. Air Force, Air National Guard or Air Force Reserve or in retired status. Selection is based upon academic ability, character, leadership, writing ability and the potential for success. The applicant must be under 25 years of age. An SAT I is required. Award requirements change regularly. Please send a self-addressed, stamped (78 cents) envelope (#10 business) to receive your application and any further instructions from the scholarship provider: Scholarship Administrator, Airmen Memorial Building, 5211 Auth Road, Suitland, MD 20746. GPA must be 3.0-4.0.

Air Force Sergeants Association (AFSA)
Scholarship Program
PO Box 50
Temple Hills, MD 20757-0050

Airmen Memorial Foundation Scholarship

AMOUNT: $1000 DEADLINE: April 15
MAJOR: All Areas of Study

The Airmen Memorial Foundation Scholarship is open to single dependent children of an enlisted member serving in the U.S. Air Force, Air National Guard or Air Force Reserve or in retired status. The applicant must be under 25 years of age. Award requirements change regularly. Please send a self-addressed, stamped (78 cents) envelope (#10 business) to receive your application and any further instructions from the scholarship provider: Scholarship Administrator, Airmen Memorial Building, 5211 Auth Road, Suitland MD 20746. No GPA requirement specified.

Air Force Sergeants Association (AFSA)
Scholarship Program
PO Box 50
Temple Hills, MD 20757-0050

Al Aigner Memorial Fund

AMOUNT: $2000 DEADLINE: March 15
MAJOR: All Fields of Study

The Al Aigner Memorial Fund is open to employees of Business Products Industry Association member firms and their families. Persons holding academic records sufficient for acceptance by accredited colleges, junior colleges or technical schools, or persons already enrolled in one of those institutions are eligible for this two-year award. Selection is made by a committee from the Student Financial Aid Department of The George Washington University, Washington, DC. Award requirements change regularly. Please send a self-addressed, stamped envelope to receive your application and any further instructions from the scholarship provider or email: info@bpia.org. No GPA requirement specified.

Business Products Industry Association
Attn: Scholarship Committee
301 North Fairfax Street
Alexandria, VA 22314-2633

Alabama G.I. Dependents Scholarship Program

AMOUNT: None Specified DEADLINE: Varies
MAJOR: All Areas of Study

The Alabama G.I. Dependents Scholarship Program is open to students who are children or spouses of eligible Alabama veterans and who attend public postsecondary educational institutions in Alabama as undergraduates. The parent must have served 90 or more days of continuous active federal military service and have been a legal resident of Alabama for a year prior to military duty. Dependents of permanently disabled service-connected veterans rated at 100 percent may also qualify after the veteran has established at least five years of permanent residency in Alabama. Award requirements change regularly. Applications and further information is available at the Veterans Affairs Office in each county of Alabama. Their offices are located in the county courthouse or in the immediate vicinity. You may also write to the address listed, including a self-addressed, stamped envelope. No GPA requirement specified.

Department of Veterans Affairs
Alabama G.I. Dependents' Scholarship
PO Box 1509
Montgomery, AL 36102-1509

Alaska Airlines Scholarship

AMOUNT: $2000 DEADLINE: July 28
MAJOR: Travel and Tourism

Awards are available to students who are enrolled in four-year colleges or universities. Applicants must submit a 500-word essay on why he/she is pursuing a career in the travel and tourism industry. The essay must also include at least two career goals. Award requirements change regularly. Write to the address listed, enclosing a self-addressed, stamped envelope for an application and further information. You can browse their website: www.astanet.com or email: myriaml@astahq.com. No GPA requirement specified.

American Society of Travel Agents
Attn: ASTA Foundation
1101 King Street, Suite 200
Alexandria, VA 22314-2944

Albert E. and Florence W. Newton Scholarship

AMOUNT: None Specified DEADLINE: April 1
MAJOR: Nursing

The Albert E. and Florence W. Newton Scholarship is open to active practicing nurses who are licensed as registered nurses in the state of Rhode Island. To be considered for the award, you must have already applied, been accepted to and matriculated into a bachelor's program in any field of study. If you have not been matriculated, you will not be eligible to receive the award. An advisory group will make their final selection based on financial need and a number of other criteria. Award requirements change regularly. No GPA requirement specified.

Rhode Island Foundation
Attn: Special Funds Office
70 Elm Street
Providence, RI 02903

65
Albuquerque Amateur Radio Club Scholarship

AMOUNT: $500 DEADLINE: February 1
MAJOR: All Areas of Study

This scholarship is available to students with any class amateur radio license who are residents of New Mexico. Applicants must be working on their undergraduate degree and submit, with their application, a one-page essay on the role Amateur Radio has played in his/her life. Possibility of more than one award per year given funding. Award requirements change regularly. Write the address provided, using a self-addressed, stamped envelope, for further information. No GPA requirement specified.

American Radio Relay League
Attn: ARRL Foundation
225 Main Street
Newington, CT 06111-1400

66
Alice Aber Smith Scholarship

AMOUNT: None Specified DEADLINE: Varies
MAJOR: All Fields of Study

The Alice Aber Smith Scholarship is open to graduating seniors at Burlington High School (Burlington, WI). Students must attend a four-year religious affiliated college. Award requirements change regularly. Please visit your Guidance Office to receive an application and any additional details. No GPA requirement specified.

Burlington High School
Attn: Guidance Office
225 Robert Street
Burlington, WI 53105

67
Alice B. Rogers Educational Fund

AMOUNT: $6000-$10000 DEADLINE: March 1
MAJOR: Advertising, Marketing, Journalism, Communications

The Alice B. Rogers Educational Fund is open to undergraduate and post-graduate students and teachers working toward a degree in advertising, marketing, journalism, graphic design, radio and television or a related communications field. You must be a Texas resident and/or attending a Houston, Texas area college, junior college or university. This award is based on academic merit, extracurricular activities and financial need. A one-page essay is required. Award requirements change regularly. No GPA requirement specified.

Houston Advertising Federation
PO Box 27592
Houston, TX 77227-7592

68
Alice Yuriko Endo Memorial Scholarship

AMOUNT: $1000-$5000 DEADLINE: April 1
MAJOR: All Fields of Study

The Alice Yuriko Endo Memorial Scholarship is open to current undergraduate students of Japanese ancestry. National Japanese American Citizens League (JACL) membership is a requirement to be considered for this award. Membership must be held either by you or your parents only. You must submit a completed application form, proof of JACL membership, a personal statement, letter of recommendation, official transcripts and a resume. Preference will be given to students residing in the Eastern District Council and/or students with an interest in public and social service. March 20 is the last day to request an application. Award requirements change regularly. Please send a self-addressed, stamped envelope to receive your application and any further instructions from the scholarship provider. Please indicate that you would like to receive an application for undergraduate awards. You may also find the scholarship application online at www.jacl.org. No GPA requirement specified.

Japanese American Citizens League - National Headquarters
Attn: National Scholarship Awards
1765 Sutter Street
San Francisco, CA 94115

69
All American Athletes Scholarship

AMOUNT: $500-$2500 DEADLINE: Varies
MAJOR: All Areas of Study

The All American Athletes Scholarship is open to high school sophomores through seniors in college. You do not have to be an athlete in order to apply, but you must be a U.S. citizen or legal resident with at least a 2.0 GPA. You must be attending, or going to attend, an accredited U.S. college or university. The respective deadline dates are April 30, August 30 and December 31. Award requirements change regularly. GPA must be 2.0-4.0.

All American Athletes Online
Attn: Scholarship Programs
1018 South 350 East
Provo, UT 84606

70
All-Teke Academic Team Recognition & John A. Courson Top Scholar Award

AMOUNT: $300-$2000 DEADLINE: February 25
MAJOR: All Areas of Study

This award is open to full-time juniors and above who have a minimum 3.5 cumulative GPA on a 4.0 scale. You must be an active member in good standing with your chapter of TKE. Selection for this award is based on your ability to balance the pursuit of a degree in higher education with the development of leadership skills, interactive extracurricular participation, and the building of a sense of social responsibility. Award requirements change regularly. GPA must be 3.5-4.0.

Alliance Francaise of Greenwich
Serge Gabriel Scholarship Chairman
299 Greenwich Avenue
Greenwich, CT 06830-6504

74
Alliance Francaise of Greenwich Undergraduate Scholarship

AMOUNT: $2000 DEADLINE: April 5
MAJOR: French

This scholarship is open to high school seniors who plan to study French in college. Eligible candidates must meet one of the following requirements: be a student in a Greenwich public or private high school, be a Greenwich resident, or be the child of a member of the Alliance Francaise for at least one year. Award requirements change regularly. For further information and an application, please contact your high school guidance counselor, call (203) 629-1340, or write to the address listed, including a self-addressed, stamped envelope. No GPA requirement specified.

Alliance Francaise of Greenwich
Serge Gabriel Scholarship Chairman
299 Greenwich Avenue
Greenwich, CT 06830-6504

75
Alma Murphey Memorial Scholarship

AMOUNT: $1000 DEADLINE: March 1
MAJOR: All Areas of Study

These scholarships are available to legally blind graduate students. Award requirements change regularly. Write to the address listed, enclosing a self-addressed envelope for an application and further information. No GPA requirement specified.

American Council of the Blind
Attn: Billie Jean Keith
1155 15th Street NW, Suite 720
Washington, DC 20005-2706

76
Alonso Martinez Scholarship

AMOUNT: None Specified DEADLINE: Varies
MAJOR: All Areas of Study

Open to Rocky Mountain High School seniors. Applicants will be considered on academic standards, financial need, and must be of Spanish surname or Hispanic background. A student statement of Hispanic origin is required - mother's surname is adequate. To be used only at Colorado colleges and universities. Application deadline, procedure, and award amount vary annually. Award requirements change regularly. Applications are available in January or February in the Rocky Mountain High School Career Center, as part of the Local Scholarship Packet. No GPA requirement specified.

Rocky Mountain High School
Scholarship Committee
1300 West Swallow Road
Fort Collins, CO 80526-2412

/Nancy Stewart

Awards are available to official representatives of ASTA Allegheny Chapter Active or Active Associate members pursuing one of ICTA's certification programs. Recipients must have at least three years of experience working in the travel industry. A letter of intent to enroll in an ICTA course within one year along with an explanation as to the benefits they hope to obtain from the ICTA program required. Award requirements change regularly. Write to the address listed, enclosing a self-addressed, stamped envelope for an application and further information. You can browse their website: www.astanet.com or email: myriaml@astahq.com. No GPA requirement specified.

American Society of Travel Agents
Attn: ASTA Foundation
1101 King Street, Suite 200
Alexandria, VA 22314-2944

72
Allen H. and Nydia Meyers Foundation Scholarship

AMOUNT: $1000 DEADLINE: March 1
MAJOR: Sciences, Allied Fields

The Allen H. and Nydia Meyers Foundation Scholarship is open to high school seniors from Lenawee County (MI). To qualify for the award, you must be planning to study science and/or an allied field. Award requirements change regularly. Please send a self-addressed, stamped envelope to receive your application and any further instructions from the scholarship provider. No GPA requirement specified.

Morenci High School
Attn: Mrs. Melissa Parnell
788 Coomer Street
Morenci, MI 49256

73
Alliance Francaise of Greenwich Graduate Scholarship

AMOUNT: $2000 DEADLINE: April 15
MAJOR: French

This scholarship is open to college graduates who plan to do graduate study in French in the U.S. or abroad. Eligible candidates must meet one of the following criteria: be a teacher in Greenwich public or private school, a Greenwich resident, or a member of the Alliance Francaise for at least one year. Award requirements change regularly. For further information, call (203) 629-1340, or write to the address listed, including a self-addressed, stamped envelope. No GPA requirement specified.

77
Alpha Delta Kappa Scholarship

AMOUNT: $500 DEADLINE: March 31
MAJOR: Teacher Education

The Alpha Delta Kappa Scholarship is open to graduating high school seniors. To be considered for the award, you must be from Lenawee County (MI) and be pursuing a career in teacher education. Award requirements change regularly. Please send a self-addressed, stamped envelope to receive your application and any further instructions from the scholarship provider. No GPA requirement specified.

Morenci High School
Attn: Mrs. Melissa Parnell
788 Coomer Street
Morenci, MI 49256

78
Alpha Gamma Delta Eta Alumnae Chapter Scholarship

AMOUNT: None Specified DEADLINE: March 15
MAJOR: All Areas of Study

This scholarship is open to members of Alpha Gamma Delta Eta Alumnae Chapter. Applicants must have a minimum 3.0 GPA, be enrolled as juniors and seniors for the upcoming year at an accredited college or university or accepted in to a post-graduate degree program. The following four criteria are used to evaluate candidates: intellectual, moral, and social commitment; scholastic ability; extracurricular activities; ability to articulate a career plan that shows motivation, initiative, and commitment. Award requirements change regularly. Please send a self-addressed, stamped envelope to receive your application and any further instructions from the scholarship provider, call (765) 653-4978, or Fax (765) 653-6385. GPA must be 3.0-4.0.

Alpha Gamma Delta Eta Alumnae Chapter Scholarship
C/O Putnam County Foundation
Two South Jackson Street, Suite 514
Greencastle, IN 46135-1514

79
Alpha Phi Alpha Fraternity-Beta Theta Lambda Chapter Scholarship

AMOUNT: $1000 DEADLINE: January 22
MAJOR: All Fields of Study

The Alpha Phi Alpha Fraternity-Beta Theta Lambda Chapter Scholarship is open to male African-American students in Durham area high schools who are committed to pursue a four-year college or university education (including a community college transfer program). Recipients are selected by the Alpha Phi Alpha Fraternity Scholarship Committee using the following criteria: scholarship, character, leadership, an essay and financial need. Award requirements change regularly. To request an application, please contact: Alpha Phi Alpha Fraternity, Inc., Beta Theta Lambda Chapter, Scholarship Committee, PO Box 3522, Durham, NC 27702. No GPA requirement specified.

East Chapel Hill High School
Attn: Career Development Coordinator
500 Weaver Dairy Road
Chapel Hill, NC 27514-1721

80
ALSC/Bound-To-Stay-Bound Books Scholarship

AMOUNT: $6000 DEADLINE: April 1
MAJOR: Library Science (Children's)

The ALSC/Bound-To-Stay-Bound Books Scholarship is open to citizens of the U.S. and Canada who are pursing a master's or advanced degree in children's librarianship. To be considered for this award, you must be accepted into (but not yet begun coursework at) an ALA-accredited library school that offers a full range of courses in children's materials and library services to children. Award recipients will be expected to become members of the ALA and the ALSC and accept positions after graduation in the field of library service to children for at least one year. Award requirements change regularly. No GPA requirement specified.

3American Library Association
HRDR/Staff Liaison - Scholarship Juries
50 East Huron Street
Chicago, IL 60611-2795

81
ALSC/Frederic G. Melcher Scholarship

AMOUNT: $6000 DEADLINE: April 1
MAJOR: Library Science (Children's)

The ALSC/Frederic G. Melcher Scholarship is open to citizens of the U.S. and Canada who are pursing a master's or advanced degree in children's librarianship. To be considered for this award, you must be accepted into (but not yet begun coursework at) an ALA-accredited library school that offers a full range of courses in children's materials and library services to children. Award recipients will be expected to become members of the ALA and the ALSC and accept positions after graduation in the field of library service to children for at least one year. Award requirements change regularly. No GPA requirement specified.

American Library Association
HRDR/Staff Liaison - Scholarship Juries
50 East Huron Street
Chicago, IL 60611-2795

82
Amarillo Area Foundation Scholarship

AMOUNT: None Specified DEADLINE: Varies
MAJOR: All Areas of Study

The Amarillo Area Foundation Scholarship Program is open to graduating high school students who live in one of the 26 northernmost counties of the Texas Panhandle. The Foundation has over 50 funding sources with a wide variety of criteria. Please contact them concerning these specifications. Applicants from the following counties are considered: Dallam; Sherman; Hansford; Ochiltree; Lipscomb; Hartley;

Moore; Hutchinson; Roberts; Hemphill; Oldham; Potter; Carson; Gray; Wheeler; Deaf Smith; Randall; Armstrong; Donley; Collingsworth; Parmer; Castro; Swisher; Briscoe; Hall; Childress. Award requirements change regularly. Please send a self-addressed, stamped envelope to receive your application and for any further instructions from the scholarship provider. No GPA requirement specified.

Amarillo Area Foundation
Attn: Scholarship Coordinator
801 South Fillmore Suite 700
Amarillo, TX 79101-3537

83
AMBUCS Scholarship for Therapists

AMOUNT: $500-$3000 DEADLINE: April 15
MAJOR: Physical Therapy, Occupational Therapy, Speech-Language Pathology, Hearing Audiology

The AMBUCS Scholarship for Therapists is open to students who are U.S. citizens at the junior level or above. You must be enrolled in an accredited health therapy program and be able to demonstrate financial need. To be eligible, you must also demonstrate good scholastic standing, express intent to enter clinical practice and submit an application, which includes a personal statement detailing why you have chosen your particular field. It is recommended, but not mandatory, that applicants seek sponsorship of a local AMBUCS chapter. Award requirements change regularly. No GPA requirement specified.

National AMBUCS, Inc.
AMBUCS Resource Center
PO Box 5127
High Point, NC 27262-5127

84
Amelia Earhart Fellowship Award

AMOUNT: $6000 DEADLINE: November 1
MAJOR: Aerospace Engineering, Aerospace Related Sciences

Open to women graduate students who have a bachelor's degree in a qualifying area of science or engineering. Must have a superior academic record with evidence of potential at a recognized university or college as verified by transcripts and recommendations. Must have completed one year of aerospace-related studies by the time the grant is awarded. Recipients will be notified on or before May 15. Award requirements change regularly. Please send stamped self-addressed envelope with request for more information to the address below. GPA must be 3.3-4.0.

Zonta International Foundation
Amelia Earhart Fellowships
557 West Randolph Street
Chicago, IL 60661-2206

85
Ameren Corporation Scholarship

AMOUNT: $2500 DEADLINE: April 15
MAJOR: All Areas of Study

This scholarship is open to enrolled, full-time undergraduates in colleges or universities in Missouri and Illinois. Applicants must be residents of Missouri and Illinois and be from households that are customers of Union Electric, now known as

AmerenUE, or Central Illinois Public Service Co., now known as AmerenCIPS. Based on financial need, academics and character. Award requirements change regularly. Information and applications will be available after January 1 to April 15. For further information, contact the scholarship provider AFTER January 1, at the address listed, include a self-addressed, stamped, business-size envelope for a reply. GPA must be 2.5-4.0.

Scholarship Foundation of St. Louis
Attn: Scholarship Coordinator
8215 Clayton Road
Saint Louis, MO 63117-1107

86
American Action Fund Scholarship

AMOUNT: $10000 DEADLINE: March 31
MAJOR: All Areas of Study

This scholarship is open to students who are legally blind and are pursuing or planning to pursue a full-time postsecondary course of study in the U.S. Selection for this award is based on academic excellence, service to the community, and financial need. Award requirements change regularly. Please contact the sponsor for further information. No GPA requirement specified.

National Federation of the Blind
Attn: Peggy Elliott, Chairman
805 5th Avenue
Grinnell, IA 50112-1653

87
American Assn. of Hispanic Certified Public Accountants Scholarship

AMOUNT: None Specified DEADLINE: September 15
MAJOR: Accounting

This scholarship is open to undergraduates of Hispanic descent who are enrolled in or have completed an intermediate-level accounting course. You must have a minimum GPA of 3.0 in accounting and overall, and be pursuing a career in accounting. Official transcripts, an essay, a letter of recommendation and a copy of your current class schedule will be required when you apply. The assessment is based on academics, financial need and community involvement. Award requirements change regularly. Please send a self-addressed, stamped envelope to receive your application. For further instructions call (626) 965-0643. GPA must be 3.0-4.0.

American Association of Hispanic Certified Public Accountants
AAHCPA Scholarship Program
19726 Colima Road #270
Rowland Heights, CA 91748-3210

88
American Association of University Women Grants

AMOUNT: None Specified DEADLINE: May 15
MAJOR: All Areas of Study

This scholarship is open to local women graduate students

who have been accepted by the school of their choice or post-college women seeking a new career or continuing professional education and enrolled in school. You must be a resident of Norwalk, Westport, Wilton, Weston or Darien (CT). Special consideration is given to members of the Norwalk-Westport Branch of the AAUW, though membership is not a prerequisite to receive this award. Award requirements change regularly. No GPA requirement specified.

American Association of University Women, Norwalk-Westport Branch
Attn: Willadean Hart, Chairperson
36 Colony Road
Westport, CT 06880-3702

American Association of University Women Scholarship

AMOUNT: None Specified DEADLINE: March 15
MAJOR: All Areas of Study

Awarded to female students entering into or already participating in a graduate school program. Candidate must be accepted or enrolled in an accredited program for a master's or doctoral degree. The grant is open to York County residents, graduates of a York County high school, or members of the York Branch of AAUW. Factors considered in choosing the recipient include academic excellence, financial need, breadth of service to school or community, and area of study and its potential for advancing the cause of women's issues. Award requirements change regularly. Write to the address listed, enclosing a self-addressed, stamped envelope for an application and further information. GPA must be 3.5-4.0.

American Association of University Women - York Branch
Attn: Marion Bowman
181 Woodland Drive
York, PA 17403-3631

American Association of University Women Scholarship - Freehold Area

AMOUNT: $1500 DEADLINE: June 15
MAJOR: All Areas of Study

The American Association of University Women Scholarship is open to female students who are residents of Monmouth County (NJ) (preference may be given to residents of western Monmouth County), enrolled in a bachelor's degree program with 60 credits completed, or enrolled in a graduate program with a semester of work completed. In order to apply, you must maintain at least a "B" average and be a minimum of 25 years of age. Award requirements change regularly. Please send a self-addressed, stamped envelope to receive your application and any further instructions from the scholarship provider. GPA must be 3.0-4.0.

American Association of University Women - Freehold Area Branch
Attn: Carol Gabriel
One Virginiana Terrace
Freehold, NJ 07728

American Board of Funeral Service Education National Scholarship

AMOUNT: $250-$500 DEADLINE: September 1
MAJOR: Funeral Service, Mortuary Science

Applicants must be enrolled in an accredited ABFSE program and be United States citizens. Applicants must have completed at least one term of study and have at least one remaining before graduation. This award is based on need, academics, extracurricular activities, recommendations and the articulateness of the application itself. Award requirements change regularly. Applications are available from each American Board School or write to the address listed for details. If writing, please indicate what school you are attending. No GPA requirement specified.

American Board of Funeral Service Education
Attn: Scholarship Committee
38 Florida Avenue
Portland, ME 04103

American Business Women's Association Scholarship

AMOUNT: $400 DEADLINE: March 15
MAJOR: All Areas of Study

Open to female Harrisonville High School seniors who are from Cass County (MO). Award requirements change regularly. Applications are available in the Harrisonville Senior High School guidance office. No GPA requirement specified.

Harrisonville Senior High School
Attn: Roy Sackman
1504 East Elm Street
Harrisonville, MO 64701-2022

American Cancer Society College Scholarship

AMOUNT: Maximum: $1000 DEADLINE: June 1
MAJOR: All Fields of Study

The American Cancer Society College Scholarship is awarded to residents of Georgia, North Carolina or South Carolina who have been diagnosed with cancer before the age of 21. To be considered for this award, you must have been accepted to a two- or four-year university or community college or vocational technical school and under the age of 21 at the time of application. Awards will be based on your possession of a combination of financial need, scholarship, leadership and community service. Priority will be given to previous American Cancer Society Scholarship recipients for scholarship renewal. Award requirements change regularly. For further information or an application, please contact the American Cancer Society at (800) 282-4914. No GPA requirement specified.

American Cancer Society — Southeast Division, Incorporated
Attn: Scholarship Chairperson
500 East Moorehead Street, Suite 211
Charlotte, NC 28202

Society

NE: April 10

are U.S. citizens and have
ge 21. Applicants must be
pplication and maintain a
be based on a combination
dership, and community ser-
vice. Consideration will be given to students pursuing an education in regionally accredited vocational technical schools.
Award requirements change regularly. For further information
and an application, please write to the address listed, including
a self-addressed, stamped envelope or call Marilyn Westley at
(800) 444-1410 ext. 405. GPA must be 2.0-4.0.

American Cancer Society - Florida Division, Inc.
College Scholarship Program
3709 West Jetton Avenue
Tampa, FL 33629-5111

95

American Cancer Society Scholarships

AMOUNT: $1000 DEADLINE: April 15
MAJOR: All Areas of Study

This scholarship is open to undergraduates who have been
diagnosed with cancer before the age of 21. Applicants must
be U.S. citizens who are residents of Michigan or Indiana
attending accredited Michigan or Indiana universities, colleges, or community colleges. Selection is based on financial
need, scholarship, community service and leadership. Priority
is given to previous American Cancer Society recipients for
scholarship renewals. Award requirements change regularly.
No GPA requirement specified.

American Cancer Society - Great Lakes Division
College Scholarship Program
1205 East Saginaw Street
Lansing, MI 48906

96

American Express Scholarship Program

AMOUNT: $500-$2000 DEADLINE: May 1
MAJOR: Hospitality Management

The American Express Scholarship Program is open to students who are enrolled or intend to enroll either full- or part-
time in an accredited undergraduate academic program leading to a degree in hospitality management. Applicants must be
actively employed (at least 20 hours per week with a minimum 12 months employment) at a hotel or motel that is a
member of the American Hotel and Motel Association or be
the dependent of an employee who meets the previous
requirement and have past employment in some capacity in
the hospitality industry. Your application will be evaluated
according to the following categories: financial need; industry-related work experience; academic record/educational
qualifications; professional, community and extracurricular
activities; personal attributes, including career goals; respons-

es to the required essay question; neatness and completeness
of the application. No GPA requirement specified.

American Hotel Foundation
Attn: Manager of Foundation Programs
1201 New York Avenue, N.W., Suite 600
Washington, DC 20005-3931

97

American Express Travel Scholarship

AMOUNT: $2500 DEADLINE: July 28
MAJOR: Travel and Tourism

Awards are available for undergraduate students who are
studying travel and tourism at any two-year or four-year
school or who are enrolled in a proprietary travel school. The
applicants must be U.S. citizens or legal residents and have a
GPA of at least 2.5. Award requirements change regularly.
Write to the address listed, enclosing a self-addressed,
stamped envelope for an application and further information.
You can browse their website: www.astanet.com or email:
myriaml@astahq.com. GPA must be 2.5.

American Society of Travel Agents
Attn: ASTA Foundation
1101 King Street, Suite 200
Alexandria, VA 22314-2944

98

American Fellowships Dissertation Fellowships

AMOUNT: $15000 DEADLINE: November 15
MAJOR: All Fields of Study Except Engineering

The American Fellowships Dissertation Fellowships are open
to women who are in the final year of a doctoral degree program at an accredited institution. To qualify, applicants must
have completed all course work, passed all required preliminary examinations and received approval for their research
proposals or plans by the fellowship application deadline. All
fields of study are acceptable with the exception of engineering. Applicants must be U.S. citizens who have achieved
scholarly excellence, have teaching experience, and are actively committed to helping women and girls through service in
their communities, professions or fields of research. Scholars
engaged in researching gender issues are encouraged to apply.
Award requirements change regularly. Please send a self-
addressed, stamped envelope to receive your application and
any further instructions from the scholarship provider or call
(319)337-1716 ext. 60 or visit www.aauw.org. No GPA
requirement specified.

AAUW Educational Foundation
Attn: Award Committee
2201 North Dodge Street - Department 60
Iowa City, IA 52243-4030

99

American General Scholarship

AMOUNT: $500-$1500 DEADLINE: Varies
MAJOR: All Areas of Study

The American General Scholarship is open to graduating high
school seniors enrolled in public high schools in the states of

Alabama, California, Florida, Georgia, Kentucky, Mississippi, North Carolina, Ohio, Pennsylvania, Texas, Tennessee or Virginia. In order to apply, you must have an above average GPA and rank in the top third of your senior class, but not in the top ten percent. You will also need to submit two recommendations and an essay. Heavy emphasis is placed on your character as demonstrated by: extracurricular activities in school; involvement in community affairs; after-school employment; and character traits such as respect, kindness and good citizenship. Award requirements change regularly. GPA must be 3.0-4.0.

American General Life and Accident Insurance Company
c/o Scholarship Program Administrators
PO Box 23737
Nashville, TN 37202-3737

100
American Indian Scholarship

AMOUNT: $500 DEADLINE: Varies
MAJOR: All Areas of Study

Applicants must be Native Americans in financial need and have a GPA of at least 2.75. NO EXCEPTIONS. Programs may be vocational training or college/university at the undergraduate or graduate level. Graduate students are eligible; however, undergraduate students are given preference. The following must be included in mailing: No EXCEPTIONS, letter giving family history, financial status, education objective, official copy of last semester transcript, or last transcript obtained and sent by previous school, three letters of recommendation from persons such as teachers, clergy or others who have personally known applicant for a minimum of two years, and proof of American Indian blood as indicated by letter or proof papers. Deadlines are July 1 and November 1. Award requirements change regularly. Write to the address listed, enclosing a self-addressed, stamped envelope for further information. GPA must be 2.8-4.0.

National Society Daughters of the American Revolution
Office of the Committees, NSDAR
1776 'D' Street NW
Washington, DC 20006-5392

101
American Meteorological Society Industry Graduate Fellowship

AMOUNT: $15000 DEADLINE: February 19
MAJOR: Meteorology, Oceanography, Hydrology, Atmospheric Sciences, Environmental Engineering, Environmental Science

Open to students entering their first year of graduate study in the fall. Applicants must be pursuing a degree in the atmospheric, oceanic, or hydrologic sciences. Award requirements change regularly. Write to the address listed, sending a self-addressed, stamped envelope for details, call AMS headquarters at (617) 227-2426, extension 235, browse their website: www.ametsoc.org/ams/amsedu/scholfel.html or contact their email: armstrong@ametsoc.org. No GPA requirement specified.

American Meteorological Society
Fellowship/Scholarship Coordinator
45 Beacon Street
Boston, MA 02108-3693

102
American Meteorological Society Minority Scholarship

AMOUNT: $3000 DEADLINE: February 12
MAJOR: Meteorology, Atmospheric Science, Hydrology, Oceanic Science

Open to graduating high school minority seniors who will be entering their freshman year of college and plan to study in one of the areas listed above. Students must plan to pursue careers in the atmospheric or related oceanic and hydrologic sciences. Award requirements change regularly. Write to the address listed, sending a self-addressed, stamped envelope for details, call AMS headquarters at (617) 227-2426, extension 235,or contact their email: armstrong@ametsoc.org. GPA must be 3.0-4.0.

American Meteorological Society
Fellowship/Scholarship Coordinator
45 Beacon Street
Boston, MA 02108-3693

103
American Meteorological Society Undergraduate Scholarship

AMOUNT: None Specified DEADLINE: June 14
MAJOR: Meteorology, Atmospheric Science, Hydrology, Oceanography

Scholarships for students entering their last year of study toward a degree in one of the fields listed above. Based on academic ability and financial need. Requires a GPA of at least 3.0 and U.S. citizenship or permanent residency. Award requirements change regularly. Write to the address listed, sending a self-addressed, stamped envelope for details, call AMS headquarters at (617) 227-2426, extension 235, browse their website: www.ametsoc.org/ams/amsedu/scholfel.html or contact their email: armstrong@ametsoc.org. GPA must be 3.0.

American Meteorological Society
Fellowship/Scholarship Coordinator
45 Beacon Street
Boston, MA 02108-3693

104
American Morgan Horse Institute Scholarships

AMOUNT: $3000 DEADLINE: March 1
MAJOR: All Areas of Study

This scholarship is open to high school graduates who completed or were involved in the AMHA Horsemastership Program, involved in 4H/FFA, won AHSA and/or AMHA medal for equitation, or placed among top finalists in open competition. This scholarship is based on ability for serious study, financial need, community service, leadership and achievement with Morgan horses. Five awards are offered annually. Award requirements change regularly. GPA must be 2.5-4.0.

American Morgan Horse Institute, Inc.
Mrs. Sally Plumley, AMHI Scholarships
PO Box 837
Shelburne, VT 05482-0519

105
American Society of Mechanical Engineers Student Loan Fund

AMOUNT: Maximum: $3000 DEADLINE: Varies
MAJOR: Mechanical Engineering

The American Society of Mechanical Engineers Student Loan Fund is available for juniors, seniors and graduate mechanical engineering and engineering technology students. To be considered for the award, you must be a member of ASME and a U.S. citizen. Loans are interest free until graduation. Award requirements change regularly. No GPA requirement specified.

American Society of Mechanical Engineers Auxiliary, Inc.
Attn: Debbie Mercer
1343 West Baltimore Pike
Media, PA 19063

106
American Society of Women Accountants Scholarship

AMOUNT: None Specified DEADLINE: April 1
MAJOR: Accounting

The American Society of Women Accountants Scholarship is open to women and men who are pursuing a bachelor's or master's degree in accounting or an equivalent designated postbaccalaureate certificate of accounting. To qualify for the award, you must have completed a minimum of 60 semester hours or 90 quarter hours with a declared major in accounting. The award also requires that you be attending an accredited college, university or professional school. You do not need to be a member of the American Society of Women Accountants to be eligible. Award requirements change regularly. Applications are made through the local chapter of the ASWA. Call ASWA at (800) 326-2163 for the name of your local chapter contact. No GPA requirement specified.

American Society of Women Accountants
Program Director
60 Revere Drive, Suite 500
Northbrook, IL 60062-1591

107
American Water Ski Educational Foundation Scholarship

AMOUNT: None Specified DEADLINE: April 1
MAJOR: All Areas of Study

This award is for active members of the American Water Ski Association/USA Water Ski or donor members of the American Water Ski Association Educational Foundation. In order to apply, you must be a full-time sophomore, junior or senior at any accredited college or university and be a U.S. citizen. Award requirements change regularly. No GPA requirement specified.

American Water Ski Educational Foundation
PO Box 2957
Winter Haven, FL 33883-2957

108
Americo Toffoli Scholarship

AMOUNT: $500 DEADLINE: May 25
MAJOR: All Areas of Study

Open to graduating high school seniors who are sons or daughters of members of a union in good standing with the Colorado AFL-CIO, or are members themselves. Based on academic achievement, extracurricular activities and a 1000-1500-word essay on political contributions. Award requirements change regularly. Contact your parent's local or write to the address listed, enclosing a self-addressed, stamped envelope for more details. GPA must be 2.8-4.0.

AFL-CIO, Colorado
Americo Toffoli Scholarship Committee 35
2460 West 26th Avenue, Bldg C
Denver, CO 80211-5308

109
Ampad Scholarship

AMOUNT: $2000 DEADLINE: March 15
MAJOR: All Fields of Study

The Ampad Scholarship is open to employees of Business Products Industry Association member firms and their families. Persons holding academic records sufficient for acceptance by accredited colleges, junior colleges or technical schools, or persons already enrolled in one of those institutions are eligible for this one-year award. Selection is made by a committee from the Student Financial Aid Department of The George Washington University, Washington, DC. Award requirements change regularly. Please send a self-addressed, stamped envelope to receive your application and any further instructions from the scholarship provider or email: info@bpia.org. No GPA requirement specified.

Business Products Industry Association
Attn: Scholarship Committee
301 North Fairfax Street
Alexandria, VA 22314-2633

110
AMS/Industry Junior Scholarship

AMOUNT: $2000 DEADLINE: February 27
MAJOR: Atmospheric Science, Oceanic Science, Hydrology, Meteorology

Scholarships are for full-time students entering their junior year who wish to pursue degrees in the fields above. Also available to those planning a career in one of the above fields. Must have at least a 3.0 GPA. Award requirements change regularly. Application forms and further information may be obtained through the AMS headquarters at the address listed, sending a self-addressed, stamped envelope, contacting their email: armstrong@ametsoc.org, or calling (617) 227-2426, extension 235. GPA must be 3.0-4.0.

American Meteorological Society
Fellowship/Scholarship Coordinator
45 Beacon Street
Boston, MA 02108-3693

111
AMVETS Auxiliary Dept. of Illinois Memorial Scholarship Award

AMOUNT: $500 DEADLINE: March 1
MAJOR: All Areas of Study

The AMVETS Auxiliary Department of Illinois Memorial Scholarship Award is open to Illinois high school seniors who have taken the American College Test (ACT). You must be an unmarried child of a veteran who served after September 15, 1940. Your parent or parents must have been honorably discharged or are presently serving in the military in order for you to apply. Award requirements change regularly. No GPA requirement specified.

AMVETS - Illinois State Headquarters
Illinois AMVETS Scholarship Program
2200 South 6th Street
Springfield, IL 62703-3454

112
AMVETS Post #94 Scholarship

AMOUNT: $500 DEADLINE: March 1
MAJOR: All Areas of Study

The AMVETS Post #94 Scholarship is open to Illinois high school seniors who have taken the American College Test (ACT). You must be an unmarried child of a veteran who served after September 15, 1940. Your parent or parents must have been honorably discharged or are presently serving in the military. Award requirements change regularly. No GPA requirement specified.

AMVETS - Illinois State Headquarters
Illinois AMVETS Scholarship Program
2200 South 6th Street
Springfield, IL 62703-3454

113
AMVETS Post #100 Scholarship

AMOUNT: $500 DEADLINE: March 1
MAJOR: All Areas of Study

The AMVETS Post #100 Scholarship is open to Illinois high school seniors who have taken the American College Test (ACT). You must be an unmarried child of a veteran who served after September 15, 1940. Your parent or parents must have been honorably discharged or are presently serving in the military in order for you to apply. Award requirements change regularly. No GPA requirement specified.

AMVETS - Illinois State Headquarters
Illinois AMVETS Scholarship Program
2200 South 6th Street
Springfield, IL 62703-3454

114
An Uncommon Legacy Foundation Scholarship

AMOUNT: $1000 DEADLINE: May 1
MAJOR: All Areas of Study

The An Uncommon Legacy Foundation Scholarship is open to lesbian undergraduates and graduates enrolled full-time in an accredited college or university. Consideration is given to academics, honors, financial need and service to the lesbian/gay community. An essay is required. Award requirements change regularly. GPA must be 3.0-4.0.

An Uncommon Legacy Foundation, Inc.
Scholarship Committee
150 W 26th Street, Rm 602
New York, NY 10001-6813

115
Anderson Development and Mitsui Chemicals America, Inc. Scholarship

AMOUNT: $1000 DEADLINE: March 31
MAJOR: Environmental Science

The Anderson Development and Mitsui Chemicals America, Inc. Scholarship is open to high school seniors from Lenawee County (MI). To qualify for the award, you must be planning to pursue a career in environmental science. Award requirements change regularly. Please send a self-addressed, stamped envelope to receive your application and any further instructions from the scholarship provider. No GPA requirement specified.

Morenci High School
Attn: Mrs. Melissa Parnell
788 Coomer Street
Morenci, MI 49256

116
Andrew W. Mellon Fellowship In Humanistic Studies

AMOUNT: None Specified DEADLINE: Varies
MAJOR: Humanities

The Andrew W. Mellon Fellowships in Humanistic Studies are awarded to exceptionally promising first-year doctoral students to help prepare them for careers of teaching and scholarship in humanistic disciplines. Fellows may take their award to any accredited graduate program in the United States or Canada. To be eligible for this award, you must be a U.S. citizen or a permanent resident. If you have received a master's (M.A.) degree in your chosen field, or are working toward one, you are eligible for the award only if the M.A. program was terminal (no Ph.D. offered). The fellowship covers graduate tuition and required fees for your first academic year and includes a stipend of $14,750. Award requirements change regularly. Foundation staff will prescreen each interested applicant before an application will be released. You may request an application via the Mellon Fellowship website at www.woodrow.org. If you have difficulty accessing the site, call (800) 899-9963. You must request an application by December 7 for the 2000 competition. Completed applications and all supplemental materials must be received by December 21. No GPA requirement specified.

Woodrow Wilson National Fellowship Foundation
CN 5281
Princeton, NJ 08543-5281

117

Angelo P. Creticos Endowed Fourth Year Student Scholarship

AMOUNT: None Specified DEADLINE: Varies
MAJOR: Podiatry

The Angelo P. Creticos Endowed Fourth Year Student Scholarship is open to forth year students attending the Scholl College of Podiatric Medicine, who meet the qualifications for the Scholl Distinguished Scholar Award (minimum GPA of 3.4, may require an essay, faculty recommendations, and evaluation of extracurricular activities), ranks in the upper quarter of the class at the end of the third year and has demonstrated the knowledge, skills and dedication necessary to provide excellence in primary foot care throughout their enrollment at the College. Award requirements change regularly. Please send a self-addressed, stamped envelope to receive your application and any further instructions from the scholarship provider or contact the Office of Student Services (800) 843-3059 or email finaid@scholl.edu. GPA must be 3.4-4.0.

Scholl College of Podiatric Medicine
Attn: Office of Student Services
1001 North Dearborn Street
Chicago, IL 60610

118

Anna and Charles Stockwitz Children and Youth Fund

AMOUNT: $2500-$5000 DEADLINE: Varies
MAJOR: All Areas of Study

The purpose of the Anna and Charles Stockwitz Children and Youth Fund is to assist Jewish children and teens with a valuable educational, social, or psychological experience, or to assist them in attending undergraduate school. The fund provides a maximum grant award of $2,500 and a maximum loan of $5,000. Grant applicants must reside in San Francisco, San Mateo, northern Santa Clara, Marin and Sonoma counties (CA). Alameda and Contra Costa county residents are also eligible for loans. Deadlines for grants vary; therefore, it is encouraged that applicants apply early. It is preferable that loan applicants submit their applications by July 1 for the fall semester and November 1 for the spring semester. Award requirements change regularly. No GPA requirement specified.

Jewish Family and Children's Services
Attn: Loans and Grants Department
2245 Post Street
San Francisco, CA 94115

119

Anna M. Winston Founders Scholarship

AMOUNT: $500 DEADLINE: December 31
MAJOR: Accounting, Finance, Business

The Anna M. Winston Founders Scholarship is available to ethnic minority accounting, finance or business undergraduates or accounting and taxation graduates. Applicants must be currently enrolled as full-time students and be paid NABA members. A minimum 3.3 GPA is required. Award requirements change regularly. Please send a self-addressed, stamped envelope to receive your application and any further instruc-

tions from the scholarship provider or call (301) 474-6222 ext. 14. GPA must be 3.3-4.0.

National Association of Black Accountants, Inc.
Attn: Scholarship Committee
7249-A Hanover Parkway
Greenbelt, MD 20770

120

Anne A. Agnew Scholarship Program

AMOUNT: $1000 DEADLINE: March 1
MAJOR: All Areas of Study

This scholarship is open to active, honorary or associate SCSEA members and children and spouses of members, or for deserving others who have completed one academic year. Primary consideration is given to academics and financial need. Character, school and community activities will also be considered. A 200-word statement will be required when you apply. Award requirements change regularly. No GPA requirement specified.

South Carolina State Employees Association
Anne A. Agnew Scholarship Foundation
PO Box 5206
Columbia, SC 29250-5206

121

Anne Maureen Whitney Barrow Memorial Scholarship

AMOUNT: $5000 DEADLINE: May 15
MAJOR: Engineering

This scholarship is open to an incoming freshman female student majoring in engineering. The applicant must be admitted to an ABET-accredited program or an SWE-approved school. The scholarship is renewable for three additional years. This award is offered once every four years. Award requirements change regularly. Please send a self-addressed, stamped envelope to receive your application and any further instructions from the scholarship provider or consult your Dean of Engineering. No GPA requirement specified.

Society of Women Engineers Headquarters
Scholarship Coordinator
120 Wall Street, FL 11
New York, NY 10005-3902

122

Anne Seaman Memorial Scholarship

AMOUNT: $250-$1000 DEADLINE: July 7
MAJOR: Landscape Management, Grounds Management, Turf Management, Irrigation Technology, Horticulture

This award is open to undergraduate and graduate students majoring in landscape management, grounds management, turf management, irrigation technology, horticulture or a closely related field. To apply, complete the scholarship application form from PGMS and submit the required materials. Extracurricular and community activities will be considered. Winners will be notified by October 1. This is a renewable award. Award requirements change regularly. Applications for the Anne Seaman Memorial Scholarship are ONLY accepted

April 3 through July 7. Please do not mail applications to the scholarship sponsor before April 3 or after July 7. GPA must be 2.5-4.0.

Professional Grounds Management Society
Attn: Scholarship Coordinator
120 Cockeysville Road, Suite 104
Hunt Valley, MD 21030

123
Annual Exhibition Prizes

AMOUNT: None Specified DEADLINE: Varies
MAJOR: Art (Sculpture)

The Annual Exhibition Prizes are given at the National Sculpture Society's annual exhibition. Entrants must be student members, colleague members, professional members of the Society at the time of submission of material. Information regarding exhibition dates and application deadlines are announced in art magazines (including Sculpture Review). Award requirements change regularly. Please send a #10 self-addressed, stamped envelope to receive the prospectus for the next annual exhibition. You may consult the website address at www.sculptor.org. Or you may call for deadlines at the National Sculpture Society office at (212) 764-5645.

National Sculpture Society
Attn: Scholarship Committee
1177 Avenue of the Americas, New York NY

124
Another Large Production Creative Excellence Scholarship

AMOUNT: $5000 DEADLINE: May 15
MAJOR: Fields Leading to a Career in Promotions and Marketing

The Another Large Production Creative Excellence Scholarship is open to college and university undergraduates at the sophomore level and above. To be considered for the award, you must be interested in a career in marketing and promotions and demonstrate creative copywriting proficiency. The scholarship application requires that you submit your transcript, a brief personal statement and a written piece that reflects your creative proficiency and copywriting skills. Award requirements change regularly. No GPA requirement specified.

PROMAX Foundation
Attn: Scholarship Coordinator
2029 Century Park East, Suite 555
Los Angeles, CA 90067-2906

125
Antonio Cirino Memorial Fund Fellowship in Arts Education

AMOUNT: $2000-$10000 DEADLINE: May 15
MAJOR: Arts Education

The Antonio Cirino Memorial Fund Fellowship in Arts Education is open to residents of Rhode Island (five or more years) who are graduate students in arts education. Preference is given to visual artists but writers, actors and composers interested in teaching are encouraged to apply. Approximately eight to ten grants are available. Rhode Island School of

Design students and graduates are not eligible. Award requirements change regularly. No GPA requirement specified.

Rhode Island Foundation
Attn: Special Funds Office
70 Elm Street
Providence, RI 02903

126
Appalachian Scholarship

AMOUNT: $100-$1500 DEADLINE: July 1
MAJOR: All Areas of Study

Scholarships for undergraduate students who are residents of Appalachia, U.S. citizens or permanent residents, and members of the Presbyterian Church (U.S.A.). Must be able to demonstrate financial need. Award requirements change regularly. Write to the address listed for information and an application enclosing a self-addressed, stamped envelope or call (502) 569-5760. No GPA requirement specified.

Presbyterian Church (U.S.A.)
Office of Financial Aid for Studies
100 Witherspoon Street
Louisville, KY 40202-1396

127
APTRA-Clete Roberts & Kathryn Dettman Memorial Journalism Scholarship

AMOUNT: $1500 DEADLINE: December 10
MAJOR: Broadcast Journalism

The APTRA-Clete Roberts and Kathryn Dettman Memorial Scholarships are open to broadcast journalism majors enrolled in a California or Nevada college or university. In order to apply, you must complete an entry form and may submit examples of broadcast-related work. Award requirements change regularly. Write to the address listed for information or call (213) 626-1200. No GPA requirement specified.

Associated Press Television-Radio Association of California/Nevada
Rachel Ambrose, The Associated Press
221 South Figueroa Street, #300
Los Angeles, CA 90012

128
Arabic Translation Contest

AMOUNT: $400-$600 DEADLINE: September 1
MAJOR: Foreign Language, Arabic

The Arabic Translation Contest is open to non-native English speakers whose first language is Arabic. The applicant will submit an essay, a translation and a resume. Award requirements change regularly. For complete details, please write to professor Margaret Larkin, translation contest chair, at the address listed. No GPA requirement specified.

American Association of Teachers of Arabic
Princeton Univ - Dept of NES
110 Jones Hall
Princeton, NJ 08540-5118

129
Arby's/Big Brothers/Big Sisters Scholarship

AMOUNT: $1000-$5000 DEADLINE: March 31
MAJOR: All Areas of Study

The Arby's/Big Brothers/Big Sisters Scholarship is open to students who were matched Little Brothers or Sisters in an affiliated Big Brothers/Big Sisters program for at least one year (the match does need not be a current match). Selection for this award takes into consideration your volunteer work, community involvement, academic achievement and financial need. Two awards at $5000 and ten awards at $1000 are offered. Award requirements change regularly. No GPA requirement specified.

Arby's Foundation & The Big Brothers/Big Sisters Foundation of America
Scholarship Coordinator
230 North 13th Street
Philadelphia, PA 19107-1538

130
Arizona Chapter Dependent/Employee Membership Scholarship

AMOUNT: $1500 DEADLINE: July 28
MAJOR: All Areas of Study

Awards are available for students in their final year of a two-year college or for juniors or seniors at a four-year institution in Arizona. A 500-word paper entitled "My Career Goals" is required. Applicants must be dependents of an ASTA Arizona Chapter Active Agency member. Award requirements change regularly. Write to the address listed, enclosing a self-addressed, stamped envelope for an application and further information. You can browse their website: www.astanet.com or email: myriaml@astahq.com. No GPA requirement specified.

American Society of Travel Agents
Attn: ASTA Foundation
1101 King Street, Suite 200
Alexandria, VA 22314-2944

131
Arkansas Academic Challenge Scholarship

AMOUNT: Maximum: $2500 DEADLINE: Varies
MAJOR: All Areas of Study

Scholarships for graduating Arkansas high school seniors. Recipients must have a GPA of at least 2.5 and an ACT composite of at least 19. For use in a public or private Arkansas college or university. Financial need is a major factor. Award requirements change regularly. Applications can be obtained in any high school counselor's office. For more information on how to apply, you may also browse the Arkansas Department of Higher Education website at www.arscholarships.com or send an email. GPA must be 2.5-4.0.

Arkansas Department of Higher Education
Financial Aid Division
114 East Capitol Avenue
Little Rock, AR 72201-3818

132
Armed Forces Health Professions Scholarship Program (HPSP)

AMOUNT: None Specified DEADLINE: March 1
MAJOR: Chemistry, Biology, Pre-Med, Pre-Health, Medicine, Dental, Osteopathy, Optometry

The Armed Forces Health Professions Scholarship Program (HPSP) is open to chemistry, biology, premed, prehealth majors or students enrolled in any year of enrollment at medical, dental, osteopathy or optometry schools. Up to four years of fully subsidized schooling is offered for qualified students enrolled in or accepted to accredited schools in the United States. Participants also receive a monthly $973 stipend (subject to regular increases) for books, equipment, lab fees and other school mandated expenses. After graduation the award recipients will go on full-time active duty as Navy physicians, dentists or optometrists. Students are required to serve one year of active duty (with a minimum of three years) for every year of fully subsidized schooling. Award requirements change regularly. Please take a moment to apply online or visit the website at www.incolor.inetnebr.com/nrdomaha for further information. No GPA requirement specified.

Navy Officer Programs, Omaha
Leads Department - Suite 400
6910 Pacific Street
Omaha, NE 68106-1085

133
Arnold Ostwald Memorial Science Scholarship

AMOUNT: $2000 DEADLINE: March 1
MAJOR: Science

This scholarship is open to entering freshmen who are legally blind and majoring in science. The award is based on academic ability. Award requirements change regularly. Please write to the address listed, enclosing a self-addressed, stamped envelope for an application and further information. No GPA requirement specified.

American Council of the Blind
Attn: Billie Jean Keith
1155 15th Street NW, Suite 720
Washington, DC 20005-2706

134
Arnold Sadler Memorial Scholarship

AMOUNT: $2500 DEADLINE: March 1
MAJOR: Service to the Disabled

Awards are available to students who are legally blind and are studying in a field of service to people with disabilities. Award requirements change regularly. Write to the address listed, enclosing a self-addressed envelope for an application and further information. No GPA requirement specified.

American Council of the Blind
Attn: Billie Jean Keith
1155 15th Street NW, Suite 720
Washington, DC 20005-2706

135

ARRL Scholarship Honoring Senator Barry Goldwater, K7UGA

AMOUNT: $5000 DEADLINE: February 1
MAJOR: All Areas of Study

This scholarship is available to students with a minimum novice class amateur radio license who are enrolled in a regionally accredited institution. The applicants must be in a study program leading to a baccalaureate or higher degree. Award requirements change regularly. Write the address provided, using a self-addressed, stamped envelope, for further information. No GPA requirement specified.

American Radio Relay League
Attn: ARRL Foundation
225 Main Street
Newington, CT 06111-1400

136

Arthur and Gladys Cervenka Scholarship Award

AMOUNT: $1250 DEADLINE: February 1
MAJOR: Manufacturing Engineering, Manufacturing Technology

Open to full-time undergraduates who are enrolled in a degree program in manufacturing engineering or technology and have completed a minimum of 30 college credit hours with a minimum GPA of 3.5. Must be seeking a career in manufacturing engineering, manufacturing engineering technology, or a closely related field. Preference will be given, but not limited, to students attending colleges or universities in the state of Florida. Award requirements change regularly. For further information, please contact Dora Murray at (313) 271-1500, ext. 1709 (email: murrdor@sme.org) or Theresa Macias, ext. 1707 (email: maciter@sme.org) You may also go to the SME website: www.sme.org. GPA must be 3.5-4.0.

Society of Manufacturing Engineering Education Foundation
PO Box 930
One SME Drive
Dearborn, MI 48121-0930

137

ARTS Recognition and Talent Search

AMOUNT: $100-$3000 DEADLINE: June 1
MAJOR: All Areas of Study

The ARTS Recognition and Talent Search is open to students in the area of fine arts: dance, jazz, music, photography, theater, visual arts, voice and writing. If you are selected for the ARTS week, you will be assigned to one of five levels of awards. About 50 students are recommended to the White House Commission on Presidential Scholars. From this group, 20 students will be selected to be Presidential Scholars in the arts. The award is open only to 17- and 18-year-old students. This is not a financial aid program, but a recognition program for students who excel in the arts. Award requirements change regularly. Please send a self-addressed, stamped envelope to receive your application and any further instructions from the scholarship provider or email: nfaa@nfaa.org You may also go to their website: www.nfaa.org. No GPA

requirement specified.

National Foundation for Advancement in the Arts (NFAA/Arts)
Attn: Programs Department
800 Brickell Avenue, Suite 500
Miami, FL 33131-2914

138

ASAE Student Engineer of the Year Scholarship

AMOUNT: $1000 DEADLINE: January 30
MAJOR: Biological, Agricultural Engineering

This scholarship is open to outstanding sophomores, juniors and seniors who are student members of ASAE. In order to apply, you must have a minimum 3.0 GPA and participate in a curriculum accredited by ABET or CEAB. This award is based on academic improvement or continued excellence, participation in school and nonschool activities, initiative and responsibility. Award requirements change regularly. GPA must be 3.0-4.0.

American Society of Agricultural Engineers
Attn: ASAE Foundation
2950 Niles Road
St. Joseph, MI 49085-9659

139

ASCLA/Century Scholarship

AMOUNT: Maximum: $2500 DEADLINE: April 1
MAJOR: Library Science

The ASCLA/Century Scholarship is open to disabled citizens of the U.S. or Canada who are library school students or students admitted to an ALA-accredited library school program. This award will fund services or accommodations not provided by law or otherwise by the university that will help enable students to successfully complete the course of study for a master's or doctorate in library science and become library or information studies professionals. To be considered for this award, you must provide medical documentation of your disability/disabilities, your need for special services and/or accommodations and demonstrate your need for financial assistance. Your application will be evaluated on the following factors: your academic credentials, financial needs, leadership and professional goals. There are no requirements on semester hours for continuing students. Award requirements change regularly. No GPA requirement specified.

American Library Association
HRDR/Staff Liaison - Scholarship Juries
50 East Huron Street
Chicago, IL 60611-2795

140

Asian American Summer Intern Grant

AMOUNT: $500 DEADLINE: Varies
MAJOR: Theology, Religious Studies, Ministry

The Asian American Summer Intern Grant is open to Asian American Baptist seminarians who want to gain ministerial experience in a church during the summer. Church pastors may nominate a seminarian. The church provides supervision during the internship. Applicants must be members of an American Baptist church for at least one year before applying for aid and enrolled at an accredited educational institution in the U.S. or Puerto Rico. U.S. citizenship is required. Award requirements change regularly. Please send a self-addressed, stamped envelope to receive your application and any further instructions from the scholarship provider. No GPA requirement specified.

American Baptist Financial Aid Program
Educational Ministries ABC/USA
PO Box 851
Valley Forge, PA 19482-0851

ASNE Scholarship Program

AMOUNT: $2500-$3500 DEADLINE: February 15
MAJOR: Naval Engineering (Marine, Mechanical, Civil, Aeronautical, Ocean, Electric, and Electronic Engineering, Naval Architecture) and the Physical Sciences

The ASNE Scholarship Program is open to undergraduate and graduate students who are naval engineering majors. Related fields of study include: marine, mechanical, civil, aeronautical, electrical and electronic engineering, naval architecture and the physical sciences. Graduate students must be members of either the American Society of Naval Engineers (ASNE) or the Society of Naval Architects and Marine Engineers (SNAME). Award requirements change regularly. Please send a self-addressed, stamped envelope to receive your application and any further instructions from the scholarship provider. You may also consult the ASNE website. No GPA requirement specified.

American Society of Naval Engineers
Scholarship Program
1452 Duke Street
Alexandria, VA 22314-3403

142
Associated General Contractors Undergraduate Scholarship

AMOUNT: $2000 DEADLINE: November 1
MAJOR: Civil Engineering/Construction

The Associated General Contractors Undergraduate Scholarship is open to college freshmen, sophomores and juniors enrolled in or planning to enroll in a full-time four-year university program of construction or civil engineering. Award requirements change regularly. No GPA requirement specified.

Associated General Contractors Education and Research Foundation
Attn: Director of Programs
333 John Carlyle Street, 2nd Floor
Alexandria, VA 22314-5743

143
Association for Women in Communications Scholarship

AMOUNT: Maximum: $1000 DEADLINE: March 17
MAJOR: Communications, Advertising, Journalism, Public Relations, Marketing, Graphics Related Field

The Washington DC. area chapter of the Association for Women in Communications awards a $1,000 scholarship to a student meeting the following criteria: a female student in your junior or senior year in a DC. area university studying communications, advertising, journalism, public relations, marketing, or graphic related field; have a minimum GPA of 3.0; have work experience in communications or related field; is active in extracurricular activities including family obligations, volunteer work, club and organization involvement that shows versatility and commitment. In order to apply, you must also submit a 500-word essay on your communications career plans and goals and at least two letters of recommendation. Award requirements change regularly. GPA must be 3.0-4.0.

Association for Women in Communications-DC. Chapter
1333 H Street NW
4th Floor
Washington, DC 20005

144
Association of State Dam Safety Officials Scholarships

AMOUNT: Maximum: $5000 DEADLINE: February 13
MAJOR: Civil Engineering, Hydrology, Geotechnics

Open to college juniors and seniors who are U.S. citizens and enrolled in an accredited civil engineering program or related field. Must have a minimum GPA of 3.0 for the first two years of college and be pursuing a career in hydraulics, hydrology or geotechnical disciplines. Based on academics, financial need and work experience/activities. Announcement of successful candidates will be made in May. Award requirements change regularly. Write to the address listed, enclosing a self-addressed, stamped envelope for an application and further information. GPA must be 3.0.

Association of State Dam Safety Officials
450 Old Vine Street, 2nd Flr.
Lexington
KY, 40507-1544

145
Assumption Program of Loans for Education

AMOUNT: $2000-$11000 DEADLINE: Varies
MAJOR: Education, Elementary & Secondary

Loan program for California students who have completed at least 60 hours of undergraduate study in the field of education. Recipients must teach full-time in a California public school in a designated subject matter shortage area for loan forgiveness. Award requirements change regularly. Write to the address below for more information or browse their website at www.casc.ca.gov. No GPA requirement specified.

California Student Aid Commission
Attn: Grants and Scholarships
PO Box 419026
Rancho Cordova, CA 95741-9026

146
Atlanta Press Club Journalism Award

AMOUNT: None Specified DEADLINE: February 1
MAJOR: Journalism

This award is open to sophomores or juniors attending a Georgia college or university and who are majoring in journalism or a related field. Applicants must be full-time students and be a U.S. citizen/resident. Applicants will be judged on skill, achievement and commitment to journalism. Award requirements change regularly. For further information, send a self-addressed, stamped envelope to the address provided or consult the press club's web page at www.atlpressclub.org. No GPA requirement specified.

Atlanta Press Club
Award Program
260 14th Street, NW, Suite 300
Atlanta, GA 30318-5360

147
Attorney-CPA Foundation Scholarships

AMOUNT: $250-$1000 DEADLINE: March 31
MAJOR: Law

This scholarship is open to law school students who will be in their third year and demonstrate commitment to the profession of accounting. In order to apply, you must have outstanding academic performance and demonstrate leadership within your school and community. Award requirements change regularly. No GPA requirement specified.

Attorney-CPA Foundation
Foundation Scholarships
24196 Alicia Pkwy, Suite K
Mission Viejo, CA 92691-3926

148
Aurora Health Care Scholarship

AMOUNT: None Specified DEADLINE: Varies
MAJOR: Health and Related Fields of Study

The Aurora Health Care Scholarship is open to graduating seniors at Burlington High School (Burlington, Wisconsin). Students must be considering a career in health or a related field. Award requirements change regularly. Please visit your Guidance Office to receive an application and any additional details. No GPA requirement specified.

Burlington High School
Attn: Guidance Office
225 Robert Street
Burlington, WI 53105

149
Automotive Hall of Fame, Inc. Scholarship

AMOUNT: None Specified DEADLINE: June 30
MAJOR: Automotive

This scholarship is open to high school seniors who have been accepted full-time in a two-year program and to current college freshmen enrolled full-time in an accredited four-year institution. In order to apply, you must show an interest in an automotive career and maintain satisfactory academic progress. Financial need will be considered but is not necessary to demonstrate in order to apply. Award requirements change regularly. For further information, call (313) 240-4000. GPA must be 2.0-4.0.

Automotive Hall of Fame, Inc
Automotive Educational Fund
21400 Oakland Blvd
Dearborn, MI 48124-4078

150
Avis Rent A Car Scholarship

AMOUNT: $2000 DEADLINE: July 28
MAJOR: Travel and Tourism

Awards are available for graduate students who have a minimum four years of full-time travel agency experience and are currently owners/officers or employees of a travel agency. Students must have a minimum 3.0 GPA and be enrolled in a minimum of two courses per semester in an accredited MBA or MS in business or equivalent graduate degree program at a four-year college/university. A 500 to 750-word essay explaining how the graduate program relates to his/her future career in the travel industry is required. Award requirements change regularly. Write to the address listed, enclosing a self-addressed, stamped envelope for an application and further information. You can browse their website: www.astanet.com or email: myriaml@astahq.com. GPA must be 3.0-4.0.

American Society of Travel Agents
Attn: ASTA Foundation
1101 King Street, Suite 200
Alexandria, VA 22314-2944

151
Bach Organ and Keyboard Music Scholarship

AMOUNT: None Specified DEADLINE: June 1
MAJOR: Music

The Bach Organ and Keyboard Music Scholarship is open to residents of Rhode Island. To be considered for this award, you must be enrolled in college as a music major and play the organ or any keyboard instrument. The award also requires that you demonstrate financial need. In addition to your scholarship application, you need to submit a letter of reference, a brief written statement detailing your career plans and past music experience, a copy of your award letter from the institute of higher education you will be attending and a copy of your most recent Student Aid Report. Award requirements change regularly. No GPA requirement specified.

Rhode Island Foundation
Attn: Special Funds Office
70 Elm Street
Providence, RI 02903

152
Bank One Scholarship

AMOUNT: $300 DEADLINE: Varies
MAJOR: Business and Related Fields of Study

The Bank One Scholarship is open to graduating seniors at Burlington High School (Burlington, Wisconsin). Students entering a postsecondary educational program that will lend to a career in a business-related field are eligible. Award requirements change regularly. Please visit your Guidance Office to receive an application and any additional details. No GPA requirement specified.

Burlington High School
Attn: Guidance Office
225 Robert Street
Burlington, WI 53105

153
Bay State Council of the Blind Scholarship

AMOUNT: $1000 DEADLINE: March 1
MAJOR: All Areas of Study

Scholarships are available to legally blind students who are residents of Massachusetts. Preference will be given to Massachusetts residents attending a Massachusetts college or university. Award requirements change regularly. Write to the address listed, enclosing a self-addressed, stamped envelope for an application and further information. No GPA requirement specified.

American Council of the Blind
Attn: Billie Jean Keith
1155 15th Street NW, Suite 720
Washington, DC 20005-2706

154
BCI Graduate Student Scholarship

AMOUNT: $500-$2500 DEADLINE: January 15
MAJOR: Speleology, Bat Research

The BCI Graduate Student Scholarship is available to support student research that will contribute new knowledge essential to conserving bats. Only projects with direct conservation relevance will be considered for funding. Some relevant research topics include roosting needs, bat feeding behavior, bat nuisance problems and bat conservation needs. Award requirements change regularly. Application information and forms are available on the sponsor's Web page. For further information contact Angela England, Educational Resources Coordinator at the address listed, enclosing a self-addressed, stamped envelope, or send an email. No GPA requirement specified.

BAT Conservation International
Attn: Angela England
PO Box 162603
Austin, TX 78716-2603

155
Be Smart Scholarship Competition

AMOUNT: $200-$5000 DEADLINE: April 16
MAJOR: All Areas of Study

This award is open to ninth through twelfth graders in Southeastern Wisconsin. The competition rewards students who identify wasteful practices at school, work, business or in the community and successfully implement projects that reduce waste. Selection will be based on your project's adherence to the purpose of waste reduction, the level of quality and sophistication, and the project's approach to real situations and implementation. Award requirements change regularly. Applications will be accepted for next year. No GPA requirement specified.

Southeast Wisconsin Waste Reduction Coalition
Be Smart Scholarship Competition
1313 West Mount Vernon Avenue
Milwaukee, WI 53233-2620

156
BEEM-Black Experience Expressed through Music-Foundation Scholarships

AMOUNT: $1000-$5000 DEADLINE: April 1
MAJOR: Music Vocal, Instrumental

The BEEM, Black Experience as Expressed through Music, Foundation has awards open to students majoring in vocal or instrumental music. Applicants must be from the Southern Califronia area and must submit an audio or video tape with the application. An audition may be required and the Foundation encourages using music from black composers. The value of the awards are approximate. PLEASE NOTE: IF YOU ARE NOT LIVING IN SOUTHERN CALIFORNIA, YOU ARE NOT ELIGIBLE TO APPLY FOR THIS SCHOLARSHIP. Award requirements change regularly. No GPA requirement specified.

BEEM Foundation for the Advancement of Music
Scholarship Coordinator
3864 Grayburn Avenue
Los Angeles, CA 90008-1941

157
Ben Delatour Foundation Scholarship

AMOUNT: $1500 DEADLINE: Varies
MAJOR: All Areas of Study

Open to Rocky Mountain High School seniors. Applicants will be considered on academic achievement, activities, and leadership in community activities. The top ten applicants will be interviewed by the Ben Delatour selection committee. Award may be used at any accredited Colorado institution. An essay may be required. Application deadline, procedure, and award amount vary annually. Award requirements change regularly. Applications are available in January or February in the Rocky Mountain High School Career Center, as part of the Local Scholarship Packet. No GPA requirement specified.

Rocky Mountain High School
Scholarship Committee
1300 West Swallow Road
Fort Collins, CO 80526-2412

158
Benton and Louise Hale Memorial Scholarship Fund Trust

AMOUNT: $1000 DEADLINE: Varies
MAJOR: All Fields of Study

The Benton and Louise Hale Memorial Scholarship Fund Trust is open to senior Burlington High School (Burlington, Wisconsin) students. Scholarship recipients must attend an accredited college, university or nursing school in Wisconsin. The scholarship provides $1000 a year for four years. Award requirements change regularly. Please visit your Guidance Office to receive an application and any additional details. No GPA requirement specified.

Burlington High School
Attn: Guidance Office
225 Robert Street
Burlington, WI 53105

159
Berna Lou Cartwright Scholarship

AMOUNT: $1500 DEADLINE: March 15
MAJOR: Mechanical Engineering

This scholarship is open to mechanical engineering students in their last year of study. If you are enrolled in a four year program, you will apply in your junior year. If enrolled in a five year program, application is in your 4th year. U.S. citizenship and enrollment in a U.S. school in an ABET-accredited mechanical engineering program is required. Selection is based on academic performance, character, need, and ASME participation. Award requirements change regularly. GPA must be 2.8-4.0.

American Society of Mechanical Engineers Auxiliary, Inc.
Attn: Alberta Cover
5425 Caldwell Mill Road
Birmingham, AL 35242

160
Bernard Berelson Award

AMOUNT: None Specified DEADLINE: December 15
MAJOR: Population Studies, Demography, Economics, Sociology, Anthropology, Geography, Public Health, and Related Areas of Study

The Bernard Berelson Award is open to candidates with a Ph.D. or an equivalent degree in demography or population studies. Fellowships will be awarded for advanced training in population studies (including demography and public health) in combination with a social science discipline, such as economics, sociology, anthropology, or geography. The awards will be made only to applicants whose proposal deals with the developing world. The typical award is for 12 months and is nonrenewable. The award consists of a monthly stipend, transportation expenses, allowances for books and supplies, and health insurance. Candidates for this fellowship are required to seek sponsorship from at least one council staff member from

the New York Office prior to submitting an application to the Fellowship Office. A letter of recommendation from the Population Council sponsor to the Fellowship Committee is required as part of the application process. For further information and an application write to the address listed (please include a self-addressed, stamped envelope); call (212) 339-0671; fax (212) 755-6052. When writing include a brief description of your academic and professional qualifications and a short statement about your research or study plans for the proposed fellowship period. No GPA requirement specified.

Population Council - Policy Research Division
Attn: Fellowship Coordinator
One Dag Hammarskjold Plaza
New York, NY 10017

161
Bernice Hollinger Memorial Scholarship

AMOUNT: None Specified DEADLINE: Varies
MAJOR: All Areas of Study

Open to high school graduates living within a 50 mile radius of Repton, AL. Award requirements change regularly. Please send a self-addressed, stamped envelope to receive your application and any further instructions from the scholarship provider. No GPA requirement specified.

George Washington Hollinger, Sr. Foundation, Inc.
Attn: Mrs. Eula J. H. Maye
PO Box 487
Monroeville, AL 36461-0487

162
Bert Smith Memorial Scholarship

AMOUNT: None Specified DEADLINE: July 1
MAJOR: Fine Arts, Theatre, Arts, Any Arts Field

Open to any York County (PA) native or resident furthering their studies in the fine arts field. Open to applicants who have completed at least one year of postsecondary education who are enrolled in a college, university or accredited specialty school. Applicant must have a declared major in an arts field. Graduate students in a qualifying field are also eligible. Award requirements change regularly. Applications and information may be obtained at the York Little Theatre office at the address provided between the hours of 9 A.M. and 5:15 P.M. on weekdays, or by calling (717) 854-3894. Applications and supporting materials must be at the York Little Theatre office by 4:30 P.M. July 1st to be considered. No GPA requirement specified.

York Little Theatre
York Little Theatre Scholarship
27 South Belmont Street
York, PA 17403-1914

163
Beta Sigma Phi Scholarship

AMOUNT: $500 DEADLINE: March 25
MAJOR: All Areas of Study

Open to all entering freshmen who are graduating or graduated from Harrisonville Senior High School (MO). Award requirements change regularly. Applications are available in the Harrisonville Senior High School guidance office. No GPA requirement specified.

Harrisonville Senior High School
Attn: Roy Sackman
1504 East Elm Street
Harrisonville, MO 64701-2022

164
Beta Sigma Phi Scholarship

AMOUNT: None Specified DEADLINE: February 1
MAJOR: All Areas of Study

The Beta Sigma Phi Scholarship is open to students who are applicants for enrollment or are currently enrolled in an accredited college or university in a program leading to an associate or baccalaureate degree. To be eligible for this award, you must also meet the following criteria: you, your mother or your grandmother is/are/was an active member in good standing, or you are officially nominated by a member in good standing, of the Beta Sigma Phi Terre Haute Council (IN); demonstrate leadership ability, mental attitude and academic achievement; maintain a minimum GPA of 2.5 or C+ equivalent. Award requirements change regularly. Please send a self-addressed, stamped envelope to receive your application and further information from the scholarship provider or call (812) 232-2234. You will also find the application online at www.wvcf.com. GPA must be 2.5-4.0.

Wabash Valley Community Foundation
Community Scholarship Program
2901 Ohio Boulevard, Suite 153
Terre Haute, IN 47803

165
Beth Ensor Memorial Scholarship

AMOUNT: $500 DEADLINE: March 10
MAJOR: Business Services Technology

The Beth Ensor Memorial Scholarship is open to Lenawee County (MI) graduating seniors. You qualify for the award if you are in the process of completing a vocational/technical business services technology program. Award requirements change regularly. Please send a self-addressed, stamped envelope to receive your application and any further instructions from the scholarship provider. No GPA requirement specified.

Morenci High School
Attn: Mrs. Melissa Parnell
788 Coomer Street
Morenci, MI 49256

166
Bette Jo Runnels Dean Scholarship Fund

AMOUNT: $500-$2500 DEADLINE: April 1
MAJOR: Ministry

Open to women in preparation for full-time ministry but not limited to women seeking ordination or serving in any particular denomination. Award requirements change regularly. GPA must be 2.0-4.0.

Community Foundation of Middle Tennessee
Scholarship Committee
210 23rd Avenue North
Nashville, TN 37203-1502

167
Betty Hildebrand Scholarship

AMOUNT: $500 DEADLINE: July 25
MAJOR: Agriculture and Related Fields

This award is open to applicants who are continuing their education in the field of agriculture or related fields. Applicants must be a member of the Hancock County Farm Bureau (OH) and must be enrolled or enrolling in a school which will further their work in agriculture. This is a renewable award. Award requirements change regularly. Please send a self-addressed, stamped envelope to receive your application and any further instructions from the scholarship provider. You may also call the Farm Bureau Office at (419) 425-1123. No GPA requirement specified.

Hancock County Farm Bureau
Betty Hildebrand Scholarship
124 West Front Street, Suite 104
Findlay, OH 45840-3471

168
Big Island Press Club Scholarship

AMOUNT: $500-$1500 DEADLINE: June 30
MAJOR: Communications, Journalism, Advertising, Broadcast, Photography

Open to students who are interested in a career in communications, journalism, advertising, broadcast, or photography, etc. Applicants must be graduates of high schools on the Island of Hawaii, or whose parents live on the Island of Hawaii, or who have attended an Island of Hawaii institution of higher education for a school year or more. Recipients can attend any college. Award requirements change regularly. For further information and an application, please write to the address listed including a self-addressed, stamped envelope. No GPA requirement specified.

Big Island Press Club
Scholarship Committee
PO Box 1920
Hilo, HI 96721-1920

169
Bishop Greco Graduate Fellowship Program

AMOUNT: Maximum: $2000 DEADLINE: May 1
MAJOR: Special Education

This fellowship is open to graduate students in a full-time program for the preparation of classroom teachers of mentally retarded children. Applicants also must be a member of the Knights in good standing or the wife, son, or daughter of a member and have a good academic record. Special consideration will be given to students who attend a Catholic graduate school. Award requirements change regularly. Write to the address listed, enclosing a self-addressed, stamped envelope for an application and further information. No GPA requirement specified.

Knights of Columbus
Rev Donald Barry SJ, Director Of Aid
PO Box 1670
New Haven, CT 06507-0901

170
Black Opal Achiever Award

AMOUNT: $2000 DEADLINE: June 1
MAJOR: All Areas of Study

The Black Opal Achiever Award is open to people of color
who are high school seniors. Your selection will be based on
academic standing, honors received, community participation,
extracurricular activities, relevant employment, hobbies and
an essay. In addition to the application, you will be required to
submit a transcript of grades, at least two letters of recommendation (from a teacher, employer, community leader or spiritual leader) and any other pertinent information that would
influence the final decision. Award requirements change regularly. Applications are available at K-Mart, CVS, Eckerd,
Rite-Aid, Sears, Wal-Mart and other stores where Black Opal
is sold. You may also write to the address listed, including a
self-addressed, stamped envelope. No GPA requirement specified.

BioCosmetic Research Labs
Black Opal Achiever Awards
PO Box 4291
Sunnyside, NY 11104-0291

171
Blackfeet Higher Education Grants Assistance Program

AMOUNT: Maximum: $3500 DEADLINE: March 1
MAJOR: All Areas of Study

Scholarships are available for members of the Blackfeet Tribe
who are actively pursuing an undergraduate degree in any area
of study. Award requirements change regularly. No GPA
requirement specified.

Blackfeet Tribe
PO Box 850
Browning, MT 59417-0850

172
Boy Scouts - Fleur-De-Lis Scholarship

AMOUNT: $500 DEADLINE: March 31
MAJOR: All Fields of Study

The Boy Scouts - Fleur-De-Lis Scholarship is open to
Lenawee County (MI) graduating seniors. To be considered
for the award, you must be an active member of a Lenape Boy
Scout Unit (including Cub Scout leader and/or Explorer
Group). Award requirements change regularly. Please send a
self-addressed, stamped envelope to receive your application
and any further instructions from the scholarship provider. No
GPA requirement specified.

Morenci High School
Attn: Mrs. Melissa Parnell
788 Coomer Street
Morenci, MI 49256

173
BPIA District 1 Scholarship

AMOUNT: $2000 DEADLINE: March 15
MAJOR: All Fields of Study

The BPIA District 1 Scholarship is open to employees of
Business Products Industry Association member firms and
their families. Persons holding academic records sufficient for
acceptance by accredited colleges, junior colleges or technical
schools, or persons already enrolled in one of those institutions are eligible for this one-year award. Selection is made by
a committee from the Student Financial Aid Department of
The George Washington University, Washington, DC. Award
requirements change regularly. Please send a self-addressed,
stamped envelope to receive your application and any further
instructions from the scholarship provider or email:
info@bpia.org. No GPA requirement specified.

Business Products Industry Association
Attn: Scholarship Committee
301 North Fairfax Street
Alexandria, VA 22314-2633

174
BPIA District 2 Scholarship

AMOUNT: $2000 DEADLINE: March 15
MAJOR: All Fields of Study

The BPIA District 2 Scholarship is open to employees of
Business Products Industry Association member firms and
their families. Persons holding academic records sufficient for
acceptance by accredited colleges, junior colleges or technical
schools, or persons already enrolled in one of those institutions are eligible for this one-year award. Selection is made by
a committee from the Student Financial Aid Department of
The George Washington University, Washington, DC. Award
requirements change regularly. Please send a self-addressed,
stamped envelope to receive your application and any further
instructions from the scholarship provider or email:
info@bpia.org. No GPA requirement specified.

Business Products Industry Association
Attn: Scholarship Committee
301 North Fairfax Street
Alexandria, VA 22314-2633

175
BPIA District 7 Scholarship

AMOUNT: $2000 DEADLINE: March 15
MAJOR: All Fields of Study

The BPIA District 7 Scholarship is open to employees of
Business Products Industry Association member firms and
their families. Persons holding academic records sufficient for
acceptance by accredited colleges, junior colleges or technical
schools, or persons already enrolled in one of those institutions are eligible for this one-year award. Selection is made by
a committee from the Student Financial Aid Department of
The George Washington University, Washington, DC. Award
requirements change regularly. Please send a self-addressed,
stamped envelope to receive your application and any further
instructions from the scholarship provider or email:
info@bpia.org. No GPA requirement specified.

Business Products Industry Association
Attn: Scholarship Committee

301 North Fairfax Street
Alexandria, VA 22314-2633

BPIA District 8 Scholarship

AMOUNT: $2000 DEADLINE: March 15
MAJOR: All Fields of Study

The BPIA District 8 Scholarship is open to employees of
Business Products Industry Association member firms and
their families. Persons holding academic records sufficient for
acceptance by accredited colleges, junior colleges or technical
schools, or persons already enrolled in one of those institutions are eligible for this one-year award. Selection is made by
a committee from the Student Financial Aid Department of
The George Washington University, Washington, DC. Award
requirements change regularly. Please send a self-addressed,
stamped envelope to receive your application and any further
instructions from the scholarship provider or email:
info@bpia.org. No GPA requirement specified.

Business Products Industry Association
Attn: Scholarship Committee
301 North Fairfax Street
Alexandria, VA 22314-2633

177
BPW Foundation Scholarship

AMOUNT: $1000 DEADLINE: May 6
MAJOR: All Areas of Study, Career-geared Curriculum

This scholarship is available to women 25 years of age or
older for use in undergraduate study. The purpose of the
scholarship to assist women in upgrading their skills for career
advancement, to train for a new career field, or to re-enter the
job market. You must demonstrate financial need and carry a
minimum of six credit hours. Award requirements change regularly. Please take a moment to apply by filling out the application online and mailing it to the address provided. No GPA
requirement specified.

Business and Professional Women's Foundation of Maryland,
Inc.
Scholarships Coordinator
282 New Mark Esplanade
Rockville, MD 20850-2733

178
Brazeway, Inc. Upward Bound
Scholarship

AMOUNT: $2000 DEADLINE: March 31
MAJOR: All Fields of Study

The Brazeway, Inc. Upward Bound Scholarship is open to
Lenawee County (MI) graduating seniors. To be considered
for the award, you must be involved in the Upward Bound
program for a minimum of two school years and two summers. The award is renewable for up to three years, provided
you meet the specified criteria. Award requirements change
regularly. Please send a self-addressed, stamped envelope to
receive your application and any further instructions from the
scholarship provider. No GPA requirement specified.

Morenci High School
Attn: Mrs. Melissa Parnell
788 Coomer Street
Morenci, MI 49256

179
Brian M. Day Scholarship

AMOUNT: Maximum: $3500 DEADLINE: February 20
MAJOR: All Areas of Study

Scholarships are available for gay minority males who have
significant financial need and who demonstrate activism in
their gay/lesbian community or minority community. Must be
residents of Seattle or surrounding area. Award requirements
change regularly. Write to the address listed, enclosing a self-
addressed, stamped envelope for an application and further
information. No GPA requirement specified.

GSBA, Pride and INBA Scholarships
Scholarship Programs
2150 North 107th Street, Suite 205
Seattle, WA 98133-9009

180
Bruce and Marjorie Sundlun
Scholarship

AMOUNT: $250-$1000 DEADLINE: June 6
MAJOR: All Areas of Study

The Bruce and Marjorie Sundlun Scholarship is available to
residents of Rhode Island with low income who are returning
to school to upgrade their potential career skills. You are a
preferred candidate if you are a single parent (male or female)
currently or previously receiving state aid. You are also preferred if you have been previously incarcerated. Award
requirements change regularly. No GPA requirement specified.

Rhode Island Foundation
Attn: Special Funds Office
70 Elm Street
Providence, RI 02903

181
Bruce B. Melchert Scholarship

AMOUNT: $600 DEADLINE: May 26
MAJOR: Political Science, Government

This scholarship is open to Tau Kappa Epsilon members who
are full-time sophomores, juniors or seniors. In order to apply,
you must be pursuing a degree in political science or government with a minimum GPA of 3.0. You must be able to
demonstrate leadership within your chapter as rush chairman,
Prytanis or other major office, as well as a leader in IFC or
other campus organizations. Award requirements change regularly. For further information, call (317) 872-6533, email:
tef@tkehq.org or visit the website at: www.tke.org. GPA must
be 3.0-4.0.

TKE Educational Foundation
Attn: Timothy L. Taschwer
8645 Founders Road
Indianapolis, IN 46268-1336

182
BT Publix Office Supplies, Inc. Scholarship

AMOUNT: $2000 DEADLINE: March 15
MAJOR: All Fields of Study

The BT Publix Office Supplies, Inc. Scholarship is open to employees of Business Products Industry Association member firms and their families. Persons holding academic records sufficient for acceptance by accredited colleges, junior colleges or technical schools, or persons already enrolled in one of those institutions are eligible for this one-year award. Selection is made by a committee from the Student Financial Aid Department of The George Washington University, Washington, DC. Award requirements change regularly. Please send a self-addressed, stamped envelope to receive your application and any further instructions from the scholarship provider or email: info@bpia.org. No GPA requirement specified.

Business Products Industry Association
Attn: Scholarship Committee
301 North Fairfax Street
Alexandria, VA 22314-2633

183
Buffalo AFL-CIO Council Scholarship

AMOUNT: $1000 DEADLINE: March 21
MAJOR: All Areas of Study

Scholarship for graduating high school seniors who are sons or daughters of affiliated members of the Buffalo Council, AFL-CIO (NY). Based on academics, extracurricular activities, recommendation, essay, and financial need. Award requirements change regularly. For further information, please contact the address provided, using a self-addressed, stamped envelope. No GPA requirement specified.

AFL-CIO Council - Buffalo NY
532 Ellicott Square Building
295 Main Street
Buffalo, NY 14203

184
Burlington Chamber of Commerce Scholarship

AMOUNT: $500 DEADLINE: Varies
MAJOR: All Fields of Study

The Burlington Chamber of Commerce Scholarship is alternately awarded to senior Burlington High School or Catholic Central High School (Burlington, WI) students with community service involvement. Award requirements change regularly. Please visit your Guidance Office to receive an application and any additional details. No GPA requirement specified.

Burlington High School
Attn: Guidance Office
225 Robert Street
Burlington, WI 53105

185
Burlington High School Scholarship

AMOUNT: None Specified DEADLINE: Varies
MAJOR: All Fields of Study

The Burlington High School Scholarship is open to graduating seniors at Burlington High School (Burlington, WI). Students must attend a two- or four-year college or university. Award requirements change regularly. Please visit your Guidance Office to receive an application and any additional details. No GPA requirement specified.

Burlington High School
Attn: Guidance Office
225 Robert Street
Burlington, WI 53105

186
Burlington Rotary Club Scholarship

AMOUNT: $1000 DEADLINE: Varies
MAJOR: All Fields of Study

The Burlington Rotary Club Scholarship is open to graduating seniors at Burlington High School (Burlington, WI) who are entering a four-year college or university. The scholarship will be awarded on the basis of service to BHS, classmates and community. Student need is also considered. Award requirements change regularly. Please visit your Guidance Office to receive an application and any additional details. No GPA requirement specified.

Burlington High School
Attn: Guidance Office
225 Robert Street
Burlington, WI 53105

187
Butrimovitz Family Endowment Fund for Jewish Education Scholarship

AMOUNT: Maximum: $500 DEADLINE: Varies
MAJOR: All Areas of Study

The Butrimovitz Family Endowment Fund for Jewish Education Scholarship is open to individuals who wish to pursue traditional Jewish education in the context of a Jewish day school, undergraduate, or graduate school setting. Applicants must demonstrate financial need. Applicants must be residents of San Francisco, San Mateo, Northern Santa Clara, Marin and Sonoma counties in California. Deadlines vary; therefore, it is encouraged that applicants apply early. Award requirements change regularly. No GPA requirement specified.

Jewish Family and Children's Services
Attn: Loans and Grants Department
2245 Post Street
San Francisco, CA 94115

188
C-Line Products, Inc. Scholarship

AMOUNT: $2000 DEADLINE: March 15
MAJOR: All Fields of Study

The C-Line Products, Inc. Scholarship is open to employees of Business Products Industry Association member firms and their families. Persons holding academic records sufficient for acceptance by accredited colleges, junior colleges or technical schools, or persons already enrolled in one of those institutions are eligible for this one-year award. Selection is made by a committee from the Student Financial Aid Department of The George Washington University, Washington, DC. Award requirements change regularly. Please send a self-addressed, stamped envelope to receive your application and any further instructions from the scholarship provider or email: info@bpia.org. No GPA requirement specified.

Business Products Industry Association
Attn: Scholarship Committee
301 North Fairfax Street
Alexandria, VA 22314-2633

189
C-Thru Ruler Company Scholarship

AMOUNT: $2000 DEADLINE: March 15
MAJOR: All Fields of Study

The C-Thru Ruler Company Scholarship is open to employees of Business Products Industry Association member firms and their families. Persons holding academic records sufficient for acceptance by accredited colleges, junior colleges or technical schools, or persons already enrolled in one of those institutions are eligible for this two-year award. Selection is made by a committee from the Student Financial Aid Department of The George Washington University, Washington, DC. Award requirements change regularly. Please send a self-addressed, stamped envelope to receive your application and any further instructions from the scholarship provider or email: info@bpia.org. No GPA requirement specified.

Business Products Industry Association
Attn: Scholarship Committee
301 North Fairfax Street
Alexandria, VA 22314-2633

190
C. B. Hughes Sr. Scholarship

AMOUNT: Maximum: $1000 DEADLINE: June 1
MAJOR: Environmental Horticulture, Landscape Architecture, Floriculture or Related Areas

Open to college students studying environmental horticulture, landscape architecture, floriculture or a closely related field are eligible to apply for a scholarship of up to $1,000. Award requirements change regularly. For an application, please send a self-addressed, stamped envelope to the address provided. For information, please call (904) 257-6012, (904) 822-5778 or (904) 423-3368. The deadline for applying is June 1st. No GPA requirement specified.

Florida Nurserymen & Growers Assn - Central East Coast Chapter
Volusia County Co-op Extension Service
3100 East New York Avenue
DeLand, FL 32724-6410

191
Cabaniss, Johnston Scholarship

AMOUNT: Maximum: $5000 DEADLINE: June 8
MAJOR: Law

This scholarship is awarded annually to a law student who is a resident of Alabama, is attending an accredited law school in the United States and will be a second year student. Award requirements change regularly. Write to the address listed, enclosing a self-addressed, stamped envelope for an application and further information or call (334) 269-1515. No GPA requirement specified.

Alabama Law Foundation, Inc.
PO Box 671
Montgomery, AL 36101-0671

192
Cal Grant Undergraduate Program

AMOUNT: None Specified DEADLINE: March 2
MAJOR: All Areas of Study

Cal Grant Undergraduate Program are available to California residents who wish to pursue an undergraduate degree at an accredited California college or university. To qualify for any of the three Cal Grants programs (Cal Grant A, B or C), you must be making satisfactory academic progress and cannot have a bachelor's degree prior to receiving a Cal Grant. Award requirements change regularly. For complete information on the Cal Grants, please write to the address listed or browse their website at www.csac.ca.gov. No GPA requirement specified.

California Student Aid Commission
Attn: Grants and Scholarships
PO Box 419026
Rancho Cordova, CA 95741-9026

193
CALAHE Scholarship

AMOUNT: $500 DEADLINE: April 15
MAJOR: All Areas of Study

The CALAHE Scholarship is open to undergraduate college students who are involved with and show commitment to activities that promote Latinos in pursuit of a college education. You must have a "B" average (3.0 college GPA), demonstrate financial need and have been accepted for admission to an accredited institution of higher education. You must also be a Connecticut residents and a U.S. citizen or permanent resident. Award requirements change regularly. For further information, please write to the address listed including, a self-addressed, stamped envelope. GPA must be 3.0-4.0.

Connecticut Association of Latin Americans in Higher Education, Inc.
Attn: Dr. Wilson Luna
P.O. Box 382
Milford, CT 06460-0382

194
California - Arizona Watermelon Academic Scholarship

AMOUNT: $1000 DEADLINE: March 1
MAJOR: Agriculture

The California - Arizona Watermelon Academic Scholarship is open to students beginning, or continuing, studies in the field of agriculture at a college or university located in the states of Arizona or California. Applicants must also be legal residents in either state. Two 300-word essays are required. Award requirements change regularly. Please send a self-addressed, stamped envelope to receive your application and any further instructions from the scholarship provider, call (805) 521-1756, or send an email to the address provided. No GPA requirement specified.

California - Arizona Watermelon Association
Scholarship Program
PO Box 606
Piru, CA 93040

195
California Groundwater Association Scholarship

AMOUNT: $1000 DEADLINE: April 1
MAJOR: Groundwater Technology

The California Groundwater Association Scholarship is open to California residents in a vocational school or college interested in some facet of groundwater technology. You must have a 2.75 GPA to enter and retain eligibility. In order to apply, you must also be nominated by a regular contractor, or a member who is a technical/manufacturer/supplier. Award requirements change regularly. GPA must be 2.8-4.0.

California Groundwater Association
Scholarship Coordinator
PO Box 14369
Santa Rosa, CA 95402-6369

196
Calumet County Professional Law Enforcement Association Scholarship

AMOUNT: $250 DEADLINE: May 15
MAJOR: Criminal Justice, Police Science, Law Enforcement

This award is granted to students currently enrolled in a criminal justice or police science program or high school seniors planning to enter such a program. The applicant must be a resident of Calumet County (WI). Award requirements change regularly. Applications will be available at the Calumet County Sheriff's Department as well as the Police Science Departments at Fox Valley Technical College in Appleton, the Moraine Park Technical College in Fond du Lac, and the Lakeshore Technical College in Cleveland. They will also be available in the following high schools: Brillion, Chilton, Hilbert, Kiel, New Holstein, and Stockbridge. For further information, send a self-addressed, stamped envelope to the address provided or call (920) 849-2335. No GPA requirement specified.

Calumet County Professional Law Enforcement Association
Calumet County Sheriff's Department
206 Court Street, Chilton WI

197
Camden-Frontier Academic Boosters Scholarship

AMOUNT: $200-$500 DEADLINE: Varies
MAJOR: All Fields of Study

The Camden-Frontier Academic Boosters Scholarship is open to seniors at Camden-Frontier School (Camden, MI) who have been officially accepted into a postsecondary school which offers either two- or four-year degrees. To be considered for this award, you must be either the valedictorian or salutatorian of your class. The valedictorian will receive a $500 scholarship and the salutatorian will receive a $200 scholarship. Award requirements change regularly. Please send a self-addressed, stamped envelope to receive your application and any further instructions from the scholarship provider. No GPA requirement specified.

Camden-Frontier Schools
Attn: Scholarship Coordinator
4971 Montgomery Road
Camden, MI 49232

198
Camden-Frontier Education Association Scholarship

AMOUNT: $500 DEADLINE: Varies
MAJOR: All Fields of Study

The Camden-Frontier Education Association Scholarship is open to seniors at Camden-Frontier School (Camden, MI) preparing to enter their first-year of a vocational school or college. The scholarship will be awarded on the basis of academic achievement, school service and financial need. To be considered for this award, you must submit an essay addressing your future goals, immediate and future plans and a short autobiography and participate in an interview. Award requirements change regularly. Please send a self-addressed, stamped envelope to receive your application and any further instructions from the scholarship provider. No GPA requirement specified.

Camden-Frontier Schools
Attn: Scholarship Coordinator
4971 Montgomery Road
Camden, MI 49232

199
Camden-Frontier School Athletic Boosters Club Scholarship

AMOUNT: $300 DEADLINE: May 1
MAJOR: All Fields of Study

The Camden-Frontier School Athletic Boosters Club Scholarship is open to seniors at Camden-Frontier School (Camden, MI). To be considered for this scholarship, you must be officially accepted into a postsecondary school which awards either two- or four-year degrees. You must also earn a varsity award in at least one sport during your senior year and have a minimum 2.5 cumulative GPA. Two award recipients will be selected: one male and one female. Award requirements change regularly. Please send a self-addressed, stamped envelope to receive your application and any further instructions from the scholarship provider. GPA must be 2.5-4.0.

Camden-Frontier Schools
Attn: Scholarship Coordinator
4971 Montgomery Road
Camden, MI 49232

200
CAMFT - Clinton E. Phillips Scholarship

AMOUNT: $1000 DEADLINE: February 26
MAJOR: Marriage/Family Counseling

This scholarship is open to students pursuing an advanced degree in marriage and family therapy, which meets the requirements of Sections 4980.37, 4980.40 and 4980.41 of the Business and Professions Code, or are licensed marriage and family therapists and are pursuing advanced training in an accredited/approved degree program. Further considerations for this award include your academic progress, degree of financial need, community activities and your commitment to the profession of marriage and family therapy. Award requirements change regularly. No GPA requirement specified.

California Association of Marriage and Family Therapists
Educational Foundation
7901 Raytheon Road
San Diego, CA 92111-1606

201
CAMFT - Educational Foundation Scholarship

AMOUNT: $1000 DEADLINE: February 26
MAJOR: Marriage/Family Therapy

This scholarship is designed for members of CAMFT who are: pursuing an advanced degree (post-master's); planning to or are conducting a research project that will advance the profession of marriage and family therapy; or participating in advanced training, education or an unpaid internship within the field of marriage and family therapy. Award requirements change regularly. No GPA requirement specified.

California Association of Marriage and Family Therapists
Educational Foundation
7901 Raytheon Road
San Diego, CA 92111-1606

202
CAMFT - Ronald D. Lunceford Scholarship

AMOUNT: $1000 DEADLINE: February 26
MAJOR: Counseling (Marriage, Family, Human Relations)

This scholarship is open to under-represented minorities for admission into an M.A., M.S. or Ph.D. program. The program should qualify you for licensure as a marriage, family and child counselor. Financial need, participation in community services and significant accomplishments will be considered. A two-page essay will also be required. Award requirements change regularly. No GPA requirement specified.

California Association of Marriage and Family Therapists
Educational Foundation
7901 Raytheon Road
San Diego, CA 92111-1606

203
Canon Environmental Scholarship

AMOUNT: $5000 DEADLINE: February 14
MAJOR: Environmental Studies

The Canon Environmental Scholarship is open to high school seniors who are pursuing a degree in environmental studies. You must be a resident of the Greater Hartford, CT, area and be able to demonstrate academic merit, community service and financial need. An essay and two recommendations are required, along with a school transcript. This is a renewable award for four years. The award amount is $5,000 per year. Award requirements change regularly. No GPA requirement specified.

Greater Hartford Jaycees Foundation, Inc.
Attn: Scholarship Committee
One Financial Plaza
Hartford, CT 06103-2608

204
Canon Technology Scholarship

AMOUNT: $5000 DEADLINE: February 14
MAJOR: All Areas of Technology

The Canon Technology Scholarship is open to high school seniors who are pursuing a degree in technology. You must be a resident of the Greater Hartford, CT, area and must be able to demonstrate academic merit, community service and financial need. An essay and two recommendations are required, along with a school transcript. This award is renewable. Award requirements change regularly. No GPA requirement specified.

Greater Hartford Jaycees Foundation, Inc.
Attn: Scholarship Committee
One Financial Plaza
Hartford, CT 06103-2608

205
Cap Lathrop Endowment Scholarship

AMOUNT: $3500 DEADLINE: June 1
MAJOR: Broadcasting, Telecommunications

The Cap Lathrop Endowment Scholarship is open to Alaska Native enrollees to the Cook Inlet Region. Applicants must be broadcast/telecommunications majors enrolled full-time in a two- or four-year undergraduate or graduate degree program. A minimum 3.0 GPA is required. Award requirements change regularly. GPA must be 3.0-4.0.

CIRI Foundation
Scholarship Coordinator
2600 Cordova Street, Suite 206
Anchorage, AK 99503-2745

206
Capitol Scholarship

AMOUNT: Maximum: $2000 DEADLINE: February 15
MAJOR: All Areas of Study

The Capitol Scholarship is open to high school seniors who are Connecticut residents. To be considered for the award, you must be in the top 20% of class or have a minimum SAT of 1200. The award also requires that you be able to demonstrate financial need. Award requirements change regularly. For information and applications, please contact your high school guidance office or the address listed. No GPA requirement specified.

Connecticut Department of Higher Education
Office of Student Financial Aid
61 Woodland Street
Hartford, CT 06105-2395

207
Career Development Program Fellow Grant

AMOUNT: Maximum: $99750 DEADLINE: September 15
MAJOR: Research in Genetics, Biology, Pharmacology, Virology and Immunology

Provides stipends to fellows who are beginning their postdoctoral research devoted to leukemia, lymphoma, Hodgkin's disease and myeloma. Fellowship is disbursed over a three-year period. Award requirements change regularly. Please send a self-addressed, stamped envelope to receive your application and any further instructions from the scholarship provider.

Preliminary application due by September 15, complete application due by October 1. No GPA requirement specified.

Leukemia Society of America
Director of Research Administration
600 Third Avenue
New York, NY 10016-1901

208
Career Development Program Scholar Award

AMOUNT: Maximum: $350000 DEADLINE: September 15
MAJOR: Research in Genetics, Biology, Pharmacology, Virology and Immunology

Provides stipends to investigators, allowing them to devote themselves to research bearing on leukemia, lymphoma, Hodgkin's disease and myeloma. Supports fundamental research in genetics, molecular and cell biology, developmental biology, structural biology, molecular pharmacology, molecular virology, and immunology. Grant is disbursed over a five-year period. Award requirements change regularly. Please send a self-addressed, stamped envelope to receive your application and any further instructions from the scholarship provider. Preliminary application due by September 15, complete application due by October 1. No GPA requirement specified.

Leukemia Society of America
Director of Research Administration
600 Third Avenue
New York, NY 10016-1901

209
Career Development Program Scholar in Clinical Research Award

AMOUNT: Maximum: $350000 DEADLINE: September 15
MAJOR: Research in Genetics, Biology, Pharmacology, Virology and Immunology

Provides stipends to investigators who have held faculty-level appointments for at least three years, allowing them to devote themselves to research bearing on leukemia, lymphoma, Hodgkin's disease and myeloma. Supports fundamental research in genetics, molecular and cell biology, developmental biology, structural biology, molecular pharmacology, molecular virology, and immunology. Must be conducting original, independent applied research, involving clinical trials, which will advance the prevention, diagnosis or treatment of the hemotologic malignancies. Grant is disbursed over a five-year period. Award requirements change regularly. Please send a self-addressed, stamped envelope to receive your application and any further instructions from the scholarship provider. Preliminary application due by September 15, complete application due by October 1. No GPA requirement specified.

Leukemia Society of America
Director of Research Administration
600 Third Avenue
New York, NY 10016-1901

210
Career Development Program Special Fellow Grant

AMOUNT: Maximum: $119100 DEADLINE: September 15
MAJOR: Research in Genetics, Biology, Pharmacology, Virology and Immunology

Provides stipends to fellows who have had two to three years of supervised postdoctoral research experience devoted to leukemia, lymphoma, Hodgkin's disease and myeloma. This Fellowship should permit the scientist to transition to an independent research program. Fellowship is disbursed over a three-year period. Award requirements change regularly. Please send a self-addressed, stamped envelope to receive your application and any further instructions from the scholarship provider. Preliminary application due by September 15, complete application due by October 1. No GPA requirement specified.

Leukemia Society of America
Director of Research Administration
600 Third Avenue
New York, NY 10016-1901

211
Cargill Scholarship

AMOUNT: $1000 DEADLINE: February 15
MAJOR: All Fields of Study

The Cargill Scholarship is available to high school seniors whose families' primary livelihood (at least 50% of their income) is derived from farming. You must be planning to enroll full-time at an accredited two- or four-year college, university or vocational-technical school. You must also be a U.S. citizen; however, you do not need to be an FFA member.

Dependents of permanent, full-time or part-time Cargill employees are not eligible. Award requirements change regularly. No GPA requirement specified.

Cargill Scholarship for Rural America
c/o National FFA Organization
Scholarship Office - PO Box 68960
Indianapolis, IN 46268-0960

212
Carl O. Koella Memorial Scholarship

AMOUNT: None Specified DEADLINE: April 1
MAJOR: Government, Politics

Open to legislative interns (public or private) currently enrolled or planning to enroll in a four-year college or university the year of the application. Extra consideration will be given to residents of Blount and Sevier Counties and to students whose extra-curricular activities are in the areas of government and politics. The committee will give weight to both merit and financial need. Award requirements change regularly. GPA must be 2.0-4.0.

Community Foundation of Middle Tennessee
Scholarship Committee
210 23rd Avenue North
Nashville, TN 37203-1502

213
Carla Thomas Memorial Scholarship Fund

AMOUNT: $500 DEADLINE: Varies
MAJOR: Elementary Education

The Carla Thomas Memorial Scholarship Fund is open to graduating seniors at Burlington High School (Burlington, WI) planning to study elementary education. The scholarship will be awarded on the basis of grades, references and projected success as an elementary teacher. Award requirements change regularly. Please visit your Guidance Office to receive an application and any additional details. No GPA requirement specified.

Burlington High School
Attn: Guidance Office
225 Robert Street
Burlington, WI 53105

214
Carolinas-Virginias Retail Hardware Scholarship

AMOUNT: Maximum: $2000 DEADLINE: February 15
MAJOR: All Areas of Study

Undergraduate scholarships to children of employees of member firms of the Carolinas-Virginias Region of the National Retail Hardware Association with a minimum GPA of 2.5. Award requirements change regularly. Write to the address listed for details, enclosing a self-addressed, stamped envelope. GPA must be 2.5-4.0.

Foundation for the Carolinas
Scholarship Program
PO Box 34769
Charlotte, NC 28234-4769

215
Carrol C. Hall Memorial Scholarship

AMOUNT: $1000 DEADLINE: May 26
MAJOR: Education, Science

If you are an undergraduate member of Tau Kappa Epsilon and earning a degree in education or science with plans to teach or pursue a professional science career, this scholarship is open to you. You must have a demonstrated record of leadership within your chapter, on campus, or in the community. Also, you must be a full-time student in good standing with a minimum cumulative GPA of 3.0. Award requirements change regularly. For further information, call (317) 872-6533, email: tef@tkehq.org or visit the website at www.tke.org. GPA must be 3.0-4.0.

TKE Educational Foundation
Attn: Timothy L. Taschwer
8645 Founders Road
Indianapolis, IN 46268-1336

216
Casper Youth Baseball Scholarship

AMOUNT: $500 DEADLINE: April 30
MAJOR: All Areas of Study

The Casper Youth Baseball Scholarship is open to residents of Casper, WY who are entering or attending college and have a history of baseball participation. Your application will be judged on the following criteria: citizenship, sportsmanship, community activities, work experience, extracurricular activities, application question responses and a written essay. The award is made by direct payment to your college of choice on your behalf. Award requirements change regularly. Please send a self-addressed, stamped envelope to receive your application and any further instructions from the scholarship provider. No GPA requirement specified.

Casper Youth Baseball
Attn: Scholarship Program
PO Box 1966
Casper, WY 82602-1966

217
Cass County Association of Educational Office Personnel Scholarship

AMOUNT: $250 DEADLINE: March 31
MAJOR: Business

This award is open to Harrisonville High School seniors who will be entering freshmen to a four-year college, two-year college, or technical school. Applicants must be pursuing a degree in the business field. Award requirements change regularly. Applications are available in the Harrisonville Senior High School guidance office. No GPA requirement specified.

Harrisonville Senior High School
Attn: Roy Sackman
1504 East Elm Street
Harrisonville, MO 64701-2022

218
Cass County Farm Bureau Scholarship

AMOUNT: $200 DEADLINE: Varies
MAJOR: Agriculture, Home Economics

Open to all entering freshmen who are graduating or graduated from Harrisonville Senior High School. Preference is given to agricultural and home economics majors. Award requirements change regularly. Applications are available in the Harrisonville Senior High School guidance office. No GPA requirement specified.

Harrisonville Senior High School
Attn: Roy Sackman
1504 East Elm Street
Harrisonville, MO 64701-2022

219
Caterpillar Scholars Award Fund

AMOUNT: $2000 DEADLINE: February 1
MAJOR: Manufacturing Engineering

Open to full-time undergraduates who have completed at least 30 credit hours with a minimum GPA of 3.0. Must be seeking a career in manufacturing engineering. Minority applicants may apply as incoming freshmen. Award requirements change regularly. For further information, please contact Dora Murray at (313) 271-1500, ext. 1709 (email: murrdor@sme.org) or Theresa Macias, ext. 1707 (email: maciter@sme.org). You may also go to the SME website: www.sme.org. GPA must be 3.0-4.0.

Society of Manufacturing Engineering Education Foundation
PO Box 930
One SME Drive
Dearborn, MI 48121-0930

220
CBCF Congressional Fellows Program

AMOUNT: $20000 DEADLINE: April 1
MAJOR: Law, Government, Political Science

The CBCF Congressional Fellows Program is open to full-time graduate or law students, recent graduates, professionals with five or more years of experience who are pursuing part-time graduate studies or college faculty members who have an interest in the legislative policy-making process. To be selected for this nine-month internship, you must have a demonstrated understanding of, and a commitment to, the process of black political empowerment. In addition to your application, you will be required to submit a resume, three letters of recommendation (one of which must be from a dean, department chairperson, faculty advisor or employer), a certificate of academic standing, official transcripts, a writing sample of up to ten pages (legal briefs will not be accepted) and three one-page essays. Award requirements change regularly. No GPA requirement specified.

Congressional Black Caucus Foundation, Inc.
Fellows Program
1004 Pennsylvania Ave SE
Washington, DC 20003-2142

221
Centennial Fellowship

AMOUNT: $10000 DEADLINE: January 15
MAJOR: Engineering, Computer Science

The Centennial Fellowship is open to full-time graduate students who are members of Tau Beta Pi. All Tau Beta Pi fellowships are awarded on the competitive basis of high scholarship, campus leadership and service and promise of future contributions to the engineering profession. The Centennial Fellowship will be awarded to a student with outstanding scholastic skill and similar dedication to Tau Beta Pi who, in the opinion of the Fellowship Board, is most outstanding. Preference is given to first-time graduate students. To be considered, you must submit an application and two letters of recommendation. Award requirements change regularly. Please send a self-addressed, stamped envelope to receive your application and any further instructions from the fellowship provider; or email dspierre@southernco.com; or find the application online at www.tbp.org. No GPA requirement specified.

Tau Beta Pi
c/o D. Stephen Pierre, Jr., P.E.
Alabama Power Company, PO Box 2247
Mobile, AL 36652-2247

222
Central Arizona Labor Council Scholarship

AMOUNT: $500-$1000 DEADLINE: Varies
MAJOR: All Areas of Study

Awards are available for undergraduates who are dependents of members of the Central Arizona Labor Council or are members themselves. The award is based on academic scholarship and a research paper. Award requirements change regularly. For more information, please write to the address provided, using a self-addressed, stamped envelope. No GPA requirement specified.

Central Arizona Labor Council
Attn: Scholarship Coordinator
5818 North 7th Street, Suite 208
Phoenix, AZ 85014-5811

223
Central Intelligence Agency Scholarship

AMOUNT: $1000 DEADLINE: February 1
MAJOR: Electrical Engineering, Computer Science

The Central Intelligence Agency Scholarship is open to entering women sophomore students. Applicants must be U.S. citizens and enrolled in, or have been accepted into, an ABET-accredited program or SWE-approved school. The applicants must have a minimum GPA of 3.5. Award requirements change regularly. Please send a self-addressed, stamped envelope to receive your application. For further instructions, please browse their website at www.swe.org or email hq@swe.org for more information. GPA must be 3.5-4.0.

Society of Women Engineers Headquarters
Scholarship Coordinator
120 Wall Street, FL 11
New York, NY 10005-3902

 224

Chapel Hill-Carrboro Chamber of Commerce Scholarship

AMOUNT: $500 DEADLINE: April 19
MAJOR: Business

The Chapel Hill-Carrboro Chamber of Commerce Scholarship is awarded to two East Chapel Hill High School (NC) seniors and two Chapel Hill High School (NC) seniors who enroll in a postsecondary program of study leading to a career in business. Applicants must: have a minimum GPA of 2.0; motivation to pursue a career in business; evidence of positive participation in school, community and/or employment and financial need and merit. Award requirements change regularly. To request an application, please contact your high school's guidance office or the Chapel Hill-Carrboro Chamber of Commerce. GPA must be 2.0-4.0.

East Chapel Hill High School
Attn: Career Development Coordinator
500 Weaver Dairy Road
Chapel Hill, NC 27514-1721

225

Chapel Hill-Carrboro Kiwanis Club Scholarship

AMOUNT: $1500 DEADLINE: Varies
MAJOR: All Fields of Study

The Chapel Hill-Carrboro Kiwanis Club Scholarship is awarded to a graduating senior at Chapel Hill High School (NC) and a graduating senior at East Chapel Hill High School (NC). Applicants must show a record of leadership and substantial personal involvement in volunteer service to the school an fellow students and/or to the Chapel Hill-Carrboro communities, a high level of academic achievement, and demonstrated contributions to the school through participation in extracurricular activities, student government or in other ways. Award requirements change regularly. To request an application, please contact your high school's guidance office or the Chapel Hill-Carrboro Kiwanis Club. No GPA requirement specified.

East Chapel Hill High School
Attn: Career Development Coordinator
500 Weaver Dairy Road
Chapel Hill, NC 27514-1721

226

Chapel Hill Service League Technical/Vocational Education Scholarship

AMOUNT: $400-$750 DEADLINE: April 16
MAJOR: Technical, Vocational

The Chapel Hill Service League Technical/Vocational Education Scholarship is open to permanent residents of Orange County, NC, who are graduating seniors at Chapel Hill High School or East Chapel Hill High School (NC). This

scholarship may be used for a one- or two-year program at any technical/vocational program or school of the recipient's choice including out-of-state schools. Selection is based on financial need, motivation, character, citizenship, scholarship and extracurricular activities. Award requirements change regularly. To request an application, please contact your high school's guidance office or the Chapel Hill Service League. No GPA requirement specified.

East Chapel Hill High School
Attn: Career Development Coordinator
500 Weaver Dairy Road
Chapel Hill, NC 27514-1721

227

Chapel Hill Woman's Club-Sallie Southall Cotten Scholarship

AMOUNT: None Specified DEADLINE: November 18
MAJOR: All Fields of Study

The Chapel Hill Woman's Club-Sallie Southall Cotten Scholarship is open to graduating seniors from Chapel Hill High School and East Chapel Hill High School (NC) who have financial need, are in the top 25% of their graduating class and will be attending a four-year college or university in North Carolina. Applicants must agree not to accept other scholarships of greater value than $5,000 each, per year. Award requirements change regularly. To request an application, please contact your high school's guidance office or the Chapel Hill Woman's Club. No GPA requirement specified.

East Chapel Hill High School
Attn: Career Development Coordinator
500 Weaver Dairy Road
Chapel Hill, NC 27514-1721

228

Chapel Hill Woman's Club Technical Training Scholarship

AMOUNT: $400 DEADLINE: April 12
MAJOR: Technical, Vocational

The Chapel Hill Woman's Club Technical Training Scholarship is open to graduating seniors from Chapel Hill High School and East Chapel Hill High School (NC) who have financial need. This scholarship is for one year and may be renewed depending upon a student's grades. Award requirements change regularly. To request an application, please contact your high school's guidance office or the Chapel Hill Woman's Club. No GPA requirement specified.

East Chapel Hill High School
Attn: Career Development Coordinator
500 Weaver Dairy Road
Chapel Hill, NC 27514-1721

229

Character Stars Scholarship

AMOUNT: $500-$1500 DEADLINE: March 1
MAJOR: All Areas of Study

This scholarship is open to graduating high school seniors in Alabama, California, Georgia, Mississippi, Pennsylvania and Tennessee. In order to apply, you are required to present two letters of recommendation that provide evidence of good character. This scholarship is based on extracurricular activities and a 250-word essay. To qualify, your family's taxable income cannot exceed $50,000. This scholarship can be used for college, university, vocational or technical schools. Award requirements change regularly. Please send a self-addressed, stamped envelope for additional information. GPA must be 2.8-4.0.

American General Life and Accident Insurance Company
c/o Scholarship Program Administrators
PO Box 23737
Nashville, TN 37202-3737

Charles and Geraldine S. Aaron, Stanley N. Gore Scholarship

AMOUNT: None Specified DEADLINE: March 1
MAJOR: Helping Professions

The Charles and Geraldine S. Aaron, Stanley N. Gore, Katherine Horwich, Joseph L. Stone-Hortense and Leo S. Singer Scholarship is open to Jewish students planning a career in the "helping professions" (nursing, teaching, etc.). You must be a resident of Cook County (IL) or the Chicago area. Award requirements change regularly. No GPA requirement specified.

Jewish Vocational Service
Attn: Scholarship Secretary
One South Franklin Street
Chicago, IL 60606-4694

231

Charles and Lucille King Family Foundation Scholarship

AMOUNT: Maximum: $2500 DEADLINE: April 15
MAJOR: Television and Film Production

The Charles and Lucille King Family Foundation Scholarship is open to juniors and seniors attending a four-year U.S. college or university majoring in television or film production. Applicants should demonstrate academic excellence, financial need and professional potential. Along with the application, which includes financial information, students must supply an official copy of the most recent transcripts, three letters of recommendation/support and a typed personal statement. If applicants are awarded a King Foundation scholarship for the junior year, they will automatically qualify for an equal amount in the senior year by maintaining a "B" average or better and verifying their grade point average by providing the Foundation office with an official transcript by no later than June 30. Award requirements change regularly. Please send a self-addressed, stamped envelope to receive your application and any further instructions from the scholarship provider; or email your request to info@kingfoundation.org; or visit the website at www.kingfoundation.org. No GPA requirement specified.

Charles and Lucille King Family Foundation
366 Madison Avenue
10th Floor
New York, NY 10017-3122

232

Charles Clarke Cordle Memorial Scholarship

AMOUNT: $1000 DEADLINE: February 1
MAJOR: All Areas of Study

This scholarship is available to students with a minimum general class amateur radio license who are residents of Georgia or Alabama. Applicants must be enrolled at a Georgia or Alabama institution and have a minimum GPA of 2.5. Award requirements change regularly. Write the address provided, using a self-addressed, stamped envelope, for further information. GPA must be 2.5-4.0.

American Radio Relay League
Attn: ARRL Foundation
225 Main Street
Newington, CT 06111-1400

233

Charles D. Mayo Student Scholarship

AMOUNT: $1000 DEADLINE: October 30
MAJOR: Textile Technology, Design, Furniture Design, Interior Decorating, Interior Design and Related Areas of Study

Applicants for the Charles D. Mayo Student Scholarship must be enrolled as full-time students and can be either current IFDA student members or nonmembers. A completed scholarship application must include: a certified transcript of all college level/advance study work which verifies full-time status and GPA; a 200-to-300-word essay describing why you joined the IFDA (if applicable), your future plans and goals, and why you believe you are deserving of this award; a letter of recommendation from a professor or instructor. Award requirements change regularly. Please send a self-addressed, stamped envelope to receive your application and any further instructions from the scholarship provider; or email your request to info@ifda.com; or visit the website at www.ifda.com. No GPA requirement specified.

International Furnishings and Design Association
Attn: Educational Foundation Office
1200 19th Street NW, Suite 300
Washington, DC 20036-2422

234

Charles E. Fahrney Foundation Scholarship

AMOUNT: $2500 DEADLINE: February 15
MAJOR: All Areas of Study

The Charles E. Fahrney Foundation Scholarship is open to residents of Wapello County, Iowa who are attending a two- or four-year Iowa college or university. Scholarships are awarded on the basis of scholastic performance and citizenship. Immediate family members of Firstar employees are not eligible for this award. Award requirements change regularly. Please send a self-addressed, stamped envelope to receive your application and any further instructions from the scholarship provider. No GPA requirement specified.

Firstar Bank - Ottumwa, Iowa
Attn: Trust Department
123 East Third Street
Ottumwa, IA 52501-8003

Charles Earp Memorial Scholarship

AMOUNT: $200 DEADLINE: March 10
MAJOR: Accounting

The Charles Earp Memorial Scholarship is open to accounting students designated the most outstanding among applicants for NSA scholarships. To be considered for this award you must be enrolled in an undergraduate degree program at a U.S.-accredited two- or four-year college or university, be majoring in accounting and have a "B" or better GPA. You must also be a U.S. or Canadian citizen. These scholarships are awarded primarily for academic merit, demonstrated leadership ability and financial need. Award requirements change regularly. Please send a self-addressed, stamped envelope to receive your application and any further instructions from the scholarship provider. Students may submit the application by email; however, fax and email transcripts or appraisal forms will not be accepted. GPA must be 3.0-4.0.

National Society of Accountants
Attn: Scholarship Foundation
1010 North Fairfax Street
Alexandria, VA 22314-1574

236
Charles G. Stott & Company Scholarship

AMOUNT: $2000 DEADLINE: March 15
MAJOR: All Fields of Study

The Charles G. Stott & Company Scholarship is open to employees of Business Products Industry Association member firms and their families. Persons holding academic records sufficient for acceptance by accredited colleges, junior colleges or technical schools, or persons already enrolled in one of those institutions are eligible for this four-year award. Selection is made by a committee from the Student Financial Aid Department of The George Washington University, Washington, DC. Award requirements change regularly. Please send a self-addressed, stamped envelope to receive your application and any further instructions from the scholarship provider or email: info@bpia.org. No GPA requirement specified.

Business Products Industry Association
Attn: Scholarship Committee
301 North Fairfax Street
Alexandria, VA 22314-2633

237
Charles Gallagher Student Financial Assistance Program

AMOUNT: $1500 DEADLINE: April 1
MAJOR: All Fields of Study

The Charles Gallagher Student Financial Assistance Program is awarded to full-time undergraduate students who are work-ing toward a first baccalaureate degree at a Missouri postsecondary school. To qualify for this award, you must be a Missouri resident, demonstrate financial need and maintain satisfactory academic progress as defined by the school. You must not be pursuing a degree in theology or divinity. Award requirements change regularly. To apply, please submit a FAFSA to your federal processor by April 1. For more information, please consult the Missouri Student Assistance Programs website at www.mocbhe.gov. No GPA requirement specified.

Missouri Department of Higher Education
Mostars Deputy Director
3515 Amazonas Drive
Jefferson City, MO 65109-5717

238
Charles Legeyt Fortescue Fellowship

AMOUNT: Maximum: $24000 DEADLINE: January 15
MAJOR: Electrical Engineering

Open to first year graduate students in electrical engineering at an engineering school of recognized standing located in the U.S. or Canada. The applicant must have a bachelor's degree from an engineering school of recognized standing. Evidence of satisfactory academic performance is required midway in the year for the recipient to continue the award. Award requirements change regularly. This award is offered every other year. Contact the address listed, enclosing a self-addressed, stamped envelope. No GPA requirement specified.

Institute of Electrical and Electronics Engineers
Attn: Lasers and Electro-Optics Society
445 Hoes Lane, PO Box 1331, Piscataway NJ

239
Charles N. Fisher Memorial Scholarship

AMOUNT: $1000 DEADLINE: February 1
MAJOR: Electronics, Communications, or Related Fields

This scholarship is available to students with any class amateur radio license and majoring in electronics, communications or a related field in a regionally-accredited institution. Applicants must be residents of: Arizona; or Los Angeles, Orange, San Diego or Santa Barbara counties in California. Award requirements change regularly. Write the address provided, using a self-addressed, stamped envelope, for further information. No GPA requirement specified.

American Radio Relay League
Attn: ARRL Foundation
225 Main Street
Newington, CT 06111-1400

240
Charles P. Bell Conservation Scholarship

AMOUNT: $500-$600 DEADLINE: January 15
MAJOR: Natural Resource Management

The Charles P. Bell Conservation Scholarship is open to juniors, seniors and graduate students who are involved or plan to be involved in the management of natural resources, specifically: fish, wildlife, forest, soil and water. You must be a Missouri resident. Preference will go to a student enrolled in a Missouri school. Award requirements change regularly. For further information and an application, please write to the address listed, including a self-addressed, stamped envelope. No GPA requirement specified.

Conservation Foundation of Missouri Charitable Trust
Bell Scholarships
728 West Main Street
Jefferson City, MO 65101-1534

241
Charles Russell Memorial Vocational Scholarship

AMOUNT: $200 DEADLINE: Varies
MAJOR: All Areas of Study

Open to Rocky Mountain High School seniors. Applicants must demonstrate an ability in general education and vocational classes by having an overall GPA of 2.8, demonstrate a desire to continue vocational training, and show financial need. An essay may be required. Application deadline, procedure, and award amount vary annually. Award requirements change regularly. Applications are available in January or February in the Rocky Mountain High School Career Center, as part of the Local Scholarship Packet. GPA must be 2.8-4.0.

Rocky Mountain High School
Scholarship Committee
1300 West Swallow Road
Fort Collins, CO 80526-2412

242
Charlotte Housing Authority Scholarship

AMOUNT: Maximum: $3400 DEADLINE: Varies
MAJOR: All Areas of Study

Scholarships for residents of Charlotte (NC) public housing who wish to attend college, technical or vocational school. Applications are due May 1 and December 1. Award requirements change regularly. Write to the address listed for details, enclosing a self-addressed, stamped envelope. No GPA requirement specified.

Foundation for the Carolinas
Scholarship Program
PO Box 34769
Charlotte, NC 28234-4769

243
Charter Fund Scholarship

AMOUNT: None Specified DEADLINE: May 12
MAJOR: All Areas of Study

The Charter Fund Scholarship is open to Colorado high school seniors who are also Colorado residents. You must be planning to attend an accredited college or university. To apply, U.S. citizenship and part-time employment is required. These scholarships are based on financial need. If you have graduated high school before Spring 2000, you are not eligible. Award requirements change regularly. No GPA requirement specified.

Charter Fund
Attn: Scholarship Administrator
370 17th Street, Suite 5300
Denver, CO 80202

244
Chateaubriand Scholarship Program

AMOUNT: None Specified DEADLINE: January 15
MAJOR: French Literature, Cinema, Humanities, Arts, History, Philosophy, Political Sciences and Related Areas

This scholarship is open to U.S. citizens currently working towards a Ph.D. at an American University. This scholarship is from the French Government to conduct research in France in the following fields of study: French literature, cinema, humanities, arts, history, philosophy, political sciences and related areas. Scholarships include a monthly stipend of 9000 francs for a period of nine months, health insurance, and a round trip ticket to France. Award requirements change regularly. For further information and an application, please write to the address listed, including a self-addressed, stamped envelope or email: new-york.culture@diplomatie.fr You may also visit their website: www.info-france-usa.org/culture. No GPA requirement specified.

Cultural Services of the French Embassy
972 5th Avenue
New York
NY, 10021-0104

245
Chevron Scholarship

AMOUNT: $2000 DEADLINE: February 1
MAJOR: Civil Engineering, Chemical Engineering, Petroleum Engineering

The Chevron Scholarship is open to women sophomore and junior students who are majoring in civil engineering, chemical engineering or petroleum engineering. The applicants must have a minimum GPA of 3.5 and be attending an ABET-accredited program or an SWE-approved school. Award requirements change regularly. Please send a self-addressed, stamped envelope to receive your application. For further instructions, please browse their website at www.swe.org or email hq@swe.org for more information. GPA must be 3.5-4.0.

Society of Women Engineers Headquarters
Scholarship Coordinator
120 Wall Street, FL 11
New York, NY 10005-3902

246
Chicago FM Club Scholarship

AMOUNT: $500 DEADLINE: February 1
MAJOR: All Areas of Study

This scholarship is available to students with a minimum technician class amateur radio license who have been accepted to a two-year or four-year college or trade school. Applicants must be residents in the FCC Ninth Call District: Indiana, Illinois or Wisconsin. Applicants must be U.S. citizens or within three months of citizenship. There are multiple awards offered annually. Award requirements change regularly. Write the address provided, using a self-addressed, stamped envelope, for further information. No GPA requirement specified.

American Radio Relay League
Attn: ARRL Foundation
225 Main Street
Newington, CT 06111-1400

247
Chicago Urban League - Jewel/Taylor C. Cotton Scholarship

AMOUNT: $2000 DEADLINE: July 15
MAJOR: Business, Engineering, Architecture

The Chicago Urban League - Jewel/Taylor C. Cotton Scholarship is open to minority business, engineering and architecture majors who are Illinois residents attending four year colleges. Priority is given to high school graduates in financial need. A minimum 2.5 GPA is required. Award requirements change regularly. Please send a self-addressed, stamped envelope to receive your application and any further instructions from the scholarship provider. GPA must be 2.5-4.0.

Chicago Urban League
Attn: Cy Fields
4510 South Michigan Avenue
Chicago, IL 60653-3819

248
Chief Justice Samuel J. Roberts Scholarship

AMOUNT: None Specified DEADLINE: May 31
MAJOR: Law

Open to students entering their first year of law studies who are residents from Erie County (PA). This scholarship is awarded annually and is based on financial need and academic achievement. Award requirements change regularly. For information or an application, please send a self-addressed, stamped envelope to the address provided or call (814) 459-3111. GPA must be 2.5-4.0.

Erie County Bar Foundation
Attn: Scholarship Director
302 West Ninth Street
Erie, PA 16502

249
Chinese American Physicians' Society Scholarship

AMOUNT: $1000-$2000 DEADLINE: October 9
MAJOR: Medicine

The Chinese American Physicians' Society Scholarship is open to medical students who can demonstrate financial need. Special consideration is given to those who are willing to serve the Chinese communities after their graduation. Selection is based on academic achievements and community service records. Award requirements change regularly. For additional information, call (415) 357-7077. No GPA requirement specified.

Chinese American Physicians Society
Scholarship Coordinator
345 Ninth Street, Suite 204
Oakland, CA 94607-4211

250
Chris Roanhouse Memorial Scholarship

AMOUNT: None Specified DEADLINE: Varies
MAJOR: All Fields of Study

The Chris Roanhouse Memorial Scholarship acknowledges the achievements of students with learning disabilities. The award is open to Burlington High School (Burlington, WI) students and can be used for a variety of activities including college or technical school, art, music or scout camp, music or drama lessons, equipment, uniforms or tools for school or employment. Students submitting an application do not have to be high school seniors. Award requirements change regularly. Please visit your Guidance Office to receive an application and any additional details. No GPA requirement specified.

Burlington High School
Attn: Guidance Office
225 Robert Street
Burlington, WI 53105

251
Christine M. Barth Scholarship

AMOUNT: $1000-$4000 DEADLINE: May 7
MAJOR: All Areas of Study

This scholarship is open to graduating high school students from Dunmore High School (PA) ONLY. The applicant must graduate in the top fifth of the class, have an SAT score of at least 1000, be involved in the community and demonstrate financial need. Award recipient will receive $1,000 per year for each of four years of postsecondary studies, for a total of $4,000. Award requirements change regularly. For further information and requirements, please write the address provided. No GPA requirement specified.

Independent Order of Odd Fellows, Thistle Lodge #512
Christine M. Barth Scholarship
22 Washington Terrace
Pittston, PA 18640

252
Christopher J. Hoy/ERT Scholarship

AMOUNT: $3000 DEADLINE: April 1
MAJOR: Library Science, Information Science

The Christopher J. Hoy/ERT Scholarship is open to citizens or permanent residents of the U.S. or Canada who have applied for admission to and will enter an ALA-accredited master's degree program in library and information studies. To be considered for this award, you cannot have completed more than 12 semester hours (or its equivalent) toward the master's degree prior to June 1. Award requirements change regularly. No GPA requirement specified.

American Library Association
HRDR/Staff Liaison - Scholarship Juries
50 East Huron Street
Chicago, IL 60611-2795

Chrysalis Scholarship Fund

AMOUNT: $750 DEADLINE: February 28
MAJOR: Geoscience Fields

Open to women who are candidates for an advanced degree in a geoscience field and whose education has been interrupted for at least one year. Applicants must be completing their thesis during the current academic year and should have contributed and will continue contributing to both the geosciences and the larger world community through her academic and personal strengths. Award requirements change regularly. For further information, please write to the address listed, including a self-addressed, stamped envelope or call (303) 534-0708. No GPA requirement specified.

Association for Women Geoscientists Foundation
G H Production Company LLC
518 17th Street, Suite 930
Denver, CO 80202-4110

254
Chrysler Corporation Freshman Scholarship

AMOUNT: $1500 DEADLINE: May 15
MAJOR: Engineering, Computer Science

This scholarship is open to a freshman female student who is majoring in engineering or computer science. You must have been accepted into an ABET-accredited program or SWE-approved school. Award requirements change regularly. Please send a self-addressed, stamped envelope to receive your application. For further instructions, please browse the SWE website at www.swe.org or send an email to hq@swe.org for further information. No GPA requirement specified.

Society of Women Engineers Headquarters
Scholarship Coordinator
120 Wall Street, FL 11
New York, NY 10005-3902

255
Chrysler Corporation Re-entry Scholarship

AMOUNT: $2000 DEADLINE: May 15
MAJOR: Engineering, Computer Science

This scholarship is open to women who are majoring in engineering or computer science at an ABET-accredited program or an SWE-approved school and who are pursuing the credentials necessary to re-enter the job market as engineers. Applicants must have been out of the engineering job market as well as out of school for a minimum of two years. Sophomore through graduate students must have minimum GPAs of 3.5. Award requirements change regularly. Please send a self-addressed, stamped envelope to receive your application. For any further instructions from the scholarship provider, please browse their website at www.swe.org or email hq@swe.org. No GPA requirement specified.

Society of Women Engineers Headquarters
Scholarship Coordinator
120 Wall Street, FL 11
New York, NY 10005-3902

Chrysler Corporation Scholarship

AMOUNT: $1750 DEADLINE: February 1
MAJOR: Engineering, Computer Science

The Chrysler Corporation Scholarship is open to female sophomores, juniors and seniors who are members of an under-represented group in the engineering or computer science field. Applicants must have a minimum GPA of 3.5 and be attending an ABET-accredited program or an SWE-approved school. Award requirements change regularly. Please send a self-addressed, stamped envelope to receive your application. For any further instructions from the scholarship provider, please browse their website at www.swe.org or email hq@swe.org. GPA must be 3.5-4.0.

Society of Women Engineers Headquarters
Scholarship Coordinator
120 Wall Street, FL 11
New York, NY 10005-3902

257
Citizens Gas Fuel Company Scholarship

AMOUNT: $1000 DEADLINE: March 10
MAJOR: Vocational, Technical Field

The Citizens Gas Fuel Company Scholarship is open to Lenawee County graduating seniors. You qualify for the award if you if you are in the process of completing a vocational or technical program. Award requirements change regularly. Please send a self-addressed, stamped envelope to receive your application and any further instructions from the scholarship provider. No GPA requirement specified.

Morenci High School
Attn: Mrs. Melissa Parnell
788 Coomer Street
Morenci, MI 49256

258
Clarence James Memorial Scholarship

AMOUNT: $500 DEADLINE: March 1
MAJOR: All Areas of Study

The Clarence James Memorial Scholarship provides financial assistance to a student of color entering college. The award is to be used for books and supplies and can be used at any four year college or university. Applicants must: be a U.S. citizen; be a resident of Western Pennsylvania; be a high school senior; have a cumulative GPA of at least 3.5 or the equivalent; have held a leadership role in a community organization or activity. Award requirements change regularly. Please send a self-addressed, stamped envelope to receive your application or call (724) 335-4027 for further instructions from the scholarship provider. GPA must be 3.5-4.0.

J.D. Hightower and Associates, Inc.
Attn: Scholarship Programs
2614 Anne Street
Lower Burrell, PA 15068

259
Cletus Ludden & Denver Area Labor Federation Scholarships

AMOUNT: $500-$1500 DEADLINE: May 28
MAJOR: All Areas of Study

Scholarships are for students who are members or children of members of a local union in the jurisdiction of the Denver area labor federation (AFL-CIO). Students whose guardians are members are also eligible. Jurisdiction: Adams, Arapahoe, Denver, Douglas, and Jefferson counties. Award requirements change regularly. Write to the address listed, enclosing a self-addressed, stamped envelope for an application and further information or have your parent contact his/her union. No GPA requirement specified.

Denver Area Labor Federation AFL-CIO
Denver Labor Center
360 Acoma Street, Rm 202
Denver, CO 80223

260
Coates, Wolff, Russell Memorial Mining Industry Scholarship

AMOUNT: $1000 DEADLINE: December 1
MAJOR: Engineering, Environmental Sciences, Mineral Extractive Disciplines

The Coates, Wolff, Russell Memorial Mining Industry Scholarship is open to Wyoming residents of sophomore, junior, or senior standing who are studying engineering, environmental sciences, or other mineral extractive disciples. To be considered for the award you must have a minimum GPA of 2.25 and submit a short essay. Recipients are eligible for award consideration through their senior year. Award requirements change regularly. For additional information and/or an application, please write to the address listed, enclosing a stamped, self-addressed envelope. GPA must be 2.3.

Society for Mining, Metallurgy, and Exploration - Wyoming Section
Attn: Scholarship Committee
800 Werner Court, Suite 201
Casper, WY 82601

261
Cogan Trust Scholarship

AMOUNT: None Specified DEADLINE: May 5
MAJOR: All Areas of Study

This scholarship is open to graduating high school seniors from Portsmouth High School, Portsmouth, NH, or St. Thomas Aquinas High School in Dover, NH. Applicants must have been residents of Portsmouth for at least four years. Based on financial need, leadership, ability and character. Approximately 15 - 17 awards offered annually. Award requirements change regularly. Contact the address listed for further information, enclosing a self-addressed, stamped envelope. No GPA requirement specified.

George T. Cogan Scholarship Trust Fund
Attn: Wyman P Boynton
82 Court Street, #418
Portsmouth, NH 03801-4414

262
Cole Scholarship

AMOUNT: $600-$2000 DEADLINE: Varies
MAJOR: All Areas of Study

Scholarships for Richmond County (NC) high school graduates. Eighteen two-year awards ($600 each) and six awards for four-year schools ($2,000 each). Award requirements change regularly. Write to the address listed for details, enclosing a self-addressed, stamped envelope. No GPA requirement specified.

Foundation for the Carolinas
Scholarship Program
PO Box 34769
Charlotte, NC 28234-4769

263
Cole/Stewart Scholarship

AMOUNT: Maximum: $3500 DEADLINE: February 20
MAJOR: All Areas of Study

Scholarships are available for undergraduate students who were raised by gay or lesbian parents who wish to pursue their education at an accredited college, university or vocational school. Must be under the age of 25 and residents of Washington. Award requirements change regularly. Write to the address listed, enclosing a self-addressed, stamped envelope for an application and further information. No GPA requirement specified.

GSBA, Pride and INBA Scholarships
Scholarship Programs
2150 North 107th Street, Suite 205
Seattle, WA 98133-9009

264
College Access Program

AMOUNT: Maximum: $1320 DEADLINE: Varies
MAJOR: All Fields of Study

The College Access Program provides grants to Kentucky residents who demonstrate financial need. To be considered for this award, you must meet the following criteria: attend a Kentucky two- or four-year public or private nonprofit college, proprietary school or publicly operated technical college; enroll for at least six semester hours (half time); and complete the FAFSA. Your total expected family contribution or EFC, which is determined by the FAFSA, cannot exceed $1,500. Award requirements change regularly. The FAFSA can be obtained from high school counselor offices, college financial aid offices, or online at www.fafsa.ed.gov. For more information, you may also visit the KHEAA website at www.kheaa.com. No GPA requirement specified.

Kentucky Higher Education Assistance Authority
Attn: Grants and Scholarship Programs
1050 U.S. 127 South
Frankfort, KY 40601-4323

265
College Bound Foundation Scholarship

AMOUNT: None Specified DEADLINE: May 19
MAJOR: All Areas of Study

The College Bound Foundation Scholarship is open to students attending Baltimore City public high schools who are planning on going to college. You must demonstrate financial need. Award requirements change regularly. No GPA requirement specified.

College Bound Foundation
Scholarship Coordinator
204 E. Lombard Street, Suite G-1
Baltimore, MD 21202-3236

266
College Bound Scholarships

AMOUNT: $500-$50000 DEADLINE: July 26
MAJOR: All Areas of Study

This scholarship is open to high school seniors. You must be a Chicago area resident and attending a Chicago area high school. If you are an economically disadvantaged student who has a strong academic ambition, good character, high motivation and wishes to attend college, this scholarship may be for you. To qualify, please see the following schedule: If your household population is 1, income may not exceed $15,780; if 2 persons, the income may not exceed $21,220; if 3 persons, the income may not exceed $26,660, if 4 persons-$32,100; if 5 persons-$37,540; if 6 persons-$42,980; if 7 persons-$48,420; if 8 persons-$53,860. For each additional person, add $5,440. Last year, there were ten awards offered. Award requirements change regularly. No GPA requirement specified.

College Bound, Inc.
Selection Committee
3715 North Richmond Street
Chicago, IL 60618

267
College Scholarship Assistance Program

AMOUNT: $400-$5000 DEADLINE: Varies
MAJOR: All Fields of Study

The College Scholarship Assistance Program is open to Virginia residents who are enrolled in Virginia's public and private colleges and universities at least half-time. To be considered for this award, you must be able to demonstrate financial need. The award is open to undergraduate students and is renewable, provided you meet certain criteria. The award also requires that you have a high school diploma or its recognized equivalent. Award requirements change regularly. To apply, you must submit the FAFSA. For further information, you may visit the State Council of Higher Education for Virginia website at www.schev.edu. No GPA requirement specified.

State Council of Higher Education in Virginia
Attn: Grant Director
101 North 14th Street, 9th Floor
Richmond, VA 23219-2638

268
Colonial Dames of America Scholarship

AMOUNT: $2000 DEADLINE: January 15
MAJOR: American History

The Colonial Dames of America Scholarship is open to junior and senior college students studying colonial American History (prior to April 18, 1775). Applicants must submit a resume, college transcript, two letters of recommendation and a one-page summary of their research project or thesis. Award requirements change regularly. Please send a self-addressed, stamped envelope to receive your application and any further instructions from the scholarship provider. No GPA requirement specified.

Colonial Dames of America
Attn: Scholarship Committee
421 East 61st Street
New York, NY 10021

269
Colonel Hayden W. Wagner Memorial Scholarship

AMOUNT: $1000 DEADLINE: March 1
MAJOR: All Areas of Study

Scholarships for daughters or granddaughters of Commissioned Officers or Warrant Officers in the U.S. Army who are on active duty, died while on active duty or retired after at least 20 years of service. For undergraduate study. Renewable. Award requirements change regularly. Write to the address listed for details. Specify the officer's name, rank, social security number, and dates of active duty when requesting an application. Be sure to include a self-addressed, stamped envelope. No GPA requirement specified.

Society of Daughters of the U.S. Army
Janet B. Otto, Scholarship Chairman
7717 Rockledge Court
West Springfield, VA 22152-3854

270
Colorado Masons Scholarship

AMOUNT: $500-$5000 DEADLINE: March 15
MAJOR: All Areas of Study

Scholarships are available to graduates of Colorado Public High Schools who will be attending Colorado colleges and universities. Selections are made without regard to Masonic affiliation. Award requirements change regularly. Applications are available from all Colorado Public High Schools between mid-November and March 15 of each year. Mailed inquiries to the sponsor cannot be answered. No GPA requirement specified.

Colorado Masons Benevolent Fund Scholarships
Scholarship Correspondent
7995 East Arapahoe Court # 1200
Englewood, CO 80112-1357

f CPAs
ion

Varies

...cation Foundation
...uate and graduate students
...lleges and universities with
...be eligible for these
merit-based awards, you must have completed at least eight
semester hours of accounting courses including one intermediate accounting course. The Foundation offers three awards:
the Gordon Sheer, Ethnic Diversity and General Scholarships.
To apply for the Gordon Sheer Scholarship, you must have at
least a 3.5/4.0 GPA and apply by June 30. To apply for the
Ethnic Diversity Scholarship, you must be a minority student,
demonstrate financial need, have a minimum GPA of 3.0/4.0
and apply by June 30. To apply for the General Scholarship,
you must have a 3.0/4.0 GPA, demonstrate financial need and
submit your application material by June 30 for the fall award
and November 30 for the winter quarter/spring semester
award. GPA must be 3.0-4.0.

Colorado Society of Certified Public Accountants
Attn: Scholarship Coordinator
7979 East Tufts Avenue, Suite 500
Denver, CO 80237-2845

272
Community College Scholarship Award

AMOUNT: $1000 DEADLINE: February 1
MAJOR: Manufacturing or a Closely Related Field

Open to full-time undergraduates who are enrolled in a degree
program in manufacturing or a closely related field with a
minimum GPA of 3.5. Applicants may be entering freshmen of
sophomore students with less than 60 college credit hours
completed. Applicants may be enrolled at a community college, trade school or other two-year degree granting institution. Award requirements change regularly. For further information, please contact Dora Murray at (313) 271-1500, ext.
1709 (email: murrdor@sme.org) or Theresa Macias, ext. 1707
(email: maciter@sme.org). You may also go to the SME website: www.sme.org. GPA must be 3.5-4.0.

Society of Manufacturing Engineering Education Foundation
PO Box 930
One SME Drive
Dearborn, MI 48121-0930

273
Community Services Block Grant

AMOUNT: $750 DEADLINE: April 1
MAJOR: All Areas of Study (Preference Is Given To High-Tech Fields)

The Community Services Block Grant is available to low
income students planning to pursue a full-time education,
preferably in (but not limited to) high-tech or "growth" fields.
Applicants must be planning to attend an accredited Illinois
school. Students must live in Bureau, Carroll, LaSalle, Lee,

Marshall, Ogle, Putnam, Stark or Whiteside Counties in
Illinois and meet low-income guidelines. A minimum 2.6 GPA
is required. Award requirements change regularly. Write to the
address listed, enclosing a self-addressed, stamped envelope
for an application and further information. Applications are
available in late January or February. GPA must be 2.6-4.0.

Tri-Counties Opportunities Council
PO Box 610
Rock Falls IL 61071-0610

274
Connecticut Building Congress Scholarship

AMOUNT: $500-$2000 DEADLINE: March 1
MAJOR: Architecture, Engineering, Construction, Planning,
Drafting, Surveying

Awards are given to graduating Connecticut high school students entering college-level programs in architecture, engineering, construction management, surveying, drafting, planning or other courses of study leading to degrees in the construction field. Awards will be given for merit, potential, and
need and may be renewable yearly based upon satisfactory
performance in school. Award requirements change regularly.
Contact your high school guidance counselor or the address
listed for further information and an application. GPA must be
3.0-4.0.

Connecticut Society of Professional Engineers
Scholarship Program
2600 Dixwell Avenue, Suite 7
Hamden, CT 06514-1800

275
Connecticut Daughters of the American Revolution Scholarship

AMOUNT: $500 DEADLINE: January 15
MAJOR: All Areas of Study

Open to high school seniors who are Connecticut residents
and plan to enter college as freshmen. Based on scholarship,
character, leadership and financial need. Students must be in
the top 25% of their senior class to be considered. Award
requirements change regularly. For further information, write
to the address listed, including a self-addressed, stamped
envelope. If you do not send the self-addressed, stamped
envelope, you will not receive the return information. The
information will provide you with your local chapter of the
DAR. You will need to write to them to request a sponsorship.
If granted, you will then receive an application. GPA must be
3.0-4.0.

Daughters of the American Revolution
State Scholarship Chairman
10 Hunters Lane
Norwalk, CT 06850-2429

276
Connecticut Education Association Minority Scholarship

AMOUNT: $500 DEADLINE: May 1
MAJOR: Teaching

Open to high school seniors and college students, who are

Connecticut residents entering a teacher preparation program. For use at two- or four-year schools. Applicants must be members of minority groups, have a minimum GPA of 2.75 and be able to demonstrate financial need. Award requirements change regularly. Write to the address listed, enclosing a self-addressed, stamped envelope for an application and further information. GPA must be 2.8-4.0.

Connecticut Education Foundation, Inc.
Attn: President
21 Oak Street #500
Hartford, CT 06106-8006

Connecticut Nurserymen's Foundation Grant

AMOUNT: $5000 DEADLINE: March 15
MAJOR: Ornamental Horticulture, Landscaping, Nursery Management, Greenhouse Management

This grant is open to Connecticut high school seniors who are accepted in a course of study beneficial to the horticulture industry at a two- or four-year college or university. This includes, but is not limited to, ornamental horticulture, landscaping, nursery management and greenhouse management. Selection will be based on academic achievement, financial need, extracurricular and community activities. You must be a Connecticut resident in order to apply, but you may attend an out-of-state institution and still remain eligible. You should be aware, however, that the University of Connecticut School of Agriculture has offered to match the CNF grant, therefore providing you with a grant totaling $7,500 per year. Award requirements change regularly. Please return in the winter for an online application. No GPA requirement specified.

Connecticut Nurserymen's Foundation, Inc.
CNF Scholarship Committee
PO Box 117
Vernon Rockville, CT 06066-0117

Connecticut Valley Office Products Association Scholarship

AMOUNT: $2000 DEADLINE: March 15
MAJOR: All Fields of Study

The Connecticut Valley Office Products Association Scholarship is open to employees of Business Products Industry Association member firms and their families. Persons holding academic records sufficient for acceptance by accredited colleges, junior colleges or technical schools, or persons already enrolled in one of those institutions are eligible for this one-year award. Selection is made by a committee from the Student Financial Aid Department of The George Washington University, Washington, DC. Award requirements change regularly. Please send a self-addressed, stamped envelope to receive your application and any further instructions from the scholarship provider or email: info@bpia.org. No GPA requirement specified.

Business Products Industry Association
Attn: Scholarship Committee
301 North Fairfax Street
Alexandria, VA 22314-2633

279
Constance A. "Connie" Howard Scholarship Illinois House District 32

AMOUNT: $500-$1500 DEADLINE: Varies
MAJOR: Technology Related

The Constance A. "Connie" Howard Scholarship Illinois House District 32 is open to minority students who are seeking a postsecondary undergraduate degree in a technology-related field. To be considered for the award, you must be a resident of Illinois District 32. A requirement of the award is that you remain enrolled as full-time student at a four-year institution, while pursuing a degree in a technology-related field. The boundaries for District 32 are roughly south of 87th Street, east of the Dan-Ryan Expressway (I-94) and north of Sibley Blvd. Award requirements change regularly. No GPA requirement specified.

Chicago Urban League
Attn: Cy Fields
4510 South Michigan Avenue
Chicago, IL 60653-3819

280
Constant Memorial Scholarship

AMOUNT: None Specified DEADLINE: June 12
MAJOR: Visual Arts, Music

The Constant Memorial Scholarship is open to deserving visual arts and music majors who are residents of Aquidneck Island, RI (documentation will be required). To be considered for this award, you must be enrolled as a sophomore in an accredited four-year postsecondary institution and must be able to demonstrate financial need. Award requirements change regularly. No GPA requirement specified.

Rhode Island Foundation
Attn: Special Funds Office
70 Elm Street
Providence, RI 02903

281
Constantinople Armenian Relief Society (C.A.R.S.) Scholarship

AMOUNT: None Specified DEADLINE: June 15
MAJOR: All Areas of Study

The Constantinople Armenian Relief Society (C.A.R.S.) Scholarship is open to Armenian students who are enrolled in an accredited college or university in the United States at the sophomore level or above. The scholarship is based mainly on merit and financial need. Award requirements change regularly. Please send a self-addressed, stamped envelope to receive your application and any further instructions from the scholarship provider; or call Berc Araz at (732) 549-8963 or Talin Sesetyan (201) 447-7048. GPA must be 3.0-4.0.

Constantinople Armenian Relief Society
Times Square Station
PO Box 769
New York, NY 10108

282

Construction Crafts Scholarship Competition

AMOUNT: None Specified DEADLINE: February 1
MAJOR: Construction Related Craft Training

The Construction Crafts Scholarship Competition is open to students currently enrolled or enrolling in a construction-related craft training program. The program must be approved by the Bureau of Apprenticeship Training or your home state's postsecondary Education Commission. You must submit a completed and signed application form, course description, extracurricular activities listing and employment history listing in order to apply Award requirements change regularly. No GPA requirement specified.

National Association of Women In Construction
NAWIC Scholarship Coordinator
327 South Adams Street
Fort Worth, TX 76104-1002

283

Continental Society Daughters of Indian Wars Scholarship

AMOUNT: $1000 DEADLINE: June 15
MAJOR: Education, Social Service

The Continental Society Daughters of Indian Wars Scholarship is open to undergraduates who are certified tribal members. Preference is given to students in their junior year. You must be planning to work on a reservation upon graduation in the field of Education or Social Service and have a career goal of working with Native Americans. Financial need is considered but not required. This award is renewable if you maintain a minimum 3.0 GPA and carry at least ten quarter hours or eight semester hours. Award requirements change regularly. GPA must be 3.0-4.0.

Continental Society Daughters of Indian Wars
Attn: Mrs. Ronald Jacobs
Route 2, Box 184
Locust Grove, OK 74352-9652

284

Continuing Education Grant

AMOUNT: $250 DEADLINE: Varies
MAJOR: Religious Studies, Ministry, Theology, Church-Related Studies

The Continuing Education Grant is open every two years to ministerial leaders who want to attend an educational event. Applicants must be listed in the current ABC Professional Registry. Applications must be submitted before attending the event/program. Applicants must be members of an American Baptist church for at least one year before applying for aid and enrolled at an accredited educational institution in the U.S. or Puerto Rico. U.S. citizenship is required. Award requirements change regularly. Please send a self-addressed, stamped envelope to receive your application and any further instructions from the scholarship provider. No GPA requirement specified.

American Baptist Financial Aid Program
Educational Ministries ABC/USA
PO Box 851
Valley Forge, PA 19482-0851

285

Continuing Education Grant for Seminarian

AMOUNT: Maximum: $100 DEADLINE: Varies
MAJOR: Religious Studies, Ministry, Theology, Church-Related Studies

The Continuing Education Grant for Seminarian is open to seminarians who want to attend a nondegree educational program. Applications must be submitted before attending the event/program. Applicants must be members of an American Baptist church for at least one year before applying for aid and enrolled at an accredited educational institution in the U.S. or Puerto Rico. U.S. citizenship is required. Award requirements change regularly. Please send a self-addressed, stamped envelope to receive your application and any further instructions from the scholarship provider. No GPA requirement specified.

American Baptist Financial Aid Program
Educational Ministries ABC/USA
PO Box 851
Valley Forge, PA 19482-0851

286

Corporate Scholarships

AMOUNT: $1000-$5000 DEADLINE: December 31
MAJOR: Accounting, Finance, Business

The Corporate Scholarship is available to ethnic minority accounting, finance or business undergraduates or accounting and taxation graduates. Applicants must be currently enrolled as full-time students and be paid NABA members. A minimum 3.3 GPA is required. Award requirements change regularly. Please send a self-addressed, stamped envelope to receive your application and any further instructions from the scholarship provider or call (301) 474-6222, ext. 14. GPA must be 3.3-4.0.

National Association of Black Accountants, Inc.
Attn: Scholarship Committee
7249-A Hanover Parkway
Greenbelt, MD 20770

287

Country Doctor Scholarship Program

AMOUNT: None Specified DEADLINE: May 1
MAJOR: Medicine

Scholarships are available for Georgia resident medical students who plan to practice medicine in a rural area of Georgia upon graduation. Applicants must demonstrate financial need and a strong commitment to practice medicine in a Board-approved Georgia community having a population of 15,000 persons or less. All recipients are required to sign a contract affirming their commitment to practice in an approved community. One year of service credits one year of scholarship. Applications available beginning in January. Award requirements change regularly. Please send a self-addressed, stamped envelope to receive your application and any further instructions from the scholarship provider or email smeb@mail.regents.peachnet.edu. No GPA requirement specified.

State Medical Education Board of Georgia
County Doctor Scholarship Program
270 Washington Street SW, Suite 7093
Atlanta, GA 30334-9009

288
Crowder Scholarship

AMOUNT: Maximum: $1000 DEADLINE: March 1
MAJOR: All Areas of Study

Scholarships for students whose parents work for construction companies in Mecklenburg County (NC). Award requirements change regularly. Write to the address listed for details, enclosing a self-addressed, stamped envelope. No GPA requirement specified.

Foundation for the Carolinas
Scholarship Program
PO Box 34769
Charlotte, NC 28234-4769

289
CTA Scholarships for Dependent Children

AMOUNT: $2000 DEADLINE: February 15
MAJOR: All Areas of Study

Open to dependent children of active, retired or deceased members of the California Teachers Association. For use by full-time undergraduate students at any accredited institution of higher learning for a degree, credential or vocational program. Based on involvement in and sensitivity to human, social and civic issues, reliability, responsibility and integrity, special achievements and academic and vocational potential. Award requirements change regularly. Please send a self-addressed, stamped envelope to receive your application and any further instructions from the scholarship provider, call (650) 697-1400, browse their website: www.cta.org and click on "Resources" for scholarship information or email: scholarships@cta.org. No GPA requirement specified.

California Teachers Association
Scholarship Committee
1705 Murchison Drive, PO Box 921
Burlingame, CA 94011-0921

290
CTA Scholarships for Members

AMOUNT: $2000 DEADLINE: February 15
MAJOR: Education

Open to active members of the California Teachers Association. For use by full-time graduate students at any accredited institution of higher learning. Based on involvement in and sensitivity to human, social and civic issues, reliability, responsibility and integrity and academic and professional achievement. Award requirements change regularly. Please send a self-addressed, stamped envelope to receive your application and any further instructions from the scholarship provider, call (650) 697-1400, browse their website: www.cta.org and click on "Resources" for scholarship infor-

mation or email: scholarships@cta.org. No GPA requirement specified.

California Teachers Association
Scholarship Committee
1705 Murchison Drive, PO Box 921
Burlingame, CA 94011-0921

291
Cultural Enrichment Grants

AMOUNT: Maximum: $300 DEADLINE: Varies
MAJOR: Visual, Literary, Performing Arts

The Cultural Enrichment Grants are open to Cook Inlet Region enrollees and descendants with a GED or high school diploma (must be at least 18 years of age.) For noncredit workshops or seminars in the performing arts that demonstrate and transmit Alaska's Eskimo, Aleut and Indian heritage. Seminars/workshops must be approved by CIRI. Applicants may apply each quarter; additional deadline dates are December 1, March 31 and June 30. Award requirements change regularly.

CIRI Foundation
Scholarship Coordinator
2600 Cordova Street, Suite 206
Anchorage, AK 99503-2745

292
D. Anita Small Science and Business Scholarship

AMOUNT: $1500 DEADLINE: May 6
MAJOR: Math, Engineering, Computer Sciences, Physical Sciences, Medical Sciences, Business

This scholarship is available to women age 21 or older, who have maintained at least a 3.0 GPA and are pursuing a bachelor's or advanced degree in one of the areas listed above. You must demonstrate financial need and carry a minimum of six credit hours. Award requirements change regularly. GPA must be 3.0-4.0.

Business and Professional Women's Foundation of Maryland, Inc.
Scholarships Coordinator
282 New Mark Esplanade
Rockville, MD 20850-2733

293
Dale Monagin Memorial Scholarship

AMOUNT: $2500 DEADLINE: March 31
MAJOR: All Fields of Study

The Dale Monagin Memorial Scholarship is open to Lenawee County (MI) graduates or graduating seniors. To qualify for the award, you must be pursuing higher education at a community college, trade school or public or private university in Michigan. Award requirements change regularly. Please send a self-addressed, stamped envelope to receive your application and any further instructions from the scholarship provider. No GPA requirement specified.

Morenci High School
Attn: Mrs. Melissa Parnell
788 Coomer Street
Morenci, MI 49256

American Legion - Maine
Department Adjutant State Headquarters
PO Box 900
Waterville, ME 04903-0900

294
Dan Klepper Outdoor Photography Scholarship

AMOUNT: Maximum: $1000 DEADLINE: December 31
MAJOR: Photography, Video Related

This scholarship is open to juniors, seniors, graduate students and active professionals who are seeking further training. In order to apply, you must be planning to enroll or are enrolled in photography or video-related courses. This award is for use at an accredited Texas college or university. Winners will be announced at the TOWA annual meeting in February in Uvalde, Texas. Award requirements change regularly. No GPA requirement specified.

Texas Outdoor Writers Association
TOWA Scholarship
P.O. Box 493
Blanco, TX 78606

295
Daniel B. Goldberg Scholarship

AMOUNT: $3500 DEADLINE: February 4
MAJOR: Finance

The Daniel B. Goldberg Scholarship is open to graduate students who are enrolled in full-time master's study preparing for a career in state and local government finance. Applicants must be citizens or permanent residents of the U.S. or Canada and have a baccalaureate degree or its equivalent. Recommendation from academic advisor or dean of the graduate program will be required. Award requirements change regularly. Applications are available in November for awards in the following spring. Please send a self-addressed, stamped envelope to receive your application and any further instructions from the scholarship provider; or email your request to Inquiries@gfoa.org; or visit the website at www.gfoa.org. No GPA requirement specified.

Government Finance Officers Association
Attn: Scholarship Committee
180 North Michigan Avenue, Suite 800
Chicago, IL 60601-7476

296
Daniel E. Lambert Memorial Scholarship

AMOUNT: $500 DEADLINE: May 1
MAJOR: All Areas of Study

This scholarship is open to high school seniors, current undergraduates and adults who are returning to school. Applicants must be residents of Maine and have at least one parent who is a veteran. Applicants must be U.S. citizens. Award requirements change regularly. Write to the address listed, enclosing a self-addressed, stamped envelope for an application and further information. No GPA requirement specified.

297
Daniel E. Mazzulla, Sr. Memorial Scholarship

AMOUNT: $500 DEADLINE: June 11
MAJOR: Parks, Recreation

Open to Rhode Island residents pursuing, full-time, a baccalaureate or a graduate degree related to the field of Parks and/or Recreation. Primary consideration given to high academics, personal qualities of initiative, leadership and professional promise. Must be able to demonstrate financial need and dedication to a Parks/Recreation career. Award requirements change regularly. Please send a self-addressed, stamped envelope to receive your application and any further instructions from the scholarship provider. GPA must be 3.0-4.0.

Rhode Island Recreation and Parks Association
Attn: Ralph S. Copps
39 North Hillview Drive
Narragansett, RI 02882-2844

298
Danish Sisterhood of America National Scholarship

AMOUNT: None Specified DEADLINE: February 28
MAJOR: Danish Heritage and Culture

Open to full-time undergraduate students who are members or dependents of members of the Danish Sisterhood of America. Recipients must have a minimum 3.0 GPA. Award requirements change regularly. Write to the address listed, enclosing a self-addressed, stamped envelope for an application and further information. GPA must be 3.0-4.0.

Danish Sisterhood of America
8004 Jasmine Blvd
Port Richey, FL 34668-3224

299
Data Match Scholarship

AMOUNT: $1000 DEADLINE: March 31
MAJOR: All Areas of Study

The Data Match Scholarship is open to FBLA (Future Business Leaders of America) members who show outstanding leadership abilities, participation in clubs, community involvement and GPA and who are high school graduates. To be considered for this award, you must plan to attend a two- or four-year accredited institution full-time. A transcript and letter of recommendation will also need to be submitted. Award requirements change regularly. Submit an application form, available by calling (800) 545-1100, or downloading it from Data Match's website: www.data-match.com. No GPA requirement specified.

Future Business Leaders of America
Attn: Scholarship Coordinator
1912 Association Drive
Reston, VA 22091

300
Davenport Foundation Scholarships In the Arts

AMOUNT: None Specified DEADLINE: July 15
MAJOR: Art, Music, Theatre

Open to Barnstable County (MA) residents who are in the last two years of undergraduate study or, preferably, graduate work in the performing or visual arts. Selection is based on need, ability, academics, and proven desire in the field of endeavor, be it theatre, music, or art. Personal interviews are an integral part of the granting process. Award requirements change regularly. For further information and an application, please write to the address listed, including a self-addressed, stamped envelope or call (508) 398-2293. No GPA requirement specified.

John K. and Thirza F. Davenport Foundation
Scholarship Committee
20 North Main Street
South Yarmouth, MA 02664-3150

301
David H. Clift Scholarship

AMOUNT: $3000 DEADLINE: April 1
MAJOR: Library Science, Information Science

The David H. Clift Scholarship is open to citizens or permanent residents of the U.S. or Canada who have applied for admission to and will enter an ALA-accredited master's degree program in library and information studies. To be considered for this award, you cannot have completed more than 12 semester hours (or its equivalent) towards the master's degree prior to June 1. Award requirements change regularly. No GPA requirement specified.

American Library Association
HRDR/Staff Liaison - Scholarship Juries
50 East Huron Street
Chicago, IL 60611-2795

302
David J. Hallissey Memorial Scholarship

AMOUNT: $2000 DEADLINE: July 28
MAJOR: Travel and Tourism

Awards are available for graduate students or professors of tourism in a college, university, or proprietary travel school. Students must submit a 500-word essay on an intended topic of research incorporating methodology and objectives. Award requirements change regularly. Write to the address listed, enclosing a self-addressed, stamped envelope for an application and further information. You can browse their website: www.astanet.com or email: myriaml@astahq.com. No GPA requirement specified.

American Society of Travel Agents
Attn: ASTA Foundation
1101 King Street, Suite 200
Alexandria, VA 22314-2944

303
David Sarnoff Research Center Scholarship

AMOUNT: $1500 DEADLINE: February 1
MAJOR: Engineering, Computer Science

This scholarship is open to women with junior standing who are majoring in engineering or computer science in an ABET-accredited program or an SWE-approved school. You must have a minimum of 3.5 GPA and be a U.S. citizen. Award requirements change regularly. Please send a self-addressed, stamped envelope to receive your application. GPA must be 3.5-4.0.

Society of Women Engineers Headquarters
Scholarship Coordinator
120 Wall Street, FL 11
New York, NY 10005-3902

304
David W. Self Scholarship

AMOUNT: Maximum: $1000 DEADLINE: June 1
MAJOR: All Fields of Study Leading to a Church-Related Career

The David W. Self Scholarship is open to United Methodist students who are entering their first year of undergraduate study. To be considered for this award, you must demonstrate participation in your local church, be pursuing a church-related career, have at least a 2.0 high school GPA and be able to establish financial need. The award is not renewable. Award requirements change regularly. Please send a self-addressed, stamped envelope between November 1 and May 15 to receive your application and any further instructions from the scholarship provider. You can also visit their website at www.umc.org/nymo/scholar.html. GPA must be 2.0-4.0.

United Methodist Church - National Youth Ministry Organization
Attn: Office of Loans and Scholarships
PO Box 840
Nashville, TN 37202-0840

305
David, Nancy and Liza Cherney Scholarship Fund

AMOUNT: Maximum: $100 DEADLINE: Varies
MAJOR: All Areas of Study

The David, Nancy and Liza Cherney Scholarship Fund is open to Jewish, female students who plan on going to college. Applicants must demonstrate financial need. Applicants must be residents of San Francisco, San Mateo, northern Santa Clara, Marin and Sonoma counties in California. Deadlines vary; therefore, it is encouraged that applicants apply early. Award requirements change regularly. No GPA requirement specified.

Jewish Family and Children's Services
Attn: Loans and Grants Department
2245 Post Street
San Francisco, CA 94115

306
Debra Levy Neimark Memorial Scholarship

AMOUNT: $1500 DEADLINE: April 1
MAJOR: All Areas of Study

This scholarship is open to female undergraduate and graduate students who attend an accredited Florida school. You must be a resident of Broward County in Florida and a U.S. citizen. This scholarship is based on merit as well as need. You are advised to enclose an essay with the application indicating any special circumstances as to the need for this scholarship and why you are applying. Award requirements change regularly. No GPA requirement specified.

Debra Levy Neimark Scholarship Foundation
Selection Committee
800 Corporate Drive, Suite 420
Fort Lauderdale, FL 33334-3621

307
Deep River Land Trust Scholarship

AMOUNT: $1000 DEADLINE: April 30
MAJOR: Conservation, Natural Science

Open to high school seniors in good standing at an accredited secondary school, and are residents of Deep River (CT) only. Interested students must submit a written statement indicating their reason for choosing their field of study. If no qualified seniors apply, award will be open to undergraduates. Award requirements change regularly. Information and application forms are available at the Deep River Public Library, the guidance department at Valley Regional High School or the address listed. GPA must be 2.5-4.0.

Deep River Land Trust, Inc.
Scholarship Coordinator
PO Box 101
Deep River, CT 06417-0101

308
DeHovitz-Senturia Campership Fund Scholarship

AMOUNT: Maximum: $600 DEADLINE: Varies
MAJOR: All Areas of Study

The purpose of the DeHovitz-Senturia Campership Fund Scholarship is to provide a Jewish summer camp experience to applicants 26 years of age or younger. Applicants must be residents of San Francisco, San Mateo, northern Santa Clara, Marin and Sonoma counties in California. Demonstrated financial need and a referral from agency caseworker are required. Deadlines vary; therefore, it is encouraged that applicants apply early. Award requirements change regularly.

Jewish Family and Children's Services
Attn: Loans and Grants Department
2245 Post Street
San Francisco, CA 94115

309
Delaware Nursing Incentive Scholarship Loan

AMOUNT: Maximum: $3000 DEADLINE: March 31
MAJOR: Nursing

Merit-based loan for undergraduate students who have an unweighted cumulative GPA of 2.5. GED recipients with a total score of 250 on the GED exam are eligible. Must be full-time students at an accredited institution in a program resulting in certification as an RN, LPN, or APN and be legal residents of Delaware. May be repaid through nursing service in a Delaware state hospital. Award requirements change regularly. Write to the address listed, enclosing a self-addressed, stamped envelope for further information, or browse their website: www.state.de.us/high-ed/nursing.htm. GPA must be 2.5-4.0.

Delaware Higher Education Commission (SCIP)
Carvel State Office Building
820 North French Street, 4th Floor
Wilmington, DE 19801-3509

310
Delaware Scholarship Incentive Program

AMOUNT: $700-$2200 DEADLINE: April 15
MAJOR: All Areas of Study

The Delaware Scholarship Incentive Program is open to Delaware residents enrolled full-time in an undergraduate degree program at a Delaware college (or Pennsylvania, if your major is unavailable in Delaware). Under certain conditions, undergraduates and graduates attending colleges in other states will be considered. To be considered for this award, you must hold at least a 2.5 GPA and be able to demonstrate substantial financial need. Award requirements change regularly. Write to the address listed, enclosing a self-addressed, stamped envelope for further information or browse their website: www.doe.state.de.us/high-ed. GPA must be 2.5-4.0.

Delaware Higher Education Commission (SCIP)
Carvel State Office Building
820 North French Street, 4th Floor
Wilmington, DE 19801-3509

311
Delbert K. Aman Memorial Scholarship

AMOUNT: $500 DEADLINE: March 1
MAJOR: All Areas of Study

Scholarships are available to legally blind students who are residents of South Dakota or who are attending a South Dakota college or university. Scholarships are for undergraduate study only. Award requirements change regularly. Write to the address listed, enclosing a self-addressed envelope for an application and further information. No GPA requirement specified.

American Council of the Blind
Attn: Billie Jean Keith
1155 15th Street NW, Suite 720
Washington, DC 20005-2706

312
Delta Kappa Gamma Scholarship

AMOUNT: $500 DEADLINE: Varies
MAJOR: Education

The Delta Kappa Gamma Scholarship is open to women who are at least juniors and attending an accredited university or college in Indiana that offers a degree in education. Recipients must be residents of Porter County, Indiana and preparing to enter the field of teaching. Award requirements change regularly. Write to the address listed, enclosing a self-addressed, stamped envelope for an application and further information. GPA must be 3.2-4.0.

Delta Kappa Gamma Society International - Alpha Gamma Chapter
Attn: Anne Egolf, Scholarship Chair
103 Mayfield Avenue
Valparaiso, IN 46383-5939

313
Dennison Stationary Products Company Scholarship

AMOUNT: $2000 DEADLINE: March 15
MAJOR: All Fields of Study

The Dennison Stationary Products Company Scholarship is open to employees of Business Products Industry Association member firms and their families. Persons holding academic records sufficient for acceptance by accredited colleges, junior colleges or technical schools, or persons already enrolled in one of those institutions are eligible for this two-year award. Selection is made by a committee from the Student Financial Aid Department of The George Washington University, Washington, DC. Award requirements change regularly. Please send a self-addressed, stamped envelope to receive your application and any further instructions from the scholarship provider or email: info@bpia.org. No GPA requirement specified.

Business Products Industry Association
Attn: Scholarship Committee
301 North Fairfax Street
Alexandria, VA 22314-2633

314
Dental Assisting Scholarship

AMOUNT: None Specified DEADLINE: Varies
MAJOR: Dental Assisting

The Dental Assisting Scholarship is open to students training for dental assisting careers in Florida. Applicants must have lived in Florida for at least two years and be enrolled in and have completed at least one grading period with a 2.5 GPA in a dental assisting program approved by the Florida Board of Dentistry. Preference is given to students from counties that the scholarship committee determines have the most need for dental assistants, who are dedicated to working in a Florida county that has a shortage of dental assistants and who are enrolled in dental assisting programs that are under enrolled. Requests for scholarships should be made at least 45 days before the date the funds are needed. Award requirements change regularly. Write to the Florida Dental Health Foundation at the address listed for details or call (850) 681-3629 ext. 119; or visit the website at www.floridadental.org.

GPA must be 2.5-4.0.

Florida Dental Association/Florida Dental Health Foundation
Attn: Scholarship and Loan Coordinator
1111 East Tennessee Street
Tallahassee, FL 32308-6914

315
Dental Hygiene Scholarship

AMOUNT: None Specified DEADLINE: Varies
MAJOR: Dental Hygiene

The Dental Hygiene Scholarship is open to students training for dental hygiene careers in Florida. Applicants must have lived in Florida for at least three years and have entered an ADA-accredited dental hygiene program in Florida. Preference is given to students from counties that the scholarship committee determines have the most need for dental hygienists, who are dedicated to working in a Florida county that has a shortage of dental hygienists and who demonstrate financial need. The deadline for the fall semester is May 1; the deadline for the spring semester is November 1. Award requirements change regularly. Write to the Florida Dental Health Foundation at the address listed for details or call (850) 681-3629, ext. 119; or visit the website at www.floridadental.org. GPA must be 2.5-4.0.

Florida Dental Association/Florida Dental Health Foundation
Attn: Scholarship and Loan Coordinator
1111 East Tennessee Street
Tallahassee, FL 32308-6914

316
Department of Nurses Scholarship

AMOUNT: $1500 DEADLINE: Varies
MAJOR: Nursing

The Department of Nurses Scholarship is open to Oregon residents who are dependents of veterans (living or dead) of the Armed Forces. To apply for this award, you must attend an accredited Hospital of Nursing. Award requirements change regularly. Please send a self-addressed, stamped envelope to receive your application and any further instructions from the scholarship provider. No GPA requirement specified.

American Legion Auxiliary - Department of Oregon
Chairman of Education
PO Box 1730
Wilsonville, OR 97070-1730

317
DeWayne Sliffe Memorial Scholarship

AMOUNT: $300 DEADLINE: May 1
MAJOR: Agriculture

Open to entering freshmen who are graduating or graduated from Harrisonville Senior High School. Preference is given to students who are majoring in agriculture. A 300-500 to word essay is required on vocational plans. Award requirements change regularly. Applications are available in the Harrisonville Senior High School guidance office. No GPA requirement specified.

Harrisonville Senior High School
Attn: Roy Sackman
1504 East Elm Street
Harrisonville, MO 64701-2022

318
Diamond State Scholarship

AMOUNT: $1000 DEADLINE: March 31
MAJOR: All Areas of Study

The Diamond State Scholarship is open to students who rank in the upper quarter of their high school class, scored a minimum 1200 on the SAT or a minimum 27 on the ACT and will be enrolling full-time at an accredited college. To be considered for this award, you must be a legal resident of Delaware. The award is based on academic merit and is renewable, provided certain criteria are maintained. Award requirements change regularly. Write to the address listed, enclosing a self-addressed, stamped envelope for further information or browse their website: www.state.de.us/high-ed/diamond.htm. No GPA requirement specified.

Delaware Higher Education Commission (SCIP)
Carvel State Office Building
820 North French Street, 4th Floor
Wilmington, DE 19801-3509

319
Dickey and Wolf Business Scholarship

AMOUNT: $250 DEADLINE: May 1
MAJOR: Business, Accounting

Open to entering freshmen who are graduating or graduated from Harrisonville Senior High School. Business and accounting majors are first choice. Award requirements change regularly. Applications are available in the Harrisonville Senior High School guidance office. No GPA requirement specified.

Harrisonville Senior High School
Attn: Roy Sackman
1504 East Elm Street
Harrisonville, MO 64701-2022

320
District 56 Graduate Scholarships

AMOUNT: Maximum: $6000 DEADLINE: April 1
MAJOR: All Areas of Study

Open to students who are graduating from Neah-Kah-Nie high school in Rockaway (OR) or any student who has graduated from this high school since 1954. Award requirements change regularly. Write to the address listed for more information. No GPA requirement specified.

Neah-Kah-Nie District 56 Graduate Scholarships, Inc.
Scholarship Coordinator
PO Box 373
Rockaway Beach, OR 97136-0373

321
Doctoral Dissertation Fellowship in Jewish Studies

AMOUNT: $7000-$10000 DEADLINE: January 3
MAJOR: Jewish Studies

The Doctoral Dissertation Fellowship in Jewish Studies is open to students who have completed all academic requirements for the doctoral degree except the dissertation. Applicants should demonstrate course work in Jewish Studies on the graduate level and must give evidence of proficiency in a Jewish language adequate for pursuing an academic career in their chosen field. Preference will be given to individuals preparing for academic careers in Jewish Studies, who demonstrate a career commitment to Jewish scholarship and who indicate that they will pursue their careers in the United States. Award requirements change regularly. Please send a self-addressed, stamped envelope to receive your application and any further instructions from the scholarship provider or send an email. No GPA requirement specified.

National Foundation for Jewish Culture
Attn: Fellowship Programs
330 Seventh Avenue, 21st Floor
New York, NY 10001

322
Doctoral Dissertation Fellowships In Law and Social Science

AMOUNT: $15000 DEADLINE: February 1
MAJOR: Law, Social Science

The Doctoral Dissertation Fellowships In Law and Social Science are available for Ph.D. candidates who have completed all doctoral requirements except the dissertation. Proposed research must be in the areas of social legal studies, social scientific approaches to law, the legal profession or legal institutions. Minority students are encouraged to apply. Award requirements change regularly. Please send a self-addressed, stamped envelope to receive your application and any further instructions from the fellowship provider. No GPA requirement specified.

American Bar Foundation
Anne Tatalovich, Assistant Director
750 North Lake Shore Drive
Chicago, IL 60611-4403

323
Doctoral Fellowship Program In Biomedical Engineering

AMOUNT: None Specified DEADLINE: December 10
MAJOR: Biomedical Engineering

Doctoral fellowships are available to support graduate students of outstanding scholarship, ability and aptitude for future achievements in biomedical engineering research. Award requirements change regularly. Write to the address listed, enclosing a self-addressed, stamped envelope for an application and further information, email: info@whitaker.org or browse their website: www.whitaker.org. No GPA requirement specified.

Whitaker Foundation
Fellowship Programs
1700 N Moore St Ste 2200
Arlington, VA 22209-1923

Doctoral Study Grant

AMOUNT: $3000 DEADLINE: March 31
MAJOR: Theology, Education

The Doctoral Study Grant is open to American Baptist students who have completed at least one year of Ph.D. studies. Students must plan to teach in a college or seminary in a field of study directly related to preparing American Baptist ministerial leaders. Applicants must demonstrate academic achievement in the first year(s) of doctoral studies. D.Min. students are not eligible. Applicants must be members of an American Baptist church for at least one year before applying for aid, enrolled at an accredited educational institution in the U.S. or Puerto Rico. U.S. citizenship is required. Award requirements change regularly. Please send a self-addressed, stamped envelope to receive your application and any further instructions from the scholarship provider. No GPA requirement specified.

American Baptist Financial Aid Program
Educational Ministries ABC/USA
PO Box 851
Valley Forge, PA 19482-0851

Dolphin Scholarship

AMOUNT: $3000 DEADLINE: April 15
MAJOR: All Areas of Study

The Dolphin Scholarship is open to children/stepchildren of members or former members of the Submarine Force who served for at least eight years. You are also eligible if your parent/stepparent served the Navy in submarine support activities for a minimum of ten years. Qualifying time must have been served on active duty. There is no minimum period of service for children of personnel who died on active duty while in the Submarine Force. To be considered for this award, you must be unmarried, under the age of 24 at the time of application and be enrolled or planning to enroll at an accredited, four-year college or university. Your application will be evaluated on the basis of your scholastic proficiency, nonscholastic activities, character, all-around ability and financial need. The award is renewable provided certain criteria are maintained. Award requirements change regularly. No GPA requirement specified.

Dolphin Scholarship Foundation
Attn: Scholarship Administrator
5040 Virginia Beach Blvd, Suite 104A
Virginia Beach, VA 23462

326

Donald A. Fisher Memorial Scholarship

AMOUNT: $1000 DEADLINE: May 26
MAJOR: All Areas of Study

If you are an undergraduate who is a member of Tau Kappa Epsilon, this scholarship is open to you. In order to apply, you must demonstrate leadership capabilities within your chapter,

on campus or in your community. Also, a minimum 2.5 GPA is required along with being a full-time student in good standing. Award requirements change regularly. For further information, call (317) 872-6533, email: tef@tkehq.org or visit the website at: www.tke.org. GPA must be 2.5-4.0.

TKE Educational Foundation
Attn: Timothy L. Taschwer
8645 Founders Road
Indianapolis, IN 46268-1336

327

Donald F. Hastings Scholarship

AMOUNT: $2500 DEADLINE: January 15
MAJOR: Welding Engineering, Welding Engineering Technology

The Donald F. Hastings Scholarship is awarded to undergraduate students pursuing a minimum four-year bachelor's degree in welding engineering or welding engineering technology. Priority will be given to welding engineering students who reside in or are attending schools in the states of Ohio or California. Applicants must have at least a GPA of 2.5. Proof of financial need is required. U.S. citizenship is required. This award is renewable. Award requirements change regularly. Please send a self-addressed, stamped envelope to receive your application and any further instructions from the scholarship provider or call (305) 445-6628. GPA must be 2.5-4.0.

American Welding Society Foundation, Inc.
National Education Scholarship Committee
550 Northwest LeJeune Road
Miami, FL 33126-4165

Donald P. Haspel Scholarship

AMOUNT: $2000 DEADLINE: March 15
MAJOR: All Fields of Study

The Donald P. Haspel Scholarship is open to employees of Business Products Industry Association member firms and their families. Persons holding academic records sufficient for acceptance by accredited colleges, junior colleges or technical schools, or persons already enrolled in one of those institutions are eligible for this one-year award. Selection is made by a committee from the Student Financial Aid Department of The George Washington University, Washington, DC. Award requirements change regularly. Please send a self-addressed, stamped envelope to receive your application and any further instructions from the scholarship provider or email: info@bpia.org. No GPA requirement specified.

Business Products Industry Association
Attn: Scholarship Committee
301 North Fairfax Street
Alexandria, VA 22314-2633

Donald F. Pike/Great Lakes Travelers Club Scholarship

AMOUNT: $2000 DEADLINE: March 15
MAJOR: All Fields of Study

The Donald F. Pike/Great Lakes Travelers Club Scholarship is open to employees of Business Products Industry Association member firms and their families. Persons holding academic records sufficient for acceptance by accredited colleges, junior colleges or technical schools, or persons already enrolled in one of those institutions are eligible for this one-year award. Selection is made by a committee from the Student Financial Aid Department of The George Washington University, Washington, DC. Award requirements change regularly. Please send a self-addressed, stamped envelope to receive your application and any further instructions from the scholarship provider or email: info@bpia.org. No GPA requirement specified.

Business Products Industry Association
Attn: Scholarship Committee
301 North Fairfax Street
Alexandria, VA 22314-2633

330
Donald Riebhoff Memorial Scholarship

AMOUNT: $1000 DEADLINE: February 1
MAJOR: International Studies

This scholarship is open to applicants with a minimum technician class amateur radio license. Applicants must be ARRL members and majoring in international studies at an accredited baccalaureate or graduate institution. Award requirements change regularly. Write the address provided, using a self-addressed, stamped envelope, for further information. No GPA requirement specified.

American Radio Relay League
Attn: ARRL Foundation
225 Main Street
Newington, CT 06111-1400

331
Dorothy Lemke Howarth Memorial Scholarship

AMOUNT: $2000 DEADLINE: February 1
MAJOR: Engineering, Computer Science

This scholarship is open to female students who are sophomores majoring in engineering or computer science. Applicants must attend an ABET-accredited program or an SWE-approved school. Applicants must be U.S. citizens and have a minimum GPA of 3.5. Award requirements change regularly. Please send a self-addressed, stamped envelope to receive your application. For any further instructions from the scholarship provider, please browse their website at www.swe.org or email hq@swe.org. GPA must be 3.5-4.0.

Society of Women Engineers Headquarters
Scholarship Coordinator
120 Wall Street, FL 11
New York, NY 10005-3902

332
Doug Spade Agriculture Scholarship

AMOUNT: $500 DEADLINE: March 31
MAJOR: Agriculture

The Doug Spade Agriculture Scholarship is open to a graduating senior from Lenawee County (MI). To qualify for the award, you must be pursuing a career related to agriculture.

Award requirements change regularly. Please send a self-addressed, stamped envelope to receive your application and any further instructions from the scholarship provider. No GPA requirement specified.

Morenci High School
Attn: Mrs. Melissa Parnell
788 Coomer Street
Morenci, MI 49256

333
Doug Spade Public Service Scholarship

AMOUNT: $500 DEADLINE: March 31
MAJOR: Public Service

The Doug Spade Public Service Scholarship is open to a graduating senior from Lenawee County (MI). To qualify for the award, you must be pursuing a career related to public service. A deciding factor in your selection will be an essay describing how you plan to make public service an important component of your life. Award requirements change regularly. Please send a self-addressed, stamped envelope to receive your application and any further instructions from the scholarship provider. No GPA requirement specified.

Morenci High School
Attn: Mrs. Melissa Parnell
788 Coomer Street
Morenci, MI 49256

334
Doug Spade Special Education Scholarship

AMOUNT: $500 DEADLINE: March 3
MAJOR: All Fields of Study

The Doug Spade Special Education Scholarship is open to a graduating senior from Lenawee County (MI). To qualify for the award, you must have been already accepted into a public or private postsecondary learning institution. The award also requires that you have been receiving special education services. Award requirements change regularly. Please send a self-addressed, stamped envelope to receive your application and any further instructions from the scholarship provider. No GPA requirement specified.

Morenci High School
Attn: Mrs. Melissa Parnell
788 Coomer Street
Morenci, MI 49256

335
Douglas K. and Doreen E. Chapman Award

AMOUNT: $2000 DEADLINE: March 15
MAJOR: All Fields of Study

The Douglas K. and Doreen E. Chapman Award is open to employees of Business Products Industry Association member firms and their families. Persons holding academic records sufficient for acceptance by accredited colleges, junior colleges or technical schools, or persons already enrolled in one of those institutions are eligible for this two-year award. Selection is made by a committee from the Student Financial

Aid Department of The George Washington University, Washington, DC. Award requirements change regularly. Please send a self-addressed, stamped envelope to receive your application and any further instructions from the scholarship provider or email: info@bpia.org. No GPA requirement specified.

Business Products Industry Association
Attn: Scholarship Committee
301 North Fairfax Street
Alexandria, VA 22314-2633

336
Dr. and Mrs. James O. Conklin Scholarship

AMOUNT: None Specified DEADLINE: February 1
MAJOR: Medicine, Music (Piano)

The Dr. and Mrs. James O. Conklin Scholarship is open to residents of Vigo County (IN) who are pursuing a degree in medicine with intention to become a physician or who are studying the piano. You must maintain a minimum 3.0 GPA. Award requirements change regularly. Please send a self-addressed, stamped envelope to receive your application and further information from the scholarship provider or call (812) 232-2234. No GPA requirement specified.

Wabash Valley Community Foundation
Community Scholarship Program
2901 Ohio Boulevard, Suite 153
Terre Haute, IN 47803

337
Dr. Charles A. Preuss Medical Award

AMOUNT: $1000-$3500 DEADLINE: April 17
MAJOR: Medicine

Open to any Sigma Alpha Epsilon brother currently attending or planning to attend medical school or who is enrolled in a course of study related to the medical profession. Candidates must be deeply committed to the study of medicine, with high moral and ethical standards. Selection will be based on academic achievement, passion for the study of medicine, and financial need. Award requirements change regularly. For further information, please write to the address listed, including a self-addressed, stamped envelope, call (847) 475-1856 ext. 223, fax (847) 475-2250, or email: rparker@sae.net. You may also visit their website: www.sae.net. GPA must be 3.0-4.0.

Sigma Alpha Epsilon Foundation
SAE Awards Committee
PO Box 1856
Evanston, IL 60204-1856

338
Dr. Daniel Hollibush Scholarship

AMOUNT: None Specified DEADLINE: Varies
MAJOR: All Fields of Study

The Dr. Daniel Hollibush Scholarship is open to graduating seniors at Burlington High School (Burlington, WI). Students must attend a two- or four-year college or university. Award requirements change regularly. Please visit your Guidance Office to receive an application and any additional details. No GPA requirement specified.

Burlington High School
Attn: Guidance Office
225 Robert Street
Burlington, WI 53105

339
Dr. George Geppner - Dr. Milo Turnbo Minority Scholarship

AMOUNT: None Specified DEADLINE: Varies
MAJOR: Podiatry

The Dr. George Geppner - Dr. Milo Turnbo Minority Scholarship is open to minority students in their second, third or fourth year at the Scholl College of Podiatric Medicine. The Scholl Scholarship and Loan Committee makes the selection based on the submission of a biographical essay by applicants. Application forms are available from the Office of Student Services during the spring prior to the award year. Award requirements change regularly. Please send a self-addressed, stamped envelope to receive your application and any further instructions from the scholarship provider or contact the Office of Student Services at (800) 843-3059 or email finaid@scholl.edu. No GPA requirement specified.

Scholl College of Podiatric Medicine
Attn: Office of Student Services
1001 North Dearborn Street
Chicago, IL 60610

340
Dr. George I. and Eunice A. Tice Scholarship

AMOUNT: $500 DEADLINE: January 15
MAJOR: Medicine, Nursing, Psychology, X-ray Technology or Related Health Care Fields

Open to students pursuing careers in the medical field at any college, medical or technical school. Must demonstrate financial need and ability to do well in their chosen medical field. Only high school graduates of north central Iowa are eligible, such as: Buena Vista, Cerra Gorde, Chickasaw, Clay, Dickinson, Emmet, Floyd, Franklin, Hancock, Hardin, Howard, Humboldt, Kossuth, Mitchell, O'Brien, Palo Alto, Pocahontas, Winnebago, Worth, and Wright counties. Award requirements change regularly. Write to the address listed, enclosing a #10 self-addressed, stamped envelope or call (515) 422-5639 for further information. No GPA requirement specified.

North Iowa Mercy Foundation
Attn: Mariann Alcorn
1000 4th Street SW
Mason City, IA 50401-2800

341
Dr. Hinesly Student Athlete Scholarship

AMOUNT: $500 DEADLINE: March 31
MAJOR: All Fields of Study

The Dr. Hinesly Student Athlete Scholarship is open to Lenawee County (MI) graduating seniors. To be considered for this award, you must be involved in athletics at your high school. Award requirements change regularly. Please send a self-addressed, stamped envelope to receive your application and any further instructions from the scholarship provider. No GPA requirement specified.

Morenci High School
Attn: Mrs. Melissa Parnell
788 Coomer Street
Morenci, MI 49256

342
Dr. James L. Lawson Memorial Scholarship

AMOUNT: $500 DEADLINE: February 1
MAJOR: Electronics, Communications or Related Fields

This scholarship is available to students with a minimum general class amateur radio license. Applicants must be residents of: Maine, Massachusetts, Vermont, Rhode Island, New Hampshire, Connecticut or New York and attend a school in one of these states. Applicants must be majoring in electronics, communications or a related area in a baccalaureate or higher institution of study. Award requirements change regularly. Write the address provided, using a self-addressed, stamped envelope, for further information. No GPA requirement specified.

American Radio Relay League
Attn: ARRL Foundation
225 Main Street
Newington, CT 06111-1400

343
Dr. Jerry C. Nims Scholarship

AMOUNT: $1000 DEADLINE: May 26
MAJOR: All Areas of Study

This scholarship is open to initiated undergraduate members of Tau Kappa Epsilon. In order to apply, you must be in good standing with your chapter, have a demonstrated record of active participation within the chapter, including officer and chairmanship leadership positions. Also, you must be active in campus organizations, be a full-time student and have a minimum 2.5 GPA. Award requirements change regularly. For further information, call (317) 872-6533, email: tef@tkehq.org or visit the website at: www.tke.org. GPA must be 2.5-4.0.

TKE Educational Foundation
Attn: Timothy L. Taschwer
8645 Founders Road
Indianapolis, IN 46268-1336

344
Dr. Mae Davidow Memorial Scholarship

AMOUNT: $1000 DEADLINE: March 1
MAJOR: All Areas of Study

This scholarship is open to entering freshmen who are legally blind and who demonstrate outstanding academic achievement. Award requirements change regularly. Write to the address listed, enclosing a self-addressed, stamped envelope for an application and further information. No GPA requirement specified.

American Council of the Blind
Attn: Billie Jean Keith
1155 15th Street NW, Suite 720
Washington, DC 20005-2706

345
Dr. Pedro Grau Undergraduate Scholarship

AMOUNT: $2500 DEADLINE: June 14
MAJOR: Meteorology, Atmospheric Science, Ocean Science, Hydrology

Scholarships for students entering their last year of study toward a degree in one of the fields listed above. Based on academic ability and financial need. Requires a GPA of at least 3.0 and U.S. citizenship or permanent residency. Award requirements change regularly. Write to the address listed, sending a self-addressed, stamped envelope for details, call AMS headquarters at (617) 227-2426, extension 235, browse their website: www.ametsoc.org/ams/amsedu/scholfel.html or contact their email: armstrong@ametsoc.org. GPA must be 3.0.

American Meteorological Society
Fellowship/Scholarship Coordinator
45 Beacon Street
Boston, MA 02108-3693

346
Dr. Robert B. Rosenberg UIFI Scholarship

AMOUNT: None Specified DEADLINE: March 1
MAJOR: Participation in the Undergraduate Interfraternity Institute

The Dr. Robert B. Rosenberg UIFI Scholarship is awarded to active members of Triangle Fraternity to support their participation in the annual Undergraduate Interfraternity Institute (UIFI). This award covers conference registration costs and up to $100 in travel costs. Award requirements change regularly. No GPA requirement specified.

Triangle Fraternity
Attn: Education Foundation
120 South Center Street
Plainfield, IN 46168-1214

347
Dr. Tom Anderson Memorial Scholarship

AMOUNT: $2000 DEADLINE: April 17
MAJOR: Travel and Tourism, Hotel/Restaurant Management

The Dr. Tom Anderson Memorial Scholarship is open to students pursuing a degree in a travel and tourism-related field. To be considered for the award, you must be a junior or senior enrolled full-time in a North American two- or four-year college. Award requirements change regularly. No GPA requirement specified.

National Tourism Foundation
PO Box 3071
546 East Main Street
Lexington, KY 40508-3071

348

Dress Barn Scholarship Program for Dress Barn Dependents

AMOUNT: $500-$5000 DEADLINE: March 15
MAJOR: All Areas of Study

The Dress Barn Scholarship Program for Dress Barn Dependents is open to the children or legal dependents of full-time Dress Barn associates who have been employed with the company for at least one year prior to February 1. You must be a high school graduate or already attending a two- or four-year program. You will be judged on your high school or college GPA; school activities and/or clubs and teams; community service or significant extracurricular accomplishments; and an essay based on your career goals and aspirations. Two types of awards will be given. One award is for dependents going to four-year accredited schools and the other award is for dependents going to two-year, vocational, technical or professional schools. If you are a child of senior management at the Vice President level and above, you are not eligible for this award. Award requirements change regularly. No GPA requirement specified.

Dress Barn, Inc. - Human Resources
Attn: Jennifer Hinck
30 Dunnigan Drive
Suffern, NY 10901

349

DuPont Challenge Science Essay Competition

AMOUNT: $50-$1500 DEADLINE: January 28
MAJOR: Science

The DuPont Challenge Science Essay Awards is open to students in grades ten to 12 (Senior Division) and grades seven to nine (Junior Division) who are attending a public or non-public school in the United States, U.S. territories or Canada. The essay must be between 700 and 1,000 words in length and discusses a scientific or technological development, event or theory that has captured the student's interest and attention. The essay must be original, unpublished and written in English. Award requirements change regularly. For complete and specific information, please visit the DuPont website at: www.glcomm.com/dupont. No GPA requirement specified.

DuPont Challenge - Science Essay Awards Program
General Learning Communications
900 Skokie Blvd, Suite 200
Northbrook, IL 60062-4028

350

Duracell/NSTA Scholarship Contest

AMOUNT: $200-$20000 DEADLINE: January 12
MAJOR: All Areas of Study

This scholarship contest for students in grades 6 through 12 who are U.S. citizens residing in the U.S. or U.S. territories. In order to apply, you must design and build working devices powered by Duracell batteries. You will also need to submit a two-page description and a schematic of the device. Awards are in the form of U.S. Savings Bonds. Award requirements change regularly. No GPA requirement specified.

National Science Teachers Association
Duracell/NSTA Scholarship Competition
1840 Wilson Blvd, FL 3
Arlington, VA 22201-3000

351

Dwight D. Gardener Scholarship

AMOUNT: $1200-$2000 DEADLINE: November 15
MAJOR: Industrial Engineering

This scholarship is open to undergraduate students who are enrolled in an industrial engineering program on a full-time basis, who are members of the institute, and have a minimum 3.4 GPA. The program enrolled in may be located in the United States and its territories, Canada or Mexico provided that the school's engineering program or equivalent is accredited by an accrediting agency recognized by IIE. The applicants must have a graduation date of May/June 2001 or later and must be nominated by their IE Department heads. Award requirements change regularly. GPA must be 3.4-4.0.

Institute of Industrial Engineers
Attn: Chapter Operations Board
25 Technology Park
Norcross, GA 30092-2988

352

E.J. Sierleja Memorial Fellowship

AMOUNT: $300 DEADLINE: November 15
MAJOR: Transportation, Rail Transportation

This scholarship is available to graduate industrial engineering majors who are enrolled on a full-time basis, members of the institute, and have minimum GPA of 3.4. Preference is given to students with career studies in the rail transportation industry. The applicants must have a graduation date of May/June 2001 or later and must be nominated by their IE Department heads. Award requirements change regularly. GPA must be 3.4-4.0.

Institute of Industrial Engineers
Attn: Chapter Operations Board
25 Technology Park
Norcross, GA 30092-2988

353

E.R. & Lillian B. Dimmette Scholarship

AMOUNT: Maximum: $2000 DEADLINE: Varies
MAJOR: All Areas of Study

Scholarships for graduating high school students from Gaston, Iredell, Mecklenburg, Rowan or Wilkes counties (NC) with significant financial need. Recommendation by your superintendent is required. Award requirements change regularly. Write to the address listed for details, enclosing a self-addressed, stamped envelope (the foundation also administers the Charlotte, Mecklenburg schools scholarship incentive program for "at risk" students). Contact your guidance office for details and application forms. GPA must be 3.3-4.0.

357
EBSCO/NMRT Scholarship

AMOUNT: $1000 DEADLINE: April 1
MAJOR: Library Science, Information Science

The EBSCO/NMRT Scholarship is open to U.S. or Canadian citizens who are members of ALA and ALA/NMRT or must join ALA/NMRT prior to accepting the award. (NMRT membership is open to individuals who have been members of ALA for ten or fewer years.) Your application will be evaluated on the following factors: your academic credentials, financial needs and professional goals. There are no requirements on semester hours for continuing students. Award requirements change regularly. No GPA requirement specified.

American Library Association
HRDR/Staff Liaison - Scholarship Juries
50 East Huron Street
Chicago, IL 60611-2795

358
Ecolab Scholarship Program

AMOUNT: $1000 DEADLINE: June 1
MAJOR: Hospitality Management

The Ecolab Scholarship Program is open to students who are enrolled or intend to enroll full-time (at least 12 hours for both the upcoming fall and spring semesters) in a U.S.-accredited baccalaureate or associate program leading to a degree in hospitality management. Your application will be evaluated according to the following categories: industry-related work experience; financial need; academic record/educational qualifications; professional, community and extracurricular activities; personal attributes, including career goals; responses to the required essay questions; neatness and completeness of the application. Award requirements change regularly. No GPA requirement specified.

American Hotel Foundation
Attn: Manager of Foundation Programs
1201 New York Avenue, N.W., Suite 600
Washington, DC 20005-3931

359
Economics for Leaders Scholarship

AMOUNT: None Specified DEADLINE: March 1
MAJOR: All Areas of Study

The Economics for Leaders Scholarship is open to high school and postsecondary teachers and PBL members enrolled in teacher education programs, as well as high school students between their junior and senior years. National experts teach the program, which helps future leaders discover how and why the world works, while giving them skills required for their future roles. The award requires that you be a national and state dues-paid member, whether you are a teacher or student. The award will cover tuition, housing and meals only for the week-long event. Award requirements change regularly. Please send a self-addressed, stamped envelope to receive your application and any further instructions to: Steve Gerhart, Vice President, Administration and Program Affairs, Foundation for Teaching Economics, 260 Russell Blvd., Suite B, Davis, CA 95616, or phone (916) 757-4630. No GPA requirement specified.

...arship

...31

...en to students who are legally blind and are pursuing or planning to pursue a full-time postsecondary course of study in the U.S. Your selection will be based on academic excellence, service to the community and financial need. Award requirements change regularly. No GPA requirement specified.

National Federation of the Blind
Attn: Peggy Elliott, Chairman
805 5th Avenue
Grinnell, IA 50112-1653

355
Earl I. Anderson Scholarship

AMOUNT: $1250 DEADLINE: February 1
MAJOR: Electronic Engineering or Related Field

This scholarship is available to students holding any class amateur radio license who are residents of and attending classes in: Illinois, Indiana, Michigan, or Florida. The applicants must be majoring in electronic engineering or a related technical field and be an ARRL member. Award requirements change regularly. Write the address provided, using a self-addressed, stamped envelope. No GPA requirement specified.

American Radio Relay League
Attn: ARRL Foundation
225 Main Street
Newington, CT 06111-1400

356
Ebell/Charles Flint Scholarship

AMOUNT: Maximum: $2000 DEADLINE: March 1
MAJOR: All Areas of Study

This scholarship is open to undergraduates attending accredited schools in Los Angeles County. In order to apply, you must be a U.S. citizen, a registered voter, have a minimum 3.25 GPA, and complete at least 12 units of credit each semester. If you receive this award, it will be renewed for three years or until your graduation, whichever comes first. You must show a financial need as determined by the financial aid portion of the application. Award requirements change regularly. GPA must be 3.2-4.0.

Ebell of Los Angeles
Attn: Scholarship Chairman
743 S. Lucerne Blvd
Los Angeles, CA 90005-3707

Future Business Leaders of America
Attn: Scholarship Coordinator
1912 Association Drive
Reston, VA 22091

360
Ed Wisnesky American Legion Scholarship

AMOUNT: $500 DEADLINE: Varies
MAJOR: All Fields of Study

The Ed Wisnesky American Legion Scholarship is open to graduating seniors at Burlington High School (Burlington, WI). Award requirements change regularly. Please visit your Guidance Office to receive an application and any additional details. No GPA requirement specified.

Burlington High School
Attn: Guidance Office
225 Robert Street
Burlington, WI 53105

361
Eddy/Peck Scholarship

AMOUNT: $1000-$2500 DEADLINE: April 10
MAJOR: Journalism

The Eddy/Peck Scholarship is open to undergraduate students in their junior or senior year who are planning a career in journalism. To be eligible for this award, you must attend a four-year accredited college in Connecticut or be a Connecticut resident enrolled in a four-year college in any state or country. You are required to submit the following material with your scholarship application: your college transcripts; writing samples, tapes or related work in any media that demonstrates your interest and competency in journalism; and a 500-word essay. Three awards will be offered; one award each at $2,500, $1,500 and $1,000. Award requirements change regularly. No GPA requirement specified.

Connecticut Society of Professional Journalists Foundation
Attn: Scholarship Committee
71 Kenwood Avenue
Fairfield, CT 06430

362
Edilia and Francois-Auguste de Montequin Fellowship

AMOUNT: $2000-$6000 DEADLINE: October 30
MAJOR: Spanish, Portuguese, Ibero-American Architectural History

Awarded each year in support of travel costs for research on Spanish, Portuguese, or Ibero-American architecture. The award consists of a $2,000 stipend for a junior scholar (awarded annually) and a $6,000 stipend for a senior scholar (awarded biannually). Judged by a committee of three who are appointed by the president of the Society. Award requirements change regularly. For information regarding submission criteria and procedures, contact the Society of Architectural Historians by telephone (312) 573-1365 or email: info@sah.org. No GPA requirement specified.

Society of Architectural Historians
Charnley-Persky House
1365 North Astor Street
Chicago, IL 60610-2144

363
Edith H. Henderson Scholarship

AMOUNT: $1000 DEADLINE: March 31
MAJOR: Landscape Architecture/Design

The Edith H. Henderson Scholarship is open to any landscape architecture student who is committed to the goal of developing practical communication skills in their role as a landscape architect. You must have participated in, or be currently participating in, a public speaking or creative writing class. A 200-400-word (maximum) essay will be required. Award requirements change regularly. No GPA requirement specified.

Landscape Architecture Foundation
Scholarship Program
636 'I' Street NW
Washington, DC 20001-3736

364
Edmond A. Metzger Scholarship

AMOUNT: $500 DEADLINE: February 1
MAJOR: Electrical Engineering

This scholarship is available to students with a minimum novice class amateur radio license and are residents of: Illinois, Indiana or Wisconsin (ARRL Central Division) and attend school in one of these states. Applicants must be ARRL members and majoring in electrical engineering in a baccalaureate or higher course of study. Award requirements change regularly. Write the address provided, using a self-addressed, stamped envelope, for further information. No GPA requirement specified.

American Radio Relay League
Attn: ARRL Foundation
225 Main Street
Newington, CT 06111-1400

365
Edna Aimes Scholarship

AMOUNT: $2000 DEADLINE: April 1
MAJOR: Mental Health

The Edna Aimes Scholarship is awarded to students who will work in the mental health field. Your professional goals must include: assisting in the prevention and treatment of mental illness, promoting mental health and the empowerment of adults, children and families whose lives have been affected by mental illness. The scholarship is open to juniors, seniors and matriculated graduate students attending school in New York State who are majoring in a mental health related field and preparing for a career in mental health. You must be a New York resident and be able to demonstrate financial need. Previous recipients of an Edna Aimes Scholarship are not eligible to apply. Award requirements change regularly. No GPA requirement specified.

Mental Health Association in New York State, Inc.
Attn: Scholarship Coordinator
194 Washington Avenue, Suite 415
Albany, NY 12210

366
Edna Meudt Memorial Scholarship

AMOUNT: $500 DEADLINE: February 15
MAJOR: Poetry

Awards open to juniors or seniors at any accredited college or university. Must submit ten original poems which are judged on or before March 31. Recipients will be announced after April 15. Award requirements change regularly. State organizations will be advertising and making available applications and information. First Class mail will only be accepted - no special deliveries to: PJ Doyle, NFSPS Edna Meudt Memorial Scholarship Committee at the address listed. No GPA requirement specified.

National Federation of State Poetry Societies (NFSPS)
PJ Doyle
4242 Stevens
Minneapolis, MN 55409-2004

367
Educational Advancement Scholarship

AMOUNT: $1500 DEADLINE: January 15
MAJOR: Nursing

Scholarships are available to AACN members who have junior or senior status in an accredited B.S.N. program. Applicants must have a minimum GPA of 3.0 and not yet be a licensed Registered Nurse. Award requirements change regularly. Please write to the address provided for complete information. GPA must be 3.0-4.0.

American Association of Critical-Care Nurses
Educational Advancement Scholarships
101 Columbia
Aliso Viejo, CA 92656-1491

368
Educational Opportunity Grant

AMOUNT: $2500 DEADLINE: March 31
MAJOR: All Areas of Study

The Educational Opportunity Grant is open to students with associate degrees or students who have already completed their first two years of college who wish to pursue four year degrees in Washington. To be considered for the award, you must demonstrate financial need and be a resident of Washington state. Award requirements change regularly. To apply, you must submit the FAFSA. For more information, you may visit the website at www.hecb.wa.gov. No GPA requirement specified.

Washington Higher Education Coordinating Board
Student Financial Aid
917 Lakeridge Way, PO Box 43430
Olympia, WA 98504-3430

369
Educational Programming and Regional Conferences Scholarship

AMOUNT: None Specified DEADLINE: March 1
MAJOR: Participation in Regional Conferences

The Educational Programming and Regional Conferences Scholarship is awarded to active members of Triangle Fraternity who wish to attend regional conferences which are either educational in nature or dedicated to leadership development. Award requirements change regularly. No GPA requirement specified.

Triangle Fraternity
Attn: Education Foundation
120 South Center Street
Plainfield, IN 46168-1214

370
Edward and Isabell Larson Memorial Fellowship

AMOUNT: $1500 DEADLINE: May 1
MAJOR: Engineering

The Edward and Isabell Larson Memorial Fellowship is open to members of Triangle fraternity who are pursuing a graduate degree in engineering. To be considered for this award, you must have graduated from an accredited undergraduate engineering program and have a minimum 3.3 cumulative undergraduate GPA. Your application will be evaluated on the basis of your academic performance, participation in Triangle activities and leadership positions, involvement in campus activities, letters of recommendation and potential for success. Award requirements change regularly. GPA must be 3.3-4.0.

Triangle Fraternity
Attn: Education Foundation
120 South Center Street
Plainfield, IN 46168-1214

371
Edward D. Stone Jr. and Associates Minority Scholarship

AMOUNT: $1000 DEADLINE: March 31
MAJOR: Landscape Architecture/Design

The Edward D. Stone Jr. and Associates Minority Scholarship is open to African-American, Hispanic, Native American, and minority students of other cultural and ethnic backgrounds who are entering their final two years of undergraduate study in landscape architecture. You will be required to submit an essay and slides or pictures of your best work. Award requirements change regularly. No GPA requirement specified.

Landscape Architecture Foundation
Scholarship Program
636 'I' Street NW
Washington, DC 20001-3736

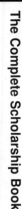

372

Edward J. Brady Scholarship

AMOUNT: $2500 DEADLINE: January 15
MAJOR: Welding Engineering, Welding Engineering Technology

The Edward J. Brady Scholarship is awarded to undergraduate students pursuing a minimum four-year bachelor's degree in welding engineering or welding engineering technology. Priority will be given to welding engineering students interested in pursuing a career with an industrial gas or welding equipment distributor by prior work experience, clubs or extracurricular activities. Applicants must reside in or attend school in the states of Alabama, Georgia or Florida. A minimum overall GPA of 2.5 is required. Demonstrated financial need is also considered. Students must have U.S. citizenship. This award is renewable. Award requirements change regularly. Please send a self-addressed, stamped envelope to receive your application and any further instructions from the scholarship provider or call (305) 445-6628. GPA must be 2.5-4.0.

American Welding Society Foundation, Inc.
National Education Scholarship Committee
550 Northwest LeJeune Road
Miami, FL 33126-4165

373

Edward Leon Duhamel Scholarship

AMOUNT: None Specified DEADLINE: May 10
MAJOR: All Fields of Study

The Edward Leon Duhamel Scholarship is open to the children, grandchildren and/or great-grandchildren of Freemason members. To be considered for this award, you must be enrolled in a college or university, show scholastic achievement and good citizenship. The award also requires that you demonstrate financial need. Preference will be given to those who are descendants of Freemason members from the Franklin Lodge in Westerly, RI. Award requirements change regularly. No GPA requirement specified.

Rhode Island Foundation
Attn: Special Funds Office
70 Elm Street
Providence, RI 02903

374

Edward O. Kallmann Scholarship

AMOUNT: $2000 DEADLINE: March 15
MAJOR: All Fields of Study

The Edward O. Kallmann Scholarship is open to employees of Business Products Industry Association member firms and their families. Persons holding academic records sufficient for acceptance by accredited colleges, junior colleges or technical schools, or persons already enrolled in one of those institutions are eligible for this one-year award. Selection is made by a committee from the Student Financial Aid Department of The George Washington University, Washington, DC. Award requirements change regularly. Please send a self-addressed, stamped envelope to receive your application and any further instructions from the scholarship provider or email: info@bpia.org. No GPA requirement specified.

Business Products Industry Association
Attn: Scholarship Committee
301 North Fairfax Street
Alexandria, VA 22314-2633

375

Edward S. Goldmacher Scholarship

AMOUNT: None Specified DEADLINE: February 28
MAJOR: Human Resource Information Management, Human Resource Management, Human Resource Systems

This scholarship is open to outstanding individuals pursuing an undergraduate or graduate degree in the field of human resource information management, human resource management, human resource systems, or a closely related field. In order to apply, you must be nominated by an IHRIM member or instructor at an accredited institution in one of the fields noted. Award requirements change regularly. Please send a self-addressed, stamped envelope to receive your application and any further instructions from the scholarship provider, call (312) 321-5141, or email: moreinfo@ihrim.org You may also visit their website: www.ihrim.org. GPA must be 3.0-4.0.

International Assn for Human Resource Information Management (IHRIM)
Attn: Kimberly Pinter
401 North Michigan Avenue
Chicago, IL 60611-4267

376

Edward T. Conroy Memorial Grant

AMOUNT: Maximum: $3480 DEADLINE: July 15
MAJOR: All Areas of Study

This grant is open to applicants who will be attending a Maryland postsecondary institution. This award is available to children of deceased or 100% disabled US Armed Forces personnel, Maryland residents who were Vietnam-era POWs and to Maryland state or local public safety personnel who are 100% disabled. Surviving spouses and children of safety personnel are also eligible. This award is renewable for up to five years full-time study or eight years part-time study. Awarded on a yearly basis. Award requirements change regularly. Write to the state scholarship administration at the address provided for more details. No GPA requirement specified.

Maryland State Higher Education Commission
Attn: State Scholarship Administration
16 Francis Street
Annapolis, MD 21401-1781

377

Edwards Group, Inc. Scholarship

AMOUNT: None Specified DEADLINE: Varies
MAJOR: Business

The Edwards Group, Inc. Scholarship is open to graduating seniors at Burlington High School (Burlington, WI). Students must be entering a business degree program. Award requirements change regularly. Please visit your Guidance Office to receive an application and any additional details. No GPA requirement specified.

Burlington High School
Attn: Guidance Office
225 Robert Street
Burlington, WI 53105

378
Eileen J. Garrett Parapsychology Research Scholarship

AMOUNT: $3000 DEADLINE: July 15
MAJOR: Parapsychology

The Eileen J. Garrett Parapsychology Research Scholarship is open to students attending accredited colleges or universities who are wishing to pursue the academic study of the science of parapsychology. You must demonstrate a previous interest in parapsychology by including a sample of writings on the subject with your application form (available from the Foundation). Letters of reference are also required from three individuals who are familiar with your work and/or study in parapsychology. Award requirements change regularly. For further information and an application, please write to the address listed, including a self-addressed, stamped envelope or call (212) 628-1550. You may also visit their website: www.parapsychology.org. No GPA requirement specified.

Parapsychology Foundation, Inc.
Eileen J Garrett Library
228 East 71st Street
New York, NY 10021-5136

379
Einar and Eva Lund Haugen Dissertation Scholarship

AMOUNT: $3000 DEADLINE: March 1
MAJOR: Arts, Humanities, Social Sciences

Open to outstanding doctoral candidates who have completed predissertation requirements within the preceding year. The dissertation shall treat a Scandinavian or Scandanavian-American topic. Based on evaluation of the applicant's academic record, three references, thesis proposal work plan and future professional goals. Awards usually made in the month of April. Award requirements change regularly. Contact the address listed for further information. There are no application forms; direct applications, together with the above described documents, must be received by March 1. GPA must be 3.0-4.0.

Norwegian-American Historical Society
Chairman Haugen, Scholarship Committee
1510 Saint Olaf Avenue
Northfield, MN 55057-1574

380
EIT Grant

AMOUNT: None Specified DEADLINE: Varies
MAJOR: Engineering

The EIT Grant is offered to reimburse the examination fee to college students who take the Fundamentals of Engineering (EIT) Examination, the first step to becoming a licensed Professional Engineer (PE). Preference is given to current student members of the California Society of Professional Engineers. Award requirements change regularly. No GPA requirement specified.

California Society of Professional Engineers
Attn: CSPE Education Foundation
8801 Folsom Boulevard, Suite 120
Sacramento, CA 95826-3249

381
ELA Foundation Fellowship

AMOUNT: $2000 DEADLINE: May 25
MAJOR: Disability Policy

The ELA Foundation Fellowship is open to female graduate students with disabilities who are studying, researching, and writing on disability policy in an accredited college or university. You must be a U.S. citizen, provide two letters of recommendation and an official transcript, and submit documentation or verification of your disability. An essay entitled "How I Will Change the Face of Disability on the Planet" is also required. Award requirements change regularly. No GPA requirement specified.

President's Committee on Employment of People With Disabilities
Recognition Program
1331 F Street NW
Washington, DC 20004-1107

382
Elaine Osborne Jacobson Award

AMOUNT: $3000 DEADLINE: January 28
MAJOR: Health Care Law

The Elaine Osborne Jacobson Award is open to female students currently enrolled in an accredited American law school on a full- or part-time basis. Candidates should demonstrate, through their law school academic and clinic work, an aptitude for and long-term commitment to a legal career of advocacy on behalf of the health care needs of children, women, the elderly or the disabled. To be considered for this award, you must be nominated by your Dean, clinical program director, or law school professor. You must also submit a current curriculum vitae, a brief personal statement, letters of recommendation and a sample of written work. A brief essay may also be required. Award requirements change regularly. Please send a self-addressed, stamped envelope to receive your application and any further instructions from the scholarship provider; or call (800) 424-2725, ext. 380; or fax (202) 965-0355. No GPA requirement specified.

Roscoe Pound Foundation
Education and Membership Coordinator
1050 31st Street NW
Washington, DC 20007

383
Eleanor Roosevelt Teacher Fellowships

AMOUNT: $1000-$9000 DEADLINE: January 10
MAJOR: Education

The Eleanor Roosevelt Teacher Fellowships are available to women K-12 public school teachers as individuals or as lead members of teams composed of teachers and administrators, including men and women. Funds support the development of innovative curriculum projects designed to encourage girl's interest and achievement in math, science, and/or technology.

Applicants must be U.S. citizens or permanent residents committed to teaching for three years including the fellowship year. Fellows are required to develop an independent study plan that may include college courses, seminars and/or professional workshops that are a part of the five-day Teacher Institute in Washington, DC. This workshop focuses on strategies to enrich the curriculum and promote gender equity in the classroom. Award requirements change regularly. Please send a self-addressed, stamped envelope to receive your application and any further instructions from the scholarship provider or call (319) 337-1716, ext. 60 or visit www.aauw.org. No GPA requirement specified.

AAUW Educational Foundation
Attn: Award Committee
2201 North Dodge Street - Department 60
Iowa City, IA 52243-4030

384
Elks Academic Scholarship

AMOUNT: $1000 DEADLINE: Varies
MAJOR: All Areas of Study

Open to Rocky Mountain High School seniors. Applicants will be considered on scholarship, leadership, and financial need. Award may be used at any degree-granting institution. Top applicants will interviewed at the local Elks Club. Application deadline, procedure, and award amount varies annually. Award requirements change regularly. Applications are available in January or February in the Rocky Mountain High School Career Center, as part of the Local Scholarship Packet. No GPA requirement specified.

Rocky Mountain High School
Scholarship Committee
1300 West Swallow Road
Fort Collins, CO 80526-2412

385
Elks Vocational Scholarship

AMOUNT: $600 DEADLINE: Varies
MAJOR: All Areas of Study

Open to Rocky Mountain High School seniors. Applicants will be considered on scholarship, leadership, financial need, and a well-defined plan for technical or other vocational employment. Must plan to attend a two-year community or junior college or a certified vocational school. Application deadline, procedure, and award amount vary annually. Award requirements change regularly. Applications are available in January or February in the Rocky Mountain High School Career Center, as part of the Local Scholarship Packet. No GPA requirement specified.

Rocky Mountain High School
Scholarship Committee
1300 West Swallow Road
Fort Collins, CO 80526-2412

386
Ellen Cushing Scholarship

AMOUNT: None Specified DEADLINE: Varies
MAJOR: Church-Related Studies, Human Service

The Ellen Cushing Scholarship is open to female American Baptist graduate students planning to enter church-related or human services vocations with preference given to students active in their school, church or region. Applicants must be members of an American Baptist church for at least one year before applying for aid and enrolled at an accredited educational institution in the U.S. or Puerto Rico. U.S. citizenship is required. Award requirements change regularly. Please send a self-addressed, stamped envelope to receive your application and any further instructions from the scholarship provider. No GPA requirement specified.

American Baptist Financial Aid Program
Educational Ministries ABC/USA
PO Box 851
Valley Forge, PA 19482-0851

387
Elmer E. Krumwiede Scholarship

AMOUNT: $2000 DEADLINE: March 15
MAJOR: All Fields of Study

The Elmer E. Krumwiede Scholarship is open to employees of Business Products Industry Association member firms and their families. Persons holding academic records sufficient for acceptance by accredited colleges, junior colleges or technical schools, or persons already enrolled in one of those institutions are eligible for this one-year award. Selection is made by a committee from the Student Financial Aid Department of The George Washington University, Washington, DC. Award requirements change regularly. Please send a self-addressed, stamped envelope to receive your application and any further instructions from the scholarship provider or email: info@bpia.org. No GPA requirement specified.

Business Products Industry Association
Attn: Scholarship Committee
301 North Fairfax Street
Alexandria, VA 22314-2633

388
Elmer H. Schmitz Memorial Scholarship

AMOUNT: $800 DEADLINE: May 26
MAJOR: All Areas of Study

This memorial scholarship is open to initiated members of Tau Kappa Epsilon. You must be from the state of Wisconsin, demonstrate leadership within your chapter, on campus or in your community. Further requirements include being a full-time student with a minimum 2.5 GPA. Award requirements change regularly. For further information, call (317) 872-6533, email: tef@tkehq.org or visit the website at: www.tke.org. GPA must be 2.5-4.0.

TKE Educational Foundation
Attn: Timothy L. Taschwer
8645 Founders Road
Indianapolis, IN 46268-1336

389
Elvin S. Douglas Jr. Scholarship

AMOUNT: $500 DEADLINE: April 15
MAJOR: Health and Medical Related Fields

Open to any Cass County (MO) citizen who is training in health or medical related fields. Award requirements change regularly. Applications are available in the Harrisonville

Senior High School guidance office. No GPA requirement specified.

Harrisonville Senior High School
Attn: Roy Sackman
1504 East Elm Street
Harrisonville, MO 64701-2022

390
Emanuel Sternberger Educational Fund Loans

AMOUNT: None Specified DEADLINE: March 31
MAJOR: All Areas of Study

The Emanuel Sternberger Educational Fund Loans are interest-free loans open to full-time juniors, seniors and graduate students who are residents of the following counties in North Carolina: Alamance, Caswell, Davidson, Davie, Forsythe, Guilford, Montgomery, Randolph, Rockingham, Stokes, Surry and Yadkin. A maximum of $1,000 is available for the first year and $2,000 for the second year. Your grades, economic situation, references, credit rating and other information may all be considered. If your application is approved, a loan agreement and note form will be sent to you sometime in June. A check for the loan proceeds will be issued in late August or early September. Award requirements change regularly. No GPA requirement specified.

Emanuel Sternberger Educational Fund
Office of the Trustee
PO Box 1735
Greensboro, NC 27402-1735

391
Emergency Secondary Education Loan

AMOUNT: Maximum: $2500 DEADLINE: April 1
MAJOR: Education

Scholarships open to full-time undergraduates or graduate students pursuing a secondary education teaching certification at an approved Arkansas school. Applicants must be Arkansas residents. Repayment of loan is forgiven at 20% for each year taught in approved subject shortage areas in Arkansas secondary schools after graduation. Award requirements change regularly. Write to the address listed, enclosing a self-addressed, stamped envelope for an application and further information. You may also browse their website: www.arscholarships.com/finsites.html. No GPA requirement specified.

Arkansas Department of Higher Education
Financial Aid Division
114 East Capitol Avenue
Little Rock, AR 72201-3818

392
Emily Gardner Munro Scholarship

AMOUNT: $500 DEADLINE: February 26
MAJOR: All Areas of Study

This scholarship is open to local women who are juniors at an accredited college or university. Award requirements change regularly. Write to the address listed, enclosing a self-addressed, stamped envelope for an application and further

information. No GPA requirement specified.

American Association of University Women-Waterbury Branch
Attn: Joan W Donald
18 Edwards Drive
Oxford, CT 06478-1523

393
Endowed Scholarships

AMOUNT: $400-$1000 DEADLINE: Varies
MAJOR: Podiatry

A number of endowed and alumni sponsored scholarships are awarded each year to eligible third and fourth year students attending the Scholl College of Podiatric Medicine. Students are considered automatically, based on financial need and academic performance by the Scholl Scholarship and Student Loan Committee. No specific application form is required. Award requirements change regularly. Please send a self-addressed, stamped envelope to receive your application and any further instructions from the scholarship provider or contact the Office of Student Services (800) 843-3059 or email finaid@scholl.edu. You may also browse the sponsor website. No GPA requirement specified.

Scholl College of Podiatric Medicine
Attn: Office of Student Services
1001 North Dearborn Street
Chicago, IL 60610

394
Energy Research Summer Fellowship

AMOUNT: $3000 DEADLINE: January 1
MAJOR: Electrochemistry and Related Fields

Awards are available for graduate students studying a field related to the objectives of the Electrochemical Society. To apply you must complete an application form and supply the following additional information: a statement of educational objectives; a statement of thesis research problem; undergraduate and graduate transcripts; two letters of recommendation including one from your research advisor. This program is supported by the U.S. Department of Energy. Winners will be announced by April 1. Award requirements change regularly. To receive a scholarship application and any further instructions, please send a self-addressed, stamped envelope to the Chairman of the Fellowship Subcommittee: Dr. Robin McCarley, Department of Chemistry, Choppin Laboratories of Chemistry, Louisiana State University, Baton Rouge, LA 70803. You can also contact Dr. McCarley by phone at (225) 388-3239; by fax at (225) 388-3458; or by email at tunnel@unix1.sncc.lsu.edu. No GPA requirement specified.

Electrochemical Society, Inc.
Attn: Honors and Awards Committee
10 South Main Street
Pennington, NJ 08534-2896

395
Engineering Council of Birmingham, Inc. Scholarship

AMOUNT: $1000 DEADLINE: April 1
MAJOR: Engineering

This scholarship is open to graduating high school students who plan on attending an ABET-EAC-accredited Alabama college or university and plan to major in engineering. In order to apply, you must be a U.S. citizen or a permanent resident and be a resident of Blount, Jefferson, St. Clair, Shelby, Bibb, Tuscaloosa or Walker counties. You must also have a minimum 3.0 GPA. The application form (with required signatures), ACT/SAT scores, an essay, two letters of recommendation, an essay and transcripts will be required. Award requirements change regularly. GPA must be 3.0-4.0.

Engineering Council of Birmingham, Inc.
Attn: Sandy Wood
7003 Alice Road
McCalla, AL 35111

396
Engineering Scholarship

AMOUNT: None Specified DEADLINE: February 15
MAJOR: Pre-Engineering

The Engineering Scholarship is open to students who are enrolled in the final year of a preengineering program in a Florida junior or community college. You must have a minimum 3.0 GPA and be recommended by an official at the college you are attending. Your selection will be based on academic performance, work experience, activities, honors, essay, and letters of recommendation, along with evidence of leadership, motivation, character, and self-reliance. Award requirements change regularly. GPA must be 3.0-4.0.

Florida Engineering Society
Attn: Win Bolton
125 South Gadsden Street
Tallahassee, FL 32301-1525

397
Engineering Scholarship

AMOUNT: $2000-$3000 DEADLINE: January 1
MAJOR: Engineering

Open to high school seniors and undergraduate students interested in pursuing engineering degrees. Five scholarship of up to $2,000 will go to high school seniors and five scholarships of up to $3,000 will go to undergraduates at accredited Michigan colleges of universities. Applicants must be U.S. citizens and Michigan residents. Minimum GPA must be a 3.0 or above and ACT score of 26. Award requirements change regularly. Please send a self-addressed, stamped envelope to receive your application and any further instructions from the scholarship provider or contact your high school counselor. GPA must be 3.0-4.0.

Michigan Society of Professional Engineers
Attn: Scholarship Coordinator
215 North Walnut Street, PO Box 15276
Lansing, MI 48901-5276

398
Ensign May High Twelve Loan Fund

AMOUNT: Maximum: $1750 DEADLINE: Varies
MAJOR: All Areas of Study

Applicants must be active or senior Demolay, Job's Daughter or Rainbow Girl in good standing. Must have a GPA of 2.75 or better and attend an approved college or university in California. Award requirements change regularly. Please send a self-addressed, stamped envelope to receive your application and any further instructions from the scholarship provider. GPA must be 2.8-4.0.

California Association of High Twelve Clubs
Norman Mykles, Secretary of the Board
PO Box 691826
Stockton, CA 95269-1826

399
Eric and Bette Friedheim Scholarship

AMOUNT: $500 DEADLINE: April 17
MAJOR: Travel and Tourism, Hotel/Restaurant Management

The Eric and Bette Friedheim Scholarship is open to juniors or seniors pursuing a degree in a travel and tourism-related field. To be considered for the award, you must be enrolled in a North American four-year college full-time. Award requirements change regularly. Please contact the sponsor for further information at (800) 682-8886. No GPA requirement specified.

National Tourism Foundation
PO Box 3071
546 East Main Street
Lexington, KY 40508-3071

400
Erna Miller Memorial Scholarship/Burlington Woman's Club

AMOUNT: $600 DEADLINE: Varies
MAJOR: Education, Nursery/Kindergarten Education

The Erna Miller Memorial Scholarship/Burlington Woman's Club is open to senior Burlington High School or Catholic Central High School (Burlington, WI) students pursuing a teaching career. Preference will be given to students with an interest in nursery/kindergarten education. The scholarship will be awarded on the basis of need and merit and applicants must have at least a 2.0 GPA. Award requirements change regularly. Please visit your Guidance Office to receive an application and any additional details. GPA must be 2.0-4.0.

Burlington High School
Attn: Guidance Office
225 Robert Street
Burlington, WI 53105

401
Ernest and Edna Aber Scholarship

AMOUNT: None Specified DEADLINE: Varies
MAJOR: All Fields of Study

The Ernest and Edna Aber Scholarship is open to graduating seniors at Burlington High School (Burlington, WI). Students must attend a four-year religious affiliated college. Award requirements change regularly. Please visit your Guidance Office to receive an application and any additional details. No GPA requirement specified.

Burlington High School
Attn: Guidance Office
225 Robert Street
Burlington, WI 53105

402
Esperanza Scholarship

AMOUNT: $500 DEADLINE: March 31
MAJOR: All Areas of Study

The Esperanza Scholarship is open to Hispanic graduating high school seniors and current full-time undergraduates who are residents of Cuyahoga County in Ohio. You must have a minimum GPA of 2.5. Award requirements change regularly. Contact the address listed, enclosing a self-addressed, stamped envelope, or call (216) 651-8289. You may also fax to (216) 651-7183. GPA must be 2.5-4.0.

Esperanza, Inc.
May Dugan Multi-Service Center
4115 Bridge Avenue, Room 107
Cleveland, OH 44113-3304

403
Esselte Pendaflex Scholarship

AMOUNT: $2000 DEADLINE: March 15
MAJOR: All Fields of Study

The Esselte Pendaflex Scholarship is open to employees of Business Products Industry Association member firms and their families. Persons holding academic records sufficient for acceptance by accredited colleges, junior colleges or technical schools, or persons already enrolled in one of those institutions are eligible for this one-year award. Selection is made by a committee from the Student Financial Aid Department of The George Washington University, Washington, DC. Award requirements change regularly. Please send a self-addressed, stamped envelope to receive your application and any further instructions from the scholarship provider or email: info@bpia.org. No GPA requirement specified.

Business Products Industry Association
Attn: Scholarship Committee
301 North Fairfax Street
Alexandria, VA 22314-2633

404
Esther Shiller Memorial Endowment Loan Fund for College Loans

AMOUNT: Maximum: $5000 DEADLINE: Varies
MAJOR: All Areas of Study

The purpose of the Esther Shiller Memorial Endowment Loan Fund for College Loans is to provide college loans for Jewish men and women who demonstrate academic promise and the ability to repay the loans. Applicants must be able to provide qualified guarantors (co-signers) that reside in the Bay Area. Applicants must be residents of San Francisco, San Mateo, northern Santa Clara, Marin, Sonoma, Alameda or Contra Costa counties in California. It is preferable that loan applicants submit their Applications by July 1 for the fall semester and November 1 for the spring semester. Award requirements change regularly. No GPA requirement specified.

Jewish Family and Children's Services
Attn: Loans and Grants Department
2245 Post Street
San Francisco, CA 94115

405
Ethan and Allan Murphy Scholarship

AMOUNT: $2000 DEADLINE: June 14
MAJOR: Atmospheric Science, Hydrologic Science, Ocean Science

Scholarships are for students entering their final year of study in hydrologic science, atmospheric science, ocean science, or related sciences with a GPA of 3.0 or better. Must be U.S. citizens or permanent residents. Award requirements change regularly. Write to the address listed, sending a self-addressed, stamped envelope for details, call AMS headquarters at (617) 227-2426, extension 235, browse their website: www.amet-soc.org/ams/amsedu/scholfel.html or contact their email: arm-strong@ametsoc.org. GPA must be 3.0.

American Meteorological Society
Fellowship/Scholarship Coordinator
45 Beacon Street
Boston, MA 02108-3693

406
Ethnic Minority Scholarship

AMOUNT: None Specified DEADLINE: March 15
MAJOR: All Fields of Study

The Ethnic Minority Scholarship is open to Kansas residents who are enrolled full-time in qualified undergraduate programs at Kansas colleges and universities. To be considered for this award, you must demonstrate financial need, be academically competitive and be a member of any of the following ethnic/racial groups: American Indian or Alaskan Native; Asian or Pacific Islander; African-American; or Hispanic. Priority will be given to recent high school graduates. Award requirements change regularly. To apply, you need to submit the FAFSA as well as a State of Kansas Student Aid Application. Please visit the Kansas Board of Regents website for more information at www.kansasregents.org. No GPA requirement specified.

Kansas Board of Regents
Attn: Student Assistance Section
700 SW Harrison Street, Suite 1410
Topeka, KS 66603-3760

407
Eugene C. Beach Memorial Scholarship

AMOUNT: $650 DEADLINE: May 26
MAJOR: All Areas of Study

This memorial scholarship is available to undergraduates who are members of Tau Kappa Epsilon. In order to apply, you must demonstrate leadership within your chapter, on campus or in your community. You must also have a minimum 2.5 GPA and be a full-time student in good standing. Award requirements change regularly. For further information, call (317) 872-6533, email: tef@tkehq.org or visit the website at: www.tke.org. GPA must be 2.5-4.0.

TKE Educational Foundation
Attn: Timothy L. Taschwer
8645 Founders Road
Indianapolis, IN 46268-1336

408
Eugene "Gene" Sallee, W4YFR Memorial Scholarship

AMOUNT: $500 DEADLINE: February 1
MAJOR: All Areas of Study

This scholarship is available to students with a minimum technician plus class amateur radio license who are residents of Georgia. Applicants must have a minimum 3.0 GPA. Award requirements change regularly. Write the address provided, using a self-addressed, stamped envelope, for further information. GPA must be 3.0-4.0.

American Radio Relay League
Attn: ARRL Foundation
225 Main Street
Newington, CT 06111-1400

409
Eugenia Bradford Roberts Memorial Fund

AMOUNT: $1000 DEADLINE: March 31
MAJOR: All Areas of Study

The Eugenia Bradford Roberts Memorial Fund is open to students who are the daughters, step-daughters, adopted daughters or granddaughters of a career commissioned officer or warrant officer of the U.S. Army. This award is based on academic standing, test scores, school and community activity and financial need. A letter of inquiry must include dates of the officer's active duty, with name, rank and social security number. The scholarship is renewable based upon continued achievement and financial need. Award requirements change regularly. Please send a self-addressed, stamped envelope to receive your application and any further instructions from the scholarship provider. No GPA requirement specified.

Daughters of the United States Army
Attn: Scholarship Chairman
7717 Rockledge Court

West Springfield, VA 22152

410
External Faculty Fellowship

AMOUNT: Maximum: $52500 DEADLINE: November 15
MAJOR: Humanities, History, Philosophy, Languages, Literature, Linguistics, Archaeology, Jurisprudence, History and Criticism of the Arts, Ethics, Comparative Religion, Cultural Anthropology, Sociology, Political Theory, International Relations

The Stanford Humanities Center awards six to eight External Faculty Fellowships annually to scholars in the humanities and scholars interested in humanistic issues. The fellowships fall into two categories: senior fellowships for well-established scholars; junior fellowships for scholars who at the beginning of their fellowship year will be at least three years beyond the receipt of the Ph.D. and normally no more than ten. The fellowships are intended primarily for persons currently teaching or affiliated with an academic institution, but others may apply. Fellows will be expected to remain in residence during the regular academic year, to live in the immediate area of the University, to take part in the life of the Center and contribute to the intellectual life of the Stanford community. Junior fellows will be offered stipends of up to $25,000 and senior fellows stipends of up to $40,000. A housing and travel allowance of up to $12,500 is offered on the basis of a fellow's needs. Please send a self-addressed, stamped envelope to receive your application and any further instructions from the scholarship provider. No GPA requirement specified.

Stanford Humanities Center - Stanford University
Attn: Fellowship Administrator
Mariposa House, 546 Salvatierra Walk
Stanford, CA 94305-8630

411
F. Charles Ruling N6FR Memorial Scholarship

AMOUNT: $1000 DEADLINE: February 1
MAJOR: Electronics, Communications or Related Areas

This scholarship is available to students with a minimum general class amateur radio license. Applicants must be studying in the areas of electronics, communications or related fields. Award requirements change regularly. Write the address provided, using a self-addressed, stamped envelope, for further information. No GPA requirement specified.

American Radio Relay League
Attn: ARRL Foundation
225 Main Street
Newington, CT 06111-1400

412
Fab 4 Scholarship

AMOUNT: $2000 DEADLINE: March 31
MAJOR: All Fields of Study

The Fab 4 Scholarship is open to Lenawee County (MI) graduating seniors pursuing higher education. To be considered for the award, you must submit an essay describing your dreams for the future and how you plan to fulfill those dreams. Award requirements change regularly. Please send a self-addressed, stamped envelope to receive your application and any further instructions from the scholarship provider. No GPA requirement specified.

Morenci High School
Attn: Mrs. Melissa Parnell
788 Coomer Street
Morenci, MI 49256

Falcon Foundation Scholarship

AMOUNT: Maximum: $3000 DEADLINE: April 30
MAJOR: Air Force Military Career

The Falcon Foundation Scholarship is open to a student who has potential for US Air Force Academy education and a desire for an Air Force career, however, needs further academic preparation before cadet appointment. The applicant must be at least 17 years old and unmarried. Award requirements change regularly. For further information, please consult the address listed. No GPA requirement specified.

Falcon Foundation
3116 Academy Drive, # 200
Usaf Academy, CO 80840-4400

414
Farver Foundation Business Scholarship

AMOUNT: $1000 DEADLINE: March 31
MAJOR: Business

The Farver Foundation Business Scholarship is open to Lenawee County (MI) graduates. You qualify for the award if you are entering your junior or senior year of college and you are majoring in business. Award requirements change regularly. Please send a self-addressed, stamped envelope to receive your application and any further instructions from the scholarship provider. No GPA requirement specified.

Morenci High School
Attn: Mrs. Melissa Parnell
788 Coomer Street
Morenci, MI 49256

415
Father James B. MacElwane Annual Awards

AMOUNT: $300 DEADLINE: June 14
MAJOR: Meteorology, Atmospheric Sciences

Awards are available from the American Meteorological Society for the top three papers submitted by undergraduate students on the subject of Atmospheric Science or Meteorology. One award is given annually. Award requirements change regularly. Write to the address listed, sending a self-addressed, stamped envelope for details, call AMS headquarters at (617) 227-2426, extension 235, browse their website: www.ametsoc.org/ams/amsedu/scholfel.html or contact their email: armstrong@ametsoc.org. GPA must be 3.0-4.0.

American Meteorological Society
Fellowship/Scholarship Coordinator
45 Beacon Street
Boston, MA 02108-3693

416
Father Joseph P. Fitzpatrick Scholarship Fund

AMOUNT: $1000 DEADLINE: February 15
MAJOR: Law

The Father Joseph P. Fitzpatrick Scholarship Fund is open to Latino students currently in a J.D. degree program at an ABA approved law school in the United States. You must demonstrate academic promise, financial need, commitment to the Latino community and be pursuing a career in public interest law. Students working towards their L.L.M. are not eligible for these awards. Award requirements change regularly. No GPA requirement specified.

Earl Warren Legal Training Program, Inc.
99 Hudson Street, Suite 1600
New York, NY 10013-2815

417
FBLA-PBL Competitive Event Award

AMOUNT: $1000-$4000 DEADLINE: April 15
MAJOR: All Areas of Study

The FBLA-PBL Competitive Event Award carries cash awards for the national winners sponsored by business partners of the association. It is open to high school seniors who plan on pursuing a full-time, two-year or four-year course of study and who have demonstrated a commitment to serve their school and/or community through activities including, but not limited to, fundraising activities. This award requires you to be a national and state dues-paying member of the FBLA. A brief description of the student, school and/or community fundraising project should be submitted to the FBLA-PBL National Center. An official transcript and two letters of recommendation must also be submitted. Award requirements change regularly. No GPA requirement specified.

Future Business Leaders of America
Attn: Scholarship Coordinator
1912 Association Drive
Reston, VA 22091

418
FDA Student Loan Fund

AMOUNT: $2000-$9000 DEADLINE: March 31
MAJOR: Dentistry

The FDA Student Loan Fund is open to dental students who have successfully completed one academic year in any accredited dental college in the United States. Applicants must have lived in Florida for three years prior to the loan application. It is possible for students to receive several loans; one for each of their sophomore, junior and senior years, or for postdoctoral study. Loans may not exceed yearly limits of $9,000 per applicant. Historically, yearly limits have been: $2,000 for sophomores, $3,000 - for juniors and postdoctoral studies, $4,000 - for seniors. Award requirements change regularly. Write to the Florida Dental Association, Task Group on Student Loans at the address below for details or call (850) 681-3629, ext. 119. No GPA requirement specified.

Florida Dental Association/Florida Dental Health Foundation
Attn: Scholarship and Loan Coordinator
1111 East Tennessee Street
Tallahassee, FL 32308-6914

419
FEEA Scholarships

AMOUNT: $300-$1500 DEADLINE: March 31
MAJOR: All Areas of Study

These scholarships are open to civilian employees (of at least three years), or dependents of civilian employees, of either the Federal Government or the U.S. Postal Service. You must have a minimum overall GPA of 3.0 or a 3.0 or better for the last full year of school. You must be enrolled in a two- or four-year school, graduate or postgraduate program. An essay will be required with your application. The number of awards may vary and are based on academic merit. Award requirements change regularly. For application requests write to Federal Employee Education & Assistance Fund (FEEA), including a self-addressed, stamped envelope. Requests for information without the return envelope included will NOT be processed. FEEA offers a merit scholarship program for civilian federal and postal employees and their legal dependents. GPA must be 3.0-4.0.

Federal Employee Education and Assistance Fund
Attn: Educational Programs
8441 West Bowles Avenue, Suite 200
Littleton, CO 80123-9501

420
Fellowes Manufacturing Company Scholarship

AMOUNT: $2000 DEADLINE: March 15
MAJOR: All Fields of Study
The Fellowes Manufacturing Company Scholarship is open to employees of Business Products Industry Association member firms and their families. Persons holding academic records sufficient for acceptance by accredited colleges, junior colleges or technical schools, or persons already enrolled in one of those institutions are eligible for this one-year award. Selection is made by a committee from the Student Financial Aid Department of The George Washington University, Washington, DC. Award requirements change regularly. Please send a self-addressed, stamped envelope to receive your application and any further instructions from the scholarship provider or email: info@bpia.org. No GPA requirement specified.

Business Products Industry Association
Attn: Scholarship Committee
301 North Fairfax Street
Alexandria, VA 22314-2633

421
Fellowship Program In Academic Medicine

AMOUNT: $500-$7000 DEADLINE: June 30
MAJOR: Biomedical Research and Academic Medicine

Scholarships, fellowships and awards for minority medical students. Minorities are defined here as African-American, Native American, Mexican-American, and mainland Puerto Rican. Applicants must be U.S. citizens. This award is for academically outstanding students to pursue careers in biomedical research and academic medicine. Award requirements change regularly. There are two deadlines: May 31 deadline is for renewal applicants and the June 30 deadline is for new applicants. Send a stamped (.55), self-addressed envelope (9x12), to the address listed for additional information. GPA must be 3.2-4.0.

National Medical Fellowships, Inc.
Scholarship Coordinator
110 West 32nd Street, FL 8
New York, NY 10001-3205

422
Fenwal Scholarship Award

AMOUNT: None Specified DEADLINE: June 1
MAJOR: Medicine, Transfusion Technology/BloodBanking

This scholarship is open to students who have an M.D. or D.O. degree who are fellows in a transfusion medicine program or training program that includes at least one continuous year in transfusion medicine training. You must submit an entry of 3,000 words or less on a subject pertaining to blood banking or a related field. Award requirements change regularly. No GPA requirement specified.

American Association of Blood Banks
Transfusion Medicine Fellows
8101 Glenbrook Road
Bethesda, MD 20814-2749

423
Fermilab Physics Fellowship for Minorities

AMOUNT: None Specified DEADLINE: August 1
MAJOR: Physics

This award is open to minority graduate students who are pursuing Ph.D.s in physics at higher-education institutions that are accredited by the Universities Research Association. Under the terms of the fellowship, Fermilab and the URA institution collaborate to provide tuition and a stipend similar to that of other first year students. Candidates are reviewed by the Summer Intern Committee. Award requirements change regularly. Please send a self-addressed, stamped envelope to receive your application and any further instructions from the scholarship provider. No GPA requirement specified.

Fermilab
Dianne M. Engram, Mgr. - EOO
Fermilab MS 117 — PO Box 500
Batavia, IL 60510

424
Fernando R. Ayuso Award

AMOUNT: Maximum: $5000 DEADLINE: July 28
MAJOR: Travel, Tourism

Open to U.S. citizens who have a high school diploma and at least two years worth of credit at an accredited college or university. Must have been involved in a professional capacity in the travel industry for a minimum of two years or have been studying the travel and tourism industry for at least two years and submit proof of American citizenship. A letter of recommendation from an employer or professor will be required, along with a 500-word essay in both Spanish and English on the topic "How the Travel Industry Can Serve to Promote Understanding Between Different Cultures" (travel between Spain and the U.S. should be used as an example). This award pays transatlantic transportation, FITUR registration, local transportation and accommodations (not to exceed $5,000) at the International Travel Fair of Madrid. Award requirements change regularly. Write to the address listed, enclosing a self-addressed, stamped envelope for an application and further information. You can browse their website: www.astanet.com or email: myriaml@astahq.com. No GPA requirement specified.

American Society of Travel Agents
Attn: ASTA Foundation
1101 King Street, Suite 200
Alexandria, VA 22314-2944

425
Ferne Salisbury Scholarship

AMOUNT: $325 DEADLINE: Varies
MAJOR: All Fields of Study

The Ferne Salisbury Scholarship is open to students who graduated from one of the Burlington, WI community high schools within two years of the date of their scholarship application. Students must be enrolling or enrolled in an accredited post-secondary course of study. Award requirements change regularly. Please visit your Guidance Office to receive an application and any additional details. No GPA requirement specified.

Burlington High School
Attn: Guidance Office
225 Robert Street
Burlington, WI 53105

426
First Catholic Slovak Ladies Association Member Scholarships

AMOUNT: $1000 DEADLINE: March 1
MAJOR: All Areas of Study

These scholarships are open to members in good standing of the First Catholic Slovak Ladies Association. You must have been a member for at least three years prior to application and your membership standing will be verified by your local branch and at the home office. In order to apply, you must be enrolled or accepted by any accredited four-year college in the U.S. or Canada and pursuing a bachelor's degree. Awards are made for one academic year. Eighty awards are offered annually. Award requirements change regularly. No GPA requirement specified.

First Catholic Slovak Ladies Association
Director of Fraternal Scholarship Aid
24950 Chagrin Blvd
Beachwood, OH 44122-5616

427
Fleet Reserve Association Scholarship

AMOUNT: None Specified DEADLINE: April 15
MAJOR: All Areas of Study

This scholarship is open to the child, grandchild or spouse of a member in good standing of the Fleet Reserve Association or the Ladies Auxiliary of the Fleet Reserve Association or of a member in good standing at the time of death. Selection is based upon financial need, scholastic standing, character and leadership qualities. Award requirements change regularly. Please write to the address listed, enclosing a self-addressed, stamped envelope for an application and further information. No GPA requirement specified.

Fleet Reserve Association
Scholarship Administrator
125 North West Street
Alexandria, VA 22314-2754

428
Florence Hefty/Lioness Club Scholarship

AMOUNT: None Specified DEADLINE: Varies
MAJOR: Art and Related Fields of Study

The Florence Hefty/Lioness Club Scholarship is open to graduating seniors at Burlington High School (Burlington, WI). Students must be studying art or a related field. Award requirements change regularly. Please visit your Guidance Office to receive an application and any additional details. No GPA requirement specified.

Burlington High School
Attn: Guidance Office
225 Robert Street
Burlington, WI 53105

429
Florida Academic Scholars Award

AMOUNT: None Specified DEADLINE: Varies
MAJOR: All Fields of Study

The Florida Academic Scholars Award is open to Florida residents who have been accepted by and enrolled in an eligible Florida public or private postsecondary institution. The award requires you to have a minimum 3.5 GPA, at least 75 hours of community service, a Florida high school diploma (or its equivalent) and also to be enrolled for at least six semester credit hours or the equivalent. You must also have a minimum composite score of 1270 on the SAT or 28 on the ACT to qualify. The award is for a possible 100% of tuition and must begin to be used within three years of high school graduation. Award requirements change regularly.

Florida Department of Education
Office of Student Financial Assistance
Turlington Building, 325 West Gaines St.
Tallahassee, FL 32399-0400

430
Florida Engineering Society High School Scholarships

AMOUNT: $1000 DEADLINE: February 15
MAJOR: Engineering

Open to high school seniors who are U.S. citizens and have a minimum GPA of 3.5. Must be enrolled in an engineering program accredited by the Engineering Accreditation Commission of the Accreditation Board for Engineering and Technology (ABET). An official transcript and a 250-word essay will also be required. Award requirements change regularly. Write to the address listed for details, include a self-addressed, stamped envelope. GPA must be 3.5-4.0.

American Consulting Engineers Council of Florida
Scholarship Coordinator
PO Box 750
Tallahassee, FL 32302-0750

431
Florida Resident Access Grant (FRAG)

AMOUNT: None Specified DEADLINE: Varies
MAJOR: All Areas of Study

Open to full-time undergraduates attending eligible independent nonprofit Florida colleges or universities. Must be a Florida resident. Award amount depends on level of funding and the number of eligible students. This award is not based on financial need. Award requirements change regularly. Contact the financial aid office at the school you plan/are attending, call (850) 488-6181 or write to the address listed, including a self-addressed, stamped envelope. You may also browse their website at www.firn.edu/doe/bin00065. No GPA requirement specified.

Florida Department of Education
Office of Student Financial Assistance
Turlington Building, 325 West Gaines St.
Tallahassee, FL 32399-0400

432
Floyd Qualls Memorial Scholarship

AMOUNT: $2500 DEADLINE: March 1
MAJOR: All Areas of Study

This scholarship is open to applicants who are legally blind and have been admitted for vocational/technical, professional, or academic studies at postsecondary levels. Award requirements change regularly. Write to the address listed, enclosing a self-addressed, stamped envelope for an application and further information. No GPA requirement specified.

American Council of the Blind
Attn: Billie Jean Keith
1155 15th Street NW, Suite 720
Washington, DC 20005-2706

433
Fogel Loan Fund

AMOUNT: Maximum: $5000 DEADLINE: Varies
MAJOR: All Areas of Study

The purpose of the Fogel Loan Fund is to provide loans to help Jewish students of all ages for college, university or vocational studies. Applicants must be able to provide qualified guarantors (co-signers) that reside in the Bay Area. Applicants must be residents of San Francisco, San Mateo, northern Santa Clara, Marin, Sonoma, Alameda or Contra Costa counties in California. It is preferable that loan applicants submit their applications by July 1 for the fall semester and November 1 for the spring semester. Award requirements change regularly. No GPA requirement specified.

Jewish Family and Children's Services
Attn: Loans and Grants Department
2245 Post Street
San Francisco, CA 94115

434
Ford Foundation Postdoctoral Fellowships for Minorities

AMOUNT: $3500 DEADLINE: January 7
MAJOR: Behavioral Sciences, Social Sciences, Physical Sciences, Life Sciences, Humanities, Engineering, Mathematics, Education

The Ford Foundation Postdoctoral Fellowships for Minorities are for U.S. citizens or U.S. nationals of African-American, Native American, Mexican American, Puerto Rican, Native Alaskan or Native Pacific Islander descent. Applicants must have earned their postdoctoral status within the last six years and no later than March 1st. Applicants are expected to be currently engaged in or planning a career in teaching and research at the college or university level. The amount of the fellowships are: $30,000 for one year; $3,000 is for travel and relocation allowance; $2,000 is for the cost-of-research at the college or university level. Award requirements change regularly. For further information and an application, please write to the address listed, enclosing a self-addressed, stamped envelope, contact their email: infofell@nas.edu, or call (202) 334-2872. Applications may be downloaded from their website or filled out online at www.fellowships.nas.edu. No GPA requirement specified.

National Research Council
Attn: Fellowship Office
2101 Constitution Avenue
Washington, DC 20418-0007

435
Fort Atkinson Piecemakers Quilt Guild Scholarship

AMOUNT: $500 DEADLINE: October 29
MAJOR: All Areas of Study

This scholarship is awarded to a nontraditional female student furthering her education at a college, technical, trade or vocational school of her choice. The applicant will have had more than a year between leaving high school and an institution of postsecondary learning. Award requirements change regularly. Please send a self-addressed, stamped envelope to receive your application and for any further instructions from the scholarship provider. No GPA requirement specified.

Fort Atkinson Piecemakers Quilt Guild
Attn: Scholarship Coordinator
301 Jackson Street
Fort Atkinson, WI 53538

Fort Collins Board of Realtors Scholarship

AMOUNT: $500 DEADLINE: Varies
MAJOR: All Areas of Study

Open to Rocky Mountain High School seniors. Applicants must have a minimum 2.5 cumulative GPA and plan to continue in postsecondary education or training in Colorado. Financial need will be considered. Application deadline, procedure, and award amount vary annually. Award requirements change regularly. Applications are available in January or February in the Rocky Mountain High School Career Center, as part of the Local Scholarship Packet. GPA must be 2.5-4.0.

Rocky Mountain High School
Scholarship Committee
1300 West Swallow Road
Fort Collins, CO 80526-2412

437
Fort Collins Soccer Club and Golden Ball Award

AMOUNT: $350 DEADLINE: Varies
MAJOR: All Areas of Study

Open to Rocky Mountain High School seniors. Applicants must be varsity soccer players from a high school in the Poudre School District fielding a soccer team. Applicants must have a minimum 3.0 cumulative GPA and be contributing members to the soccer community and club in Fort Collins. Contributions may include refereeing, coaching, and/or volunteering. To be used at any postsecondary institution. May require a letter of recommendation from soccer coach. Application deadline, procedure, and award amount vary annually. Award requirements change regularly. Applications are available in January or February in the Rocky Mountain High School Career Center, as part of the Local Scholarship Packet. GPA must be 3.0-4.0.

Rocky Mountain High School
Scholarship Committee
1300 West Swallow Road
Fort Collins, CO 80526-2412

438
Fortune Brands Scholarship

AMOUNT: $2000 DEADLINE: March 15
MAJOR: All Fields of Study

The Fortune Brands Scholarship is open to employees of Business Products Industry Association member firms and their families. Persons holding academic records sufficient for acceptance by accredited colleges, junior colleges or technical schools, or persons already enrolled in one of those institutions are eligible for this four-year award. Selection is made by a committee from the Student Financial Aid Department of The George Washington University, Washington, DC. Award

requirements change regularly. Please send a self-addressed, stamped envelope to receive your application and any further instructions from the scholarship provider or email: info@bpia.org. No GPA requirement specified.

Business Products Industry Association
Attn: Scholarship Committee
301 North Fairfax Street
Alexandria, VA 22314-2633

439
Fourth Degree Pro Deo and Pro Patria Scholarship

AMOUNT: Maximum: $1500 DEADLINE: March 1
MAJOR: All Areas of Study

This scholarship is open to high school seniors planning on attending a Catholic college in the U.S. Applicants must be members of the Knights of Columbus or children of active or deceased members. This award is renewable for up to four years. Award requirements change regularly. Write to the address listed, enclosing a self-addressed, stamped envelope for an application and further information. No GPA requirement specified.

Knights of Columbus
Rev Donald Barry SJ, Director Of Aid
PO Box 1670
New Haven, CT 06507-0901

440
Fowler Fund Alumni Scholarship

AMOUNT: None Specified DEADLINE: October 15
MAJOR: All Areas of Study

The Fowler Fund Alumni Scholarship is open to graduates of Maynard High School in Maynard, MA, for the purpose of advancing their education and training beyond high school. Applicants must submit a short personal statement of 250 words or less and a copy of the official Student Financial Aid Award Letter or proof of payment from the Treasurer's Office of the postsecondary institution that the applicants are attending. Award requirements change regularly. Please send a self-addressed, stamped envelope to receive your application and any further instructions from the scholarship provider. No GPA requirement specified.

Fowler Fund Alumni Scholarship
c/o MHS Guidance Department
1 Tiger Drive
Maynard, MA 01754

441
Francis J. Flynn Memorial Scholarship

AMOUNT: $1200 DEADLINE: May 26
MAJOR: Mathematics, Education

This memorial scholarship is open to undergraduate Tau Kappa Epsilon members who are full-time students pursuing a degree in mathematics or education with a minimum 2.75 GPA. In order to apply, you should have a record of leadership within your chapter and campus organizations. Preference will be given to members of Theta-Sigma Chapter, then open to any member of TKE. Award requirements change regularly.

For further information, call (317) 872-6533, email: tef@tkehq.org or visit the website at: www.tke.org. GPA must be 2.8-4.0.

TKE Educational Foundation
Attn: Timothy L. Taschwer
8645 Founders Road
Indianapolis, IN 46268-1336

442
Francis P. Matthews and John E. Swift Educational Trust Scholarships

AMOUNT: None Specified DEADLINE: Varies
MAJOR: All Areas of Study

This scholarship is open to applicants who are children of members of the Order who either: a) were in the military and killed or disabled in a war or conflict, or b) were policemen or firemen killed or disabled in the line of duty. Applicants must attend a Catholic school. This scholarship is for undergraduate study only. Award requirements change regularly. Write to the address listed, enclosing a self-addressed, stamped envelope for an application and further information. No GPA requirement specified.

Knights of Columbus
Rev Donald Barry SJ, Director Of Aid
PO Box 1670
New Haven, CT 06507-0901

443
Frank and Louise Groff Foundation

AMOUNT: $100-$2000 DEADLINE: April 1
MAJOR: Nursing, Medicine

Open to students who have graduated from a public school in Monmouth County (NJ) with an interest in becoming a registered nurse or medical doctor. Based on financial need and academics. Award requirements change regularly. Write to the address listed, enclosing a self-addressed, stamped envelope for an application and further information or call (908) 536-2738. No GPA requirement specified.

Frank and Louise Groff Foundation
Attn: Susan Rechel, Educational Advisor
15 Floyd Wyckoff Road
Morganville, NJ 07751-1306

444
Frank and Shirley Dick Scholarship

AMOUNT: $1000 DEADLINE: March 31
MAJOR: Health Related Field

The Frank and Shirley Dick Scholarship is open to high school seniors from Lenawee County (MI). To qualify for the award, you must be planning to pursue a career in a health-related field. The award also requires that you already be accepted at a community college or four-year institution. Award requirements change regularly. Please send a self-addressed, stamped envelope to receive your application and any further instructions from the scholarship provider. No GPA requirement specified.

Morenci High School
Attn: Mrs. Melissa Parnell
788 Coomer Street
Morenci, MI 49256

445
Frank L. Greathouse Governmental Accounting Scholarship

AMOUNT: $2000 DEADLINE: February 4
MAJOR: Accounting

The Frank L. Greathouse Governmental Accounting Scholarship is open to full-time students in the senior year of an undergraduate accounting program who are preparing for a career in state or local government finance. Applicants must be citizens or permanent residents of the U.S. or Canada. Recommendation from applicant's academic advisor or accounting program chair will be required. Award requirements change regularly. Applications are available in November for awards in the following spring. Please send a self-addressed, stamped envelope to receive your application and any further instructions from the scholarship provider; or email your request to inquiries@gfoa.org; or visit the website at www.gfoa.org. No GPA requirement specified.

Government Finance Officers Association
Attn: Scholarship Committee
180 North Michigan Avenue, Suite 800
Chicago, IL 60601-7476

446
Frank Walton Horn Memorial Scholarship

AMOUNT: $3000 DEADLINE: March 31
MAJOR: Architecture, Engineering

The Frank Walton Horn Memorial Scholarship is open to students who are legally blind and who are pursuing or planning to pursue a full-time postsecondary course of study in the U.S. Your selection will be based on academic excellence, service to the community and financial need. Preference will be given to students studying architecture or engineering. Award requirements change regularly. No GPA requirement specified.

National Federation of the Blind
Attn: Peggy Elliott, Chairman
805 5th Avenue
Grinnell, IA 50112-1653

447
Fraternal Order of Police Bobby Williams Youth Citzenship Scholarship

AMOUNT: $1000 DEADLINE: March 31
MAJOR: Criminal Justice

The Fraternal Order of Police Bobby Williams Youth Citizenship Scholarship is open to Lenawee County (MI) graduating seniors. To be considered for this award, you must be pursuing careers in the criminal justice field. This includes a career in law enforcement, probation and parole officer, social worker, etc. Award requirements change regularly. Please send a self-addressed, stamped envelope to receive your application and any further instructions from the scholarship provider. No GPA requirement specified.

Morenci High School
Attn: Mrs. Melissa Parnell
788 Coomer Street
Morenci, MI 49256

Fred C. Wikoff Jr. Scholarship

AMOUNT: Maximum: $2000 DEADLINE: March 1
MAJOR: All Areas of Study

Scholarships for children of employees of Wikoff Color Corporation or one of its subsidiaries. Award requirements change regularly. Write to the address listed for details, enclosing a self-addressed, stamped envelope. No GPA requirement specified.

Foundation for the Carolinas
Scholarship Program
PO Box 34769
Charlotte, NC 28234-4769

449
Fred R. McDaniel Memorial Scholarship

AMOUNT: $500 DEADLINE: February 1
MAJOR: Electronics, Communications or Related Fields

This scholarship is available to students with a minimum general class amateur radio license and are residents of, and attend school in, the FCC Fifth Call District. This district is comprised of: Texas, Oklahoma, Alaska, New Mexico, Louisiana and Michigan. Applicants must have a minimum GPA of 3.0 and be enrolled in a baccalaureate or higher course of study in electronics, communications or related fields. Award requirements change regularly. Write the address provided, using a self-addressed, stamped envelope, for further information. GPA must be 3.0-4.0.

American Radio Relay League
Attn: ARRL Foundation
225 Main Street
Newington, CT 06111-1400

450
Frederick W. and Grace P. Brecht Scholarship

AMOUNT: $1000 DEADLINE: March 1
MAJOR: All Areas of Study

Open to qualified, needy students who are residents of Brevard County (FL) to help them attend any Florida college or university. Applicants must enroll as undergraduates for at least 12 credit hours. Selection is based on financial need. Undergraduate students are considered automatically if they apply for financial aid. Award requirements change regularly. You may browse the UF website: www.ufsa.ufl.edu/SFA/programs/sfaschol.html. GPA must be 3.0-4.0.

University of Florida
Office for Student Financial Affairs S-1
PO Box 114025
Gainesville, FL 32611-4025

451
Freida A. Altar Scholarship

AMOUNT: $500 DEADLINE: December 29
MAJOR: Arts, Dance, Choreography, Music (Voice, Composition), Writing (Poetry, Fiction, Non-Fiction)

The Freida A. Altar Scholarship is open to current Illinois residents of Lithuanian ancestry whose major field of study will lead to a career in the arts, such as an artist, dancer, singer, writer of poetry, fiction or nonfiction, composer or choreographer. You must demonstrate financial need, have at least a 2.0 GPA and be currently enrolled in or accepted to an accredited college, university or school specializing in any of the arts. Previous recipients may reapply. Award requirements change regularly. Please send a self-addressed, stamped envelope to receive your application and any further instructions from the scholarship provider. Postage should be enough for a one ounce letter. GPA must be 2.0-4.0.

Freida A. Altar Scholarship
Attn: Scholarship Coordinator
c/o 7115 West 91st Street
Bridgeview, IL 60455-2048

452
Freshman/Sophomore Minority Grant Program

AMOUNT: Maximum: $1000 DEADLINE: Varies
MAJOR: Education

The Freshman/Sophomore Minority Grant Program is open to African-American, Asian-American and Hispanic college freshmen and sophomores enrolled into teacher education programs. You may attend two- or four-year public or private institutions of higher education in Arkansas. A requirement of the award is that you have to perform a pre-service internship in a public school setting or another appropriate activity designed to encourage you into entering a teacher education program. Award requirements change regularly. For further information, you should contact the Teacher Certifying Official at four-year institutions or the Vice-President for Academic Affairs, Academic Dean or Dean of Instruction at two-year institutions to see if your school is a participant in this program. You may also browse their website: www.arscholarships.com/finsites.html. No GPA requirement specified.

Arkansas Department of Higher Education
Financial Aid Division
114 East Capitol Avenue
Little Rock, AR 72201-3818

453
Front Range Center Outstanding Senior Science Student Award

AMOUNT: $1000 DEADLINE: Varies
MAJOR: All Areas of Study

Open to Rocky Mountain High School seniors. Applicants must have strong science grades. Top applicants will be interviewed by the Front Range Center for Brain and Spine Injury. An essay may be required. Application deadline, procedure, and award amount vary annually. Award requirements change regularly. Applications are available in January or February in the Rocky Mountain High School Career Center, as part of the

Local Scholarship Packet. No GPA requirement specified.

Rocky Mountain High School
Scholarship Committee
1300 West Swallow Road
Fort Collins, CO 80526-2412

454
G. Robert Hamrdla Award

AMOUNT: $2500 DEADLINE: April 17
MAJOR: All Areas of Study

Past ESR Bob Hamrdla, Stanford University (CAAL '60), has established this award for brothers in any field of study with transcripts that reflect more than a passing interest in nineteenth and twentieth century history. Among the pool of applicants meeting that criterion, those—if any—whose interests are shown to be modern Germany history or the two World Wars, will get preferred consideration. A cumulative G.P.A of 3.5 (4.0 scale) is required. Award requirements change regularly. For further information, please write to the address listed, including a self-addressed, stamped envelope, call (847) 475-1856 ext. 223, fax (847) 475-2250, or email: rparker@sae.net. You may also visit their website: www.sae.net. GPA must be 3.5-4.0.

Sigma Alpha Epsilon Foundation
SAE Awards Committee
PO Box 1856
Evanston, IL 60204-1856

455
GAE Scholarships for Excellence

AMOUNT: $1000 DEADLINE: March 12
MAJOR: Teaching, Education

Open to graduating seniors currently attending a fully accredited public Georgia high school who will attend a fully accredited Georgia college or university within the next 12 months. Winning candidates will show the greatest potential as a teacher, have a minimum GPA of 3.0 and be bona fide residents of Georgia. Consideration will also be given to depth of thought, clarity of expression, leadership potential, extracurricular activities, and community involvement. Award requirements change regularly. For further information and an application, please write to the address listed, including a self-addressed, stamped envelope. GPA must be 3.0-4.0.

Georgia Association of Educators
GFIE Scholarship For Excellence Awards
3951 Snapfinger Pkwy, Suite 400
Decatur, GA 30035-3203

456
Gary Krenz Memorial Scholarship

AMOUNT: $2000 DEADLINE: March 31
MAJOR: Physical Therapy

The Gary Krenz Memorial Scholarship is open to Lenawee County (MI) graduates. To qualify for the award, you must have already been accepted into a qualified physical therapy program. Award requirements change regularly. Please send a self-addressed, stamped envelope to receive your application and any further instructions from the scholarship provider. No GPA requirement specified.

Morenci High School
Attn: Mrs. Melissa Parnell
788 Coomer Street
Morenci, MI 49256

457
Gas Capital Scholarship Program

AMOUNT: None Specified DEADLINE: February 15
MAJOR: Petroleum Related

The Gas Capital Scholarship Program is open to residents of one of the counties in the Kansas portion of the Hugoton Gas Field area. To be considered for the award, you must have attended and completed at least three semesters at an accredited college or university (including postgraduate courses; and community college courses also count if such students continue their schooling at a four-year institution). Preference will be given to students pursuing a petroleum-related career. The award requires that you attend school full-time and have a minimum 2.5 GPA. Award requirements change regularly. GPA must be 2.5-4.0.

Gas Capital Scholarship Program
Scholarship Committee
630 South Main Street
Hugoton, KS 67951-2429

458
GCSAA Footsteps on the Green Award

AMOUNT: $500-$3500 DEADLINE: April 15
MAJOR: Golf/Turf Industry

The GCSAA Footsteps on the Green Award is open to undergraduates currently enrolled in a two- or four-year accredited program related to golf course/turf management. You must have successfully completed at least 12 credit hours or the equivalent of one year of full-time study (if you are studying at a two-year college, at least nine hours must be related to golf course management). You will be evaluated on academic achievement, extracurricular activities and community involvement. An original 100-word essay on why you have chosen this field of study is required for this award. For final consideration, you must be a GCSAA member. Financial need will not be a factor in the final selection. Award requirements change regularly. No GPA requirement specified.

Golf Course Superintendents Association of America
Scholarship Aid Committee
1421 Research Park Drive
Lawrence, KS 66049-3859

459
GCSAA Legacy Awards

AMOUNT: $1500 DEADLINE: April 15
MAJOR: All Areas of Study

The GCSAA Legacy Awards are open to high school seniors and undergraduates majoring in a field unrelated to golf course management. You must be accepted or enrolled full-time, attending an accredited institution and be a child or grandchild of an active GCSAA member. Your parent or grandparent must have held membership for more than five years. An essay is required. Award requirements change regularly. No GPA requirement specified.

Golf Course Superintendents Association of America
Scholarship Aid Committee
1421 Research Park Drive
Lawrence, KS 66049-3859

460
GCSAA Scholars Competition

AMOUNT: $500-$3500 DEADLINE: June 1
MAJOR: Golf/Turf Industry

The GCSAA Scholars Competition is open to outstanding undergraduates currently enrolled in a two- or four-year accredited program related to golf course management. Applicants must have successfully completed at least 24 credit hours or the equivalent of one year of full-time study. Students will be evaluated on the basis of academics, potential to become a leading professional, employment history, extracurricular activities and the recommendation of a previous superintendent and a current academic advisor. An essay is required for this award. Award requirements change regularly. No GPA requirement specified.

Golf Course Superintendents Association of America
Scholarship Aid Committee
1421 Research Park Drive
Lawrence, KS 66049-3859

461
GCSAA Student Essay Contest

AMOUNT: $400-$1000 DEADLINE: March 31
MAJOR: Turfgrass Science, Agronomy, Golf Course Management

The GCSAA Student Essay Contest is open to current undergraduates and graduate students who are pursuing degrees in turfgrass science, agronomy or any field related to golf course management. You will be required to submit an essay between 7 and 12 pages in length on the topic of golf course management. GCSAA membership is a requirement in order to apply. Award requirements change regularly. No GPA requirement specified.

Golf Course Superintendents Association of America
Scholarship Aid Committee
1421 Research Park Drive
Lawrence, KS 66049-3859

462
GCSAA Watson Fellowship Program

AMOUNT: $5000 DEADLINE: October 1
MAJOR: Golf/Turf Industry

The GCSAA Watson Fellowship Program is open to candidates for master's and doctoral degrees in fields related to turfgrass science and/or golf course management. The goal of the program is to identify and recognize outstanding postgraduates who will be the leading industry educators and researchers of tomorrow. The selection committee evaluates each applicant on: academic excellence; peer recommendations; communication skills; commitment to a career as an instructor and/or scientist; accomplishments in research and education; and the potential to contribute significantly to the industry. Award requirements change regularly. No GPA requirement specified.

Golf Course Superintendents Association of America
Scholarship Aid Committee
1421 Research Park Drive
Lawrence, KS 66049-3859

463
Gene Edmundson Scholarship

AMOUNT: None Specified DEADLINE: Varies
MAJOR: All Fields of Study

The Gene Edmundson Scholarship is open to graduating seniors at Burlington High School (Burlington, WI). Students must have participated in a varsity sport and plan on continuing their education. Award requirements change regularly. Please visit your Guidance Office to receive an application and any additional details. No GPA requirement specified.

Burlington High School
Attn: Guidance Office
225 Robert Street
Burlington, WI 53105

464
Gene Spitzer Memorial Scholarship

AMOUNT: None Specified DEADLINE: Varies
MAJOR: Science

The Gene Spitzer Memorial Scholarship is open to graduating seniors at Burlington High School (Burlington, WI). Students must be entering a four-year college or university in Wisconsin to study science. Award requirements change regularly. Please visit your Guidance Office to receive an application and any additional details. No GPA requirement specified.

Burlington High School
Attn: Guidance Office
225 Robert Street
Burlington, WI 53105

465
General Electric Fund Scholarship

AMOUNT: $1000 DEADLINE: May 15
MAJOR: Engineering

This scholarship is open to an incoming freshman woman accepted into an ABET-accredited program or SWE-approved school. The award is renewable for three years, provided that you demonstrate continued academic achievement. The fund provides an additional $500 travel grant in addition to the $1,000 award itself. This grant is used to attend the SWE National Convention. U.S. citizenship is a requirement. Award requirements change regularly. Please send a self-addressed, stamped envelope to receive your application and for any further instructions from the scholarship provider, browse the SWE website at www.swe.org or email hq@swe.org. No GPA requirement specified.

Society of Women Engineers Headquarters
Scholarship Coordinator
120 Wall Street, FL 11
New York, NY 10005-3902

General Fund Scholarship

AMOUNT: $1000 DEADLINE: February 1
MAJOR: All Areas of Study

This scholarship is available to students with any class amateur radio license who are enrolled in any area of study. Multiple awards are offered annually. Award requirements change regularly. Write the address provided, using a self-addressed, stamped envelope, for further information. No GPA requirement specified.

American Radio Relay League
Attn: ARRL Foundation
225 Main Street
Newington, CT 06111-1400

467

General Henry H. Arnold Education Grant

AMOUNT: Maximum: $1000 DEADLINE: March 17
MAJOR: All Areas of Study

This grant is open to a dependent child of an Air Force member in one of the following categories: on active duty; Title 10 Reservist on extended active duty; retired due to length of active duty service or disability; retired Guard/Reservist who is at least 60 years of age and receiving retirement pay; or deceased while on active duty or in retired status. You must have a minimum 2.0 GPA and be accepted or enrolled as a full-time student at an accredited college, university or vocational/trade school. Award requirements change regularly. For an application contact the AFAS HQ by calling (703) 607-3072 or visit their website: www.afas.org. GPA must be 2.0-4.0.

Air Force Aid Society
Education Assistance Department
1745 Jefferson Davis Hwy, Suite 202
Arlington, VA 22202-3423

468

General Motors Foundation Graduate Scholarship

AMOUNT: $1500 DEADLINE: February 1
MAJOR: Engineering Technology, Mechanical Engineering, Electrical Engineering, Chemical Engineering, Industrial Engineering, Materials Engineering, Automotive Engineering, Manufacturing Engineering

This scholarship is open to women who are entering their first year of master's level study with minimum GPAs of 3.5. Applicants must be able to demonstrate leadership abilities by holding a position of responsibility in a student organization and demonstrate career interests in the automotive industry or manufacturing environment. Applicants must be attending an ABET-accredited program or SWE-approved school. In addition to the scholarship award, the General Motors Foundation provides a $500 travel grant for each recipient to attend the SWE National Convention and Student Conference. Award requirements change regularly. Please send a self-addressed, stamped envelope to receive your application. GPA must be 3.5-4.0.

Society of Women Engineers Headquarters
Scholarship Coordinator
120 Wall Street, FL 11
New York, NY 10005-3902

469

General Motors Foundation Scholarship

AMOUNT: $1500 DEADLINE: February 1
MAJOR: Mechanical Engineering, Electrical Engineering, Chemical Engineering, Industrial Engineering, Materials Engineering, Automotive Engineering, Manufacturing Engineering, Engineering Technology

The General Motors Foundation Scholarship is open to female juniors majoring in the areas listed who are attending an ABET-accredited program or an SWE-approved school. The applicants must demonstrate leadership qualities by holding a position of responsibility in a student organization and have a career interest in the automotive industry or manufacturing environment. This award is renewable for the senior year. Applicants must have a minimum GPA of 3.5. In addition, the General Motors Foundation provides a $500 travel grant for each recipient to attend the SWE National Convention and Student Conference. Award requirements change regularly. Please send a self-addressed, stamped envelope to receive your application. For any further instructions from the scholarship provider, please browse their website at www.swe.org or email hq@swe.org. GPA must be 3.5-4.0.

Society of Women Engineers Headquarters
Scholarship Coordinator
120 Wall Street, FL 11
New York, NY 10005-3902

470

George A. Strait Minority Stipend

AMOUNT: $3500 DEADLINE: April 1
MAJOR: Library Science, Law

The George A. Strait Minority Stipend is open to college graduates with meaningful law library experience who are members of a minority group as defined by current U.S. government guidelines and are degree candidates in an ALA-accredited library school or an ABA-accredited law school. Applicants must have at least one quarter/semester remaining after the scholarship is awarded. Award requirements change regularly. Please send a self-addressed, stamped envelope to receive your application and any further instructions from the scholarship provider; or download the scholarship application and instructions from their website at www.aallnet.org/services/scholarships.asp. No GPA requirement specified.

American Association of Law Libraries
Attn: Scholarship Committee
53 West Jackson Blvd, Suite 940
Chicago, IL 60604

471

George A. Thompson Memorial Scholarship

AMOUNT: $2000 DEADLINE: March 15
MAJOR: All Fields of Study

The George A. Thompson Memorial Scholarship is open to

ry Association member
ng academic records
colleges, junior col-
lready enrolled in one
one-year award.
the Student Financial
gton University,
hange regularly. Please
e to receive your appli-
the scholarship
iPA requirement speci-

Business Products Industry Association
Attn: Scholarship Committee
301 North Fairfax Street
Alexandria, VA 22314-2633

472
George E. Allen Scholarship

AMOUNT: $1000   DEADLINE: April 1
MAJOR: All Fields of Study

The George E. Allen Scholarship is open to high school seniors from central Virginia who have demonstrated academic progress and good character. The award requires that your plans include continuing education to a university, community college or postsecondary institution. You are a preferred candidate for this award if you have overcome obstacles or special challenges and still achieved high standards of performance. In addition to your application form, you must submit two letters of recommendation (one of which must be furnished by a teacher or guidance counselor), high school transcripts, attendance records and other applicable test scores demonstrating improvement and high achievement. Award requirements change regularly. To receive an application, please visit the website at www.allenandallen.com. No GPA requirement specified.

Allen, Allen, Allen and Allen
1809 Staples Mill Road
Richmond, VA 23230

473
George Grotefend Scholarship

AMOUNT: None Specified   DEADLINE: April 20
MAJOR: All Areas of Study

Open to high school seniors and continuing students who are residents of Shasta County, CA. Applicants must have attended all four years of high school in the county. Based on financial need, an IRS 1040 form must accompany application (yours or your parents'). Renewable on an annual basis on a separate application. Award requirements change regularly. If you are in high school, contact your counselor for an application packet. If you are out of high school, you may contact the address listed (enclose a self-addressed, stamped envelope) or visit their website at www.shastalink.k12.ca.us/grotefend. No GPA requirement specified.

George Gratified Scholarship Fund
George Grotefend Scholarship Board
1644 Magnolia Avenue
Redding, CA 96001-1513

474
George H. Flint Graduating High School Senior Award

AMOUNT: $1000   DEADLINE: June 1
MAJOR: All Areas of Study

This scholarship is open to children and grandchildren of members (sponsors) who are in good standing with SWANA. In order to apply, you must be a graduating high school senior or a graduate equivalent certified candidate who has been accepted for enrollment in a junior college or a four-year college or university. Selection will be based on academics, citizenship, and extracurricular activities. Award requirements change regularly. GPA must be 2.8-4.0.

Solid Waste Association of North America (SWANA)
Mid-Atlantic Chapter Scholarship
9031 Reichs Ford Road
Frederick, MD 21704-6857

475
George H. Flint Upper Level Undergraduate Award

AMOUNT: $1000   DEADLINE: June 1
MAJOR: Solid Waste Management

This scholarship is open to children and grandchildren of members (sponsors) who are in good standing with SWANA. SWANA student members are also eligible. You must be a currently enrolled full-time college or university student who is an entering junior or senior in your undergraduate year. You will need to be pursuing a degree in environmental science, engineering, or another suitable major related to the field of solid waste management. Award requirements change regularly. GPA must be 2.8-4.0.

Solid Waste Association of North America (SWANA)
Mid-Atlantic Chapter Scholarship
9031 Reichs Ford Road
Frederick, MD 21704-6857

476
George M. Booker Collegiate Scholarship

AMOUNT: $1000-$2500   DEADLINE: April 15
MAJOR: Real Estate

Open to full-time juniors, seniors and graduate students who are enrolled in accredited institutions in the U.S. Applicants must have completed at least two courses in real estate (or intend to do so), and have a minimum GPA of 3.0. Applicants must be U.S. citizens of Alaskan Native, Native American, Asian, African-American, Mexican, Chicano, Hispanic, Puerto Rican or Pacific Islander descent. Applicants must demonstrate financial need, academic achievement, character and leadership. Award requirements change regularly. Write to the address listed, enclosing a self-addressed, stamped envelope for an application and further information, browse their website: www.irem.org/foundation/brooker.htm or email: larbette@irem.org. GPA must be 3.0-4.0.

Institute of Real Estate Management Foundation
Attn: Booker Scholarship
430 North Michigan Avenue
Chicago, IL 60611-4002

477
George McCleave Mathematics Scholarship

AMOUNT: $200 DEADLINE: Varies
MAJOR: All Areas of Study

Open to Harrisonville High School seniors who have taken four years of math and/or computer classes. Applicants must be in the upper 40% of their class. Award requirements change regularly. Applications are available in the Harrisonville Senior High School guidance office. No GPA requirement specified.

Harrisonville Senior High School
Attn: Roy Sackman
1504 East Elm Street
Harrisonville, MO 64701-2022

478
George Miller Jr. Management Leadership Endowment Fellowship

AMOUNT: Maximum: $6000 DEADLINE: Varies
MAJOR: Organizational, Corporate Management

The George Miller Jr. Management Leadership Endowment Fellowship is open to Alaska Native enrollees to the Cook Inlet Region and their descendants. Applicants must be organizational management majors who have demonstrated outstanding ability and potential to improve tribal, cultural and business leadership and management skills for career advancement. The deadline dates are June 1 and December 1, respectively. Award requirements change regularly. No GPA requirement specified.

CIRI Foundation
Scholarship Coordinator
2600 Cordova Street, Suite 206
Anchorage, AK 99503-2745

479
George R. Faenza Scholarship Fund

AMOUNT: $1000 DEADLINE: April 12
MAJOR: Space Exploration/Education

This scholarship is open to graduating American high school seniors. In order to apply, you will need to submit an essay that best describes "Why the United States Needs a Space Program," three letters of recommendation and a synopsis outlining how you have contributed to space education at the school, community, state or national level. The winner of the award will be offered an all-expense paid trip to Washington, DC. Award requirements change regularly. Please send a self-addressed, stamped envelope to receive your application and for complete instructions from the scholarship provider. No GPA requirement specified.

Society of Performers, Artists, Athletes and Celebrities for Space Exploration, Inc. (SPAACSE)
P.O. Box 4559, Grand Central Station
New York, NY 10163

480
George Reinke Scholarship

AMOUNT: $2000 DEADLINE: July 28
MAJOR: Travel and Tourism

Open to students who are attending, have attended, or will attend a proprietary school or a two-year community college in a travel agent studies program. Must submit a 500-word paper entitled "My Objectives in the Travel Agency Industry," which should also address why he/she needs the scholarship. Must also be U.S. citizens living and studying in the U.S. Applications are accepted twice yearly: July 28 and December 22. Students can only apply once each calendar year. Award requirements change regularly. Write to the address listed, enclosing a self-addressed, stamped envelope for an application and further information. You can browse their website: www.astanet.com or email: myriaml@astahq.com. No GPA requirement specified.

American Society of Travel Agents
Attn: ASTA Foundation
1101 King Street, Suite 200
Alexandria, VA 22314-2944

481
George Snow Scholarship

AMOUNT: $500-$1500 DEADLINE: March 1
MAJOR: All Areas of Study

This scholarship is open to deserving high school seniors from Palm Beach County, FL. In order to apply, you must be active in your school and/or community, have established goals and demonstrate financial need. Award requirements change regularly. Please send a self-addressed, stamped envelope to receive your application and any further instructions from the scholarship provider. No GPA requirement specified.

George Snow Scholarship Fund
Suite 203
998 South Federal Highway
Boca Raton, FL 33432

482
Georgia Press Educational Foundation (GPEF)

AMOUNT: None Specified DEADLINE: February 1
MAJOR: Journalism

This scholarship is open to undergraduates who are attending colleges or universities in Georgia and are majoring in journalism. Applicants must be residents of Georgia. Award requirements change regularly. Write to the address listed, enclosing a self-addressed, stamped envelope for an application and further information, browse their website: www.gapress.org or email: mail@gapress.org. No GPA requirement specified.

Georgia Press Foundation
Attn: Member Services
3066 Mercer University Drive, Suite 200
Atlanta, GA 30341-4137

483
Gerald Weiner Memorial Scholarship

AMOUNT: $2000 DEADLINE: March 15
MAJOR: All Fields of Study

The Gerald Weiner Memorial Scholarship is open to employees of Business Products Industry Association member firms and their families. Persons holding academic records sufficient for acceptance by accredited colleges, junior colleges or technical schools, or persons already enrolled in one of those institutions are eligible for this two-year award. Selection is made by a committee from the Student Financial Aid Department of The George Washington University, Washington, DC. Award requirements change regularly. Please send a self-addressed, stamped envelope to receive your application and any further instructions from the scholarship provider or email: info@bpia.org. No GPA requirement specified.

Business Products Industry Association
Attn: Scholarship Committee
301 North Fairfax Street
Alexandria, VA 22314-2633

484
Gerber Fellowship in Pediatric Nutrition

AMOUNT: None Specified DEADLINE: June 30
MAJOR: Pediatric Nutrition

This award is open to minority medical students and residents performing nutrition research with a special emphasis on pediatrics. Award requirements change regularly. There are two deadlines: May 31 deadline is for renewal applicants and the June 30 deadline is for new applicants. Send a stamped (.55), self-addressed envelope (9x12), to the address listed for additional information. No GPA requirement specified.

National Medical Fellowships, Inc.
Scholarship Coordinator
110 West 32nd Street, FL 8
New York, NY 10001-3205

485
Gerber Foundation Scholarship

AMOUNT: $1500 DEADLINE: February 28
MAJOR: All Areas of Study

The Gerber Foundation Scholarship is open to full-time high school seniors who will be attending college. You must be a dependent of an employee of the Gerber Company. This award is renewable with a minimum GPA of 2.0 for up to four years. At least 30 awards are offered annually. Award requirements change regularly. Please contact the Foundation at the address provided or email tgf@ncisd.net for further information. No GPA requirement specified.

Gerber Foundation
Attn: Catherine Obits
4747 West 48th Street, Suite 153
Fremont, MI 49412

486
Gilbert F. White Postdoctoral Fellowship Program

AMOUNT: None Specified DEADLINE: February 26
MAJOR: Natural Resources, Energy, Environmental Sciences

This award is open to researchers in social science or public policy programs in the areas of natural resources, energy, or the environment. Applicants must have completed doctoral requirements and preference will be given to those with teaching and/or research experience. This is a residential fellowship. Award requirements change regularly. Please send a self-addressed, stamped envelope to receive your application and any further instructions from the fellowship provider or browse their website at www.rff.org. No GPA requirement specified.

Resources for the Future
Coordinator for Academic Programs
1616 P Street NW
Washington, DC 20036-1434

487
Gilbert J. and Rose Nelson Howard Memorial Scholarship Fund Trust

AMOUNT: $500 DEADLINE: Varies
MAJOR: Nursing, Pre-Medicine, Social Work, Teaching, Business

The Gilbert J. and Rose Nelson Howard Memorial Scholarship Fund Trust is open to senior Burlington High School (Burlington, WI) students entering a postsecondary school in Wisconsin. Students preparing for careers in nursing will be given first consideration. Students pursuing careers in the following fields are also encouraged to apply: medicine, social work, teaching and business. The scholarship will be awarded on the basis of academic performance, character and financial need. Award requirements change regularly. Please visit your Guidance Office to receive an application and any additional details. No GPA requirement specified.

Burlington High School
Attn: Guidance Office
225 Robert Street
Burlington, WI 53105

488
Gilbreth Memorial Fellowship

AMOUNT: $2200 DEADLINE: November 15
MAJOR: Industrial Engineering

This fellowship is open to graduate students who are enrolled in an industrial engineering program or equivalent on a full-time basis, who are members of the institute and have a minimum 3.4 GPA. The program enrolled in may be located in the United States and its territories, Canada or Mexico. The applicants must be pursuing an advanced degree and must have a graduation date of May/June 2001 or later. Applicants must also be nominated by their IE Department heads. Award requirements change regularly. GPA must be 3.4-4.0.

Institute of Industrial Engineers
Attn: Chapter Operations Board
25 Technology Park
Norcross, GA 30092-2988

489
Gillian and Ellis Goodman Scholarship Fund

AMOUNT: None Specified DEADLINE: March 1
MAJOR: Environmental Engineering

The Gillian and Ellis Goodman Scholarship Fund is open to students who live in Cook County, Illinois or the Chicago area. Preference is given to students with career goals in engineering, focusing on environmental concerns. Award requirements change regularly. No GPA requirement specified.

Jewish Vocational Service
Attn: Scholarship Secretary
One South Franklin Street
Chicago, IL 60606-4694

490
Glamour Magazine's Top Ten College Women Competition

AMOUNT: $1000 DEADLINE: January 31
MAJOR: All Areas of Study

This competition is open to women who are college juniors at an accredited college or university and majoring in any field of study. When you apply, each entry must include: a completed application form (photo copies acceptable), an official college transcript (may be mailed separately) and a list (by year) of your activities on and off campus. Include the names of activities and organizations and briefly describe your responsibilities with and contributions to them. Also required is a 500- to 700-word essay describing your most meaningful achievements; how they relate to your field of study and your future goals. Include a photograph, no larger than 8 x 10 (for identification purposes only) and at least one letter of recommendation. Award recipients are chosen based on campus and community activities, leadership experience, unique and inspiring goals and excellent academic achievement. Award requirements change regularly. For more information, email TTCW@GLAMOUR.com or call (800) 244-GLAM. GPA must be 3.0-4.0.

Glamour Magazine
Top College Women Competition
10 Madison Avenue, #350
New York, NY 10010-3630

491
Gleaner Life Insurance Society Scholarship

AMOUNT: $1000 DEADLINE: March 10
MAJOR: Vocational/Technical

The Gleaner Life Insurance Society Scholarship is open to Lenawee County (MI) graduating seniors. You qualify for the award if you are in the process of completing a vocational or technical program. Award requirements change regularly. Please send a self-addressed, stamped envelope to receive your application and any further instructions from the scholar-

ship provider. No GPA requirement specified.

Morenci High School
Attn: Mrs. Melissa Parnell
788 Coomer Street
Morenci, MI 49256

492
Glenn Martek Memorial Scholarship

AMOUNT: $1000 DEADLINE: March 10
MAJOR: Business Services Technology, Computerized Accounting, Business Office, Computer Information Systems, Marketing Education

The Glenn Martek Memorial Scholarship is open to Lenawee County (MI) graduating seniors. To be considered for the award, you must be completing one of the following programs: business services technology, computerized accounting, business office, computer information systems or marketing education. Award requirements change regularly. Please send a self-addressed, stamped envelope to receive your application and any further instructions from the scholarship provider. No GPA requirement specified.

Morenci High School
Attn: Mrs. Melissa Parnell
788 Coomer Street
Morenci, MI 49256

493
Global Automotive Aftermarket Symposium Scholarship

AMOUNT: $1000-$2000 DEADLINE: February 28
MAJOR: Automotive

The Global Automotive Aftermarket Symposium Scholarship is open to graduating high school seniors or those who have graduated from high school within the past three years. To be considered for the award, you must be enrolled in a college level program or a National Automotive Technician Education Foundation accredited automotive technician program full-time; undergraduate part-time or graduate programs do not qualify. Priority will be given to those pursuing a career in the automotive aftermarket. Participants must be attending a program in the United States or Canada. Award requirements change regularly. No GPA requirement specified.

University of the Aftermarket
Education Committee
9237 Ward Pkwy, Suite 106
Kansas City, MO 64114-3313

Gordon K. Mortin Scholarship

AMOUNT: $2500 DEADLINE: May 1
MAJOR: Engineering, Architecture, Sciences

The Gordon K. Mortin Scholarship is open to active members of Triangle fraternity who demonstrate financial need. The award is available only to students who will be undergraduates in the school year following their application. To be considered for this award, you must submit an application, a current college transcript and two letters of recommendation. Award requirements change regularly. No GPA requirement specified.

Triangle Fraternity
Attn: Education Foundation
120 South Center Street
Plainfield, IN 46168-1214

Government Scholars Program

AMOUNT: None Specified DEADLINE: January 15
MAJOR: Municipal Government

Summer program for New York sophomores, juniors, or seniors who are interested in pursuing a career in municipal government. The program combines work experience in the mayor's office with weekly seminars. Award requirements change regularly. Write to the address listed, enclosing a self-addressed, stamped envelope for an application and further information. No GPA requirement specified.

New York City Department of Personnel
Citywide Administrative Services
One Centre Street, Rm 2425
New York, NY 10007-1602

496

Government Studies Award

AMOUNT: $1000 DEADLINE: March 1
MAJOR: American Government, Political Science

The Government Studies Award is open to two graduating high school seniors who live in the Township of Batavia, Illinois. The purpose of this award is to encourage young people to study the philosophies, forms and functions of American government. To be eligible for this award you must: have a "C" or better average, but have a "B" or better in civics, political science, government and history; have an active interest in local government and politics; have completed at least one course in civics, political science, government or history beyond classes required for graduation. You must also submit a transcript of at least seven semesters, a recommendation from a teacher or counselor and an essay. Award requirements change regularly. Please send a self-addressed, stamped envelope to receive your application and any further instructions from the scholarship provider. GPA must be 2.0-4.0. Batavia Township Board of Trustees
Attn: Jim Anderson, Township Supervisor
100 North Island Avenue
Batavia, IL 60510

497

Governor's Scholars Program

AMOUNT: Maximum: $4000 DEADLINE: March 1
MAJOR: All Areas of Study

The Governor's Scholars Program is open to Arkansas high school seniors planning to attend an approved college or university in Arkansas. To qualify to receive the award, you must be a senior with a minimum ACT score of 27, a minimum SAT score of 1100 or a minimum 3.6 GPA. The award is based on academic merit. To be a Governor's Distinguished Scholar, you must achieve a minimum ACT score of 32, a minimum SAT score of 1410 or be a National Merit Finalist. As a Governor's Distinguished Scholar, you are eligible to receive an award equal to tuition, mandatory fees, room and board at any Arkansas institution. The award is renewable for up to four years, provided you maintain a cumulative college GPA of 3.0 on a 4.0 scale and complete a minimum of 24 semester credit hours (or its equivalent) per academic year. Award requirements change regularly. Applications can be obtained at your high school counselor's office. You may also browse the Arkansas Department of Higher Education's website: www.arscholarships.com/finsites.html. No GPA requirement specified.

Arkansas Department of Higher Education
Financial Aid Division
114 East Capitol Avenue
Little Rock, AR 72201-3818

498

Governor's Scholarship

AMOUNT: Maximum: $1575 DEADLINE: Varies
MAJOR: All Areas of Study

The Governor's Scholarship is open to graduating Georgia high school seniors who chose to attend a public or private college or university in Georgia. To be considered for this award, you must be a U.S. citizen or permanent resident and be selected as a Georgia scholar by the state Department of Education or be named valedictorian, salutatorian or STAR student from an eligible Georgia high school. You are required to enroll as a full-time undergraduate freshman within seven months following your high school graduation. This award may be renewed provided you maintain a 3.0 GPA and earn 30 semester/45 quarter hours each academic year. Award requirements change regularly. A scholarship application is automatically mailed to all eligible candidates. If you have any questions, please consult your high school guidance counselor; or visit the Georgia Student Finance Commission's website at www.gsfc.org. No GPA requirement specified.

Georgia Student Finance Commission
Attn: Scholarships and Grants Division
2082 East Exchange Place
Tucker, GA 30084

Graduate Awards

AMOUNT: $600-$1500 DEADLINE: March 31
MAJOR: Economics, Business, Communications, Sociology

Three awards are available for graduate thesis and dissertations written on topics related to cooperatives. The dissertations and thesis submitted should deal with some aspect of economics, finance, operation, law, or structure of American cooperatives. Applicants must be graduate students in economics, business, communications, sociology, or other relevant field. Award requirements change regularly. Write to the address listed, enclosing a self-addressed, stamped envelope for further information or call (202) 626-8700. You may also browse their website: www.ncfc.org. GPA must be 3.0-4.0.

National Council of Farmer Cooperatives Education Foundation
NCFC Education Foundation
50-F Street NW, Suite 900
Washington, DC 20001-1530

500
Graduate Scholarship

AMOUNT: $750-$1500 DEADLINE: October 1
MAJOR: Aerospace Education, Science

This scholarship is open to graduate and doctoral students who are CAP members and majoring in aerospace education or science. Award requirements change regularly. For further information, please send a self-addressed, stamped envelope to the address provided. No GPA requirement specified.

National Board Civil Air Patrol
HQ CAP-USA/ETTC
105 South Hansell Street, Building 714
Maxwell AFB, AL 36112-6332

501
Graduate Student Scholarship

AMOUNT: $2000 DEADLINE: September 1
MAJOR: School Administration

This scholarship is open to graduate students who intend to pursue the public school superintendency as a career. Nominees must be recommended by a dean and at least one faculty member. You will also need to send supporting statements. Award requirements change regularly. Please send a self-addressed, stamped envelope to receive your application and any further instructions from the scholarship provider or email dpierce@aasa.org. No GPA requirement specified.

American Association of School Administrators
Attn: Darlene Pierce
1801 North Moore Street
Arlington, VA 22209-1813

502
Graduate Student Scholarship

AMOUNT: Maximum: $1500 DEADLINE: April 1
MAJOR: Agricultural Engineering, Agronomy, Crop and Soil Sciences, Entomology, Food Sciences, Horticulture, Plant Pathology

The Graduate Student Scholarship is granted to graduate students pursuing advanced studies which enhance the potato industry. Your selection is based on academic achievement, leadership abilities and potato-related areas of graduate study. Award requirements change regularly. Contact the address listed for further information or contact the Communications Director at (303) 773-9295. No GPA requirement specified.

National Potato Council Auxiliary Scholarship Committee
Attn: Pam Gunnerson
5690 DTC Blvd, Suite 230E
Englewood, CO 80111-3238

503
Grant M. Mack Memorial Scholarship

AMOUNT: $2000 DEADLINE: March 1
MAJOR: Business

This scholarship is open to undergraduate and graduate students who are legally blind and majoring in business. Award requirements change regularly. Write to the address listed, enclosing a self-addressed, stamped envelope for an application and further information. No GPA requirement specified.

American Council of the Blind
Attn: Billie Jean Keith
1155 15th Street NW, Suite 720
Washington, DC 20005-2706

504
Grant Program

AMOUNT: None Specified DEADLINE: Varies
MAJOR: Telepathy, Precognition, Psychokinesis, Parapsychology, Related Phenomena

The Grant Program is open to those individuals who are doing research in parapsychology (telepathy, precognition, psychokinesis and related phenomena). This award is not for travel, graduate or undergraduate studies but for persons studying parapsychology directly (not those with merely a general interest in the subject). Should you apply, you will need to submit a proposal outlining the aims of your project, the time required to achieve it and the likely expenditure; you are also requested to submit your educational record, references, past work and any publications. Award requirements change regularly. For further information, please write to the address listed, including a self-addressed, stamped envelope or call (212) 628-1550. You may also visit their website: www.parapsychology.org. No GPA requirement specified.

Parapsychology Foundation, Inc.
Eileen J. Garrett Library
228 East 71st Street
New York, NY 10021-5136

505
Grant Program for Medical Studies

AMOUNT: $500-$1500 DEADLINE: Varies
MAJOR: Medicine

Grants for medical students at the graduate level of study who are members of the Presbyterian Church (U.S.A.). Applicants must be U.S. citizens, demonstrate financial need, and be recommended by an academic advisor and church pastor. Award requirements change regularly. Write to the address listed for information and an application enclosing a self-addressed, stamped envelope or call (502) 569-5735. No GPA requirement specified.

Presbyterian Church (U.S.A.)
Office of Financial Aid for Studies
100 Witherspoon Street
Louisville, KY 40202-1396

506
Grants-In-Aid Program

AMOUNT: $500-$2000 DEADLINE: January 15
MAJOR: Petroleum Geology, Geology, Geophysics, Paleontology

The purpose of the program is to foster research in the geosciences by providing support to graduate students in the earth sciences whose research has application to the search for petroleum and energy minerals resources and to related environmental geology issues. Grants are to be applied to expenses directly related the student's thesis work, such as summer field work, lab analysis, etc. Funds are not to be used to purchase capital equipment, attend conferences, or to pay salaries, tuition, room & board during the school year. Award requirements change regularly. To receive further details, email rgriffin@aapg.org or write to the address provided to the attention of R. Griffin, Grants-In-Aid Coordinator. You may also visit their website: www.aapg.org/fdn.html. No GPA requirement specified.

American Association of Petroleum Geologists Foundation
AAPG Grants-in-Aid
PO Box 979
Tulsa, OK 74101-0979

507
Grants-In-Aid Program In Support of Anthropological Research

AMOUNT: Maximum: $20000 DEADLINE: May 1
MAJOR: Anthropology

Open to qualified scholars affiliated with accredited institutions and organizations. Awards are for individual postdoctoral research or for dissertation thesis research. Award requirements change regularly. Write to the address listed, enclosing a self-addressed, stamped envelope for an application and further, browse their website: www.wennergren.org or call (212) 683-5000. No GPA requirement specified.

Wenner-Gren Foundation for Anthropological Research
Grants Programs
220 5th Avenue
New York, NY 10001-7708

508
Graywood Youth Horsemanship Grant

AMOUNT: None Specified DEADLINE: March 1
MAJOR: Horsecare, Horsemanship, Equestrian

This grant is designed to provide a Morgan youth the opportunity to spend 3-5 days with transportation and board expense met through grant funds to: 1) further a study in the mastery of horse care and keeping 2) receive tutelage from breed professionals in the categories of breeding and management and/or horse training and/or riding or driving 3) ride and/or drive quality Morgan horses, thereby improving proficiency and 4) acquire skills and knowledge from "hands-on" experience. Award requirements change regularly. For further information, please contact the address provided. No GPA requirement specified.

American Morgan Horse Institute, Inc.
Mrs. Sally Plumley, AMHI Scholarships
PO Box 837
Shelburne, VT 05482-0519

509
Greater Hartford Jaycees Scholarship

AMOUNT: $3000 DEADLINE: February 14
MAJOR: All Areas of Study

The Greater Hartford Jaycees Scholarship is open to high school seniors who are residents of the Greater Hartford (CT) area. You must be able to demonstrate scholastic merit, community service and financial need. Also required are an essay, two recommendation letters (one from a teacher or guidance counselor) and a school transcript. The award is to be applied to tuition expenses only. Award requirements change regularly. No GPA requirement specified.

Greater Hartford Jaycees Foundation, Inc.
Attn: Scholarship Committee
One Financial Plaza
Hartford, CT 06103-2608

510
GSBA and Richard C. Rolfe Scholarships

AMOUNT: Maximum: $3500 DEADLINE: February 20
MAJOR: All Areas of Study

Scholarships are available for undergraduate students who are gay or lesbian or who were raised by gay or lesbian parents. Applicants must be Washington residents. Based on demonstrated financial need and potential leadership. Award requirements change regularly. Write to the address listed, enclosing a self-addressed, stamped envelope for an application and further information. No GPA requirement specified.

GSBA, Pride and INBA Scholarships
Scholarship Programs
2150 North 107th Street, Suite 205
Seattle, WA 98133-9009

511
GTE Foundation Scholarship

AMOUNT: $1000 DEADLINE: February 1
MAJOR: Electrical Engineering, Computer Science

The GTE Foundation Scholarship is open to sophomore and junior women majoring in electrical engineering or computer science who are attending an ABET-accredited program or an SWE-approved school. The applicants must have a minimum GPA of 3.5. Award requirements change regularly. Please send a self-addressed, stamped envelope to receive your application. For further instructions, please browse the SWE website

at www.swe.org or email hq@swe.org for more information.
GPA must be 3.5-4.0.

Society of Women Engineers Headquarters
Scholarship Coordinator
120 Wall Street, FL 11
New York, NY 10005-3902

512
Guaranteed Access Grant

AMOUNT: None Specified DEADLINE: March 1
MAJOR: All Areas of Study

The Guaranteed Access Grant is open to Maryland residents
attending a college or a designated institute of higher learning
in Maryland on a full-time basis. To qualify for the award, you
must have entered college within one year after high school,
have a GPA of at least 2.5, and be under the age of 22 (the
first year that you receive the scholarship). The award requires
that you demonstrate great financial need, with the total family income below 130% of the federal poverty level. This
award can be renewed up to three times if eligibility (a minimum 2.0 GPA) is maintained. Award requirements change
regularly. To apply, you must submit the FAFSA. For more
information, you may visit the website at
www.mhec.state.md.us. GPA must be 2.5-4.0.

Maryland State Higher Education Commission
Attn: State Scholarship Administration
16 Francis Street
Annapolis, MD 21401-1781

513
Guiliano Mazzetti Scholarship Award

AMOUNT: $1500 DEADLINE: February 1
MAJOR: Manufacturing Engineering, Technology or a Closely
Related Field

Open to full-time undergraduates who are enrolled in a degree
program in manufacturing engineering, technology or a closely related field. Applicants must have completed a minimum
of 30 college credit hours with a minimum GPA of 3.0. Award
requirements change regularly. For further information, go to
the SME website: www.sme.org. GPA must be 3.0-4.0.

Society of Manufacturing Engineering Education Foundation
PO Box 930
One SME Drive
Dearborn, MI 48121-0930

514
H. Neil Mecaskey Scholarship

AMOUNT: $500 DEADLINE: April 17
MAJOR: Travel and Tourism, Hotel/Restaurant Management

The H. Neil Mecaskey Scholarship is open to juniors or
seniors pursuing a degree in a travel and tourism-related field.
To be considered for the award, you must be enrolled in a
North American four-year college full-time. Award requirements change regularly. No GPA requirement specified.

National Tourism Foundation
PO Box 3071
546 East Main Street
Lexington, KY 40508-3071

515
Harold L. Meeker Memorial Scholarship

AMOUNT: $900 DEADLINE: Varies
MAJOR: All Areas of Study

The Harold L. Meeker Memorial Scholarship is open to
undergraduate members of Tau Kappa Epsilon. To apply, you
must be in good standing with your chapter and demonstrate a
record of active participation, including leadership in officer
and chair positions. You should also be active in campus organizations, be a full-time student and have a minimum 2.5
GPA. Award requirements change regularly. GPA must be 2.5-
4.0.

TKE Educational Foundation
Attn: Timothy L. Taschwer
8645 Founders Road
Indianapolis, IN 46268-1336

516
Harriett Barnhart Wimmer Scholarship

AMOUNT: $1000 DEADLINE: March 31
MAJOR: Landscape Architecture/Design

The Harriett Barnhart Wimmer Scholarship is open to women
entering their final year of undergraduate landscape studies. In
order to apply, you must demonstrate excellence in design
ability and sensitivity to the environment. Award requirements
change regularly. No GPA requirement specified.

Landscape Architecture Foundation
Scholarship Program
636 'I' Street NW
Washington, DC 20001-3736

517
Harrisonville N.E.T.T. Scholarship

AMOUNT: $200 DEADLINE: March 31
MAJOR: All Areas of Study

Open to Harrisonville High School (MO) seniors who exhibit
a drug/alcohol free lifestyle. Award requirements change regularly. Applications are available in the Harrisonville Senior
High School guidance office. No GPA requirement specified.

Harrisonville Senior High School
Attn: Roy Sackman
1504 East Elm Street
Harrisonville, MO 64701-2022

518
Harrisonville Teachers Association Scholarship

AMOUNT: $100 DEADLINE: May 1
MAJOR: Education

Open to Harrisonville High School (MO) seniors who are edu-
cation majors. Award requirements change regularly.
Applications are available in the Harrisonville Senior High
School guidance office. No GPA requirement specified.

American Society of Travel Agents
Attn: ASTA Foundation
1101 King Street, Suite 200
Alexandria, VA 22314-2944

...Vornick

...: Varies
... of Wood, Music

The purpose of the Harry and Florence Wornick Endowment Fund is to provide loan funds to Jewish students with higher education or vocational training, with special consideration to students pursuing careers in the use of wood, or careers in music. Applicants must be able to provide qualified guarantors (co-signers) that reside in the Bay Area. Applicants must be residents of San Francisco, San Mateo, northern Santa Clara, Marin, Sonoma, Alameda or Contra Costa counties in California. It is preferable that loan applicants submit their applications by July 1 for the fall semester and November 1 for the spring semester. Award requirements change regularly. No GPA requirement specified.

Jewish Family and Children's Services
Attn: Loans and Grants Department
2245 Post Street
San Francisco, CA 94115

520
Harry J. Donnelly Memorial Scholarship

AMOUNT: $500 DEADLINE: May 26
MAJOR: Accounting, Law

This scholarship is open to members of Tau Kappa Epsilon who are pursuing an undergraduate degree in accounting or a graduate degree in law. In order to apply, you must have a demonstrated record of leadership within your chapter, on campus or in the community. Also, a minimum 3.0 GPA and planning to be a full-time student the following academic year is required. Award requirements change regularly. For further information, call (317) 872-6533, email: tef@tkehq.org or visit the website at: www.tke.org. GPA must be 3.0-4.0.

TKE Educational Foundation
Attn: Timothy L. Taschwer
8645 Founders Road
Indianapolis, IN 46268-1336

521
Healy Scholarship

AMOUNT: $2000 DEADLINE: July 28
MAJOR: Travel and Tourism

Open to students admitted to or enrolled in a four-year college or university who are majoring in travel and tourism. Applicants will be required to submit a 500-word paper suggesting improvements in the travel industry. Award requirements change regularly. Write to the address listed, enclosing a self-addressed, stamped envelope for an application and further information. You can browse their website: www.astanet.com or email: myriaml@astahq.com. No GPA requirement specified.

522
Helen Crilly Nurses' Scholarship Fund

AMOUNT: $1000 DEADLINE: June 30
MAJOR: Nursing

Open to students who are enrolled in a nursing degree program. Applicants must have a 3.0 GPA. Applicants who are seeking a BA in nursing must have completed two years of a four-year program. Applicants who are seeking an AA in nursing must have completed one year of an associate degree program. Applicants are required to submit: a completed application form; a college transcript including GPA and class standing; a letter of recommendation from an instructor in a subject related to nursing; an essay describing the applicant's career goals with plans for achieving them; and a completed Providence Medical Center Scholarship Candidate Agreement. Award requirements change regularly. For application and other information, please send a self-addressed, stamped envelope to the address listed or call (816) 596-4872. GPA must be 3.0-4.0.

Providence Medical Center Auxiliary - Volunteer Services
Nursing Scholarship Committee
8929 Parallel Parkway
Kansas City, KS 66112

523
Helen L. Henderson Scholarship Loan Fund

AMOUNT: Maximum: $8000 DEADLINE: April 1
MAJOR: All Areas of Study

Loans are open to all Benton County residents and to all Benton Central graduates regardless of county of residence. Loans will be based on academics and financial need. Repayment begins no later than ten months after graduation, or termination of your education and are to be repaid within three years. No interest will be charged, however, on loans during this period. Award requirements change regularly. GPA must be 2.5-4.0.

Fowler State Bank
Trust Department
PO Box 511
Fowler, IN 47944-0511

524
Helen Morse Honorary Scholarship

AMOUNT: $200 DEADLINE: May 1
MAJOR: Home Economics, Human Sciences

Open to Harrisonville High School seniors who are majoring in home economics or human sciences. Award requirements change regularly. Applications are available in the Harrisonville Senior High School guidance office. No GPA requirement specified.

Harrisonville Senior High School
Attn: Roy Sackman
1504 East Elm Street
Harrisonville, MO 64701-2022

Helen N. and Harold B. Shapira Scholarship

AMOUNT: $1000 DEADLINE: April 1
MAJOR: Medicine/Medical Research

The Helen N. and Harold B. Shapira Scholarship is open to undergraduate and medical students who are enrolled at Minnesota schools specializing in diseases of the heart and blood vessel systems. You must be a resident of Minnesota. Award requirements change regularly. For an application and further information, send a self-addressed, stamped envelope to the address listed below or call the Scholarship Assistant at (612) 835-3300. No GPA requirement specified.

American Heart Association, Minnesota Affiliate Inc
Attn: Scholarship Assistance
4701 West 77th Street
Minneapolis, MN 55435-4806

Henk Hasert Soccer Scholarship

AMOUNT: $100-$500 DEADLINE: Varies
MAJOR: All Fields of Study

The Henk Hasert Soccer Scholarship is open to graduating seniors who played varsity soccer at Burlington High School (Burlington, WI). Two awards will be given: one to a male student and one to a female student. Students must be entering an accredited four-year college, university, technical or vocational school on a full-time basis by the fall semester of the current year. Award requirements change regularly. Please visit your Guidance Office to receive an application and any additional details. No GPA requirement specified.

Burlington High School
Attn: Guidance Office
225 Robert Street
Burlington, WI 53105

Henry A. Murray Dissertation Award

AMOUNT: $2500 DEADLINE: April 1
MAJOR: Social & Behavioral Sciences, Human Development, Women's Studies

The Henry A. Murray Dissertation Award is open to doctoral students. Projects should focus on some aspect of "the study of lives," concentrating on issues in human development or personality. Projects drawing on Murray Center data will be given priority, although use of the center's resources is not required. The Henry A. Murray Research Center is a national repository of social and behavioral sciences data for the study of lives over time with a special focus on the lives of American women. Award requirements change regularly. Please send a self-addressed, stamped envelope to receive your application and any further instructions from the Murray Center; or visit their website at www.radcliffe.edu/murray. No GPA requirement specified.

Radcliffe College - Henry A. Murray Research Center
Attn: Grants Program Coordinator
10 Garden Street
Cambridge, MA 02138

Henry and Tilda Shuler Scholarship Fund for Young People

AMOUNT: Maximum: $950 DEADLINE: Varies
MAJOR: All Areas of Study

The purpose of the Henry and Tilda Shuler Scholarship Fund is to provide scholarships for Jewish youths to receive vocational training, college education, or other studies. Applicants must be 26 years old or younger, demonstrate financial need and residents of San Francisco, San Mateo, northern Santa Clara, Marin or Sonoma counties in California. Deadlines vary; therefore, it is encouraged that applicants apply early. Award requirements change regularly. No GPA requirement specified.

Jewish Family and Children's Services
Attn: Loans and Grants Department
2245 Post Street
San Francisco, CA 94115

Henry Ashe Continuing Education Scholarship

AMOUNT: None Specified DEADLINE: November 1
MAJOR: Medical, Medical Related

The Henry Ashe Continuing Education Scholarship is available to students who either have graduated from Lakeland Union High School, Minocqua, Wisconsin, or who are from the area served by Lakeland Union High School or the St. Germain School District. Applicants must be enrolled in a program for medicine, dentistry, nursing, radiology, dental hygiene, physical therapy, occupational therapy, medical assisting, medical technology or other health-related fields. Award requirements change regularly. Please send a self-addressed, stamped envelope to receive your application and any further instructions from the scholarship provider. No GPA requirement specified.

Howard Young Medical Center Auxiliary
PO Box 470
Woodruff, WI 54568-0470

Henry Broughton, K2AE Memorial Scholarship

AMOUNT: $1000 DEADLINE: February 1
MAJOR: Engineering, Science or Related Areas

This scholarship is open to applicants with a minimum general class amateur radio license and a home residence within 70 miles of Schenectady, NY. Applicants must be majoring in engineering, sciences or a related area in a baccalaureate course of study at an accredited four-year college or university. At least one award per year, but multiple awards are given if funding permits. Award requirements change regularly. Please write the address provided, using a self-addressed, stamped envelope, for further information. No GPA requirement specified.

American Radio Relay League
Attn: ARRL Foundation
225 Main Street
Newington, CT 06111-1400

531
Henry J. Reilly Memorial Graduate Scholarship

AMOUNT: $500 DEADLINE: April 15
MAJOR: All Areas of Study

This scholarship is open to active or associate ROA members who have been accepted for graduate study and enrolled in two graduate courses at a regionally accredited U.S. college or university. Applicant must provide evidence of a 3.2 undergraduate GPA, GPA must be 3.3 GPA for any previous graduate work, master's degree, or acceptance into a doctoral program. Three recommendation letters and curriculum vitae required. Award requirements change regularly. For further information, please contact the address provided, using a self-addressed, stamped envelope. GPA must be 3.2-4.0.

Reserve Officers Association of the United States
Attn: Ms Mickey Hagen
One Constitution Ave NE
Washington, DC 20002-5618

532
Henry J. Reilly Memorial Undergraduate Scholarship

AMOUNT: $500 DEADLINE: April 15
MAJOR: All Areas of Study

This scholarship is open to active or associate ROA or ROAL members, their children (age 21 or under), grandchildren, or children of deceased members who were paid up at time of death. Applicant must have registered for the draft, if eligible, have good moral character and demonstrate leadership qualities. If a senior in high school, the applicant must rank in top quarter of class, have a minimum combined SAT 1 score of 1200, a minimum 3.3 GPA and submit a 500-word essay on career goals. If already in an undergraduate program, the applicant must have a minimum combined SAT 1 score of 1200, a minimum 3.0 college GPA, a minimum 3.3 high school GPA and submit a 500-word essay on career goals. Award requirements change regularly. Please consult the provider at the address listed. GPA must be 3.0-4.0.

Reserve Officers Association of the United States
Attn: Ms Mickey Hagen
One Constitution Ave NE
Washington, DC 20002-5618

533
Henry P. Epstein Award

AMOUNT: $2000 DEADLINE: March 15
MAJOR: All Fields of Study

The Henry P. Epstein Award is open to employees of Business Products Industry Association member firms and their families. Persons holding academic records sufficient for acceptance by accredited colleges, junior colleges or technical

schools, or persons already enrolled in one of those institutions are eligible for this one-year award. Selection is made by a committee from the Student Financial Aid Department of The George Washington University, Washington, DC. Award requirements change regularly. Please send a self-addressed, stamped envelope to receive your application and any further instructions from the scholarship provider or email: info@bpia.org. No GPA requirement specified.

Business Products Industry Association
Attn: Scholarship Committee
301 North Fairfax Street
Alexandria, VA 22314-2633

534
Herbert Hoover Travel Grant Program

AMOUNT: Maximum: $1500 DEADLINE: March 1
MAJOR: American History, Political Science, Public Policy

Travel grants are awarded to current graduate students, post-doctoral scholars, qualified nonacademic researchers. Priority given to proposals that have the highest probability of publication and use by educators and policymakers. This travel stipend is given to pay for travel to West Branch Iowa to use archives at Herbert Presidential Library. Award requirements change regularly. Write to the address listed or call (800) 828-0475 for details. No GPA requirement specified.

Herbert Hoover Presidential Library Association
302 Parkside Drive, PO Box 696
West Branch, IA 52358-0696

535
Hereditary Disease Foundation Huntington's Research Grant

AMOUNT: Maximum: $35000 DEADLINE: Varies
MAJOR: Hereditary Diseases, Disease Pathology

This award is open to researchers studying areas of interest regarding Huntington's Disease, including trinucleotide expansions, animal models, gene therapy, neurobiology and development of the basal ganglia, cell survival and death, and intercellular signaling in striatal neurons. Anyone accepting funding from the Hereditary Disease Foundation must agree to abide by the following policy: Propagatable materials should be freely available to other investigators following publication. Deadlines for Applications are February 15, August 15 and October 15. Thirty (30) copies of the completed application should be forwarded. If reprints are to be considered as part of the application, eight (8) copies should be provided for primary review. Award requirements change regularly. To obtain an application, please submit a letter of intent at anytime by post to the address provided or by email at the website: www.hdfoundation.org/intent.htm. No GPA requirement specified.

Hereditary Disease Foundation
Dr. Allan Tobin, Scientific Director
1427 7th Street, #2
Santa Monica, CA 90401

536
Hermione Grant Calhoun Scholarship

AMOUNT: $3000 DEADLINE: March 31
MAJOR: All Areas of Study

The Hermione Grant Calhoun Scholarship is open to female students who are legally blind and are pursuing or planning to pursue a full-time postsecondary course of study in the U.S. You will be considered based on academic excellence, service to the community and financial need. Award requirements change regularly. No GPA requirement specified.

National Federation of the Blind
Attn: Peggy Elliott, Chairman
805 5th Avenue
Grinnell, IA 50112-1653

537
Hispanic College Fund, Inc. Scholarship

AMOUNT: None Specified DEADLINE: April 15
MAJOR: Business

The Hispanic College Fund, Inc. Scholarship is open to high school seniors or full-time undergraduate college students who are U.S. citizens of Hispanic heritage. You must have a minimum GPA of 3.0, be pursuing a degree that will lead to a career in business and provide evidence of financial need. Award requirements change regularly. GPA must be 3.0-4.0.

Hispanic College Fund, Inc.
Scholarship Coordinator
One Thomas Circle NW, Suite 375
Washington, DC 20005-5802

538
Hispanic Scholarship Fund

AMOUNT: $500 DEADLINE: August 1
MAJOR: Theology, Ministry, Religious Studies

The Hispanic Scholarship Fund is open to American Baptist Hispanic students pursuing an undergraduate or first professional seminary. Applicants must demonstrate financial need and plan to serve in a church-related ministry. Applicants must be members of an American Baptist church for at least one year before applying for aid and enrolled at an accredited educational institution in the U.S. or Puerto Rico. U.S. citizenship is required. Award requirements change regularly. Please send a self-addressed, stamped envelope to receive your application and any further instructions from the scholarship provider. No GPA requirement specified.

American Baptist Financial Aid Program
Educational Ministries ABC/USA
PO Box 851
Valley Forge, PA 19482-0851

539
Hispanic Scholarship Fund, General Program

AMOUNT: $750-$2750 DEADLINE: October 15
MAJOR: All Areas of Study

The Hispanic Scholarship Fund (General Program) is open to full-time community college, four-year college and graduate school students who are at least half Hispanic (one parent fully Hispanic or both parents half Hispanic). You must be a U.S. citizen or permanent resident, have a minimum 2.7 GPA and have completed a minimum 15 semester credits of undergraduate work from an accredited college in the U.S. or Puerto Rico. Award requirements change regularly. The application period is between August 3rd and October 15th each year. You can also send a stamped, self-addressed long business envelope (9" x 4") addressed to yourself after August to the address below. GPA must be 2.7-4.0.

Hispanic Scholarship Fund (HSF)
Selection Committee
One Sansome Street, Suite 1000
San Francisco, CA 94104

540
Ho-Chunk Nation Academic Plan

AMOUNT: None Specified DEADLINE: Varies
MAJOR: All Area of Study

This assistance program helps Ho-Chunk Nation members pursuing four year or graduate degrees from accredited institutions. Students who show financial need will receive two equal payments throughout each term they are eligible. One half of award is sent at term's beginning and the second half approximately four weeks after that, after verification that recipients are still at full-time status. Award requirements change regularly. For any further questions, call (715) 284-4915 or contact Ho-Chunk at the email address: beardsj@hochunk.com. No GPA requirement specified.

Ho-Chunk Nation
PO Box 667
Education Department W9814 Airport Rd.
Black River Falls, WI 54615-0667

541
Ho-Chunk Nation Adult Continuing Education Grants

AMOUNT: None Specified DEADLINE: Varies
MAJOR: All Area of Study

This assistance program helps Ho-Chunk Nation members pursue an education or to increase their employability skills by taking up to nine credits per term at an accredited public university or technical college. Recipients must be attending classes full-time. Tribal employees qualify for job-related training such as seminars, conferences, etc. Must submit application no later than 20 days before the beginning of the first class date. Award requirements change regularly. For questions, call (715) 284-4915 or contact Ho-Chunk at the email address: beardsj@hochunk.com. No GPA requirement specified.

Ho-Chunk Nation
PO Box 667
Education Department W9814 Airport Rd.
Black River Falls, WI 54615-0667

542
Ho-Chunk Nation Pre-College Assistance

AMOUNT: None Specified DEADLINE: Varies
MAJOR: All Areas of Study

This assistance program helps Ho-Chunk Nation members with precollege expenses such as: testing fees, tuition deposits, application fees, housing and food deposits, GED/HSED testing fees and preparatory courses. Costs under $200, students will receive reimbursement. Costs above $200, direct payment may be issued to the vendor. Applications accepted on a continuous basis but must be submitted no later than 20 days before payment is due. Award requirements change regularly. For questions, call (715) 284-4915 or contact Ho-Chunk at the email address: beardsj@hochunk.com. No GPA requirement specified.

Ho-Chunk Nation
PO Box 667
Education Department W9814 Airport Rd.
Black River Falls, WI 54615-0667

543
Ho-Chunk Nation Special Requests Assistance

AMOUNT: None Specified DEADLINE: Varies
MAJOR: All Areas of Study

This assistance program helps Ho-Chunk Nation members only after all other resources have been exhausted. To be used for nondirect school-related expenses such as: required uniforms, school sponsored trips and course materials and supplies (i.e., calculators, computer programs, etc.). Award requirements change regularly. No GPA requirement specified.

Ho-Chunk Nation
PO Box 667
Education Department W9814 Airport Rd.
Black River Falls, WI 54615-0667

544
Ho-Chunk Nation Summer Session Assistance

AMOUNT: $1350 DEADLINE: Varies
MAJOR: All Area of Study

This assistance program helps Ho-Chunk Nation members continue academic progress toward graduation at an accredited public university or community/vocational/technical college. This is not for part-time students. Must submit application no later than 20 days before the beginning of the first class. Award requirements change regularly. For any further questions, call (715) 284-4915 or contact Ho-Chunk at the email address: beardsj@hochunk.com. No GPA requirement specified.

Ho-Chunk Nation
PO Box 667
Education Department W9814 Airport Rd
Black River Falls, WI 54615-0667

545
Holland America Line Research Scholarship Fund

AMOUNT: None Specified DEADLINE: July 28
MAJOR: Travel and Tourism

Open to students who wish to do research in the travel and tourism field. Applicants must submit a research project proposal on a travel and tourism topic of their choosing, or they may contact the Foundation for a suggested list of topics. The proposal should include a description of the intended topic of research, purpose of study, methodology, cost of research (provide detailed budget), objectives, and time line. This can be a school, class or individual project. Award requirements change regularly. Write to the address listed, enclosing a self-addressed, stamped envelope for an application and further information. You can browse their website: www.astanet.com or email: myriaml@astahq.com. No GPA requirement specified.

American Society of Travel Agents
Attn: ASTA Foundation
1101 King Street, Suite 200
Alexandria, VA 22314-2944

546
Holland America, Princess Cruise Scholarship

AMOUNT: $2000-$3000 DEADLINE: July 28
MAJOR: Travel and Tourism

Open to students who are currently enrolled in a travel and tourism program in either a two- or four-year college/university or proprietary school. 300 to 500-word paper on various travel/tourism topics (requirements vary slightly for each award). Award requirements change regularly. Write to the address listed, enclosing a self-addressed, stamped envelope for an application and further information. You can browse their website: www.astanet.com or email: myriaml@astahq.com. No GPA requirement specified.

American Society of Travel Agents
Attn: ASTA Foundation
1101 King Street, Suite 200
Alexandria, VA 22314-2944

547
Home Builders Association of Durham and Orange Counties Scholarship

AMOUNT: $1000 DEADLINE: March 12
MAJOR: All Areas of Study (Construction, Construction-Related preferred)

The Home Builders Association of Durham and Orange Counties Scholarship is open to graduating seniors from Durham and Orange County high schools with preference given to students who are entering a construction-related course of study or children of employees of companies in the

HBA. Selection is based on academic performance, citizenship qualities and community activities. Award requirements change regularly. To request an application, please contact your high school's guidance office or the Home Builders Association of Durham and Orange Counties. No GPA requirement specified.

East Chapel Hill High School
Attn: Career Development Coordinator
500 Weaver Dairy Road
Chapel Hill, NC 27514-1721

548
HON Company Scholarship

AMOUNT: $2000 DEADLINE: March 15
MAJOR: All Fields of Study

The HON Company Scholarship is open to employees of Business Products Industry Association member firms and their families. Persons holding academic records sufficient for acceptance by accredited colleges, junior colleges or technical schools, or persons already enrolled in one of those institutions are eligible for this one-year award. Selection is made by a committee from the Student Financial Aid Department of The George Washington University, Washington, DC. Award requirements change regularly. Please send a self-addressed, stamped envelope to receive your application and any further instructions from the scholarship provider or email: info@bpia.org. No GPA requirement specified.

Business Products Industry Association
Attn: Scholarship Committee
301 North Fairfax Street
Alexandria, VA 22314-2633

549
Hooked on Sports Scholarship

AMOUNT: $1000-$10000 DEADLINE: January 15
MAJOR: All Fields of Study

The Hooked on Sports Scholarship recognizes students who have been active in both athletics and academics. This one-time award is open to you if you are a U.S. resident who is a graduating high school senior planning to enter an accredited postsecondary educational institution in the fall. Your application will be reviewed on the basis of financial need, class rank, standardized test scores and level of sports participation. Three hundred semifinalists will be selected from the applicant pool and are required to submit additional material. Award requirements change regularly. Please send a self-addressed, stamped envelope to receive your application and any further instructions from the scholarship provider; or call (800) 521-2123; or download the application from the website at www.footaction.com. No GPA requirement specified.

Footaction USA
Attn: Scholarship Coordinator
7880 Bent Branch Drive, Suite 100
Irving, TX 75063

550
Hoosier Scholar Award

AMOUNT: $500 DEADLINE: March 1
MAJOR: All Areas of Study

Open to high school seniors at approved Indiana high schools who rank in the top 20% of their graduating class. Applicants must be Indiana residents and plan to attend an approved postsecondary institution in Indiana as a full-time student. Selection is based on academic merit. Award requirements change regularly. For further information and an application, please write to the address listed, including a self-addressed, stamped envelope. You may also visit their website: www.ai.org/ssaci. GPA must be 2.8-4.0.

State Student Assistance Commission of Indiana
Attn: Scholarship Committee
150 West Market Street, Suite 500
Indianapolis, IN 46204

551
Hoover Uncommon Student Award

AMOUNT: Maximum: $5000 DEADLINE: March 31
MAJOR: All Areas of Study

Awarded to juniors in an Iowa high school, who are planning to pursue a degree at an accredited college or university. Applicants must be junior Iowa high school students or home schooled students who are at the Junior level in the state of Iowa. Award requirements change regularly. Write to the address listed for an application and further information. You can all (800) 828-0475, browse their website: www.hooverassoc.org or email: info@hooverassoc.org. No GPA requirement specified.

Herbert Hoover Presidential Library Association
302 Parkside Drive, PO Box 696
West Branch, IA 52358-0696

552
HOPE Scholarship Program

AMOUNT: None Specified DEADLINE: Varies
MAJOR: All Areas of Study

The HOPE Scholarship Program provides scholarship and grant assistance to residents of Georgia attending eligible Georgia postsecondary institutions. The value of your award is based upon your enrollment in either a public or private institution and may be based upon your overall GPA. You may be required to submit one or more of the following: the FAFSA, the HOPE Alternate Application, the Georgia Tuition Equalization Grant Application, your college's financial aid application. Award requirements change regularly. To determine if you are eligible for a HOPE Scholarship or Grant and to find out how to apply, contact your high school's guidance office or your intended college's financial aid office; or visit the Georgia Student Finance Commission's website at www.gsfc.org. No GPA requirement specified.

Georgia Student Finance Commission
Attn: Scholarships and Grants Division
2082 East Exchange Place
Tucker, GA 30084

553
Horace Mann Scholarship

AMOUNT: $1000-$20000 DEADLINE: February 12
MAJOR: All Areas of Study

The Horace Mann Scholarship is open to children of U.S. public school employees who will be entering freshmen. In order to apply, you must have at least a 3.0 GPA, 23 ACT or 1100 SAT. You must also be accepted as a full-time student to a two- or four-year accredited college or university. One Horace Mann Scholar will receive $20,000 in scholarship funds payable over four years and five other scholars will receive up to $4,000 each in scholarship funds payable over four years. Ten additional scholars will receive $1,000 in a one-time payment. You will be judged on written essays, high school transcripts, school and community activities and letters of recommendation. Financial need is not a consideration for this award. Award requirements change regularly. GPA must be 3.0-4.0.

Horace Mann Companies
Scholarship Program
PO Box 20490
Springfield, IL 62708

554
Horatio Alger National Scholars Program

AMOUNT: None Specified DEADLINE: April 15
MAJOR: All Fields of Study

The Horatio Alger National Scholars Program is open to high school students who are planning to pursue a degree at a four-year institution. To be considered for the award, you must demonstrate critical financial need, integrity, hard work, determination and perseverance in overcoming adversity. The award also requires that you have a certain level of academic achievement (minimum 2.0 GPA) and that you are actively involved in co-curricular and community activities. A final requirement is that the high school which you attend is hosting a Horatio Alger Youth Seminar. Award requirements change regularly. GPA must be 2.0-4.0.

Horatio Alger Association
Attn: Scholarship Committee
99 Canal Center Plaza
Alexandria, VA 22314

555
Horizons Foundation Scholarship Program

AMOUNT: $500 DEADLINE: Varies
MAJOR: Engineering, Computer Science, Physics, Mathematics, Business, Law, International Relations, Political Science, Operations Research, Economics

The Horizons Foundation Scholarship Program is open to women pursuing a career in national security/national defense who are currently enrolled at an accredited university or college, either full-time or part-time. Both undergraduate and graduate students are eligible for this award. Undergraduates must have attained at least a junior level status (60 credits). Applicants must demonstrate interest in pursuing a career related to national security, have financial need, a minimum 3.25 GPA and be U.S. citizens. Application deadline is November 1 for consideration for the Spring semester and July 1 for consideration for the Fall semester. Award requirements change regularly. Please visit the website at www.wid.ndia.org or request details by sending a self-addressed, stamped envelope to the address below. Only those with the stamped envelope will be fulfilled. GPA must be 3.3-4.0.

Horizons, A Women in Defense Foundation
National Defense Industrial Association
2111 Wilson Blvd, Suite 400
Arlington, VA 22201-3061

556
Hospice of Lenawee Scholarship

AMOUNT: $1000 DEADLINE: March 31
MAJOR: All Fields of Study

The Hospice of Lenawee Scholarship is open to Lenawee County (MI) residents only. To be considered for this award, you must be the son, daughter or spouse of a Lenawee Hospice client. Award requirements change regularly. Please send a self-addressed, stamped envelope to receive your application and any further instructions from the scholarship provider. No GPA requirement specified.

Morenci High School
Attn: Mrs. Melissa Parnell
788 Coomer Street
Morenci, MI 49256

557
Howard and Barbara Wolf Scholarship

AMOUNT: $2000 DEADLINE: March 15
MAJOR: All Fields of Study

The Howard and Barbara Wolf Scholarship is open to employees of Business Products Industry Association member firms and their families. Persons holding academic records sufficient for acceptance by accredited colleges, junior colleges or technical schools, or persons already enrolled in one of those institutions are eligible for this one-year award. Selection is made by a committee from the Student Financial Aid Department of The George Washington University, Washington, DC. Award requirements change regularly. Please send a self-addressed, stamped envelope to receive your application and any further instructions from the scholarship provider or email: info@bpia.org. No GPA requirement specified.

Business Products Industry Association
Attn: Scholarship Committee
301 North Fairfax Street
Alexandria, VA 22314-2633

558
Howard Brown Rickard Scholarship

AMOUNT: $3000 DEADLINE: March 31
MAJOR: Architecture, Law, Medicine, Engineering, Natural Sciences

The Howard Brown Rickard Scholarship is open to students who are legally blind and who are pursuing or planning to pursue a full-time postsecondary course of study in the U.S. You must be majoring in law, medicine, engineering, architecture or the natural sciences. Your selection will be based on academic excellence, service to the community and financial need. Award requirements change regularly. No GPA requirement specified.

National Federation of the Blind
Attn: Peggy Elliott, Chairman
805 5th Avenue
Grinnell, IA 50112-1653

Howard E. Adkins Memorial Scholarship

AMOUNT: $2500 DEADLINE: January 15
MAJOR: Welding Engineering, Welding Engineering Technology

The Howard E. Adkins Memorial Scholarship is awarded to full-time juniors or seniors pursuing a minimum four-year bachelor's degree in welding engineering or welding engineering technology. Priority will be given to welding engineering students and those who are residing or attending school in the states of Wisconsin or Kentucky. Applicants must have a minimum overall GPA of 2.8. Financial need is not a consideration. This award is renewable. Applicants must be U.S citizens who are planning to attend an academic institution located within the U.S. Award requirements change regularly. Please send a self-addressed, stamped envelope to receive your application and any further instructions from the scholarship provider. GPA must be 2.8-4.0.

American Welding Society Foundation, Inc.
National Education Scholarship Committee
550 Northwest LeJeune Road
Miami, FL 33126-4165

Howard H. Hanks Jr. Scholarship In Meteorology

AMOUNT: $700 DEADLINE: June 14
MAJOR: Meteorology, Atmospheric Sciences, Ocean Science, Hydrology

Applicants must be entering their final year in one of the fields listed above. Must be enrolled full-time, have a minimum GPA of 3.0 and be U.S. citizens or permanent residents. Award requirements change regularly. Write to the address listed, sending a self-addressed, stamped envelope for details, call AMS headquarters at (617) 227-2426, extension 235, browse their website: www.ametsoc.org/ams/amsedu/scholfel.html or contact their email: armstrong@ametsoc.org. GPA must be 3.0-4.0.

American Meteorological Society
Fellowship/Scholarship Coordinator
45 Beacon Street
Boston, MA 02108-3693

Howard M. and Barbara Wolf Family Foundation Scholarship

AMOUNT: $2000 DEADLINE: March 15
MAJOR: All Fields of Study

The Howard M. and Barbara Wolf Family Foundation Scholarship is open to employees of Business Products Industry Association member firms and their families. Persons holding academic records sufficient for acceptance by accredited colleges, junior colleges or technical schools, or persons

already enrolled in one of those institutions are eligible for this four-year award. Selection is made by a committee from the Student Financial Aid Department of The George Washington University, Washington, DC. Award requirements change regularly. Please send a self-addressed, stamped envelope to receive your application and any further instructions from the scholarship provider or email: info@bpia.org. No GPA requirement specified.

Business Products Industry Association
Attn: Scholarship Committee
301 North Fairfax Street
Alexandria, VA 22314-2633

562

Howard M. Wolf Scholarship

AMOUNT: $2000 DEADLINE: March 15
MAJOR: All Fields of Study

The Howard M. Wolf Scholarship is open to employees of Business Products Industry Association member firms and their families. Persons holding academic records sufficient for acceptance by accredited colleges, junior colleges or technical schools, or persons already enrolled in one of those institutions are eligible for this four-year award. Selection is made by a committee from the Student Financial Aid Department of The George Washington University, Washington, DC. Award requirements change regularly. Please send a self-addressed, stamped envelope to receive your application and any further instructions from the scholarship provider or email: info@bpia.org. No GPA requirement specified.

Business Products Industry Association
Attn: Scholarship Committee
301 North Fairfax Street
Alexandria, VA 22314-2633

563

Howard Rock Foundation Scholarship Program

AMOUNT: $2500-$5000 DEADLINE: March 31
MAJOR: All Areas of Study

The Howard Rock Foundation Scholarship Program is open to Alaska Native students who are accepted/enrolled in a four-year undergraduate degree program or a degree program at an accredited college or university. This award is for students who plan on attending school full-time. Undergraduate students must have at least a 2.5 GPA and graduate students must maintain at least a 3.0 GPA. Applicants must demonstrate financial need and have a high school diploma or GED. Award requirements change regularly. GPA must be 2.5-4.0.

CIRI Foundation
Scholarship Coordinator
2600 Cordova Street, Suite 206
Anchorage, AK 99503-2745

564
Howard T. Orville Scholarship In Meteorology

AMOUNT: $2000 DEADLINE: June 14
MAJOR: Meteorology, Atmospheric Sciences, Ocean Sciences, Hydrology

Applicants must be entering their final year in one of the fields listed above. Must be enrolled full-time, have a minimum GPA of 3.0 and be U.S. citizens or permanent residents. Award requirements change regularly. Write to the address listed, sending a self-addressed, stamped envelope for details, call AMS headquarters at (617) 227-2426, extension 235, browse their website: www.ametsoc.org/ams/amsedu/scholfel.html or contact their email: armstrong@ametsoc.org. GPA must be 3.0-4.0.

American Meteorological Society
Fellowship/Scholarship Coordinator
45 Beacon Street
Boston, MA 02108-3693

565
HSF/DOE Environmental Management Scholarship

AMOUNT: $2000-$3000 DEADLINE: June 15
MAJOR: Engineering, Business Management, Science

Open to full-time Hispanic undergraduate students. Applicants must be U.S. citizens or permanent residents, have a minimum 2.8 GPA, and have completed a minimum of 12 undergraduate college credits. Must be pursuing degrees in engineering, science, business management or systems analysis and be pursuing careers supportive of the Department of Energy's goal of environmental restoration and waste management. Award requirements change regularly. To receive an application, please send a self-addressed, stamped business-sized envelope to the address listed. Applications are only available April 15 through June 15. For further information, please call (423) 576-2478, email info@hsf.net or browse their website www.hsf.net. GPA must be 2.8-4.0.

Hispanic Scholarship Fund (HSF)
Selection Committee
One Sansome Street, Suite 1000
San Francisco, CA 94104

566
Hubert H. Humphrey Doctoral Fellowships

AMOUNT: Maximum: $14000 DEADLINE: March 31
MAJOR: Arms Control, Nonproliferation and Disarmament

The Hubert H. Humphrey Doctoral Fellowships in Arms Control, Nonproliferation and Disarmament is designed to encourage specialized training and research in the arms control field. Fellowships are awarded to students from a range of academic fields including political science, economics, law, sociology, psychology, physics, chemistry, biology, public policy, philosophy, international relations, engineering and operations research. To be considered for a fellowship, you must be an advanced graduate student who has completed all of the doctoral requirements except the dissertation or a J.D. candidate in the third or fourth year of law school. You must also

be a U.S. citizen or national. Award requirements change regularly. No GPA requirement specified.

U.S. Department of State, Bureau of Arms Control
Attn: Scholarship Committee
2201 C Street NW, Room 5643
Washington, DC 20520

567
Human Resources Internship

AMOUNT: $2400 DEADLINE: Varies
MAJOR: Human Resources

The Human Resources Internship is open to currently enrolled college or university students majoring in human resources. The human resources intern will assist in the HR office by performing various HR duties. Applicants must have strong computer, interpersonal, written and organizational skills. Students must enjoy working outdoors and be able to lift at least 25 pounds. The internship duration is for twelve-weeks and students must make their own arrangements in the Washington area. FONZ (Friends of the National Zoo) can provide a listing of some lodging opportunities in Washington. The stipend for this internship is $2,400. An essay and two letters of references are required. Award requirements change regularly. For further information, please send a self-addressed, stamped envelope. No GPA requirement specified.

National Zoological Park
Human Resource Office - Internships
3001 Connecticut Avenue, NW,
Washington DC

568
Human Resources Scholarship

AMOUNT: Maximum: $500 DEADLINE: March 1
MAJOR: Human Resources

This award is open to residents of LaPorte or Porter counties (IN). You must have completed at least two years of a college program and be majoring in human resources management or in business with an emphasis in human resources. To be considered, an essay, your transcript of grades and a letter of recommendation from your college professor or advisor is required. Winners will be announced by April 30 and will be invited to attend the Association's May meeting to receive their awards. Award requirements change regularly. GPA must be 2.5-4.0.

Northern Indiana Human Resources Management Association
Purdue Univ. N. Central, Lynne Reglein
1401 South US Hwy 421
Westville, IN 46391

569
I.H. McLendon Memorial Scholarship

AMOUNT: $1000 DEADLINE: May 14
MAJOR: All Areas of Study

The I.H. McLendon Memorial Scholarship is open to high school seniors who have sickle cell disease. Applicants must be residents of Connecticut entering an accredited institution as full-time students. Students must be in the top 1/3 of their graduating class, have a minimum 3.0 GPA, participate in extracurricular activities and demonstrate good citizenship.

Applicants must submit their high school transcript, a physician's letter identifying their sickling condition, three letters of recommendation and a personal statement. Award requirements change regularly. GPA must be 3.0-4.0.

Sickle Cell Disease Association of America/Connecticut Chapter
Gengras Ambulatory Center
114 Woodland Street, Suite 2101
Hartford, CT 06105

570
IABJ Minority Scholarship Awards

AMOUNT: $1000 DEADLINE: March 31
MAJOR: Journalism, Communications

This scholarship is open to African-American second-semester freshmen, sophomores, juniors, and seniors who are studying journalism or some other aspect of communications at an accredited Indiana college or university. In order to apply, you must be attending school full-time. Award requirements change regularly. Applications are accepted year-round. No GPA requirement specified.

Indianapolis Association of Black Journalists
Minority Scholarship Awards
PO Box 441795
Indianapolis, IN 46244-1795

571
IAHPERD Scholarships

AMOUNT: $1000 DEADLINE: March 17
MAJOR: Health, Physical Education, Recreation, Dance

The IAHPERD Scholarships are open to undergraduate health, physical education, recreation and dance majors enrolled in an Iowa college/university. This award requires that you be at least a sophomore and have a minimum GPA of 2.5. Award requirements change regularly. Please send a self-addressed, stamped envelope to receive your application and any further instructions from the scholarship provider. GPA must be 2.5-4.0.

IAHPERD c/o University of Northern Iowa
Attn: Rip Marston
119 WRC
Cedar Falls, IA 50614-0241

572
Idaho Leveraging Educational Assistance Partnership (LEAP) Grant

AMOUNT: None Specified DEADLINE: Varies
MAJOR: All Areas of Study

The Idaho LEAP Grant is open to Idaho residents attending or planning to attend a college or university in Idaho. To be considered for this award, you must demonstrate financial need and submit the FAFSA. Award requirements change regularly. You will automatically be considered for this award when you complete the FAFSA. Contact the financial aid office of the school you are attending or plan to attend for information on application procedures and deadlines. No GPA requirement specified.

Idaho State Board of Education
Attn: Grant and Scholarship Programs
PO Box 83720
Boise, ID 83720-0037

573
IDEA Scholarship

AMOUNT: $500 DEADLINE: February 1
MAJOR: Electronics, Communications

This scholarship is available to students with a minimum technician class amateur radio license who are majoring in electronics or communications at any accredited Indiana college or institution. Applicants must have graduated from an Indiana high school. Award requirements change regularly. Write the address provided, using a self-addressed, stamped envelope, for further information. No GPA requirement specified.

American Radio Relay League
Attn: ARRL Foundation
225 Main Street
Newington, CT 06111-1400

574
IDF/Novartis Scholarship

AMOUNT: $500-$2000 DEADLINE: May 31
MAJOR: All Areas of Study

The IDF/Novartis Scholarship is open to students enrolled in a course of undergraduate study who have been diagnosed with a documented primary immune deficiency disease. To be considered for this award, you should also be a U.S. citizen or permanent U.S. resident. Award requirements change regularly. To receive an application or further information, contact Tamara Brown, Medical Programs Coordinator at (800) 296-4433; or send email to tb@primaryimmune.org. No GPA requirement specified.

Immune Deficiency Foundation
Attn: Scholarship Programs
25 West Chesapeake Avenue, Suite 206
Towson, MD 21204

575
IEHA Education/Scholarship Foundation Award

AMOUNT: Maximum: $500 DEADLINE: January 10
MAJOR: Facilities Management

Scholarship offered to members of the IEHA who are enrolled in a program of study leading to an undergraduate or associate degree. Application involves submitting an original manuscript on housekeeping within any industry segment. Award requirements change regularly. Please send a self-addressed, stamped envelope to receive your application and any further instructions from the scholarship provider or browse their website www.ieha.org or email excel@ieha.org. No GPA requirement specified.

International Executive Housekeepers Association
Educational Department
1001 Eastwind Drive, Suite 301
Westerville, OH 43081-3361

576
IIE Council of Fellows Undergraduate Scholarship

Amount: $600 Deadline: November 15
Major: Industrial Engineering

This scholarship is open to undergraduate students who are enrolled in an industrial engineering program on a full-time basis, who are members of the institute and have a minimum 3.4 GPA. The program enrolled in may be located in the United States and its territories, Canada or Mexico provided that the school's engineering program or equivalent is accredited by an accrediting agency recognized by IIE. The applicants must have a graduation date of May/June 2001 or later and must be nominated by their IE Department heads. Award requirements change regularly. This scholarship was created to reward outstanding academic scholarship and leadership at an undergraduate level. To apply for this scholarship, students do not have to be nominated by a department head or a faculty advisor. Students must send a written request to IIE Headquarters for the Council of Fellows Undergraduate Scholarship application forms. GPA must be 3.4-4.0.

Institute of Industrial Engineers
Attn: Chapter Operations Board
25 Technology Park
Norcross, GA 30092-2988

577
Ilinois AMVETS Auxiliary Worchid Award

Amount: $500 Deadline: March 1
Major: All Areas of Study

The Illinois AMVETS Auxiliary Worchid Award is open to Illinois high school seniors who have taken the American College Test (ACT). In order to apply, you must be an unmarried child of a veteran who served after September 15, 1940. Your parent or parents must have been honorably discharged or be presently serving in the military. Award requirements change regularly. No GPA requirement specified.

AMVETS - Illinois State Headquarters
Illinois AMVETS Scholarship Program
2200 South 6th Street
Springfield, IL 62703-3454

578
Illinois AMVETS Sad Sacks Nursing Scholarship

Amount: $500 Deadline: March 1
Major: Nursing

The Illinois AMVETS Sad Sacks Nursing Scholarships are open to students in an approved School of Nursing program in Illinois or to high school seniors who have been accepted to a nursing program. The selection criteria are based on your academics, character, interests, activity record and financial need. Priority will be given to dependents of a deceased or disabled veteran. Award requirements change regularly. No GPA requirement specified.

AMVETS - Illinois State Headquarters
Illinois AMVETS Scholarship Program
2200 South 6th Street
Springfield, IL 62703-3454

579
Illinois AMVETS Service Foundation Scholarship

Amount: $1000 Deadline: March 1
Major: All Areas of Study

The Illinois AMVETS Service Foundation Scholarship is open to Illinois high school seniors who have taken the American College Test (ACT). In order to apply, you must be an unmarried child of a veteran who served after September 15, 1940. Your parent or parents must have been honorably discharged or be presently serving in the military. Award requirements change regularly. No GPA requirement specified.

AMVETS - Illinois State Headquarters
Illinois AMVETS Scholarship Program
2200 South 6th Street
Springfield, IL 62703-3454

580
Illinois Manufactured Housing Association Scholarship

Amount: $500-$1000 Deadline: March 1
Major: All Areas of Study

The Illinois Manufactured Housing Association Scholarship is open to residents of manufactured housing communities that are members in good standing of the Illinois Manufactured Housing Association. To apply, you must be entering a program of two or more years in an accredited college or university. Award requirements change regularly. Please send a self-addressed, stamped envelope to receive your application and any further instructions from the scholarship provider. No GPA requirement specified.

Illinois Manufactured Housing Association
Attn: Scholarship Coordinator
3888 Peoria Road
Springfield, IL 62702

581
Independence Foundation of Philadelphia Scholarship

Amount: $5000-$20000 Deadline: January 15
Major: Government Service

Open to high school seniors who are planning careers in government service. This scholarship is reserved for qualifying residents of Philadelphia and its surrounding counties: Bucks, Chester, Delaware and Montgomery. Interested students are invited to write a one-page essay stating why he or she plans a career in government service including any inspiration to be derived from the leadership of George Washington in his famous crossing of the Delaware. Students must confine the essay to view points, attitudes and purpose in choice of careers. The award will be paid over a four-year period of $5,000 per year. Award requirements change regularly. For an application and further information, please write to the address listed, including a self-addressed, stamped envelope, browse their websites: www.erols.com/washcrossfdn/scholarship.htm or www.gwcf.org or email: washcrossfdn@erols.com. GPA must be 2.8-4.0.

Washington Crossing Foundation
Attn: Scholarship Administrator
PO Box 503
Levittown, PA 19058-0503

Indian American Scholarship Fund - USA Scholarship

AMOUNT: $500-$1250 DEADLINE: May 20
MAJOR: All Areas of Study

The Indian American Scholarship Fund - USA Scholarship is open to graduating high school seniors in all states other than Georgia. To be considered for this award, you must be of Indian heritage (one or both parents or grandparents from the present-day India; for purposes of these scholarships, citizens of Pakistan and Bangladesh are not included). The award requires that you provide proof of full-time admission to a four-year college, official school transcripts, SAT/ACT score reports and resume, verified by the counselor's office. This award is based on financial need. Award requirements change regularly. No GPA requirement specified.

Indian American Cultural Association
Attn: P. Ravi Sarma, M.D.
2707 Rangewood Drive
Atlanta, GA 30345-1577

583
Indian Health Service Scholarships

AMOUNT: Maximum: $30000 DEADLINE: February 19
MAJOR: Health-Related Fields

The Indian Health Service Scholarship is open to Native Americans and Alaskan Natives who are seeking an education in the health fields. A service commitment is required for scholarship participation. Award requirements change regularly. Write to the address listed, enclosing a self-addressed, stamped envelope for an application and further information or contact your school's financial aid office, or call (301) 443-6197. No GPA requirement specified.

Indian Health Service Scholarship - Twinbrook Metro Plaza
Grant Management Branch
12300 Twinbrook Parkway, Suite 100
Rockville, MD 20852-1606

584
Indiana Higher Education Grant

AMOUNT: None Specified DEADLINE: March 1
MAJOR: All Areas of Study

The Indiana Higher Education Grant is open to high school graduates and GED recipients who attend or plan to attend an eligible Indiana postsecondary institution as full-time undergraduate students. To be considered for this award, you must be an Indiana resident, demonstrate financial need and file a FAFSA by March 1 (which precedes the academic year you plan to enroll). There is no additional grant application. Award requirements change regularly. Questions about this award

should be directed to the SSACI. You may write to the address provided or send email to grants@ssaci.state.in.us. Additional information may be found online at www.state.in.us/ssaci. No GPA requirement specified.

State Student Assistance Commission of Indiana
Attn: Scholarship Committee
150 West Market Street, Suite 500
Indianapolis, IN 46204

585
Indiana Retired Teachers Association Scholarships

AMOUNT: None Specified DEADLINE: February 15
MAJOR: Education

The Indiana Retired Teachers Association Scholarships are available to juniors attending colleges or universities in Indiana. You must be an Indiana resident and the child, grand-child, legal dependents or spouse of an active, retired or deceased member of the IRTA. You must have at least a "C" average. Award requirements change regularly. For further information contact the address listed enclosing a self-addressed, stamped envelope with your request, call (317) 637-7481. GPA must be 2.0-4.0.

Indiana Retired Teachers Association
Scholarship Coordinator
150 West Market Street, Suite 610
Indianapolis, IN 46204-2812

586
Individual Seminarian Grant

AMOUNT: $500 DEADLINE: May 31
MAJOR: Theology, Religious Studies, Ministry

The Individual Seminarian Grant is open to American Baptist students who are attending a seminary not related to the American Baptist Church. Seminarians must be enrolled at least two-third time in one of the following first professional degree programs: M.Div., M.C.E., M.A.C.E., M.R.E. (D.Min. students are not eligible). Applicants must be members of an American Baptist church for at least one year before applying for aid and enrolled at an accredited educational institution in the U.S. or Puerto Rico. U.S. citizenship is required. Award requirements change regularly. Please send a self-addressed, stamped envelope to receive your application and any further instructions from the scholarship provider. No GPA requirement specified.

American Baptist Financial Aid Program
Educational Ministries ABC/USA
PO Box 851
Valley Forge, PA 19482-0851

587
International Association of Culinary Professionals Scholarship

AMOUNT: $500-$10000 DEADLINE: December 1
MAJOR: Culinary Arts

Culinary scholarships for basic, continuing and specialty education courses in the United States and abroad. Applicant must be 18 years of age and have foodservice work experience.

Award requirements change regularly. For further information please send a stamped, self-addressed envelope to the address provided. You may also consult the IACP website at www.iacp.com. No GPA requirement specified.

International Association of Culinary Professionals
Ellen McKnight, Director of Development
304 West Liberty Street, Suite 201
Louisville, KY 40202-3011

588
International Brotherhood of Electrical Workers Scholarship Fund

AMOUNT: $2000-$5000 DEADLINE: Varies
MAJOR: All Areas of Study

Scholarships for sons and daughters of members of Local Union #3 of the International Brotherhood of Electrical Workers (IBEW). Applicants must be graduating high school seniors and the qualifying parent must have been employed (or available for employment) for at least five years, by employer(s) who contribute to the Educational and Cultural Fund. Award requirements change regularly. Contact your parent's Local Union #3 or write to the address listed, including a self-addressed, stamped envelope for details. No GPA requirement specified.

Educational and Cultural Fund of the Electrical Industry
Scholarship Program
15811 Harry Van Arsdale Jr. Ave.
Fresh Meadows, NY 11365-3067

589
International Food Service Executives Association Scholarship

AMOUNT: None Specified DEADLINE: February 1
MAJOR: Foodservice, Hospitality

This scholarship is open to students enrolled in or accepted full-time at a two- or four-year college or university. In order to apply, you must be in a food service-related major. You must provide a personal statement regarding background, goals, aptitudes and interests along with your transcript of grades and letters of recommendation. Award requirements change regularly. For any further information, call (954) 977-0767. GPA must be 2.9-4.0.

International Food Service Executives Association
Scholarship Coordinator
1100 South State Road 7, Suite 103
Margate, FL 33068-4033

590
International Morgan Connection Scholarship

AMOUNT: $2000 DEADLINE: March 1
MAJOR: All Areas of Study

This scholarship is awarded annually to a student who is in one of the following three divisions: 1) Western Seat Exhibitor (including pleasure and equitation) 2) Hunter Seat Exhibitor (including pleasure and equitation) 3) Saddle Seat Exhibitor

(including pleasure, park, and equitation). In order to apply, you must be currently showing a Morgan horse in the Western Seat, Hunter Seat or Saddle Seat divisions. The scholarship will be paid directly to a college or university, trade school or vocational training program within two years after the award of the scholarship. Upon receipt of the award, you must present a written request for payment to the designated school. Award requirements change regularly. No GPA requirement specified.

American Morgan Horse Institute, Inc.
Mrs. Sally Plumley, AMHI Scholarships
PO Box 837
Shelburne, VT 05482-0519

591
Iowa Federation of Labor, AFL-CIO Scholarship

AMOUNT: $1500 DEADLINE: March 19
MAJOR: All Areas of Study

This scholarship is open to all seniors graduating from accredited high schools in Iowa. To compete for the scholarship, you must write an essay (500 to 750 words) on the following subject: "Describe two major contributions of the American Labor movement and discuss their impact on workplace justice." It is recommended that you read "The Labor Movement in the United States" by Jack Flagler prior to writing the essay. Award requirements change regularly. No GPA requirement specified.

Iowa Federation of Labor, AFL-CIO
Mark L. Smith Secretary Treasurer
2000 Walker Street, Suite A
Des Moines, IA 50317-5201

592
Iowa Tuition Grant

AMOUNT: Maximum: $3150 DEADLINE: Varies
MAJOR: All Fields of Study

The Iowa Tuition Grant is open to Iowa residents who attend private colleges and universities in Iowa. To be considered for this award, you must meet the following criteria: be a U.S. citizen, permanent resident or refugee (as defined by the U.S. Immigration and Naturalization Agency); be enrolled or plan to enroll at least part-time (three hours minimum) in an undergraduate degree program at an eligible Iowa school; submit the FAFSA; and demonstrate financial need. Priority is given to the neediest applicants. Award requirements change regularly. Submit the FAFSA as soon as possible after January 1. To be considered for this grant, you must list an eligible Iowa independent college, business school or nursing school on the original application; for priority consideration, your application should reach the processing center by April 21. You may also visit the Iowa College Student Aid Commission (ICSAC) website at www.state.ia.us. No GPA requirement specified.

Iowa College Student Aid Commission
Attn: Grant and Scholarship Programs
200 10th Street, Fourth Floor
Des Moines, IA 50309-2036

593
Irene W. Hart Scholarship

AMOUNT: $1000 DEADLINE: April 1
MAJOR: Education

This scholarship is open to undergraduate seniors in an accredited New Hampshire college or university who are graduates of a New Hampshire high school. You must apply by April 1 of your junior year. You must also demonstrate financial need and academic achievement as well as submit an essay outlining your educational goals for your profession as a teacher. Award requirements change regularly. GPA must be 2.8-4.0.

New Hampshire Retired Educators Association (NHREA)
Attn: Roland R Boucher, Chair
331 Mountain Road
Jaffrey, NH 03452-5923

594
IREX Developmental Fellowships

AMOUNT: None Specified DEADLINE: November 1
MAJOR: Eastern European Policy, Eurasian Policy, Foreign Policy

This award is a grant of two to twelve months to predoctoral and postdoctoral scholars for research at an institution in any country in Central and Eastern Europe and Eurasia. This grant is open to U.S. citizens who have a full-time affiliation with a college or university as a faculty member or doctoral candidate who has completed all the requirements for a Ph.D. except the dissertation by the time of participation. Independent scholars or recipients of professional degrees may also qualify. Normally, command of the host country language sufficient for advanced research is required of all research applicants. Award requirements change regularly. Write to the address listed below for information. No GPA requirement specified.

International Research and Exchange Board
Fellowship Program
1616 H Street NW
Washington, DC 20006-4903

595
Irving W. Cook, WA0CGS Scholarship

AMOUNT: $1000 DEADLINE: February 1
MAJOR: Electronics, Communications or Related Fields

This scholarship is available to students with any class amateur radio license who are residents of Kansas. The applicants must be pursuing a baccalaureate or higher degree in the areas of electronics, communications or related fields. Award requirements change regularly. Write the address provided, using a self-addressed, stamped envelope, for further information. No GPA requirement specified.

American Radio Relay League
Attn: ARRL Foundation
225 Main Street
Newington, CT 06111-1400

596
Isaac Lipton Memorial Scholarship

AMOUNT: $100 DEADLINE: Varies
MAJOR: All Fields of Study

The Isaac Lipton Memorial Scholarship is awarded to the valedictorian of the senior class of Burlington High School (Burlington, WI). Award requirements change regularly. Please visit your Guidance Office to receive any additional details. No GPA requirement specified.

Burlington High School
Attn: Guidance Office
225 Robert Street
Burlington, WI 53105

597
Isabel B. Watt Memorial Scholarship

AMOUNT: None Specified DEADLINE: December 1
MAJOR: Music

This memorial scholarship is open to a Connecticut high school graduate who is attending a Connecticut college or university and majoring in music. The applicant must be a sophomore, junior or senior attending school full-time. An audition by the applicant is mandatory and will be scheduled by appointment in January. Award requirements change regularly. For further information about this scholarship, please email cathysteele@home.com or send a self-addressed, stamped envelope to the address provided. No GPA requirement specified.

Plainville Choral Society
Isabel B. Watt Memorial Scholarship
25 Locust Street
Plainville, CT 06062

598
Itam Lodge No. 564 Scholarship

AMOUNT: $500 DEADLINE: May 1
MAJOR: All Areas of Study

Scholarships for Berkshire County (MA) high school seniors and continuing education students enrolled full-time at a college or university. The applicant must be a lodge member or have a parent or grandparent who belongs to Itam lodge. High School applications are due by May 1 and applicants who are continuing their education (beyond first year) and are enrolled full-time are to send in their applications by June 15. Award requirements change regularly. Please send a self-addressed, stamped envelope to receive your application and any further instructions from the scholarship provider. The address is Scholarship Committee, Itam Lodge, P.O. Box 1514, Pittsfield, MA 01202. No GPA requirement specified.

Itam Lodge No. 564
PO Box 1514
Pittsfield, MA 01202

599
Ivy Parker Memorial Scholarship

AMOUNT: $2000   DEADLINE: February 1
MAJOR: Engineering, Computer Science

The Ivy Parker Memorial Scholarship is open to junior and senior women who are majoring in engineering or computer science in an accredited ABET program or an SWE-approved school. You must be able to demonstrate financial need and have a minimum GPA of 3.5. Award requirements change regularly. Please send a self-addressed, stamped envelope to receive your application. GPA must be 3.5-4.0. Society of Women Engineers Headquarters
Scholarship Coordinator
120 Wall Street, FL 11
New York, NY 10005-3902

600
Ixtlan Technologies Scholarship

AMOUNT: $1000   DEADLINE: March 31
MAJOR: All Fields of Study

The Ixtlan Technologies Scholarship is open to high school seniors who are of Hispanic heritage. To be considered for this award, you must have graduated from a Lenawee County high school (MI). Award requirements change regularly. Please send a self-addressed, stamped envelope to receive your application and any further instructions from the scholarship provider. No GPA requirement specified.

Morenci High School
Attn: Mrs. Melissa Parnell
788 Coomer Street
Morenci, MI 49256

601
J. Russell Salisbury Memorial Scholarship

AMOUNT: $450   DEADLINE: May 26
MAJOR: All Areas of Study

This memorial scholarship is available to undergraduates who are members of Tau Kappa Epsilon. In order to apply, you must demonstrate leadership within your chapter, on campus or in the community. You must also have a minimum 2.5 GPA and be a full-time student in good standing. Award requirements change regularly. For further information, call (317) 872-6533, email: tef@tkehq.org or visit the website at: www.tke.org. GPA must be 2.5-4.0.

TKE Educational Foundation
Attn: Timothy L. Taschwer
8645 Founders Road
Indianapolis, IN 46268-1336

602
Jacob Rassen Memorial Scholarship

AMOUNT: Maximum: $1900   DEADLINE: Varies
MAJOR: All Areas of Study

The purpose of the Jacob Rassen Memorial Scholarship is to provide annual scholarships to Jewish students under 22 years of age for an Israel study trip. Applicants must demonstrate

financial need and be residents of San Francisco, San Mateo, northern Santa Clara, Marin or Sonoma counties in California. Deadlines vary; therefore, it is encouraged that applicants apply early. Award requirements change regularly. No GPA requirement specified.

Jewish Family and Children's Services
Attn: Loans and Grants Department
2245 Post Street
San Francisco, CA 94115

603
Jacobs Research Funds Small Grants Program

AMOUNT: Maximum: $1200   DEADLINE: February 15
MAJOR: Anthropology

Grants for students with any level of academic credentials who are doing research which supports the sociocultural or linguistic aspects of anthropology among living American native peoples. The primary focus of study is of the Pacific Northwest, but other areas in Canada, Mexico and the continental U.S., including Alaska, will be considered. Successful applicants will be required to conduct the research as described in their application, to keep a record as to how funding is spent, to file a final report and to deposit safe copies of field materials. This grant is made for a period of up to one year and is renewable with an application. Award requirements change regularly. Please write to the following address enclosing a self-addressed, stamped envelope. No GPA requirement specified.

Whatcom Museum
Jacobs Funds Administrator
121 Prospect Street
Bellingham, WA 98225-4401

604
James A. Finnegan Summer Internship Contest

AMOUNT: $1000-$1500   DEADLINE: February 4
MAJOR: Political Science, Government

The James A. Finnegan Summer Internship Contest is open to undergraduates attending accredited Pennsylvania colleges/universities and students from Pennsylvania attending any accredited college/university who have completed at least one semester of study. The contest provides monetary awards of $1,000-$1,500 and paid summer internships lasting between eight and ten weeks. Interns are assigned positions in state government executive offices under the governors jurisdiction and attend seminars with leading public officials and media figures. Award requirements change regularly. Please send a self-addressed, stamped envelope to receive your application and any further instructions from the scholarship provider; or visit their website at members.aol.com/JAFINNEGAN; or send email to BBAM200@aol.com. No GPA requirement specified.

James A. Finnegan Fellowship Foundation
Contest Coordinator
3600 Raymond Street
Reading, PA 19605

James A. Turner Jr. Memorial Scholarship

AMOUNT: $3000 DEADLINE: January 15
MAJOR: Business, Welding

The James A. Turner Jr. Memorial Scholarship is awarded to full-time students pursuing a minimum four-year bachelor of business degree leading to a management career in welding store operations or a welding distributorship. You must have at least a high school diploma and be employed by a welding store or distributorship at least ten hours a week. Other requirements include that you be a U.S. citizen and be planning to attend an academic institution located within the U.S. This award is renewable. Award requirements change regularly. Please send a self-addressed, stamped envelope to receive your application and any further instructions from the scholarship provider or call (305) 445-6628. No GPA requirement specified.

American Welding Society Foundation, Inc.
National Education Scholarship Committee
550 Northwest LeJeune Road
Miami, FL 33126-4165

606
James and Mary Dawson Scholarship

AMOUNT: $5000 DEADLINE: March 15
MAJOR: All Areas of Study

The James and Mary Dawson Scholarship is open to students from Scotland coming to America for graduate studies. The award is based on financial need, academic achievement and goals. Consideration is made for students who continue to enhance their knowledge of Scottish history or culture. All applicants must be able to cite their Scottish descent and must submit a statement of their plans and goals. Award requirements change regularly. Please send a self-addressed, stamped envelope to receive your application and any further instructions from the scholarship provider. You may consult the website address provided. No GPA requirement specified.

St. Andrew's Society of Washington, DC.
James Mcleod, Chairman
7012 Arandale Road
Bethesda, MD 20817-4702

607
James F. Connolly/CIS Memorial Scholarship

AMOUNT: $3000 DEADLINE: April 1
MAJOR: Law

The James F. Connolly/CIS Memorial Scholarship is open to law librarians with a degree from an ALA-accredited library school who work primarily with government documents and who are working towards a degree in an ABA-accredited law school. Award requirements change regularly. Please send a self-addressed, stamped envelope to receive your application and any further instructions from the scholarship provider; or download the scholarship application and instructions from their website at www.aallnet.org/services/scholarships.asp. No GPA requirement specified.

American Association of Law Libraries
Attn: Scholarship Committee
53 West Jackson Blvd, Suite 940
Chicago, IL 60604

608
James L. Allhands Essay Competition

AMOUNT: $2300 DEADLINE: November 1
MAJOR: Civil Engineering/Construction

The James L. Allhands Essay Competition is open to full-time seniors in a four-year ABET- or ACCE-accredited (or candidate status) university construction or construction-oriented civil engineering program. Original essays will be judged and awards totaling $2,300 will be given to the first, second and third place students and faculty. Award requirements change regularly. No GPA requirement specified.

Associated General Contractors Education and Research Foundation
Attn: Director of Programs
333 John Carlyle Street, 2nd Floor
Alexandria, VA 22314-5743

609
James Madison Junior Fellowship

AMOUNT: Maximum: $24000 DEADLINE: March 1
MAJOR: American History, Political Science, Social Studies, American Government

The James Madison Junior Fellowship is open to college seniors and graduates without teaching experience who intend to enroll in graduate study leading to one of the following master's degrees (listed in the order of the Foundation's preference): a master's degree in history or political science; a degree of Master of Arts in Teaching in history or social studies; a related master's degree in education that permits a concentration in history, government, social studies, or political science. Fellowship recipients must take at least 12 semester hours or the equivalent in topics directly related to the framing and history of the U.S. Constitution. Recipients must agree to teach American history, American government or social studies full-time in grades 7-12 for no less than one year for each full academic year of study under a fellowship. Award requirements change regularly. Please send a self-addressed, stamped envelope to receive your application and any further instructions from the scholarship provider; or call (800) 525-6928; or send email to Recogprog@act.org; or visit the website at www.jamesmadison.com. No GPA requirement specified.

James Madison Memorial Fellowship Foundation
2201 North Dodge Street
PO Box 4030
Iowa City, IA 52243-4030

610
James Madison Senior Fellowship

AMOUNT: Maximum: $24000 DEADLINE: March 1
MAJOR: American History, Political Science, Social Studies, American Government

The James Madison Senior Fellowship is open to full-time teachers of American History, American government, or social studies in grades 7-12. This fellowship allows experienced secondary school teachers to enroll in graduate study leading to one of the following master's degrees (listed in the order of the Foundation's preference): a master's degree in history or political science; a degree of Master of Arts in Teaching in history or social studies; a related master's degree in education that permits a concentration in history, government, social studies, or political science. Fellowship recipients must take at least 12 semester hours or the equivalent in topics directly related to the framing and history of the U.S. Constitution. Award requirements change regularly. Please send a self-addressed, stamped envelope to receive your application and any further instructions from the scholarship provider; or call (800) 525-6928; or send email to Recogprog@act.org; or visit the website at www.jamesmadison.com. No GPA requirement specified.

James Madison Memorial Fellowship Foundation
2201 North Dodge Street
PO Box 4030
Iowa City, IA 52243-4030

611
James T. Kane Memorial Scholarship

AMOUNT: $850 DEADLINE: May 26
MAJOR: All Areas of Study

The James T. Kane Memorial Scholarship is open to initiated undergraduate members of Tau Kappa Epsilon. In order to apply, you must be in good standing with your chapter, have a demonstrated record of active participation within the chapter, including officer and chairmanship leadership positions. Also, you must be active in campus organizations, be a full-time student and have a minimum 2.5 GPA. Award requirements change regularly. For further information, call (317) 872-6533, email: tef@tkehq.org or visit the website at: www.tke.org. GPA must be 2.5-4.0.

TKE Educational Foundation
Attn: Timothy L. Taschwer
8645 Founders Road
Indianapolis, IN 46268-1336

612
James V. Day Scholarship

AMOUNT: None Specified DEADLINE: May 1
MAJOR: All Areas of Study

Open to residents of Maine who are children or grandchildren of veterans who belong to an American Legion Post in Maine. For high school seniors, undergraduates, graduate students or nontraditional students returning to school. Must be U.S. citizens. Award requirements change regularly. Write to the address listed, enclosing a self-addressed, stamped envelope for an application and further information. No GPA requirement specified.

American Legion - Maine
Department Adjutant State Headquarters
PO Box 900
Waterville, ME 04903-0900

613
Jane Coffin Childs Fund Postdoctoral Fellowship

AMOUNT: $28000 DEADLINE: February 1
MAJOR: Cancer Research, Oncology

This fellowship is for a three-year period, with increases in stipend each year. Applicants must hold an M.D. or Ph.D. and submit a research proposal for study into the causes, origins, and treatment of cancer. No restrictions on citizenship or institution. Recipients in general should not have more than one year of postdoctoral experience. Award requirements change regularly. For further information, please write to the address listed, including a self-addressed, stamped envelope. No GPA requirement specified.

Jane Coffin Childs Memorial Fund for Medical Research
Office of the Director, PO Box 3333
333 Cedar Street
New Haven, CT 06510-0333

614
Jane Karow 1st District Nursing Scholarship/Woman's Club

AMOUNT: None Specified DEADLINE: Varies
MAJOR: Nursing

The Jane Karow 1st District Nursing Scholarship/Woman's Club is open to senior Burlington High School (Burlington, WI) students who will study nursing. Eligible students can be entering any of the following nursing program options: one-year practical nursing degree; two-year practical associate degree; three-year diploma degree; four-year Baccalaureate degree. Award requirements change regularly. Please visit your Guidance Office to receive an application and any additional details. No GPA requirement specified.

Burlington High School
Attn: Guidance Office
225 Robert Street
Burlington, WI 53105

615
Janet Romine Chatfield Business Scholarship

AMOUNT: None Specified DEADLINE: February 1
MAJOR: Business

The Janet Romine Chatfield Business Scholarship is open to graduates of North Central High School in Sullivan County (IN) who plan to pursue a degree in business. You must be entering or enrolled in an accredited college or university, maintain a minimum 3.0 GPA and demonstrate financial need. Award requirements change regularly. Please send a self-addressed, stamped envelope to receive your application and further information from the scholarship provider or call (812) 232-2234. You will also find the application online at www.wvcf.com. GPA must be 3.0-4.0.

Wabash Valley Community Foundation
Community Scholarship Program
2901 Ohio Boulevard, Suite 153
Terre Haute, IN 47803

616
Jazz Club of Sarasota Scholarships

AMOUNT: Maximum: $5000 DEADLINE: April 1
MAJOR: All Areas of Study

This scholarship is open to high school seniors and college students who are under the age of 26 and involved in jazz. In order to apply, you must submit a letter of reference from a sponsoring musician or teacher along with a videotape containing ten minutes of performance with a three-minute verbal introduction. The performance must include two tunes - one ballad and one up-tempo - plus at least 24 bars of jazz-style improvisation on the blues. Award requirements change regularly. No GPA requirement specified.

Jazz Club of Sarasota
Scholarship Committee
290 Coconut Avenue, Bldg 3
Sarasota, FL 34236-4979

617
Jeanne E. Bray Scholarship

AMOUNT: $1000 DEADLINE: November 15
MAJOR: All Areas of Study

This scholarship is open to children of law enforcement professionals, current or retired, who are members of the NRA or who lost their lives in the line of duty and were NRA members at that time. Award requirements change regularly. Please write to the address listed for more information, sending a self-addressed, stamped envelope, or visit their website at www.nra.org. GPA must be 2.5-4.0.

National Rifle Association - Field Operations Division
Attn: Event Services Coordinator
11250 Waples Mill Road
Fairfax, VA 22030-7400

618
Jeanne Humphrey Block Dissertation Award

AMOUNT: $2500 DEADLINE: April 1
MAJOR: Gender Studies, Women's Studies, Human Development, Social and Behavioral Sciences

The Jeanne Humphrey Block Dissertation Award is open to female doctoral students. Proposals should focus on sex and gender differences or some developmental issue of particular concern to women or girls. Projects drawing on Murray Center data will be given priority, although use of the center's resources is not required. The Henry A. Murray Research Center is a national repository of social and behavioral sciences data for the study of lives over time with a special focus on the lives of American women. Award requirements change regularly. Please send a self-addressed, stamped envelope to receive your application and any further instructions from the Murray Center; or visit their website at www.radcliffe.edu/murray. No GPA requirement specified.

Radcliffe College - Henry A. Murray Research Center
Attn: Grants Program Coordinator
10 Garden Street
Cambridge, MA 02138

619
Jerry Jones Scholarship

AMOUNT: $2000 DEADLINE: March 15
MAJOR: All Fields of Study

The Jerry Jones Scholarship is open to employees of Business Products Industry Association member firms and their families. Persons holding academic records sufficient for acceptance by accredited colleges, junior colleges or technical schools, or persons already enrolled in one of those institutions are eligible for this one-year award. Selection is made by a committee from the Student Financial Aid Department of The George Washington University, Washington, DC. Award requirements change regularly. Please send a self-addressed, stamped envelope to receive your application and any further instructions from the scholarship provider or email: info@bpia.org. No GPA requirement specified.

Business Products Industry Association
Attn: Scholarship Committee
301 North Fairfax Street
Alexandria, VA 22314-2633

620
Jerry Newson Scholarships

AMOUNT: $500-$2500 DEADLINE: Varies
MAJOR: Social Sciences

Open to high school graduates and adults who have been "out in the world." Applicants must be residents of Davidson County, TN, have a high school diploma or GED, be enrolled in a four-year accredited institution of higher education, and be pursuing a degree in the social sciences or areas where they will be helping and giving back to the community. Award requirements change regularly. You may call (615) 321-4939 for further information. GPA must be 2.0-4.0.

Community Foundation of Middle Tennessee
Scholarship Committee
210 23rd Avenue North
Nashville, TN 37203-1502

621
Jessica Savitch Scholarship

AMOUNT: None Specified DEADLINE: April 15
MAJOR: Communications Related

Open to full-time college sophomore, junior, senior or graduate students majoring in a communications-related field (such as English, journalism, communications, speech and theatre, law, marketing or broadcasting) at a college or university in New York, New Jersey, or Connecticut. Undergraduates must have a 3.0 GPA overall and a 3.5 or better GPA in their major and graduates must have a minimum 3.75 GPA. A 300-500-word essay exploring the theme "Did freedom of the press go too far in the coverage of President Clinton and Monica Lewinski?" will be required. Award requirements change regularly. For further information and an application, please write to the address listed, including a self-addressed, stamped envelope, call (212) 297-2133 or you may visit their website: www.nywici.org. GPA must be 3.0-4.0.

Women In Communications, Inc., New York Chapter
Scholarship Committee
355 Lexington Avenue
New York, NY 10017-6603

622

Jimmy A. Young Memorial Scholarship

AMOUNT: $1000 DEADLINE: June 30
MAJOR: Respiratory Therapy

This scholarship is open to minority students in an AMA-accepted respiratory care program. The foundation prefers that you are nominated by your schools but "any student may initiate a request of sponsorship by the school." You must have a minimum 3.0, and provide a copy of your birth certificate, social security card, immigration visa or evidence of citizenship. The award recipient will be selected by September 1. This award also includes registration for the AARC Respiratory International Congress, airfare, one night lodging and a certificate of recognition. Award requirements change regularly. GPA must be 3.0-4.0.

American Respiratory Care Foundation
Education Recognition Award
11030 Ables Lane
Dallas, TX 75229-4524

623

JJR Research Grant

AMOUNT: $2000 DEADLINE: August 2
MAJOR: Landscape Architecture

The JJR Research Grant is open to landscape architects who have been in professional practice for a minimum of five years and are interested in doing research in areas relating to sustainable development. "Sustainable development" is defined by the U.N.'s Commission on Environment and Development as development that "meets the needs of the present without compromising the ability of future generations to meet their own needs." Award requirements change regularly. If you should have any questions, please visit the sponsor's website. No GPA requirement specified.

Landscape Architecture Foundation
Scholarship Program
636 'I' Street NW
Washington, DC 20001-3736

624

Joe Ann Steele Insurance Center Scholarship

AMOUNT: Maximum: $1000 DEADLINE: March 31
MAJOR: All Fields of Study

The Joe Ann Steele Insurance Center Scholarship is open to Lenawee County (MI) residents who are seeking a new career or career enhancement. Your training may take place at a vocational center, community college, public or private college or university. You are not restricted to a Michigan institution to be eligible for the award. Award requirements change regularly. Please send a self-addressed, stamped envelope to receive your application and any further instructions from the scholarship provider. No GPA requirement specified.

Morenci High School
Attn: Mrs. Melissa Parnell
788 Coomer Street
Morenci, MI 49256

625

Joe Cribari Scholarship

AMOUNT: $1000 DEADLINE: Varies
MAJOR: All Areas of Study

Open to Rocky Mountain High School (CO) seniors. Applicants must be graduating members of one of the three Poudre School District High School football teams, have a minimum 3.5 cumulative GPA, and have goals to attend any degree-granting institution. Applicants must also have demonstrated leadership, good sportsmanship, and have excelled in the sport of football. An essay may be required. Application deadline, procedure, and award amount vary annually. Award requirements change regularly. Applications are available in January or February in the Rocky Mountain High School Career Center, as part of the Local Scholarship Packet. GPA must be 3.5-4.0.

Rocky Mountain High School
Scholarship Committee
1300 West Swallow Road
Fort Collins, CO 80526-2412

626

Joel Garcia Memorial Scholarship

AMOUNT: $250-$2000 DEADLINE: March 31
MAJOR: Journalism

This scholarship is open to Latino high school seniors and full-time undergraduates pursuing careers in journalism. In order to apply, you must be a resident of California or attend an accredited school in California. You will also need to submit samples of your work. An essay and transcripts, among other items, will be required. Award requirements change regularly. No GPA requirement specified.

California Chicano News Media Association
USC School of Journalism
3502 Watt Way, ASC G10
Los Angeles, CA 90089-0281

627

John Bayliss Broadcast Foundation Scholarship

AMOUNT: $5000 DEADLINE: April 28
MAJOR: Radio Broadcasting

The John Bayliss Broadcast Foundation Scholarships are available for outstanding junior, senior or graduate students studying for a career in radio broadcasting (not including TV broadcasting). To apply, you must have a minimum 3.0 GPA. Along with your application, you will also need to submit a transcript, three letters of recommendation evaluating your scholastic and personal strengths and an essay outlining future broadcasting goals. Award requirements change regularly. No GPA requirement specified.

John Bayliss Broadcast Foundation
Chairperson/Bayliss Scholarship
PO Box 221070
Carmel, CA 93922-1070

628

John F. and Anna Lee Stacey Scholarship

AMOUNT: $5000 DEADLINE: February 1
MAJOR: Fine Arts (Painting and Drawing)

The John F. and Anna Lee Stacey Scholarship is open to U.S. citizens between the ages of 18 and 35, who are fine art majors specializing in painting and drawing. All applicants are required to submit 35mm slides of their artwork by February 1. Award requirements change regularly. No GPA requirement specified. National Cowboy Hall of Fame and Western

Heritage Center
Attn: Scholarship Fund
1700 NE 63rd Street
Oklahoma City, OK 73111

629

John H. Litzelman Memorial Scholarship

AMOUNT: $850 DEADLINE: May 26
MAJOR: All Areas of Study

This scholarship is open to initiated undergraduate members of Tau Kappa Epsilon. In order to apply, you must be in good standing with your chapter, have a demonstrated record of active participation within the chapter, including officer and chairmanship leadership positions. Also, you must be active in campus organizations, be a full-time student and have a minimum 2.5 GPA. Award requirements change regularly. For further information, call (317) 872-6533, email: tef@tkehq.org or visit the website at: www.tke.org. GPA must be 2.5-4.0.

TKE Educational Foundation
Attn: Timothy L. Taschwer
8645 Founders Road
Indianapolis, IN 46268-1336

630

John Hebner Memorial Scholarship

AMOUNT: $600 DEADLINE: March 1
MAJOR: All Areas of Study

This scholarship is open to students who are legally blind, are employed on a full-time basis, and need additional funding for school while they are working. Award requirements change regularly. Write to the address listed, enclosing a self-addressed, stamped envelope for an application and further information. No GPA requirement specified.

American Council of the Blind
Attn: Billie Jean Keith
1155 15th Street NW, Suite 720
Washington, DC 20005-2706

631

John J. Wasmuth Postdoctoral Fellowship

AMOUNT: $23292-$35300 DEADLINE: August 15
MAJOR: Hereditary Diseases, Disease Pathology, Medicine

This award is open to researchers studying areas of interest regard Huntington's Disease, including trinucleotide expansions, animal models, gene therapy, neurobiology and development of the basal ganglia, cell survival and death, and intercellular signaling in striatal neurons. Anyone accepting funding from the Hereditary Disease Foundation must agree to abide by the following policy: Propagatable materials should be freely available to other investigators following publication. Deadlines are February 15, August 15 and October 15. Thirty (30) copies of the completed application should be forwarded. If reprints are to be considered as part of the application, eight (8) copies should be provided for primary review. Award requirements change regularly. To obtain an application, please submit a letter of intent at anytime by post to the address provided or by email at the website: www.hdfoundation.org/intent.htm. No GPA requirement specified.

Hereditary Disease Foundation
Dr. Allan Tobin, Scientific Director
1427 7th Street, #2
Santa Monica, CA 90401

632

Johnson and Wales University Scholarship

AMOUNT: $500-$10000 DEADLINE: March 1
MAJOR: All Areas of Study

The Johnson and Wales University Scholarship is open to high school seniors or current college students. To be considered for the award, you must be an FBLA (Future Business Leaders Association) national and state dues-paid member. If you are attending college, it must be a college other than Johnson and Wales. Award requirements change regularly. Please request an application form and related information from Johnson and Wales University's National Student Organizations Office at (800) DIAL-JWU (342-5598), ext. 2345. No GPA requirement specified.

Future Business Leaders of America
Attn: Scholarship Coordinator
1912 Association Drive
Reston, VA 22091

633

Jones-Laurence Award for Scholastic Achievement

AMOUNT: $1000-$3500 DEADLINE: April 17
MAJOR: All Areas of Study

Awarded annually to the junior, senior, or graduate brother who displays the most outstanding academic achievement. The selection process for each chapter's nominee should yield the most deserving candidate for the honor. Award requirements change regularly. For further information, please write to the address listed, including a self-addressed, stamped envelope, call (847) 475-1856 ext. 223, fax (847) 475-2250, or email: rparker@sae.net. You may also visit their website: www.sae.net. GPA must be 3.5-4.0.

Sigma Alpha Epsilon Foundation
SAE Awards Committee
PO Box 1856
Evanston, IL 60204-1856

634
Joseph L. Fisher Doctoral Dissertation Fellowship

AMOUNT: $12000 DEADLINE: February 26
MAJOR: Natural Resources, Energy, Environmental Sciences

Open to doctoral candidates in their final year of dissertation research in economics on issues relating to natural resources, energy, or the environment. Awards will be announced in April. Award requirements change regularly. Please send a self-addressed, stamped envelope to receive your application and any further instructions from the fellowship provider or browse their website www.rff.org. No GPA requirement specified.

Resources for the Future
Coordinator for Academic Programs
1616 P Street NW
Washington, DC 20036-1434

635
Joseph R. Stone Scholarship

AMOUNT: $2400 DEADLINE: July 28
MAJOR: Travel and Tourism

Three awards are available for undergraduates in the field of travel and tourism. Students must submit a 500-word essay on their career goals in the travel industry. One parent must also be employed in the travel industry (i.e., car rental, airlines, hotel, travel agency, etc.). Award requirements change regularly. Write to the address listed, enclosing a self-addressed, stamped envelope for an application and further information. You can browse their website: www.astanet.com or email: myriaml@astahq.com. No GPA requirement specified.

American Society of Travel Agents
Attn: ASTA Foundation
1101 King Street, Suite 200
Alexandria, VA 22314-2944

636
Josephine P. White Eagle Graduate Assistance Forgiveness Program

AMOUNT: None Specified DEADLINE: Varies
MAJOR: Law, Health, Education, Business, Social Work

This assistance program helps Ho-Chunk Nation members who have completed an undergraduate program from an accredited college or university. Must be accepted into a graduate program consistent with the anticipated professional personnel needs identified by the Ho-Chunk Nation. Recipients must work for the Ho-Chunk Nation equal to the time that funding was received from the Fellowship but not less than a two-year period. Recipients may choose to pay back the funds. April 15 is the deadline for Fall semester and October 15 is the deadline for Spring semester. Award requirements change regularly. For any further questions, call (715) 284-4915 or contact Ho-Chunk at the email address: beardsj@hochunk.com. No GPA requirement specified.

Ho-Chunk Nation
PO Box 667
Education Department W9814 Airport Rd
Black River Falls, WI 54615-0667

637
Journalism Foundation of Metropolitan St. Louis Scholarship

AMOUNT: None Specified DEADLINE: March 31
MAJOR: Journalism, Communications, Advertising, Public Relations

The Journalism Foundation of Metropolitan St. Louis Scholarships is open to full-time undergraduate or graduate students. You must also be from the St. Louis area or one of the following counties: St. Louis, Franklin, Jefferson, Lincoln, St. Charles or Warren (in Missouri), or the counties of Madison, St. Clair, Monroe, Clinton, Bond and Jersey (in Illinois). Award requirements change regularly. Please write to the address listed for further information or consult with your college's or university's financial aid office. No GPA requirement specified.

Journalism Foundation of Metropolitan St. Louis
Joseph Kenny, Scholarship Coordinator
462 North Taylor Avenue
Saint Louis, MO 63108

638
Judith Graham Poole Postdoctoral Research Fellowship

AMOUNT: Maximum: $35000 DEADLINE: July 1
MAJOR: Hemophilia Research

Postdoctorate (M.D. or Ph.D.) fellowships for hemophilia-related research. Number of awards per year dependent on available funding. Topics that the NHF has expressed an interest in are clinical or basic research on biochemical, genetic, hematologic, orthopedic, psychiatric or dental aspects of the hemophilias or Von Willebrand Disease. Award requirements change regularly. For further information please contact the grants personnel or relevant department heads in your institution. You may also write to the address listed, including a self-addressed, stamped envelope or call (800) 42HANDI ext. 3741, (212) 328-3741, fax (212) 328-3788. No GPA requirement specified.

National Hemophilia Foundation
Denise Kenny Coord of Research Program
116 West 32nd Street, FL 11
New York, NY 10001-3212

639
Judith L. and Robert D. Appelbaum Scholarship

AMOUNT: None Specified DEADLINE: March 1
MAJOR: Helping Professions

The Judith I. and Robert D. Appelbaum Scholarship is open to Jewish graduate students with career goals in the "helping professions." To be considered for this award, you must be entering or have already entered professional training. Award requirements change regularly. No GPA requirement specified.

Jewish Vocational Service
Attn: Scholarship Secretary
One South Franklin Street
Chicago, IL 60606-4694

640
Judith Resnik Memorial Scholarship

AMOUNT: $2000 DEADLINE: February 1
MAJOR: Aerospace Engineering, Aeronautical Engineering, Astronautical Engineering

The Judith Resnik Memorial Scholarship is open to female seniors who are majoring in aerospace engineering, aeronautical engineering or astronautical engineering. The applicants must be attending an ABET-accredited program or an SWE-approved school and have a minimum GPA of 3.5. Participation as an active SWE student member is required. Award requirements change regularly. Please send a self-addressed, stamped envelope to receive your application. GPA must be 3.5-4.0.

Society of Women Engineers Headquarters
Scholarship Coordinator
120 Wall Street, FL 11
New York, NY 10005-3902

641
JVS Jewish Community Scholarship Fund

AMOUNT: None Specified DEADLINE: April 15
MAJOR: All Areas of Study

Open to full-time sophomores, juniors, seniors, graduates, professional students, and students pursuing technical or vocational training. Preference is given to students attending accredited educational institutions in California. Applicants must be Jewish, U.S. citizens, and have permanent residence in Los Angeles County, CA. Award requirements change regularly. Apply online here or call Jeanie Gaynor at (323) 761-8888 ext. 122, fax (323) 761-8850, or email: jgaynor@jvsla.org. GPA must be 2.5-4.0.

JVS Jewish Community Scholarship Fund
Scholarship Coordinator
5700 Wilshire Blvd, Suite 2303
Los Angeles, CA 90036-3659

642

K2TEO Martin J. Green Sr. Memorial Scholarship

AMOUNT: $1000 DEADLINE: February 1
MAJOR: All Areas of Study

This scholarship is available to students with a minimum general class amateur radio license and who come from a "ham" family. Award requirements change regularly. Write the address provided, using a self-addressed, stamped envelope, for further information. No GPA requirement specified.

American Radio Relay League
Attn: ARRL Foundation
225 Main Street
Newington, CT 06111-1400

643
Kaminer Family Fund

AMOUNT: Maximum: $475 DEADLINE: Varies
MAJOR: All Areas of Study

The purpose of the Kaminer Family Fund is to provide a Jewish summer camp experience to students 26 years of age or younger. Grants may be made for such general and specific purposes as camperships, counseling and supportive services. Applicants must demonstrate financial need and be residents of San Francisco, San Mateo, northern Santa Clara, Marin or Sonoma counties in California. Deadlines vary; therefore, it is encouraged that applicants apply early. Award requirements change regularly. No GPA requirement specified.

Jewish Family and Children's Services
Attn: Loans and Grants Department
2245 Post Street
San Francisco, CA 94115

644
Kappa Kappa Gamma Member Scholarships and Fellowships

AMOUNT: None Specified DEADLINE: February 1
MAJOR: All Areas of Study

Graduate and undergraduate scholarships, and grants for part-time study, are available to members of Kappa Kappa Gamma. All applicants are requested to note their chapter membership on their requests. Graduates are asked to also note if they are full- or part-time students. Award requirements change regularly. For complete information and application materials, please send a self-addressed, stamped envelope to the address listed. No GPA requirement specified.

Kappa Kappa Gamma Foundation
Member Scholarships/Fellowships
PO Box 38
Columbus, OH 43216-0038

645
Katharine M. Grosscup Horticultural Scholarship

AMOUNT: Maximum: $2000 DEADLINE: February 1
MAJOR: Horticulture (Related Fields), Floriculture, Botany, Arboriculture, Landscape Design

The Katharine M. Grosscup Horticultural Scholarship is for sophomores, juniors, seniors or graduate students who are pursuing a degree in horticulture and related fields of study. Preference is given to students under the age of 35 from Ohio, Pennsylvania, West Virginia, Indiana, and Michigan. Applicants must demonstrate financial need. A "B" average is required. Award requirements change regularly. For an application and further information send a self-addressed, stamped envelope to the address provided. GPA must be 3.0-4.0.

Garden Club of America - Grosscup Scholarship Committee
Attn: Nancy C. Stevenson
11030 East Blvd.
Cleveland, OH 44106-1706

646
Kathern F. Gruber Scholarship

AMOUNT: Maximum: $2000 DEADLINE: April 15
MAJOR: All Areas of Study

This scholarship is open to children and spouses of legally blind veterans. Selection is based upon the application, transcript, three recommendations and a 300-word essay. Reapplication is required to retain scholarship. Award requirements change regularly. Write to the address listed, enclosing a self-addressed, stamped envelope for an application and further information. No GPA requirement specified.

Blinded Veterans Association
Scholarship Coordinator
477 H Street NW
Washington, DC 20001-2617

647
Kathryn M. Daugherty Scholarship for Education Majors

AMOUNT: $250-$500 DEADLINE: May 6
MAJOR: Education, Elementary Education

This scholarship is available to undergraduate women with sophomore, junior, or senior standing. You must be pursuing an education major. Preference is given to elementary education majors. You must be a full-time student with a minimum 3.0 GPA. You must demonstrate financial need in order to apply. Award requirements change regularly. GPA must be 3.0-4.0.

Business and Professional Women's Foundation of Maryland, Inc.
Scholarships Coordinator
282 New Mark Esplanade
Rockville, MD 20850-2733

648
KATU Thomas R. Dargan Minority Scholarship

AMOUNT: $4000 DEADLINE: April 30
MAJOR: Broadcasting, Communications

Scholarships available to minority freshmen through juniors residing in or attending an accredited school in Oregon or Washington. Must be U.S. citizens and have a minimum GPA of 3.0. Based on need, recommendation, personality, and essay. Award requirements change regularly. Write to the address listed, enclosing a self-addressed, stamped envelope for more information. GPA must be 3.0.

Spirit 2, KATU, Portland
Attn: Human Resources
PO Box 2
Portland, OR 97207-0002

649
Kauai County Farm Bureau Scholarships

AMOUNT: $1000 DEADLINE: April 15
MAJOR: Agriculture, Aquaculture

Open to Kauai residents majoring in an agriculture related field. Four $1,000 scholarships are available: 2 - for graduating high school seniors, 1 - for a undergraduate student, 1 - for a graduate student, and 1 - to a Kauai Farm Bureau family member in any field of study. Selection is based on scholastic achievement and participation in school and community activities. Award requirements change regularly. For further information, please write to the address listed, including a self-addressed, stamped envelope. No GPA requirement specified.

Kauai County Farm Bureau Scholarship
Attn: Mr. Herbert Keamoai
PO Box 3895
Lihue, HI 96766-6861

650
Keepers Preservation Education Fund Fellowship

AMOUNT: $500 DEADLINE: October 30
MAJOR: Historical Preservation

Awarded each year to enable a graduate student in the field of Historical Preservation to attend the annual meeting of the Society. Judged by a committee of three who are appointed by the president of the Society. A citation and an award of $500 are presented at the Annual Meeting. Award requirements change regularly. For information regarding submission criteria and procedures, contact the Society of Architectural Historians by telephone (312) 573-1365 or email: info@sah.org. No GPA requirement specified.

Society of Architectural Historians
Charnley-Persky House
1365 North Astor Street
Chicago, IL 60610-2144

651
Kellie Cannon Memorial Scholarship

AMOUNT: $1200 DEADLINE: March 1
MAJOR: Computer Science, Information Science, Data Processing

This scholarship is open to students who are legally blind and majoring in computer science or a related field. The award is based on academic ability. Award requirements change regularly. Please write to the address listed, enclosing a self-addressed, stamped envelope for an application and further information. No GPA requirement specified.

American Council of the Blind
Attn: Billie Jean Keith
1155 15th Street NW, Suite 720
Washington, DC 20005-2706

652
Kelly Carter Scholarship Fund

AMOUNT: $1000 DEADLINE: March 15
MAJOR: Physical Therapy, Occupational Therapy, Speech Therapy, Respiratory Therapy, Athletic Training, Physician's Assistant, Nursing or Any Assistant Program Related to the Above

The Kelly Carter Scholarship Fund is open to residents of Lenawee County (MI) and/or the Lenawee Intermediate School District. To qualify for the award, you must be planning to pursue a career in physical therapy, occupational therapy, speech therapy, respiratory therapy, associated assistants programs, athletic training, physician's assistant or nursing. The award also requires that you be already accepted at a community college or four-year institution. Award requirements change regularly. Please send a self-addressed, stamped envelope to receive your application and any further instructions from the scholarship provider. No GPA requirement specified.

Morenci High School
Attn: Mrs. Melissa Parnell
788 Coomer Street
Morenci, MI 49256

653
Kenai Natives Association Scholarship and Grant Fund

AMOUNT: $1000 DEADLINE: Varies
MAJOR: All Areas of Study

The Kenai Natives Association Scholarship and Grant Fund is open to Alaska Natives enrolled in the KNA, their descendants and adopted children who have a minimum GPA of 2.5. Applicants must be accepted/enrolled full-time in a two- or four-year undergraduate degree program, a graduate degree program, or a technical skills training program. The respective deadline dates are June 1 and December 1. Award requirements change regularly. GPA must be 2.5-4.0.

CIRI Foundation
Scholarship Coordinator
2600 Cordova Street, Suite 206
Anchorage, AK 99503-2745

654
Kenneth Jernigan Scholarship

AMOUNT: $21000 DEADLINE: March 31
MAJOR: All Areas of Study

The Kenneth Jernigan Scholarship is open to students who are legally blind and are pursuing or planning to pursue a full-time postsecondary course of study in the U.S. You will be considered on academic excellence, service to the community and financial need. Award requirements change regularly. No GPA requirement specified.

National Federation of the Blind
Attn: Peggy Elliott, Chairman
805 5th Avenue
Grinnell, IA 50112-1653

655
Kentucky Educational Excellence Scholarship

AMOUNT: None Specified DEADLINE: Varies
MAJOR: All Areas of Study

The Kentucky Educational Excellence Scholarship is administered by the Kentucky Higher Education Assistance Authority (KHEAA). To be considered for the award, you must have a C+ average or above. The better you do in high school, the more you are eligible to earn toward college scholarships. Award requirements change regularly. For further information, please visit the website at www.kheaa.com. GPA must be 2.5-4.0.

Kentucky Higher Education Assistance Authority
Attn: Grants and Scholarship Programs
1050 U.S. 127 South
Frankfort, KY 40601-4323

656
Kentucky Tuition Grant

AMOUNT: $50-$1500 DEADLINE: Varies
MAJOR: All Fields of Study (Except Divinity, Theology or Religious Education)

The Kentucky Tuition Grant is open to Kentucky residents who attend the Commonwealth's independent colleges. Eligible institutions must be accredited by the Southern Association of Colleges and Schools and not have institutional programs comprised solely of sectarian instruction. To be considered for this award, you must be a full-time undergraduate enrolled in an associate or baccalaureate degree program other than divinity, theology or religious education and have no past due financial obligations to KHEAA or to any Title IV program. Award requirements change regularly. The FAFSA can be obtained from high school counselor offices, college financial aid offices, or online at www.fafsa.ed.gov. For more information, you may also visit the KHEAA website at www.kheaa.com. No GPA requirement specified.

Kentucky Higher Education Assistance Authority
Attn: Grants and Scholarship Programs
1050 U.S. 127 South
Frankfort, KY 40601-4323

657
Kettle Range Conservation Group Scholarships

AMOUNT: $1000 DEADLINE: May 1
MAJOR: Conservation, Environmental Studies

Open to high school seniors in Colville, Curlew, Inchelium, Kettle Falls, Republic and Tonasket. A 350-500-word essay is required on the greatest threat to the environment today and what ideas or solutions you have to help today and in the future. Transcripts, three letters of recommendation and participation in extracurricular activities are required. Award requirements change regularly. Information and applications available from your high school counselor, the KRCG website: www.televar.com/~tcoleman or the address listed. Please send a self-addressed, stamped envelope to receive a reply. GPA must be 2.8-4.0.

Kettle Range Conservation Group
Project Scholarship
PO Box 150
Republic, WA 99166-0150

Kim Simon Award

AMOUNT: None Specified DEADLINE: February 1
MAJOR: Communication Disorders

The Kim Simon Award is available to entering freshmen who plan on majoring in communication disorders or audiology at a four-year university. Award requirements change regularly. For further information please send a self-addressed, stamped envelope to the Wisconsin Speech and Hearing Association, PO Box 1109, 330 East Lakeside Street, Madison, WI 53701, or call (800) 545-0640. No GPA requirement specified.

University of Wisconsin, Oshkosh
Financial Aid Office
800 Algoma Blvd
Oshkosh, WI 54901-8604

659
Kirby McDonald Education Endowment Scholarship Fund

AMOUNT: None Specified DEADLINE: Varies
MAJOR: Culinary Arts, Engineering, Business

The Kirby McDonald Education Endowment Scholarship Fund is open to Alaska Native enrollees to the Cook Inlet Region and their descendants. Priority is given to culinary arts, business and engineering majors enrolled in a degree program. The deadline dates are June 1 and December 1, respectively. Award requirements change regularly. No GPA requirement specified.

CIRI Foundation
Scholarship Coordinator
2600 Cordova Street, Suite 206
Anchorage, AK 99503-2745

660
Kotzebue Higher Education Scholarship

AMOUNT: None Specified DEADLINE: Varies
MAJOR: All Areas of Study

The Kotzebue Higher Education Scholarship is open to Alaskan natives of the Village of Kotzebue. Applicants must provide verification of tribal membership, an acceptance letter to a university or college, a budget/need sheet, two letters of recommendation, a personal statement of future goals and career plans and school transcripts as required. If the applicants are continuing students, they are required to have a minimum 2.0 GPA, have completed at least 12 credit hours and be full-time students. The purpose of the Kotzebue Higher Education Program is to financially assist eligible Native people enrolled to the Native Village of Kotzebue with the costs to attend a college or a university. The goal of this program is to assist Native students with the financial ability to achieve a degree in their chosen profession, thus increasing the possibility to become self-sufficient and successful individuals within the NANA Region and providing role models for future generations. For complete scholarship information, please write to

the address provided using a self-addressed, stamped envelope. No GPA requirement specified.

Kotzebue I.R.A. Council
Higher Education Program
PO Box 296
Kotzebue, AK 99752-0296

661
Kress Foundation Fellowships In the History of Art

AMOUNT: $18000 DEADLINE: November 30
MAJOR: Art History

Award for Pre-Doctoral Fellowships in the History of Art for the completion of dissertation research. Fellowships are restricted to U.S citizens or individuals matriculated at U.S. institutions. Interested individuals must be nominated by their art history department and should contact their advisor for information and an application form. Restricted to one nomination per department. Advanced dissertation research in association with a selected art historical institute in Florence, Jerusalem, Leiden, London, Munich, Nicosia, Paris, Rome, or Zurich. Applicants must be nominated by their Art History Department. For U.S. citizens to study in the above cities abroad or international students to study at American Universities. Award requirements change regularly. Write to the address listed, enclosing a self-addressed, stamped envelope for an application and further information. No GPA requirement specified.

Samuel H. Kress Foundation
Fellowship Administrator
174 East 80th Street
New York, NY 10021-0439

662
Kress Travel Fellowships

AMOUNT: $1000-$5000 DEADLINE: November 30
MAJOR: Art History

Awards for travel to view material essential for the completion of dissertation research. For U.S. citizens to travel abroad or international students at American Universities. Must be nominated by the Art History Department. Fifteen to 20 awards offered annually. Award requirements change regularly. Consult your Art History Department Advisor for further information and an application. No GPA requirement specified.

Samuel H. Kress Foundation
Fellowship Administrator
174 East 80th Street
New York, NY 10021-0439

663
Kuchler-Killian Memorial Scholarship

AMOUNT: $3000 DEADLINE: March 31
MAJOR: All Areas of Study

The Kuchler-Killian Memorial Scholarship is open to students who are legally blind and are pursuing or planning to pursue a full-time postsecondary course of study in the U.S. Your selection will be based on academic excellence, service to the community and financial need. Award requirements change regularly. No GPA requirement specified.

National Federation of the Blind
Attn: Peggy Elliott, Chairman
805 5th Avenue
Grinnell, IA 50112-1653

664
L. Gordon Bittle Memorial Scholarship

AMOUNT: $2000 DEADLINE: February 15
MAJOR: Education

Open to current "active" members of the Student California Teachers Association (SCTA) who are registered in approved teaching preparatory programs at accredited institutions of higher learning in California. Must attend school full-time and plan on careers as teachers in public education. Selection is based on academics, special achievements, involvement in and sensitivity to human, social and civic issues; and characteristics such as responsibility, reliability, and integrity. Award requirements change regularly. Please send a self-addressed, stamped envelope to receive your application and any further instructions from the scholarship provider, call (415) 697-1400, browse their website: www.cta.org and click on "Resources" for scholarship information or email: scholarships@cta.org. No GPA requirement specified.

California Teachers Association
Scholarship Committee
1705 Murchison Drive, PO Box 921
Burlingame, CA 94011-0921

665
L. Phil Wicker Scholarship

AMOUNT: $1000 DEADLINE: February 1
MAJOR: Electronics, Communications, and Related Fields

This scholarship is available to students with a minimum general class amateur radio license and majoring in electronics, communications or a related field in a baccalaureate or graduate program. Applicants must be residents of and attending school in: North Carolina, South Carolina, Virginia, or West Virginia. Award requirements change regularly. Write the address provided, using a self-addressed, stamped envelope, for further information. No GPA requirement specified.

American Radio Relay League
Attn: ARRL Foundation
225 Main Street
Newington, CT 06111-1400

666
Lake County Blue Coats, Inc. Scholarship

AMOUNT: $1000 DEADLINE: August 7
MAJOR: All Areas of Study

This award is available for children of Lake County, Ohio, police or fire department personnel (who are on active duty, retired or deceased). The applicant must be planning to continue their education and must maintain a 2.5 GPA to keep the scholarship for the full year. Award requirements change regularly. Please send a self-addressed, stamped envelope to the

address provided, or pick up the application in person. GPA must be 2.5.

Lake County Blue Coats, Inc.
M.G. Winchell, MD, Scholarship Chair
9179 Chillicothe Road
Kirtland, OH 44094

667
Laramie River Valley Rendezvous Scholarship

AMOUNT: $500 DEADLINE: Varies
MAJOR: All Areas of Study

Open to Rocky Mountain High School (CO) seniors. Applicants must have satisfactorily participated in and completed at least one Laramie River Rendezvous, and must have at least a 2.5 cumulative GPA. Awards will be decided on financial need. An essay may be required. Application deadline, procedure, and award amount vary annually. Award requirements change regularly. Applications are available in January or February in the Rocky Mountain High School Career Center, as part of the Local Scholarship Packet. GPA must be 2.5-4.0.

Rocky Mountain High School
Scholarship Committee
1300 West Swallow Road
Fort Collins, CO 80526-2412

668
Larry Francoeur Memorial Leadership Scholarship

AMOUNT: $2000 DEADLINE: March 31
MAJOR: All Fields of Study

The Larry Francoeur Memorial Leadership Scholarship is open to Lenawee County (MI) graduating seniors. To be considered for the award, you must have demonstrated leadership skills and a commitment to community service. A minimum 3.0 GPA is required. Award requirements change regularly. Please send a self-addressed, stamped envelope to receive your application and any further instructions from the scholarship provider. GPA must be 3.0-4.0.

Morenci High School
Attn: Mrs. Melissa Parnell
788 Coomer Street
Morenci, MI 49256

669
Last Dollar Scholarship

AMOUNT: $200-$3000 DEADLINE: Varies
MAJOR: All Areas of Study

The Last Dollar Scholarship is open to graduating high school seniors from one of the following high schools: John Bartram, Benjamin Franklin, University City, Gratz, Strawberry Mansion, Edison/Fareira, West Philadelphia, Kensington, Parkway Gamma, William Penn, or Germantown. To be considered for this award, you must complete a scholarship application, be accepted at an accredited two- or four-year college or university, demonstrate financial need and submit a FAFSA. The application deadline is April 28. Scholarship recipients may reapply for up to six years after their high school graduation. If you are reapplying for this award, you must submit the FAFSA and a scholarship application by May 31. Award requirements change regularly. No GPA requirement specified.

Philadelphia Scholars
Re: Last Dollar Scholarship
7 Benjamin Franklin Parkway, Suite 700
Philadelphia, PA 19103

670
Law Enforcement Officers' Dependent's Scholarship

AMOUNT: None Specified DEADLINE: May 1
MAJOR: All Areas of Study

Scholarships for Arkansas undergraduates who are dependent children or spouses of persons who were killed or permanently disabled in the line of duty as law enforcement officers in the state of Arkansas and certain highway and transportation department employees. Must be full-time students age 23 or under, at a state supported two- or four-year institution. Award requirements change regularly. Write to the address listed, enclosing a self-addressed, stamped envelope for an application and further information. You may also browse their website: www.arscholarships.com/finsites.html. No GPA requirement specified.

Arkansas Department of Higher Education
Financial Aid Division
114 East Capitol Avenue
Little Rock, AR 72201-3818

671
Law Enforcement Personnel Dependents' Scholarship

AMOUNT: None Specified DEADLINE: Varies
MAJOR: All Areas of Study

This program provides educational grants to in-need dependents and spouses of California peace officers (highway patrol, marshals, sheriffs, police officers); officers and employees of the Department of Corrections or Youth Authority; and permanent and full-time firefighters employed by California who have been killed or totally disabled in the line of duty. Award requirements change regularly. Applicants must demonstrate financial need. For further information, please write to the address provided or visit the website at www.csac.ca.gov/. No GPA requirement specified.

California Student Aid Commission
Attn: Grants and Scholarships
PO Box 419026
Rancho Cordova, CA 95741-9026

672
Law Scholarship

AMOUNT: None Specified DEADLINE: September 30
MAJOR: Law

The Law Scholarship is open to individuals pursuing an education in law who are residents of Oneida, Vilas or Forest counties in Wisconsin. This award is based on current and potential academic performance, financial need and course of study. Persons interested should apply for the scholarship by

sending a letter and resume. Award requirements change regularly. For further scholarship information, please send a self-addressed, stamped envelope to the address provided. GPA must be 3.0-4.0.

Oneida-Vilas-Foresty County Bar Association
Lawrence and Tyler
8617 Highway 51 North
Minocqua, WI 54548

673
Lawrence Luterman Memorial Scholarship

AMOUNT: $1000 DEADLINE: February 15
MAJOR: All Areas of Study

The Lawrence Luterman Memorial Scholarship is open to natural or adopted descendants of a member of the American Legion, Department of New Jersey. Two scholarships are awarded for four years, two for one year. Award requirements change regularly. Please send a self-addressed, stamped envelope to receive your application and any further instructions from the scholarship provider. No GPA requirement specified.

American Legion - Department of New Jersey
Attn: Department Adjutant
War Memorial Building
Trenton, NJ 08068

674
Lawrence Matson Memorial Endowment Scholarship

AMOUNT: None Specified DEADLINE: Varies
MAJOR: Languages, Education, Social Sciences, Arts, Communication, Law

The Lawrence Matson Memorial Endowment Scholarship is open to Alaska Native enrollees to the Cook Inlet Region and their descendants. Applicants must be language, education, social sciences, arts, communications and law majors enrolled full-time in an undergraduate or graduate degree program. The respective deadline dates are June 1 and December 1. Award requirements change regularly. No GPA requirement specified.

CIRI Foundation
Scholarship Coordinator
2600 Cordova Street, Suite 206
Anchorage, AK 99503-2745

675
Lee C. Van Wagner Scholarship

AMOUNT: None Specified DEADLINE: July 1
MAJOR: Medicine/Osteopathic Medicine

Open to residents of Chenango or Otsego county in New York state who are attending a medical or osteopathic school approved by the Association of American Medical Colleges. Recipients must agree to practice in Chenango or Otsego county for one year for each year financial assistance is received, or to pay back any monies received (plus interest) within six years following graduation from medical school or within five years following completion of residency. Award requirements change regularly. For further information, please write to the address listed, including a self-addressed, stamped envelope, call (315) 735-2204, fax (315) 735-1608, or email:

kdyman@borg.com. No GPA requirement specified.

Medical Societies of the Counties of Chenango and Otsego
Executive Vice President
4311 Middle Settlement Road
New Hartford, NY 13413-5317

676
LeGrand Smith Scholarship

AMOUNT: None Specified DEADLINE: January 20
MAJOR: All Areas of Study

The LeGrand Smith Scholarship is open to outstanding high school seniors in the 7th Congressional District of Michigan. This includes Branch, Barry, Jackson, Lenawee, Hillsdale, Calhoun, Eaton and Washtenaw. You will be awarded on the basis of academic accomplishments (a minimum 3.0 GPA) and extracurricular activities. Financial aid is not a consideration. Award requirements change regularly. Please send a self-addressed, stamped envelope to receive your application and any further instructions from the scholarship provider or contact your high school counselor. The time to apply is between October of your senior year and January 20.
GPA must be 3.0-4.0.

LeGrand Smith Scholarship
Scholarship Committee
PO Box 87
Charlotte, MI 48813-0087

677
LeGrand Smith Scholarship

AMOUNT: None Specified DEADLINE: January 20
MAJOR: All Areas of Study

The LeGrand Smith Scholarship is open to high school seniors who live in the 7th Congressional District (Barry, Branch, Calhoun, Eaton, Hillsdale, Jackson, Lenawee and Washtenaw Counties of Michigan). Awards are granted on the basis of academic and leadership accomplishments. The Scholarship Committee will select semifinalists representing all schools from which students have applied. These students will then be asked to write an essay on a given subject. Winners will be selected on the basis of the essay, academic and leadership qualifications and personal recommendations. Award requirements change regularly. Please send a self-addressed, stamped envelope to receive your application and any further instructions from the scholarship provider. No GPA
requirement specified.

LeGrand Smith Scholarship Committee
PO Box 708
Jackson, MI 49201

678
Lena and Evelyn Traut Memorial Scholarship

AMOUNT: $500 DEADLINE: Varies
MAJOR: Elementary Education

Open to Rocky Mountain High School seniors. Applicants must have at least a 3.5 cumulative GPA, currently participate in high school activities, and have plans to enter the field of education as a teacher, preferably elementary education. An essay may be required. Application deadline, procedure, and award amount vary annually. Award requirements change reg-

ularly. Applications are available in January or February in the Rocky Mountain High School Career Center, as part of the Local Scholarship Packet. GPA must be 3.5-4.0.

Rocky Mountain High School
Scholarship Committee
1300 West Swallow Road
Fort Collins, CO 80526-2412

679
Lena Chang Academic Year Internship

AMOUNT: $1250 DEADLINE: Varies
MAJOR: All Areas of Study

The Lena Chang Academic Year Internship is reserved for two academic year interns from the Santa Barbara, CA, area. In order to apply for the internship, you must commit to 200 internship hours. Each internship has a stipend of $1,250. Transportation and housing costs will be your responsibility, however. Deadlines for the Lena Chang internships are: Summer Internship 2000 - May 1, 2000; Fall Semester (Quarter) - Aug. 1, 2000. Award requirements change regularly. No GPA requirement specified.

Nuclear Age Peace Foundation
Internships Program: Chris Pizzinat
PMB 121: 1187 Coast Village Road, Ste 1
Santa Barbara, CA 93108-2794

680
Lenawee County Association of Home Builders Scholarship

AMOUNT: $1000 DEADLINE: March 10
MAJOR: Building Trades, Drafting, Computer-Aided Design

The Lenawee County Association of Home Builders Scholarship is open to Lenawee County (MI) graduating seniors. You qualify for the award if you if you are in the process of completing a vocational/technical building trades program or the architectural component of the draft/CAD program. Award requirements change regularly. Please send a self-addressed, stamped envelope to receive your application and any further instructions from the scholarship provider. No GPA
requirement specified.

Morenci High School
Attn: Mrs. Melissa Parnell
788 Coomer Street
Morenci, MI 49256

681
Lenawee County Association of School Boards Award

AMOUNT: $1000 DEADLINE: March 5
MAJOR: All Fields of Study

The Lenawee County Association of School Boards Award is open to Lenawee County (MI) graduating seniors. To qualify for the award, you must have been receiving special education services immediately prior to qualifying for graduation. The award also requires that you be accepted into a public or private postsecondary learning institution. Award requirements change regularly. Please send a self-addressed, stamped envelope to receive your application and any further instructions from the scholarship provider. No GPA requirement specified.

Morenci High School
Attn: Mrs. Melissa Parnell
788 Coomer Street
Morenci, MI 49256

682
Lenawee County Dental Community Scholarship

AMOUNT: $1000 DEADLINE: March 10
MAJOR: Dental Aide

The Lenawee County Dental Community Scholarship is open to Lenawee County (MI) students. To be considered, you must be completing either a dental aide high school or adult program at the Voc-Tech Center. Award requirements change regularly. Please send a self-addressed, stamped envelope to receive your application and any further instructions from the scholarship provider. No GPA requirement specified.

Morenci High School
Attn: Mrs. Melissa Parnell
788 Coomer Street
Morenci, MI 49256

683
Lenawee County NAACP Citizenship Scholarship

AMOUNT: $1000 DEADLINE: March 31
MAJOR: All Fields of Study

The Lenawee County NAACP Citizenship Scholarship is open to Lenawee County (MI) graduating seniors. To qualify for the award, you must be pursuing higher education at a technical school, community college or baccalaureate degree granting institution. Award requirements change regularly. Please send a self-addressed, stamped envelope to receive your application and any further instructions from the scholarship provider. No GPA requirement specified.

Morenci High School
Attn: Mrs. Melissa Parnell
788 Coomer Street
Morenci, MI 49256

684
Lenawee County Republican Party Scholarship

AMOUNT: $500 DEADLINE: March 31
MAJOR: Teaching, Education

The Lenawee County Republican Party Scholarship is open to Lenawee County (MI) high school graduates. To be considered for the award, you must be pursuing a teaching career. Award requirements change regularly. Please send a self-addressed, stamped envelope to receive your application and any further instructions from the scholarship provider. No GPA requirement specified.

Morenci High School
Attn: Mrs. Melissa Parnell
788 Coomer Street
Morenci, MI 49256

685
Lenawee Graphic Arts Association Scholarship

AMOUNT: $500 DEADLINE: March 10
MAJOR: Printing, Graphic Design

The Lenawee Graphic Arts Association Scholarship is open to Lenawee County (MI) graduating seniors who have already been accepted at a college. To be considered, you must be completing the Voc-Tech printing and design program. Award requirements change regularly. Please send a self-addressed, stamped envelope to receive your application and any further instructions from the scholarship provider. No GPA requirement specified.

Morenci High School
Attn: Mrs. Melissa Parnell
788 Coomer Street
Morenci, MI 49256

686
Lenawee Health Care Educational Fund Scholarship

AMOUNT: None Specified DEADLINE: March 31
MAJOR: Health Care

The Lenawee Health Care Educational Fund Scholarship is open to Lenawee County (MI) residents. To qualify for the award, you should be pursuing a career in the health care field and planning to return to Lenawee County. You also qualify if you are already employed in the health care field. Award requirements change regularly. Please send a self-addressed, stamped envelope to receive your application and any further instructions from the scholarship provider. No GPA requirement specified.

Morenci High School
Attn: Mrs. Melissa Parnell
788 Coomer Street
Morenci, MI 49256

687
Leonard M. Perryman Communications Scholarship for Ethnic Minorities

AMOUNT: $2500 DEADLINE: March 13
MAJOR: Communications, Journalism

The Leonard M. Perryman Communications Scholarship for Ethnic Minority Students is open to ethnic minorities and United Methodists who intend to pursue careers in religious communication and who are majoring in journalism or communication. You must be in your junior or senior year at an accredited institution of higher education in the United States. The major of communication is meant to cover such media as audiovisual, electronic and print journalism. One of the scholarships is designated for a United Methodist student. For this award, you will be judged on five criteria: 1) Christian commitment and involvement in the life of the church, 2) academic achievement as revealed by transcripts, grade-point averages and the required letters of reference, 3) journalistic experience and/or evidence of journalistic talent, 4) clarity of purpose in plans and goals for the future, 5) potential professional usefulness as a religious journalist. No GPA requirement specified.

United Methodist Communications
Fellowship Committee
810 Twelfth Avenue South
Nashville, TN 37203

688
Lillian Fried Scholarship Fund

AMOUNT: Maximum: $130 DEADLINE: Varies
MAJOR: All Areas of Study

The purpose of the Lillian Fried Scholarship Fund is to provide scholarships for Jewish women to pursue collegiate or
graduate studies. Applicants must demonstrate financial need
and be residents of San Francisco, San Mateo, northern Santa
Clara, Marin or Sonoma counties in California. Deadlines
vary; therefore, it is encouraged that applicants apply early.
Award requirements change regularly. No GPA requirement
specified.

Jewish Family and Children's Services
Attn: Loans and Grants Department
2245 Post Street
San Francisco, CA 94115

689
Lillian M. Buttolph Scholarship

AMOUNT: $1000 DEADLINE: March 31
MAJOR: Teaching, Elementary Education

The Lillian M. Buttolph Scholarship is open to graduates of
Tecumseh High School. To be considered for the award, you
must be planning to teach at the elementary school level.
Award requirements change regularly. Please send a self-
addressed, stamped envelope to receive your application and
any further instructions from the scholarship provider. No
GPA requirement specified.

Morenci High School
Attn: Mrs. Melissa Parnell
788 Coomer Street
Morenci, MI 49256

690
Lillian Moller Gilbreth Scholarship

AMOUNT: $5000 DEADLINE: February 1
MAJOR: Engineering, Computer Science

This scholarship is open to junior or senior female engineering
majors in an ABET-accredited program or SWE-approved
school. You must have a minimum 3.5 GPA in order to apply.
Award requirements change regularly. Please send a self-
addressed, stamped envelope to receive your application. For
any further instructions from the scholarship provider, please
browse their website at www.swe.org or email hq@swe.org.
GPA must be 3.5-4.0.

Society of Women Engineers Headquarters
Scholarship Coordinator
120 Wall Street, FL 11
New York, NY 10005-3902

691
Lilly Endowment Community Scholarship

AMOUNT: None Specified DEADLINE: February 1
MAJOR: All Areas of Study

The Lilly Endowment Community Scholarship is open to
entry level freshmen who graduated from an accredited
Indiana high school in the current or past two academic years.
To be considered for this award, you must intend to pursue a
baccalaureate degree in four continuous years at an Indiana
college or university accredited by the North Central
Association of Colleges and Schools, reside in or attend
school in Clay, Sullivan or Vigo Counties in Indiana and
maintain a minimum GPA of 3.0. The awards provide full-
tuition. Award requirements change regularly. Please send a
self-addressed, stamped envelope to receive your application
and further information from the scholarship provider or call
(812) 232-2234. You will also find the application online at
www.wvcf.com. GPA must be 3.0-4.0.

Wabash Valley Community Foundation
Community Scholarship Program
2901 Ohio Boulevard, Suite 153
Terre Haute, IN 47803

692
Lilly Lorenzen Scholarship

AMOUNT: $1000-$3000 DEADLINE: May 1
MAJOR: Swedish Studies

If you are a Minnesota resident and want to carry out scholarly and creative studies in Sweden, you may be eligible for this
award. You must have a working knowledge of the Swedish
language, a serious desire to make a contribution to American-
Swedish cultural exchange, and demonstrable achievement in
the selected field of study. A personal interview with the committee may be required. Award requirements change regularly.
GPA must be 2.8-4.0.

American Swedish Institute
Attn: Lilly Lorenzen Scholarship Committee
2600 Park Avenue
Minneapolis, MN 55407-1007

693
Lily and Catello Sorrentino Memorial Scholarship

AMOUNT: None Specified DEADLINE: June 6
MAJOR: All Areas of Study

The Lily and Catello Sorrentino Memorial Scholarship is
available to Rhode Island residents over 45 years of age who
are returning to a degree-conferring, nonparochial school in
Rhode Island to complete an undergraduate degree. You must
be able to demonstrate financial need. Award requirements
change regularly. No GPA requirement specified.

Rhode Island Foundation
Attn: Special Funds Office
70 Elm Street
Providence, RI 02903

694
LITA/GEAC Scholarship

AMOUNT: $2500 DEADLINE: April 1
MAJOR: Library Science, Information Science

The LITA/GEAC Scholarship is open to students who plan to pursue a career in library automation and information technology. To be considered for this award, you must have applied for admission to an ALA-accredited master's degree program in library and information studies and cannot have completed more than 12 semester hours (or its equivalent) toward the master's degree prior to June 1. This award has no citizenship requirement. Award requirements change regularly. No GPA requirement specified.

American Library Association
HRDR/Staff Liaison - Scholarship Juries
50 East Huron Street
Chicago, IL 60611-2795

695
LITA/LSSI Minority Scholarship

AMOUNT: $2500 DEADLINE: April 1
MAJOR: Library Science, Information Science

The LITA/LSSI Minority Scholarship is open to citizens or permanent residents of the U.S. or Canada who have applied for admission to an ALA-accredited master's degree program in library and information studies. In order to apply, you cannot have completed more than 12 semester hours (or its equivalent) toward the master's degree prior to June 1. You must also demonstrate a commitment to a career in library automation and information technology and be a member of one of the four largest underrepresented groups in the library profession: African-American/Canadian, Asian/Pacific Islander, Latino/Hispanic, or Native American/Canadian. Award requirements change regularly. No GPA requirement specified.

American Library Association
HRDR/Staff Liaison - Scholarship Juries
50 East Huron Street
Chicago, IL 60611-2795

696
Lockheed-Martin Corporation Scholarship

AMOUNT: $3000 DEADLINE: May 15
MAJOR: Engineering

This scholarship is open to a freshman woman student majoring in engineering. The applicant must be accepted into an ABET-accredited program or an SWE-approved school. Award requirements change regularly. Please send a self-addressed, stamped envelope to receive your application. For further instructions, please browse the SWE website at www.swe.org or email hq@swe.org. No GPA requirement specified.

Society of Women Engineers Headquarters
Scholarship Coordinator
120 Wall Street, FL 11
New York, NY 10005-3902

697
Lockheed-Martin Fort Worth Scholarship

AMOUNT: $1000 DEADLINE: February 1
MAJOR: Electrical, Mechanical Engineering

This scholarship is open to entering junior women majoring in electrical or mechanical engineering who are attending an ABET-accredited program or an SWE-approved school. The applicants must have a minimum GPA of 3.5. Award requirements change regularly. Please send a self-addressed, stamped envelope to receive your application. For further instructions, please browse their website at www.swe.org or email hq@swe.org for more information. GPA must be 3.5-4.0.

Society of Women Engineers Headquarters
Scholarship Coordinator
120 Wall Street, FL 11
New York, NY 10005-3902

698
Lottie Lisle Scholarship

AMOUNT: $100-$1000 DEADLINE: April 1
MAJOR: Mathematics, Actuarial Science

Open to women eighteen years of age or older, who are juniors and seniors attending a Virginia college or accredited four-year institution. Applicants must be studying toward a baccalaureate degree with a major in mathematics or studying for an advanced degree in mathematics of actuarial science. Applicants must be U.S. citizens, residents of Virginia and must have a GPA of 2.5 or above. Recipients will be notified by June 30. Award requirements change regularly. Write to the address listed, enclosing a self-addressed, stamped envelope for an application and further information. GPA must be 2.5-4.0.

Business and Professional Women's Foundation
Scholarship Chairman
PO Box 4842
West Mclean, VA 22103-4842

699
Louis and Fannie Sager Memorial Scholarship

AMOUNT: $500-$1000 DEADLINE: March 10
MAJOR: Accounting

The Louis and Fannie Sager Memorial Scholarship is open to graduates of public high schools in Virginia who are enrolled as undergraduate accounting majors at a Virginia college or university. To be considered for this award you must have a "B" or better GPA and be either a U.S. or Canadian citizen. These scholarships are awarded primarily for academic merit, demonstrated leadership ability and financial need. Award requirements change regularly. Please send a self-addressed, stamped envelope to receive your application and any further instructions from the scholarship provider. Students may submit the application by email; however, fax and email transcripts or appraisal forms will not be accepted. You may also download the application from the sponsor website. GPA must be 3.0-4.0.

National Society of Accountants
Attn: Scholarship Foundation
1010 North Fairfax Street
Alexandria, VA 22314-1574

Louise Dessureault Memorial Scholarship

AMOUNT: $500 DEADLINE: April 17
MAJOR: Travel and Tourism, Hotel/Restaurant Management

The Louise Dessureault Memorial Scholarship is open to Canadian juniors or seniors who are pursuing a degree in a travel and tourism-related industry. To be considered for this award, you must be enrolled full-time in a four-year college in North America. Award requirements change regularly. No GPA requirement specified.

National Tourism Foundation
PO Box 3071
546 East Main Street
Lexington, KY 40508-3071

701
Lowell Zimmerman Scholarship

AMOUNT: None Specified DEADLINE: Varies
MAJOR: All Fields of Study

The Lowell Zimmerman Scholarship is open to graduating seniors at Burlington High School (Burlington, WI). Students must attend a four-year college. Award requirements change regularly. Please visit your Guidance Office to receive an application and any additional details. No GPA requirement specified.

Burlington High School
Attn: Guidance Office
225 Robert Street
Burlington, WI 53105

702
Lucile B. Kaufman Women's Scholarship Award

AMOUNT: $1000 DEADLINE: February 1
MAJOR: Manufacturing Engineering, Manufacturing Engineering Technology

Open to full-time female undergraduates enrolled in a degree program in manufacturing engineering or manufacturing engineering technology. Applicants must have completed at least 30 college credit hours and be seeking a career in manufacturing engineering or manufacturing engineering technology and have an overall GPA of 3.5 or higher. Award requirements change regularly. For further information, please contact Dora Murray at (313) 271-1500, ext. 1709 (email: murrdor@sme.org) or Theresa Macias, ext. 1707 (email: maciter@sme.org) You may also go to the SME website: www.sme.org. GPA must be 3.5-4.0.

Society of Manufacturing Engineering Education Foundation
PO Box 930
One SME Drive
Dearborn, MI 48121-0930

703
Lucy Corbett Scholarship

AMOUNT: $1000 DEADLINE: March 31
MAJOR: Communications, Journalism

This merit award is open to juniors, seniors, and graduate students who show academic promise and are attending Michigan colleges or universities. You must be a permanent Michigan resident living in any of the following counties: Genesee, Ingham, Livingston, Macomb, Oakland, Saginaw, St. Clair, Washtenaw, or Wayne. Award requirements change regularly. GPA must be 3.0-4.0.

Women in Communications of Detroit
WIC-Detroit Scholarship Committee
PO Box 1288
Royal Oak, MI 48068-1288

704
Mabel Boland Scholarship

AMOUNT: $500 DEADLINE: Varies
MAJOR: All Areas of Study

Open to Rocky Mountain High School seniors. Applicants must demonstrate an ability for academic success and have financial need. Applicants will be considered on academics, community involvement, and evidence of career goal. Application deadline, procedure, and award amount vary annually. Award requirements change regularly. Applications are available in January or February in the Rocky Mountain High School Career Center, as part of the Local Scholarship Packet. GPA must be 2.8-4.0.

Rocky Mountain High School
Scholarship Committee
1300 West Swallow Road
Fort Collins, CO 80526-2412

705
Maine Student Incentive Scholarship Program

AMOUNT: Maximum: $1250 DEADLINE: April 15
MAJOR: All Fields of Study

The Maine Student Incentive Scholarship Program is open to Maine students who are attending degree-granting institutions in Maine. To be considered for the award, you must be able to demonstrate financial need. You may also be eligible to receive this award if you are attending a school in a state that has a reciprocity agreement with Maine. These states are Connecticut, Massachusetts, New Hampshire, Pennsylvania, Rhode Island and Vermont, as well as Washington, DC. The award also requires that you have graduated from an approved secondary school (or received a GED) and that you have not earned an undergraduate degree. The award is renewable, provided you qualify upon reapplication. Award requirements change regularly. To apply, you must complete the FAFSA. The amount of your award will be determined by this application. For more information, you may visit the Finance Authority of Maine's website. No GPA requirement specified.

Finance Authority of Maine
Attn: Education Assistance Division
1 Weston Court, 119 State House Station
Augusta, ME 04333-0119

706
MALDEF Communications Scholarship Program

AMOUNT: None Specified DEADLINE: June 30
MAJOR: Communications, Journalism, Media Communications, Law

The MALDEF Communications Scholarships are available to Latino undergraduate or graduate students who seek a career in either communications, journalism, media communications or entertainment law upon graduation. Award requirements change regularly. Write to the address listed, enclosing a self-addressed, stamped envelope for an application and further information. No GPA requirement specified.

Mexican American Legal Defense and Educational Fund
MALDEF Law School Scholarship Program
634 South Spring Street, 11th Floor
Los Angeles, CA 90014-3921

707
Marcus and Theresa Levie Educational Scholarship

AMOUNT: None Specified DEADLINE: March 1
MAJOR: Helping Professions

The Marcus and Theresa Levie Educational Scholarships are for Jewish men and women who live in Cook County (IL). You must be planning a career in the "helping professions" (nursing, teaching, etc.) and be entering at least the junior year of undergraduate study. To be considered for this award, you must be entering, or have entered, professional training. Award requirements change regularly. No GPA requirement specified.

Jewish Vocational Service
Attn: Scholarship Secretary
One South Franklin Street
Chicago, IL 60606-4694

708
Margaret M. Prickett Scholarship

AMOUNT: $1000 DEADLINE: March 31
MAJOR: All Areas of Study

This scholarship is open to daughters, stepdaughters, adopted daughters or granddaughters of a career commissioned officer or warrant officers in the U.S. Army. Selection is based upon academic standing, test scores, school and community activities and financial need. Award requirements change regularly. Write to the address listed for details. Specify the officer's name, rank, social security number, and dates of active duty when requesting an application. Please enclose a self-addressed, stamped envelope. No GPA requirement specified.

Society of Daughters of the U.S. Army
Janet B. Otto, Scholarship Chairman
7717 Rockledge Court
West Springfield, VA 22152-3854

709
Margaret S. Harter Scholarship by Harter Corporation

AMOUNT: $2000 DEADLINE: March 15
MAJOR: All Fields of Study

The Margaret S. Harter Scholarship by Harter Corporation is open to employees of Business Products Industry Association member firms and their families. Persons holding academic records sufficient for acceptance by accredited colleges, junior colleges or technical schools, or persons already enrolled in one of those institutions are eligible for this one-year award. Selection is made by a committee from the Student Financial Aid Department of The George Washington University, Washington, DC. Award requirements change regularly. Please send a self-addressed, stamped envelope to receive your application and any further instructions from the scholarship provider or email: info@bpia.org. No GPA requirement specified.

Business Products Industry Association
Attn: Scholarship Committee
301 North Fairfax Street
Alexandria, VA 22314-2633

710
Marine Corps Scholarship

AMOUNT: $500-$2500 DEADLINE: February 1
MAJOR: All Areas of Study

Candidate must be the son/daughter of an active duty or reserve Marine in good standing, or the son/daughter of a Marine honorably and/or medically discharged or deceased. Must be a high school senior, high school graduate, or college undergraduate. Gross family income must not exceed $43,000 per year. Award requirements change regularly. For further information, please send a self-addressed, stamped envelope to the address provided. No GPA requirement specified.

Marine Corps Scholarship Foundation, Inc.
Scholarship Office
PO Box 3008
Princeton, NJ 08543-3008

711
Marion T. Burr Scholarship

AMOUNT: None Specified DEADLINE: May 31
MAJOR: Human Services

The Marion T. Burr Scholarship is open to Native American students who are enrolled full-time in a college or seminary, pursuing a career in human services. Applicants must be members of an American Baptist church for at least one year before applying for aid and enrolled at an accredited educational institution in the U.S. or Puerto Rico. U.S. citizenship is required. Award requirements change regularly. Please send a self-addressed, stamped envelope to receive your application and any further instructions from the scholarship provider. No GPA requirement specified.

American Baptist Financial Aid Program
Educational Ministries ABC/USA
PO Box 851
Valley Forge, PA 19482-0851

712
Marjorie Roy Rothermel Scholarship

AMOUNT: Maximum: $2000 DEADLINE: March 15
MAJOR: Mechanical Engineering

Open to students who are working towards a master's degree at a U.S. school in an ABET-accredited mechanical engineering department. Applicants must be U.S. citizens. Selection is based on academic performance, character, need, and ASME participation. For further information and an application, please write to the address listed, including a self-addressed, stamped business size envelope or email: eprocha34D@aol.com. You may also visit their website www.amse.org/educate/aid. GPA must be 2.8-4.0.

American Society of Mechanical Engineers Auxiliary, Inc.
Attn: Mrs. Otto Prochaska
332 Valencia Street
Gulf Breeze, FL 32561-4032

713
Mark J. Schroeder Scholarship In Meteorology

AMOUNT: $5000 DEADLINE: June 14
MAJOR: Meteorology, Atmospheric Science, Ocean Science, Hydrology

Scholarships are for undergraduates entering their final year of study in meteorology, atmospheric science, oceanic science, or hydrology with a GPA of 3.0 or better. Must demonstrate financial need and be U.S. citizens or permanent residents. Award requirements change regularly. Write to the address listed, sending a self-addressed, stamped envelope for details, call AMS headquarters at (617) 227-2426, extension 235, or browse their website: www.ametsoc.org/ams/amsedu/scholfel.html or contact their email: armstrong@ametsoc.org. GPA must be 3.0.

American Meteorological Society
Fellowship/Scholarship Coordinator
45 Beacon Street
Boston, MA 02108-3693

714
Mark Miller Award

AMOUNT: $1000 DEADLINE: December 31
MAJOR: Accounting, Finance, Business, Taxation

The Mark Miller Award is available to ethnic minority accounting, finance, or business undergraduates or accounting and taxation graduates. Applicants must be currently enrolled as full-time students and be paid NABA members. A minimum 2.5 GPA is required. Award requirements change regularly. Please send a self-addressed, stamped envelope to receive your application and any further instructions from the scholarship provider or call (301) 474-6222, ext. 14. GPA must be 2.5-4.0.

National Association of Black Accountants, Inc.
Attn: Scholarship Committee
7249-A Hanover Parkway
Greenbelt, MD 20770

715
Marshall Cavendish Scholarship

AMOUNT: $3000 DEADLINE: April 1
MAJOR: Library Science, Information Science

The Marshall Cavendish Scholarship is open to citizens or permanent residents of the U.S. or Canada who have applied for admission to and will enter an ALA-accredited master's degree program in library and information studies. To be considered for this award, you cannot have completed more than 12 semester hours (or its equivalent) toward the master's degree prior to June 1. Award requirements change regularly. No GPA requirement specified.

American Library Association
HRDR/Staff Liaison - Scholarship Juries
50 East Huron Street
Chicago, IL 60611-2795

716
Martin Luther King Jr. Memorial Scholarship Fund

AMOUNT: None Specified DEADLINE: March 15
MAJOR: Education

Open to ethnic minority undergraduates and graduates. Must be active members of the California Teachers Association, dependent children of active, retired or deceased CTA members, or members of the Student California Teachers Association. For study in the fields of education or teaching. Award requirements change regularly. Please send a self-addressed, stamped envelope to receive your application and any further instructions from the scholarship provider, call (415) 697-1400, browse their website: www.cta.org and click on "Resources" for scholarship information or email: scholarships@cta.org. No GPA requirement specified.

California Teachers Association
Scholarship Committee
1705 Murchison Drive, PO Box 921
Burlingame, CA 94011-0921

717
Marvin Mundel Memorial Scholarship

AMOUNT: $800 DEADLINE: November 15
MAJOR: Industrial Engineering, Methods Engineering

This scholarship is open to undergraduate students who are enrolled in an industrial engineering program on a full-time basis, who are members of the institute and have a minimum 3.4 GPA. The program enrolled in may be located in the United States and its territories, Canada or Mexico provided that the school's engineering program or equivalent is accredited by an accrediting agency recognized by IIE. The applicants must have a graduation date of May/June 2001 or later and must be nominated by their IE Department heads. Priority consideration is given to, but not limited to, students who have a demonstrated interest in work measurement and methods engineering. Award requirements change regularly. GPA must be 3.4-4.0.

Institute of Industrial Engineers
Attn: Chapter Operations Board
25 Technology Park
Norcross, GA 30092-2988

718
Mary Butler Scholarship

AMOUNT: $1500 DEADLINE: March 31
MAJOR: Journalism, Communications

This award is open to juniors, seniors, and graduate students who have overcome a challenge or disability. You must be attending Michigan colleges or universities and a permanent Michigan resident living in any of the following counties: Genesee, Ingham, Livingston, Macomb, Oakland, Saginaw, St. Clair, Washtenaw, or Wayne. Award requirements change regularly.
Women in Communications of Detroit
WIC-Detroit Scholarship Committee
PO Box 1288
Royal Oak MI

719
Mary E. Bivins Grants

AMOUNT: None Specified DEADLINE: June 1
MAJOR: Theological Studies

Open to male residents of the northern 26 counties of the Texas Panhandle who are pursuing a ministry degree or church related vocation with a minimum GPA of 2.5. June 1 is the deadline for continuing students and July 1 for new students. Submit a letter of request including background, religious preference, reason for application and future plans. Award requirements change regularly. Write to the address listed, enclosing a self-addressed, stamped envelope for an application and further information. GPA must be 2.5-4.0.

Mary E. Bivins Foundation
President
PO Box 1727
Amarillo, TX 79105-1727

720
Mary Faye Garrett Scholarship

AMOUNT: $200 DEADLINE: April 15
MAJOR: All Areas of Study

Open to all Harrisonville High School (MO) seniors who will be entering freshmen to a college or university. Award requirements change regularly. Applications are available in the Harrisonville Senior High School guidance office. No GPA requirement specified.

Harrisonville Senior High School
Attn: Roy Sackman
1504 East Elm Street
Harrisonville, MO 64701-2022

721
Mary Labelle Scholarship

AMOUNT: None Specified DEADLINE: Varies
MAJOR: Art Photography or Related Fields of Study

The Mary Labelle Scholarship is open to graduating seniors at Burlington High School (Burlington, WI). Students must be beginning postsecondary studies in art photography or related fields of study. Award requirements change regularly. Please visit your Guidance Office to receive an application and any additional details. No GPA requirement specified.

Burlington High School
Attn: Guidance Office
225 Robert Street
Burlington, WI 53105

722
Mary Lou Brown Scholarship

AMOUNT: $2500 DEADLINE: February 1
MAJOR: All Areas of Study

This scholarship is available to students with a minimum general class amateur radio license who reside in the ARRL Northwest Division. This division includes: Alaska, Idaho, Montana, Oregon, or Washington. Applicants must have a minimum GPA of 3.0 and be pursuing a B.A. or B.S. degree or higher course of study. Applicants must also demonstrate an interest in promoting the Amateur Radio Service. Award requirements change regularly. For further information, write the address provided, using a self-addressed, stamped envelope. GPA must be 3.0-4.0.

American Radio Relay League
Attn: ARRL Foundation
225 Main Street
Newington, CT 06111-1400

723
Mary V. Gaver Scholarship

AMOUNT: $3000 DEADLINE: April 1
MAJOR: Library Science

The Mary V. Gaver Scholarship is open to graduate students who plan to specialize in the field of library youth services. To be considered for this award, you must be a citizen or permanent resident of the U.S. or Canada and have applied for admission to an ALA-accredited master's degree program in library and information studies. You cannot have completed more than 12 semester hours (or its equivalent) toward the master's degree prior to June 1. Award requirements change regularly. No GPA requirement specified.

American Library Association
HRDR/Staff Liaison - Scholarship Juries
50 East Huron Street
Chicago, IL 60611-2795

724
Maryland Chiefs of Police Association Scholarship

AMOUNT: $500 DEADLINE: June 1
MAJOR: Law Enforcement

Open to students who are at least 17 years of age and enrolled in a law enforcement course of study. Applicants must have a minimum 2.5 GPA and be a resident of the state of Maryland. Applicants are also encouraged to submit a personal statement and community references. Award requirements change regularly. Please send a self-addressed, stamped envelope to receive your application and any further instructions from the scholarship provider. GPA must be 2.5-4.0.

Maryland Chiefs of Police Association
Special Projects Coordinator
7600 Barlowe Road
Landover, MD 20785

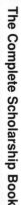

725
Masonic Temple Scholarship

AMOUNT: None Specified DEADLINE: Varies
MAJOR: All Fields of Study

The Masonic Temple Scholarship is open to graduating seniors at Burlington High School (Burlington, WI). Students must attend a four-year college. Award requirements change regularly. Please visit your Guidance Office to receive an application and any additional details. No GPA requirement specified.

Burlington High School
Attn: Guidance Office
225 Robert Street
Burlington, WI 53105

726
MassGrant

AMOUNT: $200-$1100 DEADLINE: May 1
MAJOR: All Areas of Study

The MassGrant is open to undergraduates who are residents of Massachusetts and are enrolled full-time in a program at a public institution in Massachusetts or one of the following reciprocal states: Rhode Island, New Hampshire, Connecticut, Maine, Pennsylvania, Maryland or Washington, DC. This award is based on financial need. Award requirements change regularly. To apply, you must submit the FAFSA. You may also visit the Massachusetts Office of Student Financial Assistance website. No GPA requirement specified.

Massachusetts Office of Student Financial Assistance
Public Service Grant Program
330 Stuart Street, Suite 304
Boston, MA 02116-5292

727
MASWE Memorial Scholarship

AMOUNT: $1000-$2000 DEADLINE: February 1
MAJOR: Engineering, Computer Science

The MASWE Memorial Scholarship is open to sophomore, junior and senior women in an ABET-accredited program or an SWE-approved school. You must be majoring in engineering or computer science and must demonstrate outstanding scholarship, financial need and have a minimum 3.5 GPA. Award requirements change regularly. Please send a self-addressed, stamped envelope to receive your application. For any further instructions from the scholarship provider, please browse their website at www.swe.org or email hq@swe.org. GPA must be 3.5-4.0.

Society of Women Engineers Headquarters
Scholarship Coordinator
120 Wall Street, FL 11
New York, NY 10005-3902

728
Matthew D. Lips Memorial Scholarship

AMOUNT: $500 DEADLINE: March 10
MAJOR: Building Trades, Drafting, Computer-Aided Design

The Matthew D. Lips Memorial Scholarship is open to Lenawee County (MI) graduating seniors who have already been accepted at a college. To be considered, you must be completing the Voc-Tech building trades program or the architectural component drafting/CAD program. Award requirements change regularly. Please send a self-addressed, stamped envelope to receive your application and any further instructions from the scholarship provider. No GPA requirement specified.

Morenci High School
Attn: Mrs. Melissa Parnell
788 Coomer Street
Morenci, MI 49256

729
Matthews Fellowship

AMOUNT: $10000 DEADLINE: January 15
MAJOR: Engineering, Computer Science

The Matthews Fellowship is open to full-time graduate students who are members of Tau Beta Pi. All Tau Beta Pi fellowships are awarded on the competitive basis of high scholarship, campus leadership and service, and promise of future contributions to the engineering profession. Preference is given to first-time graduate students. To be considered, you must submit an application and two letters of recommendation. Award requirements change regularly. Please send a self-addressed, stamped envelope to receive your application and any further instructions from the fellowship provider; or email dspierre@southernco.com; or find the application online at www.tbp.org. No GPA requirement specified.

Tau Beta Pi
c/o D. Stephen Pierre, Jr., P.E.
Alabama Power Company, PO Box 2247
Mobile, AL 36652-2247

730
Maurice Yonover Scholarship

AMOUNT: None Specified DEADLINE: March 1
MAJOR: Helping Professions

The Maurice Yonover Scholarship is open to Jewish men and women planning a career in the "helping professions" (nursing, teaching, etc.). You must live in the Chicago area or Northwest Indiana. You must also have already received training at the professional level. Award requirements change regularly. No GPA requirement specified.

Jewish Vocational Service
Attn: Scholarship Secretary
One South Franklin Street
Chicago, IL 60606-4694

731
Mayme and Herbert Frank Educational Fund

AMOUNT: $500-$2000 DEADLINE: October 1
MAJOR: Political Science, International Relations

Awards for students interested in creating a project that furthers the federalist principle or uniting democratic nations. For graduate study. Award requirements change regularly. Write to the address listed, enclosing a self-addressed, stamped envelope for an application and further information. No GPA requirement specified.

Association To Unite the Democracies
502 H Street SW
Washington, DC 20024-2726

732
Maynard Jenson American Legion Memorial Scholarship

AMOUNT: Maximum: $500 DEADLINE: March 1
MAJOR: All Areas of Study

Scholarships are available for Nebraska residents who attend college of university in Nebraska and are descendants of American Legion or auxiliary members, POWs, MIAs, KIAs or deceased veterans. Award requirements change regularly. Write to the address listed, enclosing a self-addressed, stamped envelope for an application and further information. No GPA requirement specified.

American Legion - Department of Nebraska
Department Adjutant
PO Box 5205
Lincoln, NE 68505-0205

733
McCurry Foundation, Inc. Scholarships

AMOUNT: $1500 DEADLINE: April 15
MAJOR: All Areas of Study

Open to public high school seniors who have a minimum GPA of 2.8. Preference is given to residents of Clay, Duval, Nassau and St. Johns counties in Florida and to residents of Watauga County, North Carolina. Factors that are considered include: financial need, academic success, leadership, work experience and community involvement and service. Applicants may be required to interview with the Scholarship Selection Committee as part of the final selection process. Award requirements change regularly. GPA must be 2.8-4.0.

McCurry Foundation, Inc.
Scholarship Selection Committee
3161 Saint Johns Bluff Rd South, Suite 4
Jacksonville, FL 32246-3741

734
McDonald's African-American Heritage Scholarship

AMOUNT: $1000-$5000 DEADLINE: March 8
MAJOR: All Areas of Study

The McDonald's African-American Heritage Scholarship is open to incoming African-American freshmen who are residents of New York, New Jersey or Connecticut and are in financial need. You must have a minimum 3.0 GPA and be involved in community activities. Winning students will receive a scholarship award of $1,000. In addition, the student displaying the most outstanding academic achievement will be awarded a $5,000 McDonald's Big Mac Valedictorian Award. The student who best demonstrates a commitment to community service will be awarded a $5,000 McDonald's Community Service Award. Award requirements change regularly. GPA must be 3.0-4.0.

MWW Group - McDonald's Tri-State
1 Meadowlands Plaza, 6th Floor
East Rutherford, NJ 07073

735
McDonald's Golden Arches Scholarship

AMOUNT: $1000-$5000 DEADLINE: March 8
MAJOR: All Areas of Study

The McDonald's Golden Arches Scholarship is open to incoming freshmen who are residents of New York, New Jersey, or Connecticut and are in financial need. You must have at least a 3.0 GPA and be involved in community activities. Winning students will receive a scholarship award of $1,000. In addition, the student displaying the most outstanding academic achievement will be awarded a $5,000 McDonald's Big Mac Valedictorian Award. The student who best demonstrates a commitment to community service will be awarded a $5,000 McDonald's Community Service Award. Award requirements change regularly. GPA must be 3.0-4.0.

MWW Group - McDonald's Tri-State
1 Meadowlands Plaza, 6th Floor
East Rutherford, NJ 07073

736
McDonald's GospelFest Music Scholarship

AMOUNT: $1000-$5000 DEADLINE: March 8
MAJOR: Music

The McDonald's GospelFest Music Scholarship is open to incoming freshmen who are music majors and residents of New York, New Jersey, or Connecticut and are in financial need. In order to apply, you must have a minimum 3.0 GPA and be involved in community activities. Award requirements change regularly. GPA must be 3.0-4.0.

MWW Group - McDonald's Tri-State
1 Meadowlands Plaza, 6th Floor
East Rutherford, NJ 07073

737
McDonald's Medallion Certificate Scholarship

AMOUNT: $200 DEADLINE: March 31
MAJOR: All Areas of Study

Open to all Harrisonville High School (MO) seniors who are planning to attend a college or technical school. Award requirements change regularly. Applications are available in the Harrisonville Senior High School guidance office. No GPA requirement specified.

Harrisonville Senior High School
Attn: Roy Sackman
1504 East Elm Street
Harrisonville, MO 64701-2022

Medical and Teaching Scholarship

AMOUNT: $1000 DEADLINE: March 25
MAJOR: Medicine, Education

The Medical and Teaching Scholarships are available to high school seniors or graduates under 20 years of age who are majoring in medicine or education. The applicant must be a New York state resident, the child or grandchild of a veteran and pursuing a career in medical or teaching fields. Award requirements change regularly. Please send a self-addressed, stamped envelope to receive your application and any further instructions from the scholarship provider. No GPA requirement specified.

American Legion - Department of New York
Attn: Adjutant
112 State Street, Suite 400
Albany, NY 12207-2015

739
Melva T. Owen Memorial Scholarship

AMOUNT: $7000 DEADLINE: March 31
MAJOR: All Areas of Study

The Melva T. Owen Memorial Scholarship is open to students who are legally blind and are pursuing or planning to pursue a full-time postsecondary course of study in the U.S. to gain financial independence. You will be considered based on academic excellence, service to the community and financial need. Award requirements change regularly. No GPA requirement specified.

National Federation of the Blind
Attn: Peggy Elliott, Chairman
805 5th Avenue
Grinnell, IA 50112-1653

740
Melva T. Owen Scholarship

AMOUNT: $3000 DEADLINE: March 1
MAJOR: All Areas of Study

These scholarships are available to legally blind undergraduate students. Award requirements change regularly. Write to the address listed, enclosing a self-addressed envelope for an application and further information. No GPA requirement specified.

American Council of the Blind
Attn: Billie Jean Keith
1155 15th Street NW, Suite 720
Washington, DC 20005-2706

741
Memphis Chapter 105 High School Incentive Scholarship Award

AMOUNT: $600 DEADLINE: February 1
MAJOR: Manufacturing Engineering, Manufacturing Engineering Technology or a Closely Related Field

Open to graduating high school seniors who intend to enroll in a manufacturing engineering or manufacturing engineering technology program. Applicants must have an overall GPA of 3.0 or higher and be residents of Memphis, TN. Award requirements change regularly. For further information, go to the SME website: www.sme.org. GPA must be 3.0-4.0.

Society of Manufacturing Engineering Education Foundation
PO Box 930
One SME Drive
Dearborn, MI 48121-0930

742
Mental Retardation Scholastic Achievement Scholarship

AMOUNT: Maximum: $1000 DEADLINE: March 15
MAJOR: Mental Retardation (Special Education, Mental Health)

This scholarship is open to juniors and seniors who are active communicant members of a Lutheran Congregation and working toward a career in the field of mental retardation. You must have a minimum 3.0 GPA and be able to document that a minimum of 100 work hours, volunteer and/or paid, have been completed to benefit people who are mentally retarded. Award requirements change regularly. For any further information, contact Kevin Keller, Coordinator of Outreach Programs and Services at (800) 369-4636, ext. 525 or email: kkeller@blhs.org. GPA must be 3.0-4.0.

Bethesda Lutheran Homes and Services, Inc.
Kevin Keller, Coordinator
700 Hoffman Drive
Watertown, WI 53094-6204

743
Merit and Memorial Scholarship

AMOUNT: Maximum: $1000 DEADLINE: March 15
MAJOR: All Areas of Study

These scholarships are open to Wisconsin residents who have a minimum GPA of 3.2, demonstrate financial need, attend an accredited school and are the child, wife or widow of a veteran. Granddaughters and great-granddaughters of veterans are eligible if they are American Legion Auxiliary members. Award requirements change regularly. Write to the address provided for additional information. GPA must be 3.2-4.0.

American Legion - Department of Wisconsin
Department Headquarters
812 East State Street
Milwaukee, WI 53202-3493

744
Merlyn and Myrna Downing Special Education Scholarship

AMOUNT: $1000 DEADLINE: March 31
MAJOR: Special Education

The Merlyn and Myrna Downing Special Education Scholarship is open to Lenawee County (MI) high school graduates. To be considered for the award, you must be pursuing a career in special education. Award requirements change regularly. Please send a self-addressed, stamped envelope to receive your application and any further instructions from the scholarship provider. No GPA requirement specified.

Morenci High School
Attn: Mrs. Melissa Parnell
788 Coomer Street
Morenci, MI 49256

745
Merlyn H. Downing Business Scholarship

AMOUNT: $1000 DEADLINE: March 31
MAJOR: Business

The Merlyn H. Downing Business Scholarship is open to
Lenawee County (MI) graduates. You qualify for the award if
you are entering your junior or senior year of college and you
are interested in pursuing a business career. A final requirement is that you plan to return to Lenawee County after you
receive your degree. Award requirements change regularly.
Please send a self-addressed, stamped envelope to receive
your application and any further instructions from the scholarship provider. No GPA requirement specified.

Morenci High School
Attn: Mrs. Melissa Parnell
788 Coomer Street
Morenci, MI 49256

746
MG James Ursano Scholarship Fund

AMOUNT: None Specified DEADLINE: February 19
MAJOR: All Areas of Study

This scholarship is open to dependent children, stepchildren,
or legally adopted children of soldiers who are on active duty,
retired, or deceased. Applicants must be unmarried U.S. citizens or permanent residents who are under the age of 22.
Must maintain a 2.0 GPA and attend school full-time. Award
requirements change regularly. For further information, please
write to the address listed, including a self-addressed, stamped
envelope or browse their website at www.aerhq.org.
Applications are only available from November 1 through
March 1. All applications must be postmarked no later than
March 1. GPA must be 2.0-4.0.

Army Emergency Relief National Headquarters
Education Department
200 Stovall Street
Alexandria, VA 22332-0001

747
MIA/KIA Dependents' Scholarship

AMOUNT: None Specified DEADLINE: May 1
MAJOR: All Areas of Study

Scholarship open to all full-time undergraduate/graduate students and high school seniors who are dependent children or
spouses of persons who were declared killed in action, missing in action or prisoners of war in 1960 or after. Must attend
an Arkansas school and be a state resident. There are four
deadlines: August 1 for the Fall Term, December 1 for the
Spring Term, May 1 for the Summer I Term and July 1 for the
Summer II Term. Award requirements change regularly. Write
to the address listed, enclosing a self-addressed, stamped

envelope for an application and further information. You may
also browse their website:
www.arscholarships.com/finsites.html. No GPA
requirement specified.

Arkansas Department of Higher Education
Financial Aid Division
114 East Capitol Avenue
Little Rock, AR 72201-3818

748
Michael J. Flosi Memorial Scholarship

AMOUNT: $500 DEADLINE: February 1
MAJOR: All Areas of Study

This scholarship is available to high school seniors with a
minimum technician class amateur radio license who have
been accepted to a postsecondary institution. Applicants must
be residents of the FCC Ninth Call District, which is comprised of Indiana, Illinois, and Wisconsin. Applicants must be
U.S. citizens or within three months of citizenship. Number of
awards varies due to funding. Award requirements change regularly. Write the address provided, using a self-addressed,
stamped envelope, for further information. No GPA
requirement specified.

American Radio Relay League
Attn: ARRL Foundation
225 Main Street
Newington, CT 06111-1400

749
Michael P. Metcalf Memorial Grant

AMOUNT: Maximum: $5000 DEADLINE: January 28
MAJOR: All Fields of Study

The Michael P. Metcalf Memorial Grant is available to legal
residents of Rhode Island who are entering their sophomore or
junior year in college. This grant helps subsidize experiences
intended to broaden students' perspectives and enhance their
personal growth. These experiences may include, but are not
limited to, travel in this country or abroad and a variety of
internship and public service programs. Traditional programs
and those that are a regular part of a student's curriculum,
such as a sponsored junior year abroad or a departmentally
sponsored summer research program, will not be funded. The
grant is not intended for the purchase of equipment or other
capital expenses. Award requirements change regularly. No
GPA requirement specified.

Rhode Island Foundation
Attn: Special Funds Office
70 Elm Street
Providence, RI 02903

750
Michael Reese Women's Board Scholarship

AMOUNT: None Specified DEADLINE: March 1
MAJOR: Medicine

The Michael Reese Women's Board Scholarship is open to
female Jewish medical students who have completed at least
one year of medical school at an accredited school by the

American Medical Association. You must have a minimum 3.0 GPA and live in Cook County (IL) or in the Chicago area. Award requirements change regularly GPA must be 3.0-4.0.

Jewish Vocational Service
Attn: Scholarship Secretary
One South Franklin Street
Chicago, IL 60606-4694

751
Michelle Gray Memorial Scholarship

AMOUNT: $250 DEADLINE: April 15
MAJOR: All Areas of Study

Open to Harrisonville High School graduating seniors who have a minimum 3.25 GPA and have been band members for at least three years. One boy and one girl are selected. Award requirements change regularly. Applications are available in the Harrisonville Senior High School guidance office. GPA must be 3.3-4.0.

Harrisonville Senior High School
Attn: Roy Sackman
1504 East Elm Street
Harrisonville, MO 64701-2022

752
Microsoft Corporation Graduate Scholarship

AMOUNT: $1000 DEADLINE: February 1
MAJOR: Computer Science, Computer Engineering

This scholarship is open to women in their first year of graduate school who are majoring in computer science or computer engineering at an ABET-accredited program or an SWE-approved school. The applicants must have minimum GPAs of 3.5. Award requirements change regularly. Please send a self-addressed, stamped envelope to receive your application. GPA must be 3.5-4.0.

Society of Women Engineers Headquarters
Scholarship Coordinator
120 Wall Street, FL 11
New York, NY 10005-3902

753
Microsoft Corporation Undergraduate Scholarship

AMOUNT: $1000 DEADLINE: February 1
MAJOR: Computer Science, Computer Engineering

This scholarship is open to entering sophomore, junior, and senior women who are majoring in computer science or computer engineering at an ABET-accredited program or an SWE-approved school. The applicants must have a minimum GPA of 3.5. Award requirements change regularly. Please send a self-addressed, stamped envelope to receive your application. For further instructions, please browse the SWE website at www.swe.org or email hq@swe.org for more information. GPA must be 3.5-4.0.

Society of Women Engineers Headquarters
Scholarship Coordinator
120 Wall Street, FL 11
New York, NY 10005-3902

754
Mid-Career Scholarship Program

AMOUNT: None Specified DEADLINE: Varies
MAJOR: Transportation

The Mid-Career Scholarship Program is open to government employees. Applicants must be U.S. citizens who wish to pursue continuing education in the traffic or transportation fields. Past scholastic and career performances will be considered. Award requirements change regularly. Contact the address below for further information or you may visit the website at www.atssa.com/fappl.htm. No GPA requirement specified.

American Traffic Safety Services Foundation
5440 Jefferson Davis Hwy
Fredericksburg, VA 22407-2627

755
MidAm Bank Scholarship

AMOUNT: $1000 DEADLINE: March 31
MAJOR: Business

The MidAm Bank Scholarship is open to Lenawee County (MI) graduating seniors. To be considered for the award, you must have a minimum 2.0 GPA and be interested in pursuing a business career. Award requirements change regularly. Please send a self-addressed, stamped envelope to receive your application and any further instructions from the scholarship provider. GPA must be 2.0-4.0.

Morenci High School
Attn: Mrs. Melissa Parnell
788 Coomer Street
Morenci, MI 49256

756
Midwest Energy Cooperative Scholarship

AMOUNT: $1000 DEADLINE: March 10
MAJOR: Vocational/Technical

The Glenn Martek Memorial Scholarship is open to Lenawee County (MI) graduating seniors. To be considered for the award, you must be completing one of the following programs: business services technology, computerized accounting, business office, computer information systems, or marketing education. Award requirements change regularly. Please send a self-addressed, stamped envelope to receive your application and any further instructions from the scholarship provider. No GPA requirement specified.

Morenci High School
Attn: Mrs. Melissa Parnell
788 Coomer Street
Morenci, MI 49256

757
Mildred McAnelly Scholarship

AMOUNT: None Specified DEADLINE: Varies
MAJOR: All Areas of Study

Open to Rocky Mountain High School seniors. Applicants must demonstrate financial need and must have maintained a high scholastic record in high school. A desire to become a teacher is a consideration in the selection process, but not a necessity. Application deadline, procedure, and award amount vary annually. Award requirements change regularly. Applications are available in January or February in the Rocky Mountain High School Career Center, as part of the Local Scholarship Packet. GPA must be 3.0-4.0.

Rocky Mountain High School
Scholarship Committee
1300 West Swallow Road
Fort Collins, CO 80526-2412

758
Mildred Monneyhand/Altrusa Scholarship

AMOUNT: $500 DEADLINE: March 19
MAJOR: All Fields of Study

The Mildred Monneyhand/Altrusa Scholarship is open to students who are graduating seniors at Chapel Hill High School, East Chapel Hill High School and Orange County High School (NC). Applicants must rank in the upper third of their class; have plans to attend and have applied to a community college, technical school, business school, a certified professional school, or a four-year college or university, have participated in service-oriented activities and demonstrated evidence of initiative toward self-support. Award requirements change regularly. To request an application, please contact your high school's guidance office or the Chapel Hill Altrusa Club. No GPA requirement specified.

East Chapel Hill High School
Attn: Career Development Coordinator
500 Weaver Dairy Road
Chapel Hill, NC 27514-1721

759
Miles Gray Memorial Scholarship

AMOUNT: $700 DEADLINE: May 26
MAJOR: All Areas of Study

This memorial scholarship is available to undergraduates who are members of Tau Kappa Epsilon. In order to apply, you must have demonstrated leadership within your chapter, on campus, or in your community. Also, you must have a minimum 2.5 GPA and be a full-time student in good standing. Award requirements change regularly. For further information, call (317) 872-6533, email: tef@tkehq.org or visit the website at: www.tke.org. GPA must be 2.5-4.0.

TKE Educational Foundation
Attn: Timothy L. Taschwer
8645 Founders Road
Indianapolis, IN 46268-1336

760
Millennium Scholarship

AMOUNT: $240-$2500 DEADLINE: Varies
MAJOR: All Fields of Study

The Millennium Scholarship is awarded to high school seniors who are Nevada residents. To be considered for this award, you must have a GPA of 3.0 or better and enroll in a public institution of higher learning in Nevada. Award requirements change regularly. For further instructions, please visit the provider's website at millennium.state.nv.us. GPA must be 3.0-4.0.

Office of the Nevada State Treasurer
555 East Washington Avenue, Suite 4600
Las Vegas, NV 89101

761
Mills Brothers Music Scholarship

AMOUNT: None Specified DEADLINE: May 17
MAJOR: Music, Performance Arts

This scholarship is open to Piqua, OH, residents who demonstrate they are pursuing a degree in music or performance arts in an accredited college, music school, or postsecondary institution. Secondary considerations are academic and extracurricular involvement. Financial need is the last consideration for the award. This is a renewable award. Award requirements change regularly. Please send a self-addressed, stamped envelope to the address provided for further information. No GPA requirement specified.

Piqua Area Chamber of Commerce
Mills Brothers Music Scholarship
326 North Main Street
Piqua, OH 45356-2316

762
Milton C. and Margaret L. Porter Special Education Scholarship

AMOUNT: $1000 DEADLINE: March 31
MAJOR: Special Education

The Milton C. and Margaret L. Porter Special Education Scholarship is open to Lenawee County (MI) high school graduates. To be considered for the award, you must be studying special education, preferably at an institution in Michigan. Award requirements change regularly. Please send a self-addressed, stamped envelope to receive your application and any further instructions from the scholarship provider. No GPA requirement specified.

Morenci High School
Attn: Mrs. Melissa Parnell
788 Coomer Street
Morenci, MI 49256

763
Milton Wexler Postdoctoral Fellowship

AMOUNT: $50000 DEADLINE: August 15
MAJOR: Hereditary Diseases, Disease Pathology, Medicine

This award is open to researchers studying areas of interest regard Huntington's Disease, including trinucleotide expansions, animal models, gene therapy, neurobiology and development of the basal ganglia, cell survival and death, and intercellular signaling in striatal neurons. Anyone accepting funding from the Hereditary Disease Foundation must agree to abide by the following policy: Propagatable materials should be freely available to other investigators following publication. Deadlines are February 15, August 15 and October 15. Thirty (30) copies of the completed application should be forwarded. If reprints are to be considered as part of the application, eight (8) copies should be provided for primary review. Award requirements change regularly. To obtain an application, please submit a letter of intent at anytime by post to the address provided or by email at the website: www.hdfounda-tion.org/intent.htm. No GPA requirement specified.

Hereditary Disease Foundation
Dr. Allan Tobin, Scientific Director
1427 7th Street, #2
Santa Monica, CA 90401

764
Minnesota State Grant

AMOUNT: $100-$7089 DEADLINE: Varies
MAJOR: All Fields of Study

The Minnesota State Grant is open to Minnesota residents who are graduates of a secondary school or its equivalent. You must be 17 years of age or older by the end of the academic year and must be enrolled as an undergraduate for at least three credits at an institution in Minnesota. This award may be renewable, but you have to reapply each year. Award require-ments change regularly. To apply, you must submit the FAFSA. For further information, please visit the Minnesota Higher Education Services Office at www.mheso.state.mn.us. No GPA requirement specified.

Minnesota Higher Education Services Office
Attn: Scholarship Coordinator
1450 Energy Park Drive, Suite 350
St. Paul, MN 55108

765
Minorities in Government Finance Scholarship

AMOUNT: $3500 DEADLINE: February 4
MAJOR: Public Administration, Accounting, Finance, Political Science, Economics, Business Administration

The Minorities in Government Finance Scholarship is open to current full- or part-time upperdivision undergraduate and graduate students in public administration (governmental) accounting, finance, political science, economics, or business administration (with a specific focus on government or non-profit management). Applicants must be citizens or permanent residents of the U.S. or Canada and belong to one of the fol-lowing groups: African-American, Native American, Hispanic, Eskimo or Aleut, Asian or Pacific Islander. Applicants are required to submit a recommendation from their academic advisor, department chair (undergraduate applicants), or dean of the graduate program (graduate applicants). Award require-ments change regularly. For an application and further infor-mation please send a self-addressed, stamped envelope to the address listed below or call (312) 977-9700. No GPA requirement specified.

Government Finance Officers Association
Attn: Scholarship Committee
180 North Michigan Avenue, Suite 800
Chicago, IL 60601-7476

766
Minority Masters Fellows Loan Program

AMOUNT: $2500-$7500 DEADLINE: June 1
MAJOR: Mathematics, Science, Foreign Languages, Education

African-American, Asian-American, and Hispanic students

who are admitted to a master's program in mathematics, the sciences or foreign languages or to African-American, Asian-American and Hispanic students in the fifth year of a teacher education program who were recipients of the minority teacher scholarship. Students must be full-time during fall/spring; can go part-time for three summers. Recipients are required to teach full-time in an Arkansas public school or institution for two years to receive total forgiveness of the loan. Award requirements change regularly. Write to the address listed, enclosing a self-addressed, stamped envelope for an application and further information. You may also browse their website: www.arscholarships.com/finsites.html. No GPA requirement specified.

Arkansas Department of Higher Education
Financial Aid Division
114 East Capitol Avenue
Little Rock, AR 72201-3818

767
Minority Scholarship Program

AMOUNT: $2500 DEADLINE: October 15
MAJOR: Psychology

The Minority Scholarship Program is open to first-year, full-time students accepted into a doctoral level psychology pro-gram in the state of California who are members of one or more of these established ethnic minority groups: Black/African American, Hispanic/Latino, Asian/Asian American, American Indian/Alaskan Native, or Pacific Islander. To be considered for this award, you must be a grad-uate from a regionally accredited undergraduate institution, demonstrate community involvement and leadership, have an academic focus on ethnic minority/cultural issues, and have financial need. Another criterion of the award is that you plan to work with direct delivery of services to a culturally diverse population in either a public or private setting. Students in ter-minal master's level programs are not eligible. Award require-ments change regularly. No GPA requirement specified.

California State Psychological Association Foundation
Attn: Scholarship Department
1022 G Street
Sacramento, CA 95814-0817

768
Minority Student Scholarship

AMOUNT: $1000 DEADLINE: May 31
MAJOR: Human Service, Church Leadership

The Minority Student Scholarship is open to full-time minori-ty freshmen students attending an American Baptist-related college or university. Preference will be given to persons preparing for careers in church leadership or human services. Recipients must maintain satisfactory academic standing. Applicants must be members of an American Baptist church for at least one year before applying for aid, enrolled at an accredited educational institution in the U.S. or Puerto Rico. U.S. citizenship is required. Award requirements change regu-larly. Please send a self-addressed, stamped envelope to receive your application and any further instructions from the scholarship provider. No GPA requirement specified.

American Baptist Financial Aid Program
Educational Ministries ABC/USA
PO Box 851
Valley Forge, PA 19482-0851

769
Minority Teacher Scholarship

AMOUNT: None Specified DEADLINE: Varies
MAJOR: Elementary Education, Secondary Education

Open to minority students pursuing a course of study allowing them to teach in elementary or secondary schools in Indiana. Colleges and universities establish eligibility criteria and filing deadlines for this program. Award requirements change regularly. For further information and an application, please contact a high school guidance counselor, a college/university financial aid office, or write to the address listed, including a self-addressed, stamped envelope. You may also visit the SSACI website: www.ai.org/ssaci. GPA must be 2.0-4.0.

State Student Assistance Commission of Indiana
Attn: Scholarship Committee
150 West Market Street, Suite 500
Indianapolis, IN 46204

770
Minority Teachers Scholarship

AMOUNT: Maximum: $5000 DEADLINE: June 1
MAJOR: Education

The Minority Teachers Scholarship is open to African-American, Asian-American, and Hispanic college juniors who are enrolled full-time at an Arkansas public or private four-year institution. You must be admitted to an approved program resulting in teacher certification. The award also requires that you have a minimum 2.5 cumulative GPA and that you are an Arkansas resident. Unless certain criteria have been met, the grant will become a loan. Award requirements change regularly. Write to the address listed, enclosing a self-addressed, stamped envelope for an application and further information. You may also browse their website: www.arscholarships.com/finsites.html. GPA must be 2.5-4.0.

Arkansas Department of Higher Education
Financial Aid Division
114 East Capitol Avenue
Little Rock, AR 72201-3818

771
Miriam L. Hornback Scholarship

AMOUNT: $3000 DEADLINE: April 1
MAJOR: Library Science, Information Science

The Miriam L. Hornback Scholarship is open to ALA or library support staff currently working in a library. To be considered for this award, you must be a citizen or permanent resident of the U.S. or Canada and have applied for admission to an ALA-accredited master's degree program in library and information studies. You cannot have completed more than 12 semester hours (or its equivalent) toward the master's degree prior to June 1. Award requirements change regularly. No GPA requirement specified.

American Library Association
HRDR/Staff Liaison - Scholarship Juries
50 East Huron Street
Chicago, IL 60611-2795

772
Miriam S. Grunfeld Scholarship Fund

AMOUNT: Maximum: $950 DEADLINE: Varies
MAJOR: All Areas of Study

The purpose of the Miriam S. Grunfeld Scholarship Fund is to provide annual grants to educate young Jewish students 26 years of age and younger who otherwise would not be able to fulfill their educational aspirations. Applicants must demonstrate financial need and be residents of San Francisco, San Mateo, northern Santa Clara, Marin or Sonoma counties in California. Deadlines vary; therefore, it is encouraged that applicants apply early. Award requirements change regularly. No GPA requirement specified.

Jewish Family and Children's Services
Attn: Loans and Grants Department
2245 Post Street
San Francisco, CA 94115

773
Mississippi Scholarship

AMOUNT: $500 DEADLINE: February 1
MAJOR: Electronics, Communications or Related Fields

This scholarship is available to students with any class amateur radio license who are residents of, and attend school in, Mississippi. Applicants must be under 30 years of age and majoring in electronics, communications or related areas at a baccalaureate or graduate institution in Mississippi. Award requirements change regularly. Write the address provided, using a self-addressed, stamped envelope, for further information. No GPA requirement specified.

American Radio Relay League
Attn: ARRL Foundation
225 Main Street
Newington, CT 06111-1400

774
Mississippi Tuition Assistance Grant

AMOUNT: $500-$1000 DEADLINE: September 15
MAJOR: All Fields of Study

The Mississippi Tuition Assistance Grant (MTAG) is available to Mississippi residents. One year residency and full-time enrollment are required. A grant of $500 per year is available for freshmen and sophomores and $1,000 per year for juniors and seniors. The grant is renewable to you based on continued full-time status, maintenance of a 2.5 GPA and resubmission of your application. If you receive this award, you will not be eligible to receive the Federal Pell Grant. Award requirements change regularly. To apply, you will need to submit a FAFSA and an MTAG application. The MTAG application can be obtained from your high school counselor or college financial aid office. For more information, please visit the Mississippi Board of Trustees of Institutions of Higher Learning at www.ihl.state.ms.us. No GPA requirement specified.

Mississippi Office of Trustees/State Institutions of Higher Learning
State Student Financial
3825 Ridgewood Road
Jackson, MS 39211-6463

775
MJSA Education Foundation Scholarship

AMOUNT: $500-$2000 DEADLINE: May 11
MAJOR: Jewelry-Related Studies

The MJSA Education Foundation Scholarship is available for residents of Rhode Island who are pursuing a jewelry-related curriculum. Your selection is based on course of study, samples of work (where appropriate), financial need, jewelry industry experience and academic achievement. In addition to your application, you will also need to submit at least one letter of recommendation, a college transcript, a written statement which includes an explanation of your career plans and, if you are a design student, you need to submit no more than three slides showing examples of current work. Award requirements change regularly. No GPA requirement specified.

Rhode Island Foundation
Attn: Special Funds Office
70 Elm Street
Providence, RI 02903

776
MLA Scholarship for Minority Students

AMOUNT: $2000 DEADLINE: December 1
MAJOR: Medical Librarianship

The MLA Scholarship for Minority Students is open to minority students entering or continuing graduate school in the area of health science librarianship. In order to apply, you must be studying in an ALA-accredited school. Award requirements change regularly. Please send a self-addressed, stamped envelope to receive your application and any further instructions from the scholarship provider, browse their website www.mlanet.org/scholarships/grants.html or email mlasal@mlahq.org. No GPA requirement specified.

Medical Library Association
Attn: Scholarship Committee
6 North Michigan Avenue, Suite 300
Chicago, IL 60602

777
Monetary Award Program

AMOUNT: Maximum: $4530 DEADLINE: Varies
MAJOR: All Fields of Study

The Monetary Award Program (MAP) provides grants to Illinois residents who demonstrate financial need. To be considered for this award, you must be a U.S. citizen or an eligible noncitizen, enrolled at least half-time as an undergraduate at a MAP-approved Illinois institution in a degree or certificate program and maintain satisfactory academic progress as determined by the college or university. You are required to submit the FAFSA, which determines your financial need and your eligibility for this award, and should list as the first school choice any MAP-approved Illinois postsecondary institution that you are considering. Award requirements change regularly. The FAFSA should be submitted as soon as possible after January 1 prior to the academic year that starts on or after July 1. Funding for the MAP grant is limited; to ensure full-year consideration for an award, apply early. ISAC may establish strict application deadlines. Check with your college or university financial aid office, high school guidance counselor or ISAC for the most current deadline information. No GPA requirement specified.

Illinois Student Assistance Commission
Attn: Scholarships and Grants Services
1755 Lake Cook Road
Deerfield, IL 60015-5209

778
Montgomery GI Bill

AMOUNT: Maximum: $6840 DEADLINE: Varies
MAJOR: All Areas of Study

The Montgomery GI Bill is open to applicants who enlist in the Army Reserves for six years. Award requirements change regularly. Please send a self-addressed, stamped envelope to receive your application and any further instructions from the scholarship provider. No GPA requirement specified.

U.S. Army Reserve
PO Box 3219
Warminster, PA 18974-9844

779
Montgomery GI Bill/Army College Fund

AMOUNT: Maximum: $30000 DEADLINE: Varies
MAJOR: All Areas of Study

The Montgomery GI Bill/Army College Fund is available to applicants who enlist in the active Army for specified critical military skills. The individual must contribute $1,200, which is deducted from the first year's pay. Award requirements change regularly. Please send a self-addressed, stamped envelope to receive your application and any further instructions from the scholarship provider. No GPA requirement specified.

U.S. Army Reserve
PO Box 3219
Warminster, PA 18974-9844

780
Morton B. Duggan Jr. Memorial Scholarship

AMOUNT: $1000 DEADLINE: June 30
MAJOR: Respiratory Therapy

This scholarship is open to students who have completed at least one semester in an AMA-approved respiratory care program. If you are from Georgia or South Carolina, you will receive preference, but applications are also accepted from students in other states. You must have a minimum 3.0 GPA and provide a photocopy of your birth certificate, social security card, immigration visa or evidence of citizenship. Recipients will be selected by September 1. The award also includes registration for the AARC Respiratory International Congress, airfare, one night lodging, and a certificate of recognition. Award requirements change regularly. GPA must be 3.0-4.0.

American Respiratory Care Foundation
Education Recognition Award
11030 Ables Lane
Dallas, TX 75229-4524

Mozelle and Willard Gold Memorial Scholarship

AMOUNT: $3000 DEADLINE: March 31
MAJOR: All Areas of Study

The Mozelle and Willard Gold Memorial Scholarship is open to students who are legally blind and are pursuing or planning to pursue a full-time postsecondary course of study in the U.S. Your selection will be based on academic excellence, service to the community and financial need. Award requirements change regularly. No GPA requirement specified.

National Federation of the Blind
Attn: Peggy Elliott, Chairman
805 5th Avenue
Grinnell, IA 50112-1653

782
Music or Recreational Therapy AMVETS Scholarship

AMOUNT: None Specified DEADLINE: March 1
MAJOR: Musical Therapy, Recreational Therapy

The Music or Recreational Therapy AMVETS Scholarship is open to Illinois high school seniors who have taken the American College Test (ACT) and plan to major in musical or recreational therapy. In order to apply, you must be an unmarried child of a veteran who served after September 15, 1940. Your parent or parents must have been honorably discharged or be presently serving in the military. Award requirements change regularly. No GPA requirement specified.

AMVETS - Illinois State Headquarters
Illinois AMVETS Scholarship Program
2200 South 6th Street
Springfield, IL 62703-3454

783
Myra Snyder Scholarship

AMOUNT: $1000 DEADLINE: May 26
MAJOR: All Areas of Study

This scholarship is open to initiated undergraduate members of Tau Kappa Epsilon. In order to apply, you must be in good standing with your chapter, have a demonstrated record of active participation within the chapter, including officer and chairmanship leadership positions. Also, you must be active in campus organizations, be a full-time student and have a minimum 2.5 GPA. Award requirements change regularly. For further information, call (317) 872-6533, email: tef@tkehq.org or visit the website at: www.tke.org. GPA must be 2.5-4.0.

TKE Educational Foundation
Attn: Timothy L. Taschwer
8645 Founders Road
Indianapolis, IN 46268-1336

784
Myrtle and Earl Walker Scholarship

AMOUNT: $1000 DEADLINE: February 1
MAJOR: Manufacturing Engineering, Manufacturing Engineering Technology

Open to full-time undergraduates enrolled in a degree program in manufacturing engineering or manufacturing engineering technology. Applicants must have an overall GPA of 3.5 or higher. Award requirements change regularly. For further information, please contact Dora Murray at (313) 271-1500, ext. 1709 (email: murrdor@sme.org) or Theresa Macias, ext. 1707 (email: maciter@sme.org). You may also go to the SME website: www.sme.org. GPA must be 3.5-4.0.

Society of Manufacturing Engineering Education Foundation
PO Box 930
One SME Drive
Dearborn, MI 48121-0930

785
NABA National Scholarship

AMOUNT: $6000 DEADLINE: December 31
MAJOR: Accounting, Finance, Business, Taxation

The NABA National Scholarship is available to ethnic minority accounting, finance or business undergraduates or accounting and taxation graduates. Applicants must be currently enrolled as full-time students and be paid NABA members. A minimum 3.3 GPA is required. Award requirements change regularly. Please send a self-addressed, stamped envelope to receive your application and any further instructions from the scholarship provider or call (301) 474-6222, ext. 14. GPA must be 3.3-4.0.

National Association of Black Accountants, Inc.
Attn: Scholarship Committee
7249-A Hanover Parkway
Greenbelt, MD 20770

786
Nagel Fellowship

AMOUNT: $10000 DEADLINE: January 15
MAJOR: Engineering, Computer Science

The Nagel Fellowship is open to full-time graduate students who are members of Tau Beta Pi. Fellowships are awarded on the competitive basis of high scholarship, campus leadership and service, and promise of future contributions to the engineering profession. Preference is given to first-time graduate students. To be considered, you must submit an application and two letters of recommendation. Award requirements change regularly. Please send a self-addressed, stamped envelope to receive your application and any further instructions from the fellowship provider; or email dspierre@southernco.com; or find the application online at www.tbp.org. No GPA requirement specified.

Tau Beta Pi
c/o D. Stephen Pierre, Jr., P.E.
Alabama Power Company, PO Box 2247
Mobile, AL 36652-22473

787
NALCO Foundation Scholarship

AMOUNT: $1050 DEADLINE: May 15
MAJOR: Chemical Engineering

The NALCO Foundation Scholarship is open to freshmen women majoring in chemical engineering. Applicants must have been accepted into an ABET-accredited program or SWE-approved school. This scholarship is renewable for three additional years and therefore is awarded only once every four years. Award requirements change regularly. Please send a self-addressed, stamped envelope to receive your application. For further instructions, please browse the SWE website at www.swe.org or email hq@swe.org. No GPA requirement specified.

Society of Women Engineers Headquarters
Scholarship Coordinator
120 Wall Street, FL 11
New York, NY 10005-3902

788
NASA Earth Science Graduate Student Research Program

AMOUNT: None Specified DEADLINE: March 15
MAJOR: Earth-Related Sciences

Fellowships for students enrolled full-time in a full-time M.Sc. and/or Ph.D. program at accredited U.S. universities and in a field supporting the study of earth as a system. Forty awards per year. Award requirements change regularly. Write to the address listed, enclosing a self-addressed, stamped envelope for an application and further information. No GPA requirement specified.

NASA Earth System Science Fellowship Program
Code Y
400 Virginia Avenue SW, Suite 700
Washington, DC 20024-2701

789
NASC/NOD Awards Program

AMOUNT: None Specified DEADLINE: March 17
MAJOR: None Specified

NASSP through the National Association of Student Councils supports the need to involve students with disabilities in cocurricular activities. The NASC/NOD Awards Program, funded by the National Organization on Disability and J.C. Penney, recognizes student councils that strive to involve students with disabilities in student activities programs. Each winning middle and high school student council will receive a $500 cash award. Please note, this is not an individual collegiate award, but an award for middle schools through high schools that meet the required criteria. Award requirements change regularly. See the website at www.nassp.org and click on student activities. No GPA requirement specified.

National Association of Secondary School Principals
Attn: Scholarship Coordinator
1900 Association Drive
Reston, VA 20191-1599

790
National Academy of Education/Spencer Postdoctoral Fellowship

AMOUNT: Maximum: $45000 DEADLINE: December 1
MAJOR: Education, Educational Research

The National Academy of Education/Spencer Postdoctoral Fellowship is designed to promote scholarship on matters relevant to the improvement of education in all its forms and is open to applicants who received their Ph.D., Ed.D., or equivalent research degree within the last five years. Applications from persons in education, the humanities, the social and behavioral sciences, or other disciplines will be accepted, provided that they describe research relevant to education. Applicants will be judged on their past research′record, the promise of early work, and the quality of the project described in the application. Fellows will receive $45,000 for one academic year of research, or $22,500 for each of two contiguous years working half-time. Award requirements change regularly. Please send a self-addressed, stamped envelope to receive your application and any further instructions from the scholarship provider; or visit the website at www.nae.nyu.edu; or call (212) 998-9035. Applications must be requested before November 18. No GPA requirement specified.

National Academy of Education
c/o NYU - School of Education
726 Broadway, Room 509
New York, NY 10003-9580

791
National Council of State Garden Clubs Scholarship

AMOUNT: Maximum: $1000 DEADLINE: July 1
MAJOR: Horticulture, Floriculture, Landscape Design, Conservation, Forestry, Botany, Agronomy, Plant Pathology, Environmental Control, City Planning, Land Management and/or Related Areas

Awards for juniors, seniors, and graduate students who are Connecticut residents attending a Connecticut school and are studying in the above areas. Applicants must have a minimum GPA of 3.0 and be able to demonstrate financial need. Award requirements change regularly. Write to the address listed, enclosing a self-addressed, stamped envelope for an application and further information. GPA must be 3.0-4.0.

Federated Garden Clubs of Connecticut, Inc.
Headquarters
PO Box 854
Branford, CT 06405-0854

792
National Federation of the Blind Computer Science Scholarship

AMOUNT: $3000 DEADLINE: March 31
MAJOR: Computer Science

The National Federation of the Blind Computer Science Scholarship is open to students who are legally blind and are pursuing or planning to pursue a full-time postsecondary course of study in the U.S. You must be majoring in a computer science field. Your selection will be based on academic excellence, service to the community, and financial need. Award requirements change regularly. No GPA requirement specified.

National Federation of the Blind
Attn: Peggy Elliott, Chairman
805 5th Avenue
Grinnell, IA 50112-1653

793
National Federation of the Blind Educator of Tomorrow Award

AMOUNT: $3000 DEADLINE: March 31
MAJOR: Elementary Education, Secondary Education, Postsecondary Education

The National Federation of the Blind Educator of Tomorrow Award is open to students who are legally blind and are pursuing or planning to pursue a full-time postsecondary course of study in the U.S. You must be planning a career in elementary, secondary, or postsecondary education. Your selection is based on academic excellence, service to the community, and financial need. Award requirements change regularly. No GPA requirement specified.

National Federation of the Blind
Attn: Peggy Elliott, Chairman
805 5th Avenue
Grinnell, IA 50112-1653

794
National Federation of the Blind Humanities Scholarship

AMOUNT: $3000 DEADLINE: March 31
MAJOR: Humanities

The National Federation of the Blind Humanities Scholarship is open to students who are legally blind and are pursuing or planning to pursue a full-time postsecondary course of study in the U.S. You must be studying in the traditional humanities such as art, English, foreign languages, history, philosophy, or religion. Your selection is based on academic excellence, service to the community and financial need. Award requirements change regularly. No GPA requirement specified.

National Federation of the Blind
Attn: Peggy Elliott, Chairman
805 5th Avenue
Grinnell, IA 50112-1653

795
National Federation of the Blind Scholarship

AMOUNT: $3000-$7000 DEADLINE: March 31
MAJOR: All Areas of Study

The National Federation of the Blind Scholarship is open to students who are legally blind and are pursuing or planning to pursue a full-time postsecondary course of study in the U.S. You will be considered on academic excellence, service to the community, and financial need. One scholarship will go to a student working full-time. Award requirements change regularly. No GPA requirement specified.

National Federation of the Blind
Attn: Peggy Elliott, Chairman
805 5th Avenue
Grinnell, IA 50112-1653

796
National Fourth Infantry (IVY) Division Association Scholarship

AMOUNT: $6000 DEADLINE: Varies
MAJOR: All Areas of Study

The National Fourth Infantry (IVY) Division Association Scholarship is open to students whose parent died in action or in the line of duty in Vietnam while attached to the Fourth Infantry Division. Award requirements change regularly. Please send a self-addressed, stamped envelope to receive your application and any further instructions from the scholarship provider. No GPA requirement specified.

National Fourth Infantry (IVY) Division Association
Attn: Scholarship Coordinator
PO Box 276
Aquebogue, NY 11931

797
National High School Poetry Contest

AMOUNT: Maximum: $1000 DEADLINE: Varies
MAJOR: All Areas of Study

The National High School Poetry Contest is open to all U.S. high school students. Poems must be of no more than 20 lines, unpublished, and the sole work of the entrant. No more than two poems will be accepted from any entrant and no email entries will be accepted. Grand prize will be a $1,000 college scholarship. There will be numerous other prizes including 12 second prizes, and 15 third prizes. Entries will be judged on creativity, originality, imagery, and artistic quality. All winning poems will be published in an upcoming anthology, which will be copyrighted by the Live Poets Society. Upon publication all rights will revert to the poet. Only the first 3,000 entries from the five geographical regions will be accepted. Award requirements change regularly. Please send a self-addressed, stamped envelope to receive your application and any further instructions from the scholarship provider or visit their website: www.geocities.com/soho/village/3801. No GPA requirement specified.

DIET-Live Poets Society
National High School Poetry Contest
PO Box 8841
Turnersville, NJ 08012

798
National Honor Society Scholarship

AMOUNT: $1000 DEADLINE: January 28
MAJOR: All Fields of Study

These scholarships are for members of the National Honor Society. Two senior students from each participating chapter may be nominated (nomination required). In order to apply, you must demonstrate that you possess outstanding character, scholarship, service, and leadership. Award requirements change regularly. Contact your high school NHS chapter advisor or principal to express your interest in this award program. Winners will be announced in May. GPA must be 3.0-4.0.

National Association of Secondary School Principals
Attn: Scholarship Coordinator
1900 Association Drive
Reston, VA 20191-1599

799
National Honor Society Scholarship

AMOUNT: None Specified DEADLINE: Varies
MAJOR: All Fields of Study

The National Honor Society Scholarship is open to graduating seniors at Burlington High School (Burlington, WI) who are members of the National Honor Society. Award requirements change regularly. Please see your NHS advisor to receive an application and any additional details. No GPA requirement specified.

Burlington High School
Attn: Guidance Office
225 Robert Street
Burlington, WI 53105

800
National Minority Scholarship Program

AMOUNT: $1500 DEADLINE: April 23
MAJOR: Public Relations, Communications

Applicants must be minority undergraduate students in public relations attending four-year accredited schools. Must have a GPA of at least 3.0. Public Relations Student Society of America membership and a major or minor of public relations is preferred. Students should have obtained at least junior status by the time the scholarship will be used. If your school does not offer a public relations degree, a major in communications or journalism is acceptable. Award requirements change regularly. Write to the address listed, enclosing a self-addressed, stamped envelope for an application and further information or browse their website: www.prsa.org. GPA must be 3.0-4.0.

Public Relations Society of America
Director Educational Affairs
33 Irving Place
New York, NY 10003-2332

801
National Presbyterian College Scholarship

AMOUNT: $500-$1400 DEADLINE: December 1
MAJOR: All Areas of Study

Scholarships for high school seniors who are members of the Presbyterian Church (U.S.A.) and are U.S. citizens or permanent residents. Applicants must take the SAT/ACT prior to December 15 of their senior year. Award requirements change regularly. Write to the address listed for information and an application enclosing a self-addressed, stamped envelope or call (502) 569-5745. No GPA requirement specified.

Presbyterian Church (U.S.A.)
Office of Financial Aid for Studies
100 Witherspoon Street
Louisville, KY 40202-1396

802
National President's Scholarship

AMOUNT: $1500-$2000 DEADLINE: March 16
MAJOR: All Areas of Study

The National President's Scholarship is available to children of veterans who served in the U.S. Armed Forces in World War I, World War II, Korea, Vietnam, Panama, Grenada, or Persian Gulf conflicts. The selection is based upon character, patriotism, leadership, academic achievement, and financial need. Award requirements change regularly. Please send a self-addressed, stamped envelope to receive your application and any further instructions from the scholarship provider. No GPA requirement specified.

American Legion Auxiliary - Department of Indiana
Sue Lifford, Department Secretary
777 North Meridian Street, Rm 107
Indianapolis, IN 46204-1117

803
National President's Scholarship

AMOUNT: $500-$2500 DEADLINE: Varies
MAJOR: All Areas of Study

The National President's Scholarship is open to high school graduates who are children of veterans (living or dead) who served in the Armed Forces during the eligibility dates for membership in the American Legion. You must be an Oregon resident and must be recommended by an American Legion Unit to be eligible. The Oregon first place winner is entered in the National Division competition. If the Oregon applicant should win on a National level, the $1,000 goes the Oregon second place winner and the alternate would then receive $500. Award requirements change regularly. Please send a self-addressed, stamped envelope to the Chairman of Education in order to receive your application and any further instructions from the scholarship provider. No GPA requirement specified.

American Legion Auxiliary - Department of Oregon
Chairman of Education
PO Box 1730
Wilsonville, OR 97070-1730

804
National Sculpture Society Scholarship

AMOUNT: $1000 DEADLINE: May 31
MAJOR: Art - Sculpture

Scholarships are awarded on a competitive basis to students showing talent in figurative or representational sculpture. Students must be enrolled in a college or art school, but may be majoring in subjects other than art. Photos of work (8 X 10 black and white preferred), brief biography, and letters of recommendation will be required. Award is based completely on the quality of sculpture submitted. Must be able to demonstrate financial need. Award requirements change regularly. No GPA requirement specified.

National Sculpture Society
Attn: Scholarship Committee
1177 Avenue of the Americas
New York, NY 10036

805
National Service Scholars Program

AMOUNT: None Specified DEADLINE: Varies
MAJOR: All Areas of Study

The National Service Scholars Program is open to college-bound high school seniors who have performed community service for at least one year. This service can include (but is not limited to) volunteer work for community organizations, service through your church or synagogue, involvement in service-oriented school organizations, and any individual efforts that help others. The Corporation for National Service is offering a matching $500 scholarship for a high school junior or senior nominated by each high school principal. The deadline for this award is the close of the school year. Award requirements change regularly. For more information, see the National Service Scholars Program web page at www.cns.gov. Application packages will be mailed to principals in March. You may also contact the Citizens' Scholarship Foundation of America, Inc., which administers the program, at (888) 275-5018. No GPA requirement specified.

Future Business Leaders of America
Attn: Scholarship Coordinator
1912 Association Drive
Reston, VA 22091

806
National Tourism Alabama/Birmingham Legacy Scholarship

AMOUNT: $1000 DEADLINE: April 17
MAJOR: Travel and Tourism, Hotel/Restaurant Management

The Alabama/Birmingham Legacy Scholarship is open to Alabama residents who are full-time juniors or seniors pursuing a degree in a travel and tourism-related field. To be considered for this award, you must be enrolled in a two- or four-year college in North America. Award requirements change regularly. No GPA requirement specified.

National Tourism Foundation
PO Box 3071
546 East Main Street
Lexington, KY 40508-3071

807
National Tourism California Scholarship Program

AMOUNT: $1000 DEADLINE: April 17
MAJOR: Travel and Tourism, Hotel/Restaurant Management

The National Tourism California Scholarship Program is open to California residents who are pursuing a degree in a travel and tourism-related field. To be considered for this award, you must be a junior or senior enrolled in a North American two- or four-year college full-time. Award requirements change regularly. No GPA requirement specified.

National Tourism Foundation
PO Box 3071
546 East Main Street
Lexington, KY 40508-3071

808
National Tourism Cleveland Legacy I Scholarship

AMOUNT: $500 DEADLINE: April 17
MAJOR: Travel and Tourism, Hotel/Motel Management

The National Tourism Cleveland Legacy I Scholarship is open to Ohio residents who are pursuing careers in a travel or tourism-related field. To be considered for this award, you must be a junior or senior enrolled in a North American four-year college full-time. Award requirements change regularly. No GPA requirement specified.

National Tourism Foundation
PO Box 3071
546 East Main Street
Lexington, KY 40508-3071

809
National Tourism Cleveland Legacy II Scholarship

AMOUNT: $500 DEADLINE: April 17
MAJOR: Travel and Tourism, Hotel/Restaurant Management

The National Tourism Cleveland Legacy II Scholarship is open to residents of Ohio who are pursuing a degree in a travel and tourism-related field. To be considered for this award, you must be a junior or senior enrolled in a North American two-year college full-time. Award requirements change regularly. No GPA requirement specified.

National Tourism Foundation
PO Box 3071
546 East Main Street
Lexington, KY 40508-3071

810
National Tourism Connecticut Scholarship Program

AMOUNT: $1000 DEADLINE: April 17
MAJOR: Travel and Tourism, Hotel/Restaurant Management

The National Tourism Connecticut Scholarship Program is open to Connecticut residents pursuing a degree in a travel and tourism-related field. To be considered for this award, you must be a junior or senior enrolled in a North American four-year college full-time. Award requirements change regularly. No GPA requirement specified.

National Tourism Foundation
PO Box 3071
546 East Main Street
Lexington, KY 40508-3071

811

National Tourism Florida Scholarship Program

AMOUNT: $500 DEADLINE: April 17
MAJOR: Travel and Tourism, Hotel/Restaurant Management

The National Tourism Florida Scholarship Program is open to Florida residents pursuing a degree in a travel or tourism-related field. To be qualified for the award, you must be a junior or senior enrolled in a North American four-year college full-time. Award requirements change regularly. No GPA requirement specified.

National Tourism Foundation
PO Box 3071
546 East Main Street
Lexington, KY 40508-3071

812

National Tourism Michigan Scholarship Program

AMOUNT: $1000 DEADLINE: April 17
MAJOR: Travel and Tourism, Hotel/Restaurant Management

The National Tourism Michigan Scholarship Program is open to Michigan residents pursuing a degree in a travel and tourism-related field. To be considered for the award, you must be a junior or senior enrolled in a Michigan four-year college full-time. Award requirements change regularly. No GPA requirement specified.

National Tourism Foundation
PO Box 3071
546 East Main Street
Lexington, KY 40508-3071

813

National Tourism Minnesota Legacy Scholarship

AMOUNT: $1000 DEADLINE: April 17
MAJOR: Travel and Tourism, Hotel/Restaurant Management

The National Tourism Minnesota Legacy Scholarship is open to Minnesota residents who are pursuing a degree in a travel and tourism-related field. To be considered for the award, you must be a junior or senior enrolled in a North American two- or four-year college full-time. Award requirements change regularly. No GPA requirement specified.

National Tourism Foundation
PO Box 3071
546 East Main Street
Lexington, KY 40508-3071

814

National Tourism Montana Scholarship Program

AMOUNT: $500 DEADLINE: April 17
MAJOR: Travel and Tourism, Hotel/Restaurant Management

The National Tourism Montana Scholarship Program is open to Montana residents pursuing a degree in a travel and tourism-related field. To be considered for this award, you must be a junior or senior enrolled in a North American two-

or four-year college full-time. Award requirements change regularly. No GPA requirement specified.

National Tourism Foundation
PO Box 3071
546 East Main Street
Lexington, KY 40508-3071

815

National Tourism Nebraska - Lois Johnson Scholarship Program

AMOUNT: $500 DEADLINE: April 17
MAJOR: Travel and Tourism, Hotel/Restaurant Management

The National Tourism Nebraska-Lois Johnson Scholarship Program is open to Nebraska residents pursuing a degree in a travel and tourism-related field. To be considered for the award, you must be a junior or senior who is enrolled in a North American two- or four-year college full-time. Award requirements change regularly. No GPA requirement specified.

National Tourism Foundation
PO Box 3071
546 East Main Street
Lexington, KY 40508-3071

816

National Tourism New Jersey I Scholarship Program

AMOUNT: $1000 DEADLINE: April 17
MAJOR: Travel and Tourism, Hotel/Restaurant Management

The National Tourism New Jersey I Scholarship Program is open to New Jersey residents pursuing a degree in a travel and tourism-related field. To be considered for the award, you must be a junior or senior enrolled in a North American four-year college full-time. Award requirements change regularly. No GPA requirement specified.

National Tourism Foundation
PO Box 3071
546 East Main Street
Lexington, KY 40508-3071

817

National Tourism New Jersey II Scholarship Program

AMOUNT: $1000 DEADLINE: April 17
MAJOR: Travel and Tourism, Hotel/Restaurant Management

The National Tourism New Jersey II Scholarship Program is open to New Jersey residents pursuing a degree in a travel and tourism-related field. To be considered for the award, you must be a junior or senior enrolled in a North American two-year college full-time. Award requirements change regularly. No GPA requirement specified.

National Tourism Foundation
PO Box 3071
546 East Main Street
Lexington, KY 40508-3071

818
National Tourism New York Scholarship Program

AMOUNT: $500 DEADLINE: April 17
MAJOR: Travel and Tourism, Hotel/Restaurant Management

The National Tourism New York Scholarship Program is open to New York residents who are pursuing a degree in a travel and tourism-related field. To be considered for this award, you must be a junior or senior enrolled in a four-year New York school full-time. Award requirements change regularly. No GPA requirement specified.

National Tourism Foundation
PO Box 3071
546 East Main Street
Lexington, KY 40508-3071

819
National Tourism North Carolina Scholarship Program

AMOUNT: $500 DEADLINE: April 17
MAJOR: Travel and Tourism, Hotel/Restaurant Management

The National Tourism North Carolina Scholarship Program is open to North Carolina residents pursuing a degree in travel or tourism-related field. To be considered for this award, you must be a junior or senior enrolled in a North American four-year college full-time. Award requirements change regularly. No GPA requirement specified.

National Tourism Foundation
PO Box 3071
546 East Main Street
Lexington, KY 40508-3071

820
National Tourism Ohio Scholarship Program

AMOUNT: $1000 DEADLINE: April 17
MAJOR: Travel and Tourism, Hotel/Restaurant Management

The National Tourism Ohio Scholarship Program is open to Ohio residents pursuing a degree in a travel and tourism-related field. To be considered for the award, you must be a junior or senior enrolled in a North American two- or four-year college full-time. Award requirements change regularly. No GPA requirement specified.

National Tourism Foundation
PO Box 3071
546 East Main Street
Lexington, KY 40508-3071

821
National Tourism Quebec Scholarship

AMOUNT: $500 DEADLINE: April 17
MAJOR: Travel and Tourism, Hotel/Restaurant Management

The National Tourism Quebec Scholarship is open to Quebec residents who are pursuing a degree in a travel or tourism-related field. To be considered for the award, you must be enrolled in a two- or four-year college in Quebec. Graduate and doctorate students are also eligible to apply. Award requirements change regularly. No GPA requirement specified.

National Tourism Foundation
PO Box 3071
546 East Main Street
Lexington, KY 40508-3071

822
National Tourism Signature Tours Scholarship

AMOUNT: $1000 DEADLINE: April 17
MAJOR: Travel and Tourism, Hotel/Restaurant Management

The National Tourism Signature Tours is open to juniors or seniors who are pursuing a degree in a travel and tourism-related field. To be considered for the award, you must be enrolled full-time in a two- or four-year college. Award requirements change regularly. No GPA requirement specified.

National Tourism Foundation
PO Box 3071
546 East Main Street
Lexington, KY 40508-3071

823
National Tourism Societe Des Casinos Du Quebec Scholarship

AMOUNT: $1000 DEADLINE: April 17
MAJOR: Travel and Tourism, Hotel/Restaurant Management

The Societe Des Casinos Du Quebec Scholarship is open to Quebec residents who are pursuing a degree in a travel or tourism-related field. To be considered for the award, you must be a junior or senior who is enrolled in a North American two- or four-year college. Award requirements change regularly. No GPA requirement specified.

National Tourism Foundation
PO Box 3071
546 East Main Street
Lexington, KY 40508-3071

824
National Tourism Tampa/Hillsborough Legacy Scholarship Program

AMOUNT: $1000 DEADLINE: April 17
MAJOR: Travel and Tourism, Hotel/Restaurant Management

The National Tourism Tampa/Hillsborough Legacy Scholarship Program is open to Florida residents pursuing a degree in a travel or tourism-related field. To be considered for this award, you must be a junior or senior enrolled in a Florida college or university full-time. Award requirements change regularly. No GPA requirement specified.

National Tourism Foundation
PO Box 3071
546 East Main Street
Lexington, KY 40508-3071

825
National Tourism Tulsa Legacy Scholarship

AMOUNT: $500 DEADLINE: April 17
MAJOR: Travel and Tourism, Hotel/Restaurant Management

The National Tourism Tulsa Legacy Scholarship is open to Oklahoma residents who are pursuing a degree in a travel or tourism-related field. To be considered for the award, you must be a junior or senior enrolled full-time in a four-year college in Oklahoma. Award requirements change regularly. No GPA requirement specified.

National Tourism Foundation
PO Box 3071
546 East Main Street
Lexington, KY 40508-3071

826
National Tourism Weeta F. Colebank Scholarship (Miss.)

AMOUNT: $1000 DEADLINE: April 17
MAJOR: Travel and Tourism, Hotel/Restaurant Management

The National Tourism Weeta F. Colebank Scholarship is available to Mississippi residents majoring in travel and tourism, hotel/motel management or restaurant management. To be considered for the award, you must be a junior or senior enrolled full-time in a four-year Mississippi college. Award requirements change regularly. No GPA requirement specified.

National Tourism Foundation
PO Box 3071
546 East Main Street
Lexington, KY 40508-3071

827
National Tourism Wyoming Scholarship Program

AMOUNT: $1000 DEADLINE: April 17
MAJOR: Travel and Tourism, Hotel/Restaurant Management

The National Tourism Wyoming Scholarship Program is open to Wyoming residents pursuing a degree in a travel and tourism-related field. To be considered for this award, you must a junior or senior enrolled in a North American two- or four-year college full-time. Award requirements change regularly. No GPA requirement specified.

National Tourism Foundation
PO Box 3071
546 East Main Street
Lexington, KY 40508-3071

828
National Wool Growers Memorial Fellowship

AMOUNT: $2500 DEADLINE: Varies
MAJOR: Sheep Industry

The National Wool Growers Memorial Fellowship is available for graduate students involved in lamb or wool research. In order to apply, you must provide proof of acceptance to a

graduate school and present two letters of reference. Award requirements change regularly. No GPA requirement specified.

American Sheep Industry Association
Attn: Memorial Fellowship
6911 South Yosemite
Englewood, CO 80112

829
National Zoo Research Traineeship Program

AMOUNT: $2400-$3000 DEADLINE: December 31
MAJOR: Animal Behavior, Reproductive Physiology, Nutrition, Genetics, Husbandry/Exhibit Interpretation, Zoo Animal Medicine, Veterinary Pathology

The National Zoo Research Traineeship Program is open to advanced undergraduates and recent graduates (except for the Zoo Animal Medicine and Veterinary Pathology fields of study which are open to veterinary college students). The stipend for the full-term is $2,400 - $3,000. The selection process focuses on the statement of interest, scholastic achievement, relevant experience, and letters of reference. Preference is given to advanced undergraduates and recent graduates. Award requirements change regularly. Please send a self-addressed, stamped envelope for further information. No GPA requirement specified.

National Zoological Park
Human Resource Office - Internships
3001 Connecticut Avenue, NW
Washington, DC 20008

830
Native American Education Grants

AMOUNT: $200-$2500 DEADLINE: June 1
MAJOR: All Areas of Study

Undergraduate grants for Alaska Natives and Native Americans pursuing college educations. Must be U.S. citizens and have completed at least one semester of work at an accredited institution of higher education. Applicants must be members of the Presbyterian Church (U.S.A.) and demonstrate financial need. Award requirements change regularly. Write to address listed for details, enclosing a self-addressed, stamped envelope or call (502) 569-5760. Specify Native American Education Grants (NAEG). No GPA requirement specified.

Presbyterian Church (U.S.A.)
Office of Financial Aid for Studies
100 Witherspoon Street
Louisville, KY 40202-1396

831
Native American Student Aid

AMOUNT: Maximum: $1750 DEADLINE: July 15
MAJOR: All Areas of Study

Open to Native Americans who are New York residents, on an official tribal roll of a New York State Tribe (or children of parent[s] who are), and attending an approved postsecondary institution in New York State. Renewable for up to four years. July 15 is the deadline for fall semester, December 31 is the deadline for spring semester, and May 20 is the deadline for the summer semester. Award requirements change regularly. Write to the address listed, enclosing a self-addressed, stamped envelope for an application and further information. No GPA requirement specified.

New York State Education Department
Attn: Native American Education Unit
478 Education Building Annex
Albany, NY 12234

832
Naval Academy Women's Club Scholarship

AMOUNT: $1000 DEADLINE: April 1
MAJOR: All Areas of Study

The Naval Academy Women's Club Scholarship is available to the child of a Navy or Marine Corps officer on active duty, retired, or deceased who is or has been stationed as a commissioned officer at the U.S. Naval Academy Complex; the child of a faculty or senior staff member presently employed at the Naval Academy; the child of a Navy or Marine Corps enlisted person presently stationed at the Academy; or a current member of the Naval Academy Women's Club. Reapplication and a satisfactory GPA is required to retain scholarship. Award requirements change regularly. Please send a self-addressed, stamped envelope to Mary R. Seymour, Scholarship Chairman, NMPC-121D Navy Department, Washington, MD 20370-5121 to receive your application and any further instructions from the scholarship provider. No GPA requirement specified.

Naval Academy Women's Club
Attn: Scholarship Programs
Box 6417
Annapolis, MD 21404

833
Navy and Nurse Reserve Officer Training Corps (NROTC) Scholarship

AMOUNT: None Specified DEADLINE: January 28
MAJOR: All Areas of Study

The Navy and Nurse Reserve Officer Training Corps (NROTC) Scholarship is open to juniors or seniors in high school. Applicants must meet navy physical standards and must apply for, and be admitted to, a college with an NROTC program. Upon graduation, NROTC midshipmen are commissioned as ensigns in the navy. The service obligation is for four years of active duty and four years of inactive duty. Recipients of the awards can withdraw from the program before starting their sophomore year with no service obligation. Recipients receive tuition, books and lab fees paid to one of over 100 colleges where NROTC is offered, and also earn a monthly stipend of $150 and the benefits of being on active duty. Applicants must have at least a 22 ACT score or 1050 (Math: 520, English: 530) SAT score. Award requirements change regularly. No GPA requirement specified.

Navy Officer Programs, Omaha
Leads Department - Suite 400
6910 Pacific Street
Omaha, NE 68106-1085

834
Navy Health Services Collegiate Program (HSCP)

AMOUNT: None Specified DEADLINE: March 1
MAJOR: Dentistry, Physician Assistant, Optometry, Health Care Administration, Industrial Hygiene, Environmental Health Specialists, Physical Therapy, Allied Health

The Navy Health Services Collegiate Program (HSCP) is open to students in the selected health care specialties mentioned above. The scholarship recipients receive many financial benefits including a monthly salary of $1,650 to $2,550, full medical and dental benefits, tax-free allowances for housing and meals, and full military benefits. Recipients' school schedules will not be affected, nor will their civilian lifestyles. Recipients will continue to wear civilian clothes on campus, but will be on active duty in the Naval Reserve. Upon graduation, the award recipients will be commissioned as officers in the Naval Reserve with a minimum length of three years active duty service in the Dental Corps or the Medical Service Corps. Award requirements change regularly. Visit the website at www.incolor.inetnebr.com/nrdomaha for further information. GPA must be 3.0-4.0.

Navy Officer Programs, Omaha
Leads Department - Suite 400
6910 Pacific Street
Omaha, NE 68106-1085

835
Navy Officer Baccalaureate Degree Completion Program (BDCP)

AMOUNT: None Specified DEADLINE: Varies
MAJOR: Science, Mathematics, Engineering

The Navy Officer Baccalaureate Degree Completion Program (BDCP) is open to civilians or enlisted inactive reservists working toward the completion of their bachelor's degree. While this program is for science, mathematics, and engineering majors, students in most curricula are eligible. Students receive a monthly salary and the benefits of active duty status. Students will pay for their tuition, books, and other school-related expenses. After earning their bachelor's degree through BDCP, graduates will be commissioned as officers in the Naval Reserve. Service obligations are for four years of active duty in the U.S. Navy. Qualified applicants may be accepted into one of several officer communities including surface warfare, aviation, SEALs, explosive ordinance disposal, supply, aeronautical maintenance duty, intelligence, cryptology, or oceanography. Award requirements change regularly. Please take a moment to apply online or visit the website at www.incolor.inetnebr.com/nrdomaha for further information. GPA must be 2.7-4.0.

Navy Officer Programs, Omaha
Leads Department - Suite 400
6910 Pacific Street
Omaha, NE 68106-1085

836
Navy Officer Financial Assistance Program For Physicians

AMOUNT: None Specified DEADLINE: Varies
MAJOR: Medicine

The Navy Officer Financial Assistance Program For Physicians offers financial benefits to qualified physicians in select specialties. Upon completion of medical residency, recipients of this program will practice medicine in the navy. Some of the benefits of this program include: no office overhead; no malpractice insurance; 30 days of vacation with pay each year; tax-free housing and subsistence allowance. Residents earn a monthly stipend of $973, an annual lump sum payment of $20,591 while keeping their current residency pay. Award requirements change regularly. Visit the website at www.incolor.inetnebr.com/nrdomaha for further information. No GPA requirement specified.

Navy Officer Programs, Omaha
Leads Department - Suite 400
6910 Pacific Street
Omaha, NE 68106-1085

837
Navy Supply Corps Foundation Scholarship

AMOUNT: $2000 DEADLINE: February 15
MAJOR: All Areas of Study

This scholarship is open to a child of a Navy Supply Corps Officer, including Warrant, or Supply Corps service member on active duty in reserve status, retired-with-pay, or deceased. Selection is based upon scholastic ability with a minimum 3.0 GPA required. Award requirements change regularly. For further information, please send a self-addressed, stamped envelope to the address provided. GPA must be 3.0-4.0.

Navy Supply Corps Foundation
Attn: Kaye Morris
1425 Prince Avenue
Athens, GA 30606-2296

838
NAWIC Undergraduate Scholarship

AMOUNT: $500-$2000 DEADLINE: February 1
MAJOR: Construction, Architecture, Engineering Technology, Landscape Architecture

Scholarships are available for freshman, sophomore, and junior students who are enrolled in a construction-related program on a full-time basis. In order to apply, you must be pursuing, or intending to pursue, a career in the construction industry. This award is based on your application, financial need, interview, and transcripts. Award requirements change regularly. No GPA requirement specified.

National Association of Women in Construction
NAWIC Scholarship Coordinator
327 South Adams Street
Fort Worth, TX 76104-1002

839
NBRC/AMP Gareth B. Gish, MS, RRT Postgraduate Education Award

AMOUNT: $1500 DEADLINE: June 30
MAJOR: Respiratory Therapy

This endowment is open to respiratory care therapists who have already earned a bachelor's degree with a minimum 3.0 GPA. You must provide proof of acceptance into an advanced degree program at a fully accredited school. The recipient will be selected by September 1. This award also includes airfare, one night lodging, and registration to attend the AARC Respiratory International Congress. Award requirements change regularly. GPA must be 3.0-4.0.

American Respiratory Care Foundation
Education Recognition Award
11030 Ables Lane
Dallas, TX 75229-4524

840
NBRC/AMP H. Frederic Helmholz Jr. Research Endowment

AMOUNT: Maximum: $3000 DEADLINE: June 30
MAJOR: Respiratory Therapy

This award is offered to support up to $3,000 for educational or credentialing research, a master's thesis or doctoral dissertation with practical value to the respiratory care profession. Award recipients will be notified by September 1. This research endowment also includes travel expenses to the AARC Respiratory International Congress in order to accept the award. Award requirements change regularly. GPA must be 3.0-4.0.

American Respiratory Care Foundation
Education Recognition Award
11030 Ables Lane
Dallas, TX 75229-4524

841
NEBHE Doctoral Scholars Program

AMOUNT: None Specified DEADLINE: Varies
MAJOR: Science, Mathematics, Engineering

Awards are available for the purpose of encouraging ethnic minority students to pursue doctoral degrees and become college level teachers in the areas of science, engineering, and mathematics. These scholarships are available to residents of Connecticut, Maine, Massachusetts, New Hampshire, Rhode Island, and Vermont. Award requirements change regularly. No GPA requirement specified.

New England Board of Higher Education
Wendy Lindsay, Assistant Director
45 Temple Place
Boston, MA 02111-1305

842
Nebraska Press Association Foundation, Inc. Scholarships

AMOUNT: $1000 DEADLINE: February 27
MAJOR: Print Journalism

This scholarship is open to graduating high school seniors planning to enroll in a college/university and for current full-time undergraduates enrolled in a print journalism program in a Nebraska college or university. Selections are based on academics, good citizenship in school and the community, as well as financial need. Your career plans must be in the field of print journalism in order for you to apply. Award requirements change regularly. GPA must be 2.8-4.0.

Nebraska Press Association Foundation, Inc.
Attn: Allen Beemann
845 'S' Street
Lincoln, NE 68508-1226

843
Nemal Electronics Scholarship

AMOUNT: $500 DEADLINE: February 1
MAJOR: Electronics, Communications or Related Areas

This scholarship is available to students with a minimum general class amateur radio license pursuing a baccalaureate or higher degree. The applicants must have a minimum GPA of 3.0 and be majoring in electronics, communications, or related areas. Included in the application process is a brief letter explaining the applicant's background and future plans. Award requirements change regularly. Write the address provided, using a self-addressed, stamped envelope, for further information. GPA must be 3.0-4.0.

American Radio Relay League
Attn: ARRL Foundation
225 Main Street
Newington, CT 06111-1400

844
Nestle/Kiwanis Scholarship

AMOUNT: $500 DEADLINE: Varies
MAJOR: All Fields of Study

The Nestle/Kiwanis Scholarship is open to senior Burlington High School (Burlington, WI) students. The scholarship will be awarded on the basis of need and performance. Award requirements change regularly. Please visit your guidance office to receive an application and any additional details. No GPA requirement specified.

Burlington High School
Attn: Guidance Office
225 Robert Street
Burlington, WI 53105

845
Nettie E. Karcher Memorial Scholarship

AMOUNT: $800 DEADLINE: Varies
MAJOR: All Fields of Study

The Nettie E. Karcher Memorial Scholarship is open to senior Burlington High School (Burlington, WI) students who will attend an accredited college or university. The scholarship provides $800 a year for four years and will be awarded on the basis of scholastic ability, financial need, and character. Award requirements change regularly. Please visit your guidance office to receive an application and any additional details. No GPA requirement specified.

Burlington High School
Attn: Guidance Office
225 Robert Street
Burlington, WI 53105

846
Nettie Tucker Yowell Scholarship

AMOUNT: $250 DEADLINE: April 1
MAJOR: All Areas of Study

Open to high school seniors who have been accepted for admission as a fall semester freshmen in a Virginia college or accredited four-year institution. Applicants must be studying toward a baccalaureate degree, in the top 25% of their class, SAT score of 900, and a 3.0 GPA. Recipients will notified by June 30. Award requirements change regularly. Write to the address listed, enclosing a self-addressed, stamped envelope for an application and further information. GPA must be 3.0-4.0.

Business and Professional Women's Foundation
Scholarship Chairman
PO Box 4842
West Mclean, VA 22103-4842

847
New England Femara Scholarship

AMOUNT: $600 DEADLINE: February 1
MAJOR: All Areas of Study

This scholarship is available to students with a minimum technician class amateur radio license who are residents of: Maine, Vermont, Connecticut, New Hampshire, Rhode Island, or Massachusetts. Multiple awards are given per year. Award requirements change regularly. Write the address provided, using a self-addressed, stamped envelope, for further information. No GPA requirement specified.

American Radio Relay League
Attn: ARRL Foundation
225 Main Street
Newington, CT 06111-1400

848
New England Regional Student Program

AMOUNT: None Specified DEADLINE: Varies
MAJOR: All Areas of Study

New England students get a break on out-of-state tuition when they enroll at public colleges and universities in the other New England states and study RSP-approved majors, majors which are not offered by public colleges in their home states. All 78 public colleges and universities in New England participate in the RSP. You must enroll as a certificate or degree student at a participating college and study a major that is offered by that college to residents of your state through the RSP. The approved majors are listed in the annual RSP catalog. Award requirements change regularly. For further information please call (617) 357-9620, fax (617) 338-1577, email: pubinfo@nebhe.org or visit their website: www.nebhe.org. Information is also available at high school guidance offices and college admissions offices. No GPA requirement specified.

New England Board of Higher Education
Wendy Lindsay, Assistant Director
45 Temple Place
Boston, MA 02111-1305

849
New England Travelers Club Scholarship

AMOUNT: $2000 DEADLINE: March 15
MAJOR: All Fields of Study

The New England Travelers Club Scholarship is open to employees of Business Products Industry Association member firms and their families. Persons holding academic records sufficient for acceptance by accredited colleges, junior colleges or technical schools, or persons already enrolled in one of those institutions are eligible for this one-year award. Selection is made by a committee from the Student Financial Aid Department of The George Washington University, Washington, DC. Award requirements change regularly. Please send a self-addressed, stamped envelope to receive your application and any further instructions from the scholarship provider or email: info@bpia.org. No GPA requirement specified.

Business Products Industry Association
Attn: Scholarship Committee
301 North Fairfax Street, Alexandria VA

850
New Hampshire Incentive Program

AMOUNT: None Specified DEADLINE: May 1
MAJOR: All Fields of Study

The New Hampshire Incentive Program is awarded to full-time students at New Hampshire institutes of higher learning or institutes in the New England area that are accredited by the New England Association of Schools and Colleges. To be considered for this award, you must be a resident of New Hampshire. The award is based on financial need. If you are an upperclassman, a minimum GPA of 2.0 is required. Award requirements change regularly. To apply for this award, please submit a FAFSA by the May 1 deadline. No GPA requirement specified.

New Hampshire postsecondary Education Commission
Attn: Scholarship Programs
Two Industrial Park Drive, Suite 7
Concord, NH 03301-8512

851
New Mexico Scholars Program

AMOUNT: None Specified DEADLINE: Varies
MAJOR: All Areas of Study

The New Mexico Scholars Program is awarded to residents of New Mexico who plan to enroll or are already attending a public or selected private nonprofit postsecondary institution in New Mexico. To be considered for this award, you must be under the age of 22 and have either graduated in the top 5% of your high school class or have a minimum score of 25 on the ACT. This award is based on financial need. Award requirements change regularly. For further information or to apply, please contact the financial aid office at your school or call (800) 279-9777. You are also required to submit a FAFSA. No GPA requirement specified.

New Mexico Commission on Higher Education
Financial Aid and Student Services
1068 Cerrillos Road
Santa Fe, NM 87501

852
New Mexico State Association of Colored Women's Clubs Scholarship

AMOUNT: None Specified DEADLINE: June 7
MAJOR: All Areas of Study

Open to graduating high school seniors with a 2.5 GPA or above. Applications must be accompanied by an official high school transcript. College students who are already scholarship recipients may reapply. Please note that if scholarships are not sent to the address given, and/or do not include an official high school transcript, the applications will not be considered. Award requirements change regularly. For more information, please send a self-addressed, stamped envelope to the address provided or call (505) 393-9837. GPA must be 2.5-4.0.

New Mexico State Association of Colored Women's Clubs
Attn: Evelyn Rising
1330 North Tasker Drive
Hobbs, NM 88240-4860

853
New Mexico Veterans Service Commission Scholarship Under Chapter 170

AMOUNT: $300 DEADLINE: Varies
MAJOR: All Areas of Study

The New Mexico Veterans Service Commission Scholarship Under Chapter 170 is open to the children of deceased veterans who were New Mexico residents at the time of entry into the service and who served during a period of armed conflict and who were killed in action or died as the result of such service. This award is also available to some children of a deceased state policeman or a deceased National Guard member. Reapplication is required to retain scholarship. Award requirements change regularly. Please send a self-addressed, stamped envelope to Alan T. Martinez of State Benefits in order to receive your application and any further instructions from the scholarship provider. No GPA requirement specified.

New Mexico Veterans' Service Commission
Scholarship Coordinator
PO Box 2324
Santa Fe, NM 87503

854
New York Council Navy League Scholarship

AMOUNT: $2500 DEADLINE: June 15
MAJOR: All Areas of Study

The New York Council Navy League Scholarship is open to children of regular/reserve navy, marine corps or coast guard service members who are serving on active duty, retired with pay, or who died in the line of duty or after retirement. To be considered for this award, you must also be a resident of Connecticut, New Jersey, or New York. To retain the scholarship, you are required to maintain a "B-" average. Award requirements change regularly. You must also submit two letters of recommendation and a copy of your academic transcript(s). GPA must be 3.0-4.0.

New York Council Navy League Scholarship Fund
c/o Intrepid Museum
One Intrepid Square, Pier 86
New York, NY 10036

855
New York Tuition Assistance Program

AMOUNT: $75-$4125 DEADLINE: May 1
MAJOR: All Fields of Study

The New York Tuition Assistance Program is awarded to residents of New York who are attending an approved postsecondary institution in New York full-time. To be considered for this award, you must be charged at least $200 for tuition per year and be in good academic standing. This award is based on financial need and type of postsecondary institution in which you are enrolled. This award is renewable, provided you meet certain criteria. Award requirements change regularly. For further information, please contact the provider at the address listed. To apply, you must submit a FAFSA. No GPA requirement specified.

New York State Higher Education Services Corporation
Attn: Scholarship Program Coordinator
99 Washington Avenue
Albany, NY 12255

856
Newhouse Scholarship/Internship Program

AMOUNT: $5000 DEADLINE: February 25
MAJOR: Print Journalism

Open to college juniors and seniors majoring in print journalism. Recipients are expected to participate in a summer internship program at a Newhouse Newspaper following their junior year. Award requirements change regularly. Please send a self-addressed, stamped envelope to receive your application and any further instructions from the scholarship provider or browse their website: www.nahj.org. No GPA requirement specified.

National Association of Hispanic Journalists (NAHJ)
Attn: Scholarship Department
1193 National Press Building
Washington, DC 20045-2101

857
NGPA Pilot Scholarship

AMOUNT: $2000 DEADLINE: April 30
MAJOR: Aviation, Aerospace, Aerodynamics, Engineering, Airport Management

This scholarship is open to students accepted or currently enrolled in an accredited college or university with an aviation-related curriculum (aerospace, aerodynamics, engineering, airport management, etc.) in pursuit of a degree leading to a career as a professional pilot; or accepted to or currently undergoing a course of study in recognized professional pilot aviation training program in an institution of higher learning, aviation technical school, or a school that provides advanced pilot training under FAR part 141. Awards are not restricted to gay or lesbian students; however, consideration will be given to students attesting to gay/lesbian community service or who have worked on behalf of gay and lesbian issues. Award requirements change regularly. Please send a self-addressed, stamped envelope to receive your application and any further instructions from the scholarship provider. No GPA requirement specified.

National Gay Pilots Association
PMB 324
150 Dorset Street
South Burlington, VT 05403-6256

858
Nicholas Van Slyck Scholarship

AMOUNT: $400 DEADLINE: Varies
MAJOR: Music

This scholarship is open to Merrimack Valley area graduating high school seniors who intend to pursue a career in music. Award requirements change regularly. Please write to the address listed, enclosing a self-addressed, stamped envelope for an application and further information. No GPA requirement specified.

Merrimack Valley Philharmonic Society, Inc.
Attn: Dorothy C Bruno
86 Pleasant Street
Methuen, MA 01844-3152

859
Nike Scholarships

AMOUNT: $2500 DEADLINE: May 11
MAJOR: Sports or Recreation Management, Marketing, Medicine or Retailing Sports, Recreation Equipment

This scholarship is open to high school seniors and undergraduates enrolled in an undergraduate degree program that focuses on sports or recreation management, marketing, medicine or retailing sports, or recreation equipment at a four-year accredited college or university in the U.S. You must be a U.S. citizen and submit documentation or verification of your disability. Also required are your high school or college transcripts and two letters of recommendation. Further, two essays are required: "Why I Want to Pursue a Career in Sports/Recreation Business and Feel I Would Succeed Upon Graduation From College" and "How My Winning This Scholarship will Help Advance Opportunities for Individuals with Disabilities." Award requirements change regularly. No GPA requirement specified.

President's Committee on Employment of People With Disabilities
Recognition Program
1331 F Street NW
Washington, DC 20004-1107

860
Ninety Nines, Inc. Scholarship (New England Chapter)

AMOUNT: $1000 DEADLINE: January 31
MAJOR: Aviation

This award is open to graduating high school seniors or continuing students who are residents of New England. Applicants must be planning a career in aviation, have prior aviation activities, and demonstrate financial need. One award goes to a woman with a private pilots license and one award goes to a man or a woman involved in aviation activities. Award requirements change regularly. For further information, please write to the address listed, including a self-addressed, stamped envelope. No GPA requirement specified.

Ninety Nines, Inc. - New England Chapter
Attn: Karla Carroll
14 Cooke Place
Warwick, RI 02888-4202

861
Ninilchik Native Association, Inc. Scholarship

AMOUNT: $1000 DEADLINE: Varies
MAJOR: All Areas of Study

The Ninilchik Native Association, Inc. (NNAI) Scholarship is open to Alaska Natives enrolled in the NNAI and their descendants who have a minimum GPA of 2.5. Applicants must be accepted/enrolled full-time in a two- or four-year or undergraduate degree program, a graduate degree program, or a technical skills training program. The respective deadlines are June 1 and December 1. Award requirements change regularly. GPA must be 2.5-4.0.

CIRI Foundation
Scholarship Coordinator
2600 Cordova Street, Suite 206
Anchorage, AK 99503-2745

862
NJSCPA Accounting Manuscript Contest

AMOUNT: $500-$1500 DEADLINE: February 4
MAJOR: Accounting

The NJSCPA Accounting Manuscript Contest is open to sophomore and junior accounting majors attending two-year or four-year New Jersey colleges or universities. You must submit an article of no more than 1,000 words. First prize includes publication of the essay in the New Jersey Business magazine. Your manuscript will be evaluated by a panel of judges for content, creativity, clarity, and ability to effectively communicate the relevance of accountancy to the topic, and ability to communicate information that is relevant to New Jersey businesses. Award requirements change regularly.

New Jersey Society of Certified Public Accountants
Scholarship Awards Committee
425 Eagle Rock Avenue
Roseland, NJ 07068-1720

863
NJSCPA College Scholarship

AMOUNT: Maximum: $2000 DEADLINE: January 14
MAJOR: Accounting

Open to the top academically ranked juniors who are majoring in accounting at New Jersey colleges. Must be nominated by your Accounting Chairperson. Based on interviews conducted by the NJSCPA Scholarship Interview Committee. The award is applied to the winner's senior year. Winners selected in January. Award requirements change regularly. Contact your department chairperson to encourage him or her to nominate you. GPA must be 3.6-4.0.

New Jersey Society of Certified Public Accountants
Scholarship Awards Committee
425 Eagle Rock Avenue
Roseland, NJ 07068-1720

864
NJSCPA High School Scholarship Program

AMOUNT: $500-$5000 DEADLINE: October 29
MAJOR: Accounting

The NJSCPA High School Scholarship Program is open to New Jersey high school seniors who intend to major in accounting in college. Applications for a one-hour accounting aptitude exam are mailed to all New Jersey guidance and business departments in September. The exam is given in November and the highest scorers receive accounting scholarships. Award requirements change regularly. No GPA requirement specified.

New Jersey Society of Certified Public Accountants
Scholarship Awards Committee
425 Eagle Rock Avenue
Roseland, NJ 07068-1720

865
Noble County Lilly Endowment Community Scholarship Program

AMOUNT: None Specified DEADLINE: March 1
MAJOR: All Areas of Study

This scholarship is open to Noble County (IN) residents who will have graduated with a diploma from an accredited Indiana High School by the end of June. Applicants must have a minimum 2.0 GPA and be entering a four-year college program for the first time as freshmen. Community/volunteer service, leadership roles, work experience, school performance, and other awards and recognitions will be strongly considered. Award requirements change regularly. For further information and an application, please write to the address listed, including a self-addressed, stamped envelope, call (219) 894-3335, or email: nccf@ligtel.com. GPA must be 2.0-4.0.

Noble County Community Foundation
Youth Program Officer
1599 Lincoln Way South
Ligonier, IN 46767

866
Nobuko R. Kodama Fong Memorial Scholarship

AMOUNT: $1000-$5000 DEADLINE: April 1
MAJOR: All Areas of Study

The Nobuko R. Kodama Fong Memorial Scholarship is open
to current undergraduate students of Japanese ancestry who
are solely provided for by a single parent. National Japanese
American Citizens League (JACL) membership is a requirement to be considered for this award. Membership must be
held either by you or your parents only. You must submit a
completed application form, proof of JACL membership, a
personal statement, letter of recommendation, official transcripts, and a resume. Preference will be given to students
from the Pacific Northwest District. March 20 is the last day
to request an application. Award requirements change regularly. Please send a self-addressed, stamped envelope to receive
your application and any further instructions from the scholarship provider. Please indicate that you would like to receive an
application for undergraduate awards. You may also find the
scholarship application online at www.jacl.org. No GPA
requirement specified.

Japanese American Citizens League - National Headquarters
Attn: National Scholarship Awards
1765 Sutter Street
San Francisco, CA 94115

867
Nordstrom Scholarship

AMOUNT: $2000 DEADLINE: May 11
MAJOR: Business

This scholarship is available for high school seniors and
undergraduates with disabilities enrolled in or planning to
enroll in a business degree program in a four-year college or
university. You must be a U.S. citizen and submit documentation or verification of your disability. Also required are your
high school or college transcripts and two letters of recommendation. Further, two essays are required: "Why I Want to
Pursue a Career in Business and Feel I Would Succeed Upon
Graduation From College" and "How My Winning This
Scholarship will Help Advance Opportunities for Individuals
with Disabilities." Award requirements change regularly. No
GPA requirement specified.

President's Committee on Employment of People With
Disabilities
Recognition Program
1331 F Street NW
Washington, DC 20004-1107

868
North Carolina League for Nursing Scholarship

AMOUNT: Maximum: $2000 DEADLINE: August 1
MAJOR: Nursing and Related Healthcare

Scholarships are for North Carolina graduate students who are
studying nursing or a related field on the graduate level.
Award requirements change regularly. Write to the address
listed for details, enclosing a self-addressed, stamped envelope. No GPA requirement specified.

Foundation for the Carolinas
Scholarship Program
PO Box 34769
Charlotte, NC 28234-4769

869
North Dakota State Student Incentive Grant Program

AMOUNT: $600 DEADLINE: April 15
MAJOR: All Fields of Study

The North Dakota State Student Incentive Grant Program is
open to North Dakota residents. To be considered for the
award, you must be attending a North Dakota college full-
time. The award also requires that you be a high school graduate or hold a GED. Award requirements change regularly. To
apply, you must submit the FAFSA. For more information,
write the North Dakota University system. No GPA requirement specified.

North Dakota University System
10th Floor, State Capitol
600 East Boulevard Avenue
Bismarck, ND 58505-0230

870
North Texas Section - Bob Nelson KB5BNU Memorial Scholarship

AMOUNT: $750 DEADLINE: February 1
MAJOR: All Areas of Study

This scholarship is open to applicants possessing any type
class of amateur radio license. The applicants must be from
the North Texas Section, may be from other Texas sections
(please write in for these areas) or Oklahoma. Applicants must
be enrolled in a full-time degree program with a minimum of
12 credit hours per semester. Deciding factors include character, humanitarianism, and active amateur radio participation.
Multiple awards are given per year when funding is available.
Award requirements change regularly. Write the address provided, using a self-addressed, stamped envelope, for further
information. No GPA requirement specified.

American Radio Relay League
Attn: ARRL Foundation
225 Main Street
Newington, CT 06111-1400

871
Northern California/Richard Epping Scholarship

AMOUNT: $2000 DEADLINE: July 28
MAJOR: Travel and Tourism

Open to students who are permanent residents of Northern California or Northern Nevada and are currently enrolled in a travel program at a college, university, or proprietary school located in Northern California or Northern Nevada. Students must submit a 500-word paper entitled "Why I Desire a Profession in the Travel and Tourism Industry." Award requirements change regularly. Write to the address listed, enclosing a self-addressed, stamped envelope for an application and further information. You can browse their website: www.astanet.com or email: myriaml@astahq.com. No GPA requirement specified.

American Society of Travel Agents
Attn: ASTA Foundation
1101 King Street, Suite 200
Alexandria, VA 22314-2944

872
Northern Colorado Artists Association Scholarship

AMOUNT: $500 DEADLINE: Varies
MAJOR: Art

Open to Rocky Mountain High School seniors. Applicants must plan to continue education or training in the field of art. An art portfolio and essay may be required. Applicants will be screened by the Rocky Mountain H.S. art teachers and must be submitted well before the deadline. Application deadline, procedure, and award amount vary annually. Award requirements change regularly. Applications are available in January or February in the Rocky Mountain High School Career Center, as part of the Local Scholarship Packet. No GPA requirement specified.

Rocky Mountain High School
Scholarship Committee
1300 West Swallow Road
Fort Collins, CO 80526-2412

873
Northrop Corporation Founders Scholarship

AMOUNT: $1000 DEADLINE: February 1
MAJOR: Engineering

This scholarship is open to sophomore women who are SWE members and majoring in engineering. You must be attending an ABET-accredited program or an SWE-approved school, have a minimum GPA of 3.5, and be a U.S. citizen. Award requirements change regularly. Please send a self-addressed, stamped envelope to receive your application. GPA must be 3.5-4.0.

Society of Women Engineers Headquarters
Scholarship Coordinator
120 Wall Street, FL 11
New York, NY 10005-3902

874
Northrop Grumman Scholarship

AMOUNT: $1000-$1500 DEADLINE: May 15
MAJOR: Engineering, Computer Science

This scholarship is open to freshmen women majoring in engineering or computer science. You must have been accepted into an ABET-accredited program or SWE-approved school. One award is offered for $1,500 and two awards are offered for $1,000. Award requirements change regularly. Please send a self-addressed, stamped envelope to receive your application. For further instructions, please browse the SWE website at www.swe.org or email hq@swe.org. No GPA requirement specified.

Society of Women Engineers Headquarters
Scholarship Coordinator
120 Wall Street, FL 11
New York, NY 10005-3902

875
Northwestern Mutual Sales Scholarship Contest

AMOUNT: $250-$2500 DEADLINE: Varies
MAJOR: Marketing Sales, Insurance

Northwestern Mutual Life Insurance Co. is sponsoring a sales scholarship contest for Fort Wayne, IN, area college students. To be considered for this award, you must submit a video of a sales presentation to the sponsor. A panel of local judges will choose the winner from all entries received. The local winner will receive a $250 certificate to their college bookstore and an opportunity for an internship with the Fort Wayne District Agency. The national competition is judged by professors from several top universities in the country. Six national winners will be chosen for the grand prize of $2,500. Award requirements change regularly. Please send a self-addressed, stamped envelope and your resume to receive your application and any further instructions from the scholarship provider. No GPA requirement specified.

Northwestern Mutual Life Insurance Co.
Alan New, Director of College Agents
127 West Berry, Suite 300
Fort Wayne, IN 46802

876
Norwest Community Scholarship Fund

AMOUNT: $1000 DEADLINE: January 15
MAJOR: All Areas of Study

The Norwest Community Scholarship Fund is open to high school seniors from Hillsboro, ND, who plan on attending college in North Dakota. Winners are selected by a local independent panel of judges. Award requirements change regularly. Please send a self-addressed, stamped envelope to receive your application and any further instructions from the scholarship provider. Applications are also available from your high school guidance counselor or at your local Norwest branch. No GPA requirement specified.

Norwest Bank Hillsboro
Attn: Kathy Larson
PO Box 280
Hillsboro, ND 58045

877
NPFDA Scholarship

AMOUNT: $1500-$2000 DEADLINE: Varies
MAJOR: Agriculture, Poultry Science, Animal Science, Food Science

The NPFDA Scholarship is open to junior or senior students majoring in poultry, food, and animal science and agriculture-related fields. To be eligible for this scholarship you must submit a one-page narrative on your goals and ambitions along with your transcript. Winners are chosen on the basis of their aspirations, extracurricular activities, and industry-related activities, as well as their academic progress. Award requirements change regularly. Please send a self-addressed, stamped envelope to receive your application and any further instructions from the scholarship provider; or send email to: info@npfda.org. No GPA requirement specified.

National Poultry and Food Distributors Association
Attn: Scholarship Committee
958 McEver Road Ext., Unit B-5
Gainesville, GA 30504

878
NRAEF Graduate Degree Scholarship

AMOUNT: $2500-$5000 DEADLINE: May 1
MAJOR: Foodservice, Hospitality

The NRAEF Graduate Degree Scholarships are open to full-time or substantially part-time foodservice and hospitality majors who are working toward postgraduate degrees in a business-related program in the U.S. or U.S. territories (American Samoa, District of Columbia, Guam, Puerto Rico, and U.S. Virgin Islands). You must have performed a minimum of 1,000 hours of restaurant or foodservice work experience verifiable by paycheck stubs or letter(s) from your employer(s); you must have at least a 3.0 GPA; and you must be a U.S. citizen or a permanent resident. Two letters of recommendation are required. Award requirements change regularly. GPA must be 3.0-4.0.

National Restaurant Association Education Foundation
Scholarship Committee
250 South Wacker Drive, Suite 1400
Chicago, IL 60606-5800

879
NRAEF Teacher Work-Study Grant

AMOUNT: $2000 DEADLINE: May 1
MAJOR: Foodservice, Hospitality

The NRAEF Teacher Work-Study Grants are available to foodservice and hospitality educators of restaurant and food-service education who wish to add hands-on work experience to gain a better understanding of day-to-day operations. You must currently be a full-time high school or college educator or administrator of a foodservice or hospitality program. You must also arrange employment in a foodservice-related line or

staff position that includes a minimum of 200 (full- or part-time hours) within a two-month period. In order to apply, you will be required to be a citizen or permanent resident of the U.S. or of the U.S. territories (American Samoa, District of Columbia, Guam, Puerto Rico, and U.S. Virgin Islands). Award requirements change regularly. No GPA requirement specified.

National Restaurant Association Education Foundation
Scholarship Committee
250 South Wacker Drive, Suite 1400
Chicago, IL 60606-5800

880
NRAEF Undergraduate Scholarships for H.S. Students

AMOUNT: $2000 DEADLINE: May 22
MAJOR: Food Service, Hospitality, Food Management, Culinary Arts

The NRAEF Undergraduate Scholarships for High School Students is open to high school seniors who have a minimum 2.75 GPA and have taken at least one foodservice-related course and/or have performed a minimum of 250 hours of restaurant and hospitality work experience in the restaurant and hospitality industry verifiable by paystubs or letters from employers. You must have applied and gained acceptance to a hospitality-related postsecondary program, either full-time or part-time in the U.S. or in a U.S. territory (American Samoa, District of Columbia, Guam, Puerto Rico, and U.S. Virgin Islands). A letter of recommendation on letterhead from a current or previous employer is also required. Award requirements change regularly. GPA must be 2.7-4.0.

National Restaurant Association Education Foundation
Scholarship Committee
250 South Wacker Drive, Suite 1400
Chicago, IL 60606-5800

881
NRAEF Undergraduate Scholarships for College Students

AMOUNT: $1000-$2000 DEADLINE: July 1
MAJOR: Food Service, Hospitality, Food Management, Culinary Arts

The NRAEF Undergraduate Scholarships for College Students is open to college students who are U.S. citizens or permanent residents and have a minimum, cumulative grade point average of 2.75; a minimum of 750 hours of restaurant or foodservice-related work experience, or are enrolled in restaurant or foodservice-related postsecondary programs either full-time or substantially part-time in the U.S. or U.S. territories (American Samoa, District of Columbia, Guam, Puerto Rico and U.S. Virgin Islands). A letter of recommendation is required. Applications are due November 1 for the December through May term; March 1 for the April through July term; and July 1 for the August through November term. Award requirements change regularly. GPA must be 2.7-4.0.

National Restaurant Association Education Foundation
Scholarship Committee
250 South Wacker Drive, Suite 1400
Chicago, IL 60606-5800

NSA Scholarship

AMOUNT: $500-$1000 DEADLINE: March 10
MAJOR: Accounting

The NSA Scholarship is open to accounting majors enrolled in an undergraduate degree program at a United States accredited two- or four-year college or university with a "B" or better GPA. To be eligible for this award you must also be a U.S. or Canadian citizen. Approximately $1,000 is awarded to students entering their third or fourth year of studies and approximately $500 is awarded to students entering their second year of studies. These scholarships are awarded primarily for academic merit, demonstrated leadership ability, and financial need. Award requirements change regularly. Please send a self-addressed, stamped envelope to receive your application and any further instructions from the scholarship provider. GPA must be 3.0-4.0.

National Society of Accountants
Attn: Scholarship Foundation
1010 North Fairfax Street
Alexandria, VA 22314-1574

883

NSA Undergraduate Training Program

AMOUNT: None Specified DEADLINE: November 30
MAJOR: Computer Science, Electrical or Computer Engineering, Language, Mathematics

This program is for high school seniors, in particular minority students or students with disabilities, who choose a full-time college major in one of the following fields: computer science, electrical or computer engineering, language or math. In order to apply for the program, you must have a minimum 3.0 GPA, a 25 ACT or SAT score of 1100, and be a U.S. citizen. Two letters of recommendation are also required. Award requirements change regularly. Please send a self-addressed, stamped envelope to receive your application and any further instructions to address listed, or contact the UTP office at (800) 669-0703. GPA must be 3.0-4.0.

National Security Agency
UTP Application S23
9800 Savage Road, Suite 6840
Fort George G. Meade, MD 20755-6840

884

Nuclear Propulsion Officer Candidate Program (NUPOC)

AMOUNT: $2000-$74000 DEADLINE: Varies
MAJOR: Engineering, Physics, Mathematics, Chemistry, Computer Science

The Nuclear Propulsion Officer Candidate Program (NUPOC) is open to qualified, full-time students and recent graduates who are majoring in all engineering areas, physics, mathematics, chemistry or computer science for highly technical positions as nuclear propulsion officers, instructors and research engineers. These positions exist both on ships and at land-based facilities. Students selected during their sophomore year, or later, begin receiving a monthly cash retainer of $2,000 (plus $8,000 signing bonus for ship-based positions). Following graduation, nuclear propulsion officers participate in an 18-month training program concentrating in the areas of nuclear, electrical, materials, and mechanical engineering. Additionally, officers undertake numerous leadership and managerial roles. Please note these are not ROTC programs. Selected applicants have no outside requirements for drill, haircuts, or uniforms. Up to $74,000 is awarded while in school. No GPA requirement specified.

Navy Officer Programs, Omaha
Leads Department - Suite 400
6910 Pacific Street
Omaha, NE 68106-1085

885

Nurse Candidate Program

AMOUNT: None Specified DEADLINE: March 1
MAJOR: Nursing

The Nurse Candidate Program is open to qualified students who have completed two years of college nursing curriculum. Recipients of the award will receive monthly stipends of $500 and become navy nurses upon graduation. The recipients will also receive a $5,000 bonus upon signing on as navy nurses. Award requirements change regularly. Visit the website at www.incolor.inetnebr.com/nrdomaha for further information. GPA must be 3.0-4.0.

Navy Officer Programs, Omaha
Leads Department - Suite 400
6910 Pacific Street
Omaha, NE 68106-1085

886

Nursing Incentive Scholarship

AMOUNT: $1000-$2000 DEADLINE: June 1
MAJOR: Nursing

Scholarships are available to Kentucky residents who have been admitted to a nursing school. Preference is given to you if you demonstrate financial need. You must agree to work as a nurse in the state of Kentucky for the same length of time for which you were funded. Award requirements change regularly. Write to the address listed, enclosing a self-addressed, stamped envelope for an application and further information. You may also browse their website: www.kbn.state.ky.us or email: darlene.chilton@mail.state.ky.us. No GPA requirement specified.

Kentucky Board of Nursing
312 Whittington Pkwy, Ste 300
Louisville, KY 40222-4925

887

Nursing Scholarship

AMOUNT: None Specified DEADLINE: Varies
MAJOR: Nursing

This scholarship is open to Indiana students admitted as full-time or part-time students to a nursing program at an eligible Indiana college or university. Recipients of these awards must also agree to work as a nurse in any type of health care setting in Indiana for at least two years after graduation. Award requirements change regularly. For further information and an application, please contact a high school guidance counselor, a college/university financial aid office, or write to the address listed, including a self-addressed, stamped envelope. You may also visit the SSACI website: www.ai.org/ssaci. GPA must be 2.0-4.0.

State Student Assistance Commission of Indiana
Attn: Scholarship Committee
150 West Market Street, Suite 500
Indianapolis, IN 46204

888
Nursing Scholastic Achievement Scholarships

AMOUNT: Maximum: $1000 DEADLINE: March 15
MAJOR: Nursing

This scholarship is open to active communicant members of Lutheran congregations who are juniors or seniors in an accredited school of nursing. You must have a minimum 3.0 GPA and be able to document that a minimum of 100 work hours, volunteer and/or paid, have been completed to benefit people who are mentally retarded. Award requirements change regularly. For any further information, contact Kevin Keller, Coordinator of Outreach Programs and Services at (800) 369-4636, ext. 525 or email: kkeller@blhs.org. GPA must be 3.0-4.0.

Bethesda Lutheran Homes and Services, Inc.
Kevin Keller, Coordinator
700 Hoffman Drive
Watertown, WI 53094-6204

889
NWSA Graduate Scholarship Award

AMOUNT: $1000 DEADLINE: February 15
MAJOR: Women's Studies

The NWSA Graduate Scholarship Award is open to a master's degree or Ph.D. candidate enrolled in a women's studies program. You must be in the research or writing stage of your thesis or dissertation. You must also be member of NWSA at the time of application. Award requirements change regularly. No GPA requirement specified.

National Women's Studies Association
University of Maryland
7100 Baltimore Avenue, Suite 500
College Park, MD 20740-3636

890
NWSA Graduate Scholarship In Lesbian Studies

AMOUNT: $500 DEADLINE: February 15
MAJOR: Women's Studies - Lesbian Studies

The NWSA Graduate Scholarship in Lesbian Studies is open to a master's degree or Ph.D. candidate enrolled in a lesbian studies program. You must be in the research or writing stage of your thesis or dissertation. Preference will be given to National Women's Studies Association members. Award requirements change regularly. No GPA requirement specified.

National Women's Studies Association
University of Maryland
7100 Baltimore Avenue, Suite 500
College Park, MD 20740-3627

891
Oakland Century B'nai B'rith Scholarship

AMOUNT: $500 DEADLINE: April 20
MAJOR: All Areas of Study

Open to Jewish undergraduates from Metropolitan Detroit, who have completed a full year of credits toward a degree. Applicants must demonstrate superior academics, financial need and campus activities that show established roots in Metropolitan Detroit. Must also demonstrate leadership qualities for the benefit of the Jewish community. Award requirements change regularly. Write to the address listed, enclosing a self-addressed, stamped envelope for an application and further information. GPA must be 3.5-4.0.

Oakland Century B'nai B'rith
Harold J Samuels Chair, Scholarship Committee
25240 Inkster Road
Southfield, MI 48034-2255

892
Observational Studies Dissertation Award

AMOUNT: $2500 DEADLINE: April 1
MAJOR: Gender and Family Studies, Social Services, Human Development

The Observational Studies Dissertation Award is open to doctoral students. Projects must use data from the Manpower Demonstration Research Corporation's Observational Studies, comprising studies of two different welfare intervention programs. The data set, which includes computer-accessible and videotaped data of mothers and their children, is available through the Murray Center. The Henry A. Murray Research Center is a national repository of social and behavioral sciences data for the study of lives over time with a special focus on the lives of American women. Award requirements change regularly. Please send a self-addressed, stamped envelope to receive your application and any further instructions from the Murray Center; or visit their website at www.radcliffe.edu/murray. No GPA requirement specified.

Radcliffe College - Henry A. Murray Research Center
Attn: Grants Program Coordinator
10 Garden Street
Cambridge, MA 02138

893
OCA Avon College Scholarship

AMOUNT: $1500 DEADLINE: Varies
MAJOR: All Areas of Study

Open to Asian Pacific American women who demonstrate financial need. Applicants must be U.S. citizens or permanent residents and have a minimum cumulative 3.0 GPA. Deadline TBA. Award requirements change regularly. For further information and an application, please write to the address listed, including a self-addressed, stamped envelope or visit their website: www.ocanatl.org/. GPA must be 3.0-4.0.

Organization of Chinese Americans
Scholarship Committee
1001 Connecticut Avenue, NW, Suite 601
Washington, DC 20036

894
OCA Chinese American Journalist Award

AMOUNT: $200-$500 DEADLINE: Varies
MAJOR: All Areas of Study

Open to Asian Pacific American journalists, young writers, and outstanding high school students. The purpose of this award is to recognize the best newspaper, magazine, or published piece on social, political, economic, or cultural issues facing Chinese Americans and/or Asian Americans. Selection will be based on completeness of story, accuracy of data used, thoroughness of analysis, importance to the understanding of Chinese Americans/Asian Americans' issues, and readability of story. Award requirements change regularly. For further information and an application, please call (202) 223-5500, or visit their website: www.ocanatl.org/. GPA must be 3.0-4.0.

Organization of Chinese Americans
Scholarship Committee
1001 Connecticut Avenue, NW, Suite 601
Washington, DC 20036

895
OCA National Youth Essay Contest

AMOUNT: $100-$400 DEADLINE: Varies
MAJOR: All Areas of Study

Essay contest open to Asian-Pacific American students in grades 9 - 12 to promote excellence in writing and communications. The essay topic will be announced along with the deadline. All essays should be 800-1,000-words long, in English, typed on 8 1/2" by 11" white bond paper, double-spaced, with full references and bibliography if applicable. Award requirements change regularly. For further information and an application, please call (202) 223-5500, or visit their website: www.ocanatl.org/. GPA must be 3.0-4.0.

Organization of Chinese Americans
Scholarship Committee
1001 Connecticut Avenue, NW, Suite 601
Washington, DC 20036

896
OCA/UPS Foundation Gold Mountain Scholarship

AMOUNT: $2000 DEADLINE: Varies
MAJOR: All Areas of Study

The OCA/UPS Foundation Gold Mountain Scholarship is awarded to Asian-Pacific American students who are in financial need and the first person in their immediate family to attend college. Applicants must be U.S. citizens or permanent residents, have a minimum cumulative 3.0 GPA, and entering their first year of college. Award requirements change regularly. For further information and an application, please write to the address listed and include a self-addressed, stamped envelope, or call (202) 223-5500. GPA must be 3.0-4.0.

Organization of Chinese Americans
Scholarship Committee
1001 Connecticut Avenue, NW, Suite 601
Washington, DC 20036

897
Odd Fellows and Rebekahs Nursing Scholarship

AMOUNT: None Specified DEADLINE: April 15
MAJOR: Nursing

This scholarship is open to Maine residents, from high school seniors to adult students returning to school, and graduate students not currently enrolled in a registered nursing program. Award requirements change regularly. Please write to the address listed, enclosing a self-addressed, stamped envelope for an application and further information. No GPA requirement specified.

Odd Fellows and Rebekahs Nursing Scholarship Program
Attn: Ms. Ellen F. Washburn
22 Munsey Avenue
Livermore Falls, ME 04254-1116

898
Ohio Instructional Grant

AMOUNT: $156-$4464 DEADLINE: October 1
MAJOR: All Areas of Study

The Ohio Instructional Grant is available to full-time undergraduates who are Ohio residents. To be considered for the award, you must be attending or planning to attend a college or university in Ohio. Awards are based on family income with consideration given to the number of dependents in the family. Award requirements change regularly. To apply, you must submit the FAFSA. No GPA requirement specified.

Ohio Board of Regents
James A. Rhodes State Office Tower
30 East Broad Street, 36th Floor
Columbus, OH 43266-0417

899
Ohio Junior Miss Scholarship Program

AMOUNT: None Specified DEADLINE: Varies
MAJOR: All Areas of Study

The Ohio Junior Miss Scholarship Program is open to female high school seniors attending Ohio high schools. The students will compete for more than $21,000 in cash scholarships. Scholastic achievement is 20 percent of the judging for the selection of Ohio's Junior Miss and the panel evaluation represents 25 percent of the judging. Other judging is based on fitness, presence, and composure (both 15 percent) and creative and performing arts, (both 25 percent). Award requirements change regularly. Please send a self-addressed, stamped envelope to receive your application and any further instructions from the scholarship provider or phone the Mount Vernon/Knox County Chamber of Commerce (740) 393-1111. No GPA requirement specified.

Ohio Junior Miss
Attn: Scholarship Program Coordinator
7 East Ohio Avenue
Mount Vernon, OH 43050

900
Ohio War Orphan Scholarship

AMOUNT: None Specified DEADLINE: July 1
MAJOR: All Areas of Study

Scholarships are available to children of veterans who served at least 90 days active duty during a period of war and must now be either disabled or deceased. The applicant must be an Ohio resident between the ages of 16 and 21 and be attending a participating Ohio college or university. Satisfactory academic progress and full-time status are required to retain the scholarship. Award requirements change regularly. Contact your school's financial aid office, your high school guidance counselor or contact the address listed for further information. No GPA requirement specified.

Ohio Board of Regents
James A. Rhodes
State Office Tower
30 East Broad Street, 36th Floor
Columbus, OH 43266-0417

901
Oklahoma Tuition Aid Grant

AMOUNT: Maximum: $1000 DEADLINE: April 30
MAJOR: All Areas of Study

The Oklahoma Tuition Aid Grant is open to Oklahoma residents who attend approved colleges, universities and vocational-technical schools in Oklahoma. Awards are approved for full-time or part-time students and undergraduate or graduate study. The award is based on financial need. You must also demonstrate satisfactory academic progress according to your respective school's policy for financial aid recipients. Award requirements change regularly. To apply, you must submit the FAFSA. The earlier you apply, the greater chance you have of receiving an award. For more information, you may visit the Oklahoma Tuition Aid Grant website at www.otag.org. No GPA requirement specified.

Oklahoma State Regents for Higher Education
State Grant and Scholarship Programs
500 Education Bldg., State Capitol
Oklahoma City, OK 73105-4503

902
Olive Lynn Salembier Scholarship

AMOUNT: $2000 DEADLINE: May 15
MAJOR: Engineering

This scholarship is open to women who are majoring in engineering at an ABET-accredited program or an SWE-approved school and who are pursuing the credentials necessary to reenter the job market as engineers. You must have been out of the engineering job market as well as out of school for a minimum of two years. You may be attending school full-time or part-time in order to be eligible. Sophomore through graduate students must have minimum GPAs of 3.5. Award requirements change regularly. Please send a self-addressed, stamped envelope to receive your application. For any further instructions from the scholarship provider, please browse their website at www.swe.org or email hq@swe.org. No GPA requirement specified.

Society of Women Engineers Headquarters
Scholarship Coordinator
120 Wall Street, FL 11
New York, NY 10005-3902

903
Operation Enterprise Program

AMOUNT: $1500 DEADLINE: February 1
MAJOR: Business

The Operation Enterprise Program is an intensive training experience that is open to students interested in business leadership. This award is sponsored by the American Management Association (AMA), and courses are taught by leading corporate executives. To be considered for this award, you must be a high school junior, senior, or postsecondary student. The value of the scholarship goes to cover tuition, room, and board for the week-long program. Award requirements change regularly. Request an application form and related information from Reg Wilson, Assistant Director, Operation Enterprise Programs, American Management Association, PO Box 88, Hamilton, NY 13346, or phone (315) 824-2000. No GPA requirement specified.

Future Business Leaders of America
Attn: Scholarship Coordinator
1912 Association Drive
Reston, VA 22091

904
Oppenheim Student's Fund, Inc. Scholarship

AMOUNT: $250-$1500 DEADLINE: May 1
MAJOR: All Areas of Study

This scholarship is open to high school seniors who are residents of Niagara County or seniors in a Niagara County high school. Award requirements change regularly. Please contact the address listed for further information or call (716) 286-4229. No GPA requirement specified.

Oppenheim Students Fund, Inc.
Barbara Joyce, Board of Education
607 Walnut Avenue
Niagara Falls, NY 14301-1729

905
Oral-B Laboratories/Juliette A. Southard Scholarship

AMOUNT: None Specified DEADLINE: January 31
MAJOR: Dental Assisting

For students accepted into an accredited dental assisting program at any level of study who are ADAA members or student members. Based on academic achievement, abilities, and interest in dental assisting as a career. Must be U.S. citizens and have a high school diploma or GED to apply. Scholarships to be awarded April 15. Award requirements change regularly. Write to the address listed, enclosing a self-addressed, stamped envelope. GPA must be 2.8-4.0.

American Dental Assistants Association
Southard/Oral B Scholarship Program
203 North LaSalle Street, Suite 1320
Chicago, IL 60601-1225

906
Orange County Chapter/Harry Jackson Scholarship Fund

AMOUNT: $250 DEADLINE: Varies
MAJOR: Travel and Tourism

Applicants must be employed by an Orange County ASTA Chapter member, and must be pursuing either an ICTA educational program or an ASTA educational program. Must have a minimum two years travel industry experience. A letter of interest and/or need and a letter of recommendation required. Award requirements change regularly. Write to the address listed, enclosing a self-addressed, stamped envelope for an application and further information. You can browse their website: www.astanet.com or email: myriaml@astahq.com. No GPA requirement specified.

American Society of Travel Agents
Attn: ASTA Foundation
1101 King Street, Suite 200
Alexandria, VA 22314-2944

907
Oregon Council of the Blind Scholarship

AMOUNT: $1000 DEADLINE: March 1
MAJOR: All Areas of Study

These scholarships are available to legally blind students who are residents of Oregon. Award requirements change regularly. Write to the address listed, enclosing a self-addressed, stamped envelope for an application and further information. No GPA requirement specified.

American Council of the Blind
Attn: Billie Jean Keith
1155 15th Street NW, Suite 720
Washington, DC 20005-2706

908
Oregon Need Grant

AMOUNT: None Specified DEADLINE: Varies
MAJOR: All Areas of Study

The Oregon Need Grant is open to Oregon residents enrolled as full-time undergraduates. To be considered for the award, you must be enrolled in a nonprofit college or university in Oregon. The award is based on demonstrated financial need and is renewable, provided you maintain satisfactory academic progress. Award requirements change regularly. To apply, you must submit the FAFSA. For more information, you may visit the Oregon Student Assistance Commission at www.ossc.state.or.us. No GPA requirement specified.

Oregon Student Assistance Commission
OSAC Grants and Scholarships Department
1500 Valley River Drive, Suite 100
Eugene, OR 97401-2130

909
Oscar Pentzke Scholarship

AMOUNT: None Specified DEADLINE: July 14
MAJOR: All Areas of Study

The Oscar Pentzke Scholarship is open to Latino/Latina graduating high school seniors and college transfer students. To be considered for this award, you must be entering a four-year college or university, be a full-time student carrying a minimum of 12 units, demonstrate financial need, and have at least a 3.0 GPA. There is no U.S. citizenship or permanent residency requirement. You will be required to submit a personal statement, transcript, and letter of recommendation with your application. Award requirements change regularly. GPA must be 3.0-4.0.

Gamma Zeta Alpha Fraternity - Beta Chapter
Attn: Scholarship Selection Committee
1680 Riverbirch Court
San Jose, CA 95131

910
Pacific Northwest Chapter/William Hunt Scholarship Fund

AMOUNT: Maximum: $1000 DEADLINE: Varies
MAJOR: Travel and Tourism

Applicants must be employed by an ASTA member organization in Area 10 (Oregon and Pacific Northwest Chapters). Also must be seeking certificates in the ASTA Certified Specialist Program, the ICTA certification programs or be taking courses at an accredited college or university offering travel/tourism. Award requirements change regularly. Write to the address listed, enclosing a self-addressed, stamped envelope for an application and further information. You can browse their website: www.astanet.com or email: myriaml@astahq.com. No GPA requirement specified.

American Society of Travel Agents
Attn: ASTA Foundation
1101 King Street, Suite 200
Alexandria, VA 22314-2944

911
Parkersburg Zonta Club Scholarship

AMOUNT: $750 DEADLINE: May 5
MAJOR: All Areas of Study

Open to female juniors and seniors attending college full-time. Applicants must have graduated from a Wood County (WV) or Belpre, OH, high school OR be current residents of Wood County (WV) or Belpre, OH. Applicants must also have a minimum 3.0 GPA, demonstrate financial need, and have a well-defined career objective. Award requirements change regularly. For further information and an application, please write to the address listed, including a self-addressed, stamped envelope. GPA must be 3.0.

Zonta Club of Parkersburg
McDonough Eddy Parsons Baylous A C
PO Box 184
Parkersburg, WV 26102-0184

912
Parrett Scholarship

AMOUNT: $1500-$2500 DEADLINE: July 31
MAJOR: Engineering, Science, Medicine, or Dentistry

This scholarship is open to residents of the state of Washington who have completed their first year of college. The applicant must be enrolled full-time. Award requirements change regularly. For further information, please contact the address provided, including a self-addressed, stamped envelope. No GPA requirement specified.

Parrett Scholarship Foundation
U S Bank of Washington Trustee
PO Box 720
Seattle, WA 98111-0720

913
Patty and Melvin Alperin First Generation Scholarship

AMOUNT: $1000 DEADLINE: May 22
MAJOR: All Areas of Study

The Patty and Melvin Alperin First Generation Scholarship is open to college-bound Rhode Island high school graduates whose parents did not have the benefit of attending college. You must be enrolled in an accredited nonprofit postsecondary institution offering either a two-year or four-year degree. This award is renewable for up to four years if you maintain a good academic record. To apply, you must submit a high school transcript, a letter of recommendation, a one-page essay detailing what it is like to be a first generation college student, a copy of your award letter from the institution you will be attending, and a completed SAR. Award requirements change regularly. No GPA requirement specified.

Rhode Island Foundation
Attn: Special Funds Office
70 Elm Street
Providence, RI 02903

914
Paul and Helen L. Grauer Scholarship

AMOUNT: $1000 DEADLINE: February 1
MAJOR: Electronics, Communications, and Related Fields

This scholarship is available to students with a minimum novice class amateur radio license who are majoring in electronics, communications, or in a related area. The applicants must be residents of the ARRL Midwest Division (Iowa, Kansas, Missouri, or Nebraska) and be participating in a baccalaureate or higher course of study in one of these states. Award requirements change regularly. For further information, write the address provided, using a self-addressed, stamped envelope or email foundation@arrl.org. No GPA requirement specified.

American Radio Relay League
Attn: ARRL Foundation
225 Main Street
Newington, CT 06111-1400

915
Paul Arnold Memorial Scholarship

AMOUNT: Maximum: $3500 DEADLINE: February 20
MAJOR: Interior, Graphic, or Fashion Design

Awards for young men and women studying interior fashion or graphic design who demonstrate originality of vision, aptitude and commitment in their chosen field. Must be residents of Washington, Oregon, Idaho, Montana and Alaska. Award requirements change regularly. Write to the address listed, enclosing a self-addressed, stamped envelope for an application and further information. No GPA requirement specified.

GSBA, Pride and INBA Scholarships
Scholarship Programs
2150 North 107th Street, Suite 205
Seattle, WA 98133-9009

916
Paul H. Kutschenreuter Scholarship

AMOUNT: $5000 DEADLINE: June 14
MAJOR: Metrology, Atmospheric Science

Scholarships for students entering their last year of study toward a degree in meteorology. Based on academics and financial need. Must have a minimum GPA of 3.0, be enrolled full-time and be U.S. citizens or permanent residents. Award requirements change regularly. Write to the address listed, sending a self-addressed, stamped envelope for details, call AMS headquarters at (617) 227-2426, extension 235, browse their website: www.ametsoc.org/ams/amsedu/scholfel.html or contact their email: armstrong@ametsoc.org. GPA must be 3.0-4.0.

American Meteorological Society
Fellowship/Scholarship Coordinator
45 Beacon Street
Boston, MA 02108-3693

917
Paul Powell Memorial AMVETS Award

AMOUNT: None Specified DEADLINE: March 1
MAJOR: All Areas of Study

The Paul Powell Memorial AMVETS Award is open to Illinois high school seniors who have taken the American College Test (ACT). In order to apply, you must be an unmarried child of a veteran who served after September 15, 1940. Your parent or parents must have been honorably discharged or be presently serving in the military. Award requirements change regularly. No GPA requirement specified.

AMVETS - Illinois State Headquarters
Illinois AMVETS Scholarship Program
2200 South 6th Street
Springfield, IL 62703-3454

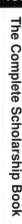

918
Pauline Gore Scholarships

AMOUNT: $500-$2500 DEADLINE: April 1
MAJOR: All Areas of Study

Open to high school seniors and current college underclassmen attending four-year colleges and universities who are from Smith County, TN. Applicants must have lived in Smith County for a majority of their precollege schooling. Award requirements change regularly. GPA must be 2.0-4.0.

Community Foundation of Middle Tennessee
Scholarship Committee
210 23rd Avenue North
Nashville, TN 37203-1502

919
Paumanauke Native American Indian Scholarship

AMOUNT: $500-$750 DEADLINE: May 1
MAJOR: All Areas of Study

Open to tribally enrolled Native American Indians attending colleges, universities, and accredited postsecondary institutions on a full-time basis. Award requirements change regularly. Apply on line. No GPA requirement specified.

Paumanauke Pow-Wow & Native American Living Arts Festival, Inc.
Native American Indian Scholarship
333 Lagoon Drive South
Copiague, NY 11726-5408

920
Pawtucket East High School Class of '42 Scholarship

AMOUNT: $500 DEADLINE: March 31
MAJOR: All Areas of Study

The Pawtucket East High School Class of '42 Scholarship is available to graduating seniors of Tolman High School in Pawtucket, RI. One award is given annually. Award requirements change regularly. No GPA requirement specified.

Rhode Island Foundation
Attn: Special Funds Office
70 Elm Street
Providence, RI 02903

921
Peeples Foundation Trust Scholarship

AMOUNT: None Specified DEADLINE: March 1
MAJOR: Nursing, Dietetics, Industrial Arts Education

This scholarship is open to graduates of Indiana high schools who are majoring in nursing (B.S., R.N., L.P.N.), dietetics, or are interested in teaching in the field of liberal arts. Preference is given first to graduates of Franklin Community High School then to graduates of other Indiana educational institutions. Selection is based on academics, recommendations, financial need, and a personal interview. Award requirements change regularly. No GPA requirement specified.

Johnson County Community Foundation
Community Scholarship Program
PO Box 217
Franklin, IN 46131

922
Penn-Mar-Va Travelers Club Scholarship

AMOUNT: $2000 DEADLINE: March 15
MAJOR: All Fields of Study

The Penn-Mar-Va Travelers Club Scholarship is open to employees of Business Products Industry Association member firms and their families. Persons holding academic records sufficient for acceptance by accredited colleges, junior colleges or technical schools, or persons already enrolled in one of those institutions are eligible for this one-year award. Selection is made by a committee from the Student Financial Aid Department of The George Washington University, Washington, DC. Award requirements change regularly. Please send a self-addressed, stamped envelope to receive your application and any further instructions from the scholarship provider or email: info@bpia.org. No GPA requirement specified.

Business Products Industry Association
Attn: Scholarship Committee
301 North Fairfax Street
Alexandria, VA 22314-2633

923
Pennsylvania State Grant

AMOUNT: Maximum: $3100 DEADLINE: May 1
MAJOR: All Fields of Study

The Pennsylvania State Grant is open to eligible Pennsylvania residents who are able to sufficiently demonstrate financial need. To be considered for the award, you must be enrolled at least half-time in a Pennsylvania Higher Education Assistance Agency (PHEAA) approved undergraduate program of study and have a high school diploma (or a GED). Though you do not necessarily have to be attending a school in Pennsylvania, your chances of receiving more aid are significantly higher if you attend an institution within the state. Award requirements change regularly. To apply, you must submit the FAFSA. For more information, you may contact the PHEAA website at www.pheaa.org. No GPA requirement specified.

Pennsylvania Higher Education Assistance Agency
Grant Programs
1200 North 7th Street
Harrisburg, PA 17102

924
Pharmacy Station Scholarship

AMOUNT: None Specified DEADLINE: Varies
MAJOR: All Fields of Study

The Pharmacy Station Scholarship is open to graduating seniors at Burlington High School (Burlington, WI). Students must attend a two- or four-year college or university. Award requirements change regularly. Please visit your guidance office to receive an application and any additional details. No GPA requirement specified.

Burlington High School
Attn: Guidance Office
225 Robert Street
Burlington, WI 53105

925
PHD ARA Scholarship

AMOUNT: $1000 DEADLINE: February 1
MAJOR: Electronic Engineering, Computer Science,
Journalism

This scholarship is available to students with any class amateur radio license who are children of deceased amateur radio operators. Applicants must be residents of Iowa, Kansas, Missouri or Nebraska majoring in journalism, computer science, or electronic engineering. Award requirements change regularly. Write the address provided, using a self-addressed, stamped envelope, for further information. No GPA requirement specified.

American Radio Relay League
Attn: ARRL Foundation
225 Main Street
Newington, CT 06111-1400

926
Phil Shanline Scholarship

AMOUNT: $500 DEADLINE: March 14
MAJOR: Mathematics, Science, Engineering, Health Services, Education, Business

This scholarship is open to students who are in fields of study leading to degrees in math, science, engineering, education, health services, or business. In order to apply, you must have completed one year of college and be registered to attend classes at a college or university located in the state of Nebraska and accredited by the North Central Association of Colleges and Schools. Award requirements change regularly. No GPA requirement specified.

American Society for Quality - Nebraska Section 1302
Leroy Umphres Scholarship Chairperson
PO Box 83335
Lincoln, NE 68501-3335

927
Pioneers of Flight Scholarship

AMOUNT: $2500 DEADLINE: November 20
MAJOR: Aviation Related Fields

Open to college students in their sophomore or junior year, at the time of application, who are intending to pursue full-time study at an accredited four-year college or university and who demonstrate an interest in pursuing a career in general aviation. Must have a GPA of 2.5 or above. Awards are for undergraduate study only. All applicants must be nominated and endorsed by a representative of a Regular or Associate Member Company of the National Air Transportation Association. Award requirements change regularly. Write the address listed or call (507) 931-1682 to obtain a National Air Transportation Association member listing by state if you are unaware of members with whom you would pursue nomination. GPA must be 2.5-4.0.

General Electric Scholarship Program
Citizens Scholarship Foundation
PO Box 297
Saint Peter, MN 56082-0297

928
Pleasant Hawaiian Holidays Scholarship

AMOUNT: $1500 DEADLINE: July 28
MAJOR: Travel and Tourism

Open to students who are residents of the U.S. enrolled in a four-year college or university and who are pursuing a degree in travel and tourism. One award goes to applicants attending school in the southern California chapter area (Los Angeles, Kern, Riverside, San Bernardino, San Luis Obispo, Santa Barbara, and Ventura counties). The other award for applicants attending school anywhere in the U.S. Applicants will be required to submit a 500-word paper entitled, "My Goals in the Travel Industry" and should include why he/she should be chosen to receive the award. Award requirements change regularly. Write to the address listed, enclosing a self-addressed, stamped envelope for an application and further information. You can browse their website: www.astanet.com or email: myriaml@astahq.com. No GPA requirement specified.

American Society of Travel Agents
Attn: ASTA Foundation
1101 King Street, Suite 200
Alexandria, VA 22314-2944

929
Pollard and A.J. (Andy) Spielman Scholarship

AMOUNT: $2000-$2500 DEADLINE: July 28
MAJOR: Travel and Tourism

Four awards are available for students in the field of travel and tourism who are attending school for the purpose of re-entering the work force in the field of travel. Students must be U.S. citizens or legal residents and have a GPA of at least 2.5. Must be enrolled (enrolling) in a proprietary travel school or two-year junior college. Award requirements change regularly. Write to the address listed, enclosing a self-addressed, stamped envelope for an application and further information. You can browse their website: www.astanet.com or email: myriaml@astahq.com. GPA must be 2.5-4.0.

American Society of Travel Agents
Attn: ASTA Foundation
1101 King Street, Suite 200
Alexandria, VA 22314-2944

930
Population Council Fellowship for Predoctoral Training

AMOUNT: None Specified DEADLINE: December 15
MAJOR: Population Studies, Demography, Economics, Sociology, Anthropology, Geography, Public Health, and Related Areas of Study

Awards are open to candidates who have completed all coursework requirements toward a Ph.D. or an equivalent degree in demography or in one of the social sciences.

Applicants requesting support for either the dissertation field-work or the dissertation writing period will be considered. Fellowships will be awarded for advanced training in population studies (including demography and public health) in combination with a social science discipline, such as economics, sociology, anthropology, or geography. Awards will be made only to applicants whose proposals deal with the developing world. The typical award is for 12 months and is nonrenewable. The scholarship consists of a monthly stipend, partial tuition payments and related fees, transportation expenses, allowances for books and supplies, and health insurance. Award requirements change regularly. For further information and an application you may: write to the address listed (please include a self-addressed, stamped envelope); call (212) 339-0671; or fax (212) 755-6052. When writing, include a brief description of your academic and professional qualifications and a short statement about your research or study plans for the proposed fellowship period. No GPA requirement specified.

Population Council - Policy Research Division
Attn: Fellowship Coordinator
One Dag Hammarskjold Plaza
New York, NY 10017

931
Population Council Fellowships for Mid-Career Training

AMOUNT: None Specified DEADLINE: December 15
MAJOR: Population Studies, Demography, Economics, Sociology, Anthropology, Geography, Public Health, and Related Areas of Study

Awards are open to candidates from the developing world with a minimum of five years of substantial professional experience in the population field. Mid-career awards are open to scholars with a Ph.D. or an equivalent degree wishing to undertake specific study in connection with a research institution. Fieldwork funds are not provided at this level. Fellowships will be awarded for advanced training in population studies (including demography and public health) in combination with a social science discipline, such as economics, sociology, anthropology, or geography. Awards will be made only to applicants whose proposals deal with the developing world. The typical award is for 12 months and is nonrenewable. This award consists of a monthly stipend, transportation expenses, allowances for books and supplies, and health insurance. Tuition at the mid-career level is not included in the award. For further information and an application write to the address listed (please include a self-addressed, stamped envelope); call (212) 339-0671, or fax (212) 755-6052. When writing include a brief description of your academic and professional qualifications and a short statement about your research or study plans for the proposed fellowship period. No GPA requirement specified.

Population Council - Policy Research Division
Attn: Fellowship Coordinator
One Dag Hammarskjold Plaza
New York NY

932
Postdoctoral Fellowships in Computational Molecular Biology

AMOUNT: $100000 DEADLINE: February 1
MAJOR: Computational Molecular Biology, Physics, Mathematics, Computer Science, Engineering

The Postdoctoral Fellowships in Computational Molecular Biology are open to U.S. citizens or legal permanent residents of the United States. Candidates must have earned their Ph.D. within the past five years or expect to earn it by June in mathematics, physics, computer science, chemistry, engineering, or other relevant fields. Awards will support up to two years of research work in an appropriate molecular biology department or laboratory in the U.S. or Canada selected by the applicant. Award requirements change regularly. Please send a self-addressed, stamped envelope to receive your application and any further instructions from the scholarship provider. You may consult the sponsor website at: www.sloan.org. No GPA requirement specified.

Alfred P. Sloan Foundation
Sloan Research Fellowships
630 5th Avenue, Suite 2550
New York, NY 10111-0100

933
Postdoctoral Fellowships In Law and Social Science

AMOUNT: $30000 DEADLINE: February 1
MAJOR: Law, Social Science

The Postdoctoral Fellowships In Law and Social Science are available to junior scholars who have completed all requirements for their Ph.D. within the past two years or are currently in the final stages of completing their dissertation. Research must be in the areas of: social scientific approaches to law, sociological studies, the legal profession, or legal institutions. Minority students are encouraged to apply. Award requirements change regularly. Please send a self-addressed, stamped envelope to receive your application and any further instructions from the fellowship provider. No GPA requirement specified.

American Bar Foundation
Anne Tatalovich, Assistant Director
750 North Lake Shore Drive
Chicago, IL 60611-4403

934
Poudre Association of School Executives Education Focus Scholarship

AMOUNT: $500 DEADLINE: Varies
MAJOR: Education

Open to Rocky Mountain High School (CO) seniors. Applicants must be prospective education majors who have at least a 3.0 cumulative GPA and also must be active in extracurricular school and community activities. Financial need may be considered. An essay may be required. Application deadline, procedure, and award amount vary annually. Award requirements change regularly. Applications are available in January or February in the Rocky Mountain

High School Career Center, as part of the Local Scholarship Packet. GPA must be 3.0-4.0.

Rocky Mountain High School
Scholarship Committee
1300 West Swallow Road
Fort Collins, CO 80526-2412

935
Poudre Association of School Executives Member Scholarship

AMOUNT: $500 DEADLINE: Varies
MAJOR: All Areas of Study

Open to Rocky Mountain High School (CO) seniors. Applicants must be children of PASE members, have at least a 3.0 cumulative GPA, and be active in extracurricular school and community activities. Financial need may be considered. An essay may be required. Application deadline, procedure, and award amount vary annually. Award requirements change regularly. Applications are available in January or February in the Rocky Mountain High School Career Center, as part of the Local Scholarship Packet. GPA must be 3.0-4.0.

Rocky Mountain High School
Scholarship Committee
1300 West Swallow Road
Fort Collins, CO 80526-2412

936
Poudre Education Association Scholarship

AMOUNT: $500 DEADLINE: Varies
MAJOR: All Areas of Study

Open to Rocky Mountain High School (CO) seniors. Applicants will be considered on academic GPA, service to the school and community, and financial need. Priority will be given to children of PEA members. An essay may be required. Top applicants will be interviewed by the PEA selection committee. Application deadline, procedure, and award amount vary annually. Award requirements change regularly. Applications are available in January or February in the Rocky Mountain High School Career Center, as part of the Local Scholarship Packet. GPA must be 3.0-4.0.

Rocky Mountain High School
Scholarship Committee
1300 West Swallow Road
Fort Collins, CO 80526-2412

937
Praxair International Scholarship

AMOUNT: $2500 DEADLINE: January 15
MAJOR: Welding Engineering, Welding Engineering Technology

The Praxair International Scholarship is awarded to full-time (minimum 12 credit hours) undergraduate students pursuing a minimum four-year bachelor's degree in welding engineering or welding engineering technology. Applicants must have at least a GPA of 2.5 and demonstrate leadership abilities through clubs, organizations, extracurricular academic activities, community involvement, etc. Applicants must be U.S. or Canadian citizens who are planning to attend an academic

institution located within the U.S. or Canada. This award is renewable. Award requirements change regularly. Please send a self-addressed, stamped envelope to receive your application and any further instructions from the scholarship provider or call (305) 445-6628. GPA must be 2.5-4.0.

American Welding Society Foundation, Inc.
National Education Scholarship Committee
550 Northwest LeJeune Road
Miami, FL 33126-4165

938
Pre-Seminary Career Counseling Matching Grant

AMOUNT: $100 DEADLINE: Varies
MAJOR: Ministerial Service

The Pre-Seminary Career Counseling Matching Grant is open to persons who are considering ministerial service. Educational Ministries will match up to $100 pledged by an American Baptist church or other sponsoring organization toward the cost of a pre-seminary career exploration at an American Baptist-related career center. Direct requests to Educational Ministries. Applicants must be members of an American Baptist church for at least one year before applying for aid and enrolled at an accredited educational institution in the U.S. or Puerto Rico. U.S. citizenship is required. Award requirements change regularly. Please send a self-addressed, stamped envelope to receive your application and any further instructions from the scholarship provider. No GPA requirement specified.

American Baptist Financial Aid Program
Educational Ministries ABC/USA
PO Box 851
Valley Forge, PA 19482-0851

939
Presbyterian Study Grant

AMOUNT: $500-$2000 DEADLINE: Varies
MAJOR: Preparation for Ministry

Open to full-time students in a PC seminary or theological institution approved by the students' Committee on Preparation for Ministry. Must be studying for the first professional degree for a church occupation or a position within one of the ecumenical agencies in which the PC participates. Award requirements change regularly. Contact the address listed for information and an application enclosing a self-addressed, stamped envelope or call (502) 569-5760. No GPA requirement specified.

Presbyterian Church (U.S.A.)
Office of Financial Aid for Studies
100 Witherspoon Street
Louisville, KY 40202-1396

940
Press Club of Houston Educational Foundation Scholarship

AMOUNT: None Specified DEADLINE: March 1
MAJOR: Journalism, Communications, Broadcasting

This award is open to college juniors or seniors majoring in journalism, broadcasting or communications, or to students who intend to pursue careers in journalism. You must have a permanent residence in the Greater Houston area or, if you live elsewhere, you must attend college in the Greater Houston area. Scholarships are awarded on the basis of financial need, academic achievement, and career goals. In order to apply, you will need to include a transcript, a financial aid report from your school's financial aid officer and two letters of recommendation. Award requirements change regularly. No GPA requirement specified.

Press Club of Houston Educational Foundation
PO Box 541038
Houston, TX, 77254-1038

941
Pride Foundation and Lee S. Burke Scholarship

AMOUNT: Maximum: $3500 DEADLINE: February 20
MAJOR: All Areas of Study

Scholarships are available for gay or lesbian residents of Washington, Oregon, Idaho, Montana, and Alaska with clear educational goals and aptitude who demonstrate financial need, community involvement, and a commitment to civil rights for all people; for any postsecondary education or training. Award requirements change regularly. Write to the address listed, enclosing a self-addressed, stamped envelope for an application and further information. No GPA requirement specified.

GSBA, Pride and INBA Scholarships
Scholarship Programs
2150 North 107th Street, Suite 205
Seattle, WA 98133-9009

942
Principals Leadership Award

AMOUNT: $1000 DEADLINE: December 10
MAJOR: All Areas of Study

This program is used for your school's principal to recognize one outstanding student leader from your senior class. School winners go on to compete on the basis of their application for 150 $1,000 scholarships. If you are a student in the United States, the District of Columbia, or Puerto Rico, you may be nominated by your school. Award requirements change regularly. Nomination forms are sent to the building principal each fall; check with the principal's office or guidance office for further information. GPA must be 3.0-4.0.

National Association of Secondary School Principals
Attn: Scholarship Coordinator
1900 Association Drive
Reston, VA 20191-1599

943
Printing Industry of Minnesota Scholarship

AMOUNT: Maximum: $1000 DEADLINE: February
MAJOR: Print Communications

The Printing Industry of Minnesota Scholarship is open to graduating high school seniors and persons who have graduated within the last five years. You must be accepted as a full-time student by an accredited technical school, college or university that offers one-, two- and four-year programs leading to a degree or graphic arts diploma. The award requires that you have a minimum 3.0 GPA, be a Minnesota resident (or the child of an employee of a Minnesota graphic arts firm), and be pursuing a career in graphic arts. Preference is given to children of full-time employees of a member of the Printing Industry of Minnesota. Awards will be announced in May. You will be eligible to compete for a second year scholarship. Award requirements change regularly. GPA must be 3.0-4.0.

Printing Industry of Minnesota Education Foundation
Scholarship Coordinator
2829 University Avenue SE, Suite 750
Minneapolis, MN 55414-3248

944
Professional Development Fellowship for Artists and Art Historians

AMOUNT: $5000 DEADLINE: January 31
MAJOR: Art, Art History

Fellowships are available for minority art and art history majors in the final year of graduate study. Applicants must be U.S. citizens or permanent residents and be able to demonstrate financial need. Award requirements change regularly. Please send a self-addressed, stamped envelope to receive your application and any further instructions from the fellowship provider, call (212) 691-1051, ext. 219 or email nyoffice@college.org. No GPA requirement specified.

College Art Association
Fellowship Program
275 7th Avenue
New York, NY 10001-6708

945
Prudential Spirit Community Award

AMOUNT: None Specified DEADLINE: October 29
MAJOR: High School Students

The Prudential Spirit Community Award is for high school students who have demonstrated exemplary self-initiated community service. Schools may select one honoree for every 1,000 students. Local honorees are then judged at the state level. One high school and one middle level student in each state, the District of Columbia, and Puerto Rico are named State Honorees and each receives a cash award, a trip to Washington, DC. and a silver medallion. Runners-up and other top finalists receive recognition. Award requirements change regularly. Information and application packets are mailed each fall to the building principal in every middle and high school in the U.S. Students and/or parents should request forms from the building principal or the guidance office. No GPA requirement specified.

National Association of Secondary School Principals
Attn: Scholarship Coordinator
1900 Association Drive
Reston, VA 20191-1599

946
Public Education and Citizenship Statewide Essay Contest

AMOUNT: $500 DEADLINE: February 15
MAJOR: All Areas of Study

This contest is open to all graduating high school seniors in the state of Florida who will be attending a Florida state supported school during the following semester. (State supported schools include any community college, university, or division of higher learning governed by the State Board of Regents). You must submit a 1,000-word essay on "Why Education is Important." All work must be original and becomes the property of the Grand Lodge of F. & A.M of Florida. Award requirements change regularly. For further information and an application please write to the address listed, including a self-addressed, stamped envelope. No GPA requirement specified.

Most Worshipful Grand Lodge F & A M of Florida
Public Education Citizenship Committee
PO Box 1020
Jacksonville, FL 32201-1020

947
Public Employee Retirement Research/Administration Scholarship

AMOUNT: $3500 DEADLINE: February 4
MAJOR: Finance, Business Administration, Social Sciences, Public Administration

The Public Employee Retirement Research and Administration Scholarship is open to graduate students intending to pursue a career in state or local government with a focus on public-sector retirement benefits. Applicants may be full- or part-time students in a graduate program in public administration, finance, business administration, or social sciences. Applicants must be citizens or permanent residents of the U.S. or Canada and have a baccalaureate degree or its equivalent. Recommendation from academic advisor or dean of the graduate program will be required. Award requirements change regularly. Applications are available in November for awards in the following spring. Please send a self-addressed, stamped envelope to receive your application and any further instructions from the scholarship provider; or email your request to inquiries@gfoa.org; or visit the website at www.gfoa.org. No GPA requirement specified.

Government Finance Officers Association
Attn: Scholarship Committee
180 North Michigan Avenue, Suite 800
Chicago, IL 60601-7476

948
Public Investor Scholarship

AMOUNT: $3000 DEADLINE: February 4
MAJOR: Public Administration, Business Administration, Finance, Social Sciences

The Public Investor Scholarship is open to graduate students with research or career interest in the efficient and productive investment of public funds. Applicants may be full- or part-time students in a graduate program in public administration, finance, business administration, or social sciences. Applicants must be citizens or permanent residents of the U.S. or Canada and have a baccalaureate degree or its equivalent. Recommendation from academic advisor or dean of the graduate program will be required. Award requirements change regularly. Applications are available in November for awards in the following spring. Please send a self-addressed, stamped envelope to receive your application and any further instructions from the scholarship provider; or email your request to inquiries@gfoa.org; or visit the website at www.gfoa.org. No GPA requirement specified.

Government Finance Officers Association
Attn: Scholarship Committee
180 North Michigan Avenue, Suite 800
Chicago, IL 60601-7476

949
Public Safety Memorial Grant

AMOUNT: None Specified DEADLINE: Varies
MAJOR: All Areas of Study

The Public Safety Memorial Grant is open to full-time undergraduates enrolled at a public college, university or technical institute in Georgia. To be considered for this award, you must be a U.S. citizen or permanent resident, a Georgia resident, and the dependent child of a Georgia law enforcement officer, fire fighter, EMT, correction officer, or prison guard who was permanently disabled or killed in the line of duty. The award, which covers the cost of attendance minus other aid, also requires that you maintain satisfactory academic progress. Award requirements change regularly. To receive an application and information about deadlines, contact your high school guidance counselor or the financial aid office of your current/intended college. No GPA requirement specified.

Georgia Student Finance Commission
Attn: Scholarships and Grants Division
2082 East Exchange Place
Tucker, GA 30084

950
Puerto Rican Bar Association (PRBA) Scholarship Award

AMOUNT: $1000 DEADLINE: February 15
MAJOR: Law

The Puerto Rican Bar Association (PRBA) Scholarship Award is open to Latino students currently in a J.D. degree program at an ABA-approved law school in the United States. You must demonstrate academic promise, financial need, commitment to the Latino community, and be pursuing a career in public interest law. Students working towards their L.L.M. are not eligible for these awards. Award requirements change regularly. No GPA requirement specified.

Earl Warren Legal Training Program, Inc.
99 Hudson Street, Suite 1600
New York, NY 10013-2815

951
Purina Mills Research Fellowship

AMOUNT: $12500 DEADLINE: February 7
MAJOR: Animal, Poultry, and Dairy Science

The Purina Mills Research Fellowships are for outstanding graduate students in the food and companion animal sciences.

Awards are made primarily in the field of nutrition and inter-related disciplines as applied to animal, dairy and poultry science. Previous winners are not eligible. The deadline date is always the first Monday in February. Award requirements change regularly. For further information and an application please write to the address listed, including a self-addressed, stamped envelope. No GPA requirement specified.

Purina Mills, Inc. - Research Awards Committee
c/o Susan Spiess - 3W
PO Box 66812
St. Louis, MO 63166-6812

952
Quartet Manufacturing Company Scholarship

AMOUNT: $2000   DEADLINE: March 15
MAJOR: All Fields of Study

The Quartet Manufacturing Company Scholarship is open to employees of Business Products Industry Association member firms and their families. Persons holding academic records sufficient for acceptance by accredited colleges, junior colleges or technical schools, or persons already enrolled in one of those institutions are eligible for this one-year award. Selection is made by a committee from the Student Financial Aid Department of The George Washington University, Washington, DC. Award requirements change regularly. Please send a self-addressed, stamped envelope to receive your application and any further instructions from the scholarship provider or email: info@bpia.org. No GPA requirement specified.

Business Products Industry Association
Attn: Scholarship Committee
301 North Fairfax Street
Alexandria, VA 22314-2633

953
Quill Corporation Scholarship

AMOUNT: $2000   DEADLINE: March 15
MAJOR: All Fields of Study

The Quill Corporation Scholarship is open to employees of Business Products Industry Association member firms and their families. Persons holding academic records sufficient for acceptance by accredited colleges, junior colleges or technical schools, or persons already enrolled in one of those institutions are eligible for this one-year award. Selection is made by a committee from the Student Financial Aid Department of The George Washington University, Washington, DC. Award requirements change regularly. Please send a self-addressed, stamped envelope to receive your application and any further instructions from the scholarship provider or email: info@bpia.org. No GPA requirement specified.

Business Products Industry Association
Attn: Scholarship Committee
301 North Fairfax Street
Alexandria, VA 22314-2633

954
Racial Ethnic Leadership Supplemental Grant

AMOUNT: $500-$1000   DEADLINE: Varies
MAJOR: Ministry

Open to full-time students who are African, Asian, Hispanic, Native Americans, or Alaska Natives. Must be enrolled in a PC seminary or theological institution approved by the students' Committee on Preparation for Ministry. Must be studying for the first professional degree for a church occupation or a position within one of the ecumenical agencies in which the PC participates. Award requirements change regularly. Contact the address listed for information and an application enclosing a self-addressed, stamped envelope or call (502) 569-5760. No GPA requirement specified.

Presbyterian Church (U.S.A.)
Office of Financial Aid for Studies
100 Witherspoon Street
Louisville, KY 40202-1396

955
Racine Education Council Achievement Scholarship

AMOUNT: $1000   DEADLINE: April 30
MAJOR: All Areas of Study

This scholarship is awarded to a graduating minority high school senior from a public or private school within the Racine Unified School District boundaries. In order to apply, you must have excelled academically and/or demonstrated leadership ability in your school, church or community. You must have a minimum 2.75 GPA and be accepted at a four-year accredited college or university. This is a nonrenewable scholarship. Award requirements change regularly. GPA must be 2.8-4.0.

Racine Education Council
310 Fifth Street, Rm 101B
Racine, WI 53403-4605

956
Radcliffe Research Support Program

AMOUNT: Maximum: $5000   DEADLINE: January 15
MAJOR: Human Development, Social and Behavioral Sciences, Women's Studies

The Radcliffe Research Support Program offers grants to post-doctoral investigators for research drawing on the Murray Center's data resources. The Henry A. Murray Research Center is a national repository of social and behavioral sciences data for the study of lives over time with a special focus on the lives of American women. At this time, funding is available for research using the center's data sets with racially and ethnically diverse samples and the observational studies data. Award requirements change regularly. Please send a self-addressed, stamped envelope to receive your application and any further instructions from the Murray Center; or visit their website at www.radcliffe.edu/murray. No GPA requirement specified.

Radcliffe College - Henry A. Murray Research Center
Attn: Grants Program Coordinator
10 Garden Street
Cambridge, MA 02138

957
Rain Bird Company Scholarship

AMOUNT: $1000 DEADLINE: March 31
MAJOR: Landscape Architecture/Design

The Rain Bird Company Scholarship is open to landscape architecture students in their final two years of undergraduate study (third, fourth or fifth years) who are in need of financial assistance. You must demonstrate commitment to the profession through participation in extracurricular activities and exemplary scholastic achievements. Award requirements change regularly. No GPA requirement specified.

Landscape Architecture Foundation
Scholarship Program
636 'I' Street NW
Washington, DC 20001-3736

958
Ralph and Valerie Thomas Scholarship

AMOUNT: $1000 DEADLINE: December 31
MAJOR: Accounting, Finance, Business, Taxation

The Ralph and Valerie Thomas Scholarship is available to ethnic minority accounting, finance or business undergraduates, or accounting and taxation graduates. Applicants must be a paid NABA members. A minimum 3.3 GPA is required. Award requirements change regularly. Please send a self-addressed, stamped envelope to receive your application and any further instructions from the scholarship provider or call (301) 474-6222, ext. 14. You may download an application by visiting the website. GPA must be 3.3-4.0.

National Association of Black Accountants, Inc.
Attn: Scholarship Committee
7249-A Hanover Parkway
Greenbelt, MD 20770

959
Ralph Hudson Environmental Fellowship

AMOUNT: $3500 DEADLINE: August 2
MAJOR: Landscape Architecture

The Ralph Hudson Environmental Fellowship is open to landscape architects who have been in professional practice for a minimum of five years (private, public and/or academic) and are full-time university professors in an ASLA-accredited program. This award is intended to advance the educational profession and academic community through research in areas relating to open space, parks, and recreation. Award requirements change regularly. If you should have any questions, please visit the sponsor's website. No GPA requirement specified.

Landscape Architecture Foundation
Scholarship Program
636 'I' Street NW
Washington, DC 20001-3736

960
Raymond E. Page Scholarship

AMOUNT: $1000 DEADLINE: March 31
MAJOR: Landscape Architecture/Design

The Raymond E. Page Scholarship is open to landscape architecture students who are in need of financial assistance, regardless of scholastic ability. A two-page description of how the money is to be used and a recommendation from a current professor will be required. Award requirements change regularly. No GPA requirement specified.

Landscape Architecture Foundation
Scholarship Program
636 'I' Street NW
Washington, DC 20001-3736

961
Raymond Mueller Farm Bureau Scholarship

AMOUNT: $500 DEADLINE: May 15
MAJOR: All Areas of Study

This award is given to any Cecil County high school graduating senior who is the son or daughter of a farm bureau member and is open to all areas of study. Award requirements change regularly. Please send a self-addressed, stamped envelope to receive your application and for any further instructions from the scholarship provider. Applications are available at all Cecil County High School Guidance Offices. No GPA requirement specified.

Cecil County Farm Bureau
Raymond Mueller Farm Bureau Scholarship
1497 Appletown Road
Elkton, MD 21921

962
Research Award in Science and Culture

AMOUNT: $3000-$5000 DEADLINE: May 15
MAJOR: Cultural Science, Natural Sciences

Bad Religion Rock Band Research Award in Science and Cultural Studies is open to high school and college students in the United States. This fund, established by the band "Bad Religion," was created to allow students to pursue field-oriented investigations in cultural or natural science. The award has an educational focus and is meant to promote self-motivated discovery, practice of the scientific method, and experience in scientific writing. There is no formal application form. However, you must submit a typed, doubled-spaced proposal that contains: a cover page; an introduction (less than two pages long); the proposal (no more than ten pages long); a description of the research (less than five pages long); the budget (detailing costs associated with each portion of the proposed work); and a description of the work's significance. Only proposals that have field-oriented research will be considered. For additional information, please visit the sponsor's website at www.badreligion.com. You may also send inquiries via email to treva@badreligion.com. No GPA requirement specified.

Bad Religion Research Fund
PO Box 4416
Ithaca, NY 14852

963
Research Grant

AMOUNT: $5000 DEADLINE: January 31
MAJOR: Horticulture (Herbs)

Grants are available for scholars with a proposed program of scientific, academic, or artistic investigation of herbal plants. Grants are given to further the knowledge and use of herbs and to contribute the results of the study and research to the records of horticulture, science, literature, history, art, and/or economics. Research must be clearly defined in 500 words or less. Announcement of recipient(s) made no later than May 1. Award requirements change regularly. For complete information on the parameters and requirements of the award, please send a self-addressed, stamped envelope to receive your application. No GPA requirement specified.

Herb Society of America, Inc.
Research and Education Grants
9019 Kirtland Chardon Road
Kirtland, OH 44094

964
Research Grants

AMOUNT: None Specified DEADLINE: February 1
MAJOR: Geology

Open to any master's or doctoral student at universities in the USA, Canada, Mexico, or Central America. Award is intended to help support thesis research. GSA membership is not required. Award requirements change regularly. Write for complete details or call (303) 447-2020, ext. 137. Application forms should be available from your department or from the campus GSA representative. If necessary, write to the Research Grants Administrator, at the address listed. No GPA requirement specified.

Geological Society of America
Attn: Research Grants Administrator
3300 Penrose Place, PO Box 9140
Boulder, CO 80301-9140

965
Rex and Mary Martin Scholarship

AMOUNT: $1000 DEADLINE: March 31
MAJOR: Teaching, Education

The Rex and Mary Martin Scholarship is open to Lenawee County (MI) high school graduates or graduating seniors. To be considered for the award, you must be pursuing a career in education. Award requirements change regularly. Please send a self-addressed, stamped envelope to receive your application and any further instructions from the scholarship provider. No GPA requirement specified.

Morenci High School
Attn: Mrs. Melissa Parnell
788 Coomer Street
Morenci, MI 49256

966
Rhode Island Advertising Scholarship

AMOUNT: $1000 DEADLINE: April 14
MAJOR: Film Making, Advertising, Television

The Rhode Island Advertising Scholarship is available for Rhode Island residents enrolled in a film making, television, or advertising program with career goals in one or more of these fields. To be considered for this award, you must be at least a college sophomore. One award is given annually. Award requirements change regularly. No GPA requirement specified.

Rhode Island Foundation
Attn: Special Funds Office
70 Elm Street
Providence, RI 02903

967
Rhode Island Association of Former Legislators Scholarship

AMOUNT: $1000 DEADLINE: April 20
MAJOR: All Fields of Study

The Rhode Island Association of Former Legislators Scholarship is available to graduating high school seniors who are Rhode Island residents. To be considered for this award, you must have distinguished yourself in academics and community or public service. The award also requires that you intend to enroll in a college or other postsecondary educational institution. To apply, submit a high school transcript, a completed application, a 500-word essay and a recommendation provided by an organizational representative. Three to five awards are available. Award requirements change regularly. No GPA requirement specified.

Rhode Island Foundation
Attn: Special Funds Office
70 Elm Street
Providence, RI 02903

968
Rhode Island State Grant Program

AMOUNT: $250-$750 DEADLINE: March 1
MAJOR: All Areas of Study

The Rhode Island State Grant Program is open to Rhode Island residents who are enrolled or accepted for enrollment in a program that leads to a degree or certificate at an eligible postsecondary institution (the institution does not necessarily have to be in Rhode Island). To be considered for the award, you must attend school on at least a half-time basis, be able to demonstrate financial need, and be a U.S. citizen or an eligible noncitizen. The award is renewable provided you are making satisfactory academic progress as defined by the school's satisfactory progress policy. Award requirements change regularly. To apply, you must submit the FAFSA. For more information, you may also browse the Rhode Island Higher Education Assistance Authority's website at www.riheaa.org. No GPA requirement specified.

Rhode Island Higher Education Assistance Authority
Scholarship and Grant Division
560 Jefferson Blvd
Warwick, RI 02886-1371

969
Rice-Cullimore Scholarship

AMOUNT: $2000 DEADLINE: February 15
MAJOR: Mechanical Engineering

Grants are available for foreign students studying mechanical engineering at a U.S. school on the graduate level. Award requirements change regularly. Applications are made through the Institute of International Education. Write to the address listed, enclosing a self-addressed, stamped business size envelope for details or visit their website www.asme.org/educate/aid. No GPA requirement specified.

American Society of Mechanical Engineers
Education Services Department
Three Park Avenue
New York, NY 10016-5990

970
Richard and Helen Hagemeyer Scholarship

AMOUNT: $3000 DEADLINE: June 14
MAJOR: Atmospheric Science, Hydrologic Science, Ocean Science

Scholarships are for students entering their final year of study in hydrologic science, atmospheric science, ocean science, or related sciences with a GPA of 3.0 or better. Must be U.S. citizens or permanent residents. Award requirements change regularly. Write to the address listed, sending a self-addressed, stamped envelope for details, call AMS headquarters at (617) 227-2426, extension 235, browse their website: www.ametsoc.org/ams/amsedu/scholfel.html or contact their email: armstrong@ametsoc.org. GPA must be 3.0.

American Meteorological Society
Fellowship/Scholarship Coordinator
45 Beacon Street
Boston, MA 02108-3693

971
Richard D. Rousher Scholarship

AMOUNT: $2000 DEADLINE: April 15
MAJOR: All Areas of Study

The Richard D. Rouser Scholarship is available to unmarried, dependent children under 23 years of age, of an Air Force Sergeants Association (AFSA) member or AFSA Auxiliary member. The selection is based on academic ability, character, leadership, writing ability, and the potential for success. Award requirements change regularly. Please send a self-addressed, stamped envelope to receive your application and any further instructions from the scholarship provider. No GPA requirement specified.

Air Force Sergeants Association (AFSA)
Scholarship Program
PO Box 50
Temple Hills, MD 20757-0050

972
Richard F. Walsh/Alfred W. Di Tolla Foundation Scholarship

AMOUNT: $1750 DEADLINE: December 31
MAJOR: All Areas of Study

The Richard F. Walsh/Alfred W. Di Tolla Foundation Scholarship is open to sons and daughters of members in good standing of the International Alliance of Theatrical Stage Employees and Moving Picture Technicians, Artists and Allied Crafts of the U.S. and Canada (IATSE). Applicants must be high school seniors planning to enroll in a full-time program at any accredited college or university. A letter of recommendation from a teacher or clergyman is required. This award is renewable for up to four years. Award requirements change regularly. Please send a self-addressed, stamped envelope to receive your application and any further instructions from the scholarship provider. No GPA requirement specified.

Richard F. Walsh/Alfred W. Di Tolla Foundation
Attn: Foundation Office
1515 Broadway, Suite 601
New York, NY 10036

973
Richard Goolsby Scholarship

AMOUNT: Maximum: $4000 DEADLINE: February 1
MAJOR: Plastics, Materials Engineering, Material Science

Scholarships for North Carolina and South Carolina students who are interested in pursuing a career in the plastics industry. Award requirements change regularly. Write to the address listed for details, enclosing a self-addressed, stamped envelope. No GPA requirement specified.

Foundation for the Carolinas
Scholarship Program
PO Box 34769
Charlotte, NC 28234-4769

974
Richard J. Kilpatrick Award

AMOUNT: $2000 DEADLINE: March 15
MAJOR: All Fields of Study

The Richard J. Kilpatrick Award is open to employees of Business Products Industry Association member firms and their families. Persons holding academic records sufficient for acceptance by accredited colleges, junior colleges or technical schools, or persons already enrolled in one of those institutions are eligible for this four-year award. Selection is made by a committee from the Student Financial Aid Department of The George Washington University, Washington, DC. Award requirements change regularly. Please send a self-addressed, stamped envelope to receive your application and any further instructions from the scholarship provider or email: info@bpia.org. No GPA requirement specified.

Business Products Industry Association
Attn: Scholarship Committee
301 North Fairfax Street
Alexandria, VA 22314-2633

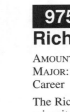

975
Richard S. Smith Scholarship

AMOUNT: Maximum: $1000 DEADLINE: June 1
MAJOR: All Fields of Study Leading to a Church-Related
Career

The Richard S. Smith Scholarship is open to racial and ethnic minority, United Methodist students who are entering their first year of undergraduate study. To be considered for this award, you must demonstrate participation in your local church, be pursuing a church-related career, have at least a 2.0 high school GPA, and be able to establish financial need. The award is not renewable. Award requirements change regularly. Please send a self-addressed, stamped envelope between November 1 and May 15 to receive an application and any further instructions from the scholarship provider. You can also visit their website at www.umc.org/nymo/scholar.html. GPA must be 2.0-4.0.

United Methodist Church - National Youth Ministry
Organization
Attn: Office of Loans and Scholarships
PO Box 840
Nashville, TN 37202-0840

976
Richmond County Medical Society Auxiliary Scholarship

AMOUNT: $2500 DEADLINE: May 31
MAJOR: Medicine

Open to medical school students who are residents of Staten Island, NY. Applicants must be in high academic standing, applying to, or already enrolled in, an American Medical Association approved medical school. Award requirements change regularly. For more information, please send a self-addressed, stamped envelope to the address provided or call (718) 442-7267. GPA must be 2.5-4.0.

Richmond County Medical Society Aux Scholarship
Committee
Bayley Seton Hospital - Building 7
Bay Street and Vanderbilt Avenue
Staten Island, NY 10304

977
RMHC/HACER Scholarship

AMOUNT: $2500-$5000 DEADLINE: March 8
MAJOR: All Areas of Study

The RMHC/HACER Scholarship is open to incoming Hispanic freshmen who are residents of New York, New Jersey, or Connecticut and are in financial need. You must have at least a 3.0 GPA and be involved in community activities. Winning students will receive a scholarship award of $2,500. In addition, the student displaying the most outstanding academic achievement will be awarded a $5,000 McDonald's Big Mac Valedictorian Award. Award requirements change regularly. GPA must be 3.0-4.0.

MWW Group - McDonald's Tri-State
1 Meadowlands Plaza, 6th Floor
East Rutherford, NJ 07073

978
Robert C. Byrd Honors Scholarship

AMOUNT: $1500 DEADLINE: April 1
MAJOR: All Areas of Study

The Robert C. Byrd Honors Scholarship is open to Connecticut high school seniors who are in the top 2% of their graduating class. You also qualify for the award if you have a minimum SAT of 1400. Award requirements change regularly. For information and applications, please contact your high school guidance office or the address listed. No GPA requirement specified.

Connecticut Department of Higher Education
Office of Student Financial Aid
61 Woodland Street
Hartford, CT 06105-2395

979
Robert Hefty Memorial Scholarship/Burlington Lion's Club

AMOUNT: $500 DEADLINE: Varies
MAJOR: Technical and Vocational Training

The Robert Hefty Memorial Scholarship/Burlington Lion's Club is open to senior Burlington High School (Burlington, WI) students enrolling in an accredited Wisconsin technical or vocational school program. Award requirements change regularly. Please visit your guidance office to receive an application and any additional details. No GPA requirement specified.

Burlington High School
Attn: Guidance Office
225 Robert Street
Burlington, WI 53105

980
Robert M. Lawrence, M.D. Scholarship

AMOUNT: $2500 DEADLINE: June 30
MAJOR: Respiratory Therapy

This scholarship is open to third and fourth year students in an accredited respiratory therapy program. In order to apply, you need a minimum 3.0 GPA, provide recommendations and an essay. You must also provide a copy of your birth certificate, social security card, immigration visa or other evidence of citizenship. The recipient will selected by September 1. This scholarship also includes registration for the AARC Respiratory International Congress, travel, one night lodging as well as a certificate of recognition. Award requirements change regularly. GPA must be 3.0-4.0.

American Respiratory Care Foundation
Education Recognition Award
11030 Ables Lane
Dallas, TX 75229-4524

981
Roberta Thumin Scholarship

AMOUNT: None Specified DEADLINE: May 1
MAJOR: English, Journalism, Communications, Speech, Theatre, Law, Marketing, Broadcasting

Open to full-time juniors and seniors attending school in Connecticut, New York, or New Jersey. Applicants must have a minimum GPA of 3.0, show evidence of involvement in communications-related activities, and submit a 300-500-word essay describing her/his need for financial assistance. Award requirements change regularly. For further information and an application, please write to the address listed, including a self-addressed, stamped envelope, call (212) 297-2133 or you may visit their website: www.nywici.org. GPA must be 3.0-4.0.

Women In Communications, Inc., New York Chapter
Scholarship Committee
355 Lexington Avenue
New York, NY 10017-6603

982
Roberts Memorial Scholarship

AMOUNT: $500 DEADLINE: Varies
MAJOR: All Fields of Study

The Roberts Memorial Scholarship is alternately awarded to senior Burlington High School or Catholic Central High School (Burlington, WI) students enrolling in postsecondary studies. Award requirements change regularly. Please visit your guidance office to receive an application and any additional details. No GPA requirement specified.

Burlington High School
Attn: Guidance Office
225 Robert Street
Burlington, WI 53105

983
Rockefeller State Wildlife Scholarship

AMOUNT: Maximum: $1000 DEADLINE: Varies
MAJOR: Forestry, Wildlife, Marine Science

The Rockefeller State Wildlife Scholarship is open to Louisiana residents who are enrolled full-time as an undergraduate or graduate student in a Louisiana public college or university. To be qualified to receive the award, you must be majoring in forestry, wildlife, or marine science with the intent on obtaining a degree in one of those fields. The award also requires that you have graduated from an accredited secondary school with at least a 2.5 GPA or that you have earned 24 or more graded college credit hours with a minimum 2.5 GPA. To continue to receive the award, certain criteria must be maintained. Award requirements change regularly. To apply, you must submit the FAFSA. For more information, you may visit the Louisiana Office of Student Financial Assistance website at www.osfa.state.la.us. GPA must be 2.5-4.0.

Louisiana Office of Student Financial Assistance
1885 Wooddale Blvd.
Baton Rouge, LA 70806

984
Rockwell International Corporation Scholarship

AMOUNT: $3000 DEADLINE: February 1
MAJOR: Engineering, Computer Science

This scholarship is open to junior minority women who are majoring in engineering or computer science in an ABET-accredited program or SWE-approved school. Applicants must have demonstrated leadership ability and have a minimum GPA of 3.5. Award requirements change regularly. Please send a self-addressed, stamped envelope to receive your application to the address provided. GPA must be 3.5-4.0.

Society of Women Engineers Headquarters
Scholarship Coordinator
120 Wall Street, FL 11
New York, NY 10005-3902

985
Rocky Mountain Chapter/Donald Estey Scholarship Fund

AMOUNT: $100-$750 DEADLINE: Varies
MAJOR: Travel and Tourism

Applicants must be either starting a travel/tourism career and attending a licensed preparatory travel program, employed by an ASTA member travel agency, in an ASTA or ICTA program or participating in another industry training program. Award requirements change regularly. Write to the address listed, enclosing a self-addressed, stamped envelope for an application and further information. You can browse their website: www.astanet.com or email: myriaml@astahq.com. No GPA requirement specified.

American Society of Travel Agents
Attn: ASTA Foundation
1101 King Street, Suite 200
Alexandria, VA 22314-2944

986
Rocky Mountain Coal Mining Institute Scholarship

AMOUNT: Maximum: $2000 DEADLINE: February 1
MAJOR: Engineering, Mining, Geology, Mineral Processing, Metallurgy

This scholarship is open to college sophomores enrolled in the above areas of study who are pursuing degrees in a mining-related field or engineering discipline. In order to apply, you must be a U.S. citizen and a resident of Arizona, Colorado, Montana, New Mexico, North Dakota, Texas, Utah, or Wyoming. You must have an interest in the coal industry in the Western states as a possible career path. Award requirements change regularly. No GPA requirement specified.

Rocky Mountain Coal Mining Institute
Attn: Assistant Executive Director
3000 Youngfield Street, Suite 324
Lakewood, CO 80215-6553

987
Roman F. and Lillian E. Arnoldy Scholarship

AMOUNT: $2500 DEADLINE: January 15
MAJOR: Welding

The Roman F. and Lillian E. Arnoldy Scholarship is awarded to full-time undergraduate students pursuing a four-year bachelor's degree in a welding program at an accredited university. Applicants must provide proof of employment (minimum eight hours per week and/or participation in a university work/study program) and have a minimum GPA of 2.0. This award is renewable. Applicants must be U.S citizens planning to attend an institution within the United States. Award requirements change regularly. Please send a self-addressed, stamped envelope to receive your application and any further instructions from the scholarship provider or call (305) 445-6628. GPA must be 2.0-4.0.

American Welding Society Foundation, Inc.
National Education Scholarship Committee
550 Northwest LeJeune Road
Miami, FL 33126-4165

988
Ron Brown Scholarship

AMOUNT: Maximum: $40000 DEADLINE: January 9
MAJOR: All Areas of Study

The Ron Brown Scholarship is open to African-American high school seniors who are academically talented and highly motivated. To be eligible for this award, you must be a U.S. citizen or a permanent resident. The award also requires that you be able to demonstrate excellent academics, exceptional leadership potential, financial need, and an impact on your community through activities and service to others. Candidates must be pursuing full-time undergraduate degrees. Awards are $10,000 per year for four years. Please note that the deadline is January 9 of your senior year. Award requirements change regularly. For further information contact the sponsor by email: franh@ronbrown.org or browse their website: www.ronbrown.org. Please visit the site to obtain an application. GPA must be 3.0-4.0.

CAP Charitable Foundation, Ron Brown Scholarship Program
Michael A Mallory, Executive Director
1160 Pepsi Place, Suite 306-B
Charlottesville, VA 22901-0807

989
Ronald Reagan Leadership Award

AMOUNT: $2500 DEADLINE: May 26
MAJOR: All Areas of Study

This leadership award is open to Tau Kappa Epsilon members for outstanding leadership as demonstrated by activities and accomplishments on campus, in the community, and within the chapter. If you are an initiated undergraduate member of Tau Kappa Epsilon, you are eligible to apply. If you are a recipient of this award, you will be required to attend an official fraternity function to accept the award. Award requirements change regularly. For further information, call (317) 872-6533, email: tef@tkehq.org or visit the website at: www.tke.org. GPA must be 2.8-4.0.

TKE Educational Foundation
Attn: Timothy L. Taschwer
8645 Founders Road
Indianapolis, IN 46268-1336

990
Rosann S. Berry Annual Meeting Fellowship

AMOUNT: $500 DEADLINE: October 30
MAJOR: Architectural History

Awarded each year to enable an advanced graduate student to attend the annual meeting of the society. Judged by a committee of three who are appointed by the president of the society. A citation and an award of $500 are presented at the annual meeting. Award requirements change regularly. For information regarding submission criteria and procedures, contact the Society of Architectural Historians by telephone (312) 573-1365 or email: info@sah.org. No GPA requirement specified.

Society of Architectural Historians
Charnley-Persky House
1365 North Astor Street
Chicago, IL 60610-2144

991
Roscoe Hogan Environmental Law Essay Contest

AMOUNT: $5000 DEADLINE: Varies
MAJOR: Environmental Law

The Roscoe Hogan Environmental Law Essay Contest is open to students currently enrolled in an accredited American law school. To be considered for this award, you must submit a legal essay on the topic "Causation Standards for Toxic Torts." Through your faculty advisor, you must file an "intent-to-enter" form by February 11 which indicates your intent to submit an essay for national judging. Your essay must be received by March 31. Essays must be written by a single author and not exceed 50 pages. Award requirements change regularly. Please send a self-addressed, stamped envelope to receive your "intent-to-enter" form and any further instructions from the scholarship provider; or call (800) 424-2725, ext. 380; or fax (202) 965-0355. No GPA requirement specified.

Roscoe Pound Foundation
Education and Membership Coordinator
1050 31st Street NW
Washington, DC 20007

992
Rotary International Foundation Scholarships

AMOUNT: $11000-$23000 DEADLINE: July 15
MAJOR: International and Cultural Studies

Scholarships are available for students interested in a period of study abroad. Scholarship terms are for the academic year, two to three full years, or three to six months. Applicants must have completed at least two years of university or college coursework and be citizens of a country in which there is a Rotary club. These scholarships are not available to Rotarian members, honorary Rotarians, an employee of a club, or relatives or spouses of the aforementioned. Award requirements change regularly. Contact your local Rotary club or call (847) 866-3000 for information. No GPA requirement specified.

Rotary International Foundation
One Rotary Center
1560 Sherman Avenue
Evanston, IL 60201

993
Rotary Scholarship - Foundation for the Carolinas

AMOUNT: Maximum: $1500 DEADLINE: April 1
MAJOR: All Areas of Study

Scholarships for graduates of CPCC who wish to pursue a bachelor's degree at a four-year college in Mecklenburg County (NC) with a minimum GPA of 3.0. Award requirements change regularly. Write to the address listed for details, enclosing a self-addressed, stamped envelope. GPA must be 3.0-4.0.

Foundation for the Carolinas
Scholarship Program
PO Box 34769
Charlotte, NC 28234-4769

994
Roy J. Ward Scholarship

AMOUNT: $2000 DEADLINE: March 1
MAJOR: All Areas of Study

Scholarships are available to legally blind undergraduates who are residents of Virginia who are attending a college or university in Virginia. Award requirements change regularly. Write to the address listed, enclosing a self-addressed, stamped envelope for an application and further information, or call (202) 467-5081 or (800) 424-8666. No GPA requirement specified.

American Council of the Blind
Attn: Billie Jean Keith
1155 15th Street NW, Suite 720
Washington, DC 20005-2706

995
Royal Chevrolet/Olds National Honor Society Scholarship

AMOUNT: $750 DEADLINE: April 15
MAJOR: All Areas of Study

Open to Harrisonville High School graduating seniors who are members in good standing of the Harrisonville National Honor Society. Award requirements change regularly. Applications are available in the Harrisonville Senior High School guidance office. No GPA requirement specified.

Harrisonville Senior High School
Attn: Roy Sackman
1504 East Elm Street
Harrisonville, MO 64701-2022

996
Rozsi and Jeno Zisovich Jewish Studies Scholarship Fund

AMOUNT: $3200 DEADLINE: Varies
MAJOR: Education (Holocaust)

The purpose of the Rozsi and Jeno Zisovich Jewish Studies Scholarship Fund is to provide scholarships to help Jewish or non-Jewish students, who hope to pursue careers which will include teaching the Holocaust to future generations, to pursue collegiate and/or graduate studies in Holocaust education. Applicants must demonstrate financial need and be residents of San Francisco, San Mateo, northern Santa Clara, Marin, or Sonoma counties in California. Deadlines vary; therefore, it is encouraged that applicants apply early. Award requirements change regularly. No GPA requirement specified.

Jewish Family and Children's Services
Attn: Loans and Grants Department
2245 Post Street
San Francisco, CA 94115

997
Ruby Marsh Eldred Scholarship

AMOUNT: None Specified DEADLINE: March 1
MAJOR: All Areas of Study

Open to high school seniors who have been residents of central or western Crawford County (PA) for at least one year. Must rank in the top 25% of class and plan to enroll in a regionally accredited two- or four-year college. Award requirements change regularly. Please send a self-addressed, stamped envelope to receive your application and any further instructions from the scholarship provider. GPA must be 3.2.

Ruby Marsh Eldred Scholarship Fund
Old Post Office Building
941 Federal Court
Meadville, PA 16335

998
Rust Scholarship

AMOUNT: $3000 DEADLINE: May 1
MAJOR: Engineering, Architecture, Sciences

The Rust Scholarship is open to active members of Triangle fraternity who demonstrate financial need. The award is available only to students who will be undergraduates in the school year following their application. To be considered for this award, you must submit an application, a current college transcript, and two letters of recommendation. Award requirements change regularly. No GPA requirement specified.

Triangle Fraternity
Attn: Education Foundation
120 South Center Street
Plainfield, IN 46168-1214

999
Ruth Roberts Scholarship Program

AMOUNT: $1000 DEADLINE: March 7
MAJOR: Law

The Ruth Roberts Scholarship Program is open to students enrolled or accepted at an accredited law school. Although academic achievement and financial need are part of the selection process, the primary focus is on your past community involvement and your plans for future involvement with an emphasis on the role of law. Preference will be given to female candidates who are residents of Tarrant County, Texas. Award requirements change regularly. No GPA requirement specified.

Black Women Lawyers Association of Tarrant County, Texas
Attn: Scholarship Committee
1402 Las Jardines Court
Arlington, TX 76013

1000
S-B Power Tool Scholarship Award Fund

AMOUNT: $1500 DEADLINE: February 1
MAJOR: Manufacturing Engineering, Technology

Open to full-time undergraduates who are enrolled in a degree program in manufacturing engineering or technology program. Applicants must have completed a minimum of 30 college credit hours with a minimum GPA of 3.5. Award requirements change regularly. For further information, please contact Dora Murray at (313) 271-1500, ext. 1709 (email: murrdor@sme.org) or Theresa Macias, ext. 1707 (email: maciter@sme.org). You may also go to the SME website: www.sme.org. GPA must be 3.5-4.0.

Society of Manufacturing Engineering Education Foundation
PO Box 930
One SME Drive
Dearborn, MI 48121-0930

1001
S.A.M.E. Lake Michigan Post Scholarship

AMOUNT: $500 DEADLINE: June 25
MAJOR: Engineering, Architecture, Applied Science

The Society of American Military Engineers Lake Michigan Post Scholarship (SAME) is open to full-time undergraduates (including entering freshmen) majoring in either engineering, architecture, or an applied science (i.e., mathematics, physics, chemistry, etc.). Applicants must be associated with the Lake Michigan (IL) post of SAME, military members, or civilian employees at Great Lakes Training Center, Glenview, Fort Sheridan, or any other DoD activities within the geographical area. Award requirements change regularly. For further information write to the address below, enclosing a self-addressed, stamped envelope, or call (847) 688-4214. You may fax your request at (847) 688-7051. No GPA requirement specified.

Society of American Military Engineers, Lake Michigan Post
Attn: Lt. Phil Carter
201 Decatur Ave., Building 1A
Great Lakes, IL 60088-5600

1002
Sabbatical Grant

AMOUNT: None Specified DEADLINE: November 1
MAJOR: Ministry

The Sabbatical Grant is open to ministerial leaders. Applicants must be members of an American Baptist church for at least one year before applying for aid and enrolled at an accredited educational institution in the U.S. or Puerto Rico. U.S. citizenship is required. Award requirements change regularly. Please send a self-addressed, stamped envelope to receive your application and any further instructions from the scholarship provider. No GPA requirement specified.

American Baptist Financial Aid Program
Educational Ministries ABC/USA
PO Box 851
Valley Forge, PA 19482-0851

1003
Sabina Farmers Exchange Scholarship

AMOUNT: $500 DEADLINE: May 1
MAJOR: Agriculture

The Premier Feeds, Premier Crop Services, and Sabina Farmers Exchange, Inc. Scholarship is open to graduating high school seniors from the southwestern Ohio area. You must be an entering freshman in a two- or four-year agricultural program at an accredited college or university. In order to apply, you must demonstrate academic merit, good character, and citizenship, seriousness of purpose, and financial need. You must also have a minimum 2.0 GPA. Award requirements change regularly. Applications may be obtained at your high school guidance office or by calling Sabina Farmers Exchange at (937) 584-4143. GPA must be 2.0-4.0.

Sabina Farmers Exchange
Scholarship Committee
219 North Howard Street
Sabina, OH 45169

1004
Sachs Foundation Scholarship

AMOUNT: $3500 DEADLINE: March 1
MAJOR: All Areas of Study

This scholarship is open to African-American high school seniors who are residents of Colorado - and have been for a minimum of five years. The award is based on academics and financial need and is renewable if you maintain a minimum 2.5 GPA and complete at least 12 credit hours per term. The average award last year was $3,500 and there were approximately 50 new applicants selected as recipients. Award requirements change regularly. GPA must be 2.9-4.0.

Sachs Foundation
Scholarship Coordinator
90 South Cascade Avenue, Suite 1410
Colorado Springs, CO 80903-1680

1005
Safe Driving Challenge

AMOUNT: $500-$1500 DEADLINE: April 15
MAJOR: All Areas of Study

This scholarship is open to enrolled 10th through 12th grade students who have completed a recognized high school or private driver training program and have a certificate of completion. You must have been issued and currently possess a valid driver's license. Your driving record must be free of moving violations (this includes no pending cases involving a moving violation). If you are a student who is a dependent of an elected AMVET state officer and if you are a student who has already competed in this program, you are not eligible. Award requirements change regularly. No GPA requirement specified.

AMVETS - Illinois State Headquarters
Illinois AMVETS Scholarship Program
2200 South 6th Street
Springfield, IL 62703-3454

1006
Salamatof Native Association, Inc. Scholarship and Grant Program

AMOUNT: $2000 DEADLINE: June 1
MAJOR: All Areas of Study

The Salamatof Native Association, Inc. Scholarship and Grant Program is open to Alaska Natives enrolled in the SNAI and their descendants, spouses, and legally adopted children who have a minimum GPA of 2.5. Applicants must be accepted/enrolled full-time in a two- or four-year undergraduate degree program, a graduate degree program, or a technical skills training program. Award requirements change regularly. GPA must be 2.5-4.0.

CIRI Foundation
Scholarship Coordinator
2600 Cordova Street, Suite 206
Anchorage, AK 99503-2745

1007
Sales Professionals of Northern Colorado Scholarship

AMOUNT: $500 DEADLINE: Varies
MAJOR: Marketing, Sales

Open to Rocky Mountain High School seniors. Applicants must be planning to study marketing and sales in college, and must have at least a 2.5 cumulative GPA. An essay and letter of recommendation may be required. Application deadline, procedure, and award amount vary annually. Award requirements change regularly. Applications are available in January or February in the Rocky Mountain High School Career Center, as part of the Local Scholarship Packet. GPA must be 2.5-4.0.

Rocky Mountain High School
Scholarship Committee
1300 West Swallow Road
Fort Collins, CO 80526-2412

1008
Sally Kress Tompkins Fellowship

AMOUNT: $7500 DEADLINE: January 13
MAJOR: Architectural History

Awarded each year jointly by the Society and the Historic American Building Survey (HABS) of the National Park Service to allow an architectural history student to work as a summer intern on a HABS project. Judged by a committee of representatives of the two organizations. A certificate is presented at the annual meeting, and a $7,500 stipend is provided in the summer. Award requirements change regularly. For information regarding submission criteria and procedures, contact the Society of Architectural Historians by telephone (312) 573-1365 or email: info@sah.org. No GPA requirement specified.

Society of Architectural Historians
Charnley-Persky House
1365 North Astor Street
Chicago, IL 60610-2144

1009
Sammy Davis Jr. Scholarship

AMOUNT: $3000 DEADLINE: February 14
MAJOR: Performing Arts

The Sammy Davis Jr. Scholarship is open to high school seniors who are pursuing a degree in the performing arts. You must be a resident of the Greater Hartford, CT, area and must be able to demonstrate academic merit, community service, and financial need. An essay and two recommendations are required along with a school transcript. This award is renewable. Award requirements change regularly. No GPA requirement specified.

Greater Hartford Jaycees Foundation, Inc.
Attn: Scholarship Committee
One Financial Plaza
Hartford, CT 06103-2608

1010
Samsung American Legion Scholarship Program

AMOUNT: None Specified DEADLINE: June 15
MAJOR: All Areas of Study

The Samsung American Legion Scholarship Program is open to undergraduates who are direct descendants of U.S. wartime veterans who served during one or more of the periods of war officially designated as eligibility dates for membership in the American Legion by the United States government. In order to apply, you must attend an accredited U.S. college or university. Selection is based on the following criteria: academic record (GPA, SAT/ACT test scores and class rank); involvement in school activities; involvement in community activities; and financial need. Additional consideration will be given to descendants of U.S. veterans of the Korean War. Award requirements change regularly. No GPA requirement specified.

American Legion - National Headquarters
700 North Pennsylvania Avenue
PO Box 1055
Indianapolis, IN 46206-1055

1011
San Diego Chapter/John Hjorth Scholarship Fund

AMOUNT: $250 DEADLINE: Varies
MAJOR: Travel and Tourism

Applicants must be employed by a San Diego ASTA Chapter member, and must be pursuing either one of the ICTA certification programs, the ICTA Destination Specialists programs, or any ASTA educational program. Must have a minimum of two years travel industry experience. A letter of interest and/or need and a letter of recommendation required. Award requirements change regularly. Write to the address listed, enclosing a self-addressed, stamped envelope for an application and further information. You can browse their website: www.astanet.com or email: myriaml@astahq.com. No GPA requirement specified.

American Society of Travel Agents
Attn: ASTA Foundation
1101 King Street, Suite 200
Alexandria, VA 22314-2944

1012
Saul Horowitz, Jr. Memorial Graduate Award

AMOUNT: $7500 DEADLINE: November 1
MAJOR: Civil Engineering/Construction

The Associated General Contractors Graduate Scholarship is open to college seniors enrolled in an undergraduate construction or civil engineering degree program, or to students possessing an undergraduate or master's degree in construction or civil engineering. You must be enrolled, or planning to enroll, in a master's or doctoral level construction or civil engineering degree program as a full-time student. U.S. citizenship or permanent residency is required to apply. This award is based on academic performance, extracurricular activities, employment experience, financial status, and a demonstrated interest in a construction industry career. Award requirements change regularly. No GPA requirement specified.

Associated General Contractors Education and Research Foundation
Attn: Director of Programs
333 John Carlyle Street, 2nd Floor
Alexandria, VA 22314-5743

1013
Schechter Foundation Grants

AMOUNT: None Specified DEADLINE: June 1
MAJOR: Physical, Occupational Therapy

Grants for graduate students enrolled in occupational and physical therapy and other graduate programs in health care and related fields at New York, Columbia, or Hahnemann Universities. Must be a U.S. citizens to apply. Based on character, ability, and financial need. The deadline to request an application is May 1. Students to be notified of decision in late July or August. Award requirements change regularly. Write to the address listed, enclosing a self-addressed, stamped envelope for an application and further information. No GPA requirement specified.

Schechter Foundation
230 Park Avenue, Suite 1000
New York, NY 10169

1014
Scholarships for Children of American Military Personnel (SCAMP)

AMOUNT: $3500-$5000 DEADLINE: July 31
MAJOR: All Areas of Study

The Scholarships for Children of American Military Personnel (SCAMP) is open to children of an American Armed Forces serviceperson who is a POW, MIA, or KIA in the Vietnam conflict or Desert Storm. The applicant must be involved in civic and community activities and maintain a minimum 2.0 in order to renew scholarship. Award requirements change regularly. Please send a self-addressed, stamped envelope to Leora M. Ostrow, Chairman of the Board, in order to receive your application and any further instructions from the scholarship provider. GPA must be 2.0-4.0.

Scholarships for Children of American Military Personnel (SCAMP)
Attn: Scholarship Coordinator
136 South Fuller Avenue
Los Angeles, CA 90036

1015
Scholarships for Children of Deceased or Disabled Veterans

AMOUNT: None Specified DEADLINE: May 1
MAJOR: All Areas of Study

Open to dependent children of deceased, 100% disabled veterans, or servicemen classified as POW/MIA for attendance at eligible postsecondary institutions. Residency requirements vary. Award equals tuition and fees for an academic year. Award requirements change regularly. Please contact the address provided for further information. No GPA requirement specified.

Florida Department of Education
Office of Student Financial Assistance
Turlington Building, 325 West Gaines St.
Tallahassee, FL 32399-0400

1016
Scholl Distinguished Scholar Awards

AMOUNT: None Specified DEADLINE: Varies
MAJOR: Podiatry

The Scholl Distinguished Scholar Award is open to first and second year students attending the Scholl College of Podiatric Medicine. First year students must have completed a minimum of 90 semester hours at the time of application for admission and have a minimum GPA of 3.4. Letters of recommendation and faculty interview evaluations may be used for making selections. Second year students must have successfully completed the current academic year and have a minimum GPA of 3.4. Requirements for selection may include an essay, faculty recommendations, and evaluation of extracurricular activities. Renewal is not guaranteed. Award requirements change regularly. Please send a self-addressed, stamped envelope to receive your application and any further instructions from the scholarship provider or contact the Office of the Associate Dean for Student Affairs or email finaid@scholl.edu. GPA must be 3.4-4.0.

Scholl College of Podiatric Medicine
Attn: Office of Student Services
1001 North Dearborn Street
Chicago, IL 60610

1017
Scholl Merit Scholar Award

AMOUNT: $1000-$3000 DEADLINE: Varies
MAJOR: Podiatry

The Scholl Merit Scholar Award is open to incoming first-year students attending the Scholl College of Podiatric Medicine. Applicants must have a minimum GPA of 3.2. Recipients are selected by the Special Scholarship Committee who may consider admission interview scores, letters of recommendation, and personal statements from the admissions application. These one-year awards are not renewable. Award requirements change regularly. Please send a self-addressed, stamped envelope to receive your application and any further instructions from the scholarship provider or contact the Office of Student Services (800) 843-3059 or email finaid@scholl.edu. GPA must be 3.2-4.0.

Scholl College of Podiatric Medicine
Attn: Office of Student Services
1001 North Dearborn Street
Chicago, IL 60610

1018
Science Fellows Program

AMOUNT: None Specified DEADLINE: February 15
MAJOR: Natural Science, Engineering

The Science Fellows Program offers natural scientists and engineers an opportunity to explore the policy dimensions of a research topic of their choosing in an interdisciplinary environment. Past research areas have included: policy issues regarding nuclear, biological, and chemical weapons and delivery systems; export controls on high technology; security issues associated with energy development; global diffusion of information technology. Fellowships are available for both postdoctoral fellows and midcareer professionals. Scientists in academic and research institutions, government and industry from both the U.S. and abroad may apply. Stipends are awarded for a 12-month period and are determined on a case-by-case basis commensurate with experience and availability of other funds. Award requirements change regularly. Please send a self-addressed, stamped envelope to receive your application and any further instructions from the scholarship provider; or send email to barbara.platt@stanford.edu; or visit the website at www.stanford.edu/group/CISAC. No GPA requirement specified.

Center for International Security and Cooperation
Attn: Fellowship Coordinator
Encina Hall
Stanford, CA 94305-6165

1019
Science Student Grant Fund

AMOUNT: $1000 DEADLINE: December 1
MAJOR: Mathematics, Science, Medicine, Engineering, Computer Science

The Science Student Grant Fund is open to disabled students entering or enrolled in graduate studies in science. These awards will be made to support a project or thesis in any field of mathematics, science, medicine, engineering, or computer science. To be considered for these awards, you must be a fourth-year undergraduate who has been accepted into graduate or professional school or a graduate student, submit an essay and two letters of recommendation from faculty. Award requirements change regularly. Please send a self-addressed, stamped envelope to receive your application and any further instructions from the scholarship provider. No GPA requirement specified.

Foundation for Science and Disability
Attn: Grant Program
503 NW 89 Street
Gainesville, FL 32607-1400

1020
Scotts Company Scholars Program

AMOUNT: $500-$2500 DEADLINE: March 1
MAJOR: Green Industry

The Scotts Company Scholars Program is open to high school seniors, college freshmen, sophomores, and juniors pursuing a career in the green industry. In order to apply, you must be accepted/enrolled in an accredited junior college, college, or university. Preference is given to students from diverse ethnic, cultural, and socioeconomic backgrounds. Five finalists are selected for summer internships, a $500 award, and an opportunity to compete for two $2,500 scholarships. You will be evaluated based on cultural diversity, academic achievement, extracurricular activities, leadership, employment potential, essay responses, and letters of recommendation. Award requirements change regularly. No GPA requirement specified.

Golf Course Superintendents Association of America
Scholarship Aid Committee
1421 Research Park Drive
Lawrence, KS 66049-3859

1021
SCS Engineers Awards

AMOUNT: $3000-$5000 DEADLINE: June 1
MAJOR: Solid Waste Management

This scholarship is open to children and grandchildren of members (sponsors) who are in good standing with SWANA. SWANA student members are also eligible. In order to apply, you must be a full-time student who is entering or currently attending graduate school pursuing a degree in environmental science, engineering, or other suitable major related to the field of solid waste management. Award requirements change regularly. GPA must be 2.8-4.0.

Solid Waste Association of North America (SWANA)
Mid-Atlantic Chapter Scholarship
9031 Reichs Ford Road
Frederick, MD 21704-6857

1022
SDMS Educational Foundation Scholarship

AMOUNT: $500-$1500 DEADLINE: November 30
MAJOR: Sonography and Vascular Technology

This scholarship is open to students in diagnostic medical sonography programs accredited by the CAAHEP in the United States or by the Canadian Medical Association in Canada. You must demonstrate financial need in excess of governmental and other available resources, provide a copy of your ACT/SAT scores (if graduated after 1992), or transcripts of a minimum 3.0 GPA (if graduated before 1992). A short essay will also be required. Additional deadline dates are November 30 and March 31. Award requirements change regularly. GPA must be 3.0-4.0.

SDMS Educational Foundation
Scholarship Coordinator
12770 Coit Road, Suite 708
Dallas, TX 75251-1314

1023
Second Effort Scholarship

AMOUNT: $1000 DEADLINE: Varies
MAJOR: All Areas of Study

Open to students who successfully pass the Arkansas High School Diploma test to enroll in an Arkansas postsecondary institution. Recipients must maintain a 2.0 GPA each year. Award requirements change regularly. Write to the address listed, enclosing a self-addressed, stamped envelope for an application and further information. You may also browse their website: www.arscholarships.com/finsites.html. GPA must be 2.0-4.0.

Arkansas Department of Higher Education
Financial Aid Division
114 East Capitol Avenue
Little Rock, AR 72201-3818

1024
Selig Fund

AMOUNT: Maximum: $5000 DEADLINE: Varies
MAJOR: All Areas of Study

The purpose of the Selig Fund is to provide college loans for the undergraduate studies of Jewish students. Applicants must provide qualified guarantors (cosigners) that reside in the Bay Area. Applicants must be residents of San Francisco, San Mateo, northern Santa Clara, Marin, Sonoma, Alameda, or Contra Costa counties in California. It is preferable that loan applicants submit their applications by July 1 for the fall semester and November 1 for the spring semester. Award requirements change regularly. No GPA requirement specified

Jewish Family and Children's Services
Attn: Loans and Grants Department
2245 Post Street
San Francisco, CA 94115

1025
Seminarian Support Program

AMOUNT: None Specified DEADLINE: August 1
MAJOR: Theology, Religious Studies, Ministry

The Seminarian Support Program is open to American Baptist students attending American Baptist seminaries. Seminarians must be enrolled at least two-third time in one of the following first professional degree programs: M.Div., M.C.E., M.A.C.E., M.R.E. (D.Min. students are not eligible). Recipients must be resident students of the American Baptist-related seminary that will award the degree. Applicants must be members of an American Baptist church for at least one year before applying for aid, and enrolled at an accredited educational institution in the U.S. or Puerto Rico. U.S. citizenship is required. Award requirements change regularly. Please send a self-addressed, stamped envelope to receive your application and any further instructions from the scholarship provider. No GPA requirement specified.

American Baptist Financial Aid Program
Educational Ministries ABC/USA
PO Box 851
Valley Forge, PA 19482-0851

1026
Share and Care Foundation Scholarship

AMOUNT: $1000 DEADLINE: May 15
MAJOR: All Areas of Study

The Share and Care Foundation Scholarship is open to graduating Asian-Indian high school seniors. You must have been accepted into an accredited four-year academic institution and have a minimum 1000 SAT or 23 ACT. You must show financial need, intellectual potential, personal integrity, enthusiasm for learning, and evidence a desire for a better humanity. Award requirements change regularly. No GPA requirement specified.

Share and Care Foundation
Scholarship Committee
21 Wynnwood Road
Chatham, NJ 07928-1755

1027
Shaw-Worth Scholarship

AMOUNT: $1000 DEADLINE: March 15
MAJOR: Animal Protection

This scholarship is open to New England high school seniors who have made meaningful contributions to the area of animal protection over a significant period of time. Actions that merit the award may include: dedicated long term direct work on behalf of animals; inspiring leadership in animal protection organizations; papers, speeches, presentations on humane topics; or heroic rescues of animals in danger. Award requirements change regularly. GPA must be 2.5-4.0.

Humane Society of the United States
New England Regional Office
PO Box 619
Jacksonville, VT 05342-0619

1028
Sheriffs' Association of Indiana Scholarships

AMOUNT: $500 DEADLINE: April 1
MAJOR: Law, Law Enforcement, Criminology, and Related Fields

Scholarships are available for members and children of members of the Indiana Sheriffs' Association. You must be an Indiana resident, a high school senior, or a full-time undergraduate at an Indiana college or university working toward a career related to law enforcement. You must also be between 17 and 23 years old and in the top 50% of your high school or college class. Award requirements change regularly. Applications are available through your local sheriff's office; the financial aid or admissions office at your college; or the guidance office of your high school. Please obtain an application from one of these sources. GPA must be 2.5-4.0.

Indiana Sheriffs Association, Inc.
Scholarship Program
PO Box 19127
Indianapolis, IN 46219-0127

1029
Short-Term Scientific Exchange Award

AMOUNT: Maximum: $5000 DEADLINE: August 1
MAJOR: Laboratory Research in Genetics, Biology, Pharmacology, Virology, and Immunology

Provides funds for grantees to travel to another laboratory to learn a specific technique and, thereby, to enhance their research program. Award to cover transportation, lodging, and out-of-pocket expenses. Award requirements change regularly. Please send a self-addressed, stamped envelope to receive your application and any further instructions from the scholarship provider. Deadlines are April 1, August 1, and December 1. No GPA requirement specified.

Leukemia Society of America
Director of Research Administration
600 Third Avenue
New York, NY 10016-1901

1030
Siler Associates, Inc. Scholarship

AMOUNT: $1000 DEADLINE: March 31
MAJOR: All Fields of Study

The Siler Associates, Inc. Scholarship is open to a graduating senior from Madison High School (MI). To qualify for the award, you must have already been accepted for attendance at a Michigan public or nonpublic institution which grants baccalaureate degrees. Award requirements change regularly. Please send a self-addressed, stamped envelope to receive your application and any further instructions from the scholarship provider. No GPA requirement specified.

Morenci High School
Attn: Mrs. Melissa Parnell
788 Coomer Street
Morenci, MI 49256

1031
Simmons Scholarship

AMOUNT: $2000 DEADLINE: July 28
MAJOR: Travel and Tourism

Awards are available for master's or doctoral students of travel and tourism at a recognized college, university, or proprietary travel school. Must be U.S. citizens or legal residents and have a GPA of at least 2.5. Award requirements change regularly. Write to the address listed including a self-addressed, stamped envelope for more information or call (703) 739-2782. GPA must be 2.5-4.0.

American Society of Travel Agents
Attn: ASTA Foundation
1101 King Street, Suite 200
Alexandria, VA 22314-2944

1032
SIOR-Northern California Chapter Scholarship

AMOUNT: $2500 DEADLINE: March 1
MAJOR: Commercial Real Estate, Business Administration

This scholarship is open to juniors and seniors in their college's School of Business who have successfully completed at least one course in real estate and who plan a career in commercial real estate. Applicants must be U.S. citizens, established residents of California, and must be attending a four-year college or university located in Northern California. A completed application, copy of college transcripts, and a written summary describing plans to enter commercial real estate are required to apply. Please include mention of extracurricular activities which are an important part of the evaluation. Award requirements change regularly. Visit their website: www.siornocalif.org/forum.html for more details. No GPA requirement specified.

Society of Industrial and Office Realtors
Craig L. Fordyce c/o Colliers Int.
1960 The Alameda, # 100
San Jose, CA 95126

1033
Six Meter Club of Chicago Scholarship

AMOUNT: $500 DEADLINE: February 1
MAJOR: All Areas of Study

This scholarship is available to undergraduates with any class amateur radio license who are residents of Illinois. The applicant must be attending a postsecondary course of study at any institution in Illinois (technical school, community college, college, or university). The award is open to applicants in the remaining states in the ARRL Central Division - Indiana and Wisconsin - if no qualified Illinois student receives the scholarship. Award requirements change regularly. Write the address provided, using a self-addressed, stamped envelope, for further information. No GPA requirement specified.

American Radio Relay League
Attn: ARRL Foundation
225 Main Street
Newington, CT 06111-1400

1034
Sloan Research Fellowships

AMOUNT: $35000 DEADLINE: September 15
MAJOR: Chemistry, Computer Science, Economics, Mathematics, Neuroscience, Physics

The Sloan Research Fellowships are for promising researchers early in their careers. Candidates are required to hold a Ph.D. (or equivalent) in chemistry, physics, mathematics, computer science, economics, neuroscience, or in a related interdisciplinary field and must be members of the regular faculty of a college in the United States or Canada. These fellowships cover a two-year period. Award requirements change regularly. For further information and a nomination form, please write to the address listed, including a self-addressed, stamped envelope. You may consult the website at: www.sloan.org. No GPA requirement specified.

Alfred P. Sloan Foundation
Sloan Research Fellowships
630 5th Avenue, Suite 2550
New York, NY 10111-0100

1035
SME Family Scholarship Award

AMOUNT: $5000-$20000 DEADLINE: February 1
MAJOR: Manufacturing Engineering, Manufacturing Engineering Technology or Closely Related Area

Open to graduating high school seniors who have at least one parent or grandparent who has been an SME member in good standing for the last four years. Applicants must pursue a degree in manufacturing engineering, manufacturing technology, or other closely related engineering fields of study at an accredited college or university. Applicants must reside in one of SME's 14 regions. Applicants must also have a minimum SAT score of 1000 and/or an ACT score of 21 and an overall GPA of 3.0 or higher. Award requirements change regularly. For further information, please contact Dora Murray at (313) 271-1500, ext. 1709 (email: murrdor@sme.org) or Theresa Macias, ext. 1707 (email: maciter@sme.org). You may also go to the SME website: www.sme.org. GPA must be 3.0-4.0.

Society of Manufacturing Engineering Education Foundation
PO Box 930
One SME Drive
Dearborn, MI 48121-0930

1036
Smithsonian Fellowship Program

AMOUNT: $3500-$27000 DEADLINE: January 15
MAJOR: Humanities, Art Studies, Anthropology, Astrophysics, Biology, History

Fellowships are available to pre- and postdoctoral scholars for research in any field of interest to the Smithsonian or in the following fields: Humanities, Art Studies, Anthropology, Astrophysics, Biology, History. Award requirements change regularly. Write to the address listed for details. Request the publication "Smithsonian Opportunities for Research and Study." No GPA requirement specified.

Smithsonian Institution
Office of Fellowships and Grants
955 L'Enfant Plaza SW, Suite 7000
Washington, DC 20024-2119

1037
Societe Generale Scholarship for Music

AMOUNT: None Specified DEADLINE: March 15
MAJOR: Conducting, Performing, Composition, Musicology

Open to U.S. citizens who are enrolled in a postgraduate program at an American University or Conservatory. This scholarship is from the French Banking and Finance conglomerate "Societe Generale" to help students further their studies in France in the following fields of study: conducting, performing, composition, and musicology. The proposed research must relate to French culture and candidates must indicate a need for their research to be conducted in France. Scholarships include a monthly stipend of 8,000 Francs (about $1,300 U.S.) for a period of nine months, health insurance, and a round trip ticket to France. Award requirements change regularly. For further information and an application, please write to the address listed, including a self-addressed, stamped envelope. You may also visit their website: www.info-france-usa.org/culture. No GPA requirement specified.

Cultural Services of the French Embassy
972 5th Avenue
New York, NY 10021-0104

1038
Society of Women Engineers, Birmingham Section Scholarship

AMOUNT: None Specified DEADLINE: April 1
MAJOR: Engineering

The Society of Women Engineers, Birmingham Section Scholarship, is open to female graduating high school seniors planning to enter an ABET-EAC-accredited Alabama college or university. You must be a U.S. citizen and a resident of Blount, Etowah, Jefferson, St. Clair, Shelby, Talladega, Tuscaloosa, or Walker counties in Alabama. Award requirements change regularly. No GPA requirement specified.

Engineering Council of Birmingham, Inc.
Attn: Sandy Wood
7003 Alice Road
McCalla, AL 35111

1039
Sophus C. Goth Memorial Scholarship

AMOUNT: $1000 DEADLINE: May 26
MAJOR: All Areas of Study

The Sophus C. Goth Memorial Scholarship is open to initiated undergraduate members of Tau Kappa Epsilon. In order to apply, you must be in good standing with your chapter, have a demonstrated record of active participation within the chapter, including officer and chairmanship leadership positions. Also, you must be active in campus organizations, be a full-time student and have a minimum 2.5 GPA. Award requirements change regularly. For further information, call (317) 872-6533, email: tef@tkehq.org or visit the website at: www.tke.org. GPA must be 2.5-4.0.

TKE Educational Foundation
Attn: Timothy L. Taschwer
8645 Founders Road
Indianapolis, IN 46268-1336

1040
Southeast Chapter Scholarship Fund

AMOUNT: $350 DEADLINE: Varies
MAJOR: Travel and Tourism

Awards are available to official representatives of an active member agency or Active Associate members in good standing of the SEASTA Chapter. Recipients must have at least three years of experience working in the travel industry. In addition, the ICTA course must be completed within three years. Award requirements change regularly. Write to the address listed, enclosing a self-addressed, stamped envelope for an application and further information. You can browse their website: www.astanet.com or email: myriaml@astahq.com. No GPA requirement specified.

American Society of Travel Agents
Attn: ASTA Foundation
1101 King Street, Suite 200
Alexandria, VA 22314-2944

1041
Southern Texas PGA Scholarships

AMOUNT: None Specified DEADLINE: April 1
MAJOR: All Areas of Study

The Southern Texas PGA Foundation scholarships are open to students who live in Southern Texas. Selection for this program is based on financial need, class ranking, GPA, entrance-exam scores, and extracurricular activities. Golf skills will not be a consideration, but a background that demonstrates an interest in golf is of importance. Award requirements change regularly. GPA must be 2.5-4.0.

Southern Texas PGA
STPGA Office
1610 Woodstead Court, Suite 110
The Woodlands, TX 77380-3403

1042
Southern Travelers Club Scholarship

AMOUNT: $2000 DEADLINE: March 15
MAJOR: All Fields of Study

The Southern Travelers Club Scholarship is open to employees of Business Products Industry Association member firms and their families. Persons holding academic records sufficient for acceptance by accredited colleges, junior colleges or technical schools, or persons already enrolled in one of those institutions are eligible for this one-year award. Selection is made by a committee from the Student Financial Aid Department of The George Washington University, Washington, DC. Award requirements change regularly. Please send a self-addressed, stamped envelope to receive your application and any further instructions from the scholarship provider or email: info@bpia.org. No GPA requirement specified.

Business Products Industry Association
Attn: Scholarship Committee
301 North Fairfax Street
Alexandria, VA 22314-2633

1043
Southwest Travelers Club Scholarship

AMOUNT: $2000 DEADLINE: March 15
MAJOR: All Fields of Study

The Southwest Travelers Club Scholarship is open to employees of Business Products Industry Association member firms and their families. Persons holding academic records sufficient for acceptance by accredited colleges, junior colleges or technical schools, or persons already enrolled in one of those institutions are eligible for this one-year award. Selection is made by a committee from the Student Financial Aid Department of The George Washington University, Washington, DC. Award requirements change regularly. Please send a self-addressed, stamped envelope to receive your application and any further instructions from the scholarship provider or email: info@bpia.org. No GPA requirement specified.

Business Products Industry Association
Attn: Scholarship Committee
301 North Fairfax Street
Alexandria, VA 22314-2633

1044
Special Education Services Scholarship

AMOUNT: None Specified DEADLINE: Varies
MAJOR: Special Education (Includes Occupational or Physical Therapy)

This scholarship is open to Indiana students pursuing a course of study that would enable them to teach special education in an accredited elementary or secondary school in Indiana or practice occupational or physical therapy in accredited schools in Indiana, in vocational rehabilitation, or community mental retardation centers or other developmental disabilities centers. Colleges and universities establish eligibility criteria and filing deadline for this program. Award requirements change regularly. For further information and an application, please contact a high school guidance counselor, a college/university financial aid office, or write to the address listed, including a self-addressed, stamped envelope. You may also visit the SSACI website: www.ai.org/ssaci. GPA must be 2.0-4.0.

State Student Assistance Commission of Indiana
Attn: Scholarship Committee
150 West Market Street, Suite 500
Indianapolis, IN 46204

1045
Speech Language Pathologist Incentive Scholarship Loan

AMOUNT: None Specified DEADLINE: March 31
MAJOR: Speech Pathology

Open to full-time graduate students who meet academic requirements and are pursuing a master's degree in speech/language pathology. Must be legal residents of

Delaware and have a GPA of at least a 3.0. May be repaid through service in a Delaware public school. Award requirements change regularly. Write to the address listed, enclosing a self-addressed, stamped envelope for further information or browse their website: www.doe.state.de.us/high-ed/. GPA must be 3.0-4.0.

Delaware Higher Education Commission (SCIP)
Carvel State Office Building
820 North French Street, 4th Floor
Wilmington, DE 19801-3509

1046
Spiegelhoff's Pick 'N Save Scholarship

AMOUNT: None Specified DEADLINE: Varies
MAJOR: All Fields of Study

The Spiegelhoff's Pick 'N Save Scholarship is open to graduating seniors at Burlington High School (Burlington, WI). Students must have participated in a varsity sport and plan on continuing their education. Award requirements change regularly. Please visit your guidance office to receive an application and any additional details. No GPA requirement specified.

Burlington High School
Attn: Guidance Office
225 Robert Street
Burlington, WI 53105

1047
Spirit of Youth Scholarship

AMOUNT: $500-$1000 DEADLINE: Varies
MAJOR: All Areas of Study

The Spirit of Youth Scholarship is open to junior members of the American Legion Auxiliary who have held their membership in the American Legion Auxiliary for the past three (3) years and hold current membership. This award is for Oregon residents. Winners will be sent to a National Division Competition. If you are not selected on the National Level, the Department winner will receive $500 (for one year). Award requirements change regularly. Please send a self-addressed, stamped envelope to receive your application and any further instructions from the scholarship provider. No GPA requirement specified.

American Legion Auxiliary - Department of Oregon
Chairman of Education
PO Box 1730
Wilsonville, OR 97070-1730

1048
Spirit Square Center for Arts & Education Scholarship

AMOUNT: Maximum: $4000 DEADLINE: Varies
MAJOR: Arts

Awarded to college juniors or seniors who are majoring in art or art-related areas. Applicants must be from North Carolina or South Carolina. Award requirements change regularly. Write to the address listed for details, enclosing a self-addressed, stamped envelope. No GPA requirement specified.

Foundation for the Carolinas
Scholarship Program
PO Box 34769
Charlotte, NC 28234-4769

1049
Sports Medicine Scholarship

AMOUNT: $250 DEADLINE: May 15
MAJOR: Physical Therapy, Athletic Training

Open to high school seniors who are residents of any of the following counties: Avon, Bloomfield, Bristol, East Hartford, Farmington, Glastonbury, Hartford, Manchester, New Britain, Simsbury, West Hartford, Windsor or Wethersfield (CT). Must be entering a four-year school. Based on academics and interest in these two fields as careers. Award requirements change regularly. Write to the address listed, enclosing a self-addressed, stamped envelope for an application and further information. GPA must be 2.7-4.0.

Physical Therapy and Sports Medicine Associates
Attn: Jill Lipson
270 Farmington Avenue, Suite 367
Farmington, CT 06032-1909

1050
St. Andrew's Society Scholarships

AMOUNT: None Specified DEADLINE: March 15
MAJOR: All Areas of Study

The Donald Malcolm MacArthur Scholarship is available to students enrolled in U.S. or Scottish institutions who are residents of Delaware, Maryland, North Carolina, New Jersey, Pennsylvania, Virginia, West Virginia, or Washington, DC. This award is based on need, academics, and goals. Amount and number of scholarships vary depending on availability of funds. Award requirements change regularly. Please send a self-addressed, stamped envelope to receive your application and any further instructions from the scholarship provider. No GPA requirement specified.

St. Andrew's Society of Washington, DC.
James Mcleod, Chairman
7012 Arandale Road
Bethesda, MD 20817-4702

1051
Stacy Ann Cox Memorial Scholarship

AMOUNT: None Specified DEADLINE: April 15
MAJOR: All Areas of Study

Open to Harrisonville High School seniors who have been choir members for at least four years. Applicants must have a minimum 3.0 GPA and enroll in a college choir class their freshman year. Award requirements change regularly. Applications are available in the Harrisonville Senior High School guidance office. GPA must be 3.0-4.0.

Harrisonville Senior High School
Attn: Roy Sackman
1504 East Elm Street
Harrisonville, MO 64701-2022

1052
Stanley H. Stearman Award

AMOUNT: $2000 DEADLINE: March 10
MAJOR: Accounting

The Stanley H. Stearman Award is open to relatives of active and retired members (living or deceased) of the National Society of Accountants. To be considered for this award you must be enrolled in an undergraduate degree program at a U.S. accredited two- or four-year college or university, be majoring in accounting and have a "B" or better GPA. You must also be a U.S. or Canadian citizen. These scholarships are awarded primarily for academic merit, demonstrated leadership ability, and financial need. Award requirements change regularly. Please send a self-addressed, stamped envelope to receive your application and any further instructions from the scholarship provider. GPA must be 3.0-4.0.

National Society of Accountants
Attn: Scholarship Foundation
1010 North Fairfax Street
Alexandria, VA 22314-1574

1053
Stanley Olson Youth Scholarship

AMOUNT: Maximum: $2500 DEADLINE: Varies
MAJOR: Liberal Arts

The Stanley Olson Youth Scholarship is awarded to Jewish undergraduates who are 26 years of age or younger and studying liberal arts. Applicants must demonstrate financial need and be residents of San Francisco, San Mateo, northern Santa Clara, Marin, or Sonoma counties in California. Deadlines vary; therefore, it is encouraged that applicants apply early. Award requirements change regularly. No GPA requirement specified.

Jewish Family and Children's Services
Attn: Loans and Grants Department
2245 Post Street
San Francisco, CA 94115

1054
State Assn. of The Daughters of Pioneers of Washington Scholarships

AMOUNT: $600 DEADLINE: April 1
MAJOR: History, Education, English

The State Association of The Daughters of Pioneers of Washington Scholarships are open to full-time juniors, seniors, and graduate students who are Washington residents and attending school in Washington. You must be a descendant of a person who established residency in one of the following regions: 1) the state of Washington during or prior to 1870; 2) the state of Oregon during or prior to 1853; 3) the state of Idaho during or prior to 1863; 4) the state of Montana (west of the crest of the Rocky Mountains) during or prior to 1863. Award requirements change regularly. No GPA requirement specified.

State Association of the Daughters of Pioneers of Washington
Scholarship Coordinator
621-141st Court SE, #103
Bellevue, WA 98007-6754

1055
State Bank of Union Grove Scholarship

AMOUNT: None Specified DEADLINE: Varies
MAJOR: Business and Related Fields of Study

The State Bank of Union Grove Scholarship is open to graduating seniors at Burlington High School (Burlington, WI) pursuing studies in a business field. Award requirements change regularly. Please visit your guidance office to receive an application and any additional details. No GPA requirement specified.

Burlington High School
Attn: Guidance Office
225 Robert Street
Burlington, WI 53105

1056
State Department Federal Credit Union Scholarship Fund

AMOUNT: Maximum: $20000 DEADLINE: April 14
MAJOR: All Fields of Study

This scholarship is open to members of SDFCU. In order to apply, you must be currently enrolled in a degree program and have completed at least 12 credit hours. A minimum 2.5 GPA is also required. Award requirements change regularly. For further information, please write to the address listed, including a self-addressed, stamped envelope, or email: sdfcu@sdfcu.org, or visit the website: www.sdfcu.org. You may also call (800) 296-8882 to have an application mailed to you. GPA must be 2.5-4.0.

State Department Federal Credit Union
Marketing Department
1630 King Street
Alexandria, VA 22314-2744

1057
Stefanie Liberti Memorial Scholarship

AMOUNT: $500-$10000 DEADLINE: March 1
MAJOR: Criminal Justice

The Stefanie Liberti Memorial Scholarship is awarded to a graduating senior from Lake Worth High School (FL) who has participated in the criminal justice program for four years and intends to pursue a career in criminal justice. Selection is not based on financial need. Award requirements change regularly. For applications and further information please contact: Community Foundation for Palm Beach and Martin Counties, Danielle Cameron, Director of Donor Services, 324 Datura Street, Suite 340, West Palm Beach, FL 33401 or call (561) 659-6800. No GPA requirement specified.

Community Foundation for Palm Beach & Martin Counties
Scholarship Program Officer
324 Datura Street, Suite 340
West Palm Beach, FL 33401-5420

1058
Stella Blum Research Grant

AMOUNT: Maximum: $3000 DEADLINE: February 1
MAJOR: Research projects in the field of North American Costume

Open to students who are members of the Costume Society and are matriculating in a degree program at an accredited institution. This award is for research projects in the field of North American Costume which is part of the degree requirement. Judging criteria will include: creativity and innovation, specific awareness and attention to costume matters, impact on the broad field of costume, awareness of the interdisciplinary field, ability to successfully implement the proposed project in a timely manner, and faculty recommendation. The award may be used toward transportation and living at the research site, photographic reproductions, film, postage, telephone, typing, computer searches, and graphics. Award requirements change regularly. For further information and an application, please write to the address listed, including a self-addressed, stamped envelope, call (410) 275-1619, or browse their website: www.costumesocietyamerica.com. No GPA requirement specified.

Costume Society of America
Stella Blum Research Grant, PO Box 73
55 Edgewater
Earleville, MD 21919-0073

1059
Stone and Webster Scholarship

AMOUNT: $1000-$1500 DEADLINE: February 1
MAJOR: Engineering, Computer Science

This scholarship is open to sophomore, junior, and senior women who are majoring in engineering or computer science at an ABET-accredited program or an SWE-approved school. You must have a minimum 3.5 GPA in order to apply. One award is for $1,500 and three awards are for $1,000. Award requirements change regularly. Please send a self-addressed, stamped envelope to receive your application. GPA must be 3.5-4.0.

Society of Women Engineers Headquarters
Scholarship Coordinator
120 Wall Street, FL 11
New York, NY 10005-3902

1060
Stone Bridge Volunteer Fire Department Scholarship

AMOUNT: $500 DEADLINE: April 20
MAJOR: All Areas of Study

The Stone Bridge Volunteer Fire Department Scholarship is available to residents of Tiverton, RI. Four to six awards are available. Award requirements change regularly. No GPA requirement specified.

Rhode Island Foundation
Attn: Special Funds Office
70 Elm Street
Providence, RI 02903

1061
Stoody-West Fellowship

AMOUNT: $6000 DEADLINE: March 15
MAJOR: Religious Journalism

The Stoody-West Fellowship is open to Christian graduate students enrolled in journalism at accredited schools who are engaged in, or plan to enter the field of, religious journalism. One of the scholarships is designated for a United Methodist applicant. The applicants will be judged on five criteria: 1) Christian commitment and involvement in the life of the church, 2) academic achievement as revealed by transcripts, grade-point averages, and the required letters of reference, 3) journalistic experience and/or evidence of journalistic talent, 4) clarity of purpose in plans and goals for the future, 5) potential professional usefulness as a religious journalist. Award requirements change regularly. No GPA requirement specified.

United Methodist Communications
Fellowship Committee
810 Twelfth Avenue South
Nashville, TN 37203

1062
Strokes for Students Scholarship

AMOUNT: $1000 DEADLINE: Varies
MAJOR: All Fields of Study

The Strokes for Students Scholarship is open to Lenawee County (MI) high school seniors. Each public high school and Lenawee Christian will designate a graduating senior to receive one scholarship. The Lenawee County Education Foundation will raise the funds through their annual Strokes for Students golf tournament. Your local district counselor will be able to notify you of the criteria. Award requirements change regularly. Please send a self-addressed, stamped envelope to receive your application and any further instructions from the scholarship provider. No GPA requirement specified.

Morenci High School
Attn: Mrs. Melissa Parnell
788 Coomer Street
Morenci, MI 49256

1063
Student Aid Award for Physically Disabled Students

AMOUNT: $2500-$5000 DEADLINE: December 31
MAJOR: All Areas of Study

This scholarship is available to students with physical disabilities. Applicants must be between the ages of 15 and 40 and demonstrate financial need. Award requirements change regularly. Please send a self-addressed, stamped envelope to receive your application and any further instructions from the scholarship provider. No GPA requirement specified.

Venture Clubs of the Americas
Suite 1000
Two Penn Center Plaza
Philadelphia, PA 19102-1721

1064
Student Aid Foundation Loans

AMOUNT: $3000-$4000 DEADLINE: Varies
MAJOR: All Areas of Study

This student loan program is for female residents of Georgia who are attending school in Georgia or for female Georgia residents attending school out-of-state. In order to apply for the loan, you must have average grades, a keen sense of responsibility, and personal integrity. This is for undergraduate or graduate study. You may be a traditional or a nontraditional student. There are three deadline dates: April 15, June 15, and October 15. Award requirements change regularly. No GPA requirement specified.

Student Aid Foundation
Suite F-180
2520 East Piedmont Road
Marietta, GA 30062-1700

1065
Student Assistance Grant

AMOUNT: $100-$600 DEADLINE: Varies
MAJOR: All Areas of Study

Applicants must be Arkansas residents who are full-time undergraduates or high school seniors. Awarded on a first-come, first-served basis by financial need. Student must be attending or planning to attend an approved Arkansas public or private postsecondary institution. Deadline date is determined by the institution the student will be attending. Award requirements change regularly. Write to the address listed, enclosing a self-addressed, stamped envelope for an application and further information. You may also browse their website: www.arscholarships.com/finsites.html. No GPA requirement specified.

Arkansas Department of Higher Education
Financial Aid Division
114 East Capitol Avenue
Little Rock, AR 72201-3818

1066
Student Council Scholarship

AMOUNT: None Specified DEADLINE: Varies
MAJOR: All Fields of Study

The Student Council Scholarship is open to graduating seniors at Burlington High School (Burlington, WI). Students do not have to be members of the Student Council to be eligible. Award requirements change regularly. Please visit your Guidance Office to receive an application and any additional details. No GPA requirement specified.

Burlington High School
Attn: Guidance Office
225 Robert Street
Burlington, WI 53105

1067
Student Loan Program

AMOUNT: None Specified DEADLINE: May 31
MAJOR: Religious Studies, Theology, Ministry

The Student Loan Program is available to full-time undergrad-uate and graduate American Baptist students. Undergraduate students may borrow up to $500 a year (four-year maximum of $2,000) and graduate students may borrow $1,000 annually (3-year maximum of $3,000). Applicants must be members of an American Baptist church for at least one year before applying for aid and enrolled at an accredited educational institution in the U.S. or Puerto Rico. U.S. citizenship is required. Award requirements change regularly. Please send a self-addressed, stamped envelope to receive your application and any further instructions from the scholarship provider. No GPA requirement specified.

American Baptist Financial Aid Program
Educational Ministries ABC/USA
PO Box 851
Valley Forge, PA 19482-0851

1068
Student Merit Scholarship

AMOUNT: $1000 DEADLINE: October 30
MAJOR: Textile Technology, Design, Furniture Design, Interior Decorating, Interior Design, and Related Areas of Study

Applicants for the Student Merit Scholarship must be enrolled as full-time students and be current IFDA student members (dues for the current membership period must be paid in full prior to submission of the scholarship application.) A completed scholarship application must include: a certified transcript of all college level/advance study work which verifies full-time status and GPA; a 200-to-300-word essay describing why you joined the IFDA, your future plans and goals, and why you believe you are deserving of this award; a letter of recommendation from a professor or instructor. Award requirements change regularly. Please send a self-addressed, stamped envelope to receive your application and any further instructions from the scholarship provider; or email your request to info@ifda.com; or visit the website at www.ifda.com. No GPA requirement specified.

International Furnishings and Design Association
Attn: Educational Foundation Office
1200 19th Street NW, Suite 300
Washington, DC 20036-2422

1069
Student Opportunity Scholarships

AMOUNT: $100-$1400 DEADLINE: April 1
MAJOR: All Areas of Study

Open to high school seniors who are African-American, Hispanic-American, Asian-American, Native American, Alaskan Natives who are Presbyterian Church U.S.A. members. Applicants must be U.S. citizens or permanent residents and be able to demonstrate financial need. Award requirements change regularly. Write to address listed for details, enclosing a self-addressed, stamped envelope or call (502) 569-5760. Specify Student Opportunity Scholarships (SOS). No GPA requirement specified.

Presbyterian Church (U.S.A.)
Office of Financial Aid for Studies
100 Witherspoon Street
Louisville, KY 40202-1396

1070
Student Research Grants In Sexuality

AMOUNT: $750 DEADLINE: September 1
MAJOR: Sexuality Studies

Three grants for students doing scholarly research on sexuality. Applicants must be enrolled in a degree-granting program. Award requirements change regularly. Write to the address listed, enclosing a self-addressed, stamped envelope for an application and more information, or call (319) 895-8407. You may also visit their website: www.ssc.edu.ssss. No GPA requirement specified.

Society for the Scientific Study of Sexuality
Attn: Ilsa L. Lottes, Ph.D.
PO Box 208
Mount Vernon, IA 52314-0208

1071
Summer Fellowship of the Electrochemical Society, Inc.

AMOUNT: None Specified DEADLINE: January 1
MAJOR: Awards are available for graduate students studying a field related to the objectives of the Electrochemical Society. To apply you must complete an application form and supply the following additional information: a statement of educational objectives; a statement of thesis research problem; undergraduate and graduate transcripts; two letters of recommendation including one from your research advisor. Award requirements change regularly. To receive a scholarship application and any further instructions, please send a self-addressed, stamped envelope to the Chairman of the Fellowship Subcommittee: Dr. Robin McCarley, Department of Chemistry, Choppin Laboratories of Chemistry, Louisiana State University, Baton Rouge, LA 70803. You can also contact Dr. McCarley by phone at (225)388-3239; by fax at (225)388-3458; or by email at tunnel@unix1.sncc.lsu.edu. No GPA requirement specified.

Electrochemical Society, Inc.
Attn: Honors and Awards Committee
10 South Main Street
Pennington, NJ 08534-2896

1072
Summer Internship Program

AMOUNT: None Specified DEADLINE: April 1
MAJOR: All Areas of Study

This is a ten-week summer internship program to provide valuable work experience for a postsecondary student who is blind. Duties include activities in the areas of public information and education, membership assistance, communications, legislative monitoring, and publications. Award requirements change regularly. Write to the address listed, enclosing a self-addressed envelope for an application and further information. No GPA requirement specified.

American Council of the Blind
Attn: Billie Jean Keith
1155 15th Street NW, Suite 720
Washington, DC 20005-2706

1073
Summer Research Fellowships In Law and Social Science

AMOUNT: $3600 DEADLINE: March 1
MAJOR: Social Science, Humanities

Fellowships are available for minority students who have completed their sophomore year. Applicants must have a minimum GPA of 3.0 and intend to pursue graduate studies in the above fields. Must be U.S. citizens or permanent residents. The program lasts ten weeks and the recipients will work at the ABF offices for 35 hours per week. Awards will be announced by April 15. Award requirements change regularly. Further information and application materials may be received by sending a 9 x 12 self-addressed, stamped envelope. This information may also be accessed from the fellowship provider's website, www.abf-sociolegal.org/mnrty.html. GPA must be 3.0-4.0.

American Bar Foundation
Anne Tatalovich, Assistant Director
750 North Lake Shore Drive
Chicago, IL 60611-4403

1074
Sybil Fong Sam Scholarship Contest

AMOUNT: $300-$1000 DEADLINE: May 14
MAJOR: All Areas of Study

The Sybil Fong Sam Scholarship Contest is open to high school seniors who have sickle cell disease and are entering an accredited four-year college or university as full-time students. You must have a minimum 3.0 GPA, be a Connecticut resident and submit a high school transcript. You will also need to submit a 900- to 1,000-word essay. Three letters of recommendation from high school teachers are also required. Award requirements change regularly. GPA must be 3.0-4.0.

Sickle Cell Disease Association of America/Connecticut Chapter
Gengras Ambulatory Center
114 Woodland Street, Suite 2101
Hartford, CT 06105

1075
Sylvia W. Farny Scholarship

AMOUNT: $1500 DEADLINE: March 15
MAJOR: Mechanical Engineering

This scholarship is open to mechanical engineering students in their last year of study. If you are enrolled in a four-year program you should apply in your junior year. If you are in a five-year program, application is in the fourth year. U.S. citizenship and enrollment in a U.S. school in an ABET-accredited mechanical engineering program is also required. Selection is based on academic performance, character, need, and ASME participation. Award requirements change regularly. GPA must be 2.8-4.0.

American Society of Mechanical Engineers Auxiliary, Inc.
Attn: Alberta Cover
5425 Caldwell Mill Road
Birmingham, AL 35242

1076
T.J. Schmitz Scholarship

AMOUNT: $1000 DEADLINE: May 26
MAJOR: All Areas of Study

This scholarship is available to undergraduates who are members of Tau Kappa Epsilon. In order to apply, you must demonstrate leadership within your chapter, on campus, or in the community. You must also have a minimum 2.5 GPA and be a full-time student in good standing. Award requirements change regularly. For further information, call (317) 872-6533, email: tef@tkehq.org or visit the website at: www.tke.org. GPA must be 2.5-4.0.

TKE Educational Foundation
Attn: Timothy L. Taschwer
8645 Founders Road
Indianapolis, IN 46268-1336

1077
Take Me Away to College Contest

AMOUNT: $500-$2500 DEADLINE: August 15
MAJOR: All Areas of Study

The Take Me Away to College Scholarship competition is open to legal residents of the U.S. and Canada who are high school seniors starting college full-time in the fall at an accredited two-year or four-year school. You may apply online by going to the Calgon website at www.takemeaway.com. The online entry form is displayed on the competition entry page at the Calgon website. For the application, you will respond to three questions posted on the website. Responses to each question should not be more than 450 characters, about 100 words. Award requirements change regularly. All rules, regulations, and an application are available at www.takemeaway.com. The website will give you more information about how to apply online and how to send an application by mail. No GPA requirement specified.

Take Me Away to College
c/o Maddenmedia
2730 Broadway, #250
Tucson, AZ 85716

1078
Talbots Women Scholarship Fund

AMOUNT: $1000-$10000 DEADLINE: March 6
MAJOR: All Areas of Study

The Talbots Women Scholarship Fund is open to women who plan to enroll in an accredited four-year college or university on a part-time or full-time basis to complete an undergraduate baccalaureate degree. You must have completed at least one semester of college a minimum of five years prior to September 30, 2000. You must also submit an essay and transcript with the application. Scholarship selection is based on a number of criteria, including your academic record, scholarship essay, potential to succeed, leadership, and participation in community activities, honors, work experience, a statement of educational and career goals, and an outside appraisal. Award requirements change regularly. No GPA requirement specified.

Talbots
Attn: Scholarship Coordinator
175 Beal Street
Hingham, MA 02043

1079
Target All-Around Scholarship

AMOUNT: $1000-$10000 DEADLINE: November 1
MAJOR: All Areas of Study

The Take Charge of Education Program is open to high school seniors and college students who are committed to their communities through volunteer service, education, and family involvement. In order to apply, you must be a U.S. citizen or permanent resident with a minimum 2.0 GPA. This scholarship is for use at a vocational, technical, two- or four-year school. The award is primarily based on your community volunteer hours, volunteer leadership awards, and honors. Applications must be postmarked from August 1 through November 1. Recipients will be notified on or about February 15. Employees of Target, Dayton Hudson Corp., Citizens' Scholarship Foundation of America, their subsidiaries, affiliates, advertising and promotion agencies, and their spouses, parents, children, siblings (and their spouses), and persons living in the same households of employees are not eligible to apply. If you are a previous recipient, you are not eligible to reapply. Applications and information available at the Target All-Around Scholarship Program display, located near the front of Target stores or browse their website www.target.com. GPA must be 2.0-4.0.

Target All-Around Scholarship
c/o CSFA
2505 Riverview Rd., P.O. Box 480
St. Peter, MN 56082-0480

1080
Target Teachers Scholarship

AMOUNT: $500-$1500 DEADLINE: November 1
MAJOR: Education

Open to legal residents of the U.S. who are full- or part-time certified teachers and administrators (principals, counselors, librarians, support staff) working at least 20 hours per week in a school that participates in "Take Charge of Education" and enroll in accredited courses through a workshop or seminar or credits toward an advanced education degree. Applications may be postmarked no later than November 1. Previous recipients are not eligible. Award requirements change regularly. Applications and information available at the Target Teachers Scholarship Program display, located near the front of Target stores or browse their website www.target.com. If you have any questions, please call (800) 537-4180.

Target All-Around Scholarship
c/o CSFA
2505 Riverview Rd., P.O. Box 480
St. Peter, MN 56082-0480

1081
Tau Beta Pi - Deuchler Fellowship

AMOUNT: $10000 DEADLINE: January 15
MAJOR: Water Supply, Waste-Water Treatment, Ecological Disciplines

The Tau Beta Pi - Deuchler Fellowship is open to full-time graduate students who are members of Tau Beta Pi. All Tau Beta Pi fellowships are awarded on the competitive basis of high scholarship, campus leadership, and service and promise of future contributions to the engineering profession. The Deuchler Fellowship will be awarded to individuals studying water supply, waste-water treatment, or ecological disciplines. Preference is given to first-time graduate students. To be considered, you must submit an application and two letters of recommendation. Award requirements change regularly. Please send a self-addressed, stamped envelope to receive your application and any further instructions from the fellowship provider; or email dspierre@southernco.com; or find the application online at www.tbp.org. No GPA requirement specified.

Tau Beta Pi
c/o D. Stephen Pierre, Jr., P.E.
Alabama Power Company, PO Box 2247
Mobile, AL 36652-2247

1082
Tau Beta Pi - Dodson Scholarship

AMOUNT: $2000 DEADLINE: January 15
MAJOR: Engineering, Computer Science

The Tau Beta Pi - Dodson Scholarship is open to full-time undergraduate seniors who are members of Tau Beta Pi. All Tau Beta Pi scholarships are awarded on the basis of high scholarship, strong faculty recommendations, extracurricular contributions and promise of substantial achievement in the field of engineering. To be considered, you must submit an application and two letters of recommendation. The scholarship is not renewable. Award requirements change regularly. Please send a self-addressed, stamped envelope to receive your application and any further instructions from the scholarship provider; or email dspierre@southernco.com; or find the application online at www.tbp.org. No GPA requirement specified.

Tau Beta Pi
c/o D. Stephen Pierre, Jr., P.E.
Alabama Power Company, PO Box 2247
Mobile, AL 36652-2247

1083
Tau Beta Pi - Fife Fellowship

AMOUNT: $10000 DEADLINE: January 15
MAJOR: Engineering, Computer Science

The Tau Beta Pi - Fife Fellowship is open to full-time graduate students who are members of Tau Beta Pi. All Tau Beta Pi fellowships are awarded on the competitive basis of high scholarship, campus leadership, and service and promise of future contributions to the engineering profession. Preference is given to first-time graduate students. To be considered, you must submit an application and two letters of recommendation. Award requirements change regularly. Please send a self-addressed, stamped envelope to receive your application and

any further instructions from the fellowship provider; or email dspierre@southernco.com; or find the application online at www.tbp.org. No GPA requirement specified.

Tau Beta Pi
c/o D. Stephen Pierre, Jr., P.E.
Alabama Power Company, PO Box 2247
Mobile, AL 36652-2247

1084
Tau Beta Pi - King Fellowship

AMOUNT: $10000 DEADLINE: January 15
MAJOR: Engineering, Computer Science

The Tau Beta Pi - King Fellowship is open to full-time graduate students who are members of Tau Beta Pi. All Tau Beta Pi fellowships are awarded on the competitive basis of high scholarship, campus leadership, and service and promise of future contributions to the engineering profession. The King Fellowship will be awarded to students whose leadership and participation in their national technical society's student branch is judged outstanding. Preference is given to first-time graduate students. To be considered, you must submit an application and two letters of recommendation. Award requirements change regularly. Please send a self-addressed, stamped envelope to receive your application and any further instructions from the fellowship provider; or email dspierre@southernco.com; or find the application online at www.tbp.org. No GPA requirement specified.

Tau Beta Pi
c/o D. Stephen Pierre, Jr., P.E.
Alabama Power Company, PO Box 2247
Mobile, AL 36652-2247

1085
Tau Beta Pi - Lenfesty Fellowship

AMOUNT: $10000 DEADLINE: January 15
MAJOR: Engineering, Computer Science

The Tau Beta Pi - Lenfesty Fellowship is open to full-time graduate students who are members of Tau Beta Pi. All Tau Beta Pi fellowships are awarded on the competitive basis of high scholarship, campus leadership, and service and promise of future contributions to the engineering profession. Preference is given to first-time graduate students. To be considered, you must submit an application and two letters of recommendation. Award requirements change regularly. Please send a self-addressed, stamped envelope to receive your application and any further instructions from the fellowship provider; or email dspierre@southernco.com; or find the application online at www.tbp.org. No GPA requirement specified.

Tau Beta Pi
c/o D. Stephen Pierre, Jr., P.E.
Alabama Power Company, PO Box 2247
Mobile, AL 36652-2247

1086
Tau Beta Pi - Maddox Fellowship

AMOUNT: $10000 DEADLINE: January 15
MAJOR: Engineering, Computer Science

The Tau Beta Pi - Maddox Fellowship is open to full-time graduate students who are members of Tau Beta Pi. All Tau

Beta Pi fellowships are awarded on the competitive basis of high scholarship, campus leadership, and service and promise of future contributions to the engineering profession. Preference is given to first-time graduate students. To be considered, you must submit an application and two letters of recommendation. Award requirements change regularly. Please send a self-addressed, stamped envelope to receive your application and any further instructions from the fellowship provider; or email dspierre@southernco.com; or find the application online at www.tbp.org. No GPA requirement specified.

Tau Beta Pi
c/o D. Stephen Pierre, Jr., P.E.
Alabama Power Company, PO Box 2247
Mobile, AL 36652-2247

1087
Tau Beta Pi - Nagel Scholarship

AMOUNT: $2000 DEADLINE: January 15
MAJOR: Engineering, Computer Science

The Tau Beta Pi - Nagel Scholarship is open to full-time undergraduate seniors who are members of Tau Beta Pi. All Tau Beta Pi scholarships are awarded on the basis of high scholarship, strong faculty recommendations, extracurricular contributions, and promise of substantial achievement in the field of engineering. To be considered, you must submit an application and two letters of recommendation. The scholarship is not renewable. Award requirements change regularly. Please send a self-addressed, stamped envelope to receive your application and any further instructions from the scholarship provider; or email dspierre@southernco.com; or find the application online at www.tbp.org. No GPA requirement specified.

Tau Beta Pi
c/o D. Stephen Pierre, Jr., P.E.
Alabama Power Company, PO Box 2247
Mobile, AL 36652-2247

1088
Tau Beta Pi - National Headquarters Fellowship

AMOUNT: $10000 DEADLINE: January 15
MAJOR: Engineering, Computer Science

The Tau Beta Pi - National Headquarters Fellowship is open to full-time graduate students who are members of Tau Beta Pi. All Tau Beta Pi fellowships are awarded on the competitive basis of high scholarship, campus leadership and service and promise of future contributions to the engineering profession. Preference is given to first-time graduate students. To be considered, you must submit an application and two letters of recommendation. Award requirements change regularly. Please send a self-addressed, stamped envelope to receive your application and any further instructions from the fellowship provider; or email dspierre@southernco.com; or find the application online at www.tbp.org. No GPA requirement specified.

Tau Beta Pi
c/o D. Stephen Pierre, Jr., P.E.
Alabama Power Company, PO Box 2247
Mobile, AL 36652-2247

1089
Tau Beta Pi - Sigma Tau Fellowship

AMOUNT: $10000 DEADLINE: January 15
MAJOR: Engineering, Computer Science

The Tau Beta Pi - Sigma Tau Fellowship is open to full-time graduate students who are members of Tau Beta Pi. All Tau Beta Pi fellowships are awarded on the competitive basis of high scholarship, campus leadership, and service and promise of future contributions to the engineering profession. Preference is given to first-time graduate students. To be considered, you must submit an application and two letters of recommendation. Award requirements change regularly. Please send a self-addressed, stamped envelope to receive your application and any further instructions from the fellowship provider; or email dspierre@southernco.com; or find the application online at www.tbp.org. No GPA requirement specified.

Tau Beta Pi
c/o D. Stephen Pierre, Jr., P.E.
Alabama Power Company, PO Box 2247
Mobile, AL 36652-2247

1090
Tau Beta Pi - Soderberg Scholarship

AMOUNT: $2000 DEADLINE: January 15
MAJOR: Engineering, Computer Science

The Tau Beta Pi - Soderberg Scholarship is open to full-time undergraduate seniors who are members of Tau Beta Pi. All Tau Beta Pi scholarships are awarded on the basis of high scholarship, strong faculty recommendations, extracurricular contributions, and promise of substantial achievement in the field of engineering. To be considered, you must submit an application and two letters of recommendation. The scholarship is not renewable. Award requirements change regularly. Please send a self-addressed, stamped envelope to receive your application and any further instructions from the scholarship provider; or email dspierre@southernco.com; or find the application online at www.tbp.org. No GPA requirement specified.

Tau Beta Pi
c/o D. Stephen Pierre, Jr., P.E.
Alabama Power Company, PO Box 2247
Mobile, AL 36652-2247

1091
Tau Beta Pi - Spencer Fellowship

AMOUNT: $10000 DEADLINE: January 15
MAJOR: Engineering, Computer Science

The Tau Beta Pi - Spencer Fellowship is open to full-time graduate students who are members of Tau Beta Pi. All Tau Beta Pi fellowships are awarded on the competitive basis of high scholarship, campus leadership and service and promise of future contributions to the engineering profession. The Spencer Fellowship will be awarded to those students whose contributions to their undergraduate chapter and college are judged most worthy of commendation. Preference is given to first-time graduate students. To be considered, you must submit an application and two letters of recommendation. Award requirements change regularly. Please send a self-addressed, stamped envelope to receive your application and any further instructions from the fellowship provider; or email dspierre@southernco.com; or find the application online at www.tbp.org. No GPA requirement specified.

Tau Beta Pi
c/o D. Stephen Pierre, Jr., P.E.
Alabama Power Company, PO Box 2247
Mobile, AL 36652-2247

1092
Tau Beta Pi - Stabile Scholarship

AMOUNT: $2000 DEADLINE: January 15
MAJOR: Engineering, Computer Science

The Tau Beta Pi - Stabile Scholarship is open to full-time undergraduate seniors who are members of Tau Beta Pi. All Tau Beta Pi scholarships are awarded on the basis of high scholarship, strong faculty recommendations, extracurricular contributions and promise of substantial achievement in the field of engineering. To be considered, you must submit an application and two letters of recommendation. The scholarship is not renewable. Award requirements change regularly. Please send a self-addressed, stamped envelope to receive your application and any further instructions from the scholarship provider; or email dspierre@southernco.com; or find the application online at www.tbp.org. No GPA requirement specified.

Tau Beta Pi
c/o D. Stephen Pierre, Jr., P.E.
Alabama Power Company, PO Box 2247
Mobile, AL 36652-2247

1093
Tau Beta Pi - Stark Fellowship

AMOUNT: $10000 DEADLINE: January 15
MAJOR: Fluid Power

The Tau Beta Pi - Stark Fellowship is open to Tau Beta Pi members doing full-time graduate study in the field of fluid power. Fellowships will be awarded on the competitive basis of high scholarship, campus leadership, and service and promise of future contributions to the engineering profession. Preference is given to first-time graduate students. To be considered, you must submit an application and two letters of recommendation. Award requirements change regularly. Please send a self-addressed, stamped envelope to receive your application and any further instructions from the fellowship provider; or find the application online at www.tbp.org. No GPA requirement specified.

Tau Beta Pi
c/o D. Stephen Pierre, Jr., P.E.
Alabama Power Company, PO Box 2247
Mobile, AL 36652-2247

1094
Tau Beta Pi - Williams Fellowship

AMOUNT: $10000 DEADLINE: January 15
MAJOR: Engineering, Computer Science

The Tau Beta Pi - Williams Fellowship is open to full-time graduate students who are members of Tau Beta Pi. All Tau

Beta Pi fellowships are awarded on the competitive basis of high scholarship, campus leadership, and service and promise of future contributions to the engineering profession. The Williams Fellowship will be awarded to students who possess outstanding cultural and ethical attributes, and plan to earn a doctoral degree and become a professor of engineering. Preference is given to first-time graduate students. To be considered, you must submit an application and two letters of recommendation. Award requirements change regularly. Please send a self-addressed, stamped envelope to receive your application and any further instructions from the fellowship provider; or email dspierre@southernco.com; or find the application online at www.tbp.org. No GPA requirement specified.

Tau Beta Pi
c/o D. Stephen Pierre, Jr., P.E.
Alabama Power Company, PO Box 2247
Mobile, AL 36652-2247

1095
TDC Scholarship

AMOUNT: $1000 DEADLINE: December 31
MAJOR: Accounting, Finance, Business, Taxation

The TDC Scholarship is available to ethnic minority accounting, finance, or business undergraduates or accounting and taxation graduates. Applicants must be currently enrolled as full-time students and be paid NABA members. A minimum 2.5 GPA is required. Award requirements change regularly. Please send a self-addressed, stamped envelope to receive your application and any further instructions from the scholarship provider or call (301) 474-6222, ext. 14. GPA must be 2.5-4.0.

National Association of Black Accountants, Inc.
Attn: Scholarship Committee
7249-A Hanover Parkway
Greenbelt, MD 20770

1096
Teach For Texas Conditional Grant Program

AMOUNT: Maximum: $5000 DEADLINE: Varies
MAJOR: All Fields of Study

The Teach For Texas Conditional Grant Program is open to Texas residents who are enrolled at an approved Texas post-secondary institution. To be considered for this award, you must have a minimum 2.5 GPA, be a junior or senior in an undergraduate degree program for educator certification and be able to demonstrate financial need. The award requires that you commit to teach full-time for at least five years following teacher certification. It is renewable, provided all criteria are met; failure to abide by the criteria may result in the grant becoming a loan, which will need to be paid back. Award requirements change regularly. For further information on how to apply, you may contact the address listed. You may also visit Texas Higher Education Coordinating Board website at www.thecb.state.tx.us. GPA must be 2.5-4.0.

Texas Higher Education Coordinating Board - Student Services
Attn: Grant Coordinator
PO Box 12788
Austin, TX 78711-2788

1097
Teacher and Administrator Grant Program

AMOUNT: None Specified DEADLINE: Varies
MAJOR: Education

Open to anyone who holds a current teacher or administrator certification from the Arkansas Department of Education and who is currently employed as a teacher or administrator in Arkansas. The Teacher and Administrator Grant Program is available for use only during summer terms. Those awarded can be reimbursed for up to three hours of coursework during the summer. Award requirements change regularly. Write to the address listed, enclosing a self-addressed, stamped envelope for an application and further information. You may also browse their website: www.arscholarships.com/finsites.html. No GPA requirement specified.

Arkansas Department of Higher Education
Financial Aid Division
114 East Capitol Avenue
Little Rock, AR 72201-3818

1098
Tennessee Student Assistance Award Program

AMOUNT: None Specified DEADLINE: May 1
MAJOR: All Areas of Study

The Tennessee Student Assistance Award Program is open to undergraduates who are Tennessee residents. To be considered for this award, you must be enrolled in an eligible Tennessee postsecondary institution. This grant is awarded on the basis of financial need. The amount of the award will not be greater than the amount of tuition and mandatory fees assessed by the institution attended. Award requirements change regularly. To apply, you must submit the FAFSA. You may also visit the Tennessee Student Assistance Corporation website at www.state.tn.us/tsac/grants.htm. No GPA requirement specified.

Tennessee Student Assistance Corporation
Parkway Towers, Suite 1900
404 James Robertson Parkway
Nashville, TN 37243

1099
Texas AFL-CIO Scholarship

AMOUNT: None Specified DEADLINE: January 31
MAJOR: All Areas of Study

The Texas AFL-CIO Scholarship is for high school seniors who are members of the AFL-CIO or for children of AFL-CIO members who are high school seniors. You must be planning to attend a university, college, or technical institute in the summer or fall term. To be considered for the award, you will need to fill out an application and participate in a test and interview conducted by your local Central Labor Council district. You will be judged on financial need, academic achievement, and your knowledge of the labor movement as determined by the test and interview. Award requirements change regularly. No GPA requirement specified.

Texas AFL-CIO
Scholarship Program
PO Box 12727
Austin, TX 78711-2727

1100
Texas Farm Bureau Young Farmer & Rancher Committee

AMOUNT: $2000 DEADLINE: June 1
MAJOR: Agriculture, Agricultural Science, Agriculture Industry

This award is open to incoming college freshmen who are graduates of Texas high schools. Applicants are to pursue some degree in the cultural field. Family must be members of Farm Bureau. Award requirements change regularly. Applications may be obtained from local county Farm Bureau offices, from the TFB website at www.txfb.com or by calling (254) 751-2286. No GPA requirement specified.

Texas Farm Bureau Youth Foundation
Scholarship Coordinator
PO Box 2689
Waco, TX 76702-2689

1101
Texas Farm Bureau Youth Foundation Scholarship

AMOUNT: Maximum: $2000 DEADLINE: June 1
MAJOR: Agriculture

Open to graduating high school seniors whose families are members of the Texas Farm Bureau. Based on academics, extracurricular activity, involvement, recommendations, and financial need. Renewable up to four years. Winner selected by committee from Baylor University and McLennan Community College. Award requirements change regularly. Contact the address listed for further information. No GPA requirement specified.

Texas Farm Bureau Youth Foundation
Scholarship Coordinator
PO Box 2689
Waco, TX 76702-2689

1102
Texas Outdoor Writers Association Scholarship

AMOUNT: $1000 DEADLINE: December 31
MAJOR: Outdoor/Environmental Conservation/Wildlife Management Communications

These scholarships are open to juniors, seniors, graduate students, and active professionals who are seeking further training. In order to apply, you must be planning to enroll or are enrolled in communications-related courses, incorporating the fields listed above, through visual, oral, or print media. This scholarship must be used at an accredited Texas college or university. Winners are announced at the TOWA annual meeting in February in Lake Jackson, Texas. Award requirements change regularly. No GPA requirement specified.

Texas Outdoor Writers Association
TOWA Scholarship
P.O. Box 493
Blanco, TX 78606

1103
Theodore S. Gary Scholarship

AMOUNT: $2000 DEADLINE: March 15
MAJOR: All Fields of Study

The Theodore S. Gary Scholarship is open to employees of Business Products Industry Association member firms and their families. Persons holding academic records sufficient for acceptance by accredited colleges, junior colleges, or technical schools, or persons already enrolled in one of those institutions are eligible for this one-year award. Selection is made by a committee from the Student Financial Aid Department of The George Washington University, Washington, DC. Award requirements change regularly. Please send a self-addressed, stamped envelope to receive your application and any further instructions from the scholarship provider or email: info@bpia.org. No GPA requirement specified.

Business Products Industry Association
Attn: Scholarship Committee
301 North Fairfax Street
Alexandria, VA 22314-2633

1104
Thirteenth Annual Christopher College Video Contest

AMOUNT: $1000-$3000 DEADLINE: June 16
MAJOR: All Areas of Study

The 13th Annual Christopher Video Contest asks you to interpret the theme "One Person Can Make a Difference" on film or video in five minutes or less (all entries must be submitted on VHS cassette). The contest is open to all postsecondary school students currently enrolled in and attending college classes—undergraduate, graduate, full- or part-time. No entries will be returned. Award requirements change regularly. For further information and an application, you are encouraged to visit their website at: www.christophers.org/vidcon2k.html. If you do not have Internet access, please write to the address listed below, including a self-addressed, stamped envelope or call (212) 759-4050. No GPA requirement specified.

The Christophers
Attn: Video Contest Coordinator
12 East 48th Street
New York, NY 10017-1008

1105
Thomas F. Seay Scholarship

AMOUNT: $2000 DEADLINE: April 1
MAJOR: Real Estate

Open to students who are enrolled in a degree program with an emphasis on real estate at any accredited college or university in the U.S. Applicants must have completed at least 30 college credit hours, have a minimum 3.5 GPA on a 5.0 scale, be U.S. citizens, and be residents of the state of Illinois. Award requirements change regularly. For further information and an application, please write to the address listed, including a self-addressed, stamped envelope. GPA must be 3.5-4.0.

Illinois Real Estate Educational Foundation
Academic Scholarships
PO Box 19457
Springfield, IL 62794

1106
Thomas Wolfe Student Essay Prize

AMOUNT: $500 DEADLINE: January 15
MAJOR: Literature, English, Writing

Undergraduate and graduate students enrolled in colleges and universities worldwide are encouraged to submit an essay (in English) about Thomas Wolfe or his works. Essays must be between eight and 15 double-spaced, typed pages. Essays will be judged on originality, style, clarity, documentation, and contribution to knowledge or understanding of Wolfe. The winning essay will be delivered at the annual Thomas Wolfe Society meeting and published in the Thomas Wolfe Review. This is not a renewable award. Award requirements change regularly. No GPA requirement specified.

Thomas Wolfe Society
Essay Contest Chair, Student Prize Committee
809 Gardner Street
Raleigh, NC 27607

1107
Timothy Bigelow and Palmer W. Bigelow, Jr. Scholarships

AMOUNT: $2500 DEADLINE: May 15
MAJOR: Landscape, Horticulture

The Timothy Bigelow and Palmer W. Bigelow, Jr. Scholarships are open to residents of: Connecticut, Maine, Massachusetts, New Hampshire, Rhode Island, and Vermont. Students must be full-time seniors in a two-year program or juniors in a four-year school with a minimum GPA of 2.25. Graduate students with a GPA of at least 3.0 are also eligible to apply. Preference is given to students who plan to work in the nursery industry following graduation and/or to applicants with financial need. Award requirements change regularly. GPA must be 2.3-4.0.

Horticultural Research Institute
Bigelow Scholarship
1250 Eye Street NW, Suite 500
Washington, DC 20005-3922

1108
TLC Community Credit Union Scholarship

AMOUNT: $1000 DEADLINE: March 31
MAJOR: All Fields of Study

The TLC Community Credit Union Scholarship is open to family members of the TLC Community Credit Union. Accounts must have been in existence for at least two years for you to be eligible. Award requirements change regularly. Please send a self-addressed, stamped envelope to receive your application and any further instructions from the scholarship provider. No GPA requirement specified.

Morenci High School
Attn: Mrs. Melissa Parnell
788 Coomer Street
Morenci, MI 49256

1109
TLMI Scholarship

AMOUNT: $5000 DEADLINE: March 31
MAJOR: Tag and Label Industry

This scholarship is open to sophomores and juniors attending an accredited college or university who have an interest in entering the tag and label industry. You must have a minimum 3.0 GPA and possess an excellent character including honesty, integrity and a solid work ethic. Award requirements change regularly. GPA must be 3.0-4.0.

Tag and Label Manufacturers Institute, Inc.
Scholarship Committee
40 Shuman Blvd, Suite 295
Naperville, IL 60563-8465

1110
Tom and Judith Comstock Scholarship

AMOUNT: $1000 DEADLINE: February 1
MAJOR: All Areas of Study

This scholarship is available to high school seniors with a minimum general class amateur radio license who have been accepted to a two-year or four-year college. Applicants must be residents of Texas or Oklahoma. Award requirements change regularly. Write the address provided, using a self-addressed, stamped envelope, for further information. No GPA requirement specified.

American Radio Relay League
Attn: ARRL Foundation
225 Main Street
Newington, CT 06111-1400

1111
Tom and Roberta Drewes Scholarship

AMOUNT: $3000 DEADLINE: April 1
MAJOR: Library Science, Information Science

The Tom and Roberta Drewes Scholarship is open to ALA or library support staff currently working in a library. To be considered for this award, you must be a citizen or permanent resident of the U.S. or Canada and have applied for admission to an ALA-accredited master's degree program in library and information studies. You cannot have completed more than 12 semester hours (or its equivalent) towards the master's degree prior to June 1. Award requirements change regularly. No GPA requirement specified.

American Library Association
HRDR/Staff Liaison - Scholarship Juries
50 East Huron Street
Chicago, IL 60611-2795

1112
Tony B. Leisner Scholarship

AMOUNT: $3000 DEADLINE: April 1
MAJOR: Library Science, Information Science

The Tony B. Leisner Scholarship is open to ALA or library support staff currently working in a library. To be considered

for this award, you must be a citizen or permanent resident of the U.S. or Canada and have applied for admission to an ALA-accredited master's degree program in library and information studies. You cannot have completed more than 12 semester hours (or its equivalent) towards the master's degree prior to June 1. Award requirements change regularly. No GPA requirement specified.

American Library Association
HRDR/Staff Liaison - Scholarship Juries
50 East Huron Street
Chicago, IL 60611-2795

1113
Tony Orlando Yellow Ribbon Scholarship

AMOUNT: $5000 DEADLINE: April 17
MAJOR: Travel and Tourism, Hotel/Restaurant Management

The Tony Orlando Yellow Ribbon Scholarship is open to students with physical or sensory disabilities who are seeking an education at any level beyond high school for use in a career in travel and tourism. If you are a high school senior, you must have a minimum 3.0 GPA; if you are a continuing college student, you must have a minimum 2.5 GPA. Award requirements change regularly. GPA must be 3.0-4.0.

National Tourism Foundation
PO Box 3071
546 East Main Street
Lexington, KY 40508-3071

1114
Tony Velonis Memorial Scholarship

AMOUNT: $500 DEADLINE: October 15
MAJOR: Ceramic Engineering, Glass Art, Ceramic Art and Design

Open to undergraduates and graduates who are in a glass, ceramic, or related curriculum including ceramic engineering, glass art, ceramic art and design, or other programs that focus on the decoration of glassware and ceramicware. Any experience in glass or ceramic design either at school or during employment is considered by the review committee along with grade, financial need, and plans for future study in the glass and ceramic field. There are two deadline dates: May 15 for the fall semester and October 15 for the spring semester. Award requirements change regularly. For more details call (202) 728-4132, or email: sgcd@sgcd.org You may also visit their website: www.sgcd.org. No GPA requirement specified.

Society of Glass and Ceramic Decorators
Scholarship Committee
1627 'K' Street NW, Suite 800
Washington, DC 20006-1702

1115
Toro Industry Advancement Award

AMOUNT: $2000 DEADLINE: August 2
MAJOR: Landscape Architecture/Design

The Toro Industry Advancement Award recognizes exemplary design projects that display effective use of irrigation techniques in creating quality environments. Projects will be evaluated on the basis of cost effectiveness, operational efficiency, transferability, water conservation, and overall contribution to environmental quality. Award requirements change regularly. No GPA requirement specified.

Landscape Architecture Foundation
Scholarship Program
636 'I' Street NW
Washington, DC 20001-3736

1116
Tourette Syndrome Association Research and Training Grants

AMOUNT: $5000-$40000 DEADLINE: Varies
MAJOR: Biochemistry, Epidemiology, Genetics, Molecular Biology, Neuroanatomy, Neurology, Neuropsychology, Neurophysiology, Pharmacology, Psychiatry, Psychology

The Tourette Syndrome Association Research and Training Grants are awarded to Ph.D. and M.D. researchers who are involved in the following areas: basic neuroscience specifically relevant to Tourette Syndrome; clinical studies related to the etiology, pathophysiology, and treatment of Tourette Syndrome. One- or two-year training postdoctoral fellowships are also available. Areas of interest include behavioral neuroscience, neuroimaging, basal ganglia physiology, neuropathology, neurochemistry, and clinical trials. Preliminary screenings are based on letters of intent. Other relevant fields are: biochemistry, epidemiology, genetics, molecular biology, neuroanatomy, neurology, neuropsychology, neurophysiology, pharmacology, psychiatry, and psychology. The letter of intent due date is October 15 and the final proposal due date is December 17. Award requirements change regularly. To receive an application packet and a review of TSA literature, call (718) 224-2999 or fax (718) 279-9596. No GPA requirement specified.

TSA Scientific Advisory Board
Neal R. Swerdlow, M.D., Ph.D., Chairman
42-40 Bell Boulevard
Bayside, NY 11361-2820

1117
Traineeships in Public Affairs, Forestry, Photography & Animal Records

AMOUNT: $2400-$3000 DEADLINE: Varies
MAJOR: Public Affairs, Forestry, Photography, and Animal Records

The Zoo Traineeships in Public Affairs, Forestry, Photography, and Animal Records is a 12-week program open to students who major in public affairs, landscaping, or zoo photography. The stipend for the full-term is $2,400 - $3,000. Students must make their own arrangements in Washington. FONZ (Friends of the National Zoo) can provide a listing of some lodging opportunities in the Washington area. The selection process focuses on the statement of interest, scholastic achievement, relevant experience, and letters of reference. Preference is given to advanced undergraduates and recent graduates. Award requirements change regularly. Please send a self-addressed, stamped envelope to receive your application and any further instructions from the scholarship provider. No GPA requirement specified.

National Zoological Park
Human Resource Office - Internships
3001 Connecticut Avenue, NW
Washington, DC 20008

1118
Translational Research Program

AMOUNT: Maximum: $324000 DEADLINE: February 15
MAJOR: Clinical Research in Genetics, Biology, Pharmacology, Virology, and Immunology

This research program was created in consultation with the National Cancer Institute to encourage and provide support for new and novel clinical research. The goal is to accelerate transfer of findings from the laboratory to clinical application. Award requirements change regularly. Please send a self-addressed, stamped envelope to receive your application and any further instructions from the scholarship provider. Preliminary application due by February 15, complete application due by March 15. No GPA requirement specified.

Leukemia Society of America
Director of Research Administration
600 Third Avenue
New York, NY 10016-1901

1119
Travis C. Tomlin Scholarship

AMOUNT: $1000 DEADLINE: December 31
MAJOR: Accounting, Finance, Business, Taxation

The Travis C. Tomlin Scholarship is available to ethnic minority accounting, finance, or business undergraduates or accounting and taxation graduates. Applicants must be currently enrolled as full-time students and be paid NABA members. Award requirements change regularly. Please send a self-addressed, stamped envelope to receive your application and any further instructions from the scholarship provider or call (301) 474-6222, ext. 14. GPA must be 3.3-4.0.

National Association of Black Accountants, Inc.
Attn: Scholarship Committee
7249-A Hanover Parkway
Greenbelt, MD 20770

1120
Treadway Inns Scholarship

AMOUNT: $500 DEADLINE: April 17
MAJOR: Travel and Tourism, Hotel/Restaurant Management

The Treadway Inns Scholarship is open to juniors or seniors pursuing a degree in a travel and tourism-related field. To be considered for the award, you must be enrolled in a North American four-year college full-time. Award requirements change regularly. No GPA requirement specified.

National Tourism Foundation
PO Box 3071
546 East Main Street
Lexington, KY 40508-3071

1121
Triangle Fraternity Student Loan Program

AMOUNT: Maximum: $3000 DEADLINE: Maximum: Varies
MAJOR: Engineering, Architecture, Sciences

The Triangle Fraternity Student Loan Program provides interest-free loans of up to $3,000 to active members of Triangle who are enrolled in a course of study leading to a degree. Repayment is made in up to 12 monthly installments and will commence on the first day of the third month following graduation or leaving school. To be considered for a loan, you must have completed at least two full academic years of school, maintained the minimum scholastic average required for graduation in your chosen major, and demonstrated financial need. You will be required to submit an application, a current college transcript, and two letters of recommendation. Award requirements change regularly. The loan application packet can be accessed online at www.triangle.org. No GPA requirement specified.

Triangle Fraternity
Attn: Education Foundation
120 South Center Street
Plainfield, IN 46168-1214

1122
TROA Scholarship 200

AMOUNT: $1000 DEADLINE: March 1
MAJOR: All Areas of Study

Applicants must be dependents of an active duty or drilling reservist member of the Army, Navy, Marine Corps, Air Force, Coast Guard, United States Public Health Service (USPHS), or National Oceanic and Atmospheric Administration (NOAA) or the dependents of a member of the National Guard. Applicants must be high school seniors or college students working on their first undergraduate degree. Applicants must be under the age of 24. Selections will be made solely on the basis of merit: scholarship, citizenship, and leadership. Award requirements change regularly. Applications will only be taken ONLINE (there are no paper applications). Go to TROA's website for complete application information: www.troa.org. Then go to "Member Services" and find "Scholarship 200." Click there. Applicants may also go to their school counselor's office or public library, or email: grant200@troa.org. GPA must be 3.0-4.0.

Retired Officers Association
Scholarship Program
200 N Washington Street # 201
Alexandria, VA 22314-2521

1123
TRW Foundation Scholarship

AMOUNT: $200-$500 DEADLINE: May 15
MAJOR: Engineering

This award is open to freshmen women majoring in engineering. Applicants must have been accepted into an ABET-accredited program or an SWE-approved school. One award is granted at $500 and ten awards are granted at $200. Award requirements change regularly. Please send a self-addressed, stamped envelope to receive your application. For any further instructions from the scholarship provider, please browse their website at www.swe.org or email hq@swe.org. No GPA requirement specified.

Society of Women Engineers Headquarters
Scholarship Coordinator
120 Wall Street, FL 11
New York, NY 10005-3902

1124
Tuition Aid Grant

AMOUNT: $844-$6674 DEADLINE: Varies
MAJOR: All Fields of Study

The Tuition Aid Grant is open to New Jersey residents who are full-time undergraduates at approved New Jersey colleges, universities and degree-granting proprietary schools. To be considered for the award, you must be able to demonstrate financial need. The award also requires that you have not received a baccalaureate degree or an associate degree if enrolled at a two-year college. You must also maintain satisfactory academic progress. Award requirements change regularly. To apply for this award, you must submit the FAFSA. For further information, you may visit the website at www.hesaa.org. No GPA requirement specified.

New Jersey Higher Education Student Assistance Authority
Scholarships, Grants and Loan Services
PO Box 540
Trenton, NJ 08625-0538

1125
Turner Family Scholarship

AMOUNT: Maximum: $5000 DEADLINE: February 15
MAJOR: All Areas of Study

Awarded to undergraduate college and vocational students who are the children of employees of National Welders Supply Company, Inc. and National Realty Sales Corporation. Award requirements change regularly. Write to the address listed for details, enclosing a self-addressed, stamped envelope. No GPA requirement specified.

Foundation for the Carolinas
Scholarship Program
PO Box 34769
Charlotte, NC 28234-4769

1126
Twin Tiers Society of Women Engineers Scholarship

AMOUNT: $1500 DEADLINE: March 18
MAJOR: Engineering, Computer Science

The Twin Tiers Society of Women Engineers Scholarship is open to female high school seniors who are enrolled or have been accepted for enrollment in an undergraduate degree program in engineering or computer science at an ABET-accredited or SWE-approved school. You must be a resident of the Twin Tiers (NY) region which includes the counties of Schuyler, Chemung, Steuben, Bradford, and Tioga. Award requirements change regularly. No GPA requirement specified.

Society of Women Engineers - Twin Tiers
Scholarship Committee
PO Box 798
Corning, NY 14830

1127
Two/Ten International Footwear Foundation Scholarship Program

AMOUNT: $200-$2000 DEADLINE: December 15
MAJOR: All Areas of Study

Open to workers or dependents of a worker whose work is related to the footwear, leather, or allied industries. Selection is based on need and academics. Applicants must have been graduated from high school within the last four years or currently be a high school senior and must attend school full-time. Award requirements change regularly. Write to the address listed for details and a preliminary application form or go to their website: www.twotenfoundation.org. No GPA requirement specified.

Two/Ten International Footwear Foundation
Scholarship Director
1466 Main Street
Waltham, MA 02451

1128
Tyonek Native Corporation Scholarship and Grant Program

AMOUNT: $1000 DEADLINE: Varies
MAJOR: All Areas of Study

The Tyonek Native Corporation Scholarship and Grant Program is open to Alaska Natives enrolled in the TNC and their descendants, or tribal members of the Native Village of Tyonek. Applicants must have a minimum GPA of 2.0 and be accepted/enrolled full-time in an approved, accredited college, university, or technical skills education program. The respective deadlines are June 1 and December 1. Award requirements change regularly. GPA must be 2.0-4.0.

CIRI Foundation
Scholarship Coordinator
2600 Cordova Street, Suite 206
Anchorage, AK 99503-2745

1129
UNA-USA National High School Essay Contest

AMOUNT: $500-$1000 DEADLINE: April 14
MAJOR: All Fields of Study

The UNA-USA National High School Essay Contest is open to students in grades 9-12. To be eligible for this monetary award, you must submit an essay of 1,500 words or less on a theme selected by the sponsor. The theme for the 2000 contest is "Culture of Peace." Your essay must be typed, double-spaced, and include endnotes and a bibliography of all sources. Your essay must be accompanied by the "Essay Cover Form" which can be found online at the sponsor's web-site. All material must be submitted to the UNA-USA Chapter or Division in your area. To find the one nearest you, please consult the Chapter and Division directory available on the website. Three national prize winners will be announced on June 30 and receive awards of $500, $750, or $1,000. Award requirements change regularly. To receive a copy of the contest application kit and any further instructions, please visit the UNA-USA website at www.unausa.org/programs/nhseckit.htm. You can

also contact your local UNA Chapter or Division. No GPA requirement specified.

United Nations Association of the United States of America
Attn: Scholarship Committee
801 Second Avenue
New York, NY 10017

1130
Undergraduate/Graduate Loans

AMOUNT: $200-$4500 DEADLINE: Varies
MAJOR: All Areas of Study

Loans for full-time undergraduate or graduate students who are U.S. citizens and members of the Presbyterian Church (U.S.A.). Based upon academic ability and demonstrated financial need. Award requirements change regularly. Write to the address for information and an application enclosing a self-addressed, stamped envelope or call (502) 569-5735. No GPA requirement specified.

Presbyterian Church (U.S.A.)
Office of Financial Aid for Studies
100 Witherspoon Street
Louisville, KY 40202-1396

1131
Undergraduate Scholarship

AMOUNT: $1000 DEADLINE: May 31
MAJOR: Human Service, Ministry

The Undergraduate Scholarship is open to full-time undergraduate students attending an American Baptist-related college or university. Preference will be given to persons preparing for careers in church leadership or human services. Recipients must maintain satisfactory academic standing. Applicants must be members of an American Baptist church for at least one year before applying for aid, enrolled at an accredited educational institution in the U.S. or Puerto Rico. U.S. citizenship is required. Award requirements change regularly. Please send a self-addressed, stamped envelope to receive your application and any further instructions from the scholarship provider. No GPA requirement specified.

American Baptist Financial Aid Program
Educational Ministries ABC/USA
PO Box 851
Valley Forge, PA 19482-0851

1132
Undergraduate Scholarship Program

AMOUNT: None Specified DEADLINE: April 30
MAJOR: Biology, Chemistry, Health Sciences, Biomedical Sciences, Life Sciences

Open to students with disadvantaged backgrounds. Recipients must demonstrate financial need or a statement indicating nonfinancial but other disadvantaged situation. Must have minimum GPA of 3.5. Must be U.S. citizens or permanent residents. Award requirements change regularly. Write to the address listed, enclosing a self-addressed, stamped envelope for an application and further information. GPA must be 3.5-4.0.

National Institutes of Health
7550 Wisconsin Avenue, Rm 102
Bethesda, MD 20814-3559

1133
Unionism In America Essay Contest

AMOUNT: None Specified DEADLINE: January 31
MAJOR: All Areas of Study

This essay contest is open to graduating high school seniors from Pennsylvania high schools or students currently attending an accredited college or graduate school. You must be a full-time student and submit a 1,500-word essay. A recommendation by a labor organization is required. Award requirements change regularly. Write to the address listed for details, enclosing a self-addressed, stamped envelope. Information may also be found in many high schools or union halls. No GPA requirement specified.

AFL-CIO, Pennsylvania
Attn: Director of Education
230 State Street
Harrisburg, PA 17101-1138

1134
United Bank and Trust Leadership Scholarship

AMOUNT: $2000 DEADLINE: March 31
MAJOR: All Fields of Study

The United Bank and Trust Leadership Scholarship is open to graduating seniors from a Lenawee County (MI) High School. To be considered for the award, you must have displayed outstanding leadership qualities. The scholarship is renewable for an additional three years. Award requirements change regularly. Please send a self-addressed, stamped envelope to receive your application and any further instructions from the scholarship provider. No GPA requirement specified.

Morenci High School
Attn: Mrs. Melissa Parnell
788 Coomer Street
Morenci, MI 49256

1135
United Church, Chapel on the Hill Scholarship

AMOUNT: $600 DEADLINE: April 18
MAJOR: All Areas of Study

This scholarship is open to high school seniors, undergraduates, and those attending technical or special training programs. You must be a resident of Oak Ridge, Anderson or Roane counties (TN). This award is based on academic ability and financial need. In order to apply for this award, your family income may not exceed $30,000 per year. Award requirements change regularly. No GPA requirement specified.

United Church, Chapel on the Hill
Scholarship Coordinator
85 Kentucky Avenue
Oak Ridge, TN 37830-5422

1136
United Parcel Service Scholarship for Minority Students

AMOUNT: $4000 DEADLINE: November 15
MAJOR: Industrial Engineering

This scholarship is open to minority undergraduate industrial engineering majors who are enrolled on a full-time basis, who are members of the institute and have a minimum 3.4 GPA. The program enrolled in may be located in the United States and its territories, Canada, or Mexico provided that the school's engineering program or equivalent is accredited by an accrediting agency recognized by IIE. The applicants must have a graduation date of May/June 2001 or later and must be nominated by their IE Department heads. Award requirements change regularly. GPA must be 3.4-4.0.

Institute of Industrial Engineers
Attn: Chapter Operations Board
25 Technology Park
Norcross, GA 30092-2988

1137
United States Senate Youth Program Award

AMOUNT: $2000 DEADLINE: Varies
MAJOR: All Areas of Study

The United States Senate Youth Program Award is available to high school juniors and seniors who are elected student officers, including student body officers, class officers, student council representatives, and student representatives to a district- or state-level civic or educational organization. This program includes an all-expense paid week in Washington, DC. and a $2,000 college scholarship. Two students from each state, the District of Columbia, and the Dept. of Defense schools overseas will be selected to participate in this intensive week of study of the United States government. Award requirements change regularly. For further information contact your high school principal or write to the address listed, enclosing a self-addressed, stamped envelope. The deadline date is in the early fall of each year. These dates vary from state to state. No GPA requirement specified.

William Randolph Hearst Foundation
Attn: Scholarship Committee
90 New Montgomery Street, Suite 1212
San Francisco, CA 94105-4504

1138
United Stationers, Inc. Scholarship

AMOUNT: $2000 DEADLINE: March 15
MAJOR: All Fields of Study

The United Stationers, Inc. Scholarship is open to employees of Business Products Industry Association member firms and their families. Persons holding academic records sufficient for acceptance by accredited colleges, junior colleges, or technical schools, or persons already enrolled in one of those institutions are eligible for this four-year award. Selection is made by a committee from the Student Financial Aid Department of The George Washington University, Washington, DC. Award requirements change regularly. Please send a self-addressed, stamped envelope to receive your application and any further instructions from the scholarship provider or email: info@bpia.org. No GPA requirement specified.

Business Products Industry Association
Attn: Scholarship Committee
301 North Fairfax Street
Alexandria, VA 22314-2633

1139
United Technologies Corporation Scholarship

AMOUNT: $1000 DEADLINE: February 1
MAJOR: Electrical Engineering, Mechanical Engineering

This scholarship is open to entering sophomore women who are majoring in electrical engineering or mechanical engineering. Applicants must be U.S. citizens and have minimum GPAs of 3.5. Renewable for two years with continued academic achievement. Applicants must be attending an ABET-accredited program or an SWE-approved school. Award requirements change regularly. Please send a self-addressed, stamped envelope to receive your application. GPA must be 3.5-4.0.

Society of Women Engineers Headquarters
Scholarship Coordinator
120 Wall Street, FL 11
New York, NY 10005-3902

1140
Universal Design Grant

AMOUNT: $2500 DEADLINE: October 22
MAJOR: Design and Related Fields of Study

The Universal Design Grant is to be awarded to an individual working independently and involved with universal design. Universal design is defined as a discipline by which to create solutions, design spaces, and develop products that suit the needs of all users throughout their lifecycle. The applicant should be involved in one of the following areas of universal design: product development, a design project, education, or marketing. Applicants must submit: a completed application; a brief statement explaining your professional goals and accomplishments; a detailed description of the project for which you are applying for grant funds. Award requirements change regularly. Please send a self-addressed, stamped envelope to receive your application and any further instructions from the scholarship provider. No GPA requirement specified.

International Furnishings and Design Association
Attn: Educational Foundation Office
1200 19th Street NW, Suite 300
Washington, DC 20036-2422

1141
University Film and Video Association Grant

AMOUNT: $1000-$4000 DEADLINE: January 1
MAJOR: Film, Video

This grant is available to undergraduates and graduate students who are film makers and video producers. You can be attending any college or university to receive this grant, and you must also be sponsored by a faculty member who is an active member of the University Film and Video Association. Works that are considered are experimental, animation, multimedia, treatments, scripts, or storyboards. Award requirements change regularly. No GPA requirement specified.

University of Baltimore - School of Communications Design
Professor Julie Simon, Chairperson
1420 North Charles Street
Baltimore, MD 21201-5720

1142
USRA Scholarship Program

AMOUNT: Maximum: $500 DEADLINE: March 1
MAJOR: Physical Sciences, Engineering, Space Research, Space Science Education, Astronomy, Biophysics, Chemistry, Astronomy, Computer Science, Geophysics, Geology, Mathematics, Physics

The purpose of the USRA Scholarship Program is to provide college scholarships to students who have shown a career interest in the physical sciences or engineering with an emphasis on space research or space science education. This includes, but is not limited to, aerospace engineering, astronomy, biophysics, chemistry, chemical engineering, computer science, electrical engineering, geophysics, geology, mathematics, mechanical engineering, and physics. In order to apply, you must have completed at least two years of college credits by the time the award is received. U.S. citizenship is required. Award requirements change regularly. No GPA requirement specified.

USRA Scholarship Program
Universities Space Research Association
10227 Wincopin Circle, Suite 212
Columbia, MD 21044-3459

1143
Van Schaik Dressage Scholarship

AMOUNT: $1000 DEADLINE: March 1
MAJOR: Horsecare, Horsemanship, Equestrian

The American Morgan Horse Institute's Van Schaik Dressage Scholarship is open to Morgan County (VT) youth who seek to preserve and work on the classic methods of horsemanship. In selecting a candidate for this scholarship, emphasis will be placed on helping a rider move from the lower levels of dressage (Training to Third Level) to Fourth Level and above. This scholarship may be used for instruction, travel, and living expenses, and instructional expenses among other things. Award requirements change regularly. For further information, please contact the address listed. No GPA requirement specified.

American Morgan Horse Institute, Inc.
Mrs. Sally Plumley, AMHI Scholarships
PO Box 837
Shelburne, VT 05482-0519

1144
Veda E. Jaqua Memorial Scholarship

AMOUNT: $500 DEADLINE: March 31
MAJOR: All Fields of Study

The Veda E. Jaqua Memorial Scholarship is open to Lenawee County (MI) graduates or graduating seniors. To qualify for the award, you must have received services for visual impairments through the Lenawee Intermediate School District. Award requirements change regularly. Please send a self-addressed, stamped envelope to receive your application and any further instructions from the scholarship provider. No GPA requirement specified.

Morenci High School
Attn: Mrs. Melissa Parnell
788 Coomer Street
Morenci, MI 49256

1145
Vercille Voss Student Scholarship

AMOUNT: $1500 DEADLINE: October 30
MAJOR: Textile Technology, Design, Furniture Design, Interior Decorating, Interior Design, and Related Areas of Study

Applicants for the Vercille Voss Student Scholarship must be enrolled as full-time students and be current IFDA student members (dues for the current membership period must be paid in full prior to submission of the scholarship application). A completed scholarship application must include: a certified transcript of all college level/advance study work which verifies full-time status and GPA; a 200-to-300-word essay describing why you joined the IFDA, your future plans and goals, and why you believe you are deserving of this award; a letter of recommendation from a professor or instructor. Award requirements change regularly. Please send a self-addressed, stamped envelope to receive your application and any further instructions from the scholarship provider; or email your request to info@ifda.com; or visit the website at www.ifda.com. No GPA requirement specified.

International Furnishings and Design Association
Attn: Educational Foundation Office
1200 19th Street NW, Suite 300
Washington, DC 20036-2422

1146
Vermont Incentive Grant

AMOUNT: $500-$6800 DEADLINE: Varies
MAJOR: All Areas of Study

The Vermont Incentive Grant is available to Vermont residents who are enrolled on a full-time basis who have not yet received a bachelor's degree. To be considered for the award, you must demonstrate financial need. You do not have to use this grant exclusively in the state of Vermont, but can be used at colleges throughout the country. The award also requires that you complete a "Financial Aid Packet for Vermont Students" form. Award requirements change regularly. To apply, you may receive your application from your respective postsecondary institution or from the Vermont Student Assistance Corporation. For further information, please visit the VSAC website at www.vsac.org. No GPA requirement specified.

Vermont Student Assistance Corporation
Attn: Scholarship Committee
Champlain Mill, PO Box 2000
Winooski, VT 05404-2601

1147
Vermont Part-Time Grant

AMOUNT: None Specified DEADLINE: Varies
MAJOR: All Areas of Study

The Vermont Part-Time Grant is available for Vermont residents who are enrolled on a part-time basis, taking fewer than 12 credit hours, who have not yet received a bachelor's degree. To be considered for this award, you must demonstrate financial need and be enrolled in a degree- or certificate-granting program. The amount of your award is dependent upon your number of credit hours. Award requirements change regularly. Applications for this grant are available at college financial aid offices or from the Vermont Student Assistance Corporation. You may also visit VSAC's website at www.vsac.org. No GPA requirement specified.

Vermont Student Assistance Corporation
Attn: Scholarship Committee
Champlain Mill, PO Box 2000
Winooski, VT 05404-2601

1148
Vernon Electric Cooperative Association Scholarship

AMOUNT: None Specified DEADLINE: February 1
MAJOR: Electrical

Awarded to Vernon County high school juniors or seniors with interest in electrical studies. Students must be members of Vernon County Electric Cooperative. Award requirements change regularly. Contact your guidance counselor for more information. No GPA requirement specified.

Vernon Electric Cooperative Association
110 North Main Street
Westby, WI 54667-1106

1149
Very Special Arts Wisconsin— Earl & Eugenia Quirk Scholarships

AMOUNT: $750 DEADLINE: April 1
MAJOR: Fine Art, Music, Dance, Drama, Visual Art, Creative Writing

Open to Wisconsin residents with disabilities who have been accepted to an accredited college or university of fine arts or a related arts-oriented program. Entering freshmen must have a minimum high school GPA of 2.5. Purpose is to provide programming in the arts, listed above, for disabled adults and children so they can serve as role models for others. Award requirements change regularly. Write to the address listed, enclosing a self-addressed, stamped envelope for an application and further information. You can browse their website: www.vsawis.org or email: vsawis@vsawis.org. GPA must be 2.5-4.0.

Very Special Arts Wisconsin
Program Coordinator
4785 Hayes Road
Madison, WI 53704-7364

1150
Veterans Dependents Educational Assistance Program

AMOUNT: Maximum: $7000 DEADLINE: Varies
MAJOR: All Areas of Study

Applicants must be surviving children or spouses of California veterans who are disabled through service-connected causes or died of service-related causes. The veteran must have served during a "qualifying war period." This fee waiver must be used at California State Universities, University of California Campuses, and California Community Colleges. Applicants may not be over 27 years of age (no age limit for unremarried surviving spouses), or currently in receipt of USDVA Chapter 35 benefits. Award requirements change regularly. No GPA requirement specified.

California Department of Veterans Affairs
Division of Veterans Services
1227 O Street #101
Sacramento, CA 95814-5840

1151
Vice Admiral E. P. Travers Scholarship

AMOUNT: Maximum: $2000 DEADLINE: March 1
MAJOR: All Areas of Study

The Vice Admiral E. P. Travers Scholarship and Loan Program is for undergraduate studies for children of active duty and retired Navy or Marine Corps service members. This award is based on need. You must be enrolled full-time and have a GPA of at least 2.0. The maximum scholarship amount is $2,000 per year and the maximum loan amount is $3,000 per year. Award requirements change regularly. There is one application for both the scholarship and the loan. GPA must be 2.0-4.0.

Navy-Marine Corps Relief Society
Education Programs
801 North Randolph Street, Suite 1228
Arlington, VA 22203-1977

1152
Vicki Carr Scholarship Fund for California Students

AMOUNT: None Specified DEADLINE: March 1
MAJOR: All Areas of Study

This scholarship is open to students who are California residents and are of Latino heritage. You must be a legal U.S. resident between the ages of 17 and 22 in order to apply. Award requirements change regularly. No GPA requirement specified.

Vikki Carr Scholarship Foundation
Scholarship Coordinator
P.O. Box 577560
Sherman Oaks, CA 91413

1153
Victor Sikevitz and the Janet and Samuel A. Goldsmith Scholarship Fund

AMOUNT: None Specified DEADLINE: March 1
MAJOR: Jewish Communal Service

The Victor Sikevitz and the Janet and Samuel A. Goldsmith Scholarship Fund is open to college students living in Cook County or the Chicago metropolitan area. To qualify for this award, you must have career goals in Jewish communal service. Award requirements change regularly. No GPA requirement specified.

Jewish Vocational Service
Attn: Scholarship Secretary
One South Franklin Street
Chicago, IL 60606-4694

1154
Virginia C. Lewis Scholarship Fund

AMOUNT: Maximum: $6000 DEADLINE: March 15
MAJOR: Art, Art History

The Virginia C. Lewis Scholarship Fund is open to art and art history undergraduates from Allegheny County (PA). Applicants must attend an accredited college or university. This award is based on academic merit, letters of commendation, and financial need. Award requirements change regularly. Please send a self-addressed, stamped envelope to receive your application and any further instructions from the scholarship provider. No GPA requirement specified.

Pittsburgh Foundation
Deborah Turner, Scholarship Coordinator
One PPG Place, FL 30
Pittsburgh, PA 15222

1155
Visiting Fellows Program

AMOUNT: None Specified DEADLINE: February 1
MAJOR: Women's Studies, Human Development, Psychology, Psychiatry, Anthropology, Political Science, Sociology, History

The Visting Fellows Program is open each year to six to eight scholars who wish to investigate some aspect of women and social change or the study of lives over time. The program offers office space and access to the facilities of Radcliffe College and Harvard University. Preference is given to researchers using the Murray Center's data resources. The Henry A. Murray Research Center is a national repository of social and behavioral sciences data for the study of lives over time with a special focus on the lives of American women. Award requirements change regularly. Please send a self-addressed, stamped envelope to receive your application and any further instructions from the Murray Center; or visit their website at www.radcliffe.edu/murray. No GPA requirement specified.

Radcliffe College - Henry A. Murray Research Center
Attn: Grants Program Coordinator
10 Garden Street
Cambridge, MA 02138

1156
Vivienne Camp Scholarship

AMOUNT: Maximum: $4350 DEADLINE: Varies
MAJOR: All Areas of Study

The Vivienne Camp Scholarship is awarded to two young
Jewish men and two young Jewish women for undergraduate
or vocational studies at a California institution. Applicants
must reside in Marin, San Francisco, San Mateo, northern
Santa Clara, or Sonoma counties in California. Students must
also demonstrate academic achievement and financial need.
Deadlines vary; therefore, it is encouraged that applicants
apply early. Award requirements change regularly. No GPA
requirement specified.

Jewish Family and Children's Services
Attn: Loans and Grants Department
2245 Post Street
San Francisco, CA 94115

1157
W. Allen Herzog Scholarship

AMOUNT: $2500 DEADLINE: May 26
MAJOR: Accounting, Finance

This scholarship is open to undergraduate Tau Kappa Epsilon
members who are full-time students pursuing a degree in
accounting or finance. In order to apply, you must have a minimum cumulative 2.75 GPA and a record of leadership within
your chapter and campus organizations. Preference will be
given to members of the Nu Chapter, with secondary consideration given to any member of TKE. Award requirements
change regularly. For further information, call (317) 872-6533,
email: tef@tkehq.org or visit the website at: www.tke.org.
GPA must be 2.8-4.0.

TKE Educational Foundation
Attn: Timothy L. Taschwer
8645 Founders Road
Indianapolis, IN 46268-1336

1158
Wal-Mart Associate Scholarships

AMOUNT: $1000 DEADLINE: March 1
MAJOR: All Areas of Study

These scholarships are open to high school seniors who work
for Wal-Mart. Also eligible under this program are children of
associates who are ineligible for the Walton Foundation
Scholarship for other reasons (e.g., for length of employment,
not working full-time, etc.). This is a one-time award. Award
requirements change regularly. Information is available from
the personnel manager at your local Wal-Mart in January. No
GPA requirement specified.

Wal-Mart Foundation
Attn: Scholarship Department
702 S.W. Eighth Street
Bentonville, AR 72716-8071

1159
Walt Bartram Memorial Education Award Fund (Region 12)

AMOUNT: Maximum: $1200 DEADLINE: February 1
MAJOR: Manufacturing Engineering

Open to graduating high school seniors who commit to enroll
in or who are full-time college or university students pursuing
a degree in manufacturing engineering or a closely related
field. Applicants must reside in Arizona, New Mexico, or
Southern California and have an overall GPA of 3.5 or higher.
All applicants must be SME members except for high school
seniors. Award requirements change regularly. For further
information, please contact Dora Murray at (313) 271-1500,
ext. 1709 (email: murrdor@sme.org) or Theresa Macias, ext.
1707 (email: maciter@sme.org). You may also go to the SME
website: www.sme.org. GPA must be 3.5-4.0.

Society of Manufacturing Engineering Education Foundation
PO Box 930
One SME Drive
Dearborn, MI 48121-0930

1160
Walter L. Kuebler American Legion Scholarship

AMOUNT: $500 DEADLINE: Varies
MAJOR: All Fields of Study

The Walter L. Kuebler American Legion Scholarship is open
to graduating seniors at Burlington High School (Burlington,
WI). Award requirements change regularly. Please visit your
guidance office to receive an application and any additional
details. No GPA requirement specified.

Burlington High School
Attn: Guidance Office
225 Robert Street
Burlington, WI 53105

1161
Walter Singer/BPIA District 9 Scholarship

AMOUNT: $2000 DEADLINE: March 15
MAJOR: All Fields of Study

The Walter Singer/BPIA District 9 Scholarship is open to
employees of Business Products Industry Association member
firms and their families. Persons holding academic records
sufficient for acceptance by accredited colleges, junior colleges or technical schools, or persons already enrolled in one
of those institutions are eligible for this one-year award.
Selection is made by a committee from the Student Financial
Aid Department of The George Washington University,
Washington, DC. Award requirements change regularly. Please
send a self-addressed, stamped envelope to receive your application and any further instructions from the scholarship
provider or email: info@bpia.org. No GPA
requirement specified.

Business Products Industry Association
Attn: Scholarship Committee
301 North Fairfax Street
Alexandria, VA 22314-2633

1162
Walton Foundation Scholarship

AMOUNT: $1500-$6000 DEADLINE: March 1
MAJOR: All Areas of Study

These scholarships are open to sons and daughters of Wal-Mart employees. In order to apply, you must be a high school senior at the time of application. Your parent or parents must work at least 28 hours per week for Wal-Mart and have worked for at least one year. This award is automatically renewable for four years and is based on ACT/SAT scores, counselor recommendations, grades, activities, and leadership qualities. Award requirements change regularly. Information is available from the personnel manager at your local Wal-Mart in January. No GPA requirement specified.

Wal-Mart Foundation
Attn: Scholarship Department
702 S.W. Eighth Street
Bentonville, AR 72716-8071

1163
Ward Bush Memorial Scholarship

AMOUNT: $1000 DEADLINE: March 31
MAJOR: All Fields of Study

The Ward Bush Memorial Scholarship is open to residents of Lenawee Intermediate School District. To be considered for the award, you must be a high school graduate or graduating senior who is pursuing a technology career at a postsecondary institution in the state of Michigan. Award requirements change regularly. Please send a self-addressed, stamped envelope to receive your application and any further instructions from the scholarship provider. No GPA requirement specified.

Morenci High School
Attn: Mrs. Melissa Parnell
788 Coomer Street
Morenci, MI 49256

1164
Warren Paul Poslusny Award for Outstanding Achievement

AMOUNT: $1000-$5000 DEADLINE: April 17
MAJOR: All Areas of Study

This award is open to any brother who is a junior, senior, or graduate student. This award has been established to recognize outstanding collegians who, by record of fraternity zeal and personal conduct, have exemplified an enthusiastic dedication to the highest ideals and values established by the founders of Sigma Alpha Epsilon. Award requirements change regularly. For further information, please write to the address listed, including a self-addressed, stamped envelope, call (847) 475-1856, ext. 223, fax (847) 475-2250, or email: rparker@sae.net. You may also visit their website: www.sae.net. GPA must be 3.0-4.0.

Sigma Alpha Epsilon Foundation
SAE Awards Committee
PO Box 1856
Evanston, IL 60204-1856

1165
Washington County Visiting Nurses' Association Fund

AMOUNT: None Specified DEADLINE: June 14
MAJOR: Nursing

This award is granted to nursing students in the second and subsequent years of nursing study. Prior scholarship recipients are eligible to reapply. All applicants must have been residents of Washington County for at least two years immediately prior to the date of application. Awards are limited to Washington County residents, but there is no limitation as to the geographic location of the school. Award requirements change regularly. Please send a self-addressed, stamped envelope to the address provided or call (724) 222-6330 to receive an application. No GPA requirement specified.

Washington County Community Foundation
Visiting Nurses' Assn Fund Scholarship
77 South Main Street
Washington, PA 15301

1166
Washington Crossing Foundation Scholarship

AMOUNT: $5000-$10000 DEADLINE: January 1
MAJOR: Government Service

Competition is open to all high school seniors who are U.S. citizens and who are planning careers in government service. Interested students are invited to write a one-page essay stating why he or she plans a career in government service including any inspiration to be derived from the leadership of George Washington in his famous crossing of the Delaware. Students must confine the essay to view points, attitudes, and purpose in choice of careers. Award requirements change regularly. For an application and further information, please write to the address listed, including a self-addressed, stamped envelope. GPA must be 2.8-4.0.

Washington Crossing Foundation
Attn: Scholarship Administrator
PO Box 503
Levittown, PA 19058-0503

1167
Washington Printing Guild Scholarship

AMOUNT: $600-$1000 DEADLINE: February 28
MAJOR: Graphic Arts Education

Open to students accepted into a graphic arts education program who are residents of the District of Columbia, Maryland, or Virginia. Must be U.S. citizens, have a minimum GPA of 2.5, and be nominated by a supervisor, counselor, or printing and Graphic Communications Association member employer. Based on financial need and references. Award requirements change regularly. Contact the address listed for more information or call (202) 682-3001. GPA must be 2.5-4.0.

American Association for the Advancement of Science
Fellowship Program
1333 H Street NW
Washington, DC 20005-4707

1168
Wayne Kay Co-Op Scholarship Award

AMOUNT: $2500 DEADLINE: February 1
MAJOR: Manufacturing Engineering, Manufacturing Engineering Technology

Open to full-time undergraduates enrolled in a manufacturing engineering or manufacturing engineering technology co-op program. Applicants must have completed at least 30 college credit hours and have an overall GPA of 3.5 or higher. Award requirements change regularly. For further information, please contact Dora Murray at (313) 271-1500, ext. 1709 (email: murrdor@sme.org) or Theresa Macias, ext. 1707 (email: maciter@sme.org). You may also go to the SME website: www.sme.org. GPA must be 3.5-4.0.

Society of Manufacturing Engineering Education Foundation
PO Box 930
One SME Drive
Dearborn, MI 48121-0930

1169
Wayne Kay Scholarship Fund

AMOUNT: $2500 DEADLINE: February 1
MAJOR: Manufacturing Engineering, Manufacturing Engineering Technology

Open to full-time undergraduates enrolled in a degree program in manufacturing engineering or technology. Applicants must have completed at least 30 college credit hours and have an overall GPA of 3.5 or higher. Award requirements change regularly. For further information, please contact Dora Murray at (313) 271-1500, ext. 1709 (email: murrdor@sme.org) or Theresa Macias, ext. 1707 (email: maciter@sme.org). You may also go to the SME website: www.sme.org. GPA must be 3.5-4.0.

Society of Manufacturing Engineering Education Foundation
PO Box 930
One SME Drive
Dearborn, MI 48121-0930

1170
Webster's New World Writing Contest

AMOUNT: $1000 DEADLINE: April 15
MAJOR: All Areas of Study

The Webster's New World Writing Contest is open to high school juniors or seniors. In order to apply, you must submit an essay of no more than 500 words, typed and double-spaced, on the following essay question: "The rise of the Internet, global commerce, and increased world travel have made international communication more important than ever. Does it follow that the world would benefit from the establishment of a single international language?" Essays must be written in English and be an original, unpublished work of the submitter. Winners of the contest will receive a $1,000 scholarship to the accredited college or school of your choice. Award requirements change regularly. No GPA requirement specified.

Webster's New World Dictionaries c/o IDG Worldwide Consumer Reference
Attn: Marketing Manager
1633 Broadway, FL 6
New York, NY 10019-6708

1171
Welsh Heritage Scholarships

AMOUNT: $1000 DEADLINE: March 1
MAJOR: All Areas of Study

The Welsh Heritage Scholarship is open to undergraduates who are of Welsh descent. Applicants must be residents of Philadelphia, PA and planning to attend any two-year or four-year institution within a 150 mile radius of Philadelphia. The selection criteria is based on ACT/SAT scores, potential, goals, extracurricular activities, recommendations, and membership in Welsh organizations. Award requirements change regularly. Write to the address listed, enclosing a self-addressed, stamped envelope for an application and further information or call (610) 527-1832. No GPA requirement specified.

Welsh Society of Philadelphia
Attn: Chairman, Scholarship Committee
PO Box 7287
Saint Davids, PA 19087-7287

1172
Wendy's High School Heisman Award

AMOUNT: None Specified DEADLINE: Varies
MAJOR: All Areas of Study

This award recognizes scholarship, citizenship, and athletic ability of students. Schools in each state and the District of Columbia may nominate two juniors-one male, one female. One-thousand twenty state finalists and 102 state winners are recognized by Wendy's International. Twelve national finalists receive a trip to New York City in December to attend Wendy's High School Heisman National Award Winners. Award requirements change regularly. Students and/or parents should inquire with the guidance office or principal for more information. Do NOT write address listed below. GPA must be 3.3-4.0.

National Association of Secondary School Principals
1900 Association Drive
Reston, VA 20191-1599

1173
West Denver Chapter of Trout Unlimited Scholarship

AMOUNT: $2000 DEADLINE: December 17
MAJOR: Fishery Biology, Fishery Management

This award will be presented to an outstanding student who has demonstrated academic excellence, highest scholarship, and potential for professional leadership in the coldwater conservation field. The award will be granted to a M.S. or Ph.D. candidate who is conducting a scholarly research project at a NCA-CIHE-accredited institution in the state of Colorado. Applicant must be currently enrolled or have been selected to matriculate as a full-time graduate student (nine semester hours) in life sciences studying fisheries, biology, fisheries management, water quality related to coldwater fisheries or conservation, with emphasis on salmonid species and their ecosystems. Award requirements change regularly. For additional information you may visit the website or email db.wdtu@mho.net. GPA must be 2.9-4.0.

West Denver Chapter of Trout Unlimited
Delwin R. Befus, Chairman
2625 South Raleigh Street
Denver, CO 80219-5727

1174
West Virginia Sheriffs Association Scholarship

AMOUNT: $1000 DEADLINE: June 12
MAJOR: Criminal Justice

Scholarship offered to West Virginia residents studying criminal justice at a college or university in West Virginia. Minimum residency requirement is one year in West Virginia. Must have at least one semester of college credit and currently enrolled. Requires an official transcript and two typed letters of recommendation from educators, employers, or community members. Award requirements change regularly. West Virginia Sheriff's Association, Scholarship Award Program, P.O. Box 3031, Charleston, WV 25331-3031 or call (304) 345-2232. No GPA requirement specified.

West Virginia Sheriff's Association
Leola R. Bateman Scholarship Coordinator
1116 Smith Street, Suite 313
Charleston, WV 25301-1314

1175
Westinghouse/Bertha Lamme Scholarship

AMOUNT: $1000 DEADLINE: May 15
MAJOR: Engineering

This scholarship is open to incoming female freshmen who are majoring in engineering and have been accepted into an ABET-accredited program or an SWE-approved school. You must be a U.S. citizen. Award requirements change regularly. Please send a self-addressed, stamped envelope to receive your application. For any further instructions from the scholarship provider, please browse their website at www.swe.org or email hq@swe.org. No GPA requirement specified.

Society of Women Engineers Headquarters
Scholarship Coordinator
120 Wall Street, FL 11
New York, NY 10005-3902

1176
Wexford County Farm Bureau Scholarship Fund

AMOUNT: None Specified DEADLINE: August 1
MAJOR: Agriculture, Agribusiness

Open to students (preferably juniors and seniors in four-year programs or seniors in two-year programs) attending college in the state of Michigan who are residents of Wexford County. Preference is given to students pursuing a degree in agriculture or agribusiness. Scholarships are to be used for tuition and books. Award requirements change regularly. Please send

a self-addressed, stamped envelope to receive your application and any further instructions from the scholarship provider. No GPA requirement specified.

Wexford County Farm Bureau
Scholarship Committee
929 N. Mitchell Street
Cadillac, MI 49601

1177
Wheatland Scholarships

AMOUNT: $1000 DEADLINE: June 1
MAJOR: Agriculture

Open to high school seniors in the Wheatland area (DuPage, Lisle, Naperville, Oswego, Plainfield, and Wheatland) or to a descendent of a family from the Wheatland or surrounding area. Applicants are required to prepare a research paper on an historical event or time in the Wheatland area to be submitted with the application form. Information and applications available at the high schools in the area. Award requirements change regularly. Contact your high school guidance office for information and applications or the address below. Please send a self-addressed, stamped envelope to receive a reply. No GPA requirement specified.

Wheatland Plowing Match Association
Scholarship Coordinator
PO Box 92
Plainfield, IL 60544-0092

1178
Wheatland Township Scholarship

AMOUNT: $1000 DEADLINE: May 1
MAJOR: All Areas of Study

Open to high school seniors who have been residents of Wheatland Township, Will County, for at least one year. Applicants must have a minimum GPA of 3.0 and demonstrate school activities which may include local government and community services. A 500-word essay on "The Importance of State Government" will also be required. Award requirements change regularly. Contact your high school administrator or the address listed for further information, enclosing a self-addressed, stamped envelope. GPA must be 3.0-4.0.

Wheatland Township Republican Organization
Donald Raue, Treasurer
28 West 118 Plainview Drive
Naperville, IL 60544-0092

1179
Wilbur C. Sensing, Jr. Scholarships

AMOUNT: $500-$2500 DEADLINE: April 1
MAJOR: Social Sciences

Open to students whose parents are employees of Enco Materials, Inc. and who are attending accredited universities, colleges, or junior colleges. Parents cannot be officers of the company. Selection is based on academic attitude, extracurricular activities, financial need, and civic and church participation. Award requirements change regularly. You may also call (615) 321-4939 for further information. GPA must be 2.0-4.0.

Community Foundation of Middle Tennessee
Scholarship Committee
210 23rd Avenue North
Nashville, TN 37203-1502

1180
William "Cal" Poppink Memorial Scholarship

AMOUNT: $1000 DEADLINE: March 31
MAJOR: All Fields of Study

The William "Cal" Poppink Memorial Scholarship is open to
Tecumseh High School graduating seniors. To qualify for the
award, you must have been accepted to a Michigan college.
Award requirements change regularly. Please send a self-
addressed, stamped envelope to receive your application and
any further instructions from the scholarship provider. No
GPA requirement specified.

Morenci High School
Attn: Mrs. Melissa Parnell
788 Coomer Street
Morenci, MI 49256

1181
William (Billbo) Boston Scholarship

AMOUNT: None Specified DEADLINE: Varies
MAJOR: Computer Science

Open to students who are Wood County residents pursuing
undergraduate degrees in computer science at an accredited
postsecondary school in West Virginia or Ohio. Recipients
will be selected on the basis of financial need, class rank,
school activities, and achievement. Applicants must have a
minimum 3.0 GPA. Award requirements change regularly.
Please send a self-addressed, stamped envelope to receive
your application and any further instructions from the scholarship provider or visit their website: www.citynet.net/person-
al/billbos. GPA must be 3.0-4.0.

Parkersburg Area Community Foundation
Scholarship Program
PO Box 1762
Parkersburg, WV 26102-1762

1182
William and Clara Bryan Scholarships

AMOUNT: $500-$2500 DEADLINE: April 1
MAJOR: All Areas of Study

Open to high school seniors, college freshmen, sophomores,
and juniors attending four-year colleges and universities who
are residents of Giles County (TN). Applicants must have
lived in Giles County (TN) for a majority of their precollege
schooling. Award requirements change regularly. You may
also call (615) 321-4939 for further information. GPA must be
2.0-4.0.

Community Foundation of Middle Tennessee
Scholarship Committee
210 23rd Avenue North
Nashville, TN 37203-1502

1183
William C. Foster Fellows Visiting Scholars Program

AMOUNT: None Specified DEADLINE: March 31
MAJOR: Fields Related to the Negotiation, Implementation,
and Verification of Arms Control; Nonproliferation, and
Disarmament Policies; Treaties, and Agreements; and
Political-Military Affairs

The William C. Foster Fellows Visiting Scholars Program
seeks visiting scholars from a number of academic fields
including biochemistry, biology, chemistry, economics, engineering, geology, history, mathematics, operations research,
physics, political science, sociology, statistics, and strategic
studies. This federal program allows college and university
faculty to spend a year actively participating in the negotiation
and implementation of arms control, nonproliferation, and disarmament treaties and agreements. U.S. citizenship is
required. Fellows will be offered a full salary and benefits
package as well as a daily stipend during their assignment.
Award requirements change regularly. No GPA
requirement specified.

U.S. Department of State, Bureau of Arms Control
Attn: Scholarship Committee
2201 C Street NW, Room 5643
Washington, DC 20520

1184
William C. Stokoe Scholarship

AMOUNT: $2000 DEADLINE: March 15
MAJOR: Deaf Education, Sign Language

The William C. Stokoe Scholarship is awarded to deaf students who have graduated from a four-year college program
and are pursuing part-time or full-time graduate studies in a
field related to sign language, or the deaf community, or deaf
graduate students who are developing a special project as one
of these topics. Award requirements change regularly. For an
application and further information, please send a self-
addressed, stamped #10 envelope to the address listed or call
(301) 587-1789 (TTY), (301) 587-1788 (Voice). No GPA
requirement specified.

National Association of the Deaf
Stokoe Scholarship Secretary
814 Thayer Avenue
Silver Spring, MD 20910-4500

1185
William E. Weisel Scholarship

AMOUNT: $1000 DEADLINE: February 1
MAJOR: Manufacturing Engineering, Technology

Open to full-time undergraduates enrolled in a manufacturing
engineering or technology program and are seeking a career in
robotics or automated systems used in manufacturing or robotics for use in the medical field. Applicants must have completed at least 30 credit hours and have an overall GPA of 3.5 or
higher. Award requirements change regularly. For further
information, please contact Dora Murray at (313) 271-1500,
ext. 1709 (email: murrdor@sme.org) or Theresa Macias, ext.
1707 (email: maciter@sme.org). You may also go to the SME
website: www.sme.org. GPA must be 3.5-4.0.

Society of Manufacturing Engineering Education Foundation
PO Box 930
One SME Drive
Dearborn, MI 48121-0930

1186
William F. Miller, M.D. Postgraduate Award

AMOUNT: $1500 DEADLINE: June 30
MAJOR: Respiratory Therapy

This award is open to respiratory care therapists who have already earned a bachelor's degree with a minimum 3.0 GPA. In order to apply, you must provide proof of acceptance into an advanced degree program at a fully accredited school. The award recipient will be selected by September 1. The award also includes airfare, one night lodging, and registration to attend the AARC Respiratory International Congress. Award requirements change regularly. GPA must be 3.0.

American Respiratory Care Foundation
Education Recognition Award
11030 Ables Lane
Dallas, TX 75229-4524

1187
William G. Corey Memorial Scholarship

AMOUNT: $1500 DEADLINE: March 1
MAJOR: All Areas of Study

These scholarships are awarded to the top applicants from Pennsylvania. Applicants must be legally blind. Award requirements change regularly. Write to the address listed, enclosing a self-addressed envelope for an application and further information. No GPA requirement specified.

American Council of the Blind
Attn: Billie Jean Keith
1155 15th Street NW, Suite 720
Washington, DC 20005-2706

1188
William Heath Educational Fund for Ministers, Priests, Missionaries

AMOUNT: $750-$1000 DEADLINE: June 30
MAJOR: Religion, Theology, Social Work

This scholarship is open to high school graduates in the southeastern U.S. who are studying ministry, missionary, or social work. In order to qualify, you must be 35 years of age or less. The application is based on character, academic ability, and financial need. Award requirements change regularly. Please write to the address listed, enclosing a self-addressed, stamped envelope for an application and further information. No GPA requirement specified.

First Florida Bank
William Heath Educational Fund
PO Box 40200
Jacksonville, FL 32203-0200

1189
William J. and Marijane E. Adams, Jr. Scholarship

AMOUNT: $1000 DEADLINE: April 15
MAJOR: Agricultural Engineering, Biological Engineering

This scholarship is open to sophomores, juniors, and seniors with a minimum 2.5 GPA. You must be a student member of ASAE, and the curriculum must be accredited by ABET or CEAB. Financial need will be taken into consideration. Award requirements change regularly. GPA must be 2.5-4.0.

American Society of Agricultural Engineers
Attn: ASAE Foundation
2950 Niles Road
St. Joseph, MI 49085-9659

1190
William J. Locklin Scholarship

AMOUNT: $1000 DEADLINE: March 31
MAJOR: Landscape Architecture/Design

The William J. Locklin Scholarship was established to stress the importance of 24-hour lighting in landscape designs. It is open to you if you are pursuing a program in lighting design or landscape architecture focusing on lighting design in studio projects. Award requirements change regularly. No GPA requirement specified.

Landscape Architecture Foundation
Scholarship Program
636 'I' Street NW
Washington, DC 20001-3736

1191
William Tasse Alexander Scholarship

AMOUNT: Maximum: $3500 DEADLINE: March 1
MAJOR: Teaching/Education

Scholarships for residents of Mecklenberg County, North Carolina, who plan to pursue teaching as a career. Applicants must be junior and senior undergraduates and have a minimum 3.0 GPA. Award requirements change regularly. Write to the address listed for details, enclosing a self-addressed, stamped envelope. GPA must be 3.0-4.0.

Foundation for the Carolinas
Scholarship Program
PO Box 34769
Charlotte, NC 28234-4769

1192
William V. Muse Scholarship

AMOUNT: $450 DEADLINE: Varies
MAJOR: All Areas of Study

The William V. Muse Scholarship is open to undergraduate members of Tau Kappa Epsilon. In order to apply, you must have a minimum cumulative 3.0 GPA and have completed at least 30 semester hours of course work. You will need to demonstrate a record of leadership within your chapter. Preference will be given to members of Epsilon-Upsilon Chapter after which the award will be open to any member of

TKE. Award requirements change regularly. GPA must be 3.0-4.0.

TKE Educational Foundation
Attn: Timothy L. Taschwer
8645 Founders Road
Indianapolis, IN 46268-1336

1193
William W. Burgin, Jr., M.D. Scholarship

AMOUNT: $2500 DEADLINE: June 30
MAJOR: Respiratory Therapy

This award is open to a second year student in an accredited respiratory therapy program leading to an Associate's Degree. You must have a GPA of at least 3.0. This award is also based on recommendations and an essay. Please provide a copy of your birth certificate, social security card, immigration visa, or other evidence of citizenship. This award also includes registration for the AARC Respiratory International Congress, travel, one night lodging, as well as a certificate of recognition. Award requirements change regularly. GPA must be 3.0-4.0.

American Respiratory Care Foundation
Education Recognition Award
11030 Ables Lane
Dallas, TX 75229-4524

1194
William Wilson Memorial and Wallace G. McCauley Memorial Scholarships

AMOUNT: $850-$900 DEADLINE: May 26
MAJOR: All Areas of Study

This scholarship is open to initiated members of Tau Kappa Epsilon who are full-time juniors or seniors. In order to apply, you should demonstrate exceptional understanding of the importance of good alumni relations to the chapter and its members. This includes excelling in the development, promotion, and execution of effective programs which have increased alumni contact, awareness, and participation in fraternity activities. Award requirements change regularly. For further information, call (317) 872-6533, email: tef@tkehq.org or visit the website at: www.tke.org. No GPA requirement specified.

TKE Educational Foundation
Attn: Timothy L. Taschwer
8645 Founders Road
Indianapolis, IN 46268-1336

1195
William Wilson Memorial Scholarship

AMOUNT: None Specified DEADLINE: Varies
MAJOR: All Fields of Study

The William Wilson Memorial Scholarship is open to graduating seniors at Burlington High School (Burlington, WI). The scholarship will be awarded on the basis of student improvement. Award requirements change regularly. Please visit your Guidance Office to receive an application and any additional details. No GPA requirement specified.

Burlington High School
Attn: Guidance Office
225 Robert Street
Burlington, WI 53105

1196
Wisconsin Higher Education Grant (WHEG)

AMOUNT: $250-$1800 DEADLINE: Varies
MAJOR: All Areas of Study

The Wisconsin Higher Education Grant (WHEG) provides assistance to undergraduate Wisconsin residents enrolled at least half-time in degree or certificate programs at the University of Wisconsin and Wisconsin Technical College institutions. To be considered for this award, you must demonstrate financial need. Your eligibility cannot exceed ten semesters. Award requirements change regularly. To apply, you must submit the FAFSA. For more information, you may visit the Wisconsin Higher Education Aids Board at www.heab.state.wi.us. No GPA requirement specified.

State of Wisconsin Higher Educational Aids Board
Attn: State Grant Coordinator
PO Box 7885
Madison, WI 53707-7885

1197
Women's Opportunity Award

AMOUNT: $300 DEADLINE: December 15
MAJOR: All Fields of Study

The Women's Opportunity Award is open to women from Des Moines, IA, and surrounding communities who are completing undergraduate degree programs or entering vocational or technical training programs. Applicants must be heads of households and indicate that further training is essential for entry or reentry into the labor market. Financial need is also a consideration. Applicants must complete an application form and submit two letters of recommendation. The local winner is submitted for regional competition for awards ranging from $3000 - $5000. Award requirements change regularly. Please send a self-addressed, stamped envelope to receive your application and any further instructions from the scholarship provider; or call (515) 278-1302. No GPA requirement specified.

Soroptimist International of Des Moines, Iowa
Attn: Scholarship Committee
4111 Aurora Avenue
Des Moines, IA 50310

1198
Wyoming Trucking Association Scholarship

AMOUNT: None Specified DEADLINE: March 3
MAJOR: Business Management, Sales Management, Computer Skills, Accounting, Office Procedures and Management, Safety, Diesel Mechanics, Truck Driving

Open to graduates of Wyoming high schools who plan to pursue a course of study which could lead to a career in the highway transportation industry. Applicants must attend a Wyoming University, Community College, or trade school approved by the WTA Scholarship Committee. Award requirements change regularly. For further information and an application, please write to the address listed, including a self-addressed, stamped envelope or call (307) 234-1579. No GPA requirement specified.

Wyoming Trucking Association
WTA Scholarship Program
PO Box 1909
Casper, WY 82602-1909

1199
Xerox Technical Minority Scholarship

AMOUNT: $4000-$5000 DEADLINE: September 15
MAJOR: Chemistry, Engineering, Physics, Material Science, Information Management

This scholarship is open to minority undergraduate or graduate students pursuing degrees in one of the following fields: chemistry, engineering, physics, material science, and information management. In order to apply, you must be a high academic achiever and of African American, Asian, Pacific Island, American Indian, Native Alaskan, or Hispanic descent. You must also be a U.S. citizen or be a visa-holding permanent resident. Award requirements change regularly. No GPA requirement specified.

Xerox Technical Minority Scholarship Program
907 Culver Road
Rochester, NY 14609-9720

1200
Young Cancer Survivor Scholarship Program

AMOUNT: $1000-$5000 DEADLINE: April 10
MAJOR: All Fields of Study

The Young Cancer Survivor Scholarship Program is open to California residents who are college bound or college-enrolled students and are also survivors of pediatric cancer. You must be under age 21 at the time you apply. If you are going to be attending college or are currently enrolled, it must be at an institution in California in order for you to be eligible. You will also need to demonstrate financial need. Two short essays and three letters of recommendation must be submitted with your application. Award requirements change regularly. GPA must be 2.5-4.0.

American Cancer Society, California Division
Research Fellowship Program
PO Box 2061
Oakland, CA 94604-2061

1201
Youth Automobile Safety Essay Competition

AMOUNT: $500 DEADLINE: March 31
MAJOR: All Areas of Study

This essay contest is open to California residents who are attending their senior year of high school in California. To apply, you must have a minimum 3.0 GPA, be accepted to an accredited two- or four-year college, university, or trade school in the U.S and intending to enroll as a full-time freshman by Fall 2000. Your parents or legal guardians must be

currently employed full-time by a government entity. If your parent or guardian is retired or deceased, they must have been employed full-time by a government entity. Selection will be based on an essay discussing ways in which the teen-age automobile accident rate can be reduced. Award requirements change regularly. GPA must be 3.0-4.0.

Civil Service Employees Insurance Company
Scholarship Contest
PO Box 7764
San Francisco, CA 94120-7764

1202
You've Got A Friend In Pennsylvania Scholarship

AMOUNT: $1000 DEADLINE: February 1
MAJOR: All Areas of Study

This scholarship is available to students with a minimum general class amateur radio license who are residents of Pennsylvania. Applicants must be members of ARRL. Award requirements change regularly. Write the address provided, using a self-addressed, stamped envelope. No GPA requirement specified.

American Radio Relay League
Attn: ARRL Foundation
225 Main Street
Newington, CT 06111-1400

1203
Zonta Club of Ashtabula County Scholarship

AMOUNT: None Specified DEADLINE: November 29
MAJOR: All Areas of Study

The Zonta Club of Ashtabula County Scholarship is open to female residents of Ashtabula County (OH) who have completed the first full year of college or a semester of nondegree training program. Applicants' parents or guardians must reside in Ashtabula County. Adult scholarships are offered also for technical school training of various lengths to women residing in Ashtabula County. Award requirements change regularly. Please send a self-addressed, stamped envelope to receive your application and any further instructions from the scholarship provider. No GPA requirement specified.

Zonta Club of Ashtabula County
c/o Elinor Sutton, Chairwoman
4257 Orchard Drive
Ashtabula, OH 44004

1204
Zonta International of Lenawee County

AMOUNT: $500-$1000 DEADLINE: March 31
MAJOR: All Fields of Study

The Zonta International of Lenawee County is open to female graduating seniors from an alternative education program. The Lenawee County (MI) chapter will award one $1,000 or two $500 scholarships. Your counselor's office has a Zonta Scholarship brochure if you have other questions. Award requirements change regularly. Please send a self-addressed, stamped envelope to receive your application and any further instructions from the scholarship provider. No GPA requirement specified.

Morenci High School
Attn: Mrs. Melissa Parnell
788 Coomer Street
Morenci, MI 49256

School Specific Awards

Adams State College

1205
Activity Grants

AMOUNT: None Specified DEADLINE: March 15
MAJOR: All Areas of Study

This scholarship is open to freshmen or continuing students at Adams State who demonstrate special skills or talents in activity areas that support or promote Adams State College. You must have a minimum 2.5 GPA. Activity grants are available in music, speech, theater, and art. Award requirements change regularly. For further information, please contact the Adams State Financial Aid Office. GPA must be 2.5-4.0.

Adams State College
Financial Aid Office
Alamosa, CO 81102

1206
Adams Scholarship

AMOUNT: $400-$1000 DEADLINE: March 15
MAJOR: All Areas of Study

This scholarship is open to both entering and continuing students at Adams State who have a 3.2 or better cumulative GPA. You must have a minimum 19 ACT or minimum 870 SAT (for freshmen only). Selection will be based on GPA, and you may reapply each year. Award requirements change regularly. GPA must be 3.2-4.0.

Adams State College
Financial Aid Office
Alamosa, CO 81102

1207
National Scholarships

AMOUNT: $2600-$2900 DEADLINE: March 15
MAJOR: All Areas of Study

This scholarship is open to non-resident undergraduates and transfer students at Adams State. In order to apply, you must have graduated in the upper one-third of your high school class or have a minimum 21 ACT or minimum 970 SAT. Selection is based on class rank or ACT/SAT score. To receive the award, you must reside in campus housing. The award may be renewed if you maintain a minimum 2.5 GPA and reside in campus housing. Award requirements change regularly. For further information, please send a self-addressed, stamped envelope to the address below. GPA must be 2.5-4.0.

Adams State College
Financial Aid Office
Alamosa, CO 81102

1208
President's Scholarships

AMOUNT: $1600-$2236 DEADLINE: March 15
MAJOR: All Areas of Study

This scholarship is open to incoming freshmen at Adams State who have a minimum 3.2 GPA, minimum 21 ACT or 970 SAT. Resident students who achieve a 3.4 GPA or higher will have the scholarship renewed. This scholarship is not renewable for non-resident students. Award requirements change regularly. For further information, please contact the Office of Financial Aid. GPA must be 3.2-4.0.

Adams State College
Financial Aid Office
Alamosa, CO 81102

Alaska Pacific University

1209
Alaska Leadership Scholarship

AMOUNT: Maximum: $1000 DEADLINE: Varies
MAJOR: All Areas of Study

This scholarship is open to high school graduates who demonstrate exemplary leadership abilities. Financial need is considered when you apply. Award requirements change regularly. No GPA requirement specified.

Alaska Pacific University
Office of Financial Aid
4101 University Drive
Anchorage, AK 99508-4672

1210
Alaska Pacific University Foreign Student Scholarship

AMOUNT: None Specified DEADLINE: Varies
MAJOR: All Areas of Study

If you are an international student alumnus of APU and are pursuing your graduate studies at APU, this may be the scholarship for you. Award requirements change regularly. No GPA requirement specified.

Alaska Pacific University
Office of Financial Aid
4101 University Drive
Anchorage, AK 99508-4672

1211
Anchorage Amateur Radio Club Scholars

AMOUNT: None Specified DEADLINE: Varies
MAJOR: All Areas of Study

This award is open to sophomores, juniors, and seniors with a GPA of at least 3.0 who are attending APU. Award requirements change regularly. GPA must be 3.0-4.0.

Alaska Pacific University
Office of Financial Aid
4101 University Drive
Anchorage, AK 99508-4672

1212
Colonel Dave and Selma Harbour Career Faith Endowed Scholarship

AMOUNT: None Specified DEADLINE: Varies
MAJOR: Religion

This scholarship is awarded to an undergraduate or graduate student with strong religious interests. Award requirements change regularly. No GPA requirement specified.

Alaska Pacific University
Office of Financial Aid
4101 University Drive
Anchorage, AK 99508-4672

1213
Distinguished Scholarship

AMOUNT: None Specified DEADLINE: Varies
MAJOR: All Areas of Study

This award is open to incoming freshmen who demonstrate exceptionally high levels of academic achievement and who are competitive. This award is based on a combination of merit and financial need and is renewable with a minimum GPA of 3.5. Award requirements change regularly. GPA must be 3.5-4.0.

Alaska Pacific University
Office of Financial Aid
4101 University Drive
Anchorage, AK 99508-4672

1214
Elizabeth (Jane) Hartman Endowed Memorial Scholarship

AMOUNT: None Specified DEADLINE: Varies
MAJOR: Literature, Creative Writing

If you are a student with a strong interest in literature and creative writing, then this scholarship may be for you. Financial need is considered when you apply. Award requirements change regularly. No GPA requirement specified.

Alaska Pacific University
Office of Financial Aid
4101 University Drive
Anchorage, AK 99508-4672

1215
F. Thomas and Gania Trotter Scholarship

AMOUNT: None Specified DEADLINE: Varies
MAJOR: All Areas of Study

This scholarship is open to full-time juniors and seniors who have completed at least two enrollment periods at APU. To apply, you must have a minimum GPA of 3.5 and not be older than 25 years old. Financial need is considered at the time of your application. Award requirements change regularly. GPA must be 3.5-4.0.

Alaska Pacific University
Office of Financial Aid
4101 University Drive
Anchorage, AK 99508-4672

1216
Hotel and Tourism Management Scholarship

AMOUNT: None Specified DEADLINE: Varies
MAJOR: Hotel/Tourism Management

This scholarship is open to students studying Hotel and Tourism Management. Merit and need is considered when you apply. Award requirements change regularly. No GPA requirement specified.

Alaska Pacific University
Office of Financial Aid
4101 University Drive
Anchorage, AK 99508-4672

1217
International Student Scholarship

AMOUNT: None Specified DEADLINE: Varies
MAJOR: All Areas of Study

This scholarship is open to undergraduate international students who demonstrate high levels of academic achievement. Financial need is considered when you apply. If you are a resident non-U.S. citizen, you are not eligible for this award. Award requirements change regularly. No GPA requirement specified.

Alaska Pacific University
Office of Financial Aid
4101 University Drive
Anchorage, AK 99508-4672

1218
Kathryn C. & Newton F. Young Scholarship

AMOUNT: None Specified DEADLINE: Varies
MAJOR: All Areas of Study

This scholarship is open to undergraduate and graduate students. Financial need is a consideration when you apply. Award requirements change regularly. No GPA requirement specified.

Alaska Pacific University
Office of Financial Aid
4101 University Drive
Anchorage, AK 99508-4672

1219
Marion Richter Nordic Ski Scholarship

AMOUNT: None Specified DEADLINE: Varies
MAJOR: All Areas of Study

This scholarship is awarded to a female undergraduate student with an interest in competitive Nordic skiing. Award requirements change regularly. This award is provided by Jim Galanis, Ski Coach. For additional information on this award, please contact him at (907) 564-8328 or email him at, apu_xc@alaskapacific.edu. No GPA requirement specified.

Alaska Pacific University
Office of Financial Aid
4101 University Drive
Anchorage, AK 99508-4672

1220
National Bank of Alaska Scholarship

AMOUNT: None Specified DEADLINE: Varies
MAJOR: Business

This scholarship is open to undergraduate and graduate students pursuing a career in Business. Award requirements change regularly. No GPA requirement specified.

Alaska Pacific University
Office of Financial Aid
4101 University Drive
Anchorage, AK 99508-4672

1221
President's Forum Scholarship

AMOUNT: None Specified DEADLINE: Varies
MAJOR: All Areas of Study

This scholarship is awarded to students who have completed at least one year of study at APU. You must have a minimum 2.5 GPA and submit a separate application with an essay. This is both a need-based and merit-based award. Award requirements change regularly. GPA must be 2.5-4.0.

Alaska Pacific University
Office of Financial Aid
4101 University Drive
Anchorage, AK 99508-4672

1222
Student Leadership Scholarship

AMOUNT: None Specified DEADLINE: Varies
MAJOR: All Areas of Study

This award is open to students at Alaska Pacific University who attain exemplary leadership positions. This is a renewable award with continued leadership participation. Award requirements change regularly. No GPA requirement specified.

Alaska Pacific University
Office of Financial Aid
4101 University Drive
Anchorage, AK 99508-4672

1223
Texaco Native Teachers Scholarship

AMOUNT: None Specified DEADLINE: Varies
MAJOR: Education

This scholarship is awarded to an Alaska Native American who is majoring in Education with the intent to become a teacher. Award requirements change regularly. No GPA requirement specified.

Alaska Pacific University
Office of Financial Aid
4101 University Drive
Anchorage, AK 99508-4672

1224
Trustees Scholarship

AMOUNT: None Specified DEADLINE: Varies
MAJOR: All Areas of Study

This award is open to continuing students or transfer students who have completed at least 32 earned Alaska Pacific semester hours, who demonstrate high levels of academic achievement, and who are competitive. Financial need is considered when you apply for this scholarship. This is a renewable award with demonstrated strong academic performance. Award requirements change regularly. No GPA requirement specified.

Alaska Pacific University
Office of Financial Aid
4101 University Drive
Anchorage, AK 99508-4672

1225
University Education Grant

AMOUNT: Maximum: $1500 DEADLINE: Varies
MAJOR: All Areas of Study

If you are an enrolled student in good standing and demonstrate financial need, you can apply for this tuition remission award. This is a renewable award as long as you demonstrate continued financial need. Award requirements change regularly. No GPA requirement specified.

Alaska Pacific University
Office of Financial Aid
4101 University Drive
Anchorage, AK 99508-4672

1226
University Scholarship

AMOUNT: None Specified DEADLINE: Varies
MAJOR: All Areas of Study

This award is open to freshman applicants who demonstrate high levels of academic and/or extracurricular achievements and who are competitive. Both merit and need will be considered when you apply. Award requirements change regularly. No GPA requirement specified.

Alaska Pacific University
Office of Financial Aid
4101 University Drive
Anchorage, AK 99508-4672

1227
Western Association of Food Chains Scholarship

AMOUNT: None Specified DEADLINE: Varies
MAJOR: Retail Food Industry; Food Merchandising, Management, and Marketing

This scholarship is open to undergraduate or graduate students who are interested in a career in the retail food industry. Award requirements change regularly. No GPA requirement specified.

Alaska Pacific University
Office of Financial Aid
4101 University Drive
Anchorage, AK 99508-4672

Alma College

1228
Alma College Scholarship

AMOUNT: $500-$50000 DEADLINE: Varies
MAJOR: All Areas of Study

The Alma College Scholarship is open to first-time freshmen and transfer students entering Alma College. In order to apply, you must have a minimum 2.5 GPA. This scholarship is based on your academic merit. Award requirements change regularly. GPA must be 2.5-4.0.

Alma College
Office of Admissions
614 West Superior Street
Alma, MI 48801

1229
Tartan Award

AMOUNT: $4500 DEADLINE: April 1
MAJOR: All Areas of Study

The Tartan Award is open to freshmen at Alma College. To be considered for this merit-based award, you must have one of the following three: a minimum 3.5 GPA; be in the top 20% of your high school class; or a minimum 25 ACT. This award is renewable for a total of four years. Award requirements change regularly. No GPA requirement specified.

Alma College
Office of Admissions
614 West Superior Street
Alma, MI 48801

1230
Trustees Honors and Presidential Scholarship

AMOUNT: $5500-$7000 DEADLINE: April 1
MAJOR: All Areas of Study

The Trustees Honors and Presidential Scholarship is open to freshmen at Alma College. To be considered for this merit-based award, you must have a minimum 3.25 GPA and have at least a 25 ACT score. The award is renewable for a total of four years. Award requirements change regularly. GPA must be 3.3-4.0.

Alma College
Office of Admissions
614 West Superior Street
Alma, MI 48801

Alverno College

1231
Alverno Freshman & Transfer Scholarship

AMOUNT: $1500-$4000 DEADLINE: Varies
MAJOR: All Areas of Study

This scholarship is open to all new freshmen and transfer Alverno students with a minimum GPA of 2.5. The scholarship amount is determined upon acceptance to the college and is renewable. Award requirements change regularly. GPA must be 2.5-4.0.

Alverno College
3401 South 29th Street
PO Box 343922
Milwaukee, WI 53234-3922

Andover College

1232
Andover College Criminal Justice Scholarship

AMOUNT: $500 DEADLINE: May 1
MAJOR: Criminal Justice, Law Enforcement

The Andover College Criminal Justice Scholarship is awarded to graduating high school seniors who have demonstrated a desire to pursue their education in the field of law enforcement. To receive this scholarship, students must be recommended by the full-time secondary criminal justice instructor (maximum of two students per school) of their high school. Award requirements change regularly. To obtain full criteria for this scholarship, please contact the Criminal Justice Department at Andover College by sending a self-addressed, stamped envelope to the address provided or emailing enroll@andovercollege.com. No GPA requirement specified.

Andover College
Office of Admissions
901 Washington Avenue
Portland, ME 04103-2737

1233
Andover College Matching Scholarship

AMOUNT: Maximum: $200 DEADLINE: Varies
MAJOR: All Areas of Study

The Andover College Matching Scholarship is for freshman full-time students who are U.S. citizens. Through this program, Andover College will match up to $200 per academic year in scholarship aid received by a student from any recognized local, state, or national scholarship-granting institutions or organizations. Each scholarship to be matched will be applied directly to the student's account at Andover College. Award requirements change regularly. Complete details can be obtained by contacting an Andover College Admissions Representative by email at enroll@andovercollege.com or by phone at (800) 639-3110. When doing so, please provide the name, mailing address with zip code, telephone number, and details of the scholarship to be matched. No GPA requirement specified.

Andover College
Office of Admissions
901 Washington Avenue
Portland, ME 04103-2737

1234
Business Education Association of Maine Regional and State Scholarship

AMOUNT: $100-$500 DEADLINE: Varies
MAJOR: Business, Business Education

The Business Education Association of Maine Regional and State Scholarship is awarded to applicants from Region "L" of the Business Education Association of Maine who participate in regional business contests. The scholarship awarded to the recipient applies only to the student's first year at Andover College; the recipient must begin classes in either July or September immediately following high school graduation. Award requirements change regularly. Please call the Admissions Office for further information at (800) 639-3110 or (207) 774-6126. No GPA requirement specified.

Andover College
Office of Admissions
901 Washington Avenue
Portland, ME 04103-2737

1235
GED and Adult Education High School Diploma Scholarship

AMOUNT: $500 DEADLINE: Varies
MAJOR: All Areas of Study

This scholarship is awarded to Maine residents who are pursuing full-time higher education at Andover College and who have earned their GED or Adult Education High School Diploma in the 12- month period prior to their application

date. Recipients are chosen by a staff and faculty committee based on an essay and recommendations submitted by the student. Award requirements change regularly. Please send a self-addressed, stamped envelope to the Admissions Office to receive your application and for any further instructions. You can also contact an Admissions Representative at Andover College by calling (800) 639-3110. No GPA requirement specified.

Andover College
Office of Admissions
901 Washington Avenue
Portland, ME 04103-2737

1236
Lee C. Jenkins Promising Scholar Program

AMOUNT: $1250-$5000 DEADLINE: April 15
MAJOR: All Areas of Study

The Lee C. Jenkins Promising Scholar Award is open to high school seniors who demonstrate a potential for success and will be attending Andover College full-time. All interested high school seniors must submit their applications to the college by the deadline date of their senior year to be considered. An interview with members of the scholarship committee is required or all finalists. Award requirements change regularly. For further information and an application, please contact your local high school guidance counselor or contact the Andover Admissions Office at the address provided. No GPA requirement specified.

Andover College
Office of Admissions
901 Washington Avenue
Portland, ME 04103-2737

Arapahoe Community College

1237
Advanced Options Scholarship

AMOUNT: None Specified DEADLINE: June 1
MAJOR: All Areas of Study

This scholarship is open to recent high school graduates who have attended Arapahoe Community College while co-enrolled in high school under the Post-Secondary Options Program. You must have graduated from high school within the last 12 months and have a minimum 2.5 GPA. Award requirements change regularly. For further information and an application, please contact the address listed, call (303) 797-5661, fax (303) 797-5663, or visit their website: www.arapahoe.edu. GPA must be 2.5-4.0.

Arapahoe Community College
Financial Aid Office
5900 South Santa Fe Drive, M 202
Littleton, CO 80160-9002

1238
Career Partnership Scholarship

AMOUNT: None Specified DEADLINE: Varies
MAJOR: All Fields of Study

The Career Partnership Scholarship is open to students who have not yet earned their GED but are planning on doing so. The award will go towards resident tuition, fees, and books as determined by the GED pre-test. You will be required to submit an essay describing your educational and career goals (including how this scholarship will benefit you) and your GED pre-test scores. You must successfully complete the GED pre-classes for the GED test fee to be waived. Award requirements change regularly. No GPA requirement specified.

Arapahoe Community College
Financial Aid Office
5900 South Santa Fe Drive, M 202
Littleton, CO 80160-9002

1239
College Bound Scholarship

AMOUNT: None Specified DEADLINE: June 1
MAJOR: All Areas of Study

This scholarship is open to students who have received their GED diploma at Arapahoe Community College with a minimum passing score and wish to continue their education. Priority will be given to students who have received and completed their GED through the Career Partnership Program. Award requirements change regularly. For further information and an application, please contact the address listed, call (303) 797-5661, fax (303) 797-5663, or visit their website: www.arapahoe.edu. No GPA requirement specified.

Arapahoe Community College
Financial Aid Office
5900 South Santa Fe Drive, M 202
Littleton, CO 80160-9002

1240
Express Personnel Services Scholarship

AMOUNT: $250-$500 DEADLINE: June 1
MAJOR: All Fields of Study

The Express Personnel Services Award is open to Colorado residents. The award requires that you have a minimum 2.5 GPA. You must also be enrolled in at least six credit hours per semester at Arapahoe Community College and must have already completed six hours of ACC curriculum. You will also be required to submit an essay. Award requirements change regularly. GPA must be 2.5-4.0.

Arapahoe Community College
Financial Aid Office
5900 South Santa Fe Drive, M 202
Littleton, CO 80160-9002

1241
James F. Weber Achievement Award

AMOUNT: None Specified DEADLINE: June 1
MAJOR: All Fields of Study

The James F. Weber Achievement Award is open to Arapahoe Community College students who have completed 18 credit hours with a cumulative 3.2 GPA. The award requires that you be able to demonstrate community leadership in volunteer activities. You will also need to submit an essay. Award requirements change regularly. GPA must be 3.2-4.0.

Arapahoe Community College
Financial Aid Office
5900 South Santa Fe Drive, M 202
Littleton, CO 80160-9002

1242
Leahbeth Barnard Scholarship

AMOUNT: None Specified DEADLINE: June 1
MAJOR: All Fields of Study

The Leahbeth Barnard Scholarship is open to students who are single parents. You will be required to write an essay describing your educational and career goals and any hardships you may have endured as a single parent; submit two letters of reference of individuals you know will attest to the fact that you can benefit from the scholarship; and demonstrate academic success and financial need. The award also requires that you have already completed one semester at ACC. Award requirements change regularly. No GPA requirement specified.

Arapahoe Community College
Financial Aid Office
5900 South Santa Fe Drive, M 202
Littleton, CO 80160-9002

1243
Nobert "Doc" Graham Scholarship

AMOUNT: None Specified DEADLINE: June 1
MAJOR: Accounting, Business Administration, Management, Computer Information Systems, Banking and Financial Services, Marketing

This scholarship is open to Colorado residents attending Arapahoe Community College who are working toward an Associate of Applied Science degree and a major in one of the following areas: accounting, business administration, management, computer information systems, banking and financial services, and marketing. You must have a minimum cumulative 3.2 GPA at the sophomore level (24 or more credit hours). Award requirements change regularly. For further information and an application, please contact the address listed, call (303) 797-5661, fax (303) 797-5663, or visit their website: www.arapahoe.edu. GPA must be 3.2-4.0.

Arapahoe Community College
Financial Aid Office
5900 South Santa Fe Drive, M 202
Littleton, CO 80160-9002

1244
Second Start Scholarship

AMOUNT: None Specified DEADLINE: June 1
MAJOR: All Areas of Study

This scholarship is open to Colorado residents who are entering Arapahoe Community College after at least a five-year absence from any type of formal education and who do not possess a college degree. Selection is based on academic promise and goals. Award requirements change regularly. For further information and an application, please contact the address listed, call (303) 797-5661, fax (303) 797-5663, or visit their website: www.arapahoe.edu. No GPA requirement specified.

Arapahoe Community College
Financial Aid Office
5900 South Santa Fe Drive, M 202
Littleton, CO 80160-9002

1245
Theodore R. Coyle, Jr., Scholarship

AMOUNT: None Specified DEADLINE: June 1
MAJOR: Computer Science

This scholarship is open to Colorado residents attending Arapahoe Community College who are pursuing a CIS degree or certificate. You must be enrolled in at least six credit hours per semester, have a minimum 3.0 GPA, and must have completed at least six credit hours of CIS curriculum. Award requirements change regularly. For further information and an application, please contact the address listed, call (303) 797-5661, fax (303) 797-5663, or visit their website: www.arapahoe.edu. GPA must be 3.0-4.0.

Arapahoe Community College
Financial Aid Office
5900 South Santa Fe Drive, M 202
Littleton, CO 80160-9002

1246
Transitions Scholarship

AMOUNT: Maximum: $300 DEADLINE: Varies
MAJOR: All Fields of Study

The Transitions Scholarship is open to students entering higher education during a transition in their lives who have not yet completed the application process for federal student aid. You will be required to provide documentation of your financial situation, an essay describing your transition (including how long you have been out of school and how the award can benefit you), and a letter of reference. This award is designed for students under special circumstances. Please do not apply if you are not in a period of transition. Award requirements change regularly. No GPA requirement specified.

Arapahoe Community College
Financial Aid Office
5900 South Santa Fe Drive, M 202
Littleton, CO 80160-9002

Arizona State University

1247
Thomas P. Papandrew Scholarship

AMOUNT: $1000 DEADLINE: March 31
MAJOR: Landscape Architecture/Design

The Thomas P. Papandrew Scholarship is open to minority students enrolled full-time at Arizona State University and pursuing a career in landscape architecture. You must be an Arizona resident and demonstrate financial need. This scholarship is renewable as long as you continue to demonstrate financial need and meet or exceed all other criteria. Award requirements change regularly. No GPA requirement specified.

Landscape Architecture Foundation
Scholarship Program
636 'I' Street NW
Washington, DC 20001-3736

Armstrong Atlantic University

1248
Armstrong Atlantic Academic Scholarship

AMOUNT: None Specified DEADLINE: Varies
MAJOR: All Areas of Study

These scholarships are awarded based on merit, need, or both. The monetary awards will be presented by a scholarship committee in the spring prior to the upcoming award year. The deadlines are the following: Incoming freshmen, February 1; returning, transfer, or graduate students, May 1. Award requirements change regularly. Other scholarships are available by various Armstrong departments. These additional scholarships will be listed throughout the year and offered through the financial aid office. Be sure to check the application procedures for these programs as well as eligibility requirements. No GPA requirement specified.

Armstrong Atlantic University
11935 Abercorn Street
Savannah, GA 31328

Art Institute of Fort Lauderdale

1249

Art Institute of Fort Lauderdale Broadcasting Scholarship

AMOUNT: None Specified DEADLINE: Varies
MAJOR: Broadcasting

The Art Institute of Fort Lauderdale Broadcasting Scholarship is open to Florida residents attending or planning to attend the Art Institute of Fort Lauderdale who are studying broadcasting. Applications are available at Florida high schools and GED testing centers. Award requirements change regularly. For further information, please send a self-addressed, stamped envelope to Art Institute of Fort Lauderdale, Eileen Northrop, Director of Admissions, 1799 SE 17th Street, Fort Lauderdale, FL 33316, or you could call (800) 275-7603 ext. 420, or (954) 527-1799 ext. 420. No GPA requirement specified.

Florida Association of Postsecondary Schools and Colleges
Attn: FAPSC Scholarship Committee
F200 West College Avenue
Tallahassee, FL 32301

1250

Art Institute of Fort Lauderdale Computer Animation Scholarship

AMOUNT: None Specified DEADLINE: Varies
MAJOR: Computer Animation

The Art Institute of Fort Lauderdale Computer Animation Scholarship is open to Florida residents attending or planning to attend the Art Institute of Fort Lauderdale who are studying computer animation. Applications are available at Florida high schools and GED testing centers. Award requirements change regularly. For further information, please send a self-addressed, stamped envelope to Art Institute of Fort Lauderdale, Eileen Northrop, Director of Admissions, 1799 SE 17th Street, Fort Lauderdale, FL 33316, or you could call (800) 275-7603 ext. 420, or (954) 527-1799 ext. 420. No GPA requirement specified.

Florida Association of Postsecondary Schools and Colleges
Attn: FAPSC Scholarship Committee
F200 West College Avenue
Tallahassee, FL 32301

1251

Art Institute of Fort Lauderdale Culinary Arts Scholarship

AMOUNT: None Specified DEADLINE: Varies
MAJOR: Culinary Arts

The Art Institute of Fort Lauderdale Culinary Arts Scholarship is open to Florida residents attending or planning to attend the Art Institute of Fort Lauderdale who are studying culinary arts. Applications are available at Florida high schools and GED testing centers. Award requirements change regularly. For further information, please send a self-addressed, stamped envelope to Art Institute of Fort Lauderdale, Eileen Northrop, Director of Admissions, 1799 SE 17th Street, Fort Lauderdale, FL 33316, or you could call (800) 275-7603 ext. 420, or (954)

527-1799 ext. 420. No GPA requirement specified.

Florida Association of Postsecondary Schools and Colleges
Attn: FAPSC Scholarship Committee
F200 West College Avenue
Tallahassee, FL 32301

1252

Art Institute of Fort Lauderdale Fashion Design Scholarship

AMOUNT: None Specified DEADLINE: Varies
MAJOR: Fashion Design

The Art Institute of Fort Lauderdale Fashion Design Scholarship is open to Florida residents attending or planning to attend the Art Institute of Fort Lauderdale who are studying fashion design. Applications are available at Florida high schools and GED testing centers. Award requirements change regularly. For further information, please send a self-addressed, stamped envelope to Art Institute of Fort Lauderdale, Eileen Northrop, Director of Admissions, 1799 SE 17th Street, Fort Lauderdale, FL 33316, or you could call (800) 275-7603 ext. 420, or (954) 527-1799 ext. 420. No GPA requirement specified.

Florida Association of Postsecondary Schools and Colleges
Attn: FAPSC Scholarship Committee
F200 West College Avenue
Tallahassee, FL 32301

1253

Art Institute of Fort Lauderdale Fashion Marketing Scholarship

AMOUNT: None Specified DEADLINE: Varies
MAJOR: Fashion Marketing

The Art Institute of Fort Lauderdale Fashion Marketing Scholarship is open to Florida residents attending or planning to attend the Art Institute of Fort Lauderdale who are studying fashion marketing. Applications are available at Florida high schools and GED testing centers. Award requirements change regularly. For further information, please send a self-addressed, stamped envelope to Art Institute of Fort Lauderdale, Eileen Northrop, Director of Admissions, 1799 SE 17th Street, Fort Lauderdale, FL 33316, or you could call (800) 275-7603 ext. 420, or (954) 527-1799 ext. 420. No GPA requirement specified.

Florida Association of Postsecondary Schools and Colleges
Attn: FAPSC Scholarship Committee
F200 West College Avenue
Tallahassee, FL 32301

1254

Art Institute of Fort Lauderdale Industrial Design Scholarship

AMOUNT: None Specified DEADLINE: Varies
MAJOR: Industrial Design Technology

The Art Institute of Fort Lauderdale Industrial Design Scholarship is open to Florida residents attending or planning to attend the Art Institute of Fort Lauderdale who are studying industrial design technology. Applications are available at Florida high schools and GED testing centers. Award requirements change regularly. For further information, please send a self-addressed, stamped envelope to Art Institute of Fort Lauderdale, Eileen Northrop, Director of Admissions, 1799 SE 17th Street, Fort Lauderdale, FL 33316, or you could call (800) 275-7603 ext. 420, or (954) 527-1799 ext. 420. No GPA requirement specified.

Florida Association of Postsecondary Schools and Colleges
Attn: FAPSC Scholarship Committee
F200 West College Avenue
Tallahassee, FL 32301

1255
Art Institute of Fort Lauderdale Interior Design Scholarship

AMOUNT: None Specified DEADLINE: Varies
MAJOR: Interior Design

The Art Institute of Fort Lauderdale Interior Design Scholarship is open to Florida residents attending or planning to attend the Art Institute of Fort Lauderdale who are studying interior design. Applications are available at Florida high schools and GED testing centers. Award requirements change regularly. For further information, please send a self-addressed, stamped envelope to Art Institute of Fort Lauderdale, Eileen Northrop, Director of Admissions, 1799 SE 17th Street, Fort Lauderdale, FL 33316, or you could call (800) 275-7603 ext. 420, or (954) 527-1799 ext. 420. No GPA requirement specified.

Florida Association of Postsecondary Schools and Colleges
Attn: FAPSC Scholarship Committee
F200 West College Avenue
Tallahassee, FL 32301

1256
Art Institute of Fort Lauderdale Multi-Media Scholarship

AMOUNT: None Specified DEADLINE: Varies
MAJOR: Multi-Media

The Art Institute of Fort Lauderdale Multi-Media Scholarship is open to Florida residents attending or planning to attend the Art Institute of Fort Lauderdale who are studying multi-media. Applications are available at Florida high schools and GED testing centers. Award requirements change regularly. For further information, please send a self-addressed, stamped envelope to Art Institute of Fort Lauderdale, Eileen Northrop, Director of Admissions, 1799 SE 17th Street, Fort Lauderdale, FL 33316, or you could call (800) 275-7603 ext. 420, or (954) 527-1799 ext. 420. No GPA requirement specified.

Florida Association of Postsecondary Schools and Colleges
Attn: FAPSC Scholarship Committee
F200 West College Avenue
Tallahassee, FL 32301

1257
Art Institute of Fort Lauderdale Photography Scholarship

AMOUNT: None Specified DEADLINE: Varies
MAJOR: Photography

The Art Institute of Fort Lauderdale Photography Scholarship is open to Florida residents attending or planning to attend the Art Institute of Fort Lauderdale who are studying photogra-phy. Applications are available at Florida high schools and GED testing centers. Award requirements change regularly. For further information, please send a self-addressed, stamped envelope to Art Institute of Fort Lauderdale, Eileen Northrop, Director of Admissions, 1799 SE 17th Street, Fort Lauderdale, FL 33316, or you could call (800) 275-7603 ext. 420, or (954) 527-1799 ext. 420. No GPA requirement specified.

Florida Association of Postsecondary Schools and Colleges
Attn: FAPSC Scholarship Committee
F200 West College Avenue
Tallahassee, FL 32301

1258
Art Institute of Fort Lauderdale Travel and Hospitality Scholarship

AMOUNT: None Specified DEADLINE: Varies
MAJOR: Travel and Hospitality

The Art Institute of Fort Lauderdale Travel and Hospitality Scholarship is open to Florida residents attending or planning to attend the Art Institute of Fort Lauderdale who are studying travel and hospitality. Applications are available at Florida high schools and GED testing centers. Award requirements change regularly. For further information, please send a self-addressed, stamped envelope to Art Institute of Fort Lauderdale, Eileen Northrop, Director of Admissions, 1799 SE 17th Street, Fort Lauderdale, FL 33316, or you could call (800) 275-7603 ext. 420, or (954) 527-1799 ext. 420. No GPA requirement specified.

Florida Association of Postsecondary Schools and Colleges
Attn: FAPSC Scholarship Committee
F200 West College Avenue
Tallahassee, FL 32301

1259
Art Institute of Fort Lauderdale Video Production Scholarship

AMOUNT: None Specified DEADLINE: Varies
MAJOR: Video Production

The Art Institute of Fort Lauderdale Video Production Scholarship is open to Florida residents attending or planning to attend the Art Institute of Fort Lauderdale who are studying video production. Applications are available at Florida high schools and GED testing centers. Award requirements change regularly. For further information, please send a self-addressed, stamped envelope to Art Institute of Fort Lauderdale, Eileen Northrop, Director of Admissions, 1799 SE 17th Street, Fort Lauderdale, FL 33316, or you could call (800) 275-7603 ext. 420, or (954) 527-1799 ext. 420. No GPA requirement specified.

Florida Association of Postsecondary Schools and Colleges
Attn: FAPSC Scholarship Committee
F200 West College Avenue
Tallahassee, FL 32301

1260

Art Institute of Fort Lauderdale Visual Communication Scholarship

AMOUNT: None Specified DEADLINE: Varies
MAJOR: Visual Communications

The Art Institute of Fort Lauderdale Visual Communication Scholarship is open to Florida residents attending or planning to attend the Art Institute of Fort Lauderdale who are studying visual communications. Applications are available at Florida high schools and GED testing centers. Award requirements change regularly. For further information, please send a self-addressed, stamped envelope to Art Institute of Fort Lauderdale, Eileen Northrop, Director of Admissions, 1799 SE 17th Street, Fort Lauderdale, FL 33316, or you could call (800) 275-7603 ext. 420, or (954) 527-1799 ext. 420. No GPA requirement specified.

Florida Association of Postsecondary Schools and Colleges
Attn: FAPSC Scholarship Committee
F200 West College Avenue
Tallahassee, FL 32301

Atlantic Coast Institute

1261

Atlantic Coast Institute Court Reporting Scholarship

AMOUNT: None Specified DEADLINE: Varies
MAJOR: Court Reporting

The Atlantic Coast Institute Court Reporting Scholarship is open to Florida residents attending or planning to attend the Atlantic Coast Institute who are studying court reporting. Applications are available at Florida high schools and GED testing centers. Award requirements change regularly. For further information, please send a self-addressed, stamped envelope to Atlantic Coast Institute, Ronald Doolely, President, 5225 West Broward Boulevard, Fort Lauderdale, FL 33317, or you could call (954) 581-2223. No GPA requirement specified.

Florida Association of Postsecondary Schools and Colleges
Attn: FAPSC Scholarship Committee
F200 West College Avenue
Tallahassee, FL 32301

1262

Atlantic Coast Institute Medical Administrative Assistant Scholarship

AMOUNT: None Specified DEADLINE: Varies
MAJOR: Medical Administrative Assistant

The Atlantic Coast Institute Medical Administrative Assistant Scholarship is open to Florida residents attending or planning to attend the Atlantic Coast Institute who are studying to be medical administrative assistants. Applications are available at Florida high schools and GED testing centers. Award requirements change regularly. For further information, please send a

self-addressed, stamped envelope to Atlantic Coast Institute, Ronald Doolely, President, 5225 West Broward Boulevard, Fort Lauderdale, FL 33317, or you could call (954) 581-2223. No GPA requirement specified.

Florida Association of Postsecondary Schools and Colleges
Attn: FAPSC Scholarship Committee
F200 West College Avenue
Tallahassee, FL 32301

1263

Atlantic Coast Institute Medical Transcription Scholarship

AMOUNT: None Specified DEADLINE: Varies
MAJOR: Medical Transcription

The Atlantic Coast Institute Medical Transcription Scholarship is open to Florida residents attending or planning to attend the Atlantic Coast Institute who are studying medical transcription. Applications are available at Florida high schools and GED testing centers. Award requirements change regularly. For further information, please send a self-addressed, stamped envelope to Atlantic Coast Institute, Ronald Doolely, President, 5225 West Broward Boulevard, Fort Lauderdale, FL 33317, or you could call (954) 581-2223. No GPA requirement specified.

Florida Association of Postsecondary Schools and Colleges
Attn: FAPSC Scholarship Committee
F200 West College Avenue
Tallahassee, FL 32301

1264

Atlantic Coast Institute Paralegal Scholarship

AMOUNT: None Specified DEADLINE: Varies
MAJOR: Paralegal

The Atlantic Coast Institute Paralegal Scholarship is open to Florida residents attending or planning to attend the Atlantic Coast Institute who are studying to become paralegals. Applications are available at Florida high schools and GED testing centers. Award requirements change regularly. For further information, please send a self-addressed, stamped envelope to Atlantic Coast Institute, Ronald Doolely, President, 5225 West Broward Boulevard, Fort Lauderdale, FL 33317, or you could call (954) 581-2223. No GPA requirement specified.

Florida Association of Postsecondary Schools and Colleges
Attn: FAPSC Scholarship Committee
F200 West College Avenue
Tallahassee, FL 32301

Baldwin-Wallace College

1265
Alumni Scholarship

AMOUNT: Maximum: $1000 DEADLINE: Varies
MAJOR: All Areas of Study

The Alumni Scholarship is awarded annually to students at Baldwin-Wallace College who are the children or grandchildren of BW alumni. Award requirements change regularly. Write to the address listed for further information or phone (877) BW APPLY. You are encouraged to visit the college's website at www.bw.edu. No GPA requirement specified.

Baldwin-Wallace College
Attn: Office of Financial Aid
275 Eastland Road
Berea, OH 44017-2088

1266
B-W Founders Scholarship

AMOUNT: Maximum: $3500 DEADLINE: Varies
MAJOR: All Areas of Study

The B-W Founders Scholarship is open to incoming freshmen at Baldwin-Wallace College whose outstanding academic skills and diverse personal qualities will enrich campus life, foster community spirit, and advance the mission of the college. A limited number of awards are available. Award requirements change regularly. Write to the address listed for further information or phone (877) BW APPLY. You are encouraged to visit the college's website at www.bw.edu. No GPA requirement specified.

Baldwin-Wallace College
Attn: Office of Financial Aid
275 Eastland Road
Berea, OH 44017-2088

1267
B-W Multicultural Scholarship

AMOUNT: Maximum: $4000 DEADLINE: Varies
MAJOR: All Areas of Study

The B-W Multicultural Scholarship is awarded to incoming freshmen at Baldwin-Wallace College who show academic promise and have demonstrated participation in high school activities coupled with leadership skills. A limited number of awards are available. Award requirements change regularly. Write to the address listed for further information or phone (877) BW APPLY. You are encouraged to visit the college's website at www.bw.edu. No GPA requirement specified.

Baldwin-Wallace College
Attn: Office of Financial Aid
275 Eastland Road
Berea, OH 44017-2088

1268
B-W Scholars Award

AMOUNT: Maximum: $4000 DEADLINE: Varies
MAJOR: All Areas of Study

The B-W Scholars Award is open to incoming freshmen at Baldwin-Wallace College who demonstrate academic ability and have actively participated and shown leadership in high school. To be considered for this award, you must be ranked in the top 20% of your class or have a minimum GPA of 3.5 or a minimum 25 ACT or 1040 SAT. A limited number of awards are available. Award requirements change regularly. Write to the address listed for further information or phone (877) BW APPLY. You are encouraged to visit the college's website at www.bw.edu. No GPA requirement specified.

Baldwin-Wallace College
Attn: Office of Financial Aid
275 Eastland Road
Berea, OH 44017-2088

1269
Dean's Award

AMOUNT: Maximum: $4000 DEADLINE: Varies
MAJOR: All Areas of Study

The Dean's Award is open to freshmen entering Baldwin-Wallace College who have strong academic potential. To be eligible for this award, you must rank in the top 30% of your graduating class or have a 3.0 minimum GPA upon high school graduation. The award may be renewed provided you maintain at least a 2.8 GPA and are enrolled full-time. Award requirements change regularly. Write to the address listed for further information or phone (877) BW APPLY. You are encouraged to visit the college's website at www.bw.edu. GPA must be 3.0-4.0.

Baldwin-Wallace College
Attn: Office of Financial Aid
275 Eastland Road
Berea, OH 44017-2088

1270
Laurels Scholarship

AMOUNT: Maximum: $5000 DEADLINE: Varies
MAJOR: All Areas of Study

The Laurels Scholarship is awarded to incoming freshmen at Baldwin-Wallace College who demonstrate academic skills, extracurricular and community involvement, leadership qualities, and the commitment to overcome obstacles. A limited number of awards are available. Award requirements change regularly. Write to the address listed for further information or phone (877) BW APPLY. You are encouraged to visit the college's website at www.bw.edu. No GPA requirement specified.

Baldwin-Wallace College
Attn: Office of Financial Aid
275 Eastland Road
Berea, OH 44017-2088

1271
Margaret Rusk Griffiths Music Scholarship

AMOUNT: $200-$3000   DEADLINE: Varies
MAJOR: Music

The Margaret Rusk Griffiths Music Scholarship is awarded to students at Baldwin-Wallace College on the basis of their musical and general academic ability. To be considered for this award, you must have a minimum 3.0 GPA in your major area of performance. An audition is required. Award requirements change regularly. Write to the address listed for further information or phone (877) BW APPLY. You are encouraged to visit the college's website at www.bw.edu. GPA must be 3.0-4.0.

Baldwin-Wallace College
Attn: Office of Financial Aid
275 Eastland Road
Berea, OH 44017-2088

1272
Presidential Honorary Scholarship

AMOUNT: Maximum: $6000   DEADLINE: Varies
MAJOR: All Areas of Study

The Presidential Honorary Scholarship is open to incoming freshmen at Baldwin-Wallace College who rank in the upper 15% of their graduating class. To be considered for this award, you must demonstrate outstanding academic ability and potential—as revealed by your ACT or SAT scores. The award may be renewed provided you maintain a minimum GPA of 3.0. Award requirements change regularly. Write to the address listed for further information or phone (877) BW APPLY. You are encouraged to visit the college's website at www.bw.edu. No GPA requirement specified.

Baldwin-Wallace College
Attn: Office of Financial Aid
275 Eastland Road
Berea, OH 44017-2088

1273
Talent Honorary Scholarship

AMOUNT: $500   DEADLINE: Varies
MAJOR: Theater, Art

The Talent Honorary Scholarship is awarded to new students at Baldwin-Wallace College who possess outstanding talent in such areas as theater and art. This award is renewable provided you maintain a minimum GPA of 2.5 and are recommended by the department. Award requirements change regularly. Write to the address listed for further information or phone (877) BW APPLY. You are encouraged to visit the college's website at www.bw.edu. No GPA requirement specified.

Baldwin-Wallace College
Attn: Office of Financial Aid
275 Eastland Road
Berea, OH 44017-2088

1274
Trustees Honor Scholarship

AMOUNT: Maximum: $5000   DEADLINE: Varies
MAJOR: All Areas of Study

The Trustees Honor Scholarship is open to students entering Baldwin-Wallace College who demonstrate strong academic potential. To be considered for this award, you must rank in the top 25% of your graduating class or have a minimum 3.2 GPA. The award may be renewed provided you maintain at least a 2.8 GPA and remain enrolled full-time. Award requirements change regularly. Write to the address listed for further information or phone (877) BW APPLY. You are encouraged to visit the college's website at www.bw.edu. GPA must be 3.2-4.0.

Baldwin-Wallace College
Attn: Office of Financial Aid
275 Eastland Road
Berea, OH 44017-2088

Beaver College

1275
Beaver College Achievement Award

AMOUNT: $1000-$6000   DEADLINE: Varies
MAJOR: All Areas of Study

Awarded to full-time Beaver College undergraduate students who have demonstrated exceptional achievement in community service, school activities, leadership, or special talent. Award requirements change regularly. Please contact the address provided, or for further information, please consult the website at www.beaver.edu. No GPA requirement specified.

Beaver College
450 South Easton Road
Glenside, PA 19038-3215

1276
Beaver College Distinguished Scholarship

AMOUNT: $1000-$16880   DEADLINE: Varies
MAJOR: All Areas of Study

Full-time freshmen and transfer students selected by the Office of Enrollment Management based upon academic credentials. Award requirements change regularly. No GPA requirement specified.

Beaver College
450 South Easton Road
Glenside, PA 19038-3215

Bemidji State University

1277
Allan Adams Memorial Scholarship

AMOUNT: None Specified DEADLINE: Varies
MAJOR: All Areas of Study - Athletics

The Allan Adams Memorial Scholarship is open to Bemidji State University students who participate in varsity sports. To be considered for this award, you must be a freshman with a minimum 3.0 GPA or an upperclassman with a minimum 2.5 GPA. Award requirements change regularly. GPA must be 3.0-4.0.

Bemidji State University
Office of Admissions and Scholarships
102 Deputy Hall, Scholarship Officer
Bemidji, MN 56601-2699

1278
Alpha Nu Omega/Alpha Tau Omega Scholarship

AMOUNT: None Specified DEADLINE: Varies
MAJOR: All Fields of Study

The Alpha Nu Omega/Alpha Tau Omega Scholarship is open to students attending Bemidji State University. To be considered for this award, you must be the relative of a member of the fraternity who attended BSU between 1962 and 1979. Current members of social fraternities and sororities will become eligible, should no relatives be identified. The award requires you to have a minimum high school GPA of 3.0 if you are a freshman and a minimum university GPA of 3.0 if you are an upperclassman or transfer student. Award requirements change regularly. GPA must be 3.0-4.0.

Bemidji State University
Office of Admissions and Scholarships
102 Deputy Hall, Scholarship Officer
Bemidji, MN 56601-2699

1279
Alumni Relative Scholarship

AMOUNT: $600 DEADLINE: Varies
MAJOR: All Areas of Study

The Alumni Relative Scholarship is open to new entering students who are relatives of active Bemidji State alumni. You may get an application form from any active alumnus or the Alumni Office. Deadline for consideration is March 1 for new freshmen and May 1 for transfer students. Award requirements change regularly. No GPA requirement specified.

Bemidji State University
Office of Admissions and Scholarships
102 Deputy Hall, Scholarship Officer
Bemidji, MN 56601-2699

1280
Anita Carlson Memorial Scholarship

AMOUNT: None Specified DEADLINE: Varies
MAJOR: Mass Communications

The Anita Carlson Memorial Scholarship is open to Bemidji State University students. To be qualified to receive the award, you must be an undergraduate mass communications major. Award requirements change regularly. No GPA requirement specified.

Bemidji State University
Office of Admissions and Scholarships
102 Deputy Hall, Scholarship Officer
Bemidji, MN 56601-2699

1281
Athletic Scholarship

AMOUNT: None Specified DEADLINE: Varies
MAJOR: All Areas of Study - Athletics

The Athletic Scholarship is open to Bemidji State University students who are participating in men's or women's athletic programs. To find out the qualifications for an athletic scholarship, you can contact the appropriate coach or the athletic director. Award requirements change regularly. No GPA requirement specified.

Bemidji State University
Office of Admissions and Scholarships
102 Deputy Hall, Scholarship Officer
Bemidji, MN 56601-2699

1282
Bertha Evenson Memorial Scholarship

AMOUNT: None Specified DEADLINE: Varies
MAJOR: Nursing

The Bertha Evenson Memorial Scholarship is open to Bemidji State University students who are nursing majors. To be considered for this award, you must be able to demonstrate financial need. The award also dictates that you be interested in continuing or establishing your career in a rural hospital, nursing home, home health care, or hospice care facility. Award requirements change regularly. No GPA requirement specified.

Bemidji State University
Office of Admissions and Scholarships
102 Deputy Hall, Scholarship Officer
Bemidji, MN 56601-2699

1283
Campus Honor Scholarship

AMOUNT: $600 DEADLINE: April 1
MAJOR: All Areas of Study

The Campus Honor Scholarship is open to graduating seniors who are in the top 15% of their class. Your application for admission to Bemidji State serves as the application for this scholarship. This is a one-time award, and you must be admitted by April 1 to be eligible. Award requirements change regularly. No GPA requirement specified.

Bemidji State University
Office of Admissions and Scholarships
102 Deputy Hall, Scholarship Officer
Bemidji, MN 56601-2699

1284
Cardinal Newman Scholarship

AMOUNT: None Specified DEADLINE: Varies
MAJOR: Humanities, Fine Arts

The Cardinal Newman Scholarship is open to students attending Bemidji State University. To be considered for this award, you must be majoring in humanities or fine arts and be actively involved in the Newman Center. Final selection will be made by the Newman Center pastor. Award requirements change regularly. GPA must be 3.0-4.0.

Bemidji State University
Office of Admissions and Scholarships
102 Deputy Hall, Scholarship Officer
Bemidji, MN 56601-2699

1285
Carl Thompson Scholarship

AMOUNT: None Specified DEADLINE: Varies
MAJOR: Music

The Carl Thompson Scholarship is open to Bemidji State University students. To be considered for the award, you must be a music major. This award is for those who have special talents. Award requirements change regularly. No GPA requirement specified.

Bemidji State University
Office of Admissions and Scholarships
102 Deputy Hall, Scholarship Officer
Bemidji, MN 56601-2699

1286
Deloitte and Touche Scholarship

AMOUNT: None Specified DEADLINE: Varies
MAJOR: Accounting

The Deloitte and Touche Scholarship is open to Bemidji State University students. To be considered for this award, you must be a junior or senior majoring in accounting. The award also requires that you have a minimum 3.0 GPA. Award requirements change regularly. GPA must be 3.0-4.0.

Bemidji State University
Office of Admissions and Scholarships
102 Deputy Hall, Scholarship Officer
Bemidji, MN 56601-2699

1287
Fred and Mabel Hamm Scholarship

AMOUNT: None Specified DEADLINE: Varies
MAJOR: All Areas of Study

The Fred and Mabel Hamm Scholarship is open to Bemidji State University sophomores, juniors, and seniors who have a minimum 3.5 GPA. You must demonstrate a high level of reading and writing competence and financial need. Award requirements change regularly. GPA must be 3.5-4.0.

Bemidji State University
Office of Admissions and Scholarships
102 Deputy Hall, Scholarship Officer
Bemidji, MN 56601-2699

1288
Full-Tuition Scholarship

AMOUNT: None Specified DEADLINE: February 1
MAJOR: All Areas of Study

The Full-Tuition Scholarship is open to new entering freshman students who were in the top 10% of their high school graduating class. You may renew the award for up to three years based on completion of at least 30 semester credits per year with a minimum 3.5 GPA. The award also requires that you have a minimum 28 on your ACT. Award requirements change regularly. No GPA requirement specified.

Bemidji State University
Office of Admissions and Scholarships
102 Deputy Hall, Scholarship Officer
Bemidji, MN 56601-2699

1289
Gurnee Bridgeman Biology Scholarship

AMOUNT: None Specified DEADLINE: Varies
MAJOR: Biology

The Gurnee Bridgeman Biology Scholarship is open to Bemidji State University students who are majoring in biology. You are eligible to receive the award if you are a graduate or undergraduate student who possesses a minimum 3.0 GPA. Award requirements change regularly. GPA must be 3.0-4.0.

Bemidji State University
Office of Admissions and Scholarships
102 Deputy Hall, Scholarship Officer
Bemidji, MN 56601-2699

1290
Harold Borchers Scholarship

AMOUNT: None Specified DEADLINE: Varies
MAJOR: Biology

The Harold Borchers Scholarship is open to Bemidji State University students who are biology majors. To be considered for the award, you must have a strong interest, work ethic, and commitment to science. Award requirements change regularly. No GPA requirement specified.

Bemidji State University
Office of Admissions and Scholarships
102 Deputy Hall, Scholarship Officer
Bemidji, MN 56601-2699

1291
Harry F. Bangberg Memorial Scholarship for Asian Studies

AMOUNT: None Specified DEADLINE: Varies
MAJOR: Asian Studies, Political Science

The Harry F. Bangberg Memorial Scholarship for Asian Studies is open to students who are interested Asian studies.

You will also be considered if you are a political science major. For more information, contact the International Studies Academic Director. Award requirements change regularly. No GPA requirement specified.

Bemidji State University
Office of Admissions and Scholarships
102 Deputy Hall, Scholarship Officer
Bemidji, MN 56601-2699

1292
Harry Moore Scholarship

AMOUNT: None Specified DEADLINE: Varies
MAJOR: All Fields of Study

The Harry Moore Scholarship is open to graduates of Bemidji High School. You are eligible for the award if you developed an academic interest late in your high school career, or if you have never accomplished academically what your potential indicates you could accomplish. Award requirements change regularly. No GPA requirement specified.

Bemidji State University
Office of Admissions and Scholarships
102 Deputy Hall, Scholarship Officer
Bemidji, MN 56601-2699

1293
Hartz Scholarship

AMOUNT: None Specified DEADLINE: Varies
MAJOR: All Areas of Study

The Hartz Scholarship is open to Bemidji State University incoming freshmen. To be considered for the award, you must have been in the top 20% of your high school graduating class. Award requirements change regularly. No GPA requirement specified.

Bemidji State University
Office of Admissions and Scholarships
102 Deputy Hall, Scholarship Officer
Bemidji, MN 56601-2699

1294
Henriques Scholarship

AMOUNT: None Specified DEADLINE: Varies
MAJOR: Foreign Studies

The Henriques Scholarship is open to current BSU students. To be considered for the award, you must be from Minnesota, have experience studying abroad, and be interested in foreign studies. Award requirements change regularly. No GPA requirement specified.

Bemidji State University
Office of Admissions and Scholarships
102 Deputy Hall, Scholarship Officer
Bemidji, MN 56601-2699

1295
Jim Cecil Political Science Scholarship

AMOUNT: None Specified DEADLINE: Varies
MAJOR: Political Science

The Jim Cecil Political Science Scholarship is open to incoming freshmen and transfer students. To be considered for the award, you must be a political science major. The award also requires that you be in the top 15% of your high school class if you are an entering freshman, or that you have a minimum 3.25 GPA if you are a transfer student. Award requirements change regularly. GPA must be 3.25-4.0.

Bemidji State University
Office of Admissions and Scholarships
102 Deputy Hall, Scholarship Officer
Bemidji, MN 56601-2699

1296
John and Anne Brady Scholarship

AMOUNT: None Specified DEADLINE: Varies
MAJOR: Elementary, Secondary, or Special Education

The John and Anne Brady Scholarship is open to Bemidji State University students. To be considered for the award, you must be an undergraduate majoring in elementary, secondary, or special education. The award also requires that you be able to demonstrate financial need. Award requirements change regularly. No GPA requirement specified.

Bemidji State University
Office of Admissions and Scholarships
102 Deputy Hall, Scholarship Officer
Bemidji, MN 56601-2699

1297
John Yourd Scholarship

AMOUNT: None Specified DEADLINE: Varies
MAJOR: Music, Education

The John Yourd Scholarship is open to Bemidji State University students. To be considered for the award, you must exhibit excellence in vocal or instrumental music and be planning a career in K-12 education. Preference is for an emphasis in history or social studies. Award requirements change regularly. No GPA requirement specified.

Bemidji State University
Office of Admissions and Scholarships
102 Deputy Hall, Scholarship Officer
Bemidji, MN 56601-2699

1298
Les Duly Scholarship

AMOUNT: None Specified DEADLINE: Varies
MAJOR: All Areas of Study

The Les Duly Scholarship is open to Bemidji State University students of color who are U.S. citizens. You must have a GPA between 2.5 and 3.25. You are a preferred student if you are female. One quality you should possess is the commitment to better yourself. Award requirements change regularly. GPA must be 2.5-3.25.

Bemidji State University
Office of Admissions and Scholarships
102 Deputy Hall, Scholarship Officer
Bemidji, MN 56601-2699

1299
Margaret Thorbeck Scholarship

AMOUNT: None Specified DEADLINE: Varies
MAJOR: English

The Margaret Thorbeck Scholarship is open to Bemidji State University students. To be considered for this award, you must be an outstanding student who is majoring in English. Award requirements change regularly. No GPA requirement specified.

Bemidji State University
Office of Admissions and Scholarships
102 Deputy Hall, Scholarship Officer
Bemidji, MN 56601-2699

1300
Marshall China Studies Fund

AMOUNT: None Specified DEADLINE: Varies
MAJOR: International Studies, Foreign Studies (China)

The Marshall China Studies Fund is open to students attending Bemidji State University. To be considered for the award, you must have an in-depth understanding of China and Chinese people. The award also requires that you demonstrate financial need. Award requirements change regularly. No GPA requirement specified.

Bemidji State University
Office of Admissions and Scholarships
102 Deputy Hall, Scholarship Officer
Bemidji, MN 56601-2699

1301
McKnight Foundation Scholarship

AMOUNT: None Specified DEADLINE: Varies
MAJOR: All Fields of Study

The McKnight Foundation Scholarship is open to an international student who has a high GPA and who has completed at least 30 semester credits. Selection will be made after each spring semester. You may contact the international student advisor and the scholarship officer for further information. Award requirements change regularly. No GPA requirement specified.

Bemidji State University
Office of Admissions and Scholarships
102 Deputy Hall, Scholarship Officer
Bemidji, MN 56601-2699

1302
Music Scholarship

AMOUNT: None Specified DEADLINE: Varies
MAJOR: Music

The Music Scholarship is open to Bemidji State University students. To be considered for this award, you must be a student who exhibits outstanding musical talent. An audition may be required; contact the Music Department for further information. Award requirements change regularly. No GPA requirement specified.

Bemidji State University
Office of Admissions and Scholarships
102 Deputy Hall, Scholarship Officer
Bemidji, MN 56601-2699

1303
Naylor Electric Scholarship

AMOUNT: None Specified DEADLINE: Varies
MAJOR: All Areas of Study

The Naylor Electric Scholarship is open to entering Bemidji State University freshmen who are in the top 15% of their graduating class. The award is also open to transfer students with a minimum 3.25 GPA. Award requirements change regularly. No GPA requirement specified.

Bemidji State University
Office of Admissions and Scholarships
102 Deputy Hall, Scholarship Officer
Bemidji, MN 56601-2699

1304
Palmer-Tarbell Scholarship

AMOUNT: None Specified DEADLINE: Varies
MAJOR: Physical Education

The Palmer-Trabell Scholarship is open to Bemidji State University females majoring in physical education. To be considered for the award, you must have a minimum 2.5 GPA. Award requirements change regularly. GPA must be 2.5-4.0.

Bemidji State University
Office of Admissions and Scholarships
102 Deputy Hall, Scholarship Officer
Bemidji, MN 56601-2699

1305
Partial Tuition Scholarship

AMOUNT: None Specified DEADLINE: Varies
MAJOR: All Areas of Study

The Partial Tuition Scholarship is open to out-of-state entering freshmen who rank in the top 15% of their graduating class and transfer students who complete an associate's degree with a minimum GPA of 3.5. An application for admission serves as your scholarship application. Award requirements change regularly. No GPA requirement specified.

Bemidji State University
Office of Admissions and Scholarships
102 Deputy Hall, Scholarship Officer
Bemidji, MN 56601-2699

1306
Peoples Natural Gas Scholarship

AMOUNT: None Specified DEADLINE: Varies
MAJOR: All Areas of Study

The Peoples Natural Gas Scholarship is open to students who will be enrolled in their second year at BSU. You must also have received a scholarship during your first year but are now without continuing scholarship support. A minimum 3.25 GPA is also required. Award requirements change regularly. GPA must be 3.25-4.0.

Bemidji State University
Office of Admissions and Scholarships
102 Deputy Hall, Scholarship Officer
Bemidji, MN 56601-2699

1307
Presidential Scholarship

AMOUNT: Maximum: $1500 DEADLINE: March 15
MAJOR: All Areas of Study

The Presidential Scholarship is open to incoming Bemidji State freshmen who are in the top 10% of their high school class. The scholarship is based on academics and extracurricular leadership activities in school, community, and the arts. If you are selected for the award, $1,500 will be awarded the first year and $1,000 will be awarded each subsequent year, as long as you maintain a GPA of 3.25 or higher. Award requirements change regularly. No GPA requirement specified.

Bemidji State University
Office of Admissions and Scholarships
102 Deputy Hall, Scholarship Officer
Bemidji, MN 56601-2699

1308
Residential Life/Dining Services Scholarship

AMOUNT: None Specified DEADLINE: Varies
MAJOR: All Areas of Study

The Residential Life/Dining Services Scholarship is open to Bemidji State University students who are campus residents, on the campus food plan, and in good academic standing. To qualify to receive the award, you must be an active contributor to the residential community. Please contact the Director of Residential Life for further information. Award requirements change regularly. No GPA requirement specified.

Bemidji State University
Office of Admissions and Scholarships
102 Deputy Hall, Scholarship Officer
Bemidji, MN 56601-2699

1309
Star Tribune-Foundation Scholarship

AMOUNT: None Specified DEADLINE: Varies
MAJOR: Mass Communications, Journalism

The Star Tribune-Foundation Scholarship is open to Bemidji State University students. To be considered for this award, you must be a Native American majoring in mass communications.

Award requirements change regularly. No GPA requirement specified.

Bemidji State University
Office of Admissions and Scholarships
102 Deputy Hall, Scholarship Officer
Bemidji, MN 56601-2699

1310
Theater Scholarship

AMOUNT: None Specified DEADLINE: Varies
MAJOR: Speech/Theater

The Theater Scholarship is open to newly entering students majoring in speech/theater. A second award is available to you if you are a returning Bemidji student who is also majoring in speech/theater. Award requirements change regularly. No GPA requirement specified.

Bemidji State University
Office of Admissions and Scholarships
102 Deputy Hall, Scholarship Officer
Bemidji, MN 56601-2699

1311
Transfer Student Scholarship

AMOUNT: $600 DEADLINE: April 1
MAJOR: All Areas of Study

The Transfer Student Scholarship is open to students transferring from a Minnesota community college to Bemidji State University. To be considered for this award, you must have completed an associate's degree with a minimum 3.5 GPA. An application for admission serves as your scholarship application. Award requirements change regularly. GPA must be 3.5-4.0.

Bemidji State University
Office of Admissions and Scholarships
102 Deputy Hall, Scholarship Officer
Bemidji, MN 56601-2699

Black Hills State University

1312
Black Hills State Scholarship

AMOUNT: $50-$10000 DEADLINE: March 1
MAJOR: All Areas of Study

You can apply for these scholarships if you are an incoming freshman who has been admitted to Black Hills State University. These scholarships are awarded based on merit and demonstrated financial need. You must be a U.S. citizen or an eligible non-citizen to apply. Award requirements change regularly. No GPA requirement specified.

Black Hills State University
The Enrollment Center
1200 University, Box 9502
Spearfish, SD 57799

Bluffton College

1313
Academic Honors Scholarship

AMOUNT: $8336 DEADLINE: Varies
MAJOR: All Areas of Study

The Bluffton College Academic Honors Scholarship is open to full-time residential students with a minimum 3.5 GPA and a class ranking in the top 10%. Applicant must have at least an 1140 SAT or 26 ACT score. Award requirements change regularly. Please send a self-addressed, stamped envelope to receive your application and any further instructions from the scholarship provider. GPA must be 3.5-4.0.

Bluffton College
Office of Admissions
280 West College Avenue
Bluffton, OH 45817-1196

1314
Bluffton College Grant

AMOUNT: Maximum: $4000 DEADLINE: April 14
MAJOR: All Areas of Study

The Bluffton College Grant is available to Bluffton undergraduates who demonstrate leadership potential, academic excellence, and outstanding character. Award requirements change regularly. Please write to the address provided for further information. GPA must be 3.0-4.0.

Bluffton College
Office of Admissions
280 West College Avenue
Bluffton, OH 45817-1196

1315
Church College Scholarship

AMOUNT: $1000 DEADLINE: Varies
MAJOR: All Areas of Study

Matching scholarships at Bluffton College for undergraduates who receive a scholarship through their church. Bluffton will match the church award up to $1000 per year. Award requirements change regularly. For further information, please write to the address listed, including a self-addressed, stamped envelope, call (800) 488-3257, or browse the Bluffton College website at www.bluffton.edu. No GPA requirement specified.

Bluffton College
Office of Admissions
280 West College Avenue
Bluffton, OH 45817-1196

1316
Leadership/Service Grants

AMOUNT: $1500-$3000 DEADLINE: Varies
MAJOR: All Areas of Study

The Bluffton College Leadership/Service Grants are available to freshmen who demonstrate strong leadership skills and service at the high school level - in church, school, or the community. Applicants must meet regular admission requirements. Award requirements change regularly. For further information, please write to the address listed, including a self-addressed, stamped envelope, call (800) 488-3257, or browse the

Bluffton College website at www.bluffton.edu. GPA must be 2.7-4.0.

Bluffton College
Office of Admissions
280 West College Avenue
Bluffton, OH 45817-1196

1317
Minister Family Grant

AMOUNT: Maximum: $4000 DEADLINE: April 14
MAJOR: All Areas of Study

The Bluffton College Minister Family Grant is open to undergraduates who are children of ministers. Award requirements change regularly. Please write to the address provided for further information. No GPA requirement specified.

Bluffton College
Office of Admissions
280 West College Avenue
Bluffton, OH 45817-1196

1318
Music Scholarship

AMOUNT: $1200 DEADLINE: April 14
MAJOR: Music

The Bluffton College Music Scholarships are available to undergraduates who plan to or are pursuing a degree in music. Award requirements change regularly. Please write to the address provided for further information. No GPA requirement specified.

Bluffton College
Office of Admissions
280 West College Avenue
Bluffton, OH 45817-1196

1319
President's Scholarships

AMOUNT: None Specified DEADLINE: April 14
MAJOR: All Areas of Study

The Bluffton College President's Scholarships are available to undergraduates who demonstrate exceptional academic ability. To qualify for the full-tuition scholarships, students must have a minimum GPA of 3.5, a class ranking in the top 10% and have at least a 1050 SAT or 26 ACT score. Award requirements change regularly. Write to the address below for details. GPA must be 3.5.

Bluffton College
Office of Admissions
280 West College Avenue
Bluffton, OH 45817-1196

Bradford College

Merit-Based/Presidential/Leadership Scholarships

AMOUNT: None Specified DEADLINE: Varies
MAJOR: Creative Arts

Open to undergraduate creative arts students at Bradford College. Must submit art portfolios and demonstrate leadership abilities and community service. Award requirements change regularly. Please send a self-addressed, stamped envelope to receive your application and any further instructions from the scholarship provider, email to admissions@bnet.bradford.edu, or visit their website at www.bradford.edu. GPA must be 2.8-4.0.

Bradford College
Admissions Office
320 South Main Street
Haverhill, MA 01835-7332

1321
Transfer Scholarship

AMOUNT: None Specified DEADLINE: Varies
MAJOR: Creative Arts

Open to undergraduate transfer students at Bradford College. Must have a minimum 3.2 GPA and be majoring in creative arts. Art portfolios required. Award requirements change regularly. Please send a self-addressed, stamped envelope to receive your application and any further instructions from the scholarship provider, email to admissions@bnet.bradford.edu, or visit their website at www.bradford.edu. GPA must be 3.2-4.0.

Bradford College
Admissions Office
320 South Main Street
Haverhill, MA 01835-7332

Bradford School

1322
Bradford School Scholarship - Houston Campus

AMOUNT: $1000 DEADLINE: Varies
MAJOR: All Areas of Study

The Bradford School (Houston) Scholarship has four $1,000 scholarships which are open to high school seniors in the Houston, TX, area who are graduating high school in 2001. To be considered for the award, you should be planning to enroll in Bradford, Houston Campus the following fall. You must take a competitive scholarship test administered at the Bradford School. Award requirements change regularly. No GPA requirement specified.

Bradford School
4669 Southwest Freeway
Houston, TX 77027

Bradley University

Bradley Legacy Scholarships

AMOUNT: $1500 DEADLINE: March 1
MAJOR: All Areas of Study

This scholarship is open to full-time incoming freshmen and transfer students whose parent(s) or grandparent(s) are Bradley graduates. This award is renewable if you remain in good academic standing. Award requirements change regularly. No GPA requirement specified.

Bradley University
Office of Financial Assistance
Peoria, IL 61625

1324
Bradley National Merit and Presidential Scholarships

AMOUNT: None Specified DEADLINE: Varies
MAJOR: All Areas of Study

This scholarship is open to incoming freshmen at Bradley University who have been designated National Merit Finalists after taking the PSAT/NMSQT test in high school during their junior year. This scholarship combines National Merit dollars, the Presidential Scholarship, and other sources of assistance to equal 100% of tuition. Renewal is contingent upon remaining a National Merit Scholar. Award requirements change regularly. For further information, please contact the Office of Financial Aid. No GPA requirement specified.

Bradley University
Office of Financial Assistance
Peoria, IL, 61625

1325
Caterpillar, Inc., Employee Dependents Scholarships

AMOUNT: $1500-$2500 DEADLINE: March 1
MAJOR: All Areas of Study

This scholarship is open to full-time undergraduate dependents of eligible employees of Caterpillar, Inc., who are attending Bradley University. Award requirements change regularly. No GPA requirement specified.

Bradley University
Office of Financial Assistance
Peoria, IL, 61625

1326
Deans-Valedictorian Scholarship

AMOUNT: $5000 DEADLINE: March 1
MAJOR: All Areas of Study

This scholarship is open to entering freshmen who rank in the top 10% of their class and have a combined SAT score of at least 1240 or an ACT of 28. Award amounts vary from $5000 to one-half of tuition. Entering freshmen who rank first in their graduating class receive a one-half tuition award. Award requirements change regularly. GPA must be 3.7-4.0.

Bradley University
Office of Financial Assistance
Peoria, IL, 61625

1327
Fine Art Scholarships

AMOUNT: $1000-$2500 DEADLINE: March 1
MAJOR: All Areas of Study

This scholarship is open to students with particular talent in the fine and performing arts, including art, music, theater, and forensics. Selection is competitive and, with the exception of forensics, requires you to declare a major in a specialty area. Auditions and/or portfolio submissions are required. Award requirements change regularly. No GPA requirement specified.

Bradley University
Office of Financial Assistance
Peoria, IL, 61625

1328
Garrett-Provost Scholars

AMOUNT: $2500-$8000 DEADLINE: March 1
MAJOR: All Areas of Study

Through this program, Bradley recognizes outstanding academic achievement of entering freshmen from multicultural or ethnically diverse backgrounds. You must be in the top 15% of your graduating class. Awards vary from $2500 to $8000 per year. Award requirements change regularly. GPA must be 3.6-4.0.

Bradley University
Office of Financial Assistance
Peoria, IL, 61625

1329
Phi Theta Kappa Scholarship

AMOUNT: Maximum: $4000 DEADLINE: May 1
MAJOR: All Areas of Study

This scholarship is open to members who are transfer students with the last 12 hours of transferable course work coming from an accredited community college. You must be enrolled for full-time study at Bradley University. Award requirements change regularly. No GPA requirement specified.

Bradley University
Office of Financial Assistance
Peoria, IL, 61625

1330
Transfer Excellence Scholarship

AMOUNT: Maximum: $5000 DEADLINE: May 1
MAJOR: All Areas of Study

This scholarship is open to transfer students with a minimum 3.5 GPA and who have acquired 45 hours of transferable course-work, the last 24 hours of credit having been earned at a community college. You must be enrolled for full-time study at Bradley University. Award requirements change regularly. GPA must be 3.5-4.0.

Bradley University
Office of Financial Assistance
Peoria, IL, 61625

Brandeis University

1331
Annenberg Scholarship

AMOUNT: Maximum: $19000 DEADLINE: Varies
MAJOR: All Areas of Study

The Annenberg Scholarships are open to incoming freshmen who have distinguished themselves both in academic studies and in the breadth of their intellectual pursuits. To be considered for this award, you must also demonstrate a commitment to a variety of activities beyond the classroom. These scholarships are renewable provided that a specific level of academic achievement is maintained. The deadline for this award is the same as the admission application deadline. Award requirements change regularly. Please send a self-addressed, stamped envelope to receive your application and any further information from the scholarship provider; or visit the website at www.brandeis.edu. No GPA requirement specified.

Brandeis University
Office of Admissions
415 South Street, MS 003
Waltham, MA 02454-9110

1332
Brandeis-Waltham Scholarship

AMOUNT: None Specified DEADLINE: Varies
MAJOR: All Areas of Study

The Brandeis-Waltham Scholarship is open to four graduating seniors from Waltham High School (Waltham, MA) who demonstrate unusually high academic potential. To be considered for this award, you must rank in the top portion of your class, earn high standardized test scores, and participate in a variety of high school and community activities. This full-tuition scholarship is renewable provided that a specific level of academic achievement is maintained. The deadline for this award is the same as the admission application deadline. Award requirements change regularly. Please send a self-addressed, stamped envelope to receive your application and any further information from the scholarship provider; or visit the website at www.brandeis.edu. No GPA requirement specified.

Brandeis University
Office of Admissions
415 South Street, MS 003
Waltham, MA 02454-9110

1333
Gilbert Grant

AMOUNT: Maximum: $19000 DEADLINE: Varies
MAJOR: All Areas of Study

The Gilbert Grant is open to incoming freshmen who demonstrate exceptional academic promise. To be considered for this award, you must rank at the top of your class, earn standardized test scores in the top 2% nationally, and have participated in intellectual activities beyond the traditional high school curriculum. These scholarships are renewable if you maintain a specific level of academic achievement. The deadline for this award is the same as the admission application deadline. Award requirements change regularly. Please send a self-addressed, stamped envelope to receive your application and any further information from the scholarship provider. No GPA requirement specified.

Brandeis University
Office of Admissions
415 South Street, MS 003
Waltham, MA 02454-9110

1334
Hiatt Challenger Memorial Scholarship

AMOUNT: None Specified DEADLINE: Varies
MAJOR: All Areas of Study

The Hiatt Challenger Memorial Scholarship is open to incoming freshmen who demonstrate unusually high academic potential. To be considered for this award, you must rank in the top portion of your class, earn high standardized test scores, and participate in a wide range of high school and community activities. The award is 75% of tuition and is renewable provided that a specific level of academic achievement is maintained. The deadline for this award is the same as the admission application deadline. Award requirements change regularly. Please send a self-addressed, stamped envelope to receive your application and any further information from the scholarship provider; or visit the website at www.brandeis.edu. No GPA requirement specified.

Brandeis University
Office of Admissions
415 South Street, MS 003
Waltham, MA 02454-9110

1335
Justice Louis D. Brandeis Scholarship

AMOUNT: Maximum: $19000 DEADLINE: Varies
MAJOR: All Areas of Study

The Justice Louis D. Brandeis Scholarship is open to incoming freshmen who demonstrate exceptional academic promise. To be considered for this award, you must rank at the top of

your class, earn standardized test scores in the top 2% nationally, and have participated in intellectual activities beyond the traditional high school curriculum. These scholarships are renewable if you maintain a specific level of academic achievement. The deadline for this award is the same as the admission application deadline. Award requirements change regularly. Please send a self-addressed, stamped envelope to receive your application and any further information from the scholarship provider; or visit the website at www.brandeis.edu. No GPA requirement specified.

Brandeis University
Office of Admissions
415 South Street, MS 003
Waltham, MA 02454-9110

1336
Norman S. Rabb Scholarship

AMOUNT: Maximum: $19000 DEADLINE: Varies
MAJOR: All Areas of Study

The Norman S. Rabb Scholarship is open to incoming freshmen who demonstrate exceptional academic promise and may be used for study abroad. To be considered for this award, you must rank at the top of your class, earn standardized test scores in the top 2% nationally, and have participated in intellectual activities beyond the traditional high school curriculum. These scholarships are renewable if you maintain a specific level of academic achievement. The deadline for this award is the same as the admission application deadline. Award requirements change regularly. Please send a self-addressed, stamped envelope to receive your application and any further information from the scholarship provider. No GPA requirement specified.

Brandeis University
Office of Admissions
415 South Street, MS 003
Waltham, MA 02454-9110

1337
Presidential Award

AMOUNT: Maximum: $11000 DEADLINE: Varies
MAJOR: All Areas of Study

The Presidential Award is open to incoming freshmen who demonstrate unusually high academic potential. To be considered for this award, you must rank in the top portion of your class, earn high standardized test scores, and participate in a wide range of high school and community activities. This scholarship is renewable provided that a specific level of academic achievement is maintained. The deadline for this award is the same as the admission application deadline. Award requirements change regularly. Please send a self-addressed, stamped envelope to receive your application and any further information from the scholarship provider; or visit the website at www.brandeis.edu. No GPA requirement specified.

Brandeis University
Office of Admissions
415 South Street, MS 003
Waltham, MA 02454-9110

Brescia University

1338
Brescia University Scholarships

AMOUNT: None Specified DEADLINE: March 15
MAJOR: All Areas of Study

Open to incoming freshmen and transfer students admitted to Brescia University who have a minimum 3.0 GPA and have applied for Federal and Kentucky State Financial Aid. Award requirements change regularly. For further information, please contact the address listed or call (877) 273-7242, (502) 686-4241. You may also visit their website: www.admissions@brescia.edu. GPA must be 3.0-4.0.

Brescia University
Office of Admissions
717 Frederica Street
Owensboro, KY 42301

Brigham Young University

1339
National Tourism Utah - Keith Griffall Scholarship

AMOUNT: $1000 DEADLINE: April 17
MAJOR: Travel and Tourism, Hotel/Restaurant Management

The National Tourism Utah-Keith Griffall Scholarship is open to students who are pursuing a degree in a travel or tourism-related field. To be considered for the award, you must be a junior or senior enrolled at either the University of Utah or Brigham Young University. Award requirements change regularly. No GPA requirement specified.

National Tourism Foundation
PO Box 3071
546 East Main Street
Lexington, KY 40508-3071

Bryan College

1340
Academic Scholarship

AMOUNT: $2500 DEADLINE: May 1
MAJOR: All Areas of Study

This scholarship is open to incoming freshmen who have 3.6 high school GPA and either a minimum 26 ACT or 1180 SAT. Transfer students may qualify based upon their high school GPA and test scores, pro-rated using the Continuance Requirements based upon their college GPA. Award requirements change regularly. GPA must be 3.6-4.0.

Bryan College
Office of Financial Aid
PO Box 7000
Dayton, TN 37321-7000

1341
Academic Scholarship

AMOUNT: $1500 DEADLINE: May 1
MAJOR: All Areas of Study

This scholarship is for incoming freshmen who have a 3.4 high school GPA and either a minimum 24 ACT or 1100 SAT. Transfer students may qualify based upon their high school GPA and test scores, pro-rated using the Continuance Requirements based upon their college GPA. Award requirements change regularly. GPA must be 3.4-4.0.

Bryan College
Office of Financial Aid
PO Box 7000
Dayton, TN 37321-7000

1342
Bryan College Music Scholarship

AMOUNT: None Specified DEADLINE: May 1
MAJOR: Music

This award is granted to incoming freshmen, transfer students, and continuing students who demonstrate musical ability and are pursuing a major or a minor in music. For the application process, you will be required to complete a Bryan College financial aid application and audition with the music faculty. Award requirements change regularly. No GPA requirement specified.

Bryan College
Office of Financial Aid
PO Box 7000
Dayton, TN 37321-7000

1343
Bryan College Scholarship

AMOUNT: $1000 DEADLINE: May 1
MAJOR: All Areas of Study

This award is for incoming freshmen who have a 3.0 high school GPA as well as a minimum 22 ACT or 1030 SAT. Transfer students may qualify based upon their high school GPA and test scores, pro-rated using the Continuance Requirements based upon their college GPA. Award requirements change regularly. GPA must be 3.0-4.0.

Bryan College
Office of Financial Aid
PO Box 7000
Dayton, TN 37321-7000

1344
Dean's Scholarship

AMOUNT: $3000 DEADLINE: May
MAJOR: All Areas of Study

This award is for incoming freshmen who compete for the Presidential Scholarship and/or the Presidential Music Award, but are not one of the recipients. You must complete a Bryan College financial aid form, submit a written essay, and interview with the faculty. Award requirements change regularly. GPA must be 3.6-4.0.

Bryan College
Office of Financial Aid
PO Box 7000
Dayton, TN 37321-7000

1345
Presidential Music Scholarship

AMOUNT: $6000 DEADLINE: May 1
MAJOR: Music

This scholarship is open to an incoming freshman with a 3.0 high school GPA. You must also have a minimum 22 ACT or a 1030 SAT. Completion of a Bryan College financial aid application, a submission of a written essay, and an audition with the music faculty are required. Award requirements change regularly. GPA must be 3.0-4.0.

Bryan College
Office of Financial Aid
PO Box 7000
Dayton, TN 37321-7000

1346
Presidential Scholarship

AMOUNT: $6000 DEADLINE: May 1
MAJOR: All Areas of Study

This scholarship is open to incoming freshmen with a high school GPA of at least 3.6. You must have a minimum 26 ACT or 1180 SAT. Completion of a Bryan College financial aid application, a written essay, and a faculty interview are required. Award requirements change regularly. GPA must be 3.6-4.0.

Bryan College
Office of Financial Aid
PO Box 7000
Dayton, TN 37321-7000

California Culinary Academy

1347
California Culinary Academy Educational Foundation Scholarship

AMOUNT: $500-$2500 DEADLINE: Varies
MAJOR: Culinary Arts

The California Culinary Academy Educational Foundation Scholarship is open to students pursing a career in food and wine. The scholarship will be awarded on the basis of academic merit, financial need, leadership, and demonstrated dedication to a career in food and wine. There are four deadline dates: January 31, April 30, July 31, and October 31. Award requirements change regularly. No GPA requirement specified.

California Culinary Academy
Educational Foundation
625 Polk Street
San Francisco, CA 94102

California State University, Fullerton

1348
Alvin Keller Excellence in Theater Scholarship

AMOUNT: $500 DEADLINE: February 11
MAJOR: Theater, Dance

The Alvin Keller Excellence in Theater Scholarship is open to continuing undergraduates and graduate students at California State University, Fullerton, who are theater or dance majors. This award requires that you have a minimum GPA of 3.25; a record of significant creative achievement; and excellence in any one area of acting, directing, dance, design, technical theater, or stage management. Financial need will be strongly considered. Award requirements change regularly. GPA must be 3.25-4.0.

California State University, Fullerton - Arts/Music Department
Attn: Scholarship Committee
800 N. State College Blvd., Room VA-199c
Fullerton, CA 92831-3599

1349
Amy Sheridan Memorial Scholarship

AMOUNT: $500 DEADLINE: February 11
MAJOR: Musical Theater

The Amy Sheridan Memorial Scholarship is open to students in the musical theater BFA program at California State University, Fullerton. This award requires that you show musical theater performance ability and evidence of creative achievement. Award requirements change regularly. No GPA requirement specified.

California State University, Fullerton - Arts/Music Department
Attn: Scholarship Committee
800 N. State College Blvd., Room VA-199c
Fullerton, CA 92831-3599

1350
Assumption Program of Loans for Education

AMOUNT: Maximum: $11000 DEADLINE: June 16
MAJOR: Education

The Assumption Program of Loans for Education is open to students obtaining their teaching credentials at California State University, Fullerton. To be considered for these funds, you must be a California resident, enrolled in 10 units in a program leading to a baccalaureate degree or in an approved teacher preparation program, have completed 60 or more units prior to the upcoming fall semester, and been approved to receive an educational loan. Additional criteria include that you intend to teach in an area of low-income families or in an area of subject need (special education, English, math, science, bilingual education, or foreign language). Award requirements change regularly. No GPA requirement specified.

California State University, Fullerton - Human
Services/Teaching
Attn: HDSC
800 N. State College Blvd., EC-324
Fullerton, CA 92831-3599

1351
Auto Club Insurance Scholarship

AMOUNT: $500 DEADLINE: March 2
MAJOR: Business

The Auto Club Insurance Scholarship is open to students at
California State University, Fullerton, who are enrolled in the
School of Business Administration and Economics. To be eligible for this award, you must be a full-time business major,
have a minimum 3.0 GPA, and show financial need. An additional requirement is that you have completed or are currently
enrolled in one or more insurance and financial services
courses. Award requirements change regularly. GPA must be
3.0-4.0.

California State University, Fullerton - Business and
Economics
Attn: Scholarship Coordinator
800 N. State College Blvd., LH-700
Fullerton, CA 92831-3599

1352
Chen-Da Su Insurance Scholarship

AMOUNT: $500 DEADLINE: March 2
MAJOR: Business

The Chen-Da Su Insurance Scholarship is open to Asian students at California State University, Fullerton, who are
enrolled in the School of Business Administration and
Economics. To be eligible for this award, you must be a full-
time business major, have a minimum 2.8 GPA, and show
financial need. Additional requirements include that you have
completed or are currently enrolled in an insurance course and
that you submit a copy of your last grade report. Award
requirements change regularly. GPA must be 2.8-4.0.

California State University, Fullerton - Business and
Economics
Attn: Scholarship Coordinator
800 N. State College Blvd., LH-700
Fullerton, CA 92831-3599

1353
Christine Lyon Dance Scholarship

AMOUNT: $500 DEADLINE: February 11
MAJOR: Dance

The Christine Lyon Dance Scholarship is open to new and
continuing dance majors at California State University,
Fullerton. This award requires that you show scholastic
achievement, evidence of creative involvement and achievement, and financial need. Award requirements change regularly. No GPA requirement specified.

California State University, Fullerton - Arts/Music Department
Attn: Scholarship Committee
800 N. State College Blvd., Room VA-199c
Fullerton, CA 92831-3599

1354
Dr. John Nichols Scholarship

AMOUNT: None Specified DEADLINE: March 2
MAJOR: Finance

The Dr. John Nichols Scholarship is open to students at
California State University, Fullerton, who are enrolled in the
School of Business Administration and Economics. To be eligible for this award, you must be a finance major, have a
strong GPA, and demonstrate financial need. Award requirements change regularly. No GPA requirement specified.

California State University, Fullerton - Business and
Economics
Attn: Scholarship Coordinator
800 N. State College Blvd., LH-700
Fullerton, CA 92831-3599

1355
Dr. Peter M. Mlynaryk Outstanding Real Estate Student Award

AMOUNT: None Specified DEADLINE: March 2
MAJOR: Real Estate

The Dr. Peter M. Mlynaryk Outstanding Real Estate Student
Award is open to students at California State University,
Fullerton, who are enrolled in the School of Business
Administration and Economics. To be eligible for this award,
you must be a real estate major and demonstrate academic
achievement and service to the department. Award requirements change regularly. No GPA requirement specified.

California State University, Fullerton - Business and
Economics
Attn: Scholarship Coordinator
800 N. State College Blvd., LH-700
Fullerton, CA 92831-3599

1356
Economics Wall Street Journal Student Award

AMOUNT: None Specified DEADLINE: March 2
MAJOR: Economics

The Economics Wall Street Journal Student Award is open to
students at California State University, Fullerton, who are
enrolled in the School of Business Administration and
Economics. To be eligible for this award, you must be an economics major. Recipients are selected on the basis of academic performance and extracurricular activities. Award requirements change regularly. No GPA requirement specified.

California State University, Fullerton - Business and
Economics
Attn: Scholarship Coordinator
800 N. State College Blvd., LH-700
Fullerton, CA 92831-3599

1357
Edith Morgan Scholarship

AMOUNT: $500 DEADLINE: February 11
MAJOR: Theater and Dance

The Edith Morgan Scholarships are open to new and continuing theater and dance majors at California State University, Fullerton. Award requirements change regularly. No GPA requirement specified.

California State University, Fullerton - Arts/Music Department
Attn: Scholarship Committee
800 N. State College Blvd., Room VA-199c
Fullerton, CA 92831-3599

1358
Experian Corporate Scholars Program

AMOUNT: $2000 DEADLINE: Varies
MAJOR: Management Information Systems

The Experian Corporate Scholars Program is open to students at California State University, Fullerton, who are enrolled in the School of Business Administration and Economics. To be considered for this award, you must be a continuing management information systems (MIS) major. The scholarship is awarded on the basis of outstanding scholarship and academic achievement. This program consists of a paid 20-hour-per-week internship in addition to a $2000 scholarship, which is paid after the recipient has completed six months working as an intern. Award requirements change regularly. To request an application contact Jim Hightower, Internship Coordinator for the MIS Department in Langsdorf Hall 540. Applicants will be prescreened by the department, and candidates will be recommended to Experian Corporation. Experian will select the award finalists. No GPA requirement specified.

California State University, Fullerton - Business and Economics
Attn: Scholarship Coordinator
800 N. State College Blvd., LH-700
Fullerton, CA 92831-3599

1359
Fannie Shaftel Scholarship

AMOUNT: $500 DEADLINE: Varies
MAJOR: Elementary Education (Multiple Subject Credential Program)

The Fannie Shaftel Scholarship is open to students accepted or enrolled in the Multiple Subject Credential Program at California State University, Fullerton. To be considered for this award, you must demonstrate a professional aptitude for teaching and have financial need. Award requirements change regularly. No GPA requirement specified.

California State University, Fullerton - Human Services/Teaching
Attn: HDSC
800 N. State College Blvd., EC-324
Fullerton, CA 92831-3599

1360
Finance Wall Street Journal Student Award

AMOUNT: None Specified DEADLINE: March 2
MAJOR: Finance

The Finance Wall Street Journal Student Award is open to students at California State University, Fullerton, who are enrolled in the School of Business Administration and Economics. To be eligible for this award, you must be a finance major, have a strong GPA, and demonstrate service to the department. Award requirements change regularly. No GPA requirement specified.

California State University, Fullerton - Business and Economics
Attn: Scholarship Coordinator
800 N. State College Blvd., LH-700
Fullerton, CA 92831-3599

1361
Francisco J. Valle Scholarship

AMOUNT: $1000 DEADLINE: March 2
MAJOR: Business

The Francisco J. Valle Scholarship is open to Hispanic students at California State University, Fullerton, who are enrolled in the School of Business Administration and Economics. To be eligible for this award, you must be a continuing business student with a minimum 2.0 GPA. Award requirements change regularly. GPA must be 2.0-4.0.

California State University, Fullerton - Business and Economics
Attn: Scholarship Coordinator
800 N. State College Blvd., LH-700
Fullerton, CA 92831-3599

1362
Front and Center Scholarship

AMOUNT: $500 DEADLINE: February 16
MAJOR: Theater and Dance

The Front and Center Scholarships are open to continuing theater and dance majors at California State University, Fullerton. There are six awards, which are allocated as follows: extraordinary contributions related to theater and dance production work in the areas of dance (one award), musical theater (one award), design/technical theater (one award), and acting/directing (one award). Two scholarships are reserved to recognize exceptional service to the department/special events and/or community outreach leadership in any area. Award requirements change regularly. No GPA requirement specified.

California State University, Fullerton - Arts/Music Department
Attn: Scholarship Committee
800 N. State College Blvd., Room VA-199c
Fullerton, CA 92831-3599

1363
International Marketing Association Scholarship

AMOUNT: None Specified DEADLINE: March 2
MAJOR: International Marketing

The International Marketing Association Scholarship is open to continuing students at California State University, Fullerton, who are enrolled in the School of Business Administration and Economics. To be eligible for this award, you must be an international marketing major, have a minimum 3.0 GPA, and be involved in extracurricular and student international activities. Award requirements change regularly. GPA must be 3.0-4.0.

California State University, Fullerton - Business and Economics
Attn: Scholarship Coordinator
800 N. State College Blvd., LH-700
Fullerton, CA 92831-3599

1364
James D. Young Founder's Scholarship

AMOUNT: $1500 DEADLINE: February 11
MAJOR: Theater and Dance

The James D. Young Founder's Scholarship is open to new and continuing theater and dance majors at California State University, Fullerton. This award requires that you show a strong interest in pursuing teaching as a career and demonstrate dedication and seriousness of purpose. Award requirements change regularly. No GPA requirement specified.

California State University, Fullerton - Arts/Music Department
Attn: Scholarship Committee
800 N. State College Blvd., Room VA-199c
Fullerton, CA 92831-3599

1365
Jeffrey and Rosalie Bacon Scholarship

AMOUNT: $2000 DEADLINE: March 2
MAJOR: Art

The Jeffrey and Rosalie Bacon Scholarship is open to full-time undergraduate and graduate art majors at California State University, Fullerton, who are U.S. citizens. Preference is given to new/incoming students. Selection is based on demonstrated talent and your portfolio review. You are required to submit a minimum of six slides of your current work. Award requirements change regularly. No GPA requirement specified.

California State University, Fullerton - Arts/Music Department
Attn: Scholarship Committee
800 N. State College Blvd., Room VA-199c
Fullerton, CA 92831-3599

1366
Jerry Goodwin Scholarship

AMOUNT: $1200 DEADLINE: February 11
MAJOR: Musical Theater

The Jerry Goodwin Scholarship is open to new and continuing musical theater majors at California State University, Fullerton. Award requirements change regularly. No GPA requirement specified.

California State University, Fullerton - Arts/Music Department
Attn: Scholarship Committee
800 N. State College Blvd., Room VA-199c
Fullerton, CA 92831-3599

1367
Maria Dolores Hernandez Fund

AMOUNT: $1000-$5000 DEADLINE: April 30
MAJOR: Nursing

The Maria Dolores Hernandez Fund is open to students who plan to enroll or have been admitted to the Nursing Department at California State University, Fullerton. Your application will be evaluated on the basis of your leadership potential and/or record of leadership in nursing. Award requirements change regularly. No GPA requirement specified.

California State University, Fullerton - Nursing Department
Attn: Scholarship Coordinator
P.O. Box 6868
Fullerton, CA 92834-6868

1368
Mercury Insurance Scholarship

AMOUNT: $500 DEADLINE: March 2
MAJOR: Business

The Mercury Insurance Scholarship is open to students at California State University, Fullerton, who are enrolled in the School of Business Administration and Economics. To be eligible for this award, you must be a full-time business major, have a minimum 3.0 GPA, and show financial need. An additional requirement is that you have completed or are currently enrolled in an insurance course. Award requirements change regularly. GPA must be 3.0-4.0.

California State University, Fullerton - Business and Economics
Attn: Scholarship Coordinator
800 N. State College Blvd., LH-700
Fullerton, CA 92831-3599

1369
Mildred Ransdorf Donoghue Credential Program Scholarship

AMOUNT: $500 DEADLINE: December 11
MAJOR: Elementary Education (Multiple Subject Credential Program)

The Mildred Ransdorf Donoghue Credential Program Scholarship is open to women enrolled in the Multiple Subject Credential Program at California State University, Fullerton. To be considered for this award, you must be a continuing elementary education student, have a bachelor's degree from an accredited American college or university, be a native-born

U.S. citizen at least 25 years of age, and be enrolled in at least 15 units. The scholarship is awarded to students of Slavic, German, Irish, Scandinavian, French, British, or Italian descent. Award requirements change regularly. No GPA requirement specified.

California State University, Fullerton - Human
Services/Teaching
Attn: HDSC
800 N. State College Blvd., EC-324
Fullerton, CA 92831-3599

1370
Minority Teaching Scholarship

AMOUNT: $1000 DEADLINE: March 3
MAJOR: Elementary and Secondary Education (Teaching Credential Program)

The Minority Teaching Scholarship is open to prospective elementary and secondary teachers who are eligible for admission to the Teaching Credential Program at California State University, Fullerton. To be considered for this award, you must be an underrepresented student and submit a personal statement and two CSUF faculty recommendations. Your application will be evaluated on the basis of your financial need, academic potential, and professional aptitude for teaching. Award requirements change regularly. No GPA requirement specified.

California State University, Fullerton - Human
Services/Teaching
Attn: HDSC
800 N. State College Blvd., EC-324
Fullerton, CA 92831-3599

1371
Myrt Purkiss Scholarship

AMOUNT: None Specified DEADLINE: Varies
MAJOR: Visual Arts

The Myrt Purkiss Scholarship is open to first-time freshmen who are entering California State University, Fullerton, as full-time visual arts majors. You are required to submit a minimum of six slides of your current work and a letter of recommendation as indication of your potential and ability to develop artistic talent and overall academic scholarship. The scholarship deadline is in mid-April. Award requirements change regularly. No GPA requirement specified.

California State University, Fullerton - Arts/Music Department
Attn: Scholarship Committee
800 N. State College Blvd., Room VA-199c
Fullerton, CA 92831-3599

1372
National Association of Hispanic Nurses Scholarship

AMOUNT: None Specified DEADLINE: November 30
MAJOR: Nursing

The National Association of Hispanic Nurses Scholarship is open to students who plan to enroll or have been admitted to the Nursing Department at California State University, Fullerton. To be considered for this award, you must have a minimum 3.0 GPA and be a resident of Orange County (CA) or be nominated by a NAHN Orange County member. Your

application will be evaluated on the basis of your potential for leadership in nursing. Award requirements change regularly. GPA must be 3.0-4.0.

California State University, Fullerton - Nursing Department
Attn: Scholarship Coordinator
P.O. Box 6868
Fullerton, CA 92834-6868

1373
New Student Music Scholarships

AMOUNT: None Specified DEADLINE: Varies
MAJOR: Music

The New Student Music Scholarships are open to incoming freshman music majors at California State University, Fullerton, and are based on auditions held in mid-March. Selection criteria for these awards include the quality of your audition, your academic record, the donors' wishes, and the department's needs. Scholarships range in value from modest assistance for one year to full-fee awards for four years. All auditioners are automatically considered for all of the music department's scholarships for which they are eligible. Scholarships are normally awarded only to prospective students who have applied to CSUF prior to March 15. Award requirements change regularly. No GPA requirement specified.

California State University, Fullerton - Arts/Music Department
Attn: Scholarship Committee
800 N. State College Blvd., Room VA-199c
Fullerton, CA 92831-3599

1374
Pacific Life Insurance Scholarship

AMOUNT: $500 DEADLINE: March 2
MAJOR: Business

The Pacific Life Insurance Scholarship is open to students at California State University, Fullerton, who are enrolled in the School of Business Administration and Economics. To be eligible for this award, you must be a full-time business major, have a minimum 3.0 GPA, and show financial need. An additional requirement is that you have completed or are currently enrolled in one or more insurance and financial services courses. Award requirements change regularly. GPA must be 3.0-4.0.

California State University, Fullerton - Business and
Economics
Attn: Scholarship Coordinator
800 N. State College Blvd., LH-700
Fullerton, CA 92831-3599

1375
Prudential/Bob Kargenian Scholarship

AMOUNT: $2000 DEADLINE: March 2
MAJOR: Finance

The Prudential/Bob Kargenian Scholarship is open to students at California State University, Fullerton, who are enrolled in the School of Business Administration and Economics. To be eligible for this award, you must be a finance major with a strong career interest in investments and financial planning and have a minimum 3.1 GPA. Award requirements change regularly. GPA must be 3.1-4.0.

California State University, Fullerton - Business and Economics
Attn: Scholarship Coordinator
800 N. State College Blvd., LH-700
Fullerton, CA 92831-3599

1376
Really Groovy Dance Scholarship

AMOUNT: $500 DEADLINE: February 11
MAJOR: Dance (Performance)

The Really Groovy Dance Scholarship is open to new and continuing dance and performance majors at California State University, Fullerton. This award requires that you be a full-time student. Pageantry students are encouraged to apply, and you need not have prior professional training. Award requirements change regularly. No GPA requirement specified.

California State University, Fullerton - Arts/Music Department
Attn: Scholarship Committee
800 N. State College Blvd., Room VA-199c
Fullerton, CA 92831-3599

1377
Robert Christianson Dance Scholarship

AMOUNT: $500 DEADLINE: February 16
MAJOR: Dance

The Robert Christianson Dance Scholarship is open to continuing undergraduate dance majors at California State University, Fullerton. The requirements for this award are that you show scholastic and creative achievement, financial need, and evidence of involvement in and service to the department. Award requirements change regularly. No GPA requirement specified.

California State University, Fullerton - Arts/Music Department
Attn: Scholarship Committee
800 N. State College Blvd., Room VA-199c
Fullerton, CA 92831-3599

1378
Robert Garrison Design/Technical Theater Scholarship

AMOUNT: $500 DEADLINE: February 16
MAJOR: Technical Theater and Design

The Robert Garrison Design/Technical Theater Scholarship is open to continuing undergraduates and graduate students at California State University, Fullerton, who are technical theater and design majors. This award requires that you show scholastic achievement and financial need, as well as demonstrate dedication to the multi-step process and success of a final design/technical product. Award requirements change regularly. No GPA requirement specified.

California State University, Fullerton - Arts/Music Department
Attn: Scholarship Committee
800 N. State College Blvd., Room VA-199c
Fullerton, CA 92831-3599

1379
Todd Muffatti Scholarship in Scene Design

AMOUNT: $500 DEADLINE: February 11
MAJOR: Theater and Dance (Scene Design)

The Todd Muffatti Scholarship in Scene Design is open to new and continuing undergraduate theater and dance majors at California State University, Fullerton, whose emphasis is scene design. This award requires that you show excellence in scene design and future potential. Award requirements change regularly. No GPA requirement specified.

California State University, Fullerton - Arts/Music Department
Attn: Scholarship Committee
800 N. State College Blvd., Room VA-199c
Fullerton, CA 92831-3599

1380
Women in International Trade Scholarship

AMOUNT: $1500 DEADLINE: March 2
MAJOR: International Business

The Women in International Trade Scholarship is open to female students at California State University, Fullerton, who are enrolled in the School of Business Administration and Economics. To be eligible for this award, you must be involved in international business or a study abroad program, be a U.S. citizen, and have a minimum 3.0 GPA. Financial need may be taken into consideration. Award requirements change regularly. Applications are available in Langsdorf Hall 700 and must be postmarked by March 2. GPA must be 3.0-4.0.

California State University, Fullerton - Business and Economics
Attn: Scholarship Coordinator
800 N. State College Blvd., LH-700
Fullerton, CA 92831-3599

California State University, Northridge

1381
Continuing Graduate Scholarship

AMOUNT: None Specified DEADLINE: March 1
MAJOR: All Areas of Study

The Continuing Graduate Scholarship is both a merit-based and need-based scholarship for students who are pursuing their first master's degree or first credential. You must have a minimum 3.0 GPA and be Classified, Conditionally Classified, or P.B. Credential (PBU students are not eligible). You must be enrolled full-time at CSUN, unless pre-approved for three-quarter time based on extenuating circumstances. If you are applying for merit-based awards, you must be pursuing your first master's degree or credential and have a minimum GPA of 3.75 (or 3.75 undergraduate GPA if applying as an entering graduate student). You must be Classified, Conditionally Classified, or P.B. Credential (PBU students are not eligible) and be enrolled full-time at CSUN. Award requirements change regularly. GPA must be 3.0-4.0.

California State University, Northridge
Office of Financial Aid
18111 Nordhoff Street
Northridge, CA 91330-8200

1382
Continuing Undergraduate Scholarship

AMOUNT: None Specified DEADLINE: March 2
MAJOR: All Areas of Study

The Continuing Undergraduate Scholarship is open on both need-based and merit-based levels. To apply for the need-based scholarship, you must have declared a major by junior class level and have a minimum 3.0 GPA. Need-based awards also require that you be enrolled full-time, unless pre-approved for three-quarter time, based on extenuating circumstances. The FAFSA must be filed by March 2. To apply for the merit-based scholarship, you must have a declared major at the time of application, have a minimum 3.6 GPA, be pursuing your first bachelor's degree, and be enrolled full-time. Award requirements change regularly. GPA must be 3.0-4.0.

California State University, Northridge
Office of Financial Aid
18111 Nordhoff Street
Northridge, CA 91330-8200

1383
First Time Freshmen and Transfer Student Scholarship

AMOUNT: None Specified DEADLINE: March 2
MAJOR: All Areas of Study

This award is open to incoming freshmen from high school and to transfer students. You must have a minimum GPA of 3.0 (as determined by the CSUN Admissions Office) and be enrolled full-time. Also, you must demonstrate financial need and file a FAFSA. The University Scholarship Program requires one application to be considered for the more than 300 scholarships available. Award requirements change regularly. GPA must be 3.0-4.0.

California State University, Northridge
Office of Financial Aid
18111 Nordhoff Street
Northridge, CA 91330-8200

Case Western Reserve University

1384
Albert W. Smith Scholarships and the Alexander Treuhaft Scholarships

AMOUNT: Maximum: $19200 DEADLINE: February 1
MAJOR: Science and Engineering

Four full-tuition scholarships are offered to qualified applicants for admission as freshmen. Awards are renewable for each of the four years of undergraduate study, provided high academic achievement is maintained. Students must already be accepted into a science or engineering program at CWRU. Award requirements change regularly. Write to the address below for details. No GPA requirement specified.

Case Western Reserve University
Undergraduate Admissions - 103 Tomlinson
10900 Euclid Avenue
Cleveland, OH 44106-7055

1385
Alden Undergraduate Fellowships in Systems Engineering

AMOUNT: Maximum: $3500 DEADLINE: February 1
MAJOR: Systems Engineering (Computer Science)

Scholarships for junior or senior undergraduates majoring in systems engineering at Case Western Reserve University. Applicants must have a minimum GPA of 3.2 for the last three semesters preceding the application. Two awards per year. Award requirements change regularly. For further information, please write to the address provided or consult the website at www.cwru.edu. GPA must be 3.2-4.0.

Case Western Reserve University
Electrical, Systems, Comp Eng & Science
10900 Euclid Ave - 407 Olin Bldg
Cleveland, OH 44106-7204

1386
Andrew Squire Scholarships and the Adelbert Alumni Scholarships

AMOUNT: Maximum: $19200 DEADLINE: February 1
MAJOR: All Areas of Study

Five full-tuition scholarships are offered to qualified applicants for admission as freshmen. Awards are renewable for each of the four years of undergraduate study, provided high academic achievement is maintained. Award requirements change regularly. Write to the address below for details. No GPA requirement specified.

Case Western Reserve University
Undergraduate Admissions - 103 Tomlinson
10900 Euclid Avenue
Cleveland, OH 44106-7055

1387
Case Alumni Association Junior and Senior Scholarships

AMOUNT: None Specified DEADLINE: February 1
MAJOR: All Areas of Study

A number of scholarships funded by the Case Alumni Association of the Case School of Engineering are awarded to juniors and seniors on the basis of academic achievement, financial need, and participation in extracurricular activities. Award requirements change regularly. For further details, please see the department chair at CWRU in your field of study. No GPA requirement specified.

Case Western Reserve University
Undergraduate Admissions - 103 Tomlinson
10900 Euclid Avenue
Cleveland, OH 44106-7055

1388
Creative Achievement Scholarship

AMOUNT: Maximum: $9600 DEADLINE: February 1
MAJOR: Art, Drama, Theater, Music

Scholarships offered to entering freshmen who demonstrate outstanding creative ability and achievement. Interested students must submit a supplemental application indicating the field(s) of interest by the deadline. Auditions/portfolio reviews will be arranged. Committee of Art's faculty will select scholarship recipients based on review of portfolios and results of auditions. Student must maintain academic eligibility for financial assistance in order for scholarship to be renewed. Scholarships are renewable for up to four years. Award requirements change regularly. Write to the address below for additional information. No GPA requirement specified.

Case Western Reserve University
Undergraduate Admissions - 103 Tomlinson
10900 Euclid Avenue
Cleveland, OH 44106-7055

1389
Frances Payne Bolton Scholarship

AMOUNT: Maximum: $9600 DEADLINE: February 1
MAJOR: Nursing

Scholarships offered to entering nursing students in the BSN program, up to one-half tuition. Student must maintain academic eligibility for financial assistance in order for scholarship to be renewed. Scholarships are renewable for up to four years. Award requirements change regularly. Please contact the address provided for further information. No GPA requirement specified.

Case Western Reserve University
Undergraduate Admissions - 103 Tomlinson
10900 Euclid Avenue
Cleveland, OH 44106-7055

1390
Full-Tuition Scholarship

AMOUNT: Maximum: $19200 DEADLINE: February 1
MAJOR: All Areas of Study

Scholarships are awarded to entering freshmen who are nominated by members of the admissions staff based on overall academic, personal, and leadership qualities. Student must maintain academic eligibility for financial assistance in order for the scholarship to be renewed. Scholarships are renewable for up to four years and are adjusted with tuition increases. Award requirements change regularly. Write to the address below for details. No GPA requirement specified.

Case Western Reserve University
Undergraduate Admissions - 103 Tomlinson
10900 Euclid Avenue
Cleveland, OH 44106-7055

1391
National Merit Scholarships at Case Western

AMOUNT: $500-$2000 DEADLINE: February 1
MAJOR: All Areas of Study

At least 25 four-year scholarships are available for National Merit Scholarship Corporation finalists who have listed Case Western Reserve University as their first-choice institution. Award requirements change regularly. Write to the address below for details. No GPA requirement specified.

Case Western Reserve University
Undergraduate Admissions - 103 Tomlinson
10900 Euclid Avenue
Cleveland, OH 44106-7055

1392
Plain Dealer Charities Scholarship

AMOUNT: Maximum: $1000 DEADLINE: February 1
MAJOR: Business Management, Print Journalism

Scholarships for entering freshmen at Case Western who are studying business management or print journalism. The applicant must have graduated in the top 20% of the high school class in Cuyahoga, Lake, Geauga, Portage, Summit, Medina, or Lorain counties (OH). Applicants must have genuine financial need (to be determined by the CWRU office of financial aid). Award requirements change regularly. Write to the address below for details. GPA must be 3.2.

Case Western Reserve University
Undergraduate Admissions - 103 Tomlinson
10900 Euclid Avenue
Cleveland, OH 44106-7055

1393
President's Scholarship

AMOUNT: Maximum: $14400 DEADLINE: February 1
MAJOR: All Areas of Study

Scholarships are awarded to entering freshmen who rank in the top 10% of their high school graduating class and who have composite SAT I scores of 1400-1490 or an ACT score (composite, single test date) of 33-34. A cumulative GPA of 3.0 is required for renewal. Scholarships are renewable for up to four years. Award requirements change regularly. Write to the address below for details. No GPA requirement specified.

Case Western Reserve University
Undergraduate Admissions - 103 Tomlinson
10900 Euclid Avenue, Cleveland OH

1394
Provost's Scholarship

AMOUNT: Maximum: $9600 DEADLINE: February 1
MAJOR: All Areas of Study

Scholarships are awarded to entering freshmen who rank in the top 15% of their high school graduating class and who have composite SAT I scores of greater than 1300 or an ACT score (composite, single test date) of at least 31. A cumulative GPA of 3.0 is required for renewal. Scholarships are renewable for up to four years. Award requirements change regularly. Write to the address below for details. GPA must be 3.4.

Case Western Reserve University
Undergraduate Admissions - 103 Tomlinson
10900 Euclid Avenue
Cleveland, OH 44106-7055

1395
Provost's Special Scholarship

AMOUNT: Maximum: $12000 DEADLINE: February 1
MAJOR: All Areas of Study

Scholarships are awarded to promising freshman applicants who will add to the diversity of the student population. Members of under-represented minority groups are encouraged to apply. Scholarships are awarded to entering freshmen who rank (mid-senior year) in the top 15% of their high school graduating classes and have earned composite SAT scores of at least 1200 or composite ACT scores of at least 28. Students must maintain academic eligibility for financial assistance in order for the scholarship to be renewed. Scholarships are renewable for up to four years. Awardees may receive additional grant support based on financial need. Award requirements change regularly. Write to the address below for details. No GPA requirement specified.

Case Western Reserve University
Undergraduate Admissions - 103 Tomlinson
10900 Euclid Avenue
Cleveland, OH 44106-7055

1396
Trustee Scholarship

AMOUNT: Maximum: $19200 DEADLINE: February 1
MAJOR: All Areas of Study

Scholarships are awarded to entering freshmen who rank in the top 10% of their high school graduating class and who have composite SAT I scores of 1500-1600 or an ACT score (composite, single test date) of 35-36. A cumulative GPA of 3.0 is required for renewal. Scholarships are renewable for up to four years. Award requirements change regularly. Write to the address below for details. No GPA requirement specified.

Case Western Reserve University
Undergraduate Admissions - 103 Tomlinson
10900 Euclid Avenue
Cleveland, OH 44106-7055

Cedar Crest College

1397
Art Scholarship

AMOUNT: $1500 DEADLINE: Varies
MAJOR: Art

The Art Scholarship is open to freshmen attending Cedar Crest College who are committed to the creative process both in making art and in looking at historical and contemporary works of art. In order to apply for this award, a portfolio review is required. To maintain your scholarship, you will be required to take a minimum of 6-8 credits in studio or art history courses each year. Award requirements change regularly. No GPA requirement specified.

Cedar Crest College
Office of Admissions: Donna Michel
100 College Drive
Allentown, PA 18104-6196

1398
Cort Grant

AMOUNT: $1000 DEADLINE: Varies
MAJOR: All Areas of Study

The Cort Grant is a scholarship open to students who attend Cedar Crest College and are active members of United Church of Christ congregations. Award requirements change regularly. No GPA requirement specified.

Cedar Crest College
Office of Admissions: Donna Michel
100 College Drive
Allentown, PA 18104-6196

1399
Girl Scout Gold Award Scholarship

AMOUNT: $1000 DEADLINE: Varies
MAJOR: All Areas of Study

The Girl Scout Gold Award is a scholarship available for students attending Cedar Crest College who have received the Girl Scout Gold Award. Award requirements change regularly. No GPA requirement specified.

Cedar Crest College
Office of Admissions: Donna Michel
100 College Drive
Allentown, PA 18104-6196

1400
Governor's Schools of Excellence Award

AMOUNT: $1000 DEADLINE: Varies
MAJOR: All Areas of Study

The Governor's Schools of Excellence Awards are open to graduates of Governor's Schools of Excellence attending Cedar Crest College. Award requirements change regularly. No GPA requirement specified.

Cedar Crest College
Office of Admissions: Donna Michel
100 College Drive
Allentown, PA 18104-6196

1401
Heritage Grant

AMOUNT: $2000 DEADLINE: Varies
MAJOR: All Areas of Study

The Heritage Grants are open to children and grandchildren of Cedar Crest College alumni. If you are a full-time traditional student attending Cedar Crest College and are a child of an alumnus, you are eligible for this award. Award requirements change regularly. No GPA requirement specified.

Cedar Crest College
Office of Admissions: Donna Michel
100 College Drive
Allentown, PA 18104-6196

1402
High School Achievement Award

AMOUNT: Maximum: $5000 DEADLINE: Varies
MAJOR: All Areas of Study

The High School Achievement Award is open to students attending Cedar Crest College who rank in the top 20% of their class and score 1150 or higher on the SAT. Award requirements change regularly. GPA must be 3.0-4.0.

Cedar Crest College
Office of Admissions: Donna Michel
100 College Drive
Allentown, PA 18104-6196

1403
Hugh O'Brian Youth (HOBY) Award

AMOUNT: $1000 DEADLINE: Varies
MAJOR: All Areas of Study

The Hugh O'Brian Youth (HOBY) Awards are open to new students who are HOBY alumnae attending Cedar Crest College. Award requirements change regularly. No GPA requirement specified.

Cedar Crest College
Office of Admissions: Donna Michel
100 College Drive
Allentown, PA 18104-6196

1404
Performing Arts Scholarship

AMOUNT: $1500 DEADLINE: Varies
MAJOR: Performing Arts

The Performing Arts Scholarship is open to freshmen attending Cedar Crest College who plan to participate in Cedar Crest Stage Company performances, serve in technical production areas, or perform with the college Dance Company. A performance audition is required. Award requirements change regularly. No GPA requirement specified.

Cedar Crest College
Office of Admissions: Donna Michel
100 College Drive
Allentown, PA 18104-6196

1405
Phi Theta Kappa Scholarship

AMOUNT: $4000 DEADLINE: Varies
MAJOR: All Areas of Study

The Phi Theta Kappa Scholarship is open to members of Phi Theta Kappa who have at least a 3.5 GPA, have completed 24 transferable credit hours, and are enrolled full-time at Cedar Crest College. Award requirements change regularly. GPA must be 3.5-4.0.

Cedar Crest College
Office of Admissions: Donna Michel
100 College Drive
Allentown, PA 18104-6196

1406
Presidential Scholarship

AMOUNT: None Specified DEADLINE: Varies
MAJOR: All Areas of Study

The Presidential Scholarship is open to entering freshmen attending Cedar Crest College who rank in the top 10% of their class and score 1150 or higher on the SAT. The amount of the freshman year award is renewable each year provided a 3.0 GPA is maintained. Award requirements change regularly. GPA must be 3.0-4.0.

Cedar Crest College
Office of Admissions: Donna Michel
100 College Drive
Allentown, PA 18104-6196

1407
Sibling Grant

AMOUNT: $1000 DEADLINE: Varies
MAJOR: All Areas of Study

If you are a student who has one or more siblings also attending Cedar Crest College, you are eligible to apply for the Sibling Grant. Award requirements change regularly. No GPA requirement specified.

Cedar Crest College
Office of Admissions: Donna Michel
100 College Drive
Allentown, PA 18104-6196

1408
Transfer Scholarship

AMOUNT: $3000 DEADLINE: Varies
MAJOR: All Areas of Study

The Transfer Scholarship is open to students who have completed at least 54 credits at another college with a minimum 3.0 GPA. Award requirements change regularly. GPA must be 3.0-4.0.

Cedar Crest College
Office of Admissions: Donna Michel
100 College Drive
Allentown, PA 18104-6196

1409
Trustee Scholarship

AMOUNT: None Specified DEADLINE: Varies
MAJOR: All Areas of Study

The Trustee Scholarship is a full-tuition scholarship during your senior year at Cedar Crest College. In order to apply, you must have a 3.55 GPA or better by the end of your junior year. You must be enrolled full-time at Cedar Crest College for three years prior to receiving this scholarship. Award requirements change regularly. GPA must be 3.5-4.0.

Cedar Crest College
Office of Admissions: Donna Michel
100 College Drive
Allentown, PA 18104-6196

Central Missouri State University

1410
Alumni Reunion Scholarship

AMOUNT: $500 DEADLINE: March 15
MAJOR: All Areas of Study

Open to high school seniors with a minimum 3.0 GPA. Must be children of a Central Missouri State University alumnus who earned a two-year, four-year, master's, or specialist degree. Award requirements change regularly. Contact the address listed, enclosing a self-addressed, stamped envelope; contact their website: www.cmsu.edu; or call (660) 543-4541 or (800) 956-0177. GPA must be 3.0-4.0.

Central Missouri State University
Scholarship Officer, Admissions Office
Administration #104
Warrensburg, MO 64093

1411
Distinguished Scholars Award

AMOUNT: None Specified DEADLINE: February 15
MAJOR: All Areas of Study

Open to high school seniors who rank in the upper 5% of their graduating class or have a minimum GPA of 3.5. Applicants must participate in the Distinguished Scholars Award Competition. Award is tuition, room, board, and book allowance. Must be admitted to CMSU. Award requirements

change regularly. Contact the address listed, enclosing a self-addressed, stamped envelope; contact their website: www.cmsu.edu; or call (660) 543-4541 or (800) 956-0177. GPA must be 3.5-4.0.

Central Missouri State University
Scholarship Officer, Admissions Office
Administration #104
Warrensburg, MO 64093

1412
High School Recognition Scholarship

AMOUNT: Maximum: $500 DEADLINE: Varies
MAJOR: All Areas of Study

Open to high school seniors who are ranked in the upper 25% of their graduating class. May not be receiving the Distinguished Scholars, University Scholar, Presidents, or National Merit Scholarships. May be renewable. Must be admitted to CMSU. Award requirements change regularly. Contact the address listed, enclosing a self-addressed, stamped envelope; contact their website: www.cmsu.edu; or call (660) 543-4541 or (800) 956-0177. GPA must be 2.7-4.0.

Central Missouri State University
Scholarship Officer, Admissions Office
Administration #104
Warrensburg, MO 64093

1413
Leadership Award for Missouri Boys State and Girls State Citizens

AMOUNT: Maximum: $1000 DEADLINE: February 15
MAJOR: All Areas of Study

Open to high school seniors who demonstrate potential or outstanding performance in a given academic area. Each department determines its own award value and selects its own recipients. Applicants must indicate their anticipated degree program on the scholarship application. Must attend CMSU. Award requirements change regularly. Contact the address listed, enclosing a self-addressed, stamped envelope; contact their website: www.cmsu.edu; or call (660) 543-4541 or (800) 956-0177. GPA must be 2.5-4.0.

Central Missouri State University
Scholarship Officer, Admissions Office
Administration #104
Warrensburg, MO 64093

1414
National Merit Finalists Scholarship

AMOUNT: None Specified DEADLINE: Varies
MAJOR: All Areas of Study

Open to high school seniors who have been designated as National Merit Finalists. Award is for tuition, room, board, and book allowance. Must be admitted to CMSU. Award requirements change regularly. Contact the address listed, enclosing a self-addressed, stamped envelope; contact their

website: www.cmsu.edu; or call (660) 543-4541 or (800) 956-

0177. GPA must be 2.5-4.0.

Central Missouri State University
Scholarship Officer, Admissions Office
Administration #104
Warrensburg, MO 64093

1415
Presidents Scholarship

AMOUNT: Maximum: $1000 DEADLINE: Varies
MAJOR: All Areas of Study

Open to high school seniors who are ranked in the upper 25% of their graduating class. May not be receiving the Distinguished Scholar, University Scholar, or National Merit Scholarships. Must be admitted to CMSU. Award requirements change regularly. Contact the address listed, enclosing a self-addressed, stamped envelope; contact their website: www.cmsu.edu; or call (660) 543-4541 or (800) 956-0177. GPA must be 2.7-4.0.

Central Missouri State University
Scholarship Officer, Admissions Office
Administration #104
Warrensburg, MO 64093

1416
Regents Scholarship

AMOUNT: Maximum: $1500 DEADLINE: Varies
MAJOR: All Areas of Study

Open to high school seniors who have been admitted to CMSU. Must be ranked in the upper 25% of their graduating class or be the valedictorian or salutatorian. The applicant may not be receiving the Distinguished Scholars, University Scholar, or National Merit Scholarships. Award requirements change regularly. Contact the address listed, enclosing a self-addressed, stamped envelope; contact their website: www.cmsu.edu; or call (660) 543-4541 or (800) 956-0177. GPA must be 2.7-4.0.

Central Missouri State University
Scholarship Officer, Admissions Office
Administration #104
Warrensburg, MO 64093

1417
University Scholar Award

AMOUNT: None Specified DEADLINE: February 15
MAJOR: All Areas of Study

Open to high school seniors who rank in the upper 5% of their graduating class or have a minimum GPA of 3.75. Applicants must participate in the Distinguished Scholars Award Competition. Award is for tuition and non-resident fees. Recipients of this award may not be receiving the Distinguished Scholars Award. Must be admitted to CMSU. Award requirements change regularly. Contact the address listed, enclosing a self-addressed, stamped envelope; contact their website: www.cmsu.edu; or call (660) 543-4541 or (800) 956-0177. GPA must be 3.75-4.0.

Central Missouri State University
Scholarship Officer, Admissions Office
Administration #104
Warrensburg, MO 64093

Christopher Newport University

1418
Alumni Society of Christopher Newport University Freshman Scholarship

AMOUNT: None Specified DEADLINE: Varies
MAJOR: All Areas of Study

The Alumni Society of Christopher Newport University Freshman Scholarship is open to Christopher Newport University full-time freshman students residing in Santoro Hall. To be considered for this award, you must have a minimum GPA of 3.0 and financial need. Preference will be given to graduates of Tidewater secondary schools. All freshmen applying for need-based financial aid will be considered for this scholarship. Award requirements change regularly. GPA must be 3.0-4.0.

Christopher Newport University
Office of Financial Aid
50 University Place
Newport News, VA 23606-2949

1419
Christopher Newport Single Parent Scholarship

AMOUNT: None Specified DEADLINE: Varies
MAJOR: All Areas of Study

The Christopher Newport Single Parent Scholarship is open to Christopher Newport University full-time juniors and seniors who are single parents. To qualify, you must have at least 30 credit hours, have a minimum GPA of 2.0, and must be able to demonstrate financial need. You must also be employed and have a dependent child (or children). Award requirements change regularly. To apply, complete Part III of the Christopher Newport University Application for Financial Aid. GPA must be 2.0-4.0.

Christopher Newport University
Office of Financial Aid
50 University Place
Newport News, VA 23606-2949

1420
Dr. Agnes Logan Braganza Scholarship

AMOUNT: None Specified DEADLINE: Varies
MAJOR: All Areas of Study

The Dr. Agnes Logan Braganza Scholarship is open to non-traditional-age (30 and above) female students. To be considered for this award, you need to be at sophomore level or higher, have at least 30 credit hours earned at Christopher Newport University, and have a minimum GPA of 2.0. To apply, you must be able to demonstrate financial need. Award requirements change regularly. GPA must be 2.0-4.0.

Christopher Newport University
Office of Financial Aid
50 University Place
Newport News, VA 23606-2949

1421
Dr. Vinod P. Maniyar Memorial Scholarship

AMOUNT: None Specified DEADLINE: Varies
MAJOR: All Areas of Study

The Dr. Vinod P. Maniyar Memorial Scholarship is awarded to juniors at Christopher Newport University. To be considered for this award, you must have a minimum GPA of 3.5 and be able to demonstrate financial need. Priority is given to academic achievement. Award requirements change regularly. GPA must be 3.5-4.0.

Christopher Newport University
Office of Financial Aid
50 University Place
Newport News, VA 23606-2949

1422
Gloria Bridges Memorial Endowment Scholarship

AMOUNT: None Specified DEADLINE: Varies
MAJOR: All Areas of Study

The Gloria Bridges Memorial Endowment Scholarship is open to Christopher Newport University seniors. To be considered for this award, you must have a minimum GPA of 2.75 and financial need. Award requirements change regularly. GPA must be 2.75-4.0.

Christopher Newport University
Office of Financial Aid
50 University Place
Newport News, VA 23606-2949

1423
James F. Draper Scholarship

AMOUNT: $1000 DEADLINE: Varies
MAJOR: All Areas of Study

The James F. Draper Scholarship is open to full-time juniors or seniors at Christopher Newport University. To qualify for this award, you must have a minimum GPA of 3.0 and be able to demonstrate financial need. Priority is based on academic achievement. Award requirements change regularly. GPA must be 3.0-4.0.

Christopher Newport University
Office of Financial Aid
50 University Place
Newport News, VA 23606-2949

City College of San Francisco

1424
Albert Ting Memorial Endowed Scholarship

AMOUNT: $250 DEADLINE: October 1
MAJOR: All Areas of Study

The Albert Ting Memorial Endowed Scholarship is open to U.S citizens and permanent residents at City College of San Francisco who are of East Indian, Japanese, Chinese, Korean, Filipino, Vietnamese, or Southeast Asian descent. To qualify for this award, you must be enrolled in at least 12 units at CCSF, have completed at least 12 units at CCSF with a minimum GPA of 3.0, and be working a minimum of 12 hours per week while attending CCSF. Award requirements change regularly. GPA must be 3.0-4.0.

City College of San Francisco
Scholarship Office
Batmale Hall, Room 366
San Francisco, CA 94112-1821

1425
Asian Coalition John Yehall Chin Scholarships

AMOUNT: $300 DEADLINE: Varies
MAJOR: All Areas of Study

The Asian Coalition John Yehall Chin Scholarships are open to credit and non-credit students at City College of San Francisco who are of Japanese, Chinese, Korean, Filipino, Thai, or Southeast Asian descent. Selection is based on financial need, academics, career goals, school and community service, potential leadership skills, and teacher evaluations. Application deadlines are usually mid-February to the end of February. Award requirements change regularly. No GPA requirement specified.

City College of San Francisco
Scholarship Office
Batmale Hall, Room 366
San Francisco, CA 94112-1821

1426
CCSF Academic Excellence Endowed Scholarship

AMOUNT: $300 DEADLINE: Varies
MAJOR: All Areas of Study

The CCSF Academic Excellence Endowed Scholarship is open to students who are enrolled in at least six units at City College of San Francisco and have completed 24 units with at least a 3.5 GPA. To qualify for this award, you must be enrolled in a university parallel or semi-professional program leading to a degree or certificate, or be transferring to a baccalaureate institution for the following semester. Application deadlines are March 3 for the spring semester and October 1 for the fall semester. Award requirements change regularly. GPA must be 3.5-4.0.

City College of San Francisco
Scholarship Office
Batmale Hall, Room 366
San Francisco, CA 94112-1821

1427
CCSF Administrators' Association Scholarship

AMOUNT: $250 DEADLINE: Varies
MAJOR: All Areas of Study

The CCSF Administrators' Association Scholarship is open to students at City College of San Francisco enrolled in at least six units of credit or ten hours per week of non-credit instruction (or the equivalent combination). To qualify for this award, you must have completed six units or more at CCSF with a minimum GPA of 2.0, or satisfactory completion of 175 hours of non-credit instruction or the equivalent combination. You are required to submit an essay on student leadership. Application deadlines are March 3 for the spring semester and October 1 for the fall semester. Award requirements change regularly. GPA must be 2.0-4.0.

City College of San Francisco
Scholarship Office
Batmale Hall, Room 366
San Francisco, CA 94112-1821

1428
CCSF Foundation Endowed Community Scholarship

AMOUNT: $1750 DEADLINE: March 3
MAJOR: All Areas of Study

The CCSF Foundation Endowed Community Scholarship is open to San Francisco high school seniors who are graduating or have recently passed the California State Proficiency Exam and are enrolling in City College of San Francisco. To qualify for this award, you must be of African-American, Latino, Native American, Pacific Islander, Vietnamese, Cambodian, Laotian, or Filipino descent. Students with disabilities are also eligible to apply. Consideration is given to your awards, activities, employment, community service, financial need, personal hardships, and evidence of significant academic improvement during your senior year in high school. This award requires that you attend City College for two years, enrolling in and completing at least nine units each semester with a minimum cumulative GPA of 2.0. Award requirements change regularly. No GPA requirement specified.

City College of San Francisco
Scholarship Office
Batmale Hall, Room 366
San Francisco, CA 94112-1821

1429
CCSF Golden Anniversary Endowed Scholarship

AMOUNT: $750 DEADLINE: March 3
MAJOR: All Areas of Study

The CCSF Golden Anniversary Endowed Scholarship is open to students enrolled in a course of study that leads to a degree or certificate at City College of San Francisco. To apply for

this award, you must have completed a minimum of 24 units with a GPA of at least 3.2, currently be enrolled in six units or more at CCSF, and be continuing a minimum of six units for the following two semesters. Award requirements change regularly. GPA must be 3.2-4.0.

City College of San Francisco
Scholarship Office
Batmale Hall, Room 366
San Francisco, CA 94112-1821

1430
CCSF Honors Program Scholarship

AMOUNT: None Specified DEADLINE: Varies
MAJOR: All Fields of Study

The CCSF Honors Program Scholarship is open to honors program graduates at City College of San Francisco who have completed 15 units in the CCSF Honors Program and have a cumulative GPA of at least 3.0. To qualify for this award, you must be transferring to UCLA, UC-Irvine, USC, Pepperdine University, or Chapman University. Award requirements change regularly. GPA must be 3.0-4.0.

City College of San Francisco
Scholarship Office
Batmale Hall, Room 366
San Francisco, CA 94112-1821

1431
CCSF Memorial Endowed Scholarships

AMOUNT: $250 DEADLINE: October 1
MAJOR: All Areas of Study

The CCSF Memorial Endowed Scholarship is open to students attending City College of San Francisco with high academics and demonstrated leadership and service to CCSF. To apply for this award, you must have completed a minimum of 24 units at CCSF with a GPA of at least 3.5, be enrolled in a university parallel or semi-professional program leading to a degree or certificate, be continuing in at least six units, or be transferring to a baccalaureate institution next semester. Application deadlines are March 3 for the spring semester and October 1 for the fall semester. Award requirements change regularly. GPA must be 3.5-4.0.

City College of San Francisco
Scholarship Office
Batmale Hall, Room 366
San Francisco, CA 94112-1821

1432
City College Faculty Association Scholarship

AMOUNT: $200 DEADLINE: March 3
MAJOR: All Areas of Study

The City College Faculty Association Scholarship is open to students currently enrolled at City College of San Francisco who have completed at least 24 units, but no more than 45 units, with a minimum GPA of 3.0. Preference is given to students who have dropped no more than two courses at CCSF. Award requirements change regularly. GPA must be 3.0-4.0.

City College of San Francisco
Scholarship Office
Batmale Hall, Room 366
San Francisco, CA 94112-1821

City College of San Francisco
Scholarship Office
Batmale Hall, Room 366
San Francisco, CA 94112-1821

1433
Hotel and Restaurant Foundation Scholarships

AMOUNT: $600-$1250 DEADLINE: March 10
MAJOR: Hotel and Restaurant Operations

The Hotel and Restaurant Foundation Scholarships are open to full-time students at City College of San Francisco who are majoring in hotel and restaurant operations. To qualify for this award, you must have a cumulative GPA of at least 2.5. Award requirements change regularly. GPA must be 2.5-4.0.

City College of San Francisco
Scholarship Office
Batmale Hall, Room 366
San Francisco, CA 94112-1821

1434
Kathleen Parker Gould Endowed Scholarship

AMOUNT: $300 DEADLINE: October 1
MAJOR: Public Health, Health Education, Biological Sciences

The Kathleen Parker Gould Endowed Scholarship is open to sophomore students at CCSF who are self-supporting mothers with one or more dependent children. To qualify for this award, you must have completed at least 44 units at CCSF with a minimum GPA of 3.0 and intend to transfer to a baccalaureate institution to pursue a bachelor's degree in health education, public health, or any biological science. Award requirements change regularly. GPA must be 3.0-4.0.

City College of San Francisco
Scholarship Office
Batmale Hall, Room 366
San Francisco, CA 94112-1821

1435
La Raza Unida Student Organization Endowed Scholarship

AMOUNT: $100 DEADLINE: Varies
MAJOR: All Areas of Study

The La Raza Unida Student Organization Endowed Scholarship is open to Latino/Latina students at City College of San Francisco who have completed at least 12 units at CCSF with a minimum GPA of 2.5, are currently enrolled in at least 12 units, and are planning to enroll in 12 units next semester. Selection is based on personal qualities and strengths with preference given to those who demonstrate commitment to enhancing the quality of life within the Latino community and demonstration of commitment to higher education by either overcoming obstacles or excelling in an academic area. Application deadlines are March 3 for the spring semester and October 1 for the fall semester. Award requirements change regularly. GPA must be 2.5-4.0.

1436
Levi Strauss Foundation/School of Business Scholarship

AMOUNT: $300 DEADLINE: Varies
MAJOR: Business

The Levi Strauss Foundation/School of Business Scholarship is open to under-represented students pursuing a course of study in business at City College of San Francisco. Under-represented groups include African Americans, Latinos, Native Americans, Pacific Islanders, Southeast Asians (Burmese, Cambodians, Vietnamese, Laotians), Filipinos, students with verifiable disabilities, or re-entry women over the age of 25. To qualify for this award, you must be currently enrolled at CCSF in at least six units of credit or ten hours per week of non-credit instruction (or the equivalent combination) in the business department or business certificate program, have completed six units of credit courses with at least a 2.0 GPA or 90 hours of non-credit classes with a passing grade, and have financial need. Application deadlines are March 3 for the spring semester and October 1 for the fall semester. Award requirements change regularly. GPA must be 2.0-4.0.

City College of San Francisco
Scholarship Office
Batmale Hall, Room 366
San Francisco, CA 94112-1821

1437
Lloyd D. Luckmann Memorial Endowed Scholarship

AMOUNT: $250 DEADLINE: March 3
MAJOR: All Areas of Study

The Lloyd D. Luckmann Memorial Endowed Scholarship is open to full-time students at City College of San Francisco who have completed a minimum of 12 units with at least a 2.5 GPA. To qualify for this award you must be enrolled in a university parallel or semi-professional program leading to a degree or certificate. Included with your application, you are required to submit verification of financial need and answers to three essay questions: a) What are your family obligations? How do you meet these responsibilities? b) What do you consider your greatest personal strength? How do you put it to use? c) What or who has had the most influence in shaping your life? Award requirements change regularly. GPA must be 2.5-4.0.

City College of San Francisco
Scholarship Office
Batmale Hall, Room 366
San Francisco, CA 94112-1821

1438
Minnie F. Reidy Liberal Arts Endowed Scholarships

AMOUNT: $300 DEADLINE: October 1
MAJOR: All Areas of Study

The Minnie F. Reidy Liberal Arts Endowed Scholarships are open to students over 50 years of age enrolled in at least six units at City College of San Francisco. You must also have completed a minimum of six college transferable units at CCSF in humanities, literature, philosophy, political science, history, the study of language and culture, art history, music theory, mathematics, biological sciences, social sciences, or earth sciences. You are required to submit proof of age, proof of current enrollment, and an unofficial transcript. Award requirements change regularly. No GPA requirement specified.

City College of San Francisco
Scholarship Office
Batmale Hall, Room 366
San Francisco, CA 94112-1821

1439
Northern California Turf and Landscape Council Scholarship

AMOUNT: Maximum: $5000 DEADLINE: October 7
MAJOR: Environmental Horticulture

The Northern California Turf and Landscape Council Scholarship is open to environmental horticulture students at City College of San Francisco or any Northern California college or to permanent residents of Northern California. Selection is based on financial need, academic achievement, extracurricular activities, and demonstrated interest or current employment in the green industry. Number and amounts of awards vary depending on available funds. Award requirements change regularly. No GPA requirement specified.

City College of San Francisco
Scholarship Office
Batmale Hall, Room 366
San Francisco, CA 94112-1821

1440
Pan-American Round Table of San Francisco Scholarships

AMOUNT: $500 DEADLINE: March 3
MAJOR: All Areas of Study

The Pan-American Round Table of San Francisco Scholarships are open to students of Hispanic descent who are from Pan America (North, Central, or South America). To qualify for this award, you must be enrolled in at least six units at CCSF in a university parallel or semi-professional program leading to a degree or certificate and have completed at least six units at CCSF with a cumulative GPA of 2.75 or higher. Selection is based on academic performance, leadership, and service. Financial need is considered. Recipients are asked to keep Pan American Round Table of San Francisco informed of their educational progress. Award requirements change regularly. GPA must be 2.8-4.0.

City College of San Francisco
Scholarship Office
Batmale Hall, Room 366
San Francisco, CA 94112-1821

1441
Ralph O. Hillsman Memorial Endowed Scholarship

AMOUNT: $500 DEADLINE: October 1
MAJOR: All Areas of Study

The Ralph O. Hillsman Memorial Endowed Scholarship is open to students at City College of San Francisco who are involved in a CCSF campus-wide student organization, activity, team sport, or collaborative creative production. To apply for this award, you must be currently enrolled in at least 6 units at CCSF and have completed at least 12 units at CCSF with a minimum cumulative GPA of 2.5. Award requirements change regularly. GPA must be 2.5-4.0.

City College of San Francisco
Scholarship Office
Batmale Hall, Room 366
San Francisco, CA 94112-1821

1442
Women's Studies Scholarship

AMOUNT: $100 DEADLINE: Varies
MAJOR: All Fields of Study

The Women's Studies Scholarship is open to students who are currently enrolled in or have completed at least one women's studies class at City College of San Francisco. To qualify for this award, you must be currently enrolled at CCSF in a women's studies class in the fall or spring semester of the current academic year and be nominated by a Women's Studies Department instructor. Award requirements change regularly. No application is necessary. No GPA requirement specified.

City College of San Francisco
Scholarship Office
Batmale Hall, Room 366
San Francisco, CA 94112-1821

Clarkson University

1443
Perry F. Hadlock Memorial Scholarship

AMOUNT: $1000 DEADLINE: February 1
MAJOR: Electronic Engineering

This scholarship is available to students with a minimum general class amateur radio license who are majoring in electronic engineering at Clarkson University. The applicant must be in a baccalaureate or graduate program. Award requirements change regularly. For further information, please send a self-addressed, stamped envelope to the address provided. No GPA requirement specified.

American Radio Relay League
Attn: ARRL Foundation
225 Main Street
Newington, CT 06111-1400

Clemson University

1444
A.B. Everett Scholarship

AMOUNT: $500 DEADLINE: February 1
MAJOR: Agronomy, Horticulture, Plant Pathology,
Entomology, Agricultural Engineering

Open to Clemson University undergraduates with a minimum
GPA of 2.5. These awards are renewable. Award requirements
change regularly. Write to the address listed, enclosing a self-
addressed, stamped envelope for an application and further
information or browse their website: www.clemson.edu. GPA
must be 2.5.

Clemson University
Office of Student Financial Aid
G01 Sikes Hall, Box 345123
Clemson, SC 29634

1445
A.U. "Buck" Priester, Jr., Scholarship

AMOUNT: $500 DEADLINE: February 1
MAJOR: Engineering

Open to Clemson University undergraduates enrolled in the
College of Engineering and Science. Award requirements
change regularly. Write to the address listed, enclosing a self-
addressed, stamped envelope for an application and further
information or browse their website: www.clemson.edu. GPA
must be 2.5.

Clemson University
Office of Student Financial Aid
G01 Sikes Hall, Box 345123
Clemson, SC 29634

1446
Adele Hane Chappell Curtis Memorial Scholarship

AMOUNT: $600 DEADLINE: February 1
MAJOR: Fine Arts

Open to Clemson University undergraduates majoring in fine
arts with a minimum GPA of 2.5. Award requirements change
regularly. Write to the address listed, enclosing a self-
addressed, stamped envelope for an application and further
information or browse their website: www.clemson.edu. GPA
must be 2.5.

Clemson University
Office of Student Financial Aid
G01 Sikes Hall, Box 345123
Clemson, SC 29634

1447
Alumni, Faculty & Staff Scholarships

AMOUNT: $1000 DEADLINE: March 1
MAJOR: All Areas of Study

Open to Clemson University entering freshmen. Renewable
for three years if recipients maintain a minimum GPA of 3.0.
Several awards offered annually. Award requirements change
regularly. Write to the address listed, enclosing a self-
addressed, stamped envelope for an application and further
information or browse their website: www.clemson.edu. GPA
must be 3.4.

Clemson University
Office of Student Financial Aid
G01 Sikes Hall, Box 345123
Clemson, SC 29634

1448
Annual Chemistry Scholarship

AMOUNT: Maximum: $2400 DEADLINE: March 1
MAJOR: Chemistry

Open to Clemson University undergraduate students majoring
in chemistry. Award requirements change regularly. Write to
the address listed, enclosing a self-addressed, stamped envelope for an application and further information or browse their
website: www.clemson.edu. GPA must be 3.0-4.0.

Clemson University
Office of Student Financial Aid
G01 Sikes Hall, Box 345123
Clemson, SC 29634

1449
Barbara Ferry Johnson Scholarship

AMOUNT: $400 DEADLINE: February 1
MAJOR: English

Open to Clemson University undergraduates majoring in
English with a minimum GPA of 2.5. Award requirements
change regularly. Write to the address listed, enclosing a self-
addressed, stamped envelope for an application and further
information or browse their website: www.clemson.edu. GPA
must be 2.5.

Clemson University
Office of Student Financial Aid
G01 Sikes Hall, Box 345123
Clemson, SC 29634

1450
Bill Hudson Family Endowment Scholarship

AMOUNT: $3800 DEADLINE: February 1
MAJOR: All Areas of Study

Open to Clemson University undergraduates with a minimum
GPA of 2.5. Recipients must be South Carolina residents and
be able to demonstrate financial need. Award is renewable.
Award requirements change regularly. Write to the address
listed, enclosing a self-addressed, stamped envelope for an

application and further information or browse their website: www.clemson.edu. GPA must be 2.5.

Clemson University
Office of Student Financial Aid
G01 Sikes Hall, Box 345123
Clemson, SC 29634

1451
Brockington G. Woodham Memorial Scholarship

AMOUNT: $2300 DEADLINE: February 1
MAJOR: Textiles

Open to Clemson University undergraduates majoring in textiles with a minimum GPA of 2.5. This award is renewable. Award requirements change regularly. Write to the address listed, enclosing a self-addressed, stamped envelope for an application and further information or browse their website: www.clemson.edu. GPA must be 2.5.

Clemson University
Office of Student Financial Aid
G01 Sikes Hall, Box 345123
Clemson, SC 29634

1452
Byron R. Ingram Memorial Scholarship

AMOUNT: $600 DEADLINE: February 1
MAJOR: Biological Science

Open to Clemson University undergraduates majoring in biological science. Recipients must have a minimum GPA of 2.5. Award requirements change regularly. Write to the address listed, enclosing a self-addressed, stamped envelope for an application and further information or browse their website: www.clemson.edu. GPA must be 2.5.

Clemson University
Office of Student Financial Aid
G01 Sikes Hall, Box 345123
Clemson, SC 29634

1453
Charles Edward Littlejohn, Jr., Memorial Scholarships

AMOUNT: $1000 DEADLINE: February 1
MAJOR: Chemical Engineering

Open to Clemson University undergraduates majoring in chemical engineering. Recipients must have a minimum GPA of 2.5. Award requirements change regularly. Write to the address listed, enclosing a self-addressed, stamped envelope for an application and further information or browse their website: www.clemson.edu. GPA must be 2.5-4.0.

Clemson University
Office of Student Financial Aid
G01 Sikes Hall, Box 345123
Clemson, SC 29634

1454
Cryovac Endowed Engineering Scholarship

AMOUNT: $1900 DEADLINE: February 1
MAJOR: Chemical, Electrical, Mechanical, or Computer Engineering

Open to Clemson University undergraduates majoring in chemical, electrical, and mechanical engineering with a minimum GPA of 2.5. These awards are renewable. Award requirements change regularly. Write to the address listed, enclosing a self-addressed, stamped envelope for an application and further information or browse their website: www.clemson.edu. GPA must be 2.5.

Clemson University
Office of Student Financial Aid
G01 Sikes Hall, Box 345123
Clemson, SC 29634

1455
Daniel Memorial Fund Endowed Scholarships

AMOUNT: None Specified DEADLINE: March 1
MAJOR: All Areas of Study

Open to Clemson University entering freshmen. Renewable if recipients maintain a minimum GPA of 3.0. Award requirements change regularly. Write to the address listed, enclosing a self-addressed, stamped envelope for an application and further information or browse their website: www.clemson.edu. GPA must be 3.0-4.0.

Clemson University
Office of Student Financial Aid
G01 Sikes Hall, Box 345123
Clemson, SC 29634

1456
Dean William H. Washington and Miriam Betts Washington Scholarship

AMOUNT: $1000 DEADLINE: February 1
MAJOR: Education

Open to Clemson University undergraduates with a minimum GPA of 2.5. Preference given to students in the Army or Air Force ROTC. Award requirements change regularly. Write to the address listed, enclosing a self-addressed, stamped envelope for an application and further information or browse their website: www.clemson.edu. GPA must be 2.5-4.0.

Clemson University
Office of Student Financial Aid
G01 Sikes Hall, Box 345123
Clemson, SC 29634

1457
Edgar J. and Emily Hesslein Scholarship

AMOUNT: $1200 DEADLINE: February 1
MAJOR: All Areas of Study

Open to Clemson University incoming freshmen who have a minimum GPA of 2.5. Recipients must be able to demonstrate financial need. This award is renewable. Award requirements change regularly. Write to the address listed, enclosing a self-addressed, stamped envelope for an application and further information or browse their website: www.clemson.edu. GPA must be 2.5-4.0.

Clemson University
Office of Student Financial Aid
G01 Sikes Hall, Box 345123
Clemson, SC 29634

1458
Frank J. Jervey Alumni Scholarships

AMOUNT: Maximum: $2500 DEADLINE: March 1
MAJOR: All Areas of Study

Open to Clemson University undergraduate students with outstanding academic potential. Award requirements change regularly. Write to the address listed, enclosing a self-addressed, stamped envelope for an application and further information or browse their website: www.clemson.edu. GPA must be 2.8-4.0.

Clemson University
Office of Student Financial Aid
G01 Sikes Hall, Box 345123
Clemson, SC 29634

1459
Frank Jefferson Julian, Sr. and Jr., Scholarships

AMOUNT: $1000 DEADLINE: February 1
MAJOR: All Areas of Study

Open to Clemson University incoming freshmen with a minimum GPA of 2.5. Award requirements change regularly. Write to the address listed, enclosing a self-addressed, stamped envelope for an application and further information or browse their website: www.clemson.edu. GPA must be 2.5-4.0.

Clemson University
Office of Student Financial Aid
G01 Sikes Hall, Box 345123
Clemson, SC 29634

1460
George R. MacDonald Trust Scholarships

AMOUNT: $1500 DEADLINE: February 1
MAJOR: All Areas of Study

This endowment provides numerous scholarships for Clemson University undergraduates. Recipients must have a minimum GPA of 2.5 and be able to demonstrate financial need. Award requirements change regularly. Write to the address listed, enclosing a self-addressed, stamped envelope for an application and further information or browse their website: www.clemson.edu. GPA must be 2.5.

Clemson University
Office of Student Financial Aid
G01 Sikes Hall, Box 345123
Clemson, SC 29634

1461
Golden Anniversary Scholarships: Classes of 1936 and 1938

AMOUNT: $2500-$3500 DEADLINE: Mrach 1
MAJOR: All Areas of Study

Open to Clemson University undergraduate students. Established by the classes of 1936 and 1938. Several awards offered annually. Award requirements change regularly. Write to the address listed, enclosing a self-addressed, stamped envelope for an application and further information or browse their website: www.clemson.edu. GPA must be 2.8-4.0.

Clemson University
Office of Student Financial Aid
G01 Sikes Hall, Box 345123
Clemson, SC 29634

1462
Hardin, Keitt, Hinton Memorial Scholarship

AMOUNT: $800 DEADLINE: February 1
MAJOR: English, Chemistry, Agronomy, Forestry, Financial Management, Accounting

Open to Clemson University juniors and seniors majoring in chemistry, English, agronomy, forest resource management, accounting, financial management, or management who have a minimum GPA of 3.0. Award requirements change regularly. Write to the address listed, enclosing a self-addressed, stamped envelope for an application and further information or browse their website: www.clemson.edu. GPA must be 3.0.

Clemson University
Office of Student Financial Aid
G01 Sikes Hall, Box 345123
Clemson, SC 29634

1463
Herbert J. Copeland Memorial Scholarship

AMOUNT: $1500 DEADLINE: February 1
MAJOR: All Areas of Study

Open to Clemson University incoming freshmen with a minimum GPA of 2.5. Preference given to students who demonstrate Christian ideals by extracurricular activities (such as involvement with the Y.M.C.A.). Award requirements change regularly. Write to the address listed, enclosing a self-addressed, stamped envelope for an application and further information or browse their website: www.clemson.edu. GPA must be 2.5-4.0.

Clemson University
Office of Student Financial Aid
G01 Sikes Hall, Box 345123
Clemson, SC 29634

1464
Howard Carlisle Copeland Memorial Scholarships

AMOUNT: $1500 DEADLINE: February 1
MAJOR: All Areas of Study

Open to Clemson University incoming freshmen with a minimum GPA of 2.5. Students must be able to demonstrate financial need. Award is renewable. Award requirements change regularly. Write to the address listed, enclosing a self-addressed, stamped envelope for an application and further information or browse their website: www.clemson.edu. GPA must be 2.5.

Clemson University
Office of Student Financial Aid
G01 Sikes Hall, Box 345123
Clemson, SC 29634

1465
PTAY Academic Scholarship

AMOUNT: $2500 DEADLINE: March 1
MAJOR: All Areas of Study

Open to Clemson University undergraduate students who do not participate in intercollegiate athletics. Several scholarships offered annually. Award requirements change regularly. Write to the address listed, enclosing a self-addressed, stamped envelope for an application and further information or browse their website: www.clemson.edu. GPA must be 2.8-4.0.

Clemson University
Office of Student Financial Aid
G01 Sikes Hall, Box 345123
Clemson, SC 29634

1466
James A. Shine, Milling Presidential Scholarships

AMOUNT: $6500 DEADLINE: March 1
MAJOR: Engineering, Industrial Management

Open to Clemson University undergraduate students majoring in engineering or industrial management. Recipients must have a minimum GPA of 3.0. Award requirements change regularly. Write to the address listed, enclosing a self-addressed, stamped envelope for an application and further information or browse their website: www.clemson.edu. GPA must be 3.0-4.0.

Clemson University
Office of Student Financial Aid
G01 Sikes Hall, Box 345123
Clemson, SC 29634

1467
Julia Folger Singleton Memorial Scholarship

AMOUNT: $1500 DEADLINE: February 1
MAJOR: All Areas of Study

Open to high school seniors in the top 10% of their graduating class. Recipients must attend Clemson University. Award requirements change regularly. Write to the address listed, enclosing a self-addressed, stamped envelope for an application and further information or browse their website: www.clemson.edu. GPA must be 3.4.

Clemson University
Office of Student Financial Aid
G01 Sikes Hall, Box 345123
Clemson, SC 29634

1468
Lewis Dameron Memorial Scholarship

AMOUNT: $800 DEADLINE: February 1
MAJOR: Agricultural Economics, Agricultural Engineering, Agricultural Mechanization, Agronomy

Open to Clemson University undergraduates majoring in agricultural and applied economics, agricultural education, agricultural mechanization and business, agronomy, animal industries, aquaculture, fisheries and wildlife biology, biosystems engineering, entomology, food science, horticulture, packaging science, or plant pathology. Award requirements change regularly. Write to the address listed, enclosing a self-addressed, stamped envelope for an application and further information or browse their website: www.clemson.edu. GPA must be 2.5.

Clemson University
Office of Student Financial Aid
G01 Sikes Hall, Box 345123
Clemson, SC 29634

1469
Marion Killian Arthur Memorial Scholarship

AMOUNT: $1900 DEADLINE: March 1
MAJOR: Engineering

Open to Clemson University undergraduate students who have a minimum GPA of 2.5. Based on financial need. Award is renewable. Award requirements change regularly. Write to the address listed, enclosing a self-addressed, stamped envelope for an application and further information or browse their website: www.clemson.edu. GPA must be 2.5.

Clemson University
Office of Student Financial Aid
G01 Sikes Hall, Box 345123
Clemson, SC 29634

1470
Minnesota Mining and Manufacturing Corporation Scholarship

AMOUNT: $3000 DEADLINE: February 1
MAJOR: Engineering, Science

Open to Clemson University undergraduates enrolled in the College of Engineering and Science. Award requirements change regularly. Write to the address listed, enclosing a self-addressed, stamped envelope for an application and further information or browse their website: www.clemson.edu. GPA must be 2.5.

Clemson University
Office of Student Financial Aid
G01 Sikes Hall, Box 345123
Clemson, SC 29634

1471
Richard Cecil Hicks Educational Fund Scholarships

AMOUNT: $2200 DEADLINE: February 1
MAJOR: Engineering, Architecture

Open to Clemson University male undergraduates with a minimum GPA of 2.5. Must be able to demonstrate financial need. Four awards offered annually. Award requirements change regularly. Write to the address listed, enclosing a self-addressed, stamped envelope for an application and further information or browse their website: www.clemson.edu. GPA must be 2.5.

Clemson University
Office of Student Financial Aid
G01 Sikes Hall, Box 345123
Clemson, SC 29634

1472
Robert C. Edwards Scholarships

AMOUNT: $3000 DEADLINE: March 1
MAJOR: All Areas of Study

Open to Clemson University entering freshmen with outstanding academic potential. Several awards offered each year. Renewable if recipients maintain a minimum GPA of 3.0. Award requirements change regularly. Write to the address listed, enclosing a self-addressed, stamped envelope for an application and further information or browse their website: www.clemson.edu. GPA must be 2.8.

Clemson University
Office of Student Financial Aid
G01 Sikes Hall, Box 345123
Clemson, SC 29634

1473
Second Robert R., Red, Ritchie Scholarship

AMOUNT: $1000 DEADLINE: February 1
MAJOR: All Areas of Study

Open to Clemson University undergraduates with a minimum GPA of 2.5. Award requirements change regularly. Write to the

address listed, enclosing a self-addressed, stamped envelope for an application and further information or browse their website: www.clemson.edu. GPA must be 2.5.

Clemson University
Office of Student Financial Aid
G01 Sikes Hall, Box 345123
Clemson, SC 29634

1474
Speck Farrar Scholarships

AMOUNT: $3000 DEADLINE: February 1
MAJOR: All Areas of Study

Open to Clemson University undergraduates with a minimum GPA of 2.5. Students must demonstrate financial need. Award requirements change regularly. Write to the address listed, enclosing a self-addressed, stamped envelope for an application and further information or browse their website: www.clemson.edu. GPA must be 2.5.

Clemson University
Office of Student Financial Aid
G01 Sikes Hall, Box 345123
Clemson, SC 29634

1475
Stephen Friendly Wyndham Memorial Scholarship

AMOUNT: $900 DEADLINE: February 1
MAJOR: All Areas of Study

Open to Clemson University incoming freshmen. Must have a minimum GPA of 2.5. This award is renewable. Award requirements change regularly. Write to the address listed, enclosing a self-addressed, stamped envelope for an application and further information or browse their website: www.clemson.edu. GPA must be 2.5-4.0.

Clemson University
Office of Student Financial Aid
G01 Sikes Hall, Box 345123
Clemson, SC 29634

1476
Terminix Scholarships

AMOUNT: $1900 DEADLINE: February 1
MAJOR: Entomology

Open to Clemson University incoming freshmen majoring in entomology. Must have a minimum GPA of 2.5. Award requirements change regularly. Write to the address listed, enclosing a self-addressed, stamped envelope for an application and further information or browse their website: www.clemson.edu. GPA must be 2.5.

Clemson University
Office of Student Financial Aid
G01 Sikes Hall, Box 345123
Clemson, SC 29634

1477
Thomas M. Hunter Endowed Scholars Scholarships

AMOUNT: $3000 DEADLINE: March 1
MAJOR: Engineering

Open to Clemson University undergraduate students majoring in engineering. These scholarships do not include a waiver of out-of-state tuition and fee differential. Award requirements change regularly. Write to the address listed, enclosing a self-addressed, stamped envelope for an application and further information or browse their website: www.clemson.edu. GPA must be 3.5-4.0.

Clemson University
Office of Student Financial Aid
G01 Sikes Hall, Box 345123
Clemson, SC 29634

1478
W.L. Abernathy, Jr., Scholarship

AMOUNT: $1500 DEADLINE: March 1
MAJOR: Agriculture, Forestry, Life Sciences

Open to Clemson University undergraduate students who are South Carolina residents. At least two recipients are entering freshmen. Award requirements change regularly. Write to the address listed, enclosing a self-addressed, stamped envelope for an application and further information or browse their website: www.clemson.edu. GPA must be 2.5.

Clemson University
Office of Student Financial Aid
G01 Sikes Hall, Box 345123
Clemson, SC 29634

1479
Walter T. Cox Presidential Scholarship

AMOUNT: $6500 DEADLINE: March 1
MAJOR: All Areas of Study

Open to Clemson University undergraduate students. Award requirements change regularly. Write to the address listed, enclosing a self-addressed, stamped envelope for an application and further information or browse their website: www.clemson.edu. GPA must be 3.8-4.0.

Clemson University
Office of Student Financial Aid
G01 Sikes Hall, Box 345123
Clemson, SC 29634

1480
William A. Kenyon Scholarships

AMOUNT: Maximum: $2500 DEADLINE: March 1
MAJOR: All Areas of Study

Open to Clemson University undergraduate students with outstanding academic potential. Several awards of up to $2500 are offered annually. Award requirements change regularly. Write to the address listed, enclosing a self-addressed, stamped envelope for an application and further information or browse their website: www.clemson.edu. GPA must be 2.8-4.0.

Clemson University
Office of Student Financial Aid
G01 Sikes Hall, Box 345123
Clemson, SC 29634

1481
William James Erwin Scholarships

AMOUNT: Maximum: $2500 DEADLINE: March 1
MAJOR: All Areas of Study

Open to Clemson University undergraduate students. Two awards are given annually. Award requirements change regularly. Write to the address listed, enclosing a self-addressed, stamped envelope for an application and further information or browse their website: www.clemson.edu. GPA must be 3.0-4.0.

Clemson University
Office of Student Financial Aid
G01 Sikes Hall, Box 345123
Clemson, SC 29634

Cogswell Polytechnical College

1482
Alumni Scholarship

AMOUNT: None Specified DEADLINE: January 24
MAJOR: All Areas of Study

The Alumni Scholarship is awarded to a U.S. citizen in financial need. In order to receive the award, you must have completed at least one full trimester prior to receiving the award and be enrolled in courses for the spring trimester. Award requirements change regularly. No GPA requirement specified.

Cogswell Polytechnical College
1175 Bordeaux Drive
Sunnyvale, CA 94089

1483
Bigglestone Scholarship

AMOUNT: None Specified DEADLINE: January 24
MAJOR: All Areas of Study

The Bigglestone Scholarship is awarded to students in the Open Learning for Fire Service Program with a minimum 3.0 GPA. You must have completed at least one full trimester and be enrolled in courses for the spring trimester. Award requirements change regularly. GPA must be 3.0-4.0.

Cogswell Polytechnical College
1175 Bordeaux Drive
Sunnyvale, CA 94089

1484
Brush Scholarship

AMOUNT: None Specified DEADLINE: January 24
MAJOR: All Areas of Study

The Brush Scholarship is awarded annually to a U.S. citizen who has completed 24 credits at Cogswell and has maintained a minimum 3.0 GPA. You must have completed at least one full trimester and be enrolled in courses for the spring trimester. Award requirements change regularly. GPA must be 3.0-4.0.

Cogswell Polytechnical College
1175 Bordeaux Drive
Sunnyvale, CA 94089

1485
Gomez Scholarship

AMOUNT: None Specified DEADLINE: January 24
MAJOR: All Areas of Study

This scholarship is awarded to a U.S. citizen, permanent resident, or refugee who is in financial need, has a 3.0 GPA, and is involved in campus activities. Scholarship candidates must have completed at least one full trimester prior to award disbursement and be enrolled in courses for the spring trimester. Award requirements change regularly. GPA must be 3.0-4.0.

Cogswell Polytechnical College
1175 Bordeaux Drive
Sunnyvale, CA 94089

1486
Robert Ewing Golden Scholarship

AMOUNT: None Specified DEADLINE: January 24
MAJOR: All Areas of Study

The Robert Ewing Golden Scholarship is awarded to an upper-division student with a minimum GPA of 3.3. To be considered for the award, you must have entered Cogswell as a freshman (31 or less credits). The award also requires that you must have completed at least one full trimester and be enrolled in courses for the spring trimester. Award requirements change regularly. GPA must be 3.3-4.0.

Cogswell Polytechnical College
1175 Bordeaux Drive
Sunnyvale, CA 94089

1487
Robinson Scholarship

AMOUNT: None Specified DEADLINE: January 24
MAJOR: All Areas of Study

The Robinson Scholarship is awarded to a U.S. citizen with severe financial need. To be considered for the award, you must have completed at least one full trimester and be enrolled in courses for the spring trimester. Award requirements change regularly. No GPA requirement specified.

Cogswell Polytechnical College
1175 Bordeaux Drive
Sunnyvale, CA 94089

1488
Sandy Scholarship

AMOUNT: None Specified DEADLINE: January 24
MAJOR: All Areas of Study

The Sandy Scholarship is awarded to a student in financial need who has at least a 3.0 GPA. To be eligible, you must have completed at least one full trimester and be enrolled in courses for the spring trimester. Award requirements change regularly. GPA must be 3.0-4.0.

Cogswell Polytechnical College
1175 Bordeaux Drive
Sunnyvale, CA 94089

1489
Smith Scholarship

AMOUNT: None Specified DEADLINE: January 24
MAJOR: All Areas of Study

The Smith Scholarship is awarded to a student in financial need who has a minimum 3.0 GPA. You must have completed at least one full trimester and be enrolled in courses for the spring trimester to be considered for the award. Award requirements change regularly. GPA must be 3.0-4.0.

Cogswell Polytechnical College
1175 Bordeaux Drive
Sunnyvale, CA 94089

1490
Taylor Scholarship

AMOUNT: None Specified DEADLINE: January 24
MAJOR: All Areas of Study

The Taylor Scholarship is awarded to a full-time Cogswell student with financial need. To be considered, you must have completed at least one full trimester and be enrolled in courses for the spring trimester. Award requirements change regularly. No GPA requirement specified.

Cogswell Polytechnical College
1175 Bordeaux Drive
Sunnyvale, CA 94089

1491
Telford Scholarship

AMOUNT: None Specified DEADLINE: January 24
MAJOR: All Areas of Study

The Telford Scholarship is awarded to a student who has demonstrated financial need and maintained a minimum 3.0 GPA or above in the trimester prior to the award. You must have completed at least one full trimester and be enrolled in courses for the spring trimester. Award requirements change regularly. GPA must be 3.0-4.0.

Cogswell Polytechnical College
1175 Bordeaux Drive
Sunnyvale, CA 94089

1492
Vierra Scholarship

AMOUNT: None Specified DEADLINE: January 24
MAJOR: All Areas of Study

The Vierra Scholarship is awarded to a student who has been a resident of Hawaii for 15 continuous years, is a graduate of a Hawaii high school, and has maintained a minimum 3.0 GPA. You must have completed at least one full trimester and be enrolled in courses for the spring trimester. Award requirements change regularly. GPA must be 3.0-4.0.

Cogswell Polytechnical College
1175 Bordeaux Drive
Sunnyvale, CA 94089

College of DuPage

1493
Advertising Design and Illustration Scholarship

AMOUNT: $1000 DEADLINE: June 1
MAJOR: Advertising Design and Illustration

The Advertising Design and Illustration Scholarship is available to students studying advertising design and illustration at the College of DuPage. The criteria for the application may include a request for information regarding academic success, credit hours completed, public/community service, or financial need. Students need to be prepared to write a paragraph or two explaining how they qualify for the scholarship. Award requirements change regularly. No applications will be mailed. No GPA requirement specified.

College of DuPage
Student Financial Aid Office
425 22nd Street, SRC - Rm 2050
Glen Ellyn, IL 60137-6599

1494
American Association of Women in Community Colleges Scholarship

AMOUNT: $500 DEADLINE: June 1
MAJOR: All Fields of Study

The American Association of Women in Community Colleges Scholarship is open to female students studying at the College of DuPage. The criteria for the application may include a request for information regarding academic success, credit hours completed, public/community service, or financial need. Students need to be prepared to write a paragraph or two explaining how they qualify for the scholarship. Award requirements change regularly. No applications will be mailed. No GPA requirement specified.

College of DuPage
Student Financial Aid Office
425 22nd Street, SRC - Rm 2050
Glen Ellyn, IL 60137-6599

1495
Aveling Memorial Student Scholarship

AMOUNT: $500-$1000 DEADLINE: Varies
MAJOR: Health Information Technology, Health Care-Related Fields

The Aveling Memorial Student Scholarship is available to students studying health information technology and health care-related fields at the College of DuPage. The criteria for the application may include a request for information regarding academic success, credit hours completed, public/community service, or financial need. Students need to be prepared to write a paragraph or two explaining how they qualify for the scholarship. Award requirements change regularly. No applications will be mailed. No GPA requirement specified.

College of DuPage
Student Financial Aid Office
425 22nd Street, SRC - Rm 2050
Glen Ellyn, IL 60137-6599

1496
Balance for Life Foundation Scholarship in Eating Disorders

AMOUNT: $500 DEADLINE: June 1
MAJOR: Human Services

The Balance for Life Foundation Scholarship in Eating Disorders is available to students studying human services at the College of DuPage. The criteria for the application may include a request for information regarding academic success, credit hours completed, public/community service, or financial need. Students need to be prepared to write a paragraph or two explaining how they qualify for the scholarship. Award requirements change regularly. No applications will be mailed. No GPA requirement specified.

College of DuPage
Student Financial Aid Office
425 22nd Street, SRC - Rm 2050
Glen Ellyn, IL 60137-6599

1497
Black Student Union Scholarship

AMOUNT: $500 DEADLINE: Varies
MAJOR: All Fields of Study

The Black Student Union Scholarship is open to African-American students attending the College of DuPage. One $500 award is offered for Winter and another $500 award is offered for Spring. November 1 is the deadline for the Winter award. The criteria for the application may include a request for information regarding academic success, credit hours completed, public/community service, or financial need. Students need to be prepared to write a paragraph or two explaining how they qualify for the scholarship. Award requirements change regularly. No applications will be mailed. No GPA requirement specified.

College of DuPage
Student Financial Aid Office
425 22nd Street, SRC - Rm 2050
Glen Ellyn, IL 60137-6599

1498
Business/Management/Marketing Scholarship

AMOUNT: $250 DEADLINE: March 1
MAJOR: Business, Management, Marketing

The Business/Management/Marketing Scholarship is available to students studying business, management, and marketing at the College of DuPage. The criteria for the application may include a request for information regarding academic success, credit hours completed, public/community service, or financial need. Students need to be prepared to write a paragraph or two explaining how they qualify for the scholarship. Award requirements change regularly. No applications will be mailed. No GPA requirement specified.

College of DuPage
Student Financial Aid Office
425 22nd Street, SRC - Rm 2050
Glen Ellyn, IL 60137-6599

1499
COD Study Abroad Scholarship

AMOUNT: Maximum: $1000 DEADLINE: Varies
MAJOR: All Fields of Study

The COD Study Abroad Scholarship is open to students attending the College of DuPage who plan on studying abroad. The scholarship has multiple deadlines: October 30 for Winter/Spring; February 20 for Summer; May 15 for Fall. The criteria for the application may include a request for information regarding academic success, credit hours completed, public/community service, or financial need. Students need to be prepared to write a paragraph or two explaining how they qualify for the scholarship. Award requirements change regularly. No applications will be mailed. No GPA requirement specified.

College of DuPage
Student Financial Aid Office
425 22nd Street, SRC - Rm 2050
Glen Ellyn, IL 60137-6599

1500
College of DuPage Cultural Guild Single Parent Scholarship

AMOUNT: $1000 DEADLINE: June 1
MAJOR: All Fields of Study

The College of DuPage Cultural Guild Single Parent Scholarship is open to students attending the College of DuPage who are single parents. The criteria for the application may include a request for information regarding academic success, credit hours completed, public/community service, or financial need. Students need to be prepared to write a paragraph or two explaining how they qualify for the scholarship. Award requirements change regularly. No applications will be mailed. No GPA requirement specified.

College of DuPage
Student Financial Aid Office
425 22nd Street, SRC - Rm 2050
Glen Ellyn, IL 60137-6599

1501
College of DuPage Foundation Achievers Scholarship

AMOUNT: $2000 DEADLINE: June 1
MAJOR: All Fields of Study

The College of DuPage Foundation Achievers Scholarship is open to students studying at the College of DuPage. The criteria for the application may include a request for information regarding academic success, credit hours completed, public/community service, or financial need. Students need to be prepared to write a paragraph or two explaining how they qualify for the scholarship. Award requirements change regularly. No applications will be mailed. No GPA requirement specified.

College of DuPage
Student Financial Aid Office
425 22nd Street, SRC - Rm 2050
Glen Ellyn, IL 60137-6599

1502
College of DuPage Foundation Freshman Scholarship

AMOUNT: $2000 DEADLINE: June 1
MAJOR: All Fields of Study

The College of DuPage Foundation Freshman Scholarship is open to freshmen attending the College of DuPage. The criteria for the application may include a request for information regarding academic success, credit hours completed, public/community service, or financial need. Students need to be prepared to write a paragraph or two explaining how they qualify for the scholarship. Award requirements change regularly. No applications will be mailed. No GPA requirement specified.

College of DuPage
Student Financial Aid Office
425 22nd Street, SRC - Rm 2050
Glen Ellyn, IL 60137-6599

1503
College of DuPage Foundation Need Based Scholarship

AMOUNT: $2000 DEADLINE: June 1
MAJOR: All Fields of Study

The College of DuPage Foundation Need Based Scholarship is open to students studying at the College of DuPage. The criteria for the application may include a request for information regarding academic success, credit hours completed, public/community service, or financial need. Students need to be prepared to write a paragraph or two explaining how they qualify for the scholarship. Award requirements change regularly. No applications will be mailed. No GPA requirement specified.

College of DuPage
Student Financial Aid Office
425 22nd Street, SRC - Rm 2050
Glen Ellyn, IL 60137-6599

1504
College of DuPage Foundation Single Parent Scholarship

AMOUNT: $2000 DEADLINE: June 1
MAJOR: All Fields of Study

The College of DuPage Foundation Single Parent Scholarship is open to students attending the College of DuPage who are single parents. The criteria for the application may include a request for information regarding academic success, credit hours completed, public/community service, or financial need. Students need to be prepared to write a paragraph or two explaining how they qualify for the scholarship. Award requirements change regularly. No applications will be mailed. No GPA requirement specified.

College of DuPage
Student Financial Aid Office
425 22nd Street, SRC - Rm 2050
Glen Ellyn, IL 60137-6599

1505
Computer Central Scholarship

AMOUNT: $1500 DEADLINE: June 1
MAJOR: Computer Science

The Computer Central Scholarship is available to students studying computer science at the College of DuPage. The criteria for application may include a request for information regarding academic success, credit hours completed, public/community service, or financial need. Students need to be prepared to write a paragraph or two explaining how they qualify for the scholarship. Award requirements change regularly. No applications will be mailed. No GPA requirement specified.

College of DuPage
Student Financial Aid Office
425 22nd Street, SRC - Rm 2050
Glen Ellyn, IL 60137-6599

1506
DuPage Chapter of F.E.M.A.L.E. Scholarship

AMOUNT: $500-$2000 DEADLINE: Varies
MAJOR: All Fields of Study

The DuPage Chapter of F.E.M.A.L.E. Scholarship is open to students studying at the College of DuPage who are mothers. The criteria for the application may include a request for information regarding academic success, credit hours completed, public/community service, or financial need. Students need to be prepared to write a paragraph or two explaining how they qualify for the scholarship. The scholarship provides $500 awarded each quarter. The deadline for the Fall quarter is June 1. Award requirements change regularly. No applications will be mailed. No GPA requirement specified.
College of DuPage
Student Financial Aid Office
425 22nd Street, SRC - Rm 2050
Glen Ellyn, IL 60137-6599

1507
DuPage County Health Improvement Association Scholarship

AMOUNT: $1000 DEADLINE: Varies
MAJOR: Health Information Technology, Health Care-Related Fields

The DuPage County Health Improvement Association Scholarship is available to students studying health information technology and health care-related fields at the College of DuPage. The criteria for the application may include a request for information regarding academic success, credit hours completed, public/community service, or financial need. Students need to be prepared to write a paragraph or two explaining how they qualify for the scholarship. Award requirements change regularly. No applications will be mailed. No GPA requirement specified.

College of DuPage
Student Financial Aid Office
425 22nd Street, SRC - Rm 2050
Glen Ellyn, IL 60137-6599

1508
Eileen Ward Textbook Scholarship Fund

AMOUNT: Maximum: $300 DEADLINE: Varies
MAJOR: All Fields of Study

The Eileen Ward Textbook Scholarship Fund is open to students attending the College of DuPage and pays the cost of textbooks for credit courses up to $300. The scholarship is awarded quarterly, and applications are due June 1 for the Fall quarter. The criteria for the application may include a request for information regarding academic success, credit hours completed, public/community service, or financial need. Students need to be prepared to write a paragraph or two explaining how they qualify for the scholarship. Award requirements change regularly. No applications will be mailed. No GPA requirement specified.

College of DuPage
Student Financial Aid Office
425 22nd Street, SRC - Rm 2050
Glen Ellyn, IL 60137-6599

1509
George O. Sinka Engineering Scholarship

AMOUNT: $1000 DEADLINE: June 1
MAJOR: Engineering

The George O. Sinka Engineering Scholarship is available to students studying engineering at the College of DuPage. The criteria for the application may include a request for information regarding academic success, credit hours completed, public/community service, or financial need. Students need to be prepared to write a paragraph or two explaining how they qualify for the scholarship. Award requirements change regularly. No applications will be mailed. No GPA requirement specified.

College of DuPage
Student Financial Aid Office
425 22nd Street, SRC - Rm 2050
Glen Ellyn, IL 60137-6599

1510
Glen Ellyn Rotary Club Single Parent Scholarship

AMOUNT: $2000 DEADLINE: Varies
MAJOR: All Fields of Study

The Glen Ellyn Rotary Club Single Parent Scholarship is open to students attending the College of DuPage who are single parents. The criteria for the application may include a request for information regarding academic success, credit hours completed, public/community service, or financial need. Students need to be prepared to write a paragraph or two explaining how they qualify for the scholarship. Applications are due in the Fall. Contact the provider for additional details regarding the application deadline. Award requirements change regularly. No applications will be mailed. No GPA requirement specified.

College of DuPage
Student Financial Aid Office
425 22nd Street, SRC - Rm 2050
Glen Ellyn, IL 60137-6599

1511
Glen Ellyn, Wheaton, Mid-America Medical Clinic CNA Scholarship

AMOUNT: $500 DEADLINE: Varies
MAJOR: Health Information Technology, Health Care-Related Fields

The Glen Ellyn, Wheaton, Mid-America Medical Clinic CNA Scholarship is available to students studying health information technology and health care-related fields at the College of DuPage. The criteria for the application may include a request for information regarding academic success, credit hours completed, public/community service, or financial need. Students need to be prepared to write a paragraph or two explaining how they qualify for the scholarship. Applications for the Fall quarter award are due June 1; applications for the Spring quarter award are due January 1. Award requirements change regularly. No applications will be mailed. No GPA requirement specified.

College of DuPage
Student Financial Aid Office
425 22nd Street, SRC - Rm 2050
Glen Ellyn, IL 60137-6599

1512
H.D. McAninch Academic Excellence Scholarship

AMOUNT: $1500 DEADLINE: June 1
MAJOR: All Fields of Study

The H.D. McAninch Academic Excellence Scholarship is open to students studying at the College of DuPage. The criteria for the application may include a request for information regarding academic success, credit hours completed, public/community service, or financial need. Students need to be prepared to write a paragraph or two explaining how they qualify for the scholarship. Award requirements change regularly. No applications will be mailed. No GPA requirement specified.

College of DuPage
Student Financial Aid Office
425 22nd Street, SRC - Rm 2050
Glen Ellyn, IL 60137-6599

1513
Harkins' Women's Scholarship for Excellence in Sociology

AMOUNT: $500 DEADLINE: May 1
MAJOR: Sociology

The Harkins' Women's Scholarship for Excellence in Sociology is open to students studying sociology at the College of DuPage. The criteria for the application may include a request for information regarding academic success, credit hours completed, public/community service, or financial need. Students need to be prepared to write a paragraph or two explaining how they qualify for the scholarship. Award requirements change regularly. No applications will be mailed. No GPA requirement specified.

College of DuPage
Student Financial Aid Office
425 22nd Street, SRC - Rm 2050
Glen Ellyn, IL 60137-6599

1514
Hawthorn Garden Club of Glen Ellyn Woods Scholarship

AMOUNT: $900 DEADLINE: June 1
MAJOR: Horticulture

The Hawthorn Garden Club of Glen Ellyn Woods Scholarship is open to students studying horticulture at the College of DuPage. The criteria for the application may include a request for information regarding academic success, credit hours completed, public/community service, or financial need. Students need to be prepared to write a paragraph or two explaining how they qualify for the scholarship. Award requirements change regularly. No applications will be mailed. No GPA requirement specified.

College of DuPage
Student Financial Aid Office
425 22nd Street, SRC - Rm 2050
Glen Ellyn, IL 60137-6599

1515
Hispanic-Latino Scholarship

AMOUNT: $500 DEADLINE: April 1
MAJOR: All Fields of Study

The Hispanic-Latino Scholarship is open to Hispanic and Latino students attending the College of DuPage. The criteria for the application may include a request for information regarding academic success, credit hours completed, public/community service, or financial need. Students need to be prepared to write a paragraph or two explaining how they qualify for the scholarship. Award requirements change regularly. No applications will be mailed. No GPA requirement specified.

College of DuPage
Student Financial Aid Office
425 22nd Street, SRC - Rm 2050
Glen Ellyn, IL 60137-6599

1516
Hospitality Administration Scholarship

AMOUNT: $500 DEADLINE: Varies
MAJOR: Travel and Tourism, Hotel Management

The Hospitality Administration Scholarship is open to students studying travel and tourism or hotel management at the College of DuPage. The criteria for the application may include a request for information regarding academic success, credit hours completed, public/community service, or financial need. Students need to be prepared to write a paragraph or two explaining how they qualify for the scholarship. Award requirements change regularly. No applications will be mailed. No GPA requirement specified.

College of DuPage
Student Financial Aid Office
425 22nd Street, SRC - Rm 2050
Glen Ellyn, IL 60137-6599

1517
Illinois Health Improvement Association Scholarship

AMOUNT: $1000 DEADLINE: Varies
MAJOR: Health Information Technology, Health Care-Related Fields

The Illinois Health Improvement Association Scholarship is available to students studying health information technology and health care-related fields at the College of DuPage. The criteria for the application may include a request for information regarding academic success, credit hours completed, public/community service, or financial need. Students need to be prepared to write a paragraph or two explaining how they qualify for the scholarship. Award requirements change regularly. No applications will be mailed. No GPA requirement specified.

College of DuPage
Student Financial Aid Office
425 22nd Street, SRC - Rm 2050
Glen Ellyn, IL 60137-6599

1518
Jodie Briggs Forensics/Theater Scholarship

AMOUNT: $500 DEADLINE: April 1
MAJOR: Speech, Drama

The Jodie Briggs Forensics/Theater Scholarship is open to students studying speech or drama at the College of DuPage. The criteria for the application may include a request for information regarding academic success, credit hours completed, public/community service, or financial need. Students need to be prepared to write a paragraph or two explaining how they qualify for the scholarship. Award requirements change regularly. No applications will be mailed. No GPA requirement specified.

College of DuPage
Student Financial Aid Office
425 22nd Street, SRC - Rm 2050
Glen Ellyn, IL 60137-6599

1519
John Belushi Memorial Choral Music Scholarship

AMOUNT: $750 DEADLINE: May 1
MAJOR: Choral Music

The John Belushi Memorial Choral Music Scholarship is available to students studying choral music at the College of DuPage. The criteria for the application may include a request for information regarding academic success, credit hours completed, public/community service, or financial need. Students need to be prepared to write a paragraph or two explaining how they qualify for the scholarship. Award requirements change regularly. No applications will be mailed. No GPA requirement specified.

College of DuPage
Student Financial Aid Office
425 22nd Street, SRC - Rm 2050
Glen Ellyn, IL 60137-6599

1520
John Belushi Memorial Jazz/Band Music Scholarship

AMOUNT: $750 DEADLINE: May 1
MAJOR: Jazz/Band Music

The John Belushi Memorial Jazz/Band Music Scholarship is available to students studying jazz/band music at the College of DuPage. The criteria for the application may include a request for information regarding academic success, credit hours completed, public/community service, or financial need. Students need to be prepared to write a paragraph or two explaining how they qualify for the scholarship. Award requirements change regularly. No applications will be mailed. No GPA requirement specified.

College of DuPage
Student Financial Aid Office
425 22nd Street, SRC - Rm 2050
Glen Ellyn, IL 60137-6599

1521
John Belushi Memorial Orchestral Music Scholarship

AMOUNT: $750 DEADLINE: May 1
MAJOR: Orchestral Music

The John Belushi Memorial Orchestral Music Scholarship is available to students studying orchestral music at the College of DuPage. The criteria for the application may include a request for information regarding academic success, credit hours completed, public/community service, or financial need. Students need to be prepared to write a paragraph or two explaining how they qualify for the scholarship. Award requirements change regularly. No applications will be mailed. No GPA requirement specified.

College of DuPage
Student Financial Aid Office
425 22nd Street, SRC - Rm 2050
Glen Ellyn, IL 60137-6599

1522
John Belushi/Second City Theater Scholarship

AMOUNT: None Specified DEADLINE: May 1
MAJOR: Theater

The John Belushi/Second City Theater Scholarship is open to students studying theater at the College of DuPage. The criteria for the application may include a request for information regarding academic success, credit hours completed, public/community service, or financial need. Students need to be prepared to write a paragraph or two explaining how they qualify for the scholarship. The scholarship provides one year of tuition, fees, and books. Award requirements change regularly. No applications will be mailed. No GPA requirement specified.

College of DuPage
Student Financial Aid Office
425 22nd Street, SRC - Rm 2050
Glen Ellyn, IL 60137-6599

1523
Kara Foundation Single Parent Scholarship

AMOUNT: $2500 DEADLINE: June 1
MAJOR: All Fields of Study

The Kara Foundation Single Parent Scholarship is open to students attending the College of DuPage who are single parents. The criteria for the application may include a request for information regarding academic success, credit hours completed, public/community service, or financial need. Students need to be prepared to write a paragraph or two explaining how they qualify for the scholarship. Award requirements change regularly. No applications will be mailed. No GPA requirement specified.

College of DuPage
Student Financial Aid Office
425 22nd Street, SRC - Rm 2050
Glen Ellyn, IL 60137-6599

1524
Kathy Marszalek Memorial Scholarship

AMOUNT: $2000 DEADLINE: June 1
MAJOR: Accounting

The Kathy Marszalek Memorial Scholarship is available to students studying accounting at the College of DuPage. The criteria for the application may include a request for information regarding academic success, credit hours completed, public/community service, or financial need. Students need to be prepared to write a paragraph or two explaining how they qualify for the scholarship. Award requirements change regularly. No applications will be mailed. No GPA requirement specified.

College of DuPage
Student Financial Aid Office
425 22nd Street, SRC - Rm 2050
Glen Ellyn, IL 60137-6599

1525
Lloyd David and Carlye Cannon Wattis Foundation Memorial Scholarship

AMOUNT: $2500 DEADLINE: June 1
MAJOR: Writing

The Lloyd David and Carlye Cannon Wattis Foundation Memorial Scholarship is open to students studying writing at the College of DuPage. The criteria for the application may include a request for information regarding academic success, credit hours completed, public/community service, or financial need. Students need to be prepared to write a paragraph or two explaining how they qualify for the scholarship. Award requirements change regularly. No applications will be mailed. No GPA requirement specified.

College of DuPage
Student Financial Aid Office
425 22nd Street, SRC - Rm 2050
Glen Ellyn, IL 60137-6599

1526
Lon A. Gault Memorial Scholarship for Academic Excellence in History

AMOUNT: $500 DEADLINE: June 1
MAJOR: History

The Lon A. Gault Memorial Scholarship for Academic Excellence in History is available to students studying history at the College of DuPage. The criteria for the application may include a request for information regarding academic success, credit hours completed, public/community service, or financial need. Students need to be prepared to write a paragraph or two explaining how they qualify for the scholarship. Award requirements change regularly. No applications will be mailed. No GPA requirement specified.

College of DuPage
Student Financial Aid Office
425 22nd Street, SRC - Rm 2050
Glen Ellyn, IL 60137-6599

1527
Mercedes Benz Scholarship

AMOUNT: $500 DEADLINE: May 1
MAJOR: Automotive Technology

The Mercedes Benz Scholarship is available to students studying automotive technology at the College of DuPage. The criteria for the application may include a request for information regarding academic success, credit hours completed, public/community service, or financial need. Students need to be prepared to write a paragraph or two explaining how they qualify for the scholarship. Award requirements change regularly. No applications will be mailed. No GPA requirement specified.

College of DuPage
Student Financial Aid Office
425 22nd Street, SRC - Rm 2050
Glen Ellyn, IL 60137-6599

1528
Natural Sciences Tuition Waiver Scholarship

AMOUNT: $500 DEADLINE: Varies
MAJOR: Natural Sciences

The Natural Sciences Tuition Waiver Scholarship is open to students studying natural sciences at the College of DuPage. The criteria for the application may include a request for information regarding academic success, credit hours completed, public/community service, or financial need. Students need to be prepared to write a paragraph or two explaining how they qualify for the scholarship. Applications are due the second Friday of spring quarter. Award requirements change regularly. No applications will be mailed. No GPA requirement specified.

College of DuPage
Student Financial Aid Office
425 22nd Street, SRC - Rm 2050
Glen Ellyn, IL 60137-6599

1529
PAQA Studio Arts Scholarship

AMOUNT: $500 DEADLINE: June 1
MAJOR: Art, Studio Art

The PAQA Studio Arts Scholarship is available to students studying art at the College of DuPage. The criteria for the application may include a request for information regarding academic success, credit hours completed, public/community service, or financial need. Students need to be prepared to write a paragraph or two explaining how they qualify for the scholarship. Award requirements change regularly. No applications will be mailed. No GPA requirement specified.

College of DuPage
Student Financial Aid Office
425 22nd Street, SRC - Rm 2050
Glen Ellyn, IL 60137-6599

1530
Richard M. Barth Engineering Scholarship

AMOUNT: None Specified DEADLINE: June 1
MAJOR: Engineering

The Richard M. Barth Engineering Scholarship is available to students studying engineering at the College of DuPage. The criteria for the application may include a request for information regarding academic success, credit hours completed, public/community service, or financial need. Students need to be prepared to write a paragraph or two explaining how they qualify for the scholarship. Award requirements change regularly. No applications will be mailed. No GPA requirement specified.

College of DuPage
Student Financial Aid Office
425 22nd Street, SRC - Rm 2050
Glen Ellyn, IL 60137-6599

1531
Robert Kerbs Memorial Scholarship

AMOUNT: $500 DEADLINE: June 1
MAJOR: Business and Manufacturing

The Robert Kerbs Memorial Scholarship is available to students studying business and manufacturing at the College of DuPage. The criteria for the application may include a request for information regarding academic success, credit hours completed, public/community service, or financial need. Students need to be prepared to write a paragraph or two explaining how they qualify for the scholarship. Award requirements change regularly. No applications will be mailed. No GPA requirement specified.

College of DuPage
Student Financial Aid Office
425 22nd Street, SRC - Rm 2050
Glen Ellyn, IL 60137-6599

1532
Ruth G. Nechoda Memorial Scholarship

AMOUNT: $1000 DEADLINE: Varies
MAJOR: Natural Sciences

The Ruth G. Nechoda Memorial Scholarship is open to students studying natural sciences at the College of DuPage. The criteria for the application may include a request for information regarding academic success, credit hours completed, public/community service, or financial need. Students need to be prepared to write a paragraph or two explaining how they qualify for the scholarship. Applications are due the second Friday of spring quarter. Award requirements change regularly. No applications will be mailed. No GPA requirement specified.

College of DuPage
Student Financial Aid Office
425 22nd Street, SRC - Rm 2050
Glen Ellyn, IL 60137-6599

1533
Social and Behavioral Sciences Continuing Student Scholarship

AMOUNT: $500 DEADLINE: April 1
MAJOR: Social and Behavioral Sciences

The Social and Behavioral Sciences Continuing Student Scholarship is open to students studying social and behavioral sciences at the College of DuPage. The criteria for the application may include a request for information regarding academic success, credit hours completed, public/community service, or financial need. Students need to be prepared to write a paragraph or two explaining how they qualify for the scholarship. Award requirements change regularly. No applications will be mailed. No GPA requirement specified.

College of DuPage
Student Financial Aid Office
425 22nd Street, SRC - Rm 2050
Glen Ellyn, IL 60137-6599

1534
Textbook Emergency Fund Scholarship

AMOUNT: Maximum: $500 DEADLINE: Varies
MAJOR: All Fields of Study

The Textbook Emergency Fund Scholarship is open to students attending the College of DuPage and pays a maximum of $150 per student per quarter towards the cost of textbooks. The scholarship funds are available approximately one week before classes begin. The criteria for the application may include a request for information regarding academic success, credit hours completed, public/community service, or financial need. Students need to be prepared to write a paragraph or two explaining how they qualify for the scholarship. Award requirements change regularly. No applications will be mailed. No GPA requirement specified.

College of DuPage
Student Financial Aid Office
425 22nd Street, SRC - Rm 2050
Glen Ellyn, IL 60137-6599

1535
UniForum Chicago Scholarship

AMOUNT: $1000 DEADLINE: June 1
MAJOR: Computer Science

The UniForum Chicago Scholarship is available to students studying computer science at the College of DuPage. The criteria for application may include a request for information regarding academic success, credit hours completed, public/community service, or financial need. Students need to be prepared to write a paragraph or two explaining how they qualify for the scholarship. Award requirements change regularly. No applications will be mailed. No GPA requirement specified.

College of DuPage
Student Financial Aid Office
425 22nd Street, SRC - Rm 2050
Glen Ellyn, IL 60137-6599

1536
W.W. Johnson Memorial Scholarship

AMOUNT: $500 DEADLINE: June 1
MAJOR: Speech, Forensics

The W.W. Johnson Memorial Scholarship is open to students studying speech or forensics at the College of DuPage. The criteria for the application may include a request for information regarding academic success, credit hours completed, public/community service, or financial need. Students need to be prepared to write a paragraph or two explaining how they qualify for the scholarship. Award requirements change regularly. No applications will be mailed. No GPA requirement specified.

College of DuPage
Student Financial Aid Office
425 22nd Street, SRC - Rm 2050
Glen Ellyn, IL 60137-6599

1537
Western Springs Women's Club Nursing Scholarship

AMOUNT: $500 DEADLINE: June 1
MAJOR: Nursing

The Western Springs Women's Club Nursing Scholarship is open to nursing students at the College of DuPage. The criteria for the application may include a request for information regarding academic success, credit hours completed, public/community service, or financial need. Students need to be prepared to write a paragraph or two explaining how they qualify for the scholarship. Award requirements change regularly. No applications will be mailed. No GPA requirement specified.

College of DuPage
Student Financial Aid Office
425 22nd Street, SRC - Rm 2050
Glen Ellyn, IL 60137-6599

1538
Winfield Area Gardeners Scholarship

AMOUNT: $500 DEADLINE: June 1
MAJOR: Horticulture

The Winfield Area Gardeners Scholarship is open to students studying horticulture at the College of DuPage. The criteria for the application may include a request for information regarding academic success, credit hours completed, public/community service, or financial need. Students need to be prepared to write a paragraph or two explaining how they qualify for the scholarship. Award requirements change regularly. No applications will be mailed. No GPA requirement specified.

College of DuPage
Student Financial Aid Office
425 22nd Street, SRC - Rm 2050
Glen Ellyn, IL 60137-6599

College of Saint Benedict\ SAINT JOHN'S UNIVERSITY

1539
Art, Music and Theater Scholarships

AMOUNT: Maximum: $2000 DEADLINE: February 1
MAJOR: Art, Music, Theater

This scholarship is available to students who have been involved in art, music, or theater in high school and wish to continue involvement during their college years at CSB or SJU. This award is renewed with continued participation in art, music, or theater. Award requirements change regularly. For further information, please visit the website at www.csbsju.edu/. No GPA requirement specified.

College of Saint Benedict
Office of Financial Aid
37 College Ave South
Saint Joseph, MN 56374-2001

1540
CSB Girl Scout Gold Award Scholarship

AMOUNT: $1000 DEADLINE: February 1
MAJOR: All Areas of Study

This scholarship is open to College of Saint Benedict applicants who have achieved the Girl Scout Gold Award. This award is automatically renewed with satisfactory academic progress. Award requirements change regularly. No GPA requirement specified.

College of Saint Benedict
Office of Financial Aid
37 College Ave South
Saint Joseph, MN 56374-2001

1541
Dean's Scholarship

AMOUNT: $3000-$5000 DEADLINE: February 1
MAJOR: All Areas of Study

This scholarship is for first-year students who have demonstrated academic excellence in high school and who have the ability to become excellent students at CBU or SJU. Applicants must have a GPA of at least 3.35 and demonstrate leadership and service. The award is renewed automatically with satisfactory academic progress. Award requirements change regularly. For further information and applications, please visit the website at www.csbsju.edu/. GPA must be 3.35-4.0.

College of Saint Benedict
Office of Financial Aid
37 College Ave South
Saint Joseph, MN 56374-2001

1542
Diversity, Leadership and Service Excellence Scholarship

AMOUNT: Maximum: $5000 DEADLINE: February 1
MAJOR: All Areas of Study

This scholarship is open to first-year students who have demonstrated diversity leadership and service. A supplemental essay is required. This scholarship is renewed automatically with satisfactory academic progress. Award requirements change regularly. No GPA requirement specified.

College of Saint Benedict
Office of Financial Aid
37 College Ave South
Saint Joseph, MN 56374-2001

1543
President's Scholarship

AMOUNT: $5500-$7500 DEADLINE: February 1
MAJOR: All Areas of Study

This scholarship is for first-year students who have demonstrated academic excellence in high school and who have the ability to become academic leaders at CBU or SJU. Applicants must have a GPA of at least 3.6 and demonstrate leadership and service. This award is renewed automatically with satisfactory academic progress. Award requirements change regularly. For further information and applications, please visit the website at www.csbsju.edu/. GPA must be 3.6-4.0.

College of Saint Benedict
Office of Financial Aid
37 College Ave South
Saint Joseph, MN 56374-2001

1544
Regents'/Trustees' Scholarship

AMOUNT: $8500 DEADLINE: February 1
MAJOR: All Areas of Study

This scholarship is for first-year students who have demonstrated superior academic achievement in high school and who have the ability to become leaders at CBU or SJU. Applicants must have a GPA of at least 3.6 and have a minimum ACT score of 30 or minimum SAT score of 1320. The applicants must also participate in a faculty interview conducted in February. This award is renewed automatically with satisfactory academic progress. Award requirements change regularly. For further information and applications, please visit the website: www.csbsju.edu/. GPA must be 3.6-4.0.

College of Saint Benedict
Office of Financial Aid
37 College Ave South
Saint Joseph, MN 56374-2001

1545
SJU Merrill Lynch Scholarship

AMOUNT: $2000 DEADLINE: February 1
MAJOR: All Areas of Study

This scholarship is for Saint John's University freshmen who demonstrate exceptional leadership in their high school and community. This scholarship is renewed automatically with satisfactory academic progress. Award requirements change regularly. For further information and applications, please visit the website at www.csbsju.edu/. No GPA requirement specified.

College of Saint Benedict
Office of Financial Aid
37 College Ave South
Saint Joseph, MN 56374-2001

College of the Atlantic

1546
College of the Atlantic Grant

AMOUNT: Maximum: $15000 DEADLINE: February 15
MAJOR: All Areas of Study

The College of the Atlantic Grant award is open to College of the Atlantic students. You may be a current student, incoming freshman, or transfer student. The award also requires that you demonstrate financial need and also have completed the FAFSA. You need a minimum 2.8 GPA and must be a U.S. citizen to qualify. Award requirements change regularly. GPA must be 2.8-4.0.

College of the Atlantic
105 Eden Street
Bar Harbor
ME, 04609

Colorado Mountain College

1547
Alpine Bank Hispanic Scholarship

AMOUNT: None Specified DEADLINE: March 31
MAJOR: All Areas of Study

To be eligible for this award, an applicant must be a Hispanic graduating senior of RE-1 School District (Basalt, Carbondale, or Glenwood Springs High School), RE-2 School District (Rifle High School), Eagle Valley High School, or Battlement High School. Applicant must demonstrate scholastic ability with a minimum GPA of 2.0 and intend to enroll full-time at Colorado Mountain College. This scholarship will cover the full cost of in-district tuition and books to a recipient who would otherwise not be able to attend college. Award requirements change regularly. For further information, contact the high school counseling office of the RE-1 School District (Basalt, Carbondale, or Glenwood Springs High School), the RE-2 School District (Rifle High School), Eagle Valley High School, or Battlement High School. GPA must be 2.0-4.0.

Colorado Mountain College Foundation
Scholarship Department
PO Box 1763
Glenwood Springs, CO 81602

1548
Central Rockies Leadership Program

AMOUNT: $100-$200 DEADLINE: Varies
MAJOR: All Areas of Study

This scholarship is available to students with financial need who are actively involved in or have applied to the Central Rockies Leadership Program at Colorado Mountain College. Award requirements change regularly. For further information, contact Bob Hartzell at Timberline Campus or send a self-addressed, stamped envelope to the address provided. No GPA requirement specified.

Colorado Mountain College Foundation
Scholarship Department
PO Box 1763
Glenwood Springs, CO 81602

1549
Dr. Armen Sarafian Endowed Scholarship

AMOUNT: None Specified DEADLINE: March 31
MAJOR: All Areas of Study

This award is open to in-district residents who have a GPA of at least 3.0. Applicants must be attending or be recently graduated from a high school within the Colorado Mountain College district. Award requirements change regularly. For further information, contact a high school counseling office in the Colorado Mountain District or a Colorado Mountain College Financial Aid/Student Services Office or send a self-addressed, stamped envelope to the address provided. GPA must be 3.0-4.0.

Colorado Mountain College Foundation
Scholarship Department
PO Box 1763
Glenwood Springs, CO 81602

1550
Freda T. Roof Memorial Scholarship

AMOUNT: $500-$1000 DEADLINE: March 31
MAJOR: All Areas of Study

This award is for in-state students who attend any Colorado Mountain College campus. The applicant must demonstrate a desire and potential to learn, have a GPA of at least 2.75, and be currently enrolled in a degree or certificate program. The awards will be based on merit and need. Award requirements change regularly. For further information, contact the Financial Aid Office or Student Services Counselor at any Colorado Mountain College campus or send a self-addressed, stamped envelope to the address provided. GPA must be 2.7-4.0.

Colorado Mountain College Foundation
Scholarship Department
PO Box 1763
Glenwood Springs, CO 81602

1551
Gavin D. Litwiller Endowed Scholarship in Law

AMOUNT: Maximum: $500 DEADLINE: March 31
MAJOR: Law, Criminal Justice, Paralegal Studies

This award will be granted based on merit and financial need. In-district students specializing in the study of law, transfer law, criminal justice, and paralegal studies at Colorado Mountain College are eligible. Preference will be given to freshmen. Applicants must enroll in at least five semester credits and have at least a 3.0 GPA. Award requirements change regularly. For further information, contact the Financial Aid Offices or the Student Services Counselors at any Colorado Mountain College campus location or send a self-addressed, stamped envelope to the address provided. GPA must be 3.0-4.0.

Colorado Mountain College Foundation
Scholarship Department
PO Box 1763
Glenwood Springs, CO 81602

1552
Goodstein/Peterson Scholarship

AMOUNT: None Specified DEADLINE: Varies
MAJOR: All Areas of Study

This award is open to displaced homemakers who wish to attend or are currently attending Roaring Fork or Rifle Campuses. Award requirements change regularly. For further information, contact the Transition Program Administrator at the Roaring Fork Campus-Glenwood Center or the Student Services Counselors at any Roaring Fork Campus location or Rifle Campus, or send a self-addressed envelope to the address provided. No GPA requirement specified.

Colorado Mountain College Foundation
Scholarship Department
PO Box 1763
Glenwood Springs, CO 81602

1553
International Student Scholarship

AMOUNT: $500-$1000 DEADLINE: Varies
MAJOR: All Areas of Study

This award is granted to second-year international students attending the Roaring Fork Campus of Colorado Mountain College, with at least a 2.5 GPA and a student visa. Award requirements change regularly. For further information, contact the Financial Aid Office at the Roaring Fork Campus-Spring Valley Center or send a self-addressed envelope to the address provided. GPA must be 2.5-4.0.

Colorado Mountain College Foundation
Scholarship Department
PO Box 1763
Glenwood Springs, CO 81602

1554
Judge and Mabelle Darrow Memorial Endowment

AMOUNT: $500-$2000 DEADLINE: March 31
MAJOR: All Areas of Study

This award is open to residents or non-residents who are entering freshmen who have enrolled or continuing sophomores. Students must carry at least 12 credit hours and have a high school GPA of at least 3.5. Students must exhibit a strong desire to continue their education and complete a certificate degree program or plan on transferring to a four-year institution. International students are not eligible for these scholarships. Award requirements change regularly. For further information, contact the Financial Aid/Student Services Offices at any Colorado Mountain College campus location or send a self-addressed envelope to the address provided. GPA must be 3.5-4.0.

Colorado Mountain College Foundation
Scholarship Department
PO Box 1763
Glenwood Springs, CO 81602

1555
Martin Family Endowed Scholarship

AMOUNT: None Specified DEADLINE: March 31
MAJOR: All Areas of Study

This award is open to any full-time student currently enrolled or seeking admission to a degree or certificate program at Colorado Mountain College. Applicant must be an in-district student and must demonstrate a desire and potential to learn, with at least a 2.75 GPA. Financial need or other barriers preventing the student from attending college will be strongly considered in giving this award. Award requirements change regularly. For further information, contact the Financial Aid Office or the Student Services Counselor at any Colorado Mountain College location or send a self-addressed, stamped envelope to the address provided. GPA must be 2.8-4.0.

Colorado Mountain College Foundation
Scholarship Department
PO Box 1763
Glenwood Springs, CO 81602

1556
Meyer Family Endowed Scholarship

AMOUNT: None Specified DEADLINE: March 31
MAJOR: All Areas of Study

This award is open to any currently enrolled part-time or full-time Colorado Mountain College student who has completed 12 hours, achieved a 3.0 GPA, and is involved in community activities. This award is based on financial need, merit, commitment, and desire. Award requirements change regularly. For further information, please contact the Financial Aid Office or the Student Services Counselors at any Colorado Mountain College campus or send a self-addressed, stamped envelope to the address provided. GPA must be 3.0-4.0.

Colorado Mountain College Foundation
Scholarship Department
PO Box 1763
Glenwood Springs, CO 81602

1557
Michelle Balcomb Scholarship

AMOUNT: $500 DEADLINE: March 31
MAJOR: Math, Science

This scholarship is designed to encourage and financially assist Colorado Mountain College students who attend class full-time, have completed 10 semester hours, and have a GPA of 3.0 or greater and are planning a career in math and/or science. Award requirements change regularly. For further information, please contact the Financial Aid Office or the Student Services Counselors at any college location, or send a self-addressed, stamped envelope to the address provided. GPA must be 3.0-4.0.

Colorado Mountain College Foundation
Scholarship Department
PO Box 1763
Glenwood Springs, CO 81602

1558
Presidential Endowed Scholarship

AMOUNT: None Specified DEADLINE: March 31
MAJOR: All Areas of Study

This award is open to residents and non-residents of the State of Colorado. Applicants must have a cumulative GPA of 3.2 and must demonstrate achievement at the college level in academic courses as evidenced by college transcripts from all institutions attended. The recipient of this award must be a full-time student taking 12 or more credits and have completed 30 semester credit hours (45 quarter hours). Students must demonstrate campus involvement, leadership and service. Financial need is not a requirement for this scholarship; however, it is a factor that will be considered among candidates whose other attributes are substantially equal. Applicants must submit two letters of recommendation. Award requirements change regularly. For further information, contact the Financial Aid Office or the Student Services Counselor at any Colorado Mountain College campus or send a self-addressed, stamped envelope to the address provided. GPA must be 3.2-4.0.

Colorado Mountain College Foundation
Scholarship Department
PO Box 1763
Glenwood Springs, CO 81602

1559
Shirley and Richard Hunt Scholarship

AMOUNT: $1000 DEADLINE: Varies
MAJOR: All Areas of Study

To be eligible for this award, applicants must be residents of Eagle, Rifle, or the Roaring Fork Valley and have completed their GED certificate. Preference will be given to individuals who are working and who plan on attending Colorado

Mountain College part-time (6 credit hours per semester). Award requirements change regularly. For further information, contact the Office of Financial Aid at the Spring Valley Campus or the Colorado Mountain College Student Services Counselors at Carbondale, Glenwood, Rifle, and Eagle, or send a self-addressed, stamped envelope to the address provided. No GPA requirement specified.

Colorado Mountain College Foundation
Scholarship Department
PO Box 1763
Glenwood Springs, CO 81602

1560
Vicki Lee Green Scholarship

AMOUNT: $500-$1000 DEADLINE: March 31
MAJOR: All Areas of Study

This award is granted to residents of Roaring Fork Valley who have earned at least a 2.5 GPA while earning an associate degree at Colorado Mountain College. This GPA must be maintained to renew the award. Applicant must live in the Roaring Fork Valley and be pursuing a baccalaureate degree. Award requirements change regularly. For further information, contact the Office of Financial Aid at the Roaring Fork Campus-Spring Valley Center or the Student Services Counselor at Rifle Campus, Carbondale Center or Glenwood Center, or send a self-addressed envelope to the address provided. GPA must be 2.5-4.0.

Colorado Mountain College Foundation
Scholarship Department
PO Box 1763
Glenwood Springs, CO 81602

Colorado Mountain College, Alpine

1561
Everett Bristol Family International Endowed Scholarship

AMOUNT: None Specified DEADLINE: March 31
MAJOR: International Business, International Affairs

This award is intended to assist students who are pursuing an education and career in international business or international affairs. Students selected to receive this scholarship will be expected to learn as much as possible about this region, our country, and the world community. The recipients will be required to share this knowledge of international cultures and issues by addressing student and community groups. Applicants must be full-time students enrolled in or applying to a two-year degree or certificate program at Alpine Campus. The award is based on financial need, student potential, and plans to pursue education and a career in international business or international affairs. Preference is given to international students who do not permanently reside in the United States. Award requirements change regularly. For further information, contact the Alpine Campus Financial Aid Office or send a stamped, self-addressed envelope to the address provided. No GPA requirement specified.

Colorado Mountain College Foundation - Alpine Campus
831 Grand Avenue
PO Box 10001
Steamboat Springs, CO 81602

1562
Nelsie J. Baskin Memorial Scholarship

AMOUNT: None Specified DEADLINE: March 31
MAJOR: Resort Industry, Hotel/Restaurant Management, Travel and Tourism

To be eligible for this award, applicants must demonstrate financial need and merit, and pursue a career in the resort industry. Applicants must attend classes at the Alpine Campus. Award requirements change regularly. For further information, contact the Alpine Campus Financial Aid Office or send a stamped, self-addressed envelope to the address provided. No GPA requirement specified.

Colorado Mountain College Foundation - Alpine Campus
831 Grand Avenue
PO Box 10001
Steamboat Springs, CO 81602

Colorado Mountain College, Roaring Fork

1563
Danielle Nicole DeKeyser Memorial Scholarship

AMOUNT: None Specified DEADLINE: March 31
MAJOR: All Areas of Study

To be eligible for this award, the applicant must attend the Roaring Fork Campus either part-time or full-time, in any academic area. This scholarship will be awarded based on merit, need, and commitment to education. Award requirements change regularly. For further information, contact the Financial Aid Office at Roaring Fork-Spring Valley Center or send a stamped, self-addressed envelope to the address provided. No GPA requirement specified.

Colorado Mountain College Foundation - Roaring Fork Campus
831 Grand Avenue
PO Box 10001
Glenwood Springs, CO 81602

1564
David Alden Cooke Memorial Endowed Scholarship

AMOUNT: None Specified DEADLINE: March 31
MAJOR: Mathematics, Science

This award is open to students who have demonstrated interest in mathematics and science, have at least a 2.5 GPA, and are attending Roaring Fork Campus-Spring Valley Center. Award requirements change regularly. For further information, contact the Financial Aid Office at Roaring Fork Campus-Spring Valley Center or send a stamped, self-addressed envelope to the address provided. GPA must be 2.5-4.0.

Colorado Mountain College Foundation - Roaring Fork Campus
831 Grand Avenue
PO Box 10001
Glenwood Springs, CO 81602

1565
Florence Frampton Gazunis Nursing Scholarship

AMOUNT: None Specified DEADLINE: March 31
MAJOR: Nursing

Applicants must be enrolled in the Colorado Mountain College Nursing Program for at least six credit hours. First consideration will be given to students who are employees of the Heritage Park Care Center who want to further their nursing careers. Other students pursuing a nursing degree will also be considered. The scholarship can be renewed. Award requirements change regularly. For further information, contact the Financial Aid Office at Roaring Fork Campus-Spring Valley Center or send a stamped, self-addressed envelope to the address provided. No GPA requirement specified.

Colorado Mountain College Foundation - Roaring Fork Campus
831 Grand Avenue
PO Box 10001
Glenwood Springs, CO 81602

1566
Jonathan Wright Memorial Endowed Scholarship

AMOUNT: None Specified DEADLINE: March 31
MAJOR: Photography

To be eligible for this award, applicants must be enrolled in the Professional Photography program at Roaring Fork Campus-Spring Valley Center and have an interest in pursuing a career in photojournalism. Recipients must be second-year students or have completed 20 semester hours in the program by the end of the semester in which the application is made. Award requirements change regularly. For further information, contact the Financial Aid Office at Roaring Fork-Spring Valley Center or send a self-addressed, stamped envelope to the address provided. No GPA requirement specified.

Colorado Mountain College Foundation - Roaring Fork Campus
831 Grand Avenue
PO Box 10001
Glenwood Springs, CO 81602

1567
R. Joan Lewis Memorial Endowed Scholarship

AMOUNT: $500-$600 DEADLINE:March 31
MAJOR: All Areas of Study

To be eligible for this award, applicants must be enrolled for at least six credit hours (half-time) and must be in-district residents attending or planning to enroll at the Roaring Fork Campus. Preference will be given to first-year students who are considered displaced homemakers. Award requirements change regularly. For further information, please contact the

Financial Aid Office at roaring Fork Campus-Spring Valley Center or send a stamped, self-addressed envelope to the address provided. No GPA requirement specified.

Colorado Mountain College Foundation - Roaring Fork Campus
831 Grand Avenue
PO Box 10001
Glenwood Springs, CO 81602

1568
Stewart Bridge Luce Memorial Endowed Scholarship

AMOUNT: None Specified DEADLINE: March 31
MAJOR: Biology, Chemistry, Computer Science, Geology, Physics, Math

This award is open to any student attending or planning to attend the Roaring Fork-Spring Valley Center and who has completed or is currently enrolled in one of the main Math/Science sequence courses: Biology, Chemistry, Computer Science, Geology, or Physics-Math. Award requirements change regularly. For further information, contact the Financial Aid Office at Roaring Fork-Spring Valley Center or send a self-addressed, stamped envelope to the address provided. No GPA requirement specified.

Colorado Mountain College Foundation - Roaring Fork Campus
831 Grand Avenue
PO Box 10001
Glenwood Springs, CO 81602

Colorado Mountain College, Summit

1569
Culinary Arts Institute Scholarship

AMOUNT: None Specified DEADLINE: Varies
MAJOR: Culinary Arts

To be eligible for this award, students must be currently enrolled in the Culinary Arts Program. Culinary scholarships are awarded on the basis of academic achievement, financial need, and excellence in the culinary workplace. Award requirements change regularly. For further information, contact the Director of Culinary Education at Keystone or the Student Services Counselor at the Breckenridge or Silverthorne Center, or send a self-addressed, stamped envelope to the address provided. No GPA requirement specified.

Colorado Mountain College Foundation - Summit Campus
831 Grand Avenue
PO Box 10001
Glenwood Springs, CO 81602

1570
John Shotton/Breckenridge Associates Real Estate Company Scholarship

AMOUNT: $800 DEADLINE: March 31
MAJOR: Business

This award is open to students who are residents of Summit County and are pursuing part-time or full-time academic studies in a Business-related degree or certificate program, including computer-related classes. Students must maintain a 2.0 GPA. Award requirements change regularly. For further information, contact the Summit Campus Financial Aid Office or the Student Services Counselors at Breckenridge or Silverthorne Centers, or send a self-addressed, stamped envelope to the address provided. GPA must be 2.0-4.0.

Colorado Mountain College Foundation - Summit Campus
831 Grand Avenue
PO Box 10001
Glenwood Springs, CO 81602

Colorado Mountain College, Timberline

1571
Hispanic Scholarship Fund of Lake County

AMOUNT: None Specified DEADLINE: March 31
MAJOR: All Areas of Study

This award is open to residents of Lake County who demonstrate financial need and scholastic ability. Students must enroll at the Timberline Campus. Award requirements change regularly. For further information, please contact the Office of Financial Aid at the Timberline Campus or send a self-addressed, stamped envelope to the address provided. No GPA requirement specified.

Colorado Mountain College Foundation - Timberline Campus
831 Grand Avenue
PO Box 10001
Glenwood Springs, CO 81602

1572
Timberline Campus Endowed Scholarship

AMOUNT: $300-$500 DEADLINE: March 31
MAJOR: All Areas of Study

This award is open to second-year degree-seeking students attending the Timberline Campus with evident involvement in campus life activities and a GPA of 3.0. Award requirements change regularly. For further information, please contact the Financial Aid Office or the Student Services Counselor at Timberline Campus, or send a self-addressed, stamped envelope to the address provided. GPA must be 3.0-4.0.

Colorado Mountain College Foundation - Timberline Campus
831 Grand Avenue
PO Box 10001
Glenwood Springs, CO 81602

Colorado Mountain College, Vail/Eagle Valley

1573
John Hazard Memorial Endowed Scholarship

AMOUNT: None Specified DEADLINE: March 31
MAJOR: All Areas of Study

This award is granted to women with dependents who are in-district residents of Eagle County. Students must exhibit financial need and commitment to attend college full- or part-time and must enroll in a program which will enable them to earn a college degree or certificate in order to become self-sufficient. Award requirements change regularly. For further information, please contact the Student Services Counselors at the Vail or Eagle Centers or send a self-addressed, stamped envelope to the address provided. No GPA requirement specified.

Colorado Mountain College Foundation - Vail/Eagle Valley Campus
831 Grand Avenue
PO Box 10001
Glenwood Springs, CO 81602

1574
Ron Johnson Memorial Scholarship

AMOUNT: None Specified DEADLINE: March 31
MAJOR: Business, Computer Science

This award is open to in-district students of Eagle County pursuing a degree in business and computer-related fields. Award requirements change regularly. For further information, contact the Student Services Counselors at the Vail or Eagle Centers or send a self-addressed, stamped envelope to the address provided. No GPA requirement specified.

Colorado Mountain College Foundation - Vail/Eagle Valley Campus
831 Grand Avenue
PO Box 10001
Glenwood Springs, CO 81602

1575
Weiss Family Scholarship

AMOUNT: $500 DEADLINE: March 31
MAJOR: Social Sciences, Education

To be eligible for this award, applicants must be residents of Eagle County, be pursuing a degree in Social Sciences or Education, and have a GPA of at least 3.5. Award requirements change regularly. For further information, please contact the Student Services Counselors at the Vail or Eagle Centers or send a self-addressed, stamped envelope to the address provided. GPA must be 3.5-4.0.

Colorado Mountain College Foundation - Vail/Eagle Valley Campus
831 Grand Avenue
PO Box 10001
Glenwood Springs, CO 81602

Colorado State University

1576
Monfort Scholarship

AMOUNT: None Specified DEADLINE: Varies
MAJOR: All Areas of Study

This award is granted to an incoming freshman of Colorado State University in any major. The applicant must be a Colorado resident who attended a Colorado high school for at least the last two years of high school. The scholarship requires that the applicant score at least 1300 on the SAT; rank in the upper 5% of the graduating class or No. 1 or No. 2 in a class fewer than 40 students; and demonstrate leadership, service to community and school, and outstanding character. Award requirements change regularly. For an application or more information, contact the Admissions Office at (970) 491-6909 or write the address provided. GPA must be 3.7-4.0.

Colorado State University
Financial Aid Office
108 Student Services
Fort Collins, CO 80523

Columbia Union College

1577
John and Mabel Livingston Memorial Fund

AMOUNT: $500-$2000 DEADLINE: May 31
MAJOR: Religion, Theology

The John and Mabel Livingston Memorial Fund Awards are for Columbia Union College students majoring in religion or theology who have a GPA of at least 2.0. Applicants must demonstrate financial need. Award requirements change regularly. Write to the address listed, enclosing a self-addressed, stamped envelope for an application and further information, or browse their website: www.cuc.edu. GPA must be 2.0-4.0.

Columbia Union College
Financial Aid Office
7600 Flower Avenue
Takoma Park, MD 20912-7796

1578
National Merit Finalist Program

AMOUNT: None Specified DEADLINE: March 31
MAJOR: All Areas of Study

Awards for National Merit Finalists who intend to enroll in Columbia Union College. Renewable if a GPA of at least 3.0 is maintained. Award requirements change regularly. Write to the address listed, enclosing a self-addressed, stamped envelope for an application and further information, or browse their website: www.cuc.edu. GPA must be 3.0-4.0.

Columbia Union College
Financial Aid Office
7600 Flower Avenue
Takoma Park, MD 20912-7796

Columbia University, Teachers College

1579
Minority Postdoctoral Fellowship Program

AMOUNT: $30000-$32000 DEADLINE: February 1
MAJOR: Education

This fellowship program aims to increase the number of minority faculty members at graduate schools of education. It provides recent doctorate recipients the opportunity to develop a program of research and participate in a mentored program at a graduate university. Applicants must have earned a doctorate in any area within the last three years and must demonstrate commitment to research and teaching in an education-related area. Duration of fellowship is one year, and the stipend is $30,000 plus $2,000 for research. Award requirements change regularly. For further information and an application, please write to Melanie Nelson at the address listed, including a self-addressed, stamped envelope, call (212) 678-3050, or email man18@columbia.edu. You may also visit their website: www.tc.columbia.edu. No GPA requirement specified.

Columbia University, Teachers College
Student Aid Office
525 West 120th Street, # 309
New York NY 10027-6625

Concorde Career Institute

1580
Concorde Career Institute Dental Assistant Scholarship (Jacksonville)

AMOUNT: None Specified DEADLINE: Varies
MAJOR: Dental Assistant

The Concorde Career Institute Dental Assistant Scholarship (Jacksonville) is open to Florida residents attending or planning to attend the Concorde Career Institute - Jacksonville Campus who are studying to become dental assistants. Applications are available at Florida high schools and GED testing centers. Award requirements change regularly. For further information, please send a self-addressed, stamped envelope to Concorde Career Institute, Cathy Gardner, Director of Admissions, 7960 Arlington Expressway, Suite #120, Jacksonville, FL 32211, or you could call (904) 725-0525. No GPA requirement specified.

Florida Association of Postsecondary Schools and Colleges
Attn: FAPSC Scholarship Committee
F200 West College Avenue
Tallahassee, FL 32301

1581
Concorde Career Institute Dental Assistant Scholarship (Lauderdale)

AMOUNT: None Specified DEADLINE: Varies
MAJOR: Dental Assistant

The Concorde Career Institute Dental Assistant Scholarship (Lauderdale) is open to Florida residents attending or planning to attend the Concorde Career Institute - Lauderdale Lakes Campus who are studying to become dental assistants. Applications are available at Florida high schools and GED testing centers. Award requirements change regularly. For further information, please send a self-addressed, stamped envelope to Concorde Career Institute, Elizabeth Boos, Director of Admissions, 4000 North State Road 7, Suite #100, Lauderdale Lakes, FL 33319, or you could call (954) 731-8880. No GPA requirement specified.

Florida Association of Postsecondary Schools and Colleges
Attn: FAPSC Scholarship Committee
F200 West College Avenue
Tallahassee, FL 32301

1582
Concorde Career Institute Dental Assistant Scholarship (Tampa)

AMOUNT: None Specified DEADLINE: Varies
MAJOR: Dental Assistant

The Concorde Career Institute Dental Assistant Scholarship (Tampa) is open to Florida residents attending or planning to attend the Concorde Career Institute - Tampa Campus who are studying to become dental assistants. Applications are available at Florida high schools and GED testing centers. Award requirements change regularly. For further information, please send a self-addressed, stamped envelope to Concorde Career Institute, Alan Spencer, Director of Admissions, 4202 West Spruce Street, Tampa, FL 33607, or you could call (813) 874-0094. No GPA requirement specified.

Florida Association of Postsecondary Schools and Colleges
Attn: FAPSC Scholarship Committee
F200 West College Avenue
Tallahassee, FL 32301

1583
Concorde Career Institute Medical Assistant Scholarship (Jacksonville)

AMOUNT: None Specified DEADLINE: Varies
MAJOR: Medical Assistant

The Concorde Career Institute Medical Assistant Scholarship (Jacksonville) is open to Florida residents attending or planning to attend the Concorde Career Institute - Jacksonville Campus who are studying to become medical assistants. Applications are available at Florida high schools and GED testing centers. Award requirements change regularly. For further information, please send a self-addressed, stamped envelope to Concorde Career Institute, Cathy Gardner, Director of Admissions, 7960 Arlington Expressway, Suite #120, Jacksonville, FL 32211, or you could call (904) 725-0525. No GPA requirement specified.

Florida Association of Postsecondary Schools and Colleges
Attn: FAPSC Scholarship Committee
F200 West College Avenue
Tallahassee, FL 32301

Concorde Career Institute Medical Assistant Scholarship (Miami)

AMOUNT: None Specified DEADLINE: Varies
MAJOR: Medical Assistant

The Concorde Career Institute Medical Assistant Scholarship (Miami) is open to Florida residents attending or planning to attend the Concorde Career Institute - Miami Campus who are studying to become medical assistants. Applications are available at Florida high schools and GED testing centers. Award requirements change regularly. For further information, please send a self-addressed, stamped envelope to Concorde Career Institute, Maritza Bedoya, Director of Admissions, 285 N.W. 199th Street, Miami, FL 33169, or you could call (305) 652-0055. No GPA requirement specified.

Florida Association of Postsecondary Schools and Colleges
Attn: FAPSC Scholarship Committee
F200 West College Avenue
Tallahassee, FL 32301

1585
Concorde Career Institute Medical Assistant Scholarship (Tampa)

AMOUNT: None Specified DEADLINE: Varies
MAJOR: Medical Assistant

The Concorde Career Institute Medical Assistant Scholarship (Tampa) is open to Florida residents attending or planning to attend the Concorde Career Institute - Tampa Campus who are studying to become medical assistants. Applications are available at Florida high schools and GED testing centers. Award requirements change regularly. For further information, please send a self-addressed, stamped envelope to Concorde Career Institute, Alan Spencer, Director of Admissions, 4202 West Spruce Street, Tampa, FL 33607, or you could call (813) 874-0094. No GPA requirement specified.

Florida Association of Postsecondary Schools and Colleges
Attn: FAPSC Scholarship Committee
F200 West College Avenue
Tallahassee, FL 32301

1586
Concorde Career Institute Medical Secretary Scholarship (Jacksonville)

AMOUNT: None Specified DEADLINE: Varies
MAJOR: Medical Secretary

The Concorde Career Institute Medical Secretary Scholarship (Jacksonville) is open to Florida residents attending or planning to attend the Concorde Career Institute - Jacksonville Campus who are studying to become medical secretaries. Applications are available at Florida high schools and GED testing centers. Award requirements change regularly. For fur-

ther information, please send a self-addressed, stamped envelope to Concorde Career Institute, Cathy Gardner, Director of Admissions, 7960 Arlington Expressway, Suite #120, Jacksonville, FL 32211, or you could call (904) 725-0525. No GPA requirement specified.

Florida Association of Postsecondary Schools and Colleges
Attn: FAPSC Scholarship Committee
F200 West College Avenue
Tallahassee, FL 32301

1587
Concorde Career Institute Medical Secretary Scholarship (Lauderdale)

AMOUNT: None Specified DEADLINE: Varies
MAJOR: Medical Secretary

The Concorde Career Institute Medical Secretary Scholarship (Lauderdale) is open to Florida residents attending or planning to attend the Concorde Career Institute - Lauderdale Lakes Campus who are studying to become medical secretaries. Applications are available at Florida high schools and GED testing centers. Award requirements change regularly. For further information, please send a self-addressed, stamped envelope to Concorde Career Institute, Elizabeth Boos, Director of Admissions, 4000 North State Road 7, Suite #100, Lauderdale Lakes, FL 33319, or you could call (954) 731-8880. No GPA requirement specified.

Florida Association of Postsecondary Schools and Colleges
Attn: FAPSC Scholarship Committee
F200 West College Avenue
Tallahassee, FL 32301

1588
Concorde Career Institute Medical Secretary Scholarship (Miami)

AMOUNT: None Specified DEADLINE: Varies
MAJOR: Medical Secretary

The Concorde Career Institute Medical Secretary Assistant Scholarship (Miami) is open to Florida residents attending or planning to attend the Concorde Career Institute - Miami Campus who are studying to become medical secretaries. Applications are available at Florida high schools and GED testing centers. Award requirements change regularly. For further information, please send a self-addressed, stamped envelope to Concorde Career Institute, Maritza Bedoya, Director of Admissions, 285 N.W. 199th Street, Miami, FL 33169, or you could call (305) 652-0055. No GPA requirement specified.

Florida Association of Postsecondary Schools and Colleges
Attn: FAPSC Scholarship Committee
F200 West College Avenue
Tallahassee, FL 32301

1589
Concorde Career Institute Patient Care Assistant Scholarship (Tampa)

AMOUNT: None Specified DEADLINE: Varies
MAJOR: Patient Care Assistant

The Concorde Career Institute Patient Care Assistant Scholarship (Tampa) is open to Florida residents attending or planning to attend the Concorde Career Institute - Tampa Campus who are studying to become patient care assistants. Applications are available at Florida high schools and GED testing centers. Award requirements change regularly. For further information, please send a self-addressed, stamped envelope to Concorde Career Institute, Alan Spencer, Director of Admissions, 4202 West Spruce Street, Tampa, FL 33607, or you could call (813) 874-0094. No GPA requirement specified.

Florida Association of Postsecondary Schools and Colleges
Attn: FAPSC Scholarship Committee
F200 West College Avenue
Tallahassee, FL 32301

Cooper Career Institute

1590
Cooper Career Institute Computer Administrative Assistant Scholarship

AMOUNT: None Specified DEADLINE: Varies
MAJOR: Computer Administrative Assistant

The Cooper Career Institute Computer Administrative Assistant Scholarship is open to Florida residents attending or planning to attend the Cooper Career Institute who are studying to become computer administrative assistants. Applications are available at Florida high schools and GED testing centers. Award requirements change regularly. For further information, please send a self-addressed, stamped envelope to Cooper Career Institute, Evelyn Kannawin, Director, 2247 Palm Beach Lakes Boulevard, West Palm Beach, FL 33409, or you could call (561) 640-6999. No GPA requirement specified.

Florida Association of Postsecondary Schools and Colleges
Attn: FAPSC Scholarship Committee
F200 West College Avenue
Tallahassee, FL 32301

1591
Cooper Career Institute Medical Office Specialist Scholarship

AMOUNT: None Specified DEADLINE: Varies
MAJOR: Medical Office Specialist

The Cooper Career Institute Medical Office Specialist Scholarship is open to Florida residents attending or planning to attend the Cooper Career Institute who are studying to become medical office specialists. Applications are available at Florida high schools and GED testing centers. Award

requirements change regularly. For further information, please send a self-addressed, stamped envelope to Cooper Career Institute, Evelyn Kannawin, Director, 2247 Palm Beach Lakes Boulevard, West Palm Beach, FL 33409, or you could call (561) 640-6999. No GPA requirement specified.

Florida Association of Postsecondary Schools and Colleges
Attn: FAPSC Scholarship Committee
F200 West College Avenue
Tallahassee, FL 32301

1592
Cooper Career Institute Paralegal Scholarship

AMOUNT: None Specified DEADLINE: Varies
MAJOR: Paralegal

The Cooper Career Institute Paralegal Scholarship is open to Florida residents attending or planning to attend the Cooper Career Institute who are studying to become paralegals. Applications are available at Florida high schools and GED testing centers. Award requirements change regularly. For further information, please send a self-addressed, stamped envelope to Cooper Career Institute, Evelyn Kannawin, Director, 2247 Palm Beach Lakes Boulevard, West Palm Beach, FL 33409, or you could call (561) 640-6999. No GPA requirement specified.

Florida Association of Postsecondary Schools and Colleges
Attn: FAPSC Scholarship Committee
F200 West College Avenue
Tallahassee, FL 32301

Creighton University

1593
Creighton Academic Scholarship

AMOUNT: None Specified DEADLINE: January 1
MAJOR: All Areas of Study

Creighton Academic Scholarships are open to incoming freshmen at Creighton University. These scholarships are based on your high school academic performance and national test scores. Your Undergraduate Application for Admissions also serves as your scholarship application. You must be admitted by January 1 of your high school senior year in order to be considered for these academic scholarships. This award is renewable with a minimum GPA, which can vary according to discipline. Award requirements change regularly. For an Undergraduate Application for Admissions and further information, you may call (402) 280-2731. No GPA requirement specified.

Creighton University
Financial Aid Office
2500 California Plaza
Omaha, NE 68178-0001

1594
Creighton Scholarship for Black and Hispanic Scholars

AMOUNT: None Specified DEADLINE: March 1
MAJOR: All Areas of Study

The Creighton Scholarship for Black and Hispanic Scholars is open to Omaha area African-American and Hispanic incoming freshmen at Creighton University. You must be admitted by March 1 of your high school senior year in order to be considered for these academic scholarships. This award is renewable by maintaining a minimum 2.5 GPA Award requirements change regularly. For an application and further information, send a self-addressed, stamped envelope to the address listed or call (402) 280-2731. No GPA requirement specified.

Creighton University
Financial Aid Office
2500 California Plaza
Omaha, NE 68178-0001

1595
Presidential Scholarship

AMOUNT: None Specified DEADLINE: January 1
MAJOR: All Areas of Study

The Presidential Scholarship is open to incoming freshmen at Creighton University. This award is based on your ACT or SAT scores, high school class rank, and leadership ability. These scholarships are renewable if you have a minimum 3.3 GPA Your Undergraduate Application for Admissions also serves as your scholarship application. You must be admitted by January 1 of your high school senior year in order to be considered for this academic scholarship. Award requirements change regularly. For an Undergraduate Application for Admissions and further information, call (402) 280-2731. No GPA requirement specified.

Creighton University
Financial Aid Office
2500 California Plaza
Omaha, NE 68178-0001

1596
Scott Scholarship

AMOUNT: None Specified DEADLINE: January 1
MAJOR: Business Administration

The Scott Scholarship is a full-tuition award that is open to top students who are planning to enroll in Creighton's College of Business Administration. The award is based on high test scores and class rank. Three awards are given annually. This award is renewable provided you maintain a minimum 3.4 GPA and continue your enrollment at the College of Business. Award requirements change regularly. For an Undergraduate Application for Admissions and further information, you may call (402) 280-2731. No GPA requirement specified.

Creighton University
Financial Aid Office
2500 California Plaza
Omaha, NE 68178-0001

DePauw University

1597
Alumni Legacy Awards

AMOUNT: $1000 DEADLINE: Varies
MAJOR: All Fields of Study

The Alumni Legacy Awards are open to students attending DePauw University whose mother, father, grandmother, or grandfather graduated from DePauw. These awards are made regardless of financial need. Award requirements change regularly. For further information and an application, please write to the address listed, including a self-addressed, stamped envelope. No GPA requirement specified.

DePauw University
Admissions Office
101 East Seminary Street
Greencastle, IN 46135-1662

1598
Holton Scholarships

AMOUNT: $1000 DEADLINE: Varies
MAJOR: All Fields of Study

The Holton Scholarships are open to students from Illinois, Indiana, Michigan, and Ohio who are attending DePauw University. Applicants must have demonstrated superior leadership and/or exceptional service to their school, family, church, or community. Applicants must also submit a 250-word essay describing their commitment to service and/or leadership. Finalists will be interviewed by a team of DePauw staff and alumni. Holton Scholarships replace other Merit Awards and are renewable. Award requirements change regularly. For further information and an application, please write to the address listed, including a self-addressed, stamped envelope. No GPA requirement specified.

DePauw University
Admissions Office
101 East Seminary Street
Greencastle, IN 46135-1662

1599
Judaic Fellows Awards

AMOUNT: $1000-$10000 DEADLINE: Varies
MAJOR: All Fields of Study

This scholarship is open to students attending DePauw University who have strong high school records, test scores, and leadership involvement in extracurricular and/or community activities. Awards range from $1,000 to $10,000, replace the Merit Awards, and are renewable. Award requirements change regularly. For further information and an application, please write to the address listed, including a self-addressed, stamped envelope. GPA must be 3.0-4.0.

DePauw University
Admissions Office
101 East Seminary Street
Greencastle, IN 46135-1662

1600
Multicultural Student Leadership Awards

AMOUNT: $1000-$10000 DEADLINE: Varies
MAJOR: All Fields of Study

Open to students attending DePauw University who have demonstrated a high level of academic achievement, community service, and leadership. Awards ranging from $1,000 to $10,000 replace merit awards and require recipients to perform community service and demonstrate civic leadership at DePauw. Selected recipients of these awards will also be offered an opportunity to benefit from a maximum of $2,500 in loans and $1,000 in on-campus employment per year. Award requirements change regularly. For further information and an application, please write to the address listed, including a self-addressed, stamped envelope. GPA must be 3.2-4.0.

DePauw University
Admissions Office
101 East Seminary Street
Greencastle, IN 46135-1662

1601
Presidential Rector Scholarship

AMOUNT: None Specified DEADLINE: Varies
MAJOR: All Areas of Study

The Presidential Rector Scholarship is open to students attending DePauw University who have demonstrated academic achievement and the potential for contribution to the intellectual climate at DePauw. Finalists for this scholarship are invited to the campus for a selection interview. This award is for four years with full-tuition grants. Award requirements change regularly. Please send a self-addressed, stamped envelope to receive your application and any further instructions from the scholarship provider. No GPA requirement specified.

DePauw University
Admissions Office
101 East Seminary Street
Greencastle, IN 46135-1662

1602
Rector Scholarship

AMOUNT: $15000 DEADLINE: Varies
MAJOR: All Areas of Study

The Rector Scholarship is open to students attending DePauw University. This award replaces Merit Awards which are awarded to students with outstanding academic achievement regardless of financial need. Award requirements change regularly. Please send a self-addressed, stamped envelope to receive your application and any further instructions from the scholarship provider. No GPA requirement specified.

DePauw University
Admissions Office
101 East Seminary Street
Greencastle, IN 46135-1662

1603
Science and Mathematics Scholarships

AMOUNT: Maximum: $11000 DEADLINE: Varies
MAJOR: Science, Mathematics

Open to students attending DePauw University who score competitively on a rigorous exam given on the DePauw campus during the Fall semester of their senior year in high school. These awards replace Merit Awards. Award requirements change regularly. For further information and an application, please write to the address listed, including a self-addressed, stamped envelope. GPA must be 2.8-4.0.

DePauw University
Admissions Office
101 East Seminary Street
Greencastle, IN 46135-1662

Eastern College

1604
Church Matching Grant

AMOUNT: $500-$1000 DEADLINE: Varies
MAJOR: All Areas of Study

Open to students admitted to Eastern College whose church donates money towards college. If your church donates up to $1,000 and there is need, Eastern will match it. Eastern will match up to $500 if there is no financial need. Award requirements change regularly. For further information, please contact the address listed, or visit their website: www.eastern.edu. No GPA requirement specified.

Eastern College
Scholarships Program
1300 Eagle Road
St. Davids, PA 19087

1605
Eastern College Academic Scholarships

AMOUNT: $1000-$6000 DEADLINE: Varies
MAJOR: All Areas of Study

Open to all students who apply to Eastern College. Selection is based on class rank, SAT scores, and GPA. Award requirements change regularly. For further information, please contact the address listed, or visit their website: www.eastern.edu. No GPA requirement specified.

Eastern College
Scholarships Program
1300 Eagle Road
St. Davids, PA 19087

1606
Honors College Scholarship

AMOUNT: $3000 DEADLINE: Varies
MAJOR: All Areas of Study

Open to all students admitted to Eastern College who meet one of the following criteria: minimum SAT score of 1250, minimum ACT English score of 30, or graduated in the top 9% of their class. Award requirements change regularly. For further information, please contact the address listed, call (800) 452-0996, or visit their website: www.eastern.edu. GPA must be 3.0-4.0.

Eastern College
Scholarships Program
1300 Eagle Road
St. Davids, PA 19087

1607
Leadership Grants

AMOUNT: $2000 DEADLINE: Varies
MAJOR: All Areas of Study

Open to all students entering Eastern College who have demonstrated their leadership and academic potential through high school, church, or community activities. Recipients must complete at least 15 hours of community service, participate in special projects and events, hold a responsible position in an on-campus group, take all required courses, maintain a 3.0 GPA, and serve as mentors in their senior years. Award requirements change regularly. For further information, please contact the address listed, or visit their website: www.eastern.edu. GPA must be 3.0-4.0.

Eastern College
Scholarships Program
1300 Eagle Road
St. Davids, PA 19087

1608
Music Scholarships

AMOUNT: $500-$5000 DEADLINE: April 1
MAJOR: Music

Open to students admitted to Eastern College who are majoring in music. Applicants must audition before April 1 to be eligible. Award requirements change regularly. For further information, please contact the address listed, or visit their website: www.eastern.edu. No GPA requirement specified.

Eastern College
Scholarships Program
1300 Eagle Road
St. Davids, PA 19087

1609
National Merit Scholarships

AMOUNT: None Specified DEADLINE: Varies
MAJOR: All Areas of Study

Open to incoming freshmen admitted to Eastern College who have been recognized by the National Merit Scholarship Competition. Award covers tuition and is renewable as long as a 3.0 GPA is maintained. Award requirements change regularly. For further information, please contact the address

listed, or visit their website: www.eastern.edu. GPA must be 3.0-4.0.

Eastern College
Scholarships Program
1300 Eagle Road
St. Davids, PA 19087

Eastern New Mexico University

1610
Accounting Information Systems Scholarship

AMOUNT: Maximum: $1000 DEADLINE: March 1
MAJOR: Accounting and Computer Information Systems

The Accounting Information Systems Scholarship is available to full-time undergraduate students who are attending Eastern New Mexico University as accounting or computer information systems majors. You must demonstrate a record of academic excellence to be eligible. This award is renewable. Award requirements change regularly. For more information or to apply, please contact the College of Business at Eastern New Mexico University at (505) 562-2808. No GPA requirement specified.

Eastern New Mexico University
ENMU College of Business
Station 49
Portales, NM 88130

1611
Albert E. and Lacy Whitehead Endowed Scholarship

AMOUNT: $750 DEADLINE: March 1
MAJOR: Marketing

The Albert E. and Lacy Whitehead Endowed Scholarship is available to undergraduate and graduate students attending the College of Business at Eastern New Mexico University as marketing majors. This award is not renewable. Award requirements change regularly. For more information or to apply, please contact the College of Business at Eastern New Mexico University at (505) 562-2808. No GPA requirement specified.

Eastern New Mexico University
ENMU College of Business
Station 49
Portales, NM 88130

1612
Albert E. and Lacy Whitehead Endowed Scholarship

AMOUNT: $750 DEADLINE: March 1
MAJOR: Theater

The Albert E. and Lacy Whitehead Endowed Scholarship is available to full-time undergraduate students who are attending Eastern New Mexico University as theater majors. This award is renewable. Award requirements change regularly. For further information, please write to the address listed, including a self-addressed, stamped envelope, or call (505) 562-

2711. No GPA requirement specified.

Eastern New Mexico University
College of Fine Arts
Station 16
Portales, NM 88130

1613
Baron M. Stuart Endowed Scholarship

AMOUNT: $1000 DEADLINE: March 1
MAJOR: Business

The Baron M. Stuart Endowed Scholarship is available to full-time undergraduate business students at Eastern New Mexico University. To qualify for this award, you must have a GPA of at least 3.0 and have successfully completed 60 credit hours by the effective date of the award. Two faculty recommendation letters are required. This award is renewable. Award requirements change regularly. For more information or to apply, please contact the College of Business at Eastern New Mexico University at (505) 562-2808. GPA must be 3.0-4.0.

Eastern New Mexico University
ENMU College of Business
Station 49
Portales, NM 88130

1614
Cattle Baron Scholarship

AMOUNT: $500 DEADLINE: March 1
MAJOR: Business Administration, Economics, Finance, Marketing, Management

The Cattle Baron Scholarship is available to full-time undergraduate students at Eastern New Mexico University who are majoring in business administration, economics, finance, marketing, or management. To apply for this award, you must have completed at least 60 hours but no more than 75 hours by the effective date of the award, have a minimum cumulative GPA of 3.0, and demonstrate financial need. This award is not renewable. Two faculty recommendation letters are required. Award requirements change regularly. For more information or to apply, please contact the College of Business at Eastern New Mexico University at (505) 562-2808. GPA must be 3.0-4.0.

Eastern New Mexico University
ENMU College of Business
Station 49
Portales, NM 88130

1615
College of Business Scholarship

AMOUNT: None Specified DEADLINE: March 1
MAJOR: College of Business

The College of Business Scholarship is available to full-time undergraduate students at Eastern New Mexico University who are attending the College of Business. To apply for this award, you must demonstrate financial need and academic excellence. Preference will be given to graduates of New Mexico high schools. This award is not renewable. Two faculty recommendation letters are required. Award requirements change regularly. For more information or to apply, please contact the College of Business at Eastern New Mexico

University at (505) 562-2808. No GPA requirement specified.

Eastern New Mexico University
ENMU College of Business
Station 49
Portales, NM 88130

1616
Dena Dutton Memorial Scholarship

AMOUNT: $400 DEADLINE: March 1
MAJOR: Home Economics

The Dena Dutton Memorial Scholarship is open to undergraduate and graduate students who are attending Eastern New Mexico University as home economics majors. To apply for this award, you must be residents of Roosevelt County, New Mexico, and demonstrate financial need. This scholarship is not renewable. Award requirements change regularly. For further information, please write to the address listed, including a self-addressed, stamped envelope, or call (505) 562-2443. No GPA requirement specified.

Eastern New Mexico University
College of Education and Technology
Station 25
Portales, NM 88130

1617
Dollar Rent-A-Car Endowed Scholarship

AMOUNT: $500 DEADLINE: March 1
MAJOR: Business Education, Business Administration

The Dollar Rent-A-Car Endowed Scholarship is open to full-time students who are attending Eastern New Mexico University as business education or business administration majors. You must be a graduate of a Roosevelt County, New Mexico, high school, with preference given to those students from Dora, Elida, or Floyd, in order to apply. Eligibility requirements include two faculty recommendation letters, a minimum GPA of 3.0, and demonstrated desire to complete a college degree. Selection is based on financial need. This award is renewable. Award requirements change regularly. For more information or to apply, please contact the College of Business at Eastern New Mexico University at (505) 562-2808. GPA must be 3.0-4.0.

Eastern New Mexico University
ENMU College of Business
Station 49
Portales, NM 88130

1618
Dr. William Baldwin Award

AMOUNT: None Specified DEADLINE: March 1
MAJOR: Psychology

The Dr. William Baldwin Award is available to upper division and graduate students who are attending Eastern New Mexico University as psychology majors. To apply for this award, you must have a GPA of 3.2. This scholarship is not renewable. Award requirements change regularly. For more information or to apply, please call (501) 562-2443, or you can browse the university's website. GPA must be 3.2-4.0.

Eastern New Mexico University
College of Education and Technology
Station 25
Portales, NM 88130

1619
Euola Cox Scholarship

AMOUNT: $125 DEADLINE: March 1
MAJOR: Education (Teaching)

The Euola Cox Scholarship is available to minority students at Eastern New Mexico University who are pursuing a teaching career. Selection is based on financial need. You must provide one faculty recommendation letter. This award is not renewable. Award requirements change regularly. For further information, please write to the address listed, including a self-addressed, stamped envelope, or call (505) 562-2443. No GPA requirement specified.

Eastern New Mexico University
College of Education and Technology
Station 25
Portales, NM 88130

1620
Garland Tillery Memorial Scholarship in Business

AMOUNT: $600 DEADLINE: March 1
MAJOR: Business

The Garland Tillery Memorial Scholarship in Business is available to full-time undergraduate business students at Eastern New Mexico University. To qualify for this award, you must have a GPA of at least 3.0 and be a sophomore by the effective date of the award. To apply for this award, you must be a New Mexico resident with a family history of New Mexico residency. Two faculty recommendation letters are required. This award is renewable. Award requirements change regularly. For more information or to apply, please contact the College of Business at Eastern New Mexico University at (505) 562-2808. GPA must be 3.0-4.0.

Eastern New Mexico University
ENMU College of Business
Station 49
Portales, NM 88130

1621
Gilbert May Endowed Scholarship

AMOUNT: $1000 DEADLINE: March 1
MAJOR: Accounting

The Gilbert May Endowed Scholarship is available to full-time undergraduate students who are attending Eastern New Mexico University as accounting majors. To apply for this award, you must demonstrate academic excellence and be a resident of the Roswell area. Two faculty recommendation letters are required. This award is renewable. Award requirements change regularly. For more information or to apply, please contact the College of Business at Eastern New Mexico University at (505) 562-2808.

Eastern New Mexico University
ENMU College of Business
Station 49
Portales, NM 88130

1622
Hal Reed Tunnell Scholarship in Education

AMOUNT: $400 DEADLINE: March 1
MAJOR: Education (Teaching)

The Hal Reed Tunnell Scholarship in Education is available to students at Eastern New Mexico University who are pursuing a teaching career. One faculty recommendation letter is required. This award is not renewable. Award requirements change regularly. For further information, please write to the address listed, including a self-addressed, stamped envelope, or call (505) 562-2443. No GPA requirement specified.

Eastern New Mexico University
College of Education and Technology
Station 25
Portales, NM 88130

1623
I.V. Payne Endowed Scholarship

AMOUNT: $600-$1000 DEADLINE: March 1
MAJOR: Education Administration

The I.V. Payne Endowed Scholarship is available to graduate students in the master of education program with an emphasis on education administration at Eastern New Mexico University. To apply for this award, you must be enrolled in at least six hours per semester, have at least one year of successful teaching experience in a public school, and have strong recommendations from the administrators in your present or last school and also from an ENMU professor in education. Selection is based on educational leadership, stated desire to become an administrator, and financial need. This award is not renewable. Award requirements change regularly. For further information, please write to the address listed, including a self-addressed, stamped envelope, or call (505) 562-2443. No GPA requirement specified.

Eastern New Mexico University
College of Education and Technology
Station 25
Portales, NM 88130

1624
J. Henry Young Endowed Scholarship

AMOUNT: $500 DEADLINE: March 1
MAJOR: Accounting

The J. Henry Young Endowed Scholarship is available to full-time undergraduate and graduate students who are attending Eastern New Mexico University as accounting majors. To apply for this award, you must have a GPA of at least 3.0 and have completed ACCT 301 by the effective date of the award. Two faculty recommendation letters are required. This award is not renewable. Award requirements change regularly. For more information or to apply, please contact the College of Business at Eastern New Mexico University at (505) 562-2808. GPA must be 3.0-4.0.

Eastern New Mexico University
ENMU College of Business
Station 49
Portales, NM 88130

1625

Lorraine Schula Endowed Scholarship in Music

AMOUNT: $700 DEADLINE: March 1
MAJOR: Music

The Lorraine Schula Endowed Scholarship in Music is available to sophomore level students or above at Eastern New Mexico University who are majoring in music and are participants in an ensemble. To apply for this award, you must attach an essay explaining professional goals, why funding is deserved, and career objectives. You are also required to submit a cassette tape with 3-5 minutes of performance skills (must have been made within the last year and from a recital or performance within the School of Music). Financial need is a consideration. Four faculty recommendation letters and a minimum 3.0 GPA are required. This award is not renewable. Award requirements change regularly. For further information, please write to the address listed, including a self-addressed, stamped envelope, or call (505) 562-2376. GPA must be 3.0-4.0.

Eastern New Mexico University
College of Education and Technology
Station 25
Portales, NM 88130

1626

Malott Music Scholarship

AMOUNT: $500 DEADLINE: March 1
MAJOR: Vocal Music

The Malott Music Scholarship is available to students who are attending Eastern New Mexico University as choral education or vocal performance majors and are actively participating in choral ensembles. Three faculty recommendation letters are required. Selection is based on academic excellence, performance, ensemble participation, leadership, character, and commitment to music. This award is not renewable. Award requirements change regularly. For further information, please write to the address listed, including a self-addressed, stamped envelope, or call (505) 562-2376. No GPA requirement specified.

Eastern New Mexico University
College of Education and Technology
Station 25
Portales, NM 88130

1627

Marry L. Peed Scholarship

AMOUNT: $1500-$3000 DEADLINE: March 1
MAJOR: Music

The Marry L. Peed Scholarship is available to full-time students who are attending Eastern New Mexico University as music majors and have a GPA of at least 3.0. To apply for this award, you must be a resident of New Mexico and provide three faculty recommendation letters. This award is renewable. Financial need is a factor. Award requirements change

regularly. For further information, please write to the address listed, including a self-addressed, stamped envelope, or call (505) 562-2376. GPA must be 3.0-4.0.

Eastern New Mexico University
College of Education and Technology
Station 25
Portales, NM 88130

1628

Myrtle Moore Women in Business Scholarship

AMOUNT: None Specified DEADLINE: March 1
MAJOR: College of Business

The Myrtle Moore Women in Business Scholarship is available to full-time female sophomore business students at Eastern New Mexico University. To qualify for this award, you must have a minimum GPA of 3.0 and have successfully completed 27-40 credit hours by the effective date of the award. This award is for in-state tuition, fees, room, board, and books. Two faculty recommendation letters are required. This award is renewable. Award requirements change regularly. For more information or to apply, please contact the College of Business at Eastern New Mexico University at (505) 562-2808. GPA must be 3.0-4.0.

Eastern New Mexico University
ENMU College of Business
Station 49
Portales, NM 88130

1629

New Mexico Society of Public Accountants, A.J. Groebner Memorial Scholarship

AMOUNT: $600 DEADLINE: March 1
MAJOR: Accounting

The A.J. Groebner Memorial Scholarship is available to full-time undergraduate accounting students at Eastern New Mexico University. To qualify for this award, you must have a 3.0 minimum GPA, have successfully completed 60 credit hours, and be a graduate of a New Mexico high school. You must be planning to pursue a career in public accounting, provide two faculty recommendation letters, and demonstrate financial need. This award is not renewable. Award requirements change regularly. For more information or to apply, please contact the College of Business at Eastern New Mexico University at (505) 562-2808. GPA must be 3.0-4.0.

Eastern New Mexico University
ENMU College of Business
Station 49
Portales, NM 88130

1630
Ronald K. Payne/KPMG Peat Marwick Scholarship

AMOUNT: $750 DEADLINE: March 1
MAJOR: Accounting

The Ronald K. Payne/KPMG Peat Marwick Scholarship is available to full-time undergraduates at Eastern New Mexico University. To qualify for this award, you must be an accounting major, have a minimum GPA of 3.0, and have completed both semesters of intermediate accounting. Two faculty recommendation letters are required. This award is renewable. Award requirements change regularly. For more information or to apply, please contact the College of Business at Eastern New Mexico University at (505) 562-2808. GPA must be 3.0-4.0.

Eastern New Mexico University
ENMU College of Business
Station 49
Portales, NM 88130

1631
Steven R. Hudson Scholarship

AMOUNT: $1000 DEADLINE: March 1
MAJOR: Accounting

The Steven R. Hudson Scholarship is open to full-time undergraduate students who are attending Eastern New Mexico University as accounting majors. To apply for this award, you must have completed a minimum of 50 hours by the effective date of the award and demonstrate academic excellence. Two faculty recommendation letters are required. This award is renewable. Award requirements change regularly. For more information or to apply, please contact the College of Business at Eastern New Mexico University at (505) 562-2808. No GPA requirement specified.

Eastern New Mexico University
College of Education and Technology
Station 25
Portales, NM 88130

1632
Tremewan Family Scholarship

AMOUNT: $500 DEADLINE: March 1
MAJOR: College of Business

The Tremewan Family Scholarship is available to full-time undergraduate students attending the College of Business at Eastern New Mexico University. To apply for this award, you must demonstrate academic excellence and financial need and provide two faculty recommendation letters. This award is renewable. Award requirements change regularly. For more information or to apply, please contact the College of Business at Eastern New Mexico University at (505) 562-2808. No GPA requirement specified.

Eastern New Mexico University
ENMU College of Business
Station 49
Portales, NM 88130

Eastern Washington University

1633
Beginning Freshmen Academic Scholarship

AMOUNT: $500-$3500 DEADLINE: February 1
MAJOR: All Areas of Study

The Beginning Freshmen Academic Scholarship is open to incoming freshmen at EWU who have a minimum 3.5 GPA. The selection criteria is based on academic excellence. Several awards are available. For priority consideration applicants must apply by February 1. Award requirements change regularly. GPA must be 3.5-4.0.

Eastern Washington University
Office of Admissions, Sutton Hall
148 5th Street
Cheney, WA 99004-1522

1634
Continuing Eastern Students and Transfer Students Academic Scholarship

AMOUNT: $500-$3500 DEADLINE: February 1
MAJOR: All Areas of Study

The Continuing Eastern Students and Transfer Students Academic Scholarship is open to continuing and transfer students at EWU who have a minimum 3.5 GPA. The selection process is based on academic excellence. Several awards are available. The eligibility criteria vary slightly for each award. Award requirements change regularly. GPA must be 3.5-4.0.

Eastern Washington University
Office of Admissions, Sutton Hall
148 5th Street
Cheney, WA 99004-1522

1635
Graduate Student Academic Scholarship

AMOUNT: $500-$3500 DEADLINE: February 1
MAJOR: All Areas of Study

The Graduate Student Academic Scholarship is open to graduate students at EWU who have a minimum 3.5 GPA. The selection process is based on academic excellence. Several awards are available. The eligibility criteria vary slightly for each award. Award requirements change regularly. GPA must be 3.5-4.0.

Eastern Washington University
Office of Admissions, Sutton Hall
148 5th Street
Cheney, WA 99004-1522

Elizabethtown College

1636
Elizabethtown College Presidential Scholarships

AMOUNT: $10000 DEADLINE: Varies
MAJOR: All Areas of Study

Awarded to academically superior Elizabethtown College entering freshmen. Students must rank in the top 2% of their secondary school class; have taken a very challenging curriculum; have a combined recentered SAT score of at least 1300; plan to enroll in the College full-time (12 credit hours or more); and display good academic promise, citizenship, and extracurricular achievement. Award requirements change regularly. Contact the address listed for further information or call (717) 361-1400. GPA must be 3.8-4.0.

Elizabethtown College
M. Clarke Paine - Dir of Financial Aid
One Alpha Drive
Elizabethtown, PA 17022-2298

1637
Elizabethtown College Provost Scholarship

AMOUNT: $5500-$8000 DEADLINE: Varies
MAJOR: All Areas of Study

Awarded to Elizabethtown College entering students. Students must rank in the upper 10% of their secondary school class; have taken a challenging curriculum; have a combined recentered SAT score of at least 1150; plan to enroll in the College full-time (12 credit hours or more); and display good academic promise, citizenship, and extracurricular achievement. Award requirements change regularly. Contact the address listed for further information or call (717) 361-1400. GPA must be 3.0-4.0.

Elizabethtown College
M. Clarke Paine - Dir of Financial Aid
One Alpha Drive
Elizabethtown, PA 17022-2298

1638
Elmer Esbenshade Scholarship

AMOUNT: None Specified DEADLINE: March 15
MAJOR: All Areas of Study

Awarded to Elizabethtown College students from Lancaster County who exhibit financial needs, academic abilities, and leadership potential, and who actively participate in campus activities. Award requirements change regularly. Contact the address listed for further information or call (717) 361-1400. No GPA requirement specified.

Elizabethtown College
M. Clarke Paine - Dir of Financial Aid
One Alpha Drive
Elizabethtown, PA 17022-2298

1639
Ernst/Young Alumni Endowment Fund

AMOUNT: None Specified DEADLINE: March 1
MAJOR: Accounting

Awarded to Elizabethtown College outstanding, incoming freshmen majoring in accounting. Award requirements change regularly. Contact the address listed for further information or call (717) 361-1400. No GPA requirement specified.

Elizabethtown College
M. Clarke Paine - Dir of Financial Aid
One Alpha Drive
Elizabethtown, PA 17022-2298

1640
Girl Scout Gold Award Scholarship

AMOUNT: $1000 DEADLINE: Varies
MAJOR: All Areas of Study

Four-year scholarships are available to Girl Scout Gold Award recipients who are enrolled at Elizabethtown College. Applicants must demonstrate financial need. Award requirements change regularly. For further information, please call (717) 361-1400, or write to the address listed, including a self-addressed, stamped envelope. No GPA requirement specified.

Elizabethtown College
M. Clarke Paine - Dir of Financial Aid
One Alpha Drive
Elizabethtown, PA 17022-2298

Elmhurst College

1641
Elmhurst College Freshman Academic Achievement Scholarship

AMOUNT: $6950 DEADLINE: January 15
MAJOR: All Areas of Study

The Elmhurst College Freshman Academic Achievement Scholarship is open to incoming freshmen who are planning to attend Elmhurst College. You must rank in the upper 20% of your high school graduating class and have composite scores of at least 25 on the ACT or 1140 on the SAT. This award is renewable if you maintain a minimum 3.0 GPA. Award requirements change regularly. Please send a self-addressed, stamped envelope to Elmhurst College for additional information. GPA must be 3.0-4.0.

Elmhurst College
Office of Admissions
190 Prospect Ave
Elmhurst, IL 60126-3271

1642
Elmhurst College Presidential Scholarship

AMOUNT: $9260 DEADLINE: January 15
MAJOR: All Areas of Study

The Elmhurst College Presidential Scholarship is open to incoming freshmen who plan to attend Elmhurst College. You must demonstrate the highest combination of GPA, class standing, and composite ACT or SAT scores. This award is renewable each year if you maintain a minimum cumulative GPA of 3.25. Award requirements change regularly. Please send a self-addressed, stamped envelope to Elmhurst College for additional information. GPA must be 3.3-4.0.

Elmhurst College
Office of Admissions
190 Prospect Ave
Elmhurst, IL 60126-3271

1643
Elmhurst College Transfer Academic Achievement Scholarship

AMOUNT: $6950 DEADLINE: January 15
MAJOR: All Areas of Study

The Elmhurst College Transfer Academic Achievement Scholarship is open to students transferring to Elmhurst College. You must have earned at least 32 semester hours of credit with a minimum cumulative 3.5 GPA. This scholarship is renewable each year if you maintain a minimum 3.0 GPA. Award requirements change regularly. GPA must be 3.5-4.0.

Elmhurst College
Office of Admissions
190 Prospect Ave
Elmhurst, IL 60126-3271

1644
Elmhurst College United Church of Christ Scholarship

AMOUNT: $4630 DEADLINE: May 1
MAJOR: All Areas of Study

The United Church of Christ Scholarships are open to freshmen and transfer students at Elmhurst College who are members of a United Church of Christ congregation. Renewable each year, provided that recipients remain enrolled full-time and are in good academic standing at the college. Your pastor must submit a letter of nomination to the Director of Financial Aid for you to be considered. Award requirements change regularly. No GPA requirement specified.

Elmhurst College
Office of Admissions
190 Prospect Ave
Elmhurst, IL 60126-3271

1645
Enrichment Scholarship

AMOUNT: $5000 DEADLINE: April 15
MAJOR: All Areas of Study

The Enrichment Scholarships are open to full-time traditionally underrepresented freshmen attending Elmhurst College with at least a 2.5 GPA. Award requirements change regularly. GPA must be 2.5-4.0.

Elmhurst College
Office of Admissions
190 Prospect Ave
Elmhurst, IL 60126-3271

1646
Music Talent Scholarship

AMOUNT: $1000 DEADLINE: Varies
MAJOR: All Areas of Study

The Music Talent Scholarship is open to students at Elmhurst College who demonstrate exceptional talent in auditions. Scholarships are for $1,000 per year for four years and are offered upon the recommendation of the Department of Music. Award requirements change regularly. No GPA requirement specified.

Elmhurst College
Office of Admissions
190 Prospect Ave
Elmhurst, IL 60126-3271

1647
Phi Theta Kappa Scholarship

AMOUNT: $9260 DEADLINE: March 15
MAJOR: All Areas of Study

The Phi Theta Kappa Scholarship is open to students transferring to Elmhurst College who are members of Phi Theta Kappa. This award is a two-thirds-tuition scholarship. Award requirements change regularly. No GPA requirement specified.

Elmhurst College
Office of Admissions
190 Prospect Ave
Elmhurst, IL 60126-3271

Elon College

1648
Presidential Scholarship

AMOUNT: $1500 DEADLINE: February 15
MAJOR: All Areas of Study

This scholarship is available to Elon College incoming freshmen with superior academics and ACT or SAT test scores. Based on class rank and/or GPA and SAT/ACT scores, scholarships are automatically awarded to students who meet the necessary criteria. This is a renewable award. Award requirements change regularly. For an application and further information, send a self-addressed, stamped envelope to the address listed, email web@numen.elon.edu, or browse their website: www.elon.edu.admissions/aid.html. GPA must be 3.0-4.0.

Elon College
Office of Financial Planning
2700 Campus Box
Elon College, NC 27244-2010

Science Fellows Scholarship

AMOUNT: $2000 DEADLINE: February 1
MAJOR: Biology, Chemistry, Computer Science, Mathematics, Physics, Science

Awards are available for incoming freshmen who are admitted to Elon College in the areas of study listed above. This scholarship is based on academics, recommendations, and an on-campus interview. Nominations to compete for a Science Fellows Scholarship are made by the Office of Admissions. This is a renewable award. Award requirements change regularly. For an application and further information, send a self-addressed, stamped envelope to the address listed, email web@numen.elon.edu, or browse their website: www.elon.edu/math-scince/scfel.htm.

Elon College
Office of Financial Planning
2700 Campus Box
Elon College, NC 27244-2010

Eureka College

Alumni Grant

AMOUNT: $500 DEADLINE: Varies
MAJOR: All Areas of Study

The Alumni Grant is open to students attending Eureka College. To qualify for this award, you must demonstrate financial need by submitting a FAFSA by the appropriate deadline. Award requirements change regularly. For more information or to apply, please call Eureka College at (309) 467-3721. No GPA requirement specified.

Eureka College - Admissions Office
Attn: Scholarship Programs
300 East College Avenue
Eureka, IL 61530-1562

1651
Christian Church (Disciples of Christ) Grant

AMOUNT: $2500-$3000 DEADLINE: Varies
MAJOR: All Areas of Study

The Christian Church (Disciples of Christ) Grant is open to Eureka College students. To qualify for this award, you must be a member of the Christian Church (Disciples of Christ). Award requirements change regularly. For more information or to apply, please call Eureka College at (309) 467-3721. No GPA requirement specified.

Eureka College - Admissions Office
Attn: Scholarship Programs
300 East College Avenue
Eureka, IL 61530-1562

1652
Dean's Scholarship

AMOUNT: $7000 DEADLINE: Varies
MAJOR: All Areas of Study

The Dean's Scholarship is open to freshmen at Eureka College. To be considered for this award, you must meet two of the following criteria: 80% class rank, a minimum 25 ACT score, and/or a minimum 3.5 GPA. Award requirements change regularly. For more information or to apply, please call Eureka College at (309) 467-3721. GPA must be 3.5-4.0.

Eureka College - Admissions Office
Attn: Scholarship Programs
300 East College Avenue
Eureka, IL 61530-1562

1653
Family Grant

AMOUNT: $500 DEADLINE: Varies
MAJOR: All Areas of Study

The Family Grant is open to siblings attending Eureka College. To qualify for this award, you must be one of two or more full-time dependent siblings attending Eureka College at the same time. Award requirements change regularly. For more information or to apply, please call Eureka College at (309) 467-3721. No GPA requirement specified.

Eureka College - Admissions Office
Attn: Scholarship Programs
300 East College Avenue
Eureka, IL 61530-1562

1654
Fine and Performing Arts Scholarship

AMOUNT: $1000-$6000 DEADLINE: February 15
MAJOR: Vocal, Keyboard Music, Art, Theater

The Fine and Performing Arts Scholarship is open to Eureka College students who are pursuing a major in vocal music, keyboard music, art, or theater. To qualify for this award, you must demonstrate a high level of accomplishment in one of these areas competitively through auditions and/or interviews. Award requirements change regularly. For more information or to apply, please call Eureka College at (309) 467-3721. No GPA requirement specified.

Eureka College - Admissions Office
Attn: Scholarship Programs
300 East College Avenue
Eureka, IL 61530-1562

1655
Legacy Grant

AMOUNT: $500-$1000   DEADLINE: Varies
MAJOR: All Areas of Study

The Legacy Grant is open to full-time students at Eureka College who are dependent children of Eureka College alumni. Award requirements change regularly. For more information or to apply, please call Eureka College at (309) 467-3721. No GPA requirement specified.

Eureka College - Admissions Office
Attn: Scholarship Programs
300 East College Avenue
Eureka, IL 61530-1562

1656
Level Three Transfer Scholarship

AMOUNT: $2500-$3000   DEADLINE: Varies
MAJOR: All Areas of Study

The Level Three Transfer Scholarship is awarded to transfer students at Eureka College. To qualify for this award, you must have a minimum 2.8 transferable GPA in at least 24 semester hours. Award requirements change regularly. For more information or to apply, please call Eureka College at (309) 467-3721. GPA must be 2.5-4.0.

Eureka College - Admissions Office
Attn: Scholarship Programs
300 East College Avenue
Eureka, IL 61530-1562

1657
Level Two Transfer Scholarship

AMOUNT: $4000-$5700   DEADLINE: Varies
MAJOR: All Areas of Study

The Level Two Transfer Scholarship is awarded to transfer students. To qualify for this award, you must have a minimum 3.0 transferable GPA in at least 24 semester hours. Award requirements change regularly. For more information or to apply, please call Eureka College at (309) 467-3721. GPA must be 3.0-4.0.

Eureka College - Admissions Office
Attn: Scholarship Programs
300 East College Avenue
Eureka, IL 61530-1562

1658
Minister's Dependents Grant

AMOUNT: $3500-$4000   DEADLINE: Varies
MAJOR: All Areas of Study

The Minister's Dependents Grant is awarded to students at Eureka College. To qualify for this award, you must be a dependent of a minister with standing in the Christian Church (Disciples of Christ). Award requirements change regularly. For more information or to apply, please call Eureka College at (309) 467-3721. No GPA requirement specified.

Eureka College - Admissions Office
Attn: Scholarship Programs
300 East College Avenue
Eureka, IL 61530-1562

1659
Phi Theta Kappa Scholarship

AMOUNT: $7500   DEADLINE: Varies
MAJOR: All Areas of Study

The Phi Theta Kappa Scholarship is open to transfer students at Eureka College. To qualify for this award, you must have a minimum 3.5 GPA in 24 semester hours, and you must be in good standing in Phi Theta Kappa. Award requirements change regularly. For more information or to apply, please call Eureka College at (309) 467-3721. GPA must be 3.5-4.0.

Eureka College - Admissions Office
Attn: Scholarship Programs
300 East College Avenue
Eureka, IL 61530-1562

1660
Presidential Scholarship

AMOUNT: $9000   DEADLINE: Varies
MAJOR: All Areas of Study

The Presidential Scholarship is open to freshmen at Eureka College. To qualify for this award, you must have two of the following: a minimum ACT score of 27, a 90% class rank, and/or a 3.7 GPA. Award requirements change regularly. For more information or to apply, please call Eureka College at (309) 467-3721. GPA must be 3.7-4.0.

Eureka College - Admissions Office
Attn: Scholarship Programs
300 East College Avenue
Eureka, IL 61530-1562

1661
Raymond W. McCallister Fellowship

AMOUNT: None Specified   DEADLINE: Varies
MAJOR: Ministry

The Raymond W. McCallister Fellowship is awarded to students at Eureka College. To qualify for this award, you must demonstrate academic excellence, service, and commitment to enter the Christian Church (Disciples of Christ) Ministry. Award requirements change regularly. For more information or to apply, please call Eureka College at (309) 467-3721. No GPA requirement specified.

Eureka College - Admissions Office
Attn: Scholarship Programs
300 East College Avenue
Eureka, IL 61530-1562

1662
Ronald W. Reagan Scholarship

AMOUNT: None Specified   DEADLINE: December 1
MAJOR: All Areas of Study

The Ronald W. Reagan Scholarship is open to incoming freshmen at Eureka College. To be considered for this award, you must demonstrate leadership potential, commitment to service, and academic excellence. Award requirements change regularly. For further information from the scholarship provider, call (309) 467-3721. No GPA requirement specified.

Eureka College - Admissions Office
Attn: Scholarship Programs
300 East College Avenue
Eureka, IL 61530-1562

1663
Transfer Scholarship

AMOUNT: $4000-$5000 DEADLINE: May 1
MAJOR: All Areas of Study

The Transfer Scholarship is open to transfer students at Eureka College who have a minimum 3.3 transferable GPA in at least 24 semester hours. Award requirements change regularly. Please send a self-addressed, stamped envelope to receive your application and any further instructions from the scholarship provider, or call (309) 467-3721. GPA must be 3.3-4.0.

Eureka College - Admissions Office
Attn: Scholarship Programs
300 East College Avenue
Eureka, IL 61530-1562

1664
U.S. Johnson Fellowship

AMOUNT: Maximum: $8000 DEADLINE: Varies
MAJOR: Ministry

The U.S. Johnson Fellowship is awarded to students at Eureka College. To qualify for this award, you must demonstrate academic merit, service, and commitment to pursue a career in ministry. Award requirements change regularly. For more information or to apply, please call Eureka College at (309) 467-3721. No GPA requirement specified.

Eureka College - Admissions Office
Attn: Scholarship Programs
300 East College Avenue
Eureka, IL 61530-1562

Fairmont State College

1665
Alan B. Mollohan Scholarship

AMOUNT: $750 DEADLINE: Varies
MAJOR: All Areas of Study

This award is open to an incoming freshman who is a resident of West Virginia. The applicant must have a GPA of at least 3.5 and be enrolled in a four-year program. This award is non-renewable. Award requirements change regularly. Please send a self-addressed, stamped envelope to receive your application and any further instructions from the scholarship provider. GPA must be 3.5-4.0.

Fairmont State College
Director of Scholarships
1201 Locust Avenue
Fairmont, WV 26554

1666
Blanche Kinney Fine Arts Scholarship

AMOUNT: None Specified DEADLINE: Varies
MAJOR: Fine Arts, Art, Music, Speech, Drama

This award is open to students with outstanding talent in art, music, speech, or drama. Selection will be made by the Chairperson of the School of Fine Arts. Award requirements change regularly. Please send a self-addressed, stamped envelope to receive your application and any further instructions from the scholarship provider. No GPA requirement specified.

Fairmont State College
Director of Scholarships
1201 Locust Avenue
Fairmont, WV 26554

1667
Edward Kaprelian Memorial Scholarship

AMOUNT: $1250 DEADLINE: Varies
MAJOR: All Areas of Study

This award is open to a full-time student who demonstrates a mature sense of ethics, honesty, concern for human dignity, and financial need. Recommendations are made by the faculty, and selections are made by the financial aid office. Award requirements change regularly. Please send a self-addressed, stamped envelope to receive your application and any further instructions from the scholarship provider. No GPA requirement specified.

Fairmont State College
Director of Scholarships
1201 Locust Avenue
Fairmont, WV 26554

1668
Fairmont Concert Association Scholarship

AMOUNT: None Specified DEADLINE: Varies
MAJOR: Music

This award is granted to a student who excels in academic performance and musical capabilities. The award winner will be selected by the Music Faculty Scholarship Committee. Award requirements change regularly. Please send a self-addressed, stamped envelope to receive your application and any further instructions from the scholarship provider. GPA must be 3.0-4.0.

Fairmont State College
Director of Scholarships
1201 Locust Avenue
Fairmont, WV 26554

1669
Fairmont State College Alumni Scholarship

AMOUNT: $500 DEADLINE: Varies
MAJOR: All Areas of Study

This award is open to a junior or senior who is the son or daughter of a Fairmont State College alumnus. The applicant must have at least a 2.5 GPA and have full-time student status. Award requirements change regularly. Please send a self-addressed, stamped envelope to receive your application and any further instructions from the scholarship provider. GPA must be 2.5-4.0.

Fairmont State College
Director of Scholarships
1201 Locust Avenue
Fairmont, WV 26554

1670
Fairmont State College Outstanding International Student Scholarship

AMOUNT: None Specified DEADLINE: Varies
MAJOR: All Areas of Study

This award is open to newly admitted international students with outstanding academic records. The applicant may renew the scholarship by reapplying to the International Education Committee for a maximum of eight semesters. The recipient receives partial tuition. Award requirements change regularly. Please send a self-addressed, stamped envelope to receive your application and any further instructions from the scholarship provider. GPA must be 3.0-4.0.

Fairmont State College
Director of Scholarships
1201 Locust Avenue
Fairmont, WV 26554

1671
Fairmont Undergraduate Scholarship

AMOUNT: None Specified DEADLINE: Varies
MAJOR: All Areas of Study

This award is open to undergraduates who demonstrate high academic performance based on ACT or SAT, GPA, and rank in class. To renew the award, the student must maintain a minimum 3.0 GPA. The award recipient receives partial tuition. Award requirements change regularly. Please send a self-addressed, stamped envelope to receive your application and any further instructions from the scholarship provider. GPA must be 3.0-4.0.

Fairmont State College
Director of Scholarships
1201 Locust Avenue
Fairmont, WV 26554

1672
Fairmont Undergraduate Scholarship - Commerce

AMOUNT: None Specified DEADLINE: Varies
MAJOR: Commerce, Business, Economics

This award is open to undergraduates with outstanding academic performance or potential in the field of Commerce. The award winner must maintain a full-time status and a minimum 3.0 GPA. To renew, the student must apply yearly for a maximum of eight semesters. Award requirements change regularly. Please send a self-addressed, stamped envelope to receive your application and any further instructions from the scholarship provider. GPA must be 3.0-4.0.

Fairmont State College
Director of Scholarships
1201 Locust Avenue
Fairmont, WV 26554

1673
Fairmont Undergraduate Scholarship - Education

AMOUNT: None Specified DEADLINE: Varies
MAJOR: Education

This award is open to an undergraduate in Education with outstanding academic performance and potential. To renew the scholarship, the student must maintain full-time status and have a 3.0 GPA. The student can apply yearly to renew, for a maximum of eight semesters. The scholarship covers partial tuition. Award requirements change regularly. Please send a self-addressed, stamped envelope to receive your application and any further instructions from the scholarship provider. GPA must be 3.0-4.0.

Fairmont State College
Director of Scholarships
1201 Locust Avenue
Fairmont, WV 26554

1674
Fairmont Undergraduate Scholarship - Fine Arts

AMOUNT: None Specified DEADLINE: Varies
MAJOR: Fine Arts

This award is for an undergraduate in the Fine Arts with outstanding academic performance, potential, and talent. To renew the scholarship, the student must maintain full-time status and a 3.0 GPA. The student can apply yearly to renew, for a maximum of eight semesters. The scholarship covers partial tuition. Award requirements change regularly. Please send a self-addressed, stamped envelope to receive your application and any further instructions from the scholarship provider. GPA must be 3.0-4.0.

Fairmont State College
Director of Scholarships
1201 Locust Avenue
Fairmont, WV 26554

1675
Fairmont Undergraduate Scholarship - Health Career

AMOUNT: None Specified DEADLINE: Varies
MAJOR: Health, Health Administration, Nursing

This award is for an undergraduate interested in the area of Health and Health Issues with an outstanding academic performance and potential. To renew the scholarship, the student must maintain full-time status and a 3.0 GPA. The student can apply yearly to renew, for a maximum of eight semesters. The scholarship covers partial tuition. Award requirements change regularly. Please send a self-addressed, stamped envelope to receive your application and any further instructions from the scholarship provider. GPA must be 3.0-4.0.

Fairmont State College
Director of Scholarships
1201 Locust Avenue
Fairmont, WV 26554

1676
Fairmont Undergraduate Scholarship - Language and Literature

AMOUNT: None Specified DEADLINE: Varies
MAJOR: Language, Literature

This award is for an undergraduate in Language and Literature with outstanding academic performance and potential. To renew the scholarship, the student must maintain full-time status and a 3.0 GPA. The student can apply yearly to renew, for a maximum of eight semesters. The scholarship covers partial tuition. Award requirements change regularly. Please send a self-addressed, stamped envelope to receive your application and any further instructions from the scholarship provider. GPA must be 3.0-4.0.

Fairmont State College
Director of Scholarships
1201 Locust Avenue
Fairmont, WV 26554

1677
Fairmont Undergraduate Scholarship - Math and Science

AMOUNT: None Specified DEADLINE: Varies
MAJOR: Math, Science

This award is for an undergraduate in Math and/or Science with outstanding academic performance and potential. To renew the scholarship, the student must maintain full-time status and a 3.0 GPA. The student can apply yearly to renew, for a maximum of eight semesters. The scholarship covers partial tuition. Award requirements change regularly. Please send a self-addressed, stamped envelope to receive your application and any further instructions from the scholarship provider. GPA must be 3.0-4.0.

Fairmont State College
Director of Scholarships
1201 Locust Avenue
Fairmont, WV 26554

1678
Fairmont Undergraduate Scholarship - Physical Education

AMOUNT: None Specified DEADLINE: Varies
MAJOR: Physical Education

This award is for an undergraduate in Physical Education with outstanding academic performance and potential. To renew the scholarship, the student must maintain full-time status and a 3.0 GPA. The student can apply yearly to renew, for a maximum of eight semesters. The scholarship covers partial tuition. Award requirements change regularly. Please send a self-addressed, stamped envelope to receive your application and any further instructions from the scholarship provider. GPA must be 3.0-4.0.

Fairmont State College
Director of Scholarships
1201 Locust Avenue
Fairmont, WV 26554

1679
Fairmont Undergraduate Scholarship - Social Science

AMOUNT: None Specified DEADLINE: Varies
MAJOR: Social Science

This award is for an undergraduate in Social Science with outstanding academic performance and potential. To renew the scholarship, the student must maintain full-time status and a 3.0 GPA. The student can apply yearly to renew, for a maximum of eight semesters. The scholarship covers partial tuition. Award requirements change regularly. Please send a self-addressed, stamped envelope to receive your application and any further instructions from the scholarship provider. GPA must be 3.0-4.0.

Fairmont State College
Director of Scholarships
1201 Locust Avenue
Fairmont, WV 26554

1680
Fairmont Undergraduate Scholarship - Technology

AMOUNT: None Specified DEADLINE: Varies
MAJOR: Technology

This award is for an undergraduate in Technology with outstanding academic performance and potential. To renew the scholarship, the student must maintain full-time status and a 3.0 GPA. The student can apply yearly to renew, for a maximum of eight semesters. The scholarship covers partial tuition. Award requirements change regularly. Please send a self-addressed, stamped envelope to receive your application and any further instructions from the scholarship provider. GPA must be 3.0-4.0.

Fairmont State College
Director of Scholarships
1201 Locust Avenue
Fairmont, WV 26554

1681
Governor's Honors Academy Scholarship

AMOUNT: None Specified DEADLINE: Varies
MAJOR: All Areas of Study

This award is open to entering freshmen who are Governor's Honors Academy participants. To renew the scholarship, students must maintain full-time status and a minimum overall GPA of 3.0 after freshman year, 3.2 after sophomore year, and 3.4 after junior year. Award requirements change regularly. Please send a self-addressed, stamped envelope to receive your application and any further instructions from the scholarship provider. GPA must be 3.5-4.0.

Fairmont State College
Director of Scholarships
1201 Locust Avenue
Fairmont, WV 26554

1682
Governor's School for the Arts Scholarship

AMOUNT: None Specified DEADLINE: Varies
MAJOR: Fine Arts

This award is open to entering freshman who were participants in the Governor's School for the Arts at FSC Performance Audition. To renew this scholarship, the students must maintain full-time status, and a minimum overall GPA of 3.0 after freshman year, 3.2 after sophomore year, and 3.4 after junior year. Award requirements change regularly. Please send a self-addressed, stamped envelope to receive your application and any further instructions from the scholarship provider. GPA must be 3.0-4.0.

Fairmont State College
Director of Scholarships
1201 Locust Avenue
Fairmont, WV 26554

1683
Jean Billingslea Johnson Scholarship

AMOUNT: $700 DEADLINE: Varies
MAJOR: All Areas of Study

The Jean Billingslea Johnson Scholarship is open to students attending Fairmont State College. The applicant's financial need is taken into consideration. Award requirements change regularly. Please send a self-addressed, stamped envelope to receive your application and any further instructions from the scholarship provider. No GPA requirement specified.

Fairmont State College
Director of Scholarships
1201 Locust Avenue
Fairmont, WV 26554

1684
Letterman's Scholarship

AMOUNT: None Specified DEADLINE: Varies
MAJOR: Athletics

This award is open to a Fairmont State College student who has demonstrated outstanding athletic performance. Selection of the award recipient will be made by the Athletic Director and athletic coaches. Award requirements change regularly. Please send a self-addressed, stamped envelope to receive your application and any further instructions from the scholarship provider. No GPA requirement specified.

Fairmont State College
Director of Scholarships
1201 Locust Avenue
Fairmont, WV 26554

1685
Louis Schoolnic Scholarship

AMOUNT: $400 DEADLINE: Varies
MAJOR: Business, Economics

This award is open to a resident of West Virginia majoring in a field within the School of Business and Economics. The selection of the recipient is made by the Business and Economics Department faculty. Award requirements change regularly. Please send a self-addressed, stamped envelope to receive your application and any further instructions from the scholarship provider. No GPA requirement specified.

Fairmont State College
Director of Scholarships
1201 Locust Avenue
Fairmont, WV 26554

1686
Marjorie R. Hoult Lough Scholarship

AMOUNT: $500 DEADLINE: Varies
MAJOR: Education (Teaching Concentration)

This award is open to an education major with an emphasis in teaching. Applicant must have a GPA of at least 3.4. The recipient of this award cannot receive any other college-sponsored scholarships. This is a non-renewable scholarship. Award requirements change regularly. Please send a self-addressed, stamped envelope to receive your application and any further instructions from the scholarship provider. GPA must be 3.4-4.0.

Fairmont State College
Director of Scholarships
1201 Locust Avenue
Fairmont, WV 26554

1687
Mary B. Jaynes Scholarship

AMOUNT: $900 DEADLINE: Varies
MAJOR: Business, Economics

This award is open to an outstanding senior in the School of Business and Economics. The award recipient will be selected by the Business and Economics Department faculty. Award requirements change regularly. Please send a self-addressed, stamped envelope to receive your application and any further instructions from the scholarship provider. No GPA requirement specified.

Fairmont State College
Director of Scholarships
1201 Locust Avenue
Fairmont, WV 26554

1688
Mary Reitz Leeming Memorial Scholarship

AMOUNT: $550 DEADLINE: Varies
MAJOR: Nursing

This award is open to Fairmont State College students majoring in Nursing. The award winner is selected by the Nursing faculty. This award is non-renewable. Award requirements change regularly. Please send a self-addressed, stamped envelope to receive your application and any further instructions from the scholarship provider. No GPA requirement specified.

Fairmont State College
Director of Scholarships
1201 Locust Avenue
Fairmont, WV 26554

1689
T.J. & Madge Herndon Pearse Memorial Scholarship

AMOUNT: $250 DEADLINE: Varies
MAJOR: Elementary Education, Science Education

This award is open to a junior or senior majoring in elementary or science education. Applicant must have a GPA of at least 3.0. Recommendation is made by the education, science, or math faculty. Final selection is made by the financial aid office. Award requirements change regularly. Please send a self-addressed, stamped envelope to receive your application and any further instructions from the scholarship provider. GPA must be 3.0-4.0.

Fairmont State College
Director of Scholarships
1201 Locust Avenue
Fairmont, WV 26554

1690
Virgina Palmer Wellock/Richard P. Wellock Music Scholarship Fund

AMOUNT: None Specified DEADLINE: Varies
MAJOR: Music

This award is granted to a student with strong academic performance and musical capabilities who demonstrates financial need. The selection of the award winner is made by the Scholarship Committee of the music faculty. Award requirements change regularly. Please send a self-addressed, stamped envelope to receive your application and any further instructions from the scholarship provider. GPA must be 2.5-4.0.

Fairmont State College
Director of Scholarships
1201 Locust Avenue
Fairmont, WV 26554

Faulkner University

1691
Bible Award

AMOUNT: $2000 DEADLINE: April 15
MAJOR: Biblical Studies

Open to enrolled students who have completed at least 60 hours toward a Bible degree. Renewable if recipients demonstrate satisfactory academic progress. Applicants must be Alabama residents. Maximum award from all university sources cannot exceed $3000. Award requirements change regularly. For further information please call (334) 260-6200. GPA must be 2.5-4.0.

Faulkner University
Office of Admissions
5345 Atlanta Highway
Montgomery, AL 36109

1692
Bible Bowl Award

AMOUNT: $500 DEADLINE: April 15
MAJOR: All Areas of Study

Open to admitted incoming freshmen who are/were Bible Bowl team members. Renewable if recipients demonstrate satisfactory academic progress. Applicants must also be Alabama residents. Award requirements change regularly. For further information please call (334) 260-6200, or visit the sponsor's website. No GPA requirement specified.

Faulkner University
Office of Admissions
5345 Atlanta Highway
Montgomery, AL 36109

1693
Faulkner University Scholarship

AMOUNT: None Specified DEADLINE: March 15
MAJOR: All Areas of Study

The Faulkner University Scholarship is open to valedictorians or salutatorians admitted as full-time students at Faulkner University. You must have a minimum ACT score of 26 or a minimum SAT score of 1190 and be an Alabama resident. The award consists of tuition, room, and board. A minimum GPA of 3.4 is required to renew the award. Award requirements change regularly. For further information, please call (334) 260-6200. No GPA requirement specified.

Faulkner University
Office of Admissions
5345 Atlanta Highway
Montgomery, AL 36109

1694
Minister's Child Award

AMOUNT: $500 DEADLINE: April 15
MAJOR: All Areas of Study

This scholarship is open to incoming freshmen who are Alabama residents. You must have a parent who is a minister and deriving at least 50% of the family income from church work. Award requirements change regularly. No GPA requirement specified.

Faulkner University
Office of Admissions
5345 Atlanta Highway
Montgomery, AL 36109

1695
President's List Scholarship

AMOUNT: $500 DEADLINE: April 15
MAJOR: All Areas of Study

Open to students enrolled at Faulkner with a minimum GPA of 3.90 for two consecutive semesters. The 3.90 must have been earned at Faulkner and maintained to keep the award. Award requirements change regularly. For further information please call (334) 260-6200. GPA must be 3.9-4.0.

Faulkner University
Office of Admissions
5345 Atlanta Highway
Montgomery, AL 36109

Florida Gulf Coast University

1696
Florence Hecht Endowed Scholarship Fund

AMOUNT: None Specified DEADLINE: March 10
MAJOR: All Areas of Study

The Florence Hecht Endowed Scholarship Fund is open to employees of the Naples-Fort Myers Greyhound Track and the Flagler Greyhound Track and their relatives. Applicants must attend Florida Gulf Coast University. Award requirements change regularly. Please send a self-addressed, stamped envelope to receive your application and any further instructions from the scholarship provider. You may browse the sponsor website at condor.fgcu.edu/ES/FASO/. GPA must be 3.0-4.0.

Florida Gulf Coast University
Financial Aid and Scholarship Office
10501 FGCU Blvd., South
Fort Myers, FL 33965-6565

1697
General Scholarship Fund

AMOUNT: None Specified DEADLINE: March 1
MAJOR: All Areas of Study

The General Scholarship Fund is open to students selected by the scholarship committee who are attending Florida Gulf Coast University. Award requirements change regularly. Please send a self-addressed, stamped envelope to receive your application and any further instructions from the scholarship provider. You may browse the sponsor website at condor.fgcu.edu/ES/FASO/. GPA must be 3.0-4.0.

Florida Gulf Coast University
Financial Aid and Scholarship Office
10501 FGCU Blvd., South
Fort Myers, FL 33965-6565

1698
Golden Apple Teacher Recognition Program Scholarship Fund

AMOUNT: None Specified DEADLINE: March 1
MAJOR: Teaching

The Golden Apple Teacher Recognition Program Scholarship Fund is open to teachers in the public schools of Lee County, Florida. Recipients must wish to take a course or courses to enhance their classroom skills. The application should be sent to the Golden Apple Teacher Recognition program. Awards will be made in an effort to cover the costs of the desired course(s) and related books and supplies. Applicants must plan on attending Florida Gulf Coast University. Award requirements change regularly. Please send a self-addressed, stamped envelope to receive your application and any further instructions from the scholarship provider. You may browse the sponsor website at condor.fgcu.edu/ES/FASO/. No GPA requirement specified.

Florida Gulf Coast University
Financial Aid and Scholarship Office
10501 FGCU Blvd., South
Fort Myers, FL 33965-6565

1699
Joe A. and "Tippy" Hillard Scholarship Fund

AMOUNT: None Specified DEADLINE: March 1
MAJOR: All Areas of Study

The Joe A. and "Tippy" Hillard Scholarship Fund is open to residents of Hendry and Lee Counties in Florida. Preference for this scholarship should be given to non-traditional students and single parents on the basis of need. Award requirements change regularly. Please send a self-addressed, stamped envelope to receive your application and any further instructions from the scholarship provider. You may browse the sponsor website at condor.fgcu.edu/ES/FASO/. GPA must be 3.0-4.0.

Florida Gulf Coast University
Financial Aid and Scholarship Office
10501 FGCU Blvd., South
Fort Myers, FL 33965-6565

1700
Muriel K. Hudson Endowed Nursing Scholarship Fund

AMOUNT: None Specified DEADLINE: March 1
MAJOR: Nursing

The Muriel K. Hudson Endowed Nursing Scholarship Fund is open to nursing majors attending Florida Gulf Coast University. A minimum 3.0 GPA is required in addition to community service. Award requirements change regularly. Please send a self-addressed, stamped envelope to receive your application and any further instructions from the scholarship provider. You may browse the sponsor website at condor.fgcu.edu/. GPA must be 3.0-4.0.

Florida Gulf Coast University
Financial Aid and Scholarship Office
10501 FGCU Blvd., South
Fort Myers, FL 33965-6565

1701
W. Thomas Howard/Gannett Foundation Scholarship Fund

AMOUNT: None Specified DEADLINE: March 1
MAJOR: All Areas of Study

The W. Thomas Howard/Gannett Foundation Scholarship Fund is open to residents of the Greater Fort Myers, Florida, area attending Florida Gulf Coast University. Applicants must be valedictorians or runner-ups. Award requirements change regularly. Please send a self-addressed, stamped envelope to receive your application and any further instructions from the scholarship provider. You may browse the sponsor website at condor.fgcu.edu/. No GPA requirement specified.

Florida Gulf Coast University
Financial Aid and Scholarship Office
10501 FGCU Blvd., South
Fort Myers, FL 33965-6565

Fort Lewis College

1702
Academic Excellence Award

AMOUNT: $1000 DEADLINE: Varies
MAJOR: All Fields of Study

The Academic Excellence Award is open to continuing undergraduates at Fort Lewis College. You must have completed a minimum 30 credit hours during the preceding fall and winter terms. You must also have a 3.5 cumulative GPA and not qualify for other academic scholarships. Former recipients of the Deans or Presidential Scholarships are automatically considered. Award requirements change regularly. There is no scholarship application. Students meeting the stated criteria are automatically considered. GPA must be 3.5-4.0.

Fort Lewis College
Attn: Office of Financial Aid
101 Miller Student Ctr. - 1000 Rim Drive
Durango, CO 81301-3999

1703
Alice Admire Memorial Scholarship

AMOUNT: $300 DEADLINE: Varies
MAJOR: English

The Alice Admire Memorial Scholarship is open to English majors at Fort Lewis College. You must have completed a minimum of 60 credit hours and have a 3.0 cumulative GPA. Award requirements change regularly. No application is required. English Department faculty selects scholarship recipients. GPA must be 3.0-4.0.

Fort Lewis College
Attn: Office of Financial Aid
101 Miller Student Ctr. - 1000 Rim Drive
Durango, CO 81301-3999

1704
American Association of University Women (AAUW) Scholarship

AMOUNT: $500 DEADLINE: April 14
MAJOR: All Fields of Study

The American Association of University Women (AAUW) Scholarship is open to female students at Fort Lewis College. You must be a non-traditional student at least 25 years of age and a resident of La Plata, San Juan, Archuleta, Montezuma, or San Miguel Counties in Colorado. You must also have earned a minimum 30 credit hours and have a 2.5 cumulative GPA. Award requirements change regularly. To receive an application and further instructions, please send a self-addressed, stamped envelope to Foundation Office, 109 Kroeger Building at Fort Lewis College; or call (970) 247-7425. GPA must be 2.5-4.0.

Fort Lewis College
Attn: Office of Financial Aid
101 Miller Student Ctr. - 1000 Rim Drive
Durango, CO 81301-3999

1705
Carleno Memorial Scholarship

AMOUNT: $750 DEADLINE: April 14
MAJOR: All Fields of Study

The Carleno Memorial Scholarship is open to students at Fort Lewis College (FLC). You must be enrolled in a minimum of 12 credit hours per term, have a 3.0 cumulative high school or college GPA, and be enrolled in a major leading to any medical field. Preference will be given to residents of Durango, La Plata County, Southwest Colorado, or Colorado (in order preferred by FLC). Award requirements change regularly. To receive an application and further instructions, please send a self-addressed, stamped envelope to the scholarship provider; or apply online at the FLC website: www.fortlewis.edu. GPA must be 3.0-4.0.

Fort Lewis College
Attn: Office of Financial Aid
101 Miller Student Ctr. - 1000 Rim Drive
Durango, CO 81301-3999

1706
Carroll Peterson Scholarship

AMOUNT: $800 DEADLINE: Varies
MAJOR: English

The Carroll Peterson Scholarship is open to junior English majors at Fort Lewis College. You must have completed a minimum of 60 credit hours and have a 3.0 cumulative GPA. Award requirements change regularly. No application is required. English Department faculty selects scholarship recipients. GPA must be 3.0-4.0.

Fort Lewis College
Attn: Office of Financial Aid
101 Miller Student Ctr. - 1000 Rim Drive
Durango, CO 81301-3999

1707
Colorado Diversity Grant

AMOUNT: $2500 DEADLINE: April 14
MAJOR: All Fields of Study

The Colorado Diversity Grant is open to Colorado residents attending Fort Lewis College full-time. Priority is given to students entering FLC for the first time and students who are members of an underrepresented group that will promote diversity (African-American, Asian-American, or Hispanic students and/or students with a disability). Secondary consideration will be given to non-traditional students (defined as 24 years or older and who are single parents). You will be required to submit the FAFSA. The award is renewable. Award requirements change regularly. To receive an application and further instructions, please send a self-addressed, stamped envelope to the scholarship provider. No GPA requirement specified.

Fort Lewis College
Attn: Office of Financial Aid
101 Miller Student Ctr. - 1000 Rim Drive
Durango, CO 81301-3999

1708
Continuing Student Scholarship

AMOUNT: $1500 DEADLINE: Varies
MAJOR: All Fields of Study

The Continuing Student Scholarship is open to students at Fort Lewis College (FLC). You must be a Colorado resident, have a minimum 3.75 cumulative GPA, have completed at least 24 credit hours at FLC during the preceding fall and winter terms, and be enrolled for a minimum of 12 credit hours for fall term of the upcoming year. Students who are within one term of graduation or who have accumulated more than 110 credit hours will not be considered. Award requirements change regularly. No application is required. Please refer all questions to the Office of Financial Aid at Fort Lewis College. GPA must be 3.75-4.0.

Fort Lewis College
Attn: Office of Financial Aid
101 Miller Student Ctr. - 1000 Rim Drive
Durango, CO 81301-3999

1709
Dean Ernest H. Bader Memorial Scholarship

AMOUNT: Maximum: $500 DEADLINE: April 14
MAJOR: All Fields of Study

The Dean Ernest H. Bader Memorial Scholarship is open to seniors at Fort Lewis College (FLC). You must be enrolled in a minimum of 12 credit hours per term, have a 2.0 cumulative GPA, and demonstrate financial need. You must also submit an essay stating your participation in extracurricular activities, honors, awards, and leadership experience. You will be required to submit a FAFSA. Preference is given to students who are descendents of FLC alumni. Award requirements change regularly. To receive an application and further instructions, please send a self-addressed, stamped envelope to the scholarship provider; or apply online at the FLC website: www.fortlewis.edu. GPA must be 2.0-4.0.

Fort Lewis College
Attn: Office of Financial Aid
101 Miller Student Ctr. - 1000 Rim Drive
Durango, CO 81301-3999

1710
Deans Scholarship

AMOUNT: $600 DEADLINE: Varies
MAJOR: All Fields of Study

The Deans Scholarship is open to first-time freshmen at Fort Lewis College. You must be a Colorado resident, have a 3.0 cumulative high school GPA, and have a minimum 24 ACT or 1060 SAT. The award is not renewable. Award requirements change regularly. There is no scholarship application. Students meeting the stated criteria are automatically considered. GPA must be 3.0-4.0.

Fort Lewis College
Attn: Office of Financial Aid
101 Miller Student Ctr. - 1000 Rim Drive
Durango, CO 81301-3999

1711
Don and Helen James Family Scholarship

AMOUNT: $500 DEADLINE: April 14
MAJOR: All Fields of Study

The Don and Helen James Family Scholarship is open to students at Fort Lewis College who have completed at least 30 credit hours. You must be a Colorado resident and have a minimum cumulative GPA of 3.0. Award selection is based on academic GPA, financial need, and outside activities. Award requirements change regularly. To receive an application and further instructions, please send a self-addressed, stamped envelope to Foundation Office, 109 Kroeger Building at Fort Lewis College; or call (970) 247-7425. GPA must be 3.0-4.0.

Fort Lewis College
Attn: Office of Financial Aid
101 Miller Student Ctr. - 1000 Rim Drive
Durango, CO 81301-3999

1712
Durango 100 Club Scholarship

AMOUNT: $1000 DEADLINE: April 14
MAJOR: All Fields of Study

The Durango 100 Club Scholarship is open to students at Fort Lewis College (FLC). You must have one parent employed by the City of Durango Police or Fire Department, Colorado State Patrol, or La Plata County Sheriff's Office or be the child of a parent killed in the line of duty. You must also have a 2.7 cumulative high school or FLC GPA. Award requirements change regularly. To receive an application and further instructions, please send a self-addressed, stamped envelope to Jasper Welch, Durango 100 Club, PO Box 3146, Durango, CO, 81302. GPA must be 2.7-4.0.

Fort Lewis College
Attn: Office of Financial Aid
101 Miller Student Ctr. - 1000 Rim Drive
Durango, CO 81301-3999

1713
Fern and Walter Holmquist Scholarship

AMOUNT: $500 DEADLINE: April 14
MAJOR: Pre-Medicine, Education, Law Enforcement, Computer Science, Sciences

The Fern and Walter Holmquist Scholarship is open to Native American students at Fort Lewis College (FLC). Preference is given to students studying pre-med, teacher licensing, law enforcement, computer science, and the sciences. You must have at least a GPA of 2.5. Award requirements change regularly. To receive an application and further instructions, please send a self-addressed, stamped envelope to Foundation Office, 109 Kroeger Building at Fort Lewis College; call (970) 247-7425; or apply online at the FLC website: www.fortlewis.edu. GPA must be 2.5-4.0.

Fort Lewis College
Attn: Office of Financial Aid
101 Miller Student Ctr. - 1000 Rim Drive
Durango, CO 81301-3999

1714
First Generation College Student Award

AMOUNT: None Specified DEADLINE: April 14
MAJOR: All Fields of Study

The First Generation College Student Award is open to incoming freshmen at Fort Lewis College (FLC). You must be accepted to FLC as a full-time degree-seeking student, be a Colorado resident, and be a first-generation college student (neither parent earned a bachelor's degree). You will be required to submit the FAFSA. The award provides the amount of in-state tuition and mandatory fees and is renewable for a maximum of 10 terms of continuous attendance, not including summer. Award requirements change regularly. To receive an application and further instructions, please send a self-addressed, stamped envelope to the scholarship provider. No GPA requirement specified.

Fort Lewis College
Attn: Office of Financial Aid
101 Miller Student Ctr. - 1000 Rim Drive
Durango, CO 81301-3999

1715
Fort Lewis Alumni Scholarship

AMOUNT: $250 DEADLINE: April 14
MAJOR: All Fields of Study

The Fort Lewis Alumni Scholarship is open to students at Fort Lewis College (FLC). You must be the child or grandchild of an FLC alumnus and have a cumulative GPA of 2.7. Preference is given to students enrolled in at least 15 credit hours a term. The award provides between $250 and the amount of in-state tuition. Award requirements change regularly. To receive an application and further instructions, please send a self-addressed, stamped envelope to Daniel Ziesmer, Alumni Office, Admissions Building at Fort Lewis College. GPA must be 2.7-4.0.

Fort Lewis College
Attn: Office of Financial Aid
101 Miller Student Ctr. - 1000 Rim Drive
Durango, CO 81301-3999

1716
Garrett Family Scholarship

AMOUNT: $500 DEADLINE: April 14
MAJOR: All Fields of Study

The Garrett Family Scholarship is open to students at Fort Lewis College who transferred from Pueblo Community College, Southwest Branch. Award requirements change regularly. To receive an application and further instructions, please send a self-addressed, stamped envelope to Foundation Office, 109 Kroeger Building at Fort Lewis College; or call (970) 247-7425. No GPA requirement specified.

Fort Lewis College
Attn: Office of Financial Aid
101 Miller Student Ctr. - 1000 Rim Drive
Durango, CO 81301-3999

1717
Helen Kroeger-Faris Scholarship

AMOUNT: None Specified DEADLINE: April 14
MAJOR: All Fields of Study

The Helen Kroeger-Faris Scholarship is open to students at Fort Lewis College. Students must have the following cumulative GPAs: incoming freshmen - 2.0; sophomores - 2.5; juniors - 2.75; seniors - 3.0. You must be a graduate of any high school in the drainage area of the San Juan or Dolores River Basins in either Colorado or New Mexico. You must also complete 15 credit hours per term. The award provides the amount of in-state tuition and may be renewable. Award requirements change regularly. To receive an application and further instructions, please send a self-addressed, stamped envelope to the scholarship provider. GPA must be 2.0-4.0.

Fort Lewis College
Attn: Office of Financial Aid
101 Miller Student Ctr. - 1000 Rim Drive
Durango, CO 81301-3999

1718
Helen Sloan Daniels Scholarship

AMOUNT: Maximum: $400 DEADLINE: June 1
MAJOR: Southwest Studies

The Helen Sloan Daniels Scholarship is open to senior Southwest Studies majors at Fort Lewis College. You must be a full-time student and demonstrate academic promise. Award requirements change regularly. To receive an application and further instructions, please send a self-addressed, stamped envelope to Dr. Richard Ellis, Chair, Southwest Studies Department, 152 Sage Hall at Fort Lewis College. No GPA requirement specified.

Fort Lewis College
Attn: Office of Financial Aid
101 Miller Student Ctr. - 1000 Rim Drive
Durango, CO 81301-3999

1719
James Mark Jones Memorial Scholarship

AMOUNT: None Specified DEADLINE: April 14
MAJOR: All Fields of Study

The James Mark Jones Memorial Scholarship is open to students at Fort Lewis College. Award requirements change regularly. To receive information and an application, please send a self-addressed, stamped envelope to Foundation Office, 109 Kroeger Building at Fort Lewis College; or call (970) 247-7425. No GPA requirement specified.

Fort Lewis College
Attn: Office of Financial Aid
101 Miller Student Ctr. - 1000 Rim Drive
Durango, CO 81301-3999

1720
Jesse Brown Memorial Scholarship

AMOUNT: $500 DEADLINE: April 14
MAJOR: All Fields of Study

The Jesse Brown Memorial Scholarship is open to students at Fort Lewis College (FLC). You must be a Colorado resident. You must also be a member, or immediate family of a member, of the Colorado Timber Industry Association or an employee, or immediate family of an employee, of Koppers Industries. Preference is given to students who have completed a minimum of 32 credit hours at FLC. Award requirements change regularly. To receive an application and further instructions, please send a self-addressed, stamped envelope to Foundation Office, 109 Kroeger Building at Fort Lewis College; or call (970) 247-7425. No GPA requirement specified.

Fort Lewis College
Attn: Office of Financial Aid
101 Miller Student Ctr. - 1000 Rim Drive
Durango, CO 81301-3999

1721
Joan Sanders Memorial Scholarship

AMOUNT: None Specified DEADLINE: April 14
MAJOR: All Fields of Study

The Joan Sanders Memorial Scholarship is open to students at Fort Lewis College. Award requirements change regularly. To receive an application and further instructions, please send a self-addressed, stamped envelope to Foundation Office, 109 Kroeger Building at Fort Lewis College; or call (970) 247-7425. No GPA requirement specified.

Fort Lewis College
Attn: Office of Financial Aid
101 Miller Student Ctr. - 1000 Rim Drive
Durango, CO 81301-3999

1722
Julian H. Murphy Scholarship

AMOUNT: Maximum: $500 DEADLINE: April 14
MAJOR: All Fields of Study

The Julian H. Murphy Scholarship is open to students at Fort Lewis College (FLC) who have completed a minimum of 60 credit hours. You must have attended FLC the previous term and have a cumulative GPA of 3.0. Preference will be given to students who have shown academic improvement. Award requirements change regularly. To receive an application and further instructions, please send a self-addressed, stamped envelope to the scholarship provider. GPA must be 3.0-4.0.

Fort Lewis College
Attn: Office of Financial Aid
101 Miller Student Ctr. - 1000 Rim Drive
Durango, CO 81301-3999

1723
La Plata Electric Scholarship

AMOUNT: None Specified DEADLINE: April 14
MAJOR: Accounting, Business, Management, Engineering, Related Fields

The La Plata Electric Scholarship is open to students at Fort Lewis College. You must select a major that leads to a career in the Rural Co-op Electric Association, such as accounting, business, management, engineering, or related fields. The scholarship is renewable provided you complete 15 credit hours per term and maintain a 2.0 GPA in the first year of the award, a 2.5 GPA in the second year, and a 3.0 GPA in the third and fourth years. The award is valued at the amount of in-state tuition and books. Award requirements change regularly. To receive an application and further instructions, please send a self-addressed, stamped envelope to Foundation Office, 109 Kroeger Building at Fort Lewis College; call (970) 247-7425; or contact Jeannie Bennett at La Plata Electric Association. No GPA requirement specified.

Fort Lewis College
Attn: Office of Financial Aid
101 Miller Student Ctr. - 1000 Rim Drive
Durango, CO 81301-3999

1724
LeRoy Goodwin Scholarship

AMOUNT: None Specified DEADLINE: April 14
MAJOR: Political Science, Government, Law, Political Theory

The LeRoy Goodwin Scholarship is open to students at Fort Lewis College who demonstrate an interest in politics, public opinion, government, law, and political theory. You do not have to be a political science major. You must have a minimum 3.0 GPA. Award requirements change regularly. To receive an application and further instructions, please send a self-addressed, stamped envelope to Foundation Office, 109 Kroeger Building at Fort Lewis College; or call (970) 247-7425.

Fort Lewis College
Attn: Office of Financial Aid
101 Miller Student Ctr. - 1000 Rim Drive
Durango, CO 81301-3999

1725
MaryMaureen Katheryn Anderson Scholarship

AMOUNT: $500 DEADLINE: April 14
MAJOR: All Fields of Study

The MaryMaureen Katheryn Anderson Scholarship is open to all class levels of students at Fort Lewis College (FLC). You must have pressing economic need and high moral character. You will be required to submit a FAFSA and a faculty/staff recommendation. Award requirements change regularly. To receive an application and further instructions, please send a self-addressed, stamped envelope to Foundation Office, 109 Kroeger Building at Fort Lewis College; call (970) 247-7425; or apply online at the FLC website: www.fortlewis.edu. No GPA requirement specified.

Fort Lewis College
Attn: Office of Financial Aid
101 Miller Student Ctr. - 1000 Rim Drive
Durango, CO 81301-3999

1726
Michael Bodo Trust Scholarship

AMOUNT: Maximum: $1000 DEADLINE: April 14
MAJOR: All Fields of Study

The Michael Bodo Trust Scholarship is open to students at Fort Lewis College (FLC). Preference is given to those whose recent grades indicate an improvement. You must have a 2.0 cumulative GPA and not be eligible for need-based financial aid. You will be required to submit a FAFSA. Award requirements change regularly. To receive an application and further instructions, please send a self-addressed, stamped envelope to the scholarship provider; or apply online at the FLC website: www.fortlewis.edu. GPA must be 2.0-4.0.

Fort Lewis College
Attn: Office of Financial Aid
101 Miller Student Ctr. - 1000 Rim Drive
Durango, CO 81301-3999

1727
Nora Horan Leadership Award

AMOUNT: $1000 DEADLINE: April 14
MAJOR: Business

The Nora Horan Leadership Award is open to seniors at Fort Lewis College who intend to graduate within one calendar year. Preference is given to students studying business who meet the following additional criteria (listed in order of importance for consideration): you must have overcome or currently be overcoming a major obstacle in obtaining your degree; you must have a cumulative 3.0 GPA; you must demonstrate campus leadership. Award requirements change regularly. To receive an application and further instructions, please send a self-addressed, stamped envelope to Foundation Office, 109 Kroeger Building at Fort Lewis College; or call (970) 247-7425. GPA must be 3.0-4.0.

Fort Lewis College
Attn: Office of Financial Aid
101 Miller Student Ctr. - 1000 Rim Drive
Durango, CO 81301-3999

1728
Old Fort Special Scholarship

AMOUNT: $250 DEADLINE: April 14
MAJOR: All Fields of Study

The Old Fort Special Scholarship is open to students at Fort Lewis College (FLC) who are children or grandchildren of FLC alumni. Preference is given to children and grandchildren of Old Fort Alumni who have completed 30 credit hours at the time of application. The scholarship amount varies from $250 to the cost of in-state tuition. Award requirements change regularly. To receive an application and further instructions, please send a self-addressed, stamped envelope to Foundation Office, 109 Kroeger Building at Fort Lewis College; or call (970) 247-7425. No GPA requirement specified.

Fort Lewis College
Attn: Office of Financial Aid
101 Miller Student Ctr. - 1000 Rim Drive
Durango, CO 81301-3999

1729
Performing Arts Scholarship for Art

AMOUNT: None Specified DEADLINE: Varies
MAJOR: Art

The Performing Arts Scholarship for Art is open to full-time degree-seeking students at Fort Lewis College. You must be a declared art major, have a 3.0 cumulative GPA, and have completed a minimum of 45 credit hours. You must also provide a portfolio of eight to ten art works from college-level courses. The award provides the approximate value of in-state tuition. Award requirements change regularly. To receive an application and further instructions, please send a self-addressed, stamped envelope to Mark Reber, Art Department, Room 101 Art Building at Fort Lewis College. GPA must be 3.0-4.0.

Fort Lewis College
Attn: Office of Financial Aid
101 Miller Student Ctr. - 1000 Rim Drive
Durango, CO 81301-3999

1730
Presidential Scholarship

AMOUNT: $1500 DEADLINE: Varies
MAJOR: All Fields of Study

The Presidential Scholarship is open to first-time freshmen at Fort Lewis College (FLC). You must have a 3.5 cumulative high school GPA. Rank in class and test scores are also considered. Preference will be given to Colorado residents, although a small number of awards are reserved for students paying non-resident tuition. The award is not renewable. Award requirements change regularly. There is no scholarship application. Your application for admission is automatically screened to determine if you meet the qualifications. Students admitted to FLC by the end of April receive first consideration. GPA must be 3.5-4.0.

Fort Lewis College
Attn: Office of Financial Aid
101 Miller Student Ctr. - 1000 Rim Drive
Durango, CO 81301-3999

1731
Ronnie Thomas Anthropology Memorial Term Fund

AMOUNT: $200-$500 DEADLINE: April 7
MAJOR: Anthropology

The Ronnie Thomas Anthropology Memorial Term Fund is open to full-time degree-seeking students at Fort Lewis College. You must be enrolled in at least 12 credit hours, have a 3.0 cumulative GPA, and have earned a minimum of 45 credit hours, including at least 16 credit hours of anthropology coursework. Award requirements change regularly. To receive an application and further instructions, please send a self-addressed, stamped envelope to David Kozak, Anthropology Club, Room 134 Hesperus Hall at Fort Lewis College. GPA must be 3.0-4.0.

Fort Lewis College
Attn: Office of Financial Aid
101 Miller Student Ctr. - 1000 Rim Drive
Durango, CO 81301-3999

1732
Sandy Heizer Memorial Scholarship

AMOUNT: $300 DEADLINE: Varies
MAJOR: English

The Sandy Heizer Memorial Scholarship is open to junior and senior English majors at Fort Lewis College. You must have completed a minimum of 60 credit hours and have a 3.0 cumulative GPA. Award requirements change regularly. No application is required. English Department faculty selects scholarship recipients. GPA must be 3.0-4.0.

Fort Lewis College
Attn: Office of Financial Aid
101 Miller Student Ctr. - 1000 Rim Drive
Durango, CO 81301-3999

1733
Scarlet Letters Scholarship

AMOUNT: $300 DEADLINE: Varies
MAJOR: English

The Scarlet Letters Scholarship is open to full-time students at Fort Lewis College. You must have completed a minimum of 12 credit hours, have a 3.0 cumulative GPA, and be a member of the Scarlet Letters Club. Award requirements change regularly. No application is required. English Department faculty selects scholarship recipients. Students with questions should contact Paul Pavich, English Department, 239 Noble Hall at Fort Lewis College. GPA must be 3.0-4.0.

Fort Lewis College
Attn: Office of Financial Aid
101 Miller Student Ctr. - 1000 Rim Drive
Durango, CO 81301-3999

1734
Suzanne Jones Memorial Scholarship

AMOUNT: $200 DEADLINE: April 14
MAJOR: All Fields of Study

The Suzanne Jones Memorial Scholarship is open to students at Fort Lewis College who have a minimum cumulative GPA of 2.5. Award requirements change regularly. To receive an application and further instructions, please send a self-addressed, stamped envelope to Foundation Office, 109 Kroeger Building at Fort Lewis College; or call (970) 247-7425. GPA must be 2.5-4.0.

Fort Lewis College
Attn: Office of Financial Aid
101 Miller Student Ctr. - 1000 Rim Drive
Durango, CO 81301-3999

Full Sail Real World Education

1735
Full Sail Real World Education Digital Media Scholarship

AMOUNT: None Specified DEADLINE: Varies
MAJOR: Digital Media

The Full Sail Real World Education Digital Media Scholarship is open to Florida residents attending or planning to attend the Full Sail Real World Education who are studying digital media. Applications are available at Florida high schools and GED testing centers. Award requirements change regularly. For further information, please send a self-addressed, stamped envelope to Full Sail Real World Education, Sharon R. Griffith, Assistant Director of Financial Aid, 3300 University Boulevard, Winter Park, FL 32792, or you could call (407) 679-6333. No GPA requirement specified.

Florida Association of Postsecondary Schools and Colleges
Attn: FAPSC Scholarship Committee
F200 West College Avenue
Tallahassee, FL 32301

1736

Full Sail Real World Education Film and Video Scholarship

AMOUNT: None Specified DEADLINE: Varies
MAJOR: Film and Video

The Full Sail Real World Education Film and Video Scholarship is open to Florida residents attending or planning to attend the Full Sail Real World Education who are studying film and video. Applications are available at Florida high schools and GED testing centers. Award requirements change regularly. For further information, please send a self-addressed, stamped envelope to Full Sail Real World Education, Sharon R. Griffith, Assistant Director of Financial Aid, 3300 University Boulevard, Winter Park, FL 32792, or you could call (407) 679-6333. No GPA requirement specified.

Florida Association of Postsecondary Schools and Colleges
Attn: FAPSC Scholarship Committee
F200 West College Avenue
Tallahassee, FL 32301

1737

Full Sail Real World Education Recording Arts Scholarship

AMOUNT: None Specified DEADLINE: Varies
MAJOR: Recording Arts

The Full Sail Real World Education Recording Arts Scholarship is open to Florida residents attending or planning to attend the Full Sail Real World Education who are studying recording arts. Applications are available at Florida high schools and GED testing centers. Award requirements change regularly. For further information, please send a self-addressed, stamped envelope to Full Sail Real World Education, Sharon R. Griffith, Assistant Director of Financial Aid, 3300 University Boulevard, Winter Park, FL 32792, or you could call (407) 679-6333. No GPA requirement specified.

Florida Association of Postsecondary Schools and Colleges
Attn: FAPSC Scholarship Committee
F200 West College Avenue
Tallahassee, FL 32301

Furman University

1738

Alden Pre-Engineering Scholarship

AMOUNT: None Specified DEADLINE: February 1
MAJOR: Pre-Engineering

This award is open to entering freshmen who are enrolled in the pre-engineering program. Award requirements change regularly. Please write to the address provided for more information or consult the website at www.furman.edu. No GPA requirement specified.

Furman University
Admissions Office
3300 Poinsett Hwy
Greenville, SC 29613-0002

1739

Dow Chemical Company Foundation and Dreyfus Foundation Scholarships

AMOUNT: None Specified DEADLINE: February 1
MAJOR: Chemistry

This award is open to students who are planning a career in the chemical industry or planning to pursue a Ph.D. in chemistry. Award requirements change regularly. Please write to the address below for more information or consult the website at www.furman.edu. No GPA requirement specified.

Furman University
Admissions Office
3300 Poinsett Hwy
Greenville, SC 29613-0002

1740

Furman Teacher Education Scholarship

AMOUNT: None Specified DEADLINE: February 1
MAJOR: Education

This award is open to entering freshmen who have indicated teaching as their career goal. Award requirements change regularly. Please write to the address below for more information or consult the website at www.furman.edu. No GPA requirement specified.

Furman University
Admissions Office
3300 Poinsett Hwy
Greenville, SC 29613-0002

1741

Liberty Scholarship

AMOUNT: None Specified DEADLINE: February 1
MAJOR: Business, Economics, Computer Science

This scholarship is open to entering freshmen who intend to major in business, economics, or computer science. Award requirements change regularly. Please write to the address provided for more information or consult the website at www.furman.edu. No GPA requirement specified.

Furman University
Admissions Office
3300 Poinsett Hwy
Greenville, SC 29613-0002

1742

Wylie Math Scholarship

AMOUNT: None Specified DEADLINE: February 1
MAJOR: Math, All Areas of Study

This scholarship is open to entering freshmen who have outstanding mathematical ability and a combined SAT score of at least 1300. Award requirements change regularly. Please write to the address provided for more information or consult the website at www.furman.edu. No GPA requirement specified.

Furman University
Admissions Office
3300 Poinsett Hwy
Greenville, SC 29613-0002

Georgia Military College

1743
Georgia Military College State Service Scholarship

AMOUNT: None Specified DEADLINE: February 1
MAJOR: All Fields of Study

The Georgia Military College State Service Scholarship is open to high school graduates interested in a military career. To be considered for this scholarship you must be a Georgia resident planning to attend Georgia Military College in Milledgeville and be nominated by a member of the General Assembly who represents a district within the U.S. congressional district where you reside. You must also have at least a 2.5 GPA, a minimum 800 combined SAT score, and successfully meet the mental and physical health standard required for enlistment in the Georgia National Guard. The award provides full tuition, fees, room and board, books, and supplies and requires a commitment of service, upon graduation, in the Georgia National Guard. Award requirements change regularly. Please send a self-addressed, stamped envelope to receive your application and any further instructions from the scholarship provider or phone (770) 724-9040. GPA must be 2.5-4.0.

Georgia Student Finance Commission
Attn: Scholarships and Grants Division
2082 East Exchange Place
Tucker, GA 30084

Gonzaga University

1744
Charlotte Y. Martin Scholarship

AMOUNT: Maximum: $20000 DEADLINE: February 1
MAJOR: All Areas of Study

This scholarship is open to graduating Montana high school seniors who will be attending Gonzaga University. You must complete the Application for Admission to Gonzaga and the Charlotte Y. Martin Scholarship application by the deadline listed. Also, you must have a minimum 3.5 GPA; demonstrate academic achievement; be involved in your school and community; submit one recommendation from a high school teacher, counselor, or administrator; and submit an essay of not more than two pages explaining how your outlook on life has been shaped by your community. Award requirements change regularly. GPA must be 3.5-4.0.

Gonzaga University
Office of Admission
Spokane, WA 99258-0102

1745
Christopher M. West Memorial Scholarship

AMOUNT: None Specified DEADLINE: February 1
MAJOR: All Areas of Study

This scholarship is open to full-time incoming degree-seeking freshmen to Gonzaga University who are Spokane County, WA, residents. In order to apply, you must demonstrate humanitarianism through membership in honorary service clubs, participate in community service, organizations, exhibit unusual individual humanitarian interests or deeds, and submit two letters of recommendation from individuals who can speak about your ideals, community involvement, and character. You must be a resident of Spokane County, WA. Award requirements change regularly. No GPA requirement specified.

Gonzaga University
Christopher M. West Scholarship Committee
AD Box 72
Spokane, WA 99258

1746
Dauna Leigh Bauer Scholarship

AMOUNT: $2000-$8000 DEADLINE: February 1
MAJOR: All Areas of Study

This scholarship is open to full-time incoming freshmen at Gonzaga University who can demonstrate financial need. You will be required to submit an application for financial aid and a one-page essay describing your career goals and how you might use your goals to contribute to society. The donor has directed that preference be given to students who will consider repaying the amount of the scholarship to the University. This is so the University can award similar scholarships to other students after you have been established in your career or occupation. Award requirements change regularly. No GPA requirement specified.

Gonzaga University - Admissions Office
Dauna Leigh Bauer Scholarship
AD Box 64
Spokane, WA 99258

1747
Gonzaga University Diversity Scholarship

AMOUNT: Maximum: $10000 DEADLINE: February 1
MAJOR: All Areas of Study

This scholarship is open to graduating high school seniors who will be attending Gonzaga University. You must complete the Application for Admission to Gonzaga and the Diversity Scholarship application by the deadline listed. Also, you must have a minimum 3.0 GPA; demonstrate academic achievement; be involved in your school and community; submit one recommendation from a high school teacher, counselor, or administrator; and submit a one-page essay which describes an experience you had working or otherwise interacting with someone of a different race and how the experience affected you. Award requirements change regularly. GPA must be 3.0-4.0.

Gonzaga University
Office of Admission
Spokane, WA 99258-0102

1748
Joseph C. Metcalfe Memorial Scholarship

AMOUNT: None Specified DEADLINE: February 1
MAJOR: All Areas of Study

This scholarship symbolizes and respects the wishes of students with disabilities who choose to pursue an education at Gonzaga University, and encourages these students to develop their talents and personalities. You will be selected as a scholarship recipient based on demonstrating financial need and maintaining a minimum 2.0 GPA. You must have a physical disability and use the scholarship for tuition payment only. The scholarship will be evenly divided among the fall and spring semesters. Please submit two letters of recommendation with your application. Award requirements change regularly. GPA must be 2.0-4.0.

Gonzaga University - Admissions Office
Associate Director of Financial Aid
AD Box 72
Spokane, WA 99258

1749
Joseph M. Cataldo, S.J., Scholarship

AMOUNT: Maximum: $20000 DEADLINE: February 1
MAJOR: All Areas of Study

This scholarship is open to graduating high school seniors who attend Catholic high schools and will be attending Gonzaga University. You must complete the Application for Admission to Gonzaga University and the Joseph M. Cataldo Scholarship application by the deadline listed. In order to apply, you must also meet the following criteria: have a minimum 3.5 GPA; demonstrate academic achievement; be involved in your school and community; and submit one recommendation from a high school teacher, counselor, or administrator. An additional requirement is that you submit an essay (no more than one page) on a topic concerning an area of the world where religious persecution has taken place, or is taking place, and the resultant issues that surround this. Award requirements change regularly. GPA must be 3.5-4.0.

Gonzaga University
Office of Admission
Spokane, WA 99258

Herzing College of Business and Technology

1750
Herzing Computer Information System Technology Scholarship (Orlando)

AMOUNT: None Specified DEADLINE: Varies
MAJOR: Computer Information System Technology

The Herzing Computer Information System Technology Scholarship (Orlando) is open to Florida residents attending or planning to attend the Herzing College of Business and Technology - Orlando Campus who are studying computer information system technology. Applications are available at Florida high schools and GED testing centers. Award requirements change regularly. For further information, please send a self-addressed, stamped envelope to Herzing College of Business and Technology - Orlando Campus, Ron Rountree, Director, 1300 North Semoran Boulevard, Suite 103, Orlando, FL 32807, or you could call (407) 380-6315. No GPA requirement specified.

Florida Association of Postsecondary Schools and Colleges
Attn: FAPSC Scholarship Committee
F200 West College Avenue
Tallahassee, FL 32301

1751
Herzing Institute Business Administration Scholarship (Melbourne)

AMOUNT: None Specified DEADLINE: Varies
MAJOR: Business Administration

The Herzing Institute Business Administration Scholarship (Melbourne) is open to Florida residents attending or planning to attend the Herzing College of Business and Technology - Melbourne Campus who are studying business administration. Applications are available at Florida high schools and GED testing centers. Award requirements change regularly. For further information, please send a self-addressed, stamped envelope to Herzing College of Business and Technology - Melbourne Campus, Darlene Wohl, Director, 1270 North Wickham Road, Suite 51, Melbourne, FL 32935, or you could call (407) 255-9232. No GPA requirement specified.

Florida Association of Postsecondary Schools and Colleges
Attn: FAPSC Scholarship Committee
F200 West College Avenue
Tallahassee, FL 32301

Holy Names College

1752
President's Scholarships

AMOUNT: None Specified DEADLINE: March 2
MAJOR: All Areas of Study

This scholarship is open to entering freshmen with a minimum 3.0 GPA. Selections are based on academics and your contributions to school or the community and is renewable if you maintain a minimum 3.0 GPA and complete at least 30 units each academic year. Award requirements change regularly. GPA must be 3.0-4.0.

Holy Names College
Financial Aid Office
3500 Mountain Blvd
Oakland, CA 94619-1627

1753
Regent's Scholarships

AMOUNT: None Specified DEADLINE: March 2
MAJOR: All Areas of Study

This scholarship is open to entering freshmen and transfer students at Holy Names College who have a minimum 3.5 GPA. The award is based on academics, leadership, and contributions to your school or community and is renewable if you maintain a minimum GPA of 3.0 and complete a minimum of 30 units each academic year. Awards are 100% of tuition for students living on campus and up to 75% of tuition for students living off campus. Award requirements change regularly. GPA must be 3.5-4.0.

Holy Names College
Financial Aid Office
3500 Mountain Blvd
Oakland, CA 94619-1627

Hope International University

1754
Bible Bowl Scholarship

AMOUNT: None Specified DEADLINE: March 2
MAJOR: All Fields of Study

The Bible Bowl Scholarship is open to students who plan to attend Hope International University. To be considered for this award, you must participate in a preaching competition. If you finish on the first-place team, you are eligible for 50% of tuition; if you are on the second-place team, you are eligible for 25% of tuition. The award is granted according to the Bible Bowl results at the annual North American Christian Convention. Award requirements change regularly. No GPA requirement specified.

Hope International University
Attn: Financial Aid
2500 E. Nutwood Avenue
Fullerton, CA 92831

1755
Family Tuition Grant

AMOUNT: None Specified DEADLINE: March 2
MAJOR: All Areas of Study

The Family Tuition Grant is open to families having two or more dependents enrolled full-time at Hope International University. The award is for up to 12.5% of tuition costs per student. It is renewable, though an application and documentation must be submitted each year. Award requirements change regularly. No GPA requirement specified.

Hope International University
Attn: Financial Aid
2500 E. Nutwood Avenue
Fullerton, CA 92831

1756
Minister's Dependent Tuition Grant

AMOUNT: None Specified DEADLINE: March 2
MAJOR: All Areas of Study

The Minister's Dependent Tuition Grant is open to students whose parent or parents are full-time paid ministers in a church. Verification is required. The grant is renewable at the dollar amount initially granted, though a new application and documentation must be submitted each year. You may receive up to 25% of HIU's tuition costs. Award requirements change regularly. No GPA requirement specified.

Hope International University
Attn: Financial Aid
2500 E. Nutwood Avenue
Fullerton, CA 92831

1757
Missionary Dependent Tuition Grant

AMOUNT: None Specified DEADLINE: March 2
MAJOR: All Areas of Study

The Missionary Dependent Tuition Grant is open to students whose parent or parents are missionaries. Verification is required. The grant is renewable at the dollar amount initially granted, though a new application and documentation must be submitted each year. You may receive up to 25% of HIU's tuition costs. Award requirements change regularly. No GPA requirement specified.

Hope International University
Attn: Financial Aid
2500 E. Nutwood Avenue
Fullerton, CA 92831

1758
New and Continuing Student Tuition Grant

AMOUNT: $300-$2100 DEADLINE: March 2
MAJOR: All Fields of Study

The New and Continuing Student Tuition Grant is open to students who plan to attend Hope International University. To be considered for this award, you must demonstrate financial need and have a high GPA. Awards are made to eligible applicants as funds are available. Award requirements change regularly. No GPA requirement specified.

Hope International University
Attn: Financial Aid
2500 E. Nutwood Avenue
Fullerton, CA 92831

1759
Presidential Scholarship for Academic Achievement

AMOUNT: None Specified DEADLINE: March 2
MAJOR: All Fields of Study

The Presidential Scholarship for Academic Achievement is open to new freshman students who plan to attend Hope International University. The amount of the award will be in direct correlation to your standardized test scores, where the higher your score, the greater the amount of money you are eligible to receive, up to 75% of tuition. The award is renewable for up to four years, provided you maintain a minimum 3.25 GPA. Award requirements change regularly. No GPA requirement specified.

Hope International University
Attn: Financial Aid
2500 E. Nutwood Avenue
Fullerton, CA 92831

1760
Presidential Scholarship with Honors

AMOUNT: None Specified DEADLINE: March 2
MAJOR: All Fields of Study

The Presidential Scholarship with Honors is open to students who plan to attend Hope International University. To be considered for this award, you must demonstrate leadership, excellence in the classroom, and involvement in your church or community. The award requires you to have a minimum 3.0 GPA. It is renewable for up to four years, provided you maintain a minimum 3.0 GPA. Award requirements change regularly. GPA must be 3.0-4.0.

Hope International University
Attn: Financial Aid
2500 E. Nutwood Avenue
Fullerton, CA 92831

1761
Sealbearer's Scholarship

AMOUNT: Maximum: $200 DEADLINE: March 2
MAJOR: All Fields of Study

The Sealbearer's Scholarship is open to students who plan to attend Hope International University. To be considered for this award, you must supply a copy of your high school diploma showing the Sealbearer's Seal from the California Scholarship Federation. The award is renewable, provided you maintain continuous full-time enrollment and a minimum 3.0 GPA. Award requirements change regularly. No GPA requirement specified.

Hope International University
Attn: Financial Aid
2500 E. Nutwood Avenue
Fullerton, CA 92831

1762
Senior Citizen Tuition Grant

AMOUNT: None Specified DEADLINE: March 2
MAJOR: All Areas of Study

The Senior Citizen Tuition Grant is open to students who are age 55 and older. To be considered for this award, you must be either retired or unemployed and enrolled in the traditional on-campus program. The award requires that you submit a driver's license the first year of the grant. If you are between the ages of 55 and 61, you are eligible for 50% of tuition costs; if you are age 62 or over, you are eligible for 100%. Award requirements change regularly. No GPA requirement specified.

Hope International University
Attn: Financial Aid
2500 E. Nutwood Avenue
Fullerton, CA 92831

Houston Community College

1763
George Foundation Scholarship

AMOUNT: None Specified DEADLINE: May 14
MAJOR: All Areas of Study

This award is for students planning to attend the Houston Community College System (any campus) during the academic year. Students must be Fort Bend residents who are graduating high school seniors, new students, or returning HCCS students. Returning HCCS students must have a 2.0 GPA. Award requirements change regularly. The application is available at the HCCS Southwest College Stafford Campus Counseling Office, Room 108N. The phone number for this office is (713) 718-6711. You may also write the address provided for further information. No GPA requirement specified.

George Foundation
HCCS Southwest College Counseling Office
1014 Cash Road
Stafford, TX 77477-4408

Huron State University

1764
Huron State University Scholarship

AMOUNT: $1500 DEADLINE: July 15
MAJOR: All Areas of Study

Huron State University will offer $1,500 scholarships to the first 200 South Dakota applicants. Available to new full-time students enrolling as freshmen or as transfer students planning to live in the dormitories. Each scholarship will be applied against the cost of a double occupancy room for the 2001-2002 academic year. To be eligible for the scholarship, a student must complete the enrollment process before the July 15 deadline. Award requirements change regularly. Please send a self-addressed, stamped envelope to receive your application and for any further instructions from the scholarship provider. No GPA requirement specified.

Huron State University
Admissions Office
333 Ninth Street SW
Huron, SD 57350

Illinois Institute of Technology

1765
Heald Scholarship

AMOUNT: $10000 DEADLINE: Varies
MAJOR: All Majors at Illinois Institute of Technology (IIT)

The Heald Scholarship is open to first-time freshmen entering IIT for full-time undergraduate studies in one of the following majors: architecture, engineering (aerospace, architectural, chemical, civil, computer, electrical, environmental, mechanical, metallurgical, and materials), computer science, biology, chemistry, computer information systems, mathematics, molecular biochemistry and biophysics, physics, political science, professional and technical communication, or psychology. To be considered for this award, you must have a minimum 3.5 GPA, at least a 29 ACT or 1280 SAT, rank in the top 25% of your graduating class, and submit a completed application for undergraduate admission. This award provides $10,000 a year for four years, or five years if you are a student in the College of Architecture. Award requirements change regularly. There is no separate scholarship application for this award. Freshmen admitted to IIT will automatically be considered. IIT admits students and awards this scholarship on a rolling basis. To receive an application for undergraduate admission, please write to the address provided. GPA must be 3.5-4.0.

Illinois Institute of Technology
Office of Admission - 101 Perlstein Hall
10 West 33rd Street
Chicago, IL 60616

1766
Transfer Tuition Scholarship

AMOUNT: $2000-$6000 DEADLINE: Varies
MAJOR: All Majors at Illinois Institute of Technology (IIT)

The Transfer Tuition Scholarship is open to transfer students entering IIT for full-time undergraduate studies in one of the following majors: architecture, engineering (aerospace, architectural, chemical, civil, computer, electrical, environmental, mechanical, metallurgical, and materials), computer science, biology, chemistry, computer information systems, mathematics, molecular biochemistry and biophysics, physics, political science, professional and technical communication, or psychology. To be eligible for this award, you must be a U.S. citizen or permanent resident, have a minimum 3.0 GPA, and submit a completed application for transfer admission. This award provides $2000 to $6000 an academic year for the time required to complete your undergraduate degree. Award requirements change regularly. There is no separate scholarship application for this award. Transfer students admitted to IIT will automatically be considered. To receive an application for transfer admission, please write to the address provided. The recommended deadlines for admission are July 1 for the fall semester and November 1 for the spring semester. GPA must be 3.0-4.0.

Illinois Institute of Technology
Office of Admission - 101 Perlstein Hall
10 West 33rd Street
Chicago, IL 60616

Illinois Valley Community College

1767
Albino Bruno Memorial Scholarship

AMOUNT: $300 DEADLINE: March 19
MAJOR: All Fields of Study

The Albino Bruno Memorial Scholarship is open to full-time students at Illinois Valley Community College. To be considered for this award, you must be an IVCC District resident and have a minimum 3.0 GPA. Award requirements change regularly. Please send a self-addressed, stamped envelope to receive your application and any further instructions from the scholarship provider. These materials are available after December 1. GPA must be 3.0-4.0.

Illinois Valley Community College
Attn: Financial Aid Office
815 North Orlando Smith Avenue
Oglesby, IL 61348

1768
Barbara Hoover Hammerich Memorial Scholarship

AMOUNT: $500 DEADLINE: March 19
MAJOR: Education (Elementary, Secondary)

The Barbara Hoover Hammerich Memorial Scholarship is open to full-time students at Illinois Valley Community College. To be considered for this award, you must be a life-long IVCC District resident, be a sophomore student planning a career in elementary or secondary education, and have a minimum 3.0 GPA. Award requirements change regularly. Please send a self-addressed, stamped envelope to receive your application and any further instructions from the scholarship provider. These materials are available after December 1. GPA must be 3.0-4.0.

Illinois Valley Community College
Attn: Financial Aid Office
815 North Orlando Smith Avenue
Oglesby, IL 61348

1769
Carol Korter Nursing Scholarship

AMOUNT: $500 DEADLINE: march 19
MAJOR: Nursing

The Carol Korter Nursing Scholarship is open to students at Illinois Valley Community College. To be considered for this award, you must have formal admission into the IVCC nursing program (RN or LPN) and have demonstrated volunteer service in the community. In order to receive the full award, you must be enrolled in at least eight hours per semester. Award requirements change regularly. Please send a self-addressed, stamped envelope to receive your application and any further instructions from the scholarship provider. These materials are available after December 1. No GPA requirement specified.

Illinois Valley Community College
Attn: Financial Aid Office
815 North Orlando Smith Avenue
Oglesby, IL 61348

1770
Cellular One/Jacquelyn Margis Scholarship

AMOUNT: $300 DEADLINE: March 19
MAJOR: All Fields of Study

The Cellular One/Jacquelyn Margis Scholarship is open to full-time students at Illinois Valley Community College. To be considered for this award, you must be a single mother and an IVCC District resident. Award requirements change regularly. Please send a self-addressed, stamped envelope to receive your application and any further instructions from the scholarship provider. These materials are available after December 1. No GPA requirement specified.

Illinois Valley Community College
Attn: Financial Aid Office
815 North Orlando Smith Avenue
Oglesby, IL 61348

1771
Clifton Gunderson Accounting Scholarship

AMOUNT: $500 DEADLINE: March 19
MAJOR: Accounting

The Clifton Gunderson Accounting Scholarship is open to full-time students at Illinois Valley Community College. To be considered for this award, you must be an accounting student graduating with an Associate's degree at the end of the

upcoming fall or spring semester, have attended IVCC for a year prior to graduation, and be an IVCC District resident. Your application will be evaluated on the basis of scholarship ability, leadership, and extracurricular activities. Award requirements change regularly. Please send a self-addressed, stamped envelope to receive your application and any further instructions from the scholarship provider. These materials are available after December 1. No GPA requirement specified.

Illinois Valley Community College
Attn: Financial Aid Office
815 North Orlando Smith Avenue
Oglesby, IL 61348

1772
D. Russell Sheedy Memorial Scholarship

AMOUNT: $700 DEADLINE: March 19
MAJOR: All Fields of Study

The D. Russell Sheedy Memorial Scholarship is open to students at Illinois Valley Community College. To be considered for this award, you must have earned a GED from IVCC and received a score of at least 242. Students do not have to be enrolled full-time. Award requirements change regularly. Please send a self-addressed, stamped envelope to receive your application and any further instructions from the scholarship provider. These materials are available after December 1. No GPA requirement specified.

Illinois Valley Community College
Attn: Financial Aid Office
815 North Orlando Smith Avenue
Oglesby, IL 61348

1773
Donna Jo Adrian Memorial Scholarship

AMOUNT: $275 DEADLINE: March 19
MAJOR: Art

The Donna Jo Adrian Memorial Scholarship is open to full-time art students at Illinois Valley Community College. To be considered for this award, you must be a returning sophomore student, be an IVCC District resident, and have at least a 3.0 GPA. Award requirements change regularly. To receive an application and any further information, please contact Mr. David Bergsieker at (815) 224-2720, ext. 342, or Ms. Dana Collins at (815) 224-2720, ext. 351. GPA must be 3.0-4.0.

Illinois Valley Community College
Attn: Financial Aid Office
815 North Orlando Smith Avenue
Oglesby, IL 61348

1774
Duguid-Muhich Theater Scholarship

AMOUNT: $200 DEADLINE: March 19
MAJOR: Theater

The Duguid-Muhich Theater Scholarship is open to full-time students at Illinois Valley Community College. To be considered for this award, you must be an entering or enrolled IVCC theater student (performance or technical); have a 3.0 GPA;

and provide an audition, resume, or portfolio review of previous theater involvement and all theater-related experience. Award requirements change regularly. To receive an application and any further information, please contact Mr. David Kuester in the IVCC Theater Department at (815) 224-2720, ext. 352. GPA must be 3.0-4.0.

Illinois Valley Community College
Attn: Financial Aid Office
815 North Orlando Smith Avenue
Oglesby, IL 61348

Frances Rabenstein Memorial Scholarship

AMOUNT: $200 DEADLINE: March 19
MAJOR: Theater

The Frances Rabenstein Memorial Scholarship is open to entering freshmen at Illinois Valley Community College. To be considered for this award, you must be a full-time theater student and provide an audition, resume, or portfolio review of previous theater involvement and all theater-related experience. Award requirements change regularly. To receive an application and any further information, please contact Mr. David Kuester in the IVCC Theater Department at (815) 224-2720, ext. 352. No GPA requirement specified.

Illinois Valley Community College
Attn: Financial Aid Office
815 North Orlando Smith Avenue
Oglesby, IL 61348

1776
Frank H. and Marion L. Costello Memorial Scholarship

AMOUNT: $400 DEADLINE: March 19
MAJOR: All Fields of Study

The Frank H. and Marion L. Costello Memorial Scholarship is open to full-time students at Illinois Valley Community College. Award requirements change regularly. Please send a self-addressed, stamped envelope to receive your application and any further instructions from the scholarship provider. These materials are available after December 1. No GPA requirement specified.

Illinois Valley Community College
Attn: Financial Aid Office
815 North Orlando Smith Avenue
Oglesby, IL 61348

1777
GED Scholarship

AMOUNT: None Specified DEADLINE: March 19
MAJOR: All Fields of Study

The GED Scholarship is open to full-time students at Illinois Valley Community College. To be considered for this award, you must be an IVCC GED graduate with a score of at least 300 on the GED examination. Award requirements change regularly. To receive an application and any further information, please contact Ms. Lynn Reha at (815) 224-2720, ext. 345. No GPA requirement specified.

Illinois Valley Community College

Attn: Financial Aid Office
815 North Orlando Smith Avenue
Oglesby, IL 61348

1778
Gladys Koehler Memorial Scholarship for Journalism

AMOUNT: $150 DEADLINE: March 19
MAJOR: All Fields of Study - For Students with an Interest or Background in Journalism

The Gladys Koehler Memorial Scholarship for Journalism is open to full-time students at Illinois Valley Community College. To be considered for this award, you must be an entering freshman, be an IVCC District resident, and have a minimum 3.0 GPA. Award requirements change regularly. Please send a self-addressed, stamped envelope to receive your application and any further instructions from the scholarship provider. These materials are available after December 1. GPA must be 3.0-4.0.

Illinois Valley Community College
Attn: Financial Aid Office
815 North Orlando Smith Avenue
Oglesby, IL 61348

1779
Harry L. Wilmot Memorial Scholarship

AMOUNT: $200 DEADLINE: March 19
MAJOR: All Fields of Study

The Harry L. Wilmot Memorial Scholarship is open to full-time students at Illinois Valley Community College. To be considered for this award, you must be an IVCC District resident and have a minimum 2.0 GPA. Award requirements change regularly. Please send a self-addressed, stamped envelope to receive your application and any further instructions from the scholarship provider. These materials are available after December 1. GPA must be 2.0-4.0.

Illinois Valley Community College
Attn: Financial Aid Office
815 North Orlando Smith Avenue
Oglesby, IL 61348

1780
Helen and Joseph Marchesi Memorial Scholarship

AMOUNT: $400 DEADLINE: March 19
MAJOR: Personnel Management, Industrial Relations

The Helen and Joseph Marchesi Memorial Scholarship is open to full-time students at Illinois Valley Community College. To be considered for this award, you must be a graduate of an IVCC District high school and have a minimum 3.0 GPA. Preference is given to applicants who seek to enter the personnel management or industrial relations fields. Award requirements change regularly. Please send a self-addressed, stamped envelope to receive your application and any further instructions from the scholarship provider. These materials are available after December 1. GPA must be 3.0-4.0.

Illinois Valley Community College
Attn: Financial Aid Office
815 North Orlando Smith Avenue
Oglesby, IL 61348

1781
Helen Taylor Memorial Scholarship

AMOUNT: $500-$750 DEADLINE: March 19
MAJOR: All Fields of Study

The Helen Taylor Memorial Scholarship is open to full-time students at Illinois Valley Community College. To be considered for this award, you must be a graduating valedictorian or salutatorian of an IVCC District high school and a district resident. The award provides $750 for valedictorians and $500 for salutatorians. Award requirements change regularly. To receive an application and any further information, please contact your high school guidance office. No GPA requirement specified.

Illinois Valley Community College
Attn: Financial Aid Office
815 North Orlando Smith Avenue
Oglesby, IL 61348

1782
High School Writing (Essay) Competition Scholarship

AMOUNT: $50-$125 DEADLINE: Varies
MAJOR: None Specified

The High School Writing (Essay) Competition Scholarship is open to full-time students at Illinois Valley Community College. To be considered for this award, you must be an entering freshman and complete a written essay competition exam at IVCC in February. Award requirements change regularly. To receive an application and any further information, please contact Mr. Randy Rambo at (815) 224-2720, ext. 338, or your high school English teacher(s). No GPA requirement specified.

Illinois Valley Community College
Attn: Financial Aid Office
815 North Orlando Smith Avenue
Oglesby, IL 61348

1783
High School Writing (Journalism) Competition Scholarship

AMOUNT: $50-$125 DEADLINE: Varies
MAJOR: None Specified

The High School Writing (Journalism) Competition Scholarship is open to full-time students at Illinois Valley Community College. To be considered for this award, you must be an entering freshman and complete a written journalism competition exam at IVCC in February. Award requirements change regularly. To receive an application and any further information, please contact Ms. Rose Marie Lynch at (815) 224-2720, ext. 209, or your high school English or journalism teacher(s). No GPA requirement specified.

Illinois Valley Community College
Attn: Financial Aid Office
815 North Orlando Smith Avenue
Oglesby, IL 61348

1784
Howard C. Ryan Scholarship

AMOUNT: $600 DEADLINE: March 19
MAJOR: All Fields of Study Leading to a Career in Law, Law Enforcement, Criminal Justice, or a Government-Related Field

The Howard C. Ryan Scholarship is open to full-time students at Illinois Valley Community College. To be considered for this award, you must be an IVCC District resident and have a minimum 2.0 GPA. Preference is given to students who demonstrate career plans that will lead to work in law, law enforcement, criminal justice, or a government-related field. Award requirements change regularly. Please send a self-addressed, stamped envelope to receive your application and any further instructions from the scholarship provider. These materials are available after December 1. GPA must be 2.0-4.0.

Illinois Valley Community College
Attn: Financial Aid Office
815 North Orlando Smith Avenue
Oglesby, IL 61348

1785
Illinois Society of Professional Engineers Scholarship

AMOUNT: $500 DEADLINE: March 19
MAJOR: Pre-Engineering, Engineering

The Illinois Society of Professional Engineers Scholarship is open to full-time sophomores at Illinois Valley Community College. To be considered for this award, you must be enrolled in pre-engineering, be committed to entering a Bachelor of Science degree program at a four-year institution, and have a minimum 3.0 GPA. You are required to submit verification of your ACT scores, and preference is given to students with at least a composite score of 28. Award requirements change regularly. Please send a self-addressed, stamped envelope to receive your application and any further instructions from the scholarship provider. These materials are available after December 1. GPA must be 3.0-4.0.

Illinois Valley Community College
Attn: Financial Aid Office
815 North Orlando Smith Avenue
Oglesby, IL 61348

1786
Illinois Valley Community Hospital Auxiliary Scholarship

AMOUNT: $500 DEADLINE: March 19
MAJOR: Health Care-Related Disciplines

The Illinois Valley Community Hospital Auxiliary Scholarship is open to students at Illinois Valley Community College. To be considered for this award, you must be pursuing studies in a health care-related discipline, be an IVCC District resident, and have a minimum 3.0 GPA. Students officially accepted into, and actively enrolled in, the nursing program may receive this award provided they are enrolled in at least eight hours per semester. All other applicants must be enrolled full-time. Award requirements change regularly. Please send a self-addressed, stamped envelope to receive your application and any further instructions from the scholarship provider. These materials are available after December 1. GPA must be 3.0-4.0.

Illinois Valley Community College
Attn: Financial Aid Office
815 North Orlando Smith Avenue
Oglesby, IL 61348

1787
IVCC Agriculture Scholarship

AMOUNT: $200 DEADLINE: March 19
MAJOR: Agriculture

The IVCC Agriculture Scholarship is open to full-time agriculture students at Illinois Valley Community College. To be considered for this award, you must be an entering freshman. Award requirements change regularly. To receive an application and any further information, please contact Mr. Doug Stockley in the IVCC Agriculture Department at (815) 224-2720, ext. 217. No GPA requirement specified.

Illinois Valley Community College
Attn: Financial Aid Office
815 North Orlando Smith Avenue
Oglesby, IL 61348

1788
IVCC Automotive Skills Scholarship

AMOUNT: $300 DEADLINE: Varies
MAJOR: Automotive Technology

The IVCC Automotive Skills Scholarship is open to full-time automotive students at Illinois Valley Community College. To be considered for this award, you must be an entering freshman and complete a competition exam at IVCC in April. Award requirements change regularly. To receive an application and any further information, please contact Mr. Dan O'Connor at (815) 224-2720, ext. 219, or Mr. Art Koudelka at (815) 224-2720, ext. 220. No GPA requirement specified.

Illinois Valley Community College
Attn: Financial Aid Office
815 North Orlando Smith Avenue
Oglesby, IL 61348

1789
IVCC Criminal Justice Scholarship

AMOUNT: $300 DEADLINE: March 19
MAJOR: Criminal Justice

The IVCC Criminal Justice Scholarship is open to full-time students at Illinois Valley Community College. To be considered for this award, you must be a criminal justice student, have completed at least 12 credits (6 of which are in criminal justice), and have a minimum 3.0 GPA. Award requirements change regularly. To receive an application and any further information, please contact Ms. Rebecca Donna in the Criminal Justice Department at (815) 224-2720, ext. 202. GPA must be 3.0-4.0.

Illinois Valley Community College
Attn: Financial Aid Office
815 North Orlando Smith Avenue
Oglesby, IL 61348

1790
IVCC Freshman Criminal Justice Scholarship

AMOUNT: $300 DEADLINE: March 19
MAJOR: Criminal Justice

The IVCC Freshman Criminal Justice Scholarship is open to full-time students at Illinois Valley Community College. To be considered for this award, you must be an entering freshman criminal justice student and have a minimum 3.0 GPA. You are required to show evidence of leadership qualities as demonstrated through involvement in extracurricular activities and community service. Award requirements change regularly. To receive an application and any further information, please contact Ms. Rebecca Donna in the Criminal Justice Department at (815) 224-2720, ext. 202. GPA must be 3.0-4.0.

Illinois Valley Community College
Attn: Financial Aid Office
815 North Orlando Smith Avenue
Oglesby, IL 61348

1791
John N. Barron Memorial Scholarship

AMOUNT: $400 DEADLINE: March 19
MAJOR: All Fields of Study - For Students with an Interest or Background in Journalism or Creative Writing

The John N. Barron Memorial Scholarship is open to full-time students at Illinois Valley Community College. To be considered for this award, you must have an interest or background in journalism or creative writing and have a minimum 3.0 GPA. Award requirements change regularly. Please send a self-addressed, stamped envelope to receive your application and any further instructions from the scholarship provider. These materials are available after December 1. GPA must be 3.0-4.0.

Illinois Valley Community College
Attn: Financial Aid Office
815 North Orlando Smith Avenue
Oglesby, IL 61348

1792
Karen Wisgoski Weber Memorial Scholarship

AMOUNT: $500 DEADLINE: March 19
MAJOR: Science Education

The Karen Wisgoski Weber Memorial Scholarship is open to full-time students at Illinois Valley Community College. To be considered for this award, you must be a science education student and have a minimum 3.0 GPA. Award requirements change regularly. Please send a self-addressed, stamped envelope to receive your application and any further instructions from the scholarship provider. These materials are available after December 1. GPA must be 3.0-4.0.

Illinois Valley Community College
Attn: Financial Aid Office
815 North Orlando Smith Avenue
Oglesby, IL 61348

1793
Louis and Minnie Faletti Memorial Scholarship

AMOUNT: $400 DEADLINE: March 19
MAJOR: Law, Pre-Law

The Louis and Minnie Faletti Memorial Scholarship is open to full-time students at Illinois Valley Community College. To be considered for this award, you must have a minimum 3.0 GPA and should be interested in the law and taking pre-law courses. Award requirements change regularly. Please send a self-addressed, stamped envelope to receive your application and any further instructions from the scholarship provider. These materials are available after December 1. GPA must be 3.0-4.0.

Illinois Valley Community College
Attn: Financial Aid Office
815 North Orlando Smith Avenue
Oglesby, IL 61348

1794
Murray Crowder Ecology Scholarship

AMOUNT: $1500 DEADLINE: March 19
MAJOR: Ecology- and Conservation-Related Disciplines

The Murray Crowder Ecology Scholarship is open to full-time students at Illinois Valley Community College. To be considered for this award, you must be enrolled in an ecology- or conservation-related discipline, be an IVCC District resident, and rank in the top 20% of your high school graduating class or have a minimum 2.5 GPA at IVCC after completing at least 12 credit hours. Award requirements change regularly. Please send a self-addressed, stamped envelope to receive your application and any further instructions from the scholarship provider. These materials are available after December 1. GPA must be 2.5-4.0.

Illinois Valley Community College
Attn: Financial Aid Office
815 North Orlando Smith Avenue
Oglesby, IL 61348

1795
New Beginnings Scholarship

AMOUNT: $1000 DEADLINE: March 19
MAJOR: All Fields of Study

The New Beginnings Scholarship is open to full-time students at Illinois Valley Community College. To be considered for this award, you must be a single mother, complete the FAFSA, and have a minimum 2.0 GPA. Award requirements change regularly. Please send a self-addressed, stamped envelope to receive your application and any further instructions from the scholarship provider. These materials are available after December 1. GPA must be 2.0-4.0.

Illinois Valley Community College
Attn: Financial Aid Office
815 North Orlando Smith Avenue
Oglesby, IL 61348

1796
Peru Rotary Scholarship

AMOUNT: $500 DEADLINE: March 19
MAJOR: All Fields of Study

The Peru Rotary Scholarship is open to full-time students at Illinois Valley Community College. To be considered for this award, you must be a resident of Peru, Illinois, and have a minimum 2.75 GPA. Award requirements change regularly. Please send a self-addressed, stamped envelope to receive your application and any further instructions from the scholarship provider. These materials are available after December 1. GPA must be 2.75-4.0.

Illinois Valley Community College
Attn: Financial Aid Office
815 North Orlando Smith Avenue
Oglesby, IL 61348

1797
Philosophy Scholarship

AMOUNT: $100 DEADLINE: March 19
MAJOR: Philosophy

The Philosophy Scholarship is open to full-time, second-year students at Illinois Valley Community College. To be considered for this award, you must submit an essay that will be evaluated by IVCC Philosophy faculty. Award requirements change regularly. To receive an application and any further information, please contact Mr. Steve Rhoades at (815) 224-2720, ext. 319. No GPA requirement specified.

Illinois Valley Community College
Attn: Financial Aid Office
815 North Orlando Smith Avenue
Oglesby, IL 61348

1798
R. Earl and Florence Trobaugh Scholarship

AMOUNT: $300 DEADLINE: March 19
MAJOR: English, French, German, Spanish

The R. Earl and Florence Trobaugh Scholarship is open to full-time students at Illinois Valley Community College. To be considered for this award, you must be an English or foreign language student with a minimum 3.0 GPA. Award requirements change regularly. Please send a self-addressed, stamped envelope to receive your application and any further instructions from the scholarship provider. These materials are available after December 1. GPA must be 3.0-4.0.

Illinois Valley Community College
Attn: Financial Aid Office
815 North Orlando Smith Avenue
Oglesby, IL 61348

1799
Rhea Crowder Health Care Scholarship

AMOUNT: $1500 DEADLINE: March 19
MAJOR: Health Care-Related Disciplines

The Rhea Crowder Health Care Scholarship is open to students at Illinois Valley Community College. To be considered for this award, you must be pursuing studies in a health care-related discipline, be an IVCC District resident, and rank in the top 20% of your high school graduating class or have a minimum 2.5 GPA after completing at least 12 credit hours at IVCC. Students officially accepted into, and actively enrolled in, the nursing program may receive this award provided they are enrolled in at least 8 hours per semester. All other applicants must be enrolled full-time. Award requirements change regularly. Please send a self-addressed, stamped envelope to receive your application and any further instructions from the scholarship provider. These materials are available after December 1. GPA must be 2.5-4.0.

Illinois Valley Community College
Attn: Financial Aid Office
815 North Orlando Smith Avenue
Oglesby, IL 61348

1800
Rick Publow Memorial Scholarship

AMOUNT: $250 DEADLINE: March 19
MAJOR: All Fields of Study

The Rick Publow Memorial Scholarship is open to full-time students at Illinois Valley Community College. To be considered for this award, you must be a currently enrolled IVCC student who has taken either an English or Philosophy course at IVCC. You must submit a copy of a writing assignment from that course and a letter of recommendation from the course's instructor. Award requirements change regularly. Please send a self-addressed, stamped envelope to receive your application and any further instructions from the scholarship provider. These materials are available after December 1. No GPA requirement specified.

Illinois Valley Community College
Attn: Financial Aid Office
815 North Orlando Smith Avenue
Oglesby, IL 61348

1801
Rita Wisgoski Memorial Scholarship

AMOUNT: $500 DEADLINE: March 19
MAJOR: Education

The Rita Wisgoski Memorial Scholarship is open to full-time students at Illinois Valley Community College. To be considered for this award, you must be planning on a career in teaching, be a GED recipient, and have a minimum 3.0 GPA. Preference is given to female students. Award requirements change regularly. Please send a self-addressed, stamped envelope to receive your application and any further instructions from the scholarship provider. These materials are available after December 1. GPA must be 3.0-4.0.

Illinois Valley Community College
Attn: Financial Aid Office
815 North Orlando Smith Avenue
Oglesby, IL 61348

1802
Samuel B. McCartney Memorial Scholarship

AMOUNT: $300 DEADLINE: March 19
MAJOR: Political Science, History

The Samuel B. McCartney Scholarship is open to full-time students at Illinois Valley Community College. To be considered for this award, you must be an IVCC District resident planning a career in history or political science, be a graduate of LaSalle-Peru High School, and have a minimum 3.0 GPA. Award requirements change regularly. Please send a self-addressed, stamped envelope to receive your application and any further instructions from the scholarship provider. These materials are available after December 1. GPA must be 3.0-4.0.

Illinois Valley Community College
Attn: Financial Aid Office
815 North Orlando Smith Avenue
Oglesby, IL 61348

Indiana University

1803
Ambrose and Miriam Rubey Scholarship

AMOUNT: None Specified DEADLINE: February 1
MAJOR: All Fields of Study

The Ambrose and Miriam Rubey Scholarship is open to students who will attend Indiana University. You must demonstrate academic achievement, activities, and work experience; maintain a minimum 3.0 GPA; and demonstrate financial need. Award requirements change regularly. Please send a self-addressed, stamped envelope to receive your application and further information from the scholarship provider or call (812) 232-2234. No GPA requirement specified.

Wabash Valley Community Foundation
Community Scholarship Program
2901 Ohio Boulevard, Suite 153
Terre Haute, IN 47803

1804
Indiana Retired Teachers Association Scholarship

AMOUNT: None Specified DEADLINE: February 15
MAJOR: Teacher Education

The Indiana Retired Teachers Association Scholarships are available to juniors attending colleges or universities in Indiana. You must be an Indiana resident and the child or grandchild of an active, retired, or deceased member of the IRTA. You must have at least a "C" average. Award requirements change regularly. Contact the Indiana Retired Teachers Association, 150 West Market Street, Indianapolis, IN 46204 for more information, or call (317) 637-7481. GPA must be 2.0-4.0.

Indiana University/Purdue University
799 West Michigan Street
Indianapolis, IN 46202-5195

Institute of Career Education

1805
Institute of Career Education Business Accounting Scholarship

AMOUNT: None Specified DEADLINE: Varies
MAJOR: Business Accounting

The Institute of Career Education Business Accounting Scholarship is open to Florida residents attending or planning to attend the Institute of Career Education who are studying business accounting. Applications are available at Florida high schools and GED testing centers. Award requirements change regularly. For further information, please send a self-addressed, stamped envelope to Institute of Career Education, Don Schaefer, President, 1750 45th Street, West Palm Beach, FL 33407, or you could call (561) 881-0220. No GPA requirement specified.

Florida Association of Postsecondary Schools and Colleges
Attn: FAPSC Scholarship Committee
F200 West College Avenue
Tallahassee, FL 32301

1806
Institute of Career Education Medical Assistant Scholarship

AMOUNT: None Specified DEADLINE: Varies
MAJOR: Medical Assistant

The Institute of Career Education Medical Assistant Scholarship is open to Florida residents attending or planning to attend the Institute of Career Education who are studying to become medical assistants. Applications are available at Florida high schools and GED testing centers. Award requirements change regularly. For further information, please send a self-addressed, stamped envelope to Institute of Career Education, Don Schaefer, President, 1750 45th Street, West Palm Beach, FL 33407, or you could call (561) 881-0220. No GPA requirement specified.

Florida Association of Postsecondary Schools and Colleges
Attn: FAPSC Scholarship Committee
F200 West College Avenue
Tallahassee, FL 32301

1807
Institute of Career Education Medical Office Specialist Scholarship

AMOUNT: None Specified DEADLINE: Varies
MAJOR: Medical Office Specialist

The Institute of Career Education Medical Office Specialist Scholarship is open to Florida residents attending or planning to attend the Institute of Career Education who are studying to become medical office specialists. Applications are available at Florida high schools and GED testing centers. Award requirements change regularly. For further information, please send a self-addressed, stamped envelope to Institute of Career Education, Don Schaefer, President, 1750 45th Street, West Palm Beach, FL 33407, or you could call (561) 881-0220. No GPA requirement specified.

Florida Association of Postsecondary Schools and Colleges
Attn: FAPSC Scholarship Committee
F200 West College Avenue
Tallahassee, FL 32301

1808
Institute of Career Education Travel Industry Specialist Scholarship

AMOUNT: None Specified DEADLINE: Varies
MAJOR: Travel Industry Specialist

The Institute of Career Education Travel Industry Specialist Scholarship is open to Florida residents attending or planning to attend the Institute of Career Education who are studying to become travel industry specialists. Applications are available at Florida high schools and GED testing centers. Award requirements change regularly. For further information, please send a self-addressed, stamped envelope to Institute of Career Education, Don Schaefer, President, 1750 45th Street, West Palm Beach, FL 33407, or you could call (561) 881-0220. No GPA requirement specified.

Florida Association of Postsecondary Schools and Colleges
Attn: FAPSC Scholarship Committee
F200 West College Avenue
Tallahassee, FL 32301

Institute of Food Technologists

1809
Graduate Scholarships and Fellowships

AMOUNT: $1250-$5000 DEADLINE: February 1
MAJOR: Food Science and Technology

Graduate fellowships to encourage and support research in food science and technology at accredited institutions in the U.S. or Canada. In addition, the Arthur T. Schramm Fellowship will provide tuition assistance for Ph.D. candidates who need financial assistance. Award requirements change regularly. Write to the address listed for details, enclosing a self-addressed, stamped envelope. Please specify your year in school or what degree you are pursuing. You may request information and an application via phone at (312) 782-8424 or "fax on demand" (800) 234-0270. Graduates must request document #3440. No GPA requirement specified.

Institute of Food Technologists
Attn: Scholarship Department
221 North LaSalle Street, Suite 300
Chicago, IL 60601-1291

1810
Undergraduate Scholarship

AMOUNT: $1000-$2250 DEADLINE: February 1
MAJOR: Food Science, Technology

Scholarships open to undergraduates enrolled in a food science and technology curriculum. Applicants must have a GPA of at least 2.5. February 1 is the deadline for juniors and seniors; February 15 is the deadline for freshmen; and March 1 is the deadline for sophomores. Must be enrolled/planning to enroll in an IFT-approved food science/technology program. When requesting an application by phone or fax, you will automatically receive a list of IFT-approved programs. Award requirements change regularly. Write to the address listed for details, enclosing a self-addressed, stamped envelope, and specify your year in school. You may request information via phone at (312) 782-8424 or "fax on demand" (800) 234-0270. Freshmen request document #3410. Sophomores request document #3420. Juniors and seniors request document #3430. GPA must be 2.5.

Institute of Food Technologists
Attn: Scholarship Department
221 North LaSalle Street, Suite 300
Chicago, IL 60601-1291

INTERNATIONAL ACADEMY OF MERCHANDISING AND DESIGN

1811
International Academy Advertising and Design Scholarship

AMOUNT: None Specified DEADLINE: Varies
MAJOR: Advertising and Design

The International Academy Advertising and Design Scholarship is open to Florida residents attending or planning to attend the International Academy of Merchandising and Design who are studying advertising and design. Applications are available at Florida high schools and GED testing centers. Award requirements change regularly. For further information, please send a self-addressed, stamped envelope to International Academy of Merchandising and Design, Marilyn Westropp, High School Relations Coordinator, 5225 Memorial Highway, Tampa, FL 33634, or you could call (813) 881-0007. No GPA requirement specified.

Florida Association of Postsecondary Schools and Colleges
Attn: FAPSC Scholarship Committee
F200 West College Avenue
Tallahassee, FL 32301

1812
International Academy Interior Design Scholarship

AMOUNT: None Specified DEADLINE: Varies
MAJOR: Interior Design

The International Academy Interior Design Scholarship is open to Florida residents attending or planning to attend the International Academy of Merchandising and Design who are studying interior design. Applications are available at Florida high schools and GED testing centers. Award requirements change regularly. For further information, please send a self-addressed, stamped envelope to International Academy of Merchandising and Design, Marilyn Westropp, High School Relations Coordinator, 5225 Memorial Highway, Tampa, FL 33634, or you could call (813) 881-0007. No GPA requirement specified.

Florida Association of Postsecondary Schools and Colleges
Attn: FAPSC Scholarship Committee
F200 West College Avenue
Tallahassee, FL 32301

1813
International Academy Merchandising Management Scholarship

AMOUNT: None Specified DEADLINE: Varies
MAJOR: Merchandising Management

The International Academy Merchandising Management Scholarship is open to Florida residents attending or planning to attend the International Academy of Merchandising and Design who are studying merchandising management. Applications are available at Florida high schools and GED testing centers. Award requirements change regularly. For further information, please send a self-addressed, stamped envelope to International Academy of Merchandising and Design, Marilyn Westropp, High School Relations Coordinator, 5225 Memorial Highway, Tampa, FL 33634, or you could call (813) 881-0007. No GPA requirement specified.

Florida Association of Postsecondary Schools and Colleges
Attn: FAPSC Scholarship Committee
F200 West College Avenue
Tallahassee, FL 32301

International College

1814
International College Accounting Scholarship

AMOUNT: None Specified DEADLINE: Varies
MAJOR: Accounting

The International College Accounting Scholarship is open to Florida residents attending or planning to attend International College to study accounting. Applications are available at Florida high schools and GED testing centers. Award requirements change regularly. For further information, please send a self-addressed, stamped envelope to International College, Buddy Cantwell, Director of Enrollment Management, 2654 Tamiami Trail East, Naples, FL 34103, or you could call (941) 774-4700. No GPA requirement specified.

Florida Association of Postsecondary Schools and Colleges
Attn: FAPSC Scholarship Committee
F200 West College Avenue
Tallahassee, FL 32301

1815
International College Business Administration Scholarship

AMOUNT: None Specified DEADLINE: Varies
MAJOR: Business Administration

The International College Business Administration Scholarship is open to Florida residents attending or planning to attend International College to study business administration. Applications are available at Florida high schools and GED testing centers. Award requirements change regularly. For further information, please send a self-addressed, stamped envelope to International College, Buddy Cantwell, Director of Enrollment Management, 2654 Tamiami Trail East, Naples, FL 34103, or you could call (941) 774-4700. No GPA requirement specified.

Florida Association of Postsecondary Schools and Colleges
Attn: FAPSC Scholarship Committee
F200 West College Avenue
Tallahassee, FL 32301

1816
International College Health Information Scholarship

AMOUNT: None Specified DEADLINE: Varies
MAJOR: Health Information

The International College Health Information Scholarship is open to Florida residents attending or planning to attend International College to study health information. Applications are available at Florida high schools and GED testing centers. Award requirements change regularly. For further information, please send a self-addressed, stamped envelope to International College, Buddy Cantwell, Director of Enrollment Management, 2654 Tamiami Trail East, Naples, FL 34103, or you could call (941) 774-4700. No GPA requirement specified.

Florida Association of Postsecondary Schools and Colleges
Attn: FAPSC Scholarship Committee
F200 West College Avenue
Tallahassee, FL 32301

1817
International College Medical Assisting Scholarship

AMOUNT: None Specified DEADLINE: Varies
MAJOR: Medical Assisting

The International College Medical Assisting Scholarship is open to Florida residents attending or planning to attend International College to study medical assisting. Applications are available at Florida high schools and GED testing centers. Award requirements change regularly. For further information, please send a self-addressed, stamped envelope to International College, Buddy Cantwell, Director of Enrollment Management, 2654 Tamiami Trail East, Naples, FL 34103, or you could call (941) 774-4700. No GPA requirement specified.

Florida Association of Postsecondary Schools and Colleges
Attn: FAPSC Scholarship Committee
F200 West College Avenue
Tallahassee, FL 32301

1818
International College Paralegal Scholarship

AMOUNT: None Specified DEADLINE: Varies
MAJOR: Paralegal

The International College Paralegal Scholarship is open to Florida residents attending or planning to attend International College who are studying to become a paralegal. Applications are available at Florida high schools and GED testing centers. Award requirements change regularly. For further information, please send a self-addressed, stamped envelope to International College, Buddy Cantwell, Director of Enrollment Management, 2654 Tamiami Trail East, Naples, FL 34103, or you could call (941) 774-4700. No GPA requirement specified.

Florida Association of Postsecondary Schools and Colleges
Attn: FAPSC Scholarship Committee
F200 West College Avenue
Tallahassee, FL 32301

Iowa State University

1819
Agronomic Freshmen Scholarship

AMOUNT: $500 DEADLINE: April 30
MAJOR: Agronomy

The Agronomic Freshmen Scholarship is available to freshmen at Iowa State University who are studying agronomy. This award is based on extracurricular activities, leadership potential, scholastic abilities, and work/community experiences. Award requirements change regularly. Write to the address listed, enclosing a self-addressed, stamped envelope, or call (515) 294-3846 for further information. GPA must be 2.5-4.0.

Iowa State University - Department of Agronomy
Attn: Scholarship Coordinator
1126C Agronomy
Ames, IA 50011

1820
Animal Science Scholarship

AMOUNT: $500 DEADLINE: March 14
MAJOR: Animal Science, Preveterinary Medicine

The Animal Science Scholarship is to open to entering freshmen admitted to Iowa State University, majoring in animal science or animal science-preveterinary medicine. The award is based on academics, leadership, and interest in the animal industry. Award requirements change regularly. For further information contact the address listed, enclosing a self-addressed, stamped envelope or call (515) 294-6614. GPA must be 2.7-4.0.

Iowa State University
Associate Dean of Academic Programs
Ames, IA 50011

1821
Beverly J. and Jewell Crabtree Scholarship

AMOUNT: None Specified DEADLINE: January 2
MAJOR: Apparel Merchandising/Design, Dietetics, Early Childhood Education, Food Science, Nutritional Science, Hotel/Restaurant Management

The Beverly J. and Jewell Crabtree Scholarship is open to incoming freshman majors in the College of Family and Consumer Sciences at Iowa State University with a minimum ACT of 24 or who rank in the top 10% of their high school graduating class. Recipients must assume and reflect leadership qualities related specifically to the mission of Family and Consumer Sciences. Award requirements change regularly. Contact the address listed for further information, enclosing a self-addressed, stamped envelope. GPA must be 3.3-4.0.

Iowa State University - College of Family and Consumer Sciences
Attn: Letha Demos
122A Mackay Hall
Ames, IA 50011

1822
Biology Teacher Scholarship

AMOUNT: $500 DEADLINE: February 19
MAJOR: Biology

The Biology Teacher Scholarship is open to freshman biology majors admitted to Iowa State University who are committed to teaching biology at the high school level. The award is based on academic achievement and is renewable provided the student completes 14 or more credits in the first semester and maintains a minimum GPA of 3.0. Award requirements change regularly. Contact the address listed for further information, enclosing a self-addressed, stamped envelope or call (515) 294-2223. GPA must be 3.0-4.0.

Iowa State University - Biology Department
Attn: Warren D. Dolphin
201 Bessey Hall
Ames, IA 50011

1823
Biotechnology Scholarship in Agriculture

AMOUNT: None Specified DEADLINE: December 1
MAJOR: Agriculture

The Biotechnology Scholarship in Agriculture is available to freshmen at Iowa State University who are studying agriculture. The award is based on scholarship, ACT and SAT scores, and an interest in science. Award requirements change regularly. For further information contact the address listed, enclosing a self-addressed, stamped envelope. No GPA requirement specified.

Iowa State University
Associate Dean of Academic Programs
Ames, IA 50011

1824
Christina Hixson Opportunity Award

AMOUNT: $2500 DEADLINE: February 15
MAJOR: All Areas of Study

The Christina Hixson Opportunity Award is open to incoming freshmen accepted at Iowa State University who are Iowa residents. The award is based on financial need, family circumstances, and potential for success. Award requirements change regularly. For further information contact your high school guidance counselor, Iowa State University Extension Office, or the address listed - please enclose a self-addressed, stamped envelope - or call (515) 294-6545. GPA must be 2.5-4.0.

Iowa State University
Christina Hixson Opportunity Award
314 Alumni Hall
Ames, IA 50011

1825
Clair B. Watson Design Scholarship

AMOUNT: $1000 DEADLINE: February 10
MAJOR: Architecture, Regional Planning, Graphic Design, Interior Design, Landscape Architecture

The Clair B. Watson Design Scholarship is open to entering freshmen enrolled in/admitted to the College of Design at Iowa State University. The award is based on high school ranking, ACT scores, and a self-authored essay. A portfolio may be submitted for consideration, but it is not required. Award requirements change regularly. Contact the address listed for further information, including a self-addressed, stamped envelope. GPA must be 3.0-4.0.

Iowa State University - College of Design
Roger Baer, Assistant Dean
134 College of Design
Ames, IA 50011

1826
College of Design Minority Scholarship

AMOUNT: $1000 DEADLINE: March 31
MAJOR: Design

The College of Design Minority Scholarships are sponsoring awards for entering freshmen of African-American, Asian-American, Hispanic, Native American, or Alaskan descent. The award is based on academic achievement, high school records, and statements of interests and abilities. This scholarship is open to majors in a College of Design curriculum. Award requirements change regularly. For further information contact the address below, enclosing a self-addressed, stamped envelope. No GPA requirement specified.

Iowa State University - College of Design
Michael Chinn, Interim Assistant Dean
134 College of Design
Ames, IA 50011

1827
College of Education Minority Scholarship

AMOUNT: $250 DEADLINE: January 30
MAJOR: Education

The College of Education Minority Scholarship is open to minority undergraduates enrolled in the College of Education at Iowa State University who are residents of Iowa. The award is based on academic achievement and financial need. Consideration is given to students who significantly contribute to programs in college. Award requirements change regularly. Contact the address listed for further information, enclosing a self-addressed, stamped envelope or call (515) 294-2223. You may consult the address provided. GPA must be 2.5-4.0.

Iowa State University
Education Student Services
E105 Lagomarcino Hall
Ames, IA 50011

1828
Computer Science Freshman Scholarship

AMOUNT: $500-$1000 DEADLINE: December 15
MAJOR: Computer Science

The Computer Science Freshman Scholarship is open to incoming freshmen admitted to Iowa State University who were in the top 5% of their graduating classes and have a minimum ACT score of 29. Consideration will be given to high school preparation in Math and Science. The award is renewable if the student earns 12 or more graded credits with a minimum GPA of 2.75 in the first semester. Award requirements change regularly. Contact the address listed for further information, enclosing a self-addressed, stamped envelope or call (515) 294-2223. GPA must be 2.8-4.0.

Iowa State University
Computer Science Advising
223 Atanasoff Hall
Ames, IA 50011

1829
Dean's Advisory Council Scholarships

AMOUNT: $5000 DEADLINE: Varies
MAJOR: Business

The Dean's Advisory Council Scholarship is available to entering African-American, Hispanic, and Native American freshmen who demonstrate academic achievement and financial need. Award requirements change regularly. Contact the address below for further information, enclosing a self-addressed, stamped envelope. No GPA requirement specified.

Iowa State University - College of Business
Attn: Ann Coppernoll Farni
204 Carver Hall
Ames, IA 50011

1830
Dow-Goetz and Noble Hines Scholarship

AMOUNT: $500-$1000 DEADLINE: February 15
MAJOR: Chemistry

The Dow-Goetz and Noble Hines Scholarship is open to incoming freshmen at Iowa State University who have an ACT composite score of 27 or better, a 3.5 GPA, an aptitude for science and mathematics, and a general interest in being a chemistry major. Award requirements change regularly. Contact the address listed for further information, enclosing a self-addressed, stamped envelope. GPA must be 3.5-4.0.

Iowa State University - Department of Chemistry
Chemistry Undergraduate Office
1608 Gilman Hall
Ames, IA 50011

1831
Dudley Chittenden Memorial Scholarship

AMOUNT: None Specified DEADLINE: March 15
MAJOR: Horticulture

The Dudley Chittenden Memorial Scholarship is open to entering freshmen based on academic achievement, extracurricular activities, leadership, and financial need in the area of Horticulture. Award requirements change regularly. Contact the address below for further information, enclosing a self-addressed, stamped envelope. No GPA requirement specified.

Iowa State University - Department of Horticulture
Chair, Scholarship Committee
106 Horticulture Hall
Ames, IA 50011

1832
Edward F. and Phoebe H. Knipling Scholarships

AMOUNT: None Specified DEADLINE: December 1
MAJOR: Agriculture

The Edward F. and Phoebe H. Knipling Scholarships are open to enrolled or admitted students pursuing degrees in agriculture. Award is renewable. Award requirements change regularly. Please call (515) 294-6614 for any further information. GPA must be 2.8-4.0.

Iowa State University
Associate Dean of Academic Programs
Ames, IA 50011

1833
Excellence in Agriculture Scholarship

AMOUNT: None Specified DEADLINE: December 1
MAJOR: Agriculture

The Excellence in Agriculture Scholarship is open to entering freshmen admitted to Iowa State University with a minimum GPA of 3.5 and a minimum ACT score of 28 or an SAT score of 1160 or higher. The applicant must have the potential to make a significant contribution to society as demonstrated by extracurricular activities or employment experiences. Award requirements change regularly. Contact the address listed for further information, enclosing a self-addressed, stamped envelope or call (515) 294-6614. GPA must be 3.5-4.0.

Iowa State University
Associate Dean of Academic Programs
Ames, IA 50011

1834
Floyd Andre Scholarship

AMOUNT: None Specified DEADLINE: December 1
MAJOR: Agriculture

The Floyd Andre Scholarship is open to entering Iowa resident freshmen admitted to Iowa State University. The award is based on extracurricular activities and leadership potential in the area of agriculture. Award requirements change regularly. Contact the address listed, enclosing a self-addressed, stamped envelope or call (515) 294-6614 for further information. GPA must be 2.5-4.0.

Iowa State University
Associate Dean of Academic Programs
Ames, IA 50011

1835
Forestry Scholarship

AMOUNT: $500-$1000 DEADLINE: January 31
MAJOR: Forestry

The Forestry Scholarship is open to entering freshmen admitted to Iowa State University. The award is based on academic achievement and extracurricular activities. A high school transcript and a one-page essay on how the applicant became interested in forestry will be required. Award requirements change regularly. Contact the address listed, enclosing a self-addressed, stamped envelope or call (515) 294-2223 for further information. GPA must be 3.0-4.0.

Iowa State University - Department of Forestry
Dr. Steven Jungst
251 Bessey Hall
Ames, IA 50011

1836
J.S. Latta, Jr., Education Scholarship

AMOUNT: Maximum: $1000 DEADLINE: January 30
MAJOR: Education

The J.S. Latta, Jr., Education Scholarship is open to full-time undergraduates majoring in a program of Teacher Education at Iowa State University. This award is renewable if recipients maintain a minimum GPA of 3.0, remain full-time, and are able to demonstrate financial need. Award requirements change regularly. Contact the address listed for further information, enclosing a self-addressed, stamped envelope or call (515) 294-2223. GPA must be 3.0-4.0.

Iowa State University
Education Student Services
E105 Lagomarcino Hall
Ames, IA 50011

1837
Jeanne Verne Blahnik Scholarship

AMOUNT: None Specified DEADLINE: January 2
MAJOR: Apparel Merchandising/Design, Dietetics, Early Childhood Education, Food Science, Nutritional Science, Hotel/Restaurant Management

The Jeanne Verne Blahnik Scholarship is open to incoming freshman majors in the College of Family and Consumer Sciences at Iowa State University with a minimum ACT of 24 or who rank in the top 10% of their high school graduating class. The award is based on demonstrated leadership qualities and financial need. Award requirements change regularly. Contact the address listed for further information, enclosing a self-addressed, stamped envelope. GPA must be 3.3-4.0.

Iowa State University - College of Family and Consumer Sciences
Attn: Letha Demos
122A Mackay Hall
Ames, IA 50011

1838
Journalism Alumni Scholarship

AMOUNT: $400-$1000 DEADLINE: February 1
MAJOR: Journalism

The Journalism Alumni Scholarship is open to journalism students at Iowa State University. The award is based on academic achievement and extracurricular activities in print or broadcast media (newspaper, yearbook, radio, TV). Award requirements change regularly. Contact the address listed for further information, enclosing a self-addressed, stamped envelope. GPA must be 3.5-4.0.

Iowa State University
Scholarship Committee
Room 40 Memorial Union
Ames, IA 50014

1839
Liberal Arts and Sciences Alumni Scholarship

AMOUNT: None Specified DEADLINE: February 1
MAJOR: Liberal Arts

The Liberal Arts and Sciences Alumni Scholarship is open to freshmen at Iowa State University planning to major in the area of Liberal Arts & Sciences who rank in the 10% of their high school class or have an ACT of 29 or above. The selection is based on academic excellence, leadership in school, and community activities. Award requirements change regularly. Contact the address listed for further information, enclosing a self-addressed, stamped envelope or call (515) 294-2223. GPA must be 3.5-4.0.

Iowa State University - LAS School Coordinator
Attn: Anne Johnson
243 Catt Hall
Ames, IA 50011

1840
Margaret and Barton Morgan Scholarship

AMOUNT: $600 DEADLINE: January 30
MAJOR: Education, School Administration

The Margaret and Barton Morgan Scholarship is open to full-time undergraduates admitted to Iowa State University, who are preparing to become teachers or school administrators. Applicants must have a minimum GPA of 3.0 and must demonstrate financial need. Award requirements change regularly. Contact the address listed for further information, enclosing a self-addressed, stamped envelope or call (515) 294-2223. GPA must be 3.0-4.0.

Iowa State University
Education Student Services
E105 Lagomarcino Hall
Ames, IA 50011

1841
Marian Daniels Mathematics Scholarship

AMOUNT: $500-$1000 DEADLINE: February 15
MAJOR: Mathematics

The Marian Daniels Mathematics Scholarship is open to incoming freshmen admitted to Iowa State University. The award is based on academic achievement and mathematical interests and abilities. Applicants must submit a high school transcript, one or two letters of recommendation (one from a mathematics teacher), ACT or SAT scores, and scores from the American High School Mathematics Contest (if available). Award requirements change regularly. Contact the address listed, enclosing a self-addressed, stamped envelope or call (515) 294-2223 for further information. GPA must be 2.8-4.0.

Iowa State University - Mathematics Department
Richard Tondra, Undergrad Coordinator
490 Carver
Ames, IA 50011

1842
Naomi Wilkinson Scott Endowed Scholarship

AMOUNT: None Specified DEADLINE: January 2
MAJOR: Apparel Merchandising/Design, Dietetics, Early Childhood Education, Food Science, Nutritional Science, Hotel/Restaurant Management

The Naomi Wilkinson Scott Endowed Scholarship is open to incoming freshman majors in the College of Family and Consumer Sciences at Iowa State University with a minimum ACT of 24 or who rank in the 10% of their high school graduating class. Award requirements change regularly. Contact the address listed for further information, enclosing a self-addressed, stamped envelope. GPA must be 3.3-4.0.

Iowa State University - College of Family and Consumer Sciences
Attn: Letha Demos
122A Mackay Hall
Ames, IA 50011

1843
Outstanding Freshman Scholarship

AMOUNT: Maximum: $750 DEADLINE: January 30
MAJOR: Industrial Education/Technology

The Outstanding Freshman Scholarship is open to entering freshmen enrolled in the Department of Industrial Education and Technology at Iowa State University. The award is based on academic performance. Award requirements change regularly. Contact the address listed for further information, enclosing a self-addressed, stamped envelope or call (515) 294-2223. No GPA requirement specified.

Iowa State University
Attn: Dr. John Dugger
114 Industrial Education and Tech Dept
Ames, IA 50011

1844
Robert E. and Patricia A. Jester Scholarship

AMOUNT: None Specified DEADLINE: December 1
MAJOR: Agronomy, Animal Ecology/Science, Biochemistry, Biophysics, Entomology, Food Science and Human Nutrition, Zoology/Genetics, Horticulture, Microbiology, Plant Pathology

The Robert E. and Patricia A. Jester Scholarship is open to entering freshmen majoring in entomology, food science, human nutrition, forestry, genetics, horticulture, microbiology, or plant pathology at Iowa State University. The applicant must have a minimum GPA of 3.0. Award requirements change regularly. For further information contact the address listed, enclosing a self-addressed, stamped envelope. GPA must be 3.0-4.0.

Iowa State University
Associate Dean of Academic Programs
Ames, IA 50011

1845
Ruth and J.R. Underwood Scholarship

AMOUNT: Maximum: $3479 DEADLINE: January 30
MAJOR: Elementary Education, Secondary Education

The Ruth and J.R. Underwood Scholarship is open to resident incoming freshmen accepted at Iowa State University, majoring in Elementary or Secondary Education. This award is based on academic excellence, extracurricular activities, enthusiasm for teaching, and financial need. The applicant must have a minimum GPA of 3.0. Awards are half annual tuition, room, and board. Award requirements change regularly. Contact the address listed for further information, including a self-addressed, stamped envelope or call (515) 294-2223. GPA must be 3.0-4.0.

Iowa State University
Education Student Services
E105 Lagomarcino Hall
Ames, IA 50011

1846
Veishea Leadership Scholarship

AMOUNT: $500 DEADLINE: February 1
MAJOR: All Areas of Study

The Veishea Leadership Scholarship is open to entering freshmen admitted to Iowa State University who have a minimum ACT score of 26, or at least an SAT combined verbal and math score of 1070, and are in the top 15% of their graduating class. Award requirements change regularly. Contact the address listed, enclosing a self-addressed, stamped envelope, or call (515) 294-6545 for further information. GPA must be 3.1-4.0.

Iowa State University
Scholarship Committee
Room 40 Memorial Union
Ames, IA 50014

1847
Vincent V. Malcolm Scholarship

AMOUNT: None Specified DEADLINE: December 1
MAJOR: Agriculture

The Vincent V. Malcolm Scholarship is open to students enrolled in or admitted to Iowa State University. Applicants must be pursuing a degree in agriculture. Award requirements change regularly. For further information contact the address provided. Please include a self-addressed, stamped envelope or call (515) 294-6614. GPA must be 2.8-4.0.

Iowa State University
Associate Dean of Academic Programs
Ames, IA 50011

1848
Virgil and Dorothy Lagomarcino Scholarship

AMOUNT: $500 DEADLINE: January 30
MAJOR: Education

The Virgil and Dorothy Lagomarcino Scholarship is open to full-time undergraduates enrolled in at least 12 credit hours per semester in the College of Education at Iowa State University. This award is based on outstanding academics and financial need. The applicant must have a minimum GPA of 3.0. Award requirements change regularly. Contact the address listed for further information, enclosing a self-addressed, stamped envelope or call (515) 294-2223. GPA must be 3.0-4.0.

Iowa State University
Education Student Services
E105 Lagomarcino Hall
Ames, IA 50011

1849
W. Price and Lucille Manatt Scholarship

AMOUNT: $500 DEADLINE: January 30
MAJOR: Education

The W. Price and Lucille Manatt Scholarship is open to full-time undergraduates enrolled in the College of Education at Iowa State University. The applicant must possess strong character and academic ability and demonstrate financial need. Award requirements change regularly. Contact the address listed for further information, enclosing a self-addressed, stamped envelope or call (515) 294-2223. GPA must be 2.8-4.0.

Iowa State University
Education Student Services
E105 Lagomarcino Hall
Ames, IA 50011

Jacksonville University

1850
Davin Loan

AMOUNT: Maximum: $3000 DEADLINE: Varies
MAJOR: All Areas of Study

The Davin Loan is available to Jacksonville University students who demonstrate financial need. Award requirements change regularly. File Free Application for Federal Student Aid (FAFSA), contact the financial aid office at the address listed, or call (800) 558-3467 for further information. No GPA requirement specified.

Jacksonville University
Financial Aid Office
2800 University Blvd North
Jacksonville, FL 32211-3321

1851
Fine Arts Scholarship

AMOUNT: None Specified DEADLINE: Varies
MAJOR: Art, Theater, Dance, Music

The Fine Arts Scholarship is available to students of outstanding achievement in art, dance, music, and theater at Jacksonville University. This award is renewable for four years. Award requirements change regularly. For further information, please write the address provided or call (800) 558-3467. No GPA requirement specified.

Jacksonville University
Attn: William J. McNeiland
College of Fine Arts/Division of Music
Jacksonville, FL 32211

1852
Junior College Scholarship

AMOUNT: None Specified DEADLINE: Varies
MAJOR: All Areas of Study

The Junior College Scholarship is available to junior college graduates who have never attended a four-year college and are transferring to Jacksonville University. This award is renewable, and the award amount varies. Award requirements change regularly. Contact your high school guidance counselor or the financial aid office at the address listed for details, enclosing a self-addressed, stamped envelope, or call (800) 558-3467 for further information. No GPA requirement specified.

Jacksonville University
Financial Aid Office
2800 University Blvd North
Jacksonville, FL 32211-3321

1853
Knabb Scholarship

AMOUNT: $1000 DEADLINE: Varies
MAJOR: All Areas of Study

The Knabb Scholarship is available to Jacksonville University students from Baker and Duval counties. Award requirements change regularly. File Free Application for Federal Student Aid (FAFSA). Contact the financial aid office at the address listed or call (800) 558-3467 for further information. No GPA requirement specified.

Jacksonville University
Financial Aid Office
2800 University Blvd North
Jacksonville, FL 32211-3321

1854
Multiple Family Member Discount

AMOUNT: None Specified DEADLINE: Varies
MAJOR: All Areas of Study

The Multiple Family Member Discount is open to families supporting two or more full-time undergraduates attending Jacksonville University. One student pays full tuition; the second receives a 15% discount; additional students receive 30% discounts. Award requirements change regularly. Please send a self-addressed, stamped envelope to receive your application and for any further instructions from the scholarship provider. You can also call (800) 558-3467 to reach the Jacksonville University Financial Aid Office. No GPA requirement specified.

Jacksonville University
Financial Aid Office
2800 University Blvd North
Jacksonville, FL 32211-3321

1855
President's and University Scholarship

AMOUNT: None Specified DEADLINE: January 15
MAJOR: All Areas of Study

The President's and University Scholarship is available to graduating Florida seniors from high schools in Clay, Duval, Baker, St. Johns, and Nassau counties who have been accepted to Jacksonville University. Renewable for four years if student maintains a 3.0 GPA. The award amount is full tuition for the President's Scholarship and 3/4 tuition for the University Scholarship, Award requirements change regularly. Contact your high school guidance counselor or the financial aid office at the address listed for details, enclosing a self-addressed, stamped envelope, or call (800) 558-3467 for further details. GPA must be 3.0-4.0.

Jacksonville University
Financial Aid Office
2800 University Blvd North
Jacksonville, FL 32211-3321

1856
Service Awards at Jacksonville University

AMOUNT: None Specified DEADLINE: Varies
MAJOR: All Areas of Study

The Service Awards at Jacksonville University are for Jacksonville University students who participate in various campus activities (e.g., student publications, student government, etc.). The amount of this award varies. Award requirements change regularly. Contact your high school guidance counselor or the financial aid office at the address listed for details, enclosing a self-addressed, stamped envelope, or call (800) 558-3467 for further information. No GPA requirement specified.

Jacksonville University
Financial Aid Office
2800 University Blvd North
Jacksonville, FL 32211-3321

1857
Trustee Scholarship Program

AMOUNT: None Specified DEADLINE: Varies
MAJOR: All Areas of Study

The Trustee Scholarship Program is open to incoming Jacksonville University freshmen. This award is based on grades and SAT or ACT scores. Award requirements change regularly. Contact your high school guidance counselor or the financial aid office at the address listed for details, enclosing a self-addressed, stamped envelope, or call (800) 558-3467 for further information. GPA must be 2.5-4.0.

Jacksonville University
Financial Aid Office
2800 University Blvd North
Jacksonville, FL 32211-3321

1858
Williams Memorial Scholarship

AMOUNT: None Specified DEADLINE: January 15
MAJOR: All Areas of Study

The Williams Memorial Scholarship is open to graduating seniors who will be attending Jacksonville University. Qualified applicants must be Florida or Georgia residents and must have a minimum GPA of 3.5, a minimum ACT score of 29, or a minimum SAT score of 1270. The award amount is full-tuition, room and board, fees and books. This award is renewable. Award requirements change regularly. Please send a self-addressed, stamped envelope to receive your application and for any further instructions from the scholarship provider. GPA must be 3.5-4.0.

Jacksonville University
Financial Aid Office
2800 University Blvd North
Jacksonville, FL 32211-3321

Jamestown College

1859
Honors Scholarship

AMOUNT: $16000 DEADLINE: Varies
MAJOR: All Areas of Study

The Honors Scholarship is open to freshmen attending Jamestown College. To be considered for this award you must demonstrate academic strength; leadership skills; and involvement in extracurricular activities in school, community, or church. The award provides $16,000 over four years of study. Award requirements change regularly. Please send a self-addressed, stamped envelope to receive your application and any further instructions from the scholarship provider. You

may also browse the website at www.jc.edu. No GPA requirement specified.

Jamestown College - Admissions Office
Attn: Scholarship Programs
6081 College Lane
Jamestown, ND 58405

1860
Leadership Scholarship

AMOUNT: $12000 DEADLINE: Varies
MAJOR: All Areas of Study

The Leadership Scholarship is open to freshmen attending Jamestown College. To be considered for this award you must demonstrate academic strength; leadership skills; and involvement in extracurricular activities in school, community, or church. The award provides $12,000 over four years of study. Award requirements change regularly. Please send a self-addressed, stamped envelope to receive your application and any further instructions from the scholarship provider. You may also consult the website at www.jc.edu. No GPA requirement specified.

Jamestown College - Admissions Office
Attn: Scholarship Programs
6081 College Lane
Jamestown, ND 58405

1861
Melvin R. Arnold Chemistry Scholarship

AMOUNT: $5000 DEADLINE: March 1
MAJOR: Chemistry

The Melvin R. Arnold Chemistry Scholarship is open to freshmen chemistry majors enrolled at Jamestown College. This $5,000 award is renewable for up to four years. To be considered for this award you must demonstrate academic strength; leadership skills; and involvement in extracurricular activities in school, community, or church. Award requirements change regularly. Please send a self-addressed, stamped envelope to receive your application and any further instructions from the scholarship provider. You may also browse the website at www.jc.edu. No GPA requirement specified.

Jamestown College - Admissions Office
Attn: Scholarship Programs
6081 College Lane
Jamestown, ND 58405

1862
Presidential Scholarship

AMOUNT: $20000 DEADLINE: Varies
MAJOR: All Areas of Study

The Presidential Scholarship is open to freshmen attending Jamestown College. To be considered for this award, you must demonstrate academic strength; leadership skills; and involvement in extracurricular activities in school, community, or church. The award provides $20,000 over four years of study. Award requirements change regularly. Please send a self-addressed, stamped envelope to receive your application and any further instructions from the scholarship provider. You may consult the website at www.jc.edu. No GPA requirement specified.

Jamestown College - Admissions Office
Attn: Scholarship Programs
6081 College Lane
Jamestown, ND 58405

Wilson Scholarship

AMOUNT: None Specified DEADLINE: February 1
MAJOR: All Areas of Study

The Wilson Scholarship is open to freshmen attending
Jamestown College. The scholarship provides full tuition for
four years. To be considered for this award you must demonstrate academic strength; leadership skills; and involvement in
extracurricular activities in school, community, or church.
Award requirements change regularly. Please send a self-
addressed, stamped envelope to receive your application and
any further instructions from the scholarship provider. You
may also consult the website at www.jc.edu. No GPA requirement specified.

Jamestown College - Admissions Office
Attn: Scholarship Programs
6081 College Lane
Jamestown, ND 58405

John Brown University

1864
Academic Achievement Award

AMOUNT: $1200 DEADLINE: May 1
MAJOR: All Areas of Study

The Academic Achievement Award is open to entering freshmen enrolled at John Brown University. The applicant must
have at least a 27 ACT and 1170 SAT score in order to qualify. Award requirements change regularly. Please send a self-
addressed, stamped envelope to receive your application and
for any further instructions from the scholarship provider. No
GPA requirement specified.

John Brown University
Admissions Office
2000 West University Street
Siloam Springs, AR 72761

1865
Academic Scholarship

AMOUNT: $1000-$5000 DEADLINE: May 1
MAJOR: All Areas of Study

The JBU Academic Scholarship is available to JBU freshmen
who demonstrate superior academics. The applicant must have
scored well on the ACT/SAT tests, and high school class ranking is also considered for this scholarship. This award is
renewable by maintaining a GPA as defined by the criteria of
the award. Award requirements change regularly. Please write
to the address listed for details, sending a self-addressed,
stamped envelope, or email finaid@adm.jbu.edu. You can also
call (800) 634-6969 or browse the website at www.jbu.edu.
GPA must be 3.0-4.0.

John Brown University
Admissions Office
2000 West University Street
Siloam Springs, AR 72761

Athletic Scholarship

AMOUNT: None Specified DEADLINE: Varies
MAJOR: All Areas of Study

Athletic Scholarships are available to full-time JBU students
who are recommended by a coach. Award amounts vary but
cannot exceed tuition, room, and board costs. Award requirements change regularly. Contact the Athletic Department at
(501) 524-7305 or browse the web at www.jbu.edu for further
information. No GPA requirement specified.

John Brown University
Admissions Office
2000 West University Street
Siloam Springs, AR 72761

1867
Dean's Award

AMOUNT: $1500 DEADLINE: May 1
MAJOR: All Areas of Study

The Dean's Award is open to freshman students at John
Brown University with an ACT composite range of 28-29 and
an SAT math/verbal combined range of 1240-1310. This
award is not available to transfer students. Award requirements change regularly. Please send a self-addressed, stamped
envelope to receive your application and for any further
instructions from the scholarship provider. No GPA requirement specified.

John Brown University
Admissions Office
2000 West University Street
Siloam Springs, AR 72761

1868
Divisional Scholarship

AMOUNT: $3000 DEADLINE: January 15
MAJOR: All Areas of Study

This scholarship is open to JBU freshmen who demonstrate
superior academics and leadership potential and who have a
minimum 3.5 GPA. Applicants must be in the top 10% of their
graduating class and placed in the top 90 percentile on the
ACT/SAT exams. This award is renewable by maintaining an
appropriate GPA. Applicants must have a strong Christian testimony and have demonstrated leadership ability. Award
requirements change regularly. Please write to the address provided for further information, including a self-addressed,
stamped envelope. GPA must be 3.5-4.0.

John Brown University
Admissions Office
2000 West University Street
Siloam Springs, AR 72761

1869
Engineering Achievement Award

AMOUNT: $3000 DEADLINE: May 1
MAJOR: Engineering

This award is open to incoming full-time JBU freshmen enrolled as engineering majors and placed in the top 90 percentile on the ACT/SAT exams. Applicant must also demonstrate strong Christian testimony and demonstrate leadership abilities. Awards are renewable by maintaining appropriate GPA and continuing as engineering majors. Award requirements change regularly. For further information, please send a self-addressed, stamped envelope. No GPA requirement specified.

John Brown University
Admissions Office
2000 West University Street
Siloam Springs, AR 72761

1870
Family Christian Service Award

AMOUNT: $300 DEADLINE: Varies
MAJOR: All Areas of Study

The Family Christian Service Award is open to the children of parents employed in full-time Christian service positions. Award requirements change regularly. Please send a self-addressed, stamped envelope to receive your application and for any further instructions from the scholarship provider. No GPA requirement specified.

John Brown University
Admissions Office
2000 West University Street
Siloam Springs, AR 72761

1871
JBU Donor and Endowed Scholarship

AMOUNT: None Specified DEADLINE: March 1
MAJOR: All Areas of Study

Available to full-time JBU students with financial need. Most awards are given to continuing students. Applicants must file applications for Federal Student Aid (FAFSA). Award requirements change regularly. Write to the address listed for details and send a self-addressed, stamped envelope; call (800) 634-6969; send email to finaid@adm.jbu.edu; or browse the web at www.jbu.edu for further information. No GPA requirement specified.

John Brown University
Admissions Office
2000 West University Street
Siloam Springs, AR 72761

1872
JBU Leadership Scholarship

AMOUNT: $500-$1000 DEADLINE: Varies
MAJOR: All Areas of Study

The JBU Leadership Scholarship is open to high school graduates who will attend John Brown University. The applicant must have at least a 3.0 GPA and demonstrate campus, church, or community leadership ability. This award is renewable if the student maintains a 3.0 GPA. Award requirements change regularly. Please send a self-addressed, stamped envelope to receive your application and for any further instructions from the scholarship provider. GPA must be 3.0-4.0.

John Brown University
Admissions Office
2000 West University Street
Siloam Springs, AR 72761

1873
Missionary Children's Scholarship

AMOUNT: $2000 DEADLINE: Varies
MAJOR: All Areas of Study

Available to JBU students with at least one parent who is a full-time missionary. Award requirements change regularly. Write to the address listed for details and send a self-addressed, stamped envelope; call (800) 634-6969; email finaid@adm.jbu.edu; or browse the web at www.jbu.edu. No GPA requirement specified.

John Brown University
Admissions Office
2000 West University Street
Siloam Springs, AR 72761

1874
Music/Choral Scholarship

AMOUNT: None Specified DEADLINE: Varies
MAJOR: Music

Available to full-time JBU students who are pursuing a degree in the music field. Applicant will audition with the music department. Award amounts vary. Award requirements change regularly. Contact address listed for details, sending a self-addressed, stamped envelope; email finaid@adm.jbu.edu; call (800) 634-6969; or browse the web at www.jbu.edu for further information. No GPA requirement specified.

John Brown University
Admissions Office
2000 West University Street
Siloam Springs, AR 72761

1875
Presidential Scholarship

AMOUNT: $9000 DEADLINE: January 15
MAJOR: All Areas of Study

This scholarship is open to entering JBU freshmen who demonstrate superior academics and leadership potential with a minimum high school GPA of 3.9. You must be in the top 5% of your graduating class and be placed in the top 95th percentile on the ACT/SAT exams. Applicants must have a strong Christian testimony and demonstrated leadership ability. Award requirements change regularly. For further information, please write to the address provided, using a self-addressed, stamped envelope. GPA must be 3.9-4.0.

John Brown University
Admissions Office
2000 West University Street
Siloam Springs, AR 72761

1876
Provost Scholarship

AMOUNT: $5000 DEADLINE: January 1
MAJOR: All Areas of Study

The Provost Scholarship is open to freshmen attending John Brown University with a 95% or above on the ACT/SAT and at least a 3.8 high school GPA. The student must demonstrate leadership abilities, and, a strong Christian testimony and be in the top 5% in the high school class. The scholarship is renewable provided the applicant maintains the appropriate GPA. This award is not open to transfer students. Award requirements change regularly. Please send a self-addressed, stamped envelope to receive your application and for any further instructions from the scholarship provider. GPA must be 3.8-4.0.

John Brown University
Admissions Office
2000 West University Street
Siloam Springs, AR 72761

1877
Sibling Award

AMOUNT: $300 DEADLINE: Varies
MAJOR: All Areas of Study

The Sibling Award is open to siblings of current John Brown University students. Award requirements change regularly. Please send a self-addressed, stamped envelope to receive your application and any further instructions from the scholarship provider. No GPA requirement specified.

John Brown University
Admissions Office
2000 West University Street
Siloam Springs, AR 72761

1878
Trustee's Award

AMOUNT: $2000 DEADLINE: May 1
MAJOR: All Areas of Study

The Trustee's Award is open to freshmen and transfer students attending John Brown University. Freshman applicants must have at least a 97% on ACT/SAT. Transfer students must have at least a 3.6 GPA with 24 or more hours of transfer credit. This award is renewable provided the GPA is maintained. Award requirements change regularly. Please send a self-addressed, stamped envelope to receive your application and for any further instructions from the scholarship provider. No GPA requirement specified.

John Brown University
Admissions Office
2000 West University Street
Siloam Springs, AR 72761

Johnson and Wales University

1879
Johnson and Wales Business Management Scholarship (Florida)

AMOUNT: None Specified DEADLINE: Varies
MAJOR: Business Management

The Johnson and Wales Business Management Scholarship (Florida) is open to Florida residents attending or planning to attend Johnson and Wales University in Florida to study business management. Applications are available at Florida high schools and GED testing centers. Award requirements change regularly. For further information, please send a self-addressed, stamped envelope to Johnson and Wales University, Jeffery Greenip, Associate Director of Admissions, 1701 NE 127th Street, North Miami, FL 33181, or call (305) 892-7600. No GPA requirement specified.

Florida Association of Postsecondary Schools and Colleges
Attn: FAPSC Scholarship Committee
F200 West College Avenue
Tallahassee, FL 32301

Kansas City Art Institute

1880
Kansas City Art Institute Competitive Scholarship

AMOUNT: None Specified DEADLINE: Varies
MAJOR: All Areas of Study

This scholarship is open to students who are attending the Kansas City Art Institute. Applicants must demonstrate exceptional artistic and academic ability and be nominated by their regional coordinator of admissions. The deadline is January 15 for freshmen and March 15 for transfer students. Award requirements change regularly. For additional information please write to the address listed, enclosing a self-addressed, stamped envelope, or call (816) 561-4852 or (800) 522-5224 for more information or email admiss@kcai.edu. GPA must be 3.0-4.0.

Kansas City Art Institute
Ron Cattelino, Exec VP Administration
4415 Warwick Blvd
Kansas City, MO 64111-1820

1881
Kansas City Art Institute Scholarships and Merit Awards

AMOUNT: $2500-$8000 DEADLINE: Varies
MAJOR: All Areas of Study

This scholarship is open to undergraduate students attending the Kansas City Art Institute. Scholarships are awarded based on academic excellence and a portfolio evaluation. First priority deadline date for the Merit Award is January 15. Second priority deadline is February 15. Third priority deadline is

March 15. Award requirements change regularly. For further information please write to the address listed, enclosing a self-addressed, stamped envelope, or call (816) 561-4852 or (800) 522-5224 for more information or email admiss@kcai.edu. GPA must be 2.8-4.0.

Kansas City Art Institute
Ron Cattelino, Exec VP Administration
4415 Warwick Blvd
Kansas City, MO 64111-1820

Keiser College

1882

Keiser College Accounting Scholarship (Ft. Lauderdale)

AMOUNT: None Specified DEADLINE: Varies
MAJOR: Accounting

The Keiser College Accounting Scholarship (Ft. Lauderdale) is open to Florida residents attending or planning to attend the Keiser College - Fort Lauderdale Campus to study accounting. Applications are available at Florida high schools and GED testing centers. Award requirements change regularly. For further information, please send a self-addressed, stamped envelope to Keiser College, Carole Fuller, Director, 1500 NW 49th Street, Fort Lauderdale, FL 33309, or call (954) 776-4456. No GPA requirement specified.

Florida Association of Postsecondary Schools and Colleges
Attn: FAPSC Scholarship Committee
F200 West College Avenue
Tallahassee, FL 32301

1883

Keiser College Accounting Scholarship (Melbourne)

AMOUNT: None Specified DEADLINE: Varies
MAJOR: Accounting

The Keiser College Accounting Scholarship (Melbourne) is open to Florida residents attending or planning to attend the Keiser College - Melbourne Campus to study accounting. Applications are available at Florida high schools and GED testing centers. Award requirements change regularly. For further information, please send a self-addressed, stamped envelope to Keiser College, Shirley Simoni, Director of Admissions, 701 South Babcock Street, Melbourne, FL 32901, or call (407) 255-2255. No GPA requirement specified.

Florida Association of Postsecondary Schools and Colleges
Attn: FAPSC Scholarship Committee
F200 West College Avenue
Tallahassee, FL 32301

1884

Keiser College Accounting Scholarship (Sarasota)

AMOUNT: None Specified DEADLINE: Varies
MAJOR: Accounting

The Keiser College Accounting Scholarship (Sarasota) is open to Florida residents attending or planning to attend the Keiser College - Sarasota Campus to study accounting. Applications are available at Florida high schools and GED testing centers. Award requirements change regularly. For further information, please send a self-addressed, stamped envelope to Keiser College, Barbara Doran, Director of Admissions, 332 Sarasota Quay, Sarasota, FL 34235, or call (941) 954-0954. No GPA requirement specified.

Florida Association of Postsecondary Schools and Colleges
Attn: FAPSC Scholarship Committee
F200 West College Avenue
Tallahassee, FL 32301

1885

Keiser College Accounting Scholarship (Tallahassee)

AMOUNT: None Specified DEADLINE: Varies
MAJOR: Accounting

The Keiser College Accounting Scholarship (Tallahassee) is open to Florida residents attending or planning to attend the Keiser College - Tallahassee Campus to study accounting. Applications are available at Florida high schools and GED testing centers. Award requirements change regularly. For further information, please send a self-addressed, stamped envelope to Keiser College, Lisa Sharp, Director of Admissions, 1700 Halstead Boulevard, Tallahassee, FL 32308, or call (850) 906-9494. No GPA requirement specified.

Florida Association of Postsecondary Schools and Colleges
Attn: FAPSC Scholarship Committee
F200 West College Avenue
Tallahassee, FL 32301

1886

Keiser College Business Administration Scholarship (Daytona Beach)

AMOUNT: None Specified DEADLINE: Varies
MAJOR: Business Administration

The Keiser College Business Administration Scholarship (Daytona Beach) is open to Florida residents attending or planning to attend the Keiser College - Daytona Beach Campus to study business administration. Applications are available at Florida high schools and GED testing centers. Award requirements change regularly. For further information, please send a self-addressed, stamped envelope to Keiser College, James Wallis, Director of Admissions, 1800 West International Speedway, Building #3, Daytona Beach, FL 32114, or call (904) 255-1707. No GPA requirement specified.

Florida Association of Postsecondary Schools and Colleges
Attn: FAPSC Scholarship Committee
F200 West College Avenue
Tallahassee, FL 32301

1887
Keiser College Business Administration Scholarship (Ft. Lauderdale)

AMOUNT: None Specified DEADLINE: Varies
MAJOR: Business Administration

The Keiser College Business Administration Scholarship (Ft. Lauderdale) is open to Florida residents attending or planning to attend the Keiser College - Fort Lauderdale Campus to study business administration. Applications are available at Florida high schools and GED testing centers. Award requirements change regularly. For further information, please send a self-addressed, stamped envelope to Keiser College, Carole Fuller, Director, 1500 NW 49th Street, Fort Lauderdale, FL 33309, or call (954) 776-4456. No GPA requirement specified.

Florida Association of Postsecondary Schools and Colleges
Attn: FAPSC Scholarship Committee
F200 West College Avenue
Tallahassee, FL 32301

1888
Keiser College Business Administration Scholarship (Melbourne)

AMOUNT: None Specified DEADLINE: Varies
MAJOR: Business Administration

The Keiser College Business Administration Scholarship (Melbourne) is open to Florida residents attending or planning to attend the Keiser College - Melbourne Campus to study business administration. Applications are available at Florida high schools and GED testing centers. Award requirements change regularly. For further information, please send a self-addressed, stamped envelope to Keiser College, Shirley Simoni, Director of Admissions, 701 South Babcock Street, Melbourne, FL 32901, or call (407) 255-2255. No GPA requirement specified.

Florida Association of Postsecondary Schools and Colleges
Attn: FAPSC Scholarship Committee
F200 West College Avenue
Tallahassee, FL 32301

1889
Keiser College Business Administration Scholarship (Sarasota)

AMOUNT: None Specified DEADLINE: Varies
MAJOR: Business Administration

The Keiser College Business Administration Scholarship (Sarasota) is open to Florida residents attending or planning to attend the Keiser College - Sarasota Campus to study business administration. Applications are available at Florida high schools and GED testing centers. Award requirements change regularly. For further information, please send a self-addressed, stamped envelope to Keiser College, Barbara Doran, Director of Admissions, 332 Sarasota Quay, Sarasota, FL 34235, or call (941) 954-0954. No GPA requirement specified.

Florida Association of Postsecondary Schools and Colleges
Attn: FAPSC Scholarship Committee
F200 West College Avenue
Tallahassee, FL 32301

1890
Keiser College Business Administration Scholarship (Tallahassee)

AMOUNT: None Specified DEADLINE: Varies
MAJOR: Business Administration

The Keiser College Business Administration Scholarship (Tallahassee) is open to Florida residents attending or planning to attend the Keiser College - Tallahassee Campus to study business administration. Applications are available at Florida high schools and GED testing centers. Award requirements change regularly. For further information, please send a self-addressed, stamped envelope to Keiser College, Lisa Sharp, Director of Admissions, 1700 Halstead Boulevard, Tallahassee, FL 32308, or call (850) 906-9494. No GPA requirement specified.

Florida Association of Postsecondary Schools and Colleges
Attn: FAPSC Scholarship Committee
F200 West College Avenue
Tallahassee, FL 32301

1891
Keiser College Computer Graphics and Design Scholarship (Daytona Beach)

AMOUNT: None Specified DEADLINE: Varies
MAJOR: Computer Graphics and Design

The Keiser College Computer Graphics and Design Scholarship (Daytona Beach) is open to Florida residents attending or planning to attend the Keiser College - Daytona Beach Campus to study computer graphics and design. Applications are available at Florida high schools and GED testing centers. Award requirements change regularly. For further information, please send a self-addressed, stamped envelope to Keiser College, James Wallis, Director of Admissions, 1800 West International Speedway, Building #3, Daytona Beach, FL 32114, or call (904) 255-1707. No GPA requirement specified.

Florida Association of Postsecondary Schools and Colleges
Attn: FAPSC Scholarship Committee
F200 West College Avenue
Tallahassee, FL 32301

1892
Keiser College Computer Graphics and Design Scholarship (Ft. Lauderdale)

AMOUNT: None Specified DEADLINE: Varies
MAJOR: Computer Graphics and Design

The Keiser College Computer Graphics and Design Scholarship (Ft. Lauderdale) is open to Florida residents attending or planning to attend the Keiser College - Fort Lauderdale Campus to study computer graphics and design. Applications are available at Florida high schools and GED testing centers. Award requirements change regularly. For further information, please send a self-addressed, stamped envelope to Keiser College, Carole Fuller, Director, 1500 NW 49th Street, Fort Lauderdale, FL 33309, or call (954) 776-4456. No GPA requirement specified.

Florida Association of Postsecondary Schools and Colleges
Attn: FAPSC Scholarship Committee
F200 West College Avenue
Tallahassee, FL 32301

1893
Keiser College Computer Graphics and Design Scholarship (Melbourne)

AMOUNT: None Specified DEADLINE: Varies
MAJOR: Computer Graphics and Design

The Keiser College Computer Graphics and Design Scholarship (Melbourne) is open to Florida residents attending or planning to attend the Keiser College - Melbourne Campus to study computer graphics and design. Applications are available at Florida high schools and GED testing centers. Award requirements change regularly. For further information, please send a self-addressed, stamped envelope to Keiser College, Shirley Simoni, Director of Admissions, 701 South Babcock Street, Melbourne, FL 32901, or call (407) 255-2255. No GPA requirement specified.

Florida Association of Postsecondary Schools and Colleges
Attn: FAPSC Scholarship Committee
F200 West College Avenue
Tallahassee, FL 32301

1894
Keiser College Computer Graphics and Design Scholarship (Sarasota)

AMOUNT: None Specified DEADLINE: Varies
MAJOR: Computer Graphics and Design

The Keiser College Computer Graphics and Design Scholarship (Sarasota) is open to Florida residents attending or planning to attend the Keiser College - Sarasota Campus to study computer graphics and design. Applications are available at Florida high schools and GED testing centers. Award requirements change regularly. For further information, please send a self-addressed, stamped envelope to Keiser College, Barbara Doran, Director of Admissions, 332 Sarasota Quay, Sarasota, FL 34235, or call (941) 954-0954. No GPA requirement specified.

Florida Association of Postsecondary Schools and Colleges
Attn: FAPSC Scholarship Committee
F200 West College Avenue
Tallahassee, FL 32301

1895
Keiser College Computer Graphics and Design Scholarship (Tallahassee)

AMOUNT: None Specified DEADLINE: Varies
MAJOR: Computer Graphics and Design

The Keiser College Computer Graphics and Design Scholarship (Tallahassee) is open to Florida residents attending or planning to attend the Keiser College - Tallahassee Campus to study computer graphics and design. Applications are available at Florida high schools and GED testing centers. Award requirements change regularly. For further information, please send a self-addressed, stamped envelope to Keiser College, Lisa Sharp, Director of Admissions, 1700 Halstead Boulevard, Tallahassee, FL 32308, or call (850) 906-9494. No GPA requirement specified.

Florida Association of Postsecondary Schools and Colleges
Attn: FAPSC Scholarship Committee
F200 West College Avenue
Tallahassee, FL 32301

1896
Keiser College Computer Network Administration Scholarship (Melbourne)

AMOUNT: None Specified DEADLINE: Varies
MAJOR: Computer Network Administration

The Keiser College Computer Network Administration Scholarship (Melbourne) is open to Florida residents attending or planning to attend the Keiser College - Melbourne Campus to study computer network administration. Applications are available at Florida high schools and GED testing centers. Award requirements change regularly. For further information, please send a self-addressed, stamped envelope to Keiser College, Shirley Simoni, Director of Admissions, 701 South Babcock Street, Melbourne, FL 32901, or call (407) 255-2255. No GPA requirement specified.

Florida Association of Postsecondary Schools and Colleges
Attn: FAPSC Scholarship Committee
F200 West College Avenue
Tallahassee, FL 32301

1897
Keiser College Computer Programming Scholarship (Ft. Lauderdale)

AMOUNT: None Specified DEADLINE: Varies
MAJOR: Computer Programming

The Keiser College Computer Programming Scholarship (Ft. Lauderdale) is open to Florida residents attending or planning to attend the Keiser College - Fort Lauderdale Campus to study computer programming. Applications are available at Florida high schools and GED testing centers. Award requirements change regularly. For further information, please send a self-addressed, stamped envelope to Keiser College, Carole Fuller, Director, 1500 NW 49th Street, Fort Lauderdale, FL 33309, or call (954) 776-4456. No GPA requirement specified.

Florida Association of Postsecondary Schools and Colleges
Attn: FAPSC Scholarship Committee
F200 West College Avenue
Tallahassee, FL 32301

1898
Keiser College Computer Programming Scholarship (Melbourne)

AMOUNT: None Specified DEADLINE: Varies
MAJOR: Computer Programming

The Keiser College Computer Programming Scholarship (Melbourne) is open to Florida residents attending or planning to attend the Keiser College - Melbourne Campus to study computer programming. Applications are available at Florida high schools and GED testing centers. Award requirements change regularly. For further information, please send a self-addressed, stamped envelope to Keiser College, Shirley Simoni, Director of Admissions, 701 South Babcock Street, Melbourne, FL 32901, or call (407) 255-2255. No GPA requirement specified.

Florida Association of Postsecondary Schools and Colleges
Attn: FAPSC Scholarship Committee
F200 West College Avenue
Tallahassee, FL 32301

1899
Keiser College Computer Programming Scholarship (Sarasota)

AMOUNT: None Specified DEADLINE: Varies
MAJOR: Computer Programming

The Keiser College Computer Programming Scholarship (Sarasota) is open to Florida residents attending or planning to attend the Keiser College - Sarasota Campus to study computer programming. Applications are available at Florida high schools and GED testing centers. Award requirements change regularly. For further information, please send a self-addressed, stamped envelope to Keiser College, Barbara Doran, Director of Admissions, 332 Sarasota Quay, Sarasota, FL 34235, or call (941) 954-0954. No GPA requirement specified.

Florida Association of Postsecondary Schools and Colleges
Attn: FAPSC Scholarship Committee
F200 West College Avenue
Tallahassee, FL 32301

1900
Keiser College Computer Programming Scholarship (Tallahassee)

AMOUNT: None Specified DEADLINE: Varies
MAJOR: Computer Programming

The Keiser College Computer Programming Scholarship (Tallahassee) is open to Florida residents attending or planning to áttend the Keiser College - Tallahassee Campus to study computer programming. Applications are available at Florida high schools and GED testing centers. Award requirements change regularly. For further information, please send a

self-addressed, stamped envelope to Keiser College, Lisa Sharp, Director of Admissions, 1700 Halstead Boulevard, Tallahassee, FL 32308, or call (850) 906-9494. No GPA requirement specified.

Florida Association of Postsecondary Schools and Colleges
Attn: FAPSC Scholarship Committee
F200 West College Avenue
Tallahassee, FL 32301

1901
Keiser College Computer-Aided Drafting Scholarship (Ft. Lauderdale)

AMOUNT: None Specified DEADLINE: Varies
MAJOR: Computer-Aided Drafting and Design/CAD

The Keiser College Computer-Aided Drafting Scholarship (Ft. Lauderdale) is open to Florida residents attending or planning to attend the Keiser College - Fort Lauderdale Campus to study computer-aided drafting and design/CAD. Applications are available at Florida high schools and GED testing centers. Award requirements change regularly. For further information, please send a self-addressed, stamped envelope to Keiser College, Carole Fuller, Director, 1500 NW 49th Street, Fort Lauderdale, FL 33309, or call (954) 776-4456. No GPA requirement specified.

Florida Association of Postsecondary Schools and Colleges
Attn: FAPSC Scholarship Committee
F200 West College Avenue
Tallahassee, FL 32301

1902
Keiser College Film and Video Production Scholarship (Daytona Beach)

AMOUNT: None Specified DEADLINE: Varies
MAJOR: Film and Video Production

The Keiser College Film and Video Production Scholarship (Daytona Beach) is open to Florida residents attending or planning to attend the Keiser College - Daytona Beach Campus to study film and video production. Applications are available at Florida high schools and GED testing centers. Award requirements change regularly. For further information, please send a self-addressed, stamped envelope to Keiser College, James Wallis, Director of Admissions, 1800 West International Speedway, Building #3, Daytona Beach, FL 32114, or call (904) 255-1707. No GPA requirement specified.

Florida Association of Postsecondary Schools and Colleges
Attn: FAPSC Scholarship Committee
F200 West College Avenue
Tallahassee, FL 32301

1903
Keiser College Health Services Administration Scholarship (Melbourne)

AMOUNT: None Specified DEADLINE: Varies
MAJOR: Health Services Administration

The Keiser College Health Services Administration Scholarship (Melbourne) is open to Florida residents attending or planning to attend the Keiser College - Melbourne Campus to study health services administration. Applications are available at Florida high schools and GED testing centers. Award requirements change regularly. For further information, please send a self-addressed, stamped envelope to Keiser College, Shirley Simoni, Director of Admissions, 701 South Babcock Street, Melbourne, FL 32901, or call (407) 255-2255. No GPA requirement specified.

Florida Association of Postsecondary Schools and Colleges
Attn: FAPSC Scholarship Committee
F200 West College Avenue
Tallahassee, FL 32301

1904
Keiser College Health Services Administration Scholarship (Sarasota)

AMOUNT: None Specified DEADLINE: Varies
MAJOR: Health Services Administration

The Keiser College Health Services Administration Scholarship (Sarasota) is open to Florida residents attending or planning to attend the Keiser College - Sarasota Campus to study health services administration. Applications are available at Florida high schools and GED testing centers. Award requirements change regularly. For further information, please send a self-addressed, stamped envelope to Keiser College, Barbara Doran, Director of Admissions, 332 Sarasota Quay, Sarasota, FL 34235, or call (941) 954-0954. No GPA requirement specified.

Florida Association of Postsecondary Schools and Colleges
Attn: FAPSC Scholarship Committee
F200 West College Avenue
Tallahassee, FL 32301

1905
Keiser College Hospitality Management Scholarship (Ft. Lauderdale)

AMOUNT: None Specified DEADLINE: Varies
MAJOR: Hospitality Management

The Keiser College Hospitality Management Scholarship (Ft. Lauderdale) is open to Florida residents attending or planning to attend the Keiser College - Fort Lauderdale Campus to study hospitality management. Applications are available at Florida high schools and GED testing centers. Award requirements change regularly. For further information, please send a self-addressed, stamped envelope to Keiser College, Carole Fuller, Director, 1500 NW 49th Street, Fort Lauderdale, FL 33309, or call (954) 776-4456. No GPA requirement specified.

Florida Association of Postsecondary Schools and Colleges
Attn: FAPSC Scholarship Committee
F200 West College Avenue
Tallahassee, FL 32301

1906
Keiser College Medical Assisting Scholarship (Daytona Beach)

AMOUNT: None Specified DEADLINE: Varies
MAJOR: Medical Assisting

The Keiser College Medical Assisting Scholarship (Daytona Beach) is open to Florida residents attending or planning to attend the Keiser College - Daytona Beach Campus to study medical assisting. Applications are available at Florida high schools and GED testing centers. Award requirements change regularly. For further information, please send a self-addressed, stamped envelope to Keiser College, James Wallis, Director of Admissions, 1800 West International Speedway, Building #3, Daytona Beach, FL 32114, or call (904) 255-1707. No GPA requirement specified.

Florida Association of Postsecondary Schools and Colleges
Attn: FAPSC Scholarship Committee
F200 West College Avenue
Tallahassee, FL 32301

1907
Keiser College Medical Assisting Scholarship (Ft. Lauderdale)

AMOUNT: None Specified DEADLINE: Varies
MAJOR: Medical Assisting

The Keiser College Medical Assisting Scholarship (Ft. Lauderdale) is open to Florida residents attending or planning to attend the Keiser College - Fort Lauderdale Campus to study medical assisting. Applications are available at Florida high schools and GED testing centers. Award requirements change regularly. For further information, please send a self-addressed, stamped envelope to Keiser College, Carole Fuller, Director, 1500 NW 49th Street, Fort Lauderdale, FL 33309, or call (954) 776-4456. No GPA requirement specified.

Florida Association of Postsecondary Schools and Colleges
Attn: FAPSC Scholarship Committee
F200 West College Avenue
Tallahassee, FL 32301

1908
Keiser College Medical Assisting Scholarship (Melbourne)

AMOUNT: None Specified DEADLINE: Varies
MAJOR: Medical Assisting

The Keiser College Medical Assisting Scholarship (Melbourne) is open to Florida residents attending or planning to attend the Keiser College - Melbourne Campus to study medical assisting. Applications are available at Florida high schools and GED testing centers. Award requirements change regularly. For further information, please send a self-addressed, stamped envelope to Keiser College, Shirley Simoni, Director of Admissions, 701 South Babcock Street, Melbourne, FL 32901, or call (407) 255-2255. No GPA requirement specified.

Florida Association of Postsecondary Schools and Colleges
Attn: FAPSC Scholarship Committee
F200 West College Avenue
Tallahassee, FL 32301

1909
Keiser College Medical Assisting Scholarship (Sarasota)

AMOUNT: None Specified DEADLINE: Varies
MAJOR: Medical Assisting

The Keiser College Medical Assisting Scholarship (Sarasota) is open to Florida residents attending or planning to attend the Keiser College - Sarasota Campus to study medical assisting. Applications are available at Florida high schools and GED testing centers. Award requirements change regularly. For further information, please send a self-addressed, stamped envelope to Keiser College, Barbara Doran, Director of Admissions, 332 Sarasota Quay, Sarasota, FL 34235, or call (941) 954-0954. No GPA requirement specified.

Florida Association of Postsecondary Schools and Colleges
Attn: FAPSC Scholarship Committee
F200 West College Avenue
Tallahassee, FL 32301

1910
Keiser College Medical Assisting Scholarship (Tallahassee)

AMOUNT: None Specified DEADLINE: Varies
MAJOR: Medical Assisting

The Keiser College Medical Assisting Scholarship (Tallahassee) is open to Florida residents attending or planning to attend the Keiser College - Tallahassee Campus to study medical assisting. Applications are available at Florida high schools and GED testing centers. Award requirements change regularly. For further information, please send a self-addressed, stamped envelope to Keiser College, Lisa Sharp, Director of Admissions, 1700 Halstead Boulevard, Tallahassee, FL 32308, or call (850) 906-9494. No GPA requirement specified.

Florida Association of Postsecondary Schools and Colleges
Attn: FAPSC Scholarship Committee
F200 West College Avenue
Tallahassee, FL 32301

1911
Keiser College Network Administration Scholarship (Sarasota)

AMOUNT: None Specified DEADLINE: Varies
MAJOR: Computer Network Administration

The Keiser College Computer Network Administration Scholarship (Sarasota) is open to Florida residents attending or planning to attend the Keiser College - Sarasota Campus to study computer network administration. Applications are available at Florida high schools and GED testing centers. Award requirements change regularly. For further information, please send a self-addressed, stamped envelope to Keiser College, Barbara Doran, Director of Admissions, 332 Sarasota Quay, Sarasota, FL 34235, or call (941) 954-0954. No GPA requirement specified.

Florida Association of Postsecondary Schools and Colleges
Attn: FAPSC Scholarship Committee
F200 West College Avenue
Tallahassee, FL 32301

1912
Keiser College Network Administration Scholarship (Tallahassee)

AMOUNT: None Specified DEADLINE: Varies
MAJOR: Computer Network Administration

The Keiser College Computer Network Administration Scholarship (Tallahassee) is open to Florida residents attending or planning to attend the Keiser College - Tallahassee Campus to study computer network administration. Applications are available at Florida high schools and GED testing centers. Award requirements change regularly. For further information, please send a self-addressed, stamped envelope to Keiser College, Lisa Sharp, Director of Admissions, 1700 Halstead Boulevard, Tallahassee, FL 32308, or call (850) 906-9494. No GPA requirement specified.

Florida Association of Postsecondary Schools and Colleges
Attn: FAPSC Scholarship Committee
F200 West College Avenue
Tallahassee, FL 32301

1913
Keiser College Paralegal Studies Scholarship (Daytona Beach)

AMOUNT: None Specified DEADLINE: Varies
MAJOR: Paralegal

The Keiser College Paralegal Studies Scholarship (Daytona Beach) is open to Florida residents attending or planning to attend the Keiser College - Daytona Beach Campus to study to become a paralegal. Applications are available at Florida high schools and GED testing centers. Award requirements change regularly. For further information, please send a self-addressed, stamped envelope to Keiser College, James Wallis, Director of Admissions, 1800 West International Speedway, Building #3, Daytona Beach, FL 32114, or call (904) 255-1707. No GPA requirement specified.

Florida Association of Postsecondary Schools and Colleges
Attn: FAPSC Scholarship Committee
F200 West College Avenue
Tallahassee, FL 32301

1914
Keiser College Paralegal Studies Scholarship (Ft. Lauderdale)

AMOUNT: None Specified DEADLINE: Varies
MAJOR: Paralegal

The Keiser College Paralegal Studies Scholarship (Ft. Lauderdale) is open to Florida residents attending or planning to attend the Keiser College - Fort Lauderdale Campus to study to become a paralegal. Applications are available at Florida high schools and GED testing centers. Award requirements change regularly. For further information, please send a self-addressed, stamped envelope to Keiser College, Carole Fuller, Director, 1500 NW 49th Street, Fort Lauderdale, FL 33309, or call (954) 776-4456. No GPA requirement specified.

Florida Association of Postsecondary Schools and Colleges
Attn: FAPSC Scholarship Committee
F200 West College Avenue
Tallahassee, FL 32301

1915
Keiser College Paralegal Studies Scholarship (Melbourne)

AMOUNT: None Specified   DEADLINE: Varies
MAJOR: Paralegal Studies

The Keiser College Paralegal Studies Scholarship (Melbourne) is open to Florida residents attending or planning to attend the Keiser College - Melbourne Campus to study to become a paralegal. Applications are available at Florida high schools and GED testing centers. Award requirements change regularly. For further information, please send a self-addressed, stamped envelope to Keiser College, Shirley Simoni, Director of Admissions, 701 South Babcock Street, Melbourne, FL 32901, or call (407) 255-2255. No GPA requirement specified.

Florida Association of Postsecondary Schools and Colleges
Attn: FAPSC Scholarship Committee
F200 West College Avenue
Tallahassee, FL 32301

1916
Keiser College Paralegal Studies Scholarship (Sarasota)

AMOUNT: None Specified   DEADLINE: Varies
MAJOR: Paralegal

The Keiser College Paralegal Studies Scholarship (Sarasota) is open to Florida residents attending or planning to attend the Keiser College - Sarasota Campus who are studying to become paralegals. Applications are available at Florida high schools and GED testing centers. Award requirements change regularly. For further information, please send a self-addressed, stamped envelope to Keiser College, Barbara Doran, Director of Admissions, 332 Sarasota Quay, Sarasota, FL 34235, or call (941) 954-0954. No GPA requirement specified.

Florida Association of Postsecondary Schools and Colleges
Attn: FAPSC Scholarship Committee
F200 West College Avenue
Tallahassee, FL 32301

1917
Keiser College Paralegal Studies Scholarship (Tallahassee)

AMOUNT: None Specified   DEADLINE: Varies
MAJOR: Paralegal

The Keiser College Paralegal Studies Scholarship (Tallahassee) is open to Florida residents attending or planning to attend the Keiser College - Tallahassee Campus who are studying to become a paralegal. Applications are available

at Florida high schools and GED testing centers. Award requirements change regularly. For further information, please send a self-addressed, stamped envelope to Keiser College, Lisa Sharp, Director of Admissions, 1700 Halstead Boulevard, Tallahassee, FL 32308, or call (850) 906-9494. No GPA requirement specified.

Florida Association of Postsecondary Schools and Colleges
Attn: FAPSC Scholarship Committee
F200 West College Avenue
Tallahassee, FL 32301

Kendall College of Art & Design

1918
Kendall College Merit Scholarship

AMOUNT: $1000-$5000   DEADLINE: February 15
MAJOR: Art, Design

The Kendall College Merit Scholarship is open to incoming freshmen and transfer students at Kendall College of Art & Design who have a minimum 3.0 GPA. Awards can range from $1000 to $5000 per year and are renewable if you maintain a 3.0 GPA and demonstrate continued artistic growth. Award requirements change regularly. GPA must be 3.0-4.0.

Kendall College of Art & Design
Financial Aid Office
111 Division Avenue, North
Grand Rapids, MI 49503-3102

Kent State University

1919
AFROTC Incentive Scholarship

AMOUNT: $500-$1000   DEADLINE: July 1
MAJOR: Aerospace Studies

The AFROTC Incentive Scholarship is open to freshmen aerospace majors attending Kent State University. This award is based on academic record and ACT/SAT scores. You must enroll in Air Force ROTC for one year and meet AFROTC scholarship retention criteria. No further military obligation is incurred. This award is for U.S. citizens or those applying for citizenship. Award requirements change regularly. For further information contact the Unit Admissions Officer: (330) 672-2182. No GPA requirement specified.

Kent State University
Student Financial Aid
PO Box 5190
Kent, OH 44242-0001

1920
American Greeting Card Scholarship

AMOUNT: None Specified DEADLINE: Varies
MAJOR: Graphic Design, Illustration

The American Greeting Card Scholarship is open to undergraduates attending Kent State University who are graphic design and illustration majors. This award is not available to incoming freshmen. Selection is based on artistic merit. Award requirements change regularly. For an application and further information, please contact J. Charles Walker: (330) 672-7856. No GPA requirement specified.

Kent State University
Student Financial Aid
PO Box 5190
Kent, OH 44242-0001

1921
Art Scholarship for Incoming Freshmen

AMOUNT: $500 DEADLINE: October 1
MAJOR: Art

The Art Scholarship for Incoming Freshmen is open to incoming freshmen at Kent State University who are majoring in art. Selection is based on your portfolio, merit, and financial need. This award is renewable. Award requirements change regularly. For an application and further information, please contact Joseph Fry: (330) 672-2192. No GPA requirement specified.

Kent State University
Student Financial Aid
PO Box 5190
Kent, OH 44242-0001

1922
Athletic Scholarship

AMOUNT: $200-$14766 DEADLINE: August 15
MAJOR: All Areas of Study

The Athletic Scholarship is open to varsity athletes who are recommended by their head coach. This award applies to undergraduates attending Kent State University. Award requirements change regularly. For further information contact Judy Devine at (330) 672-5976. No GPA requirement specified.

Kent State University
Student Financial Aid
PO Box 5190
Kent, OH 44242-0001

1923
Black Alumni Council Scholarship

AMOUNT: $500 DEADLINE: February 27
MAJOR: All Areas of Study

The Black Alumni Council Scholarship is open to African-American students at Kent State University who have a high level of participation and involvement in community service activities. You must be a sophomore, junior, or senior and

have a minimum 2.5. GPA. Award requirements change regularly. For an application and further information, please contact the Alumni Association: (330) 672-5368. GPA must be 2.5-4.0.

Kent State University
Student Financial Aid
PO Box 5190
Kent, OH 44242-0001

1924
Chagrin Valley Junior Women's Club Award

AMOUNT: $1000 DEADLINE: March 30
MAJOR: All Areas of Study

The Chagrin Valley Junior Women's Club Award is open to adult females 25 years or older at Kent Campus whose education has been deferred by child rearing or marriage. In order to apply, you should be planning to earn an undergraduate degree that will qualify you for employment or will upgrade your skills. Award requirements change regularly. For an application and further information, please contact the Office of Adult Services: (330) 672-7933. No GPA requirement specified.

Kent State University
Student Financial Aid
PO Box 5190
Kent, OH 44242-0001

1925
General Foundation Scholarship

AMOUNT: $1000-$1500 DEADLINE: Varies
MAJOR: All Areas of Study

The General Foundation Scholarship is open to incoming full-time freshmen and transfer students who are in their second year of study at Kent State University, Tuscarawas Campus. Demonstration of your superior academic record is required. The preferred application deadline for the fall semester is April 1 of the preceding spring for new students and June 1 for returning students or new transfer students. This award is nonrenewable. Award requirements change regularly. For an application and further information, please contact Agnes Swigart, Tuscarawas Campus: (330) 339-3391. No GPA requirement specified.

Kent State University
Student Financial Aid
PO Box 5190
Kent, OH 44242-0001

1926
Idabelle Hoose Memorial Scholarship

AMOUNT: $500 DEADLINE: March 1
MAJOR: All Areas of Study

The Idabelle Hoose Memorial Scholarship is open to female undergraduates enrolled full-time at Kent State University. To be considered for this award, you must have a minimum 3.25 GPA and demonstrate achievement under some type of disability (physical, financial, etc.). The amount of your financial need will be determined by the FAFSA. This award is not renewable. Award requirements change regularly. Please contact Kent State for more information on how to apply. GPA must be 3.25-4.0.

Kent State University
Student Financial Aid
PO Box 5190
Kent, OH 44242-0001

1927
James Martin Education Scholarship

AMOUNT: $300 DEADLINE: February 27
MAJOR: Education

The James Martin Education Scholarship is open to Kent State University students of sophomore, junior, or senior standing. You must have officially declared education as a major and demonstrate financial need. A minimum 3.0 GPA is required. Award requirements change regularly. For an application and further information, please contact the Alumni Association at (330) 672-5368. GPA must be 3.0-4.0.

Kent State University
Student Financial Aid
PO Box 5190
Kent, OH 44242-0001

1928
James R. Fako Memorial Scholarship

AMOUNT: $500-$750 DEADLINE: February 15
MAJOR: Accounting

The James R. Fako Memorial Scholarship is open to accounting majors at Kent State University. You must have sophomore standing for the initial award. You must demonstrate financial need and scholastic ability. This award is renewable. Award requirements change regularly. For an application and further information, please contact Dr. Stephens, Accounting Chair, at (330) 672-2545. No GPA requirement specified.

Kent State University
Student Financial Aid
PO Box 5190
Kent, OH 44242-0001

1929
Joseph Wheeler Accounting Technology Foundation Scholarship

AMOUNT: $1500 DEADLINE: April 1
MAJOR: Accounting Technology

The Joseph Wheeler Accounting Technology Foundation Scholarship is open to incoming freshmen accounting technology majors attending Kent State University, Tuscarawas Campus. This award is based on full-time enrollment and superior academic record. The preferred application deadline for the fall semester is April 1 of the preceding spring for new students. This award is nonrenewable. Award requirements change regularly. For an application and further information, please contact Agnes Swigart, Tuscarawas Campus: (330) 339-3391. No GPA requirement specified.

Kent State University
Student Financial Aid
PO Box 5190
Kent, OH 44242-0001

1930
Kent State University Scholarship for Excellence

AMOUNT: $1000 DEADLINE: March 1
MAJOR: All Areas of Study

The Kent State University Scholarship for Excellence is open to full-time Kent State University incoming freshmen who are valedictorians or co-valedictorians of an Ohio high school. This award is renewable as long as you maintain a 3.0 GPA. Award requirements change regularly. For an application and further information, please contact Student Financial Aid at (330) 672-2444. No GPA requirement specified.

Kent State University
Student Financial Aid
PO Box 5190
Kent, OH 44242-0001

1931
Mary Hanhart Foundation Scholarship

AMOUNT: $1500 DEADLINE: Varies
MAJOR: All Areas of Study

The Mary Hanhart Foundation Scholarship is open to full-time incoming freshmen attending Kent State University, Tuscarawas Campus. You must demonstrate a superior academic record in order to apply. This award is not renewable. Award requirements change regularly. For an application and further information, please contact Agnes Swigart, Tuscarawas Campus: (330) 339-3391. No GPA requirement specified.

Kent State University
Student Financial Aid
PO Box 5190
Kent, OH 44242-0001

1932
Mary Miller Shaw Award

AMOUNT: $1000 DEADLINE: February 1
MAJOR: All Areas of Study

The Mary Miller Shaw Award is open to non-traditional, adult female students pursuing a baccalaureate degree at Kent State University. You must have completed a minimum of nine hours of undergraduate coursework after returning to school, and you must have earned a minimum 3.0 GPA before applying. Proof of adult community leadership and/or service is required. Award requirements change regularly. For an application and further information, please contact the Office of Adult Services, (330) 672-7933. GPA must be 3.0-4.0.

Kent State University
Student Financial Aid
PO Box 5190
Kent, OH 44242-0001

1933
Mason Scholarship

AMOUNT: $1250 DEADLINE: March 1
MAJOR: All Areas of Study

The Mason Scholarship is open to Kent State University and regional campus students. To be eligible to receive the award, you must be an Ohio resident with demonstrated scholastic ability. This renewable award is based on financial need as determined by the FAFSA. Masonic affiliation is not required. Award requirements change regularly. Please contact Kent State for more information on how to apply. No GPA requirement specified.

Kent State University
Student Financial Aid
PO Box 5190
Kent, OH 44242-0001

1934
Minority Foundation Scholarship (Incoming Freshmen)

AMOUNT: $1500 DEADLINE: April 1
MAJOR: All Areas of Study

The Minority Foundation Scholarship (Incoming Freshmen) is open to full-time incoming freshmen attending Kent State University, Tuscarawas Campus. Priority is given to minority students for this award. The preferred application deadline for the fall semester is April 1 of the preceding spring. Award requirements change regularly. For an application and further information, please contact Agnes Swigart, Tuscarawas Campus, at (330) 339-3391. No GPA requirement specified.

Kent State University
Student Financial Aid
PO Box 5190
Kent, OH 44242-0001

1935
Minority Incentive Scholarship

AMOUNT: $2000-$3500 DEADLINE: May 1
MAJOR: All Areas of Study

The Minority Incentive Scholarship is open to African-American, Hispanic, or Native American transfers attending Kent State University. The award requires that you have junior status in a Kent major and are able to demonstrate financial need. This scholarship is renewable for one year provided you maintain certain criteria. Award requirements change regularly. Please contact Kent State for further information on how to apply. No GPA requirement specified.

Kent State University
Student Financial Aid
PO Box 5190
Kent, OH 44242-0001

1936
Minority Uplift Scholarship

AMOUNT: $1000 DEADLINE: July 15
MAJOR: All Areas of Study

The Minority Uplift Scholarship is open to students at Kent State University, Ashtabula Campus, who are African-American, Native American, Alaskan Native, Hispanic, Asian, or Pacific Islander. You must be enrolled in a minimum of six hours per semester. If you are an incoming freshman, you must have a minimum 2.5 GPA (or be in the top 30% of your high school graduating class). If you are a GED recipient, you must have a composite of 250, with a standard score of 50. If you are a transfer or continuing student, you must have a minimum 3.0 GPA. This award is renewable. Award requirements change regularly. For an application and further information, please contact the Director of Student Services, Ashtabula Campus, (440) 964-3322. GPA must be 2.5-4.0.

Kent State University
Student Financial Aid
PO Box 5190
Kent, OH 44242-0001

1937
Nursing Alumni Council Scholarship

AMOUNT: $500 DEADLINE: April 23
MAJOR: Nursing

The Nursing Alumni Council Scholarship is open to freshman nursing majors attending Kent State University. You must also have a minimum 3.0 GPA in order to apply. Award requirements change regularly. For an application and further information, please contact the Alumni Association at (330) 672-5368. GPA must be 3.0-4.0.

Kent State University
Student Financial Aid
PO Box 5190
Kent, OH 44242-0001

1938
President's Grant

AMOUNT: None Specified DEADLINE: March 1
MAJOR: All Areas of Study

The President's Grant is open to incoming Kent State University full-time freshmen. You must be a child of a Kent State alumni and be an out-of-state resident. The award is renewable. Award requirements change regularly. For an application and further information, please contact the Admissions Office at (330) 672-2444. No GPA requirement specified.

Kent State University
Student Financial Aid
PO Box 5190
Kent, OH 44242-0001

1939
President's Scholarship

AMOUNT: None Specified DEADLINE: March 1
MAJOR: All Areas of Study

The President's Scholarship is open to incoming Kent State University freshmen enrolled full-time with a minimum 24 ACT or 1050 SAT. You must have a minimum 3.0 high school GPA (top 20% of high school class) and be an out-of-state resident. This award is renewable. Award requirements change regularly. For an application and further information, please contact the Admissions Office at (330) 672-2444. GPA must be 3.0-4.0.

Kent State University
Student Financial Aid
PO Box 5190
Kent, OH 44242-0001

1940
Preston Memorial Foundation Scholarship

AMOUNT: $1500 DEADLINE: April 1
MAJOR: All Areas of Study

The Preston Memorial Foundation Scholarship is open to incoming freshmen attending Kent State University, Tuscarawas Campus, who demonstrate superior academic records. This award is nonrenewable. Award requirements change regularly. For further information contact Agnes Swigart, Tuscarawas Campus, at (330) 339-3391. No GPA requirement specified.

Kent State University
Student Financial Aid
PO Box 5190
Kent, OH 44242-0001

1941
Professional Officer Corps Incentive Scholarship

AMOUNT: None Specified DEADLINE: Varies
MAJOR: Aerospace Studies

The Professional Officer Corps Incentive Scholarship is open to AFROTC cadets at Kent State University and its campuses who have completed summer field training. This award is based on merit and the recommendation of a professor of aerospace studies. You must have a minimum 2.0 cumulative GPA and a minimum 2.35 term GPA. The amount of this award is $850 for tuition and $150 for books per semester and a $150-per-month stipend. Award requirements change regularly. For an application and further information, please contact Unit Admissions Officer: (330) 672-2182. GPA must be 2.0-4.0.

Kent State University
Student Financial Aid
PO Box 5190
Kent, OH 44242-0001

1942
R. J. Wean Scholarship

AMOUNT: $100-$1600 DEADLINE: Varies
MAJOR: All Areas of Study

The R. J. Wean Scholarship is open to Kent State University, Trumbull Campus, students. The deadline for the fall semester is May 1; for the spring semester the deadline is December 1. A minimum GPA of 3.0 is required for this renewable award. Award requirements change regularly. For further information contact Nina J. Conner, Trumbull Campus, at (330) 847-0571. GPA must be 3.0-4.0.

Kent State University
Student Financial Aid
PO Box 5190
Kent, OH 44242-0001

1943
Richard Demuth Foundation Scholarship

AMOUNT: $1500 DEADLINE: Varies
MAJOR: All Areas of Study

The Richard Demuth Foundation Scholarship is open to incoming full-time freshmen attending Kent State University, Tuscarawas Campus. You must demonstrate a superior academic record. The preferred application deadline for the fall semester is April 1 of the preceding spring for new students. This award is not renewable. Award requirements change regularly. For an application and further information, please contact Agnes Swigart, Tuscarawas Campus: (330) 339-3391. No GPA requirement specified.

Kent State University
Student Financial Aid
PO Box 5190
Kent, OH 44242-0001

1944
School of Theater Scholarship

AMOUNT: $200-$600 DEADLINE: April 1
MAJOR: Theater

The School of Theater Scholarship is open to Kent State University campus undergraduate and graduate students who are majoring in theater. Undergraduates must have a minimum 2.5 GPA, and graduates must have a minimum 3.0 GPA. To be considered for this award, you must demonstrate creative and/or scholarly potential. You are required to have a written application and recommendation for this award as an incoming student. If you are not an incoming student, you are recommended by nomination. This award is not renewable. Award requirements change regularly. For an application and further information, please contact Director, School of Theater, at (330) 672-2082. GPA must be 2.5-4.0.

Kent State University
Student Financial Aid
PO Box 5190
Kent, OH 44242-0001

1945
Training Awards Program

AMOUNT: None Specified DEADLINE: December 15
MAJOR: All Areas of Study

The Training Awards Program is open to adult female students at Kent State University who need additional or different skills to enter or return to the job market. In order to apply, you must be entering vocational or technical training or completing an undergraduate degree. You must show characteristics of maturity in the following areas: adaptability to new situations, motivation to improve, and acceptance of responsibility. You must also be the head of your household with financial responsibility for dependent(s) as well as demonstrate a need for specific educational training and financial assistance. Award requirements change regularly. For an application and further information, please contact the Office of Adult Services: (330) 672-7933. No GPA requirement specified.

Kent State University
Student Financial Aid
PO Box 5190
Kent, OH 44242-0001

1946
Trustee Scholarship

AMOUNT: $1000-$1500 DEADLINE: March 1
MAJOR: All Areas of Study

The Trustee Scholarship is open to incoming freshmen attending Kent State University. This award is based on a minimum 3.25 GPA, national test scores, and leadership ability. In order to apply, you must complete a FAFSA. This award is renewable. Award requirements change regularly. For an application and further information, please contact the Admissions Office: (330) 672-2444. GPA must be 3.25-4.0.

Kent State University
Student Financial Aid
PO Box 5190
Kent, OH 44242-0001

1947
TRW Foundation Minority Scholarship

AMOUNT: $2500 DEADLINE: April 1
MAJOR: Mathematics, Science, Engineering

The TRW Foundation Minority Scholarship is open to Kent State University campus African-American, Hispanic, or Native American sophomores and juniors. To be considered for the award, you must be pursuing a degree in mathematics, science, or engineering with a minimum 3.0 GPA. This renewable award is based on financial need as determined by the FAFSA. Award requirements change regularly. Please contact Kent State for further information on how to apply. GPA must be 3.0-4.0.

Kent State University
Student Financial Aid
PO Box 5190
Kent, OH 44242-0001

1948
W. P. Litchfield Award

AMOUNT: $750 DEADLINE: March 1
MAJOR: All Areas of Study

The W. P. Litchfield Award is open to students attending Kent State University and the regional campuses. One of your parents must be an employee with five or more years of service with, or a retiree of, Goodyear Tire and Rubber Company or one of its domestic subsidiaries. This renewable award is based on your academic records, national test scores, and financial need. Award requirements change regularly. For an application and further information, please contact the Admissions Office: (330) 672-2444. No GPA requirement specified.

Kent State University
Student Financial Aid
PO Box 5190
Kent, OH 44242-0001

1949
Washington Program in National Issues (WPNI) Scholarship

AMOUNT: $500 DEADLINE: Varies
MAJOR: All Areas of Study

The Washington Program in National Issues (WPNI) Scholarship is open to Kent State University juniors participating in the spring semester study/internship program in Washington, D.C. You must have a minimum 3.0 GPA in order to apply. Award requirements change regularly. For further information contact the Williamson Alumni Center: (330) 672-5368. GPA must be 3.0-4.0.

Kent State University
Student Financial Aid
PO Box 5190
Kent, OH 44242-0001

Kent State University, Tuscarawas

1950
Bank One Book Scholarship

AMOUNT: Maximum: $200 DEADLINE: Varies
MAJOR: All Areas of Study

The Bank One Book Scholarship is open to full- or part-time students at Kent State, Tuscarawas Campus, who are Tuscarawas County residents. You must demonstrate financial need. The application deadline for the fall semester is April 1 of the preceding spring for new students and June 1 for returning students or new transfer students. This award is not renewable. Award requirements change regularly. For an application and further information, please contact Agnes Swigart, Tuscarawas Campus: (330) 339-3391. No GPA requirement specified.

Kent State University, Tuscarawas Campus
Financial Aid Office
330 University Drive, NE
New Philadelphia, OH 44663

1951
Chestnut Society Scholarships

AMOUNT: $200-$400 DEADLINE: April 1
MAJOR: All Areas of Study

The Chestnut Society seeks to provide funds for non-traditional students who have prior college experience and a minimum 3.0 GPA. Must be Tuscarawas County residents who have completed at least 12 hours of coursework, be at least 21 years of age, and be able to demonstrate financial need. Application deadline for the fall semester is April 1 of the preceding spring for new students and June 1 for returning students or new transfer students. Not renewable. Award requirements change regularly. For an application and further information, please contact Agnes Swigart, Tuscarawas Campus: (330) 339-3391. GPA must be 3.0-4.0.

Kent State University, Tuscarawas Campus
Financial Aid Office
330 University Drive, NE
New Philadelphia, OH 44663

1952
Daniel J. Steiner Scholarship

AMOUNT: $1000 DEADLINE: Varies
MAJOR: Nursing

The Daniel J. Steiner Scholarship is open to female graduates of New Philadelphia High School or Tuscarawas Central Catholic High School who are enrolled in a nursing program at Kent State University, Tuscarawas Campus. You must demonstrate financial need. The preferred application deadline for the fall semester is April 1 of the preceding spring for new students and June 1 for returning students. Award requirements change regularly. For further information contact Agnes Swigart, Tuscarawas Campus, at (330) 339-3391. No GPA requirement specified.

Kent State University, Tuscarawas Campus
Financial Aid Office
330 University Drive, NE
New Philadelphia, OH 44663

1953
Dorothy M. and Mildred G. Lucke Scholarship for Nutrition/Dietetics

AMOUNT: $750-$1000 DEADLINE: January 1
MAJOR: Nutrition, Dietetics

The Dorothy M. and Mildred G. Lucke Scholarship for Nutrition/Dietetics is available to one undergraduate junior and two graduate students. Undergraduates must have completed organic chemistry. A minimum GPA of 3.0 for undergraduates and 3.5, for graduate students is required. Recipients must be able to demonstrate work experience related to the field and submit a goal statement and a list of extracurricular activities. Award requirements change regularly. For an application and further information, please contact the Director, Family and Consumer Studies: (330) 672-2197. GPA must be 3.0-4.0.

Kent State University, Tuscarawas Campus
Financial Aid Office
330 University Drive, NE
New Philadelphia, OH 44663

1954
Errington Memorial Scholarship

AMOUNT: $200 DEADLINE: Varies
MAJOR: Nursing

The Errington Memorial Scholarship is open to Tuscarawas County, Ohio, residents enrolled in the nursing program at Kent State University, Tuscarawas Campus. The application deadline for the fall semester is April 1 of the preceding spring for new students and June 1 for returning students or new transfer students. This nonrenewable award is based on a superior academic record. Award requirements change regularly. For an application and further information, please contact Agnes Swigart, Tuscarawas Campus: (330) 339-3391. No GPA requirement specified.

Kent State University, Tuscarawas Campus
Financial Aid Office
330 University Drive, NE
New Philadelphia, OH 44663

1955
Food Service Board Plan

AMOUNT: None Specified DEADLINE: May 1
MAJOR: All Areas of Study

The Food Service Board Plan is open to returning Kent State University, Tuscarawas Campus, students. In order to apply, you must have registered for the Food Service Board Plan in the current academic year. This award is based on need as determined by FAFSA and is not renewable. A minimum 2.5 GPA is required. Award requirements change regularly. For an application and further information, please contact University Food Services at (330) 672-2594. GPA must be 2.5-4.0.

Kent State University, Tuscarawas Campus
Financial Aid Office
330 University Drive, NE
New Philadelphia, OH 44663

1956
Foundation Part-Time Scholarship

AMOUNT: $500 DEADLINE: Varies
MAJOR: All Areas of Study

The Foundation Part-Time Scholarship is open to part-time students (enrolled 6 to 11 hours) at Kent State University, Tuscarawas Campus. You must be in financial need and have a superior academic record. The preferred application deadline for the fall semester is April 1 of the preceding spring for new students and June 1 for returning students or new transfer students. This award is nonrenewable. Award requirements change regularly. For an application and further information, please contact Agnes Swigart, Tuscarawas Campus: (330) 339-3391. No GPA requirement specified.

Kent State University, Tuscarawas Campus
Financial Aid Office
330 University Drive, NE
New Philadelphia, OH 44663

1957

Frances Schwebel Solomon Food Service Management Scholarship

AMOUNT: $500-$1000 DEADLINE: September 15
MAJOR: Food Service Management, Hospitality

The Frances Schwebel Solomon Food Service Management Scholarship is open to full-time Kent State University freshmen majoring in hospitality or food service management. Applicants must have a minimum GPA of 3.0 and faculty recommendations. Recipients must also demonstrate extracurricular activities and food service work experience. One to two awards are offered annually. Award requirements change regularly. For an application and further information, please contact the Director, Family and Consumer Studies: (330) 672-2197. GPA must be 3.0-4.0.

Kent State University, Tuscarawas Campus
Financial Aid Office
330 University Drive, NE
New Philadelphia, OH 44663

1958

General Food Service Scholarship

AMOUNT: None Specified DEADLINE: May 1
MAJOR: All Areas of Study

The General Food Service Scholarship is open to returning Kent State University, Tuscarawas Campus, students with a minimum 2.5 GPA. This award is nonrenewable and is based on need as determined by FAFSA. Award requirements change regularly. For an application and further information, please contact University Food Services at (330) 672-2594. GPA must be 2.5-4.0.

Kent State University, Tuscarawas Campus
Financial Aid Office
330 University Drive, NE
New Philadelphia, OH 44663

1959

Gross Family Scholarship

AMOUNT: $300 DEADLINE: March 1
MAJOR: Business

The Gross Family Scholarship is open to sophomore, junior, and senior business majors at Kent State University. You must have a minimum GPA of 2.25 in order to apply. Award requirements change regularly. For further information contact the College of Business Administration at (330) 672-2755, ext. 231. GPA must be 2.25-4.0.

Kent State University, Tuscarawas Campus
Financial Aid Office
330 University Drive, NE
New Philadelphia, OH 44663

1960

Hannah Pittis Schoenbrunn Grange Scholarship

AMOUNT: $200 DEADLINE: Varies
MAJOR: Nursing, Agriculture (Agriculture Related)

The Hannah Pittis Schoenbrunn Grange Scholarship is open to female students attending Kent State University, Tuscarawas Campus, who are pursuing a degree in nursing and for male students studying agriculture. The preferred application deadline for the fall semester is April 1 of the preceding spring for new students and June 1 for returning students or new transfer students. Award requirements change regularly. For an application and further information, please contact Agnes Swigart, Tuscarawas Campus: (330) 339-3391. No GPA requirement specified.

Kent State University, Tuscarawas Campus
Financial Aid Office
330 University Drive, NE
New Philadelphia, OH 44663

1961

Harold E. Stokey Scholarship

AMOUNT: None Specified DEADLINE: April 1
MAJOR: Engineering Technology

The Harold E. Stokey Scholarship is open to incoming freshmen at Kent State University, Tuscarawas Campus. You must be an engineering technology major with a strong high school academic record and demonstrated financial need. This award is renewable. Award requirements change regularly. For an application and further information, please contact Agnes Swigart, Tuscarawas Campus: (330) 339-3391. No GPA requirement specified.

Kent State University, Tuscarawas Campus
Financial Aid Office
330 University Drive, NE
New Philadelphia, OH 44663

1962

Hospitality Food Service Major Scholarship

AMOUNT: None Specified DEADLINE: May 1
MAJOR: All Areas of Study

The Hospitality Food Service Major Scholarship is open to Kent State University, Tuscarawas Campus, students who have a minimum 2.5 GPA. This nonrenewable award is based on need as determined by FAFSA. Award requirements change regularly. For an application and further information, please contact University Food Services at (330) 672-2594. GPA must be 2.5-4.0.

Kent State University, Tuscarawas Campus
Financial Aid Office
330 University Drive, NE
New Philadelphia, OH 44663

1963
Lillian Stollar Memorial and Gertrude Kaderly Memorial Scholarship

AMOUNT: $1000 DEADLINE: April 1
MAJOR: All Areas of Study

The Lillian Stollar Memorial and Gertrude Kaderly Memorial Scholarship is open to students at Kent State University, Tuscarawas Campus, who are residents of Tuscarawas County, Ohio, and students from a Tuscarawas County public or county school system. The application deadline for the fall semester is April 1 of the preceding spring for new students and June 1 for returning or new transfer students. You must be able to demonstrate financial need. This award is nonrenewable. Award requirements change regularly. For an application and further information, please contact Agnes Swigart, Tuscarawas Campus: (330) 339-3391. No GPA requirement specified.

Kent State University, Tuscarawas Campus
Financial Aid Office
330 University Drive, NE
New Philadelphia, OH 44663

1964
Mabel Hammersley Nursing Foundation Scholarship

AMOUNT: $1500 DEADLINE: April 1
MAJOR: Nursing

The Mabel Hammersley Nursing Scholarship is open to beginning nursing students attending Kent State University, Tuscarawas Campus. You must have a superior academic record. This award is nonrenewable. Award requirements change regularly. For an application and further information, please contact Agnes Swigart, Tuscarawas Campus: (330) 339-3391. No GPA requirement specified.

Kent State University, Tuscarawas Campus
Financial Aid Office
330 University Drive, NE
New Philadelphia, OH 44663

1965
Mahavir Scholarship

AMOUNT: $500 DEADLINE: April 1
MAJOR: All Areas of Study

The Mahavir Scholarship is open to students at Kent State University, Tuscarawas Campus, who are residents of Tuscarawas County, Ohio. You must have continuous enrollment in NRST, a minimum 3.0 GPA, and demonstrated financial need. The preferred deadline for fall semester is April 1 of the preceding spring for new students and June 1 for returning or new transfer students. This award is renewable. Award requirements change regularly. For an application and further information, please contact Agnes Swigart, Tuscarawas Campus: (330) 339-3391. GPA must be 3.0-4.0.

Kent State University, Tuscarawas Campus
Financial Aid Office
330 University Drive, NE
New Philadelphia, OH 44663

1966
Manley Scholarship

AMOUNT: None Specified DEADLINE: Varies
MAJOR: All Areas of Study

The Manley Scholarship is open to incoming full-time freshmen at Kent State University, Tuscarawas Campus, who are residents of Tuscarawas County, Ohio. In order to apply, you must have a minimum ACT score of 25, be in the top 15% of your graduating class, and have a minimum 3.5 GPA. The application deadline for the fall semester is April 1 of the preceding spring for new students and June 1 for returning students or new transfer students. This award is renewable. Award requirements change regularly. For an application and further information, please contact Agnes Swigart, Tuscarawas Campus: (330) 339-3391. GPA must be 3.5-4.0.

Kent State University, Tuscarawas Campus
Financial Aid Office
330 University Drive, NE
New Philadelphia, OH 44663

1967
New Philadelphia Rotary Club Scholarship

AMOUNT: $250-$500 DEADLINE: Varies
MAJOR: All Areas of Study

The New Philadelphia Rotary Club Scholarship is open to full- or part-time students at Kent State University, Tuscarawas Campus, who are residents of New Philadelphia or the New Philadelphia school district. You will need to demonstrate financial need and a superior academic record in order to apply. The preferred application deadline for the fall semester is April 1 of the preceding spring for new students and June 1 for returning or new transfer students. This award is renewable. Award requirements change regularly. For an application and further information, please contact Agnes Swigart, Tuscarawas Campus: (330) 339-3391. No GPA requirement specified.

Kent State University, Tuscarawas Campus
Financial Aid Office
330 University Drive, NE
New Philadelphia, OH 44663

1968
Office Technology Scholarship

AMOUNT: $1500 DEADLINE: April 1
MAJOR: Office Technology

The Office Technology Scholarship is open to office technology majors attending Kent State University, Tuscarawas Campus. In order to apply, you must have a superior academic record. This award is nonrenewable. Award requirements change regularly. For an application and further information, please contact Agnes Swigart, Tuscarawas Campus: (330) 339-3391. No GPA requirement specified.

Kent State University, Tuscarawas Campus
Financial Aid Office
330 University Drive, NE
New Philadelphia, OH 44663

1969
Roy A. Wilson and Ruth A. Wilson Memorial Fund Award

AMOUNT: None Specified DEADLINE: April 1
MAJOR: All Areas of Study

The Roy A. Wilson and Ruth A. Wilson Memorial Fund Award is open to full-time students at Kent State University, Tuscarawas Campus, who were residents of the Claymont School District when they graduated from high school. Preference is given to incoming freshmen who demonstrate financial need. The application deadline for the fall semester is April 1 of the preceding spring for new students and June 1 for returning students or transfer students. Award requirements change regularly. For an application and further information, please contact Agnes Swigart, Tuscarawas Campus: (330) 339-3391. No GPA requirement specified.

Kent State University, Tuscarawas Campus
Financial Aid Office
330 University Drive, NE
New Philadelphia, OH 44663

1970
Samuel H. Winston Memorial Scholarship

AMOUNT: $1000 DEADLINE: Varies
MAJOR: Sciences

The Samuel H. Winston Memorial Scholarship is for full-time students at Kent State University, Tuscarawas Campus, who graduated from Tuscarawas County High School and are studying any of the sciences. The application deadline for the fall semester is April 1 of the preceding spring for new students and June 1 for returning students or new transfer students. This award is nonrenewable. Award requirements change regularly. For an application and further information, please contact Agnes Swigart, Tuscarawas Campus: (330) 339-3391. No GPA requirement specified.

Kent State University, Tuscarawas Campus
Financial Aid Office
330 University Drive, NE
New Philadelphia, OH 44663

1971
Student Employee Scholarship

AMOUNT: None Specified DEADLINE: May 1
MAJOR: All Areas of Study

The Student Employee Scholarship is open to returning Kent State University campus students who have a minimum 2.5 GPA. In order to apply, you must be an employee in good standing with at least 200 hours of Auxiliary Services employment history. This award is based on need as determined by FAFSA. Award requirements change regularly. For an application and further information, please contact University Food Services at (330) 672-2594. GPA must be 2.5-4.0.

Kent State University, Tuscarawas Campus
Financial Aid Office
330 University Drive, NE
New Philadelphia, OH 44663

1972
Tech Prep Scholarship

AMOUNT: $1000 DEADLINE: April 1
MAJOR: Technology

The Tech Prep Scholarship is open to students at Kent State University, Tuscarawas Campus. You must be a high school graduate from the Tech Prep program at the Tuscarawas Campus. This award is nonrenewable. Award requirements change regularly. For an application and further information, please contact Agnes Swigart, Tuscarawas Campus: (330) 339-3391. No GPA requirement specified.

Kent State University, Tuscarawas Campus
Financial Aid Office
330 University Drive, NE
New Philadelphia, OH 44663

1973
Wesley E. Tolle Mathematics Scholarship

AMOUNT: None Specified DEADLINE: Varies
MAJOR: Mathematics, Mathematics Education

The Wesley E. Tolle Mathematics Scholarship is open to full-time Kent State University, Tuscarawas Campus, students. You must be pursuing a B.A. or a B.S. in mathematics or a B.S. in mathematics education with a minimum 3.5 GPA. Demonstration of financial need is also required. The application deadline for fall is April 1 of the preceding spring for new students and June 1 for returning or new transfer students. This award is nonrenewable. Award requirements change regularly. For an application and further information, please contact Agnes Swigart, Tuscarawas Campus: (330) 339-3391. GPA must be 3.5-4.0.

Kent State University, Tuscarawas Campus
Financial Aid Office
330 University Drive, NE
New Philadelphia, OH 44663

1974
Willie P. Morrow Memorial Scholarship

AMOUNT: $500 DEADLINE: Varies
MAJOR: All Areas of Study

The Willie P. Morrow Memorial Scholarship is open to African-American students at Kent State University, Tuscarawas Campus, who are residents of Tuscarawas County, Ohio. This award is based on financial need and academic potential. The preferred application deadline for the fall semester is April 1 of the preceding spring for new students and June 1 for returning students or new transfer students. This award is nonrenewable. Award requirements change regularly. For an application and further information, please contact Agnes Swigart, Tuscarawas Campus: (330) 339-3391. No GPA requirement specified.

Kent State University, Tuscarawas Campus
Financial Aid Office
330 University Drive, NE
New Philadelphia, OH 44663

Keystone College

Keystone College
Office of Admissions
1 College Green - Sisson Hall
La Plume, PA 18440-0200

1975
Drinko Criminal Justice Award

AMOUNT: Maximum: $4000 DEADLINE: Varies
MAJOR: Criminal Justice

The Drinko Criminal Justice Award is open to full-time students enrolled in the criminal justice program at Keystone College. To be eligible for this award, you must demonstrate financial need and submit the FAFSA. The award provides up to $4,000 per year for four years. Award requirements change regularly. There is no separate application for this scholarship. Students admitted to Keystone College who meet the award criteria will automatically be considered. To request an admission application, please contact the Office of Admissions or apply online at www.keystone.edu. No GPA requirement specified.

Keystone College
Office of Admissions
1 College Green - Sisson Hall
La Plume, PA 18440-0200

1976
Endowed Scholarships and Grants

AMOUNT: None Specified DEADLINE: Varies
MAJOR: All Areas of Study

Endowed Scholarships and Grants are awarded to full-time students with or without financial need at Keystone College. The awards are granted through benefactors of Keystone College. Award requirements change regularly. There is no separate application for this scholarship. Students admitted to Keystone College who meet the award criteria will automatically be considered. To request an admission application, please contact the Office of Admissions or apply online at www.keystone.edu. No GPA requirement specified.

Keystone College
Office of Admissions
1 College Green - Sisson Hall
La Plume, PA 18440-0200

1977
Keystone College Grant

AMOUNT: Maximum: $5000 DEADLINE: Varies
MAJOR: All Areas of Study

Keystone College Grants are awarded to full-time students at Keystone College. To be eligible for this award, you must demonstrate financial need and submit the FAFSA. The award provides up to $5,000 per year. Award requirements change regularly. There is no separate application for this scholarship. Students admitted to Keystone College who meet the award criteria will automatically be considered. To request an admission application, please contact the Office of Admissions or apply online at www.keystone.edu. No GPA requirement specified.

1978
Leadership Award

AMOUNT: Maximum: $3000 DEADLINE: Varies
MAJOR: All Areas of Study

The Leadership Award is open to full-time students enrolled in a major course of study at Keystone College. The award provides up to $3,000 per year for four years. Financial need is not a consideration. Award requirements change regularly. There is no separate application for this scholarship. Students admitted to Keystone College who meet the award criteria will automatically be considered. To request an admission application, please contact the Office of Admissions or apply online at www.keystone.edu. No GPA requirement specified.

Keystone College
Office of Admissions
1 College Green - Sisson Hall
La Plume, PA 18440-0200

1979
Pennsylvania State Grant

AMOUNT: Maximum: $2900 DEADLINE: May 1
MAJOR: All Areas of Study

The Pennsylvania State Grant is available to Pennsylvania residents attending Keystone College part- or full-time who demonstrate financial need. In order to receive this grant, you must have submitted the Free Application for Federal Student Aid (FAFSA) prior to applying. Award requirements change regularly. There is no separate application for this scholarship. Students admitted to Keystone College who meet the award criteria will automatically be considered. To request an admission application, please contact the Office of Admissions or apply online at www.keystone.edu. No GPA requirement specified.

Keystone College
Office of Admissions
1 College Green - Sisson Hall
La Plume, PA 18440-0200

1980
Presidential Scholarship

AMOUNT: Maximum: $5000 DEADLINE: Varies
MAJOR: All Areas of Study

The Presidential Scholarship is open to academically talented, full-time entering freshmen at Keystone College. The award provides up to $5,000 per year for four years. Financial need is not a consideration. Award requirements change regularly. There is no separate application for this scholarship. Students admitted to Keystone College who meet the award criteria will automatically be considered. To request an admission application, please contact the Office of Admissions or apply online at www.keystone.edu. No GPA requirement specified.

Keystone College
Office of Admissions
1 College Green - Sisson Hall
La Plume, PA 18440-0200

1981
Professional Human Resource Manager's Scholarship

AMOUNT: Maximum: $4000 DEADLINE: Varies
MAJOR: Human Resource Management

The Human Resource Manager's Scholarship is open to full-time students enrolled in the human resource management program at Keystone College. To be eligible for this award, you must demonstrate financial need and submit the FAFSA. The award provides up to $4,000 per year for four years. Award requirements change regularly. There is no separate application for this scholarship. Students admitted to Keystone College who meet the award criteria will automatically be considered. To request an admission application, please contact the Office of Admissions or apply online at www.keystone.edu. No GPA requirement specified.

Keystone College
Office of Admissions
1 College Green - Sisson Hall
La Plume, PA 18440-0200

1982
Program Scholarship

AMOUNT: Maximum: $2000 DEADLINE: April 1
MAJOR: All Areas of Study

The Program Scholarship is open to full-time students enrolled in a major course of study at Keystone College. The award provides up to $2,000 per year for four years. Financial need is not a consideration. Award requirements change regularly. There is no separate application for this scholarship. Students admitted to Keystone College who meet the award criteria will automatically be considered. To request an admission application, please contact the Office of Admissions or apply online at www.keystone.edu. No GPA requirement specified.

Keystone College
Office of Admissions
1 College Green - Sisson Hall
La Plume, PA 18440-0200

1983
Residence Hall Grant

AMOUNT: Maximum: $1200 DEADLINE: Varies
MAJOR: All Areas of Study

The Residence Hall Grant is awarded to full-time residential students at Keystone College. You may receive up to $1,200 per year. Award requirements change regularly. There is no separate application for this scholarship. Students admitted to Keystone College who meet the award criteria will automatically be considered. To request an admission application, please contact the Office of Admissions or apply online at www.keystone.edu. No GPA requirement specified.

Keystone College
Office of Admissions
1 College Green - Sisson Hall
La Plume, PA 18440-0200

1984
Salutatorian Scholarship

AMOUNT: None Specified DEADLINE: Varies
MAJOR: All Areas of Study

The Salutatorian Scholarship is open to entering freshmen at Keystone College. To be considered for this award, you must be the documented salutatorian of your high school. This award provides one-half tuition. Award requirements change regularly. There is no separate application for this scholarship. Students admitted to Keystone College who meet the award criteria will automatically be considered. To request an admission application, please contact the Office of Admissions or apply online at www.keystone.edu. No GPA requirement specified.

Keystone College
Office of Admissions
1 College Green - Sisson Hall
La Plume, PA 18440-0200

1985
Shoney's Culinary Arts Award

AMOUNT: Maximum: $4000 DEADLINE: Varies
MAJOR: Culinary Arts

The Shoney's Culinary Arts Award is open to full-time students enrolled in the Culinary Arts program at Keystone College. To be eligible for this award, you must demonstrate financial need and submit the FAFSA. The award provides up to $4,000 per year for four years. Award requirements change regularly. There is no separate application for this scholarship. Students admitted to Keystone College who meet the award criteria will automatically be considered. To request an admission application, please contact the Office of Admissions or apply online at www.keystone.edu. No GPA requirement specified.

Keystone College
Office of Admissions
1 College Green - Sisson Hall
La Plume, PA 18440-0200

1986
Trustees Scholarship

AMOUNT: Maximum: $4000 DEADLINE: Varies
MAJOR: All Areas of Study

The Trustees Scholarship is open to academically talented, full-time entering freshmen at Keystone College. The award provides up to $4,000 per year for four years. Financial need is not a consideration. Award requirements change regularly. There is no separate application for this scholarship. Students admitted to Keystone College who meet the award criteria will automatically be considered. To request an admission application, please contact the Office of Admissions or apply online at www.keystone.edu. No GPA requirement specified.

Keystone College
Office of Admissions
1 College Green - Sisson Hall
La Plume, PA 18440-0200

1987
Valedictorian Scholarship

AMOUNT: None Specified DEADLINE: Varies
MAJOR: All Areas of Study

The Valedictorian Scholarship is open to entering freshmen at Keystone College. To be considered for this award, you must be the documented valedictorian of your high school. This award provides full tuition. Award requirements change regularly. There is no separate application for this scholarship. Students admitted to Keystone College who meet the award criteria will automatically be considered. To request an admission application, please contact the Office of Admissions or apply online at www.keystone.edu. No GPA requirement specified.

Keystone College
Office of Admissions
1 College Green - Sisson Hall
La Plume, PA 18440-0200

Lake Land College

1988
Effingham County Farm Bureau Foundation Scholarship

AMOUNT: $1000 DEADLINE: March 30
MAJOR: Agriculture

The Effingham County Farm Bureau Foundation Scholarship is open to Effingham County (IL) high school graduates. To be considered for the award, you must be the son or daughter of a Farm Bureau member. The award also requires that you be majoring in an agriculture field. It is not automatically renewed; you will have to reapply at the end of one year. Award requirements change regularly. No GPA requirement specified.

Lake Land College
Attn: LLC Foundation
5001 Lake Land Blvd.
Mattoon, IL 61938

1989
Farmers Grain Company of Dorans Scholarship

AMOUNT: $250-$500 DEADLINE: March 30
MAJOR: Agriculture

The Farmers Grain Company of Dorans Scholarship is open to students attending Lake Land College. To be considered for the award, you must be pursuing a degree in agriculture. This scholarship is not automatically renewed; you must reapply each semester. Award requirements change regularly. No GPA requirement specified.

Lake Land College
Attn: LLC Foundation
5001 Lake Land Blvd.
Mattoon, IL 61938

1990
Gary and Theresa Melvin Scholarship

AMOUNT: $250-$500 DEADLINE: March 30
MAJOR: Agriculture

The Gary and Theresa Melvin Scholarship is open to students who have graduated from Sullivan High School. To be considered for the award, you must be pursuing a degree in agriculture. This scholarship is not automatically renewed; you must reapply each semester. Award requirements change regularly. No GPA requirement specified.

Lake Land College
Attn: LLC Foundation
5001 Lake Land Blvd.
Mattoon, IL 61938

1991
Gary E. Lee Scholarship

AMOUNT: None Specified DEADLINE: March 30
MAJOR: Agriculture

The Gary E. Lee Scholarship is open to students attending Lake Land College. To be considered for the award, you must be pursuing a degree in agriculture. This scholarship is not automatically renewed; you must reapply each semester. Award requirements change regularly. No GPA requirement specified.

Lake Land College
Attn: LLC Foundation
5001 Lake Land Blvd.
Mattoon, IL 61938

1992
John Deere Company Scholarship

AMOUNT: $1000 DEADLINE: March 30
MAJOR: Agricultural Technology, Agricultural Sales

The John Deere Company Scholarship is open to students attending Lake Land College. To be considered for the award, you must be enrolled in the John Deere agricultural technology or agricultural sales program. The awards will be evenly split between the ten recipients from these two disciplines. This scholarship is not automatically renewed; you must reapply each year. Award requirements change regularly. No GPA requirement specified.

Lake Land College
Attn: LLC Foundation
5001 Lake Land Blvd.
Mattoon, IL 61938

1993
Lake Land College Agriculture Fund Scholarship

AMOUNT: None Specified DEADLINE: March 30
MAJOR: Agriculture

The Lake Land College Agriculture Fund Scholarship is open to students attending Lake Land College. To be considered for the award, you must be pursuing a degree in agriculture. The award also requires you to demonstrate financial need. It is not automatically renewed; you must reapply when it expires. Award requirements change regularly. No GPA requirement specified.

Lake Land College
Attn: LLC Foundation
5001 Lake Land Blvd.
Mattoon, IL 61938

1994
Mid-America Designs - Bernie Wendt Memorial Scholarship

AMOUNT: $250-$500 DEADLINE: March 30
MAJOR: Agriculture

The Mid-America Designs - Bernie Wendt Memorial Scholarship is open to students from Effingham County (IL). To be considered for the award, you must be pursuing a degree in agriculture. This scholarship is not automatically renewed; you must reapply each semester. Award requirements change regularly. No GPA requirement specified.

Lake Land College
Attn: LLC Foundation
5001 Lake Land Blvd.
Mattoon, IL 61938

1995
Niebrugge Ag Service Scholarship

AMOUNT: $250-$500 DEADLINE: March 30
MAJOR: Agriculture

The Niebrugge Ag Service Scholarship is open to students from Effingham, Jasper, or Cumberland Counties (IL). To be considered for the award, you must be pursuing a degree in agriculture. This scholarship is not automatically renewed; you must reapply each semester. Award requirements change regularly. No GPA requirement specified.

Lake Land College
Attn: LLC Foundation
5001 Lake Land Blvd.
Mattoon, IL 61938

1996
Patricia Speer Memorial Scholarship

AMOUNT: $250-$500 DEADLINE: March 30
MAJOR: Agriculture

The Patricia Speer Memorial Scholarship is open to high school graduates from Edgar County (IL). To be considered for the award, you must be pursuing a degree in agriculture. This scholarship is not automatically renewed; you must reapply each semester. Award requirements change regularly. No GPA requirement specified.

Lake Land College
Attn: LLC Foundation
5001 Lake Land Blvd.
Mattoon, IL 61938

1997
Staley Grain, Inc. - Coles Elevator Scholarship

AMOUNT: $250-$500 DEADLINE: March 30
MAJOR: Agriculture

The Staley Grain, Inc. - Coles Elevator Scholarship is open to students attending Lake Land College. To be considered for the award, you must be pursuing a degree in agriculture. This scholarship is not automatically renewed; you must reapply each semester. Award requirements change regularly. No GPA requirement specified.

Lake Land College
Attn: LLC Foundation
5001 Lake Land Blvd.
Mattoon, IL 6193

Lee College

1998
A. E. (Gene) Griffin Memorial Scholarship

AMOUNT: None Specified DEADLINE: March 15
MAJOR: All Fields of Study

The A. E. (Gene) Griffin Memorial Scholarship is open to students attending or planning to attend Lee College. Students are only required to fill out one application to be considered for all of the Foundation Scholarships, including those with special selection criteria. Award requirements change regularly. Applications are available at the Financial Aid Office in Moler Hall. For further information, please call (281) 425-6389. No GPA requirement specified.

Lee College
Attn: Scholarship Committee
Corner of Lee Dr. & Gulf St., PO Box 818
Baytown, TX 77522-0818

1999
A. Zellner Foundation Scholarship

AMOUNT: None Specified DEADLINE: March 15
MAJOR: Applied Sciences

The A. Zellner Foundation Scholarship is open to students attending or planning to attend Lee College and majoring in one of the applied sciences. Students are only required to fill out one application to be considered for all of the Foundation Scholarships, including those with special selection criteria. Award requirements change regularly. Applications are available at the Financial Aid Office in Moler Hall. For further information, please call (281) 425-6389. No GPA requirement specified.

Lee College
Attn: Scholarship Committee
Corner of Lee Dr. & Gulf St., PO Box 818
Baytown, TX 77522-0818

2000
American Association of University Women Scholarship

AMOUNT: None Specified DEADLINE: Varies
MAJOR: All Fields of Study

The American Association of University Women Scholarship is open to female Lee College graduates intending to transfer to a university. Students interested in this scholarship should contact their instructors and/or dean. Award requirements change regularly. Please send a self-addressed, stamped envelope to receive your application and any further instructions from the scholarship provider; call (281) 425-6389. No GPA requirement specified.

Lee College
Attn: Scholarship Committee
Corner of Lee Dr. & Gulf St., PO Box 818
Baytown, TX 77522-0818

2001
Barbara McDonald Rhodes Scholarship for the Handicapped

AMOUNT: None Specified DEADLINE: March 15
MAJOR: All Fields of Study

The Barbara McDonald Rhodes Scholarship for the Handicapped is open to students with disabilities attending or planning to attend Lee College. Students are only required to fill out one application to be considered for all of the Foundation Scholarships, including those with special selection criteria. Award requirements change regularly. Applications are available at the Financial Aid Office in Moler Hall. For further information, please call (281) 425-6389. No GPA requirement specified.

Lee College
Attn: Scholarship Committee
Corner of Lee Dr. & Gulf St., PO Box 818
Baytown, TX 77522-0818

2002
Baytown Recycling Works Scholarship

AMOUNT: None Specified DEADLINE: March 15
MAJOR: Environmental Science

The Baytown Recycling Works Scholarship is open to students attending or planning to attend Lee College as environmental science majors. Students are only required to fill out one application to be considered for all of the Foundation Scholarships, including those with special selection criteria. Award requirements change regularly. Applications are available at the Financial Aid Office in Moler Hall. For further information, please call (281) 425-6389. No GPA requirement specified.

Lee College
Attn: Scholarship Committee
Corner of Lee Dr. & Gulf St., PO Box 818
Baytown, TX 77522-0818

2003
Baytown Sun Scholarship

AMOUNT: None Specified DEADLINE: March 15
MAJOR: All Fields of Study

The Baytown Sun Scholarship is open to students attending or planning to attend Lee College. Students are only required to fill out one application to be considered for all of the Foundation Scholarships, including those with special selection criteria. Award requirements change regularly. Applications are available at the Financial Aid Office in Moler Hall. For further information, please call (281) 425-6389. No GPA requirement specified.

Lee College
Attn: Scholarship Committee
Corner of Lee Dr. & Gulf St., PO Box 818
Baytown, TX 77522-0818

2004
Charles Bonner Memorial Scholarship

AMOUNT: None Specified DEADLINE: March 15
MAJOR: All Fields of Study

The Charles Bonner Memorial Scholarship is open to students attending or planning to attend Lee College. Students are only required to fill out one application to be considered for all of the Foundation Scholarships, including those with special selection criteria. Award requirements change regularly. Applications are available at the Financial Aid Office in Moler Hall. For further information, please call (281) 425-6389. No GPA requirement specified.

Lee College
Attn: Scholarship Committee
Corner of Lee Dr. & Gulf St., PO Box 818
Baytown, TX 77522-0818

2005
Dan Stallworth Memorial Scholarship

AMOUNT: None Specified DEADLINE: March 15
MAJOR: All Fields of Study

The Dan Stallworth Memorial Scholarship is open to students attending or planning to attend Lee College with preference given to students who have participated in athletics. Students are only required to fill out one application to be considered for all of the Foundation Scholarships, including those with special selection criteria. Award requirements change regularly. Applications are available at the Financial Aid Office in Moler Hall. For further information, please call (281) 425-6389. No GPA requirement specified.

Lee College
Attn: Scholarship Committee
Corner of Lee Dr. & Gulf St., PO Box 818
Baytown, TX 77522-0818

2006
Edna Gray Scholarship

AMOUNT: None Specified DEADLINE: March 15
MAJOR: All Fields of Study

The Edna Gray Scholarship is open to students attending or planning to attend Lee College. Students are only required to fill out one application to be considered for all of the Foundation Scholarships, including those with special selection criteria. Award requirements change regularly. Applications are available at the Financial Aid Office in Moler Hall. For further information, please call (281) 425-6389. No GPA requirement specified.

Lee College
Attn: Scholarship Committee
Corner of Lee Dr. & Gulf St., PO Box 818
Baytown, TX 77522-0818

2007
Ethel Huggins Scholarship

AMOUNT: None Specified DEADLINE: March 15
MAJOR: All Fields of Study

The Ethel Huggins Scholarship is open to students attending or planning to attend Lee College. Students are only required to fill out one application to be considered for all of the Foundation Scholarships, including those with special selection criteria. Award requirements change regularly. Applications are available at the Financial Aid Office in Moler Hall. For further information, please call (281) 425-6389. No GPA requirement specified.

Lee College
Attn: Scholarship Committee
Corner of Lee Dr. & Gulf St., PO Box 818
Baytown, TX 77522-0818

2008
Holly McLemore Scholarship

AMOUNT: None Specified DEADLINE: March 15
MAJOR: All Fields of Study

The Holly McLemore Scholarship is open to students attending or planning to attend Lee College. Students are only required to fill out one application to be considered for all of the Foundation Scholarships, including those with special selection criteria. Selection for this award is based on scholarship. Award requirements change regularly. Applications are available at the Financial Aid Office in Moler Hall. For further information, please call (281) 425-6389. No GPA requirement specified.

Lee College
Attn: Scholarship Committee
Corner of Lee Dr. & Gulf St., PO Box 818
Baytown, TX 77522-0818

2009
Jane M. and John B. Tucker Scholarship

AMOUNT: None Specified DEADLINE: March 15
MAJOR: All Fields of Study

The Jane M. and John B. Tucker Scholarship is open to students attending or planning to attend Lee College. Students are only required to fill out one application to be considered for all of the Foundation Scholarships, including those with special selection criteria. Award requirements change regularly. Applications are available at the Financial Aid Office in Moler Hall. For further information, please call (281) 425-6389. No GPA requirement specified.

Lee College
Attn: Scholarship Committee
Corner of Lee Dr. & Gulf St., PO Box 818
Baytown, TX 77522-0818

2010
Joanne Horeczy Young Music Scholarship

AMOUNT: None Specified DEADLINE: March 15
MAJOR: Music

The Joanne Horeczy Young Music Scholarship is open to students attending or planning to attend Lee College as music majors. Students are only required to fill out one application to be considered for all of the Foundation Scholarships, including those with special selection criteria. Award requirements change regularly. Applications are available at the Financial Aid Office in Moler Hall. For further information, please call (281) 425-6389. No GPA requirement specified.

Lee College
Attn: Scholarship Committee
Corner of Lee Dr. & Gulf St., PO Box 818
Baytown, TX 77522-0818

2011
Judy Tate Barber Memorial Scholarship

AMOUNT: None Specified DEADLINE: March 15
MAJOR: All Fields of Study

The Judy Tate Barber Memorial Scholarship is open to students attending or planning to attend Lee College. Students are only required to fill out one application to be considered for all of the Foundation Scholarships, including those with special selection criteria. Preference is given to students demonstrating distinguished academic achievement with intent to transfer to a university. Award requirements change regularly. Applications are available at the Financial Aid Office in Moler Hall. For further information, please call (281) 425-6389. No GPA requirement specified.

Lee College
Attn: Scholarship Committee
Corner of Lee Dr. & Gulf St., PO Box 818
Baytown, TX 77522-0818

2012
Kenneth Scheffler Business Scholarship

AMOUNT: None Specified DEADLINE: March 15
MAJOR: Business

The Kenneth Scheffler Business Scholarship is open to students attending or planning to attend Lee College as business majors. Students are only required to fill out one application to be considered for all of the Foundation Scholarships, including those with special selection criteria. Award requirements change regularly. Applications are available at the Financial Aid Office in Moler Hall. For further information, please call (281) 425-6389. No GPA requirement specified.

Lee College
Attn: Scholarship Committee
Corner of Lee Dr. & Gulf St., PO Box 818
Baytown, TX 77522-0818

2013
Kevin Hendon Model of Courage Scholarship

AMOUNT: None Specified DEADLINE: March 15
MAJOR: All Fields of Study

The Kevin Hendon Model of Courage Scholarship is open to students attending or planning to attend Lee College. Students are only required to fill out one application to be considered for all of the Foundation Scholarships, including those with special selection criteria. Award requirements change regularly. Applications are available at the Financial Aid Office in Moler Hall. For further information, please call (281) 425-6389. No GPA requirement specified.

Lee College
Attn: Scholarship Committee
Corner of Lee Dr. & Gulf St., PO Box 818
Baytown, TX 77522-0818

2014
Lacy Taylor Scholarship for the Handicapped

AMOUNT: None Specified DEADLINE: March 15
MAJOR: All Fields of Study

The Lacy Taylor Scholarship for the Handicapped is open to students with disabilities attending or planning to attend Lee College. Students are only required to fill out one application to be considered for all of the Foundation Scholarships, including those with special selection criteria. Award requirements change regularly. Applications are available at the Financial Aid Office in Moler Hall. For further information, please call (281) 425-6389. No GPA requirement specified.

Lee College
Attn: Scholarship Committee
Corner of Lee Dr. & Gulf St., PO Box 818
Baytown, TX 77522-0818

2015
Lindon M. Williams American Studies Scholarship

AMOUNT: None Specified DEADLINE: March 15
MAJOR: American Studies

The Lindon M. Williams American Studies Scholarship is open to students attending or planning to attend Lee College as American Studies majors. Students are only required to fill out one application to be considered for all of the Foundation Scholarships, including those with special selection criteria. Award requirements change regularly. Applications are available at the Financial Aid Office in Moler Hall. For further information, please call (281) 425-6389. No GPA requirement specified.

Lee College
Attn: Scholarship Committee
Corner of Lee Dr. & Gulf St., PO Box 818
Baytown, TX 77522-0818

2016
Maggie J. Coffey Memorial Scholarship

AMOUNT: None Specified DEADLINE: March 15
MAJOR: All Fields of Study

The Maggie J. Coffey Memorial Scholarship is open to students attending or planning to attend Lee College. Students are only required to fill out one application to be considered for all of the Foundation Scholarships, including those with special selection criteria. Award requirements change regularly. Applications are available at the Financial Aid Office in Moler Hall. For further information, please call (281) 425-6389. No GPA requirement specified.

Lee College
Attn: Scholarship Committee
Corner of Lee Dr. & Gulf St., PO Box 818
Baytown, TX 77522-0818

2017
Margie Hartrick Scholarship for Young Mothers

AMOUNT: None Specified DEADLINE: Varies
MAJOR: All Areas of Study

The Margie Hartrick Scholarship for Young Mothers is open to female students attending Lee College as return college students who have children in the Goose Creek Consolidated Independent School District. This award is in the amount of the student's tuition and fees. Award requirements change regularly. Please send a self-addressed, stamped envelope to receive your application and any further instructions from the scholarship provider; call (281) 425-6389. No GPA requirement specified.

Lee College
Attn: Scholarship Committee
Corner of Lee Dr. & Gulf St., PO Box 818
Baytown, TX 77522-0818

2018
Maude Moler Scholarship

AMOUNT: None Specified DEADLINE: March 15
MAJOR: All Fields of Study

The Maude Moler Scholarship is open to students attending or planning to attend Lee College. Students are only required to fill out one application to be considered for all of the Foundation Scholarships, including those with special selection criteria. Award requirements change regularly. Applications are available at the Financial Aid Office in Moler Hall. For further information, please call (281) 425-6389. No GPA requirement specified.

Lee College
Attn: Scholarship Committee
Corner of Lee Dr. & Gulf St., PO Box 818
Baytown, TX 77522-0818

2019
Musical Instrumentalist Scholarship

AMOUNT: None Specified DEADLINE: March 15
MAJOR: All Areas of Study

The Music Instrumentalist Scholarship is open to graduating seniors from Goose Creek Consolidated Independant School District who are band or orchestra instrumentalists planning to attend Lee College. Students are only required to fill out one application to be considered for all of the Foundation Scholarships, including those with special selection criteria. Award requirements change regularly. Applications are available at the Financial Aid Office in Moler Hall. For further information, please call (281) 425-6389. No GPA requirement specified.

Lee College
Attn: Scholarship Committee
Corner of Lee Dr. & Gulf St., PO Box 818
Baytown, TX 77522-0818

2020
P. Walter Henckell Scholarship

AMOUNT: None Specified DEADLINE: March 15
MAJOR: Liberal Arts

The P. Walter Henckell Scholarship is open to students attending or planning to attend Lee College as liberal arts majors. Preference is given to students who demonstrate distinguished academic achievement with intent to transfer to a university. Students are only required to fill out one application to be considered for all of the Foundation Scholarships, including those with special selection criteria. Award requirements change regularly. Applications are available at the Financial Aid Office in Moler Hall. For further information, please call (281) 425-6389. No GPA requirement specified.

Lee College
Attn: Scholarship Committee
Corner of Lee Dr. & Gulf St., PO Box 818
Baytown, TX 77522-0818

2021
Priscilla Massengale Memorial Scholarship

AMOUNT: None Specified DEADLINE: March 15
MAJOR: Agriculture, Technical or Vocational

The Priscilla Massengale Memorial Scholarship is open to students attending or planning to attend Lee College as technical or vocational agricultural majors. Students are only required to fill out one application to be considered for all of the Foundation Scholarships, including those with special selection criteria. Award requirements change regularly. Applications are available at the Financial Aid Office in Moler Hall. For further information, please call (281) 425-6389. No GPA requirement specified.

Lee College
Attn: Scholarship Committee
Corner of Lee Dr. & Gulf St., PO Box 818
Baytown, TX 77522-0818

2022
Rotary Club Scholarship (Rotaract)

AMOUNT: None Specified DEADLINE: March 15
MAJOR: All Fields of Study

The Rotary Club Scholarship (Rotaract) is open to students attending or planning to attend Lee College who are members of the Lee College chapter of Rotaract. Students are only required to fill out one application to be considered for all of the Foundation Scholarships, including those with special selection criteria. Award requirements change regularly. Applications are available at the Financial Aid Office in Moler Hall. For further information, please call (281) 425-6389. No GPA requirement specified.

Lee College
Attn: Scholarship Committee
Corner of Lee Dr. & Gulf St., PO Box 818
Baytown, TX 77522-0818

2023
Rufo Sanchez Memorial Scholarship

AMOUNT: None Specified DEADLINE: March 15
MAJOR: All Fields of Study

The Rufo Sanchez Memorial Scholarship is open to Hispanic students attending or planning to attend Lee College. Students are only required to fill out one application to be considered for all of the Foundation Scholarships, including those with special selection criteria. Award requirements change regularly. Applications are available at the Financial Aid Office in Moler Hall. For further information, please call (281) 425-6389. No GPA requirement specified.

Lee College
Attn: Scholarship Committee
Corner of Lee Dr. & Gulf St., PO Box 818
Baytown, TX 77522-0818

2024
Sam Bramlett Memorial Foundation Scholarship

AMOUNT: None Specified DEADLINE: March 15
MAJOR: All Fields of Study

The Sam Bramlett Memorial Foundation Scholarship is open to students who are high school graduates of Saint Mark's United Methodist Church attending or planning to attend Lee College. Students are only required to fill out one application to be considered for all of the Foundation Scholarships, including those with special selection criteria. Award requirements change regularly. Applications are available at the Financial Aid Office in Moler Hall. For further information, please call (281) 425-6389. No GPA requirement specified.

Lee College
Attn: Scholarship Committee
Corner of Lee Dr. & Gulf St., PO Box 818
Baytown, TX 77522-0818

2025
Sarah Mitchell Young Scholarship

AMOUNT: None Specified DEADLINE: March 15
MAJOR: All Fields of Study

The Sarah Mitchell Young Scholarship is open to students attending or planning to attend Lee College. You are only required to fill out one application to be considered for all of the Foundation Scholarships, including those with special selection criteria. Award requirements change regularly. Applications are available at the Financial Aid Office in Moler Hall. For further information, please call (281) 425-6389. No GPA requirement specified.

Lee College
Attn: Scholarship Committee
Corner of Lee Dr. & Gulf St., PO Box 818
Baytown, TX 77522-0818

2026
Snyder Endowment Scholarship

AMOUNT: None Specified DEADLINE: March 15
MAJOR: All Fields of Study

The Sarah Snyder Endowment Scholarship is open to female graduates of a Goose Creek Consolidated Independant School District high school who are attending or planning to attend Lee College with intent to transfer to a university. This scholarship is automatically renewed for a second year at Lee College. Students are only required to fill out one application to be considered for all of the Foundation Scholarships, including those with special selection criteria. Award requirements change regularly. Applications are available at the Financial Aid Office in Moler Hall. For further information, please call (281) 425-6389. No GPA requirement specified.

Lee College
Attn: Scholarship Committee
Corner of Lee Dr. & Gulf St., PO Box 818
Baytown, TX 77522-0818

2027
Stella Pepper Journalism Foundation Scholarship

AMOUNT: None Specified DEADLINE: March 15
MAJOR: Journalism

The Stella Pepper Journalism Foundation Scholarship is open to a student attending or planning to attend Lee College as a journalism major. The student is only required to fill out one application to be considered for all of the Foundation Scholarships, including those with special selection criteria. This award is intended for the editor of the *Lantern*. Award requirements change regularly. Applications are available at the Financial Aid Office in Moler Hall. For further information, please call (281) 425-6389. No GPA requirement specified.

Lee College
Attn: Scholarship Committee
Corner of Lee Dr. & Gulf St., PO Box 818
Baytown, TX 77522-0818

2028
Tim and Kelly Bell Memorial Scholarship

AMOUNT: None Specified DEADLINE: March 15
MAJOR: All Fields of Study

The Tim and Kelly Bell Memorial Scholarship is open to students attending or planning to attend Lee College. Students are only required to fill out one application to be considered for all of the Foundation Scholarships, including those with special selection criteria. Award requirements change regularly. Applications are available at the Financial Aid Office in Moler Hall. For further information, please call (281) 425-6389. No GPA requirement specified.

Lee College
Attn: Scholarship Committee
Corner of Lee Dr. & Gulf St., PO Box 818
Baytown, TX 77522-0818

2029
W. A. and Jerri Read Communications Scholarship

AMOUNT: None Specified DEADLINE: March 15
MAJOR: Communications

The W. A. and Jerri Read Communications Scholarship is open to students attending or planning to attend Lee College as communications majors. Students are only required to fill out one application to be considered for all of the Foundation Scholarships, including those with special selection criteria. Award requirements change regularly. Applications are available at the Financial Aid Office in Moler Hall. For further information, please call (281) 425-6389. No GPA requirement specified.

Lee College
Attn: Scholarship Committee
Corner of Lee Dr. & Gulf St., PO Box 818
Baytown, TX 77522-0818

Life University

2030
Angelfire Datatel Scholars Foundation Scholarship

AMOUNT: $700-$2000 DEADLINE: Februrary 8
MAJOR: All Areas of Study

Open to students who are military veterans of the Vietnam War; children of Vietnam War veterans; or Vietnamese, Cambodian, or Laotian refugees who entered the U.S. between 1964 and 1975. Based on academics, personal motivation, and involvement in external activities, including employment. Award requirements change regularly. If you should have any further questions, please call (770) 426-2975.

Life University
Melody Maziar, Scholarship Coordinator
1269 Barclay Circle SE
Marietta, GA 30060-2903

Louisiana State University

2031
American Bank & Trust Company/J. Clifford Ourso Scholarship

AMOUNT: None Specified DEADLINE: February 1
MAJOR: Ourso College of Business Administration

The American Bank & Trust Company/J. Clifford Ourso Scholarship is open to students enrolled or planning to enroll in the Ourso College of Business Administration at Louisiana State University. To be eligible for this award, you must be a resident of East Baton Rouge or adjacent parishes in Louisiana and demonstrate scholarship, financial need, and civic or community involvement. Award requirements change regularly. For an application and further information, contact

the Ourso College of Business Administration or visit their website at www.bus.lsu.edu. No GPA requirement specified.

Louisiana State University - Ourso College of Business Administration
Attn: Scholarship Programs
3139 CEBA Building
Baton Rouge, LA 70803

2032
Amoco Foundation Scholarship

AMOUNT: None Specified DEADLINE: February 1
MAJOR: Ourso College of Business Administration

The Amoco Foundation Scholarship is open to students in the Ourso College of Business Administration at Louisiana State University. Award requirements change regularly. For an application and further information, contact the Ourso College of Business Administration or visit their website at www.bus.lsu.edu. No GPA requirement specified.

Louisiana State University - Ourso College of Business Administration
Attn: Scholarship Programs
3139 CEBA Building
Baton Rouge, LA 70803

2033
Arthur Andersen and Company Scholarship

AMOUNT: $200 DEADLINE: Varies
MAJOR: Accounting

The Arthur Andersen and Company Scholarship is awarded by the Department of Accounting at Louisiana State University to the most active member of Beta Alpha Psi, an honorary and professional fraternity for students of accountancy. Award requirements change regularly. For further information, contact the Department of Accounting or visit the Ourso College of Business Administration website at www.bus.lsu.edu. No GPA requirement specified.

Louisiana State University - Ourso College of Business Administration
Attn: Scholarship Programs
3139 CEBA Building
Baton Rouge, LA 70803

2034
Arthur Young and Company Award

AMOUNT: $400 DEADLINE: Varies
MAJOR: Taxation

The Arthur Young and Company Award is open to juniors and master's degree students studying taxation at Louisiana State University. Award requirements change regularly. For an application and further information, contact the Department of Accounting or visit the Ourso College of Business Administration website at www.bus.lsu.edu. No GPA requirement specified.

Louisiana State University - Ourso College of Business Administration
Attn: Scholarship Programs
3139 CEBA Building
Baton Rouge, LA 70803

2035
Beta Alpha Psi Award

AMOUNT: None Specified DEADLINE: Varies
MAJOR: Accounting

The Beta Alpha Psi Award is open to junior and senior accounting majors at Louisiana State University. A certificate of merit is awarded to the senior with the highest overall GPA, and a U.S. Savings Bond is awarded to the top-ranking junior. Award requirements change regularly. For further information, contact the Department of Accounting or visit the Ourso College of Business Administration website at www.bus.lsu.edu. No GPA requirement specified.

Louisiana State University - Ourso College of Business Administration
Attn: Scholarship Programs
3139 CEBA Building
Baton Rouge, LA 70803

2036
Capital Bank and Trust Company Banking and Finance Scholarship

AMOUNT: $1000 DEADLINE: February 1
MAJOR: Finance, Commercial Banking

The Capital Bank and Trust Company Banking and Finance Scholarship is open to juniors and seniors majoring in finance or commercial banking at Louisiana State University. To be considered for this award, you must be a Louisiana resident, have a minimum GPA of 3.0, and demonstrate financial need. Award requirements change regularly. For an application and further information, contact your department or visit the Ourso College of Business Administration website at www.bus.lsu.edu. GPA must be 3.0-4.0.

Louisiana State University - Ourso College of Business Administration
Attn: Scholarship Programs
3139 CEBA Building
Baton Rouge, LA 70803

2037
Capital Bank and Trust/Allison R. Kolb Scholarship

AMOUNT: None Specified DEADLINE: February 1
MAJOR: Finance

The Capital Bank and Trust/Allison R. Kolb Scholarship is open to juniors and seniors majoring in finance at Louisiana State University. To be considered for this award, you must have a minimum 3.0 GPA. Award requirements change regularly. For an application and further information, contact your department or visit the Ourso College of Business Administration website at www.bus.lsu.edu. GPA must be 3.0-4.0.

Louisiana State University - Ourso College of Business Administration
Attn: Scholarship Programs
3139 CEBA Building
Baton Rouge, LA 70803

2038
Capital Bank and Trust/Embree K. Easterly Scholarship

AMOUNT: $500 DEADLINE: February 1
MAJOR: Finance, Commercial Banking

The Capital Bank and Trust/Embree K. Easterly Scholarship is open to juniors and seniors majoring in finance or commercial banking at Louisiana State University. To be considered for this award, you must be a Louisiana resident, have a minimum 3.0 GPA, and demonstrate financial need. Award requirements change regularly. For an application and further information, contact your department or visit the Ourso College of Business Administration website at www.bus.lsu.edu. GPA must be 3.0-4.0.

Louisiana State University - Ourso College of Business Administration
Attn: Scholarship Programs
3139 CEBA Building
Baton Rouge, LA 70803

2039
Century 21 Brokers of Louisiana Scholarship

AMOUNT: None Specified DEADLINE: February 1
MAJOR: Ourso College of Business Administration (Interest in Real Estate)

The Century 21 Brokers of Louisiana Scholarship is open to juniors and seniors in the Ourso College of Business Administration at Louisiana State University. To be considered for this award, you must have an interest in real estate and be a resident of Louisiana. Award requirements change regularly. For an application and further information, contact the Ourso College of Business Administration or visit their website at www.bus.lsu.edu. No GPA requirement specified.

Louisiana State University - Ourso College of Business Administration
Attn: Scholarship Programs
3139 CEBA Building
Baton Rouge, LA 70803

2040
Coopers and Lybrand Award

AMOUNT: $500 DEADLINE: February 1
MAJOR: Accounting

The Coopers and Lybrand Award is open to juniors in the Department of Accounting at Louisiana State University. To be considered for this award, you must demonstrate outstanding academic qualifications, extracurricular activities, leadership, and character. Award requirements change regularly. For further information, contact your department or visit the Ourso College of Business Administration website at www.bus.lsu.edu. No GPA requirement specified.

Louisiana State University - Ourso College of Business
Administration
Attn: Scholarship Programs
3139 CEBA Building
Baton Rouge, LA 70803

David Harper Garland Memorial Scholarship

AMOUNT: None Specified DEADLINE: February 1
MAJOR: Business Administration

The David Harper Garland Memorial Scholarship is open to
undergraduate students majoring in business administration at
Louisiana State University. To be considered for this award,
you must demonstrate academic ability and financial need.
Award requirements change regularly. For an application and
further information, contact the Ourso College of Business
Administration or visit their website at www.bus.lsu.edu. No
GPA requirement specified.

Louisiana State University - Ourso College of Business
Administration
Attn: Scholarship Programs
3139 CEBA Building
Baton Rouge, LA 70803

2042
Dupont Minority Education Grant

AMOUNT: None Specified DEADLINE: February 1
MAJOR: Ourso College of Business Administration

The Dupont Minority Education Grant is open to minority students in the Ourso College of Business Administration at
Louisiana State University. Award requirements change regularly. For an application and further information, contact the
Ourso College of Business Administration or visit their website at www.bus.lsu.edu. No GPA requirement specified.

Louisiana State University - Ourso College of Business
Administration
Attn: Scholarship Programs
3139 CEBA Building
Baton Rouge, LA 70803

2043
Greater Baton Rouge Society for Human Resource Management Scholarship

AMOUNT: $800 DEADLINE: February 1
MAJOR: Management (Human Resources)

The Greater Baton Rouge Society for Human Resource
Management Scholarship is open to juniors and seniors majoring in management with an emphasis in human resources at
Louisiana State University. To be considered for this award,
you must apply each semester and have the highest GPA in the
major. Award requirements change regularly. For an application and further information, contact your department or visit
the Ourso College of Business Administration website at
www.bus.lsu.edu. No GPA requirement specified.

Louisiana State University - Ourso College of Business
Administration
Attn: Scholarship Programs
3139 CEBA Building
Baton Rouge, LA 70803

2044
Hawthorne, Waymouth and Carroll Scholarship

AMOUNT: $250 DEADLINE: February 1
MAJOR: Accounting

The Hawthorne, Waymouth and Carroll Scholarship is open to
senior accounting majors at Louisiana State University. To be
considered for this award, you must demonstrate the ability to
succeed in public accountancy as a local practitioner. Award
requirements change regularly. For an application and further
information, contact your department or visit the Ourso
College of Business Administration website at
www.bus.lsu.edu. No GPA requirement specified.

Louisiana State University - Ourso College of Business
Administration
Attn: Scholarship Programs
3139 CEBA Building
Baton Rouge, LA 70803

2045
IABC-Baton Rouge Business Communications Scholarship

AMOUNT: None Specified DEADLINE: February 1
MAJOR: Communications

The IABC-Baton Rouge Business Communications
Scholarship is open to seniors pursuing studies in a communications field at Louisiana State University. Award requirements change regularly. For an application and further information, contact your department or visit the Ourso College of
Business Administration website at www.bus.lsu.edu. No GPA
requirement specified.

Louisiana State University - Ourso College of Business
Administration
Attn: Scholarship Programs
3139 CEBA Building
Baton Rouge, LA 70803

2046
International Paper Scholarship

AMOUNT: None Specified DEADLINE: February 1
MAJOR: Information Systems and Decision Sciences

The International Paper Scholarship is open to information
systems and decision sciences majors at Louisiana State
University. Award requirements change regularly. For an
application and further information, contact your department
or visit the Ourso College of Business Administration website
at www.bus.lsu.edu. No GPA requirement specified.

Louisiana State University - Ourso College of Business
Administration
Attn: Scholarship Programs
3139 CEBA Building
Baton Rouge, LA 70803

2047
Kitty B. Strain Endowed Scholarship

AMOUNT: None Specified DEADLINE: February 1
MAJOR: Ourso College of Business Administration

The Kitty B. Strain Endowed Scholarship is open to female juniors and seniors in the Ourso College of Business Administration at Louisiana State University. To be considered for this award, you must have a minimum 3.0 GPA. Award requirements change regularly. For an application and further information, contact the Ourso College of Business Administration or visit their website at www.bus.lsu.edu. GPA must be 3.0-4.0.

Louisiana State University - Ourso College of Business Administration
Attn: Scholarship Programs
3139 CEBA Building
Baton Rouge, LA 70803

2048
L.A. Champagne Memorial Scholarship

AMOUNT: $800 DEADLINE: February 1
MAJOR: Accounting

The L.A. Champagne Memorial Scholarship is open to sophomores majoring in accounting at Louisiana State University. To be considered for this award, you must have a minimum 2.7 GPA. The award may be renewed for three years. Award requirements change regularly. For an application and further information, contact your department or visit the Ourso College of Business Administration website at www.bus.lsu.edu. GPA must be 2.7-4.0.

Louisiana State University - Ourso College of Business Administration
Attn: Scholarship Programs
3139 CEBA Building
Baton Rouge, LA 70803

2049
Lewis Gottlieb Fellowship

AMOUNT: $1500 DEADLINE: February 1
MAJOR: Business Administration, Finance

The Lewis Gottlieb Fellowship is open to full-time graduate students working towards a master's degree in finance or an MBA degree at Louisiana State University. Award requirements change regularly. For an application and further information, contact your department or visit the Ourso College of Business Administration website at www.bus.lsu.edu. No GPA requirement specified.

Louisiana State University - Ourso College of Business Administration
Attn: Scholarship Programs
3139 CEBA Building
Baton Rouge, LA 70803

2050
Lonnie H. Bearry Scholarship

AMOUNT: None Specified DEADLINE: February 1
MAJOR: Accounting

The Lonnie H. Bearry Scholarship is open to sophomore and junior accounting majors in the Ourso College of Business Administration at Louisiana State University. Award requirements change regularly. For an application and further information, contact the Department of Accounting or visit the Ourso College of Business Administration website at www.bus.lsu.edu. No GPA requirement specified.

Louisiana State University - Ourso College of Business Administration
Attn: Scholarship Programs
3139 CEBA Building
Baton Rouge, LA 70803

2051
Louisiana Consumer Finance Association Award

AMOUNT: $250 DEADLINE: February 1
MAJOR: Ourso College of Business Administration

The Louisiana Consumer Finance Association Award is open to juniors and seniors in the Ourso College of Business Administration at Louisiana State University. Award requirements change regularly. For an application and further information, contact the Ourso College of Business Administration or visit their website at www.bus.lsu.edu. No GPA requirement specified.

Louisiana State University - Ourso College of Business Administration
Attn: Scholarship Programs
3139 CEBA Building
Baton Rouge, LA 70803

2052
Louisiana Motor Transport Association-Baton Rouge Chapter Award

AMOUNT: $440 DEADLINE: February 1
MAJOR: Business Administration

The Louisiana Motor Transport Association-Baton Rouge Chapter Award is open to freshmen planning to major in business administration at Louisiana State University. Award requirements change regularly. For an application and further information, contact the Ourso College of Business Administration or visit their website at www.bus.lsu.edu. No GPA requirement specified.

Louisiana State University - Ourso College of Business Administration
Attn: Scholarship Programs
3139 CEBA Building
Baton Rouge, LA 70803

2053
Mack H. Hornbeak Scholarship

AMOUNT: $1000 DEADLINE: February 1
MAJOR: Ourso College of Business Administration

The Mack H. Hornbeak Scholarship is open to outstanding students in the Ourso College of Business Administration at Louisiana State University. To be considered for this award, you must have financial need. Preference is given to students majoring in finance or concentrating in commercial banking. Award requirements change regularly. For an application and further information, contact your department or visit the Ourso College of Business Administration website at www.bus.lsu.edu. No GPA requirement specified.

Louisiana State University - Ourso College of Business Administration
Attn: Scholarship Programs
3139 CEBA Building
Baton Rouge, LA 70803

2054
Marathon Oil Foundation Minority Scholarship

AMOUNT: $1500 DEADLINE: February 1
MAJOR: Accounting, Geology, Petroleum Engineering

The Marathon Oil Foundation Minority Scholarship is open to undergraduate students majoring in accounting, geology, or petroleum engineering at Louisiana State University. Award requirements change regularly. For an application and further information, contact your department or the Chancellor's Office. No GPA requirement specified.

Louisiana State University
Attn: Scholarship Programs
3139 CEBA Building
Baton Rouge, LA 70803

2055
Mr. and Mrs. R. Irby Didier, Sr., Memorial Scholarship

AMOUNT: None Specified DEADLINE: February 1
MAJOR: Banking

The Mr. and Mrs. R. Irby Didier, Sr., Memorial Scholarship is open to senior banking majors at Louisiana State University. To be considered for this award, you must be a native and resident of Louisiana and demonstrate financial need. Award requirements change regularly. For an application and further information, contact your department or visit the Ourso College of Business Administration website at www.bus.lsu.edu. No GPA requirement specified.

Louisiana State University - Ourso College of Business Administration
Attn: Scholarship Programs
3139 CEBA Building
Baton Rouge, LA 70803

2056
Paul and Ellen Arst Scholarship

AMOUNT: $1000 DEADLINE: February 1
MAJOR: Risk Management, Insurance

The Paul and Ellen Arst Scholarship is open to students in the Ourso College of Business Administration at Louisiana State University. To be considered for this award, you must be a junior or senior in the risk and insurance curriculum. Award requirements change regularly. For an application and further information, contact the Ourso College of Business Administration or visit their website at www.bus.lsu.edu. No GPA requirement specified.

Louisiana State University - Ourso College of Business Administration
Attn: Scholarship Programs
3139 CEBA Building
Baton Rouge, LA 70803

2057
Paul and Theresa Hendershot Scholarship

AMOUNT: None Specified DEADLINE: February 1
MAJOR: Marketing

The Paul and Theresa Hendershot Scholarship is open to senior marketing majors at Louisiana State University. To be considered for this award, you must have a minimum 3.0 GPA and demonstrate financial need. Award requirements change regularly. For an application and further information, contact your department or visit the Ourso College of Business Administration website at www.bus.lsu.edu. GPA must be 3.0-4.0.

Louisiana State University - Ourso College of Business Administration
Attn: Scholarship Programs
3139 CEBA Building
Baton Rouge, LA 70803

2058
Peat, Marwick, Mitchell and Company Award

AMOUNT: $300 DEADLINE: Varies
MAJOR: Enrolled in Auditing Course in the Ourso College of Business Administration

The Peat, Marwick, Mitchell and Company Award is given to an outstanding student in a basic auditing course at Louisiana State University. Award requirements change regularly. For further information, contact the Department of Accounting. No GPA requirement specified.

Louisiana State University - Ourso College of Business Administration
Attn: Scholarship Programs
3139 CEBA Building
Baton Rouge, LA 70803

2059
Phi Kappa Phi Outstanding Senior Award

AMOUNT: None Specified DEADLINE: Varies
MAJOR: Ourso College of Business Administration

The Phi Kappa Phi Outstanding Senior Award is a certificate given to the senior in the Ourso College of Business Administration at Louisiana State University with the highest GPA. Award requirements change regularly. For further information, contact your department. No GPA requirement specified.

Louisiana State University - Ourso College of Business Administration
Attn: Scholarship Programs
3139 CEBA Building
Baton Rouge, LA 70803

2060
Price Waterhouse and Company Award

AMOUNT: $500 DEADLINE: February 1
MAJOR: Accounting

The Price Waterhouse and Company Award is open to junior accounting students in the Ourso College of Business Administration at Louisiana State University. Award requirements change regularly. For an application and further information, contact your department or visit the Ourso College of Business Administration website at www.bus.lsu.edu. No GPA requirement specified.

Louisiana State University - Ourso College of Business Administration
Attn: Scholarship Programs
3139 CEBA Building
Baton Rouge, LA 70803

2061
Quinn M. Coco Scholarship

AMOUNT: None Specified DEADLINE: February 1
MAJOR: Accounting

The Quinn M. Coco Scholarship is open to accounting majors in the Ourso College of Business Administration at Louisiana State University. Award requirements change regularly. For an application and further information, contact your department or visit the Ourso College of Business Administration website at www.bus.lsu.edu. No GPA requirement specified.

Louisiana State University - Ourso College of Business Administration
Attn: Scholarship Programs
3139 CEBA Building
Baton Rouge, LA 70803

2062
Reymond Holmes Bussie Pope Scholarship

AMOUNT: None Specified DEADLINE: February 1
MAJOR: Ourso College of Business Administration

The Reymond Holmes Bussie Pope Scholarship is open to full-time students in the Ourso College of Business Administration at Louisiana State University. To be considered for this award, you must be a resident of Louisiana and have a minimum 3.0 GPA. Award requirements change regularly. For an application and further information, contact the Ourso College of Business Administration or visit their website at www.bus.lsu.edu. GPA must be 3.0-4.0.

Louisiana State University - Ourso College of Business Administration
Attn: Scholarship Programs
3139 CEBA Building
Baton Rouge, LA 70803

2063
Russell Sledge Scholarship

AMOUNT: None Specified DEADLINE: February 1
MAJOR: Ourso College of Business Administration

The Russell Sledge Scholarship is open to full-time sophomores, juniors, and seniors in the Ourso College of Business Administration at Louisiana State University. To be considered for this award, you must demonstrate academic achievement and financial need. Award requirements change regularly. For an application and further information, contact the Ourso College of Business Administration or visit their website at www.bus.lsu.edu. No GPA requirement specified.

Louisiana State University - Ourso College of Business Administration
Attn: Scholarship Programs
3139 CEBA Building
Baton Rouge, LA 70803

2064
Society of Louisiana CPAs - Baton Rouge Chapter Scholarship

AMOUNT: $300 DEADLINE: February 1
MAJOR: Accounting

The Society of Louisiana CPAs - Baton Rouge Chapter Scholarship is open to senior accounting students in the Ourso College of Business Administration at Louisiana State University. Award requirements change regularly. For an application and further information, contact your department or visit the Ourso College of Business Administration website at www.bus.lsu.edu. No GPA requirement specified.

Louisiana State University - Ourso College of Business Administration
Attn: Scholarship Programs
3139 CEBA Building
Baton Rouge, LA 70803

2065
Southern Scrap Company Scholarship in Operations Management

AMOUNT: None Specified DEADLINE: February 1
MAJOR: Information Systems and Decision Sciences

The Southern Scrap Company Scholarship in Operations Management is open to information systems and decision sciences majors at Louisiana State University. To be considered for this award, you must be a junior or senior, be a Louisiana resident, and have a minimum 2.5 GPA. You are required to submit a 250-word (or less) essay on the role of operations management in a modern organization and a 100-word (or less) autobiography. Award requirements change regularly. For an application and further information, contact your department or visit the Ourso College of Business Administration website at www.bus.lsu.edu. GPA must be 2.5-4.0.

Louisiana State University - Ourso College of Business Administration
Attn: Scholarship Programs
3139 CEBA Building
Baton Rouge, LA 70803

2066
Tenneco Gas Scholarship

AMOUNT: $750 DEADLINE: February 1
MAJOR: Information Systems and Decision Sciences

The Tenneco Gas Scholarship is open to full-time information systems and decision sciences majors at Louisiana State University. To be considered for this award, you must be a U.S. citizen, have a minimum cumulative GPA of 3.0, and have one or two regular semesters remaining in the undergraduate program. The award provides $750 per semester. Award requirements change regularly. For an application and further information, contact your department or visit the Ourso College of Business Administration website at www.bus.lsu.edu. GPA must be 3.0-4.0.

Louisiana State University - Ourso College of Business Administration
Attn: Scholarship Programs
3139 CEBA Building
Baton Rouge, LA 70803

2067
Texaco Marketing and Refining, Inc., Scholarship

AMOUNT: None Specified DEADLINE: February 1
MAJOR: Information Systems and Decision Sciences

The Texaco Marketing and Refining, Inc., Scholarship is open to information systems and decision sciences majors at Louisiana State University. Award requirements change regularly. For an application and further information, contact your department or visit the Ourso College of Business Administration website at www.bus.lsu.edu. No GPA requirement specified.

Louisiana State University - Ourso College of Business Administration
Attn: Scholarship Programs
3139 CEBA Building
Baton Rouge, LA 70803

2068
Tommy Doiron and Jimmy Webb Memorial Scholarship

AMOUNT: None Specified DEADLINE: February 1
MAJOR: Ourso College of Business Administration

The Tommy Doiron and Jimmy Webb Memorial Scholarship is open to sophomores in the Ourso College of Business Administration at Louisiana State University. To be considered for this award, you must have a minimum 2.5 GPA and demonstrate financial need. Award requirements change regularly. For an application and further information, contact the Ourso College of Business Administration or visit their website at www.bus.lsu.edu. GPA must be 2.5-4.0.

Louisiana State University - Ourso College of Business Administration
Attn: Scholarship Programs
3139 CEBA Building
Baton Rouge, LA 70803

2069
Travis Varner Memorial Scholarship

AMOUNT: $500 DEADLINE: February 1
MAJOR: Accounting, Information Systems and Decision Sciences

The Travis Varner Memorial Scholarship is open to undergraduates at Louisiana State University. To be considered for this award, you must be an accounting or information systems and decision sciences major. Award requirements change regularly. For an application and further information, contact your department or visit the Ourso College of Business Administration website at www.bus.lsu.edu. No GPA requirement specified.

Louisiana State University - Ourso College of Business Administration
Attn: Scholarship Programs
3139 CEBA Building
Baton Rouge, LA 70803

Maharishi University of Management

2070
DeRoy C. Thomas Scholarship

AMOUNT: None Specified DEADLINE: May 15
MAJOR: All Areas of Study

Open to African-American undergraduates at the Maharishi University of Management who have a minimum 3.0 GPA. Award covers tuition, double room, and board when used with any available grants. One new recipient is chosen when the previous recipient graduates. Award is only available every four years. Award requirements change regularly. For further information and an application, please contact the address listed, call (515) 472-1156, or email finaid@mum.edu. You may also visit their website: www.mum.edu/welcome.html. GPA must be 3.0-4.0.

Maharishi University of Management
Office of Financial Aid
1000 North 4th Street, DB 1127
Fairfield, IA 52557

2071
Girl Scout Gold Award

AMOUNT: $1500 DEADLINE: July 31
MAJOR: All Areas of Study

Open to Girl Scout Gold Award recipients attending Maharishi University of Management who have graduated from high school within the last two years. Renewable for four years. Award requirements change regularly. For further information and an application, please contact the address listed, call (515) 472-1156, or email finaid@mum.edu. You may also visit their website: www.mum.edu/welcome.html. No GPA rquirement specified.

Maharishi University of Management
Office of Financial Aid
1000 North 4th Street, DB 1127
Fairfield, IA 52557

2072
Shelley Hoffman Scholarship Fund

AMOUNT: $500-$2000 DEADLINE: May 31
MAJOR: Creative Writing (Preferred)

This scholarship is open to students who have cerebral palsy and/or will be enrolling in a creative writing program at the Maharishi University of Management. Funds received by you are to be used for the payment of expenses relating to both the undergraduate education and the Transcendental Meditation-Sidhi program. Award requirements change regularly. No GPA requirement specified.

Maharishi University of Management
Office of Financial Aid
1000 North 4th Street, DB 1127
Fairfield, IA 52557

2073
Walter Koch Scholarship

AMOUNT: None Specified DEADLINE: Varies
MAJOR: Engineering

This scholarship is open to outstanding upperclassmen at the Maharishi University of Management. You must be majoring in engineering. Award requirements change regularly. No GPA requirement specified.

Maharishi University of Management
Office of Financial Aid
1000 North 4th Street, DB 1127
Fairfield, IA 52557

McIntosh College

2074
Delta Epsilon Chi - Business Leader Scholarships

AMOUNT: $500 DEADLINE: April 15
MAJOR: All Areas of Study

One award is open to first-year McIntosh students who served in a high school DECA, FBLA, VICA, Student Council, or other leadership position. The second award is open to second-year students who were participating members in Delta Epsilon Chi during the first year of study at McIntosh College. Selection is based on financial need, academic achievement, and leadership within the leadership organization. Award requirements change regularly. Please send a self-addressed, stamped envelope to receive your application and any further instructions from the scholarship provider. GPA must be 3.0-4.0.

McIntosh College
Attn: Scholarship Committee
23 Cataract Avenue
Dover, NH 03820-3908

2075
International Student Scholarships

AMOUNT: $500 DEADLINE: Varies
MAJOR: All Areas of Study

Open to international students entering McIntosh College directly from their country of citizenship. To be considered for this scholarship, you must have the following on file at the college: an application for admission; all required documentation for Form I-20 issuance; proof of English proficiency; full-time degree program of study selected; a clearly defined career objective; a copy of high school records stating graduation; an explanation of any achievements, awards, activities, or community involvement; and at least one personal reference. Award requirements change regularly. Please send a self-addressed, stamped envelope to receive your application and any further instructions from the scholarship provider. GPA must be 2.8-4.0.

McIntosh College
Attn: Scholarship Committee
23 Cataract Avenue
Dover, NH 03820-3908

2076
President's Scholarships

AMOUNT: $750 DEADLINE: April 15
MAJOR: All Areas of Study

Open to freshman students entering McIntosh College directly upon high school graduation. Criteria used to consider applicants for this scholarship include academic achievement or a significant record of academic improvement, school and/or community involvement, clearly defined college and career objectives, and academic and personal references. Award requirements change regularly. Please send a self-addressed, stamped envelope to receive your application and any further instructions from the scholarship provider. GPA must be 3.0-4.0.

McIntosh College
Attn: Scholarship Committee
23 Cataract Avenue
Dover, NH 03820-3908

McMurry University

2077
Endowed Scholarship

AMOUNT: None Specified DEADLINE: March 15
MAJOR: All Areas of Study

The Endowed Scholarship is open to full-time students at McMurry University with a GPA of 3.0 or better. Individual award restrictions may apply. Award requirements change regularly. Please send a self-addressed, stamped envelope to receive your application and any further information from the scholarship provider or visit the website at www.mcm.edu. GPA must be 3.0-4.0.

McMurry University
Attn: Student Financial Aid
McMurry Station Box 278
Abilene, TX 79697-0278

2078
International Scholarship

AMOUNT: None Specified DEADLINE: March 15
MAJOR: All Areas of Study Except Nursing

The International Scholarship is awarded to the top incoming international applicant at McMurry University. The award provides full tuition and fees and residence hall accommodation. Award requirements change regularly. Contact the Admissions Office for additional information or visit the website at www.mcm.edu. No GPA requirement specified.

McMurry University
Attn: Student Financial Aid
McMurry Station Box 278
Abilene, TX 79697-0278

2079
McMurry Grant

AMOUNT: $1500-$3000 DEADLINE: March 15
MAJOR: All Areas of Study

The McMurry Grant is open to entering freshmen at McMurry University. To be considered for this award, you must have a minimum 2.9 high school GPA and at least a 20 ACT or 950 SAT. Award requirements change regularly. Contact the Admissions Office for additional information or visit the website at www.mcm.edu. GPA must be 2.9-4.0.

McMurry University
Attn: Student Financial Aid
McMurry Station Box 278
Abilene, TX 79697-0278

2080
McMurry Honors Program

AMOUNT: None Specified DEADLINE: February 1
MAJOR: All Areas of Study Except Nursing

The McMurry Honors Program is open to entering freshmen at McMurry University. To be considered for this award, you must be in the top 5% of your high school graduating class and have at least a 27 ACT/1220 SAT score. An on-campus interview is required. The award provides full tuition and fees. Award requirements change regularly. Contact the Admissions Office for additional information or visit the website at www.mcm.edu. GPA must be 3.7-4.0.

McMurry University
Attn: Student Financial Aid
McMurry Station Box 278
Abilene, TX 79697-0278

2081
Ministerial Scholarship

AMOUNT: $2200 DEADLINE: March 15
MAJOR: All Areas of Study

The Ministerial Scholarship is open to McMurry University students who are ministers, or the dependents of ministers and those pursuing a church-related vocation. To be considered for this award, you must be enrolled full-time with a GPA of 2.0 or better. Award requirements change regularly. Please send a self-addressed, stamped envelope to receive your application and any further information from the scholarship provider or visit the website at www.mcm.edu. GPA must be 2.0-4.0.

McMurry University
Attn: Student Financial Aid
McMurry Station Box 278
Abilene, TX 79697-0278

2082
Phi Theta Kappa Scholarship

AMOUNT: $2000 DEADLINE: March 15
MAJOR: All Areas of Study Except Nursing

The Phi Theta Kappa Scholarship is open to incoming transfer students at McMurry University. To be considered for this award, you must be a member of Phi Theta Kappa. Award requirements change regularly. Contact the Admissions Office for additional information or visit the website at www.mcm.edu. No GPA requirement specified.

McMurry University
Attn: Student Financial Aid
McMurry Station Box 278
Abilene, TX 79697-0278

2083
Presidential Scholar Award

AMOUNT: $5000 DEADLINE: March 15
MAJOR: All Areas of Study

The Presidential Scholar Award is open to entering freshmen at McMurry University. To be considered for this award, you must be enrolled full-time, have at least a 3.7 high school GPA, and have a minimum 27 ACT or 1200 SAT. Award requirements change regularly. Please send a self-addressed, stamped envelope to receive your application and any further information from the scholarship provider or visit the website at www.mcm.edu. GPA must be 3.7-4.0.

McMurry University
Attn: Student Financial Aid
McMurry Station Box 278
Abilene, TX 79697-0278

2084
Transfer Scholarship

AMOUNT: $1500-$2500 DEADLINE: March 15
MAJOR: All Areas of Study Except Nursing

The Transfer Scholarship is open to incoming transfer students at McMurry University. To be considered for this award, you must have a minimum 3.0 GPA. Your transferable GPA determines the value of your award: a 3.0 GPA is worth $750 per semester; a GPA must be 3.4 GPA is $1,000 per semester; and a 3.7 GPA is $1,250 per semester. Award requirements change regularly. Contact the Admissions Office for additional information or visit the website at www.mcm.edu. GPA must be 3.0-4.0.

McMurry University
Attn: Student Financial Aid
McMurry Station Box 278
Abilene, TX 79697-0278

2085
Trustee Scholar Award

AMOUNT: $5000-$7000 DEADLINE: March 15
MAJOR: All Areas of Study

The Trustee Scholar Award is open to entering freshmen at McMurry University. To be considered for this award, you must be in the top 5% of your high school graduating class, have at least a 27 ACT or 1220 SAT, and qualify and participate in the Honors Program. Award requirements change regularly. Contact the Admissions Office for additional information or visit the website at www.mcm.edu. GPA must be 3.7-4.0.

McMurry University
Attn: Student Financial Aid
McMurry Station Box 278
Abilene, TX 79697-0278

2086
University Scholar Award

AMOUNT: $3000 DEADLINE: March 15
MAJOR: All Areas of Study Except Nursing

The University Scholar Award is open to entering freshmen at McMurry University. To be considered for this award, you must be enrolled full-time, have at least a 3.3 high school GPA, and have a minimum 22 ACT or 1050 SAT. Award requirements change regularly. Please send a self-addressed, stamped envelope to receive your application and any further information from the scholarship provider or visit the website at www.mcm.edu. GPA must be 3.3-4.0.

McMurry University
Attn: Student Financial Aid
McMurry Station Box 278
Abilene, TX 79697-0278

Middle Tennessee State University

2087
Academic Service Scholarship

AMOUNT: $2600-$3000 DEADLINE: March 15
MAJOR: All Areas of Study

The Academic Service Scholarship is open to freshmen entering the Middle Tennessee State University. Applicants must have a minimum ACT score of 20 or equivalent SAT score. ACT/SAT scores and high school GPAs are weighted equally. A work obligation of five hours a week is required. This award is renewable for eight semesters providing the student maintains a minimum GPA of 2.5 the first semester and a minimum GPA of 2.9 beginning the second semester. Transfer students from a Tennessee Board of Regents institution are also eligible to apply for this scholarship. Award requirements change regularly. Please send a self-addressed, stamped envelope to receive your application and any further instructions from the scholarship provider or visit www.mtsu.edu. GPA must be 2.5-4.0.

Middle Tennessee State University
Office of Admissions
Cope 208 Administration Bldg
Murfreesboro, TN 37132

2088
Archie Hartwell Nash Memorial Scholarship

AMOUNT: $500-$2500 DEADLINE: April 1
MAJOR: All Areas of Study

Open to students of sophomore standing or above (including graduate students) who are attending Middle Tennessee State University full-time. Applicants must work a minimum of 20 hours per week and maintain a C average or better. Award requirements change regularly. You may call (615) 321-4939 or (888) 540-5200 toll-free for further information. GPA must be 2.0-4.0.

Community Foundation of Middle Tennessee
Scholarship Committee
210 23rd Avenue North
Nashville, TN 37203-1502

2089
Enrichment Scholarship

AMOUNT: None Specified DEADLINE: March 1
MAJOR: All Areas of Study

The Enrichment Scholarship is open to entering freshmen, transfer students, and currently enrolled students at the Middle Tennessee State University. Applicants receiving adequate financial aid from other sources may not be considered. Considerations are based on potential, academic achievement, and financial need. Entering freshmen must have a minimum ACT score of 21 and a minimum GPA of 3.0. Currently enrolled and transfer students must have a minimum GPA of 2.5. Recipients must maintain a minimum GPA of 2.5 and must reapply for this award annually. Award requirements change regularly. Please send a self-addressed, stamped envelope to receive your application and any further instructions from the scholarship provider or visit www.mtsu.edu. GPA must be 3.0-4.0.

Middle Tennessee State University
Office of Admissions
Cope 208 Administration Bldg
Murfreesboro, TN 37132

2090
James M. Buchanan Scholarship

AMOUNT: $1000 DEADLINE: Varies
MAJOR: All Fields of study

The James M. Buchanan Scholarship is open to first-time freshmen entering the Middle Tennessee State University who have qualified for the Presidential Scholarship or the Otis L. Floyd Academic Excellence Scholarship. Award requirements change regularly. Please send a self-addressed, stamped envelope to receive your application and any further instructions from the scholarship provider, call the Admissions Office at (615) 898-2111, or visit www.mtsu.edu. GPA must be 3.8-4.0.

Middle Tennessee State University
Office of Admissions
Cope 208 Administration Bldg
Murfreesboro, TN 37132

2091
Leadership/Performance Scholarship

AMOUNT: $2000 DEADLINE: March 1
MAJOR: All Areas of Study

The Leadership/Performance Scholarship is open to outstanding freshmen entering the Middle Tennessee State University and is based on academic achievement, extracurricular activities, and leadership. This award is renewable for eight semesters provided the student maintains a minimum GPA of 2.8. Award requirements change regularly. Please send a self-addressed, stamped envelope to receive your application and any further instructions from the scholarship provider or visit www.mtsu.edu. No GPA requirement specified.

Middle Tennessee State University
Office of Admissions
Cope 208 Administration Bldg
Murfreesboro, TN 37132

2092
Matching Scholarship Program

AMOUNT: None Specified DEADLINE: March 1
MAJOR: All Areas of Study

The Matching Scholarship Program is available to African-American U.S. citizens who are qualified for admission to or are currently enrolled at the Middle Tennessee State University. This award is based on potential, area of specialization, and economic status. Award requirements change regularly. Please send a self-addressed, stamped envelope to receive your application and any further instructions from the scholarship provider or visit www.mtsu.edu. No GPA requirement specified.

Middle Tennessee State University
Office of Admissions
Cope 208 Administration Bldg
Murfreesboro, TN 37132

2093
Otis L. Floyd Academic Excellence Scholarship

AMOUNT: $4000 DEADLINE: March 1
MAJOR: All Areas of Study

The Otis L. Floyd Academic Excellence Scholarship is open to first-time freshmen entering the Middle Tennessee State University who have a minimum ACT score of 25 and a minimum GPA of 3.2 after the seventh semester of high school. This award is automatically renewable for eight semesters by earning a minimum GPA of 2.5 the first semester and a minimum GPA of 3.0 every following semester. Applicants offered the scholarship must notify Middle Tennessee State University by May 1 of their intention to accept the award. Award requirements change regularly. Please send a self-addressed, stamped envelope to receive your application and any further instructions from the scholarship provider, call the Admissions Office at (615) 898-2111, or visit www.mtsu.edu. GPA must be 3.2-4.0.

Middle Tennessee State University
Office of Admissions
Cope 208 Administration Bldg
Murfreesboro, TN 37132

2094
Presidential Scholarship

AMOUNT: $4000 DEADLINE: March 1
MAJOR: All Areas of Study

The Presidential Scholarship is open to first-time freshmen entering the Middle Tennessee State University who have a minimum ACT score of 29, minimum combined SAT score of 1280, and a minimum GPA of 3.75, although National Merit Finalists automatically qualify regardless of GPA or ACT score. This award is automatically renewable for eight semesters by earning a minimum GPA of 2.5 the first semester and a minimum GPA of 3.0 every following semester. Applicants offered the scholarship must notify Middle Tennessee State University by May 1 of their intention to accept it. Award requirements change regularly. Please send a self-addressed, stamped envelope to receive your application and any further instructions from the scholarship provider, call the Admissions Office at (615) 898-2111, or visit www.mtsu.edu. GPA must be 3.75-4.0.

Middle Tennessee State University
Office of Admissions
Cope 208 Administration Bldg
Murfreesboro, TN 37132

2095
Provost Scholarship

AMOUNT: None Specified DEADLINE: March 1
MAJOR: All Fields of Study

The Provost Scholarship is open to first-time attendees at Middle Tennessee State University. Entering freshmen must have a minimum ACT score of 20 and a minimum GPA of

2.8. Transfer students must have a minimum GPA of 2.0. This scholarship is awarded at the discretion of the Admission Review Committee and is only guaranteed for one year. Students must earn a minimum GPA of 2.5 the first semester to receive the award the second semester. Award requirements change regularly. Please send a self-addressed, stamped envelope to receive your application and any further instructions from the scholarship provider or visit www.mtsu.edu. GPA must be 2.8-4.0.

Middle Tennessee State University
Office of Admissions
Cope 208 Administration Bldg
Murfreesboro, TN 37132

2096
Scholastic Achievement Scholarship

AMOUNT: $2600-$3000 DEADLINE: March 1
MAJOR: All Areas of Study

The Scholastic Achievement Scholarship is open to first-time freshmen entering the Middle Tennessee State University. Applicants must be African-American U.S. citizens who scored a minimum of 21 on the ACT tests and have a minimum high school GPA of 3.0. Preference may be given to students with the highest GPA and/or test score. This award is renewable for eight semesters provided students maintain a minimum GPA of 2.5 the first semester and a minimum GPA of 2.8 each semester beginning with the second semester. Award requirements change regularly. Please send a self-addressed, stamped envelope to receive your application and any further instructions from the scholarship provider, call the Admissions Office at (615) 898-2111, or visit www.mtsu.edu. GPA must be 3.0-4.0.

Middle Tennessee State University
Office of Admissions
Cope 208 Administration Bldg
Murfreesboro, TN 37132

Mills College

2097
Arthur Vining Davis Science Scholarship

AMOUNT: Maximum: $2000 DEADLINE: February 15
MAJOR: Science, Mathematics, Computer Science

Scholarship for entering Mills College freshmen or transfer students who have demonstrated strong ability and interest in science, mathematics, or computer science. Award based on merit and is renewable as long as the student stays in the same field of study and maintains a 3.0 GPA. Award requirements change regularly. Write to the address listed, enclosing a self-addressed, stamped envelope for an application and further information. You can browse their website: www.mills.edu or email finaid@mills.edu. GPA must be 3.0-4.0.

Mills College
Office of Financial Aid
5000 MacArthur Blvd
Oakland, CA 94613-1301

2098
Barbara Hazelton Floyd Scholarship in Music

AMOUNT: Maximum: $5000 DEADLINE: February 15
MAJOR: Music

Scholarship for entering Mills College freshman women or undergraduate transfer students who have demonstrated superior music talent. Applicants must audition in person or on tape. Renewable with a 3.2 GPA and full-time enrollment. Preference is given to piano students. Award requirements change regularly. Write to the address listed, enclosing a self-addressed, stamped envelope for an application and further information. You can browse their website: www.mills.edu or email finaid@mills.edu. No GPA requirement specified.

Mills College
Office of Financial Aid
5000 MacArthur Blvd
Oakland, CA 94613-1301

2099
Carroll Donner Commemorative Scholarship in Music

AMOUNT: Maximum: $5000 DEADLINE: February 15
MAJOR: Music

Scholarship for entering Mills College freshman women or undergraduate transfer students who have demonstrated superior music talent. Applicants must audition in person or on tape. Renewable with a 3.2 GPA and full-time enrollment. Award requirements change regularly. Write to the address listed, enclosing a self-addressed, stamped envelope for an application and further information. You can browse their website: www.mills.edu or email finaid@mills.edu. No GPA requirement specified.

Mills College
Office of Financial Aid
5000 MacArthur Blvd
Oakland, CA 94613-1301

2100
Regional Scholarships

AMOUNT: $5000-$7500 DEADLINE: February 15
MAJOR: All Areas of Study

Awards for entering Mills College freshman women who have demonstrated superior scholastic achievement and distinguished themselves in their extracurricular activities or personal interests. Students must have a GPA of 3.2 from high school and an SAT score of at least 1100. Based on both merit and financial need. Ten awards offered annually. Award requirements change regularly. Write to the address listed, enclosing a self-addressed, stamped envelope for an application and further information. You can browse their website: www.mills.edu or email finaid@mills.edu. GPA must be 3.2-4.0.

Mills College
Office of Financial Aid
5000 MacArthur Blvd
Oakland, CA 94613-1301

Transfer Scholarships

AMOUNT: Maximum: $5000 DEADLINE: April 1
MAJOR: All Areas of Study

Awards for Mills College transfer students who have demonstrated superior scholastic achievement, leadership ability, and/or a significant contribution to their previous educational institution. Renewable with a 3.2 GPA and full-time enrollment. Based on academics and financial need. Renewable if recipients maintain pre-set standards. Award requirements change regularly. Write to the address listed, enclosing a self-addressed, stamped envelope for an application and further information. You can browse their website: www.mills.edu or email finaid@mills.edu. GPA must be 3.2-4.0.

Mills College
Office of Financial Aid
5000 MacArthur Blvd
Oakland, CA 94613-1301

2102
Trustee Scholarships

AMOUNT: Maximum: $10000 DEADLINE: February 15
MAJOR: All Areas of Study

Awards for entering Mills College freshman women who have demonstrated superior scholastic achievement and distinguished themselves in their extracurricular activities or personal interests. Students must have a GPA of 3.5 from high school and an SAT score of at least 1200. Based on merit and financial need. Award requirements change regularly. Write to the address listed, enclosing a self-addressed, stamped envelope for an application and further information. You can browse their website: www.mills.edu or email finaid@mills.edu. GPA must be 3.5-4.0.

Mills College
Office of Financial Aid
5000 MacArthur Blvd
Oakland, CA 94613-1301

Minneapolis Drafting School

2103
Minneapolis Drafting School Scholarships

AMOUNT: $500-$1000 DEADLINE: April 25
MAJOR: Architectural/Structural CAD Drafting, Mechanical/Electronic CAD Drafting

Open to undergraduates who are seeking careers in CAD drafting. Applicants will be required to have a letter of recommendation from a drafting teacher or counselor and a sample of drafting work to be presented during their personal interview. Award requirements change regularly. No GPA requirement specified.

Minneapolis Drafting School
Attn: Ron Bauleke
5700 West Broadway Avenue
Minneapolis, MN 55428-3568

Missouri Valley College

2104
Chamber of Commerce Scholarships

AMOUNT: $500 DEADLINE: Varies
MAJOR: All Areas of Study

Open to residents of Saline County, Missouri, graduates of Marshall High School, and non-traditional students. Must be first-time students at Missouri Valley College. Award requirements change regularly. Contact the address listed for further information or call (816) 831-4114. You may also visit their website: www.moval.edu. No GPA requirement specified

Missouri Valley College
Director of Admissions
500 East College Street
Marshall, MO 65340-3109

2105
Horatio Alger Scholarships

AMOUNT: Maximum: $7900 DEADLINE: Varies
MAJOR: All Areas of Study

Open to high school seniors accepted to Missouri Valley College who participated in the competitive scholarship sponsored by the Horatio Alger Association. Must be a national winner or runner-up to qualify. Award requirements change regularly. Contact the address listed for further information or call (816) 831-4114. You may also visit their website: www.moval.edu. No GPA requirement specified.

Missouri Valley College
Director of Admissions
500 East College Street
Marshall, MO 65340-3109

2106
Missouri Valley College Alumni Scholarships

AMOUNT: $2000 DEADLINE: Varies
MAJOR: All Areas of Study

Open to high school seniors accepted to Missouri Valley College who have been recommended by a friend or relative who graduated from MVC. Award requirements change regularly. Contact the address listed for further information or call (816) 831-4114. You may also visit their website: www.moval.edu. GPA must be 3.0-4.0.

Missouri Valley College
Director of Admissions
500 East College Street
Marshall, MO 65340-3109

2107
Missouri Valley College American Humanics Scholarships

AMOUNT: $5000 DEADLINE: Varies
MAJOR: All Areas of Study

Open to high school seniors accepted to Missouri Valley College who are/have been members or participants of Scouts, YMCA/YWCA, Big Brothers/Big Sisters, 4-H, Boys Club of America, Junior Achievement, Campfire, Goodwill Industries, or American Red Cross. A letter of reference from the organization will be required. Award requirements change regularly. Contact the address listed for further information or call (816) 831-4114. You may also visit their website: www.moval.edu. No GPA requirement specified.

Missouri Valley College
Director of Admissions
500 East College Street
Marshall, MO 65340-3109

2108
Missouri Valley College Board of Trustees Scholarships

AMOUNT: $5000 DEADLINE: Varies
MAJOR: All Areas of Study

Open to high school seniors accepted to Missouri Valley College who have been recommended by a member of the Board of Trustees. Award requirements change regularly. Contact the address listed for further information or call (816) 831-4114. You may also visit their website: www.moval.edu. GPA must be 3.0-4.0.

Missouri Valley College
Director of Admissions
500 East College Street
Marshall, MO 65340-3109

2109
Missouri Valley College Boy/Girl State Scholarships

AMOUNT: None Specified DEADLINE: Varies
MAJOR: All Areas of Study

Open to high school seniors accepted to Missouri Valley College who have been participants of Boy's State or Girl's State. Award is cost of room and board. Award requirements change regularly. Contact the address listed for further information or call (816) 831-4114. You may also visit their website: www.moval.edu. No GPA requirement specified.

Missouri Valley College
Director of Admissions
500 East College Street
Marshall, MO 65340-3109

2110
Missouri Valley College National Merit Scholarships

AMOUNT: $250-$2000 DEADLINE: Varies
MAJOR: All Areas of Study

Open to high school seniors accepted to Missouri Valley College who were finalists in the National Merit Competition. Award requirements change regularly. Contact the address listed for further information or call (816) 831-4114. You may also visit their website: www.moval.edu. No GPA requirement specified.

Missouri Valley College
Director of Admissions
500 East College Street
Marshall, MO 65340-3109

2111
Missouri Valley College National Presbyterian Scholarships

AMOUNT: $2000 DEADLINE: December 1
MAJOR: All Areas of Study

Open to high school senior accepted to Missouri Valley College who are members of the Presbyterian Church. Award requirements change regularly. Contact the address listed for further information or call (816) 831-4114. You may also visit their website: www.moval.edu. No GPA requirement specified.

Missouri Valley College
Director of Admissions
500 East College Street
Marshall, MO 65340-3109

2112
Missouri Valley College Presidential Scholarships

AMOUNT: None Specified DEADLINE: Varies
MAJOR: All Areas of Study

Open to high school seniors accepted to Missouri Valley who are residents of Missouri. Applicants must have a minimum 3.5 GPA and an ACT score of at least 30 or 1300 SAT. The award is equal to tuition. Award requirements change regularly. Contact the address listed for further information or call (816) 831-4114. You may also visit their website: www.moval.edu. GPA must be 3.5.

Missouri Valley College
Director of Admissions
500 East College Street
Marshall, MO 65340-3109

2113
Missouri Valley College Talent Scholarships

AMOUNT: None Specified DEADLINE: Varies
MAJOR: All Areas of Study

Open to high school seniors accepted to Missouri Valley College who have various talents including, but not limited to, academics, art, music, leadership, athletics, and spirit squad abilities. Award requirements change regularly. Contact the address listed for further information or call (816) 831-4114. You may also visit their website: www.moval.edu. No GPA requirement specified.

Missouri Valley College
Director of Admissions
500 East College Street
Marshall, MO 65340-3109

Moorhead State University

2114
Academic Excellence Award

AMOUNT: $3000 DEADLINE: June 30
MAJOR: All Areas of Study

The Academic Excellence Awards are open to incoming freshmen admitted to Moorhead State University who are National Merit Finalists. This award is renewable for three years based on GPA. Award requirements change regularly. For further information, please call the financial aid office or mail in a request, including a self-addressed, stamped envelope. No GPA requirement specified.

Moorhead State University
Office of Scholarship and Financial Aid
1104 7th Avenue South, Owens Hall Rm 107
Moorhead, MN 56563

2115
Athletic Scholarships

AMOUNT: None Specified DEADLINE: Varies
MAJOR: All Areas of Study

The Athletic Scholarships are open to incoming freshmen attending Moorhead State University who demonstrate exceptional athletic talent. Award requirements change regularly. For further information, please call the financial aid office or mail in a request, including a self-addressed, stamped envelope. No GPA requirement specified.

Moorhead State University
Office of Scholarship and Financial Aid
1104 7th Avenue South, Owens Hall Rm 107
Moorhead, MN 56563

2116
Community College Transfer Scholarship

AMOUNT: $500-$750 DEADLINE: May 30
MAJOR: All Areas of Study

This scholarship is available to Moorhead State University students who have completed two years of community college. You must have a minimum 3.5 GPA in order to apply. Award requirements change regularly. GPA must be 3.5-4.0.

Moorhead State University
Office of Scholarship and Financial Aid
1104 7th Avenue South, Owens Hall Rm 107
Moorhead, MN 56563

2117
Dragon Scholarship

AMOUNT: $1000 DEADLINE: Varies
MAJOR: All Areas of Study

The Dragon Scholarship is open to incoming freshmen admitted to Moorhead State University. You must have either a minimum 28 ACT or a ranking in the top 10% of your high school graduating class. This award is not renewable. Award requirements change regularly. No GPA requirement specified.

Moorhead State University
Office of Scholarship and Financial Aid
1104 7th Avenue South, Owens Hall Rm 107
Moorhead, MN 56563

2118
Honors Apprenticeship Scholarships

AMOUNT: $3000 DEADLINE: February 1
MAJOR: All Areas of Study

The Honors Apprenticeship Scholarships are open to incoming freshmen admitted to Moorhead State University who have demonstrated academic excellence. In order to apply, you must rank in the top 5% of your high school graduating class or in the top 5th percentile on the ACT/SAT. Opportunities to apprentice in an area of academic interest under the supervision of a faculty member are available. Award requirements change regularly. For further information, please call the financial aid office or mail in a request, including a self-addressed, stamped envelope. No GPA requirement specified.

Moorhead State University
Office of Scholarship and Financial Aid
1104 7th Avenue South, Owens Hall Rm 107
Moorhead, MN 56563

2119
Minority Scholarship

AMOUNT: $500-$2200 DEADLINE: April 1
MAJOR: All Areas of Study

The Minority Scholarships are open to minorities at Moorhead State University who are in the top 25% of their high school graduating class and score well on standardized tests. Award requirements change regularly. No GPA requirement specified.

Moorhead State University
Office of Scholarship and Financial Aid
1104 7th Avenue South, Owens Hall Rm 107
Moorhead, MN 56563

2120
President's Scholarships

AMOUNT: $500 DEADLINE: March 1
MAJOR: All Areas of Study

The President's Scholarships are open to incoming freshmen admitted to Moorhead State University. You must rank in the top 25% of your high school graduating class and have an ACT score between 24 and 27. The selection criteria are also based on academics and community service. You will need to maintain a minimum 3.0 GPA to receive the award in your second year. Award requirements change regularly. For further information, please call the financial aid office or mail in a request, including a self-addressed, stamped envelope. GPA must be 3.0-4.0.

Moorhead State University
Office of Scholarship and Financial Aid
1104 7th Avenue South, Owens Hall Rm 107
Moorhead, MN 56563

2121
Second Start Scholarship

AMOUNT: $500 DEADLINE: May 30
MAJOR: All Areas of Study

Scholarships are available to Moorhead State University students who are at least 25 years of age and enrolled for a minimum of eight credit hours per semester in an undergraduate program. You must not have attended an institution of higher education as a full-time student within the last three years. Award requirements change regularly. No GPA requirement specified.

Moorhead State University
Office of Scholarship and Financial Aid
1104 7th Avenue South, Owens Hall Rm 107
Moorhead, MN 56563

2122
Talent Scholarships

AMOUNT: None Specified DEADLINE: Varies
MAJOR: Art, Music, Theater, Speech

The Talent Scholarships are open to students at Moorhead State University who demonstrate exceptional talent in the areas of art, music, speech, or theater arts. Recipients of this award are selected by the department faculty. Award requirements change regularly. For further information, please call the financial aid office or mail in a request, including a self-addressed, stamped envelope. No GPA requirement specified.

Moorhead State University
Office of Scholarship and Financial Aid
1104 7th Avenue South, Owens Hall Rm 107
Moorhead, MN 56563

2123
University Scholarships

AMOUNT: $500 DEADLINE: Varies
MAJOR: All Areas of Study

The University Scholarships are open to incoming freshmen admitted to Moorhead State University. In order to apply, you must rank in the top 25% of your high school graduating class or have a minimum composite 24 ACT. This award is nonrenewable. Award requirements change regularly. No GPA requirement specified.

Moorhead State University
Office of Scholarship and Financial Aid
1104 7th Avenue South, Owens Hall Rm 107
Moorhead, MN 56563

2124
Upperclass Academic Scholarships

AMOUNT: None Specified DEADLINE: February 1
MAJOR: All Areas of Study

This scholarship is open to currently enrolled Moorhead State University undergraduate students who have completed 15 MSU credits and have a minimum 3.5 GPA. Award requirements change regularly. For further information, please call the financial aid office or mail in a request, including a self-addressed, stamped envelope. GPA must be 3.5-4.0.

Moorhead State University
Office of Scholarship and Financial Aid
1104 7th Avenue South, Owens Hall Rm 107
Moorhead, MN 56563

2125
Upperclass Minority Scholarship

AMOUNT: None Specified DEADLINE: April 1
MAJOR: All Areas of Study

This scholarship is open to currently enrolled MSU minority students who have a minimum GPA of 2.5. You must be enrolled for at least 12 credits per term. Award requirements change regularly. For further information, please call the financial aid office or mail in a request, including a self-addressed, stamped envelope. GPA must be 2.5-4.0.

Moorhead State University
Office of Scholarship and Financial Aid
1104 7th Avenue South, Owens Hall Rm 107
Moorhead, MN 56563

Morehead State University

2126
Alumni Award

AMOUNT: $500-$750 DEADLINE: March 15
MAJOR: All Areas of Study

This scholarship is open to admitted entering freshmen or transfer students who have at least one parent or grandparent who is an alumni and who also is an active member of the MSU Alumni Association. Freshmen must have an Admission Index of at least 500, and transfer students must have a minimum GPA of 3.0. May be renewed if recipients achieve a minimum GPA of 2.75 during each of the first two semesters and a 3.0 GPA for each semester thereafter. Transfer students must maintain the minimum 3.0 with which they entered MSU. Award requirements change regularly. Please write to the address listed for more information or call (800) 585-6781. GPA must be 2.75-4.0.

Morehead State University
Office of Admissions
301 Howell-McDowell
Morehead, KY 40351

2127
Leadership Award

AMOUNT: Maximum: $650 DEADLINE: March 15
MAJOR: All Areas of Study

Open to incoming freshmen admitted to MSU. Must have exhibited strong leadership and achievement capabilities through school and community activities. Must have a minimum GPA of 2.5. May be renewed if recipients maintain a minimum GPA of 2.5. Award requirements change regularly. Contact the address listed for further information or call (800) 585-6781. GPA must be 2.5-4.0.

Morehead State University
Office of Admissions
301 Howell-McDowell
Morehead, KY 40351

2128
Minority Student Leadership Award

AMOUNT: $650 DEADLINE: March 15
MAJOR: All Areas of Study

Open to admitted entering freshmen who are African-American, Native American, Hispanic-American, Asian-American, Alaskan Native, or Pacific Islander. Applicant must be a Kentucky resident who has demonstrated achievement in academics and/or extracurricular activities. This award is renewable if recipient maintains a minimum GPA of 2.5. Award requirements change regularly. Please contact the address listed for further information or call (800) 585-6781. GPA must be 2.5-4.0.

Morehead State University
Office of Admissions
301 Howell-McDowell
Morehead, KY 40351

2129
Presidential Scholarship

AMOUNT: $2000-$6000 DEADLINE: March 15
MAJOR: All Areas of Study

This scholarship is open to students who have been admitted as freshmen and meet one of the following requirements: 1) a National Merit Scholar/Finalist; 2) your school's valedictorian with a minimum 30 ACT; 3) your school's salutatorian with a minimum ACT score of 30; 4) a National Merit Semi-Finalist with a minimum 28 ACT; 5) a Kentucky Governor's Scholar with a minimum ACT of 28; or 6) a minimum GPA of 3.75 and an ACT score of at least 28. Award requirements change regularly. Contact the address listed for further information or call (800) 585-6781. GPA must be 3.7-4.0.

Morehead State University
Office of Admissions
301 Howell-McDowell
Morehead, KY 40351

2130
Regents Scholarship

AMOUNT: $750-$2000 DEADLINE: March 15
MAJOR: All Areas of Study

Scholarships are available to entering freshmen admitted to MSU. Must have a minimum ACT score of 20. Renewable if recipients achieve a minimum cumulative GPA of 2.75 during each of the first two semesters and at least a 3.0 GPA for each semester thereafter. Award requirements change regularly. Write to the address listed for more information or call (800) 585-6781. GPA must be 3.0-4.0.

Morehead State University
Office of Admissions
301 Howell-McDowell
Morehead, KY 40351

2131
Regional Honors Scholarship

AMOUNT: Maximum: $3000 DEADLINE: Varies
MAJOR: All Areas of Study

The Regional Honors Scholarship is open to an entering freshman at MSU who graduated from a high school within MSU's Kentucky service region. The applicant must be recommended by the high school, be the highest ranking or second highest ranking academic achiever from that high school coming to MSU, and have at least a cumulative 3.5 high school GPA (on a 4.0 scale) with the academic work based on seven semesters of academics. Award requirements change regularly. Please send a self-addressed, stamped envelope to receive your application and for any further instructions from the scholarship provider. GPA must be 3.5-4.0.

Morehead State University
Office of Admissions
301 Howell-McDowell
Morehead, KY 40351

2132
Transfer Student Award

AMOUNT: $300-$1000 DEADLINE: Varies
MAJOR: All Areas of Study

The Transfer Student Award is open to undergraduate transfer students from any accredited college or university who plan to attend Morehead State University. Award requirements change regularly. Meanwhile you may visit the sponsor's website for further information. No GPA requirement specified.

Morehead State University
Office of Admissions
301 Howell-McDowell
Morehead, KY 40351

2133
Tuition Assistance Grant

AMOUNT: Maximum: $2000 DEADLINE: Varies
MAJOR: All Areas of Study

The Tuition Assistance Grant is for out-of-state students who have been admitted to MSU as freshmen or as a new transfer student. The applicant must have a minimum ACT composite of 20, have at least 12 hours of completed college work if a, transfer student, and have the following Admission Indexes: 500-549 for a $1,200 award; 500-599 for a $1,500 award; 600 and over for a $2,000 award. New transfer students must have a transfer GPA of 3.0 for $1,200; 3.25 for $1,500; 3.5 for $2,000. Award requirements change regularly. Please send a self-addressed, stamped envelope to receive your application and for any further instructions from the scholarship provider. GPA must be 3.0-4.0.

Morehead State University
Office of Admissions
301 Howell-McDowell
Morehead, KY 40351

Nazareth College

2134
Art Scholarship

AMOUNT: None Specified DEADLINE: February 15
MAJOR: Art

The Art Scholarships are open to art majors at Nazareth College. You must submit your portfolio for review. This award is renewable. Award requirements change regularly. Please send a self-addressed, stamped envelope to receive your application and any further instructions from the college, or call (716) 389-2310. No GPA requirement specified.

Nazareth College
Financial Aid Office
4245 East Avenue
Rochester, NY 14618-3790

2135
Campus Diversity Scholarship

AMOUNT: $2500 DEADLINE: Varies
MAJOR: All Areas of Study

The Campus Diversity Scholarships are open to undergraduates attending Nazareth College. You must represent family backgrounds, life experiences, or academic interests atypical of full-time undergraduate students at Nazareth College. Award requirements change regularly. Please send a self-addressed, stamped envelope to receive your application and any further instructions from the college, or call (716) 389-2310. No GPA requirement specified.

Nazareth College
Financial Aid Office
4245 East Avenue
Rochester, NY 14618-3790

2136
Dean's Scholarship

AMOUNT: $10000 DEADLINE: Varies
MAJOR: All Areas of Study

The Dean's Scholarship is open to Nazareth College full-time freshmen. You must have at least a 3.75 GPA, 1300 SAT, or 29 ACT and rank in the top 5% of your high school graduating class. This award is renewable for eight semesters if you maintain a minimum 3.25 GPA in the freshmen year and 3.5 thereafter. Award requirements change regularly. Please send a

self-addressed, stamped envelope to receive your application and any further instructions from the college, or call (716) 389-2310. GPA must be 3.75-4.0.

Nazareth College
Financial Aid Office
4245 East Avenue
Rochester, NY 14618-3790

2137
Founders Scholarship

AMOUNT: None Specified DEADLINE: Varies
MAJOR: All Areas of Study

The Founders Scholarship is open to Nazareth College full-time freshmen. You must have at least a 3.5 GPA, 1170 SAT, or 26 ACT and be in the top 25% or your high school graduating class. This award is renewable for eight semesters if you maintain a minimum 3.0 GPA. Award requirements change regularly. Please send a self-addressed, stamped envelope to receive your application and any further instructions from the college, or call (716) 389-2310. GPA must be 3.5-4.0.

Nazareth College
Financial Aid Office
4245 East Avenue
Rochester, NY 14618-3790

2138
Heritage Award

AMOUNT: $2500 DEADLINE: Varies
MAJOR: All Areas of Study

The Heritage Award is open to Nazareth College incoming freshmen. You must be the child of an alumnus who received a bachelor's degree or master's degree from Nazareth College. This award is renewable for eight full-time undergraduate semesters provided you remain in good academic standing. The $40 application fee is also waived. Award requirements change regularly. Please send a self-addressed, stamped envelope to receive your application and any further instructions from the college, or call (716) 389-2310. No GPA requirement specified.

Nazareth College
Financial Aid Office
4245 East Avenue
Rochester, NY 14618-3790

2139
Music Scholarship

AMOUNT: None Specified DEADLINE: Varies
MAJOR: Music

The Music Scholarships are open to Nazareth College undergraduates and graduates majoring in music. You must perform at an audition in order to qualify for this award. This award is renewable. Award requirements change regularly. Please send a self-addressed, stamped envelope to receive your application and any further instructions from the college, or call (716) 389-2310. No GPA requirement specified.

Nazareth College
Financial Aid Office
4245 East Avenue
Rochester, NY 14618-3790

2140
Nazareth Family Grant

AMOUNT: $500 DEADLINE: Varies
MAJOR: All Areas of Study

The Nazareth Family Grant is available to Nazareth College full-time students. You must have a sibling attending Nazareth College on a full-time basis. Award requirements change regularly. Please send a self-addressed, stamped envelope to receive your application and any further instructions from the college, or call (716) 389-2310. No GPA requirement specified.

Nazareth College
Financial Aid Office
4245 East Avenue
Rochester, NY 14618-3790

2141
Nazareth Scholar Award

AMOUNT: $7500 DEADLINE: Varies
MAJOR: All Areas of Study

The Nazareth Scholar Award is open to Nazareth College full-time freshmen. You must have at least a 3.75 GPA, 1220 SAT, or 27 ACT and rank in the top 10% of your high school graduating class. This award is renewable for eight semesters if you maintain a minimum 3.2 GPA. Award requirements change regularly. Please send a self-addressed, stamped envelope to receive your application and any further instructions from the college, or call (716) 389-2310. GPA must be 3.75-4.0.

Nazareth College
Financial Aid Office
4245 East Avenue
Rochester, NY 14618-3790

2142
Nazareth Scholarship

AMOUNT: None Specified DEADLINE: Varies
MAJOR: All Areas of Study

The Nazareth Scholarship is available to Nazareth College full-time undergraduate students. This award is renewable for eight semesters if you maintain a minimum 3.0 GPA. Award requirements change regularly. Please send a self-addressed, stamped envelope to receive your application and any further instructions from the college, or call (716) 389-2310. No GPA requirement specified.

Nazareth College
Financial Aid Office
4245 East Avenue
Rochester, NY 14618-3790

2143
Physical Therapy Scholarship

AMOUNT: $5000-$7500 DEADLINE: Varies
MAJOR: Physical Therapy

The Physical Therapy Scholarships are open to Nazareth College full-time freshmen. You must have at least a 3.75 GPA, a minimum 1250 SAT, or 28 ACT and rank in the top 10% of your high school graduating class. This award is renewable for eight semesters if you maintain a minimum 3.2 GPA. It is also renewable at the graduate level at the completion of the B.S. degree program. Award requirements change regularly. Please send a self-addressed, stamped envelope to receive your application and any further instructions from the college, or call (716) 389-2310. GPA must be 3.75-4.0.

Nazareth College
Financial Aid Office
4245 East Avenue
Rochester, NY 14618-3790

2144
Presidential Scholarship

AMOUNT: None Specified DEADLINE: Varies
MAJOR: All Areas of Study

The Presidential Scholarship is open to full-time freshmen attending Nazareth College. You must have at least a 3.9 GPA, 1400 SAT, or 32 ACT and be in the top 1% of your high school graduating class. This award is renewable for eight semesters, provided you maintain a minimum 3.25 GPA for your freshman year and a minimum 3.5 GPA thereafter. Award requirements change regularly. Please send a self-addressed, stamped envelope to receive your application and any further instructions from the college, or call (716) 389-2310. GPA must be 3.9-4.0.

Nazareth College
Financial Aid Office
4245 East Avenue
Rochester, NY 14618-3790

2145
Purple and Gold Award

AMOUNT: None Specified DEADLINE: Varies
MAJOR: All Areas of Study

The Gold and Purple Awards are open to full-time students attending Nazareth College. You must be in financial need. This award is renewable for eight semesters. Award requirements change regularly. Please send a self-addressed, stamped envelope to receive your application and any further instructions from the college, or call (716) 389-2310. No GPA requirement specified.

Nazareth College
Financial Aid Office
4245 East Avenue
Rochester, NY 14618-3790

2146
Regional Scholarship

AMOUNT: $2500 DEADLINE: Varies
MAJOR: All Areas of Study

The Regional Scholarships are open to Nazareth College full-time freshmen. You must live outside of New York State or live further than 300 miles from Nazareth College or attend a high school that has never before been represented at Nazareth. This award is renewable provided you maintain at least a 3.0 GPA. Award requirements change regularly. Please send a self-addressed, stamped envelope to receive your application and any further instructions from the college, or call (716) 389-2310. No GPA requirement specified.

Nazareth College
Financial Aid Office
4245 East Avenue
Rochester, NY 14618-3790

2147
Theater Arts Scholarship

AMOUNT: None Specified DEADLINE: February 1
MAJOR: Theater, Drama

The Theater Arts Scholarship is open to Nazareth College undergraduates majoring in theater arts. You must have an interview and perform at an audition. Award requirements change regularly. Please send a self-addressed, stamped envelope to receive your application and any further instructions from the college, or call (716) 389-2310. No GPA requirement specified.

Nazareth College
Financial Aid Office
4245 East Avenue
Rochester, NY 14618-3790

2148
Transfer Student Scholarship

AMOUNT: None Specified DEADLINE: Varies
MAJOR: All Areas of Study

The Transfer Student Scholarships are available to transfer students attending Nazareth College. This award is renewable depending on the number of credits transferred to Nazareth and the maintenance of a minimum 3.0 GPA. Award requirements change regularly. Please send a self-addressed, stamped envelope to receive your application and any further instructions from the college, or call (716) 389-2310. No GPA requirement specified.

Nazareth College
Financial Aid Office
4245 East Avenue
Rochester, NY 14618-3790

2149
Trustee Scholarship

AMOUNT: $3000 DEADLINE: Varies
MAJOR: All Areas of Study

The Trustee Scholarships are open to Nazareth College full-time freshmen who do not receive other merit scholarships. You must rank in the top 25% of your high school graduating class and have a minimum 1120 SAT or 25 ACT. If your high school does not have a ranking system, you must have a minimum 3.4 GPA. This award is renewable for eight semesters if you maintain a minimum 3.0 GPA. Award requirements change regularly. Please send a self-addressed, stamped envelope to receive your application and any further instructions from the college, or call (716) 389-2310. GPA must be 3.4-4.0.

Nazareth College
Financial Aid Office
4245 East Avenue
Rochester, NY 14618-3790

New Mexico State University

2150
D. B. Jett Memorial Scholarship

AMOUNT: None Specified DEADLINE: March 1
MAJOR: Engineering

The D. B. Jett Memorial Scholarship is awarded to engineering majors at New Mexico State University. You must be a junior or senior in good academic standing and demonstrate professional potential. Award requirements change regularly. For an application and further information call (505) 646-4593. No GPA requirement specified.

New Mexico State University
College of Engineering
Complex I, Box 30001, Dept 3449
Las Cruces, NM 88003

2151
Dr. Louis and Jane Kazda Scholarship

AMOUNT: None Specified DEADLINE: March 1
MAJOR: Electrical Engineering

The Dr. Louis and Jane Kazda Scholarship is open to electrical engineering majors at New Mexico State University. You must have a minimum 3.5 GPA and have completed at least one semester at NMSU. This award is renewable if you maintain a 3.5 GPA. U.S. citizenship is required. Award requirements change regularly. For an application and further information call (505) 646-4593. GPA must be 3.5-4.0.

New Mexico State University
College of Engineering
Complex I, Box 30001, Dept 3449
Las Cruces, NM 88003

2152
George W. Lucky Scholarship

AMOUNT: None Specified DEADLINE: March 1
MAJOR: Electrical Engineering

The George W. Lucky Scholarship is open to junior and senior full-time students who are majoring in electrical engineering at New Mexico State University. You must be a U.S. citizen, have completed 50 credits toward the electrical engineering degree, and be a member of EEE and HKN with at least a 2.75 GPA. Award requirements change regularly. For an application and further information call (505) 646-4593. GPA must be 2.75-4.0.

New Mexico State University
College of Engineering
Complex I, Box 30001, Dept 3449
Las Cruces, NM 88003

2153
Honeywell Scholarship

AMOUNT: None Specified DEADLINE: March 1
MAJOR: Electrical or Manufacturing Engineering

The Honeywell Scholarship is awarded to New Mexico State University electrical or manufacturing engineering majors who are either female or members of an ethnic minority. You must be a junior, senior, or graduate student with a minimum 3.0 GPA. U.S. citizenship is required. Award requirements change regularly. For an application and further information call (505) 646-4593. GPA must be 3.0-4.0.

New Mexico State University
College of Engineering
Complex I, Box 30001, Dept 3449
Las Cruces, NM 88003

2154
Ideas in Science and Electronics Scholarship

AMOUNT: None Specified DEADLINE: March 1
MAJOR: Electrical Engineering

The Ideas in Science and Electronics Scholarship is awarded to New Mexico State University electrical engineering majors of junior standing. This award requires that you be a New Mexico resident. Award requirements change regularly. For an application and further information call (505) 646-4593. No GPA requirement specified.

New Mexico State University
College of Engineering
Complex I, Box 30001, Dept 3449
Las Cruces, NM 88003

2155
Intel Corporation Scholarship

AMOUNT: $3000 DEADLINE: March 1
MAJOR: Electrical/Computer, Chemical, Industrial, and Mechanical Engineering

The Intel Corporation Scholarship is awarded to full-time chemical, electrical/computer, industrial, or mechanical engineering majors at New Mexico State University. You must be a sophomore, junior, or senior and a U.S. citizen with at least a 3.2 GPA. Award requirements change regularly. For an application and further information call (505) 646-4593. GPA must be 3.2-4.0.

New Mexico State University
College of Engineering
Complex I, Box 30001, Dept 3449
Las Cruces, NM 88003

2156
Kenneth Hill Scholarship

AMOUNT: None Specified DEADLINE: March 1
MAJOR: Engineering Technology

The Kenneth Hill Scholarship is open to New Mexico State University engineering technology majors. This award requires that you be a continuing student with a minimum 2.5 GPA. Award requirements change regularly. For an application and further information call (505) 646-4593. GPA must be 2.5-4.0.

New Mexico State University
College of Engineering
Complex I, Box 30001, Dept 3449
Las Cruces, NM 88003

2157
Keyes Scholarship

AMOUNT: $500 DEADLINE: March 1
MAJOR: Civil Engineering

The Keyes Scholarship is open to New Mexico State University full-time civil engineering majors. You must be a continuing student who is active in CAGE student organizations. Award requirements change regularly. For an application and further information call (505) 646-4593. No GPA requirement specified.

New Mexico State University
College of Engineering
Complex I, Box 30001, Dept 3449
Las Cruces, NM 88003

2158
Lucent Technologies Scholarship

AMOUNT: $1000 DEADLINE: March 1
MAJOR: Electrical Engineering, Engineering Technology

The Lucent Technologies Scholarship is open to electrical engineering/engineering technology majors at New Mexico State University. You must be a minority sophomore, junior, or senior or first-year graduate student with a minimum 3.0 GPA. Award requirements change regularly. For an application and further information call (505) 646-4593. GPA must be 3.0-4.0.

New Mexico State University
College of Engineering
Complex I, Box 30001, Dept 3449
Las Cruces, NM 88003

2159

Mr. and Mrs. Richard L. Leza Scholarship

AMOUNT: None Specified DEADLINE: March 1
MAJOR: Chemical, Civil, Electrical/Computer, and Mechanical Engineering

The Mr. and Mrs. Richard L. Leza Scholarship is open to chemical, civil, electrical/computer, and mechanical engineering majors at New Mexico State University. You must be Hispanic, a junior student, and a U.S. citizen with at least a 3.0 GPA. Residency requirements are restricted to Arizona, California, or New Mexico. Award requirements change regularly. For an application and further information call (505) 646-4593. GPA must be 3.0-4.0.

New Mexico State University
College of Engineering
Complex I, Box 30001, Dept 3449
Las Cruces, NM 88003

2160

Paul W. Klipsch Engineering Scholarship

AMOUNT: None Specified DEADLINE: March 1
MAJOR: Engineering

The Paul W. Klipsch Engineering Scholarship is open to New Mexico State University engineering majors. You must be a continuing student who shows financial need, character, practicality, leadership, and active participation in a religious faith. Award requirements change regularly. For an application and further information call (505) 646-4593. No GPA requirement specified.

New Mexico State University
College of Engineering
Complex I, Box 30001, Dept 3449
Las Cruces, NM 88003

2161

Paul W. Klipsch Graduate Scholarship

AMOUNT: None Specified DEADLINE: March 1
MAJOR: Engineering

The Paul W. Klipsch Graduate Scholarship is open to New Mexico State University engineering majors. You must be a graduate student who has returned to school after a five-year absence. Tau Beta Pi membership and participation in R.O.T.C. is recommended. Award requirements change regularly. For an application and further information call (505) 646-4593. No GPA requirement specified.

New Mexico State University
College of Engineering
Complex I, Box 30001, Dept 3449
Las Cruces, NM 88003

2162

Paul W. Klipsch Scholarship for Electrical and Mechanical Engineering

AMOUNT: None Specified DEADLINE: March 1
MAJOR: Electrical and Mechanical Engineering

The Paul W. Klipsch Scholarship for Electrical and Mechanical Engineering is open to New Mexico State University electrical and mechanical engineering majors. You must be a junior who shows financial need, character, practicality, leadership, and active participation in a religious faith. Award requirements change regularly. For an application and further information call (505) 646-4593. No GPA requirement specified.

New Mexico State University
College of Engineering
Complex I, Box 30001, Dept 3449
Las Cruces, NM 88003

2163

Paul W. Klipsch Scholarship/Tau Beta Pi Scholarship

AMOUNT: None Specified DEADLINE: March 1
MAJOR: Engineering

The Paul W. Klipsch Scholarship/Tau Beta Pi Scholarship is open to New Mexico State University engineering majors. You must be a graduating senior who is a member of Tau Beta Pi. Your good character, leadership potential, and active participation in a religious faith will be considered. Award requirements change regularly. For an application and further information call (505) 646-4593. No GPA requirement specified.

New Mexico State University
College of Engineering
Complex I, Box 30001, Dept 3449
Las Cruces, NM 88003

2164

Paul W. Klipsch/Eta Kappa Nu Scholarship

AMOUNT: None Specified DEADLINE: March 1
MAJOR: Electrical Engineering

The Paul W. Klipsch/Eta Kappa Nu Scholarship is open to New Mexico State University electrical engineering majors. You must be a junior who shows financial need, character, leadership potential, and active participation in a religious faith. You do not have to be an Eta Kappa Nu member or pledge. Award requirements change regularly. For an application and further information call (505) 646-4593. No GPA requirement specified.

New Mexico State University
College of Engineering
Complex I, Box 30001, Dept 3449
Las Cruces, NM 88003

2165
Robert E. and Evelyn McKee Foundation Scholarship

AMOUNT: None Specified DEADLINE: March 1
MAJOR: Civil, Electrical, and Mechanical Engineering

The Robert E. and Evelyn McKee Foundation Scholarship is open to upper-division engineering students at New Mexico State University. You must be a civil, electrical, or mechanical engineering major who is interested in the construction industry. Award requirements change regularly. For an application and further information call (505) 646-4593. No GPA requirement specified.

New Mexico State University
College of Engineering
Complex I, Box 30001, Dept 3449
Las Cruces, NM 88003

2166
William Townsley Scholarship

AMOUNT: None Specified DEADLINE: March 1
MAJOR: Chemical Engineering

The William Townsley Scholarship is for a chemical engineering major attending NMSU. You must be either a sophomore, junior, or senior student. Award requirements change regularly. For an application and further information call (505) 646-4593. No GPA requirement specified.

New Mexico State University
College of Engineering
Complex I, Box 30001, Dept 3449
Las Cruces, NM 88003

New Mexico Tech

2167
Competitive Scholarship

AMOUNT: $700 DEADLINE: March 1
MAJOR: All Areas of Study

This scholarship is open to NMT entering freshmen who have a high school GPA of at least 3.0, an ACT score of at least 27, or an SAT recentered score of 1200 or higher. Preference is given to transfer students with a GPA of at least 3.25 and a past high school GPA of at least 3.0. This award is for non-residents of New Mexico. Award requirements change regularly. Write to the address listed for further information, browse their website: www.nmt.edu, or email admission@admin.nmt.edu. GPA must be 3.0-4.0.

New Mexico Tech
Admissions Office
801 Leroy Place
Socorro, NM 87801-4681

2168
Counselor's Choice Scholarship

AMOUNT: $1500 DEADLINE: March 1
MAJOR: All Areas of Study

This scholarship is open to NMT entering freshmen from New Mexico who are nominated by their high school counselor. Applicants must have a GPA of at least 2.5, ACT scores of 21, or SAT scores of 860 or better. This award is for U.S. citizens enrolled in full-time study and is renewable. Award requirements change regularly. Write to the address listed for further information, browse their website: www.nmt.edu, or email admission@admin.nmt.edu. GPA must be 2.5-4.0.

New Mexico Tech
Admissions Office
801 Leroy Place
Socorro, NM 87801-4681

2169
Gold Merit Scholarship

AMOUNT: $5000 DEADLINE: March 1
MAJOR: All Areas of Study

Scholarships for NMT entering freshmen who are National Merit finalists and have a high school GPA of 3.0. Must be U.S. citizens or permanent residents and carry at least 12 graded credit hours per semester. Award requirements change regularly. Write to the address listed for further information, browse their website: www.nmt.edu, or email admission@admin.nmt.edu. GPA must be 3.0-4.0.

New Mexico Tech
Admissions Office
801 Leroy Place
Socorro, NM 87801-4681

2170
Presidential Scholarship

AMOUNT: $2700 DEADLINE: March 1
MAJOR: All Areas of Study

This scholarship is open to NMT entering freshmen who have a high school GPA of at least 3.0, an ACT score of at least 27, or a recentered SAT score of 1200 or higher. Applicants must be U.S. citizens and enrolled in full-time study. This award is renewable. Award requirements change regularly. Write to the address listed for further information, browse their website: www.nmt.edu, or email admission@admin.nmt.edu. GPA must be 3.0-4.0.

New Mexico Tech
Admissions Office
801 Leroy Place
Socorro, NM 87801-4681

2171
Regents' Scholarship

AMOUNT: $2000 DEADLINE: March 1
MAJOR: All Areas of Study

This scholarship is open to NMT entering freshmen and transfer students. Freshmen and transfer students with less than 30 credits must have a GPA of at least 3.0, ACT scores of 25, and a recentered SAT score of 1130 or better. Transfer students

with over 30 credits must have a collegiate GPA of at least 3.0. Applicants must be full-time students and U.S. citizens. Award requirements change regularly. Write to the address listed for further information, browse their website: www.nmt.edu, or email admission@admin.nmt.edu. GPA must be 3.0-4.0.

New Mexico Tech
Admissions Office
801 Leroy Place
Socorro, NM 87801-4681

2172
Silver Scholar Scholarship

AMOUNT: $4000 DEADLINE: March 1
MAJOR: All Areas of Study

Scholarships for NMT entering freshmen who have a high school GPA of at least 3.5, an ACT score of 30 or higher, or a recentered SAT score of 1320 or better. Applicants must be U.S. citizens and enrolled in full-time study. This award is renewable. Award requirements change regularly. Write to the address listed for further information, browse their website: www.nmt.edu, or email admission@admin.nmt.edu. GPA must be 3.5-4.0.

New Mexico Tech
Admissions Office
801 Leroy Place
Socorro, NM 87801-4681

North Arkansas College

2173
Allbright-Moore Memorial Scholarship

AMOUNT: $1000 DEADLINE: May 1
MAJOR: All Fields of Study

The Allbright-Moore Memorial Scholarship is open to Arkansas residents attending North Arkansas College. To be considered for this award, you must have an ACT composite score of at least 27 with all subtest scores of 21 or better. The award provides $500 per semester and is renewable if you complete 24 hours during the first year with a 3.25 GPA. Award requirements change regularly. Please send a self-addressed, stamped envelope to receive your application and any further instructions from the scholarship provider; or visit the website at pioneer.northark.cc.ar.us. No GPA requirement specified.

North Arkansas College
Attn: Financial Aid Office
1515 Pioneer Drive
Harrison, AR 72601

2174
Arkansas Fiddlers' Association Scholarship

AMOUNT: $500 DEADLINE: August 1
MAJOR: Performing Arts

The Arkansas Fiddlers' Association Scholarship is open to full-time students at North Arkansas College. To be considered for this award, you must demonstrate financial need and academic promise. Preference is given to performing arts majors. The award provides $250 per semester. Award requirements change regularly. Please send a self-addressed, stamped envelope to receive your application and any further instructions from the scholarship provider; or visit the website at pioneer.northark.cc.ar.us. No GPA requirement specified.

North Arkansas College
Attn: Financial Aid Office
1515 Pioneer Drive
Harrison, AR 72601

2175
Art Department Scholarship

AMOUNT: None Specified DEADLINE: April 1
MAJOR: Art

The Art Department Scholarship is open to full-time students at North Arkansas College. To be considered for this award, you must enroll in at least one art class per semester, maintain an overall GPA of 3.0, and present a positive image as established by North Arkansas College. The award provides the cost of tuition. Award requirements change regularly. To receive your application and any further instructions, please send a self-addressed, stamped envelope to the attention of the Art Department; or visit the website at pioneer.northark.cc.ar.us. GPA must be 3.0-4.0.

North Arkansas College
Attn: Financial Aid Office
1515 Pioneer Drive
Harrison, AR 72601

2176
Barbara and Thelma Muller Nursing Scholarship

AMOUNT: None Specified DEADLINE: August 1
MAJOR: Nursing

The Barbara and Thelma Muller Nursing Scholarship is open to full-time students at North Arkansas College. To be considered for this award, you must be enrolled in the RN program, have a minimum GPA of 2.0 in high school and at North Arkansas College, and not receive any other North Arkansas College scholarships. Award requirements change regularly. Please send a self-addressed, stamped envelope to receive your application and any further instructions from the scholarship provider; or visit the website at pioneer.northark.cc.ar.us. GPA must be 2.0-4.0.

North Arkansas College
Attn: Financial Aid Office
1515 Pioneer Drive
Harrison, AR 72601

2177
Chapter AG, PEO and Wanda Coffman Memorial Scholarship

AMOUNT: None Specified DEADLINE: August 1
MAJOR: All Fields of Study

The Chapter AG, PEO and Wanda Coffman Memorial Scholarship is open to female students at North Arkansas College. To be considered for this award, you must be a resident of Boone, Marion, Newton, Carroll, or Searcy (AR) counties, have been out of school for one year or more (a GED is acceptable), and demonstrate financial need. Chapter AG, PEO awards the scholarship for the first semester, and the Wanda Coffman Memorial Scholarship is given during the second semester provided you have maintained a minimum GPAof 2.0. Award requirements change regularly. Please send a self-addressed, stamped envelope to receive your application and any further instructions from the scholarship provider; or visit the website at pioneer.northark.cc.ar.us. No GPA requirement specified.

North Arkansas College
Attn: Financial Aid Office
1515 Pioneer Drive
Harrison, AR 72601

2178
Clara Benson Memorial Nursing Scholarship

AMOUNT: None Specified DEADLINE: August 1
MAJOR: Nursing

The Clara Benson Memorial Nursing Scholarship is open to full-time students at North Arkansas College. To be considered for this award, you must be accepted into the RN or LPN program, be a resident of Arkansas, and not receive any other North Arkansas College-funded scholarships. The award is renewable for the second year of the program. Award requirements change regularly. Please send a self-addressed, stamped envelope to receive your application and any further instructions from the scholarship provider; or visit the website at pioneer.northark.cc.ar.us. No GPA requirement specified.

North Arkansas College
Attn: Financial Aid Office
1515 Pioneer Drive
Harrison, AR 72601

2179
Doris Cecil Baker Memorial Scholarship

AMOUNT: None Specified DEADLINE: August 1
MAJOR: Humanities, Arts

The Doris Cecil Baker Memorial Scholarship is open to on-campus, full-time students at North Arkansas College. To be considered for this award, you must be interested in the humanities and/or the arts. Athletic scholarship recipients are not eligible for this two-semester award. Award requirements change regularly. Please send a self-addressed, stamped envelope to receive your application and any further instructions from the scholarship provider; or visit the website at pioneer.northark.cc.ar.us. No GPA requirement specified.

North Arkansas College
Attn: Financial Aid Office
1515 Pioneer Drive
Harrison, AR 72601

2180
Dr. Jean Gladden Memorial Nursing Scholarship

AMOUNT: None Specified DEADLINE: August 1
MAJOR: Nursing

The Dr. Jean Gladden Memorial Nursing Scholarship is open to students at North Arkansas College. To be considered for this award, you must be a resident of Arkansas and be enrolled in the RN program. Preference is given to residents of Boone and contiguous counties. You must also demonstrate a genuine concern and desire to provide quality nursing care and an intention to remain and provide nursing services in the Harrison area after graduation. Award requirements change regularly. Please send a self-addressed, stamped envelope to receive your application and any further instructions from the scholarship provider; or visit the website at pioneer.northark.cc.ar.us. No GPA requirement specified.

North Arkansas College
Attn: Financial Aid Office
1515 Pioneer Drive
Harrison, AR 72601

2181
Dr. Joe Bennett Radiology Technology Scholarship

AMOUNT: None Specified DEADLINE: August 1
MAJOR: Radiology Technology

The Dr. Joe Bennett Radiology Technology Scholarship is open to students at North Arkansas College. To be considered for this award, you must be a resident of Arkansas, be admitted to the radiology technology program, and not receive any other tuition scholarship given by North Arkansas College. The award provides one semester of tuition. Award requirements change regularly. Please send a self-addressed, stamped envelope to receive your application and any further instructions from the scholarship provider; or visit the website at pioneer.northark.cc.ar.us. No GPA requirement specified.

North Arkansas College
Attn: Financial Aid Office
1515 Pioneer Drive
Harrison, AR 72601

2182
Dr. O.B. McCoy Memorial Scholarship

AMOUNT: None Specified DEADLINE: August 1
MAJOR: Nursing, Paramedics, Dentistry, Related Medical Fields

The Dr. O.B. McCoy Memorial Scholarship is open to full-time students at North Arkansas College. To be considered for this award, you must be a resident of Arkansas, have a cumulative high school or college GPA of 2.8, and have a major preference in the fields of nursing, paramedics, dentistry, or other related fields of medicine. You must also demonstrate financial need and submit a personal statement. Award requirements change regularly. Please send a self-addressed, stamped envelope to receive your application and any further instructions from the scholarship provider; or visit the website at pioneer.northark.cc.ar.us. GPA must be 2.8-4.0.

North Arkansas College
Attn: Financial Aid Office
1515 Pioneer Drive
Harrison, AR 72601

2183
Drama Department Scholarship

AMOUNT: None Specified DEADLINE: August 1
MAJOR: Drama

The Drama Department Scholarship is open to full-time students at North Arkansas College. To be considered for this award, you must enroll in at least one drama class per semester, audition for all drama productions at the college, maintain an overall GPA of 3.0, and present a positive image as established by North Arkansas College. The award provides the cost of tuition. Award requirements change regularly. Please send a self-addressed, stamped envelope to receive your application and any further instructions from the scholarship provider; or visit the website at pioneer.northark.cc.ar.us. GPA must be 3.0-4.0.

North Arkansas College
Attn: Financial Aid Office
1515 Pioneer Drive
Harrison, AR 72601

2184
Ernest H. Cecil Memorial Scholarship

AMOUNT: None Specified DEADLINE: August 1
MAJOR: Health Sciences, Theology

The Ernest H. Cecil Memorial Scholarship is open to students at North Arkansas College. To be considered for this award, you must be pursuing a course of study in health sciences or theology. Award requirements change regularly. Please send a self-addressed, stamped envelope to receive your application and any further instructions from the scholarship provider; or visit the website at pioneer.northark.cc.ar.us. No GPA requirement specified.

North Arkansas College
Attn: Financial Aid Office
1515 Pioneer Drive
Harrison, AR 72601

2185
Garrison Motor Freight Scholarship

AMOUNT: None Specified DEADLINE: August 1
MAJOR: All Fields of Study

The Garrison Motor Freight Scholarship is open to full-time students at North Arkansas College. To be considered for this award, you must have an ACT composite score of 21 or better, be in the top 20% of your graduating high school class, or have a high school or college GPA of at least 3.0. You must also be a resident of Boone County (AR) and demonstrate

financial need. Award requirements change regularly. Please send a self-addressed, stamped envelope to receive your application and any further instructions from the scholarship provider; or visit the website at pioneer.northark.cc.ar.us. No GPA requirement specified.

North Arkansas College
Attn: Financial Aid Office
1515 Pioneer Drive
Harrison, AR 72601

2186
Gladys Carlton Scholarship

AMOUNT: None Specified DEADLINE: August 1
MAJOR: All Fields of Study

The Gladys Carlton Scholarship is open to students at North Arkansas College. To be considered for this award, you must be a resident of Boone County (AR) and demonstrate financial need. Award requirements change regularly. Please send a self-addressed, stamped envelope to receive your application and any further instructions from the scholarship provider; or visit the website at pioneer.northark.cc.ar.us. No GPA requirement specified.

North Arkansas College
Attn: Financial Aid Office
1515 Pioneer Drive
Harrison, AR 72601

2187
Honors Scholarship

AMOUNT: None Specified DEADLINE: August 1
MAJOR: All Fields of Study

The Honors Scholarship is open to full-time students at North Arkansas College. To be considered for this award, you must be an Arkansas resident, rank in the top 10% of your high school graduating class, and have a minimum ACT composite score of 20. The scholarship provides the cost of tuition, must be used the fall semester following your high school graduation, and is renewable if you complete 30 hours during the academic year with a 3.25 GPA. Award requirements change regularly. Please send a self-addressed, stamped envelope to receive your application and any further instructions from the scholarship provider; or visit the website at pioneer.northark.cc.ar.us. No GPA requirement specified.

North Arkansas College
Attn: Financial Aid Office
1515 Pioneer Drive
Harrison, AR 72601

2188
Jackson Davis Reeves Scholarship

AMOUNT: None Specified DEADLINE: August 1
MAJOR: Nursing

The Jackson Davis Reeves Scholarship is open to full-time students at North Arkansas College. To be considered for this award, you must be an Arkansas resident and demonstrate financial need. Preference is given to nursing students. The award is renewable for four semesters and pays for tuition, books, and supplies. Award requirements change regularly. Please send a self-addressed, stamped envelope to receive your application and any further instructions from the scholarship provider; or visit the website at pioneer.northark.cc.ar.us. No GPA requirement specified.

North Arkansas College
Attn: Financial Aid Office
1515 Pioneer Drive
Harrison, AR 72601

2189
Kiwanis-LPN Scholarship

AMOUNT: $125 DEADLINE: Varies
MAJOR: Nursing

The Kiwanis-LPN Scholarship is open to students at North Arkansas College. To be considered for this award, you must be an Arkansas resident and be accepted into the LPN program. The award provides $125 for two semesters. The application deadline is August 1 for students entering the program in the fall semester and December 1 for students entering in the spring semester. Award requirements change regularly. Please send a self-addressed, stamped envelope to receive your application and any further instructions from the scholarship provider; or visit the website at pioneer.northark.cc.ar.us. No GPA requirement specified.

North Arkansas College
Attn: Financial Aid Office
1515 Pioneer Drive
Harrison, AR 72601

2190
Kiwanis-RN Scholarship

AMOUNT: $125 DEADLINE: August 1
MAJOR: Nursing

The Kiwanis-RN Scholarship is open to students at North Arkansas College. To be considered for this award, you must be an Arkansas resident and be accepted into the RN program. The award provides $125 for two semesters. Award requirements change regularly. Please send a self-addressed, stamped envelope to receive your application and any further instructions from the scholarship provider; or visit the website at pioneer.northark.cc.ar.us. No GPA requirement specified.

North Arkansas College
Attn: Financial Aid Office
1515 Pioneer Drive
Harrison, AR 72601

2191
Learning Resource Center Scholarship

AMOUNT: None Specified DEADLINE: August 1
MAJOR: All Fields of Study with an Interest in Audio-Visual Work

The Learning Resource Center Scholarship is open to students at North Arkansas College. To be considered for this award, you must have an interest in audio-visual equipment (such as 16-mm projectors, slide projectors, videotape equipment) and/or be willing to be trained. You must also have a high school GPA of at least 2.3 and maintain this GPA and a minimum of 12 college credit hours per semester. The scholarship pays tuition. Recipients must be dependable and willing to

work flexible hours including days, nights, weekends and holidays. Award requirements change regularly. Please send a self-addressed, stamped envelope to receive your application and any further instructions from the scholarship provider; or visit the website at pioneer.northark.cc.ar.us. GPA must be 2.3-4.0.

North Arkansas College
Attn: Financial Aid Office
1515 Pioneer Drive
Harrison, AR 72601

2192
North Arkansas Medical Center (NAMC) Auxiliary Scholarship

AMOUNT: None Specified DEADLINE: Varies
MAJOR: Nursing

The North Arkansas Medical Center (NAMC) Auxiliary Scholarship is open to students at North Arkansas College. To be considered for this award, you must show proof of acceptance into the RN clinical program or the LPN program, have at least a 2.5 GPA, and carry a minimum of ten credit hours per semester. Preference is given to students receiving no other financial assistance. The scholarship covers the cost of Boone County resident tuition. LPN scholarships will be awarded after the first 18 weeks of classes have been successfully completed. RN scholarships will be awarded to applicants successfully completing two semesters of study. Award requirements change regularly. Applications and information on application deadlines can be obtained at the NAMC gift shop. GPA must be 2.5-4.0.

North Arkansas College
Attn: Financial Aid Office
1515 Pioneer Drive
Harrison, AR 72601

2193
Presidential Scholarship

AMOUNT: None Specified DEADLINE: August 1
MAJOR: All Fields of Study

The Presidential Scholarship is open to full-time students at North Arkansas College. To be considered for this award, you must be a first-time entering freshman, be an Arkansas resident, have graduated from an Arkansas high school or received an Arkansas GED, and have an ACT composite score of at least 22. You must submit a copy of your ACT scores and a letter indicating your educational goals, financial need, and ways you plan to fund the remainder of your educational expenses. Award requirements change regularly. Please send a self-addressed, stamped envelope to receive your application and any further instructions from the scholarship provider; or visit the website at pioneer.northark.cc.ar.us. No GPA requirement specified.

North Arkansas College
Attn: Financial Aid Office
1515 Pioneer Drive
Harrison, AR 72601

2194
Radiology Associates of North Arkansas Scholarship

AMOUNT: $912 DEADLINE: August 1
MAJOR: Radiology Technology

The Radiology Associates of North Arkansas Scholarship is open to full-time students at North Arkansas College. To be considered for this award, you must be an Arkansas resident, be enrolled in the radiology technology program, and not receive any other tuition scholarship given by North Arkansas College. The award provides $456 per semester. Award requirements change regularly. Please send a self-addressed, stamped envelope to receive your application and any further instructions from the scholarship provider; or visit the website at pioneer.northark.cc.ar.us. No GPA requirement specified.

North Arkansas College
Attn: Financial Aid Office
1515 Pioneer Drive
Harrison, AR 72601

2195
Theater Company Performing Arts Scholarship

AMOUNT: None Specified DEADLINE: August 1
MAJOR: All Fields of Study with Participation in Theater Company Productions

The Theater Company Performing Arts Scholarship is open to full-time students at North Arkansas College. The award is applied toward the fall semester tuition of students who have participated in the cast, crew, or orchestra of a Theater Company production during the previous school year. To be considered for this award, you must have and maintain a 2.5 GPA and demonstrate financial need. Auditions, interviews, letters of recommendation, or other presentations may be required in the selection process. Award requirements change regularly. Please send a self-addressed, stamped envelope to receive your application and any further instructions from the scholarship provider; or visit the website at pioneer.northark.cc.ar.us. GPA must be 2.5-4.0.

North Arkansas College
Attn: Financial Aid Office
1515 Pioneer Drive
Harrison, AR 72601

2196
Tyson Foundation, Inc., Scholarship

AMOUNT: None Specified DEADLINE: August 1
MAJOR: Air Conditioning, Heating and Refrigeration, Business, Electronics Technology, Practical Nursing, Machine Technology, Welding

The Tyson Foundation, Inc., Scholarship is open to students at North Arkansas College. To be considered for this award, you must be enrolled in one of the following programs: air conditioning, heating and refrigeration, business, electronics technology, practical nursing, machine technology, or welding. Preference is given to Tyson employees and the dependents of employees or growers. Other criteria include a desire to succeed in your chosen vocation, scholastic achievement and

attendance, financial need, character, reputation, and leadership qualities. Award requirements change regularly. Please send a self-addressed, stamped envelope to receive your application and any further instructions from the scholarship provider; or visit the website at pioneer.northark.cc.ar.us. No GPA requirement specified.

North Arkansas College
Attn: Financial Aid Office
1515 Pioneer Drive
Harrison, AR 72601

North Georgia College and State University

2197
North Georgia College and State University Military Scholarship

AMOUNT: None Specified DEADLINE: January 3
MAJOR: All Fields of Study

The North Georgia College and State University Military Scholarship is open to high school graduates interested in a military career. To be considered for this scholarship you must be a resident of Georgia planning to attend North Georgia College and State University in Dahlonega. You must also have at least a 3.0 GPA, have a minimum 1010 combined SAT (a minimum verbal score of 480 and 440 math), and successfully meet the mental and physical health standards required for enlistment in the Georgia National Guard. The award provides full tuition, fees, room and board, books, and supplies and requires a commitment of service, upon graduation, in the Georgia National Guard. Award requirements change regularly. Please send a self-addressed, stamped envelope to receive your application and any further instructions from the scholarship provider or phone (770) 724-9040. GPA must be 3.0-4.0.

Georgia Student Finance Commission
Attn: Scholarships and Grants Division
2082 East Exchange Place
Tucker, GA 30084

Northeast Iowa Community College, Calmar

2198
Community First Bank of Decorah Scholarship

AMOUNT: None Specified DEADLINE: November 10
MAJOR: Agriculture

The Community First Bank of Decorah Scholarship is open to students at Northeast Iowa Community College, Calmar Campus, enrolled full-time in an agricultural program. You must be able to demonstrate financial need and a strong interest in pursuing an agricultural program and future employment. Award requirements change regularly. No GPA requirement specified.

Northeast Iowa Community College, Calmar
Financial Aid Office
PO Box 400
Calmar, IA 52132-0400

2199
Crow's Hybrid Corn Company Scholarship

AMOUNT: None Specified DEADLINE: April 14
MAJOR: Vocational, Technical Programs

The Crow's Hybrid Corn Company Scholarship is open to full-time students enrolled in a vocational-technical program at Northeast Iowa Community College, Calmar. You must be an employee or the descendant of an employee (or dealer) of Crow's Hybrid Corn Company. The award also requires that you demonstrate financial need and that you maintain good academic standing. Award requirements change regularly. No GPA requirement specified.

Northeast Iowa Community College, Calmar
Financial Aid Office
PO Box 400
Calmar, IA 52132-0400

2200
Dollars for Scholars Collegiate Partners Program

AMOUNT: None Specified DEADLINE: April 14
MAJOR: All Areas of Study

Northeast Iowa Community College and the Citizens Scholarship Foundation of America are working together to sponsor the Dollars for Scholars Collegiate Partners Program. NICC is a matching source of funds for you if you have received awards from your local chapter. You may contact the Financial Aid office for further information on matching awards if you are eligible. Award requirements change regularly. No GPA requirement specified.

Northeast Iowa Community College, Calmar
Financial Aid Office
PO Box 400
Calmar, IA 52132-0400

2201
Donaldson Company, Inc., Scholarship

AMOUNT: $1500 DEADLINE: July 2
MAJOR: Computer Science

The Donaldson Company, Inc., Scholarship is open to students attending Northeast Iowa Community College, Calmar Campus, who are enrolled full-time in a computer or computer-related program. The applicants must be able to demonstrate financial need and a commitment to being successful in academic and post-graduation pursuits. Applicants must be residents of the Oelwein area. If there are no Oelwein area applicants, preference will be given to Cresco area residents. Award requirements change regularly. No GPA requirement specified.

Northeast Iowa Community College, Calmar
Financial Aid Office
PO Box 400
Calmar, IA 52132-0400

2202
Evenson Brothers Scholarship

AMOUNT: None Specified DEADLINE: April 14
MAJOR: Agriculture

The Evenson Brothers Scholarship is open to students attending Northeast Iowa Community College, Calmar Campus. You must be enrolled full-time in an agricultural program and show financial need. Award requirements change regularly. No GPA requirement specified.

Northeast Iowa Community College, Calmar
Financial Aid Office
PO Box 400
Calmar, IA 52132-0400

2203
Fel Pro Automotive Scholarship

AMOUNT: None Specified DEADLINE: Varies
MAJOR: Automotive Technology

The Fel Pro Automotive Scholarship is open to automotive technology majors at Northeast Iowa Community College, Calmar Campus. Applications are sent to NICC and distributed to the program. Award requirements change regularly. No GPA requirement specified.

Northeast Iowa Community College, Calmar
Financial Aid Office
PO Box 400
Calmar, IA 52132-0400

2204
Industrial Technology, Coffee Pot, Scholarship

AMOUNT: None Specified DEADLINE: November 10
MAJOR: Industrial Technology

The Industrial Technology "Coffee Pot" Scholarship is open to students attending Northeast Iowa Community College, Calmar Campus. You must be enrolled full-time in an industrial technology program and be able to demonstrate financial need. The award also requires that you have completed at least one semester. Award requirements change regularly. No GPA requirement specified.

Northeast Iowa Community College, Calmar
Financial Aid Office
PO Box 400
Calmar, IA 52132-0400

2205
Kermit Teig Scholarship

AMOUNT: None Specified DEADLINE: November 10
MAJOR: All Areas of Study

The Kermit Teig Scholarship is open to full-time students enrolled in a degree program at Northeast Iowa Community College, Calmar. You must have successfully completed one semester in your major and have a minimum GPA of 3.0. You must also be able to demonstrate leadership potential and involvement in school and community activities. Award requirements change regularly. GPA must be 3.0-4.0.

Northeast Iowa Community College, Calmar
Financial Aid Office
PO Box 400
Calmar, IA 52132-0400

2206
KOEL Ag Scholarship

AMOUNT: None Specified DEADLINE: November 10
MAJOR: Agriculture

The KOEL Ag Scholarship is open to students at Northeast Iowa Community College, Calmar Campus, enrolled in an agricultural division program. You must be able to demonstrate financial need and a strong desire to be successful in your educational program and employment efforts and goals. The award also requires that you be a resident of Iowa, Minnesota, or Wisconsin. Award requirements change regularly. No GPA requirement specified.

Northeast Iowa Community College, Calmar
Financial Aid Office
PO Box 400
Calmar, IA 52132-0400

2207
Land O' Lakes, Inc., Scholarship

AMOUNT: None Specified DEADLINE: April 14
MAJOR: Agribusiness

The Land O' Lakes, Inc., Scholarship is open to students at Northeast Iowa Community College, Calmar Campus. You must be enrolled full-time in an agribusiness technology program. The award also requires that you have already successfully completed the first year of the program. Award requirements change regularly. No GPA requirement specified.

Northeast Iowa Community College, Calmar
Financial Aid Office
PO Box 400
Calmar, IA 52132-0400

2208
Maquoketa Valley Agricultural Scholarship

AMOUNT: None Specified DEADLINE: April 14
MAJOR: Dairy Herd Program

The Maquoketa Valley Agricultural Scholarship is open to students at Northeast Iowa Community College, Calmar Campus. You must be a Maquoketa Valley student enrolled in the Dairy Herd Program. If there are no applicants with an agricultural background or interest, the scholarship will be awarded to another deserving person. Award requirements change regularly. No GPA requirement specified.

Northeast Iowa Community College, Calmar
Financial Aid Office
PO Box 400
Calmar, IA 52132-0400

2209
Marlys Seitz Memorial Scholarship

AMOUNT: None Specified DEADLINE: April 14
MAJOR: Nursing

The Marlys Seitz Memorial Scholarship is open to students at Northeast Iowa Community College, Calmar Campus. You must be enrolled in a nursing program and be entering or already into your second year. You are a preferred candidate if you are from the MFL-Mar Mac school district. A minimum 3.0 GPA is needed. Award requirements change regularly. GPA must be 3.0-4.0.

Northeast Iowa Community College, Calmar
Financial Aid Office
PO Box 400
Calmar, IA 52132-0400

2210
Mavis G. Young Scholarship

AMOUNT: None Specified DEADLINE: November 10
MAJOR: All Areas of Study

The Mavis G. Young Scholarship is open to students at Northeast Iowa Community College, Calmar. You must have worked primarily in the home, be currently unemployed, and have lost your source of financial support. You will also need to state your specific reasons for submitting the application and a statement that also explains how you meet the criteria for a displaced homemaker. Award requirements change regularly. No GPA requirement specified.

Northeast Iowa Community College, Calmar
Financial Aid Office
PO Box 400
Calmar, IA 52132-0400

2211
Medical Associates Foundation Scholarship

AMOUNT: None Specified DEADLINE: Varies
MAJOR: Nursing, Radiological Technician, Respiratory Therapy Technology, Medical Records Technician, Medical Transcription

The Medical Associates Foundation Scholarship is open to full-time students at Northeast Iowa Community College, Peosta and Calmar Campuses, who are nursing, radiological technology, respiratory therapy, or medical records and/or medical transcription majors. Applicants must have completed at least one semester in their program with a minimum GPA of 2.5. This award is only for residents from the following areas: Dubuque, Delaware, Clayton, Jackson, or Jones Counties in Iowa; Grant, Iowa, LaFayette, or Crawford Counties in Wisconsin; or Jo Daviess County in Illinois. Award requirements change regularly. GPA must be 2.5-4.0.

Northeast Iowa Community College, Calmar
Financial Aid Office
PO Box 400
Calmar, IA 52132-0400

2212
Nelson Dairy Consultants Scholarship

AMOUNT: $250 DEADLINE: November 26
MAJOR: Dairy Herd Management

The Nelson Dairy Consultants Scholarship is open to students at Northeast Iowa Community College, Calmar Campus, who are enrolled in dairy herd management. Applicants must demonstrate financial need, show strong interest in pursuing the dairy herd management program, and show a commitment to be successful in future agricultural employment. Award requirements change regularly. No GPA requirement specified.

Northeast Iowa Community College, Calmar
Financial Aid Office
PO Box 400
Calmar, IA 52132-0400

2213
NICC Academic Scholarship

AMOUNT: None Specified DEADLINE: April 14
MAJOR: All Areas of Study

The NICC Academic Scholarship is open to high school seniors accepted at Northeast Iowa Community College, Calmar, in a degree program full-time. You must have a minimum 3.5 GPA, show leadership potential, and participate in school and community activities. Award requirements change regularly. GPA must be 3.5-4.0.

Northeast Iowa Community College, Calmar
Financial Aid Office
PO Box 400
Calmar, IA 52132-0400

2214
NICC Board of Trustees Scholarship

AMOUNT: None Specified DEADLINE: April 14
MAJOR: All Areas of Study

The NICC Board of Trustees Scholarship is open to high school seniors who have been accepted at NICC, Calmar. The award requires that you be an Iowa resident, preferably living in the NICC school district. You must also have good academic standing, citizenship, leadership/community service roles, and a minimum 2.5 GPA. Award requirements change regularly. GPA must be 2.5-4.0.

Northeast Iowa Community College, Calmar
Financial Aid Office
PO Box 400
Calmar, IA 52132-0400

2215
NICC Departmental Scholarship

AMOUNT: None Specified DEADLINE: November 10
MAJOR: All Areas of Study

The NICC Departmental Scholarship is open to students attending Northeast Iowa Community College, Calmar Campus. You must have completed at least one semester with a minimum GPA of 2.5. You must also show good citizenship

abilities, strong academics, and successful leadership and community service roles. Award requirements change regularly. GPA must be 2.5-4.0.

Northeast Iowa Community College, Calmar
Financial Aid Office
PO Box 400
Calmar, IA 52132-0400

2216
NICC Insurance Advisory Committee Scholarship

AMOUNT: None Specified DEADLINE: April 14
MAJOR: All Areas of Study

The NICC Insurance Advisory Committee Scholarship is open to full-time students at Northeast Iowa Community College, Calmar. The award requires that you be an Iowa resident, preferably from the NICC school district. You must also have good academic standing, citizenship, and leadership/community service roles and a minimum 3.0 GPA. Award requirements change regularly. GPA must be 3.0-4.0.

Northeast Iowa Community College, Calmar
Financial Aid Office
PO Box 400
Calmar, IA 52132-0400

2217
NICC Staff Scholarship

AMOUNT: None Specified DEADLINE: November 10
MAJOR: All Areas of Study

The NICC Staff Scholarship is open to students attending Northeast Iowa Community College, Calmar. You must have at least a 3.0 GPA, have completed one academic semester, and maintain a "student in good standing" status. Award requirements change regularly. GPA must be 3.0-4.0.

Northeast Iowa Community College, Calmar
Financial Aid Office
PO Box 400
Calmar, IA 52132-0400

2218
President's Leadership Scholarship

AMOUNT: None Specified DEADLINE: April 14
MAJOR: All Areas of Study

The President's Leadership Scholarship is open to high school seniors planning to attend Northeast Iowa Community College, Calmar. You must be either a student government president or a senior class president within the NICC district to qualify for this award. Award requirements change regularly. No GPA requirement specified.

Northeast Iowa Community College, Calmar
Financial Aid Office
PO Box 400
Calmar, IA 52132-0400

2219
Robert A. Klimesh Family Memorial Automotive Scholarship

AMOUNT: None Specified DEADLINE: April 14
MAJOR: Automotive Technology, Automotive Collision Repair

The Robert A. Klimesh Family Memorial Automotive Scholarship is open to students enrolled in an automotive technology program at Northeast Iowa Community College, Calmar Campus. You must show a strong interest and desire for employment in the fields of automotive technology and automotive collision repair upon graduation. Award requirements change regularly. No GPA requirement specified.

Northeast Iowa Community College, Calmar
Financial Aid Office
PO Box 400
Calmar, IA 52132-0400

2220
Ruth Lembke Scholarship

AMOUNT: None Specified DEADLINE: November 10
MAJOR: Accounting

The Ruth Lembke Scholarship is open to second-year accounting students at Northeast Iowa Community College, Calmar Campus. You must have a minimum 3.0 GPA in the first year of the NICC program. Award requirements change regularly. GPA must be 3.0-4.0.

Northeast Iowa Community College, Calmar
Financial Aid Office
PO Box 400
Calmar, IA 52132-0400

2221
Sara Lee Bakery Scholarship

AMOUNT: None Specified DEADLINE: Varies
MAJOR: Business, Accounting

The Sara Lee Bakery Scholarship is open to students at Northeast Iowa Community College, Calmar Campus, who are enrolled full-time with a minimum GPA of 3.0. Applicants must demonstrate leadership potential. Sara Lee distributes application forms to NICC in March. Award requirements change regularly. GPA must be 3.0-4.0.

Northeast Iowa Community College, Calmar
Financial Aid Office
PO Box 400
Calmar, IA 52132-0400

2222
Security Bank and Trust Scholarship

AMOUNT: None Specified DEADLINE: November 10
MAJOR: All Areas of Study

The Security Bank and Trust Scholarship is open to students at Northeast Iowa Community College, Calmar Campus. You must be a resident of Winneshiek County, Iowa, and be enrolled in a degree-seeking program. This is a random-drawing scholarship. Award requirements change regularly. No GPA requirement specified.

Northeast Iowa Community College, Calmar
Financial Aid Office
PO Box 400
Calmar, IA 52132-0400

2223
Wilder Scholarship

AMOUNT: None Specified DEADLINE: April 14
MAJOR: All Areas of Study

The Wilder Scholarship is open to full-time second-year students at Northeast Iowa Community College, Calmar. You must be an Iowa resident with a minimum 2.5 GPA. You must also meet the standards of good citizenship, excellence in academic achievements, leadership, and service. Award requirements change regularly. GPA must be 2.5-4.0.

Northeast Iowa Community College, Calmar
Financial Aid Office
PO Box 400
Calmar, IA 52132-0400

2224
Winneshiek County Memorial Hospital Scholarship

AMOUNT: None Specified DEADLINE: Varies
MAJOR: Health Fields

The Winneshiek County Memorial Hospital Scholarship is open to residents of Winneshiek County who are attending Northeast Iowa Community College, Calmar Campus. Students must be enrolled full-time in a health career program. Applicants must demonstrate financial need. Application forms are distributed to NICC in March. Award requirements change regularly. No GPA requirement specified.

Northeast Iowa Community College, Calmar
Financial Aid Office
PO Box 400
Calmar, IA 52132-0400

Northeast Iowa Community College, Peosta

2225
40 and 8 Nursing Scholarship

AMOUNT: None Specified DEADLINE: Varies
MAJOR: Nursing - ADN or LPN

The 40 and 8 Nursing Scholarship is open to all nursing students at Northeast Iowa Community College, Peosta Campus, who are veterans or related to veterans. Award requirements change regularly. No GPA requirement specified.

Northeast Iowa Community College, Peosta
Financial Aid Office
10250 Sundown Road
Peosta, IA 52068-9776

2226
Adams Company Scholarship

AMOUNT: None Specified DEADLINE: November 15
MAJOR: Industrial Technology

The Adams Company Scholarship is open to students at Northeast Iowa Community College, Peosta Campus, enrolled in an industrial technology program. You must have completed at least one term in the program and be in good academic standing. You are a preferred candidate if you are without financial aid. Award requirements change regularly. No GPA requirement specified.

Northeast Iowa Community College, Peosta
Financial Aid Office
10250 Sundown Road
Peosta, IA 52068-9776

2227
B & PW Scholarship

AMOUNT: None Specified DEADLINE: Varies
MAJOR: All Areas of Study

The B & PW Scholarship is open to Iowa residents who are non-traditional students at Northeast Iowa Community College, Peosta Campus. Award requirements change regularly. No GPA requirement specified.

Northeast Iowa Community College, Peosta
Financial Aid Office
10250 Sundown Road
Peosta, IA 52068-9776

2228
Carver Scholarship

AMOUNT: None Specified DEADLINE: Varies
MAJOR: All Areas of Study

The Carver Scholarship is open to full-time students at Northeast Iowa Community College, both campuses, who are in their second year and plan to transfer to one of the three regent's universities or one of the 24 four-year private colleges under the membership of the Iowa College Foundation. Applicants must have a minimum GPA of 2.8. (Do not use the NICC application form when applying for this scholarship.) Award requirements change regularly. GPA must be 2.8-4.0.

Northeast Iowa Community College, Peosta
Financial Aid Office
10250 Sundown Road
Peosta, IA 52068-9776

2229
Crow's Hybrid Corn Company Scholarship

AMOUNT: None Specified DEADLINE: April 15
MAJOR: Vocational, Technical Programs

The Crow's Hybrid Corn Company Scholarship is open to full-time students enrolled in a vocational-technical program at Northeast Iowa Community College, Peosta. You must be an employee or descendant of employees (or dealers) of Crow's Hybrid Corn Company. You must also remain in good academic standing and be in financial need. Award requirements change regularly. No GPA requirement specified.

Northeast Iowa Community College, Peosta
Financial Aid Office
10250 Sundown Road
Peosta, IA 52068-9776

2230
Dubuque Advertiser Marketing Scholarship

AMOUNT: None Specified DEADLINE: April 15
MAJOR: Marketing

The Dubuque Advertiser Marketing Scholarship is open to students attending Northeast Iowa Community College, Peosta Campus. You must have completed at least one semester in the Marketing Management Program, and you must have a minimum 2.5 GPA. Award requirements change regularly. GPA must be 2.5-4.0.

Northeast Iowa Community College, Peosta
Financial Aid Office
10250 Sundown Road
Peosta, IA 52068-9776

2231
Dubuque Home Builders and Associates Scholarship

AMOUNT: None Specified DEADLINE: November 15
MAJOR: Carpentry

The Dubuque Home Builders and Associates Scholarship is open to students at Northeast Iowa Community College, Peosta Campus, enrolled in a carpentry program. You must have completed at least one academic semester and have a minimum 2.5 GPA. You must also be a resident of Dubuque County, Iowa, and be able to prove financial need. Award requirements change regularly. GPA must be 2.5-4.0.

Northeast Iowa Community College, Peosta
Financial Aid Office
10250 Sundown Road
Peosta, IA 52068-9776

2232
DUPACO Credit Union Scholarship

AMOUNT: None Specified DEADLINE: Varies
MAJOR: All Areas of Study

The DUPACO Credit Union Scholarship is open to first-year students at Northeast Iowa Community College, Peosta Campus, who are customers of the DUPACO Credit Union. Notices will be sent to NICC, and applications are available through DUPACO. Award requirements change regularly. No GPA requirement specified.

Northeast Iowa Community College, Peosta
Financial Aid Office
10250 Sundown Road
Peosta, IA 52068-9776

2233
Edith Kritz Scholarship

AMOUNT: None Specified DEADLINE: Varies
MAJOR: Nursing - ADN and LPN

The Edith Kritz Scholarship is open to nursing students at Northeast Iowa Community College, Peosta Campus, who have completed at least one semester of their nursing program. Award requirements change regularly. No GPA requirement specified.

Northeast Iowa Community College, Peosta
Financial Aid Office
10250 Sundown Road
Peosta, IA 52068-9776

2234
Farmers and Merchants Savings Bank Scholarship

AMOUNT: None Specified DEADLINE: Varies
MAJOR: All Areas of Study

The Farmers and Merchants Savings Bank Scholarship is open to residents of Delaware County, Iowa, at Northeast Iowa Community College, Peosta Campus, who have completed at least one semester with a minimum GPA of 3.0. Applicants must be able to demonstrate financial need. Award requirements change regularly. GPA must be 3.0-4.0.

Northeast Iowa Community College, Peosta
Financial Aid Office
10250 Sundown Road
Peosta, IA 52068-9776

2235
Iowa Society for Respiratory Technicians Scholarship

AMOUNT: None Specified DEADLINE: Varies
MAJOR: Respiratory Therapy Technician

The Iowa Society for Respiratory Technicians Scholarship is open to students attending Northeast Iowa Community College, both campuses. Applicants must have completed the first year of their program. Award requirements change regularly. No GPA requirement specified.

Northeast Iowa Community College, Peosta
Financial Aid Office
10250 Sundown Road
Peosta, IA 52068-9776

2236
Jerry Fischer Memorial Scholarship

AMOUNT: $600 DEADLINE: October 1
MAJOR: Industrial Technology, Associates Arts

The Jerry Fischer Memorial Scholarship is open to students attending Northeast Iowa Community College, Peosta Campus, who are enrolled full-time in an industrial technology or associate in arts program. Applicants must have completed at least one full year and must be entering the second year and anticipating graduation at the completion of the current academic year. Preference given to students who do not already have financial aid. Award requirements change regularly. No GPA requirement specified.

Northeast Iowa Community College, Peosta
Financial Aid Office
10250 Sundown Road
Peosta, IA 52068-9776

2237
John and Mabel Heinen Family Award

AMOUNT: None Specified DEADLINE: April 15
MAJOR: All Areas of Study

The John and Mabel Heinen Family Award is open to students at Northeast Iowa Community College, Peosta. You must be enrolled at least half-time (6 credits) and in financial need. Award requirements change regularly. No GPA requirement specified.

Northeast Iowa Community College, Peosta
Financial Aid Office
10250 Sundown Road
Peosta, IA 52068-9776

2238
John Deere Dubuque/Genesis Systems Welding Scholarship

AMOUNT: None Specified DEADLINE: November 15
MAJOR: Welding

The John Deere Dubuque/Genesis Systems Welding Scholarship is open to students attending Northeast Iowa Community College, Peosta, enrolled full-time in the welding program. You must have completed at least one semester in the program and have at least a GPA of 2.5. Award requirements change regularly. GPA must be 2.5-4.0.

Northeast Iowa Community College, Peosta
Financial Aid Office
10250 Sundown Road
Peosta, IA 52068-9776

2239
Lowe's Community Scholarship

AMOUNT: None Specified DEADLINE: April 15
MAJOR: Carpentry, Heating and Air Conditioning

The Lowe's Community Scholarship is open to students at Northeast Iowa Community College, Peosta. You must be a student in one of the carpentry or heating and air conditioning programs. Award requirements change regularly. No GPA requirement specified.

Northeast Iowa Community College, Peosta
Financial Aid Office
10250 Sundown Road
Peosta, IA 52068-9776

2240
Mary Lou Kurt Memorial Nursing Scholarship

AMOUNT: None Specified DEADLINE: April 15
MAJOR: Nursing

The Mary Lou Kurt Memorial Nursing Scholarship is open to students at Northeast Iowa Community College, Peosta, enrolled full-time in the ADN program. You must be a high school graduate from Dubuque or Jones Counties in Iowa. You must also complete one semester of nursing, maintaining a 2.8 GPA, and be able to demonstrate financial need. The award also requires that you submit one nursing faculty recommendation (it is optional for you to include recommendations from the arts and science faculty). An interview with the selection committee may be required. Award requirements change regularly. GPA must be 2.8-4.0.

Northeast Iowa Community College, Peosta
Financial Aid Office
10250 Sundown Road
Peosta, IA 52068-9776

2241
Mavis G. Young Award

AMOUNT: None Specified DEADLINE: April 15
MAJOR: All Areas of Study

The Mavis G. Young Award is open to students at Northeast Iowa Community College, Peosta. You must have worked primarily in the home, be currently unemployed, and lost your source of financial support. When submitting your application, also be sure to include your reasons for making this application and in what ways you qualify as a displaced homemaker. Award requirements change regularly. No GPA requirement specified.

Northeast Iowa Community College, Peosta
Financial Aid Office
10250 Sundown Road
Peosta, IA 52068-9776

2242
National Society of Public Accountants Scholarship

AMOUNT: None Specified DEADLINE: Varies
MAJOR: Accounting

The National Society of Public Accountants Scholarship is open to full-time students at Northeast Iowa Community College, both campuses, who are majoring in accounting. Applicants must be planning to transfer to a four-year college to continue their education in accounting. Award requirements change regularly. No GPA requirement specified.

Northeast Iowa Community College, Peosta
Financial Aid Office
10250 Sundown Road
Peosta, IA 52068-9776

2243
NICC Board of Trustees Scholarship

AMOUNT: None Specified DEADLINE: April 15
MAJOR: All Areas of Study

The NICC Board of Trustees Scholarship is open to current high school seniors. You must be an Iowa resident (preferably from the NICC school district) with a minimum 2.5 GPA. You must also demonstrate good citizenship abilities, strong academic achievements, and leadership/community service roles. A continuous "student in good standing" status will be required. Award requirements change regularly. GPA must be 2.5-4.0.

Northeast Iowa Community College, Peosta
Financial Aid Office
10250 Sundown Road
Peosta, IA 52068-9776

2244
NICC Foundation Scholarship

AMOUNT: None Specified DEADLINE: April 15
MAJOR: All Areas of Study

The NICC Foundation Scholarship is open to students attending Northeast Iowa Community College, Peosta. You must have completed at least one semester at NICC and be in financial need. A minimum 3.0 GPA and good academic standing are also required. Award requirements change regularly. GPA must be 3.0-4.0.

Northeast Iowa Community College, Peosta
Financial Aid Office
10250 Sundown Road
Peosta, IA 52068-9776

2245
NICC Insurance Advisory Committee Scholarship

AMOUNT: None Specified DEADLINE: April 15
MAJOR: All Areas of Study

The NICC Insurance Advisory Committee Scholarship is open to full-time second-year students at Northeast Iowa Community College, Peosta. You must be an Iowa resident from the NICC school district with a minimum 3.0 GPA. You must also show good citizenship abilities, strong academic achievements, and leadership/community service roles. You are also required to have and maintain a "student in good standing" status by maintaining a 3.0 minimum GPA. Award requirements change regularly. GPA must be 3.0-4.0.

Northeast Iowa Community College, Peosta
Financial Aid Office
10250 Sundown Road
Peosta, IA 52068-9776

2246
NICC/Loras-Fidelity Bank Partnership Scholarship

AMOUNT: $1500 DEADLINE: December 3
MAJOR: Business

The NICC/Loras-Fidelity Bank Partnership Scholarship is open to students attending Northeast Iowa Community College (NICC), Peosta, who have completed at least one year of an Associate Degree program (currently enrolled in their second year) and plan to transfer to Loras College. Applicants must have maintained a minimum GPA of 3.3 at NICC. The scholarship awards $500 while at NICC and $1,000 upon registering at Loras College. Award requirements change regularly. GPA must be 3.3-4.0.

Northeast Iowa Community College, Peosta
Financial Aid Office
10250 Sundown Road
Peosta, IA 52068-9776

2247
Northeast Iowa Community College Academic Scholarship

AMOUNT: None Specified DEADLINE: April 15
MAJOR: All Areas of Study

The Northeast Iowa Community College Academic Scholarship is open to high school seniors planning to attend Northeast Iowa Community College, Peosta. You must show leadership potential and participation in school and community activities and be planning to attend full-time. A minimum 3.8 GPA is needed. Award requirements change regularly. GPA must be 3.8-4.0.

Northeast Iowa Community College, Peosta
Financial Aid Office
10250 Sundown Road
Peosta, IA 52068-9776

2248
Northeast Iowa Community College Staff Scholarship

AMOUNT: None Specified DEADLINE: April 15
MAJOR: All Areas of Study

The Northeast Iowa Community College Staff Scholarship is open to students at Northeast Iowa Community College, Peosta. You must have completed one semester, have a minimum 3.0 GPA, and maintain a "student in good standing" status. Award requirements change regularly. GPA must be 3.0-4.0.

Northeast Iowa Community College, Peosta
Financial Aid Office
10250 Sundown Road
Peosta, IA 52068-9776

2249
President's Leadership Scholarship

AMOUNT: None Specified DEADLINE: April 15
MAJOR: All Areas of Study

The President's Leadership Scholarship is open to high school seniors planning to attend Northeast Iowa Community College, Peosta. You must be either a student government president or a senior class president within the NICC district. Award requirements change regularly. No GPA requirement specified.

Northeast Iowa Community College, Peosta
Financial Aid Office
10250 Sundown Road
Peosta, IA 52068-9776

2250

Robert Preitauer Memorial Scholarship

AMOUNT: None Specified DEADLINE: November 15
MAJOR: Business, Carpentry

The Robert Preitauer Memorial Scholarship is open to students at Northeast Iowa Community College, Peosta Campus. You must be either a business or carpentry major. Of the two scholarships that will be awarded, one will go to a business major, and the other one will go to a carpentry major. Award requirements change regularly. No GPA requirement specified.

Northeast Iowa Community College, Peosta
Financial Aid Office
10250 Sundown Road
Peosta, IA 52068-9776

2251
Rotary Club of Dubuque-Key City Scholarship

AMOUNT: $500 DEADLINE: Varies
MAJOR: All Areas of Study

The Rotary Club of Dubuque-Key City Scholarship is open to students at Northeast Iowa Community College, Peosta Campus, who are enrolled full-time. Applicants must be able to demonstrate leadership potential and financial need. Award requirements change regularly. No GPA requirement specified.

Northeast Iowa Community College, Peosta
Financial Aid Office
10250 Sundown Road
Peosta, IA 52068-9776

2252

Scott Sieverding Memorial Scholarship

AMOUNT: None Specified DEADLINE: November 15
MAJOR: Respiratory Therapy Technology

The Scott Sieverding Memorial Scholarship is open to students attending Northeast Iowa Community College, Peosta Campus. You must be enrolled full-time in the Respiratory Therapy Technologist or Technician programs. You must have completed one academic semester, and your GPA must be a minimum 2.75. Award requirements change regularly. GPA must be 2.75-4.0.

Northeast Iowa Community College, Peosta
Financial Aid Office
10250 Sundown Road
Peosta, IA 52068-9776

Sherry Oldenburg Scholarship

AMOUNT: None Specified DEADLINE: April 15
MAJOR: Accounting

The Sherry Oldenburg Scholarship is open to full-time students attending Northeast Iowa Community College (NICC), Peosta Campus. You must have completed at least one semester in the Accounting Specialist program, have a minimum 2.8 GPA, and be enrolled full-time. Financial need will not be a factor in the selection. Award requirements change regularly. GPA must be 2.8-4.0.

Northeast Iowa Community College, Peosta
Financial Aid Office
10250 Sundown Road
Peosta, IA 52068-9776

2254
Tri-State Data Processing Association Scholarship

AMOUNT: None Specified DEADLINE: Varies
MAJOR: Data Processing

The Tri-State Data Processing Association Scholarship is open to students attending Northeast Iowa Community College, Peosta Campus, who are enrolled in the data processing program. Applicants must be residents of Dubuque County, Iowa; Grant County, Wisconsin; or Jo Daviess County, Illinois. Award requirements change regularly. No GPA requirement specified.

Northeast Iowa Community College, Peosta
Financial Aid Office
10250 Sundown Road
Peosta, IA 52068-9776

2255
Trilog, Inc., Scholarship

AMOUNT: None Specified DEADLINE: April 15
MAJOR: Accounting, Marketing Management, Business, Business Computer Systems, Administrative Assistance

The Trilog, Inc., Scholarship is open to full-time students attending Northeast Iowa Community College, Peosta Campus. You must have a minimum GPA of 2.7, be from the Dubuque or the surrounding (Iowa) area, and submit a one-page essay stating your long-term goals. Award requirements change regularly. GPA must be 2.7-4.0.

Northeast Iowa Community College, Peosta
Financial Aid Office
10250 Sundown Road
Peosta, IA 52068-9776

2256
Virginia Heim Memorial Nursing Scholarship

AMOUNT: None Specified DEADLINE: April 15
MAJOR: Nursing

The Virginia Heim Memorial Nursing Scholarship is open to ADN nursing students attending Northeast Iowa Community College, Peosta Campus. You must be enrolled in the second year of the ADN nursing program. You are a preferred candidate if you have limited or no financial aid. Your GPA scores will be considered, but will not be a mandatory guideline. Award requirements change regularly. No GPA requirement specified.

Northeast Iowa Community College, Peosta
Financial Aid Office
10250 Sundown Road
Peosta, IA 52068-9776

2257
W. T. Raisbeck Memorial Scholarship

AMOUNT: None Specified DEADLINE: April 15
MAJOR: Mechanical Technology

The W. T. Raisbeck Memorial Scholarship is open to full-time mechanical technology majors attending Northeast Iowa Community College, Peosta Campus. You must have completed the first year of the program and have a minimum GPA of 2.5. Award requirements change regularly. GPA must be 2.5-4.0.

Northeast Iowa Community College, Peosta
Financial Aid Office
10250 Sundown Road
Peosta, IA 52068-9776

2258
Wilder Scholarship

AMOUNT: None Specified DEADLINE: April 15
MAJOR: All Areas of Study

The Wilder Scholarship is open to second-year students at Northeast Iowa Community College, Peosta. You must display good citizenship qualities, academic achievements, leadership, and service. You should be an Iowa resident, and your GPA score should be at least 2.5. Award requirements change regularly. GPA must be 2.5-4.0.

Northeast Iowa Community College, Peosta
Financial Aid Office
10250 Sundown Road
Peosta, IA 52068-9776

2259
Women in Construction Scholarship

AMOUNT: None Specified DEADLINE: February 20
MAJOR: Construction Trade

The Women in Construction Scholarship is open to male and female students attending Northeast Iowa Community College, Peosta Campus, who are residents of the Dubuque area and are enrolled in the construction trade area. Award requirements change regularly. No GPA requirement specified.

Northeast Iowa Community College, Peosta
Financial Aid Office
10250 Sundown Road
Peosta, IA 52068-9776

2260
Women in Management Scholarship

AMOUNT: None Specified DEADLINE: Varies
MAJOR: Business, Management

The Women in Management Scholarship is open to Northeast Iowa Community College, Peosta Campus, students who have completed the first year of their business and management majors. Preference given to students who plan to transfer to a four-year college. Award requirements change regularly. No GPA requirement specified.

Northeast Iowa Community College, Peosta
Financial Aid Office
10250 Sundown Road
Peosta, IA 52068-9776

Northwood University

2261
Northwood University DECA Scholarships

AMOUNT: $1000-$2500 DEADLINE: Varies
MAJOR: All Areas of Study

Scholarships for all national and state officers and first-place winners by category. Scholarships are also available for all other active DECA students with a minimum GPA of 2.75. Award requirements change regularly. GPA must be 2.75-4.0.

Northwood University
Office of Admissions
3225 Cook Road
Midland, MI 48640-2311

2262
Northwood University Free-Enterprise Scholarships

AMOUNT: $4000 DEADLINE: Varies
MAJOR: All Areas of Study

Scholarships available to incoming full-time freshmen. Must have at least a 20 score on the ACT, 950 on the SAT, and a minimum GPA of 2.70. Renewable if recipients maintain a 2.70 GPA. Award requirements change regularly. GPA must be 2.7-4.0.

Northwood University
Office of Admissions
3225 Cook Road
Midland, MI 48640-2311

2263
Northwood University Freedom Scholarships

AMOUNT: $5000 DEADLINE: Varies
MAJOR: All Areas of Study

Scholarships available for incoming full-time freshmen. Must have at least a score of 25 on the ACT, 1150 on the SAT, and a minimum GPA of 3.0. Renewable if recipients maintain a 3.0 GPA. Award requirements change regularly. GPA must be 3.0-4.0.

Northwood University
Office of Admissions
3225 Cook Road
Midland, MI 48640-2311

2264
Northwood University Transfer Scholarships

AMOUNT: $3000 DEADLINE: May 1
MAJOR: All Areas of Study

Scholarship available for students transferring to Northwood as full-time juniors who will be enrolled for a minimum of two years. Applicants must have an Associate Degree and a minimum GPA of 2.70. Award requirements change regularly. GPA must be 2.7-4.0.

Northwood University
Office of Admissions
3225 Cook Road
Midland, MI 48640-2311

Nossi College of Art

2265
Mahtaban Art Scholarship

AMOUNT: $1800 DEADLINE: Varies
MAJOR: Commercial Art

The Mahtaban Art Scholarship is for students enrolling in the Nossi College of Art's Commercial Art Program directly from high school. You must have demonstrated to your high school art instructors and counselors an exceptional ability in art and a promising future as a commercial artist. You must submit a one-page essay, your high school transcript, a letter of recommendation, and two original art projects to be determined by the college. Award requirements change regularly. No GPA requirement specified.

Nossi College of Art
Attn: Scholarship Programs
907 Two Mile Parkway, E6
Goodlettsville, TN 37072

2266
Mahtaban Art Scholarship for Rural Counties

AMOUNT: $1800 DEADLINE: Varies
MAJOR: Commercial Art

The Mahtaban Art Scholarship for Rural Counties is for students enrolling in the Nossi College of Art's Commercial Art Program. You must live in the rural counties of Tennessee, demonstrate an exceptional creativity in visual art, and pursue your career in commercial art. In addition, you must submit a one-page essay, your high school transcript, a letter of recommendation, and two original art projects to be determined by the college. Award requirements change regularly. No GPA requirement specified.

Nossi College of Art
Attn: Scholarship Programs
907 Two Mile Parkway, E6
Goodlettsville, TN 37072

2267
Mahtaban Scholarship for Out-of-State Residents

AMOUNT: $1800 DEADLINE: Varies
MAJOR: Commercial Art

The Mahtaban Scholarship for Out-of-State Residents is for out-of-state students enrolling in the Nossi College of Art's Commercial Art Program. You must demonstrate an exceptional ability and creativity in art and wish to pursue a career as a commercial artist. Also required are a one-page essay, your high school transcript, a letter of recommendation, and two original art projects to be determined by the college. Award requirements change regularly. No GPA requirement specified.

Nossi College of Art
Attn: Scholarship Programs
907 Two Mile Parkway, E6
Goodlettsville, TN 37072

Occidental College

2268
A. W. Bodine Sunkist Memorial Scholarship

AMOUNT: Maximum: $3000 DEADLINE: April 30
MAJOR: All Fields of Study

The A. W. Bodine Sunkist Memorial Scholarship is open to applicants attending Occidental College whose families have a background in Arizona or California agriculture. Award requirements change regularly. Please send a self-addressed, stamped envelope to receive your application and any further instructions from the scholarship provider, or call (323) 259-2548. No GPA requirement specified.

Occidental College
Financial Aid Office
1600 Campus Road
Los Angeles, CA 90041

2269
AICPA John L. Carey Scholarship Program

AMOUNT: $5000 DEADLINE: April 1
MAJOR: Accounting

The AICPA John L. Carey Scholarship Program is open to liberal arts degree holders who wish to pursue a CPA certification at Occidental College. Scholarships are contingent upon acceptance in a graduate accounting program. This award is renewable. Award requirements change regularly. Please send a self-addressed, stamped envelope to receive your application and any further instructions from the scholarship provider, or call (323) 259-2548. No GPA requirement specified.

Occidental College
Financial Aid Office
1600 Campus Road
Los Angeles, CA 90041

2270
American Bar Association Summer Research Fellowships

AMOUNT: None Specified DEADLINE: March 1
MAJOR: Law, Social Sciences

The American Bar Association Summer Research Fellowships are open to minority sophomores and juniors attending Occidental College as law or social sciences majors. Award requirements change regularly. Please send a self-addressed, stamped envelope to receive your application and any further instructions from the scholarship provider, or call (323) 259-2548. No GPA requirement specified.

Occidental College
Financial Aid Office
1600 Campus Road
Los Angeles, CA 90041

2271
American Chemical Society Scholarship

AMOUNT: Maximum: $2500 DEADLINE: February 15
MAJOR: Chemical Sciences

The American Chemical Society Scholarship is open to African-American, Hispanic, and Native American students attending Occidental College who are interested in pursuing undergraduate degrees in the chemical sciences. Award requirements change regularly. Please send a self-addressed, stamped envelope to receive your application and any further instructions from the scholarship provider, or call (323) 259-2548. No GPA requirement specified.

Occidental College
Financial Aid Office
1600 Campus Road
Los Angeles, CA 90041

2272
American Industrial Real Estate Association Scholarships

AMOUNT: None Specified DEADLINE: Varies
MAJOR: Real Estate, Real Estate-Related

The American Industrial Real Estate Association Scholarships are open to juniors, seniors, and graduate students attending Occidental College who are pursuing careers in real estate or real estate-related fields of study. Award requirements change regularly. Please send a self-addressed, stamped envelope to receive your application and any further instructions from the scholarship provider, or call (323) 259-2548. No GPA requirement specified.

Occidental College
Financial Aid Office
1600 Campus Road
Los Angeles, CA 90041

2273
American Psychological Association - Minority Fellowship Program

AMOUNT: None Specified DEADLINE: January 15
MAJOR: Neuroscience

The American Psychological Association Minority Fellowship Program is open to minority students attending Occidental College who are interested in neuroscience. Areas of study would include research on humans, vertebrate and invertebrate animals, and isolated biological systems. Award requirements change regularly. Please send a self-addressed, stamped envelope to receive your application and any further instructions from the scholarship provider, or call (323) 259-2548. No GPA requirement specified.

Occidental College
Financial Aid Office
1600 Campus Road
Los Angeles, CA 90041

2274
Bernice Simon Memorial Scholarship

AMOUNT: $1000 DEADLINE: May 1
MAJOR: All Areas of Study

The Bernice Simon Memorial Scholarship is open to women 35 years of age or older returning to school to learn a skill for economic independence. This award is for students planning to attend Occidental College. Award requirements change regularly. Please send a self-addressed, stamped envelope to receive your application and any further instructions from the scholarship provider, or call (323) 259-2548. No GPA requirement specified.

Occidental College
Financial Aid Office
1600 Campus Road
Los Angeles, CA 90041

2275
Board of Higher Education and Ministry Scholarship

AMOUNT: None Specified DEADLINE: Varies
MAJOR: All Areas of Study

The Board of Higher Education and Ministry Scholarship is open to full, active members of the United Methodist Church (for at least one year) attending Occidental College. The eligibility requirements differ for each scholarship, but only one application is needed. Applicants will be considered for all scholarship funds. Award requirements change regularly. Please send a self-addressed, stamped envelope to receive your application and any further instructions from the scholarship provider, or call (323) 259-2548. No GPA requirement specified.

Occidental College
Financial Aid Office
1600 Campus Road
Los Angeles, CA 90041

2276
Bureau of Indian Affairs/Office of Indian Education Programs

AMOUNT: None Specified DEADLINE: Varies
MAJOR: All Areas of Study

The Bureau of Indian Affairs/Office of Indian Education Programs are open to members of a federally recognized Native American tribe who are attending Occidental College. These programs base eligibility on financial need. Award requirements change regularly. Please send a self-addressed, stamped envelope to receive your application and any further instructions from the scholarship provider, or call (323) 259-2548 No GPA requirement specified.

Occidental College
Financial Aid Office
1600 Campus Road
Los Angeles, CA 90041

2277
California State Psychological Association Foundation Scholarship

AMOUNT: $2500 DEADLINE: October 15
MAJOR: Psychology

The California State Psychological Association Foundation Scholarship is open to first-year, full-time, ethnic minority students accepted into a doctoral level psychology program at Occidental College. Priority will be given to those who demonstrate community involvement with an ethnic minority/cultural issues focus within your graduate program, plan to work with direct delivery of services to a culturally diverse population either publicly or privately, and show financial need. Award requirements change regularly. Please send a self-addressed, stamped envelope to receive your application and any further instructions from the scholarship provider, or call (323) 259-2548. No GPA requirement specified.

Occidental College
Financial Aid Office
1600 Campus Road
Los Angeles, CA 90041

2278
Charles M. Goethe Scholarship Fund

AMOUNT: None Specified DEADLINE: June 10
MAJOR: Genetics, Biological and Life Sciences

The Charles M. Goethe Scholarship Fund is open to students attending Occidental College who are genetics or biological and life sciences majors. You must be a member or senior member of the Order of Demolay or the child of a living or deceased member of a constituent Masonic Lodge or the Grand Lodge of the Free and Accepted Masons of California to apply for this award. Award requirements change regularly. Please send a self-addressed, stamped envelope to receive your application and any further instructions from the scholarship provider, or call (323) 259-2548. No GPA requirement specified.

Occidental College
Financial Aid Office
1600 Campus Road
Los Angeles, CA 90041

2279
College Women's Club of Pasadena Scholarship Foundation

AMOUNT: None Specified DEADLINE: February 15
MAJOR: All Areas of Study

The College Women's Club of Pasadena Scholarship Foundation is open to female applicants in their sophomore year or higher who are attending Occidental College. Award requirements change regularly. Please send a self-addressed, stamped envelope to receive your application and any further instructions from the scholarship provider, or call (323) 259-2548. No GPA requirement specified.

Occidental College
Financial Aid Office
1600 Campus Road
Los Angeles, CA 90041

2280
Dennis W. Cabaret Scholarship

AMOUNT: None Specified DEADLINE: February 26
MAJOR: All Areas of Study

The Dennis W. Cabaret Scholarship is open to students attending Occidental College who are Orange County-area residents. Applicants must have clear roots of activism in the Orange County lesbian and gay community. Award requirements change regularly. Please send a self-addressed, stamped envelope to receive your application and any further instructions from the scholarship provider, or call (323) 259-2548. No GPA requirement specified.

Occidental College
Financial Aid Office
1600 Campus Road
Los Angeles, CA 90041

2281
Hae Won Park Memorial Scholarship

AMOUNT: None Specified DEADLINE: March 30
MAJOR: All Areas of Study

The Hae Won Park Memorial Scholarship is open to women of Korean ancestry attending Occidental College who have demonstrated a commitment to serve their community. Applicants must be undergraduates and residents of Los Angeles, California. Award requirements change regularly. Please send a self-addressed, stamped envelope to receive your application and any further instructions from the scholarship provider, or call (323) 259-2548. No GPA requirement specified.

Occidental College
Financial Aid Office
1600 Campus Road
Los Angeles, CA 90041

2282
Jewish Community Scholarship Fund

AMOUNT: None Specified DEADLINE: April 15
MAJOR: All Areas of Study

The Jewish Community Scholarship Fund is open to Jewish students attending Occidental College who are legal residents of Los Angeles County, California. Applicants must be at sophomore level or above. Award requirements change regularly. Please send a self-addressed, stamped envelope to receive your application and any further instructions from the scholarship provider, or call (323) 259-2548. No GPA requirement specified.

Occidental College
Financial Aid Office
1600 Campus Road
Los Angeles, CA 90041

2283
June Miller Nursing Education Scholarship

AMOUNT: $500 DEADLINE: May 1
MAJOR: Nursing

The June Miller Nursing Education Scholarship is open to female nursing students attending Occidental College. Award requirements change regularly. Please send a self-addressed, stamped envelope to receive your application and any further instructions from the scholarship provider, or call (323) 259-2548. No GPA requirement specified.

Occidental College
Financial Aid Office
1600 Campus Road
Los Angeles, CA 90041

2284
JVS Jewish Community Scholarship Fund

AMOUNT: None Specified DEADLINE: April 15
MAJOR: All Areas of Study

The JVS Jewish Community Scholarship Fund is open to Jewish students attending Occidental College who are legal residents of Los Angeles County, California. Applicants must be at sophomore level or above. Award requirements change regularly. Please send a self-addressed, stamped envelope to receive your application and any further instructions from the scholarship provider, or call (323) 259-2548. No GPA requirement specified.

Occidental College
Financial Aid Office
1600 Campus Road
Los Angeles, CA 90041

2285
Lesbian, Gay and Bisexual Task Force Scholarships

AMOUNT: $250-$1000 DEADLINE: Varies
MAJOR: All Areas of Study

The Lesbian, Gay and Bisexual Task Force Scholarships are open to lesbian, gay, and bisexual students attending Occidental College. The eligibility criteria differ for each scholarship. Award requirements change regularly. Please send a self-addressed, stamped envelope to receive your application and any further instructions from the scholarship provider, or call (323) 259-2548. No GPA requirement specified.

Occidental College
Financial Aid Office
1600 Campus Road
Los Angeles, CA 90041

2286
National Black MBA Association, Inc., Fellowship

AMOUNT: None Specified DEADLINE: March 31
MAJOR: Business

The National Black MBA Association, Inc., Fellowship is open to minority students attending Occidental College as full-time doctoral business management majors. Award requirements change regularly. Please send a self-addressed, stamped envelope to receive your application and any further instructions from the scholarship provider, or call (323) 259-2548. No GPA requirement specified.

Occidental College
Financial Aid Office
1600 Campus Road
Los Angeles, CA 90041

2287
National Federation of Music Clubs Scholarships and Awards

AMOUNT: None Specified DEADLINE: Varies
MAJOR: Music

The National Federation of Music Clubs Scholarships and Awards are open to music majors attending Occidental College. You must be interested in a professional music career to be eligible for this award. Award requirements change regularly. Please send a self-addressed, stamped envelope to receive your application and any further instructions from the scholarship provider, or call (323) 259-2548. You may also visit the college's website. No GPA requirement specified.

Occidental College
Financial Aid Office
1600 Campus Road
Los Angeles, CA 90041

2288
Pasadena Arts Council Scholarship

AMOUNT: None Specified DEADLINE: March 1
MAJOR: Art

The Pasadena Arts Council Scholarship is open to art majors attending Occidental College. Students must be nominated by faculty members. Award requirements change regularly. Please send a self-addressed, stamped envelope to receive your application and any further instructions from the scholarship provider, or call (323) 259-2548. No GPA requirement specified.

Occidental College
Financial Aid Office
1600 Campus Road
Los Angeles, CA 90041

2289
Sol Goldberg Childcare Subsidy

AMOUNT: $1000 DEADLINE: May 1
MAJOR: All Areas of Study

The Sol Goldberg Childcare Subsidy is intended to ease the financial burden of child care for women entering or returning to Occidental College. Award requirements change regularly. Please send a self-addressed, stamped envelope to receive your application and any further instructions from the scholarship provider, or call (323) 259-2548. No GPA requirement specified.

Occidental College
Financial Aid Office
1600 Campus Road
Los Angeles, CA 90041

2290
Soroptimist International of Los Angeles Fellowship

AMOUNT: $3000 DEADLINE: March 15
MAJOR: All Areas of Study

The Soroptimist International of Los Angeles Fellowship is open to outstanding women graduates who are residents of California. The field of study is open, but consideration will be given to those students who have the greatest potential for contributing to society. Award requirements change regularly. Please send a self-addressed, stamped envelope to receive your application and any further instructions from the scholarship provider, or call (323) 259-2548. No GPA requirement specified.

Occidental College
Financial Aid Office
1600 Campus Road
Los Angeles, CA 90041

2291
Women of the Evangelical Lutheran Church in America Scholarship

AMOUNT: None Specified DEADLINE: March 1
MAJOR: All Areas of Study

The Women of the Evangelical Lutheran Church in America Scholarships are open to Lutheran women attending Occidental College. Award requirements change regularly. Please send a self-addressed, stamped envelope to receive your application and any further instructions from the scholarship provider, or call (323) 259-2548. No GPA requirement specified.

Occidental College
Financial Aid Office
1600 Campus Road
Los Angeles, CA 90041

2292
Women's Overseas Service League Scholarship

AMOUNT: $500-$1000 DEADLINE: March 1
MAJOR: Military, Public Service

The Women's Overseas Service League Scholarship is open to women who are committed to advancement in the military or in other public service careers. Awards are renewable for a second year. Award requirements change regularly. Please send a self-addressed, stamped envelope to receive your application and any further instructions from the scholarship provider, or call (323) 259-2548. No GPA requirement specified.

Occidental College
Financial Aid Office
1600 Campus Road
Los Angeles, CA 90041

Ohio State University

2293
Alga, Peg, Weaver 4-H Scholarship

AMOUNT: $900 DEADLINE: Varies
MAJOR: College of Human Ecology

Applicants must be 4-H members, seniors in high school during the year of application, and planning to enroll in the College of Human Ecology at Ohio State University. A minimum GPA of 2.0 or above is required. Award requirements change regularly. Please send a self-addressed, stamped envelope to receive your application and any further instructions from the scholarship provider, or you may email them at finaid@fa.adm.ohio-state.edu. You may consult the sponsor website: www.ag.ohio-state.edu/. GPA must be 2.0-4.0.

Ohio State University
Financial Aid, Lincoln Tower
1800 Cannon Drive, Office 517
Columbus, OH 43210-1230

2294
All American Youth Horse Show Foundation 4-H Scholarship

AMOUNT: $1000 DEADLINE: Varies
MAJOR: All Areas of Study

The All American Youth Horse Show Foundation 4-H Scholarship is open to high school seniors. To be considered for this award, you must be a current 4-H horse member who is planning to enroll in the fall semester at Ohio State University in any course of study. Award requirements change regularly. Please send a self-addressed, stamped envelope to receive your application and any further instructions from the scholarship provider. No GPA requirement specified.

Ohio State University
Financial Aid, Lincoln Tower
1800 Cannon Drive, Office 517
Columbus, OH 43210-1230

2295
Ashley Brittany Calhoon 4-H Leadership Scholarship

AMOUNT: $500 DEADLINE: Varies
MAJOR: All Areas of Study

The Ashley Brittany Calhoon 4-H Leadership Scholarship is open to 4-H members who are seniors in high school during the year of application. You are a preferred candidate if you are from Franklin County, Ohio. Award requirements change regularly. Please send a self-addressed, stamped envelope to receive your application and any further instructions from the scholarship provider, or email them at finaid@fa.adm.ohio-state.edu. No GPA requirement specified.

Ohio State University
Financial Aid, Lincoln Tower
1800 Cannon Drive, Office 517
Columbus, OH 43210-1230

2296
Bea Cleveland 4-H Scholarship

AMOUNT: $1000 DEADLINE: Varies
MAJOR: College of Human Ecology

The Bea Cleveland 4-H Scholarship is open to 4-H members who are seniors in high school during the year of application. You must be planning to enroll as a freshman for the autumn quarter in the College of Human Ecology at Ohio State University, Columbus, or any of its regional campuses. Award requirements change regularly. Please send a self-addressed, stamped envelope to receive your application and any further instructions from the scholarship provider, or email them at finaid@fa.adm.ohio-state.edu. No GPA requirement specified.

Ohio State University
Financial Aid, Lincoln Tower
1800 Cannon Drive, Office 517
Columbus, OH 43210-1230

2297
Bob Evans Farms 4-H Scholarship

AMOUNT: $1000 DEADLINE: Varies
MAJOR: Natural Resources

The Bob Evans Farms 4-H Scholarship is open to 4-H members who are seniors in high school during the year of application. You must be planning to enroll in the College of Food, Agricultural and Environmental Sciences at Ohio State University in the autumn quarter. You are a preferred candidate if you are a natural resources major. Award requirements change regularly. Please send a self-addressed, stamped envelope to receive your application and any further instructions from the scholarship provider, or email them at finaid@fa.adm.ohio-state.edu. No GPA requirement specified.

Ohio State University
Financial Aid, Lincoln Tower
1800 Cannon Drive, Office 517
Columbus, OH 43210-1230

2298
Freshman Foundation Program

AMOUNT: None Specified DEADLINE: Varies
MAJOR: All Areas of Study

The Freshman Foundation Program is open to freshmen at OSU who are Ohio residents with a minimum 2.7 GPA. You must be African-American, Appalachian-American, Asian-American, Hispanic-American, or Native-American to qualify to receive this award. Your final selection is based on financial need. Award requirements change regularly. Please send a self-addressed, stamped envelope to receive your application and any further instructions from the scholarship provider. GPA must be 2.7-4.0.

Ohio State University
Financial Aid, Lincoln Tower
1800 Cannon Drive, Office 517
Columbus, OH 43210-1230

2299
Henderson Family 4-H Scholarship

AMOUNT: $500 DEADLINE: Varies
MAJOR: All Areas of Study

The Henderson Family 4-H Scholarship is open to high school seniors. To be considered for the award, you must be a 4-H member attending or planning to attend Ohio State University in the fall. Award requirements change regularly. Please send a self-addressed, stamped envelope to receive your application and any further instructions from the scholarship provider, or email them at finaid@fa.adm.ohio-state.edu. No GPA requirement specified.

Ohio State University
Financial Aid, Lincoln Tower
1800 Cannon Drive, Office 517
Columbus, OH 43210-1230

2300
John L. Ryant 4-H Scholarship

AMOUNT: $1000 DEADLINE: Varies
MAJOR: College of Food, Agricultural and Environmental Sciences

The John L. Ryant 4-H Scholarship is open to high school seniors who are 4-H members enrolled in the College of Food, Agricultural and Environmental Sciences at Ohio State University in the fall. Preference is given to residents of Delaware County, Ohio, who demonstrate qualities of leadership. Award requirements change regularly. Please send a self-addressed, stamped envelope to receive your application and any further instructions from the scholarship provider, or email them at finaid@fa.adm.ohio-state.edu. You may browse through the sponsor website: www.ag.ohio-state.edu/. No GPA requirement specified.

Ohio State University
Financial Aid, Lincoln Tower
1800 Cannon Drive, Office 517
Columbus, OH 43210-1230

2301
Jonard Family 4-H Scholarship

AMOUNT: $1000 DEADLINE: Varies
MAJOR: All Areas of Study

The Jonard Family 4-H Scholarship is open to high school seniors who are present or former 4-H members attending or planning to attend Ohio State University in the fall. You are a preferred candidate if you are a resident of Harrison, Jefferson, and Delaware Counties in Ohio. Award requirements change regularly. Please send a self-addressed, stamped envelope to receive your application and any further instructions from the scholarship provider or email them at finaid@fa.adm.ohio-state.edu. No GPA requirement specified.

Ohio State University
Financial Aid, Lincoln Tower
1800 Cannon Drive, Office 517
Columbus, OH 43210-1230

2302
Kathryn Beich 4-H Scholarship

AMOUNT: $500 DEADLINE: Varies
MAJOR: All Areas of Study

The Kathryn Beich 4-H Scholarship is open to current 4-H members. To be considered for the award, you must reside within one of the counties participating in a Nestle-Beich candy fund-raising program. Award requirements change regularly. Please send a self-addressed, stamped envelope to receive your application and any further instructions from the scholarship provider, or email them at finaid@fa.adm.ohio-state.edu. No GPA requirement specified.

Ohio State University
Financial Aid, Lincoln Tower
1800 Cannon Drive, Office 517
Columbus, OH 43210-1230

2303
Mabel Sarbaugh 4-H Scholarship

AMOUNT: $1000 DEADLINE: Varies
MAJOR: College of Human Ecology

The Mabel Sarbaugh 4-H Scholarship is open to 4-H members who are seniors in high school planning to enroll in the College of Human Ecology for the Autumn Quarter as freshmen at Ohio State University or any of its regional campuses. Award requirements change regularly. Please send a self-addressed, stamped envelope to receive your application and any further instructions from the scholarship provider. You may browse through the sponsor website: www.ag.ohio-state.edu/. No GPA requirement specified.

Ohio State University
Financial Aid, Lincoln Tower
1800 Cannon Drive, Office 517
Columbus, OH 43210-1230

2304
Mary E. Border Ohio 4-H Scholarship

AMOUNT: $1000 DEADLINE: Varies
MAJOR: All Areas of Study

The Mary E. Border Ohio 4-H Scholarship is open to high school seniors. To be considered for the award, you must be a current 4-H horse member who is planning to enroll in the fall at Ohio State University. The course of study you choose will have no bearing on your scholarship eligibility. Award requirements change regularly. Please send a self-addressed, stamped envelope to receive your application and any further instructions from the scholarship provider, or email them at finaid@fa.adm.ohio-state.edu. No GPA requirement specified.

Ohio State University
Financial Aid, Lincoln Tower
1800 Cannon Drive, Office 517
Columbus, OH 43210-1230

2305
Minority Scholars Distinction Scholarship

AMOUNT: $12900 DEADLINE: December 15
MAJOR: All Areas of Study

The Minority Scholars Distinction Scholarship is open to incoming freshmen admitted to OSU who have a minimum 3.75 GPA and rank in the top 5% of their high school graduating class. To be considered for the award, you must be African-American, Asian-American, Hispanic-American, or Native-American. The award includes full in-state tuition, room and board, book allowance, and miscellaneous expenses. Award requirements change regularly. Please send a self-addressed, stamped envelope to receive your application and any further instructions from the scholarship provider.

Ohio State University
Financial Aid, Lincoln Tower
1800 Cannon Drive, Office 517
Columbus, OH 43210-1230

2306
Minority Scholars Excellence Scholarship

AMOUNT: $4137 DEADLINE: December 15
MAJOR: All Areas of Study

The Minority Scholars Excellence Scholarship is open to incoming freshmen admitted to OSU. You qualify if you have a minimum 3.0 GPA and rank in the top 20% of your high school graduating class. To be considered, you must also be African-American, Asian-American, Hispanic-American, or Native-American. The award includes full in-state tuition. Award requirements change regularly. Please send a self-addressed, stamped envelope to receive your application and any further instructions from the scholarship provider. GPA must be 3.0-4.0

Ohio State University
Financial Aid, Lincoln Tower
1800 Cannon Drive, Office 517
Columbus, OH 43210-1230

2307
Minority Scholars Prestigious Scholarship

AMOUNT: $4637 DEADLINE: December 15
MAJOR: All Areas of Study

The Minority Scholars Prestigious Scholarship is open to incoming freshmen admitted to OSU. You qualify if you have a minimum 3.5 GPA and rank in the top 10% of your high school graduating class. You must also be African-American, Asian-American, Hispanic-American, or Native-American. The award includes full in-state tuition and an additional $500. Award requirements change regularly. Please send a self-addressed, stamped envelope to receive your application and any further instructions from the scholarship provider. GPA must be 3.5-4.0.

Ohio State University
Financial Aid, Lincoln Tower
1800 Cannon Drive, Office 517
Columbus, OH 43210-1230

Minority Scholars Program

AMOUNT: None Specified DEADLINE: December 15
MAJOR: All Areas of Study

The Minority Scholars Program is open to African-Americans, Asian-Americans, Hispanics, or Native-Americans who are attending the Ohio State University, Columbus campus. Your selection is based on test scores, extracurricular activities, and leadership potential. Award requirements change regularly. Please send a self-addressed, stamped envelope to receive your application and any further instructions from the scholarship provider. No GPA requirement specified.

Ohio State University
Financial Aid, Lincoln Tower
1800 Cannon Drive, Office 517
Columbus, OH 43210-1230

2309
Mr. and Mrs. G. Deming Seymour Scholarship

AMOUNT: $1000 DEADLINE: Varies
MAJOR: All Areas of Study

The Mr. and Mrs. G. Deming Seymour Scholarship is open to 4-H members who are seniors in high school planning to enroll as freshmen in the fall at Ohio State University or Mansfield Regional Campus in any academic area. Preference will be given to residents of Richland County, Ohio. Award requirements change regularly. Please send a self-addressed, stamped envelope to receive your application and any further instructions from the scholarship provider, or email them at finaid@fa.adm.ohio-state.edu. You may also consult the website: www.ag.ohio-state.edu/. No GPA requirement specified.

Ohio State University
Financial Aid, Lincoln Tower
1800 Cannon Drive, Office 517
Columbus, OH 43210-1230

2310
OSU Campus Scholarship

AMOUNT: None Specified DEADLINE: Varies
MAJOR: All Areas of Study

The OSU Campus Scholarship is open to sophomores at the Ohio State University, Columbus campus. To be considered for this award, you must have completed your freshman year. The award also requires that you demonstrate academic excellence. Award requirements change regularly. For further information, please write to the address listed, including a self-addressed, stamped envelope. No GPA requirement specified.

Ohio State University
Financial Aid, Lincoln Tower
1800 Cannon Drive, Office 517
Columbus, OH 43210-1230

2311
OSU Distinction Scholarship

AMOUNT: $12900 DEADLINE: December 15
MAJOR: All Areas of Study

The OSU Distinction Scholarship is open to African-Americans, Asian-Americans, Hispanics, or Native-Americans who are attending the Ohio State University, Columbus campus. To be considered for the award, you must have a minimum 3.75 GPA and average in the top 5% of your high school graduating class. The award is for full in-state tuition, room and board, book allowance, and miscellaneous expenses. Award requirements change regularly. For further information, please write to the address listed, including a self-addressed, stamped envelope. GPA must be 3.75-4.0.

Ohio State University
Financial Aid, Lincoln Tower
1800 Cannon Drive, Office 517
Columbus, OH 43210-1230

2312
OSU Excellence Scholarship

AMOUNT: $4137 DEADLINE: December 15
MAJOR: All Areas of Study

The OSU Excellence Scholarship is open to African-Americans, Asian-Americans, Hispanics, or Native-Americans who are attending the Ohio State University, Columbus campus. To be considered for the award, you must have a minimum 3.0 GPA and rank in the top 20% of your high school graduating class. The award is for full in-state tuition. Award requirements change regularly. For further information, please write to the address listed, including a self-addressed, stamped envelope. GPA must be 3.0-4.0.

Ohio State University
Financial Aid, Lincoln Tower
1800 Cannon Drive, Office 517
Columbus, OH 43210-1230

2313
OSU Prestigious Scholarship

AMOUNT: $4637 DEADLINE: December 15
MAJOR: All Areas of Study

The OSU Prestigious Scholarship is open to incoming students who are African-American, Asian-American, Hispanic, or Native-American who are attending the Ohio State University, Columbus campus. To be considered for the award, you must have a minimum 3.5 GPA and rank in the top 10% of your high school graduating class. The amount of the award is for full in-state tuition and an additional $500. Award requirements change regularly. For further information, please write to the address listed, including a self-addressed, stamped envelope. GPA must be 3.5-4.0.

Ohio State University
Financial Aid, Lincoln Tower
1800 Cannon Drive, Office 517
Columbus, OH 43210-1230

2314
Scarlet and Gray Scholarship

AMOUNT: None Specified DEADLINE: Varies
MAJOR: All Areas of Study

The Scarlet and Gray Scholarship is open to entering freshmen and continuing students at the Ohio State University, Columbus campus. The amount of the award will be based on your financial need. If you were a recipient of the University, Trustees, and/or Campus Scholarship, you may be eligible for this award. Award requirements change regularly. For further information, please write to the address listed, including a self-addressed, stamped envelope. No GPA requirement specified.

Ohio State University
Financial Aid, Lincoln Tower
1800 Cannon Drive, Office 517
Columbus, OH 43210-1230

2315
University Scholarship

AMOUNT: $1200 DEADLINE: Varies
MAJOR: All Areas of Study

The University Scholarship is open to incoming freshmen admitted to Ohio State University. To be qualified to receive this award, you must rank in the top 3% of your high school graduating class. The award also requires that you possess a minimum ACT score of 29 or SAT score of 1300. Award requirements change regularly. For further information, please write to the address listed, including a self-addressed, stamped envelope. No GPA requirement specified.

Ohio State University
Financial Aid, Lincoln Tower
1800 Cannon Drive, Office 517
Columbus, OH 43210-1230

2316
Vance Family 4-H Scholarship

AMOUNT: $1000 DEADLINE: Varies
MAJOR: Agriculture, Home Economics

The Vance Family 4-H Scholarship is open to students who are present or former 4-H members currently enrolled or planning to enroll in the fall at Ohio State University, ATI, or any of its regional campuses, majoring in home economics or agriculture. Award requirements change regularly. Please send a self-addressed, stamped envelope to receive your application and any further instructions from the scholarship provider, or email them at finaid@fa.adm.ohio-state.edu. You may consult the sponsor website: www.ag.ohio-state.edu/. No GPA requirement specified.

Ohio State University
Financial Aid, Lincoln Tower
1800 Cannon Drive, Office 517
Columbus, OH 43210-1230

2317
William E. Goos Memorial Scholarship

AMOUNT: $1000 DEADLINE: Varies
MAJOR: All Areas of Study

The William E. Goos Memorial Scholarship is open to high school seniors who are 4-H members attending or planning to attend Ohio State University during the autumn quarter. You are a preferred candidate if you are a resident of Butler, Preble, and Hamilton Counties in Ohio. You can reapply for this scholarship after freshman year. Award requirements change regularly. Please send a self-addressed, stamped envelope to receive your application and any further instructions from the scholarship provider, or email them at finaid@fa.adm.ohio-state.edu. No GPA requirement specified.

Ohio State University
Financial Aid, Lincoln Tower
1800 Cannon Drive, Office 517
Columbus, OH 43210-1230

PacE University

2318
President's Scholarship

AMOUNT: None Specified DEADLINE: Varies
MAJOR: All Areas of Study

The President's Scholarship is open to entering students enrolled full-time in an undergraduate degree program at Pace University. This award is based on your academic record and scholarship interview. Priority is given to you if you have completed the application process, filed a FAFSA by February 8, and participated in the Scholarship Weekend the last weekend in February. Renewal is automatic provided you maintain a minimum 3.0 GPA and full-time status. This award is for incoming freshmen and transfer students. Award requirements change regularly. For an application and further information, please send a self-addressed, stamped envelope to the address provided, or call (914) 773-3200. No GPA requirement specified.

Pace University
Office of Student Financial Aid
861 Bedford Road
Pleasantville, NY 10570-2700

Pacific Lutheran University

2319
PLU Matching Scholarships (PLUMS)

AMOUNT: $100-$1000 DEADLINE: Varies
MAJOR: All Areas of Study

The PLU Matching Scholarships are open to full-time undergraduates attending PLU who have received scholarships between $100 to $1,000 from any Christian church congregation. Award requirements change regularly. Please send a self-addressed, stamped envelope to receive your application and any further instructions from the scholarship provider, or call (253) 535-7151. No GPA requirement specified.

Pacific Lutheran University
Attn: Scholarship Coordinator
Office of Admissions
Tacoma, WA 98447

Parsons School of Design

2320
Adolf Klein Scholarship

AMOUNT: None Specified DEADLINE: Varies
MAJOR: Fashion Design

The Adolf Klein Scholarship is open to senior fashion design students at Parsons School of Design. Award requirements change regularly. If you meet the criteria of this award or any other restricted scholarship/award(s), please write to the Office of Financial Aid and enclose a self-addressed, stamped envelope to receive any further instructions; or visit the website at www.parsons.edu. No GPA requirement specified.

Parsons School of Design
Attn: Office of Financial Aid
65 Fifth Avenue
New York, NY 10003

2321
Alice Robinson Student Scholarship and Loan Fund

AMOUNT: None Specified DEADLINE: Varies
MAJOR: All Fields of Study at Parsons

The Alice Robinson Student Scholarship and Loan Fund awards aid to students at Parsons School of Design. To be considered for financial aid from Parsons, you must complete the FAFSA and any other requested application forms by April 1 for fall semester (priority deadline) and December 1 for spring semester. Award requirements change regularly. Applicants for financial aid will be considered for all scholarships but may wish to express their interest in particular awards. If you meet the criteria of this award or any other restricted scholarship/award(s), please write to the Office of Financial Aid and enclose a self-addressed, stamped envelope to receive any further instructions; or visit the website at www.parsons.edu. No GPA requirement specified.

Parsons School of Design
Attn: Office of Financial Aid
65 Fifth Avenue
New York, NY 10003

2322
Anatol Shulkin Memorial Scholarship

AMOUNT: None Specified DEADLINE: Varies
MAJOR: Fine Arts

The Anatol Shulkin Memorial Scholarship is open to undergraduate students at Parsons School of Design studying fine arts. To be considered for this award, you must be a resident of New York State, display artistic promise, and demonstrate financial need. Students requesting financial aid from Parsons must complete the FAFSA and any other requested application forms by April 1 for fall semester (priority deadline) and December 1 for spring semester. Award requirements change regularly. Applicants for financial aid will be considered for all scholarships but may wish to express their interest in particular awards. If you meet the criteria of this award or any other restricted scholarship/award(s), please write to the Office of Financial Aid and enclose a self-addressed, stamped envelope to receive any further instructions; or visit the website at www.parsons.edu. No GPA requirement specified.

Parsons School of Design
Attn: Office of Financial Aid
65 Fifth Avenue
New York, NY 10003

2323
Arnold and Sheila Aronson Scholarship

AMOUNT: None Specified DEADLINE: Varies
MAJOR: Fashion Design, Design Marketing, Environmental Design

The Arnold and Sheila Aronson Scholarship is open to undergraduate students at Parsons School of Design. This scholarship is awarded annually on the basis of financial need to students in fashion design, design marketing, and environmental design. To be considered for financial aid from Parsons, you must complete the FAFSA and any other requested application forms by April 1 for fall semester (priority deadline) and December 1 for spring semester. Award requirements change regularly. Applicants for financial aid will be considered for all scholarships but may wish to express their interest in particular awards. If you meet the criteria of this award or any other restricted scholarship/award(s), please write to the Office of Financial Aid and enclose a self-addressed, stamped envelope to receive any further instructions; or visit the website at www.parsons.edu. No GPA requirement specified.

Parsons School of Design
Attn: Office of Financial Aid
65 Fifth Avenue
New York, NY 10003

2324
Arthur Rothstein Photography Scholarship

AMOUNT: None Specified DEADLINE: Varies
MAJOR: Photography

The Arthur Rothstein Photography Scholarship is open to undergraduate students at Parsons School of Design. This scholarship is awarded annually to a photography student on the basis of merit, financial need, and the submission of a portfolio. To be considered for financial aid from Parsons, you must complete the FAFSA and any other requested application forms by April 1 for fall semester (priority deadline) and December 1 for spring semester. Award requirements change regularly. Applicants for financial aid will be considered for all scholarships but may wish to express their interest in particular awards. If you meet the criteria of this award or any other restricted scholarship/award(s), please write to the Office of Financial Aid and enclose a self-addressed, stamped envelope to receive any further instructions; or visit the website at www.parsons.edu. No GPA requirement specified.

Parsons School of Design
Attn: Office of Financial Aid
65 Fifth Avenue
New York, NY 10003

2325
Bernard and Erna Mechur Scholarship

AMOUNT: None Specified DEADLINE: Varies
MAJOR: All Fields of Study at Parsons

The Bernard and Erna Mechur Scholarship is open to students at Parsons School of Design who demonstrate merit and financial need. To be considered for financial aid from Parsons, you must complete the FAFSA and any other requested application forms by April 1 for fall semester (priority deadline) and December 1 for spring semester. Award requirements change regularly. Applicants for financial aid will be considered for all scholarships but may wish to express their interest in particular awards. If you meet the criteria of this award or any other restricted scholarship/award(s), please write to the Office of Financial Aid and enclose a self-addressed, stamped envelope to receive any further instructions; or visit the website at www.parsons.edu. No GPA requirement specified.

Parsons School of Design
Attn: Office of Financial Aid
65 Fifth Avenue
New York, NY 10003

2326
Betty and Malcolm B. Smith Scholarship Fund

AMOUNT: None Specified DEADLINE: Varies
MAJOR: All Fields of Study at Parsons

The Betty and Malcolm B. Smith Scholarship Fund is awarded to an undergraduate or graduate student at Parsons School of Design in any major who is physically disabled or visually or hearing impaired. Award requirements change regularly. If you meet the criteria of this award or any other restricted scholarship/award(s), please write to the Office of Financial Aid and enclose a self-addressed, stamped envelope to receive any further instructions; or visit the website at www.parsons.edu. No GPA requirement specified.

Parsons School of Design
Attn: Office of Financial Aid
65 Fifth Avenue
New York, NY 10003

2327
Brunschwig and Fils International Scholarship

AMOUNT: None Specified DEADLINE: Varies
MAJOR: Parsons Summer Program in Paris

The Brunschwig and Fils International Scholarship is open to students at Parsons School of Design. This scholarship provides assistance to students participating in the Parsons Summer Program in Paris. Award requirements change regularly. If you meet the criteria of this award or any other

restricted scholarship/award(s), please write to the Office of Financial Aid and enclose a self-addressed, stamped envelope to receive any further instructions; or visit the website at www.parsons.edu. No GPA requirement specified.

Parsons School of Design
Attn: Office of Financial Aid
65 Fifth Avenue
New York, NY 10003

2328
C.V. Starr Scholarship

AMOUNT: None Specified DEADLINE: Varies
MAJOR: All Fields of Study at Parsons

The C.V. Starr Scholarship is open to international undergraduate students at Parsons School of Design and is awarded on the basis of merit and financial need. Award requirements change regularly. If you meet the criteria of this award or any other restricted scholarship/award(s), please write to the Office of Financial Aid and enclose a self-addressed, stamped envelope to receive any further instructions; or visit the website at www.parsons.edu. No GPA requirement specified.

Parsons School of Design
Attn: Office of Financial Aid
65 Fifth Avenue
New York, NY 10003

2329
Carole Little Scholarship

AMOUNT: None Specified DEADLINE: Varies
MAJOR: Fashion Design

The Carole Little Scholarship is open to upperclassmen in the Fashion Design Department at Parsons School of Design. Award requirements change regularly. If you meet the criteria of this award or any other restricted scholarship/award(s), please write to the Office of Financial Aid and enclose a self-addressed, stamped envelope to receive any further instructions; or visit the website at www.parsons.edu. No GPA requirement specified.

Parsons School of Design
Attn: Office of Financial Aid
65 Fifth Avenue
New York, NY 10003

2330
Chaim Gross Sculpture Award

AMOUNT: None Specified DEADLINE: Varies
MAJOR: Sculpture

The Chaim Gross Sculpture Award is open to students in the MFA sculpture program at Parsons School of Design. Award requirements change regularly. If you meet the criteria of this award or any other restricted scholarship/award(s), please write to the Office of Financial Aid and enclose a self-addressed, stamped envelope to receive any further instructions; or visit the website at www.parsons.edu. No GPA requirement specified.

Parsons School of Design
Attn: Office of Financial Aid
65 Fifth Avenue
New York, NY 10003

2331
Chester Weinberg Scholarship

AMOUNT: None Specified DEADLINE: Varies
MAJOR: Fashion Design

The Chester Weinberg Scholarship is open to an outstanding senior studying fashion design at Parsons School of Design. Award requirements change regularly. If you meet the criteria of this award or any other restricted scholarship/award(s), please write to the Office of Financial Aid and enclose a self-addressed, stamped envelope to receive any further instructions; or visit the website at www.parsons.edu. No GPA requirement specified.

Parsons School of Design
Attn: Office of Financial Aid
65 Fifth Avenue
New York, NY 10003

2332
Cipe Pineles Scholarship in Communication Design

AMOUNT: None Specified DEADLINE: Varies
MAJOR: Communication Design

The Cipe Pineles Scholarship in Communication Design is open to undergraduate students at Parsons School of Design. This award provides partial assistance to students in the Communication Design Department and is based on design ability and financial need. To be considered for financial aid from Parsons, you must complete the FAFSA and any other requested application forms by April 1 for fall semester (priority deadline) and December 1 for spring semester. Award requirements change regularly. Applicants for financial aid will be considered for all scholarships but may wish to express their interest in particular awards. If you meet the criteria of this award or any other restricted scholarship/award(s), please write to the Office of Financial Aid and enclose a self-addressed, stamped envelope to receive any further instructions; or visit the website at www.parsons.edu. No GPA requirement specified.

Parsons School of Design
Attn: Office of Financial Aid
65 Fifth Avenue
New York, NY 10003

2333
David C. Levy Scholarship

AMOUNT: None Specified DEADLINE: Varies
MAJOR: All Fields of Study at Parsons

The David C. Levy Scholarship is open to students at Parsons School of Design. This scholarship is awarded annually and is based on merit and financial need. To be considered for financial aid from Parsons, you must complete the FAFSA and any other requested application forms by April 1 for fall semester (priority deadline) and December 1 for spring semester. Award requirements change regularly. Applicants for financial aid will be considered for all scholarships but may wish to express their interest in particular awards. If you meet the criteria of this award or any other restricted scholarship/award(s), please write to the Office of Financial Aid and enclose a self-addressed, stamped envelope to receive any further instruc

tions; or visit the website at www.parsons.edu. No GPA requirement specified.

Parsons School of Design
Attn: Office of Financial Aid
65 Fifth Avenue
New York, NY 10003

2334
David Warren Memorial Scholarship

AMOUNT: None Specified DEADLINE: Varies
MAJOR: Fashion Design

The David Warren Memorial Scholarship is open to students studying fashion design at Parsons School of Design. This award is based on merit and financial need. To be considered for financial aid from Parsons, you must complete the FAFSA and any other requested application forms by April 1 for fall semester (priority deadline) and December 1 for spring semester. Award requirements change regularly. Applicants for financial aid will be considered for all scholarships but may wish to express their interest in particular awards. If you meet the criteria of this award or any other restricted scholarship/award(s), please write to the Office of Financial Aid and enclose a self-addressed, stamped envelope to receive any further instructions; or visit the website at www.parsons.edu. No GPA requirement specified.

Parsons School of Design
Attn: Office of Financial Aid
65 Fifth Avenue
New York, NY 10003

2335
Designer Critics Scholarship Fund

AMOUNT: None Specified DEADLINE: Varies
MAJOR: Fashion Design

The Designer Critics Scholarship Fund is open to undergraduate students at Parsons School of Design. To be considered for this award, you must be an outstanding student in the Fashion Design Department. Award requirements change regularly. If you meet the criteria of this award or any other restricted scholarship/award(s), please write to the Office of Financial Aid and enclose a self-addressed, stamped envelope to receive any further instructions; or visit the website at www.parsons.edu. No GPA requirement specified.

Parsons School of Design
Attn: Office of Financial Aid
65 Fifth Avenue
New York, NY 10003

2336
Fashion Design Competition Scholarship

AMOUNT: None Specified DEADLINE: Varies
MAJOR: Fashion Design

The Fashion Design Competition Scholarships are open to undergraduate students at Parsons School of Design. The following companies present a design problem and award three finalists with scholarship money to be applied to their senior year: The Gap, Inc.; The Mohair Council; Hanes Hosiery; Lord and Taylor. The Gap, Inc., also arranges for the finalists to intern in their organization. Award requirements change regularly. If you meet the criteria of this award or any other restricted scholarship/award(s), please write to the Office of Financial Aid and enclose a self-addressed, stamped envelope to receive any further instructions; or visit the website at www.parsons.edu. No GPA requirement specified.

Parsons School of Design
Attn: Office of Financial Aid
65 Fifth Avenue
New York, NY 10003

2337
Gordon Parks Photography Award

AMOUNT: None Specified DEADLINE: Varies
MAJOR: Photography

The Gordon Parks Photography Award is open to undergraduate students at Parsons School of Design. This scholarship is awarded annually to a photography student on the basis of merit, financial need, and the submission of a portfolio. To be considered for financial aid from Parsons, you must complete the FAFSA and any other requested application forms by April 1 for fall semester (priority deadline) and December 1 for spring semester. Award requirements change regularly. Applicants for financial aid will be considered for all scholarships but may wish to express their interest in particular awards. If you meet the criteria of this award or any other restricted scholarship/award(s), please write to the Office of Financial Aid and enclose a self-addressed, stamped envelope to receive any further instructions; or visit the website at www.parsons.edu. No GPA requirement specified.

Parsons School of Design
Attn: Office of Financial Aid
65 Fifth Avenue
New York, NY 10003

2338
Inner-City Scholarship Fund in the Arts

AMOUNT: None Specified DEADLINE: Varies
MAJOR: Fields Leading to a Career in the Arts (Music, Visual Arts, Writing, Theater, Dance)

The Inner-City Scholarship Fund in the Arts is open to students at Parsons School of Design. The award provides assistance to students from low-income, inner-city neighborhoods in the U.S. who are entering any undergraduate degree program and are interested in pursing a career in the arts - music, visual arts, writing, theater, or dance. Recipients are selected by the Office of the President upon the recommendation of the Deans. Award requirements change regularly. If you meet the criteria of this award or any other restricted scholarship/award(s), please write to the Office of Financial Aid and enclose a self-addressed, stamped envelope to receive any further instructions; or visit the website at www.parsons.edu. No GPA requirement specified.

Parsons School of Design
Attn: Office of Financial Aid
65 Fifth Avenue
New York, NY 10003

2339
Isabel and Irving Tolkin Scholarship

AMOUNT: None Specified DEADLINE: Varies
MAJOR: Fashion Design

The Isabel and Irving Tolkin Scholarship is open to students studying fashion design at Parsons School of Design. This award is based on ability and financial need. To be considered for financial aid from Parsons, you must complete the FAFSA and any other requested application forms by April 1 for fall semester (priority deadline) and December 1 for spring semester. Award requirements change regularly. Applicants for financial aid will be considered for all scholarships but may wish to express their interest in particular awards. If you meet the criteria of this award or any other restricted scholarship/award(s), please write to the Office of Financial Aid and enclose a self-addressed, stamped envelope to receive any further instructions; or visit the website at www.parsons.edu. No GPA requirement specified.

Parsons School of Design
Attn: Office of Financial Aid
65 Fifth Avenue
New York, NY 10003

2340
Joan Steers Scholarship

AMOUNT: None Specified DEADLINE: Varies
MAJOR: Fashion Design

The Joan Steers Scholarship provides partial assistance to students in the Fashion Design Department at Parsons School of Design. Award requirements change regularly. If you meet the criteria of this award or any other restricted scholarship/award(s), please write to the Office of Financial Aid and enclose a self-addressed, stamped envelope to receive any further instructions; or visit the website at www.parsons.edu. No GPA requirement specified.

Parsons School of Design
Attn: Office of Financial Aid
65 Fifth Avenue
New York, NY 10003

2341
Joseph Breitenbach Photography Scholarship

AMOUNT: None Specified DEADLINE: Varies
MAJOR: Photography

The Joseph Breitenbach Photography Scholarship is open to undergraduate students at Parsons School of Design. This scholarship is awarded annually to a photography student on the basis of merit, financial need, and the submission of a portfolio. To be considered for financial aid from Parsons, you must complete the FAFSA and any other requested application forms by April 1 for fall semester (priority deadline) and December 1 for spring semester. Award requirements change regularly. Applicants for financial aid will be considered for all scholarships but may wish to express their interest in particular awards. If you meet the criteria of this award or any other restricted scholarship/award(s), please write to the Office of Financial Aid and enclose a self-addressed, stamped envelope to receive any further instructions; or visit the website at www.parsons.edu. No GPA requirement specified.

Parsons School of Design
Attn: Office of Financial Aid
65 Fifth Avenue
New York, NY 10003

2342
Katty Dunn Memorial Scholarship

AMOUNT: None Specified DEADLINE: Varies
MAJOR: Communication Design

The Katty Dunn Memorial Scholarship is open to undergraduate students at Parsons School of Design. The award is given to an outstanding student, generally a young woman, entering the first year of the Communication Design Department and is based on merit and financial need. The award may be renewed through the final year of study in the department. To be considered for financial aid from Parsons, you must complete the FAFSA and any other requested application forms by April 1 for fall semester (priority deadline) and December 1 for spring semester. Award requirements change regularly. Applicants for financial aid will be considered for all scholarships but may wish to express their interest in particular awards. If you meet the criteria of this award or any other restricted scholarship/award(s), please write to the Office of Financial Aid and enclose a self-addressed, stamped envelope to receive any further instructions; or visit the website at www.parsons.edu. No GPA requirement specified.

Parsons School of Design
Attn: Office of Financial Aid
65 Fifth Avenue
New York, NY 10003

2343
Laverne Neil Scholarship

AMOUNT: None Specified DEADLINE: Varies
MAJOR: All Fields of Study at Parsons

The Laverne Neil Scholarship is open to students at Parsons School of Design who demonstrate merit and financial need. To be considered for financial aid from Parsons, you must complete the FAFSA and any other requested application forms by April 1 for fall semester (priority deadline) and December 1 for spring semester. Award requirements change regularly. Applicants for financial aid will be considered for all scholarships but may wish to express their interest in particular awards. If you meet the criteria of this award or any other restricted scholarship/award(s), please write to the Office of Financial Aid and enclose a self-addressed, stamped envelope to receive any further instructions; or visit the website at www.parsons.edu. No GPA requirement specified.

Parsons School of Design
Attn: Office of Financial Aid
65 Fifth Avenue
New York, NY 10003

2344
Lerman International Studies Award

AMOUNT: None Specified DEADLINE: Varies
MAJOR: Fashion Design

The Lerman International Studies Award is open to undergraduate students at Parsons School of Design. To be considered for this award, you must be a student in the Fashion Design Department and be recommended by the Chair of the department. This award is for study in the Parsons Summer Program in Paris. Award requirements change regularly. If you meet the criteria of this award or any other restricted scholarship/award(s), please write to the Office of Financial Aid and enclose a self-addressed, stamped envelope to receive any further instructions; or visit the website at www.parsons.edu. No GPA requirement specified.

Parsons School of Design
Attn: Office of Financial Aid
65 Fifth Avenue
New York, NY 10003

2345
Lester Martin Scholarship

AMOUNT: None Specified DEADLINE: Varies
MAJOR: Bachelor of Fine Arts Program

The Lester Martin Scholarship is open to undergraduate students in the BFA program at Parsons School of Design. Award requirements change regularly. If you meet the criteria of this award or any other restricted scholarship/award(s), please write to the Office of Financial Aid and enclose a self-addressed, stamped envelope to receive any further instructions; or visit the website at www.parsons.edu. No GPA requirement specified.

Parsons School of Design
Attn: Office of Financial Aid
65 Fifth Avenue
New York, NY 10003

2346
Marty Forscher Photography Award

AMOUNT: None Specified DEADLINE: Varies
MAJOR: Photography

The Marty Forscher Photography Award is open to undergraduate students at Parsons School of Design. The award provides financial assistance to a young, professional photographer who demonstrates a talent for humanistic photography. The recipient will present a lecture on his/her work to high school and junior college students. Award requirements change regularly. If you meet the criteria of this award or any other restricted scholarship/award(s), please write to the Office of Financial Aid and enclose a self-addressed, stamped envelope to receive any further instructions; or visit the website at www.parsons.edu. No GPA requirement specified.

Parsons School of Design
Attn: Office of Financial Aid
65 Fifth Avenue
New York, NY 10003

2347
Melanie Kahane Scholarship

AMOUNT: None Specified DEADLINE: Varies
MAJOR: All Fields of Study at Parsons

The Melanie Kahane Scholarships are for students at Parsons School of Design. These scholarships are awarded annually and are open to all applicants with financial need. To be considered for financial aid from Parsons, you must complete the FAFSA and any other requested application forms by April 1 for fall semester (priority deadline) and December 1 for spring semester. Award requirements change regularly. Applicants for financial aid will be considered for all scholarships but may wish to express their interest in particular awards. If you meet the criteria of this award or any other restricted scholarship/award(s), please write to the Office of Financial Aid and enclose a self-addressed, stamped envelope to receive any further instructions; or visit the website at www.parsons.edu. No GPA requirement specified.

Parsons School of Design
Attn: Office of Financial Aid
65 Fifth Avenue
New York, NY 10003

2348
NAMSB Foundation Award

AMOUNT: None Specified DEADLINE: Varies
MAJOR: Fashion Design

The NAMSB Foundation Award is open to undergraduates at Parsons School of Design. To be considered for this award, you must be a fashion design student who has demonstrated excellence in men's wear design. Award requirements change regularly. If you meet the criteria of this award or any other restricted scholarship/award(s), please write to the Office of Financial Aid and enclose a self-addressed, stamped envelope to receive any further instructions; or visit the website at www.parsons.edu. No GPA requirement specified.

Parsons School of Design
Attn: Office of Financial Aid
65 Fifth Avenue
New York, NY 10003

2349
Natalie R. Pion Scholarship

AMOUNT: None Specified DEADLINE: Varies
MAJOR: All Fields of Study at Parsons

The Natalie R. Pion Scholarship is open to students at Parsons School of Design who demonstrate merit and financial need. To be considered for financial aid from Parsons, you must complete the FAFSA and any other requested application forms by April 1 for fall semester (priority deadline) and December 1 for spring semester. Award requirements change regularly. Applicants for financial aid will be considered for all scholarships but may wish to express their interest in particular awards. If you meet the criteria of this award or any other restricted scholarship/award(s), please write to the Office of Financial Aid and enclose a self-addressed, stamped envelope to receive any further instructions; or visit the website at www.parsons.edu. No GPA requirement specified.

Parsons School of Design
Attn: Office of Financial Aid
65 Fifth Avenue
New York, NY 10003

2350
Oscar Kolin Fellowship Fund

AMOUNT: None Specified DEADLINE: Varies
MAJOR: Painting, Decorative Arts, Parsons Summer Program in Paris

The Oscar Kolin Fellowship Fund provides two distinct awards to students at Parsons School of Design. The first is awarded to an outstanding second-year student in the MFA painting program. The second award goes to a student in each of the following programs: the MFA painting program, the MFA decorative arts program, and the Parsons Summer Program in Paris. Selections for this second award are based on merit and financial need. To be considered for financial aid from Parsons, you must complete the FAFSA and any other requested application forms by April 1 for fall semester (priority deadline) and December 1 for spring semester. Award requirements change regularly. Applicants for financial aid will be considered for all scholarships but may wish to express their interest in particular awards. If you meet the criteria of this award or any other restricted scholarship/award(s), please write to the Office of Financial Aid and enclose a self-addressed, stamped envelope to receive any further instructions; or visit the website at www.parsons.edu. No GPA requirement specified.

Parsons School of Design
Attn: Office of Financial Aid
65 Fifth Avenue
New York, NY 10003

2351
Perry Ellis Scholarships I and II

AMOUNT: None Specified DEADLINE: Varies
MAJOR: Fashion Design

The Perry Ellis Scholarships I and II are two distinct awards for undergraduate students in the Fashion Design Department at Parsons School of Design. The first is awarded to an outstanding upperclassman. The second award goes to an outstanding student of any year who is recommended by the Chair of the department. Award requirements change regularly. If you meet the criteria of this award or any other restricted scholarship/award(s), please write to the Office of Financial Aid and enclose a self-addressed, stamped envelope to receive any further instructions; or visit the website at www.parsons.edu. No GPA requirement specified.

Parsons School of Design
Attn: Office of Financial Aid
65 Fifth Avenue
New York, NY 10003

2352
Richard Taubin Memorial Award

AMOUNT: $200-$500 DEADLINE: Varies
MAJOR: Design, Fine Arts, Photography, Illustration

The Richard Taubin Memorial Award is open to undergraduate students at Parsons School of Design. Recipients will be selected on the basis of a portfolio and academic record review by faculty. This award is supported by annual gifts from the Art Directors Club of New York. Award requirements change regularly. If you meet the criteria of this award or any other restricted scholarship/award(s), please write to the Office of Financial Aid and enclose a self-addressed, stamped envelope to receive any further instructions; or visit the website at www.parsons.edu. No GPA requirement specified.

Parsons School of Design
Attn: Office of Financial Aid
65 Fifth Avenue
New York, NY 10003

2353
Risa Blanche Sussman Scholarship Fund

AMOUNT: None Specified DEADLINE: Varies
MAJOR: Fine Arts in the Parsons Summer Program in Paris

The Risa Blanche Sussman Scholarship Fund is open to students studying fine arts in the Parsons School of Design Summer Program in Paris. This award is based on merit and financial need. To be considered for financial aid from Parsons, you must complete the FAFSA and any other requested application forms by April 1 for fall semester (priority deadline) and December 1 for spring semester. Award requirements change regularly. Applicants for financial aid will be considered for all scholarships but may wish to express their interest in particular awards. If you meet the criteria of this award or any other restricted scholarship/award(s), please write to the Office of Financial Aid and enclose a self-addressed, stamped envelope to receive any further instructions; or visit the website at www.parsons.edu. No GPA requirement specified.

Parsons School of Design
Attn: Office of Financial Aid
65 Fifth Avenue
New York, NY 10003

2354
Sanyo Shokai Ltd. Scholarship Fund

AMOUNT: None Specified DEADLINE: Varies
MAJOR: All Fields of Study at Parsons

The Sanyo Shokai Ltd. Scholarship Fund provides financial assistance to Japanese students studying at Parsons School of Design. Award requirements change regularly. If you meet the criteria of this award or any other restricted scholarship/award(s), please write to the Office of Financial Aid and enclose a self-addressed, stamped envelope to receive any further instructions; or visit the website at www.parsons.edu. No GPA requirement specified.

Parsons School of Design
Attn: Office of Financial Aid
65 Fifth Avenue
New York, NY 10003

2355
Sergeant Boyd W. Anderson Memorial Scholarship

AMOUNT: None Specified DEADLINE: Varies
MAJOR: Environmental Design

The Sergeant Boyd W. Anderson Memorial Scholarship is open to undergraduate students at Parsons School of Design. This scholarship is awarded annually to an outstanding environmental design student based on recommendations by the faculty of the Architecture & Environmental Design Department and the Scholarship Committee. Award requirements change regularly. If you meet the criteria of this award or any other restricted scholarship/award(s), please write to the Office of Financial Aid and enclose a self-addressed, stamped envelope to receive any further instructions; or visit the website at www.parsons.edu. No GPA requirement specified.

Parsons School of Design
Attn: Office of Financial Aid
65 Fifth Avenue
New York, NY 10003

2356
Stanley H. Curtis Scholarship Fund

AMOUNT: None Specified DEADLINE: Varies
MAJOR: All Fields of Study at Parsons

The Stanley H. Curtis Scholarship Fund is open to students at Parsons School of Design. This scholarship provides support based on merit and financial need. To be considered for financial aid from Parsons, you must complete the FAFSA and any other requested application forms by April 1 for fall semester (priority deadline) and December 1 for spring semester. Award requirements change regularly. Applicants for financial aid will be considered for all scholarships but may wish to express their interest in particular awards. If you meet the criteria of this award or any other restricted scholarship/award(s), please write to the Office of Financial Aid and enclose a self-addressed, stamped envelope to receive any further instructions; or visit the website at www.parsons.edu. No GPA requirement specified.

Parsons School of Design
Attn: Office of Financial Aid
65 Fifth Avenue
New York, NY 10003

2357
Thomas and Andrew Schultz Memorial Scholarship Fund

AMOUNT: None Specified DEADLINE: Varies
MAJOR: All Fields of Study at Parsons

The Thomas and Andrew Schultz Memorial Scholarship Fund provides financial assistance to students studying at Parsons School of Design. Award requirements change regularly. If you meet the criteria of this award or any other restricted scholarship/award(s), please write to the Office of Financial Aid and enclose a self-addressed, stamped envelope to receive any further instructions; or visit the website at www.parsons.edu. No GPA requirement specified.

Parsons School of Design
Attn: Office of Financial Aid
65 Fifth Avenue
New York, NY 10003

2358
University Scholars Program

AMOUNT: None Specified DEADLINE: Varies
MAJOR: All Fields of Study at Parsons

The University Scholars Program is open to selected minority students with financial need at Parsons School of Design. African-American and Hispanic applicants are encouraged to apply by requesting consideration, in writing, to the Committee on Admissions and Financial Aid. To be considered for financial aid from Parsons, you must complete the FAFSA and any other requested application forms by April 1 for fall semester (priority deadline) and December 1 for spring semester. Award requirements change regularly. Applicants for financial aid will be considered for all scholarships but may wish to express their interest in particular awards. If you meet the criteria of this award or any other restricted scholarship/award(s), please write to the Office of Financial Aid and enclose a self-addressed, stamped envelope to receive any further instructions; or visit the website at www.parsons.edu. No GPA requirement specified.

Parsons School of Design
Attn: Office of Financial Aid
65 Fifth Avenue
New York, NY 10003

Philadelphia College of Bible

2359
Alumni Award

AMOUNT: $1000 DEADLINE: Varies
MAJOR: All Areas of Study

The Alumni Award is open to dependent children of Philadelphia College of Bible graduates. This award is divided into each semester. Award requirements change regularly. Please send a self-addressed, stamped envelope to receive your application and any further instructions from the scholarship provider. No GPA requirement specified.

Philadelphia College of Bible
Financial Aid Department
200 Manor Avenue
Langhorne, PA 19047-2943

2360
Canadian Award

AMOUNT: None Specified DEADLINE: Varies
MAJOR: All Areas of Study

The Canadian Award is open to full-time Canadian students attending Philadelphia College of Bible. There is a rate-of-exchange discount for this award at the beginning of each semester. Award requirements change regularly. Please send a self-addressed, stamped envelope to receive your application and any further instructions from the scholarship provider. No GPA requirement specified.

Philadelphia College of Bible
Financial Aid Department
200 Manor Avenue
Langhorne, PA 19047-2943

2361
Christian Worker Award

AMOUNT: Maximum: $7317 DEADLINE: Varies
MAJOR: All Areas of Study

The Christian Worker Award is open to dependent children of full-time Christian workers who are the heads of the household. A 50% discount is awarded on the student's tuition and room and board charges, which is equivalent to up to $7,317. The student must attend Philadelphia College of Bible. The Free Application for Federal Student Aid form must be filled out prior to the first day of enrollment. Award requirements change regularly. Please send a self-addressed, stamped envelope to receive your application and any further instructions from the scholarship provider. No GPA requirement specified.

Philadelphia College of Bible
Financial Aid Department
200 Manor Avenue
Langhorne, PA 19047-2943

2362
Church Matching Grant

AMOUNT: Maximum: $500 DEADLINE: August 15
MAJOR: All Areas of Study

The Church Matching Grant is open to students who are enrolled at Philadelphia College of Bible. Applicants who receive gifts from their home church will have that amount matched with the college's fund up to $500 annually. Award requirements change regularly. Please send a self-addressed, stamped envelope to receive your application and any further instructions from the scholarship provider. No GPA requirement specified.

Philadelphia College of Bible
Financial Aid Department
200 Manor Avenue
Langhorne, PA 19047-2943

2363
Dean's Scholar Award

AMOUNT: $1000 DEADLINE: Varies
MAJOR: All Areas of Study

The Dean's Scholar Award is open to first-year, full-time freshman students entering Philadelphia College of Bible, whose SAT score is 1100 or above, or whose composite ACT score is a 23 or above. The applicant must be enrolled in an academic program in high school with a minimum GPA of 3.0. Students must achieve a 3.0 cumulative GPA by the end of their first year and by the end of each subsequent semester to retain the scholarship. Award requirements change regularly. Please send a self-addressed, stamped envelope to receive your application and any further instructions from the scholarship provider. GPA must be 3.0-4.0.

Philadelphia College of Bible
Financial Aid Department
200 Manor Avenue
Langhorne, PA 19047-2943

2364
Dean's Scholar Award for Transfer Students

AMOUNT: $1000 DEADLINE: Varies
MAJOR: All Areas of Study

The Dean's Scholar Award for Transfer Students is open to full-time students who transfer from another college/university to enter Philadelphia College of Bible. Applicants who have completed 30 or more semester hours and have a GPA of 3.0 are eligible. Students must achieve a 3.0 cumulative GPA by the end of their first year and by the end of each subsequent semester to retain the scholarship. Award requirements change regularly. Please send a self-addressed, stamped envelope to receive your application and any further instructions from the scholarship provider. GPA must be 3.0-4.0.

Philadelphia College of Bible
Financial Aid Department
200 Manor Avenue
Langhorne, PA 19047-2943

2365
Distinguished Christian High School Student Scholarship

AMOUNT: $1000 DEADLINE: Varies
MAJOR: All Areas of Study

The Distinguished Christian High School Student Scholarship is open to students who attend Philadelphia College of Bible. Applicants must be nominated by their Christian high school as being distinguished in their junior or senior year. A nomination from the Association of Christian Schools International is also required. This award is divided into each semester. Award requirements change regularly. Please send a self-addressed, stamped envelope to receive your application and any further instructions from the scholarship provider. No GPA requirement specified.

Philadelphia College of Bible
Financial Aid Department
200 Manor Avenue
Langhorne, PA 19047-2943

2366
Family Award

AMOUNT: $800-$1200 DEADLINE: Varies
MAJOR: All Areas of Study

The Family Award is available to additional students who are dependent children from the same family attending Philadelphia College of Bible simultaneously. This award does not apply to married students. Award requirements change regularly. Please send a self-addressed, stamped envelope to receive your application and any further instructions from the scholarship provider. No GPA requirement specified.

Philadelphia College of Bible
Financial Aid Department
200 Manor Avenue
Langhorne, PA 19047-2943

2367
Home Schooler's Award

AMOUNT: $1000 DEADLINE: Varies
MAJOR: All Areas of Study

The Home Schooler's Award is open to full-time students who have completed at least their junior and senior years as home-schooled students. Applicants must attend Philadelphia College of Bible. This award is not renewable. Award requirements change regularly. Please send a self-addressed, stamped envelope to receive your application and any further instructions from the scholarship provider. No GPA requirement specified.

Philadelphia College of Bible
Financial Aid Department
200 Manor Avenue
Langhorne, PA 19047-2943

2368
Jack Turney Discover Your Mind Scholarship

AMOUNT: $250 DEADLINE: Varies
MAJOR: All Areas of Study

The Jack Turney Discover Your Mind Scholarship is open to students who memorize the book of Galatians. The applicant must be a student at Philadelphia College of Bible. Award requirements change regularly. Please send a self-addressed, stamped envelope to receive your application and any further instructions from the scholarship provider. No GPA requirement specified.

Philadelphia College of Bible
Financial Aid Department
200 Manor Avenue
Langhorne, PA 19047-2943

2369
Merit Scholarship

AMOUNT: None Specified DEADLINE: Varies
MAJOR: All Areas of Study

The Merit Scholarship is open to students who will attend Philadelphia College of Bible. This award is based on need and recognition of outstanding achievement. The scholarship is divided into each semester and is not renewable. Award requirements change regularly. Please send a self-addressed, stamped envelope to receive your application and any further instructions from the scholarship provider. No GPA requirement specified.

Philadelphia College of Bible
Financial Aid Department
200 Manor Avenue
Langhorne, PA 19047-2943

Music Competition Scholarship

AMOUNT: $3000-$15000 DEADLINE: Varies
MAJOR: Voice, Piano, Organ, Strings, Brass, Woodwinds, Percussion, and Composition

The Music Competition Scholarship is open to music majors entering Philadelphia College of Bible with an interest in the categories of voice, piano, organ, strings, brass, woodwinds, percussion, or composition. One-fifth of the award is applied toward the students' tuition each year they remain in the music program. An audition with the Music Department is required. Award requirements change regularly. Please send a self-addressed, stamped envelope to receive your application and any further instructions from the scholarship provider. No GPA requirement specified.

Philadelphia College of Bible
Financial Aid Department
200 Manor Avenue
Langhorne, PA 19047-2943

2371
Pioneer Caterers Award

AMOUNT: $250 DEADLINE: Varies
MAJOR: All Areas of Study

The Pioneer Caterers Award is available to full-time Philadelphia College of Bible students working for the college dining commons at least two consecutive semesters. Scholarships are awarded during finals week. Award requirements change regularly. Please send a self-addressed, stamped envelope to receive your application and any further instructions from the scholarship provider. No GPA requirement specified.

Philadelphia College of Bible
Financial Aid Department
200 Manor Avenue
Langhorne, PA 19047-2943

2372
President's Scholarship

AMOUNT: $2400 DEADLINE: Varies
MAJOR: All Areas of Study

The President's Scholarship is open to first-year, full-time freshmen entering Philadelphia College of Bible with an SAT score of 1180 or above or whose composite ACT is at least 25. The applicant must be enrolled in an academic program in high school and have at least a 3.5 GPA. Students must achieve a 3.0 cumulative GPA by the end of their first year and by the end of each subsequent semester to retain the scholarship. Award requirements change regularly. Please send a self-addressed, stamped envelope to receive your application and any further instructions from the scholarship provider. GPA must be 3.5-4.0.

Philadelphia College of Bible
Financial Aid Department
200 Manor Avenue
Langhorne, PA 19047-2943

2373
Raymond G. and Ada M. Cornelius Scholarship

AMOUNT: $200-$800 DEADLINE: April 30
MAJOR: All Areas of Study

The Raymond G. and Ada M. Cornelius Scholarship is open to students enrolled at Philadelphia College of Bible who contribute positively to student life and maintain at least a 2.0 GPA. This award is based on financial need. Award requirements change regularly. Please send a self-addressed, stamped envelope to receive your application and any further instructions from the scholarship provider. GPA must be 2.0-4.0.

Philadelphia College of Bible
Financial Aid Department
200 Manor Avenue
Langhorne, PA 19047-2943

2374
Samuel and Mary Jeffries and Daniel F. Smith's Leadership Scholarship

AMOUNT: $200-$1000 DEADLINE: Varies
MAJOR: All Areas of Study

The Samuel and Mary Jeffries and Daniel F. Smith's Leadership Scholarship is open to freshman and transfer full-time students entering Philadelphia College of Bible. Applicants must meet all of the enrollment requirements and be outstanding leaders in academic, extracurricular, church, or community endeavors. Applicants must maintain a cumulative 2.5 GPA each semester and submit a renewal application demonstrating leadership in at least one area of the college to retain the scholarship. Award requirements change regularly. Please send a self-addressed, stamped envelope to receive your application and any further instructions from the scholarship provider. The application must be submitted prior to the first day of enrollment. GPA must be 2.5-4.0.

Philadelphia College of Bible
Financial Aid Department
200 Manor Avenue
Langhorne, PA 19047-2943

2375
Top Bible Graduate Scholarship

AMOUNT: $1000 DEADLINE: Varies
MAJOR: All Areas of Study

The Top Bible Graduate Scholarship is open to graduating seniors from Christian high schools who have demonstrated excellence in Bible courses and who attend Philadelphia College of Bible. A recommendation from a high school administrator is required. This award is not renewable. Award requirements change regularly. Please send a self-addressed, stamped envelope to receive your application and any further instructions from the scholarship provider. No GPA requirement specified.

Philadelphia College of Bible
Financial Aid Department
200 Manor Avenue
Langhorne, PA 19047-2943

2376
Transfer Scholarship

AMOUNT: $1000-$2000 DEADLINE: Varies
MAJOR: All Areas of Study

The Transfer Scholarship is available to students transferring from New Jersey Campus, Ravencrest Chalet, Wisconsin Wilderness Campus, or Word of Life Bible Institute to Philadelphia College of Bible. This award is based on academic performance, personal motivation for ministry, and financial aid. This award is divided into each semester. Award requirements change regularly. Please send a self-addressed, stamped envelope to receive your application and any further instructions from the scholarship provider. No GPA requirement specified.

Philadelphia College of Bible
Financial Aid Department
200 Manor Avenue
Langhorne, PA 19047-2943

2377
W. W. Smith Charitable Trust

AMOUNT: $2000 DEADLINE: Varies
MAJOR: All Areas of Study

The W.W. Smith Charitable Trust is available to full-time students who attend Philadelphia College of Bible. Applicants must meet the trust requirements. Students are selected by the college's Financial Aid Office. This award is based on financial need. Award requirements change regularly. Please send a self-addressed, stamped envelope to receive your application and any further instructions from the scholarship provider. No GPA requirement specified.

Philadelphia College of Bible
Financial Aid Department
200 Manor Avenue
Langhorne, PA 19047-2943

2378
Who's Who Scholarship

AMOUNT: $1000 DEADLINE: Varies
MAJOR: All Areas of Study

The Who's Who Scholarship is open to high school seniors listed in *Who's Who Among American High School Students* and who attend Philadelphia College of Bible immediately following graduation. This award is not renewable and is divided into each semester. A letter of recognition must be presented to the Financial Aid Office prior to the first date of enrollment. Award requirements change regularly. Please send a self-addressed, stamped envelope to receive your application and any further instructions from the scholarship provider. No GPA requirement specified.

Philadelphia College of Bible
Financial Aid Department
200 Manor Avenue
Langhorne, PA 19047-2943

Portland State University

2379
American Concrete Institute - Oregon Chapter

AMOUNT: $1000 DEADLINE: Varies
MAJOR: Engineering, Concrete Technology

This scholarship is open to students enrolled in at least nine hours with a minimum 2.5 GPA. The following will be considered in your application: financial need, residency/citizenship, enrollment in an applicable program, and contribution in the field of concrete technology. Award requirements change regularly. GPA must be 2.5-4.0.

Portland State University-Engineering
Civil Engineering Department
138 Science Building 2
Portland, OR 97207

2380
American Public Works - Oregon Section

AMOUNT: $1000 DEADLINE: May 1
MAJOR: Civil Engineering

This award is open to full-time students enrolled in the department of civil engineering at Portland State University. You must have been an Oregon resident for at least four years. Financial need is a consideration for this award. Award requirements change regularly. No GPA requirement specified.

Portland State University-Engineering
Civil Engineering Department
138 Science Building 2
Portland, OR 97207

2381
American Society of Civil Engineers Scholarship - Oregon Section

AMOUNT: $1500 DEADLINE: May 1
MAJOR: Civil Engineering

This award is open to full-time students at Portland State University enrolled in the Department of Civil Engineering who will complete their junior year in June of the year the application is made. You must have a minimum 3.0 GPA. Preference will be given to a student who has participated in ASCE Student Chapter activities. Award requirements change regularly. GPA must be 3.0-4.0.

Portland State University-Engineering
Civil Engineering Department
138 Science Building 2
Portland, OR 97207

2382
American Water Works Association Scholarship

AMOUNT: None Specified DEADLINE: May 1
MAJOR: Water Works

This scholarship is open to junior, senior, or first-year graduate students enrolled in courses directly relating to the water works field. The award covers tuition, books, and related fees. Awards are based on academic achievement, but there are no stated minimum requirements. Strong favor will be shown to those indicating interest in the water works field. Award requirements change regularly. No GPA requirement specified.

Portland State University-Engineering
Civil Engineering Department
138 Science Building 2
Portland, OR 97207

2383
Arthur M. James Scholarship

AMOUNT: $1500-$2000 DEADLINE: March 15
MAJOR: Engineering

This award is open to students who are accepted into the Civil Engineering Department as a junior or senior. You must be a U.S. citizen, show financial need, and have a GPA of 2.8 or higher. Some awards will give special preference to those specializing in structural engineering. Award requirements change regularly. GPA must be 2.8-4.0.

Portland State University-Engineering
Civil Engineering Department
138 Science Building 2
Portland, OR 97207

2384
Boeing Engineering Scholarship

AMOUNT: $3000 DEADLINE: March 15
MAJOR: Engineering

This scholarship is open to full-time undergraduate students at Portland State University who are majoring in engineering. You must have achieved or shown the potential to achieve satisfactory or better academic accomplishments. Other requirements include the authorization to work in the United States on a full-time basis for other than training. This award is not renewable. Award requirements change regularly. GPA must be 3.0-4.0.

Portland State University-Engineering/Applied Science
School of Engineering & Applied Science
4th Ave Bldg Suite 20
Portland, OR 92707-0751

2385
Carl E. Green Graduate Fellowship

AMOUNT: $1000 DEADLINE: May 1
MAJOR: Environmental Engineering, Geotechnical Engineering, Environmental Geology

This scholarship is open to graduate students specializing in environmental/geotechnical engineering or environmental geology. You must have a minimum 3.0 GPA, and demonstrate financial need and a potential for success in this area. Award requirements change regularly. GPA must be 3.0-4.0.

Portland State University-Engineering
Civil Engineering Department
138 Science Building 2
Portland, OR 97207

2386
CG Fanger Mechanical Engineering Scholarship

AMOUNT: $750 DEADLINE: March 15
MAJOR: Mechanical Engineering

This award is open to outstanding mechanical engineering students and is based on scholarship, potential for success, and financial need. Award requirements change regularly. No GPA requirement specified.

Portland State University-Engineering/Applied Science
School of Engineering & Applied Science
4th Ave Bldg Suite 20
Portland, OR 92707-0751

2387
Coral Sales Company/D.P. Daniels Civil Engineering Scholarship

AMOUNT: $800 DEADLINE: May 1
MAJOR: Highway/Transportation Engineering, Highway Construction

This scholarship is open to students who intend to pursue a career in highway/transportation engineering or highway construction. Demonstrated leadership qualities and participation in civic and professional activities will be considered. Evidence of your work experience in the highway/transportation field is also an asset. You must have lived in the Northwest for at least ten years and be a junior or senior in college. Two awards are offered annually. Award requirements change regularly. No GPA requirement specified.

Portland State University-Engineering/Applied Science
School of Engineering & Applied Science
4th Ave Bldg Suite 20
Portland, OR 92707-0751

2388
David Evans & Associates Civil Engineering Scholarship

AMOUNT: $1000 DEADLINE: May 1
MAJOR: Civil Engineering

This scholarship is open to students majoring in civil engineering at Portland State University. Requirements for this award include U.S. citizen or permanent residency, a minimum 3.0 GPA, and demonstration of financial need. Three awards are offered annually. Award requirements change regularly. GPA must be 3.0-4.0.

Portland State University-Engineering/Applied Science
School of Engineering & Applied Science
4th Ave Bldg Suite 20
Portland, OR 92707-0751

2389
Electrical Engineering Endowment

AMOUNT: None Specified DEADLINE: Varies
MAJOR: Electrical Engineering

At the end of the academic year the faculty nominates and awards the scholarship to a student who will be returning the following academic year to the undergraduate or graduate program in electrical engineering at Portland State University. Award requirements change regularly. For further information, please consult the Engineering and Applied Science Department. No GPA requirement specified.

Portland State University-Engineering/Applied Science
School of Engineering & Applied Science
4th Ave Bldg Suite 20
Portland, OR 92707-0751

2390
H.C.M Erzurumlu Scholarship

AMOUNT: None Specified DEADLINE: March 15
MAJOR: Engineering or Computer Science

The H.C.M. Erzurumlu Scholarship is open to upper division students majoring in engineering or computer science. Criteria for this award are based on academic excellence, financial need, and your potential for success. The award amount is for one year of resident tuition and fees. This award is not renewable. Award requirements change regularly. GPA must be 3.0-4.0.

Portland State University-Engineering/Applied Science
School of Engineering & Applied Science
4th Ave Bldg Suite 20
Portland, OR 92707-0751

2391
Harry J. and Rhoda White Scholarship

AMOUNT: None Specified DEADLINE: March 15
MAJOR: Engineering, Computer Science

The Harry J. and Rhoda White Scholarship is open to students majoring in engineering or computer science at Portland State University. The award is for one year of resident tuition and fees. Award requirements change regularly. No GPA requirement specified.

Portland State University-Engineering/Applied Science
School of Engineering & Applied Science
4th Ave Bldg Suite 20
Portland, OR 92707-0751

2392
Henry & Janice Schuette Engineering Scholarship

AMOUNT: $1200 DEADLINE: March 15
MAJOR: Engineering, Mechanical Engineering

The Henry & Janice Schuette Engineering Scholarship is open to engineering students at Portland State University. The award is based on academic achievement, financial need, and demonstration of leadership qualities in civic and professional activities. Preference will be given to those studying mechanical engineering. Award requirements change regularly. No GPA requirement specified.

Portland State University-Engineering/Applied Science
School of Engineering & Applied Science
4th Ave Bldg Suite 20
Portland, OR 92707-0751

2393
J. W. Coombs Scholarship

AMOUNT: $200 DEADLINE: March 15
MAJOR: Engineering

The J. W. Coombs Scholarship is open to engineering students at Portland State University. The recipient will be chosen from a pool of candidates by the Engineering and Applied Science scholarship committee. This award is not renewable. Award requirements change regularly. No GPA requirement specified.

Portland State University-Engineering/Applied Science
School of Engineering & Applied Science
4th Ave Bldg Suite 20
Portland, OR 92707-0751

2394
Julie & Bill Reiersgaard Mechanical Engineering Scholarship

AMOUNT: None Specified DEADLINE: March 15
MAJOR: Mechanical Engineering

This award is open to female students who are majoring in mechanical engineering, working part-time, and have a minimum 3.0 GPA. You must intend to remain in Oregon after graduation. Award requirements change regularly. GPA must be 3.0-4.0.

Portland State University-Engineering/Applied Science
School of Engineering & Applied Science
4th Ave Bldg Suite 20
Portland, OR 92707-0751

2395
LSI Logic Scholarship

AMOUNT: $2000 DEADLINE: March 15
MAJOR: Electrical Engineering, Computer Engineering, Mechanical Engineering, Computer Science

This scholarship is open to upper-division students pursuing a major in electrical engineering, computer engineering, computer science, or mechanical engineering. You must also be interested in working in the semiconductor field, including the fields of process, manufacturing, modeling, and/or circuit and systems design. Other requirements include U.S. citizenship or permanent residency and a minimum 3.0 GPA in both core courses and overall course work. Prior work history, financial need, and leadership experience in civic or professional associations will also be considered. Winners will be required to complete an internship at LSI as part of the award. This award may be renewable. Award requirements change regularly. GPA must be 3.0-4.0.

Portland State University-Engineering/Applied Science
School of Engineering & Applied Science
4th Ave Bldg Suite 20
Portland, OR 92707-0751

2396
Maria Balogh Scholarship

AMOUNT: $500 DEADLINE: March 15
MAJOR: Computer Science

The Maria Balogh Scholarship is open to undergraduate computer science students at Portland State University. Award requirements change regularly. No GPA requirement specified.

Portland State University
Department of Computer Science
120 PCAT Building
Portland, OR 97207

2397
PacifiCorp Environmental Engineering Scholarship

AMOUNT: $2000-$3000 DEADLINE: March 15
MAJOR: Environmental Engineering

This scholarship is open to students studying environmental engineering. One award is given to a graduate student, and one award is given to an undergraduate student. Award requirements change regularly. No GPA requirement specified.

Portland State University-Engineering
Civil Engineering Department
138 Science Building 2
Portland, OR 97207

2398
Professional Engineers of Oregon Scholarship

AMOUNT: $1000 DEADLINE: March 15
MAJOR: Engineering, Computer Science

The Professional Engineers of Oregon Scholarship is open to students majoring in engineering or computer science with upper division standing. You must have graduated from an Oregon high school, be an Oregon resident, and be a U.S. citizen. This award is not renewable. Award requirements change regularly. No GPA requirement specified.

Portland State University-Engineering/Applied Science
School of Engineering & Applied Science
4th Ave Bldg Suite 20
Portland, OR 92707-0751

2399
Richard Apfel Engineering Scholarship

AMOUNT: $2000 DEADLINE: March 15
MAJOR: Engineering

The Richard Apfel Engineering Scholarship is open to upper division engineering students at Portland State University. This award is not renewable. Award requirements change regularly. No GPA requirement specified.

Portland State University-Engineering/Applied Science
School of Engineering & Applied Science
4th Ave Bldg Suite 20
Portland, OR 92707-0751

2400
Structural Engineers Association of Oregon Scholarship

AMOUNT: $2100 DEADLINE: May 1
MAJOR: Structural Engineering

This scholarship is open to students who are specializing in structural engineering and will complete their junior year in June of the year the application is made. You must also have been an Oregon resident for at least four years prior to receiving the award. Other requirements include a minimum 3.0 GPA, U.S. citizenship, and demonstration of financial need. Award requirements change regularly. GPA must be 3.0-4.0.

Portland State University-Engineering
Civil Engineering Department
138 Science Building 2
Portland, OR 97207

2401
Women in Engineering Scholarship

AMOUNT: $1000 DEADLINE: March 15
MAJOR: Engineering

The Women in Engineering Scholarship is awarded to an upper division woman studying engineering at Portland State University. The award amount is one year resident tuition and fees. This scholarship is non-renewable. Award requirements change regularly. No GPA requirement specified.

Portland State University-Engineering/Applied Science
School of Engineering & Applied Science
4th Ave Bldg Suite 20
Portland, OR 92707-0751

Purdue University

2402
Agronomy Freshmen Scholarship

AMOUNT: $500 DEADLINE: Varies
MAJOR: Agronomy

The Agronomy Freshmen Scholarship is open to entering freshmen or transfer students at Purdue University. To be considered for the award, you must have already been accepted to the Department of Agronomy. Your selection is based on scholastic ability, leadership, and demonstrated interest in agronomy. A minimum 2.5 GPA is also required. Award requirements change regularly. Write to the address listed, enclosing a self-addressed, stamped envelope for an application and further information or call (765) 494-6374. GPA must be 2.5-4.0.

Purdue University - Department of Agronomy
Undergraduate Teaching Coordinator
Lilly Hall of Life Sciences
West Lafayette, IN 47907

2403
Award of Excellence Scholarship

AMOUNT: $1500 DEADLINE: February 15
MAJOR: All Agriculture Programs of Study

The Award of Excellence Scholarship is available to high school seniors who have been accepted to the School of Agriculture at Purdue University. You should be in the top 10% of your class and have a minimum combined SAT score of 1100. The award also requires that you be an Indiana resident and have a minimum 3.5 GPA. Award requirements change regularly. Please write to the address listed, enclosing a self-addressed, stamped envelope for an application and further information or call (765) 494-8470. GPA must be 3.5-4.0.

Purdue University - School of Agriculture
Attn: Thomas W. Atkinson
Agricultural Administration Bldg, Rm 121
West Lafayette, IN 47907

2404
Bill and Mary Earle Scholarship

AMOUNT: $1000 DEADLINE: February 1
MAJOR: All Agricultural Programs

The Bill and Mary Earle Scholarship is open to students enrolled in the School of Agriculture at Purdue University. You must have a minimum 2.2 GPA and be an essentially self-supporting student. Award requirements change regularly. Write to the address listed, enclosing a self-addressed, stamped envelope for an application and further information or call (765) 494-8470. GPA must be 2.2-4.0.

Purdue University - School of Agriculture
Attn: Thomas W. Atkinson
Agricultural Administration Bldg, Rm 121
West Lafayette, IN 47907

2405
Bratton-Brown Scholarship

AMOUNT: None Specified DEADLINE: February 15
MAJOR: Agriculture

The Bratton-Brown Scholarship is open to high school seniors who have been accepted to the School of Agriculture at Purdue University. In order to apply, you must be a resident of Huntington or Montgomery counties in Indiana and living in a single-parent household. Selection is based on academics and financial need. This scholarship is renewable as long as you remain in good academic standing. A minimum 2.8 GPA is required. Award requirements change regularly. Write to the address listed, enclosing a self-addressed, stamped envelope for an application and further information or call (765) 494-8470. GPA must be 2.8-4.0.

Purdue University - School of Agriculture
Attn: Thomas W. Atkinson
Agricultural Administration Bldg, Rm 121
West Lafayette, IN 47907

2406
Bruce E. Hardy Scholarship

AMOUNT: $1000 DEADLINE: April 1
MAJOR: Crop Science

The Bruce E. Hardy Scholarship is open to undergraduates at Purdue University who are crop science majors. You must be an Indiana resident and have a good scholastic record to be considered for the award. A minimum 2.5 GPA is also required. Award requirements change regularly. Write to the address listed, enclosing a self-addressed, stamped envelope for an application and further information or call (765) 494-6374. GPA must be 2.5-4.0.

Purdue University - Department of Agricultural Economics
Professor Lawrence P. Bohl
Krannert Building, Rm 681
West Lafayette, IN 47907

2407
Central Soya Freshman Scholarship

AMOUNT: $1000 DEADLINE: January 15
MAJOR: Food Science

The Central Soya Freshman Scholarship is open to high school seniors planning to enroll in food science at Purdue University. In order to apply, you must have a minimum 23 ACT or 1000 SAT and be ranked in the top 20% of your graduating class. This award is based on scholastics and extracurricular activities. Award requirements change regularly. No GPA requirement specified.

Purdue University - Department of Food Science
Jennifer Lawrence, Academic Coordinator
1160 Food Science Building
West Lafayette, IN 47907

2408
Chicago Farmers Scholarship

AMOUNT: $1000 DEADLINE: October 1
MAJOR: Agriculture

The Chicago Farmers Scholarship is available to juniors in the School of Agriculture at Purdue University. Your selection will be based on academics, participation in agricultural/community activities, and participation in Purdue organizations. One award is offered annually. A minimum 2.8 GPA is required. Award requirements change regularly. Write to the address listed, enclosing a self-addressed, stamped envelope for an application and further information or call (765) 494-8470. GPA must be 2.8-4.0.

Purdue University - School of Agriculture
Attn: Thomas W. Atkinson
Agricultural Administration Bldg, Rm 121
West Lafayette, IN 47907

2409
Cohee Crop and Soil Science Award

AMOUNT: $900 DEADLINE: April 1
MAJOR: Crop Science, Soil Science

The Cohee Crop and Soil Science Award is open to juniors and seniors at Purdue University. To be considered for the award, you must be a crop and soil science major. Your selection will be based on your scholastic record. A minimum 2.5 GPA is required. Award requirements change regularly. Write to the address listed, enclosing a self-addressed, stamped envelope for an application and further information or call (765) 494-6374. GPA must be 2.5-4.0.

Purdue University - Department of Agricultural Economics
Professor Lawrence P. Bohl
Krannert Building, Rm 681
West Lafayette, IN 47907

2410
Colonel Fletcher P. Jaquess Scholarship

AMOUNT: $1000 DEADLINE: February 15
MAJOR: Agriculture and Related Areas

The Colonel Fletcher P. Jaquess Scholarship is open to high school seniors from Gibson, Posey, Vanderburgh, and Warrick counties in Indiana. You must be enrolling in the School of Agriculture at Purdue University. Award requirements change regularly. Write to the address listed, enclosing a self-addressed, stamped envelope for an application and further information or call (765) 494-8470. No GPA requirement specified.

Purdue University - School of Agriculture
Attn: Thomas W. Atkinson
Agricultural Administration Bldg, Rm 121
West Lafayette, IN 47907

2411
Denton Food Science Scholarship

AMOUNT: $1500 DEADLINE: January 15
MAJOR: Food Science

The Denton Food Science Scholarship is open to high school seniors planning to enroll in food science at Purdue University. In order to apply, you must have a minimum 23 ACT or 1000 SAT score and be ranked in the top 20% of your graduating class. This award is based on scholastic abilities and extracurricular activities. Award requirements change regularly. No GPA requirement specified.

Purdue University - Department of Food Science
Jennifer Lawrence, Academic Coordinator
1160 Food Science Building
West Lafayette, IN 47907

2412
Dow AgroSciences Agricultural Economics Scholarship

AMOUNT: $1000 DEADLINE: February 1
MAJOR: Agricultural Economics

The Dow AgroSciences Agricultural Economics Scholarship is open to juniors and seniors in the School of Agriculture at Purdue University. You must be majoring in agricultural economics, have completed AGEC 331, and have a minimum 3.0 GPA. Award requirements change regularly. Write to the address listed, enclosing a self-addressed, stamped envelope for an application and further information or call (765) 494-8470. GPA must be 3.0-4.0.

Purdue University - School of Agriculture
Attn: Thomas W. Atkinson
Agricultural Administration Bldg, Rm 121
West Lafayette, IN 47907

2413
Dow AgroSciences Graduate Scholarship

AMOUNT: $1000 DEADLINE: February 1
MAJOR: Plant Science, Plant Pathology, Weed Science, Forestry, Wildlife, Fisheries

The Dow AgroSciences Graduate Scholarship is open to graduate students in the School of Agriculture at Purdue University who are concentrating in any of these areas: plant science, plant pathology, weed science, forestry, wildlife, or fisheries. In order to apply, you must be a U.S. citizen and have been at PU for at least one year. Preference is given to doctoral students, and one award is given to a graduate teaching assistant. Award requirements change regularly. Write to the address listed, enclosing a self-addressed, stamped envelope for an application and further information or call (765) 494-8470. No GPA requirement specified.

Purdue University - School of Agriculture
Dean K. G. Brandt
Agricultural Administration Bldg, Rm 121
West Lafayette, IN 47907

2414
Dow AgroSciences Minority Scholarship

AMOUNT: $1000 DEADLINE: February 1
MAJOR: All Agricultural Programs

The Dow AgroSciences Minority Scholarship is open to minority sophomores, juniors, or seniors who have completed 30, 60, or 90 hours, respectively, at Purdue or Vincennes University. To apply, you must also have a minimum 2.5 GPA. Award requirements change regularly. Write to the address listed, enclosing a self-addressed, stamped envelope for an application and further information or call (765) 494-8470. GPA must be 2.5-4.0.

Purdue University - School of Agriculture
Attn: Thomas W. Atkinson
Agricultural Administration Bldg, Rm 121
West Lafayette, IN 47907

2415
Dow AgroSciences Plant Science/Pest Management Scholarship

AMOUNT: $1000 DEADLINE: February 1
MAJOR: Plant Science, Pest Management, Agricultural Communications, Agronomy, Botany, Entomology, Horticulture

The Dow AgroSciences Plant Science/Pest Management Scholarship is open to juniors and seniors in the School of Agriculture at Purdue University who are majoring in any of these areas: plant science, pest management, agricultural communications, agronomy, botany, entomology, or horticulture. In order to apply, you must have a minimum 3.0 GPA and have completed 60 hours if you are a junior and 90 hours if you are a senior. Award requirements change regularly. Write to the address listed, enclosing a self-addressed, stamped envelope for an application and further information or call (765) 494-8470. GPA must be 3.0-4.0.

Purdue University - School of Agriculture
Attn: Thomas W. Atkinson
Agricultural Administration Bldg, Rm 121
West Lafayette, IN 47907

2416
Dow AgroSciences Purdue Scholar Scholarship

AMOUNT: None Specified DEADLINE: April 1
MAJOR: Agricultural Economics, Biochemistry, Entomology, Horticulture, Agronomy, Botany, Plant Pathology

The Dow AgroSciences Purdue Scholar Scholarship award is available to minority Indiana high school seniors who have been accepted to the School of Agriculture at Purdue University. In order to apply, you must enroll in agricultural economics, biochemistry, entomology, horticulture, agronomy, botany, or plant pathology. Selection is based on academics, references, and an interview. This award pays for fees, tuition, room and board, and book allowance. A minimum 2.8 GPA is required. Award requirements change regularly. Write to the address listed, enclosing a self-addressed, stamped envelope for an application and further information or call Karla Hay at (765) 494-8470. GPA must be 2.8-4.0.

Purdue University - School of Agriculture
Dean K. G. Brandt
Agricultural Administration Bldg, Rm 121
West Lafayette, IN 47907

2417
Farm Credit Services Scholarship

AMOUNT: $1000 DEADLINE: October 1
MAJOR: All Agricultural Programs

The Farm Credit Services Scholarship is open to sophomores, juniors, and seniors enrolled in the School of Agriculture at Purdue University. You must be an Indiana resident who has not won this award before and who is not receiving more than $2,500 in other awards. Selection is based on academics, evidence of citizenship, and demonstration of leadership. A minimum 2.7 GPA is required. Award requirements change regularly. Write to the address listed, enclosing a self-addressed,

stamped envelope for an application and further information or call (765) 494-8470. GPA must be 2.7.

Purdue University - School of Agriculture
Attn: Thomas W. Atkinson
Agricultural Administration Bldg, Rm 121
West Lafayette, IN 47907

2418
Fluid Power Scholarship

AMOUNT: None Specified DEADLINE: March 1
MAJOR: Agricultural Engineering, Biological Engineering

The Fluid Power Scholarship is open to agricultural or biological engineering majors at Purdue University. To qualify for consideration, you must have completed one fluid power or fluid mechanics engineering course. Award requirements change regularly. Write to the address listed, enclosing a self-addressed, stamped envelope for an application and further information or call (765) 494-1172. No GPA requirement specified.

Purdue University - Department of Agricultural/Biological Engineering
Student Academic Center
Agricultural/Biological Engineering #201
West Lafayette, IN 47907

2419
Fred J. Babel Memorial Scholarship

AMOUNT: $1500 DEADLINE: January 15
MAJOR: Food Science

The Fred J. Babel Memorial Scholarship is open to high school seniors planning to enroll in food science at Purdue University. In order to apply, you must have a minimum 23 ACT or 1000 SAT score and be ranked in the top 20% of your graduating class. This award is based on scholastic abilities and extracurricular activities. Award requirements change regularly. No GPA requirement specified.

Purdue University - Department of Food Science
Jennifer Lawrence, Academic Coordinator
1160 Food Science Building
West Lafayette, IN 47907

2420
General Mills Food Process Engineering Scholarship

AMOUNT: $1000 DEADLINE: February 1
MAJOR: Food Process Engineering

The General Mills Food Process Engineering Scholarship is open to sophomores and juniors currently enrolled at Purdue University. To be considered for the award, you must be a food process engineering major. Award requirements change regularly. Write to the address listed, enclosing a self-addressed, stamped envelope for an application and further information or call (765) 494-1172. No GPA requirement specified.

Purdue University - Department of Agricultural/Biological Engineering
Student Academic Center
Agricultural/Biological Engineering #201
West Lafayette, IN 47907

2421
General Mills Freshman Scholarship

AMOUNT: $1000   DEADLINE: January 15
MAJOR: Food Science

The General Mills Freshman Scholarship is open to high school seniors planning to enroll in food science at Purdue University. In order to apply, you must have a minimum ACT score of 23 or 1000 SAT score and be ranked in the top 20% of your graduating class. Your application will also be assessed on scholastic abilities, extracurricular activities, and leadership activities. Award requirements change regularly. No GPA requirement specified.

Purdue University - Department of Food Science
Jennifer Lawrence, Academic Coordinator
1160 Food Science Building
West Lafayette, IN 47907

2422
Gerber Scholarship

AMOUNT: $2500   DEADLINE: January 15
MAJOR: Food Science

The Gerber Scholarship is open to high school seniors planning to enroll in food science at Purdue University. In order to apply, you must have a minimum 23 ACT or 1000 SAT score and be ranked in the top 20% of your graduating class. This award is based on scholastics and extracurricular activities. Award requirements change regularly. No GPA requirement specified.

Purdue University - Department of Food Science
Jennifer Lawrence, Academic Coordinator
1160 Food Science Building
West Lafayette, IN 47907

2423
Institute of Food Technologists Freshman Scholarship

AMOUNT: $750-$1000   DEADLINE: February 15
MAJOR: Food Science

The Institute of Food Technologists Freshman Scholarship is open to incoming freshmen who have been accepted into an accredited food science program at Purdue University. In order to apply, you must show outstanding scholastic ability and have a well-rounded personality. Selection for this award is based on scholastic record, extracurricular activities, and leadership activities. A minimum 2.7 GPA is required. Award requirements change regularly. GPA must be 2.7-4.0.

Purdue University - Department of Food Science
Jennifer Lawrence, Academic Coordinator
1160 Food Science Building
West Lafayette, IN 47907

2424
Institute of Food Technologists Scholarship

AMOUNT: $750-$2000   DEADLINE: February 15
MAJOR: Food Science

The Institute of Food Technologists Scholarship is open to sophomores, juniors, and seniors in the Department of Food Science at Purdue University. In order to apply, you need to demonstrate outstanding scholastic ability and have a well-rounded personality. Your final selection will be based on leadership and extracurricular activities. A minimum 2.7 GPA is required. Award requirements change regularly. GPA must be 2.7-4.0.

Purdue University - Department of Food Science
Jennifer Lawrence, Academic Coordinator
1160 Food Science Building
West Lafayette, IN 47907

2425
John F. Benham Citizenship and Leadership Scholarship

AMOUNT: $1000   DEADLINE: February 1
MAJOR: Agriculture

The John F. Benham Citizenship and Leadership Scholarship is available to seniors in the School of Agriculture at Purdue University who have completed 90 hours of course work, with at least 60 taken at a Purdue Campus. You must have at least 15 hours remaining in your course work and be able to demonstrate financial need. One award is offered annually. Award requirements change regularly. Write to the address listed, enclosing a self-addressed, stamped envelope for an application and further information or call (765) 494-8470. No GPA requirement specified.

Purdue University - School of Agriculture
Attn: Thomas W. Atkinson
Agricultural Administration Bldg, Rm 121
West Lafayette, IN 47907

2426
Kellogg Freshman Scholarship

AMOUNT: $3000   DEADLINE: January 15
MAJOR: Food Science

The Kellogg Freshman Scholarship is open to high school seniors planning to enroll in food science at Purdue University. In order to apply, you must have a minimum 23 ACT or 1000 SAT and be ranked in the top 10% of your graduating class. The award is based on scholastics, extracurricular activities, and leadership activities. Award requirements change regularly. No GPA requirement specified.

Purdue University - Department of Food Science
Jennifer Lawrence, Academic Coordinator
1160 Food Science Building
West Lafayette, IN 47907

2427
Kellogg's Freshmen Food Engineering Scholarship

AMOUNT: $3000 DEADLINE: April 1
MAJOR: Food Engineering

The Kellogg's Freshmen Food Engineering Scholarship is open to incoming freshmen accepted to Purdue University who will be enrolling in the food process engineering program. In order to be considered, you should have a good scholastic record and a well-rounded personality. A minimum 2.5 GPA is required. Award requirements change regularly. Write to the address listed, enclosing a self-addressed, stamped envelope for an application and further information or call (765) 494-1172. GPA must be 2.5-4.0.

Purdue University - Department of Agricultural/Biological Engineering
Student Academic Center
Agricultural/Biological Engineering #201
West Lafayette, IN 47907

2428
Kroger Freshman Scholarship

AMOUNT: $1000 DEADLINE: January 15
MAJOR: Food Science

The Kroger Freshman Scholarship is open to high school seniors planning to enroll in food science at Purdue University. You must have a minimum 23 ACT or 1000 SAT and be ranked in the top 10% of your graduating class. This award is based on scholastic abilities and extracurricular activities. Award requirements change regularly. No GPA requirement specified.

Purdue University - Department of Food Science
Jennifer Lawrence, Academic Coordinator
1160 Food Science Building
West Lafayette, IN 47907

2429
McCormick Freshman Scholarship

AMOUNT: $1000 DEADLINE: January 15
MAJOR: Food Science

The McCormick Freshman Scholarship is open to high school seniors planning to enroll in food science at Purdue University. In order to apply, you must have a minimum 23 ACT or 1000 SAT score and be ranked in the top 20% of your graduating class. This award is based on scholastic abilities and extracurricular activities. Award requirements change regularly. No GPA requirement specified.

Purdue University - Department of Food Science
Jennifer Lawrence, Academic Coordinator
1160 Food Science Building
West Lafayette, IN 47907

2430
National Pest Control Association Scholarship

AMOUNT: None Specified DEADLINE: Varies
MAJOR: Entomology, Pest Control

The National Pest Control Association Scholarship is open to upperclass entomology majors at Purdue University who have completed at least two semesters. For final consideration, you will be judged on scholastic accomplishments, character, and financial need. A minimum 2.5 GPA is required. Award requirements change regularly. Please write to the address listed, enclosing a self-addressed, stamped envelope for an application and further information or call (765) 494-4553. GPA must be 2.5-4.0.

Purdue University - Department of Entomology
Prof. Gary W. Bennett-Sondra L. Lindsey
Entomology Hall
West Lafayette, IN 47907

2431
Paul Girton Food Engineering Scholarship

AMOUNT: $3000 DEADLINE: February 1
MAJOR: Food Process Engineering

The Paul Girton Food Engineering Scholarship is open to junior and senior students at Purdue University. To be considered for the award, you must be a food process engineering major. The award amount is $2,500 plus $500 for travel to the Worldwide Food Expo. Award requirements change regularly. Write to the address listed, enclosing a self-addressed, stamped envelope for an application and further information or call (765) 494-1172. No GPA requirement specified.

Purdue University - Department of Agricultural/Biological Engineering
Student Academic Center
Agricultural/Biological Engineering #201
West Lafayette, IN 47907

2432
Richard D. and Emma F. Schweikhardt Memorial Scholarship

AMOUNT: $500 DEADLINE: February 1
MAJOR: Agriculture and Related Areas

The Richard D. and Emma F. Schweikhardt Memorial Scholarship is open to undergraduates at Purdue University who are residents of Henry or Rush counties in Indiana. In order to apply, you must have a minimum 3.0 GPA. Selection is also based on academic scholarship, leadership, community service on campus, and community service at home. Award requirements change regularly. Write to the address listed, enclosing a self-addressed, stamped envelope for an application and further information or call (765) 494-8470. GPA must be 3.0-4.0.

Purdue University - School of Agriculture
Attn: Thomas W. Atkinson
Agricultural Administration Bldg, Rm 121
West Lafayette, IN 47907

2433
Southern States Scholarship

AMOUNT: $800 DEADLINE: February 15
MAJOR: Agriculture, Related Areas

The Southern States Scholarship is open to incoming freshmen who have been accepted to Purdue University. In order to apply, you must be a son or daughter of an Indiana producer of agricultural products. You are a preferred candidate for this scholarship if you are a student with two or more years of 4-H or National FFA participation. Academic scholarship and leadership are also selection factors. This award is renewable. Award requirements change regularly. Write to the address listed, enclosing a self-addressed, stamped envelope for an application and further information or call (765) 494-8470. No GPA requirement specified.

Purdue University - School of Agriculture
Attn: Thomas W. Atkinson
Agricultural Administration Bldg, Rm 121
West Lafayette, IN 47907

2434
Universal Flavors Freshman Scholarship

AMOUNT: $1000 DEADLINE: January 15
MAJOR: Food Science

The Universal Flavors Freshman Scholarship is open to high school seniors planning to enroll in food science at Purdue University. In order to apply, you must have a minimum 23 ACT or 1000 SAT score and be ranked in the top 20% of your graduating class. This award is based on scholastic abilities and extracurricular activities. Award requirements change regularly. No GPA requirement specified.

Purdue University - Department of Food Science
Jennifer Lawrence, Academic Coordinator
1160 Food Science Building
West Lafayette, IN 47907

2435
William J. Adams, Jr., and Maryanne E. Adams Scholarship

AMOUNT: None Specified DEADLINE: Varies
MAJOR: Agricultural Engineering, Biological Engineering, Agricultural Machinery Design

The William J. Adams, Jr., and Maryanne E. Adams Scholarship is open to agricultural or biological engineering majors at Purdue University. In order to apply, you must have an interest in agricultural machinery design and be a student member of the American Society of Agricultural Engineers. Award requirements change regularly. Write to the address listed, enclosing a self-addressed, stamped envelope for an application and further information or call (765) 494-1172. No GPA requirement specified.

Purdue University - Department of Agricultural/Biological Engineering
Student Academic Center
Agricultural/Biological Engineering #201
West Lafayette, IN 47907

Quincy University

2436
Endowed Scholarships and Annual Awards

AMOUNT: None Specified DEADLINE: Varies
MAJOR: All Areas of Study

The Endowed Scholarships and Annual Awards are open to students attending Quincy University. The criteria vary with each award. Award requirements change regularly. Please send a self-addressed, stamped envelope to receive your application and any further instructions from the scholarship provider or call (217) 222-8020. No GPA requirement specified.

Quincy University
Office of Financial Aid
1800 College
Quincy, IL 62301

2437
Merit and Talent Based Awards

AMOUNT: $500-$8500 DEADLINE: Varies
MAJOR: All Areas of Study

The Merit and Talent Based Awards are open to students attending Quincy University who show academic merit. These renewable awards are based on a combination of the ACT/SAT scores and high school grade point averages. Academic awards are renewable for up to three years for incoming freshmen, and up to two years for transfers, providing the student meets the required GPA for renewal. Award requirements change regularly. Please send a self-addressed, stamped envelope to receive your application and any further instructions from the scholarship provider or call (217) 222-8020. No GPA requirement specified.

Quincy University
Office of Financial Aid
1800 College
Quincy, IL 62301

2438
OFM Grants

AMOUNT: $500 DEADLINE: Varies
MAJOR: All Areas of Study

The OFM Grants are awarded to students attending Quincy University who are the nieces or nephews of members of the Order of Friars Minor, Sacred Heart Province. These awards are renewable for up to three consecutive years. Award requirements change regularly. Please send a self-addressed, stamped envelope to receive your application and any further instructions from the scholarship provider or call (217) 222-8020. No GPA requirement specified.

Quincy University
Office of Financial Aid
1800 College
Quincy, IL 62301

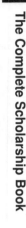

2439
QU Art Scholarships

AMOUNT: $350-$1250 DEADLINE: Varies
MAJOR: Art

The QU Art Scholarships are open to art majors attending Quincy University. These scholarships are awarded annually by the Division of Fine Arts faculty after the submission and review of a portfolio. Participation in departmental activities is required. Award requirements change regularly. Please send a self-addressed, stamped envelope to receive your application and any further instructions from the scholarship provider or call (217) 222-8020. No GPA requirement specified.

Quincy University
Office of Financial Aid
1800 College
Quincy, IL 62301

2440
QU Athletic Scholarships

AMOUNT: $500 DEADLINE: Varies
MAJOR: Athletic Participation

The QU Athletic Scholarships are open to students attending Quincy University who are involved in the following sports: men's baseball, soccer, basketball, football, and volleyball and women's basketball, soccer, softball, tennis, and volleyball. Eligibility and amounts are determined by the coaches of the individual sports. Award requirements change regularly. Please send a self-addressed, stamped envelope to receive your application and any further instructions from the scholarship provider or call (217) 222-8020. No GPA requirement specified.

Quincy University
Office of Financial Aid
1800 College
Quincy, IL 62301

2441
QU Music Scholarships

AMOUNT: $250 DEADLINE: Varies
MAJOR: All Areas of Study

The QU Music Scholarships are open to students who demonstrate musical talent, whether instrumentally or vocally. Awards are determined by the faculty in the Division of Fine Arts after auditions are conducted and any additional requirement are met. While participation in music events is required for these scholarships, it is not necessary to be a music major in order to earn an award. Award requirements change regularly. Please send a self-addressed, stamped envelope to receive your application and any further instructions from the scholarship provider or call (217) 222-8020. No GPA requirement specified.

Quincy University
Office of Financial Aid
1800 College
Quincy, IL 62301

Quinnipiac College

2442
Dean's Scholarship

AMOUNT: $3000-$6000 DEADLINE: Varies
MAJOR: All Areas of Study

The Quinnipiac College Dean's Scholarship is open to accepted freshmen at Quinnipiac College. Applicants must be in the top 10% of their high school class and demonstrate academic promise. An admissions application must be on file by February 15. A minimum 1200 SAT score is required. Applicants must maintain full-time status and maintain a 3.0 GPA. Award requirements change regularly. Please send a self-addressed, stamped envelope to receive your application and any further instructions from the scholarship provider. No GPA requirement specified.

Quinnipiac College
Admissions Office
275 Mount Carmel Avenue
Hamden, CT 06518

2443
Diversity Scholarship

AMOUNT: None Specified DEADLINE: Varies
MAJOR: All Areas of Study

The Quinnipiac College Diversity Scholarship is open to accepted minority freshmen at Quinnipiac College. Some awards are based on academic achievement and others on financial need. Applicants must have a completed admissions application on file by February 15 and the Quinnipiac Application for Financial Assistance on file by March 1. This award is renewable provided the students maintain full-time status and satisfactory academic progress. Award requirements change regularly. Please send a self-addressed, stamped envelope to receive your application and any further instructions from the scholarship provider. No GPA requirement specified.

Quinnipiac College
Admissions Office
275 Mount Carmel Avenue
Hamden, CT 06518

Radcliffe College

2444
Undergraduate Research Award Program

AMOUNT: Maximum: $500 DEADLINE: April 1
MAJOR: Social and Behavioral Sciences

The Undergraduate Research Award Program is open to Harvard University undergraduate students in the social and behavioral sciences. Data from the Murray Center can be used to develop and answer research questions related to course work and senior theses. The Henry A. Murray Research Center is a national repository of social and behavioral sciences data for the study of lives over time with a special focus on the lives of American women. Award requirements change regularly. Please send a self-addressed, stamped envelope to receive your application and any further instructions from the Murray Center; or visit their website at www.radcliffe.edu/murray. No GPA requirement specified.

Radcliffe College - Henry A. Murray Research Center
Attn: Grants Program Coordinator
10 Garden Street
Cambridge, MA 02138

Rochester Institute of Technology

2445
Abe Lincoln Scholarship Fund for Minorities

AMOUNT: None Specified DEADLINE: Varies
MAJOR: All Fields of Study

The Abe Lincoln Scholarship Fund for Minorities is awarded to a worthy and needy black student at Rochester Institute of Technology and may be granted to the same student for consecutive years as long as the student maintains at least a C+ average. Should a qualified black scholar not be available, the award may be given to another minority student. To be considered for this scholarship, please file your FAFSA by the priority deadline (March 15 for new students and April 1 for continuing students). Award requirements change regularly. Please send a self-addressed, stamped envelope to receive your application and any further instructions from the scholarship provider, or you may visit the sponsor's website. GPA must be 2.8-4.0.

Rochester Institute of Technology
Attn: Office of Financial Aid
56 Lomb Memorial Drive
Rochester, NY 14623-5604

2446
Ann Conway Powers Memorial Scholarship

AMOUNT: None Specified DEADLINE: Varies
MAJOR: All Fields of Study

The Ann Conway Powers Memorial Scholarship is open to students at Rochester Institute of Technology, with preference given to young men from broken homes. To be considered for this scholarship, please file your FAFSA by the priority deadline (March 15 for new students and April 1 for continuing students). Award requirements change regularly. Please send a self-addressed, stamped envelope to receive your application and any further instructions from the scholarship provider, or you may visit the sponsor's website. No GPA requirement specified.

Rochester Institute of Technology
Attn: Office of Financial Aid
56 Lomb Memorial Drive
Rochester, NY 14623-5604

2447
Barlow Endowed Scholarship Fund

AMOUNT: None Specified DEADLINE: Varies
MAJOR: Medical Technology

The Barlow Endowed Scholarship Fund is open to students majoring in medical technology at Rochester Institute of Technology's National Institute for the Deaf. To be considered for this scholarship, please file your FAFSA by the priority deadline (March 15 for new students and April 1 for continuing students). Award requirements change regularly. Please send a self-addressed, stamped envelope to receive your application and any further instructions from the scholarship provider. No GPA requirement specified.

Rochester Institute of Technology
Attn: Office of Financial Aid
56 Lomb Memorial Drive
Rochester, NY 14623-5604

2448
Clara Louise Andrews Hale Memorial Scholarship

AMOUNT: None Specified DEADLINE: Varies
MAJOR: All Fields of Study

The Clara Louise Andrews Hale Memorial Scholarship is open to students enrolled in any area of study at Rochester Institute of Technology who demonstrate financial need and have a minimum GPA of 3.0. This award is renewable as long as you maintain the minimum level of academic achievement. To be considered for this scholarship, please file your FAFSA by the priority deadline (March 15 for new students and April 1 for continuing students). Award requirements change regularly. Please send a self-addressed, stamped envelope to receive your application and any further instructions from the scholarship provider. GPA must be 3.0-4.0.

Rochester Institute of Technology
Attn: Office of Financial Aid
56 Lomb Memorial Drive
Rochester, NY 14623-5604

2449
Curtice-Burns Endowed Scholarship

AMOUNT: None Specified DEADLINE: Varies
MAJOR: All Fields of Study

The Curtice-Burns Endowed Scholarship is open to incoming freshmen at Rochester Institute of Technology who demonstrate academic excellence and financial need. This award is renewable for up to four years, as long as you maintain a reasonable academic record. To be considered for this scholarship, please file your FAFSA by the priority deadline (March 15 for new students and April 1 for continuing students). Award requirements change regularly. Please send a self-addressed, stamped envelope to receive your application and any further instructions from the scholarship provider. No GPA requirement specified.

Rochester Institute of Technology
Attn: Office of Financial Aid
56 Lomb Memorial Drive
Rochester, NY 14623-5604

Eastman Kodak Company Scholar Awards

AMOUNT: None Specified DEADLINE: Varies
MAJOR: Disciplines of Interest to Eastman Kodak

The Eastman Kodak Company Scholar Awards are open to
sophomores and juniors at Rochester Institute of Technology
who are in a discipline of interest to Eastman Kodak.
Selection is based on academic merit. To renew this award,
you must maintain at least a B average. Summer employment
(for a minimum of ten consecutive weeks) is required after the
first year in which tuition has been paid by Eastman Kodak.
To be considered for this scholarship, please file your FAFSA
by the priority deadline (March 15 for new students and April
1 for continuing students). Award requirements change regularly. Please send a self-addressed, stamped envelope to
receive your application and any further instructions from the
scholarship provider. No GPA requirement specified.

Rochester Institute of Technology
Attn: Office of Financial Aid
56 Lomb Memorial Drive
Rochester, NY 14623-5604

2451
Eisenhart Memorial Scholarship

AMOUNT: None Specified DEADLINE: Varies
MAJOR: All Fields of Study

The Eisenhart Memorial Scholarship is open to students at
Rochester Institute of Technology who demonstrate financial
need and have attained a minimum GPA of 3.2. To be considered for this scholarship, please file your FAFSA by the priority deadline (March 15 for new students and April 1 for continuing students). Award requirements change regularly. Please
send a self-addressed, stamped envelope to receive your application and any further instructions from the scholarship
provider. GPA must be 3.2-4.0.

Rochester Institute of Technology
Attn: Office of Financial Aid
56 Lomb Memorial Drive
Rochester, NY 14623-5604

2452
Ezra Randall Andrews Memorial Scholarship

AMOUNT: None Specified DEADLINE: Varies
MAJOR: All Fields of Study

The Ezra Randall Andrews Memorial Scholarship is open to
students enrolled in any area of study at Rochester Institute of
Technology who demonstrate financial need and have a minimum GPA of 3.0. This award is renewable as long as you
maintain the minimum level of academic achievement. To be
considered for this scholarship, please file your FAFSA by the
priority deadline (March 15 for new students and April 1 for
continuing students). Award requirements change regularly.
Please send a self-addressed, stamped envelope to receive

your application and any further instructions from the scholarship provider. GPA must be 3.0-4.0.

Rochester Institute of Technology
Attn: Office of Financial Aid
56 Lomb Memorial Drive
Rochester, NY 14623-5604

Frank Horton Endowed Graduate Scholarship

AMOUNT: None Specified DEADLINE: Varies
MAJOR: All Fields of Study

The Frank Horton Endowed Graduate Scholarship is open to
graduate students at Rochester Institute of Technology. To
qualify for this award, you must be a full-time student in good
academic standing and demonstrate financial need. Candidates
are recommended by the Dean of Graduate Studies. To be
considered for this scholarship, please file your FAFSA by the
priority deadline (March 15 for new students and April 1 for
continuing students). Award requirements change regularly.
Please send a self-addressed, stamped envelope to receive
your application and any further instructions from the scholarship provider. No GPA requirement specified.

Rochester Institute of Technology
Attn: Office of Financial Aid
56 Lomb Memorial Drive
Rochester, NY 14623-5604

2454
G. Sherwin Haxton Memorial Scholarship

AMOUNT: None Specified DEADLINE: Varies
MAJOR: All Fields of Study

The G. Sherwin Haxton Memorial Scholarship is open to students from the Oakfield/Alabama area of New York State at
Rochester Institute of Technology. To be considered for this
scholarship, please file your FAFSA by the priority deadline
(March 15 for new students and April 1 for continuing students). Award requirements change regularly. Please send a
self-addressed, stamped envelope to receive your application
and any further instructions from the scholarship provider. No
GPA requirement specified.

Rochester Institute of Technology
Attn: Office of Financial Aid
56 Lomb Memorial Drive
Rochester, NY 14623-5604

2455
Hakes School Association Scholarship

AMOUNT: None Specified DEADLINE: Varies
MAJOR: All Fields of Study

The Hakes School Association Scholarship is open to entering
female students who are funding their own education at
Rochester Institute of Technology. To be considered for this
scholarship, please file your FAFSA by the priority deadline
(March 15 for new students and April 1 for continuing students). Award requirements change regularly. Please send a
self-addressed, stamped envelope to receive your application

and any further instructions from the scholarship provider. No GPA requirement specified.

Rochester Institute of Technology
Attn: Office of Financial Aid
56 Lomb Memorial Drive
Rochester, NY 14623-5604

2456
Helen and Frederick Blaessig Annual Memorial Scholarship

AMOUNT: None Specified DEADLINE: Varies
MAJOR: All Fields of Study

The Helen and Frederick Blaessig Annual Memorial Scholarship is open to disabled veterans and spouses, children, and grandchildren of service-connected veterans who are either full-time or part-time students at Rochester Institute of Technology. To qualify for this award, you must maintain a high level of academic achievement, possess qualities of "strong motivation, and character" and demonstrate financial need. To be considered for this scholarship, please file your FAFSA by the priority deadline (March 15 for new students and April 1 for continuing students). Award requirements change regularly. Please send a self-addressed, stamped envelope to receive your application and any further instructions from the scholarship provider. No GPA requirement specified.

Rochester Institute of Technology
Attn: Office of Financial Aid
56 Lomb Memorial Drive
Rochester, NY 14623-5604

2457
Isaac L. Jordan, Sr., Endowed Memorial Fund

AMOUNT: None Specified DEADLINE: Varies
MAJOR: All Fields of Study

The Isaac L. Jordan, Sr., Endowed Memorial Fund is open to students at Rochester Institute of Technology. One award is given to an incoming freshman based on a writing contest on a diversity topic. The second scholarship is given to a returning student who has demonstrated an understanding of the concept of diversity through overt contributions in this area. The recipients will be invited to become involved with the Commission for Promoting Pluralism. To be considered for this scholarship, please file your FAFSA by the priority deadline (March 15 for new students and April 1 for continuing students). Award requirements change regularly. Please send a self-addressed, stamped envelope to receive your application and any further instructions from the scholarship provider. No GPA requirement specified.

Rochester Institute of Technology
Attn: Office of Financial Aid
56 Lomb Memorial Drive
Rochester, NY 14623-5604

2458
John D. and Rachael E. Hromi Endowed Scholarship

AMOUNT: None Specified DEADLINE: Varies
MAJOR: Quality and Applied Statistics

The John D. and Rachael E. Hromi Endowed Scholarship is open to full-time or part-time graduate students at Rochester Institute of Technology who by virtue of merit, need, and interest aspire to professional careers in quality standards and statistical methods. To qualify for this award, you must have an undergraduate GPA of 3.0 or higher in engineering, science, or business. To be considered for this scholarship, please file your FAFSA by the priority deadline (March 15 for new students and April 1 for continuing students). Award requirements change regularly. Please send a self-addressed, stamped envelope to receive your application and any further instructions from the scholarship provider. GPA must be 3.0-4.0.

Rochester Institute of Technology
Attn: Office of Financial Aid
56 Lomb Memorial Drive
Rochester, NY 14623-5604

2459
Kathleen M. Keyes Memorial Scholarship

AMOUNT: None Specified DEADLINE: Varies
MAJOR: All Fields of Study

The Kathleen M. Keyes Memorial Scholarship is open to student leaders and participants in organizations under the student government umbrella at Rochester Institute of Technology. To qualify for this award, you must have a minimum GPA of 2.75; demonstrate financial need; make meaningful contributions to campus life; and exhibit the qualities of dedication, open-mindedness, friendliness, and willingness to help others. To be considered for this scholarship, please file your FAFSA by the priority deadline (March 15 for new students and April 1 for continuing students). Award requirements change regularly. Please send a self-addressed, stamped envelope to receive your application and any further instructions from the scholarship provider. GPA must be 2.75-4.0.

Rochester Institute of Technology
Attn: Office of Financial Aid
56 Lomb Memorial Drive
Rochester, NY 14623-5604

2460
Lomb People's Award

AMOUNT: None Specified DEADLINE: Varies
MAJOR: All Fields of Study

The Lomb People's Award is open to students in all areas of study at Rochester Institute of Technology. To be considered for this scholarship, please file your FAFSA by the priority deadline (March 15 for new students and April 1 for continuing students). Award requirements change regularly. Please send a self-addressed, stamped envelope to receive your application and any further instructions from the scholarship provider. No GPA requirement specified.

Rochester Institute of Technology
Attn: Office of Financial Aid
56 Lomb Memorial Drive
Rochester, NY 14623-5604

2461
Maurice and Maxine Forman Scholarship Fund

AMOUNT: None Specified DEADLINE: Varies
MAJOR: All Fields of Study

The Maurice and Maxine Forman Scholarship Fund is open to students at Rochester Institute of Technology's National Institute for the Deaf who plan to pursue baccalaureate degrees in RIT professional programs. To be considered for this scholarship, Please file your FAFSA by the priority deadline (March 15 for new students and April 1 for continuing students). Award requirements change regularly. Please send a self-addressed, stamped envelope to receive your application and any further instructions from the scholarship provider. No GPA requirement specified.

Rochester Institute of Technology
Attn: Office of Financial Aid
56 Lomb Memorial Drive
Rochester, NY 14623-5604

2462
Quality Cup Scholarships

AMOUNT: $1000-$7000 DEADLINE: February 1
MAJOR: All Fields of Study

The Quality Cup Scholarships are open to students at Rochester Institute of Technology and are not dependent on financial need. These awards are based on your academic record, recommendations, activities, and the requirements for your major. You must apply for admission to RIT by February 1 to be considered. You may renew these awards as long as you maintain a GPA of at least 3.0. Award requirements change regularly. Please send a self-addressed, stamped envelope to receive your application and any further instructions from the scholarship provider. No GPA requirement specified.

Rochester Institute of Technology
Attn: Office of Financial Aid
56 Lomb Memorial Drive
Rochester, NY 14623-5604

2463
Residence Halls Association Leadership Scholarship

AMOUNT: None Specified DEADLINE: Varies
MAJOR: All Fields of Study

The Residence Halls Association Leadership Scholarship is open to incoming freshmen at Rochester Institute of Technology who live in the residence halls. To qualify for this award, you must have a high school GPA of at least 3.0 and demonstrate leadership abilities and interest. To be considered for this scholarship, please file your FAFSA by the priority deadline (March 15 for new students and April 1 for continuing students). Award requirements change regularly. Please send a self-addressed, stamped envelope to receive your application and any further instructions from the scholarship provide. GPA must be 3.0-4.0.

Rochester Institute of Technology
Attn: Office of Financial Aid
56 Lomb Memorial Drive
Rochester, NY 14623-5604

2464
RIT Minority Transfer Scholarship

AMOUNT: $2500 DEADLINE: Varies
MAJOR: All Fields of Study

The RIT Minority Transfer Scholarship is open to African-American, Hispanic, or Native American students at Rochester Institute of Technology. This renewable award is based on your academic achievement, leadership potential, and financial need. To be considered for this scholarship, please file your FAFSA by the priority deadline (March 15 for new students and April 1 for continuing students). Applications filed after these dates will receive consideration as long as funds are available. Award requirements change regularly. Please send a self-addressed, stamped envelope to receive your application and any further instructions from the scholarship provider. No GPA requirement specified.

Rochester Institute of Technology
Attn: Office of Financial Aid
56 Lomb Memorial Drive
Rochester, NY 14623-5604

2465
RIT National Merit Scholarships

AMOUNT: $1000-$7000 DEADLINE: February 1
MAJOR: All Fields of Study

The RIT National Merit Scholarships are open to students at Rochester Institute of Technology and are not dependent on financial need. These awards are based on your academic record, recommendations, activities, and the requirements for your major. You must apply for admission to RIT by February 1 to be considered. You may renew these awards as long as you maintain a GPA of at least 3.0. Award requirements change regularly. Please send a self-addressed, stamped envelope to receive your application and any further instructions from the scholarship provider. No GPA requirement specified.

Rochester Institute of Technology
Attn: Office of Financial Aid
56 Lomb Memorial Drive
Rochester, NY 14623-5604

2466
RIT Phi Theta Kappa Scholarships

AMOUNT: $2000 DEADLINE: Varies
MAJOR: All Fields of Study

The RIT Phi Theta Kappa Scholarships are open to full-time students transferring to Rochester Institute of Technology who had been elected to Phi Theta Kappa at their previous college. You are required to document your Phi Theta Kappa membership. These award are renewable for up to seven quarters as long as you maintain at least a 3.0 GPA. Award requirements change regularly. Please send a self-addressed, stamped envelope to receive your application and any further instructions from the scholarship provider. No GPA requirement specified.

Rochester Institute of Technology
Attn: Office of Financial Aid
56 Lomb Memorial Drive
Rochester, NY 14623-5604

2467
RIT/ROTC Grant Subsidy Scholarship

AMOUNT: $5000 DEADLINE: Varies
MAJOR: All Fields of Study

The RIT/ROTC Grant Subsidy Scholarship is open to holders of Air Force ROTC Type II or Type VIII or Army Tier I cadets attending Rochester Institute of Technology who hold certain Air Force or Army scholarships. To be considered for these scholarships, please file your FAFSA by the priority deadline (March 15 for new students and April 1 for continuing students). Applications filed after these dates will receive consideration as long as funds are available. Award requirements change regularly. Please send a self-addressed, stamped envelope to receive your application and any further instructions from the scholarship provider. No GPA requirement specified.

Rochester Institute of Technology
Attn: Office of Financial Aid
56 Lomb Memorial Drive
Rochester, NY 14623-5604

2468
Rochester Institute of Technology International Alumni Scholarship

AMOUNT: None Specified DEADLINE: Varies
MAJOR: All Fields of Study

The Rochester Institute of Technology International Alumni Scholarship is open to worthy, bright, and needy international students at Rochester Institute of Technology. Preference is given to students in their junior and senior years. Award requirements change regularly. Please send a self-addressed, stamped envelope to receive your application and any further instructions from the scholarship provider. No GPA requirement specified.

Rochester Institute of Technology
Attn: Office of Financial Aid
56 Lomb Memorial Drive
Rochester, NY 14623-5604

2469
Sarah Shelton Scholarship

AMOUNT: None Specified DEADLINE: Varies
MAJOR: All Fields of Study

The Sarah Shelton Scholarship is open to worthy and needy students in all areas of study at Rochester Institute of Technology. To be considered for this scholarship, please file your FAFSA by the priority deadline (March 15 for new students and April 1 for continuing students). Award requirements change regularly. Please send a self-addressed, stamped envelope to receive your application and any further instructions from the scholarship provide. No GPA requirement specified.

Rochester Institute of Technology
Attn: Office of Financial Aid
56 Lomb Memorial Drive
Rochester, NY 14623-5604

2470
Warren L. (Dusty) Rhodes Memorial Scholarship

AMOUNT: None Specified DEADLINE: Varies
MAJOR: All Fields of Study

The Warren L. (Dusty) Rhodes Memorial Scholarship is open to students at Rochester Institute of Technology. To be considered for this scholarship, please file your FAFSA by the priority deadline (March 15 for new students and April 1 for continuing students). Award requirements change regularly. Please send a self-addressed, stamped envelope to receive your application and any further instructions from the scholarship provider. No GPA requirement specified.

Rochester Institute of Technology
Attn: Office of Financial Aid
56 Lomb Memorial Drive
Rochester, NY 14623-5604

2471
William F. and Mildred Feinbloom Scholarship

AMOUNT: None Specified DEADLINE: Varies
MAJOR: All Fields of Study

The William F. and Mildred Feinbloom Scholarship is open to worthy international students attending Rochester Institute of Technology. In the absence of a qualified international student, preference is given to art students in textiles and weaving, or to students in the College of Business. Award requirements change regularly. Please send a self-addressed, stamped envelope to receive your application and any further instructions from the scholarship provider. No GPA requirement specified.

Rochester Institute of Technology
Attn: Office of Financial Aid
56 Lomb Memorial Drive
Rochester, NY 14623-5604

2472
Xerox Scholarship

AMOUNT: None Specified DEADLINE: Varies
MAJOR: All Fields of Study

The Xerox Scholarship is open to students at Rochester Institute of Technology who demonstrate financial need. To be considered for this scholarship, please file your FAFSA by the priority deadline (March 15 for new students and April 1 for continuing students). Award requirements change regularly. Please send a self-addressed, stamped envelope to receive your application and any further instructions from the scholarship provider, or you may visit the sponsor's website. No GPA requirement specified.

Rochester Institute of Technology
Attn: Office of Financial Aid
56 Lomb Memorial Drive
Rochester, NY 14623-5604

Saint John's University

2473
Art, Music and Theater Scholarships

AMOUNT: Maximum: $2000 DEADLINE: February 1
MAJOR: Art, Music, Theater

This scholarship is available to students who have been involved in art, music, or theater in high school and wish to continue involvement during their college years at College of Sto Benedict or SJU. This award is renewed with continued participation in art, music, or theater. Award requirements change regularly. For further information, please visit the website at www.csbsju.edu/. No GPA requirement specified.

Saint John's University
Office of Financial Aid
Collegeville, MN 56321

2474
Dean's Scholarship

AMOUNT: $3000-$5000 DEADLINE: February 1
MAJOR: All Areas of Study

This scholarship is for first-year students who have demonstrated academic excellence in high school and who have the ability to become excellent students at CBU or SJU. Applicants must have a GPA of at least 3.35, and demonstrate leadership and service. The award is renewed automatically with satisfactory academic progress. Award requirements change regularly. For further information and applications, please visit the website at www.csbsju.edu/. GPA must be 3.35-4.0.

Saint John's University
Office of Financial Aid
Collegeville, MN 56321

2475
Diversity, Leadership and Service Excellence Scholarship

AMOUNT: Maximum: $5000 DEADLINE: February 1
MAJOR: All Areas of Study

This scholarship is open to first-year students who have demonstrated diversity leadership and service. A supplemental essay is required. This scholarship is renewed automatically with satisfactory academic progress. Award requirements change regularly. No GPA requirement specified.

Saint John's University
Office of Financial Aid
Collegeville, MN 56321

2476
Eagle Scout Scholarship

AMOUNT: $1000 DEADLINE: February 1
MAJOR: All Areas of Study

This scholarship is available to Eagle Scout members attending the College of St. Benedict. This award is not renewable. Award requirements change regularly. For further information and applications, please visit the website at www.csbsju.edu/. No GPA requirement specified.

Saint John's University
Office of Financial Aid
Collegeville, MN 56321

2477
President's Scholarship

AMOUNT: $5500-$7500 DEADLINE: February 1
MAJOR: All Areas of Study

This scholarship is for first-year students who have demonstrated academic excellence in high school and who have the ability to become academic leaders at CBU or SJU. Applicants must have a GPA of at least 3.6, and demonstrate leadership and service. This award is renewed automatically with satisfactory academic progress. Award requirements change regularly. For further information and applications, please visit the website at www.csbsju.edu/. GPA must be 3.6-4.0.

Saint John's University
Office of Financial Aid
Collegeville, MN 56321

2478
Regents'/Trustees' Scholarship

AMOUNT: $8500 DEADLINE: February 1
MAJOR: All Areas of Study

This scholarship is for first-year students who have demonstrated superior academic achievement in high school and who have the ability to become leaders at CBU or SJU. Applicants must have a GPA of at least 3.6 and have a minimum ACT score of 30 or minimum SAT score of 1320. The applicants must also participate in a faculty interview conducted in February. This award is renewed automatically with satisfactory academic progress. Award requirements change regularly. For further information and applications, please visit the website: www.csbsju.edu/. GPA must be 3.6-4.0.

Saint John's University
Office of Financial Aid
Collegeville, MN 56321

2479
SJU Merrill Lynch Scholarship

AMOUNT: $2000 DEADLINE: February 1
MAJOR: All Areas of Study

This scholarship is for Saint John's University freshmen who demonstrate exceptional leadership in their high school and community. This scholarship is renewed automatically with satisfactory academic progress. Award requirements change regularly. For further information and applications, please visit the website at www.csbsju.edu/. No GPA requirement specified.

Saint John's University
Office of Financial Aid
Collegeville, MN 56321

Sauk Valley Community College

2480
Allied Locke Industries Scholarship

AMOUNT: None Specified DEADLINE: Varies
MAJOR: All Areas of Study

This scholarship is open to full-time students at SVCC who are current employees, or whose parents are current employees, of Allied Locke Industries. In order to apply, you must have a minimum 2.0 GPA. Scholarships cover tuition and fees and can only be received for a maximum of four semesters. The deadline is June 1 for the fall semester and October 15 for the spring semester. Award requirements change regularly. GPA must be 2.0-4.0.

Sauk Valley Community College
Financial Aid Office
173 Illinois Route 2
Dixon, IL 61021

2481
Alvin J. Dimond Scholarship

AMOUNT: None Specified DEADLINE: Varies
MAJOR: All Areas of Study

This scholarship is open to SVCC athletes who graduated from in-district high schools. Scholarship covers tuition and fees. The deadline is June 1 for the fall semester and October 15 for the spring semester. Award requirements change regularly. No GPA requirement specified.

Sauk Valley Community College
Financial Aid Office
173 Illinois Route 2
Dixon, IL 61021

2482
Amcore Bank of Rock River Scholarship

AMOUNT: $500 DEADLINE: Varies
MAJOR: All Areas of Study

This scholarship is open to students at SVCC who are current employees, or whose parents are current employees, of Amcore Bank of Rock River. In order to apply, you must live within the SVCC district, attend school full-time, and demonstrate financial need and scholastic achievement. The deadline is June 1 for the fall semester and October 15 for the spring semester. Award requirements change regularly. GPA must be 2.0-4.0.

Sauk Valley Community College
Financial Aid Office
173 Illinois Route 2
Dixon, IL 61021

2483
Bauder Foundation Scholarship

AMOUNT: None Specified DEADLINE: Varies
MAJOR: All Areas of Study

This scholarship is open to students at SVCC who demonstrate financial need and academic achievement. The scholarship covers tuition, fees, and books. The deadline is June 1 for the fall semester and October 15 for the spring semester. Award requirements change regularly. GPA must be 2.5-4.0.

Sauk Valley Community College
Financial Aid Office
173 Illinois Route 2
Dixon, IL 61021

2484
Broderick/Harrison Memorial Scholarship

AMOUNT: $500 DEADLINE: Varies
MAJOR: All Areas of Study

This scholarship is open to second-year non-traditional women students at SVCC who demonstrate academic excellence. The deadline is June 1 for the fall semester and October 15 for the spring semester. Award requirements change regularly. GPA must be 3.0-4.0.

Sauk Valley Community College
Financial Aid Office
173 Illinois Route 2
Dixon, IL 61021

2485
Burton Lindgren Memorial Scholarship

AMOUNT: $500 DEADLINE: Varies
MAJOR: Accounting

This scholarship is open to students at SVCC who are enrolled in the Associate in Applied Science in Accounting Degree program. In order to apply, you must be from the communities of Sterling, Rock Falls, or Dixon. If you are an award recipient, you will be requested to provide a biography for publicity purposes. The deadline is June 1 for the fall semester and October 15 for the spring semester. Award requirements change regularly. No GPA requirement specified.

Sauk Valley Community College
Financial Aid Office
173 Illinois Route 2
Dixon, IL 61021

2486
Carl Sommers Memorial Scholarship

AMOUNT: $750 DEADLINE: Varies
MAJOR: Criminal Justice

This scholarship is open to students at SVCC who are enrolled in the criminal justice program. The deadline is June 1 for the fall semester and October 15 for the spring semester. Award requirements change regularly. No GPA requirement specified.

Sauk Valley Community College
Financial Aid Office
173 Illinois Route 2
Dixon, IL 61021

2487
Dixon Community Trust Scholarship

AMOUNT: $500 DEADLINE: Varies
MAJOR: All Areas of Study

This scholarship is open to selected graduates of Dixon High School who attend SVCC and demonstrate financial need. The deadline is June 1 for the fall semester and October 15 for the spring semester. Award requirements change regularly. No GPA requirement specified.

Sauk Valley Community College
Financial Aid Office
173 Illinois Route 2
Dixon, IL 61021

2488
Jerry Weston Memorial Scholarship

AMOUNT: $500 DEADLINE: Varies
MAJOR: Health Care

This scholarship is open to students at SVCC who are enrolled in a fine arts program. The deadline is June 1 for the fall semester and October 15 for the spring semester. Award requirements change regularly. No GPA requirement specified.

Sauk Valley Community College
Financial Aid Office
173 Illinois Route 2
Dixon, IL 61021

2489
KSB Health Care Fund

AMOUNT: $500 DEADLINE: Varies
MAJOR: Health Care

This fund is open to students at SVCC who are studying in the health care field. In order to apply, you must demonstrate scholastic achievement. The deadline is June 1 for the fall semester and October 15 for the spring semester. Award requirements change regularly. GPA must be 2.5-4.0.

Sauk Valley Community College
Financial Aid Office
173 Illinois Route 2
Dixon, IL 61021

2490
KSB Hospital Auxiliary Scholarship

AMOUNT: $750 DEADLINE: Varies
MAJOR: Allied Health

This scholarship is open to students at SVCC who are in the allied health program. The deadline is June 1 for the fall semester and October 15 for the spring semester. Award requirements change regularly. No GPA requirement specified.

Sauk Valley Community College
Financial Aid Office
173 Illinois Route 2
Dixon, IL 61021

2491
Marine Corps League of Dixon Scholarship

AMOUNT: $350 DEADLINE: Varies
MAJOR: All Areas of Study

This scholarship is open to students at SVCC who are honorably discharged veterans, reservists, or members of the active duty. The deadline is June 1 for the fall semester and October 15 for the spring semester. Award requirements change regularly. No GPA requirement specified.

Sauk Valley Community College
Financial Aid Office
173 Illinois Route 2
Dixon, IL 61021

2492
Mercantile Bank of Sterling Scholarship

AMOUNT: $500 DEADLINE: Varies
MAJOR: Business

This scholarship is open to students at SVCC who are enrolled in the business degree program on a full-time basis. In order to apply, you must demonstrate financial need. The deadline is June 1 for the fall semester and October 15 for the spring semester. Award requirements change regularly. No GPA requirement specified.

Sauk Valley Community College
Financial Aid Office
173 Illinois Route 2
Dixon, IL 61021

2493
Minority Scholarship

AMOUNT: $500 DEADLINE: Varies
MAJOR: All Areas of Study

This scholarship is open to minority students at SVCC who demonstrate financial need and academic achievement. The deadline is June 1 for the fall semester and October 15 for the spring semester. Award requirements change regularly. GPA must be 2.5-4.0.

Sauk Valley Community College
Financial Aid Office
173 Illinois Route 2
Dixon, IL 61021

2494
Morrison Rotary Club Scholarship

AMOUNT: $500 DEADLINE: Varies
MAJOR: All Areas of Study

This scholarship is open to full-time students at SVCC who graduated from Morrison High School. The deadline is June 1 for the fall semester and October 15 for the spring semester. Award requirements change regularly. No GPA requirement specified.

Sauk Valley Community College
Financial Aid Office
173 Illinois Route 2
Dixon, IL 61021

2495
National Manufacturing Company Scholarship

AMOUNT: None Specified DEADLINE: Varies
MAJOR: All Areas of Study

This scholarship is open to full-time students at SVCC who are current employees, or whose parents are current employees, at National Manufacturing Company. In order to apply, you must have a minimum 3.0 GPA. Scholarships cover tuition, books, and fees. The deadline is June 1 for the fall semester and October 15 for the spring semester. Award requirements change regularly. GPA must be 3.0-4.0.

Sauk Valley Community College
Financial Aid Office
173 Illinois Route 2
Dixon, IL 61021

2496
Prophetstown Lions Club Scholarship

AMOUNT: $400 DEADLINE: Varies
MAJOR: All Areas of Study

This scholarship is open to students at SVCC who graduated from Prophetstown High School. In order to apply, you must demonstrate financial need and scholastic achievement. The deadline is June 1 for the fall semester and October 15 for the spring semester. Award requirements change regularly. GPA must be 2.5-4.0.

Sauk Valley Community College
Financial Aid Office
173 Illinois Route 2
Dixon, IL 61021

2497
Raynor Manufacturing Scholarship

AMOUNT: None Specified DEADLINE: Varies
MAJOR: All Areas of Study

This scholarship is open to students at SVCC whose parents are current employees of Raynor Manufacturing. In order to apply, you must attend school full-time and be in good academic standing. Scholarships cover tuition and fees. The deadline is June 1 for the fall semester and October 15 for the spring semester. Award requirements change regularly. GPA must be 2.5-4.0.

Sauk Valley Community College
Financial Aid Office
173 Illinois Route 2
Dixon, IL 61021

2498
Robert L. Wentz Memorial Scholarship

AMOUNT: $500 DEADLINE: Varies
MAJOR: Business

This scholarship is open to students at SVCC who are studying business. In order to apply, you must demonstrate scholastic achievement. The deadline is June 1 for the fall semester and October 15 for the spring semester. Award requirements change regularly. GPA must be 2.5-4.0.

Sauk Valley Community College
Financial Aid Office
173 Illinois Route 2
Dixon, IL 61021

2499
Sterling Beta Sigma Phi Scholarship

AMOUNT: $200 DEADLINE: Varies
MAJOR: All Areas of Study

This scholarship is open to non-traditional women students at SVCC who demonstrate financial need. The deadline is June 1 for the fall semester and October 15 for the spring semester. Award requirements change regularly. No GPA requirement specified.

Sauk Valley Community College
Financial Aid Office
173 Illinois Route 2
Dixon, IL 61021

2500
Tim Sullivan Memorial Award

AMOUNT: $500 DEADLINE: Varies
MAJOR: All Areas of Study

This award is open to students at SVCC who demonstrate financial need and academic achievement. The deadline is June 1 for the fall semester and October 15 for the spring semester. Award requirements change regularly. GPA must be 2.5-4.0.

Sauk Valley Community College
Financial Aid Office
173 Illinois Route 2
Dixon, IL 61021

2501
Tony Given Business Award

AMOUNT: $150 DEADLINE: Varies
MAJOR: Business

This award is open to selected graduates of Morrison High School who attend SVCC and are studying business. The deadline is June 1 for the fall semester and October 15 for the spring semester. Award requirements change regularly. No GPA requirement specified.

Sauk Valley Community College
Financial Aid Office
173 Illinois Route 2
Dixon, IL 61021

2502
Whiteside County Mounted Patrol Scholarship

AMOUNT: $500 DEADLINE: Varies
MAJOR: All Areas of Study

This scholarship is open to selected students at SVCC. Whiteside County will review the applications. The deadline is June 1 for the fall semester and October 15 for the spring semester. Award requirements change regularly. GPA must be 2.5-4.0.

Sauk Valley Community College
Financial Aid Office
173 Illinois Route 2
Dixon, IL 61021

2503
YMCA Racial Justice Scholarship

AMOUNT: $250 DEADLINE: Varies
MAJOR: Arts and Sciences

This scholarship is open to second-year minority women at SVCC who are enrolled in either the Associate in Science, Associate in Arts, or Associate in Applied Science Degree program. The deadline is June 1 for the fall semester and October 15 for the spring semester. Award requirements change regularly. No GPA requirement specified.

Sauk Valley Community College
Financial Aid Office
173 Illinois Route 2
Dixon, IL 61021

Silver Lake College

2504
Presidential Honor Scholarship

AMOUNT: $2000 DEADLINE: April 15
MAJOR: All Areas of Study

The Presidential Honor Scholarship is open to new undergraduate, full-time, on-campus students attending Silver Lake College. To be eligible for this award you must have a minimum GPA of 3.5 and demonstrate involvement in school and community affairs. The award is renewable based on your cumulative GPA. Award requirements change regularly. Please

send a self-addressed, stamped envelope to receive your application and any further instructions from the scholarship provider; email your request to smbkor@sl.edu; or visit the website at www.sl.edu. GPA must be 3.5-4.0.

Silver Lake College
Financial Aid Office
2406 South Alverno Road
Manitowoc, WI 54220

2505
Presidential Scholarship

AMOUNT: $1200 DEADLINE: April 15
MAJOR: All Areas of Study

The Presidential Scholarship is open to new undergraduate, full-time, on-campus students attending Silver Lake College. To be eligible for this award you must have a minimum GPA of 3.0 and demonstrate involvement in school and community affairs. The award is renewable based on your cumulative GPA. Award requirements change regularly. Please send a self-addressed, stamped envelope to receive your application and any further instructions from the scholarship provider; email your request to smbkor@sl.edu; or visit the website at www.sl.edu. GPA must be 3.0-3.5.

Silver Lake College
Financial Aid Office
2406 South Alverno Road
Manitowoc, WI 54220

2506
Religious Service Award

AMOUNT: $500 DEADLINE: April 15
MAJOR: All Areas of Study

The Religious Service Award is open to new undergraduate, full-time, on-campus students attending Silver Lake College. To be eligible for this award you must be currently involved in religious service activities. The award is renewable. Award requirements change regularly. Please send a self-addressed, stamped envelope to receive your application and any further instructions from the scholarship provider; email your request to admslc@silver.sl.edu; or visit the website at www.sl.edu. No GPA requirement specified.

Silver Lake College
Financial Aid Office
2406 South Alverno Road
Manitowoc, WI 54220

Slippery Rock University

2507
A. Craig Succop Scholarship

AMOUNT: None Specified DEADLINE: Varies
MAJOR: Metalsmithing

The A. Craig Succop Scholarship is open to freshmen art majors who are studying metalsmithing at Slippery Rock University. The amount of this award varies. Award requirements change regularly. Please send a self-addressed, stamped envelope to receive your application and any further instruc-

tions from the scholarship provider. No GPA requirement specified.

Slippery Rock University
Office of Financial Aid
107 Maltby Center
Slippery Rock, PA 16057

2508
Academic Affairs Scholarship

AMOUNT: $2500 DEADLINE: Varies
MAJOR: All Areas of Study

The Academic Affairs Scholarship is open to freshman residents of Mercer County who demonstrate superior academic achievement, financial need, and good moral character who will attend Slippery Rock University. The applicant must include three letters of recommendation with the application. It is required that two of the letters come from high school teachers who have taught the student and the other from the high school principal or guidance counselor. Award requirements change regularly. Please send a self-addressed, stamped envelope to receive your application and any further instructions from the scholarship provider. GPA must be 3.5-4.0.

Slippery Rock University
Office of Financial Aid
107 Maltby Center
Slippery Rock, PA 16057

2509
American Legion Post 393 Scholarship

AMOUNT: $500 DEADLINE: Varies
MAJOR: All Areas of Study

The American Legion Post 393 Scholarship is available to Slippery Rock Area High School graduates who demonstrate financial need and will attend Slippery Rock University. Award requirements change regularly. Please send a self-addressed, stamped envelope to receive your application and any further instructions from the scholarship provider. No GPA requirement specified.

Slippery Rock University
Office of Financial Aid
107 Maltby Center
Slippery Rock, PA 16057

2510
Biology Honors Scholarship

AMOUNT: $500-$1000 DEADLINE: Varies
MAJOR: Biology

The Biology Honors Scholarship is offered to a freshman biology major planning to attend Slippery Rock University, who is in the top 20% of the high school graduating class or has a combined SAT score of at least 1,000 or a composite ACT score of 23 or better. Applicants are required to send three letters of recommendation with their application. These letters should attest to the applicant's character, potential for academic success, dependability, and emotional maturity. A handwritten statement describing your long-range goals, both professional and personal, should be attached to your application. Award requirements change regularly. Please send a self-addressed, stamped envelope to receive your application and

any further instructions from the scholarship provider. No GPA requirement specified.

Slippery Rock University
Office of Financial Aid
107 Maltby Center
Slippery Rock, PA 16057

2511
Blase Scarnati Endowment Scholarship

AMOUNT: None Specified DEADLINE: April 15
MAJOR: Music, Marching Band

The Blase Scarnati Endowment Scholarship is open to a musically talented Slippery Rock University Marching Band member. Applicants are required to complete their musical audition prior to consideration for a scholarship. The award amount of this scholarship varies. Award requirements change regularly. Please send a self-addressed, stamped envelope to receive your application and any further instructions from the scholarship provider. No GPA requirement specified.

Slippery Rock University
Office of Financial Aid
107 Maltby Center
Slippery Rock, PA 16057

2512
Board of Governors Scholarship

AMOUNT: None Specified DEADLINE: Varies
MAJOR: All Areas of Study

The Board of Governors Scholarship is open to freshman minority students, academically talented students, and students who demonstrate leadership qualities and students in the performing arts at Slippery Rock University. The award is equal to tuition and can be received for eight semesters. Award requirements change regularly. Please send a self-addressed, stamped envelope to receive your application and any further instructions from the scholarship provider. No GPA requirement specified.

Slippery Rock University
Office of Financial Aid
107 Maltby Center
Slippery Rock, PA 16057

2513
Bonnie Winder Scholarship

AMOUNT: None Specified DEADLINE: April 15
MAJOR: Music

The Bonnie Winder Scholarship is available to outstanding musically-talented, incoming freshmen majoring in music who will be attending Slippery Rock University. Students are required to complete their musical audition prior to consideration for a scholarship. The amount of this scholarship varies. Award requirements change regularly. Please send a self-addressed, stamped envelope to receive your application and any further instructions from the scholarship provider. No GPA requirement specified.

Slippery Rock University
Office of Financial Aid
107 Maltby Center
Slippery Rock, PA 16057

2514
Charles Sheetz Scholarship

AMOUNT: $1000 DEADLINE: Varies
MAJOR: All Areas of Study

The Charles Sheetz Scholarship is available to high school students from Blair County attending Slippery Rock University (SRU). This award is renewable for up to seven additional semesters with a minimum overall GPA of 2.5 at SRU. Award requirements change regularly. Please send a self-addressed, stamped envelope to receive your application and any further instructions from the scholarship provider. GPA must be 2.5-4.0.

Slippery Rock University
Office of Financial Aid
107 Maltby Center
Slippery Rock, PA 16057

2515
Dean's Scholarship

AMOUNT: $1000 DEADLINE: Varies
MAJOR: All Areas of Study

The Dean's Scholarship is open to the highest-ranking freshmen for admission to Slippery Rock University. Students must have at least a 3.5 GPA and achieved at least a 1200 SAT or 26 ACT score. Award requirements change regularly. Please send a self-addressed, stamped envelope to receive your application and any further instructions from the scholarship provider. GPA must be 3.5-4.0.

Slippery Rock University
Office of Financial Aid
107 Maltby Center
Slippery Rock, PA 16057

2516
Dr. Robert Marcus Scholarship

AMOUNT: $1000 DEADLINE: Varies
MAJOR: All Areas of Study

The Dr. Robert Marcus Scholarship is open to minority high school students from Dauphin County who will attend Slippery Rock University. The scholarship recipient must demonstrate financial need and a commitment to community service. This award is renewable for up to three additional years. Award requirements change regularly. Please send a self-addressed, stamped envelope to receive your application and any further instructions from the scholarship provider. No GPA requirement specified.

Slippery Rock University
Office of Financial Aid
107 Maltby Center
Slippery Rock, PA 16057

2517
Dwight Baker Memorial Scholarship

AMOUNT: None Specified DEADLINE: April 15
MAJOR: Music, Pianist or String

The Dwight Baker Memorial Scholarship is available to talented freshman pianists or string players who are majoring in music and attending Slippery Rock University. Applicants are required to complete their musical audition prior to consideration for a scholarship. The amount of this scholarship varies. Award requirements change regularly. Please send a self-addressed, stamped envelope to receive your application and any further instructions from the scholarship provider. No GPA requirement specified.

Slippery Rock University
Office of Financial Aid
107 Maltby Center
Slippery Rock, PA 16057

2518
Eberly Family Scholarship

AMOUNT: $2500-$3000 DEADLINE: Varies
MAJOR: All Areas of Study

The Eberly Family Scholarship is open to freshman residents of Fayette County who will be attending Slippery Rock University and demonstrate superior academic achievement, financial need, and good moral character. Award requirements change regularly. Please send a self-addressed, stamped envelope to receive your application and any further instructions from the scholarship provider. GPA must be 3.5-4.0.

Slippery Rock University
Office of Financial Aid
107 Maltby Center
Slippery Rock, PA 16057

2519
First National Bank of Slippery Rock Scholarship

AMOUNT: $1500 DEADLINE: Varies
MAJOR: Information Science, Business Administration

The First National Bank of Slippery Rock Scholarship is open to full-time freshmen who are permanent residents of Butler, Lawrence, Mercer, or Venango counties of Pennsylvania. Applicants must be College of Information Science or Business Administration majors at Slippery Rock University, have a high school GPA of 3.0, and demonstrate financial need. This award is renewable for up to three additional years. Award requirements change regularly. Please send a self-addressed, stamped envelope to receive your application and any further instructions from the scholarship provider. GPA must be 3.0-4.0.

Slippery Rock University
Office of Financial Aid
107 Maltby Center
Slippery Rock, PA 16057

2520
General Music Scholarship

AMOUNT: None Specified DEADLINE: April 15
MAJOR: Music

The General Music Scholarship is open to incoming freshman music majors. The student must attend Slippery Rock University. Applicants are required to complete their musical audition prior to consideration for a scholarship. The amount of this scholarship varies. Award requirements change regularly. Please send a self-addressed, stamped envelope to receive your application and any further instructions from the scholarship provider. No GPA requirement specified.

Slippery Rock University
Office of Financial Aid
107 Maltby Center
Slippery Rock, PA 16057

2521
Governor's School Merit Scholarship

AMOUNT: $1000 DEADLINE: Varies
MAJOR: All Areas of Study

The Governor's School Merit Scholarship is open to students who have graduated from Governor's School of Excellence, earned at least a 3.0 high school GPA and have an SAT of 1,000 or an ACT score of 22, and who attend Slippery Rock University. Applicants should submit a 500-word essay with their application describing their experience at PGSE and how they plan to apply what they have learned to their college or professional career. Award requirements change regularly. Please send a self-addressed, stamped envelope to receive your application and any further instructions from the scholarship provider. GPA must be 3.0-4.0.

Slippery Rock University
Office of Financial Aid
107 Maltby Center
Slippery Rock, PA 16057

2522
Grace H. "Arky" Vaughan Memorial Scholarship

AMOUNT: $1500 DEADLINE: Varies
MAJOR: Physical Education

The Grace H. "Arky" Vaughan Memorial Scholarship is open to students graduating from Robert E. Lee High School, Springfield, Virginia, and to women who plan on majoring in physical education at Slippery Rock University. Applicants must have a high school GPA of 3.0 and demonstrate financial need. This award is renewable. Award requirements change regularly. Please send a self-addressed, stamped envelope to receive your application and any further instructions from the scholarship provider. GPA must be 3.0-4.0.

Slippery Rock University
Office of Financial Aid
107 Maltby Center
Slippery Rock, PA 16057

2523
Helen Brua Gettig Memorial Scholarship

AMOUNT: None Specified DEADLINE: Varies
MAJOR: Education

The Helen Brua Gettig Memorial Scholarship is open to eligible freshmen majoring in education from any high school in Lawrence or Beaver County, Pennsylvania, who will be attending Slippery Rock University. The student must have at least a 3.5 GPA. The award is full tuition. Award requirements change regularly. Please send a self-addressed, stamped envelope to receive your application and any further instructions from the scholarship provider. GPA must be 3.5-4.0.

Slippery Rock University
Office of Financial Aid
107 Maltby Center
Slippery Rock, PA 16057

2524
James Steel Memorial Scholarship

AMOUNT: $500-$1000 DEADLINE: Varies
MAJOR: Biology

The James Steel Memorial Scholarship is offered to a freshman biology major planning to attend Slippery Rock University, who is in the top 20% of the high school graduating class or has a combined SAT score of at least 1,000 or a composite ACT score of 23 or better. Applicants are required to send three letters of recommendation with their application. These letters should attest to the applicant's character, potential for academic success, dependability, and emotional maturity. A handwritten statement describing your long-range goals, both professional and personal, should be attached to your application. Award requirements change regularly. Please send a self-addressed, stamped envelope to receive your application and any further instructions from the scholarship provider. GPA must be 3.0-4.0.

Slippery Rock University
Office of Financial Aid
107 Maltby Center
Slippery Rock, PA 16057

2525
John and Helen Williams Endowed Scholarship

AMOUNT: $1000 DEADLINE: Varies
MAJOR: Education

The John and Helen Williams Endowed Scholarship is open to students graduating from Conneaut Valley High School who will major in education at Slippery Rock University. The applicant must have a minimum high school GPA of 3.0 and demonstrated financial need. Award requirements change regularly. Please send a self-addressed, stamped envelope to receive your application and any further instructions from the scholarship provider. GPA must be 3.0-4.0.

Slippery Rock University
Office of Financial Aid
107 Maltby Center
Slippery Rock, PA 16057

2526

Kris Chapin Memorial Flute Scholarship

AMOUNT: None Specified DEADLINE: April 15
MAJOR: Music

The Kris Chapin Memorial Flute Scholarship is available to talented incoming freshman flutists majoring in music at Slippery Rock University. Applicants are required to complete their musical audition prior to consideration for the scholarship. The amount of this scholarship varies. Award requirements change regularly. Please send a self-addressed, stamped envelope to receive your application and any further instructions from the scholarship provider. No GPA requirement specified.

Slippery Rock University
Office of Financial Aid
107 Maltby Center
Slippery Rock, PA 16057

2527

Lawrence Tillack Memorial Scholarship

AMOUNT: $500 DEADLINE: Varies
MAJOR: Computer Science, Natural Science

The Lawrence Tillack Memorial Scholarship is open to North Allegheny High School graduates majoring in computer science and natural science who will be attending Slippery Rock University. Award requirements change regularly. Please send a self-addressed, stamped envelope to receive your application and any further instructions from the scholarship provider. No GPA requirement specified.

Slippery Rock University
Office of Financial Aid
107 Maltby Center
Slippery Rock, PA 16057

2528

Mable Eichler Vincent Scholarship

AMOUNT: $500 DEADLINE: Varies
MAJOR: Theater

The Mable Eichler Vincent Scholarship is open to freshman students majoring in theater with a minimum high school GPA of 3.0 and a minimum SAT score of 1100 or ACT score of 22 who will be attending Slippery Rock University. This award is renewable for up to three additional years. Award requirements change regularly. Please send a self-addressed, stamped envelope to receive your application and any further instructions from the scholarship provider. GPA must be 3.0-4.0.

Slippery Rock University
Office of Financial Aid
107 Maltby Center
Slippery Rock, PA 16057

2529

Madrigal Dinner Scholarship

AMOUNT: None Specified DEADLINE: April 15
MAJOR: Music, Vocal

The Madrigal Dinner Scholarship is open to talented incoming freshmen who are voice majors. The student must attend Slippery Rock University. Applicants are required to complete their musical audition prior to consideration for a scholarship. The amount of this scholarship varies. Award requirements change regularly. Please send a self-addressed, stamped envelope to receive your application and any further instructions from the scholarship provider. No GPA requirement specified.

Slippery Rock University
Office of Financial Aid
107 Maltby Center
Slippery Rock, PA 16057

2530

Michael J. Estocin '54 Memorial Scholarship

AMOUNT: $500 DEADLINE: Varies
MAJOR: All Areas of Study

The Michael J. Estocin '54 Memorial Scholarship is open to incoming freshmen attending Slippery Rock University who have at least a 3.5 GPA, are in the top 20% of their graduating class, and are in financial need. The application must be accompanied by a two-paragraph statement written by the applicant outlining his/her educational goals. Award requirements change regularly. Please send a self-addressed, stamped envelope to receive your application and any further instructions from the scholarship provider. GPA must be 3.5-4.0.

Slippery Rock University
Office of Financial Aid
107 Maltby Center
Slippery Rock, PA 16057

2531

Nate and Irene Maruca Education Scholarship

AMOUNT: None Specified DEADLINE: Varies
MAJOR: All Areas of Study

The Nate and Irene Maruca Education Scholarship is open to academically talented high school students from Avonworth and Quaker Valley High School who demonstrate financial need. The specific eligibility criteria for this scholarship are set by the Slippery Rock University Scholarship Committee and are revised annually. The amount of this award varies and can be renewed. Award requirements change regularly. Please send a self-addressed, stamped envelope to receive your application and any further instructions from the scholarship provider. No GPA requirement specified.

Slippery Rock University
Office of Financial Aid
107 Maltby Center
Slippery Rock, PA 16057

2532
Phillips Scholarship

AMOUNT: $1000 DEADLINE: Varies
MAJOR: All Areas of Study

The Phillips Scholarship is open to high school students from Venango, Armstrong, Butler, Clarion, Crawford, Erie, Forest, Lawrence, Mercer, or Warren County in Pennsylvania. A minimum SAT score of 1000 or ACT of 22 and a minimum cumulative GPA of a B average for 13 or more of the recommended college preparatory units are required by all applicants. This award is renewable for four years. Award requirements change regularly. Please send a self-addressed, stamped envelope to receive your application and any further instructions from the scholarship provider. GPA must be 3.0-4.0.

Slippery Rock University
Office of Financial Aid
107 Maltby Center
Slippery Rock, PA 16057

2533
President's Scholarship

AMOUNT: $1500 DEADLINE: Varies
MAJOR: All Areas of Study

The President's Scholarship is open to high school students ranked number one in their class at the end of their junior year in high school. The applicant must attend Slippery Rock University. Award requirements change regularly. Please send a self-addressed, stamped envelope to receive your application and any further instructions from the scholarship provider. GPA must be 3.5-4.0.

Slippery Rock University
Office of Financial Aid
107 Maltby Center
Slippery Rock, PA 16057

2534
Robert N. Aebersold Scholarship

AMOUNT: None Specified DEADLINE: Varies
MAJOR: All Areas of Study

The Robert N. Aebersold Scholarship is a four-year scholarship open to freshmen attending Slippery Rock University with at least a 1200 SAT or equivalent ACT score and in the top 10% of the high school class. This scholarship is equal to tuition and can be received for eight semesters. Award requirements change regularly. Please send a self-addressed, stamped envelope to receive your application and any further instructions from the scholarship provider. GPA must be 3.5-4.0.

Slippery Rock University
Office of Financial Aid
107 Maltby Center
Slippery Rock, PA 16057

2535
Ruth Vaughan Coon Scholarship

AMOUNT: $1200 DEADLINE: Varies
MAJOR: Physical Education

The Ruth Vaughan Coon Scholarship is open to students majoring in physical education with a minimum high school GPA of 3.0 and who demonstrate financial need. The applicants must be permanent residents of Beaver County, Pennsylvania. This award is renewable. Award requirements change regularly. Please send a self-addressed, stamped envelope to receive your application and any further instructions from the scholarship provider. GPA must be 3.0-4.0.

Slippery Rock University
Office of Financial Aid
107 Maltby Center
Slippery Rock, PA 16057

2536
Thomas H. John Scholarship

AMOUNT: $500-$1000 DEADLINE: Varies
MAJOR: Biology

The Thomas H. John Scholarship is offered to a freshman biology major planning to attend Slippery Rock University, who is in the top 20% of the high school graduating class or has a combined SAT score of at least 1,000 or a composite ACT score of 23 or better. Applicants are required to send three letters of recommendation with their application. These letters should attest to the applicant's character, potential for academic success, dependability, and emotional maturity. A handwritten statement describing your long-range goals, both professional and personal, should be attached to your application. Award requirements change regularly. Please send a self-addressed, stamped envelope to receive your application and any further instructions from the scholarship provider. GPA must be 3.0-4.0.

Slippery Rock University
Office of Financial Aid
107 Maltby Center
Slippery Rock, PA 16057

2537
University Academic Scholarship

AMOUNT: None Specified DEADLINE: Varies
MAJOR: All Areas of Study

The University Academic Scholarship is open to first-time freshmen at SRU who have attained at least a 3.5 high school GPA and have achieved at least a 1200 SAT or 26 ACT score. Award requirements change regularly. Please send a self-addressed, stamped envelope to receive your application and any further instructions from the scholarship provider. GPA must be 3.5-4.0.

Slippery Rock University
Office of Financial Aid
107 Maltby Center
Slippery Rock, PA 16057

2538
Watson Family Scholarship for Butler, Lawrence or Allegheny Graduates

AMOUNT: $500 DEADLINE: Varies
MAJOR: Elementary Education, Secondary Education

The Watson Family Scholarship is open to high school graduates from Butler, Lawrence, or Allegheny counties, majoring in elementary or secondary education at Slippery Rock University. Applicants must be ranked in the top quarter of their high school class and demonstrate leadership potential by activities and community service. Award requirements change regularly. Please send a self-addressed, stamped envelope to receive your application and any further instructions from the scholarship provider. No GPA requirement specified.

Slippery Rock University
Office of Financial Aid
107 Maltby Center
Slippery Rock, PA 16057

2539
Watson Family Scholarship for Slippery Rock Area High School Graduates

AMOUNT: $500 DEADLINE: Varies
MAJOR: Biology

The Watson Family Scholarship is open to Slippery Rock area high school graduates attending Slippery Rock University. Award requirements change regularly. Please send a self-addressed, stamped envelope to receive your application and any further instructions from the scholarship provider. No GPA requirement specified.

Slippery Rock University
Office of Financial Aid
107 Maltby Center
Slippery Rock, PA 16057

2540
Wolves Club of Coraopolis Scholarship

AMOUNT: $1800 DEADLINE: Varies
MAJOR: All Areas of Study

The Wolves Club of Coraopolis Scholarship is open to students graduating from Cornell, Montour, and Moon school districts in Pennsylvania who will be attending Slippery Rock University. This award is based on high school performance and demonstrated financial need. Award requirements change regularly. Please send a self-addressed, stamped envelope to receive your application and any further instructions from the scholarship provider. No GPA requirement specified.

Slippery Rock University
Office of Financial Aid
107 Maltby Center
Slippery Rock, PA 16057

2541
Wolves Club of New Castle Scholarship

AMOUNT: $1000 DEADLINE: Varies
MAJOR: All Areas of Study

The Wolves Club of New Castle Scholarship is open to students who are permanent residents of Lawrence County, Pennsylvania, and who will be attending Slippery Rock University. High school academic performance and demonstrated financial need are considerations. This award is renewable for up to three additional years. Award requirements change regularly. Please pick up your application from the Wolves Club of New Castle. No GPA requirement specified.

Slippery Rock University
Office of Financial Aid
107 Maltby Center
Slippery Rock, PA 16057

Sonoma State University

2542
Presidential Scholarship at Entrance Program

AMOUNT: $1000 DEADLINE: February 15
MAJOR: All Areas of Study

The Presidential Scholarship at Entrance is for incoming freshmen attending Sonoma State University. Applicants must have a cumulative weighted high school GPA of at least 4.0. Award requirements change regularly. GPA must be 4.0.

Sonoma State University
Kay Ashbrook, Scholarship Coordinator
1801 East Cotati Avenue
Rohnert Park, CA 94928

Southeastern Illinois College

2543
Privately Endowed Scholarship

AMOUNT: None Specified DEADLINE: February 1
MAJOR: All Areas of Study

The Privately Endowed Scholarship is open to students at Southeastern Illinois College. Private scholarships are based on criteria determined by the sponsors of the awards. The spring deadline date is February 1. Fall deadline date is September 1. Should you complete one application, it will constitute application to all the scholarships. Selections are made by a local committee or a designee of the donor. You may revise your application by completing a new one. Award requirements change regularly. No GPA requirement specified.

Southeastern Illinois College
Financial Aid Office
3575 College Road
Harrisburg, IL 62946-4925

Southern Illinois University, CARBONDALE

2544
Delyte and Dorothy Morris Doctoral Fellowship Program

AMOUNT: $15000 DEADLINE: January 14
MAJOR: Arts and Sciences, Business Administration, Communications, Education, Engineering, and Rehabilitation

The Delyte and Dorothy Morris Doctoral Fellowship Program is open to outstanding college seniors or post-baccalaureate students at Southern Illinois University at Carbondale. Candidates should be in one of the following fields: Arts and Sciences, Business Administration, Communications, Education, Engineering, or Rehabilitation. The stipend for this award is $15,000 over 12 months. In addition, SIUC tuition will be waived. Award requirements change regularly. Please send a self-addressed, stamped envelope to receive your application and any further instructions from the scholarship provider. No GPA requirement specified.

Southern Illinois University
Morris Doctoral Fellowship Program
Graduate School, Mailcode 4716
Carbondale, IL 62901-4716

Southern Illinois University, Edwardsville

2545
Bessie May Briggs Mason Scholarship

AMOUNT: $2000 DEADLINE: February 10
MAJOR: Primary Education, Secondary Education, and Teaching Certificate

The Bessie May Briggs Mason Scholarship is available to freshmen attending SIUE as primary or secondary education majors or students who plan to obtain their teaching certificate. Applicants must be graduates of Alton Senior High School in Illinois. The selection criteria are based on academic merit and financial need. Award requirements change regularly. For further information please write to the address listed, including a self-addressed, stamped envelope. No GPA requirement specified.

Southern Illinois University, Edwardsville
Student Financial Aid
2308 Rendleman Hall
Edwardsville, IL 62026-1060

2546
Campus Residence Honors Scholarship

AMOUNT: $500-$1000 DEADLINE: February 10
MAJOR: All Areas of Study

The Campus Residence Honors Scholarship is available to first-time undergraduate students with strong academic records pursuing a baccalaureate degree. Applicants must be enrolled in SIUE for a minimum of 12 hours per session and must live in university housing during the period of the award. Incoming freshmen should have at least a 26 ACT and rank in the top 90th percentile of their high school class. Transfer students should have at least a 2.75 GPA. This award is not renewable. Award requirements change regularly. For further information please write to the address listed, including a self-addressed, stamped envelope. No GPA requirement specified.

Southern Illinois University, Edwardsville
Student Financial Aid
2308 Rendleman Hall
Edwardsville, IL 62026-1060

2547
Chancellor's Scholarship Program

AMOUNT: None Specified DEADLINE: February 1
MAJOR: All Areas of Study

The Chancellor's Scholarship Program is available to freshmen with outstanding academic credentials attending SIUE. Each scholarship covers tuition and fees for up to four years of undergraduate study at SIUE. The application deadline is February 1, but it is preferred that candidates apply for the scholarship and admission by January 1. Award requirements change regularly. For further information please write to the address listed, including a self-addressed, stamped envelope. No GPA requirement specified.

Southern Illinois University, Edwardsville
Student Financial Aid
2308 Rendleman Hall
Edwardsville, IL 62026-1060

2548
Dennis Wade Smith Memorial Scholarship

AMOUNT: None Specified DEADLINE: March 1
MAJOR: Education, Humanities, Nursing, Social Sciences or Sciences

The Dennis Wade Smith Memorial Scholarship is available to full-time junior or senior students at SIUE who graduated from public high schools in St. Clair County, Illinois. Applicants must have declared majors in education, humanities, nursing, social sciences, or sciences and a GPA of 3.0 throughout high school and college. The selection is based on financial need. The recommended date for submission of the application is March 1, but applications are accepted until May 1. Award requirements change regularly. For further information please write to the address listed, including a self-addressed, stamped envelope. GPA must be 3.0-4.0.

Southern Illinois University, Edwardsville
Student Financial Aid
2308 Rendleman Hall
Edwardsville, IL 62026-1060

2549
Farmer's Insurance Group of Companies Scholarship

AMOUNT: $500 DEADLINE: February 10
MAJOR: Insurance, Mathematics, Business Administration, Personnel, or Areas Related to the Insurance Industry

The Farmer's Insurance Group of Companies Scholarship is available to students who are attending SIUE as insurance (or in areas related to the insurance industry), mathematics, business administration, and personnel majors. Applicants must have a GPA of 2.5. The selection process is based on financial need. Award requirements change regularly. For further information please write to the address listed, including a self-addressed, stamped envelope. GPA must be 2.5-4.0.

Southern Illinois University, Edwardsville
Student Financial Aid
2308 Rendleman Hall
Edwardsville, IL 62026-1060

2550
FEW Mary E. McGregor Memorial Scholarship

AMOUNT: $250 DEADLINE: February 10
MAJOR: All Areas of Study

The FEW Mary E. McGregor Memorial Scholarship is available to SIUE students who are members of the Federally Employed Women, Federal Civilian, or Military Employees of Scott Air Force Base or their dependents. Applicants must be completing their first undergraduate degree, have a cumulative and semester GPA of 2.5, and be enrolled for at least six hours. The selection criteria is based on financial need. Award requirements change regularly. For further information please write to the address listed, including a self-addressed, stamped envelope. GPA must be 2.5-4.0.

Southern Illinois University, Edwardsville
Student Financial Aid
2308 Rendleman Hall
Edwardsville, IL 62026-1060

2551
Harbert Memorial Scholarship

AMOUNT: None Specified DEADLINE: February 10
MAJOR: All Areas of Study

The Harbert Memorial Scholarship is available to students who are attending SIUE. This scholarship is awarded to students who are graduates of Centralia High School in Illinois and have superior academic records. This award is renewable as long as the student continues to meet the criteria. Award requirements change regularly. For further information please write to Assistant Vice Chancellor for Enrollment Management, Box 1610, SIUE, Edwardsville, Illinois 62026, including a self-addressed, stamped envelope. No GPA requirement specified.

Southern Illinois University, Edwardsville
Student Financial Aid
2308 Rendleman Hall
Edwardsville, IL 62026-1060

2552
James M. and Aune P. Nelson Minority Student Grant

AMOUNT: None Specified DEADLINE: February 10
MAJOR: All Areas of Study

The James M. and Aune P. Nelson Minority Student Grant is available to minority students attending SIUE who require financial assistance. This scholarship is awarded to minority students who are graduates of Alton Secondary Schools with a 2.0 GPA in high school and 2.5 GPA in college. Award requirements change regularly. For further information please write to the address listed, including a self-addressed, stamped envelope. GPA must be 2.0-4.0.

Southern Illinois University, Edwardsville
Student Financial Aid
2308 Rendleman Hall
Edwardsville, IL 62026-1060

2553
James R. Anderson Housing Scholarship

AMOUNT: $500 DEADLINE: February 10
MAJOR: All Areas of Study

The James R. Anderson Housing Scholarship is available to students attending SIUE. Applicants must have a GPA of 3.0 and demonstrate civic leadership through community service that focuses on leadership development, whole person development, and the value of family. Preference will be given to applicants from the Chicago area who have demonstrated a sincere pursuit of their educational goals and have been involved in University Housing Activities. Award requirements change regularly. For further information please write to the address listed, including a self-addressed, stamped envelope. GPA must be 3.0-4.0.

Southern Illinois University, Edwardsville
Student Financial Aid
2308 Rendleman Hall
Edwardsville, IL 62026-1060

2554
John A. Baker Memorial Scholarship

AMOUNT: None Specified DEADLINE: February 10
MAJOR: All Areas of Study

The John A. Baker Memorial Scholarship is available to SIUE students entering their junior or senior year who have a strong desire to complete a degree. The selection criteria are based on financial need. Award requirements change regularly. For further information please write to the address listed, including a self-addressed, stamped envelope. No GPA requirement specified.

Southern Illinois University, Edwardsville
Student Financial Aid
2308 Rendleman Hall
Edwardsville, IL 62026-1060

2555
Johnetta Haley Scholarship Program

AMOUNT: $600-$2200 DEADLINE: March 1
MAJOR: Engineering, Physical and Biological Sciences, Nursing, Teacher Education, Computer Science

The Johnetta Haley Scholarship Program is available to minority students attending SIUE as engineering, physical and biological sciences, nursing, teacher education or or computer science majors. The selection criteria are based on financial need and academic merit. The application deadline is March 1 for new students. Award requirements change regularly. For further information please write to Johnetta Haley Scholars Academy, Box 1610, SIUE, Edwardsville, Illinois 62026, including a self-addressed, stamped envelope. No GPA requirement specified.

Southern Illinois University, Edwardsville
Student Financial Aid
2308 Rendleman Hall
Edwardsville, IL 62026-1060

2556
Joseph (Cobby) Rodriguez Memorial Scholarship

AMOUNT: $250 DEADLINE: February 10
MAJOR: All Areas of Study

The Joseph (Cobby) Rodriguez Memorial Scholarship is available to SIUE students who are police officers or the children or spouses of a police officer. Applicants must be residents of St. Clair County, Illinois. The selection criteria are based on academic merit and financial need. Award requirements change regularly. For further information please write to the address listed, including a self-addressed, stamped envelope. No GPA requirement specified.

Southern Illinois University, Edwardsville
Student Financial Aid
2308 Rendleman Hall
Edwardsville, IL 62026-1060

2557
Leo and Hilda Kolb Memorial Scholarship

AMOUNT: $500 DEADLINE: February 10
MAJOR: All Areas of Study

The Leo and Hilda Kolb Memorial Scholarship is available to students attending SIUE. Applicants must be residents of Madison County, Illinois, with preference given to residents of Marine Township. The selection criteria are based on financial need. Award requirements change regularly. For further information please write to the address listed, including a self-addressed, stamped envelope. No GPA requirement specified.

Southern Illinois University, Edwardsville
Student Financial Aid
2308 Rendleman Hall
Edwardsville, IL 62026-1060

2558
Martha Huckelberry Memorial Grant

AMOUNT: $500 DEADLINE: February 10
MAJOR: All Areas of Study

The Martha Huckelberry Memorial Grant is available to single-parent undergraduates who are attending SIUE. Applicants must pursue a degree and have a 2.5 cumulative GPA. This award is also based on financial need. Award requirements change regularly. For further information please write to the address listed, including a self-addressed, stamped envelope. GPA must be 2.5-4.0.

Southern Illinois University, Edwardsville
Student Financial Aid
2308 Rendleman Hall
Edwardsville, IL 62026-1060

2559
Maurice and Catherine Sessel Alton Student Grant

AMOUNT: None Specified DEADLINE: February 10
MAJOR: All Areas of Study

The Maurice and Catherine Sessel Alton Student Grant is available to students attending SIUE. This scholarship is awarded to students who are graduates of Alton secondary schools with a 2.5 GPA in high school and college. The selection criteria are based on financial need. Award requirements change regularly. For further information please write to the address listed, including a self-addressed, stamped envelope. GPA must be 2.5-4.0.

Southern Illinois University, Edwardsville
Student Financial Aid
2308 Rendleman Hall
Edwardsville, IL 62026-1060

2560
Phi Theta Kappa Scholarship

AMOUNT: None Specified DEADLINE: February 10
MAJOR: All Areas of Study

The Phi Theta Kappa Scholarship is available to transfer undergraduate students who are attending SIUE. Applicants must be members of Phi Theta Kappa and U.S citizens. Students must also have completed an associate of arts or science degree from an Illinois community college prior to using the award. The selection criteria are based on academic merit. Award requirements change regularly. For further information please write to the address listed, including a self-addressed, stamped envelope. No GPA requirement specified.

Southern Illinois University, Edwardsville
Student Financial Aid
2308 Rendleman Hall
Edwardsville, IL 62026-1060

Provost's Scholarship

AMOUNT: $500 DEADLINE: February 10
MAJOR: All Areas of Study

The Provost's Scholarship is available to continuing SIUE undergraduates with a 3.25 cumulative GPA enrolled for six or more hours each term. The selection criteria is based on demonstrated academic achievement, service contributions (to the university or the community), financial need, excellence in undergraduate course work, and contributions to the workplace. Award requirements change regularly. For further information please write to the address listed, including a self-addressed, stamped envelope. GPA must be 3.25-4.0.

Southern Illinois University, Edwardsville
Student Financial Aid
2308 Rendleman Hall
Edwardsville, IL 62026-1060

2562
Thelma Thompson Memorial Scholarship

AMOUNT: None Specified DEADLINE: February 10
MAJOR: All Areas of Study

The Thelma Thompson Memorial Scholarship is available to students attending SIUE. Applicants must have a minimum GPA of 2.0. The selection criteria are based on academic merit and financial need. Award requirements change regularly. For further information please write to the address listed, including a self-addressed, stamped envelope. GPA must be 2.0-4.0.

Southern Illinois University, Edwardsville
Student Financial Aid
2308 Rendleman Hall
Edwardsville, IL 62026-1060

Southwest Florida College of Business

2563
Southwest Florida Accounting/Computer Operations Scholarship

AMOUNT: None Specified DEADLINE: Varies
MAJOR: Accounting/Computer Operations

The Southwest Florida Accounting/Computer Operations Scholarship is open to Florida residents attending or planning to attend Southwest Florida College of Business to study Accounting and Computer Operations. Applications are available at Florida high schools and GED testing centers. Award requirements change regularly. For further information, please send a self-addressed, stamped envelope to Southwest Florida College of Business, Gregory H. Jones, Chief Fiscal Officer,

1685 Medical Lane, Suite 200, Fort Myers, FL 33907, or call (941) 939-4766. No GPA requirement specified.

Florida Association of Postsecondary Schools and Colleges
Attn: FAPSC Scholarship Committee
F200 West College Avenue
Tallahassee, FL 32301

2564
Southwest Florida Management and Marketing Scholarship

AMOUNT: None Specified DEADLINE: Varies
MAJOR: Management and Marketing

The Southwest Florida Management and Marketing Scholarship is open to Florida residents attending or planning to attend Southwest Florida College of Business to study management and marketing. Applications are available at Florida high schools and GED testing centers. Award requirements change regularly. For further information, please send a self-addressed, stamped envelope to Southwest Florida College of Business, Gregory H. Jones, Chief Fiscal Officer, 1685 Medical Lane, Suite 200, Fort Myers, FL 33907, or call (941) 939-4766. No GPA requirement specified.

Florida Association of Postsecondary Schools and Colleges
Attn: FAPSC Scholarship Committee
F200 West College Avenue
Tallahassee, FL 32301

2565
Southwest Florida Medical Administration Scholarship

AMOUNT: None Specified DEADLINE: Varies
MAJOR: Medical Administration

The Southwest Florida Medical Administration Scholarship is open to Florida residents attending or planning to attend Southwest Florida College of Business to study medical administration. Applications are available at Florida high schools and GED testing centers. Award requirements change regularly. For further information, please send a self-addressed, stamped envelope to Southwest Florida College of Business, Gregory H. Jones, Chief Fiscal Officer, 1685 Medical Lane, Suite 200, Fort Myers, FL 33907, or call (941) 939-4766. No GPA requirement specified.

Florida Association of Postsecondary Schools and Colleges
Attn: FAPSC Scholarship Committee
F200 West College Avenue
Tallahassee, FL 32301

2566
Southwest Florida Medical Transcription Scholarship

AMOUNT: None Specified DEADLINE: Varies
MAJOR: Medical Transcription

The Southwest Florida Medical Transcription Scholarship is open to Florida residents attending or planning to attend Southwest Florida College of Business to study medical transcription. Applications are available at Florida high schools and GED testing centers. Award requirements change regularly. For further information, please send a self-addressed, stamped envelope to Southwest Florida College of Business,

Gregory H. Jones, Chief Fiscal Officer, 1685 Medical Lane, Suite 200, Fort Myers, FL 33907, or call (941) 939-4766. No GPA requirement specified.

Florida Association of Postsecondary Schools and Colleges
Attn: FAPSC Scholarship Committee
F200 West College Avenue
Tallahassee, FL 32301

2567
Southwest Florida Office Administration Scholarship

AMOUNT: None Specified DEADLINE: Varies
MAJOR: Office Administration

The Southwest Florida Office Administration Studies Scholarship is open to Florida residents attending or planning to attend Southwest Florida College of Business to study office administration. Applications are available at Florida high schools and GED testing centers. Award requirements change regularly. For further information, please send a self-addressed, stamped envelope to Southwest Florida College of Business, Gregory H. Jones, Chief Fiscal Officer, 1685 Medical Lane, Suite 200, Fort Myers, FL 33907, or call (941) 939-4766. No GPA requirement specified.

Florida Association of Postsecondary Schools and Colleges
Attn: FAPSC Scholarship Committee
F200 West College Avenue
Tallahassee, FL 32301

2568
Southwest Florida Paralegal Studies Scholarship

AMOUNT: None Specified DEADLINE: Varies
MAJOR: Paralegal

The Southwest Florida Paralegal Studies Scholarship is open to Florida residents attending or planning to attend Southwest Florida College of Business who are studying to become paralegals. Applications are available at Florida high schools and GED testing centers. Award requirements change regularly. For further information, please send a self-addressed, stamped envelope to Southwest Florida College of Business, Gregory H. Jones, Chief Fiscal Officer, 1685 Medical Lane, Suite 200, Fort Myers, FL 33907, or call (941) 939-4766. No GPA requirement specified.

Florida Association of Postsecondary Schools and Colleges
Attn: FAPSC Scholarship Committee
F200 West College Avenue
Tallahassee, FL 32301

Southwest Missouri State University

2569
Albert L. Verweire Memorial Scholarship

AMOUNT: $75 DEADLINE: Varies
MAJOR: Music (Flute)

The Albert L. Verweire Memorial Scholarship is open to outstanding senior music majors at SMSU who are studying applied flute. The award is a $75 savings bond. Award requirements change regularly. Contact the Music Department at (417) 836-5648 for a special application and audition information. You may also visit the SMSU website at www.smsu.edu. No GPA requirement specified.

Southwest Missouri State University - Arts and Letters
Financial Aid Office
901 South National Avenue
Springfield, MO 65804

2570
A.L. Hagale Memorial Scholarship

AMOUNT: $1000 DEADLINE: Varies
MAJOR: All Areas of Study

This scholarship is open to dependent children of Hagale Industries employees who are attending SMSU. You must rank in the top 15% of your high school graduating class and maintain a minimum 3.0 GPA in order to renew. Award requirements change regularly. Contact the Personnel Office at Hagale Industries for information. GPA must be 3.3-4.0.

Southwest Missouri State University - General Scholarships
Financial Aid Office
901 South National Avenue
Springfield, MO 65804

2571
Anna B. Jefferson Memorial Scholarship

AMOUNT: $350 DEADLINE: March 31
MAJOR: All Areas of Study

This scholarship is open to juniors and seniors attending SMSU who demonstrate satisfactory scholarship and financial need. You must complete the FAFSA by March 31. Award requirements change regularly. For further information, please write to the address listed, including a self-addressed, stamped envelope. GPA must be 2.5-4.0.

Southwest Missouri State University - General Scholarships
Financial Aid Office
901 South National Avenue
Springfield, MO 65804

2572
Basil Boritzki Academic Achievement Scholarship

AMOUNT: $2100 DEADLINE: Varies
MAJOR: All Areas of Study

This scholarship is open to active members of the Alpha Rho Chapter of Sigma Pi Fraternity who are attending SMSU. To apply, you must be a full-time student and maintain satisfactory academic progress to renew. Two awards are offered annually. Award requirements change regularly. Contact the Greek Life Office at (417) 836-5501 for more information. No GPA requirement specified.

Southwest Missouri State University - General Scholarships
Financial Aid Office
901 South National Avenue
Springfield, MO 65804

2573
Board of Governors Scholarship

AMOUNT: $3400 DEADLINE: March 1
MAJOR: All Areas of Study

The Board of Governors Scholarship is open to freshmen who have a minimum 28 ACT or 1240 SAT. In order to apply, you must also be in the top 10% of your graduating high school class or have a minimum 3.8 GPA. Renewability is based on completing 30 semester hours each year with a minimum 3.4 GPA. Award requirements change regularly. Please apply for admission by March 1 for consideration. For an application and further information, write to the address listed, including a self-addressed, stamped envelope. GPA must be 3.8-4.0.

Southwest Missouri State University - Freshmen Scholarships
Financial Aid Office
901 South National Avenue
Springfield, MO 65804

2574
Community College Scholarship

AMOUNT: $1500 DEADLINE: May 1
MAJOR: All Areas of Study

This award is based on a nomination from a Missouri public community college president. The college president may nominate two students, who are attending or will be attending SMSU, to receive this scholarship. Award requirements change regularly. For an application and further information, write to the address listed, including a self-addressed, stamped envelope. Feel free to browse the SMSU website at www.smsu.edu. GPA must be 3.3-4.0.

Southwest Missouri State University - Transfer Scholarships
Financial Aid Office
901 South National Avenue
Springfield, MO 65804

2575
Continue the Tradition Scholarship

AMOUNT: None Specified DEADLINE: Varies
MAJOR: All Areas of Study

This scholarship is open to entering students who are classified as non-residents for fee purposes and have at least one parent or grandparent who is an SMSU graduate. If you are an entering freshman, you must rank in the upper 25% of your class - or have a minimum 3.5 GPA - and have a minimum 24 ACT. If you are a transfer student, you must have completed at least 24 hours with a minimum GPA of 3.25. Award requirements change regularly. Contact the Office of Alumni Relations at (417) 836-5654 for information and an application. GPA must be 3.25-4.0.

Southwest Missouri State University - Freshmen Scholarships
Financial Aid Office
901 South National Avenue
Springfield, MO 65804

2576
Floyd M. and Bertha E. Holt Scholarship

AMOUNT: $200 DEADLINE: March 31
MAJOR: All Areas of Study

This scholarship is open to seniors attending SMSU. You must have a minimum 2.5 GPA and demonstrate financial need. Award requirements change regularly. For further information and an application, please write to the address listed, including a self-addressed, stamped envelope. GPA must be 2.5-4.0.

Southwest Missouri State University - General Scholarships
Financial Aid Office
901 South National Avenue
Springfield, MO 65804

2577
Freshman Academic Scholarship

AMOUNT: $2000 DEADLINE: March 1
MAJOR: All Areas of Study

The Freshman Academic Scholarship is open to SMSU freshmen who have a minimum 26 ACT or 1170 SAT. You must also rank in the top 20% of your high school class or have a minimum 3.6 GPA. If you are class valedictorian or salutatorian you are also eligible. Renewability is based on completing 30 hours each year with a minimum 3.25 GPA. This award is not available to recipients of the Governors Scholarship. Award requirements change regularly. Please apply for admission by March 1 for consideration. For an application and further information, write to the address listed, including a self-addressed, stamped envelope. GPA must be 3.6-4.0.

Southwest Missouri State University - Freshmen Scholarships
Financial Aid Office
901 South National Avenue
Springfield, MO 65804

2578
Freshman Achievement Scholarship

AMOUNT: $1000 DEADLINE: March 1
MAJOR: All Areas of Study

The Freshman Achievement Scholarship is open to SMSU freshmen who have a minimum 24 ACT or 1090 SAT. You must also be in the top 10% of your high school class or have a minimum 3.8 GPA. Renewability is based on completing 24 hours each year with a minimum 2.75 GPA. This award is not available to recipients of the Freshman Academic Scholarship. Award requirements change regularly. Please apply for admission by March 1 for consideration. For an application and further information, write to the address listed, including a self-addressed, stamped envelope. GPA must be 3.8-4.0.

Southwest Missouri State University - Freshmen Scholarships
Financial Aid Office
901 South National Avenue
Springfield, MO 65804

2579
Greek Scholarship

AMOUNT: $275 DEADLINE: Varies
MAJOR: All Areas of Study

This scholarship is open to full-time sophomores or above who are attending SMSU. You must be an active member of the SMSU Greek community and have a minimum 3.0 GPA. Award requirements change regularly. Contact the Greek Office at (417) 836-5501 for further information. GPA must be 3.0.

Southwest Missouri State University - General Scholarships
Financial Aid Office
901 South National Avenue
Springfield, MO 65804

2580
Homer and Dorothy Mace Kesterson Scholarship

AMOUNT: $450 DEADLINE: March 31
MAJOR: Biology, Educational Administration, English, Mathematics, Modern/Classical Languages

This scholarship is open to full-time juniors or above who are attending SMSU. You must be majoring in biology, educational administration, English, math, or modern and classical languages and have a minimum cumulative 3.0 GPA and a 3.5 GPA in your major. Enrollment of at least 12 hours is required if you are an undergraduate and 6 hours if you are a graduate student. Award requirements change regularly. For further information, please write to the address listed, including a self-addressed, stamped envelope. GPA must be 3.0-4.0.

Southwest Missouri State University - General Scholarships
Financial Aid Office
901 South National Avenue
Springfield, MO 65804

2581
Hutchens Industries Scholarship

AMOUNT: $1600 DEADLINE: Varies
MAJOR: All Areas of Study

This scholarship is open to SMSU students who are dependent children of Hutchens Industries employees and who demonstrate financial need. You must maintain satisfactory academic progress in order to renew this scholarship. Award requirements change regularly. Contact the Personnel Office at Hutchens Industries for information. No GPA requirement specified.

Southwest Missouri State University - General Scholarships
Financial Aid Office
901 South National Avenue
Springfield, MO 65804

2582
International Students Activity Scholarship

AMOUNT: $150 DEADLINE: Varies
MAJOR: All Areas of Study

This scholarship is open to students attending SMSU who are active members of the Association of International Students. Selections are based on GPA and participation in intercultural activities. Award requirements change regularly. Contact the International Student Services office, Carrington Hall #302, for further information or call (417) 836-6618. GPA must be 2.8-4.0.

Southwest Missouri State University - General Scholarships
Financial Aid Office
901 South National Avenue
Springfield, MO 65804

2583
Jerry Fortner Memorial Scholarship

AMOUNT: $200 DEADLINE: March 31
MAJOR: All Areas of Study

This scholarship is open to students attending SMSU who are in good academic standing and demonstrate financial need. To apply, you must complete the FAFSA by March 31. Award requirements change regularly. For further information and an application, please contact the address listed, including a self-addressed, stamped envelope. GPA must be 2.8-4.0.

Southwest Missouri State University - General Scholarships
Financial Aid Office
901 South National Avenue
Springfield, MO 65804

2584
Joseph N. Boyce/Wall Street Journal Public Affairs Award

AMOUNT: $1000 DEADLINE: March 31
MAJOR: Public Affairs

This scholarship is open to full-time juniors and seniors attending SMSU who are in good academic standing with a record of service and leadership. Award requirements change regularly. For an application and further information, please contact the address listed, including a self-addressed, stamped envelope. GPA must be 2.8-4.0.

Southwest Missouri State University - General Scholarships
Financial Aid Office
901 South National Avenue
Springfield, MO 65804

2585
Midwest Student Exchange Program (MSEP)

AMOUNT: $2000 DEADLINE: March 1
MAJOR: All Areas of Study

Awards for non-resident students who are from Kansas, Michigan, Minnesota, or Nebraska enrolled full-time. Entering freshmen must rank in the upper 25% of their class (or 3.5 GPA) and have an ACT score of at least 24. Transfer students must have completed at least 24 hours and have a minimum 3.25 GPA. Recipients of the Out-of-State Fee Stipend are not eligible for this award. Award requirements change regularly. Please apply for admission by March 1 for consideration. For an application and further information, write to the address listed, including a self-addressed, stamped envelope. Feel free to browse the SMSU website at www.smsu.edu. GPA must be 3.5-4.0.

Southwest Missouri State University - General Scholarships
Financial Aid Office
901 South National Avenue
Springfield, MO 65804

2586
Missouri Higher Education Academic Scholarship (Bright Flight)

AMOUNT: $2000 DEADLINE: July 31
MAJOR: All Areas of Study

Missouri Higher Education Academic Scholarship (Bright Flight) is open to Missouri residents who are freshmen entering SMSU. You must have an SAT or ACT score in the top 3% of Missouri students to be eligible for this award. Renewability is based on full-time enrollment and the maintenance of satisfactory academic progress. Award requirements change regularly. For further information, contact your high school counselor or the Missouri Student Assistance Resource Services (MOSTAR) at (800) 473-6757. No GPA requirement specified.

Southwest Missouri State University - Freshmen Scholarships
Financial Aid Office
901 South National Avenue
Springfield, MO 65804

2587
Multicultural Leadership Scholarship for Transfer Students

AMOUNT: None Specified DEADLINE: March 1
MAJOR: All Areas of Study

Awards for SMSU transferring minority students who have completed at least 24 hours with a minimum GPA of 2.75. Recipients must be able to demonstrate leadership in the

minority community through involvement in school or community organizations. Award requirements change regularly. Please complete the Multicultural Leadership Application and return to Minority Student Services by March 1. For further information, write to the address listed, including a self-addressed, stamped envelope. Feel free to browse their website at www.smsu.edu. GPA must be 2.75-4.0.

Southwest Missouri State University - Transfer Scholarships
Financial Aid Office
901 South National Avenue
Springfield, MO 65804

2588
Multicultural Leadership Scholarship

AMOUNT: $3400 DEADLINE: March 1
MAJOR: All Areas of Study

The Multicultural Leadership Scholarship is open to SMSU freshmen who have graduated in the upper 50% of their class. You must demonstrate leadership in the minority community through involvement in various school and community organizations. Renewability is based on completing 24 hours each year with a minimum 2.75 GPA. Award requirements change regularly. Please complete the Multicultural Leadership Application and return it to Minority Student Services by March 1. For further information, write to the address listed, including a self-addressed, stamped envelope. GPA must be 2.0-4.0.

Southwest Missouri State University - Freshmen Scholarships
Financial Aid Office
901 South National Avenue
Springfield, MO 65804

2589
Out-of-State Fee Stipend

AMOUNT: $2000 DEADLINE: March 1
MAJOR: All Areas of Study

This scholarship is open to entering students classified as non-residents. If you are an entering freshman, you must rank in the upper 25% of your class - or have a minimum 3.5 GPA - and have scored at least a 24 ACT. If you are a transfer student, you must have completed at least 24 hours with a minimum GPA of 3.25. Award requirements change regularly. Please apply for admission by March 1 for consideration. For an application and further information, write to the address listed, including a self-addressed, stamped envelope. GPA must be 3.25-4.0.

Southwest Missouri State University - Freshmen Scholarships
Financial Aid Office
901 South National Avenue
Springfield, MO 65804

2590
Phi Theta Kappa Scholarship

AMOUNT: $2000 DEADLINE: March 31
MAJOR: All Areas of Study

Open to entering students who are current members of Phi Theta Kappa. Award requirements change regularly. Please complete the Phi Theta Kappa application and return it to the Financial Aid Office by March 31. You may also write to the address listed, including a self-addressed, stamped envelope. Feel free to browse their website at www.smsu.edu. GPA must be 3.3-4.0.

Southwest Missouri State University - Transfer Scholarships
Financial Aid Office
901 South National Avenue
Springfield, MO 65804

2591
Presidential Scholarship

AMOUNT: $9000 DEADLINE: January 15
MAJOR: All Areas of Study

The Presidential Scholarship is open to freshmen who rank in the upper 10% of their class and have a minimum 30 ACT or 1320 SAT. You may also apply if you have been selected as National Merit finalists or semifinalists. Renewability is based on completing 30 hours per year with a minimum 3.4 GPA. Note: The December ACT is the last score accepted for consideration. Award requirements change regularly. Please complete the Presidential Scholarship Application and return it to the Office of Admissions by January 15. For an application and further information, write to the address listed, including a self-addressed, stamped envelope. GPA must be 3.6-4.0.

Southwest Missouri State University - Freshmen Scholarships
Financial Aid Office
901 South National Avenue
Springfield, MO 65804

2592
SMSU Leadership Scholarship

AMOUNT: $1000 DEADLINE: May 1
MAJOR: All Areas of Study

For this scholarship, Southwest Missouri high schools may recommend one student for every 100 graduates. The Southwest district includes schools in the following counties: Barry, Barton, Cedar, Christian, Dade, Dallas, Douglas, Greene, Howell, Jasper, Laclede, Lawrence, McDonald, Newton, Oregon, Ozark, Polk, Shannon, Stone, Taney, Texas, Vernon, Webster, and Wright. Renewability is based on completing 30 hours each year with a minimum 3.25 GPA. Award requirements change regularly. For an application and further information, write to the address listed, including a self-addressed, stamped envelope. High schools must submit nomination forms to the Financial Aid office by May 1. No GPA requirement specified.

Southwest Missouri State University - Freshmen Scholarships
Financial Aid Office
901 South National Avenue
Springfield, MO 65804

2593
Transfer Academic Scholarship

AMOUNT: $1500 DEADLINE: March 31
MAJOR: All Areas of Study

Open to students transferring from community college. Must have completed 45 hours with a minimum GPA of 3.5. Recipients of the Phi Theta Kappa scholarship are not eligible for this award. Award requirements change regularly. Please apply for admission by March 31 for consideration. For an application and further information, write to the address listed,

including a self-addressed, stamped envelope. Feel free to browse their website at www.smsu.edu. GPA must be 3.5-4.0.

Southwest Missouri State University - Transfer Scholarships
Financial Aid Office
901 South National Avenue
Springfield, MO 65804

2594
Wilda F. Looney Residence Life Leadership Scholarship

AMOUNT: $800 DEADLINE: Varies
MAJOR: All Areas of Study

This scholarship is open to full-time undergraduates attending SMSU who are living in a university residence life facility. You must have completed at least 12 hours at SMSU with a minimum cumulative GPA of 2.5. Award requirements change regularly. Contact the Residence Life and Services Office in Hammons House at (417) 836-5536 for more information. GPA must be 2.5-4.0.

Southwest Missouri State University - General Scholarships
Financial Aid Office
901 South National Avenue
Springfield, MO 65804

Southwest Texas State University

2595
Foster Care Initiative Endowed Scholarship

AMOUNT: None Specified DEADLINE: Varies
MAJOR: All Areas of Study

The Foster Care Initiative Endowed Scholarship is open to students attending SWT who have foster care in their background. This award provides funds for room and board. Award requirements change regularly. No GPA requirement specified.

Southwest Texas State University
Attn: Scholarship Coordinator
601 University Dr. - JC Kellam Bldg. 220
San Marcos, TX 78666-4602

2596
LBJ Achievement Scholarship

AMOUNT: $2000 DEADLINE: February 1
MAJOR: All Areas of Study

This award is open to full-time freshmen (less than 30 credit hours) at SWT who are living on campus. Applicants must have been in the top 25% of their graduating high school class and must be either a prior Upward Bound, Talent Search, or Educational Opportunity Center participant. Award requirements change regularly. GPA must be 3.0-4.0.

Southwest Texas State University
Attn: Scholarship Coordinator
601 University Dr. - JC Kellam Bldg. 220
San Marcos, TX 78666-4602

2597
Louise Lindsey Merrick Scholarship

AMOUNT: $1000-$3000 DEADLINE: February 1
MAJOR: All Areas of Study

This scholarship is open to academically talented high school seniors and junior college transfer students. Traditionally, high school seniors must have a minimum ACT score of 28 or SAT score of 1260. Transfer students must have a minimum GPA of 3.25 to apply. This award is renewable with a minimum GPA of 3.25. Non-Texas residents who receive this award may be eligible to pay resident tuition. Award requirements change regularly. GPA must be 3.25-4.0.

Southwest Texas State University
Attn: Scholarship Coordinator
601 University Dr. - JC Kellam Bldg. 220
San Marcos, TX 78666-4602

2598
MLK-Rivera Scholarship

AMOUNT: $1500-$2000 DEADLINE: February 1
MAJOR: All Areas of Study

This award is open to transfer students who are Texas residents and demonstrate financial need. To qualify, you must be prior Upward Bound, Talent Search, TRIO, or free school lunch participants. Graduate students must have obtained their undergraduate degree from SWT with a minimum 3.0 GPA. Undergraduate transfer students, in order to qualify, must be continuously enrolled at the university for a minimum of 12 semester hours. Award requirements change regularly. GPA must be 3.0-4.0.

Southwest Texas State University
Attn: Scholarship Coordinator
601 University Dr. - JC Kellam Bldg. 220
San Marcos, TX 78666-4602

2599
New Braunfels Junior Chamber of Commerce Scholarship

AMOUNT: $1000 DEADLINE: February 1
MAJOR: All Areas of Study

This scholarship is open to students at SWT who are graduates of Comal County High Schools and/or are the children of past or present New Braunfels Jaycees. Preference for this award is given to non-freshmen who can demonstrate financial need and who have a minimum 24 ACT or 1000 SAT score. Award requirements change regularly. GPA must be 3.4-4.0.

Southwest Texas State University
Attn: Scholarship Coordinator
601 University Dr. - JC Kellam Bldg. 220
San Marcos, TX 78666-4602

2600
President's Endowed Scholarships

AMOUNT: $1000 DEADLINE: February 1
MAJOR: All Areas of Study

This scholarship is open to entering freshmen who are admitted to SWT. You must have a minimum ACT score of 24 and a minimum SAT of 1000. Several scholarships are available, and criteria may vary slightly for each award. Award requirements change regularly. GPA must be 3.4-4.0.

Southwest Texas State University
Attn: Scholarship Coordinator
601 University Dr. - JC Kellam Bldg. 220
San Marcos, TX 78666-4602

2601
Roy F. and Joann C. Mitte Foundation Scholarship

AMOUNT: $5050 DEADLINE: February 1
MAJOR: All Areas of Study

The Roy F. and Joann C. Mitte Foundation Scholarship is open to first-time freshmen who are commended students, semi-finalists or finalists in the National Merit competition, valedictorians, salutatorians, or in the top 5% of their graduating class. All scholarship applicants must submit a resume, an essay, and three letters of recommendation. This scholarship may be renewable. Award requirements change regularly. No GPA requirement specified.

Southwest Texas State University
Attn: Scholarship Coordinator
601 University Dr. - JC Kellam Bldg. 220
San Marcos, TX 78666-4602

2602
University Scholars Scholarship

AMOUNT: $2100 DEADLINE: February 1
MAJOR: All Areas of Study

This award is open to high school seniors with a minimum ACT score of 27 and SAT of 1230. Selections are based on GPA and ACT/SAT scores, and a personal interview with the college selection committee is required. Scholarships are awarded by each of the university's seven undergraduate colleges and the College of General Studies. These scholarships are renewable for up to three years. Non-Texas residents who receive this scholarship may be eligible to pay resident tuition. Award requirements change regularly. No GPA requirement specified.

Southwest Texas State University
Attn: Scholarship Coordinator
601 University Dr. - JC Kellam Bldg. 220
San Marcos, TX 78666-4602

St. Matthew's University

2603
Colonel Harry E. Walmer Memorial Scholarship

AMOUNT: $500-$2500 DEADLINE: Varies
MAJOR: Medicine, Chemistry, Biology, and related areas

The Colonel Harry E. Walmer Memorial Scholarship is open to a beginning medical student at St. Matthew's University School of Medicine. To be considered for the award, you must demonstrate through references and community involvement that you are honest, giving, compassionate, and deeply committed to helping others. The renewal of the award is dependent upon your continuing commitment to these qualities, as well as being in the top 50% of your class. Award requirements change regularly. GPA must be 2.5-4.0.

St. Matthew's University
School of Medicine
PO Box 730
Liberty Lake, WA 99019-0730

Stanford University

2604
Stanford Financial Need Scholarships

AMOUNT: None Specified DEADLINE: Varies
MAJOR: All Areas of Study

If Stanford determines that an applicant for financial aid cannot meet the year's standard educational budget from personal, family, and outside resources, Stanford will offer or recommend financial aid resources to meet those costs. In awarding financial aid, Stanford first includes "self-help" (i.e., student loans and anticipated job earnings). If the computed need is greater than this self-help expectation, Stanford will award scholarship funds to meet the remaining need. With the exception of aid to student-athletes awarded under the rules of the NCAA, all scholarship aid at Stanford is based on demonstrated financial need. Stanford students do not apply for individual scholarships. Scholarships are assigned to each student in whatever amount is required to cover the need that remains after that student's other resources have been taken into consideration. Award requirements change regularly. Contact Stanford's Admission Office (650) 723-2091 or Stanford's Financial Aid Office (650) 723-3058 for more information. You may also visit their website: www.stanford.edu. No GPA requirement specified.

Stanford University
Financial Aid Office
520 Lasuen Mall, Old Union, Room 322
Stanford, CA 94305

State University of West Georgia

2605
A & M Scholarship

AMOUNT: None Specified DEADLINE: March 1
MAJOR: All Fields of Study

The A & M Scholarship is open to full-time students attending the State University of West Georgia who demonstrate academic ability and financial need, with preference given to descendants of A & M School Alumni. To be eligible for this award, you must be an incoming freshman, transfer, or continuing student and have a minimum GPA of 3.5. Incoming freshmen must have a minimum 1100 SAT score with at least a 580 verbal score, or a minimum 24 ACT score with at least a 23 verbal score. Award requirements change regularly. GPA must be 3.5-4.0.

State University of West Georgia
Attn: Financial Aid Office
1600 Maple Avenue
Carrollton, GA 30118

2606
Amos and Leona Caswell Scholarship

AMOUNT: None Specified DEADLINE: March 1
MAJOR: All Fields of Study

The Amos and Leona Caswell Scholarship is open to students attending the State University of West Georgia. To be eligible for this award, you must be an incoming freshman, transfer, or continuing student; have a minimum GPA of 3.5; and demonstrate financial need. Incoming freshmen must have a minimum 1100 SAT score with at least a 580 verbal score or a minimum 24 ACT score with at least a 23 verbal score. Award requirements change regularly. GPA must be 3.5-4.0.

State University of West Georgia
Attn: Financial Aid Office
1600 Maple Avenue
Carrollton, GA 30118

2607
Artist/Scholar Award

AMOUNT: $1450 DEADLINE: Varies
MAJOR: Art

The Artist/Scholar Award is open to students majoring in art at the State University of West Georgia. If you are an entering freshman you must have a minimum of 1000 SAT and a high school GPA of 3.25. You must present a portfolio of at least 10 works of art and two letters of recommendation to the art department. Letters of recommendation may be from the student's high school art teacher, principal, or another teacher. This scholarship is renewable if you maintain a minimum GPA of 3.5 in art with an overall minimum GPA of 3.0. If you are an outstanding sophomore or junior you may be eligible for a full-tuition award. Award requirements change regularly. Please send a self-addressed, stamped envelope to receive your application and any further instructions from the scholarship provider, or call (770) 836-6521. You may also browse the university's website at www.westga.edu. GPA must be

3.25-4.0.

State University of West Georgia
Attn: Financial Aid Office
1600 Maple Avenue
Carrollton, GA 30118

2608
Betty Reynolds Cobb Scholarship

AMOUNT: None Specified DEADLINE: March 1
MAJOR: All Fields of Study

The Betty Reynolds Cobb Scholarship is open to freshmen attending the State University of West Georgia who demonstrate financial need. To be considered for this award, you must have a minimum SAT score of 1100 with at least a 580 verbal score or a minimum ACT score of 24 with at least a 23 verbal score and a minimum GPA of 3.5. Award requirements change regularly. GPA must be 3.5-4.0.

State University of West Georgia
Attn: Financial Aid Office
1600 Maple Avenue
Carrollton, GA 30118

2609
Charles Wadsworth Music Scholarship

AMOUNT: $1500 DEADLINE: Varies
MAJOR: Music (Piano, Organ, Vocal, Wind, Brass, Percussion)

The Charles Wadsworth Music Scholarship is open to incoming State University of West Georgia music majors. You must demonstrate artistic excellence and potential as an instrumentalist or vocalist at an audition. You must also participate in the choral and instrumental ensembles at the university. This award is renewable for up to four years. Award requirements change regularly. Please send a self-addressed, stamped envelope to the Music Department at the address listed to receive your application and any further instructions, or call (770) 836-6516. You may also apply online at www.westga.edu/~musicdpt/form.html. No GPA requirement specified.

State University of West Georgia
Attn: Financial Aid Office
1600 Maple Avenue
Carrollton, GA 30118

2610
Connie Wright Gunter Scholarship in Early Childhood Education

AMOUNT: None Specified DEADLINE: February 18
MAJOR: Early Childhood Education

The Connie Wright Gunter Scholarship in Early Childhood Education is awarded approximately every four years to the top academic incoming freshman at the State University of West Georgia. You must be an early childhood education major. Award requirements change regularly. Please send a self-addressed, stamped envelope to the Dean's Office at the College of Education to receive your application and any fur-

ther instructions or call (770) 836-6570. No GPA requirement specified.

State University of West Georgia
Attn: Financial Aid Office
1600 Maple Avenue
Carrollton, GA 30118

2611
Davenport-Cadenhead Scholarship

AMOUNT: None Specified DEADLINE: March 1
MAJOR: All Fields of Study

The Davenport-Cadenhead Scholarship is open to students attending the State University of West Georgia who demonstrate academic ability and financial need. To be eligible for this award, you must be an incoming freshman, transfer, or continuing student and have a minimum GPA of 3.5. Incoming freshmen must have a minimum 1100 SAT score with at least a 580 verbal score, or a minimum 24 ACT score with at least a 23 verbal score. Award requirements change regularly. GPA must be 3.5-4.0.

State University of West Georgia
Attn: Financial Aid Office
1600 Maple Avenue
Carrollton, GA 30118

2612
Dr. Robert M. Reeves Scholarship

AMOUNT: $150 DEADLINE: February 18
MAJOR: Physical Education, Recreation

The Dr. Robert M. Reeves Scholarship is open to rising seniors majoring in physical education or recreation at the State University of West Georgia. You must demonstrate academic achievement, activities, and leadership. Award requirements change regularly. Please send a self-addressed, stamped envelope to the Dean's Office at the College of Education to receive your application and any further instructions or call (770) 836-6570. No GPA requirement specified.

State University of West Georgia
Attn: Financial Aid Office
1600 Maple Avenue
Carrollton, GA 30118

2613
Elizabeth Gellerstedt Wright Scholarship

AMOUNT: None Specified DEADLINE: Varies
MAJOR: Music

The Elizabeth Gellerstedt Wright Scholarship is open to graduate and undergraduate students majoring in music at the State University of West Georgia. You must perform at an audition. Award requirements change regularly. Please send a self-addressed, stamped envelope to receive your application and any further instructions to the Music Department at the address listed, or call (770) 836-6516. You may also browse the university's website at www.westga.edu. No GPA requirement specified.

State University of West Georgia
Attn: Financial Aid Office
1600 Maple Avenue
Carrollton, GA 30118

2614
Felton Denney Scholarship

AMOUNT: None Specified DEADLINE: March 1
MAJOR: All Fields of Study

The Felton Denney Scholarship is open to full-time students attending the State University of West Georgia who demonstrate financial need. To be eligible for this award, you must be an incoming freshman, transfer, or continuing student and have a minimum GPA of 3.5. Incoming freshmen must have a minimum 1100 SAT score with at least a 580 verbal score, or a minimum 24 ACT score with at least a 23 verbal score. Award requirements change regularly. GPA must be 3.5-4.0.

State University of West Georgia
Attn: Financial Aid Office
1600 Maple Avenue
Carrollton, GA 30118

2615
Geology Scholarship

AMOUNT: None Specified DEADLINE: Varies
MAJOR: Geology, Earth Science

The Geology Scholarship is open to promising undergraduates at the State University of West Georgia. You must be a geology or earth science major. Award requirements change regularly. Please send a self-addressed, stamped envelope to receive your application and any further instructions from the scholarship provider, or call (770) 836-6421. You may also browse the university's website at www.westga.edu. No GPA requirement specified.

State University of West Georgia
Attn: Financial Aid Office
1600 Maple Avenue
Carrollton, GA 30118

2616
Grace Talley Richards Scholarship Fund

AMOUNT: None Specified DEADLINE: Varies
MAJOR: Art

The Grace Talley Richards Scholarship Fund is open to art majors and minors at the State University of West Georgia. You must be enrolled in one of the Art History Museum Seminar courses. This award is to help defray travel expenses associated with these courses. You will be judged based on financial need and academic aptitude. Award requirements change regularly. Please send a self-addressed, stamped envelope to receive your application and any further instructions to the Art Department at the address listed or call (770) 836-6520. Feel free to browse the university's website at www.westga.edu. No GPA requirement specified.

State University of West Georgia
Attn: Financial Aid Office
1600 Maple Avenue
Carrollton, GA 30118

2617
Henry Lumpkin Memorial Scholarship

AMOUNT: None Specified DEADLINE: March 1
MAJOR: All Fields of Study

The Henry Lumpkin Memorial Scholarship is open to women over 30 with financial need who are attending the State University of West Georgia. Both full- and part-time students are eligible. To be considered for this award, you must be an incoming freshman, transfer, or continuing student and have a minimum GPA of 3.5. Incoming freshmen must have a minimum 1100 SAT score with at least a 580 verbal score, or a minimum 24 ACT score with at least a 23 verbal score. Award requirements change regularly. GPA must be 3.5-4.0.

State University of West Georgia
Attn: Financial Aid Office
1600 Maple Avenue
Carrollton, GA 30118

2618
Ingram Scholarship Fund of the Forties

AMOUNT: None Specified DEADLINE: March 1
MAJOR: All Fields of Study

The Ingram Scholarship Fund of the Forties is open to students attending the State University of West Georgia who demonstrate academic ability and financial need. To be eligible for this award, you must be an incoming freshman, transfer, or continuing student and have a minimum GPA of 3.5. Incoming freshmen must have a minimum 1100 SAT score with at least a 580 verbal score, or a minimum 24 ACT score with at least a 23 verbal score. Award requirements change regularly. GPA must be 3.5-4.0.

State University of West Georgia
Attn: Financial Aid Office
1600 Maple Avenue
Carrollton, GA 30118

2619
Jewell Miles Burson German Language Internship

AMOUNT: $500 DEADLINE: Varies
MAJOR: Foreign Language, German

The Jewell Miles Burson German Language Internship is open to students enrolled in the State University of West Georgia. You must be a German language major. This award is to be used for some travel expenses. Award requirements change regularly. Please send a self-addressed, stamped envelope to receive your application and any further instructions to Dr. Caryl Lloyd, Foreign Languages Department, or call (770) 836-6515. You may also browse the university's website at www.westga.edu. No GPA requirement specified.

State University of West Georgia
Attn: Financial Aid Office
1600 Maple Avenue
Carrollton, GA 30118

2620
Joe M. Ward Memorial Scholarship

AMOUNT: None Specified DEADLINE: March 1
MAJOR: All Fields of Study

The Joe M. Ward Memorial Scholarship is open to students attending the State University of West Georgia. Preference will be given to descendents of graduates of the A & M School. To be eligible for this award, you must be an incoming freshman, transfer, or continuing student and have a minimum GPA of 3.5. Incoming freshmen must have a minimum 1100 SAT score with at least a 580 verbal score, or a minimum 24 ACT score with at least a 23 verbal score. Award requirements change regularly. GPA must be 3.5-4.0.

State University of West Georgia
Attn: Financial Aid Office
1600 Maple Avenue
Carrollton, GA 30118

2621
L. Wayne Brown Scholarship

AMOUNT: None Specified DEADLINE: March 1
MAJOR: All Fields of Study

The L. Wayne Brown Scholarship is open to outstanding students attending the State University of West Georgia. To be eligible for this award, you must be an incoming freshman, transfer, or continuing student and have a minimum GPA of 3.5. Your financial need may be taken into consideration. Incoming freshmen must have a minimum 1100 SAT score with at least a 580 verbal score, or a minimum 24 ACT score with at least a 23 verbal score. Award requirements change regularly. GPA must be 3.5-4.0.

State University of West Georgia
Attn: Financial Aid Office
1600 Maple Avenue
Carrollton, GA 30118

2622
MacGregor Flanders Scholarship

AMOUNT: None Specified DEADLINE: March 1
MAJOR: All Fields of Study

The MacGregor Flanders Scholarship is open to students attending the State University of West Georgia. To be eligible for this award, you must be an incoming freshman, transfer, or continuing student and have a minimum GPA of 3.5. Incoming freshmen must have a minimum 1100 SAT score with at least a 580 verbal score, or a minimum 24 ACT score with at least a 23 verbal score. Award requirements change regularly. GPA must be 3.5-4.0.

State University of West Georgia
Attn: Financial Aid Office
1600 Maple Avenue
Carrollton, GA 30118

2623
McDonald's of Carrollton Scholarship

AMOUNT: None Specified DEADLINE: March 1
MAJOR: All Fields of Study

The McDonald's of Carrollton Scholarship is open to deserving students attending the State University of West Georgia who need financial assistance. To be eligible for this award, you must be an incoming freshman, transfer, or continuing student and have a minimum GPA of 3.5. Incoming freshmen must have a minimum 1100 SAT score with at least a 580 verbal score, or a minimum 24 ACT score with at least a 23 verbal score. Award requirements change regularly. GPA must be 3.5-4.0.

State University of West Georgia
Attn: Financial Aid Office
1600 Maple Avenue
Carrollton, GA 30118

2624
National Society of Public Accountants Stanley H. Stearman Award

AMOUNT: $2000 DEADLINE: March 1
MAJOR: Accounting

The National Society of Public Accountants Stanley H. Stearman Award is open to accounting majors at the State University of West Georgia who are sons, daughters, grandchildren, nieces, or nephews of an NSPA member or deceased member. You must have a minimum GPA of 2.0 with a minimum GPA of 3.0 in accounting and demonstrate leadership ability and financial need. Award requirements change regularly. Please send a self-addressed, stamped envelope to receive your application and any further instructions from the scholarship provider, or call (770) 836-6421. GPA must be 2.0-4.0.

State University of West Georgia
Attn: Financial Aid Office
1600 Maple Avenue
Carrollton, GA 30118

2625
Pathfinders Civitan Scholarship

AMOUNT: None Specified DEADLINE: February 18
MAJOR: Special Education/Teacher Education

The Pathfinders Civitan Scholarship is awarded to a special education major who has been accepted into the teacher education program at the State University of West Georgia. You must show merit and financial need. Award requirements change regularly. Please send a self-addressed, stamped envelope to the Dean's Office at the College of Education to receive your application and any further instructions or call (770) 836-6570. No GPA requirement specified.

State University of West Georgia
Attn: Financial Aid Office
1600 Maple Avenue
Carrollton, GA 30118

2626
Phi Kappa Phi Scholarship

AMOUNT: None Specified DEADLINE: March 1
MAJOR: All Fields of Study

The Phi Kappa Phi Scholarship is open to graduate and undergraduate students at the State University of West Georgia and is awarded on the basis of academic achievement. Preference is given to Phi Kappa Phi members. To be eligible for this award, you must be an incoming freshman, transfer, continuing, or graduate student and have a minimum GPA of 3.5. Incoming freshmen must have a minimum 1100 SAT score with at least a 580 verbal score, or a minimum 24 ACT score with at least a 23 verbal score. Award requirements change regularly. GPA must be 3.5-4.0.

State University of West Georgia
Attn: Financial Aid Office
1600 Maple Avenue
Carrollton, GA 30118

2627
Presidential Scholarships

AMOUNT: None Specified DEADLINE: March 1
MAJOR: All Fields of Study

The Presidential Scholarships are open to entering freshmen at the State University of West Georgia who have exceptional academic ability. All entering freshmen are considered for these awards as they apply for admission. To be considered for these awards, you must have a minimum high school GPA of 3.5 and a minimum SAT score of 1250 with a verbal score of 610. These scholarships are renewed annually provided that you continue to participate in the program. Award requirements change regularly. To receive an application for admission, please contact the Office of Admission; or visit the university's website at www.westga.edu. GPA must be 3.5-4.0.

State University of West Georgia
Attn: Financial Aid Office
1600 Maple Avenue
Carrollton, GA 30118

2628
Regents Scholarship

AMOUNT: None Specified DEADLINE: March 1
MAJOR: All Fields of Study

The Regents Scholarship is open to residents of Georgia who are full-time graduate and undergraduate students attending the State University of West Georgia. To be eligible for this award, you must be an incoming freshman, transfer, continuing, or graduate student and have a minimum GPA of 3.5. Incoming freshmen must have a minimum 1100 SAT score with at least a 580 verbal score, or a minimum 24 ACT score with at least a 23 verbal score. Selection is based on academics and financial need with preference given to prior recipients. Recipients must work in the state of Georgia for a year for each $1000 they receive or else the scholarship becomes a loan that must be repaid to UWG. Award requirements change regularly. GPA must be 3.5-4.0.

State University of West Georgia
Attn: Financial Aid Office
1600 Maple Avenue
Carrollton, GA 30118

2629
Regents' Scholarship/Loan

AMOUNT: None Specified DEADLINE: March 1
MAJOR: All Fields of Study

The Regents' Scholarship/Loan is open to graduate and undergraduate students at the State University of West Georgia. You must demonstrate financial need, be in good academic standing, and rank in the upper 25% of the class. This award is for Georgia residents. Award requirements change regularly. For further information, please contact the Dean's office at (770) 836-6419. Applications are available online at www.westga.edu/~gradsch/ and should be returned to The Graduate School, Cobb Hall, State University of West Georgia, Carrollton, GA 30118-4160. You may also browse the university's website at www.westga.edu. No GPA requirement specified.

State University of West Georgia
Attn: Financial Aid Office
1600 Maple Avenue
Carrollton, GA 30118

2630
Thomas R. Luck, Jr., Scholarship

AMOUNT: None Specified DEADLINE: March 1
MAJOR: Political Science, Mass Communications (Print Emphasis - Journalism)

The Thomas R. Luck, Jr., Scholarship is open to full-time undergraduates at the State University of West Georgia who are majoring in political science or mass communications (print emphasis-journalism). To be eligible for this award, you must be an incoming freshman, transfer, or continuing student, have a minimum GPA of 3.5 and demonstrate financial need. Incoming freshmen must have a minimum 1100 SAT score with at least a 580 verbal score, or a minimum 24 ACT score with at least a 23 verbal score. Award requirements change regularly. GPA must be 3.5-4.0.

State University of West Georgia
Attn: Financial Aid Office
1600 Maple Avenue
Carrollton, GA 30118

2631
Worthy Family Scholarship

AMOUNT: None Specified DEADLINE: March 1
MAJOR: All Fields of Study

The Worthy Family Scholarship is awarded to a well-rounded, outstanding student with academic potential who is attending the State University of West Georgia. To be eligible for this award, you must be an incoming freshman, transfer, or continuing student and have a minimum GPA of 3.5. Incoming freshmen must have a minimum 1100 SAT score with at least a 580 verbal score, or a minimum 24 ACT score with at least a 23 verbal score. Award requirements change regularly. GPA must be 3.5-4.0.

State University of West Georgia
Attn: Financial Aid Office
1600 Maple Avenue
Carrollton, GA 30118

Syracuse University

2632
Newhouse Graduate Newspaper Fellowship/Internship for Minorities

AMOUNT: $1100 DEADLINE: February 1
MAJOR: Newspaper Journalism

This award is open to African-American, Asian, Native American, and Hispanic/Latino students who are U.S. citizens at the master's level in newspaper journalism at the Newhouse School of Public Communications. Applicants must have an undergraduate degree in a field other than journalism and have a minimum GPA of 3.0. The award consists of a $1,100 monthly stipend, moving expenses to Syracuse, travel/academic expenses, and health insurance coverage. Award requirements change regularly. For further information, please write to the address, including a self-addressed, stamped envelope; call (315) 443-1124; fax (315) 443-3946; or email jalorrai@suadmin.syr.edu. Or you can browse their website at sumweb.syr.edu/financial_aid/. GPA must be 3.0-4.0.

Syracuse University
Attn: Ms Lorraine Newhouse
305 Jane Drive
Syracuse, NY 13219-2815

Tampa Technical Institute

2633
Tampa Technical Commercial Art and Video Production Scholarship

AMOUNT: None Specified DEADLINE: Varies
MAJOR: Commercial Art and Video Production

The Tampa Technical Commercial Art and Video Production Scholarship is open to Florida residents attending or planning to attend Tampa Technical Institute to study commercial art and video production. Applications are available at Florida high schools and GED testing centers. Award requirements change regularly. For further information, please send a self-addressed, stamped envelope to Tampa Technical Institute, Keith A. Cravens, Director of Admissions, 2410 East Busch Boulevard, Tampa, FL 33612, or call (813) 935-5700. No GPA requirement specified.

Florida Association of Postsecondary Schools and Colleges
Attn: FAPSC Scholarship Committee
F200 West College Avenue
Tallahassee, FL 32301

2634
Tampa Technical Electronic and Computer Engineering Scholarship

AMOUNT: None Specified DEADLINE: Varies
MAJOR: Electronic and Computer Engineering Technology

The Tampa Technical Electronic and Computer Engineering Scholarship is open to Florida residents attending or planning to attend Tampa Technical Institute to study electronic and computer engineering technology. Applications are available at Florida high schools and GED testing centers. Award requirements change regularly. For further information, please send a self-addressed, stamped envelope to Tampa Technical Institute, Keith A. Cravens, Director of Admissions, 2410 East Busch Boulevard, Tampa, FL 33612, or call (813) 935-5700. No GPA requirement specified.

Florida Association of Postsecondary Schools and Colleges
Attn: FAPSC Scholarship Committee
F200 West College Avenue
Tallahassee, FL 32301

2635
Tampa Technical Institute Business Administration Scholarship

AMOUNT: None Specified DEADLINE: Varies
MAJOR: Business Administration

The Tampa Technical Institute Business Administration Scholarship is open to Florida residents attending or planning to attend Tampa Technical Institute to study business administration. Applications are available at Florida high schools and GED testing centers. Award requirements change regularly. For further information, please send a self-addressed, stamped envelope to Tampa Technical Institute, Keith A. Cravens, Director of Admissions, 2410 East Busch Boulevard, Tampa, FL 33612, or call (813) 935-5700. No GPA requirement specified.

Florida Association of Postsecondary Schools and Colleges
Attn: FAPSC Scholarship Committee
F200 West College Avenue
Tallahassee, FL 32301

2636
Tampa Technical Institute Commercial Art Scholarship

AMOUNT: None Specified DEADLINE: Varies
MAJOR: Commercial Art

The Tampa Technical Institute Commercial Art Scholarship is open to Florida residents attending or planning to attend Tampa Technical Institute to study commercial art. Applications are available at Florida high schools and GED testing centers. Award requirements change regularly. For further information, please send a self-addressed, stamped envelope to Tampa Technical Institute, Keith A. Cravens, Director of Admissions, 2410 East Busch Boulevard, Tampa, FL 33612, or call (813) 935-5700. No GPA requirement specified.

Florida Association of Postsecondary Schools and Colleges
Attn: FAPSC Scholarship Committee
F200 West College Avenue
Tallahassee, FL 32301

2637
Tampa Technical Institute Computer Information Systems Scholarship

AMOUNT: None Specified DEADLINE: Varies
MAJOR: Computer Information Systems

The Tampa Technical Institute Computer Information Systems Scholarship is open to Florida residents attending or planning to attend Tampa Technical Institute to study computer information systems. Applications are available at Florida high schools and GED testing centers. Award requirements change regularly. For further information, please send a self-addressed, stamped envelope to Tampa Technical Institute, Keith A. Cravens, Director of Admissions, 2410 East Busch Boulevard, Tampa, FL 33612, or call (813) 935-5700. No GPA requirement specified.

Florida Association of Postsecondary Schools and Colleges
Attn: FAPSC Scholarship Committee
F200 West College Avenue
Tallahassee, FL 32301

Texas A & M University

2638
Sul Ross/Corps Scholarship

AMOUNT: $500-$2000 DEADLINE: Varies
MAJOR: All Areas of Study

Open to entering first-year cadets. Based upon academic performance and demonstrated leadership potential. Some of these scholarships are weighted more toward those demonstrating financial need. Award requirements change regularly. Write to the Office of the Commandant at the address listed for details. No GPA requirement specified.

Texas A & M University
Office of the Commandant
College Station, TX 77843

Tulane University

2639
Athletic Undergraduate Scholarships

AMOUNT: None Specified DEADLINE: Varies
MAJOR: All Areas of Study

The Athletic Undergraduate Scholarships for male undergraduates are in the following sports: football, golf, basketball, baseball, tennis, cross-country, and track. The scholarships for female undergraduates are in the following sports: volleyball, tennis, basketball, golf, cross-country and track, and soccer. Award requirements change regularly. Contact the address list-

ed for further information; call (504) 865-5500; or email finaid@pulse.tcs.tulane.edu. You may also browse the website at www.tulane.edu./~finaid. No GPA requirement specified.

Tulane University - Athletic Department
Attn: Scholarship Coordinator
New Orleans, LA 70118

United States International University

2640
Athletic Scholarship

AMOUNT: None Specified DEADLINE: March 2
MAJOR: Soccer, Tennis, Cross Country

For USIU full-time undergraduate students. Awarded annually to selected team members. For men's and women's soccer, tennis, and cross-country running teams. Award amounts vary. Scholarships are reviewed annually. Award requirements change regularly. Contact the Athletic Department for more information or call (619) 635-4630. No GPA requirement specified.

United States International University
Financial Aid Office
10455 Pomerado Road
San Diego, CA 92131-1717

2641
First Time Freshman Student Grant

AMOUNT: $750-$6500 DEADLINE: Varies
MAJOR: All Areas of Study

Open to incoming freshmen who are U.S. citizens or permanent residents. The award ranges from $750 to $6,500 depending on incoming GPA and on- or off-campus residency. Renewable if recipients maintain a minimum GPA of 2.0. Award requirements change regularly. For further information, call (619) 635-4772 or visit the website at www.usiu.edu. No GPA requirement specified.

United States International University
Financial Aid Office
10455 Pomerado Road
San Diego, CA 92131-1717

2642
First Time Freshmen Scholarship

AMOUNT: $3000-$8000 DEADLINE: Varies
MAJOR: All Areas of Study

Open to first-time freshmen who are U.S. citizens or permanent residents. The scholarship awards range from $3,000 to $8,000 depending on the incoming GPA, SAT/ACT scores, and on- or off-campus residency. Renewable if recipients maintain a minimum GPA of 3.0. Award requirements change regularly. For further information, call (619) 635-4772, or visit the website at www.usiu.edu. No GPA requirement specified.

United States International University
Financial Aid Office
10455 Pomerado Road
San Diego, CA 92131-1717

2643
Undergraduate International Student Scholarship

AMOUNT: $1500-$2000 DEADLINE: Varies
MAJOR: All Areas of Study

Open to incoming international undergraduates who have a minimum GPA of 3.0. The scholarship awards range from $1,500 to $2,000 depending on the incoming GPA and on- or off-campus residency. Renewable if recipients maintain a minimum GPA of 3.0. Award requirements change regularly. For further information, call (619) 635-4772 or visit the website at www.usiu.edu. GPA must be 3.0-4.0.

United States International University
Financial Aid Office
10455 Pomerado Road
San Diego, CA 92131-1717

2644
Undergraduate Transfer Student Grant

AMOUNT: $1000-$3000 DEADLINE: Varies
MAJOR: All Areas of Study

Open to undergraduate transfer students who are U.S. citizens or permanent residents. The award ranges from $1,000 to $3,000 depending on incoming GPA and on- or off-campus residency. Award requirements change regularly. For further information, call (619) 635-4772 or visit the website at www.usiu.edu. No GPA requirement specified.

United States International University
Financial Aid Office
10455 Pomerado Road
San Diego, CA 92131-1717

2645
Undergraduate Transfer Student Scholarship

AMOUNT: $3000-$7000 DEADLINE: Varies
MAJOR: All Areas of Study

Open to incoming transfer students who are U.S. citizens or permanent residents. The scholarship awards range from $3000 to $7000 depending on the incoming GPA and on- or off-campus residency. Renewable if recipients maintain a minimum GPA of 3.0. Award requirements change regularly. For further information, call (619) 635-4772 or visit the website at www.usiu.edu. No GPA requirement specified.

United States International University
Financial Aid Office
10455 Pomerado Road
San Diego, CA 92131-1717

University of Arkansas, Fayetteville

2646
Sturgis Fellowships

AMOUNT: Maximum: $11000 DEADLINE: February 1
MAJOR: All Areas of Study

This fellowship is open to University of Arkansas, Fayetteville, students who are outstanding incoming freshmen. You must be pursuing a four-year program of honors studies. While doing so, you must complete a broad interdisciplinary core curriculum of honors courses in the arts, humanities, and sciences in addition to the honors course work in your field of study. Academically superior results in your college prep high school curriculum and on your SAT/ACT tests are required. Award requirements change regularly. No GPA requirement specified.

University of Arkansas, Fayetteville
Director of Honors Studies
Old Main 517
Fayetteville, AR 72701

University of Arkansas, Pine Bluff

2647
Chancellor's Scholarship

AMOUNT: $2500 DEADLINE: Varies
MAJOR: All Areas of Study

The Chancellor's Scholarship is a four-year award which is open to students (preferably incoming freshmen) attending the University of Arkansas, Pine Bluff. Applicants must carry a minimum of 15 credit hours per semester, maintain a minimum GPA of 3.5, possess good moral character, and be involved in extracurricular activities. Award requirements change regularly. Please send a self-addressed, stamped envelope to receive your application and any further instructions from the scholarship provider. GPA must be 3.5-4.0.

University of Arkansas, Pine Bluff - Relations and Development
Attn: Scholarship Committee
1200 North University - PO Box 4981
Pine Bluff, AR 71611

2648
Charles and Nadine Baum Scholarship

AMOUNT: None Specified DEADLINE: Varies
MAJOR: All Areas of Study

The Charles and Nadine Baum Scholarship is open to students attending the University of Arkansas, Pine Bluff, who have a minimum GPA of 2.85 and demonstrate financial need. Entering freshmen must have a minimum GPA of 3.0 and/or a minimum ACT score of 22. Award requirements change regularly. Please send a self-addressed, stamped envelope to receive your application and any further instructions from the scholarship provider. GPA must be 3.0-4.0.

University of Arkansas, Pine Bluff - Relations and Development
Attn: Scholarship Committee
1200 North University - PO Box 4981
Pine Bluff, AR 71611

2649
Corliss H. Latimore/Celeste Ragan Mays Award

AMOUNT: $350 DEADLINE: Varies
MAJOR: All Areas of Study

The Corliss H. Latimore/Celeste Ragan Mays Award is open to students attending the University of Arkansas, Pine Bluff, who have achieved academic excellence and demonstrated qualities of leadership, good citizenship, and good professional promise. Award requirements change regularly. Please send a self-addressed, stamped envelope to receive your application and any further instructions from the scholarship provider. No GPA requirement specified.

University of Arkansas, Pine Bluff - Relations and Development
Attn: Scholarship Committee
1200 North University - PO Box 4981
Pine Bluff, AR 71611

2650
Dorothy Fairchild Bennett Scholarship

AMOUNT: None Specified DEADLINE: Varies
MAJOR: All Areas of Study

The Dorothy Fairchild Bennett Scholarship is open to students attending the University of Arkansas, Pine Bluff, who have demonstrated achievement, leadership qualities, and financial need. Award requirements change regularly. Please send a self-addressed, stamped envelope to receive your application and any further instructions from the scholarship provider. No GPA requirement specified.

University of Arkansas, Pine Bluff - Relations and Development
Attn: Scholarship Committee
1200 North University - PO Box 4981
Pine Bluff, AR 71611

2651
Erma Jean Bien-Aime Scholarship

AMOUNT: $4000 DEADLINE: Varies
MAJOR: All Areas of Study

The Erma Jean Bien-Aime Scholarship is open to students attending the University of Arkansas, Pine Bluff, who exemplify scholarship, leadership, and service and demonstrate a dedication to higher education. Applicants must have a minimum GPA of 3.5. Award requirements change regularly. Please send a self-addressed, stamped envelope to receive your application and any further instructions from the scholarship provider. GPA must be 3.5-4.0.

University of Arkansas, Pine Bluff - Relations and Development
Attn: Scholarship Committee
1200 North University - PO Box 4981
Pine Bluff, AR 71611

2652
Etta Nall Bates Memorial Award

AMOUNT: $200 DEADLINE: Varies
MAJOR: All Areas of Study

The Etta Nall Bates Memorial Award '48 is open to students attending the University of Arkansas, Pine Bluff, who have achieved academic excellence and demonstrated qualities of leadership, good citizenship, and good professional promise. Award requirements change regularly. Please send a self-addressed, stamped envelope to receive your application and any further instructions from the scholarship provider. No GPA requirement specified.

University of Arkansas, Pine Bluff - Relations and Development
Attn: Scholarship Committee
1200 North University - PO Box 4981
Pine Bluff, AR 71611

2653
Gabe Meyer Endowment Fund

AMOUNT: None Specified DEADLINE: Varies
MAJOR: All Areas of Study

The Gabe Meyer Endowment Fund is open to students attending the University of Arkansas, Pine Bluff, who are in good academic standing, exhibit leadership qualities, and provide evidence of involvement in extracurricular activities. Award requirements change regularly. Please send a self-addressed, stamped envelope to receive your application and any further instructions from the scholarship provider. No GPA requirement specified.

University of Arkansas, Pine Bluff - Relations and Development
Attn: Scholarship Committee
1200 North University - PO Box 4981
Pine Bluff, AR 71611

2654
Gateway Alumni Annual Scholarship

AMOUNT: $1000 DEADLINE: Varies
MAJOR: All Areas of Study

The Gateway Alumni Annual Scholarship is open to students attending the University of Arkansas, Pine Bluff, who have a minimum GPA of 2.85, exhibit outstanding leadership qualities, possess a good strong value system, have high moral character, and demonstrate good citizenship. Financial need is a consideration but not a requirement. Restrictions on major fields of study may change from year to year. Award requirements change regularly. Please send a self-addressed, stamped envelope to receive your application and any further instructions from the scholarship provider. GPA must be 2.85-4.0.

University of Arkansas, Pine Bluff - Relations and
Development
Attn: Scholarship Committee
1200 North University - PO Box 4981
Pine Bluff, AR 71611

2655
Gerber Foundation Scholarship for Single Mothers

AMOUNT: None Specified DEADLINE: Varies
MAJOR: All Areas of Study

The Gerber Foundation Scholarship for Single Mothers is
open to underprivileged mothers attending the University of
Arkansas, Pine Bluff. Award requirements change regularly.
Please send a self-addressed, stamped envelope to receive
your application and any further instructions from the scholarship provider. No GPA requirement specified.

University of Arkansas, Pine Bluff - Relations and
Development
Attn: Scholarship Committee
1200 North University - PO Box 4981
Pine Bluff, AR 71611

2656
Gilmore/Usher Endowment Scholarship

AMOUNT: None Specified DEADLINE: Varies
MAJOR: All Areas of Study

The Gilmore/Usher Endowment Scholarship is open to students attending the University of Arkansas, Pine Bluff, who
are in good academic standing, exhibit leadership qualities,
and provide evidence of involvement in extracurricular activities. Award requirements change regularly. Please send a self-
addressed, stamped envelope to receive your application and
any further instructions from the scholarship provider. No
GPA requirement specified.

University of Arkansas, Pine Bluff - Relations and
Development
Attn: Scholarship Committee
1200 North University - PO Box 4981
Pine Bluff, AR 71611

2657
Hosea King Washington Scholarship

AMOUNT: $1000 DEADLINE: Varies
MAJOR: All Areas of Study

The Hosea King Washington Scholarship is open to students
attending the University of Arkansas, Pine Bluff, who exemplify scholarship, leadership, and service and demonstrate a
dedication to higher education. Applicants must have a minimum GPA of 2.5. Award requirements change regularly.
Please send a self-addressed, stamped envelope to receive
your application and any further instructions from the scholarship provider. GPA must be 2.5-4.0.

University of Arkansas, Pine Bluff - Relations and
Development
Attn: Scholarship Committee
1200 North University - PO Box 4981
Pine Bluff, AR 71611

2658
Jewell Minnis Endowment Scholarship

AMOUNT: None Specified DEADLINE: Varies
MAJOR: All Areas of Study

The Jewell Minnis Endowment Scholarship is open to first-
time freshmen entering the University of Arkansas, Pine Bluff,
who have demonstrated academic achievement, qualities of
leadership, good citizenship, and professional promise.
Applicants must have a minimum GPA of 2.5 and a minimum
ACT score of 19. Award requirements change regularly.
Please send a self-addressed, stamped envelope to receive
your application and any further instructions from the scholarship provider. GPA must be 2.5-4.0.

University of Arkansas, Pine Bluff - Relations and
Development
Attn: Scholarship Committee
1200 North University - PO Box 4981
Pine Bluff, AR 71611

2659
John Edgar Washington Memorial Scholarship

AMOUNT: $4000 DEADLINE: Varies
MAJOR: All Areas of Study

The John Edgar Washington Memorial Scholarship is open to
students attending the University of Arkansas, Pine Bluff, who
exemplify scholarship, leadership, and service; demonstrate
compassion and consideration for others; and hold the belief
that these can provide meaning and direction in life.
Applicants must have a minimum GPA of 2.0. Award requirements change regularly. Please send a self-addressed, stamped
envelope to receive your application and any further instructions from the scholarship provider. GPA must be 2.0-4.0.

University of Arkansas, Pine Bluff - Relations and
Development
Attn: Scholarship Committee
1200 North University - PO Box 4981
Pine Bluff, AR 71611

2660
National Alumni Association Scholarship

AMOUNT: None Specified DEADLINE: Varies
MAJOR: All Areas of Study

The National Alumni Association Scholarship is open to high
school seniors entering the University of Arkansas, Pine Bluff,
who have shown leadership ability in high school by participation in various worthwhile campus organizations and community activities. Applicants must have a minimum GPA of
3.0 and demonstrate a need for financial assistance. This is a
full scholarship which covers in-state tuition, room, and board
and is renewable for up to four years. Award requirements

change regularly. Please send a self-addressed, stamped envelope to receive your application and any further instructions from the scholarship provider or call the Alumni Association at (870) 536-2309. GPA must be 3.0-4.0.

University of Arkansas, Pine Bluff - Relations and Development
Attn: Scholarship Committee
1200 North University - PO Box 4981
Pine Bluff, AR 71611

2661
Robert Adams, William Moore and S. Trice Families Scholarship

AMOUNT: $240 DEADLINE: Varies
MAJOR: All Areas of Study

The Robert Adams, William Moore and S. Trice Families Scholarship is open to students attending the University of Arkansas, Pine Bluff, who have achieved academic excellence, and demonstrated qualities of leadership, good citizenship, and good professional promise. Award requirements change regularly. Please send a self-addressed, stamped envelope to receive your application and any further instructions from the scholarship provider. No GPA requirement specified.

University of Arkansas, Pine Bluff - Relations and Development
Attn: Scholarship Committee
1200 North University - PO Box 4981
Pine Bluff, AR 71611

2662
ROTC Scholarship

AMOUNT: Maximum: $16450 DEADLINE: Varies
MAJOR: All Areas of Study

The ROTC Scholarships are open to freshman and sophomore students attending the University of Arkansas, Pine Bluff. Applicants must take military science classes. Scholarships are awarded based on merit to the most outstanding students who apply. Award requirements change regularly. Please send a self-addressed, stamped envelope to receive your application and any further instructions from the scholarship provider or contact University of Arkansas, Pine Bluff, Army ROTC at (870) 543-8445. No GPA requirement specified.

University of Arkansas, Pine Bluff - Relations and Development
Attn: Scholarship Committee
1200 North University - PO Box 4981
Pine Bluff, AR 71611

2663
Snowie and Tommie Brown Endowed Scholarship

AMOUNT: None Specified DEADLINE: Varies
MAJOR: Music, Teacher Education, Business Administration

The Snowie and Tommie Brown Endowed Scholarship is open to students majoring in music, teacher education, or business administration at the University of Arkansas, Pine Bluff, who have a minimum GPA of 2.8. Award requirements change regularly. Please send a self-addressed, stamped envelope to

receive your application and any further instructions from the scholarship provider. GPA must be 2.8-4.0.

University of Arkansas, Pine Bluff - Relations and Development
Attn: Scholarship Committee
1200 North University - PO Box 4981
Pine Bluff, AR 71611

2664
Union Pacific Foundation Endowed Scholarship

AMOUNT: Maximum: $1000 DEADLINE: Varies
MAJOR: All Areas of Study

The Union Pacific Foundation Endowed Scholarship is open to students attending the University of Arkansas, Pine Bluff, who maintain a minimum GPA of 2.85 and demonstrate financial need. Entering freshmen must have a minimum GPA of 3.0 and/or a minimum ACT score of 22. Award requirements change regularly. Please send a self-addressed, stamped envelope to receive your application and any further instructions from the scholarship provider. GPA must be 3.0-4.0.

University of Arkansas, Pine Bluff - Relations and Development
Attn: Scholarship Committee
1200 North University - PO Box 4981
Pine Bluff, AR 71611

2665
Wal-Mart Competitive Edge Scholarship

AMOUNT: $5000 DEADLINE: Varies
MAJOR: Science, Engineering, Computer-related Fields

The Wal-Mart Competitive Edge Scholarship is open to students majoring in science, engineering, or computer-related fields. This scholarship pays $5,000 a year for four years to students who are selected by universities. Award requirements change regularly. Please send a self-addressed, stamped envelope to receive your application and any further instructions from the scholarship provider or call the Office of Financial Aid at (870) 543-8302. No GPA requirement specified.

University of Arkansas, Pine Bluff - Relations and Development
Attn: Scholarship Committee
1200 North University - PO Box 4981
Pine Bluff, AR 71611

2666
Wiley Branton Endowed Scholarship

AMOUNT: None Specified DEADLINE: Varies
MAJOR: Social Science, Physical Science

The Wiley Branton Endowed Scholarship is open to students (preferably incoming freshmen) attending the University of Arkansas, Pine Bluff. Applicants must exhibit exemplary academic achievement and exceptional leadership abilities in the social and physical sciences. This award is renewable for a maximum of four years contingent upon sustained exceptional performance. Award requirements change regularly. Please send a self-addressed, stamped envelope to receive your application and any further instructions from the scholarship provider. No GPA requirement specified.

University of Arkansas, Pine Bluff - Relations and Development
Attn: Scholarship Committee
1200 North University - PO Box 4981
Pine Bluff, AR 71611

University of California, Berkeley

2667
Alumni Leadership Scholarship

AMOUNT: $1000 DEADLINE: Varies
MAJOR: All Areas of Study

The Alumni Leadership Scholarship is open to freshmen and junior transfers who will enter UC Berkeley in either the fall or spring semester. If you are a freshman, the last school you attended must be in the United States, and you need to have a minimum GPA of 3.3. If you are a junior transfer, the last school you attended must be in California, and you need a minimum 3.0 GPA. To be eligible for the award, you must apply for admission to UC Berkeley by November 30. Scholarship applications are due February 1 and should include a copy of your admission application, a personal statement, and a description of up to three activities in which you participated in the last four years and demonstrated significant leadership. The award requires that you be a U.S. citizen or permanent resident and be available for an interview. Award requirements change regularly. Please send a self-addressed, stamped envelope to receive your application and any further instructions from the scholarship provider. GPA must be 3.3-4.0.

California Alumni Association
Attn: Berkeley Alumni Scholarship Office
Alumni House #7520
Berkeley, CA 94720-7520

2668
Regents' Scholarships, Chancellor's Scholarships

AMOUNT: None Specified DEADLINE: March 2
MAJOR: All Areas of Study

Scholarships are available at the University of California, Berkeley, for entering freshmen and transfer students with a GPA of at least 3.8 who demonstrate academic ability and future potential. Award requirements change regularly. Please write to the address listed, enclosing a self-addressed, stamped envelope for an application and further information. GPA must be 3.8-4.0.

University of California, Berkeley
Office of Financial Aid
210 Sproul Hall
Berkeley, CA 94720-1964

University of Central Oklahoma

2669
Freshmen Achievement Scholarship

AMOUNT: $1500 DEADLINE: March 1
MAJOR: All Areas of Study

The Freshmen Achievement Scholarship is open to incoming freshmen at UCO who are Oklahoma residents. You must have a minimum 3.25 GPA and a minimum 27 ACT. This award is renewable for four years. Award requirements change regularly. GPA must be 3.25-4.0.

University of Central Oklahoma
Prospective Student Services/Scholarship
University Center, Room 136
Edmond, OK 73034

2670
Merit Graduate Scholarship

AMOUNT: $500 DEADLINE: March 1
MAJOR: All Areas of Study

This scholarship is open to graduate students at UCO who have a minimum 3.5 GPA. You must be an Oklahoma resident, be enrolled for a minimum of six credit hours, and have completed at least six college hours at the time of your application. Award requirements change regularly. GPA must be 3.5-4.0.

University of Central Oklahoma
Prospective Student Services/Scholarship
University Center, Room 136
Edmond, OK 73034

2671
Merit Undergraduate Scholarship

AMOUNT: $500 DEADLINE: March 1
MAJOR: All Areas of Study

The Merit Undergraduate Scholarship is open to incoming freshmen and undergraduates at UCO who are Oklahoma residents and have a minimum 22 ACT. Incoming freshmen must have a minimum 3.25 GPA and be enrolled six credit hours per semester. Continuing students must have a minimum 3.4 GPA, have at least 12 college hours completed, and also be enrolled six credit hours per semester. Award requirements change regularly. GPA must be 3.25-4.0.

University of Central Oklahoma
Prospective Student Services/Scholarship
University Center, Room 136
Edmond, OK 73034

2672
Minority Achievement Award

AMOUNT: $1500 DEADLINE: March 1
MAJOR: All Areas of Study

The Minority Achievement Award is open to incoming minority freshmen at UCO who are Oklahoma residents. You must have a minimum 3.25 GPA and a minimum 24 ACT. This award is renewable for four years. Award requirements change regularly. GPA must be 3.25-4.0.

University of Central Oklahoma
Prospective Student Services/Scholarship
University Center, Room 136
Edmond, OK 73034

2673
Muticultural Achievement Award

AMOUNT: Maximum: $1000 DEADLINE: March 1
MAJOR: All Areas of Study

This award is open to continuing minority undergraduates and graduate students at UCO who have completed 12 college hours. You must have a minimum 2.5 GPA, be an Oklahoma resident, and be enrolled a minimum of six hours per semester. Award requirements change regularly. GPA must be 2.5-4.0.

University of Central Oklahoma
Multicultural Student Services
University Center, Room 140
Edmond, OK 73034

2674
Phi Theta Kappa In-State Transfer Scholarship

AMOUNT: $1500 DEADLINE: March 1
MAJOR: All Areas of Study

The Phi Theta Kappa In-State Transfer Scholarship is open to incoming transfer students admitted to UCO who are members of Phi Theta Kappa. You must have a minimum of 24 transferable hours (maximum-90), be an Oklahoma resident, and have a minimum 3.4 GPA. Award requirements change regularly. GPA must be 3.4-4.0.

University of Central Oklahoma
Prospective Student Services/Scholarship
University Center, Room 136
Edmond, OK 73034

2675
UCO Baccalaureate Scholarship

AMOUNT: None Specified DEADLINE: March 1
MAJOR: All Areas of Study

This scholarship is open to incoming freshmen at UCO who are Oklahoma residents. You must have a minimum 3.5 GPA and an ACT score of at least 30. This award is for tuition plus $3,000 per year and is renewable for four years. Award requirements change regularly. GPA must be 3.5-4.0.

University of Central Oklahoma
Prospective Student Services/Scholarship
University Center, Room 136
Edmond, OK 73034

2676
UCO Foundation Scholarship

AMOUNT: $250-$5000 DEADLINE: March 1
MAJOR: All Areas of Study

This scholarship is open to incoming freshmen, undergraduates, and graduate students at UCO who have a minimum 2.5 GPA. Campus participation, GPA, financial need, and work, community, and family obligations are all considered for this award. Award requirements change regularly. GPA must be 2.5-4.0.

University of Central Oklahoma
Prospective Student Services/Scholarship
University Center, Room 136
Edmond, OK 73034

University of Colorado at Boulder

2677
Alpha Omicron Pi Arthritis Scholarship

AMOUNT: $200 DEADLINE: March 1
MAJOR: All Areas of Study

The Alpha Omicron Pi Arthritis Scholarship is open to students attending the University of Colorado, Boulder, who have been diagnosed with arthritis or arthritis-related illness documented by a letter from an M.D. In replacement of the standard essay, an essay on how arthritis has impacted the applicant's life is required. Award requirements change regularly. Please send a self-addressed, stamped envelope to receive your application and any further instructions from the scholarship provider. No GPA requirement specified.

University of Colorado at Boulder - General
Office of Financial Aid
Campus Box 106
Boulder, CO 80309-0106

2678
Alumni Association and Parents Association Scholars Award

AMOUNT: $1000 DEADLINE: April 13
MAJOR: All Areas of Study

The Alumni Association and Parents Association Scholars Award is open to sophomores, juniors, and seniors enrolled full-time with at least a 3.5 GPA. This award is for students attending the University of Colorado, Boulder, and is based on merit, leadership, and involvement with the university and community programs. Applications from qualified students are reviewed by the alumni clubs from the applicant's home towns or Parents Association if there are no alumni clubs. This award is renewable through competitive reapplication. Award requirements change regularly. Please send a self-addressed, stamped envelope to receive your application and any further instructions from the scholarship provider. GPA must be 3.5-4.0.

University of Colorado at Boulder - General
Office of Financial Aid
Campus Box 106
Boulder, CO 80309-0106

2679
Arnold Scholarship

AMOUNT: $1000 DEADLINE: March 1
MAJOR: All Areas of Study

The Arnold Scholarship is open to entering freshmen attending University of Colorado, Boulder. This award is based on academic excellence, leadership, and community involvement. Applicants must have at least a 2.5 GPA. The award is renewable for up to four years with full-time enrollment. Students receive automatic consideration for this scholarship but must be admitted to CU-Boulder by March 1. No separate application is required. Award requirements change regularly. For further information, please contact the Financial Aid office at the address provided. GPA must be 2.5-4.0.

University of Colorado at Boulder - General
Office of Financial Aid
Campus Box 106
Boulder, CO 80309-0106

University of Connecticut

2680
Actuarial Science Scholarship

AMOUNT: Maximum: $5000 DEADLINE: Varies
MAJOR: Actuarial Science

The Actuarial Science Scholarship is open to incoming full-time freshmen and full-time undergraduates attending the University of Connecticut who are majoring in actuarial science. Applicants must demonstrate academic success, have an aptitude for mathematics, and be planning a career in actuarial science. This scholarship is for Connecticut residents. A minimum 3.0 GPA is required. Award requirements change regularly. Write to the address listed, enclosing a self-addressed, stamped envelope for an application and further information. You may also send an email to request information at vinson@math.uconn.edu, or consult the website address at www.math.uconn.edu. GPA must be 3.0-4.0.

University of Connecticut
Charles Vinsonhaler, Department Head
Department of Mathematics U-3009
Storrs, CT 06269

University of Evansville

2681
Academic Scholarships

AMOUNT: $4500-$8000 DEADLINE: February 15
MAJOR: All Areas of Study

Awards for students applying for admission to the University of Evansville. Based on strength of academic record, SAT score of at least 1130 or 25 on the ACT, etc. Students who rank first or second in their high school class will be considered for a $5,000 academic scholarship. National Merit Finalists will receive an award worth 75% tuition. Award requirements change regularly. Write to the address listed, enclosing a self-addressed, stamped envelope for an application and further information. You can browse their website: www.evansville.edu or email faidweb@evansville.edu. GPA must be 3.0-4.0.

University of Evansville
Office of Financial Aid
1800 Lincoln Avenue
Evansville, IN 47714-1506

2682
Art, Music and Theater Scholarship

AMOUNT: $4500-$8000 DEADLINE: February 15
MAJOR: Art, Music, and Theater

Academic scholarship that takes into account artistic and performing talent as well as academic achievement at the University of Evansville. Auditions or portfolio presentations are required as part of the application. Award requirements change regularly. Write to the address listed, enclosing a self-addressed, stamped envelope for an application and further information. You can browse their website: www.evansville.edu or email faidweb@evansville.edu. No GPA requirement specified.

University of Evansville
Office of Financial Aid
1800 Lincoln Avenue
Evansville, IN 47714-1506

2683
Indiana Honors Diploma Scholarships

AMOUNT: Maximum: $2500 DEADLINE: February 15
MAJOR: All Areas of Study

Awards for University of Evansville students who graduate with an Indiana academic honors diploma from high school. Renewable. Award requirements change regularly. Write to the address listed, enclosing a self-addressed, stamped envelope for an application and further information. You can browse their website: www.evansville.edu or email faidweb@evansville.edu. No GPA requirement specified.

University of Evansville
Office of Financial Aid
1800 Lincoln Avenue
Evansville, IN 47714-1506

2684
Leadership Activity Awards

AMOUNT: Maximum: $3000 DEADLINE: February 15
MAJOR: All Areas of Study

Awards for students applying for admission to the University of Evansville. Based on strength of academic record, SAT score of at least 970 or 21 on the ACT, and activities and involvements in high school. Renewable. Award requirements change regularly. Write to the address listed, enclosing a self-addressed, stamped envelope for an application and further information. You can browse their website: www.evansville.edu or email faidweb@evansville.edu. GPA must be 2.0-4.0.

University of Evansville
Office of Financial Aid
1800 Lincoln Avenue
Evansville, IN 47714-1506

2685
Legacy Scholarships

AMOUNT: Maximum: $5000 DEADLINE: February 15
MAJOR: All Areas of Study

Awards for children and grandchildren of University of Evansville graduates. Award requirements change regularly. Write to the address listed, enclosing a self-addressed, stamped envelope for an application and further information. You can browse their website: www.evansville.edu or email faidweb@evansville.edu. GPA must be 2.5-4.0.

University of Evansville
Office of Financial Aid
1800 Lincoln Avenue
Evansville, IN 47714-1506

2686
Multicultural Scholars Awards

AMOUNT: $4500-$8000 DEADLINE: February 15
MAJOR: All Areas of Study

Awards for students of color applying for admission to the University of Evansville. Based on strength of academic record and leadership abilities. Renewable. Award requirements change regularly. Write to the address listed, enclosing a self-addressed, stamped envelope for an application and further information. You can browse their website: www.evansville.edu or email faidweb@evansville.edu. No GPA requirement specified.

University of Evansville
Office of Financial Aid
1800 Lincoln Avenue
Evansville, IN 47714-1506

2687
Sibling Scholarship

AMOUNT: $1000-$1500 DEADLINE: February 15
MAJOR: All Areas of Study

Awards for current students who have a brother or sister who will enroll at University of Evansville. It is $1,500 a year for the first student attending University of Evansville and is given to each for as long as both remain full-time. Entering twins or triplets would each receive $1,000 a year. Award requirements change regularly. Write to the address listed, enclosing a self-addressed, stamped envelope for an application and further information. You can browse their website: www.evansville.edu or email faidweb@evansville.edu. No GPA requirement specified.

University of Evansville
Office of Financial Aid
1800 Lincoln Avenue
Evansville, IN 47714-1506

University of Florida

2688
Albert Gilchrist Memorial Scholarship

AMOUNT: $200 DEADLINE: Varies
MAJOR: All Areas of Study

Open to juniors and seniors at the University of Florida who demonstrate scholastic ability and financial need. Undergraduate students are considered automatically if they apply for financial aid. There is no special application required. Award requirements change regularly. You may browse the website: www.ufsa.ufl.edu/SFA/programs/sfaschol.html. GPA must be 3.0-4.0.

University of Florida
Office for Student Financial Affairs S-1
PO Box 114025
Gainesville, FL 32611-4025

2689
Alfred I. duPont Scholarship

AMOUNT: $450 DEADLINE: Varies
MAJOR: All Areas of Study

Undergraduates showing high academic achievement and financial need are eligible for these scholarships. Undergraduate students are considered automatically if they apply for financial aid. There is no special application required. Award requirements change regularly. You may browse the website: www.ufsa.ufl.edu/SFA/programs/sfaschol.html. GPA must be 3.0-4.0.

University of Florida
Office for Student Financial Affairs S-1
PO Box 114025
Gainesville, FL 32611-4025

2690
Arthur Henderson Memorial Scholarship

AMOUNT: $450 DEADLINE: Varies
MAJOR: All Areas of Study

Open to students at the University of Florida who demonstrate financial need and academic achievement. The number of recipients depends on the income of the fund. Undergraduate students are considered automatically if they apply for financial aid. There is no special application required. Award requirements change regularly. You may browse the website: www.ufsa.ufl.edu/SFA/programs/sfaschol.html. GPA must be 3.0-4.0.

University of Florida
Office for Student Financial Affairs S-1
PO Box 114025
Gainesville, FL 32611-4025

2691
Barbara and William Mickelberry Scholarship

AMOUNT: None Specified DEADLINE: Varies
MAJOR: All Areas of Study

Scholarships are awarded in recognition of academic achievement and financial need. Preference is given to students in the fields of special education, art education, or the fine arts. Undergraduate students are considered automatically if they apply for financial aid. There is no special application required. Award requirements change regularly. You may browse the website: www.ufsa.ufl.edu/SFA/programs/sfaschol.html. GPA must be 3.0-4.0.

University of Florida
Office for Student Financial Affairs S-1
PO Box 114025
Gainesville, FL 32611-4025

2692
Benito Agrello, Christina Holt Memorial Scholarship

AMOUNT: None Specified DEADLINE: Varies
MAJOR: All Areas of Study

Open to students attending the University of Florida who have a minimum 3.0 GPA and are able to demonstrate financial need. Award amounts will be based on the availability of funds. Undergraduate students are considered automatically if they apply for financial aid. There is no special application required. Award requirements change regularly. You may browse the UF website: www.ufsa.ufl.edu/SFA/programs/sfaschol.html. GPA must be 3.0-4.0.

University of Florida
Office for Student Financial Affairs S-1
PO Box 114025
Gainesville, FL 32611-4025

2693
Calvin Ira Baird Memorial Scholarship

AMOUNT: None Specified DEADLINE: Varies
MAJOR: All Areas of Study

Open to students attending the University of Florida. Selection is based on financial need and superior academic performance. Awards vary. Undergraduate students are considered automatically if they apply for financial aid. There is no special application required. Award requirements change regularly. You may browse the UF website: www.ufsa.ufl.edu/SFA/programs/sfaschol.html. GPA must be 3.0-4.0.

University of Florida
Office for Student Financial Affairs S-1
PO Box 114025
Gainesville, FL 32611-4025

2694
Coite and Mildred Hill Scholarship

AMOUNT: $2000 DEADLINE: Varies
MAJOR: All Areas of Study

Recipients must apply to and are selected by the Orange County School System. Undergraduate students are considered automatically if they apply for financial aid. There is no special application required. Award requirements change regularly. You may browse the website: www.ufsa.ufl.edu/SFA/programs/sfaschol.html. GPA must be 3.0-4.0.

University of Florida
Office for Student Financial Affairs S-1
PO Box 114025
Gainesville, FL 32611-4025

2695
Dolly and Robert L. Secrist, Sr., Scholarship

AMOUNT: $2500 DEADLINE: Varies
MAJOR: All Areas of Study

Open to sophomores at the University of Florida who have shown outstanding academic achievement and have demonstrated financial need. Award is renewable for three years, depending upon maintenance of a 3.0 GPA and continued financial need. Undergraduate students are considered automatically if they apply for financial aid. There is no special application required. Award requirements change regularly. You may browse the UF website: www.ufsa.ufl.edu/SFA/programs/sfaschol.html. GPA must be 3.0-4.0.

University of Florida
Office for Student Financial Affairs S-1
PO Box 114025
Gainesville, FL 32611-4025

2696
Earl W. Halsey Scholarship

AMOUNT: None Specified DEADLINE: Varies
MAJOR: All Areas of Study

Open to students at the University of Florida who are financially needy. Must demonstrate superior academic performance. Award amounts vary. Undergraduate students are considered automatically if they apply for financial aid. There is
no special application required. Award requirements change
regularly. You may browse the website:
www.ufsa.ufl.edu/SFA/programs/sfaschol.html. GPA must be
3.0-4.0.

University of Florida
Office for Student Financial Affairs S-1
PO Box 114025
Gainesville, FL 32611-4025

2697
Erma R. Ayres Scholarship

AMOUNT: None Specified DEADLINE: Varies
MAJOR: All Areas of Study

Open to students attending the University of Florida who have
a minimum 3.0 GPA and are able to demonstrate financial
need. The number of students awarded will be based on the
availability of funds. Undergraduate students are considered
automatically if they apply for financial aid. There is no special application required. Award requirements change regularly. You may browse the UF website:
www.ufsa.ufl.edu/SFA/programs/sfaschol.html. GPA must be
3.0-4.0.

University of Florida
Office for Student Financial Affairs S-1
PO Box 114025
Gainesville, FL 32611-4025

2698
Flora and Richard Ward Scholarship

AMOUNT: None Specified DEADLINE: Varies
MAJOR: All Areas of Study

This scholarship provides assistance to academically qualified
juniors and seniors with financial need. Preference is given to
students in the fine arts (including creative writing) or the military sciences, with strong preference given to students over
the age of 24 (independent students) or to students who are
parents (have dependents). Undergraduate students are considered automatically if they apply for financial aid. There is no
special application required. Award requirements change regularly. You may browse the website:
www.ufsa.ufl.edu/SFA/programs/sfaschol.html. GPA must be
3.0-4.0.

University of Florida
Office for Student Financial Affairs S-1
PO Box 114025
Gainesville, FL 32611-4025

2699
George R. Greene Scholarship

AMOUNT: None Specified DEADLINE: Varies
MAJOR: All Areas of Study

Awarding is based on financial need and a GPA of 3.0 or better. Undergraduate students are considered automatically if
they apply for financial aid. There is no special application
required. Award requirements change regularly. You may
browse the website:
www.ufsa.ufl.edu/SFA/programs/sfaschol.html. GPA must be
3.0-4.0.

University of Florida
Office for Student Financial Affairs S-1
PO Box 114025
Gainesville, FL 32611-4025

2700
Herbert and Jeffrey Galernter Memorial Scholarship

AMOUNT: $800 DEADLINE: Varies
MAJOR: All Areas of Study

Open to undergraduates at the University of Florida who
demonstrate financial need and academic achievement.
Undergraduate students are considered automatically if they
apply for financial aid. There is no special application
required. Award requirements change regularly. You may
browse the website:
www.ufsa.ufl.edu/SFA/programs/sfaschol.html. GPA must be
3.0-4.0.

University of Florida
Office for Student Financial Affairs S-1
PO Box 114025
Gainesville, FL 32611-4025

2701
Irene B. Kirbo Scholarship

AMOUNT: $750-$1000 DEADLINE: Varies
MAJOR: All Areas of Study

The university nominates students to receive these scholarships, and the administrators of the scholarship fund select
recipients. Undergraduate students are considered automatically if they apply for financial aid. There is no special application required. Award requirements change regularly. You may
browse the website:
www.ufsa.ufl.edu/SFA/programs/sfaschol.html. GPA must be
3.0-4.0.

University of Florida
Office for Student Financial Affairs S-1
PO Box 114025
Gainesville, FL 32611-4025

2702
J. Hillis Miller Memorial Scholarship

AMOUNT: $1000 DEADLINE: Varies
MAJOR: All Areas of Study

Open to students at the University of Florida who have a minimum 3.0 GPA and demonstrate financial need. Undergraduate students are considered automatically if they apply for financial aid. There is no special application required. Award requirements change regularly. You may browse the website: www.ufsa.ufl.edu/SFA/programs/sfaschol.html. GPA must be 3.0-4.0.

University of Florida
Office for Student Financial Affairs S-1
PO Box 114025
Gainesville, FL 32611-4025

2703
James K. Steiner Endowed Scholarship

AMOUNT: $2500 DEADLINE: Varies
MAJOR: All Areas of Study

Open to incoming freshmen admitted to the University of Florida. Applicants must demonstrate financial need, high academic achievement, and a strong interest in service to others. Award is renewable for three years. Undergraduate students are considered automatically if they apply for financial aid. There is no special application required. Award requirements change regularly. You may browse the UF website: www.ufsa.ufl.edu/SFA/programs/sfaschol.html. GPA must be 3.0-4.0.

University of Florida
Office for Student Financial Affairs S-1
PO Box 114025
Gainesville, FL 32611-4025

2704
Jessie Ball duPont, Alfred I. duPont Scholarships

AMOUNT: $400-$450 DEADLINE: Varies
MAJOR: All Areas of Study

Open to undergraduates at the University of Florida who have demonstrated high academic achievement and financial need. Undergraduate students are considered automatically if they apply for financial aid. There is no special application required. Award requirements change regularly. You may browse the UF website: www.ufsa.ufl.edu/SFA/programs/sfaschol.html. GPA must be 3.0-4.0.

University of Florida
Office for Student Financial Affairs S-1
PO Box 114025
Gainesville, FL 32611-4025

2705
Lillian P. Mosbacher Scholarship

AMOUNT: None Specified DEADLINE: Varies
MAJOR: All Areas of Study

Open to female students at the University of Florida who might be unable to pay tuition and other college expenses. Must demonstrate financial need and academic achievement. Undergraduate students are considered automatically if they apply for financial aid. There is no special application required. Award requirements change regularly. You may browse the website: www.ufsa.ufl.edu/SFA/programs/sfaschol.html. GPA must be 3.0-4.0.

University of Florida
Office for Student Financial Affairs S-1
PO Box 114025
Gainesville, FL 32611-4025

2706
P.I. Eschbach Scholarship

AMOUNT: $650 DEADLINE: Varies
MAJOR: All Areas of Study

Open to Brevard Community College students who are transferring to the University of Florida. Undergraduate students are considered automatically if they apply for financial aid. There is no special application required. Award requirements change regularly. You may browse the website: www.ufsa.ufl.edu/SFA/programs/sfaschol.html. GPA must be 3.0-4.0.

University of Florida
Office for Student Financial Affairs S-1
PO Box 114025
Gainesville, FL 32611-4025

2707
Philip B. Glancy Scholarship

AMOUNT: None Specified DEADLINE: Varies
MAJOR: All Areas of Study

Open to students at the University of Florida. Selection is based on financial need and a minimum 3.0 GPA. Priority is given to residents of Sarasota County. Undergraduate students are considered automatically if they apply for financial aid. There is no special application required. Award requirements change regularly. You may browse the website: www.ufsa.ufl.edu/SFA/programs/sfaschol.html. GPA must be 3.0-4.0.

University of Florida
Office for Student Financial Affairs S-1
PO Box 114025
Gainesville, FL 32611-4025

2708
Robert D. and Flora E. Fuhrman Scholarship

AMOUNT: $2000 DEADLINE: Varies
MAJOR: All Areas of Study

Open to students at the University of Florida who have a minimum 3.0 GPA. Must demonstrate financial need.

Undergraduate students are considered automatically if they apply for financial aid. There is no special application required. Award requirements change regularly. You may browse the website: www.ufsa.ufl.edu/SFA/programs/sfaschol.html. GPA must be 3.0-4.0.

University of Florida
Office for Student Financial Affairs S-1
PO Box 114025
Gainesville, FL 32611-4025

2709
Timer E. Powers Scholarship

AMOUNT: None Specified DEADLINE: Varies
MAJOR: All Areas of Study

This scholarship was established for awarding need-based scholarships to entering or enrolled undergraduate and/or graduate students who are Native Americans and members of either the Miccosukee or Seminole Indian tribes of Florida. Undergraduate students are considered automatically if they apply for financial aid. There is no special application required. Award requirements change regularly. You may browse the website: www.ufsa.ufl.edu/SFA/programs/sfaschol.html. GPA must be 3.0-4.0.

University of Florida
Office for Student Financial Affairs S-1
PO Box 114025
Gainesville, FL 32611-4025

2710
University of Florida Student Memorial Scholarship

AMOUNT: $1000 DEADLINE: Varies
MAJOR: All Areas of Study

Open to undergraduates at the University of Florida who have a minimum 3.5 GPA and demonstrate financial need. Priority is given to seniors. Undergraduate students are considered automatically if they apply for financial aid. There is no special application required. Award requirements change regularly. You may browse the website: www.ufsa.ufl.edu/SFA/programs/sfaschol.html. GPA must be 3.5-4.0.

University of Florida
Office for Student Financial Affairs S-1
PO Box 114025
Gainesville, FL 32611-4025

2711
University Women's Club Scholarship

AMOUNT: $1000 DEADLINE: Varies
MAJOR: All Areas of Study

This scholarship is designated for full-time undergraduates based on financial need. Undergraduate students are considered automatically if they apply for financial aid. There is no special application required. Award requirements change regularly. You may browse the website:

www.ufsa.ufl.edu/SFA/programs/sfaschol.html. GPA must be 3.0-4.0.

University of Florida
Office for Student Financial Affairs S-1
PO Box 114025
Gainesville, FL 32611-4025

2712
Victor Garnett Campbell Eubank Scholarship

AMOUNT: $450 DEADLINE: Varies
MAJOR: All Areas of Study

Open to undergraduates at the University of Florida who demonstrate high academic achievement and financial need. Undergraduate students are considered automatically if they apply for financial aid. There is no special application required. Award requirements change regularly. You may browse the website: www.ufsa.ufl.edu/SFA/programs/sfaschol.html. GPA must be 3.0-4.0.

University of Florida
Office for Student Financial Affairs S-1
PO Box 114025
Gainesville, FL 32611-4025

2713
Winifred Todd Parker Scholarship

AMOUNT: $450 DEADLINE: Varies
MAJOR: Social Science

Open to undergraduates at the University of Florida who are majoring in the social sciences. Must demonstrate financial need. Undergraduate students are considered automatically if they apply for financial aid. There is no special application required. Award requirements change regularly. You may browse the website: www.ufsa.ufl.edu/SFA/programs/sfaschol.html. GPA must be 3.0-4.0.

University of Florida
Office for Student Financial Affairs S-1
PO Box 114025
Gainesville, FL 32611-4025

University of Hawaii

2714
Graduate Degree Fellowships

AMOUNT: None Specified DEADLINE: October 15
MAJOR: Economics Studies, Politics and Security Studies, Environmental Studies, Population and Health Studies

The Graduate Degree Fellowships are open to individuals interested in participating in the educational and research programs at the East-West Center while pursuing graduate degree studies at the University of Hawaii. Preference is given to master's degree applicants, but outstanding doctoral applicants will be considered. The degree fellowships offer opportunities for involvement in the Center's research program, focused in several thematic areas: economics studies, politics and security studies, environmental studies, and population and health studies. Award requirements change regularly. Send a self-addressed, stamped envelope to the address listed for more information or visit their website at www.ewc.hawaii.edu/et/et1.htm. No GPA requirement specified.

East-West Center
Awards Services
1601 East-West Road
Honolulu, HI 96848-1601

University of Illinois, Champaign-Urbana

2715
Morgan L. Fitch Scholarship

AMOUNT: $2000 DEADLINE: April 1
MAJOR: Real Estate

Open to students who are enrolled in a degree program with an emphasis on real estate at the University of Illinois, Champaign-Urbana, College of Commerce and Business Administration or College of Liberal Arts and Sciences. Applicants must have completed at least 60 college credit hours, be U.S. citizens, have a minimum 3.5 GPA on a 5.0 scale, and be residents of the state of Illinois. Award requirements change regularly. For further information and an application, please write to the address listed, including a self-addressed, stamped envelope. GPA must be 3.5-4.0.

Illinois Real Estate Educational Foundation
Academic Scholarships
PO Box 19457
Springfield, IL 62794

University of Iowa

2716
Iowa Federation of Labor, AFL-CIO Graduate Assistantship

AMOUNT: Maximum: $6660 DEADLINE: April 9
MAJOR: All Areas of Study

This assistantship is open to graduate students accepted into or attending the University of Iowa. You must be a member or a child of a member in good standing (active, deceased, or retired) of any local Iowa union affiliated with the Iowa Federation of Labor, AFL-CIO. In order to apply, you must demonstrate financial need; have an interest in working in the industrial relations or labor education area; and take part in the teaching, researching, and/or service activities of the Labor Education Program. In order to meet the requirements of this award, you will be participating in ten hours of professional activities a week. The annual stipend is $6,600. Award requirements change regularly. No GPA requirement specified.

Iowa Federation of Labor, AFL-CIO
University of Iowa
100 Oakdale Campus, Rm M210
Iowa City, IA 52242-5000

2717
Minority American Science Scholarship

AMOUNT: None Specified DEADLINE: Varies
MAJOR: Natural Science, Mathematics, Statistics, Actuarial Science

Scholarships are available at the University of Iowa for entering minority freshmen. Applicants must be of Hispanic, African-American, Native American, or Southeast Asian descent and plan to major in one of the listed fields. Applicants must be U.S. citizens with a GPA of at least 3.0. Award requirements change regularly. Write to the address listed for an application and further information. You may also visit their website: www.uiowa.edu/~finaid or email financial-aid@uiowa.edu. GPA must be 3.0-4.0.

University of Iowa
Office of Student Financial Aid
208 Calvin Hall
Iowa City, IA 52242-1315

University of Mary

2718
Academic/Involvement Scholarship/Grant

AMOUNT: None Specified DEADLINE: Varies
MAJOR: Music, Speech, Drama/Theater, Athletics

The Academic/Involvement Scholarship/Grant is open to students who are planning to attend University of Mary. To be considered for this award, you must have a minimum ACT score of 23; have a minimum 3.0 GPA; and plan to be involved in music, speech, drama, or sports. Award requirements change regularly. GPA must be 3.0-4.0.

University of Mary
Attn: Admissions
7500 University Drive
Bismarck, ND 58504

2719
Athletic/Music Scholarship Grant

AMOUNT: None Specified DEADLINE: Varies
MAJOR: Music, Athletics

The Athletic/Music Scholarship Grant is open to students who are planning to attend University of Mary. To be considered for this award, you must be planning to be involved in music or athletics. Award requirements change regularly. No GPA requirement specified.

University of Mary
Attn: Admissions
7500 University Drive
Bismarck, ND 58504

2720
Pacesetter Grant

AMOUNT: None Specified DEADLINE: Varies
MAJOR: All Fields of Study

The Pacesetter Grant is open to students who are planning to attend the University of Mary. Award requirements change regularly. No GPA requirement specified.

University of Mary
Attn: Admissions
7500 University Drive
Bismarck, ND 58504

2721
Presidential Scholar Award

AMOUNT: Maximum: $24000 DEADLINE: Varies
MAJOR: All Fields of Study

The Presidential Scholar Award is open to entering freshmen who are planning to attend University of Mary. To be considered for this award, you must have a minimum ACT score of 28 and a minimum 3.85 GPA. This award also requires you to participate in an interview. Award requirements change regularly. GPA must be 3.85-4.0.

University of Mary
Attn: Admissions
7500 University Drive
Bismarck, ND 58504

University of Minnesota, Morris

2722
National Merit Scholarship Program

AMOUNT: $1000 DEADLINE: Varies
MAJOR: All Areas of Study

The National Merit Scholarship Program is open to National Merit Finalists and Commended Scholars in the National Merit Scholarship Competition. Finalists are eligible for a four-year full-tuition scholarship. Finalists must indicate UMM as their first-choice school to the National Merit Corporation. Commended scholars are eligible for a $1,000 scholarship for four years. These awards are limited, and priority will be given to those first confirming their enrollment at UMM. Award requirements change regularly. Students will automatically be reviewed for this scholarship upon admission to UMM. Students may be required to submit documentation and verification of their Finalist/Commended Scholar status. Please consult with an admission counselor for further details. No GPA requirement specified.

University of Minnesota, Morris
Admissions and Financial Aid Office
105 Behmler Hall, 600 East 4th Street
Morris, MN 56267

2723
President's Outstanding Minority Scholarship

AMOUNT: Maximum: $3000 DEADLINE: April 7
MAJOR: All Areas of Study

The President's Outstanding Minority Scholarship is open to ethnic minority students admitted to UMM. This scholarship can be worth up to $3000 depending on financial need and is renewable for up to four years. You must file the FAFSA in order to apply. Award requirements change regularly. No GPA requirement specified.

University of Minnesota, Morris
Admissions and Financial Aid Office
105 Behmler Hall, 600 East 4th Street
Morris, MN 56267

2724
Transfer Academic Scholarship

AMOUNT: None Specified DEADLINE: Varies
MAJOR: All Areas of Study

The Transfer Academic Scholarship is open to students transferring to UMM from an accredited institution with at least one year's worth of credits. If students have a GPA of at least 3.75, they qualify for a one-half tuition scholarship. Students with at least a 3.5 GPA qualify for a one-quarter tuition scholarship. These scholarships can be used during the student's first year at UMM and are based on resident tuition. Award requirements change regularly. Students will automatically be reviewed for this scholarship upon admission to UMM. Please consult with an admission counselor for further details. GPA must be 3.5-4.0.

University of Minnesota, Morris
Admissions and Financial Aid Office
105 Behmler Hall, 600 East 4th Street
Morris, MN 56267

University of Mississippi

2725
General Freshman Scholarship

AMOUNT: None Specified DEADLINE: February 1
MAJOR: All Areas of Study

This scholarship is open to high school seniors who apply for admission to the University of Mississippi. You must send in your scholarship request form by February 1. Most awards are based on academics, but leadership and financial need may be factors. You must also file the FAFSA by February 15. Award requirements change regularly. GPA must be 2.8-4.0.

University of Mississippi
Admissions Office
117 Lyceum
University, MS 38677

University of Missouri, Rolla

2726
Curators Scholarship

AMOUNT: $3500 DEADLINE: November 1
MAJOR: All Areas of Study

This scholarship is open to graduating seniors who are Missouri residents with a minimum GPA of 3.25 and ranked in the top 5% of their graduating class. Renewable if recipients maintain a GPA of at least 3.25. Award requirements change regularly. For further information, please contact your high school guidance counselor or the financial aid office at UMR, or browse their website at www.umr.edu/admissions/afford.html. GPA must be 3.25-4.0.

University of Missouri, Rolla
G-1 Parker Hall
1870 Miner Circle
Rolla, MO 65409

2727
Midwest Student Exchange Program Awards

AMOUNT: None Specified DEADLINE: February 1
MAJOR: Nuclear/Petroleum/Mining/Metallurgical/Geological Engineering, Geology, Geophysics, Mathematics, Physics, Chemistry, English

Open to incoming freshmen and new transfer students from Kansas, Michigan, Minnesota, and Nebraska in the top 15% of their class. Applicants must have a minimum GPA of 2.5 to renew the award. Award requirements change regularly. For further information, please contact your high school guidance counselor or the financial aid office at UMR, or browse their website at www.umr.edu/admissions/afford.html. GPA must be 3.4.

University of Missouri, Rolla
G-1 Parker Hall
1870 Miner Circle
Rolla, MO 65409

2728
Minority Engineering Award

AMOUNT: None Specified DEADLINE: December 31
MAJOR: Engineering

Scholarships for entering minority freshmen or minority transfer students - Native American, African-American, or Hispanic-American - at UMR. This award is based on academics and professional interest. Applicants must be U.S. citizens. Award requirements change regularly. For further information, please contact your high school guidance counselor or the financial aid office at UMR, or browse their website at www.umr.edu/admissions/afford.html. No GPA requirement specified.

University of Missouri, Rolla
G-1 Parker Hall
1870 Miner Circle , Rolla MO

2729
National Merit Scholarships

AMOUNT: $750-$2000 DEADLINE: Varies
MAJOR: All Areas of Study

This scholarship is open to students at the UMR who were classified as finalists in the National Merit Scholarship Competition and have listed UMR as their first choice of schools. Award requirements change regularly. For further information, please contact your high school guidance counselor or the financial aid office at UMR, or browse their website at www.umr.edu/admissions/afford.html. No GPA requirement specified.

University of Missouri, Rolla
G-1 Parker Hall
1870 Miner Circle
Rolla, MO 65409

2730
Scholarships for Outstanding Freshmen (Bright Flight)

AMOUNT: $2000 DEADLINE: July 15
MAJOR: All Areas of Study

This scholarship is open to entering freshmen at UMR who are Missouri residents in the top 3% of their graduating class. Renewable if recipients maintain a minimum GPA of 2.25. Award requirements change regularly. For further information, please contact your high school guidance counselor or the financial aid office at UMR, or browse their website at www.umr.edu/admissions/afford.html. GPA must be 3.7-4.0.

University of Missouri, Rolla
G-1 Parker Hall
1870 Miner Circle
Rolla, MO 65409

2731
Women in Engineering Program

AMOUNT: $500 DEADLINE: January 15
MAJOR: Engineering, Computer Science

This scholarship is open to women who are either entering freshmen or transfer students at UMR, pursuing an engineering or computer science degree. This scholarship is not renewable. Award requirements change regularly. For further information, please contact your high school guidance counselor or the financial aid office at UMR, or browse their website at www.umr.edu/admissions/afford.html. No GPA requirement specified.

University of Missouri, Rolla
G-1 Parker Hall
1870 Miner Circle
Rolla, MO 65409

University of Nevada, Reno

2732
University of Nevada, Reno, Scholarship

AMOUNT: None Specified DEADLINE: February 1
MAJOR: All Areas of Study

The University of Nevada, Reno, is offering several scholarships for continuing and returning University of Nevada, Reno, students. In order to apply, you will need to complete only one application form to be considered for all the awards that are offered through the University. If you are an entering freshman or transfer student, you must apply using the application in the admissions booklet. Award requirements change regularly. No GPA requirement specified.

University of Nevada, Reno
Office of Financial Aid
Mail Stop 076, 200 TSSC
Reno, NV 89557

University of North Dakota

2733
La Verne Noyes Scholarship

AMOUNT: None Specified DEADLINE: March 15
MAJOR: All Areas of Study

Scholarships for students who are attending the University of North Dakota and are direct descendents of veterans of World War I. Please note the veteran must have been honorably discharged. Applicant must also show financial need and meet the general scholarship criteria. Award requirements change regularly. Contact the office of student financial aid or write to the address below for details. GPA must be 3.5-4.0.

University of North Dakota
Student Financial Aid Office
PO Box 8371
Grand Forks, ND 58202-8371

University of North Texas

2734
Annell Roberts Barentine ('59) Memorial Scholarship

AMOUNT: None Specified DEADLINE: March 31
MAJOR: English Education

The Annell Roberts Barentine ('59) Memorial Scholarship is open to students at UNT planning to teach English at the high school level. If you are an incoming freshman, you must have a minimum 1270 SAT or 29 ACT and rank in the top 25% of your high school graduating class. Continuing and transfer students must have a minimum GPA of 3.25. Award requirements change regularly. Contact the address listed for further

information, enclosing a self-addressed, stamped envelope, or call (940) 565-2302.

University of North Texas
Scholarship & Financial Aid Office
PO Box 311370
Denton, TX 76203-1370

2735
Association of Old Crows Scholarship (Dallas Chapter)

AMOUNT: $1500 DEADLINE: March 31
MAJOR: Computer Science, Physics

The Association of Old Crows Scholarship (Dallas Chapter) is open to juniors and seniors at UNT majoring in physics and computer science. You must have at least a 3.0 GPA. Award requirements change regularly. Contact the address listed for further information, enclosing a self-addressed, stamped envelope, or call (940) 565-2302. GPA must be 3.0-4.0.

University of North Texas
Scholarship & Financial Aid Office
PO Box 311370
Denton, TX 76203-1370

2736
Auxiliary Services Scholarship

AMOUNT: None Specified DEADLINE: March 1
MAJOR: All Areas of Study

The Auxiliary Services Scholarship is open to full-time graduate students at UNT who are employed by UNT's auxiliary services division. You must continue employment while receiving this scholarship and maintain a minimum 3.0 GPA. Award requirements change regularly. Contact the address listed for further information, enclosing a self-addressed, stamped envelope, or call (940) 565-2302. GPA must be 3.0-4.0.

University of North Texas
Scholarship & Financial Aid Office
PO Box 311370
Denton, TX 76203-1370

2737
Barney Hilton/Frito-Lay Scholarship

AMOUNT: None Specified DEADLINE: March 31
MAJOR: Chemistry

The Barney Hilton/Frito-Lay Scholarship is open to junior chemistry majors at UNT. You must have at least a 3.0 GPA in order to apply. Award requirements change regularly. Contact the address listed for further information, enclosing a self-addressed, stamped envelope, or call (940) 565-2302. GPA must be 3.0-4.0.

University of North Texas
Scholarship & Financial Aid Office
PO Box 311370
Denton, TX 76203-1370

2738
Beta Alpha Rho Beta Scholarship

AMOUNT: None Specified DEADLINE: March 31
MAJOR: All Areas of Study

The Beta Alpha Rho Beta Scholarships are open to all undergraduates at UNT. If you are an incoming freshman you must have at least a 24 ACT or 1100 SAT and rank in the top 25% of your high school graduating class. If you are a continuing or transfer student you must have a minimum 3.0 GPA. Award requirements change regularly. Contact the address listed for further information, enclosing a self-addressed, stamped envelope, or call (940) 565-2302.

University of North Texas
Scholarship & Financial Aid Office
PO Box 311370
Denton, TX 76203-1370

2739
Bettie J. Lillard Memorial Scholarship

AMOUNT: None Specified DEADLINE: March 31
MAJOR: All Areas of Study

The Bettie J. Lillard Memorial Scholarship is open to sons and daughters of K-12 teachers. If you are an incoming freshman, you must have at least a 24 ACT or 1100 SAT. You must have a minimum 3.0 GPA if you are a continuing or transfer student. Award requirements change regularly. Contact the address listed for further information, enclosing a self-addressed, stamped envelope, or call (940) 565-2302.

University of North Texas
Scholarship & Financial Aid Office
PO Box 311370
Denton, TX 76203-1370

2740
Beulah Harriss Memorial Scholarships

AMOUNT: $500-$1000 DEADLINE: March 31
MAJOR: Health Related, Physical Education

The Beulah Harriss Memorial Scholarships are open to undergraduate women at UNT majoring in a health-related field or physical education. Incoming freshmen must have at least a 24 ACT or 1100 SAT. Continuing and transfer students must have at least a 3.0 GPA. Award requirements change regularly. Contact the address listed for further information, enclosing a self-addressed, stamped envelope, or call (940) 565-2302.

University of North Texas
Scholarship & Financial Aid Office
PO Box 311370
Denton, TX 76203-1370

2741
Bobby E. Franklin Memorial Scholarship

AMOUNT: None Specified DEADLINE: March 31
MAJOR: Foreign Languages, Education

The Bobby E. Franklin Memorial Scholarship is open to high school seniors in the Denton Independent School District planning on attending the University of North Texas. You must be planning to major in foreign languages or pursue a career in education. You must also have at least a 24 ACT or 1100 SAT. Award requirements change regularly. Contact the address listed for further information, enclosing a self-addressed, stamped envelope, or call (940) 565-2302.

University of North Texas
Scholarship & Financial Aid Office
PO Box 311370
Denton, TX 76203-1370

2742
Brent Korol Memorial Scholarships

AMOUNT: None Specified DEADLINE: March 31
MAJOR: Interior Design

The Brent Korol Memorial Scholarships are open to UNT interior design majors. Incoming freshmen must have at least a 24 ACT or 1100 SAT. Continuing and transfer students must have a minimum 3.0 GPA. Award requirements change regularly. Contact the address listed for further information, enclosing a self-addressed, stamped envelope, or call (940) 565-2302.

University of North Texas
Scholarship & Financial Aid Office
PO Box 311370
Denton, TX 76203-1370

2743
Brownlee-Moore Scholarship

AMOUNT: None Specified DEADLINE: March 31
MAJOR: All Areas of Study

The Brownlee-Moore Scholarship is open to undergraduates enrolled at UNT. Under some circumstances, descendants of the donors will be given preference. If you are an incoming freshman you must have at least a 24 ACT or 1100 SAT and rank in the top 25% of your high school graduating class. If you are a continuing or transfer student you must have a minimum 3.0 GPA. Award requirements change regularly. Contact the address listed for further information, enclosing a self-addressed, stamped envelope, or call (940) 565-2302.

University of North Texas
Scholarship & Financial Aid Office
PO Box 311370
Denton, TX 76203-1370

2744
C. J. "Red" Davidson Scholarship

AMOUNT: None Specified DEADLINE: March 31
MAJOR: All Areas of Study

The C. J. "Red" Davidson Scholarship is open to outstanding undergraduates at UNT who are Texas residents. Incoming freshmen must have at least a 24 ACT or 1100 SAT. Continuing and transfer students must have a minimum 3.0 GPA. Award requirements change regularly. Contact the address listed for further information, enclosing a self-addressed, stamped envelope, or call (940) 565-2302.

University of North Texas
Scholarship & Financial Aid Office
PO Box 311370
Denton, TX 76203-1370

2745
Casey President's Council Award

AMOUNT: $250 DEADLINE: March 31
MAJOR: All Areas of Study

The Casey President's Council Award is open to students attending UNT. If you are an incoming freshman you must have at least a 24 ACT or 1100 SAT and rank in the top 25% of your high school graduating class. A minimum 3.0 GPA is needed if you are a continuing or transfer student. You must also participate in extracurricular activities or be working in order to be eligible for this award. Award requirements change regularly. Contact the address listed for further information, enclosing a self-addressed, stamped envelope, or call (940) 565-2302.

University of North Texas
Scholarship & Financial Aid Office
PO Box 311370
Denton, TX 76203-1370

2746
Charles "Choc" Sportsman Memorial Scholarships

AMOUNT: None Specified DEADLINE: March 31
MAJOR: All Areas of Study

The Charles "Choc" Sportsman Memorial Scholarships are open to students at UNT who are members of the men's and women's varsity cross country and track programs. If you are an incoming freshman you must have at least a 24 ACT or 1100 SAT. If you are a continuing or transfer student you must have a minimum 3.0 GPA. Award requirements change regularly. Contact the address listed for further information, enclosing a self-addressed, stamped envelope, or call (940) 565-2302.

University of North Texas
Scholarship & Financial Aid Office
PO Box 311370
Denton, TX 76203-1370

2747
Charles E. and Joanna E. Bond Presidential Scholarship

AMOUNT: None Specified DEADLINE: March 31
MAJOR: All Areas of Study

The Charles E. and Joanna E. Bond Presidential Scholarship is open to students at UNT. If you are an incoming freshman you must have at least a 24 ACT or 1100 SAT and rank in the top 25% of your high school graduating class. If you are a continuing or transfer student you must have a minimum 3.0 GPA. Award requirements change regularly. Contact the address listed for further information, enclosing a self-addressed, stamped envelope, or call (940) 565-2302.

University of North Texas
Scholarship & Financial Aid Office
PO Box 311370
Denton, TX 76203-1370

2748
Chris Athens Scholarship

AMOUNT: None Specified DEADLINE: March 31
MAJOR: All Areas of Study

The Chris Athens Scholarship is open to students at UNT. You must participate in the varsity football program. If you are an incoming freshman you must have at least a 24 ACT or 1100 SAT and rank in the top 25% of your high school graduating class. If you are a continuing or transfer student you must have a minimum 3.0 GPA. Award requirements change regularly. Contact the address listed for further information, enclosing a self-addressed, stamped envelope, or call (940) 565-2302.

University of North Texas
Scholarship & Financial Aid Office
PO Box 311370
Denton, TX 76203-1370

2749
Colin Caruthers Memorial Scholarship

AMOUNT: None Specified DEADLINE: March 31
MAJOR: All Areas of Study

The Colin Caruthers Memorial Scholarship is open to members of the Theta Chi fraternity at UNT. If you are an entering freshman, you must have a minimum 24 ACT or 1100 SAT and rank in the top 25% of your high school graduating class. If you are a continuing or transfer student, you must have a minimum 3.0 GPA. Award requirements change regularly. Contact the address listed for further information, enclosing a self-addressed, stamped envelope, or call (940) 565-2302. GPA must be 3.0-4.0.

University of North Texas
Scholarship & Financial Aid Office
PO Box 311370
Denton, TX 76203-1370

2750
Dallas Chapter, Chartered Property & Casualty Underwriters Scholarship

AMOUNT: $500 DEADLINE: Varies
MAJOR: Insurance

The Dallas Chapter, Chartered Property & Casualty Underwriters (CPCU) Scholarship is open to junior or senior insurance students at UNT. You must have a minimum GPA of 3.0 and prove financial need. Award requirements change regularly. For further information call Dr. Imre Karafiath at (940) 565-3050. GPA must be 3.0-4.0.

University of North Texas
Financial Aid Office
PO Box 311370
Denton, TX 76203-1370

2751
Dallas-Fort Worth Chapter of RIMS Scholarship

AMOUNT: $1000 DEADLINE: Varies
MAJOR: Insurance

The Dallas-Fort Worth Chapter of Risk and Insurance Management Society (RIMS) Scholarships are open to undergraduate insurance students. You must demonstrate financial need. Your work experience and activities are also considered. Award requirements change regularly. For further information call Dr. Imre Karafiath at (940) 565-3050. You may also browse the department's website. No GPA requirement specified.

University of North Texas
Financial Aid Office
PO Box 311370
Denton, TX 76203-1370

2752
Direct Marketing Association Scholarship

AMOUNT: None Specified DEADLINE: March 31
MAJOR: Merchandising, Journalism, Marketing

The Direct Marketing Association Scholarship is open to undergraduates at UNT majoring in merchandising, journalism, or marketing. Incoming freshmen must have at least a 24 ACT or 1100 SAT. Continuing and transfer students must have a minimum 3.0 GPA. Award requirements change regularly. Contact the address listed for further information, enclosing a self-addressed, stamped envelope, or call (940) 565-2302.

University of North Texas
Scholarship & Financial Aid Office
PO Box 311370
Denton, TX 76203-1370

2753
E. J. Milam Memorial Scholarship

AMOUNT: None Specified DEADLINE: March 31
MAJOR: All Areas of Study

The E. J. Milam Memorial Scholarship is open to undergraduates at UNT with outstanding academic records. Incoming freshmen must have at least a 24 ACT or 1100 SAT. Continuing and transfer students must have a minimum 3.0 GPA. Award requirements change regularly. Contact the address listed for further information, enclosing a self-addressed, stamped envelope, or call (940) 565-2302.

University of North Texas
Scholarship & Financial Aid Office
PO Box 311370
Denton, TX 76203-1370

2754
Eagle Escapades Scholarships

AMOUNT: None Specified DEADLINE: March 31
MAJOR: All Areas of Study

The Eagle Escapades Scholarships are open to high school seniors in the Denton Independent School District who plan to attend the University of North Texas. You must have a minimum 1100 SAT or 24 ACT. Award requirements change regularly. Contact the address listed for further information, enclosing a self-addressed, stamped envelope, or call (940) 565-2302. No GPA requirement specified.

University of North Texas
Scholarship & Financial Aid Office
PO Box 311370
Denton, TX 76203-1370

2755
Edith Lanier Clark Scholarship

AMOUNT: None Specified DEADLINE: March 31
MAJOR: Education, Teaching Certification

The Edith Lanier Clark Scholarships are open to female graduate students at UNT. You must be a student majoring in education, a teacher returning to campus to pursue graduate work towards a higher degree, or a female UNT student with an undergraduate degree seeking teacher certification. Award requirements change regularly. Contact the address listed for further information, enclosing a self-addressed, stamped envelope, or call (940) 565-2302. No GPA requirement specified.

University of North Texas
Scholarship & Financial Aid Office
PO Box 311370
Denton, TX 76203-1370

2756
FMA (Financial Management Association) Scholarship

AMOUNT: None Specified DEADLINE: Varies
MAJOR: Finance

The FMA (Financial Management Association) Scholarship is open to finance majors. You must be an undergraduate student at UNT. Award requirements change regularly. For further information call Dr. Imre Karafiath at (940) 565-3050. No GPA requirement specified.

University of North Texas
Financial Aid Office
PO Box 311370
Denton, TX 76203-1370

2757
Foley's/Federated Foundation Scholarship

AMOUNT: None Specified DEADLINE: March 31
MAJOR: Marketing, Merchandising, Fashion Design, Journalism, Retailing

The Foley's/Federated Foundation Scholarship is open to juniors at UNT majoring in marketing, merchandising, fashion design, or journalism. You must be planning to pursue a career in retailing. A minimum 3.0 GPA is required. This award varies and is for use in the senior year. Award requirements change regularly. Contact the address listed for further information, enclosing a self-addressed, stamped envelope, or call (940) 565-2302. GPA must be 3.0-4.0.

University of North Texas
Scholarship & Financial Aid Office
PO Box 311370
Denton, TX 76203-1370

2758
Fraiser McConnell Memorial Scholarship

AMOUNT: None Specified DEADLINE: March 31
MAJOR: Library and Information Sciences

The Fraiser McConnell Memorial Scholarship is open to graduate students at UNT. You must be a library or information sciences major. Award requirements change regularly. Contact the address listed for further information, enclosing a self-addressed, stamped envelope, or call (940) 565-2302. No GPA requirement specified.

University of North Texas
Scholarship & Financial Aid Office
PO Box 311370
Denton, TX 76203-1370

2759
Fred Coffey Class of 1925 Memorial Scholarship

AMOUNT: None Specified DEADLINE: March 31
MAJOR: All Areas of Study

The Fred Coffey Class of 1925 Memorial Scholarship is open to graduate students at UNT who have learning disabilities or physical disabilities. Award requirements change regularly. Contact the address listed for further information, enclosing a self-addressed, stamped envelope, or call (940) 565-2302. No GPA requirement specified.

University of North Texas
Scholarship & Financial Aid Office
PO Box 311370
Denton, TX 76203-1370

2760
George Christy Scholarship

AMOUNT: None Specified DEADLINE: Varies
MAJOR: Finance

The George Christy Scholarship is open to undergraduate finance majors at UNT. You must have achieved a 3.5 GPA in at least nine hours of finance course work. Award requirements change regularly. For further information call Dr. Imre Karafiath at (940) 565-3050. You may also browse the department's website. GPA must be 3.5-4.0.

University of North Texas
Financial Aid Office
PO Box 311370
Denton, TX 76203-1370

2761
Good Neighbor Scholarship

AMOUNT: None Specified DEADLINE: March 31
MAJOR: All Areas of Study

The Good Neighbor Scholarship is open to graduate students attending UNT. You must be a citizen of a Western Hemisphere nation besides the U.S. in order to apply. Award requirements change regularly. Contact the address listed for further information, enclosing a self-addressed, stamped envelope, or call (940) 565-2302. No GPA requirement specified.

University of North Texas
Scholarship & Financial Aid Office
PO Box 311370
Denton, TX 76203-1370

2762
Government Employees Insurance Company (GEICO) Scholarship

AMOUNT: $1000 DEADLINE: Varies
MAJOR: Insurance

The Government Employees Insurance Company (GEICO) Scholarship is open to undergraduate and graduate insurance students at UNT. You must have an outstanding academic record and demonstrate financial need. Both work experience and activities are considered. Award requirements change regularly. For further information call Dr. Imre Karafiath at (940) 565-3050. No GPA requirement specified.

University of North Texas
Financial Aid Office
PO Box 311370
Denton, TX 76203-1370

2763
Helen J. Audrain Scholarship

AMOUNT: None Specified DEADLINE: March 31
MAJOR: Pre-Med

The Helen J. Audrain Scholarship is open to students at UNT majoring in pre-med with outstanding academic credentials. If you are an incoming freshman you must have at least a 24 ACT or 1100 SAT and rank in the top 25% of your high school graduating class. If you are a continuing or transfer student you must have a minimum 3.0 GPA. Award requirements change regularly. Contact the address listed for further information, enclosing a self-addressed, stamped envelope, or call (940) 565-2302.

University of North Texas
Scholarship & Financial Aid Office
PO Box 311370
Denton, TX 76203-1370

2764
Hideaki Oku/Houston General Insurance Company Scholarship

AMOUNT: None Specified DEADLINE: March 31
MAJOR: Insurance

The Hideaki Oku/Houston General Insurance Company Scholarship is open to a student at UNT in the College of Business pursuing a career in the insurance profession. If you are an incoming freshman you must have at least a 24 ACT or 1100 SAT. If you are a continuing or transfer student you must have a minimum 3.0 GPA. Award requirements change regularly. Contact the address listed for further information, enclosing a self-addressed, stamped envelope, or call (940) 565-2302. No GPA requirement specified.

University of North Texas
Scholarship & Financial Aid Office
PO Box 311370
Denton, TX 76203-1370

2765
Hsaio-Pei Yang Memorial Scholarship

AMOUNT: None Specified DEADLINE: March 31
MAJOR: All Areas of Study

The Hsaio-Pei Yang Memorial Scholarship is open to graduate students of UNT. You must have published your research or presented research papers at a national professional conference. A minimum 3.5 GPA is needed. Award requirements change regularly. Contact the address listed for further information, enclosing a self-addressed, stamped envelope, or call (940) 565-2302. GPA must be 3.5-4.0.

University of North Texas
Scholarship & Financial Aid Office
PO Box 311370
Denton, TX 76203-1370

2766
Hugh M. Ayer Scholarship

AMOUNT: None Specified DEADLINE: March 31
MAJOR: All Areas of Study

The Hugh M. Ayer Scholarship is open to incoming freshmen and continuing students at UNT with exceptional academic potential. If you are an incoming freshman you must have at least a 24 ACT or 1100 SAT and rank in the top 25% of your high school class. If you are a continuing student you must have a minimum 3.0 GPA. Award requirements change regularly. Contact the address listed for further information, enclosing a self-addressed, stamped envelope, or call (940) 565-2302.

University of North Texas
Scholarship & Financial Aid Office
PO Box 311370
Denton, TX 76203-1370

2767
Insurance Women of Dallas Scholarship

AMOUNT: None Specified DEADLINE: Varies
MAJOR: Insurance

The Insurance Women of Dallas (IWD) Scholarship is open to undergraduate insurance students at UNT. You must show financial need. Your work experience, career goals, and activities are considered. Award requirements change regularly. For further information call Dr. Imre Karafiath at (940) 565-3050. No GPA requirement specified.

University of North Texas
Financial Aid Office
PO Box 311370
Denton, TX 76203-1370

2768
International Education Committee Scholarship

AMOUNT: $200 DEADLINE: March 31
MAJOR: All Areas of Study

The International Education Committee Scholarship is open to graduate students at UNT. In order to apply, you must show, through your field of study or extracurricular activities, a strong commitment to furthering world understanding. Award requirements change regularly. Contact the address listed for further information, enclosing a self-addressed, stamped envelope, or call (940) 565-2302. No GPA requirement specified.

University of North Texas
Scholarship & Financial Aid Office
PO Box 311370
Denton, TX 76203-1370

2769
John and Louvenia Knight Scholarships

AMOUNT: None Specified DEADLINE: March 31
MAJOR: All Areas of Study

The John and Louvenia Knight Scholarships are open to UNT graduates of Collin County high schools. Preference is given to you if you are from a smaller school district. In order to apply, you must have at least a 24 ACT or 1100 SAT. Award requirements change regularly. Contact the address listed for further information, enclosing a self-addressed, stamped envelope, or call (940) 565-2302. No GPA requirement specified.

University of North Texas
Scholarship & Financial Aid Office
PO Box 311370
Denton, TX 76203-1370

John Houston Douglass Scholarships

AMOUNT: None Specified DEADLINE: March 3
MAJOR: Elementary Education

The John Houston Douglass Scholarships are open to juniors and seniors at UNT planning careers in elementary education. You must have a minimum 3.0 GPA in order to apply. Award requirements change regularly. Contact the address listed for further information, enclosing a self-addressed, stamped envelope, or call (940) 565-2302. GPA must be 3.0-4.0.

University of North Texas
Scholarship & Financial Aid Office
PO Box 311370
Denton, TX 76203-1370

2771
Ken Bahnsen Scholarship

AMOUNT: None Specified DEADLINE: March 31
MAJOR: All Areas of Study

The Ken Bahnsen Scholarship is open to students at UNT who are members of the varsity tennis program. If you are an incoming freshman you must have at least a 24 ACT or 1100 SAT and rank in the top 25% of your high school graduating class. If you are a continuing or transfer student you must have a minimum 3.0 GPA. Award requirements change regularly. Contact the address listed for further information, enclosing a self-addressed, stamped envelope, or call (940) 565-2302.

University of North Texas
Scholarship & Financial Aid Office
PO Box 311370
Denton, TX 76203-1370

2772
Kirby Keas Scholarships

AMOUNT: None Specified DEADLINE: March 31
MAJOR: All Areas of Study

The Kirby Keas Scholarships are open to undergraduates participating in the soccer program at UNT. Incoming freshmen must have at least a 24 ACT or 1100 SAT. Continuing and transfer students must have at least a 3.0 GPA. Award requirements change regularly. Contact the address listed for further information, enclosing a self-addressed, stamped envelope, or call (940) 565-2302.

University of North Texas
Scholarship & Financial Aid Office
PO Box 311370
Denton, TX 76203-1370

2773
Laotian Scholarship Fund Award

AMOUNT: None Specified DEADLINE: March 31
MAJOR: All Areas of Study

The Laotian Scholarship Fund Award is open to U.S. citizens or permanent residents at UNT who are of Laotian descent. You must be a U.S. citizen or permanent resident. If you are an incoming freshman, you must have at least a 24 ACT or

1100 SAT. A minimum 3.0 GPA will be required if you are a continuing or transfer student. Award requirements change regularly. Contact the address listed for further information, enclosing a self-addressed, stamped envelope, or call (940) 565-2302.

University of North Texas
Scholarship & Financial Aid Office
PO Box 311370
Denton, TX 76203-1370

2774
Lauream Christian Robertson Fellowship

AMOUNT: None Specified DEADLINE: March 31
MAJOR: Education

The Lauream Christian Robertson Fellowship is open to UNT graduate students in the College of Education. You must be in the process of writing your thesis or dissertation. Award requirements change regularly. Contact the address listed for further information, enclosing a self-addressed, stamped envelope, or call (940) 565-2302. No GPA requirement specified.

University of North Texas
Scholarship & Financial Aid Office
PO Box 311370
Denton, TX 76203-1370

2775
Linda J. Carter Scholarship

AMOUNT: None Specified DEADLINE: March 31
MAJOR: All Areas of Study

The Linda J. Carter Scholarship is open to members of the women's varsity basketball program at UNT. If you are an incoming freshman you must have at least a 24 ACT or 1100 SAT and rank in the top 25% of your high school graduating class. If you are a continuing or transfer student you must have a minimum 3.0 GPA. Award requirements change regularly. Contact the address listed for further information, enclosing a self-addressed, stamped envelope, or call (940) 565-2302.

University of North Texas
Scholarship & Financial Aid Office
PO Box 311370
Denton, TX 76203-1370

2776
Lucille Murchison Graduate Scholarship

AMOUNT: None Specified DEADLINE: March 31
MAJOR: All Areas of Study

The Lucille Murchison Graduate Scholarships are open to graduate students of UNT. You must have a minimum 3.0 GPA. Award requirements change regularly. Contact the address listed for further information, enclosing a self-addressed, stamped envelope, or call (940) 565-2302. GPA must be 3.0-4.0.

University of North Texas
Scholarship & Financial Aid Office
PO Box 311370
Denton, TX 76203-1370

2777
Mary Arden Scholarship

AMOUNT: None Specified DEADLINE: March 31
MAJOR: English

The Mary Arden Scholarship is open to juniors and seniors at UNT. You must be a female English major with at least a 3.0 GPA. Award requirements change regularly. Contact the address listed for further information, enclosing a self-addressed, stamped envelope, or call (940) 565-2302. GPA must be 3.0-4.0.

University of North Texas
Scholarship & Financial Aid Office
PO Box 311370
Denton, TX 76203-1370

2778
Men's Golf Scholarship

AMOUNT: None Specified DEADLINE: March 31
MAJOR: All Areas of Study

The Men's Golf Scholarship is open to students at UNT who are participants in the men's varsity golf program. If you are an incoming freshman you must have at least a 24 ACT or 1100 SAT. If you are a continuing or transfer student you must have a minimum 3.0 GPA. Award requirements change regularly. Contact the address listed for further information, enclosing a self-addressed, stamped envelope, or (940) 565-2302.

University of North Texas
Scholarship & Financial Aid Office
PO Box 311370
Denton, TX 76203-1370

2779
Nadine Core Scholarships

AMOUNT: None Specified DEADLINE: March 31
MAJOR: Education

The Nadine Core Scholarships are open to undergraduates at UNT majoring in education. Incoming freshmen must have at least a 24 ACT or 1100 SAT. Continuing and transfer students must have a minimum 3.0 GPA. Award requirements change regularly. Contact the address listed for further information, enclosing a self-addressed, stamped envelope, or call (940) 565-2302.

University of North Texas
Scholarship & Financial Aid Office
PO Box 311370
Denton, TX 76203-1370

2780
Paramount Hotel Corporation Inn-Dow Scholarship

AMOUNT: None Specified DEADLINE: March 31
MAJOR: All Areas of Study

The Paramount Hotel Corporation Inn-Dow Scholarship is open to all UNT qualified undergraduates. Incoming freshmen must have at least a 24 ACT or 1100 SAT. Continuing and transfer students must have a minimum 3.0 GPA. Award requirements change regularly. Contact the address listed for

further information, enclosing a self-addressed, stamped envelope, or call (940) 565-2302.

University of North Texas
Scholarship & Financial Aid Office
PO Box 311370
Denton, TX 76203-1370

2781
Pat McLeod Scholarship

AMOUNT: None Specified DEADLINE: March 31
MAJOR: Vocational/Technical, Career Counseling

The Pat McLeod Scholarship is open to UNT graduate students. You must be working in the area of vocational guidance in the College of Education. Award requirements change regularly. Contact the address listed for further information, enclosing a self-addressed, stamped envelope, or call (940) 565-2302.

University of North Texas
Scholarship & Financial Aid Office
PO Box 311370
Denton, TX 76203-1370

2782
Pete Shands Scholarship

AMOUNT: None Specified DEADLINE: March 31
MAJOR: All Areas of Study

The Pete Shands Scholarship is open to students at UNT who are participants in the varsity basketball program. If you are an incoming freshman you must have at least a 24 ACT or 1100 SAT. If you are a continuing or transfer student you must have a minimum 3.0 GPA. Award requirements change regularly. Contact the address listed for further information, enclosing a self-addressed, stamped envelope, or call (940) 565-2302.

University of North Texas
Scholarship & Financial Aid Office
PO Box 311370
Denton, TX 76203-1370

2783
President's Council Scholarships

AMOUNT: None Specified DEADLINE: March 31
MAJOR: All Areas of Study

The President's Council Scholarships are open to all UNT qualified undergraduates. Incoming freshmen must have at least a 24 ACT or 1100 SAT. Continuing and transfer students must have a minimum 3.0 GPA. Award requirements change regularly. Contact the address listed for further information, enclosing a self-addressed, stamped envelope, or call (940) 565-2302.

University of North Texas
Scholarship & Financial Aid Office
PO Box 311370
Denton, TX 76203-1370

2784
Rauscher Pierce Refsnes, Inc., Finance Scholarship

AMOUNT: None Specified DEADLINE: Varies
MAJOR: Finance

The Rauscher Pierce Refsnes, Inc., Finance Scholarship is open to finance majors. You must be a student at UNT. Award requirements change regularly. For further information call Dr. Imre Karafiath at (940) 565-3050. No GPA requirement specified.

University of North Texas
Financial Aid Office
PO Box 311370
Denton, TX 76203-1370

2785
Republic Insurance Companies Scholarship

AMOUNT: None Specified DEADLINE: Varies
MAJOR: Insurance

The Republic Insurance Companies Scholarship is open to insurance majors. You must be an undergraduate at UNT with an excellent academic record. Work experience and activities are considered. Award requirements change regularly. For further information call Dr. Imre Karafiath at (940) 565-3050. No GPA requirement specified.

University of North Texas
Financial Aid Office
PO Box 311370
Denton, TX 76203-1370

2786
S. J. and Elena Boyd Scholarship

AMOUNT: $600 DEADLINE: March 31
MAJOR: All Areas of Study

The S. J. and Elena Boyd Scholarship is open to all undergraduates at UNT who have demonstrated academic excellence. If you are an incoming freshman you will need a minimum 24 ACT or 1100 SAT and rank in the top 25% of your high school graduating class. If you are a continuing or transfer student you must have a minimum 3.0 GPA. Award requirements change regularly. Contact the address listed for further information, enclosing a self-addressed, stamped envelope, or call (940) 565-2302.

University of North Texas
Scholarship & Financial Aid Office
PO Box 311370
Denton, TX 76203-1370

2787
Shaun Burns Memorial Scholarship

AMOUNT: $250 DEADLINE: March 31
MAJOR: All Areas of Study

The Shaun Burns Memorial Scholarship is open to undergraduates enrolled at UNT. If you are an incoming freshman you must have at least a 24 ACT or 1100 SAT and rank in the top

25% of your high school graduating class. If you are a continuing or transfer student you must have a minimum 3.0 GPA. Award requirements change regularly. Contact the address listed for further information, enclosing a self-addressed, stamped envelope, or call (940) 565-2302.

University of North Texas
Scholarship & Financial Aid Office
PO Box 311370
Denton, TX 76203-1370

2788
Steinsick/Egly Scholarship Fund and Women's Golf Scholarship

AMOUNT: None Specified DEADLINE: March 31
MAJOR: All Areas of Study

The Steinsick/Egly Scholarship Fund and Women's Golf Scholarship is open to students at UNT who are participants in the women's golf program. If you are an incoming freshman you must have at least a 24 ACT or 1100 SAT. If you are a continuing or transfer student you must have a minimum 3.0 GPA. Award requirements change regularly. Contact the address listed for further information, enclosing a self-addressed, stamped envelope, or call (940) 565-2302.

University of North Texas
Scholarship & Financial Aid Office
PO Box 311370
Denton, TX 76203-1370

2789
Tom and Cornez Bussey Memorial Scholarship

AMOUNT: None Specified DEADLINE: March 31
MAJOR: Elementary and Secondary Education

The Tom and Cornez Bussey Memorial Scholarship is open to elementary or secondary education majors at UNT. You must be a high school graduate of the Birdville Independent School District. You must also have a minimum 24 ACT or 1100 SAT. Award requirements change regularly. Contact the address listed for further information, enclosing a self-addressed, stamped envelope, or call (940) 565-2302. No GPA requirement specified.

University of North Texas
Scholarship & Financial Aid Office
PO Box 311370
Denton, TX 76203-1370

2790
Tony and Linda Altermann Scholarship Endowment for Theater/Visual Arts

AMOUNT: None Specified DEADLINE: March 31
MAJOR: Theater Arts, Visual Arts

The Tony and Linda Altermann Scholarship Endowment for Theater/Visual Arts is open to visual arts and theater majors at UNT. If you are an incoming freshman you must have at least a 24 ACT or 1100 SAT and rank in the top 25% of your high school graduating class. If you are a continuing or transfer student you must have a minimum 3.0 GPA. The scholarship is awarded to theater arts majors in even years and visual arts majors in odd years. Award requirements change regularly. Contact the address listed for further information, enclosing a self-addressed, stamped envelope, or call (940) 565-2302.

University of North Texas
Scholarship & Financial Aid Office
PO Box 311370
Denton, TX 76203-1370

2791
UNT Alumni Association Scholarship

AMOUNT: None Specified DEADLINE: March 31
MAJOR: All Areas of Study

Awards open to all UNT students who are relatives of UNT Alumni Association members. If you are an incoming freshman you must have at least a 24 ACT or 1100 SAT. If you are a continuing or transfer student you must have a minimum 3.0 GPA. Award requirements change regularly. Contact the address listed for further information, enclosing a self-addressed, stamped envelope, or call (940) 565-2302.

University of North Texas
Scholarship & Financial Aid Office
PO Box 311370
Denton, TX 76203-1370

2792
UNT Financial Professionals Scholarship

AMOUNT: $500 DEADLINE: Varies
MAJOR: Business, Finance

The UNT Financial Professionals Scholarships are open to full-time minority students from the Dallas Independent School District who are business majors concentrating in finance at UNT. You must be enrolled in a four-year program and maintain a 2.25 GPA overall and a 2.5 GPA in your major. Award requirements change regularly. For further information call Dr. Imre Karafiath at (940) 565-3050. No GPA requirement specified.

University of North Texas
Financial Aid Office
PO Box 311370
Denton, TX 76203-1370

2793
UNT Library Staff Scholarship

AMOUNT: None Specified DEADLINE: March 31
MAJOR: All Areas of Study

The UNT Library Staff Scholarships are open to graduate students attending UNT. You must be an employee of the UNT libraries. Award requirements change regularly. Contact the address listed for further information, enclosing a self-addressed, stamped envelope, or call (940) 565-2302. No GPA requirement specified.

University of North Texas
Scholarship & Financial Aid Office
PO Box 311370
Denton, TX 76203-1370

2794
William Joseph Augustus Nobles Family Trust Scholarships

AMOUNT: None Specified DEADLINE: March 31
MAJOR: All Areas of Study

The William Joseph Augustus Nobles Family Trust Scholarships are open to all undergraduates at UNT who meet the University Scholarship Committee's requirements. Incoming freshmen must have at least a 24 ACT or 1100 SAT. Continuing and transfer students must have a minimum 3.0 GPA. Award requirements change regularly. Contact the address listed for further information, enclosing a self-addressed, stamped envelope, or call (940) 565-2302.

University of North Texas
Scholarship & Financial Aid Office
PO Box 311370
Denton, TX 76203-1370

University of Northern Iowa

2795
Army ROTC Scholarship

AMOUNT: None Specified DEADLINE: April 15
MAJOR: All Areas of Study

The Army ROTC Scholarship is available to freshmen and transfer students who are attending the University of Northern Iowa. Selection is based on academic merit, health, citizenship, and moral character. Scholarship covers full tuition, books, fees, and a stipend of $150 per month. Award requirements change regularly. For further information, please write to the address listed, including a self-addressed, stamped envelope; contact Department of Military Science at (319) 273-6337 or (319) 273-6178; send email to fin-aid@uni.edu; or browse the UNI website at www.uni.edu/finaid/scholarships/ftother.html. No GPA requirement specified.

University of Northern Iowa, General and Miscellaneous Scholarships
Financial Aid Office
116 Gilchrist Hall
Cedar Falls, IA 50614-0024

2796
Association for Facilities Engineering Scholarship

AMOUNT: $500 DEADLINE: May 1
MAJOR: Pre-Engineering

The Association for Facilities Engineering Scholarship is available to students who are attending the University of Northern Iowa as pre-engineering majors or are currently employed in the facilities management or maintenance field. Applicants must be high school graduates with a 2.5 or above

GPA and residents of a county where a chapter #132 member resides. Award requirements change regularly. For further information, please write to the address listed, including a self-addressed, stamped envelope; contact A.F.E. Cedar Valley Chapter #132, Joe Zachar, Jr., 1203 Forest Glen Ct. SE, Cedar Rapids, IA 52403; call (319) 364-4740; send email to fin-aid@uni.edu; or browse the UNI website at www.uni.edu/finaid/scholarships/ftother.html; or fax (319) 365-0541. GPA must be 2.5-4.0.

University of Northern Iowa, General and Miscellaneous Scholarships
Financial Aid Office
116 Gilchrist Hall
Cedar Falls, IA 50614-0024

2797
Athletic Scholarship

AMOUNT: None Specified DEADLINE: Varies
MAJOR: All Areas of Study

The Athletic Scholarship is available to students who are attending the University of Northern Iowa. Applicants must be admissible to UNI, meet all NCAA initial eligibility requirements for Division I, and be recruited by UNI coaching staff. All athletic scholarship are awarded by the coaching staff for each individual sport. Scholarships range in value from partial tuition to full tuition, room and board, and books. Award requirements change regularly. For further information, please write to the address listed, including a self-addressed, stamped envelope; contact The Athletic Department NW, UNI Dome, Cedar Falls, IA 50614-0314, (319) 273-2470; send email to fin-aid@uni.edu; or browse the UNI website at www.uni.edu/finaid/scholarships/ftother.html. No GPA requirement specified.

University of Northern Iowa, General and Miscellaneous Scholarships
Financial Aid Office
116 Gilchrist Hall
Cedar Falls, IA 50614-0024

2798
Benton County Soil and Water Conservation District Scholarship

AMOUNT: $250 DEADLINE: March 1
MAJOR: Resource Conservation and Management

The Benton County Soil and Water Conservation District Scholarship is open to incoming freshmen and current students at the University of Northern Iowa who are majoring in the various fields of resource conservation and management. Applicants must be current or former residents of Benton County, Iowa. Award requirements change regularly. For further information, please write to the address listed, including a self-addressed, stamped envelope; contact Benton Soil and Water Conservation District, 1705 West D Street, Vinton, IA 52349; call (319) 472-2161; send email to fin-aid@uni.edu; or browse the UNI website at www.uni.edu/finaid/scholarships/ftother.html. No GPA requirement specified.

University of Northern Iowa, General and Miscellaneous Scholarships
Financial Aid Office
116 Gilchrist Hall
Cedar Falls, IA 50614-0024

2799
Carver Scholarship

AMOUNT: $3800 DEADLINE: April 1
MAJOR: All Areas of Study

The Carver Scholarship is open to Iowa high school graduates who are transfer students planning to attend the University of Northern Iowa. Applicants must have junior standing and a minimum GPA of 2.8. Currently enrolled students at UNI are also eligible. Financial need is required. Applicants must demonstrate they have overcome obstacles or barriers in life. An essay and two letters of reference are required. This award is renewable for one year. Award requirements change regularly. For further information, please write to the address listed, including a self-addressed, stamped envelope; call (319) 273-2700 or (800) 772-2736; email at fin-aid@uni.edu; or browse the UNI website at www.uni.edu/finaid/scholarships/ftother.html. GPA must be 2.8-4.0.

University of Northern Iowa, General and Miscellaneous Scholarships
Financial Aid Office
116 Gilchrist Hall
Cedar Falls, IA 50614-0024

2800
Joseph L. Marion Memorial Golf Scholarship

AMOUNT: None Specified DEADLINE: Varies
MAJOR: All Areas of Study

The Joseph L. Marion Memorial Golf Scholarship is available to students who are attending the University of Northern Iowa. The men's golf scholarship is awarded to a freshman recruited athlete or a letter winner as referred to the head golf coach for men. No application is necessary. Award requirements change regularly. For further information, please write to the address listed, including a self-addressed, stamped envelope; contact John Bermel, UNI-Dome, Cedar Falls, IA 50614-0314; call (319) 273-3100; send email to fin-aid@uni.edu; or browse the UNI website at www.uni.edu/finaid/scholarships/ftother.html. No GPA requirement specified.

University of Northern Iowa, General and Miscellaneous Scholarships
Financial Aid Office
116 Gilchrist Hall
Cedar Falls, IA 50614-0024

2801
Multicultural Achievement Scholarship

AMOUNT: $500-$1000 DEADLINE: January 1
MAJOR: All Areas of Study

The Multicultural Achievement Scholarship is open to incoming ethnic minority freshmen and transfer students, enrolling in the University of Northern Iowa directly from high school, who self-identify as Black/African American, Hispanic/Latino, Native American, or Asian American. Applicants must rank in the top 25% of their class and achieve a composite score of at least 23 on the ACT. Transfer students must have earned a minimum of 45 semester hours of transferable credit with a minimum GPA of 2.75. Award requirements change regularly. For further information, please contact Juanita Wright or Ron Green, Office of Admissions, 120 Gilchrist Hall, University of Northern Iowa, Cedar Falls, IA 50614-0018 or call (319) 273-2281. You may also email fin-aid@uni.edu or browse the UNI website at www.uni.edu/finaid. GPA must be 3.0-4.0.

University of Northern Iowa, General and Miscellaneous Scholarships
Financial Aid Office
116 Gilchrist Hall
Cedar Falls, IA 50614-0024

2802
Northern Iowa Foundation Scholarships

AMOUNT: $100-$2686 DEADLINE: January 1
MAJOR: All Areas of Study

The Northern Iowa Foundation Scholarships are mostly available to incoming full-time freshmen admitted to the University of Northern Iowa. Most of the selection criteria are based on academic achievement, leadership, and financial need. For some scholarships, geographic location or field of study are stipulated. To apply for the Foundation Scholarships, students should complete the FAFSA and multicultural scholarship application as soon as possible after January 1. The University will then match students with any available scholarships for which they are qualified. Award requirements change regularly. For further information, please write to the address listed, including a self-addressed, stamped envelope, or call (319) 273-2281. You may also email fin-aid@uni.edu or browse the UNI website at www.uni.edu/finaid. No GPA requirement specified.

University of Northern Iowa, General and Miscellaneous Scholarships
Financial Aid Office
116 Gilchrist Hall
Cedar Falls, IA 50614-0024

2803
One Year Resident Scholar Award

AMOUNT: $200-$500 DEADLINE: January 1
MAJOR: All Areas of Study

The One Year Resident Scholar Award is open to incoming freshmen and students transferring to the University of Northern Iowa. Selection is based on class rank, ACT scores, GPA, and financial aid. Award requirements change regularly. Contact the address listed for further information or call (319) 273-2281. No GPA requirement specified.

University of Northern Iowa, General and Miscellaneous Scholarships
Financial Aid Office
116 Gilchrist Hall
Cedar Falls, IA 50614-0024

2804
Patrick and Irma Freely Scholarship

AMOUNT: $1500 DEADLINE: March 1
MAJOR: All Areas of Study

The Patrick and Irma Freely Scholarship is available to freshmen student-athletes who are attending the University of Northern Iowa. Students recommended by their head coach may apply. This award is renewable up to three additional years based on GPA criteria and good team standing. Award requirements change regularly. For further information, please write to the address listed, including a self-addressed, stamped envelope; contact Jack Wilkinson, Faculty Athletic Representative, c/o the Math Department; call (319) 273-2515; send email to fin-aid@uni.edu; or browse the UNI website at www.uni.edu/finaid/scholarships/ftother.html. No GPA requirement specified.

University of Northern Iowa, General and Miscellaneous Scholarships
Financial Aid Office
116 Gilchrist Hall
Cedar Falls, IA 50614-0024

2805
Phi Theta Kappa Scholarship

AMOUNT: $1000-$2000 DEADLINE: April 1
MAJOR: All Areas of Study

The Phi Theta Kappa Scholarship is open to transfer students who are members of the Phi Theta Kappa honorary society at the community college from which they are transferring. Applicants must demonstrate leadership, and campus and/or community involvement. Must have a minimum GPA of 3.5. Awards are $1000 per year for two years for Iowa residents and $1000 to $2000 per year for two years for non-residents. This award is renewable for the second year by maintaining a 3.0 GPA. Five in-state and five out-of-state scholarships will be awarded. Award requirements change regularly. For further information, please write to the address listed, including a self-addressed, stamped envelope or call (319) 273-2281. You may also email fin-aid@uni.edu or browse the UNI website at www.uni.edu/finaid. GPA must be 3.5-4.0.

University of Northern Iowa, General and Miscellaneous Scholarships
Financial Aid Office
116 Gilchrist Hall
Cedar Falls, IA 50614-0024

2806
Presidential Scholarship

AMOUNT: $6900-$11600 DEADLINE: October 1
MAJOR: All Areas of Study

The Presidential Scholarship is available to freshmen who are enrolling directly from high school to the University of Northern Iowa. Applicants must rank in the upper 10 percent of their high school graduating class and have a minimum ACT composite score of 29. Selection is based on academic excellence, extracurricular achievements, leadership, and demonstrated potential for making a significant contribution to society. The final screening will include an interview with members of the Presidential Scholars Board and the writing of an essay during a visit to the Northern Iowa campus. This award is renewable each year for four years by maintaining a minimum 3.50 GPA. Award requirements change regularly. For further information, please write to the address listed, including a self-addressed, stamped envelope; contact Carol Geiger, Office of the Vice President for Educational and Student Services, SSC 103, University of Northern Iowa, Cedar Falls, IA 50614-0382; call (319) 273-2331; email at fin-aid@uni.edu; browse the UNI website at www.uni.edu/finaid/scholarships/prezscholar.html; or fax (319) 273-5832. No GPA requirement specified.

University of Northern Iowa, General and Miscellaneous Scholarships
Financial Aid Office
116 Gilchrist Hall
Cedar Falls, IA 50614-0024

2807
Provost Scholarship

AMOUNT: $2900-$7500 DEADLINE: October 1
MAJOR: All Areas of Study

The Provost Scholarship is available to freshmen who are attending the University of Northern Iowa. Applicants must rank in the upper 10 percent of their high school graduating class and have an ACT composite score of 29. Selection is based on academic excellence, extracurricular achievements, leadership, and demonstrated potential for making a signifi-cant contribution to society. The final screening will include an interview with members of the Presidential Scholars Board and the writing of an essay during a visit to the Northern Iowa campus. This award is renewable each year for four years by maintaining a 3.25 GPA. Award requirements change regular-ly. For further information, please write to the address listed, including a self-addressed, stamped envelope; contact Carol Geiger, Office of the Vice President for Educational and Student Services, SSC 103, University of Northern Iowa, Cedar Falls, IA 50614-0382; call (319) 273-2331; email at fin-aid@uni.edu; browse the UNI website at www.uni.edu/finaid/scholarships/prezscholar.html; or fax (319) 273-5832. No GPA requirement specified.

University of Northern Iowa, General and Miscellaneous Scholarships
Financial Aid Office
116 Gilchrist Hall
Cedar Falls, IA 50614-0024

2808
State of Iowa Scholarship

AMOUNT: None Specified DEADLINE: Varies
MAJOR: All Areas of Study

The State of Iowa Scholarship is available to incoming fresh-men who are attending the University of Northern Iowa. Selection is based on ACT scores and high school class rank. The scholarship is awarded by the Iowa College Aid Commission. This scholarship is for $200 a semester for one year. Award requirements change regularly. For further infor-mation, please write to the address listed, including a self-addressed, stamped envelope; contact Iowa College Aid Commission, 201 Jewett Building, Des Moines, IA 50309, (515) 281-3501; send email to fin-aid@uni.edu; or browse the UNI website at www.uni.edu/finaid/scholarships/ftother.html.

You may also contact your guidance counselor. No GPA requirement specified.

University of Northern Iowa, General and Miscellaneous Scholarships
Financial Aid Office
116 Gilchrist Hall
Cedar Falls, IA 50614-0024

2809
University Scholarship

AMOUNT: $1000 DEADLINE: October 1
MAJOR: All Areas of Study

The University Scholarship is available to freshmen who are attending the University of Northern Iowa. Applicants must rank in the upper 10 percent of their high school graduating class and have an ACT composite score of 29. Selection is based on academic excellence, extracurricular achievements, leadership, and demonstrated potential for making a signifi-cant contribution to society. The final screening will include an interview with members of the Presidential Scholars Board and the writing of an essay during a visit to the Northern Iowa campus. This award is renewable each year for four years by maintaining a 3.0 GPA. Award requirements change regularly. For further information, please write to the address listed, including a self-addressed, stamped envelope; contact Carol Geiger, Office of the Vice President for Educational and Student Services, SSC 103, University of Northern Iowa, Cedar Falls, IA 50614-0382; call (319) 273-2331; email at fin-aid@uni.edu or feel free to browse the UNI website at www.uni.edu/finaid/scholarships/prezscholar.html; fax (319) 273-5832. No GPA requirement specified.

University of Northern Iowa, General and Miscellaneous Scholarships
Financial Aid Office
116 Gilchrist Hall
Cedar Falls, IA 50614-0024

University of Oregon

2810
General University Scholarship

AMOUNT: $1500-$4200 DEADLINE: February 1
MAJOR: All Areas of Study

The General University Scholarship is open to incoming freshmen, current undergraduates, and graduate students attending the University of Oregon. The scholarship commit-tee considers many factors in making awards, including your academic performance, test scores, extracurricular involve-ment, and writing ability and creativity, as demonstrated in the required scholarship questions and essay. You must also have a minimum 3.5 GPA. Award requirements change regularly. When you submit this scholarship application you will auto-matically be considered for other University of Oregon schol-arships. GPA must be 3.5-4.0.

University of Oregon - Student Financial Aid Office
1278 University of Oregon
260 Oregon Hall
Eugene, OR 97403-1205

Laurel Scholarship

AMOUNT: $1500-$4200 DEADLINE: February 1
MAJOR: All Areas of Study

The Laurel Scholarship is open to incoming freshmen, current undergraduates, and graduate students attending the University of Oregon. The scholarship committee considers many factors in making awards, including your academic performance, test scores, extracurricular involvement, and writing ability and creativity, as demonstrated in the required scholarship questions and essay. You must also have a minimum 3.50 GPA. Award requirements change regularly. If you submit this scholarship application you will automatically be considered for other University of Oregon scholarships. GPA must be 3.5-4.0.

University of Oregon - Student Financial Aid Office
1278 University of Oregon
260 Oregon Hall
Eugene, OR 97403-1205

2812

Presidential Scholarship

AMOUNT: $1500-$4200 DEADLINE: February 1
MAJOR: All Areas of Study

The Presidential Scholarship is open to incoming freshman, current undergraduates, and graduate students attending the University of Oregon. The scholarship committee considers many factors in making awards, including your academic performance, test scores, extracurricular involvement, and writing ability and creativity, as demonstrated in the required scholarship questions and essay. You must also have a minimum 3.50 GPA. Award requirements change regularly. If you submit this scholarship application you will automatically be considered for other University of Oregon scholarships. GPA must be 3.5-4.0.

University of Oregon - Student Financial Aid Office
1278 University of Oregon
260 Oregon Hall
Eugene, OR 97403-1205

2813

U-Lane-O Scholarship

AMOUNT: $4000 DEADLINE: February 1
MAJOR: All Areas of Study

The U-Lane-O Scholarship is open to undergraduates attending the University of Oregon. You should demonstrate academic excellence, financial need, and contributions to the community in which you live. You must have a minimum 3.0 GPA. You are also required to submit the FAFSA to the federal processor by February 1. Award requirements change regularly. If you submit this scholarship application you will automatically be considered for other University of Oregon scholarships. GPA must be 3.0-4.0.

University of Oregon - Student Financial Aid Office
1278 University of Oregon
260 Oregon Hall
Eugene, OR 97403-1205

University of South Florida

Carl A. Gelin Endowed Fellowship

AMOUNT: None Specified DEADLINE: Varies
MAJOR: Health Policy and Management (College of Public Health)

The Carl A. Gelin Endowed Fellowship is open to students attending the University of South Florida who are enrolled in the Department of Health Policy and Management in the College of Public Health. Nominations will be made by the Department of Health Policy and Management. Award requirements change regularly. No GPA requirement specified.

University of South Florida - College of Public Health
Attn: Scholarship Coordinator
13201 Bruce B. Downs Blvd., MDC 56
Tampa, FL 33612-3805

2815

College Work Study Program

AMOUNT: None Specified DEADLINE: Varies
MAJOR: College of Public Health

The College Work Study Program offers part-time employment for the College of Public Health graduate students attending the University of South Florida. Award requirements change regularly. No GPA requirement specified.

University of South Florida - College of Public Health
Attn: Scholarship Coordinator
13201 Bruce B. Downs Blvd., MDC 56
Tampa, FL 33612-3805

2816

Delores A. Auzenne Fellowship

AMOUNT: $5000 DEADLINE: Varies
MAJOR: College of Public Health

The Delores A. Auzenne Fellowship is open to African-American students attending the College of Public Health at the University of South Florida. Award requirements change regularly. No GPA requirement specified.

University of South Florida - College of Public Health
Attn: Scholarship Coordinator
13201 Bruce B. Downs Blvd., MDC 56
Tampa, FL 33612-3805

2817

Graduate Assistantships

AMOUNT: None Specified DEADLINE: April 1
MAJOR: College of Public Health

Graduate Assistantships offer graduate students attending the College of Public Health at University of South Florida biweekly stipends and potential qualification to receive tuition waivers. The recipients may perform research or teaching functions, assist in the production seminars and workshops, or do other work related to their specific disciplines. Assistantships are awarded on a competitive basis for up to four semesters for Master's candidates and up to six for

Doctoral candidates. Applicants must have a GPA of 3.0 or better in their upper division coursework and must be degree-seeking and enrolled full-time. Application deadline dates are Fall - April 1, Spring - November 1, Summer - February 1. Award requirements change regularly. GPA must be 3.0-4.0.

University of South Florida - College of Public Health
Attn: Scholarship Coordinator
13201 Bruce B. Downs Blvd., MDC 56
Tampa, FL 33612-3805

2818
Graduate Educational Opportunity Grant (GEOG)

AMOUNT: $3000 DEADLINE: Varies
MAJOR: College of Public Health

The Graduate Educational Opportunity Grant (GEOG) is open to African-American graduate students who are U.S. citizens or permanent residents and who are attending the College of Public Health at the University of South Florida. This award provides stipends to applicants formally admitted to a graduate program and nominated to the Dean of the Graduate School by the chair or director of that program and the dean of the college in which the program is located. Priority is given to new students. Applicants must have at least a 3.0 GPA in the last two years of undergraduate work and a minimum GRE score of 900 or a minimum GMAT score of 450. Nomination forms are forwarded by the Office of Academics after acceptance by the Graduate School. Award requirements change regularly. GPA must be 3.0-4.0.

University of South Florida - College of Public Health
Attn: Scholarship Coordinator
13201 Bruce B. Downs Blvd., MDC 56
Tampa, FL 33612-3805

2819
Maternal-Child Health (MCH) Traineeship

AMOUNT: None Specified DEADLINE: Varies
MAJOR: Maternal and Child Health (College of Public Health)

The Maternal-Child Health (MCH) Traineeship is open to students admitted to the Master of Public Health or Master of Science in Public Health degree programs in MCH within the Department of Community and Family Health. Traineeships provide student stipends and/or financial assistance toward tuition costs. Applicants should 1) hold a degree recognized by their own profession as conferring professional status in an MCH relevant field, 2) have at least two years of professional experience related to MCH, and 3) have career goals consonant with a commitment to MCH. The availability of MCH Traineeships is dependent upon annual funding and is open to both Florida resident and nonresident students. Award requirements change regularly. No GPA requirement specified.

University of South Florida - College of Public Health
Attn: Scholarship Coordinator
13201 Bruce B. Downs Blvd., MDC 56
Tampa, FL 33612-3805

2820
McKnight Foundation Black Doctoral Fellowship Program

AMOUNT: $11000 DEADLINE: Varies
MAJOR: Arts and Sciences, Mathematics, Business, Engineering

The McKnight Foundation Black Doctoral Fellowship Program is open to minority American citizens who are studying in the fields of arts and sciences, mathematics, business, and engineering while pursuing a Ph.D. at the University of South Florida. This Fellowship provides full tuition plus an $11,000 stipend. Award requirements change regularly. No GPA requirement specified.

University of South Florida - College of Public Health
Attn: Scholarship Coordinator
13201 Bruce B. Downs Blvd., MDC 56
Tampa, FL 33612-3805

2821
NIOSH Traineeship

AMOUNT: None Specified DEADLINE: Varies
MAJOR: Industrial Hygiene/Safety Management

The National Institute of Occupational Safety and Health (NIOSH) offers traineeships to students who have been accepted in the Industrial Hygiene/Safety Management program at USF. The traineeship award includes a tuition waiver for nine semester hours as well as a stipend. Traineeship applications are forwarded to all applicants once the application for admission to graduate school is received. Award requirements change regularly. No GPA requirement specified.

University of South Florida - College of Public Health
Attn: Scholarship Coordinator
13201 Bruce B. Downs Blvd., MDC 56
Tampa, FL 33612-3805

2822
Special Summer Program for Black Students

AMOUNT: $1300 DEADLINE: April 1
MAJOR: All Areas of Study

The Special Summer Program for Black Students is open to African-American graduate students attending the College of Public Health at the University of South Florida. The award provides a $1,300 stipend during the summer term. Candidates must have submitted a formal application to the university. This program is primarily for new students. Candidates are selected in April of each year. Award requirements change regularly. No GPA requirement specified.

University of South Florida - College of Public Health
Attn: Scholarship Coordinator
13201 Bruce B. Downs Blvd., MDC 56
Tampa, FL 33612-3805

University of South Florida, St. Petersburg

2823
Allstate Minority Scholarship

AMOUNT: $500 DEADLINE: Varies
MAJOR: All Areas of Study

The Allstate Minority Scholarship is open to degree-seeking, USF St. Petersburg students in good standing. To be considered for the award, you must be a minority student, which is defined as African-American, Hispanic, Asian/Pacific Islander, or American Indian/Alaskan Native, and have a minimum GPA of 3.0. You must also be enrolled at least half-time (six hours undergraduate, five hours graduate) during the semester for which the award is given. Award requirements change regularly. GPA must be 3.0-4.0.

University of South Florida, St. Petersburg Campus
Attn: Scholarship Coordinator
140 7th Avenue South
St. Petersburg, FL 33701

2824
Amanda Cole Scholarship

AMOUNT: $500 DEADLINE: Varies
MAJOR: All Areas of Study

This award is given to a degree-seeking USF St. Petersburg student in good standing with a minimum GPA of 3.0. The applicant must be a transfer student with an associate degree from St. Petersburg Junior College and be a resident of St. Petersburg. Two of the three required letters of recommendation must come from an SPJC faculty member. The applicant must also be enrolled at least half time (six hours undergraduate, five hours graduate) during the semester for which the award is given. Financial need will be considered. Award requirements change regularly. GPA must be 3.0-4.0.

University of South Florida, St. Petersburg Campus
Attn: Scholarship Coordinator
140 7th Avenue South
St. Petersburg, FL 33701

2825
Barnett Bank/Martin Luther King, Jr., Scholarship

AMOUNT: $500 DEADLINE: Varies
MAJOR: All Areas of Study

The award is open to a degree-seeking USF St. Petersburg campus student in good standing who is African-American and a resident of Florida. Applicant must demonstrate leadership and service to the campus and community organizations. Preference given to College of Arts & Sciences students. Applicant must be enrolled at least half-time (six hours undergraduate, five hours graduate) and have a minimum GPA of 3.0. Award requirements change regularly. GPA must be 3.0-4.0.

University of South Florida, St. Petersburg Campus
Attn: Scholarship Coordinator
140 7th Avenue South
St. Petersburg, FL 33701

2826
Charles Haslam Award for Study in the Liberal Arts

AMOUNT: $750 DEADLINE: Varies
MAJOR: College of Arts and Sciences or College of Education

Applicant must be degree-seeking USF St. Petersburg campus students in good standing who are enrolled full-time (12 hours undergraduate) and have a minimum GPA of 3.0. The applicant must be a major in the College of Arts and Sciences or College of Education and be of senior standing when the award is granted. Requirements include submitting a 300-500- word essay discussing the value of literature in today's technological world and the names of two St. Petersburg campus faculty members as references. Award requirements change regularly. GPA must be 3.0-4.0.

University of South Florida, St. Petersburg Campus
Attn: Scholarship Coordinator
140 7th Avenue South
St. Petersburg, FL 33701

2827
Demetrios Karamesoutis Endowed Memorial Scholarship

AMOUNT: $2000 DEADLINE: Varies
MAJOR: All Areas of Study

This award is for degree-seeking USF St. Petersburg campus students with preference given to students of Greek heritage. The applicant must be enrolled full-time (12 hours undergraduate or 9 hours graduate) and submit three letters of recommendation from USF St. Petersburg faculty. Financial need for this scholarship will be considered. Finalists will be interviewed by the USF St. Petersburg Scholarship Committee. Award requirements change regularly. No GPA requirement specified.

University of South Florida, St. Petersburg Campus
Attn: Scholarship Coordinator
140 7th Avenue South
St. Petersburg, FL 33701

2828
Donald A. Haney Memorial Scholarship

AMOUNT: $250 DEADLINE: Varies
MAJOR: All Areas of Study

This award is open to a degree-seeking USF St. Petersburg campus student in good standing who has completed at least one semester on the St. Petersburg campus. Student must demonstrate service to the campus and/or community and have a minimum GPA of 3.0. The student must also be enrolled at least half-time (six hours undergraduate, five hours graduate). Financial need will be considered for this scholarship. Award requirements change regularly. GPA must be 3.0-4.0.

University of South Florida, St. Petersburg Campus
Attn: Scholarship Coordinator
140 7th Avenue South
St. Petersburg, FL 33701

2829
First Union Bank Scholarship

AMOUNT: $400-$800 DEADLINE: Varies
MAJOR: Business

Award is open to a degree-seeking USF St. Petersburg campus student in good standing. Student must be enrolled at least half time (six hours undergraduate, five hours graduate), be a College of Business Administration major, and have completed at least one semester on the St. Petersburg campus. Financial need and campus/community involvement will be considered for the scholarship. A 3.0 minimum GPA is required. Award requirements change regularly. GPA must be 3.0-4.0.

University of South Florida, St. Petersburg Campus
Attn: Scholarship Coordinator
140 7th Avenue South
St. Petersburg, FL 33701

2830
Frances G. Elvidge Scholarship

AMOUNT: None Specified DEADLINE: Varies
MAJOR: All Areas of Study

This award is open to degree-seeking campus students at USF St. Petersburg. Both GPA and financial need will be considered for this scholarship, though no GPA is specified. Service to campus and community will be considered. Scholarship may be renewable. Award requirements change regularly. No GPA requirement specified.

University of South Florida, St. Petersburg Campus
Attn: Scholarship Coordinator
140 7th Avenue South
St. Petersburg, FL 33701

2831
Gelin Memorial Scholarship

AMOUNT: $1000-$2000 DEADLINE: Varies
MAJOR: All Areas of Study Excluding Social Sciences

Award is open to a degree-seeking USF St. Petersburg campus student. Student must be enrolled full-time (12 hours undergraduate, 9 hours graduate). All majors, excluding social sciences, will be considered for this scholarship. Finalists for this scholarship will be interviewed by the USF St. Petersburg Scholarship Committee. A minimum GPA of 3.5 is required, and financial need will be taken into consideration. Award requirements change regularly. GPA must be 3.5-4.0.

University of South Florida, St. Petersburg Campus
Attn: Scholarship Coordinator
140 7th Avenue South
St. Petersburg, FL 33701

2832
GTE Minority Scholarship

AMOUNT: $500 DEADLINE: Varies
MAJOR: All Areas of Study

Award is open to a degree-seeking USF St. Petersburg campus student who is a Florida resident. Student must be enrolled at least half-time (six hours undergraduate, five hours graduate) with a minimum GPA of 3.0 and be a minority student.

Preference for this scholarship will be given to a student in the math or science fields. Student must be transferring or have transferred with an associate degree from any Florida community/junior college. Award requirements change regularly. GPA must be 3.0-4.0.

University of South Florida, St. Petersburg Campus
Attn: Scholarship Coordinator
140 7th Avenue South
St. Petersburg, FL 33701

2833
Howard Paulson Memorial Scholarship

AMOUNT: $500 DEADLINE: Varies
MAJOR: Political Science

Award is open to a degree-seeking USF St. Petersburg campus student with preference given to students entering their senior year. The applicant must be a Political Science major and demonstrate public service. Financial need will be considered, and a minimum GPA of 3.0 is required. Award requirements change regularly. GPA must be 3.0-4.0.

University of South Florida, St. Petersburg Campus
Attn: Scholarship Coordinator
140 7th Avenue South
St. Petersburg, FL 33701

2834
Lena M. Brown Book Scholarship

AMOUNT: $100 DEADLINE: Varies
MAJOR: All Areas of Study

Student must be a degree-seeking USF St. Petersburg student in good standing. Preference is given to an African-American student enrolled at least half-time. Applicant must have a minimum 2.5 GPA. Financial need will be considered for this scholarship. Award requirements change regularly. GPA must be 2.5-4.0.

University of South Florida, St. Petersburg Campus
Attn: Scholarship Coordinator
140 7th Avenue South
St. Petersburg, FL 33701

2835
Lowell E. Davis Endowed Scholarship

AMOUNT: $250-$500 DEADLINE: Varies
MAJOR: All Areas of Study

Applicants must be degree-seeking USF St. Petersburg students in good standing who have completed at least one semester on the St. Petersburg campus. Applicants must be enrolled during the semester for which the award is given and be international or minority students. Applicants must also be full-time undergraduates (12 hours) and have a GPA of 3.0. Award requirements change regularly. GPA must be 3.0-4.0.

University of South Florida, St. Petersburg Campus
Attn: Scholarship Coordinator
140 7th Avenue South
St. Petersburg, FL 33701

2836
Marilynn S. Bach Brace Alumni Scholarship

AMOUNT: $300 DEADLINE: Varies
MAJOR: Nursing

This award is open to a Registered Nurse matriculated in the R.N./B.S. sequence at USF St. Petersburg's College of Nursing who is practicing in Pinellas County, Florida. A minimum 3.0 GPA or financial need is required. One of three letters of recommendation must be written by a current nursing instructor or major advisor, and students must demonstrate voluntary service to the campus and/or community. Award requirements change regularly. GPA must be 3.0-4.0.

University of South Florida, St. Petersburg Campus
Attn: Scholarship Coordinator
140 7th Avenue South
St. Petersburg, FL 33701

2837
NationsBank Scholarship

AMOUNT: $500-$1000 DEADLINE: Varies
MAJOR: Business Administration

Award is open to a degree-seeking USF St. Petersburg campus student in good standing. Student must be enrolled at least half-time (six hours undergraduate, five hours graduate), be a major in the College of Business Administration, and have completed at least one semester on the St. Petersburg campus. A minimum 3.0 GPA is required, and the applicant must demonstrate voluntary service to the campus and/or community. Financial need will be considered for the scholarship. Award requirements change regularly. GPA must be 3.0-4.0.

University of South Florida, St. Petersburg Campus
Attn: Scholarship Coordinator
140 7th Avenue South
St. Petersburg, FL 33701

2838
Raymund Endowed Scholarship

AMOUNT: $2000-$2300 DEADLINE: Varies
MAJOR: All Areas of Study

Award is open to a degree-seeking USF St. Petersburg campus student in good standing who is African American, Hispanic, Asian/Pacific Islander, or American Indian/Alaskan Native. The applicant must be enrolled full-time (12 hours undergraduate, 9 hours graduate) with a minimum GPA of 2.0. The student must have completed at least one semester on the St. Petersburg campus and be enrolled during the semester for which the award is given. Financial need will be considered. Award requirements change regularly. GPA must be 2.0-4.0.

University of South Florida, St. Petersburg Campus
Attn: Scholarship Coordinator
140 7th Avenue South
St. Petersburg, FL 33701

2839
Raymund Foundation for Minorities Scholarship

AMOUNT: $250 DEADLINE: Varies
MAJOR: All Areas of Study

Award is open to a degree-seeking USF St. Petersburg campus student in good standing who is African American, Hispanic, Asian/Pacific Islander, or American Indian/Alaskan Native. The applicant must be enrolled full-time (12 hours undergraduate, 9 hours graduate) with a minimum GPA of 2.0. The student must have completed at least one semester on the St. Petersburg campus and be enrolled during the semester for which the award is given. Financial need will be considered. Award requirements change regularly. GPA must be 2.0-4.0.

University of South Florida, St. Petersburg Campus
Attn: Scholarship Coordinator
140 7th Avenue South
St. Petersburg, FL 33701

2840
Raymund SAO Book Scholarship

AMOUNT: $100 DEADLINE: Varies
MAJOR: Accounting

The Raymund SAO Book Scholarship is open to accounting majors attending the University of South Florida, St. Petersburg. Applicants must have completed at least one semester on the St. Petersburg campus and be enrolled during the semester for which the award is given. A minimum 2.0 GPA is required, and financial aid is considered. Award requirements change regularly. GPA must be 2.0-4.0.

University of South Florida, St. Petersburg Campus
Attn: Scholarship Coordinator
140 7th Avenue South
St. Petersburg, FL 33701

2841
SEA/SCEC Scholarship

AMOUNT: $500 DEADLINE: Varies
MAJOR: Education

Award is open to degree-seeking USF St. Petersburg campus students in good standing who are College of Education majors. Students must be seniors in Level III internships and demonstrate involvement with SEA and/or SCEC, as verified with a letter from the organization's adviser. One of three required letters of reference must come from a practicum classroom teacher or Level I or II internship. A minimum GPA of 3.5 is required. Award requirements change regularly. GPA must be 3.5-4.0.

University of South Florida, St. Petersburg Campus
Attn: Scholarship Coordinator
140 7th Avenue South
St. Petersburg, FL 33701

2842
Three-Year B.A. Scholarship

AMOUNT: $250-$500 DEADLINE: Varies
MAJOR: All Areas of Study

Award is open to degree-seeking USF St. Petersburg campus students in good standing. Applicants must be enrolled full-time (12 hours undergraduate, 9 hours graduate) and have a minimum 2.0 GPA. Academic standing will be a priority consideration. Award requirements change regularly. GPA must be 2.0-4.0.

University of South Florida, St. Petersburg Campus
Attn: Scholarship Coordinator
140 7th Avenue South
St. Petersburg, FL 33701

2843
USF St. Petersburg Faculty/Staff Scholarship

AMOUNT: $250-$500 DEADLINE: Varies
MAJOR: All Areas of Study

Award is open to a degree-seeking USF St. Petersburg campus student in good standing with a minimum GPA of 2.0. The applicant must be enrolled full-time (12 hours undergraduate, 9 hours graduate). Academic standing will be a priority consideration. Applicant must also submit three letters of recommendation from USF St. Petersburg faculty. Award requirements change regularly. GPA must be 2.0-4.0.

University of South Florida, St. Petersburg Campus
Attn: Scholarship Coordinator
140 7th Avenue South
St. Petersburg, FL 33701

University of Southern California

2844
Asian Pacific American Support Group Scholarships

AMOUNT: $1000-$2500 DEADLINE: March 26
MAJOR: All Areas of Study

Scholarships for Asian Pacific American students at the University of Southern California. Based on academic achievement, personal merit, and financial need. Must be U.S. citizens or permanent residents enrolled in full-time study and have a GPA of 3.0 or better. Award requirements change regularly. Write to the address listed for an application and further information, email apass@usc.edu, or call Jeff Murakami at (213) 740-4999. GPA must be 3.0.

Asian Pacific American Support Group Scholarship Committee
University of Southern California
Student Union 410, University Park
Los Angeles, CA 90089

2845
Mexican American Alumni Association Scholarships

AMOUNT: $400-$4500 DEADLINE: June 30
MAJOR: All Areas of Study

Scholarships available at USC for Hispanic undergraduate master's candidates. Awards given on the basis of academic achievement and demonstrated financial aid eligibility. Award requirements change regularly. Write to the address listed, enclosing a self-addressed, stamped envelope for information or call (213) 740-4735. GPA must be 2.7-4.0.

University of Southern California (USC)
Mexican American Programs Office
Student Union 203
Los Angeles, CA 90089

University of St. Francis

2846
Biology Fellows Scholarship

AMOUNT: $3000 DEADLINE: Varies
MAJOR: All Fields of Study

The Biology Fellows Scholarship is open to incoming freshmen who will be attending USF on a full-time basis who are interested in the sciences. To be considered for this award, you must meet two of the following criteria: have an ACT score of 25 or higher, be in the top 20% of your graduating class, or have a cumulative minimum 3.5 GPA. The scholarship is renewable and is awarded in addition to any other USF academic scholarships. Award requirements change regularly. No GPA requirement specified.

University of St. Francis
Attn: Director of Financial Aid
500 Wilcox Street
Joliet, IL 60435

2847
Community College Scholarship

AMOUNT: $1000-$3000 DEADLINE: Varies
MAJOR: All Fields of Study

The Community College Scholarship is open to all community college transfer students. To be considered for this award, you must be attending full-time, be transferring with at least 60 credits, and have a minimum 3.0 cumulative GPA. The higher your GPA, the higher the amount of the award you will receive. Award requirements change regularly. GPA must be 3.0-4.0.

University of St. Francis
Attn: Director of Financial Aid
500 Wilcox Street
Joliet, IL 60435

2848
Enhanced Academic Scholarship

AMOUNT: Maximum: $2000 DEADLINE: Varies
MAJOR: All Fields of Study

The Enhanced Academic Scholarship is open to all full-time transfer students who have already received the Community College or Transfer Scholarship. The award is based on a referral from the counseling staff and is received from the Director of Transfer Admission. Award requirements change regularly. GPA must be 3.0-4.0.

University of St. Francis
Attn: Director of Financial Aid
500 Wilcox Street
Joliet, IL 60435

2849
Illinois Educator's Grant

AMOUNT: Maximum: $1000 DEADLINE: Varies
MAJOR: All Fields of Study

The Illinois Educator's Grant is open to students who are children of currently employed or retired teachers, administrators, and counselors at elementary or secondary schools who enroll at USF on a full-time basis. To be considered for the award, you must submit a letter from the parent's employer verifying retirement/full-time employment status. The letter should include the official school seal. Award requirements change regularly. GPA must be 2.5-4.0.

University of St. Francis
Attn: Director of Financial Aid
500 Wilcox Street
Joliet, IL 60435

2850
Minority Achievement/Low Income Scholarship

AMOUNT: Maximum: $2000 DEADLINE: Varies
MAJOR: All Fields of Study

The Minority Achievement/Low Income Scholarship is open to full-time students who meet two of the three following criteria: must be of African-American, Hispanic, Asian, or Native American descent; must have achieved a 3.0 GPA on a 4.0 scale and rank in the upper half of your class (if you are a transfer student, you should have 30 or more transferable hours at a 2.5 GPA); must have a total family income of less than $15,000 per year in the year prior to applying. The award is renewable, provided a minimum 2.5 GPA is maintained. If you receive this award, you are not eligible to receive any other athletic or academic scholarship. Award requirements change regularly. GPA must be 3.0-4.0.

University of St. Francis
Attn: Director of Financial Aid
500 Wilcox Street
Joliet, IL 60435

2851
Phi Theta Kappa Scholarship

AMOUNT: $6000 DEADLINE: Varies
MAJOR: All Fields of Study

The Phi Theta Kappa Scholarship is open to all community college transfer students who are Phi Theta Kappa members. To be considered for this award, you must be entering USF as a full-time student. If you are eligible to receive this award, you are not eligible to receive any other USF academic scholarships. Award requirements change regularly. No GPA requirement specified.

University of St. Francis
Attn: Director of Financial Aid
500 Wilcox Street
Joliet, IL 60435

2852
President's Leadership Award

AMOUNT: $500-$2000 DEADLINE: Varies
MAJOR: All Fields of Study

The President's Leadership Award is open to prospective full-time transfer students who have exhibited leadership in academics, spiritual or civic involvement, or extracurricular activities. If you are to receive this award, you may not be receiving any other athletic or academic scholarship. Award requirements change regularly. GPA must be 2.5-4.0.

University of St. Francis
Attn: Director of Financial Aid
500 Wilcox Street
Joliet, IL 60435

2853
Presidential Scholarship

AMOUNT: $4000-$6000 DEADLINE: Varies
MAJOR: All Fields of Study

The Presidential Scholarship is open to high school seniors who will be attending USF on a full-time basis. The award is based on an institutional formula factoring ACT/SAT scores and class rank. To qualify, you must complete the Application for Freshman Admission. If you are already receiving an athletic scholarship, you qualify to receive a maximum of $4,000 from this award. Award requirements change regularly. GPA must be 2.5-4.0.

University of St. Francis
Attn: Director of Financial Aid
500 Wilcox Street
Joliet, IL 60435

2854
Schola Cantorum Scholarship

AMOUNT: Maximum: $2000 DEADLINE: Varies
MAJOR: All Fields of Study

The Schola Cantorum Scholarship is open to incoming students for participation in the choir. To be considered for the award, you must audition with the Director of the Schola Cantorum. Availability for these awards is limited. Award requirements change regularly. No GPA requirement specified.

University of St. Francis
Attn: Director of Financial Aid
500 Wilcox Street
Joliet, IL 60435

2855
Transfer Scholarship

AMOUNT: $1000-$3000 DEADLINE: Varies
MAJOR: All Fields of Study

The Transfer Scholarship is open to full-time transfer students who have transferred from a four-year college or university. To be considered for this award, you must have a minimum 3.0 cumulative GPA. The higher your GPA, the higher your award will be. The award also requires you to complete the equivalent of College Writing I and math competencies at college algebra level or higher. Award requirements change regularly. GPA must be 3.0-4.0.

University of St. Francis
Attn: Director of Financial Aid
500 Wilcox Street
Joliet, IL 60435

2856
Trustee Scholarship

AMOUNT: $2000-$5000 DEADLINE: Varies
MAJOR: All Fields of Study

The Trustee Scholarship is open to high school seniors who will be attending USF on a full-time basis. The award is based on an institutional formula factoring ACT/SAT scores and class rank. To qualify, you must complete the Application for Freshman Admission. If you are already receiving an athletic scholarship, you qualify to receive a maximum of $2,000 from this scholarship. Award requirements change regularly. GPA must be 2.5-4.0.

University of St. Francis
Attn: Director of Financial Aid
500 Wilcox Street
Joliet, IL 60435

2857
University Full Tuition Scholarship

AMOUNT: None Specified DEADLINE: Varies
MAJOR: All Fields of Study

The University Full Tuition Scholarship is open to high school seniors who will be attending USF on a full-time basis. The award is based on previous academic achievement and an essay submitted by you which your high school English teacher has certified. The award is renewable, provided you maintain criteria listed under the USF Satisfactory Progress Policy. Award requirements change regularly. GPA must be 2.5-4.0.

University of St. Francis
Attn: Director of Financial Aid
500 Wilcox Street
Joliet, IL 60435

2858
University Half Tuition Scholarship

AMOUNT: None Specified DEADLINE: Varies
MAJOR: All Fields of Study

The University Half Tuition Scholarship is open to high school seniors who will be attending USF on a full-time basis. The award is based on previous academic achievement and an essay submitted by you which your high school English teacher has certified. The award is renewable, provided you maintain criteria listed under the USF Satisfactory Progress Policy. Award requirements change regularly. GPA must be 2.5-4.0.

University of St. Francis
Attn: Director of Financial Aid
500 Wilcox Street
Joliet, IL 60435

2859
University Scholarship for Adult Students

AMOUNT: None Specified DEADLINE: Varies
MAJOR: All Fields of Study

The University Scholarship for Adult Students is a full-tuition scholarship open to first-time distinguished adult transfer students. To be considered for this award, you must be accepted to USF as a full-time student, be seeking a degree, have 60 hours of transferable credit, have a minimum 3.5 GPA in your most recent 30 semester hours, and have already applied for federal and state aid. The award also requires that you be at least 24 years old. Two awards are given, one in the fall semester and one in the spring semester.. Award requirements change regularly. GPA must be 3.5-4.0.

University of St. Francis
Attn: Director of Financial Aid
500 Wilcox Street
Joliet, IL 60435

2860
University Three-Quarter Tuition Scholarship

AMOUNT: None Specified DEADLINE: Varies
MAJOR: All Fields of Study

The University Three-Quarter Tuition Scholarship is open to high school seniors who will be attending USF on a full-time basis. The award is based on previous academic achievement and an essay submitted by you which your high school English teacher has certified. The award is renewable, provided you maintain criteria listed under the USF Satisfactory Progress Policy. Award requirements change regularly. GPA must be 2.5-4.0.

University of St. Francis
Attn: Director of Financial Aid
500 Wilcox Street
Joliet, IL 60435

2861
University Transfer Scholarship

AMOUNT: None Specified DEADLINE: Varies
MAJOR: All Fields of Study

The University Transfer Scholarship is a full-tuition scholarship open to first-time distinguished transfer students. To be considered for this award, you must be accepted to USF as a full-time student, be seeking a degree, have 60 hours of transferable credit, have a minimum 3.9 cumulative GPA, have already applied for federal and state aid, and have demonstrated work/service in the community. One award is presented during each fall and spring semester. Award requirements change regularly. GPA must be 3.9-4.0.

University of St. Francis
Attn: Director of Financial Aid
500 Wilcox Street
Joliet, IL 60435

2862
USF Monetary Award

AMOUNT: $3500-$4000 DEADLINE: Varies
MAJOR: All Fields of Study

The USF Monetary Award is open to high school seniors who will be attending USF on a full-time basis. The award is based on an institutional formula factoring ACT/SAT scores and class rank. To qualify, you must complete the Application for Freshman Admission. If you are already receiving an athletic scholarship, you do not qualify to receive this scholarship. Award requirements change regularly. GPA must be 2.5-4.0.

University of St. Francis
Attn: Director of Financial Aid
500 Wilcox Street
Joliet, IL 60435

University of Tennessee, Knoxville

2863
Alumni Achievement Scholarship

AMOUNT: $1500 DEADLINE: Varies
MAJOR: All Areas of Study

The Alumni Achievement Scholarship is open to students at all undergraduate campuses of the University of Tennessee who have a minimum GPA of 3.0 and an ACT score of 28. Students must be admitted to a campus of The University of Tennessee prior to February 1. Financial need may be considered. Award requirements change regularly. Please send a self-addressed, stamped envelope to receive your application and any further instructions from the scholarship provider. GPA must be 3.0- 4.0.

University of Tennessee, Knoxville
Office of Undergraduate Admissions
350 Student Services Building
Knoxville, TN 37996

2864
Alumni First-Year Scholarship

AMOUNT: $1100-$1500 DEADLINE: Varies
MAJOR: All Areas of Study

The Alumni First-Year Scholarship is open to freshmen attending the University of Tennessee, Knoxville. Award requirements change regularly. Please send a self-addressed, stamped envelope to receive your application and any further instructions from the scholarship provider. No GPA requirement specified.

University of Tennessee, Knoxville
Office of Undergraduate Admissions
350 Student Services Building
Knoxville, TN 37996

2865
Alumni National Merit Scholarship

AMOUNT: $800-$2000 DEADLINE: Varies
MAJOR: All Areas of Study

The Alumni National Merit Scholarship is open to students at all undergraduate campuses of UT who are National Merit Finalists. The selection criteria are based on academic merit and leadership. A National Merit Scholar must select a campus of the University of Tennessee as his/her "First Choice" to be considered for this UT alumni-funded scholarship. Award requirements change regularly. Please send a self-addressed, stamped envelope to receive your application and any further instructions from the scholarship provider. No GPA requirement specified.

University of Tennessee, Knoxville
Office of Undergraduate Admissions
350 Student Services Building
Knoxville, TN 37996

2866
Fred M. Roddy Merit Scholarship

AMOUNT: $3000 DEADLINE: Varies
MAJOR: All Areas of Study

The Fred M. Roddy Merit Scholarship is open to freshmen at UTK who have an average GPA of 4.0, an average ACT score of 33, and an average SAT score of 1450. This award is based on academic merit and leadership. Selections are made in Spring by the UTK General Scholarship Committee. Award requirements change regularly. Please send a self-addressed, stamped envelope to receive your application and any further instructions from the scholarship provider. GPA must be 4.0.

University of Tennessee, Knoxville
Office of Undergraduate Admissions
350 Student Services Building
Knoxville, TN 37996

2867
Frederick T. Bonham Scholarship

AMOUNT: $4000 DEADLINE: Varies
MAJOR: All Areas of Study

The Frederick T. Bonham Scholarship is open to freshmen at UTK who have an average GPA of 4.0, an average ACT score of 31, and an average SAT score of 1360. This award is based on academic merit. Selections are made in Spring by the UTK General Scholarship Committee. Award requirements change regularly. Please send a self-addressed, stamped envelope to receive your application and any further instructions from the scholarship provider. GPA must be 4.0.

University of Tennessee, Knoxville
Office of Undergraduate Admissions
350 Student Services Building
Knoxville, TN 37996

2868
Herbert S. Walters Scholarship

AMOUNT: None Specified DEADLINE: Varies
MAJOR: All Areas of Study

The Herbert S. Walters Scholarship is open to freshmen at UTK who have an average GPA of 3.8, an average ACT score of 28, and an average SAT score of 1240. Applicants must be East Tennessee residents. The selection criteria is based on academic merit, financial need, and work experience. The award is in-state tuition. Award requirements change regularly. Please send a self-addressed, stamped envelope to receive your application and any further instructions from the scholarship provider. GPA must be 3.8-4.0.

University of Tennessee, Knoxville
Office of Undergraduate Admissions
350 Student Services Building
Knoxville, TN 37996

2869
Manning Scholars Scholarship

AMOUNT: $7000 DEADLINE: January 15
MAJOR: All Areas of Study

The Manning Scholars Scholarship is open to graduating high school seniors who are nominated in writing (by a teacher, principal, or friend of the University) by December 15. Applicants must have a minimum GPA of 3.5, a minimum ACT score of 27, or an SAT score of 1200. An essay, transcripts, ACT/SAT scores, and letter of recommendation will be required. Manning Scholars will be selected among the Whittle Scholars finalists and will be interviewed on campus in early March. Award requirements change regularly. For further information send a self-addressed, stamped envelope to the address listed. GPA must be 3.5-4.0.

University of Tennessee, Knoxville
University Honors Program
F101 Melrose Hall
Knoxville, TN 37996-4352

2870
Minority Teaching Fellows Program

AMOUNT: $5000-$20000 DEADLINE: May 15
MAJOR: All Areas of Study

The Minority Teaching Fellows Program is open to minority entering freshmen attending a Tennessee college or university with a minimum 2.5 GPA, at least an 18 on the ACT or at least 850 on the SAT. Applicants must agree to teach at a K-12 level in a Tennessee public school one year for each year the award is received. This award is for Tennessee residents only. Award requirements change regularly. For further information contact your high school guidance office or the Financial Aid Office. GPA must be 2.5-4.0.

University of Tennessee - Knoxville - Office of Financial Aid
Attn: Scholarship Coordinator
115 Student Services Building
Knoxville, TN 37996-0210

2871
Ned McWherter Scholars Program

AMOUNT: Maximum: $6000 DEADLINE: Varies
MAJOR: All Areas of Study

The Ned McWherter Scholars Program is open to entering freshmen at any eligible Tennessee institution who have a 3.5 high school GPA and a minimum ACT of 29 or SAT of 1280. Award requirements change regularly. Please send a self-addressed, stamped envelope to receive your application and any further instructions from the scholarship provider. GPA must be 3.5-4.0.

University of Tennessee, Knoxville
Office of Undergraduate Admissions
350 Student Services Building
Knoxville, TN 37996

2872
Robert C. Byrd Honors Scholarship

AMOUNT: $1500 DEADLINE: April 1
MAJOR: All Areas of Study

The Robert C. Byrd Honors Scholarship Program is open to high school seniors who have a GPA of 3.5 in high school or an average GED score of 57 or higher. Students with at least a GPA of 3.0 in high school, a minimum ACT score of 24, or an SAT score of 1090 may also apply. This award is for Tennessee residents only. Award requirements change regularly. Please send a self-addressed, stamped envelope to receive your application and any further instructions from the scholarship provider. GPA must be 3.0-3.5

University of Tennessee, Knoxville
Office of Undergraduate Admissions
350 Student Services Building
Knoxville, TN 37996

2873
Robert R. Neyland Scholarship

AMOUNT: $5000 DEADLINE: Varies
MAJOR: All Areas of Study

The Robert R. Neyland Scholarship is open to freshmen at UTK who have an average GPA of 4.0, an average ACT score of 31, and an average SAT score of 1360. The selection criteria are based on academic merit and leadership. Selections are made in Spring by the UTK General Scholarship Committee. Award requirements change regularly. Please send a self-addressed, stamped envelope to receive your application and any further instructions from the scholarship provider. GPA must be 4.0.

University of Tennessee, Knoxville
Office of Undergraduate Admissions
350 Student Services Building
Knoxville, TN 37996

2874
Tennessee Scholars Scholarship

AMOUNT: $4000 DEADLINE: January 15
MAJOR: All Areas of Study

The Tennessee Scholars Scholarship is open to graduating high school seniors and transfer students. An essay, high school transcript, ACT/SAT scores, and two letters of recommendation (one from a teacher) will be required. Applicants must have a minimum GPA of 3.5, a minimum ACT score of 27, or an SAT score of 1200. Recipients must take four honors courses during their first two years and complete a senior project. The selection criteria are based on merit, extracurricular/community activities, and creativity. Award requirements change regularly. For further information send a self-addressed, stamped envelope to the address listed. GPA must be 3.5-4.0.

University of Tennessee, Knoxville
University Honors Program
F101 Melrose Hall
Knoxville, TN 37996-4352

2875
UTK African-American Achievers Scholarship

AMOUNT: None Specified DEADLINE: Varies
MAJOR: All Areas of Study

The UTK African-American Achievers Scholarship is open to incoming African-American freshmen at UTK who have a minimum high school GPA of 3.4, a minimum ACT Composite score of 23, and an SAT score of 1060. Applicants must be U.S citizens and fully admitted to UTK by February 1 prior to fall semester of enrollment. Award requirements change regularly. For further information send a self-addressed, stamped envelope to the address listed. GPA must be 3.4-4.0.

University of Tennessee, Knoxville
Office of Undergraduate Admissions
350 Student Services Building
Knoxville, TN 37996

2876
UTK Bicentennial Scholarship

AMOUNT: None Specified DEADLINE: Varies
MAJOR: All Areas of Study

The UTK Bicentennial Scholarship is open to incoming freshmen at UTK who have a minimum high school GPA of 3.75, a minimum ACT Composite score of 31, or an SAT score of 1360. Applicants must be Tennessee residents and fully admitted to UTK by February 1 prior to fall semester of enrollment. Award requirements change regularly. Please send a self-addressed, stamped envelope to receive your application and any further instructions from the scholarship provider. GPA must be 3.8-4.0.

University of Tennessee, Knoxville
Office of Undergraduate Admissions
350 Student Services Building
Knoxville, TN 37996

2877
Whittle Scholars Scholarship

AMOUNT: $7000 DEADLINE: January 15
MAJOR: All Areas of Study

The Whittle Scholars Scholarship is open to graduating high school seniors who are nominated in writing (by a teacher, guidance counselor, or a friend of the University) by December 15. Applicants must have a minimum GPA of 3.5, a minimum ACT score of 27, or an SAT score of 1200. An essay, transcripts, ACT/SAT scores, and two letters of recommendation will be required. The 25 finalists will be invited for campus interviews in March. Award requirements change regularly. For further information send a self-addressed, stamped envelope to the address listed. GPA must be 3.5-4.0.

University of Tennessee, Knoxville
University Honors Program
F101 Melrose Hall
Knoxville, TN 37996-4352

University of Tennessee, Martin

2878
Alumni Valedictorian Scholarship

AMOUNT: $1500 DEADLINE: Varies
MAJOR: All Areas of Study

The Alumni Valedictorian Scholarship is available to all Tennessee valedictorians from each high school in the state of Tennessee attending any undergraduate campus of the University of Tennessee. Award requirements change regularly. Please send a self-addressed, stamped envelope to receive your application and any further instructions from the scholarship provider. No GPA requirement specified.

University of Tennessee, Martin
Office of Financial Assistance
205 Administration Building
Martin, TN 38238

Army ROTC Scholarship

AMOUNT: None Specified DEADLINE: Varies
MAJOR: All Areas of Study

The Army ROTC Scholarship is available to students at UTM. Award requirements change regularly. Please send a self-addressed, stamped envelope to receive your application and any further instructions from the scholarship provider. No GPA requirement specified.

University of Tennessee, Martin
Office of Financial Assistance
205 Administration Building
Martin, TN 38238

2880
Band Scholarship

AMOUNT: $375-$660 DEADLINE: Varies
MAJOR: All Areas of Study

The Band Scholarship is available to students at UTM. This scholarship is awarded by audition to students regardless of major and is renewable each academic year. Award requirements change regularly. Please send a self-addressed, stamped envelope to receive your application and any further instructions from the scholarship provider. No GPA requirement specified.

University of Tennessee, Martin
Office of Financial Assistance
205 Administration Building
Martin, TN 38238

2881
Chancellor's Award

AMOUNT: None Specified DEADLINE: March 1
MAJOR: All Areas of Study

The Chancellor's Award is open to full-time students attending UTM who have a minimum 3.5 GPA and an ACT score of 28. This award is renewable if recipients maintain a 3.2 GPA at the end of two semesters and thereafter. Recipients must participate in seminars and attend lectures with distinguished campus visitors each year. Award requirements change regularly. Please send a self-addressed, stamped envelope to receive your application and any further instructions from the scholarship provider. GPA must be 3.5-4.0.

University of Tennessee, Martin
Office of Financial Assistance
205 Administration Building
Martin, TN 38238

2882
Deans Scholarship/Workship

AMOUNT: $1500 DEADLINE: Varies
MAJOR: All Areas of Study

The Deans Scholarship/Workship is open to students at UTM who have a minimum 3.5 GPA and an ACT score of 25. This award is renewable. Award requirements change regularly. Please send a self-addressed, stamped envelope to receive your application and any further instructions from the scholarship provider. GPA must be 3.5-4.0.

University of Tennessee, Martin
Office of Financial Assistance
205 Administration Building
Martin, TN 38238

2883
Fine Arts Scholarship

AMOUNT: None Specified DEADLINE: Varies
MAJOR: All Areas of Study

The Fine Arts Scholarship is open to art students at UTM. Scholarships are available through the Division of Fine and Performing Arts (Music, Band, and Dance). Award requirements change regularly. Please send a self-addressed, stamped envelope to receive your application and any further instructions from the scholarship provider. No GPA requirement specified.

University of Tennessee, Martin
Office of Financial Assistance
205 Administration Building
Martin, TN 38238

2884
Girl Scout Gold Award Scholarship

AMOUNT: $800 DEADLINE: Varies
MAJOR: All Areas of Study

The Girl Scout Gold Award Scholarship is available to students at the UTM who are Girl Scouts of America's Gold Award recipients. Applicants must live in the residence halls, have an ACT score of at least 21, and have a minimum 3.0 GPA. Award requirements change regularly. Please send a self-addressed, stamped envelope to receive your application and any further instructions from the scholarship provider. GPA must be 3.0-4.0.

University of Tennessee, Martin
Admissions Office
200 Administration Building
Martin, TN 38238

2885
Gooch Scholarship

AMOUNT: $300-$500 DEADLINE: Varies
MAJOR: All Areas of Study

The Gooch Scholarship is open to students at UT Martin and UT Center for Health Sciences in Memphis. The selection is based on financial need and academic performance. Award requirements change regularly. Please send a self-addressed, stamped envelope to receive your application and any further instructions from the scholarship provider. No GPA requirement specified.

University of Tennessee, Martin
Office of Financial Assistance
205 Administration Building
Martin, TN 38238

H.O.B.Y. Scholarship

AMOUNT: None Specified DEADLINE: Varies
MAJOR: All Areas of Study

The H.O.B.Y. Scholarship is open to students at UTM. Students who have participated in the Hugh O' Brien Youth Leadership program are selected to participate in the Leaders-in-Residence program. Priority is given to applicants who are student council presidents, Beta Club and/or Honor Society presidents, state officers in any student organizations, JROTC Battalion Commanders, and four selected freshmen entering ROTC. Applicants must have a minimum 2.6 GPA or an ACT score of 19. Recipients must participate in a special leadership development program and live in the residence halls. Award requirements change regularly. Please send a self-addressed, stamped envelope to receive your application and any further instructions from the scholarship provider. GPA must be 2.6-4.0.

University of Tennessee, Martin
Office of Financial Assistance
205 Administration Building
Martin, TN 38238

2887
Harold Conner African-American Scholarship

AMOUNT: $3000 DEADLINE: Varies
MAJOR: All Areas of Study

The Harold Conner African-American Scholarship is open to African-American Tennessee high school graduates who are planning to attend UTM. Applicants must have a minimum 3.25 GPA and an ACT score of 21. The selection criteria are based on high school academics, leadership, and ACT scores. Award requirements change regularly. Please send a self-addressed, stamped envelope to receive your application and any further instructions from the scholarship provider. GPA must be 3.3-4.0.

University of Tennessee, Martin
Office of Financial Assistance
205 Administration Building
Martin, TN 38238

2888
Honors Seminar Scholarship/Workship

AMOUNT: $1500 DEADLINE: March 1
MAJOR: All Areas of Study

The Honors Seminar Scholarship/Workship is open to full-time freshman, sophomore, junior, and senior students at UTM who have a minimum 3.5 GPA and an ACT score of 25. This award is renewable if recipients maintain a 3.2 GPA at the end of two semesters and thereafter. Students will be

required to work on campus nine hours per week. Award requirements change regularly. Please send a self-addressed, stamped envelope to receive your application and any further instructions from the scholarship provider. GPA must be 3.5-4.0.

University of Tennessee, Martin
Office of Financial Assistance
205 Administration Building
Martin, TN 38238

2889
Leaders-in-Residence Program

AMOUNT: $1000 DEADLINE: Varies
MAJOR: All Areas of Study

The Leaders-in-Residence Program is open to students at UTM who are student council presidents, Beta Club and/or Honor Society presidents, state officers in any student organizations, JROTC Battalion Commanders, and four selected freshmen entering ROTC. Applicants must have a minimum 2.6 GPA or an ACT score of 19. Recipients must participate in a special leadership development program and live in the residence halls. Award requirements change regularly. Please send a self-addressed, stamped envelope to receive your application and any further instructions from the scholarship provider. GPA must be 2.6-4.0.

University of Tennessee, Martin
Office of Financial Assistance
205 Administration Building
Martin, TN 38238

Music Scholarship

AMOUNT: $300-$750 DEADLINE: Varies
MAJOR: Music

The Music Scholarship is available to students at UTM who are majoring in music. This scholarship is awarded by audition and is renewable each year by meeting renewal criteria. Award requirements change regularly. Please send a self-addressed, stamped envelope to receive your application and any further instructions from the scholarship provider. No GPA requirement specified.

University of Tennessee, Martin
Office of Financial Assistance
205 Administration Building
Martin, TN 38238

2891
Salutatorian Freshman Award

AMOUNT: $1000 DEADLINE: Varies
MAJOR: All Areas of Study

The Salutatorian Freshman Award is available to salutatorian freshmen at UTM. Award requirements change regularly. Please send a self-addressed, stamped envelope to receive your application and any further instructions from the scholarship provider. No GPA requirement specified.

University of Tennessee, Martin
Office of Financial Assistance
205 Administration Building
Martin, TN 38238

2892
University Scholars Scholarship

AMOUNT: $3600 DEADLINE: Varies
MAJOR: All Areas of Study

The University Scholars Scholarship is open to students at UTM who have a minimum 3.5 GPA and an ACT score of 28. This award is renewable if recipients maintain a minimum 3.3 cumulative GPA and participate in the special ten-semester-hour curriculum for University Scholar students. Award requirements change regularly. Please send a self-addressed, stamped envelope to receive your application and any further instructions from the scholarship provider. GPA must be 3.5-4.0.

University of Tennessee, Martin
Office of Financial Assistance
205 Administration Building
Martin, TN 38238

2893
UT Martin Freshman Scholarship

AMOUNT: None Specified DEADLINE: Varies
MAJOR: All Areas of Study

The UT Martin Freshman Scholarship is open to freshmen at UTM who have a minimum 3.0 GPA and an ACT score of 20. Selection is based on leadership and academic achievement. Award requirements change regularly. Please send a self-addressed, stamped envelope to receive your application and any further instructions from the scholarship provider. GPA must be 3.0-4.0.

University of Tennessee, Martin
Office of Financial Assistance
205 Administration Building
Martin, TN 38238

2894
UTM - Community College Scholarship

AMOUNT: $1500 DEADLINE: Varies
MAJOR: All Areas of Study

The UTM - Community College Scholarship is open to juniors and seniors from community colleges who are attending the University of Tennessee, Martin. Applicants must have a minimum 60 hours or 90 quarter hours with a minimum 3.5 GPA. Recipients will be required to maintain a 3.2 GPA during their semesters at UTM and have the option of participating in the Honors Seminar program by enrolling in Honors Seminars courses. Award requirements change regularly. Please send a self-addressed, stamped envelope to receive your application and any further instructions from the scholarship provider.GPA must be 3.5-4.0.

University of Tennessee, Martin
Office of Financial Assistance
205 Administration Building
Martin, TN 38238

University of Utah

2895
AIME/SME Coal Division Scholarship

AMOUNT: $1500 DEADLINE: Varies
MAJOR: Mining Engineering

The AIME/SME Coal Division Scholarship is available to resident juniors at the University of Utah who intend to major in mining engineering with a coal specialization. Applicants must be members of SME. Award requirements change regularly. For further information write to the address listed enclosing a self-addressed, stamped envelope or call (801) 581-8603. No GPA requirement specified.

University of Utah
Attn: Dr. M.K. McCarter
135 South 1460 East, Room 313
Salt Lake City, UT 84112-0113

2896
Achievement Award for Culturally Diverse Students

AMOUNT: None Specified DEADLINE: Varies
MAJOR: All Areas of Study

The Achievement Award for Culturally Diverse Students is available to matriculated freshmen or transfer students at the University of Utah who, on account of their geographical, ethnic, or cultural background, will contribute to an educationally diverse environment at the University. Freshmen must apply before February 1, and transfer students must apply before April 1. Award requirements change regularly. For further information write to the address listed, enclosing a self-addressed, stamped envelope, or call (801) 581-6211. No GPA requirement specified.

University of Utah - Financial Aid and Scholarship Office
Attn: Scholarship Coordinator
201 South 1460 East, Room 105
Salt Lake City, UT 84112-8910

2897
Air Force Association Scholarship

AMOUNT: $1500 DEADLINE: Varies
MAJOR: Engineering, Mathematics, Chemistry, Physics

The Air Force Association Scholarship is available to juniors and seniors at the University of Utah who are majoring in engineering, mathematics, chemistry, or physics. The selection process is based on grade point average. Award requirements change regularly. For further information write to the address listed, enclosing a self-addressed, stamped envelope, or call (801) 581-6211. No GPA requirement specified.

University of Utah - Financial Aid and Scholarship Office
Attn: Scholarship Coordinator
201 South 1460 East, Room 105
Salt Lake City, UT 84112-8910

2898
Daughters of Minos Scholarship

AMOUNT: None Specified DEADLINE: February 15
MAJOR: All Areas of Study

The Daughters of Minos Scholarship is open to students who are of Cretan-Greek descent attending the University of Utah. Award requirements change regularly. For further information write to the address listed, enclosing a self-addressed, stamped envelope, or call (801) 581-6211. No GPA requirement specified.

University of Utah - Financial Aid and Scholarship Office
Attn: Scholarship Coordinator
201 South 1460 East, Room 105
Salt Lake City, UT 84112-8910

2899
Departmental Scholarships

AMOUNT: None Specified DEADLINE: Varies
MAJOR: All Areas of Study

The Departmental Scholarships are available at the University of Utah for full-time entering freshmen and transfer students who have declared a major. You must be a Utah resident. The respective deadline dates are February 1 and March 31. Award requirements change regularly. Write to the address listed for further information, enclosing a self-addressed, stamped envelope, or call (801) 581-6211. No GPA requirement specified.

University of Utah - Financial Aid and Scholarship Office
Attn: Scholarship Coordinator
201 South 1460 East, Room 105
Salt Lake City, UT 84112-8910

2900
Dorothy Rich, Brent Scott Presidential Scholarship

AMOUNT: None Specified DEADLINE: February 1
MAJOR: All Areas of Study

The Dorothy Rich, Brent Scott Presidential Scholarship is available to non-resident high school seniors and transfer students who plan on attending the University of Utah. Award requirements change regularly. Write to the address listed for further information, or call (801) 581-6211. No GPA requirement specified.

University of Utah - Financial Aid and Scholarship Office
Attn: Scholarship Coordinator
201 South 1460 East, Room 105
Salt Lake City, UT 84112-8910

2901
Endowment Pool Scholarships

AMOUNT: None Specified DEADLINE: February 15
MAJOR: All Areas of Study

The Endowment Pool Scholarships are available to students at the University of Utah who can demonstrate financial need. Many awards are available. Requirements may vary slightly for each award. Award requirements change regularly. Write to the address listed for further information, enclosing a self-addressed, stamped envelope, or call (801) 581-6211. No GPA requirement specified.

University of Utah - Financial Aid and Scholarship Office
Attn: Scholarship Coordinator
201 South 1460 East, Room 105
Salt Lake City, UT 84112-8910

2902
Honors at Entrance Scholarship

AMOUNT: None Specified DEADLINE: February 1
MAJOR: All Areas of Study

The Honors at Entrance Scholarship is available at the University of Utah for entering National Merit Finalist freshmen. You must meet one of the following criteria: an SAT or ACT composite score of 28, a minimum 3.9 high school GPA, or an admissions index of 128 or higher. Preference is given to you if you are a Utah resident. Award requirements change regularly. Write to the address listed for further information, enclosing a self-addressed, stamped envelope, or call (801) 581-6211. GPA must be 3.9-4.0.

University of Utah - Financial Aid and Scholarship Office
Attn: Scholarship Coordinator
201 South 1460 East, Room 105
Salt Lake City, UT 84112-8910

2903
Honors at Entrance Scholarship/Early Admission

AMOUNT: None Specified DEADLINE: July 10
MAJOR: All Areas of Study

The Honors at Entrance Scholarship/Early Admission is available at the University of Utah for entering National Merit Finalist freshmen who have an admission index of 130 or higher. You must maintain a minimum cumulative GPA of 3.7 and complete 24 hours of course work every two semesters. Award requirements change regularly. Write to the address listed for further information, enclosing a self-addressed, stamped envelope, or call (801) 581-6211. No GPA requirement specified.

University of Utah - Financial Aid and Scholarship Office
Attn: Scholarship Coordinator
201 South 1460 East, Room 105
Salt Lake City, UT 84112-8910

2904
Ichiji Motoki Scholarship

AMOUNT: None Specified DEADLINE: February 15
MAJOR: All Areas of Study

The Ichiji Motoki Scholarship is available at the University of Utah for students of Japanese descent. Award requirements change regularly. For further information write to the address listed, enclosing a self-addressed, stamped envelope, or call (801) 581-6211.No GPA requirement specified.

University of Utah - Financial Aid and Scholarship Office
Attn: Scholarship Coordinator
201 South 1460 East, Room 105
Salt Lake City, UT 84112-8910

2905
John A. Moran Scholarship

AMOUNT: None Specified DEADLINE: Varies
MAJOR: All Areas of Study

The John A. Moran Scholarship is available to matriculated freshmen or transfer students at the University of Utah, who on account of their geographical, ethnic, or cultural background, will contribute to an educationally diverse environment at the University. Freshmen must apply before February 1, and transfer students must apply before April 1. Award requirements change regularly. For further information write to the address listed, enclosing a self-addressed, stamped envelope, or call (801) 581-6211. No GPA requirement specified.

University of Utah - Financial Aid and Scholarship Office
Attn: Scholarship Coordinator
201 South 1460 East, Room 105
Salt Lake City, UT 84112-8910

2906
John Alden and Amelia Wright Bowers Scholarship

AMOUNT: None Specified DEADLINE: February 15
MAJOR: All Areas of Study

The John Alden and Amelia Wright Bowers Scholarship is available to all students at the University of Utah who can demonstrate financial need. Award requirements change regularly. For further information write to the address listed, enclosing a self-addressed, stamped envelope, or call (801) 581-6211. No GPA requirement specified.

University of Utah - Financial Aid and Scholarship Office
Attn: Scholarship Coordinator
201 South 1460 East, Room 105
Salt Lake City, UT 84112-8910

2907
Josephine Beam Scholarship

AMOUNT: Maximum: $2000 DEADLINE: February 15
MAJOR: Engineering, Mines and Earth Science

The Josephine Beam Scholarship is available to continuing engineering students matriculated in the College of Engineering or the College of Mines and Earth Sciences at the University of Utah. You must demonstrate financial need. Award requirements change regularly. Write to the address listed for further information, enclosing a self-addressed, stamped envelope, or call (801) 581-6211. No GPA requirement specified.

University of Utah - Financial Aid and Scholarship Office
Attn: Scholarship Coordinator
201 South 1460 East, Room 105
Salt Lake City, UT 84112-8910

2908
Josephine Beam Scholarships

AMOUNT: Maximum: $2000 DEADLINE: February 15
MAJOR: Geology, Geophysics, Metallurgy, Meteorology, and Related Fields

The Josephine Beam Scholarships are available at the University of Utah for students matriculated in the College of Mines and Earth Sciences. Applicants must demonstrate financial need. Award requirements change regularly. For further information contact the College of Mines and Earth Sciences. No GPA requirement specified.

University of Utah - Financial Aid and Scholarship Office
Attn: Scholarship Coordinator
201 South 1460 East, Room 105
Salt Lake City, UT 84112-8910

2909
Ken Winsness Scholarship

AMOUNT: None Specified DEADLINE: February 15
MAJOR: All Areas of Study

The Ken Winsness Scholarship is available to students at the University of Utah who can demonstrate financial need. Award requirements change regularly. Write to the address listed for further information, enclosing a self-addressed, stamped envelope, or call (801) 581-6211. No GPA requirement specified.

University of Utah - Financial Aid and Scholarship Office
Attn: Scholarship Coordinator
201 South 1460 East, Room 105
Salt Lake City, UT 84112-8910

2910
Kennecott Scholarship

AMOUNT: $2500 DEADLINE: February 15
MAJOR: All Areas of Study

The Kennecott Scholarship is open to undergraduates selected by each college from among its majors within the University of Utah. If you win this award you will become a member of the Honor Society of Kennecott Scholars. Award requirements change regularly. Write to the address listed for further information, or call (801) 581-6211. No GPA requirement specified.

University of Utah - Financial Aid and Scholarship Office
Attn: Scholarship Coordinator
201 South 1460 East, Room 105
Salt Lake City, UT 84112-8910

2911
Leadership Scholarship

AMOUNT: None Specified DEADLINE: Varies
MAJOR: All Areas of Study

The Leadership Scholarship is open to incoming freshmen and transfer students with associate degrees, or the equivalent in quarter or semester hours from a Utah two-year college. You must have at least a 3.0 GPA and demonstrate outstanding leadership abilities. The respective deadline dates are February 1 for entering freshmen and April 1 for transfer students. Priority is given to you if you are a Utah resident. Award requirements change regularly. Write to the address listed for further information, enclosing a self-addressed, stamped envelope, or call (801) 581-6211. GPA must be 3.0-4.0.

University of Utah - Financial Aid and Scholarship Office
Attn: Scholarship Coordinator
201 South 1460 East, Room 105
Salt Lake City, UT 84112-8910

2912
Madelyn S. Silver Scholarship

AMOUNT: None Specified DEADLINE: February 15
MAJOR: Literature, Biblical Literature

The Madelyn S. Silver Scholarship is available at the University of Utah for students with high academic achievement who demonstrate a substantial interest in literature, preferably Biblical literature. An essay is required. Award requirements change regularly. Write to the address listed for further information, enclosing a self-addressed, stamped envelope, or call (801) 581-6211. No GPA requirement specified.

University of Utah - Financial Aid and Scholarship Office
Attn: Scholarship Coordinator
201 South 1460 East, Room 105
Salt Lake City, UT 84112-8910

2913
Margaret E. Oser Foundation Scholarship

AMOUNT: None Specified DEADLINE: Varies
MAJOR: All Areas of Study

The Margaret E. Oser Foundation Scholarship is available to matriculated freshmen or transfer students at the University of Utah who, on account of their geographical, ethnic, or cultural background, will contribute to an educationally diverse environment at the University. Freshmen must apply before February 1, and transfer students must apply before April 1. Award requirements change regularly. For further information write to the address listed, enclosing a self-addressed, stamped envelope, or call (801) 581-6211. No GPA requirement specified.

University of Utah - Financial Aid and Scholarship Office
Attn: Scholarship Coordinator
201 South 1460 East, Room 105
Salt Lake City, UT 84112-8910

2914
Meritorious Award for Culturally Diverse Students

AMOUNT: None Specified DEADLINE: Varies
MAJOR: All Areas of Study

The Meritorious Award for Culturally Diverse Students is available to matriculated freshmen or transfer students at the University of Utah who, on account of their geographical, ethnic, or cultural background, will contribute to an educationally diverse environment at the University. Freshmen must apply before February 1, and transfer students must apply before April 1. Award requirements change regularly. For further information write to the address listed, enclosing a self-addressed, stamped envelope, or call (801) 581-6211. No GPA requirement specified.

University of Utah - Financial Aid and Scholarship Office
Attn: Scholarship Coordinator
201 South 1460 East, Room 105
Salt Lake City, UT 84112-8910

2915
Nonresident Academic Full Tuition Scholarship

AMOUNT: None Specified DEADLINE: February 1
MAJOR: All Areas of Study

The Nonresident Academic Full Tuition Scholarships are available at the University of Utah for full-time nonresident entering freshmen. Your cumulative GPA and ACT/SAT scores, and proven leadership abilities, activities, and accomplishments will be considered. This award is renewable if you maintain a minimum 3.7 GPA and complete 24 hours of course work (20 of which must be graded) every two semesters. Award requirements change regularly. Write to the address listed for further information, enclosing a self-addressed, stamped envelope, or call (801) 581-6211. No GPA requirement specified.

University of Utah - Financial Aid and Scholarship Office
Attn: Scholarship Coordinator
201 South 1460 East, Room 105
Salt Lake City, UT 84112-8910

2916
Nonresident Academic Partial Tuition Scholarship

AMOUNT: None Specified DEADLINE: February 1
MAJOR: All Areas of Study

The Nonresident Academic Partial Tuition Scholarship is available at the University of Utah for full-time nonresident entering freshmen. Your scholastic record will be considered. This award is renewable. Award requirements change regularly. Write to the address listed for further information, or call (801) 581-6211. No GPA requirement specified.

University of Utah - Financial Aid and Scholarship Office
Attn: Scholarship Coordinator
201 South 1460 East, Room 105
Salt Lake City, UT 84112-8910

2917
Nonresident Leadership Scholarship

AMOUNT: None Specified DEADLINE: February 1
MAJOR: All Areas of Study

The Nonresident Leadership Scholarship is available to nonresident incoming freshmen attending the University of Utah. You must have a minimum 3.0 GPA, and outstanding leadership abilities, activities, and achievements. This award is non-renewable. Award requirements change regularly. Write to the address listed for further information, or call (801) 581-6211. GPA must be 3.0-4.0.

University of Utah - Financial Aid and Scholarship Office
Attn: Scholarship Coordinator
201 South 1460 East, Room 105
Salt Lake City, UT 84112-8910

2918
Nonresident Transfer Student Merit Scholarship

AMOUNT: None Specified DEADLINE: April 1
MAJOR: All Areas of Study

The Nonresident Transfer Student Merit Scholarship is available to nonresident transfer students at the University of Utah with a minimum 3.8 GPA. You must have completed a two-year college associate degree program or its equivalent in quarter or semester hours in a state contiguous with Utah. Award requirements change regularly. Write to the address listed for further information, enclosing a self-addressed, stamped envelope or call (801) 581-6211. GPA must be 3.8-4.0.

University of Utah - Financial Aid and Scholarship Office
Attn: Scholarship Coordinator
201 South 1460 East, Room 105
Salt Lake City, UT 84112-8910

2919
Olga V. Alexandria (Logan) Scholarship

AMOUNT: Maximum: $2000 DEADLINE: February 15
MAJOR: Ballet, Theater, Business, Law, Medicine

The Olga V. Alexandria (Logan) Scholarship is available to women at the University of Utah who are majoring in ballet, theater, business, law, or medicine. Applicants must demonstrate financial need. Award requirements change regularly. For further information write to the address listed, enclosing a self-addressed, stamped envelope, or call (801) 581-6211. No GPA requirement specified.

University of Utah - Financial Aid and Scholarship Office
Attn: Scholarship Coordinator
201 South 1460 East, Room 105
Salt Lake City, UT 84112-8910

2920
President's Scholarship

AMOUNT: $12000 DEADLINE: February 1
MAJOR: All Areas of Study

The President's Scholarship is open to Utah resident incoming freshmen who are semifinalists for the Honors at Entrance Scholarship (you must be a National Merit Finalist in order to qualify for that award). The selection process is based on academic excellence, leadership, and civic activities. In order to qualify for a renewal, you must maintain a minimum cumulative GPA of 3.7 and complete 24 hours of course work. Award requirements change regularly. Write to the address listed for further information, enclosing a self-addressed, stamped envelope, or call (801) 581-6211. No GPA requirement specified.

University of Utah - Financial Aid and Scholarship Office
Attn: Scholarship Coordinator
201 South 1460 East, Room 105
Salt Lake City, UT 84112-8910

2921
Sigma Phi Epsilon Scholarship

AMOUNT: $50-$600 DEADLINE: February 15
MAJOR: All Areas of Study

The Sigma Phi Epsilon Scholarship is available to male entering freshmen at the University of Utah. The selection criteria are based on high school grades. Awards are provided by the Lewis A. Kingsley Foundation. Award requirements change regularly. Write to the address listed for further information, enclosing a self-addressed, stamped envelope, or call (801) 581-6211. No GPA requirement specified.

University of Utah - Financial Aid and Scholarship Office
Attn: Scholarship Coordinator
201 South 1460 East, Room 105
Salt Lake City, UT 84112-8910

2922
Stephanie Papanikolas Scholarship

AMOUNT: None Specified DEADLINE: February 15
MAJOR: All Areas of Study

The Stephanie Papanikolas Scholarship is available at the University of Utah for students who are of Greek-Orthodox descent. Award requirements change regularly. For further information write to the address listed, enclosing a self-addressed, stamped envelope, or call (801) 581-6211. No GPA requirement specified.

University of Utah - Financial Aid and Scholarship Office
Attn: Scholarship Coordinator
201 South 1460 East, Room 105
Salt Lake City, UT 84112-8910

2923
Transfer Student Merit Scholarship

AMOUNT: None Specified DEADLINE: April 1
MAJOR: All Areas of Study

The Transfer Student Merit Scholarship is open to Utah transfer students with a cumulative GPA of 3.8 or higher who have completed a Utah two-year college program or its equivalent. You must maintain a 3.7 GPA and complete 24 hours of course work. The amount of this award is resident tuition. Award requirements change regularly. Please send a self-addressed, stamped envelope to receive your application and any further instructions from the scholarship provider, or call (801) 581-6211. GPA must be 3.8-4.0.

University of Utah - Financial Aid and Scholarship Office
Attn: Scholarship Coordinator
201 South 1460 East, Room 105
Salt Lake City, UT 84112-8910

2924
University of Utah Merit Scholarship

AMOUNT: $500 DEADLINE: February 1
MAJOR: All Areas of Study

The University of Utah Merit Scholarship is open to entering freshmen admitted to the University of Utah who are National Merit Finalists and are non-residents of Utah. This award is renewable if you maintain a minimum 2.0 GPA and complete 24 hours of course work (20 of which must be graded) every two semesters. Award requirements change regularly. Check with your high school counseling center for detailed application procedures. No GPA requirement specified.

University of Utah - Financial Aid and Scholarship Office
Attn: Scholarship Coordinator
201 South 1460 East, Room 105
Salt Lake City, UT 84112-8910

2925
University of Utah Merit Scholarship with Presidential Honors

AMOUNT: None Specified DEADLINE: Varies
MAJOR: All Areas of Study

The University of Utah Merit Scholarship with Presidential Honors is open to incoming freshmen admitted to the University of Utah who qualify for both the Merit Scholarship and the President's Scholarship. You must be a resident of Utah and a National Merit Finalist. This award is renewable if you maintain a cumulative 3.7 GPA and complete 24 hours of course work (20 of which must be graded) every year. Award requirements change regularly. Write to the address listed for further information, or call (801) 581-6211. No GPA requirement specified.

University of Utah - Financial Aid and Scholarship Office
Attn: Scholarship Coordinator
201 South 1460 East, Room 105
Salt Lake City, UT 84112-8910

2926
University President's Club Nonresident Scholarship

AMOUNT: $1800 DEADLINE: February 1
MAJOR: All Areas of Study

The University President's Club Nonresident Scholarship is available at the University of Utah for full-time nonresident entering freshmen. Your cumulative GPA and ACT/SAT scores and proven leadership abilities, activities, and accomplishments will be considered. The scholarship is renewable if you maintain a minimum 3.7 GPA and complete 24 hours of course work (20 of which must be graded) every two semesters. The amount of this award is full nonresident tuition and a $1,800 cash award. Award requirements change regularly. Write to the address listed for further information, or call (801) 581-6211. No GPA requirement specified.

University of Utah - Financial Aid and Scholarship Office
Attn: Scholarship Coordinator
201 South 1460 East, Room 105
Salt Lake City, UT 84112-8910

University of Wisconsin, Eau Claire

2927
Ade and Margaret Olson Scholarship

AMOUNT: $400 DEADLINE: April 1
MAJOR: All Areas of Study

The Ade and Margaret Olson Scholarship is open to seniors (male or female) who have participated in men's or women's athletics while attending the University of Wisconsin, Eau Claire. Award requirements change regularly. Application/nomination forms are available in the Department of Kinesiology and Athletics. For further information call (715) 836-2546. No GPA requirement specified.

University of Wisconsin - Eau Claire - Financial Aid Office
Attn: Scholarship Programs
105 Garfield Avenue
Eau Claire, WI 54701-4004

2928
AVL List (Graz) Scholarship

AMOUNT: None Specified DEADLINE: Varies
MAJOR: All Areas of Study

The AVL List (Graz) Scholarship is open to Austrian students from Karl-Franzens-Universitat in Graz, Austria, who are at the University of Wisconsin, Eau Claire, under the exchange program. The Center for International Education coordinates this exchange and the scholarship designation. The funds are paid after the student arrives in Eau Claire and begins the fall semester. Award requirements change regularly. Please send a self-addressed, stamped envelope to receive your application and any further instructions from the scholarship provider. No GPA requirement specified.

University of Wisconsin - Eau Claire - Financial Aid Office
Attn: Scholarship Programs
105 Garfield Avenue
Eau Claire, WI 54701-4004

2929
Berniece Wagner Nursing Scholarship

AMOUNT: $1000 DEADLINE: April 1
MAJOR: Nursing

The Berniece Wagner Nursing Scholarship is open to nursing students admitted to the Nursing program who are in good academic standing with both the School of Nursing and the university. A minimum "B+" academic competence in previous college course work is required. This award is for students attending the University of Wisconsin, Eau Claire. Award requirements change regularly. For further information contact Elaine Wendt at (715) 836-5007. GPA must be 3.0-4.0.

University of Wisconsin - Eau Claire - Financial Aid Office
Attn: Scholarship Programs
105 Garfield Avenue
Eau Claire, WI 54701-4004

2930
Bill and Virginia Zorn Scholarship Fund

AMOUNT: $600 DEADLINE: April 1
MAJOR: All Areas of Study

The Bill and Virginia Zorn Scholarship Fund is open to students who have participated and demonstrated leadership in extracurricular activities and of a physical nature (athletics, recreation, pompom squad, cheerleading squad, etc.). Applicants must have at least a 2.5 GPA, a minimum sophomore standing, and demonstrated outstanding service to the university or community. Award requirements change regularly. Application/nomination forms are available in the Department of Kinesiology and Athletics. For further information call (715) 836-2546. GPA must be 2.5-4.0.

University of Wisconsin - Eau Claire - Financial Aid Office
Attn: Scholarship Programs
105 Garfield Avenue
Eau Claire, WI 54701-4004

2931
Carson W. Proctor Voice Scholarship

AMOUNT: $600 DEADLINE: April 1
MAJOR: Music (Voice)

The Carson W. Proctor Voice Scholarship is open to full-time music voice majors attending the University of Wisconsin, Eau Claire. A minimum 2.5 cumulative GPA in all course work and a minimum 2.75 GPA in music courses are required. Students must register for a major choral ensemble and for applied voice. Application forms are available in the Department of Music and Theater Arts Office. Award requirements change regularly. For further information contact Dr. David Baker, Music and Theater Arts Department Chair, at (715) 836-2284. GPA must be 2.5-4.0.

University of Wisconsin - Eau Claire - Financial Aid Office
Attn: Scholarship Programs
105 Garfield Avenue
Eau Claire, WI 54701-4004

2932
Charles Campbell Art Scholarship

AMOUNT: None Specified DEADLINE: Varies
MAJOR: Art

The Charles Campbell Art Scholarship is open to entering freshmen majoring in either the BA or BFA degree programs in Art at UWEC. Students must demonstrate by performance a serious interest in art: outstanding ability, discipline, and dedication. An essay is required for this award. Award requirements change regularly. For further information contact Stephen Katrosits, Art Department Chair. No GPA requirement specified.

University of Wisconsin - Eau Claire - Financial Aid Office
Attn: Scholarship Programs
105 Garfield Avenue
Eau Claire, WI 54701-4004

2933
Daniel Kincaid Pre-Medicine Scholarship

AMOUNT: $500 DEADLINE: March 20
MAJOR: Pre-Medicine

The Daniel Kincaid Pre-Medicine Scholarship is open to pre-med majors attending the University of Wisconsin, Eau Claire. Applicants must be second-semester freshmen, sophomores, or juniors. A minimum 3.5 GPA in sciences is required along with a minimum overall GPA of 3.5. An essay and two recommendations are also required. Award requirements change regularly. Application forms should be obtained from pre-medicine coordinator Dr. Thomas Rouse, or call the Financial Aid Office at (715) 836-3373. GPA must be 3.5-4.0.

University of Wisconsin - Eau Claire - Financial Aid Office
Attn: Scholarship Programs
105 Garfield Avenue
Eau Claire, WI 54701-4004

2934
Dr. Harold and Helena Ray Huston Nursing Scholarship

AMOUNT: $1400 DEADLINE: Varies
MAJOR: Nursing

The Dr. Harold and Helena Ray Huston Nursing Scholarship is open to nursing majors attending the University of Wisconsin, Eau Claire, who are of at least sophomore standing. Financial need may be a consideration. Award requirements change regularly. For further information contact Elaine Wendt at (715) 836-5007. No GPA requirement specified.

University of Wisconsin - Eau Claire - Financial Aid Office
Attn: Scholarship Programs
105 Garfield Avenue
Eau Claire, WI 54701-4004

2935
Edward B. Blackorby Book Award

AMOUNT: None Specified DEADLINE: Varies
MAJOR: History

The Edward B. Blackorby Book Award is open to outstanding history majors attending the University of Wisconsin, Eau Claire. The award is based on the following criteria: overall GPA, history GPA, performance in the required historiography courses, and recommendations from the history faculty. Award requirements change regularly. Please send a self-addressed, stamped envelope to receive your application and any further instructions from the scholarship provider, or call (715) 836-5501. No GPA requirement specified.

University of Wisconsin - Eau Claire - Financial Aid Office
Attn: Scholarship Programs
105 Garfield Avenue
Eau Claire, WI 54701-4004

2936
Florence M. and Fred R. Nelson Keyboard Scholarship

AMOUNT: $500-$2500 DEADLINE: Varies
MAJOR: Music (Keyboard)

The Florence M. and Fred R. Nelson Keyboard Scholarship is open to keyboard music majors attending the University of Wisconsin, Eau Claire. Selection is based on a high potential for success and contribution as a performer, inside or outside the academic arena, and is judged on a competition either through audition, jury performance, or UWEC recital. Award requirements change regularly. For further information contact Dr. David Baker, Music and Theater Arts Department Chair at (715) 836-2284. No GPA requirement specified.

University of Wisconsin - Eau Claire - Financial Aid Office
Attn: Scholarship Programs
105 Garfield Avenue
Eau Claire, WI 54701-4004

2937
George C. Barland Scholarship Fund

AMOUNT: $2000 DEADLINE: Varies
MAJOR: Music

The George C. Barland Scholarship Fund is open to full-time music majors attending the University of Wisconsin, Eau Claire. Applicants must have a minimum cumulative GPA of 2.5 in all course work, a minimum 2.75 GPA in music courses, and be registered for a major choral ensemble and for applied voice. Award requirements change regularly. For further information contact Dr. David Baker, Music and Theater Arts Department Chair at (715) 836-2284. GPA must be 2.5-4.0.

University of Wisconsin - Eau Claire - Financial Aid Office
Attn: Scholarship Programs
105 Garfield Avenue
Eau Claire, WI 54701-4004

2938
Hank Aaron Merit Scholarship

AMOUNT: $500 DEADLINE: March 1
MAJOR: All Areas of Study

The Hank Aaron Merit Scholarship is open to African American, Asian American, Native American, and Hispanic students who have shown substantial leadership ability and involvement at the University of Wisconsin, Eau Claire. Applicants must be in good academic standing and either a junior or senior. Award requirements change regularly. Please send a self-addressed, stamped envelope to receive your application and any further instructions from the scholarship provider, or call (715) 836-3373. No GPA requirement specified.

University of Wisconsin - Eau Claire - Financial Aid Office
Attn: Scholarship Programs
105 Garfield Avenue
Eau Claire, WI 54701-4004

2939
Ihle Family Award for Caring

AMOUNT: $800 DEADLINE: March 1
MAJOR: Nursing

The Ihle Family Award for Caring is open to students, alumna or members of the faculty of the School of Nursing at the University of Wisconsin, Eau Claire. Any student, alumna or faculty member of the School of Nursing may nominate an individual for this award. Award requirements change regularly. For further information contact Elaine Wendt at (715) 836-5007. No GPA requirement specified.

University of Wisconsin - Eau Claire - Financial Aid Office
Attn: Scholarship Programs
105 Garfield Avenue
Eau Claire, WI 54701-4004

2940
Jan and Maria Taminiau Memorial Scholarship

AMOUNT: None Specified DEADLINE: May 1
MAJOR: History, Art, Music

The Jan and Maria Taminiau Memorial Scholarship is open to sophomore level and above students who are history, art, or music majors attending the University of Wisconsin, Eau Claire. Special emphasis is placed on candidates who have a record of community involvement and service. Award requirements change regularly. Nominations/applications should be submitted to Dr. Stephen Gosch, Department of History at (715) 836-5501. No GPA requirement specified.

University of Wisconsin - Eau Claire - Financial Aid Office
Attn: Scholarship Programs
105 Garfield Avenue
Eau Claire, WI 54701-4004

2941
Leonard and Dorellen Haas Scholarship

AMOUNT: $5000 DEADLINE: May 1
MAJOR: All Areas of Study

The Leonard and Dorellen Haas Scholarship is open to full-time students attending the University of Wisconsin, Eau Claire. Applicants must demonstrate high academic achievement. One semester of study abroad experience with a UW-Eau Claire program prior to the application is required. Award requirements change regularly. Application forms are available in the Center for International Education, Schofield Hall 111. Call the Financial Aid Office at (715) 836-3373 for further information. No GPA requirement specified.

University of Wisconsin - Eau Claire - Financial Aid Office
Attn: Scholarship Programs
105 Garfield Avenue
Eau Claire, WI 54701-4004

2942
Lyla Flagler Scholarship

AMOUNT: $900 DEADLINE: May 1
MAJOR: All Areas of Study

The Lyla Flagler Scholarship is open to mature individuals who formerly attended the University of Wisconsin, Eau Claire, without graduating and returned to complete their degrees. Recipients must have financial need and should have had an above-average scholastic record when they first attended the University. Award requirements change regularly. Applications may be picked up from the Adult Opportunity Office, Schofield 240. For further information contact Rita Webb at (715) 836-3259. No GPA requirement specified.

University of Wisconsin - Eau Claire - Financial Aid Office
Attn: Scholarship Programs
105 Garfield Avenue
Eau Claire, WI 54701-4004

2943
Mari Jo S. Janke University Ambassador Service Award

AMOUNT: $250 DEADLINE: October 31
MAJOR: All Areas of Study

The Mari Jo S. Janke University Ambassador Service Award is open to active members of the University Ambassadors who have demonstrated exceptional service to the university. To be considered for the award, you must have demonstrated financial need. The award is to be used for school-related expenses. Award requirements change regularly. Application forms are available in the Alumni Association office. No GPA requirement specified.

University of Wisconsin - Eau Claire - Financial Aid Office
Attn: Scholarship Programs
105 Garfield Avenue
Eau Claire, WI 54701-4004

2944
Ormsby L. Harry Scholarship

AMOUNT: $500 DEADLINE: March 15
MAJOR: All Areas of Study

The Ormsby L. Harry Scholarship is open to students attending University of Wisconsin, Eau Claire. To be considered for this award, you must demonstrate exceptional scholarship, leadership, service to the university, and service to the community. The award also requires that you participate in the Honors Week Steering Committee. Financial need will not be a consideration. Award requirements change regularly. Application forms are available in the Office of the Dean of Students. No GPA requirement specified.

University of Wisconsin - Eau Claire - Financial Aid Office
Attn: Scholarship Programs
105 Garfield Avenue
Eau Claire, WI 54701-4004

2945
Ralph and Peggy Hudson Pre-Medicine Scholarship

AMOUNT: $500 DEADLINE: March 20
MAJOR: Pre-Medicine

The Ralph and Peggy Hudson Pre-Medicine Scholarship is open to pre-med majors attending the University of Wisconsin, Eau Claire. Applicants must be second semester freshmen, sophomores, or juniors. A minimum 3.5 GPA in sciences is required, along with a minimum overall GPA of 3.5. An essay and two recommendations are also required. Award requirements change regularly. Application forms should be obtained from pre-medicine coordinator Dr. Thomas Rouse, or call the Financial Aid Office at (715) 836-3373. GPA must be 3.5-4.0.

University of Wisconsin - Eau Claire - Financial Aid Office
Attn: Scholarship Programs
105 Garfield Avenue
Eau Claire, WI 54701-4004

2946
Rodaynah Obaid Nursing Scholarship

AMOUNT: $2500 DEADLINE: April 1
MAJOR: Nursing

The Rodaynah Obaid Nursing Scholarship is open to nursing students attending the School of Nursing at the University of Wisconsin, Eau Claire. Recipients must be nursing students who exhibit high academic achievement and a record of service and caring. Award requirements change regularly. For further information contact Elaine Wendt at (715) 836-5007. No GPA requirement specified.

University of Wisconsin - Eau Claire - Financial Aid Office
Attn: Scholarship Programs
105 Garfield Avenue
Eau Claire, WI 54701-4004

2947
Roma Hoff Scholarship

AMOUNT: $1500 DEADLINE: April 1
MAJOR: Foreign Language (Spanish)

The Roma Hoff Scholarship is open to Spanish language majors who have completed one semester of study at the Universidad de Valladolid or Universidad de Oviedo. Students must have 90 credits of course work completed and a cumulative 3.0 GPA with a 3.5 GPA in Spanish courses. An essay is required. Award requirements change regularly. Application forms are available in the Department of Foreign Languages Office; call (715) 836-4287. GPA must be 3.0-4.0.

University of Wisconsin - Eau Claire - Financial Aid Office
Attn: Scholarship Programs
105 Garfield Avenue
Eau Claire, WI 54701-4004

2948
Veda Stone Native American Art Scholarship

AMOUNT: $600 DEADLINE: October 15
MAJOR: Art

The Veda Stone Native American Art Scholarship is open to Native American art majors attending UWEC. Preference will be shown for Wisconsin residents and members of Wisconsin tribes. Applicants must be in good academic standing, demonstrate artistic talent, and be pursuing a degree program in an artistic discipline. A portfolio of work and two letters of recommendation are required. Award requirements change regularly. Application forms are available from the American Indian Program, UW-Eau Claire, WI 54702-4004. Please send a self-addressed, stamped envelope. No GPA requirement specified.

University of Wisconsin - Eau Claire - Financial Aid Office
Attn: Scholarship Programs
105 Garfield Avenue
Eau Claire, WI 54701-4004

2949
W. Parker Clark Scholarship

AMOUNT: $500 DEADLINE: April 10
MAJOR: Physics

The W. Parker Clark Scholarship is open to junior physics majors who have earned at least 60 credits toward graduation by the end of the spring semester and have completed or have registered for a 300-level physics course at the time of application. This award is for students attending the University of Wisconsin, Eau Claire, and is based on high GPAs. Award requirements change regularly. Applications should be completed and turned in to the Physics and Astronomy Department Office. For further information contact the Financial Aid Office at (715) 836-3373. No GPA requirement specified.

University of Wisconsin - Eau Claire - Financial Aid Office
Attn: Scholarship Programs
105 Garfield Avenue
Eau Claire, WI 54701-4004

2950
Wilhelm and Ingrid Brauner Award

AMOUNT: $1000 DEADLINE: December 1
MAJOR: Foreign Languages and Studies (German)

The Wilhelm and Ingrid Brauner Award is open to sophomore level and above German language or German studies majors. Preference will be given to students enrolled in the School of Arts and Sciences who are involved in university and community life and have a demonstrated interest in the study of arts, culture, languages, and societies. Particular preference is given to a student who plans a minimum of one full semester of study in Austria (preferably an institute in Vienna). A minimum 3.5 GPA is required. Award requirements change regularly. Applicants for this award should file formal application forms with the Viennese Ball Committee. For an application form contact Ada Bors, Coordinator-Viennese Ball, Room 133 in the Davies Center. GPA must be 3.5-4.0.

University of Wisconsin - Eau Claire - Financial Aid Office
Attn: Scholarship Programs
105 Garfield Avenue
Eau Claire, WI 54701-4004

University of Wisconsin, Platteville

2951
Alpha Lambda Delta Joanne Trow Scholarship

AMOUNT: $1000 DEADLINE: April 1
MAJOR: All Areas of Study

The Alpha Lambda Delta Joanne Trow Scholarship is awarded to full-time UW - Platteville students who have already been inducted into the UWP chapter. To qualify, you must have maintained a cumulative GPA of at least 3.5. The UWP chapter will select one application to forward to the national competition. Award requirements change regularly. A special application must be picked up from advisor Darla Banfi, 308 Warner Hall, after February 1. GPA must be 3.5-4.0.

University of Wisconsin - Platteville, General Scholarships
Financial Aid Office
1 University Plaza, 204 Brigham Hall
Platteville, WI 53818

2952
Alpha Lambda Delta, UW - Platteville Chapter Scholarship

AMOUNT: $200 DEADLINE: March 1
MAJOR: All Fields of Study

The Alpha Lambda Delta, UW - Platteville Chapter Scholarship is awarded to students at UW - Platteville who have received an invitation to join Alpha Lambda Delta at the current year's induction ceremony and plan on continuing their education in the fall semester. Your selection is based on academic achievement, financial need, and university/community service. Award requirements change regularly. No GPA requirement specified.

University of Wisconsin - Platteville, General Scholarships
Financial Aid Office
1 University Plaza, 204 Brigham Hall
Platteville, WI 53818

2953
Helen Harms Anderson Scholarship

AMOUNT: $250 DEADLINE: February 15
MAJOR: All Areas of Study

The Helen Harms Anderson Scholarship is available to full-time undergraduate women continuing at University of Wisconsin - Platteville who demonstrate financial need. You must also file a FAFSA to be eligible. Award requirements change regularly. No GPA requirement specified.

University of Wisconsin - Platteville, General Scholarships
Financial Aid Office
1 University Plaza, 204 Brigham Hall
Platteville, WI 53818

2954
Leo E. Boebel Memorial Scholarship

AMOUNT: None Specified DEADLINE: February 15
MAJOR: Biology, Human Health, Liberal Arts (Social Work, Psychology, Social Services)

The Leo E. Boebel Memorial Scholarship is available to undergraduate students with high academic achievement who graduated from a high school in Grant, Iowa, Lafayette, Richland, Crawford, or Vernon counties in Wisconsin. You should be planning to enter into the biology or human health fields (with a liberal arts major). The award of full resident tuition is renewable for the duration of your entire undergraduate program. Award requirements change regularly. No GPA requirement specified.

University of Wisconsin - Platteville, New Freshman Scholarships
Financial Aid Office
1 University Plaza, 204 Brigham Hall
Platteville, WI 53818

2955
Patricia Doyle Scholarship

AMOUNT: $200 DEADLINE: February 15
MAJOR: Health or Physical Education

The Patricia Doyle Scholarship is awarded to females of at least sophomore standing at UW - Platteville. You must be majoring or minoring in health or physical education, be participating in student activities, and have a GPA of at least 2.5 to be eligible for this need-based award. Award requirements change regularly. GPA must be 2.5-4.0.

University of Wisconsin - Platteville, General Scholarships
Financial Aid Office
1 University Plaza, 204 Brigham Hall
Platteville, WI 53818

2956
Roger L. Davies Scholarship

AMOUNT: $175 DEADLINE: February 15
MAJOR: Astronomy, Biology, Chemistry, Geography, Physics

The Roger L. Davies Scholarship is available to full-time students at UW - Platteville. To qualify for this award, you must demonstrate financial need, have a GPA of 3.0 or greater, and have a major in the natural sciences (includes astronomy, biology, chemistry, geography, and physics). Award requirements change regularly. GPA must be 3.0-4.0.

University of Wisconsin - Platteville, College of EMS Scholarships
Financial Aid Office
1 University Plaza, 204 Brigham Hall
Platteville, WI 53818

2957
Tharold Dorn Scholarship

AMOUNT: $200 DEADLINE: February 15
MAJOR: All Areas of Study

The Tharold Dorn Scholarship is available to continuing students at UW - Platteville. To be considered for the award, you must demonstrate character, have high scholastic achievement, and participate in extracurricular activities. Award requirements change regularly. No GPA requirement specified.

University of Wisconsin - Platteville, General Scholarships
Financial Aid Office
1 University Plaza, 204 Brigham Hall
Platteville, WI 53818

University of Wisconsin, Oshkosh

2958
Ann Beier Scholarship

AMOUNT: $2500 DEADLINE: May 1
MAJOR: Nursing

The Ann Beier Scholarship is open to full-time freshmen at UWO. You must be a nursing major. The award amount is $2500 over four years. Award requirements change regularly. Please send a self-addressed, stamped envelope to receive your application and any further instructions from the scholarship provider. No GPA requirement specified.

University of Wisconsin, Oshkosh
Financial Aid Office
800 Algoma Blvd
Oshkosh, WI 54901-8604

2959
Annual Short Story Competition

AMOUNT: $150-$300 DEADLINE: February 3
MAJOR: All Areas of Study

The Annual Short Story Competition is open to students at the University of Wisconsin, Oshkosh, campus. Awards are presented to first- and second-place winners. Award requirements change regularly. For an application and further information send a self-addressed, stamped envelope to the attention of the University of Wisconsin Oshkosh Foundation. No GPA requirement specified.

University of Wisconsin, Oshkosh
Financial Aid Office
800 Algoma Blvd
Oshkosh, WI 54901-8604

2960
Army Four-Year ROTC Scholarship

AMOUNT: Maximum: $16000 DEADLINE: Varies
MAJOR: All Areas of Study

The Army Four-Year ROTC Scholarship is open to incoming freshmen between the ages of 17 and 23 attending the University of Wisconsin, Oshkosh, campus. You must be a high school graduate and a U.S. citizen with a minimum GPA of 2.5. This award includes up to $16,000 in tuition, fees, and books and a $150 monthly stipend. Award requirements change regularly. The deadline for this award is in February. For further information, please contact the Department of Military Science. GPA must be 2.5-4.0.

University of Wisconsin, Oshkosh
Financial Aid Office
800 Algoma Blvd
Oshkosh, WI 54901-8604

2961
Chancellor's Freshman Academic Award

AMOUNT: $1000 DEADLINE: March 1
MAJOR: All Areas of Study

The Chancellor's Freshman Academic Award is available to full-time entering freshmen admitted to UW Oshkosh who rank in the top quarter of their graduating class (top 20% for athletics). You must be able to demonstrate outstanding academics and potential in your chosen field of study. Award requirements change regularly. Please send a self-addressed, stamped envelope to the Admissions Office at the address listed for more details, or call (920) 424-0202. No GPA requirement specified.

University of Wisconsin, Oshkosh
Financial Aid Office
800 Algoma Blvd
Oshkosh, WI 54901-8604

2962
Chancellor's Freshman Leadership Scholarship

AMOUNT: $1000 DEADLINE: March 1
MAJOR: All Areas of Study

The Chancellor's Freshman Leadership Scholarship is available to entering freshmen admitted to UW Oshkosh who rank in the top quarter of their class (top 20% for athletes). You must also have had significant leadership experience (excluding leadership roles in athletic participation). Award requirements change regularly. For further information, please contact the Admissions Office. GPA must be 3.0-4.0.

University of Wisconsin, Oshkosh
Financial Aid Office
800 Algoma Blvd
Oshkosh, WI 54901-8604

2963
Class Gift Scholarship

AMOUNT: $300 DEADLINE: February 15
MAJOR: All Areas of Study

The Class Gift Scholarship is open to full-time students at UWO who demonstrate involvement in at least three university or community volunteer activities. You must be a second-semester freshman, sophomore, or junior or a first-semester senior with at least a 3.0 GPA. Award requirements change regularly. Please send a self-addressed, stamped envelope to the attention of Sheryl Hanson, Office of Alumni Affairs, to receive your application and any further instructions. GPA must be 3.0-4.0.

University of Wisconsin, Oshkosh
Financial Aid Office
800 Algoma Blvd
Oshkosh, WI 54901-8604

2964
David J. Lippert Memorial Scholarship

AMOUNT: $1000 DEADLINE: Varies
MAJOR: Journalism

The David J. Lippert Memorial Scholarship is open to UW Oshkosh students with a strong career interest in the news editorial side of journalism. You must be either a sophomore or junior with a minimum 3.0 GPA. Award requirements change regularly. The deadline for this award is in early March. Please send a self-addressed, stamped envelope to the Journalism Department at the address listed for more details. GPA must be 3.0-4.0.

University of Wisconsin, Oshkosh
Financial Aid Office
800 Algoma Blvd
Oshkosh, WI 54901-8604

2965
Diversity in Journalism Scholarship

AMOUNT: $500 DEADLINE: March 15
MAJOR: Journalism

The Diversity in Journalism Scholarship is open to incoming freshmen and new transfer students (with a journalism major) at UW Oshkosh who are minorities as defined by affirmative action guidelines. A 500-word essay will be required along with the completed application form. Award requirements change regularly. For an application and further information, please send a self-addressed, stamped envelope to the attention of Mike Cowling, Department of Journalism, UWO, at the address listed, or call (920) 424-7144. No GPA requirement specified.

University of Wisconsin, Oshkosh
Financial Aid Office
800 Algoma Blvd
Oshkosh, WI 54901-8604

2966
Edwin J. and Dorothy M. Hartman Scholarship

AMOUNT: $500 DEADLINE: February 25
MAJOR: All Areas of Study

The Edwin J. and Dorothy M. Hartman Scholarship is open to full-time undergraduate female students at UWO. You must have an interest in small business and/or family business and have a commendable scholastic record. You must also be involved in extracurricular activities. Award requirements change regularly. Please send a self-addressed, stamped envelope to receive your application and any further instructions from the scholarship provider. GPA must be 2.5-4.0.

University of Wisconsin, Oshkosh
Financial Aid Office
800 Algoma Blvd
Oshkosh, WI 54901-8604

2967
Freshman Scholarship in Geology

AMOUNT: $500 DEADLINE: March 1
MAJOR: Geology, Earth Science

The Freshman Scholarship in Geology is for entering freshmen at UW Oshkosh who have a strong interest in geology or earth science. You must be ranked in the top 25% of your high school graduating class in addition to completing three years each of math and science. You must be either a U.S. citizen or permanent resident to qualify. Award requirements change regularly. Please send a self-addressed, stamped envelope to William D. Mode, Geology Department, at the address listed for more details. In addition, you may call (920) 424-4460. No GPA requirement specified.

University of Wisconsin, Oshkosh
Financial Aid Office
800 Algoma Blvd
Oshkosh, WI 54901-8604

2968
Harris N. Liechti Award

AMOUNT: None Specified DEADLINE: March 1
MAJOR: Film, Television, Radio

The Harris N. Liechti Award is open to full-time radio, television, and film majors at UW Oshkosh. To be considered, you must submit a production, paper, or project in any format with a letter explaining its significance. Award requirements change regularly. Please send a self-addressed, stamped envelope to the Communications Department Office at the address listed for more information. No GPA requirement specified.

University of Wisconsin, Oshkosh
Financial Aid Office
800 Algoma Blvd
Oshkosh, WI 54901-8604

2969
Jon C. Pierce Memorial Scholarship

AMOUNT: $1500 DEADLINE: April 15
MAJOR: Pre-Engineering, Nursing

The Jon C. Pierce Memorial Scholarship is available to entering freshmen at UW Oshkosh who are employees or children of full-time employees of Oshkosh Truck, Inc. You must have a record of academic achievement. Preference is given to students in pre-engineering or nursing. Award requirements change regularly. Please send a self-addressed, stamped envelope to the Office of Admissions at the address listed for more information. No GPA requirement specified.

University of Wisconsin, Oshkosh
Financial Aid Office
800 Algoma Blvd
Oshkosh, WI 54901-8604

2970
Lanore Netzer Scholarship

AMOUNT: $500 DEADLINE: March 1
MAJOR: Education

The Lanore Netzer Scholarship is open to upperclassmen and graduate students at UW Oshkosh who are majoring in teacher education. Academic performance and financial need will also be considered in determining award recipients. Award requirements change regularly. Please send a self-addressed, stamped envelope to the Curriculum and Instruction Department at the address listed for more details. No GPA requirement specified.

University of Wisconsin, Oshkosh
Financial Aid Office
800 Algoma Blvd
Oshkosh, WI 54901-8604

2971
Lucile Morton-Grams Scholarship

AMOUNT: $750 DEADLINE: Varies
MAJOR: All Areas of Study

The Lucile Morton-Grams Scholarship is open to full-time undergraduates at UW Oshkosh who have a minimum GPA of 2.5 and have filed a FAFSA. In order to be considered, you cannot be eligible for grants. Award requirements change regularly. The deadline for this award is in February. Please send a self-addressed, stamped envelope to the address listed for more details. GPA must be 2.5-4.0.

University of Wisconsin, Oshkosh
Financial Aid Office
800 Algoma Blvd
Oshkosh, WI 54901-8604

2972
Mary Ellen Frenzel Memorial Scholarship

AMOUNT: $100 DEADLINE: March 1
MAJOR: Elementary or Secondary Education

The Mary Ellen Frenzel Memorial Scholarship is open to non-traditional sophomore students at UW Oshkosh who are majoring in elementary education or secondary education english or art. You must have a minimum 2.75 GPA and participate in extracurricular activities (excluding athletic participation) in the community and the university. You must also demonstrate financial need. Award requirements change regularly. Please send a self-addressed, stamped envelope to receive your application and any further instructions to the Department of Curriculum and Instruction, or call (920) 424-2477. GPA must be 2.75-4.0.

University of Wisconsin, Oshkosh
Financial Aid Office
800 Algoma Blvd
Oshkosh, WI 54901-8604

2973
Minority Honors Scholarship

AMOUNT: Maximum: $2500 DEADLINE: March 15
MAJOR: All Areas of Study

The Minority Honors Scholarship is open to entering freshmen at UW Oshkosh who are of Native American, African-American, Hispanic/Latino, Cambodian, Laotian, or Vietnamese descent. You must demonstrate a strong academic record and be a U.S. citizen or permanent resident. Award requirements change regularly. Please send a self-addressed, stamped envelope to the Admissions Office at the address listed for more information. No GPA requirement specified.

University of Wisconsin, Oshkosh
Financial Aid Office
800 Algoma Blvd
Oshkosh, WI 54901-8604

2974
Music Department Scholarship for Freshmen

AMOUNT: None Specified DEADLINE: January 13
MAJOR: Music

The Music Department Scholarship for Freshmen is open to incoming freshmen at UW Oshkosh. You must demonstrate musical talent in brass, string, woodwind, percussion, voice, or keyboard and submit a letter of recommendation. Award requirements change regularly. Please send a self-addressed, stamped envelope to the Music Department at the address listed for more details. No GPA requirement specified.

University of Wisconsin, Oshkosh
Financial Aid Office
800 Algoma Blvd
Oshkosh, WI 54901-8604

2975
Oshkosh Fine Arts Association Scholarship

AMOUNT: $250 DEADLINE: February 10
MAJOR: Art

The Oshkosh Fine Arts Association Scholarship is open to full-time UW Oshkosh freshman, sophomore, and junior art majors. Award requirements change regularly. Please send a self-addressed, stamped envelope to the address listed for further information. No GPA requirement specified.

University of Wisconsin, Oshkosh
Financial Aid Office
800 Algoma Blvd
Oshkosh, WI 54901-8604

2976
Philip and Jean C. Nelson Alumni Scholarship

AMOUNT: $500 DEADLINE: April 1
MAJOR: All Areas of Study

The Philip and Jean C. Nelson Alumni Scholarship is open to freshmen entering UW Oshkosh whose parents or grandparents are UW Oshkosh alumni. You must have a record of academic achievement and extracurricular involvement (excluding athletic participation). U.S. citizenship or permanent residency is also required. Award requirements change regularly. Please send a self-addressed, stamped envelope to the Office of Admissions at the address listed for more details. No GPA requirement specified.

University of Wisconsin, Oshkosh
Financial Aid Office
800 Algoma Blvd
Oshkosh, WI 54901-8604

2977
Ruth Rowland Award

AMOUNT: $900 DEADLINE: Varies
MAJOR: Physical Education

The Ruth Rowland Award is open to female physical education majors attending UW Oshkosh who are full-time students. To qualify, you must be a second semester freshman with a minimum GPA of 2.75. Award requirements change regularly. The deadline for this award is in March. Please send a self-addressed, stamped envelope to the Health and Physical Education Department at the address listed for more information. GPA must be 2.75-4.0.

University of Wisconsin, Oshkosh
Financial Aid Office
800 Algoma Blvd
Oshkosh, WI 54901-8604

2978
Sentry Insurance Leadership Scholarship

AMOUNT: $2000-$8000 DEADLINE: March 15
MAJOR: Business, Math, Computer Science

The Sentry Insurance Leadership Scholarship is open to entering freshmen at UW Oshkosh who are majoring in business, math, or computer science. You must rank in the top 15% of your class, demonstrate outstanding leadership potential, and be a U.S. citizen or permanent resident. Award requirements change regularly. Please send a self-addressed, stamped envelope to the address listed for more information. No GPA requirement specified.

University of Wisconsin, Oshkosh
Financial Aid Office
800 Algoma Blvd
Oshkosh, WI 54901-8604

2979
SHRM Student Chapter, Outstanding Service Award

AMOUNT: $100 DEADLINE: February 25
MAJOR: Human Resources Management

The SHRM Student Chapter, Outstanding Service Award is open to full-time UW Oshkosh juniors and seniors who are majoring in human resources management. Selection is based on academic achievement and extracurricular activities (excluding athletic participation). Award requirements change regularly. Please send a self-addressed, stamped envelope to the College of Business, SHRM Advisor, at the address listed for more information. No GPA requirement specified.

University of Wisconsin, Oshkosh
Financial Aid Office
800 Algoma Blvd
Oshkosh, WI 54901-8604

2980
Virginia A. Sokolowski Memorial Scholarship

AMOUNT: $200 DEADLINE: Varies
MAJOR: Journalism

The Virginia A. Sokolowski Memorial Scholarship is open to full-time UW Oshkosh students with a career interest in the news editorial side of journalism. You must be a sophomore or a junior and have a minimum 3.0 GPA. Award requirements change regularly. The deadline for this award is in early March. Please send a self-addressed, stamped envelope to Margaret Davidson, Chair of the Journalism Department, at the address listed for further information. GPA must be 3.0-4.0.

University of Wisconsin, Oshkosh
Financial Aid Office
800 Algoma Blvd
Oshkosh, WI 54901-8604

2981
William Patrick Niederberger Memorial Award

AMOUNT: $125 DEADLINE: February 10
MAJOR: Photography, Fine Art

The William Patrick Niederberger Memorial Award is available to full-time UW Oshkosh sophomores and juniors with a declared major in photography or fine art. You must also demonstrate skills in unrelated areas of expertise to qualify. Award requirements change regularly. Please send a self-addressed, stamped envelope to the Art Department at the address listed for more information. No GPA requirement specified.

University of Wisconsin, Oshkosh
Financial Aid Office
800 Algoma Blvd
Oshkosh, WI 54901-8604

University of Wyoming

2982
Hearst Minority Scholarship

AMOUNT: None Specified DEADLINE: April 30
MAJOR: All Areas of Study

Scholarships for minority students at the University of Wyoming who have a minimum 2.5 GPA. Must be entering freshmen, undergraduate transfer students, or current Hearst Minority Scholars. Must be U.S. citizens or permanent residents and be of American ethnic minority background (American Indian, Asian, Hispanic, or African-American). Award requirements change regularly. Send a self-addressed, stamped envelope to the address listed; call (307) 766-6189; or browse their website at siswww.uwyo.edu/sfa/homepage.htm. GPA must be 2.5-4.0.

University of Wyoming
Minority Affairs Office
PO Box 3808
Laramie, WY 82071-3808

Valdosta State University

 2983
A. B. "Sonny" Martin Scholarship

AMOUNT: None Specified DEADLINE: May 1
MAJOR: Education

The A. B. "Sonny" Martin Scholarship is open to students at VSU who are pursuing a masters of education degree. Award requirements change regularly. No GPA requirement specified.

Valdosta State University
Financial Aid Office
1500 North Patterson Street
Valdosta, GA 31698-0167

2984
Air Force ROTC Scholarship

AMOUNT: None Specified DEADLINE: May 1
MAJOR: All Areas of Study

The Air Force ROTC Scholarship is open to ROTC students at VSU. This award is based on your performance, academic achievement, and leadership potential. Award requirements change regularly. For more information on how to apply, please contact the Valdosta State University Office of Admissions. No GPA requirement specified.

Valdosta State University
Financial Aid Office
1500 North Patterson Street
Valdosta, GA 31698-0167

2985
Applied Music Scholarships

AMOUNT: $1000-$2500 DEADLINE: May 1
MAJOR: Music

The Applied Music Scholarships are open to all music majors at VSU. If you are an incoming freshman you must have at least a 1230 SAT or 28 ACT. If you are a transfer student, your GPA score will be considered. This award is renewable if you maintain a 3.0 GPA. You must perform at an audition between February 12 and April 15. Award requirements change regularly. For an application and further information please apply online at www.valdosta.edu/music/scholarships.html. No GPA requirement specified.

Valdosta State University
Financial Aid Office
1500 North Patterson Street
Valdosta, GA 31698-0167

2986
Athletic Scholarships

AMOUNT: None Specified DEADLINE: May 1
MAJOR: All Areas of Study

The Athletic Scholarships are open to students attending VSU. You must participate in campus athletics. Award requirements change regularly. No GPA requirement specified.

Valdosta State University
Financial Aid Office
1500 North Patterson Street
Valdosta, GA 31698-0167

2987
Band Assistance

AMOUNT: $1000-$2500 DEADLINE: May 1
MAJOR: Music

Band Assistance is available to new undergraduate music majors at VSU. If you are an incoming freshman you must have at least a 1230 SAT or 28 ACT. If you are a transfer student your GPA will be considered. This award is renewable if you maintain a 3.0 GPA. You must perform at an audition between February 12 and April 15. Award requirements change regularly. For an application and further information please apply online at www.valdosta.edu/music/scholarships.html. No GPA requirement specified.

Valdosta State University
Financial Aid Office
1500 North Patterson Street
Valdosta, GA 31698-0167

2988
Bank of America Scholarship

AMOUNT: None Specified DEADLINE: May 1
MAJOR: Business

The Bank of America Scholarship is open to business majors at VSU. You must be in good academic standing. Award requirements change regularly. No GPA requirement specified.

Valdosta State University
Financial Aid Office
1500 North Patterson Street
Valdosta, GA 31698-0167

2989
Barbara Pearlman Soshnik Scholarship

AMOUNT: None Specified DEADLINE: May 1
MAJOR: All Areas of Study

The Barbara Pearlman Soshnik Scholarship is open to deserving students at VSU. You must demonstrate financial need. Award requirements change regularly. No GPA requirement specified.

Valdosta State University
Financial Aid Office
1500 North Patterson Street
Valdosta, GA 31698-0167

2990
Belk-Hudson Management Scholarship

AMOUNT: None Specified DEADLINE: May 1
MAJOR: Management

The Belk-Hudson Management Scholarship is open to management majors at VSU. You must be pursuing a B.B.A. This award is renewable if you maintain a 2.75 GPA. Award requirements change regularly. No GPA requirement specified.

Valdosta State University
Financial Aid Office
1500 North Patterson Street
Valdosta, GA 31698-0167

2991
Bernard L. Linger Memorial Fine Arts Scholarship

AMOUNT: None Specified DEADLINE: May 1
MAJOR: Music, Art, Communication Art

The Bernard L. Linger Memorial Fine Arts Scholarship is open to music, art, and communication arts majors at VSU. You must be a sophomore, junior, or senior who has carried a minimum of 15 credit hours per semester prior to the application. A minimum 3.5 GPA is required. Award requirements change regularly. GPA must be 3.5-4.0.

Valdosta State University
Financial Aid Office
1500 North Patterson Street
Valdosta, GA 31698-0167

2992
Catherine Hensley McDonald Memorial Scholarship

AMOUNT: None Specified DEADLINE: April 1
MAJOR: Business/Vocational Education

The Catherine Hensley McDonald Memorial Scholarship is open to students enrolled in the business/vocational education program at VSU. You must have at least a 2.5 GPA and prove financial need. This award is renewable provided you maintain a 2.5 GPA. Award requirements change regularly. For more information on how to apply, please contact the Valdosta State University Office of Admissions. GPA must be 2.5-4.0.

Valdosta State University
Financial Aid Office
1500 North Patterson Street
Valdosta, GA 31698-0167

2993
Citizens Community Bank Scholarship

AMOUNT: None Specified DEADLINE: May 1
MAJOR: College of Business Administration

The Citizens Community Bank Scholarship is open to students enrolled in the College of Business Administration at VSU. You must have at least a 1000 SAT and a minimum high school 2.5 GPA. Award requirements change regularly. GPA must be 2.5-4.0.

Valdosta State University
Financial Aid Office
1500 North Patterson Street
Valdosta, GA 31698-0167

2994
Dr. Joseph Durrenberger Scholarship

AMOUNT: None Specified DEADLINE: May 1
MAJOR: All Areas of Study

The Dr. Joseph Durrenberger Scholarship is open to undergraduate students at VSU. Preference is given to you if you are considered non-traditional, at least 25 years of age, and enrolled full-time with a 2.5 GPA. This award is renewable. Award requirements change regularly. GPA must be 2.5-4.0.

Valdosta State University
Financial Aid Office
1500 North Patterson Street
Valdosta, GA 31698-0167

2995
Elene D. Dorminy Scholarship

AMOUNT: None Specified DEADLINE: May 1
MAJOR: Music

The Elene D. Dorminy Scholarship is open to undergraduate music majors at VSU. Your musical ability and potential will be considered. You must audition for this award between February 12 and April 15. Award requirements change regularly. For more information on how to apply, please contact the Valdosta State University Office of Admissions. No GPA requirement specified.

Valdosta State University
Financial Aid Office
1500 North Patterson Street
Valdosta, GA 31698-0167

2996
Eva Carroll Herndon Scholarship

AMOUNT: None Specified DEADLINE: May 1
MAJOR: Education, Art and Sciences (Pre-Med), Nursing, Ministry

The Eva Carroll Herndon Scholarship is open to education, pre-med, and nursing students and ministry majors at VSU. You must have at least a "C+" or better GPA and demonstrate financial need. Award requirements change regularly. GPA must be 2.5-4.0.

Valdosta State University
Financial Aid Office
1500 North Patterson Street
Valdosta, GA 31698-0167

2997
Frances Wood Wilson Foundation, Inc., Scholarship

AMOUNT: None Specified DEADLINE: May 1
MAJOR: All Areas of Study

The Frances Wood Wilson Foundation, Inc., Scholarship is open to students attending VSU. You must be in good academic standing and prove financial need. Award requirements change regularly. No GPA requirement specified.

Valdosta State University
Financial Aid Office
1500 North Patterson Street
Valdosta, GA 31698-0167

2998
Gail Aberson Scholarship

AMOUNT: None Specified DEADLINE: May 1
MAJOR: Education, Science

The Gail Aberson Scholarship is open to students at VSU majoring in education. You must be a teacher at the graduate level in your professional development/certification as teacher support specialists (mentors) and science teachers K-12. The award will provide you with assistance from member school systems in the Okefenokee RESA. Award requirements change regularly. For more information on how to apply, please contact the Valdosta State University Office of Admissions. No GPA requirement specified.

Valdosta State University
Financial Aid Office
1500 North Patterson Street
Valdosta, GA 31698-0167

2999
Georgia Gulf Sulfur Business-Athlete Scholarship

AMOUNT: None Specified DEADLINE: May 1
MAJOR: College of Business Administration

The Georgia Gulf Sulfur Business-Athlete Scholarship is open to incoming freshmen at VSU. This award recognizes outstanding performance in the classroom and in the field of competition. You must be enrolled in the College of Business Administration and participating in one of VSU's intercollegiate athletic teams. You need a minimum 950 SAT. This award is renewable if you maintain a 2.5 GPA. Award requirements change regularly. No GPA requirement specified.

Valdosta State University
Financial Aid Office
1500 North Patterson Street
Valdosta, GA 31698-0167

3000
Golden Circle Theater Scholarship

AMOUNT: None Specified DEADLINE: May
MAJOR: Theater

The Golden Circle Theater Scholarship is open to undergraduate theater majors at VSU. You will be judged on your academic achievement and audition or portfolio presentation. Award requirements change regularly. For more information on how to apply, please contact the Valdosta State University Office of Admissions. No GPA requirement specified.

Valdosta State University
Financial Aid Office
1500 North Patterson Street
Valdosta, GA 31698-0167

3001
Griffin L.L.C. Scholarship

AMOUNT: None Specified DEADLINE: April 1
MAJOR: All Areas of Study

The Griffin L.L.C. Scholarship is open to the dependent children of a Griffin Associate at VSU. You must be an incoming freshman. This award is renewable provided you maintain a 15-credit-hour enrollment and a 2.5 GPA. This scholarship is renewable. Award requirements change regularly. For more information on how to apply, please contact the Valdosta State University Office of Admissions. No GPA requirement specified.

Valdosta State University
Financial Aid Office
1500 North Patterson Street
Valdosta, GA 31698-0167

3002
Harold S. Gulliver, Sr., Memorial Scholarship

AMOUNT: None Specified DEADLINE: May 1
MAJOR: English, Humanities

The Harold S. Gulliver, Sr., Memorial Scholarship is open to English and humanities majors at Valdosta State University. To determine your eligibility to receive the award, your academic ability and financial need will be considered. Award requirements change regularly. No GPA requirement specified.

Valdosta State University
Financial Aid Office
1500 North Patterson Street
Valdosta, GA 31698-0167

3003
HOPE Scholarship

AMOUNT: None Specified DEADLINE: May 1
MAJOR: All Areas of Study

The HOPE Scholarship is open to undergraduate students at VSU. You must be a Georgia resident with at least a 3.0 GPA. Your GPA will be reviewed at the 30th, 60th, and 90th attempted hour. HOPE covers tuition, fees, and a book allowance ($150 for six hours or more; $75 for five hours or less). Award requirements change regularly. GPA must be 3.0-4.0.

Valdosta State University
Financial Aid Office
1500 North Patterson Street
Valdosta, GA 31698-0167

3004
HOPE Teacher Scholarship

AMOUNT: None Specified DEADLINE: May 1
MAJOR: Education

The HOPE Teacher Scholarship program provides financial assistance to teachers, counselors, and individuals who are seeking advanced degrees in critical fields of study. You must agree to teach in a Georgia public school at the preschool, elementary, or secondary level after graduation or else the scholarship becomes a loan which must be repaid in cash with interest. Award requirements change regularly. For more information on how to apply, please contact the Valdosta State University Office of Admissions. No GPA requirement specified.

Valdosta State University
Financial Aid Office
1500 North Patterson Street
Valdosta, GA 31698-0167

3005
James E. Martin Scholarship

AMOUNT: None Specified DEADLINE: May 1
MAJOR: Physics

The James E. Martin Scholarship is open to a physics major at VSU. You must be a student pursuing a B.S. degree. This award is renewable provided you maintain a 3.0 GPA in all courses required for the physics major. Award requirements change regularly. For more information on how to apply, please contact the Valdosta State University Office of Admissions. No GPA requirement specified.

Valdosta State University
Financial Aid Office
1500 North Patterson Street
Valdosta, GA 31698-0167

3006
James L. Dewar, Sr. - Park Avenue Bank Scholarship

AMOUNT: None Specified DEADLINE: May 1
MAJOR: Business Administration

The James L. Dewar, Sr. - Park Avenue Bank Scholarship is open to business administration students at VSU. You must be a high school graduate from a Lowndes County school. Award requirements change regularly. No GPA requirement specified.

Valdosta State University
Financial Aid Office
1500 North Patterson Street
Valdosta, GA 31698-0167

3007
Jim and Mary Threatte Scholarship

AMOUNT: None Specified DEADLINE: May 1
MAJOR: Education

The Jim and Mary Threatte Scholarship is open to outstanding students at VSU. You must be enrolled in the College of Education. Award requirements change regularly. For more information on how to apply, please contact the Valdosta State University Office of Admissions. No GPA requirement specified.

Valdosta State University
Financial Aid Office
1500 North Patterson Street
Valdosta, GA 31698-0167

3008
John and Gertrude Odum Scholarship

AMOUNT: None Specified DEADLINE: May 1
MAJOR: All Areas of Study

The John and Gertrude Odum Scholarship is open to freshmen and transfer students attending Valdosta State University. Over the course of your selection process, various criteria are considered, such as SAT or ACT scores and high school or junior college grades. Award requirements change regularly. There is no application needed, as eligible students are automatically selected and notified by the Office of Admissions. No GPA requirement specified.

Valdosta State University
Financial Aid Office
1500 North Patterson Street
Valdosta, GA 31698-0167

3009
John Henry Dorminy Scholarship

AMOUNT: None Specified DEADLINE: May 1
MAJOR: Business Administration

The John Henry Dorminy Scholarship is open to incoming freshmen at VSU. You must be enrolled in the College of Business Administration. This award is renewable for up to three years provided you maintain a 3.0 GPA. Award requirements change regularly. No GPA requirement specified.

Valdosta State University
Financial Aid Office
1500 North Patterson Street
Valdosta, GA 31698-0167

3010
LaForrest Eberhardt Theater Scholarship

AMOUNT: None Specified DEADLINE: May 1
MAJOR: Theater

The LaForrest Eberhardt Theater Scholarship is open to undergraduate theater majors at VSU. You will be judged on your academic achievement and audition or portfolio presentation. Award requirements change regularly. For more information on how to apply, please contact the Valdosta State University Office of Admissions. No GPA requirement specified.

Valdosta State University
Financial Aid Office
1500 North Patterson Street
Valdosta, GA 31698-0167

3011
Lee M. Bennett Art Scholarship

AMOUNT: None Specified DEADLINE: May 1
MAJOR: Art

The Lee M. Bennett Art Scholarship is open to art majors at VSU. Award requirements change regularly. For more information on how to apply, please contact the Valdosta State.

University Office of Admissions. No GPA requirement specified.

Valdosta State University
Financial Aid Office
1500 North Patterson Street
Valdosta, GA 31698-0167

3012
Lettie Pate Whitehead Foundation Scholarship

AMOUNT: None Specified DEADLINE: May 1
MAJOR: Nursing

The Lettie Pate Whitehead Foundation Scholarship is open to nursing undergraduate students at VSU. You must be a female student in good academic standing and in financial need. Award requirements change regularly. No GPA requirement specified.

Valdosta State University
Financial Aid Office
1500 North Patterson Street
Valdosta, GA 31698-0167

3013
Lorene Joiner Memorial Scholarship

AMOUNT: None Specified DEADLINE: May 1
MAJOR: All Areas of Study

The Lorene Joiner Memorial Scholarship is open to students attending VSU. You must prove financial need. Award requirements change regularly. No GPA requirement specified.

Valdosta State University
Financial Aid Office
1500 North Patterson Street
Valdosta, GA 31698-0167

3014
Louise Sawyer Theater Scholarship

AMOUNT: None Specified DEADLINE: May 1
MAJOR: Theater Arts

The Louise Sawyer Theater Scholarship is open to theater art majors at VSU. You must be pursuing a degree in this major. Award requirements change regularly. For more information on how to apply, please contact the Valdosta State University Office of Admissions. No GPA requirement specified.

Valdosta State University
Financial Aid Office
1500 North Patterson Street
Valdosta, GA 31698-0167

3015
Lucy Martin Stewart Scholarship

AMOUNT: $1000-$2500 DEADLINE: May 1
MAJOR: Vocal Music

The Lucy Martin Stewart Scholarship is open to voice majors at VSU. If you are an incoming freshman you must have at least a 1230 SAT or 28 ACT. If you are a transfer student,

your GPA score will be considered. This award is renewable if you maintain a 3.0 GPA. You must be a Georgia resident. Award requirements change regularly. For more information on how to apply, please contact the Valdosta State University Office of Admissions. No GPA requirement specified.

Valdosta State University
Financial Aid Office
1500 North Patterson Street
Valdosta, GA 31698-0167

3016
Margaret H. Hiers Scholarship

AMOUNT: None Specified DEADLINE: May 1
MAJOR: All Areas of Study

The Margaret H. Hiers Scholarship is open to students at VSU. Award requirements change regularly. No GPA requirement specified.

Valdosta State University
Financial Aid Office
1500 North Patterson Street
Valdosta, GA 31698-0167

3017
Max Stephenson Scholarship

AMOUNT: None Specified DEADLINE: May 1
MAJOR: Business Administration

The Max Stephenson Scholarship is open to business administration majors at VSU. You must be in good academic standing. Award requirements change regularly. No GPA requirement specified.

Valdosta State University
Financial Aid Office
1500 North Patterson Street
Valdosta, GA 31698-0167

3018
Melvene D. Hardee Scholarship

AMOUNT: None Specified DEADLINE: May 1
MAJOR: All Areas of Study

The Melvene D. Hardee Scholarship is open to freshmen and transfer students attending Valdosta State University. Over the course of your selection process, various criteria are considered, such as SAT or ACT scores and high school or junior college grades. Award requirements change regularly. There is no application needed, as eligible students are automatically selected and notified by the Office of Admissions. No GPA requirement specified.

Valdosta State University
Financial Aid Office
1500 North Patterson Street
Valdosta, GA 31698-0167

3019
Milton M. Ratnor Foundation Scholarship

AMOUNT: None Specified DEADLINE: May 1
MAJOR: All Areas of Study

The Milton M. Ratnor Foundation Scholarship is open to students attending VSU. You must be in good academic standing and prove financial need. Award requirements change regularly. No GPA requirement specified.

Valdosta State University
Financial Aid Office
1500 North Patterson Street
Valdosta, GA 31698-0167

3020
Ola Lee Means Scholarship

AMOUNT: None Specified DEADLINE: May 1
MAJOR: English, College of Arts

The Ola Lee Means Scholarship is open to students at Valdosta State University. To be considered for this award, you must be an English major or a student enrolled in the College of Arts. Award requirements change regularly. No GPA requirement specified.

Valdosta State University
Financial Aid Office
1500 North Patterson Street
Valdosta, GA 31698-0167

3021
Ola M. Brown Minority Scholarship

AMOUNT: None Specified DEADLINE: May 1
MAJOR: Education

The Ola M. Brown Minority Scholarship is open to minority education majors at VSU. You must be in good academic standing and be in financial need. Award requirements change regularly. No GPA requirement specified.

Valdosta State University
Financial Aid Office
1500 North Patterson Street
Valdosta, GA 31698-0167

3022
R.B. Whitehead Scholarship

AMOUNT: None Specified DEADLINE: May 1
MAJOR: All Areas of Study

The R.B. Whitehead Scholarship is open to freshmen and transfer students attending Valdosta State University. Over the course of your selection process, various criteria are considered, such as SAT or ACT scores and high school or junior college grades. Award requirements change regularly. There is no application needed, as eligible students are automatically selected and notified by the Office of Admissions. No GPA requirement specified.

Valdosta State University
Financial Aid Office
1500 North Patterson Street
Valdosta, GA 31698-0167

3023
Robert F. Barr Scholarship

AMOUNT: $1000-$2500 DEADLINE: May 1
MAJOR: Instrumentalist, Wind, String, and Percussion Music and Music Education

The Robert F. Barr Scholarship is open to wind, string, percussion, and instrumentalist music and music education majors at VSU. If you are an incoming freshman you must have at least a 1230 SAT or 28 ACT. If you are a transfer student, your GPA score will be considered. This award is renewable if you maintain a 3.0 GPA. You must perform at an audition between February 12 and April 15. Award requirements change regularly. For more information on how to apply, please contact the Valdosta State University Office of Admissions. No GPA requirement specified.

Valdosta State University
Financial Aid Office
1500 North Patterson Street
Valdosta, GA 31698-0167

3024
Saralyn Sammons Scholarship

AMOUNT: None Specified DEADLINE: April 1
MAJOR: Business/Vocational Education

The Saralyn Sammons Scholarship is open to students enrolled in the Department of Business and Vocational Education at VSU. You must have completed at least 30 hours and have a minimum 3.0 GPA. Award requirements change regularly. For more information on how to apply, please contact the Valdosta State University Office of Admissions. GPA must be 3.0-4.0.

Valdosta State University
Financial Aid Office
1500 North Patterson Street
Valdosta, GA 31698-0167

3025
Speech and Hearing Scholarship

AMOUNT: None Specified DEADLINE: May 1
MAJOR: Speech, Hearing

The Speech and Hearing Scholarship is open to students at VSU. You must major in speech and hearing and have completed at least 50 semester hours with a minimum 2.5 GPA. Award requirements change regularly. For more information on how to apply, please contact the Valdosta State University Office of Admissions. GPA must be 2.5-4.0.

Valdosta State University
Financial Aid Office
1500 North Patterson Street
Valdosta, GA 31698-0167

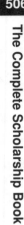

3026
Tammy Lee Fortner Scholarship

AMOUNT: None Specified DEADLINE: May 1
MAJOR: Art

The Tammy Lee Fortner Scholarship is open to art majors at VSU. You must be a sophomore, junior, or senior. This award is renewable. Award requirements change regularly. For more information on how to apply, please contact the Valdosta State University Office of Admissions. No GPA requirement specified.

Valdosta State University
Financial Aid Office
1500 North Patterson Street
Valdosta, GA 31698-0167

3027
Thomas H. Moseley, M.D., Nursing Scholarship

AMOUNT: None Specified DEADLINE: May 1
MAJOR: Nursing

The Thomas H. Moseley, M.D., Nursing Scholarship is open to senior nursing majors at VSU. Your academics and financial need will be considered. Award requirements change regularly. No GPA requirement specified.

Valdosta State University
Financial Aid Office
1500 North Patterson Street
Valdosta, GA 31698-0167

3028
Walter R. and Dorothy S. Salter Scholarship

AMOUNT: None Specified DEADLINE: May 1
MAJOR: Pre-Medicine

The Walter R. and Dorothy S. Salter Scholarship is open to undergraduates at VSU who are enrolled in a pre-medical program of study. You must be enrolled full-time, have a minimum 3.0 GPA, and be a declared pre-med major having completed two major-level courses in both chemistry and biology (four courses). Award requirements change regularly. GPA must be 3.0-4.0.

Valdosta State University
Financial Aid Office
1500 North Patterson Street
Valdosta, GA 31698-0167

3029
Wesley Ren Christie Scholarship

AMOUNT: None Specified DEADLINE: May 1
MAJOR: Communication Arts

The Wesley Ren Christie Scholarship is open to high school seniors accepted at VSU. You must be a communication art major with a minimum SAT score of 1100. Award requirements change regularly. For more information on how to apply, please contact the Valdosta State University Office of Admissions. No GPA requirement specified.

Valdosta State University
Financial Aid Office
1500 North Patterson Street
Valdosta, GA 31698-0167

3030
Wine and Spirits Wholesalers of Georgia Scholarship

AMOUNT: None Specified DEADLINE: May 1
MAJOR: All Areas of Study

The Wine and Spirits Wholesalers of Georgia Scholarship is open to undergraduate students at VSU. You must be a Georgia resident with superior academic achievement and financial need. This is a full-tuition scholarship, and it is awarded throughout the state of Georgia on a rotating basis. Award requirements change regularly. No GPA requirement specified.

Valdosta State University
Financial Aid Office
1500 North Patterson Street
Valdosta, GA 31698-0167

Virginia Commonwealth University

3031
Dean's Scholarship

AMOUNT: None Specified DEADLINE: January 1
MAJOR: All Areas of Study

The Dean's Scholarship is open to outstanding entering freshmen at VCU. The award is for half in-state tuition and fees and is based on academics, not financial need. Applicants will be required to submit an essay, and no other application is necessary. Award requirements change regularly. Please send a self-addressed, stamped envelope to receive your application and any further instructions from the scholarship provider. GPA must be 3.0-4.0.

Virginia Commonwealth University
Undergraduate Admissions Office
821 West Franklin Street
Richmond, VA 23284-2526

3032
Dianne Nunnally Hoppes Scholarship

AMOUNT: None Specified DEADLINE: January 1
MAJOR: All Areas of Study

The Dianne Nunnally Hoppes Scholarship is open to outstanding entering freshmen at VCU. The award is for in-state tuition, fees, room, board, and books and is based on academics and not financial need. Applicants will be required to submit an essay, and no other application is necessary. This scholarship is awarded every four years. Award requirements change regularly. Please send a self-addressed, stamped envelope to receive your application and any further instructions from the scholarship provider. GPA must be 3.0-4.0.

Virginia Commonwealth University
Undergraduate Admissions Office
821 West Franklin Street
Richmond, VA 23284-2526

3033
Phi Theta Kappa Scholarship

AMOUNT: None Specified DEADLINE: January 1
MAJOR: All Areas of Study

The Phi Theta Kappa Scholarship is open to outstanding entering freshmen at VCU. The applicant must be a Phi Theta Kappa member at any Virginia community college who then transfers to VCU and has earned a minimum of 45 semester credit hours. The award is for half in-state tuition and fees and is based on academics, not financial need. Applicants will be required to submit an essay, and no other application is necessary. Award requirements change regularly. Please send a self-addressed, stamped envelope to receive your application and any further instructions from the scholarship provider. GPA must be 3.0-4.0.

Virginia Commonwealth University
Undergraduate Admissions Office
821 West Franklin Street
Richmond, VA 23284-2526

3034
Presidential Scholarship

AMOUNT: None Specified DEADLINE: January 1
MAJOR: All Areas of Study

The Presidential Scholarship is open to outstanding entering freshmen at VCU. The award is for in-state tuition, fees, room, and board. This award is based on academics and not financial need. Applicants will be required to submit an essay, and no other application is necessary. Award requirements change regularly. Please send a self-addressed, stamped envelope to receive your application and any further instructions from the scholarship provider. GPA must be 3.0-4.0.

Virginia Commonwealth University
Undergraduate Admissions Office
821 West Franklin Street
Richmond, VA 23284-2526

3035
Provost Scholarship

AMOUNT: None Specified DEADLINE: January 1
MAJOR: All Areas of Study

The Provost Scholarship is open to outstanding entering freshmen at VCU. The award is for in-state tuition and fees, and is based on academics, not financial need. The applicant will be required to submit an essay, and no other application is necessary. Award requirements change regularly. Please send a self-addressed, stamped envelope to receive your application and any further instructions from the scholarship provider. GPA must be 3.0-4.0.

Virginia Commonwealth University
Undergraduate Admissions Office
821 West Franklin Street
Richmond, VA 23284-2526

3036
Reynolds Metals Scholarship

AMOUNT: None Specified DEADLINE: January 1
MAJOR: All Areas of Study

The Reynolds Metals Scholarship is open to outstanding entering freshmen at VCU. The applicant must be a dependent of eligible Reynolds Metals employees in Virginia. The award is for in-state tuition and fees and is based on academics, not financial need. Applicants will be required to submit an essay, and no other application is necessary. Award requirements change regularly. Please send a self-addressed, stamped envelope to receive your application and any further instructions from the scholarship provider. GPA must be 3.0-4.0.

Virginia Commonwealth University
Undergraduate Admissions Office
821 West Franklin Street
Richmond, VA 23284-2526

Virginia Intermont College

3037
A. J. Coyle Memorial Scholarship

AMOUNT: None Specified DEADLINE: Varies
MAJOR: Equine Studies

The A. J. Coyle Memorial Scholarship is open to students at Virginia Intermont College (VIC). To be considered for this award, you must be enrolled in the Equine Studies Department at VIC. Award requirements change regularly. For more information, call the Financial Aid office at (800) 451-1842. No GPA requirement specified.

Virginia Intermont College
1013 Moore Street
Bristol, VA 24201

3038
Academic I Scholarship

AMOUNT: $4500-$6000 DEADLINE: Varies
MAJOR: All Areas of Study

The Academic I Scholarship is open to students at Virginia Intermont College. To be considered for this award, you must have a minimum GPA of 3.5 and have an on-campus interview. Award requirements change regularly. For more information, call the Financial Aid office at (800) 451-1842. GPA must be 3.5-4.0.

Virginia Intermont College
1013 Moore Street
Bristol, VA 24201

3039
Academic II Scholarship

AMOUNT: $3000-$4000 DEADLINE: Varies
MAJOR: All Areas of Study

The Academic II Scholarship is open to students at Virginia Intermont College who have a GPA of 3.25 or higher. To be considered for this award, you must have an on-campus interview. Award requirements change regularly. For more information, call the Financial Aid office at (800) 451-1842. GPA must be 3.25-4.0.

Virginia Intermont College
1013 Moore Street
Bristol, VA 24201

3040
Academic III Scholarship

AMOUNT: $2500-$3000 DEADLINE: Varies
MAJOR: All Areas of Study

The Academic III Scholarship is open to students at Virginia Intermont College who have a GPA of 3.0 or higher. To be considered for this award you must have an on-campus interview. Award requirements change regularly. For more information, call the Financial Aid office at (800) 451-1842. GPA must be 3.0-4.0.

Virginia Intermont College
1013 Moore Street
Bristol, VA 24201

3041
Alumni Association Scholarship

AMOUNT: None Specified DEADLINE: Varies
MAJOR: All Areas of Study

The Alumni Association Scholarship is open to students at Virginia Intermont College. To qualify for this award, you must demonstrate academic achievement and campus contribution. Award requirements change regularly. For more information, call the Financial Aid office at (800) 451-1842. No GPA requirement specified.

Virginia Intermont College
1013 Moore Street
Bristol
VA, 24201

3042
Barton Edward Smith Memorial Scholarship

AMOUNT: None Specified DEADLINE: Varies
MAJOR: Photography

The Barton Edward Smith Memorial Scholarship is open to students at Virginia Intermont College. To qualify for this award, you must be majoring in photography. Award requirements change regularly. For more information, call the Financial Aid office at (800) 451-1842. No GPA requirement specified.

Virginia Intermont College
1013 Moore Street
Bristol, VA 24201

3043
Bristol Art Guild Award

AMOUNT: None Specified DEADLINE: Varies
MAJOR: Art

The Bristol Art Guild Award is awarded to students at Virginia Intermont College. To be considered for this award, you must

be majoring in art. Award requirements change regularly. For more information, call the Financial Aid office at (800) 451-1842. No GPA requirement specified.

Virginia Intermont College
1013 Moore Street
Bristol, VA 24201

3044
Bristol Morning Rotary Club Scholarship

AMOUNT: None Specified DEADLINE: Varies
MAJOR: All Areas of Study

The Bristol Morning Rotary Club Scholarship is awarded to deserving students at Virginia Intermont College. To qualify for this award, you must be from one of Bristol's local high schools. Award requirements change regularly. For more information, call the Financial Aid office at (800) 451-1842. No GPA requirement specified.

Virginia Intermont College
1013 Moore Street
Bristol, VA 24201

3045
Catherine Doran White Memorial Scholarship

AMOUNT: None Specified DEADLINE: Varies
MAJOR: All Areas of Study

The Catherine Doran White Memorial Scholarship is open to students at Virginia Intermont College. Preference will be given to returning female students from Connecticut. Award requirements change regularly. For more information, call the Financial Aid office at (800) 451-1842. No GPA requirement specified.

Virginia Intermont College
1013 Moore Street
Bristol, VA 24201

3046
Cobra Award

AMOUNT: $500-$2000 DEADLINE: Varies
MAJOR: All Areas of Study

The Cobra Award is open to students at Virginia Intermont College. To be considered for the award, you must have a GPA of 2.5 or higher. Award requirements change regularly. For more information, call the Financial Aid office at (800) 451-1842. GPA must be 2.5-4.0.

Virginia Intermont College
1013 Moore Street
Bristol, VA 24201

3047
Doctor W.C. Elliott Memorial Scholarship

AMOUNT: None Specified DEADLINE: Varies
MAJOR: Natural Science, Social Work

The Doctor W.C. Elliott Memorial Scholarship is open to students at Virginia Intermont College. Preference will be given to students who are majoring in natural science or social work. Award requirements change regularly. For more information, call the Financial Aid office at (800) 451-1842. No GPA requirement specified.

Virginia Intermont College
1013 Moore Street
Bristol, VA 24201

3048
Equine Studies Scholarship Award

AMOUNT: Maximum: $1500 DEADLINE: Varies
MAJOR: Equine Studies

The Equine Studies Scholarship Award is open to students at Virginia Intermont College. To qualify for this award, you must audition. Award requirements change regularly. For more information, call the Financial Aid office at (800) 451-1842. No GPA requirement specified.

Virginia Intermont College
1013 Moore Street
Bristol, VA 24201

3049
Erskrine Parks Scholarship

AMOUNT: None Specified DEADLINE: Varies
MAJOR: Business

The Erskrine Parks Scholarship is open to students at Virginia Intermont College. To qualify for the award, you must be majoring in business. Award requirements change regularly. For more information, call the Financial Aid office at (800) 451-1842. No GPA requirement specified.

Virginia Intermont College
1013 Moore Street
Bristol, VA 24201

3050
Greater Roanoke Valley Alumni Chapter Scholarship

AMOUNT: None Specified DEADLINE: Varies
MAJOR: All Areas of Study

The Greater Roanoke Valley Alumni Chapter Scholarship is open to students at Virginia Intermont College. To be considered for this award, you must be a Roanoke Valley student. Award requirements change regularly. For more information, call the Financial Aid office at (800) 451-1842. No GPA requirement specified.

Virginia Intermont College
1013 Moore Street
Bristol, VA 24201

3051
Janette Montgomery Newman Dance Award

AMOUNT: None Specified DEADLINE: Varies
MAJOR: Dance

The Janette Montgomery Newman Dance Award is open to students at Virginia Intermont College. To be considered for

this award, you must be majoring in dance. The recipient will be selected by the faculty and college administration. Award requirements change regularly. For more information, call the Financial Aid office at (800) 451-1842. No GPA requirement specified.

Virginia Intermont College
1013 Moore Street
Bristol, VA 24201

3052
Kathe Carman Peyton Memorial Scholarship

AMOUNT: None Specified DEADLINE: Varies
MAJOR: All Areas of Study

The Kathe Carman Peyton Memorial Scholarship is open to students at Virginia Intermont College. To qualify for this award, you must be from West Virginia. Award requirements change regularly. For more information, call the Financial Aid office at (800) 451-1842. No GPA requirement specified.

Virginia Intermont College
1013 Moore Street
Bristol, VA 24201

3053
Lettie Pate Whitehead Foundation Scholarship

AMOUNT: None Specified DEADLINE: Varies
MAJOR: All Areas of Study

The Lettie Pate Whitehead Foundation Scholarship is open to students at Virginia Intermont College. To be considered for this award you will need to demonstrate financial need by submitting a FAFSA. This scholarship is awarded to Christian women from the nine southern states. Award requirements change regularly. For more information, call the Financial Aid office at (800) 451-1842. No GPA requirement specified.

Virginia Intermont College
1013 Moore Street
Bristol, VA 24201

3054
Marjorie DeFriece Scholarship

AMOUNT: None Specified DEADLINE: Varies
MAJOR: Visual Arts

The Marjorie DeFriece Scholarship is open to upper-class students at Virginia Intermont College. To be considered for this award, you must be a resident of Virginia and be majoring in visual arts. The award covers full tuition, room, and board. Award requirements change regularly. For more information, call the Financial Aid office at (800) 451-1842. No GPA requirement specified.

Virginia Intermont College
1013 Moore Street
Bristol, VA 24201

3055
Marry Lou Smith Secretarial Studies Scholarship

AMOUNT: None Specified DEADLINE: Varies
MAJOR: Office Administration

The Marry Lou Smith Secretarial Studies Scholarship is open to outstanding juniors at Virginia Intermont College (VIC). To qualify for this award, you must be majoring in office administration at VIC. Award requirements change regularly. For more information, call the Financial Aid office at (800) 451-1842. No GPA requirement specified.

Virginia Intermont College
1013 Moore Street
Bristol, VA 24201

3056
Peggy M. Leonard Memorial Scholarship

AMOUNT: $5000 DEADLINE: Varies
MAJOR: Business Administration

The Peggy M. Leonard Memorial Scholarship is open to full-time students at Virginia Intermont College. To qualify for this award, you must be majoring in business administration. Applicants are selected by the President based on faculty recommendation. Award requirements change regularly. For more information, call the Financial Aid office at (800) 451-1842. No GPA requirement specified.

Virginia Intermont College
1013 Moore Street
Bristol, VA 24201

3057
Performing Arts Scholarship Award

AMOUNT: Maximum: $1500 DEADLINE: Varies
MAJOR: All Areas of Study

The Performing Arts Scholarship Award is open to students at Virginia Intermont College. To qualify for this award, you must audition in musical theater, music, theater, or dance. Award requirements change regularly. For more information, call the Financial Aid office at (800) 451-1842. No GPA requirement specified.

Virginia Intermont College
1013 Moore Street
Bristol, VA 24201

3058
Phi Theta Kappa Scholarship

AMOUNT: Maximum: $4500 DEADLINE: Varies
MAJOR: All Areas of Study

The Phi Theta Kappa Scholarship is open to students at Virginia Intermont College. To qualify for this award, you must be a Phi Theta Kappa member, have a minimum 3.5 GPA, and have 60 transferable hours. Award requirements change regularly. For more information, call the Financial Aid office at (800) 451-1842. GPA must be 3.5-4.0.

Virginia Intermont College
1013 Moore Street
Bristol, VA 24201

3059
Phil Pinkerton Award

AMOUNT: None Specified DEADLINE: Varies
MAJOR: Photography

The Phil Pinkerton Award scholarship is open to rising junior and senior students at Virginia Intermont College. To qualify for this award you must be majoring in photography. Award requirements change regularly. For more information, call the Financial Aid office at (800) 451-1842. No GPA requirement specified.

Virginia Intermont College
1013 Moore Street
Bristol, VA 24201

3060
Photography Scholarship Award

AMOUNT: Maximum: $1500 DEADLINE: Varies
MAJOR: All Areas of Study

The Photography Scholarship Award is open to students at Virginia Intermont College. To qualify for this award, you must present a portfolio. Award requirements change regularly. For more information, call the Financial Aid office at (800) 451-1842. No GPA requirement specified.

Virginia Intermont College
1013 Moore Street
Bristol, VA 24201

3061
Robert and Minne Lee Barnhill Scholarship

AMOUNT: None Specified DEADLINE: Varies
MAJOR: Liberal Arts

The Robert and Minne Lee Barnhill Scholarship is open to students at Virginia Intermont College. To qualify for this award, you must be majoring in liberal arts and have a GPA of 2.5. Award requirements change regularly. For more information, call the Financial Aid office at (800) 451-1842. No GPA requirement specified.

Virginia Intermont College
1013 Moore Street
Bristol, VA 24201

3062
Roy C. Brown Memorial Scholarship

AMOUNT: None Specified DEADLINE: Varies
MAJOR: Public Speaking

The Roy C. Brown Memorial Scholarship is open to returning students at Virginia Intermont College. To qualify for this award, you must exhibit excellence in public speaking. Award requirements change regularly. For more information, call the Financial Aid office at (800) 451-1842. No GPA requirement specified.

Virginia Intermont College
1013 Moore Street
Bristol, VA 24201

3063
Transfer Scholarship

AMOUNT: $1500-$4000 DEADLINE: Varies
MAJOR: All Areas of Study

The Transfer Scholarship is open to transfer students at
Virginia Intermont College. To qualify for this award, you
must have a GPA of 2.5 or higher. Award requirements change
regularly. For more information, call the Financial Aid office
at (800) 451-1842. GPA must be 2.5-4.0.

Virginia Intermont College
1013 Moore Street
Bristol, VA 24201

3064
Worrell Presidential Scholarship

AMOUNT: None Specified DEADLINE: Varies
MAJOR: All Areas of Study

The Worrell Presidential Scholarship is open to students at
Virginia Intermont College who have a GPA of 3.8, an ACT
score of 27, and an SAT score of 1200. To be considered, you
must submit an essay. The total amount of the award is full
tuition. Award requirements change regularly. For more information on how to apply, call the Financial Aid office at (800)
451-1842. GPA must be 3.8-4.0.

Virginia Intermont College
1013 Moore Street
Bristol, VA 24201

Virginia Tech

3065
Agricultural and Applied Economics Scholarship

AMOUNT: $500-$1500 DEADLINE: Varies
MAJOR: Agricultural and Applied Economics

The Agricultural and Applied Economics Scholarship is available to students attending Virginia Tech as agricultural and
applied economics majors. Award requirements change regularly. Please send a self-addressed, stamped envelope to Dr. L.
Leon Geyer, 206-B Hutcheson Hall, College of Agriculture
and Life Sciences, Virginia Tech, Blacksburg, VA 24061; or
call (540) 231-7720; or email geyer@vt.edu. No GPA requirement specified.

Virginia Tech - College of Agriculture and Life Sciences
Dr. John M. White, Associate Dean
1060 Litton Reaves Hall
Blacksburg, VA 24061

3066
Agricultural Education Scholarship

AMOUNT: $500-$1000 DEADLINE: March 1
MAJOR: Agricultural Education

The Agricultural Education Scholarship is available to students attending Virginia Tech as agricultural education majors.
Award requirements change regularly. Please send a self-
addressed, stamped envelope to Dr. William G. Camp, 288
Litton Reaves Hall, College of Agriculture and Life Sciences,
Virginia Tech, Blacksburg, VA 24061; call (540) 231-8188; or
email wgcamp@vt.edu. No GPA requirement specified.

Virginia Tech - College of Agriculture and Life Sciences
Dr. John M. White, Associate Dean
1060 Litton Reaves Hall
Blacksburg, VA 24061

3067
Animal and Poultry Sciences Scholarship

AMOUNT: $500-$1000 DEADLINE: Varies
MAJOR: Animal and Poultry Sciences

The Animal and Poultry Sciences Scholarship is available to
students attending Virginia Tech as animal and poultry sciences majors. At least two scholarships are available for new
students in the poultry major (a separate application is
required). Award requirements change regularly. Please send a
self-addressed, stamped envelope to Dr. Dan Eversole, 3400
Litton Reaves Hall, College of Agriculture and Life Sciences,
Virginia Tech, Blacksburg, VA 24061; call (540) 231-4738; or
email at deversol@vt.edu. . No GPA requirement specified.

Virginia Tech - College of Agriculture and Life Sciences
Dr. John M. White, Associate Dean
1060 Litton Reaves Hall
Blacksburg, VA 24061

3068
Atlantic Rural Exposition Scholarship

AMOUNT: $1000 DEADLINE: May 1
MAJOR: College of Agriculture and Life Sciences

The Atlantic Rural Exposition Scholarship is available to FFA
or 4-H freshmen attending Virginia Tech as College of
Agriculture and Life Sciences majors. Applicants must be
Virginia residents. The selections are based on high school
academic achievement, character, leadership potential, and
financial need. Award requirements change regularly. For further instructions, please contact the scholarship provider at
dascweb@vt.edu or feel free to browse the VT website at
www.cals.vt.edu/scholarships/collegescholarships.html. No
GPA requirement specified.

Virginia Tech - College of Agriculture and Life Sciences
Dr. John M. White, Associate Dean
1060 Litton Reaves Hall
Blacksburg, VA 24061

3069

Biological Systems Engineering Scholarship

AMOUNT: $1000-$1500 DEADLINE: Varies
MAJOR: Biological Systems Engineering

The Biological Systems Engineering Scholarship is available to students attending Virginia Tech as biological systems engineering majors. Award requirements change regularly. Please send a self-addressed, stamped envelope to Dr. Theo Dillaha, 310 Seitz Hall, College of Agriculture and Life Sciences, Virginia Tech, Blacksburg, VA 24061; call (540) 231-6813; or email at dillaha@vt.edu. No GPA requirement specified.

Virginia Tech - College of Agriculture and Life Sciences
Dr. John M. White, Associate Dean
1060 Litton Reaves Hall
Blacksburg, VA 24061

3070

Charles W. Wampler, Sr., Scholarship

AMOUNT: $1000 DEADLINE: May 1
MAJOR: College of Agriculture and Life Sciences

The Charles W. Wampler, Sr., Scholarship is available to students who are attending Virginia Tech as College of Agriculture and Life Sciences majors. Selection is based on scholastic achievement, good character, financial need, and demonstrated leadership ability. Award requirements change regularly. For further instructions, please contact the scholarship provider at dascweb@vt.edu or feel free to browse the VT website at www.cals.vt.edu/scholarships/collegescholarships.html. No GPA requirement specified.

Virginia Tech - College of Agriculture and Life Sciences
Dr. John M. White, Associate Dean
1060 Litton Reaves Hall
Blacksburg, VA 24061

3071

Cyrus H. McCormick Undergraduate Scholarship

AMOUNT: $1000 DEADLINE: May 1
MAJOR: Agriculture, Life Sciences, Biological Systems, Engineering, Agricultural Education

The Cyrus H. McCormick Undergraduate Scholarship is available to freshmen and outstanding returning undergraduates who are attending Virginia Tech as majors in agriculture and life sciences, including biological systems engineering and agricultural education. Selection is based on academic merit, financial need, and extracurricular achievements. Award requirements change regularly. For further instructions, please contact the scholarship provider at dascweb@vt.edu or feel free to browse the VT website at www.cals.vt.edu/scholarships/collegescholarships.html. No GPA requirement specified.

Virginia Tech - College of Agriculture and Life Sciences
Dr. John M. White, Associate Dean
1060 Litton Reaves Hall
Blacksburg, VA 24061

3072

Dairy Industry Scholarship

AMOUNT: $1000 DEADLINE: Varies
MAJOR: Dairy Science

The Dairy Industry Scholarship is available to students attending Virginia Tech as dairy science majors. The selection criteria consist of academic performance and extracurricular activities. Preference is given in some cases to members of these respective organizations: Dairy Farmers of America, Maryland-Virginia Milk Producers, Cooperative Milk Producers, Valley of Virginia Milk Producers, Petersburg-Hopewell Milk Producers, Virginia Ayrshire Breeders Association, Virginia State Dairymen's Association, and Virginia Jersey Foundation. Award requirements change regularly. Please send a self-addressed, stamped envelope to Dr. R.E. James, Department of Dairy Science, Virginia Tech, Blacksburg, VA 24061-0315; call (540) 231-4770; or email jamesre@vt.edu. Feel free to browse the VT website at www.dasc.vt.edu. No GPA requirement specified.

Virginia Tech - College of Agriculture and Life Sciences
Dr. John M. White, Associate Dean
1060 Litton Reaves Hall
Blacksburg, VA 24061

3073

Dean James R. Nichols Scholarship

AMOUNT: $1500 DEADLINE: May 1
MAJOR: College of Agriculture and Life Sciences

The Dean James R. Nichols Scholarship is available to freshmen and returning students attending Virginia Tech as College of Agriculture and Life Sciences majors. The selection criteria are based on scholarship, leadership, and financial need. Award requirements change regularly. For further instructions, please contact the scholarship provider at dascweb@vt.edu or feel free to browse the VT website at www.cals.vt.edu/scholarships/collegescholarships.html. No GPA requirement specified.

Virginia Tech - College of Agriculture and Life Sciences
Dr. John M. White, Associate Dean
1060 Litton Reaves Hall
Blacksburg, VA 24061

3074

Dean L.B. Dietrick Freshman Merit Scholarship

AMOUNT: $1000 DEADLINE: May 1
MAJOR: College of Agriculture and Life Sciences

The Dean L.B. Dietrick Freshman Merit Scholarship is available to freshmen attending Virginia Tech as College of Agriculture and Life Sciences majors. The selection criteria consist of academic merit, leadership potential, and extracurricular activities in high school. Award requirements change regularly. For further instructions, please contact the scholarship provider at dascweb@vt.edu or feel free to browse the VT website at www.cals.vt.edu/scholarships/collegescholarships.html. No GPA requirement specified.

Virginia Tech - College of Agriculture and Life Sciences
Dr. John M. White, Associate Dean
1060 Litton Reaves Hall
Blacksburg, VA 24061

3075
Entomology Scholarship

AMOUNT: None Specified DEADLINE: Varies
MAJOR: Entomology, Urban Pest Management

The Entomology Scholarship is available to students attending Virginia Tech as entomology majors with an emphasis in urban pest management. Award requirements change regularly. Please send a self-addressed, stamped envelope to Dr. Rick Fell, 324 Prince Hall, College of Agriculture and Life Sciences, Virginia Tech, Blacksburg, VA 24061; call (540) 231-7207; or email rfell@vt.edu. No GPA requirement specified.

Virginia Tech - College of Agriculture and Life Sciences
Dr. John M. White, Associate Dean
1060 Litton Reaves Hall
Blacksburg, VA 24061

3076
Hackman Foundation Scholarship

AMOUNT: $1000 DEADLINE: Varies
MAJOR: Dairy Science

The Hackman Foundation Scholarship is available to students attending Virginia Tech as dairy science majors. The selection criteria consist of academic performance and extracurricular activities. Award requirements change regularly. Please send a self-addressed, stamped envelope to Dr. R.E. James, Department of Dairy Science, Virginia Tech, Blacksburg, VA 24061-0315; call (540) 231-4770; or email jamesre@vt.edu. Feel free to browse the VT website at www.dasc.vt.edu. No GPA requirement specified.

Virginia Tech - College of Agriculture and Life Sciences
Dr. John M. White, Associate Dean
1060 Litton Reaves Hall
Blacksburg, VA 24061

3077
John Lee Pratt Animal Nutrition Senior Research Scholarship

AMOUNT: $1500 DEADLINE: May 1
MAJOR: College of Agriculture and Life Sciences

The John Lee Pratt Animal Nutrition Senior Research Scholarship is available to seniors attending Virginia Tech as College of Agriculture and Life Sciences majors. The scholarship is awarded annually to rising seniors to aid in conducting senior research projects under the guidance of faculty advisors. A research proposal and letter of application from the student and his or her faculty advisor are required. Award requirements change regularly. For further instructions, please contact the scholarship provider at dascweb@vt.edu or feel free to browse the VT website at www.cals.vt.edu/scholarships/collegescholarships.html. No GPA requirement specified.

Virginia Tech - College of Agriculture and Life Sciences
Dr. John M. White, Associate Dean
1060 Litton Reaves Hall
Blacksburg, VA 24061

3078
John Lee Pratt Freshman Merit Scholarship

AMOUNT: $1000 DEADLINE: May 1
MAJOR: College of Agriculture and Life Sciences

The John Lee Pratt Freshman Merit Scholarship is available to freshmen attending Virginia Tech as College of Agriculture and Life Sciences majors. Selection is based on academic achievement, leadership, school and community service, and extracurricular activities. Award requirements change regularly. For further instructions, please contact the scholarship provider at dascweb@vt.edu or feel free to browse the VT website at www.cals.vt.edu/scholarships/collegescholarships.html. No GPA requirement specified.

Virginia Tech - College of Agriculture and Life Sciences
Dr. John M. White, Associate Dean
1060 Litton Reaves Hall
Blacksburg, VA 24061

3079
Maury A. Hubbard Scholarship

AMOUNT: $1000 DEADLINE: May 1
MAJOR: College of Agriculture and Life Sciences

The Maury A. Hubbard Scholarship is available to incoming freshmen and returning or transfer students who are attending Virginia Tech as College of Agriculture and Life Sciences majors. The selection criteria are based on academic merit, financial need, and extracurricular activities. Award requirements change regularly. For further instructions, please contact the scholarship provider at dascweb@vt.edu or feel free to browse the VT website at www.cals.vt.edu/scholarships/collegescholarships.html. No GPA requirement specified.

Virginia Tech - College of Agriculture and Life Sciences
Dr. John M. White, Associate Dean
1060 Litton Reaves Hall
Blacksburg, VA 24061

3080
Philip D. Digges Scholarship

AMOUNT: $1250 DEADLINE: Varies
MAJOR: Dairy Science

The Philip D. Digges Scholarship is available to freshmen attending Virginia Tech as dairy science majors. The selection criteria consist of high school academic performance and leadership achievements. Applicants must reside in the states of Virginia, Pennsylvania, or Maryland with preference given to students residing in Northern Virginia. Award requirements change regularly. Please send a self-addressed, stamped envelope to Dr. R.E. James, Department of Dairy Science, Virginia Tech, Blacksburg, VA 24061-0315; call (540) 231-4770; or email jamesre@vt.edu. Feel free to browse the VT website at www.dasc.vt.edu. No GPA requirement specified.

Virginia Tech - College of Agriculture and Life Sciences
Dr. John M. White, Associate Dean
1060 Litton Reaves Hall
Blacksburg, VA 24061

3081
Special New Student Scholarship

AMOUNT: $1000 DEADLINE: Varies
MAJOR: Dairy Science

The Special New Student Scholarship is available to outstanding FFA, 4-H freshmen or transfer students who are attending Virginia Tech as dairy science majors. Selection is based on 4-H, FFA, or college activities and evidence of leadership potential. Award requirements change regularly. Please send a self-addressed, stamped envelope to Dr. R.E. James, Department of Dairy Science, Virginia Tech, Blacksburg, VA 24061-0315; call (540) 231-4770; or email jamesre@vt.edu. Feel free to browse the VT website at www.dasc.vt.edu. No GPA requirement specified.

Virginia Tech - College of Agriculture and Life Sciences
Dr. John M. White, Associate Dean
1060 Litton Reaves Hall
Blacksburg, VA 24061

3082
State of Virginia Diversity Enhancement Scholarship

AMOUNT: $2500-$5000 DEADLINE: May 1
MAJOR: College of Agriculture and Life Sciences

The State of Virginia Diversity Enhancement Scholarship is available to underrepresented students attending Virginia Tech as College of Agriculture and Life Sciences majors. Priority is given to residents of Virginia. Award requirements change regularly. For further instructions, please contact the scholarship provider at dascweb@vt.edu or feel free to browse the VT website at www.cals.vt.edu/scholarships/collegescholarships.html. No GPA requirement specified.

Virginia Tech - College of Agriculture and Life Sciences
Dr. John M. White, Associate Dean
1060 Litton Reaves Hall
Blacksburg, VA 24061

3083
United States Department of Agriculture Multicultural Scholarship

AMOUNT: $5750 DEADLINE: May 1
MAJOR: College of Agriculture and Life Sciences

The United States Department of Agriculture Multicultural Scholarship is available to highly qualified minority students attending Virginia Tech as College of Agriculture and Life Sciences majors. The availability of these scholarships to the college depends on the successful competitive proposals to the USDA every other year by the Office of Academic Programs. Award requirements change regularly. For further instructions, please contact the scholarship provider at dascweb@vt.edu or feel free to browse the VT website at

www.cals.vt.edu/scholrships/collegescholarships.html. No GPA requirement specified.

Virginia Tech - College of Agriculture and Life Sciences
Dr. John M. White, Associate Dean
1060 Litton Reaves Hall
Blacksburg, VA 24061

3084
Virginia Pest Control Association Scholarship

AMOUNT: $1000 DEADLINE: May 1
MAJOR: Agriculture Technology, Entomology

The Virginia Pest Control Association Scholarship is available to students attending Virginia Tech. One scholarship is awarded to students in the Agricultural Technology Program, and the other scholarship is awarded to entomology majors (B.S. degree students). Award requirements change regularly. For further instructions, please contact the scholarship provider at dascweb@vt.edu or feel free to browse the VT website at www.cals.vt.edu/scholarships/collegescholarships.html. No GPA requirement specified.

Virginia Tech - College of Agriculture and Life Sciences
Dr. John M. White, Associate Dean
1060 Litton Reaves Hall
Blacksburg, VA 24061

3085
Walter S. Newman Memorial Scholarship

AMOUNT: $1000 DEADLINE: May 1
MAJOR: College of Agriculture and Life Sciences

The Walter S. Newman Memorial Scholarship is available to freshmen attending Virginia Tech as College of Agriculture and Life Sciences majors. Applicants must be from Southwest Virginia and from a rural background. The selection criteria are based on academic achievement, financial need, extracurricular activities, and leadership potential. Award requirements change regularly. For further instructions, please contact the scholarship provider at dascweb@vt.edu or feel free to browse the VT website at www.cals.vt.edu/scholarships/collegescholarships.html. No GPA requirement specified.

Virginia Tech - College of Agriculture and Life Sciences
Dr. John M. White, Associate Dean
1060 Litton Reaves Hall
Blacksburg, VA 24061

3086
William M. Etgen Memorial Scholarship

AMOUNT: None Specified DEADLINE: Varies
MAJOR: Dairy Science

The William M. Etgen Memorial Scholarship is available to sophomores or junior students attending Virginia Tech as dairy science majors. Award requirements change regularly. Please send a self-addressed, stamped envelope to Dr. R.E. James, Department of Dairy Science, Virginia Tech, Blacksburg, VA 24061-0315; call (540) 231-4770; or email jamesre@vt.edu.

Feel free to browse the VT website at www.dasc.vt.edu. No GPA requirement specified.

Virginia Tech - College of Agriculture and Life Sciences
Dr. John M. White, Associate Dean
1060 Litton Reaves Hall
Blacksburg, VA 24061

3087
William R. Powell Scholarship

AMOUNT: $1000 DEADLINE: May 1
MAJOR: College of Agriculture and Life Sciences

The William R. Powell Scholarship is available to freshmen and returning or transfer students attending Virginia Tech as College of Agriculture and Life Sciences majors. The selection criteria are based on academic performance, service, and financial need. Award requirements change regularly. For further instructions, please contact the scholarship provider at dascweb@vt.edu or feel free to browse the VT website at www.cals.vt.edu/scholarships/collegescholarships.html. No GPA requirement specified.

Virginia Tech - College of Agriculture and Life Sciences
Dr. John M. White, Associate Dean
1060 Litton Reaves Hall
Blacksburg, VA 24061

Washington University

3088
M/M Spencer Olin Fellowship for Women in Graduate or Professional Studies

AMOUNT: None Specified DEADLINE: February 1
MAJOR: All Areas of Study

Awards for women who have already obtained their bachelor's degree, who are about to start graduate or professional school at Washington University-St. Louis. All applicants must have obtained their bachelor's degree from any college or university in the United States. Applicants with a bachelor's degree from foreign countries will not be considered. Award requirements change regularly. Please write to the address listed, enclosing a self-addressed, stamped envelope, for further information. No GPA requirement specified.

Washington University
Graduate School of Arts and Sciences Campus
One Brookings Drive, #1187
Saint Louis, MO 63130-4862

Webster College

3089
Webster Business Administration/Accounting Scholarship (Holiday)

AMOUNT: None Specified DEADLINE: Varies
MAJOR: Business Administration (Accounting Emphasis)

The Webster Business Administration/Accounting Scholarship (Holiday) is open to Florida residents attending or planning to attend Webster College - Holiday Campus to study business administration with an accounting emphasis. Applications are available at Florida high schools and GED testing centers. Award requirements change regularly. For further information, please send a self-addressed, stamped envelope to Webster College, Vicki DeSosa, High School Coordinator, 2127 Grand Boulevard, Holiday, FL 34691, or call (813) 942-0069. No GPA requirement specified.

Florida Association of Postsecondary Schools and Colleges
Attn: FAPSC Scholarship Committee
F200 West College Avenue
Tallahassee, FL 32301

3090
Webster Business Administration/Accounting Scholarship (Ocala)

AMOUNT: None Specified DEADLINE: Varies
MAJOR: Business Administration (Accounting Emphasis)

The Webster Business Administration/Accounting Scholarship (Ocala) is open to Florida residents attending or planning to attend Webster College - Ocala Campus to study business administration with an accounting emphasis. Applications are available at Florida high schools and GED testing centers. Award requirements change regularly. For further information, please send a self-addressed, stamped envelope to Webster College, Judy Chuds, High School Coordinator, 1530 SW Third Avenue, Ocala, FL 34474, or call (352) 629-1941. No GPA requirement specified.

Florida Association of Postsecondary Schools and Colleges
Attn: FAPSC Scholarship Committee
F200 West College Avenue
Tallahassee, FL 32301

3091
Webster Business Administration/Computer Scholarship (Holiday)

AMOUNT: None Specified DEADLINE: Varies
MAJOR: Business Administration (Computer Emphasis)

The Webster Business Administration/Computer Scholarship (Holiday) is open to Florida residents attending or planning to attend Webster College - Holiday Campus to study business administration with a computer emphasis. Applications are available at Florida high schools and GED testing centers. Award requirements change regularly. For further information, please send a self-addressed, stamped envelope to Webster College, Vicki DeSosa, High School Coordinator, 2127 Grand Boulevard, Holiday, FL 34691, or call (813) 942-0069. No GPA requirement specified.

Florida Association of Postsecondary Schools and Colleges
Attn: FAPSC Scholarship Committee
F200 West College Avenue
Tallahassee, FL 32301

3092
Webster Business Administration/Computer Scholarship (Ocala)

AMOUNT: None Specified DEADLINE: Varies
MAJOR: Business Administration (Computer Emphasis)

The Webster Business Administration/Computer Scholarship (Ocala) is open to Florida residents attending or planning to attend Webster College - Ocala Campus to study business administration with a computer emphasis. Applications are available at Florida high schools and GED testing centers. Award requirements change regularly. For further information, please send a self-addressed, stamped envelope to Webster College, Judy Chuds, High School Coordinator, 1530 SW Third Avenue, Ocala, FL 34474, or call (352) 629-1941. No GPA requirement specified.

Florida Association of Postsecondary Schools and Colleges
Attn: FAPSC Scholarship Committee
F200 West College Avenue
Tallahassee, FL 32301

3093
Webster Business Administration/Legal Scholarship (Holiday)

AMOUNT: None Specified DEADLINE: Varies
MAJOR: Business Administration (Legal Emphasis)

The Webster Business Administration/Legal Scholarship (Holiday) is open to Florida residents attending or planning to attend Webster College - Holiday Campus to study business administration with a legal emphasis. Applications are available at Florida high schools and GED testing centers. Award requirements change regularly. For further information, please send a self-addressed, stamped envelope to Webster College, Vicki DeSosa, High School Coordinator, 2127 Grand Boulevard, Holiday, FL 34691, or call (813) 942-0069. No GPA requirement specified.

Florida Association of Postsecondary Schools and Colleges
Attn: FAPSC Scholarship Committee
F200 West College Avenue
Tallahassee, FL 32301

3094
Webster Business Administration/Legal Scholarship (Ocala)

AMOUNT: None Specified DEADLINE: Varies
MAJOR: Business Administration (Legal Emphasis)

The Webster Business Administration/Legal Scholarship (Ocala) is open to Florida residents attending or planning to attend Webster College - Ocala Campus to study business administration with a legal emphasis. Applications are available at Florida high schools and GED testing centers. Award requirements change regularly. For further information, please send a self-addressed, stamped envelope to Webster College, Judy Chuds, High School Coordinator, 1530 SW Third Avenue, Ocala, FL 34474, or call (352) 629-1941. No GPA requirement specified.

Florida Association of Postsecondary Schools and Colleges
Attn: FAPSC Scholarship Committee
F200 West College Avenue
Tallahassee, FL 32301

3095
Webster College Medical Assisting Scholarship (Holiday)

AMOUNT: None Specified DEADLINE: Varies
MAJOR: Medical Assisting

The Webster College Medical Assisting Scholarship (Holiday) is open to Florida residents attending or planning to attend Webster College - Holiday Campus to study medical assisting. Applications are available at Florida high schools and GED testing centers. Award requirements change regularly. For further information, please send a self-addressed, stamped envelope to Webster College, Vicki DeSosa, High School Coordinator, 2127 Grand Boulevard, Holiday, FL 34691, or call (813) 942-0069. No GPA requirement specified.

Florida Association of Postsecondary Schools and Colleges
Attn: FAPSC Scholarship Committee
F200 West College Avenue
Tallahassee, FL 32301

3096
Webster College Medical Assisting Scholarship (Ocala)

AMOUNT: None Specified DEADLINE: Varies
MAJOR: Medical Assisting

The Webster College Medical Assisting Scholarship (Ocala) is open to Florida residents attending or planning to attend Webster College - Ocala Campus to study medical assisting. Applications are available at Florida high schools and GED testing centers. Award requirements change regularly. For further information, please send a self-addressed, stamped envelope to Webster College, Judy Chuds, High School Coordinator, 1530 SW Third Avenue, Ocala, FL 34474, or call (352) 629-1941. No GPA requirement specified.

Florida Association of Postsecondary Schools and Colleges
Attn: FAPSC Scholarship Committee
F200 West College Avenue
Tallahassee, FL 32301

3097
Webster College Travel and Tourism Scholarship (Holiday)

AMOUNT: None Specified DEADLINE: Varies
MAJOR: Travel and Tourism

The Webster College Travel and Tourism Scholarship (Holiday) is open to Florida residents attending or planning to attend Webster College - Holiday Campus to study travel and tourism. Applications are available at Florida high schools and GED testing centers. Award requirements change regularly. For further information, please send a self-addressed, stamped envelope to Webster College, Vicki DeSosa, High School Coordinator, 2127 Grand Boulevard, Holiday, FL 34691, or call (813) 942-0069. No GPA requirement specified.

Florida Association of Postsecondary Schools and Colleges
Attn: FAPSC Scholarship Committee
F200 West College Avenue
Tallahassee, FL 32301

3098
Webster College Travel and Tourism Scholarship (Ocala)

AMOUNT: None Specified DEADLINE: Varies
MAJOR: Travel and Tourism

The Webster College Travel and Tourism Scholarship (Ocala) is open to Florida residents attending or planning to attend Webster College - Ocala Campus to study travel and tourism. Applications are available at Florida high schools and GED testing centers. Award requirements change regularly. For further information, please send a self-addressed, stamped envelope to Webster College, Judy Chuds, High School Coordinator, 1530 SW Third Avenue, Ocala, FL 34474, or call (352) 629-1941. No GPA requirement specified.

Florida Association of Postsecondary Schools and Colleges
Attn: FAPSC Scholarship Committee
F200 West College Avenue
Tallahassee, FL 32301

Wells College

3099
21st Century Leadership Award

AMOUNT: $5000-$20000 DEADLINE: May 1
MAJOR: All Areas of Study

This scholarship is awarded based on a student's exceptional leadership skills. In order to demonstrate these skills, the applicant will need to list all organizations that she is affiliated with or ones of which she is a member. The applicant should also list involvement in extracurricular activities and organizations, clearly noting positions of leadership within these areas. One student per high school receives this award, and the recipient will receive $5000 per year for four years. Award requirements change regularly. Please send a self-addressed, stamped envelope to receive your application and for any further instructions from the scholarship provider. GPA must be 3.0-4.0.

Wells College
Director of Admissions
170 Main Street
Aurora, NY 13026

3100
Henry Wells Scholarship

AMOUNT: None Specified DEADLINE: February 1
MAJOR: All Areas of Study

Recipients of the Henry Wells Scholarship will have a top 90% cumulative grade point average and a minimum 1150 SAT or 28 ACT score. Award recipients will receive a guaranteed first-year internship or related experience, after which they will be guaranteed the opportunity to participate in a $3000 paid internship or experiential learning program later in their college career. Award requirements change regularly.

Please send a self-addressed, stamped envelope to receive your application and any further instructions from the scholarship provider. GPA must be 3.0-4.0.

Wells College
Director of Admissions
170 Main Street
Aurora, NY 13026

3101
Legacy Award

AMOUNT: $2500-$10000 DEADLINE: Varies
MAJOR: All Areas of Study

This award is open to the daughter or granddaughter of an alumna of Wells College. The award recipient will receive $2500 a year for four years. Applicant must be a full-time college student. Award requirements change regularly. Please send a self-addressed, stamped envelope to receive your application and for any further instructions from the scholarship provider. No GPA requirement specified.

Wells College
Director of Admissions
170 Main Street
Aurora, NY 13026

Wheeling Jesuit College

3102
Academic Achievement Scholarship

AMOUNT: None Specified DEADLINE: Varies
MAJOR: All Areas of Study

Open to entering freshmen, admitted to WJU, who are National Merit Semi-Finalists or Finalists. Award requirements change regularly. Write to the address listed, enclosing a self-addressed, stamped envelope for more information or call (304) 243-2304 or (800) 624-6992. No GPA requirement specified.

Wheeling Jesuit College
Student Financial Planning
316 Washington Avenue
Wheeling, WV 26003-6243

3103
Biery (Guy and Marie Paul) Memorial Scholarship

AMOUNT: None Specified DEADLINE: Varies
MAJOR: All Areas of Study

Awards for needy Ohio County (WV) residents, with preference to Central Catholic students at WJU. Award requirements change regularly. Write to the address listed, enclosing a self-addressed, stamped envelope for more information or call (304) 243-2304 or (800) 624-6992. No GPA requirement specified.

Wheeling Jesuit College
Student Financial Planning
316 Washington Avenue
Wheeling, WV 26003-6243

3104
Byzantine Rite Scholarships

AMOUNT: $1500 DEADLINE: Varies
MAJOR: All Areas of Study

Awards for WJU students who live in West Virginia, Pennsylvania, or Ohio and attend Byzantine parishes. Recipients must be nominated by their pastor in order to be considered for this award. Award requirements change regularly. Write to the address listed, enclosing a self-addressed, stamped envelope for more information or call (304) 243-2304 or (800) 624-6992. GPA must be 2.7-4.0.

Wheeling Jesuit College
Student Financial Planning
316 Washington Avenue
Wheeling, WV 26003-6243

3105
Campion Grants

AMOUNT: None Specified DEADLINE: Varies
MAJOR: All Areas of Study

Awards for WJU students in intercollegiate athletics. Varsity sports for men include basketball, soccer, track, swimming, cross country, and golf. Those for women include basketball, soccer, track, cross country, volleyball, golf, and swimming. Award requirements change regularly. Write to the address listed, enclosing a self-addressed, stamped envelope for more information or call (304) 243-2304 or (800) 624-6992. No GPA requirement specified.

Wheeling Jesuit College
Student Financial Planning
316 Washington Avenue
Wheeling, WV 26003-6243

3106
Carrigan Alumni Scholarship

AMOUNT: None Specified DEADLINE: Varies
MAJOR: All Areas of Study

Award for children or grandchildren of WJU alumni with a GPA of at least 2.5. Also based on the qualities of compassion and commitment. Award requirements change regularly. Write to the address listed, enclosing a self-addressed, stamped envelope for more information or call (304) 243-2304 or (800) 624-6992. GPA must be 2.5.

Wheeling Jesuit College
Student Financial Planning
316 Washington Avenue
Wheeling, WV 26003-6243

3107
Greene County Scholarship

AMOUNT: $1000-$2000 DEADLINE: $1000-$2000
MAJOR: All Areas of Study

Awards for residents of Greene County in Pennsylvania. Must have a GPA of at least 2.5 at WJU. Recipients must be nominated by their local counselors or priests. Based on financial need. Award requirements change regularly. Write to the address listed, enclosing a self-addressed, stamped envelope for more information or call (304) 243-2304 or (800) 624-6992. GPA must be 2.5.

Wheeling Jesuit College
Student Financial Planning
316 Washington Avenue
Wheeling, WV 26003-6243

3108
Halloran and Ditrapano Scholarships

AMOUNT: None Specified DEADLINE: Varies
MAJOR: All Areas of Study

Awards for WJU needy students from the Charleston area. Preference is given to Charleston Catholic High School graduates. Award requirements change regularly. Write to the address listed, enclosing a self-addressed, stamped envelope for more information or call (304) 243-2304 or (800) 624-6992. No GPA requirement specified.

Wheeling Jesuit College
Student Financial Planning
316 Washington Avenue
Wheeling, WV 26003-6243

3109
Hodges Scholarship

AMOUNT: None Specified DEADLINE: Varies
MAJOR: All Areas of Study

Awards for WJU students based on need and academics. Award requirements change regularly. Write to the address listed, enclosing a self-addressed, stamped envelope for more information or call (304) 243-2304 or (800) 624-6992. GPA must be 2.7.

Wheeling Jesuit College
Student Financial Planning
316 Washington Avenue
Wheeling, WV 26003-6243

3110
James B. Chambers Memorial Scholarship

AMOUNT: None Specified DEADLINE: Varies
MAJOR: All Areas of Study

Awards for Ohio County (WV) residents who are younger than 21 years of age. Based on need rather than merit. Recipients must attend WJU. Award requirements change regularly. Write to the address listed, enclosing a self-addressed, stamped envelope for more information or call (304) 243-2304 or (800) 624-6992. No GPA requirement specified.

Wheeling Jesuit College
Student Financial Planning
316 Washington Avenue
Wheeling, WV 26003-6243

3111
Knights of Columbus Scholarships

AMOUNT: None Specified DEADLINE: Varies
MAJOR: All Areas of Study

Awards for West Virginia students attending WJU whose fathers are K of C members in good standing. Award requirements change regularly. Contact the state or local K of C organizations for more information or call (304) 243-2304 or (800) 624-6992. No GPA requirement specified.

Wheeling Jesuit College
Student Financial Planning
316 Washington Avenue
Wheeling, WV 26003-6243

3112
McConnell Scholarship

AMOUNT: None Specified DEADLINE: Varies
MAJOR: All Areas of Study

Awards for Wheeling, West Virginia, students attending WJU who can demonstrate financial need. Award requirements change regularly. Write to the address listed, enclosing a self-addressed, stamped envelope for more information or call (304) 243-2304 or (800) 624-6992. No GPA requirement specified.

Wheeling Jesuit College
Student Financial Planning
316 Washington Avenue
Wheeling, WV 26003-6243

3113
Pastor's Scholarships

AMOUNT: $500 DEADLINE: Varies
MAJOR: All Areas of Study

Awards for WJU students who live in the Wheeling-Charleston Diocese and have demonstrated academic achievement. The college sends nomination forms to the pastors in this district each fall, and those interested in this scholarship should contact their pastors. Award requirements change regularly. Write to the address listed, enclosing a self-addressed, stamped envelope for more information or call (304) 243-2304 or (800) 624-6992. No GPA requirement specified.

Wheeling Jesuit College
Student Financial Planning
316 Washington Avenue
Wheeling, WV 26003-6243

3114
Presidential Scholarships

AMOUNT: $500-$5000 DEADLINE: Varies
MAJOR: All Areas of Study

Open to entering freshmen admitted to WJU. Based on high school GPA, class ranking, and test scores. Award requirements change regularly. Write to the address listed, enclosing a self-addressed, stamped envelope for more information or call (304) 243-2304 or (800) 624-6992. GPA must be 2.7.

Wheeling Jesuit College
Student Financial Planning
316 Washington Avenue
Wheeling, WV 26003-6243

3115
Pride Scholarship

AMOUNT: None Specified DEADLINE: Varies
MAJOR: All Areas of Study

Awards for minority students at WJU based on academics and leadership. Award requirements change regularly. Write to the address listed, enclosing a self-addressed, stamped envelope for more information or call (304) 243-2304 or (800) 624-6992. No GPA requirement specified.

Wheeling Jesuit College
Student Financial Planning
316 Washington Avenue
Wheeling, WV 26003-6243

3116
Stifel Nursing Scholarship

AMOUNT: None Specified DEADLINE: Varies
MAJOR: Nursing

Awards for residents of Ohio County (WV) who are attending WJU. Preference will be given to graduates of the Ohio County Public School system. Award requirements change regularly. Write to the address listed, enclosing a self-addressed, stamped envelope for more information or call (304) 243-2304 or (800) 624-6992. No GPA requirement specified.

Wheeling Jesuit College
Student Financial Planning
316 Washington Avenue
Wheeling, WV 26003-6243

3117
Szitar Memorial Scholarship

AMOUNT: None Specified DEADLINE: Varies
MAJOR: All Areas of Study

Awards for WJU needy and deserving students, Catholic or non-Catholic, from Belmont County (WV). Award requirements change regularly. Write to the address listed for more information or call (304) 243-2304 or (800) 624-6992. No GPA requirement specified.

Wheeling Jesuit College
Student Financial Planning
316 Washington Avenue
Wheeling, WV 26003-6243

3118
Teen of the Week Scholarship

AMOUNT: $250 DEADLINE: Varies
MAJOR: All Areas of Study

Awards for WJU entering freshmen from Wheeling, WV, who are selected weekly by the News Register and from the recommendation of high school counselors or principals. Award requirements change regularly. Write to the address listed, enclosing a self-addressed, stamped envelope for more information or call (304) 243-2304 or (800) 624-6992. No GPA requirement specified.

Wheeling Jesuit College
Student Financial Planning
316 Washington Avenue
Wheeling, WV 26003-6243

3119
Theodora Eich Memorial Scholarship

AMOUNT: None Specified DEADLINE: Varies
MAJOR: All Areas of Study

Awards for residents of Ohio or Belmont counties in West Virginia attending WJU. Award requirements change regularly. Write to the address listed, enclosing a self-addressed, stamped envelope for more information or call (304) 243-2304 or (800) 624-6992. No GPA requirement specified.

Wheeling Jesuit College
Student Financial Planning
316 Washington Avenue
Wheeling, WV 26003-6243

3120
Troy Memorial Scholarship

AMOUNT: $1200 DEADLINE: Varies
MAJOR: All Areas of Study

Awards funded by contributions from WJU faculty/staff. Awarded to needy, local students. Must make a "difference" in their financial situation and enable them to attend or continue study at WJU. Award requirements change regularly. Write to the address listed, enclosing a self-addressed, stamped envelope for more information or call (304) 243-2304 or (800) 624-6992. No GPA requirement specified.

Wheeling Jesuit College
Student Financial Planning
316 Washington Avenue
Wheeling, WV 26003-6243

3121
Washington County Scholarship

AMOUNT: $1000-$2000 DEADLINE: Varies
MAJOR: All Areas of Study

Awards for students from Washington County, PA, who have a GPA of at least 2.5 at WJU. Must be nominated by their local priests or high school counselors. Award requirements change regularly. Write to the address listed, enclosing a self-addressed, stamped envelope for more information or call (304) 243-2304 or (800) 624-6992. GPA must be 2.5.

Wheeling Jesuit College
Student Financial Planning
316 Washington Avenue
Wheeling, WV 26003-6243

3122
Woomer Scholarship

AMOUNT: None Specified DEADLINE: Varies
MAJOR: All Areas of Study

Awards for students at WJU based on academic performance and leadership. Award requirements change regularly. Write to the address listed, enclosing a self-addressed, stamped envelope for more information or call (304) 243-2304 or (800) 624-6992. GPA must be 2.7.

Wheeling Jesuit College
Student Financial Planning
316 Washington Avenue
Wheeling, WV 26003-6243

Whitworth College

3123
Alice Woodhead Scholarship

AMOUNT: $400 DEADLINE: April 1
MAJOR: All Areas of Study

This scholarship is open to students who have attended Whitworth for at least a year with a minimum GPA of 2.75. In order to apply, you must be able to demonstrate high financial need, creativity, initiative, and ambition in pursuing educational and career objectives. This award is not renewable. Award requirements change regularly. GPA must be 2.75-4.0.

Whitworth College
Financial Aid Office
300 West Hawthorne Road
Spokane, WA 99251-2515

3124
Alumni Association Scholarship

AMOUNT: $1000 DEADLINE: March 31
MAJOR: All Areas of Study

This scholarship is open to full-time undergraduate students at Whitworth College whose parents graduated from Whitworth College. You must have a minimum GPA of 3.0 and an active leadership role on campus. Award requirements change regularly. GPA must be 3.0-4.0.

Whitworth College
Financial Aid Office
300 West Hawthorne Road
Spokane, WA 99251-2515

3125
B. Camp Sanford Scholarship

AMOUNT: $500 DEADLINE: April 1
MAJOR: International Studies

This scholarship is open to students at Whitworth College who are pursuing degrees in international studies and have a minimum GPA of 3.0. You must have maintained a membership in a Christian church in order to apply. Financial need will be considered. This award is not renewable. Award requirements change regularly. GPA must be 3.0-4.0.

Whitworth College
Financial Aid Office
300 West Hawthorne Road
Spokane, WA 99251-2515

3126
Beulah Wilkie Scholarship

AMOUNT: $500-$2000 DEADLINE: April 15
MAJOR: All Areas of Study

This scholarship is open to full-time undergraduate students at Whitworth College who graduated from Davenport High School and are members of the United Presbyterian Church. Financial need will be considered. This award may be renewed. Three or four awards are given annually. Award requirements change regularly. GPA must be 3.0-4.0.

Whitworth College
Financial Aid Office
300 West Hawthorne Road
Spokane, WA 99251-2515

3127
C.W. and Madeline Anderson Scholarship

AMOUNT: $1000 DEADLINE: March 1
MAJOR: All Areas of Study

This scholarship is open to full-time undergraduate students at Whitworth College who are residents of the Pacific Northwest. In order to apply, your Christian faith must be an integral part of your life, and you must have a minimum 3.25 GPA. Financial need will be considered. This award is not renewable. Award requirements change regularly. GPA must be 3.3-4.0.

Whitworth College
Financial Aid Office
300 West Hawthorne Road
Spokane, WA 99251-2515

3128
d'Urbal Writing Scholarship

AMOUNT: $500 DEADLINE: March 15
MAJOR: Writing

This scholarship is open to upperclassmen at Whitworth College pursuing an English-Writing major. In order to apply, you must have a minimum 3.3 GPA. Financial need will be considered. Award requirements change regularly. GPA must be 3.3-4.0.

Whitworth College
Financial Aid Office
300 West Hawthorne Road
Spokane, WA 99251-2515

3129
Eileen "Mom" Hendrick Scholarship

AMOUNT: $200 DEADLINE: March 15
MAJOR: All Areas of Study

The Eileen "Mom" Hendrick Scholarship is open to students at Whitworth College who have had at least one year of residency on campus. You must demonstrate a strong sense of service to the Whitworth community. Financial need is considered when applying for this award. Award requirements change regularly. No GPA requirement specified.

Whitworth College
Financial Aid Office
300 West Hawthorne Road
Spokane, WA 99251-2515

3130
Estella Baldwin Scholarships for International Students

AMOUNT: $1000 DEADLINE: April 15
MAJOR: All Areas of Study

This scholarship is open to international students accepted at Whitworth College with a minimum 2.75 GPA and a high financial need. This award may be renewable. Award requirements change regularly. GPA must be 2.75-4.0.

Whitworth College
Financial Aid Office
300 West Hawthorne Road
Spokane, WA 99251-2515

3131
Gowdy Memorial Scholarship

AMOUNT: $500 DEADLINE: April 1
MAJOR: All Areas of Study

This scholarship is open to upperclassmen at Whitworth College who exhibit social service, college/community involvement, and leadership. You must have a minimum GPA of 3.25. Award requirements change regularly. GPA must be 3.25-4.0.

Whitworth College
Financial Aid Office
300 West Hawthorne Road
Spokane, WA 99251-2515

3132
James Family Scholarships

AMOUNT: $500-$1000 DEADLINE: April 1
MAJOR: International Business/Relations, Political Science

This scholarship is open to students who have completed at least one year at Whitworth College majoring in international business/relations or political science. You must have a minimum 3.0 GPA and have a solid Christian commitment. Financial need is not a consideration for this award. Award requirements change regularly. GPA must be 3.0-4.0.

Whitworth College
Financial Aid Office
300 West Hawthorne Road
Spokane, WA 99251-2515

3133
Lisa M. Plotkin Scholarships

AMOUNT: $500 DEADLINE: April 15
MAJOR: Education

This award is open to sophomores and juniors at Whitworth College with high academics, college community involvement, and service to others. In order to apply you must have a disability or be majoring in a field to benefit the developmentally disabled. This scholarship may be renewable. Award requirements change regularly. No GPA requirement specified.

Whitworth College
Financial Aid Office
300 West Hawthorne Road
Spokane, WA 99251-2515

3134
Lynda Sittser Memorial Scholarship

AMOUNT: $1000 DEADLINE: April 1
MAJOR: Music, Religion

This scholarship is open to juniors and seniors at Whitworth College who have a proven interest and experience in ministry and/or church music. You must have a minimum GPA of 3.3 in order to apply. This award is not based on financial need. Award requirements change regularly. GPA must be 3.3-4.0.

Whitworth College
Financial Aid Office
300 West Hawthorne Road
Spokane, WA 99251-2515

3135
Martha Estelle Frimoth Scholarship

AMOUNT: $500 DEADLINE: March 15
MAJOR: All Areas of Study

This award is open to students at Whitworth College. You must have attended Whitworth College for at least one year, have a minimum 2.75 GPA, and demonstrate community involvement and good academic standards. Award requirements change regularly. GPA must be 2.75-4.0.

Whitworth College
Financial Aid Office
300 West Hawthorne Road
Spokane, WA 99251-2515

3136
Myrna Wittwer Scholarship

AMOUNT: $500 DEADLINE: March 15
MAJOR: Computer Science, Mathematics

This scholarship is open to female students at Whitworth College with a minimum GPA of 3.0. You must have attended Whitworth for at least a year in order to apply. Financial need

will be considered. Award requirements change regularly. GPA must be 3.0-4.0.

Whitworth College
Financial Aid Office
300 West Hawthorne Road
Spokane, WA 99251-2515

3137
Nalos Scholarships

AMOUNT: $700 DEADLINE: March 31
MAJOR: Religion

This scholarship is open to juniors and seniors who have attended Whitworth for at least one year with a minimum GPA of 3.0. Other majors besides religion will be considered if your goal is a career in full-time Christian ministry. This award is not renewable. Award requirements change regularly. GPA must be 3.0.

Whitworth College
Financial Aid Office
300 West Hawthorne Road
Spokane, WA 99251-2515

3138
Rev. Edward E. Baird Scholarship

AMOUNT: $800 DEADLINE: March 31
MAJOR: Philosophy

This scholarship is open to upperclassmen at Whitworth College who have a declared philosophy major or minor. You must have a minimum GPA of 3.0 and have attended Whitworth for at least one year. Financial need is a consideration. Award requirements change regularly. GPA must be 3.0-4.0.

Whitworth College
Financial Aid Office
300 West Hawthorne Road
Spokane, WA 99251-2515

3139
Sheryl Fardel-Winget Scholarship

AMOUNT: $1000 DEADLINE: March 1
MAJOR: Teacher Education, Special Education

This scholarship is open to students who have attended Whitworth College for at least one year with a minimum GPA of 3.0. Financial need is a consideration but not a necessity. Award requirements change regularly. GPA must be 3.0-4.0.

Whitworth College
Financial Aid Office
300 West Hawthorne Road
Spokane, WA 99251-2515

3140
Sophie Anderson Scholarship

AMOUNT: $350-$500 DEADLINE: October 1
MAJOR: Nursing, Pre-Med, Education, History, Liberal Arts

This scholarship is open to juniors and seniors accepted at Whitworth College who are Washington residents, have a minimum GPA of 3.25, and can demonstrate high financial need. Award requirements change regularly. GPA must be 3.25-4.0.

Whitworth College
Financial Aid Office
300 West Hawthorne Road
Spokane, WA 99251-2515

3141
Synod of Alaska-Northwest Scholarship for Native Americans

AMOUNT: $900 DEADLINE: April 1
MAJOR: All Areas of Study

This scholarship is open to students at Whitworth College who are of Native American descent and belong to the Presbyterian Church. Financial need is considered for this award. Award requirements change regularly.

Whitworth College
Financial Aid Office
300 West Hawthorne Road
Spokane, WA 99251-2515

3142
United Parcel Service Scholarship

AMOUNT: $1325 DEADLINE: April 15
MAJOR: All Areas of Study

This scholarship is open to full-time undergraduates accepted at Whitworth College with a minimum 3.0 GPA. In order to apply, you must be able to demonstrate financial need. This award is not renewable. Award requirements change regularly. GPA must be 3.0-4.0.

Whitworth College
Financial Aid Office
300 West Hawthorne Road
Spokane, WA 99251-2515

3143
Winner/Christiansen Scholarship

AMOUNT: $700 DEADLINE: April 15
MAJOR: Journalism

This scholarship is open to students at Whitworth who are interested in careers in journalism. Requirements include involvement/commitment to campus media, a minimum GPA of 3.0, and financial need. Award requirements change regularly. GPA must be 3.0-4.0.

Whitworth College
Financial Aid Office
300 West Hawthorne Road
Spokane, WA 99251-2515

William Rainey Harper College

3144
A&T Philia Scholarship

AMOUNT: Maximum: $1200 DEADLINE: April 14
MAJOR: All Fields of Study

The A&T Philia Scholarship is open to full-time students enrolled in an academic program, vocational education, or certificate program at William Rainey Harper College. Award requirements change regularly. No GPA requirement specified.

William Rainey Harper College
Office of Student Financial Assistance
1200 West Algonquin Road
Palatine, IL 60067-7398

3145
Access To Opportunity Scholarship

AMOUNT: $1000-$1500 DEADLINE: March 24
MAJOR: All Fields of Study

The Access To Opportunity Scholarship is open to students at William Rainey Harper College who demonstrate financial need. You must submit a typewritten letter detailing your current financial situation in order to be considered for this award. Two awards will be given in the amount of $1500 and two in the amount of $1000. Award requirements change regularly. No GPA requirement specified.

William Rainey Harper College
Office of Student Financial Assistance
1200 West Algonquin Road
Palatine, IL 60067-7398

3146
Amersham Endowment Scholarship

AMOUNT: Maximum: $1000 DEADLINE: March 24
MAJOR: Technology, Mathematics, Physical Science, Life and Human Services, Business and Social Science

The Amersham Endowment Scholarship is open to second-year students who have shown excellent achievement in academics, extracurricular activities, and community service while attending William Rainey Harper College. To apply for this award, you must have at least a 3.5 GPA, have 24 earned credit hours at Harper College, be enrolled either full- or part-time during the award year, and be eligible for graduation during the following spring semester. Award requirements change regularly. GPA must be 3.5-4.0.

William Rainey Harper College
Office of Student Financial Assistance
1200 West Algonquin Road
Palatine, IL 60067-7398

3147
Architectural Technology Scholarship

AMOUNT: None Specified DEADLINE: April 14
MAJOR: Architectural Technology

The Architectural Technology Scholarship is open to students from high schools in districts 211, 214, or 220, who are enrolling in architectural technology courses at William Rainey Harper College. To apply for this award, you must be taking or have taken drafting or architectural drafting classes in high school. This award is for the summer term only. You must have at least a 2.5 GPA to apply for a second award. Award requirements change regularly. No GPA requirement specified.

William Rainey Harper College
Office of Student Financial Assistance
1200 West Algonquin Road
Palatine, IL 60067-7398

3148
Beverly Kiss Memorial Scholarship

AMOUNT: $1000 DEADLINE: March 24
MAJOR: Participation in the Women's Program

The Beverly Kiss Memorial Scholarship is open to non-traditional students participating in the Women's Program at William Rainey Harper College. To qualify for this award, you must demonstrate high motivation in returning to college. Award requirements change regularly. No GPA requirement specified.

William Rainey Harper College
Office of Student Financial Assistance
1200 West Algonquin Road
Palatine, IL 60067-7398

3149
Business/Social Science Fund Scholarship

AMOUNT: $500 DEADLINE: March 24
MAJOR: Business

The Business/Social Science Fund Scholarship is open to graduating high school seniors who are enrolling as business majors at William Rainey Harper College. To apply for this award, you must have at least a 2.5 GPA, be enrolling in Introduction to Business Organization, and show financial need by submitting a typewritten letter detailing your current financial situation. Award requirements change regularly. GPA must be 2.5-4.0.

William Rainey Harper College
Office of Student Financial Assistance
1200 West Algonquin Road
Palatine, IL 60067-7398

3150
Cheryl M. Dwyer Memorial Endowed Scholarship

AMOUNT: Maximum: $1000 DEADLINE: March 24
MAJOR: Cardio-Technology Program

The Cheryl M. Dwyer Memorial Endowed Scholarship is open to second-year students enrolled at William Rainey Harper College in the cardio-technology program with a specialization in cardio-diagnostics. You must submit a short essay detailing how this scholarship will effect your educational goals and be available for an interview. Award requirements change regularly. No GPA requirement specified.

William Rainey Harper College
Office of Student Financial Assistance
1200 West Algonquin Road
Palatine, IL 60067-7398

3151
Chicago Chapter CPCU Society Scholarship

AMOUNT: $1000 DEADLINE: March 24
MAJOR: Electronic Insurance

The Chicago Chapter CPCU Society Scholarship is open to students who are enrolled in an electronic insurance course at William Rainey Harper College. To apply for this award, you must be a graduating high school senior or a currently enrolled Harper student and supply three letters of recommendation. Award requirements change regularly. No GPA requirement specified.

William Rainey Harper College
Office of Student Financial Assistance
1200 West Algonquin Road
Palatine, IL 60067-7398

3152
Displaced Homemakers Scholarship

AMOUNT: $300 DEADLINE: March 24
MAJOR: All Fields of Study

The Displaced Homemakers Scholarship is open to students enrolled at William Rainey Harper College. The requirements for this award are that you be a Harper District resident and that you verify "displaced homemaker" status by interviewing with the Women's Program Staff. Award requirements change regularly. No GPA requirement specified.

William Rainey Harper College
Office of Student Financial Assistance
1200 West Algonquin Road
Palatine, IL 60067-7398

3153
Education to Careers Scholarship

AMOUNT: $500 DEADLINE: March 24
MAJOR: Electronics

The Education to Careers Scholarship is open to graduating seniors enrolled in a high school electronics program who are enrolling in a degree or certificate program at William Rainey

Harper College. To qualify for this award, you must show financial need by submitting an essay detailing your current financial status. Full- and part-time students are eligible to apply. Award requirements change regularly. No GPA requirement specified.

William Rainey Harper College
Office of Student Financial Assistance
1200 West Algonquin Road
Palatine, IL 60067-7398

3154
Edward Moran Memorial Computer Science Scholarship

AMOUNT: $500 DEADLINE: March 24
MAJOR: Computer Science

The Edward Moran Memorial Computer Science Scholarship is open to students at William Rainey Harper College who are enrolled in computer science course 121 or 122. To qualify for this award, you must be enrolled in at least six credit hours, have a cumulative GPA of at least 2.5, have a GPA of 3.0 or higher in computer courses, and submit three letters of recommendation. Award requirements change regularly. GPA must be 2.5-4.0.

William Rainey Harper College
Office of Student Financial Assistance
1200 West Algonquin Road
Palatine, IL 60067-7398

3155
Elizabeth Schmik Hull Scholarship

AMOUNT: $500 DEADLINE: March 24
MAJOR: All Fields of Study

The Elizabeth Schmik Hull Scholarship is open to students at William Rainey Harper College who have completed a GED certificate and are now enrolled in the Harper Honors Program. One scholarship will be awarded per semester. Award requirements change regularly. No GPA requirement specified.

William Rainey Harper College
Office of Student Financial Assistance
1200 West Algonquin Road
Palatine, IL 60067-7398

3156
Eugenia S. Chapman Memorial Endowment Scholarship

AMOUNT: None Specified DEADLINE: April 14
MAJOR: All Fields of Study

The Eugenia S. Chapman Memorial Endowment Scholarship is open to part-time William Rainey Harper College students who are residents of the Harper District. To apply for this award, you must be taking credit courses leading to a degree or certificate and submit a short essay on the impact of this scholarship as related to your educational goals. This scholarship covers in-district tuition and related fees and is renewable. Award requirements change regularly. No GPA requirement specified.

William Rainey Harper College
Office of Student Financial Assistance
1200 West Algonquin Road
Palatine, IL 60067-7398

3157
Fine Arts Scholarship

AMOUNT: $1000 DEADLINE: March 24
MAJOR: Art, Music, Theater

The Fine Arts Scholarship is open to graduating high school seniors and currently enrolled students at William Rainey Harper College who are in art, music, or theater programs. To qualify for this award, you must have at least a 3.0 GPA, be enrolled in at least 12 credit hours, present a portfolio or audition for the selection committee, submit two letters of recommendation, and write a brief essay about your educational and professional goals. Award requirements change regularly. GPA must be 3.0-4.0.

William Rainey Harper College
Office of Student Financial Assistance
1200 West Algonquin Road
Palatine, IL 60067-7398

3158
Garden Club of Inverness Plant Science Technology Scholarship

AMOUNT: $250 DEADLINE: March 24
MAJOR: Plant Science Technology

The Garden Club of Inverness Plant Science Technology Scholarship is open to full- and part-time students currently enrolled in or planning to enroll in a plant science technology course at William Rainey Harper College. Award requirements change regularly. No GPA requirement specified.

William Rainey Harper College
Office of Student Financial Assistance
1200 West Algonquin Road
Palatine, IL 60067-7398

3159
Harper College General Endowment Scholarship

AMOUNT: None Specified DEADLINE: April 14
MAJOR: All Fields of Study

The Harper College General Endowment Scholarship is open to graduating high school students enrolling at William Rainey Harper College. To qualify for this award, you must have maintained a minimum GPA of 2.5 and submit your official high school academic transcript. This award will provide in-district tuition and fees. Award requirements change regularly. GPA must be 2.5-4.0.

William Rainey Harper College
Office of Student Financial Assistance
1200 West Algonquin Road
Palatine, IL 60067-7398

3160
Harper Nursing Student Endowment Scholarship

AMOUNT: Maximum: $500 DEADLINE: April 28
MAJOR: Nursing

The Harper Nursing Student Endowment Scholarship is open to students at William Rainey Harper College who are currently enrolled in or have completed NUR 101. To apply for this award, you must have at least a 2.0 GPA, demonstrate financial need, and have satisfactory ratings for clinical performance. Two recommendations from nursing program faculty and a 100-word essay noting what this scholarship means to you are required. Award requirements change regularly. GPA must be 2.0-4.0.

William Rainey Harper College
Office of Student Financial Assistance
1200 West Algonquin Road
Palatine, IL 60067-7398

3161
Illinois CPA Society - O'Hare Chapter Scholarship

AMOUNT: $500 DEADLINE: March 24
MAJOR: Accounting

The Illinois CPA Society - O'Hare Chapter Scholarship is open to second-year accounting students at William Rainey Harper College. To qualify for this award, you must have at least a 3.0 GPA and be a full-time student. Award requirements change regularly. GPA must be 3.0-4.0.

William Rainey Harper College
Office of Student Financial Assistance
1200 West Algonquin Road
Palatine, IL 60067-7398

3162
International Air Cargo Association of Chicago Scholarship

AMOUNT: $600 DEADLINE: March 24
MAJOR: Business

The International Air Cargo Association of Chicago Scholarship is open to students at William Rainey Harper College who are enrolled in any business course and enrolled for a minimum of six credit hours. You must have at least a 2.5 GPA to qualify. This scholarship is renewable provided you meet the established renewal criteria. Award requirements change regularly. GPA must be 2.5-4.0.

William Rainey Harper College
Office of Student Financial Assistance
1200 West Algonquin Road
Palatine, IL 60067-7398

3163
James J. McGrath Humanities Scholarship

AMOUNT: $1000 DEADLINE: March 24
MAJOR: Humanities

The James J. McGrath Humanities Scholarship is open to humanities majors at William Rainey Harper College who are graduating in the spring with an AA degree and transferring to a four-year college. To qualify for this award, you must have at least a 3.5 GPA, supply three letters of recommendation, and interview with the humanities selection committee. This scholarship is forwarded to the recipient's transfer institution upon verification of enrollment. Award requirements change regularly. GPA must be 3.5-4.0.

William Rainey Harper College
Office of Student Financial Assistance
1200 West Algonquin Road
Palatine, IL 60067-7398

3164
John W. Davis Spanish Travel Scholarship

AMOUNT: $1000 DEADLINE: March 24
MAJOR: Spanish

The John W. Davis Spanish Travel Scholarship is open to students studying Spanish at William Rainey Harper College. To be considered for this award, you must have completed two Spanish language classes and plan to study abroad in a Spanish-speaking country. Award requirements change regularly. No GPA requirement specified.

William Rainey Harper College
Office of Student Financial Assistance
1200 West Algonquin Road
Palatine, IL 60067-7398

3165
Kathleen N. Graber Scholarship

AMOUNT: $500 DEADLINE: April 14
MAJOR: All Fields of Study

The Kathleen N. Graber Scholarship is open to second-semester students with at least a 2.5 GPA at William Rainey Harper College. The purpose of this award is to encourage and reward students who did not do well academically in high school but have demonstrated significant improvement during their first experience with college. To qualify for this award, you must be a U.S. citizen, have earned 12 or more college credits (at least nine must be in non-remedial courses), and have graduated in the bottom 40% of your high school class. A brief essay on how you achieved success by changing your behavior, habits, attitude, or some other aspect of your life is required. Award requirements change regularly. GPA must be 2.5-4.0.

William Rainey Harper College
Office of Student Financial Assistance
1200 West Algonquin Road
Palatine, IL 60067-7398

3166
Marilyn Shiely Coste Memorial Scholarship

AMOUNT: $500 DEADLINE: March 24
MAJOR: Fashion Design or Literature

The Marilyn Shiely Coste Memorial Scholarship is open to full- and part-time William Rainey Harper College students who are enrolled in the fashion design program or a course in literature. To apply for this award, you must be a U.S. citizen or permanent resident and have a minimum GPA of 2.5. Award requirements change regularly. GPA must be 2.5-4.0.

William Rainey Harper College
Office of Student Financial Assistance
1200 West Algonquin Road
Palatine, IL 60067-7398

3167
Mary Ellen Klotz Scholarship for Art Students

AMOUNT: $2000 DEADLINE: March 24
MAJOR: Art

The Mary Ellen Klotz Scholarship for Art Students is open to seniors graduating from an accredited high school who intend to major in art at William Rainey Harper College. To apply for this award, you must be in the upper 75% of your class, have at least a 2.75 GPA, submit two letters of recommendation, provide a statement of educational and professional goals, and submit a portfolio of work. You must also have financial need and are required to submit an essay detailing your current financial situation. Award requirements change regularly. GPA must be 2.75-4.0.

William Rainey Harper College
Office of Student Financial Assistance
1200 West Algonquin Road
Palatine, IL 60067-7398

3168
Motorola Award for Excellence

AMOUNT: $1000 DEADLINE: March 24
MAJOR: All Fields of Study

The Motorola Award for Excellence is open to full- and part-time students enrolled at William Rainey Harper College who have a minimum GPA of 3.5 and have completed at least 24 credit hours by the end of this spring's semester. To qualify for this award, you must be eligible to graduate and must participate in the graduation exercise next spring. Award requirements change regularly. GPA must be 3.5-4.0.

William Rainey Harper College
Office of Student Financial Assistance
1200 West Algonquin Road
Palatine, IL 60067-7398

3169
Northrop Grumman Engineering Scholarship

AMOUNT: Maximum: $1000 DEADLINE: September 1
MAJOR: Pre-Engineering

The Northrop Grumman Engineering Scholarship is open to students enrolled in the pre-engineering program at William Rainey Harper College who intend to continue their studies toward a Baccalaureate degree in engineering. To qualify for this award, you must have a GPA of at least 3.5 and exhibit exceptional achievement in areas other than science. This award provides a maximum of $500 for tuition per semester and is renewable for a second semester as long as you maintain at least a 3.5 GPA. Preference will be given to engineering students; however, all students enrolled in transfer programs within the Technology, Mathematics, and Physical Science division may apply. Award requirements change regularly. GPA must be 3.5-4.0.

William Rainey Harper College
Office of Student Financial Assistance
1200 West Algonquin Road
Palatine, IL 60067-7398

3170
Pepper Engineering Scholarship

AMOUNT: $750 DEADLINE: March 24
MAJOR: Engineering

The Pepper Engineering Scholarship is open to students at William Rainey Harper College who are enrolled or planning to enroll in an engineering program. To qualify for this award, you must be a returning student at least 21 years of age. Award requirements change regularly. No GPA requirement specified.

William Rainey Harper College
Office of Student Financial Assistance
1200 West Algonquin Road
Palatine, IL 60067-7398

3171
Roy G. Kearns Memorial Scholarship

AMOUNT: None Specified DEADLINE: October 27
MAJOR: Physical Education, Health/Fitness

The Roy G. Kearns Memorial Scholarship is open to full-time students majoring in physical education and/or health/fitness at William Rainey Harper College. To qualify for this award, you must have completed at least 24 credit hours as a full-time student and have a minimum GPA of 2.5. This scholarship covers tuition and fees for the entire fall semester. Award requirements change regularly. GPA must be 2.5-4.0.

William Rainey Harper College
Office of Student Financial Assistance
1200 West Algonquin Road
Palatine, IL 60067-7398

3172
Sharlene Marchiori Memorial Nursing Scholarship

AMOUNT: $500 DEADLINE: March 24
MAJOR: Nursing

The Sharlene Marchiori Memorial Nursing Scholarship is open to students currently enrolled in or accepted to the nursing program at William Rainey Harper College. To qualify for this award, you must have at least a 2.5 GPA, be in the upper 50% of your graduating class, and demonstrate financial need. Three letters of reference, an essay detailing your current financial status, and an interview with the selection committee are required. Award requirements change regularly. GPA must be 2.5-4.0.

William Rainey Harper College
Office of Student Financial Assistance
1200 West Algonquin Road
Palatine, IL 60067-7398

3173
William Rainey Harper Employee Transfer Scholarship

AMOUNT: $1000 DEADLINE: March 29
MAJOR: All Fields of Study

The William Rainey Harper Employee Transfer Scholarship is open to dependents and spouses of current William Rainey Harper College employees. To apply for this award, you must be graduating from Harper College, transferring to a four-year college, and participating in the spring graduation ceremony. Award requirements change regularly. No GPA requirement specified.

William Rainey Harper College
Office of Student Financial Assistance
1200 West Algonquin Road
Palatine, IL 60067-7398

William Woods University

3174
Departmental Award

AMOUNT: $500-$5000 DEADLINE: March 1
MAJOR: Juvenile Justice, Sports Medicine, Performing Arts, Art, Graphic Arts, Journalism/Mass Communication, Equestrian Studies

The Departmental Award is open to students attending William Woods University. To be considered for the award, you must be majoring in juvenile justice, sports medicine, performing arts, art, graphic arts, journalism/mass communication, or equestrian studies. The amount will vary depending on whether you are a full-time student versus a part-time student, where less than 12 credit hours is part-time. Award requirements change regularly. No GPA requirement specified.

William Woods University
Office of Admissions
200 West 12th Street
Fulton, MO 65251-1004

3175
LEAD Award

AMOUNT: Maximum: $5000 DEADLINE: March 1
MAJOR: All Fields of Study

The LEAD Award is open to students attending William Woods University. To be considered for the award, you must be active in university life outside the classroom. The award is granted based on a signed commitment to participate in LEAD activities during the year. It is renewable, contingent upon satisfying the prior year's commitment. The amount will vary depending on your student status; you may earn more being a full-time student versus a part-time student (where less than 12 credit hours is part-time) or being a residential student versus a commuter student. The residential award is $5,000; the commuter award is $2,500. Award requirements change regularly. No GPA requirement specified.

William Woods University
Office of Admissions
200 West 12th Street
Fulton, MO 65251-1004

Williams Baptist College

3176
Baptist Associational Scholarship

AMOUNT: $500 DEADLINE: Varies
MAJOR: All Areas of Study

This scholarship is open to Southern Baptist students who are nominated by Directors of Associational Missions. The Director of Missions of each Arkansas Southern Baptist Association is encouraged to recommend one student from the association for the scholarship. Upon selection, you must enroll or be enrolled full-time at Williams for the semester following your selection. Arkansas residency is also required. Award requirements change regularly. For further information and an application, please write to the address listed, including a self-addressed, stamped envelope or call (800) 722-4434. No GPA requirement specified.

Williams Baptist College
Financial Aid Office
PO Box 3661
Walnut Ridge, AR 72476-4661

York College of Pennsylvania

3177
York College Scholarships

AMOUNT: None Specified DEADLINE: February 1
MAJOR: All Areas of Study

Open to entering full-time freshmen admitted to York College and current students who have completed 12 credit hours with a minimum GPA of 3.25. There is only one application form, which is applicable to all the awards offered. Award criteria and amounts vary. Award requirements change regularly. Write to address listed for additional information, enclosing a self-addressed, postage-paid envelope. GPA must be 3.25-4.0.

York College of Pennsylvania
Director of Admissions
Country Club Road
York, PA 17405

INDEXES

Major/Career Objective Index

Special Criteria Index

School Specific Index

Major/Career Objective Index

Academic Medicine, 421

Accounting, 53, 87, 106, 119, 152, 235, 271, 286, 319, 445, 492, 520, 699, 714, 785, 862, 863, 864, 882, 958, 1052, 1095, 1119, 1152, 1198

Acting (*see also* Drama, Theatre) 50, 291

Actuarial Science, 28, 698

Actuarial/Computer Science (*see also* Actuarial Science, Computer Science), 28

Advanced Practice Nursing (*see also* Nursing, Nurse Practitioner), 230

Advertising, 67, 143, 168, 637, 966

Advertising Art, 143

Aeronautics, 84, 141, 640

Aerospace Education, 84, 500, 857

Aerospace Engineering (*see also* Space, Space Related Engineering), 84, 500, 640, 857

Aerospace History, 84

African/African-American Studies, 20

Agribusiness (*see also* Agriculture, Agronomy), 21, 167, 1176

Agricultural Economics, 167, 194, 218

Agricultural Education, 167

Agricultural Engineering, 138, 167, 194, 218, 316, 332, 502, 649, 877, 1189

Agriculture; Communications; Systems, 21, 167, 194, 218, 316, 332, 649, 877, 1003, 1101, 1176, 1177

Agronomy (*see also* Agribusiness, Agriculture), 167, 461, 502, 791

Aircraft (*see also* Aviation, Aeronautics), 857

Allergy/Immunology Medical Research (*see* Immunology, Virology, Medicine)

Allied Health, 834

American Government (*see* Government; American)

American History (*see also* History), 268, 534, 609, 610

American Studies (*see also* American History, History), 268, 496, 534, 609, 610

Animals (*see also* Zoology): Behavior, 829; Protection, 1027; Record, 1117; Science, 21, 877, 951

Anthropology (*see also* Humanities, Science?), 160, 410, 507, 603, 930, 931, 1036, 1155

Applied Mathematics (*see* Mathematics)

Applied Physical Sciences (*see* Physical Science)

Applied Science (*see* Science)

Aquatic Sciences (*see* Ocean Sciences, Science)

Arboriculture (*see also* Landscape Architecture/Design, Forestry), 645

Arc Welding, 57, 327, 372, 559, 605, 937, 987

Archaeology, 410

Architecture, 247, 274, 446, 494, 558, 838, 998, 1001, 1121; History of, 990, 1008

Arms Control, 566, 1183

Art, 50, 123, 143, 162, 244, 280, 291, 300, 379, 428, 451, 674, 721, 804, 872, 944, 1048, 1154

Art Education (*see also* Art), 125, 1048

Art History (*see also* Art), 162, 410, 428, 661, 662, 944, 1048, 1154

Art Studies (*see also* Art), 162, 244, 379, 428, 1036, 1048

Art Theory (*see also* Art), 162, 1048

Arts and Literature (*see* Art, Literature, Humanities, Liberal Arts)

Arts and Sciences (*see* Art, Humanities, Science)

Astronomy, 1142

Astronautical Engineering (*see also* Aereonuatical Engineering, Space Related), 640

Astrophysics (*see also* Science), 1036

Athletic Training, 652, 1049

Atmospheric Science (*see also* Meteorology), 101, 102, 103, 110, 345, 405, 415, 560, 564, 713, 916, 970

Audiology, 658

Automotive Aftermarket, 34, 149, 493

Special Criteria Index

Disability

Ethnic

Gay, Lesbian, Bisexual, Transgendered

Graduate/Postgraduate/Research Fellowships

Men

Membership in Club/Organization

Parents Employed By/Depedent Of

Present Occupation

Teacher, 26, 383, 1080

Wal-Mart Employee, 1158

Military

Air Force, 55, 59, 60, 413, 971, 1122

Army, 1, 2, 269, 778, 779, 1122

Coast Guard, 1122

Marines, 1122

Military, 45, 62

Navy, 1122

ROTC, 48

Religion

American Baptist, 538, 586, 768, 1002, 1025, 1131

Jewish, 31, 118, 187, 230, 305, 308, 405, 433, 519, 528, 602, 639, 641, 643, 688, 707, 730, 750, 772, 891, 1024, 1053, 1156

Lutheran, 742, 888

Presbyterian, 505, 801, 1069, 1130

United Methodist Church, 687, 975

Women

3, 8, 16, 17, 18, 19, 20, 33, 84, 88, 89, 90, 92, 98, 121, 143, 166, 177, 223, 253, 254, 255, 256, 292, 303, 305, 306, 312, 331, 381, 382, 383, 386, 392, 435, 465, 468, 490, 511, 516, 536, 555, 618, 640, 647, 688, 690, 696, 697, 698, 702, 727, 750, 752, 753, 874, 893, 899, 911, 1038, 1059, 1078, 1123, 1126, 1175, 1197, 1204

School Specific Index

Adams State College, 1205-1208

Alaska Pacific University, 1209-1227

Alma College, 1228-1230

Alverno College, 1231

Andover College, 1232-1236

Arapahoe Community College, 1237-1246

Arizona State University, 1247

Armstrong Atlantic University, 1248

Art Institute of Fort Lauderdale, 1249-1260

Atlantic Coast Institute, 1261-1264

Baldwin-Wallace College, 1265-1274

Beaver College, 1275-1276

Bemidji State University, 1277-1311

Black Hills State University, 1312

Bluffton College, 1313-1319

Bradford College, 1320-1321

Bradford School, 1322

Bradley University, 1323-1330

Bradeis University, 1331-1338

Brescia University, 1339

Brighamd Young University, 1340

Bryan College, 1341-1347

California Culinary Academy, 1348

California State Univeristy, Fullerton, 1349-1381

California State University, Northridge, 1382-1384

Case Western Reserve University, 1385-1397

Cedar Crest College, 1398-1410

Central Missouri State University, 1411-1418

Christopher Newport University, 1419-1424

City College of San Francisco, 1425-1443

Clarkson University, 1444

Clemson University, 1445-1482

Cogswell Polytechnical College, 1483-1493

College of Dupage, 1494-1539

College of Saint Benedict/Saint Johnís University, 1540-1546

College of the Atlantic, 1547

Colorado Mountain College, 1548-1561

Colorado Mountain College, Alpine, 1562-1563

Colorado Mountain College, Roaring Fork, 1564-1569

Colorado Mountain College, Summit, 1570-1571

Colorado Mountain College, Timberline, 1572-1573

Colorado Mountain College, Vail/Eagle, 1574-1576

Colorado State University, 1577

Columbia Union College, 1578-1579

Columbia University, Teachers College, 1580

Concorde Career Institute, 1581-1590

Cooper Career Institute, 1591-1593

Creighton University, 1594-1597

DePauw University, 1598-1604

Eastern College, 1605-1610

Eastern New Mexico University, 1611-1633

Eastern Washington University, 1634-1636

Elizabethtown College, 1637-1641

Elmhurst College, 1642-1648

Elon College, 1649-1650

Eureka College, 1651-1665

Fairmont State College, 1666-1691

Faulkner University, 1692-1696

Florida Gulf Coast University, 1697-1702

Fort Lewis College, 1703-1736

Full Sail Real World Education, 1737-1739

Furman University, 1740-1744

Georgia Military College, 1745

Gonzaga University, 1746-1751

Herzing College of Business and Technology, 1752-1753

Holy Names College, 1754-1755

Hope International University, 1756-1764

Houston Community College, 1765

Huron State University, 1766

Illinois Institute of Technology, 1767-1768

Illinois Valley Community College, 1769-1804

Indiana University, 1805-1806

Institute of Career Education, 1807-1810

Institute of Food Technologists, 1811-1812

International Academy of Merchandising and Design, 1813-1815

International College, 1816-1820

Iowa State University, 1821-1851

Jacksonville University, 1852-1865

John Brown University, 1866-1880

Johnson and Wales University, 1881

Kansas City Art Institute, 1882-1883

Keiser College, 1884-1920

Kendall College of Art and Design, 1921

Kent State University, 1922-1952

Kent State University, Tuscarawas, 1953-1977

Keystone College, 1978-1990

Lakeland College, 1991-2000

Lee College, 2001-2032

Life University, 2033

Louisiana State University, 2034-2072

Maharishi University of Management, 2073-2076

McIntosh College, 2077-2079

McMurry University, 2080-2089

Middle Tennessee State University, 2090-2102

Mills College, 2103-2108

Minneapolis Drafting School, 2109

Missouri Valley College, 2110-2119

Moorhead State University, 2120-2131

Morehead State University, 2132-2139

Nazareth College, 2140-2155

New Mexico State University, 2156-2172

New Mexico Tech, 2173-2178

North Arkansas College, 2179-2202

North Georgia College and State University, 2203

Northeast Iowa Community College, Calmar, 2204-2230

Northeast Iowa Community College, Peosta, 2231-2266

Northwood University, 2267-2270